THE FIRST AMENDMENT

AND

THE FIFTH ESTATE

REGULATION OF ELECTRONIC MASS MEDIA

By

T. BARTON CARTER
Professor of Communication and Law
Boston University

MARC A. FRANKLIN
Frederick I. Richman Professor of Law, Emeritus
Stanford University

JAY B. WRIGHT
Professor of Journalism
S.I. Newhouse School of Public Communications
Syracuse University

SIXTH EDITION

FOUNDATION PRESS
New York, New York
2003

COPYRIGHT © 1986, 1989, 1993, 1996, 1999 FOUNDATION PRESS
COPYRIGHT © 2003 By FOUNDATION PRESS
395 Hudson Street
New York, NY 10014
Phone Toll Free 1–877–888–1330
Fax (212) 367–6799
fdpress.com
Printed in the United States of America

ISBN 1–58778–571–4

 TEXT IS PRINTED ON 10% POST CONSUMER RECYCLED PAPER

For Alison, Jonathan, and Richard

*

PREFACE TO THE SIXTH EDITION

The shared power in the English Parliament of the three estates of the realm—the Lords Spiritual, the Lords Temporal and the Commons—was long ago recognized as being in some ways matched by the special powers of the Reporters' Gallery. Journalism thus came to be known as the Fourth Estate. *Broadcasting & Cable* magazine and others have referred to the world of the electronic mass media as the Fifth Estate.

It was in recognition of the special importance and influence of the electronic mass media that we wrote the first edition of this book—a companion to our earlier book, *The First Amendment and the Fourth Estate.*

Since the last edition four years ago, electronic mass media regulation has continued its rapid change and development. For example, as this book was going to press, the F.C.C. substantially changed many of its media concentration rules, see Appendix D. Meanwhile, technological developments, especially digital television and the Internet, have raised a host of new legal questions.

This Sixth Edition continues to reflect our belief that a proper understanding of this subject is possible only through examination of the opinions and decisions of the governmental bodies most directly responsible for the laws and regulations that apply to the electronic mass media: Congress, the Federal Communications Commission and the courts.

The book is divided into three parts. Chapters I and II serve as an introduction to the legal, technological and economic structure that has produced our system of electronic media regulation. Chapters III through XII detail the laws and regulations that apply specifically to the electronic media. Finally, Chapters XIII through XVI outline some of the more important laws applicable to both print and electronic media.

We have used the earlier editions of the book in teaching undergraduate, graduate, and law students and have incorporated what we have learned from that experience, but we welcome, of course, comments about ways of using the book or improving it.

Thanks are due to the American Law Institute for excerpts from the Restatement (Second) of Torts. Joel Baras, Spencer Cordell, Chris Powers and Jacqueline Rutigliano deserve special thanks for their help with the research for this edition.

T. Barton Carter
Marc A. Franklin
Jay B. Wright

June, 2003

*

v

SUMMARY OF CONTENTS

*

TABLE OF CONTENTS

TABLE OF CASES

Principal cases are in bold type. Non-principal cases are in roman type. References are to Pages.

———————

xxiii

*

THE FIRST AMENDMENT

AND

THE FIFTH ESTATE

REGULATION OF ELECTRONIC MASS MEDIA

*

Chapter I

INTRODUCTION

The rapidly changing law and regulation of electronic media in the United States presents a challenge both to communications students and to law school students. This casebook surveys the law and regulation with which both types of students need to become familiar.

Law school students will typically have had such courses as constitutional law, contracts, torts and civil procedure before they undertake the more specialized study of electronic media law. They need to know the specialized law in this area if they, as practicing attorneys, are to give advice to media clients.

Most students in communications schools, on the other hand, will be *consumers* of legal advice. They will need to know when to ask for such advice and how to be guided by it. Presumably, an intelligent professional in any aspect of communications should know enough about law and public policy to make on-the-spot judgments. This is particularly true in the electronic media, where deadline pressures often require quick decision-making. The competent professional also needs to know enough to alert a superior when a potential legal problem is spotted and should know, particularly after reaching management level, how to use an attorney's advice in arriving at a decision.

With some experience, the consumer of legal advice learns how to take the attorney's advice. Some attorneys are much more cautious than others, and they will tend to give advice discouraging clients from airing some controversial materials that could lead to law suits. Other attorneys, particularly those who represent major media, may be much more daring and may say to a client, "Air what you need to. You're the journalist, and you know best what you think has to be aired. If you get sued, it will be my responsibility to defend you."

Newcomers are sometimes surprised to discover how unclear the law seems to be. Many questions have never been anticipated by legislators nor been answered by the courts. This is especially true with the electronic media, where technological developments are constantly raising new issues. Sometimes in two similar cases in different parts of the country, different courts have reached different conclusions. Bright attorneys disagree when they predict the outcomes of cases. Judges— even the nine justices of the Supreme Court of the United States— frequently disagree with one another and arrive at split decisions based on 5–4 or 6–3 votes. Newcomers to the law may be surprised to find, after they have read the opinion of the majority of the Court and agreed with it, that they also agree with points made in the dissenting opinion. It should not be quite so surprising that frequently there are good arguments on *both* sides of a dispute that has reached the Supreme Court.

Textbooks like this one give heavy emphasis to opinions of the Supreme Court because those opinions influence the application of the law in the courts below and they influence out-of-court settlements made on a much less formal basis. They also, of course, have an impact on rules and regulations imposed on electronic media by the Federal Communications Commission. It should be recognized, however, that a case that reaches the Supreme Court is an unusual case rather than a typical one. If, for example, we were to examine 1,000 instances in which the electronic media had aired something erroneous about individuals, we would probably find that most of the resulting "disputes" were resolved by the media's retracting the erroneous statements or by the unhappy individuals' being advised that they did not have libel cases because they really suffered no reputational harm as a result of the errors, or by the individuals' deciding that they did not have the time, inclination or money to file a lawsuit. Even if 100 of those disputes resulted in lawsuits, the odds would still favor an out-of-court settlement or a decision by a trial court without getting into the appellate courts. If a single one of those 100 lawsuits reached the Supreme Court it would be surprising. For the last few years, the Court has handed down only about 75 decisions per year.

If Supreme Court cases are so relatively rare, one might ask, why not study the "ordinary" cases instead? The answer, of course, is that the way communications professionals and attorneys assess their chances of winning or losing a suit, and thereby decide whether to pursue it in court or to settle out of court, is by applying the principles from decisions in the major cases.

In this chapter we look not just at the Supreme Court cases but at a variety of sources of law in America and at the way legal cases proceed.

A. THE LAW

Law has always been an important force in American life—and courts have always been at the center of our legal system. All state constitutions created state court systems. The United States Constitution established the Supreme Court of the United States and empowered Congress to create lower federal courts. Many critical national questions have been addressed and resolved in court, from sedition questions after the Revolutionary War to the treatment of blacks after the Civil War, from school desegregation beginning in the 1930s, '40s and '50s to questions of Presidential behavior in office. Hindsight shows that not all judicial decisions over 200 years have been correct, nor have they all been popular. But the overall respect Americans have for the legal system, even when they may disagree with particular decisions or dislike particular judges, has allowed the country to solve most major problems without violent upheavals. In general terms, the law is a system of rules of conduct that individuals and institutions are expected to follow, rules given force by a community's decision to punish those who violate them.

1. SOURCES AND STRUCTURE OF LAW AND THE LEGAL PROCESS

a. *Sources of Law*

In the United States, laws and sanctions for disobeying them come from four major sources: constitutions, statutes, administrative decisions and the judge-made law called the common law.

Constitutions. Although much of our legal system was borrowed from Great Britain, that country has no written constitution. This important form of law was developed in the United States. Not only is there a federal constitution, but each state has one. These documents decree governmental organization, describe the duties and responsibilities of governmental branches and officials and frequently specify certain individual rights, such as freedom of expression.

A constitution is written to allow flexibility as social conditions change. As new questions arise courts must ascertain whether the document permits or requires certain conduct. For instance, the First Amendment to the United States Constitution reads in part: "Congress shall make no law . . . abridging the freedom of speech, or of the press. . . ." As simple as this seems, our study of electronic media law will show the complexity of these words.

Statutes. Another source of law is the array of statutes passed by Congress, state legislatures, and city and county governments. The law we inherited from Great Britain generally served as basic authority in the early days of the United States. After that, statutes adopted by legislative bodies began to be more important than judicially developed law. Today, statutes are the dominant form of lawmaking. Much judicial time is spent interpreting these laws and deciding how they apply to specific situations. Statutes are general in scope and prospective in operation.

Statutes are also used to create administrative agencies, specifying exactly how much authority they have. For example, the Communications Act of 1934 created the Federal Communications Commission. All criminal laws in this country are now statutory. Crimes must be described carefully so that people know precisely what is forbidden. Case law could rarely provide sufficient guidance.

Administrative Regulations and Decisions. Much law comes from decisions of administrative agencies. These were first developed by Congress as a way to bring expertise to bear on areas under the legislature's responsibility. The first administrative agency was the Interstate Commerce Commission, but today such agencies are numerous. The Federal Communications Commission and the Federal Trade Commission, both of which affect electronic media law, are just two of the federal agencies. Administrative agencies also exist on the state and city levels. Much more law is created by these agencies through their delegated lawmaking powers than by all the courts in the country. We will return to administrative law and some of these agencies later in this chapter.

Common Law. The term "common law" is sometimes used to distinguish the Anglo–American legal system from the "civil law" systems of continental Europe. More commonly, the term refers to those areas of law in which no statutes exist and, thus, in which courts are expected to chart their own decisional course without legislative direction. The product of this process, law based on cases alone, is called common law. It is the ever growing result of specific but principled decisions in individual disputes rather than a written body of prospective general rules set down by a legislature.

The common law came from England, where the term first was used to distinguish law made by the King's courts from that made by ecclesiastical courts. But if the law were made by courts, not following a written statute, could not each court—each judge—decide similar cases in different ways? Not only would this cause consternation among citizens who would not know how to act, but judges might totally reconsider whole areas of law as each case arose. The concept of *stare decisis* emerged from these concerns. This is the doctrine of precedent under which judges refer to previous decisions involving basically similar legal issues and facts in order to decide the case at hand. It is then possible to look at previous cases and decisions to see how a court is likely to decide future cases. However, courts are not strictly bound by *stare decisis*. They can "distinguish" a current case from previous cases and refuse to follow the guidance of the past if they find the facts sufficiently different. Or, in an unusual situation, a court can overrule precedents and explicitly embark on a new approach to the legal area. In general, though, judges work within the boundaries of *stare decisis*.

Although the common law was dominant at the time of the Revolution, the increasing complexity of our society and other factors have brought about legislation in almost all areas—and a consequent reduction in the role of the common law. It still retains importance for us, however, in the areas of defamation and privacy.

b. Hierarchy

There is a hierarchy among these four sources of law. Within a state the state constitution is dominant. If a question is not answered in the constitution, an appropriate statute, as interpreted by the courts, will be the final word. But a statute in conflict with the constitution will be struck down by the courts.

Within the spheres of their statutory authority, administrative agency rulings have the force of a statute and will be upheld by courts unless the ruling violates the constitution, the agency has violated its own rules in making the decision or the agency is arbitrary and capricious. Courts examine decisions by zoning commissions and public utility commissions according to these criteria.

When no constitution or statute or administrative agency ruling controls, courts will apply common law principles to decide a dispute.

c. *Federalism*

The hierarchy just discussed applies within a single state. But the federal structure of the United States creates a second hierarchy of legal sources that must be explored. When the United States Constitution was written, most space was devoted to creating the three branches of government—Legislature in Article I, Executive in Article II and Judiciary in Article III. Those articles dealt only with how the federal government should conduct its internal affairs. In this respect, the federal government's structure resembled that of a state government.

However, the nature of federalism required that some attention be paid to the relationship between the existing state governments and the new federal government. This was addressed in Article VI, Section 2, the Supremacy Clause, which provides that:

> This Constitution, and the Laws of the United States which shall be made in pursuance thereof . . . shall be the supreme Law of the Land; and the Judges in every State shall be bound thereby, any Thing in the Constitution or Laws of any State to the Contrary notwithstanding.

This aspect of federalism becomes important because some of our cases involve claims that state laws are invalid because they conflict with some federally protected right. Notice also that state court judges are obligated to declare state laws invalid if they conflict with federal provisions.

Finally, notice how important the courts are at every stage of the legal system. Although courts act only to resolve specific disputes that the parties cannot settle, the judicial power permeates every layer of the two hierarchies. When a constitutional provision is relied upon by one of the parties to the dispute, the court must interpret the provision's meaning and its application to the dispute before it. When one party relies upon a statute, the court may have to interpret it—and may also have to decide whether it is consistent with the state's constitution. When an administrative ruling is involved in the dispute, the court must decide whether the agency acted constitutionally, acted within its statutory authority, followed its own rules, and acted without being arbitrary or capricious. When none of these sources appears to have a bearing on the litigation, the court turns to common-law decisionmaking.

When federalism is involved, state and federal courts are obligated to assure that in cases of conflict proper scope is given to the federal provisions in resolving the case before them.

d. Litigation

The judicial system must deal with several kinds of controversies.

Some controversies, for example, arise out of decisions by federal administrative agencies like the Federal Communications Commission. Throughout its history, the FCC has made decisions on issues ranging from the initial granting of licenses to broadcasters to, more recently, auctions for spectrum space. The Commission makes rules and regulations. It decides whether broadcasters have violated those rules and regulations. Like the decisions of other regulatory agencies, FCC decisions are subject to appeal, and appellate courts may be called upon to decide whether the FCC acted appropriately. These matters are normally civil; that is, there is usually no allegation of criminal behavior on the part of the broadcaster.

A variety of other civil matters are also addressed by the judicial system. When one party sues another for breach of contract, it is a civil case. When a decision must be made as to whether a journalist is protected from having to divulge secret sources or other confidential information, it is a civil matter. When one party sues another because the second party somehow harmed the first, the party suing is alleging that the defendant committed a *tort*—a civil wrong or injury. Libel, slander and several kinds of invasion of privacy are examples of torts for which plaintiffs can bring civil lawsuits that must be decided by the judicial system. If one party were to go to court and ask for an order to stop the other party from doing something, that action (i.e., seeking an injunction), is also a civil matter. If one thought that a statute were unconstitutional, one could initiate a lawsuit to have the statute so declared; that, too, would be a civil matter. Or, one might go to court to seek an injunction to stop government authorities from enforcing such a law; that, too, would be a civil matter.

The judicial system also, of course, concerns itself with criminal law—cases in which defendants are alleged to have committed crimes. Although there are certainly instances in which people in the media commit crimes, such cases are obviously much less frequent than the civil cases in which people in the media find themselves. In criminal law, facts are disputed: can the victim accurately identify the defendant or is the jury persuaded by the defendant's alibi witnesses? In conventional criminal cases, the parties agree on the legal rules but they disagree about the facts—and a trial is needed to determine the facts governed by these rules.

In most of the cases in this book, and most First Amendment cases generally, the crucial questions that will determine the outcome do not depend on disputed facts. Rather, the parties usually disagree over what legal rule applies to an accepted set of facts. Such a dispute raises legal questions to be resolved by a judge, often with no need for a trial.

The dispute will be brought in one of two court systems—state or federal. Before the United States Constitution was adopted, each state had its own court system—with trial and appellate courts. These systems survived. As a result of the adoption of the United States Constitution, and early action of Congress, a second court system—the federal system—was created.

When one party sues another party in the same state, under state libel law, for example, the trial—if there is one—will take place in a state court. When the parties are individuals or corporations in different states, questions beyond our present concerns arise about whether the litigation will take place in a state or federal court. Regardless, the trial will provide the opportunity for the presentation of evidence, including testimony by witnesses. Usually a jury would hear the case, but in some instances the trial judge will decide the case alone.

If there has been a trial, or if the judge has made a legal ruling on a motion on an agreed upon set of facts, either or both of the parties may be dissatisfied. They may believe that errors were made—either errors in procedure or errors in substantive law. If they choose to appeal to a higher (appellate) court, they will submit a transcript of the lower court proceedings and a *brief,* a document explaining the alleged errors, to the appellate court. Virtually every system permits the right to one appeal. However, although one is entitled to one's "day in court" and even a second day in an appellate court, higher courts often do not have to take cases for review unless they choose to do so.

Depending on the size of the state and the complexity of the state system, state judgments might be appealed to one or more levels of appellate courts before reaching the highest court in the state—typically, but not always, called the supreme court. In the federal system, decisions from the trial court, called the U.S. District Court, are appealed to a regional court of appeals and then to the Supreme Court of the United States. Federal administrative agency decisions are appealed directly to a court of appeals.

The Supreme Court performs two distinct roles. As the final appellate court for litigants who have lost cases in *federal* courts, it is the apex of the federal system. As such, it construes federal statutes just as state courts construe state statutes. In a discussion on obscenity and indecency, for example, we will encounter cases in which defendants have been prosecuted for violating *federal* statutes. Some other cases are tried in federal courts because the parties in the case are from different states. When such a *diversity of citizenship* exists, the federal court may provide a more neutral forum for the resolution of the dispute than a state court might, but the federal court applies the law of the state in which the court is located. The second distinct role that the Supreme Court performs is in hearing appeals on cases from the *state* courts: states and state courts have obligations imposed upon them by the United States Constitution, and the Supreme Court is sometimes called upon to decide if those obligations have been met. For example, Article I, Section 10, of the Constitution states that no state may adopt an *ex post facto* law or coin its own currency. Other limitations are imposed by the Supremacy

Clause of Article VI, Section 2, which declares that when federal and state law conflict, the federal law is supreme—and the judges of the state courts are required to recognize that supremacy. The Supreme Court of the United States has the power to review the actions of state courts to assure that states are complying with federal obligations.

Some of the cases we consider have come to the Supreme Court from the state courts. The losing party has usually claimed that the decision of the state courts has incorrectly interpreted the First Amendment—which applies to the states because of the Fourteenth Amendment, as will be explained shortly. Although state courts may render decisions interpreting the First and Fourteenth Amendments, the Supreme Court is the *final* authority on the meaning of the United States Constitution.

If a case poses an important question involving the First Amendment or some other part of the United States Constitution, it can wind up in the Supreme Court whether it starts in the state courts or in the federal courts.

In most instances the Supreme Court has been given discretion by Congress to choose what cases it will hear, and of the many thousands of cases that are brought each year, the Court accepts fewer than 200 for hearing and decision. To seek review by the Supreme Court, the litigant who lost the case in the lower court files what is called a "petition for *certiorari*" stating the nature of the dispute, the decision below, and the reasons why the Court should review this case. Because a case usually reaches the Supreme Court only after several lower courts, state or federal, have considered it, it rarely suffices for the petitioner to allege that the judges below made a mistake—a better reason is necessary. A serious claim that a state law violates the First Amendment is such a reason.

After the petition for *certiorari* is filed, the party who won below will usually file a memorandum trying to persuade the Court either that the case is not important, that there is no conflict with other decisions or that the decision is clearly correct in light of previous Supreme Court cases. In deciding whether or not to grant a petition for *certiorari*, all the justices will meet in conference and vote. The Court follows the so-called "rule of four" under which, if four justices believe the case should be heard, the petition for *certiorari* will be granted.

If the Supreme Court decides not to hear the case, it will usually not state its reasons and will issue an order that says simply "The petition for *certiorari* is denied." In this book that procedure is indicated when "*certiorari* denied" is part of the citation. Although this outcome favors the party that won in the lower court, the legal effect is different from having the Supreme Court listen to the case on the merits and decide to affirm the decision of the lower court. When the Supreme Court denies *certiorari*, all that is clear is that the Court did not think the case worthy of full consideration. This does not mean that the Court believes that the case was correctly decided below. It may mean only that the Court does not think the issue is important enough to justify further attention.

When the Supreme Court decides it will listen to a case, it will generally issue an order "granting" the petition for *certiorari* and directing the parties to file formal briefs arguing the merits of the controversy. The losing party below, the petitioner, prepares a brief, trying to persuade the Court to decide the case on the merits in petitioner's favor. The respondent's brief seeks to persuade the Court to affirm the result reached by the lower court.

The Court will schedule oral arguments at which the attorneys representing both parties have a limited period of time before the justices of the Court to make the best arguments they can for their clients and to answer questions posed by the justices. Because new evidence is not presented at the appellate level, and witnesses are not heard, the parties to the case need not even be present. In a sense, the discussion is about whether errors have been made in the trial court below, and it is not necessary to hear from the witnesses. The witnesses' testimony and other evidence is already reflected in the transcripts of the case filed with the Court, so the oral argument should, as the name suggests, focus on the attempts to persuade the justices as to the outcome of the case.

Following the oral arguments in the case, the justices meet privately to discuss the case and to indicate how they expect to vote. In the Supreme Court, if the Chief Justice is a member of the majority, he may assign the writing of the majority opinion to himself or to any of the other justices in the majority. Similarly, the senior justice among the dissenters may assign the dissenting opinion. When the Chief Justice is dissenting, the senior justice among the majority assigns the majority opinion. Drafts of opinions, written by the justices and their clerks, are circulated privately among the justices. Agreement is reached where possible, but the justices may publish their own opinions if they choose. In the "Pentagon Papers" case (see discussion of New York Times Co. v. United States later in this chapter), to use a most unusual example, all nine justices wrote opinions.

A single opinion that has the support of a majority of the participating justices is denominated an "opinion of the Court." As such it becomes binding on the Court, establishing a precedent for subsequent decisions (unless later overruled by the Court itself). Sometimes, however, while a majority of the Court agree on the outcome of a case, they do so for different reasons. For example, six of the nine justices might vote to affirm a lower court decision, but four could be doing so for one reason and two could be doing so for a different reason. In such a case, the opinion written by the four justices is a "plurality" opinion, not a majority opinion. Such an opinion is entitled to substantially less precedential value than an opinion of the Court. The first line of the reported decision will indicate the nature of the opinion—a named justice either delivers the "opinion of the Court" or announces "the judgment of the Court and an opinion joined by" up to three other justices. The "judgment of the Court" means the bare result, such as affirmance or reversal. The reasons for the judgment are found in the opinions.

2. READING THE LAW

Supreme Court decisions obviously are not written for readers who are totally unfamiliar with legal language. Typically, they refer to, or *cite,* earlier cases that you may or may not have to read. Not surprisingly, some of the justices are better writers than others. The meaning of some paragraphs may be perfectly clear, but some confuse even the best lawyers and require subsequent cases to resolve the confusion. Although reading Supreme Court decisions may seem difficult at first, it usually becomes easier as you become more familiar with the language and gradually develop some background in reading the law.

As you read the cases, note the names. When the losing party in the lower court files a petition for *certiorari*, the petitioner's name comes first in the title of the case. The initial plaintiff thus may later become the *respondent* and be listed second in the title in the Supreme Court. A few other appellate courts follow the practice of putting the losing party's name first. As you read the appellate cases in this book, do not assume that the party named first in the title was the original plaintiff.

On a related point, every title of a case is followed by a group of numbers and abbreviations called a "citation." This tells which volumes in the law library contain the full report of the opinions in the case. For example, the citation to Cox Broadcasting Corp. v. Cohn, 420 U.S. 469, 95 S.Ct. 1029, 43 L.Ed.2d 328, 1 Med.L.Rptr. 1819 (1975), means that the case can be found in volume 420 of the official *United States Reports* at page 469, and also in volume 95 of the *Supreme Court Reporter* at page 1029, and also in volume 43 of *United States Supreme Court Reports (Lawyers' Edition, 2d Series)* at page 328 and also in volume 1 of *Media Law Reporter* at page 1819. Opinions of the United States Court of Appeals are found in the *Federal Reporter Third Series* (F.3d). Decisions of the United States District Courts are found in the *Federal Supplement Second Series* (F.Supp.2d). State decisions usually have two citations: one to a state reporter and one to a private service that groups state decisions in regional volumes. Thus, in Taylor v. KTVB, 96 Idaho 202, 525 P.2d 984 (1974), the first reference is to volume 96 of the official *Idaho Reports* at page 202, and the second is to volume 525 of the *Pacific Reporter, Second Series*, page 984, where the Idaho case will also be found.

In addition to citing judicial opinions, we will cite the *U.S. Code Annotated* (U.S.C.A.), an unofficial publication of federal statutes. The comparable official publication is the *U.S. Code* (U.S.C.) but U.S.C.A. includes useful comments and references to judicial decisions. We will also cite the *Code of Federal Regulations* (C.F.R.), which contains rules and regulations of the federal regulatory agencies, including the FCC.

There are certain reporting services of special importance to electronic media regulation. The FCC's official reports from 1986 and earlier, the *FCC Reports*, are referred to by volume number, F.C.C. or

F.C.C.2d, followed by page number. Beginning with materials from October 1986, the Commission's official record, including decisions, reports, public notices and other documents, is the *FCC Record*. It is cited by volume number, F.C.C.Rcd. and the page number. When the Commission proposes rules for possible adoption, formal notice of the pending action must be given to the public. This is done through the *Federal Register* (Fed.Reg. or F.R.). The register is organized chronologically and covers all federal agencies and departments. An unofficial service of Pike & Fischer, Inc., reports on Commission rulemaking and case decisions as well as court decisions. Known for many years as *Radio Regulation*, it is cited as R.R. or R.R.2d, or sometimes as P & F Radio Reg. Despite its name, the service has long included television decisions as well as telephone and other common carrier decisions. In December 1995 it was renamed *Communications Regulation*, cited as Communications Reg. (P & F) or C.R.

The foregoing discussion of litigation and the role of the Supreme Court has necessarily been general and abstract. As we turn to actual cases, you should review this information if some aspect of a case puzzles you. Any unusual matters will be discussed in the introduction to the case or in the notes that follow the opinions.

Some of the terms used in the texts, particularly the Latin ones, may be unfamiliar to you at first. Although there are a variety of legal dictionaries published, some in paperback, you will probably find most of the terms defined in any good collegiate dictionary. As you see them used in the cases, they will become part of your legal vocabulary.

B. THE FIRST AMENDMENT

In the United States, regulation of the mass media is different from the regulation of any other industry. What distinguishes it is the First Amendment to the Constitution of the United States: "Congress shall make no law . . . abridging the freedom of speech, or of the press. . . ." A brief examination of the historical roots of the First Amendment and its interpretation by the courts is necessary for an understanding of electronic mass media regulation.

1. INTRODUCTION TO FREEDOM OF EXPRESSION

a. *The English Background*

In England repression of ideas antithetical to the government was in operation by the 13th century. In 1275 and again in 1379, Parliament made it criminal to speak against the state. Later known as "seditious libel," words that questioned the crown in any way were punished by the King's Council sitting in the "starred chamber." Ecclesiastical laws forbidding heresy already existed, thus making it dangerous to say anything in opposition to the Church or the state.

With the advent of printing, around 1500, the government became even more concerned about statements that questioned the secular powers. To prevent the wider dissemination that the printing press made possible, the Crown established a system of censorship, similar to the one already used by the Church, for all publications. This repression lasted until almost 1700. The core of the censorship system was licensing. Unlicensed publication could lead to severe punishment and to charges of criminal libel.

In addition to criminal prosecutions for libel, the English government found taxation to be an effective way to control the press. The purpose of the Stamp Act of 1711 and later laws was to reduce the circulation of newspapers. Half of England's newspapers went out of business in the first year of the Act.

Despite such measures, it was possible for Great Britain still to contend that freedom of the press existed. Sir William Blackstone, the most famous compiler of the common law, wrote in the late 1760s:

> [w]here blasphemous, immoral, treasonable, schismatical, seditious, or scandalous libels are punished by the English law . . . the liberty of the press, properly understood, is by no means infringed or violated. The liberty of the press is indeed essential to the nature of a free estate; but this consists in laying no previous restraints upon publications, and not in freedom from censure for criminal matter when published. Every freeman has an undoubted right to lay what sentiments he pleases before the press: to forbid this is to destroy the freedom of the press: but if he publishes what is improper, mischievous, or illegal, he must take the consequences of his own temerity. . . .

W. Blackstone, 4 Commentaries on the Laws of England 151–52 (1765–69).

Blackstone is central to this analysis because he was a major influence on English and American legal thinking in the period when our Constitution was taking shape. His definition of freedom of the press as the absence of "previous restraints upon publications," and the distinction between liberty thus defined, and licentiousness, for which punishment was considered legitimate, made clear that freedom of expression meant, at a minimum, rejection of prior restraint. Uncertainty remains as to the legitimacy of subsequent punishment for seditious libel, and as to what types of expression constitute punishable "licentiousness."

b.   The Colonial Experience

Those who drafted and adopted the United States Constitution and the Bill of Rights were well aware of this background of repression in Great Britain. They also knew of, and had experienced, similar restrictions on freedom of expression imposed by Britain on the colonies. The British Stamp Act of 1765 was directed specifically against the colonies and was meant to offset "the expense of defending, protecting and securing" the colonies. In fact, the Act served more to anger colonists than to raise revenue. The colonists saw the Act as "taxation without representation" and rebelled against it.

Prior to that, however, laws that applied to the press in England during the 17th and 18th centuries were also applied to the emerging colonial press, and the licensing of presses in the colonies closely paralleled the English practice. The colonies saw printers jailed and their books burned for publishing without permission.

In 1734 John Peter Zenger, who printed the *Weekly Journal,* was charged with seditious libel by the Governor General of New York, whom Zenger had criticized. Zenger spent almost a year in jail awaiting trial. By the traditional common law standards he was surely guilty because he had published the articles in question, and the law did not recognize truth as a defense. Zenger's lawyer, Andrew Hamilton, convinced the jury that the only question in the case involved the liberty to write the truth, and the jury, despite the judge's instructions, acquitted Zenger. Although the verdict set no precedent (because a jury verdict is not a ruling on the law), it did signal a change in the political climate.

After the American Revolution, the governments of the former colonies sought to come together to form a nation. Even before the war was ended, the colonies had attempted to form a national government under the Articles of Confederation, devised in 1783. This document allowed the states to retain much power, leaving little for the central government. The Articles contained no mention of freedom of expression, but many argued such a clause was not necessary. Because the federal government had no power to interfere with citizens, there was no need to forbid it from exercising power it did not have. Additionally, most states had some form of bill of rights in their own constitutions.

The new Constitution, formulated at the Constitutional Convention of 1787, created the national government with three branches. Some states in their own constitutions had protected citizens against state government action, but the federal Constitution was not primarily concerned with that problem. The omission led some critics to oppose ratification because the new government itself might threaten the freedom of citizens of the new country.

Although the records of the Constitutional Convention are sketchy, it is known that discussion of a bill of rights did not take place until the last few days of the meeting. That short-lived debate was inconclusive. The Constitution was promulgated without a bill of rights and sent to the states for ratification.

During ratification debates there was much enthusiasm for freedom of the press but no clear idea of exactly how it should be protected or how far it should extend.

Even though 13 states ratified the Constitution, five expressed concern that a bill of rights had been omitted.

As a result of this dissatisfaction, James Madison introduced a set of amendments to the Constitution when the First Congress met. The House of Representatives approved an amendment that protected freedom of speech and press from infringement "by any state." The Senate struck the provision limiting the powers of the states and the final version provided that "Congress shall make no law . . . abridging the freedom of speech, or of the press. . . ." This was the third of 12 amendments submitted to the states for ratification. When the first two failed at that time, this became the First Amendment to the United States Constitution.

Although it was later argued that the Bill of Rights was intended to protect citizens against invasions by the state as well as the federal government, this was rejected in Barron v. Baltimore, 32 U.S. (7 Pet.) 243 (1833) when the Supreme Court decided that the Bill of Rights applied solely against the federal government. Constraints on the states were those specified in Article I, Section 10 and in such other provisions as the Supremacy Clause.

Though on its face the First Amendment appears to bind only the Congress, it is well established today that the prohibitions of the First Amendment extend to all branches of both the federal and state governments by way of the "due process" clause of the Fourteenth Amendment. The First Amendment guarantees, the Supreme Court has held, are a fundamental element of the "liberty" protected by the Fourteenth Amendment. Gitlow v. New York, 268 U.S. 652 (1925).

As a result, what Congress may not do because of the First Amendment, a state may not do because of the Fourteenth Amendment. The Constitution restrains only governments, not private individuals from interfering with the exercise of freedom of expression.

In Free Speech in the United States (1941), Professor Zechariah Chafee, Jr., acknowledging that little was said at the time about the meaning of freedom of speech, reviewed some contemporary statements that suggest that in the years before the First Amendment "freedom of speech was conceived as giving a wide and genuine protection for all sorts of discussion of public matters." He argued that "such a widely recognized right must mean something," and that merely reaffirming the freedom of the press from previous censorship would have been pointless. During the 18th century, besides the narrow legal meaning of liberty of the press, there existed "a definite popular meaning: the right of unrestricted discussion of public affairs," and Chafee thought the framers were aware of basic differences between Great Britain and the former colonies.

2. BASES FOR FREEDOM OF COMMUNICATION

Professor Thomas I. Emerson, in The System of Freedom of Expression 6–9 (1970), asserted that "the system of freedom of expression in a democratic society" is based on four premises:

(1) freedom of expression facilitates self-fulfillment,

(2) it is an essential tool for advancing knowledge and discovering truth,

(3) it is a way to achieve a more stable and adaptable community, and

(4) it permits individuals to be involved in the democratic decision-making process.

Perhaps the most powerful judicial statement of the justifications for free expression is that of Justice Louis Brandeis, concurring in Whitney v. California, 274 U.S. 357, 375–77 (1927):

> Those who won our independence believed that the final end of the State was to make men free to develop their faculties; and that in its government the deliberative forces should prevail over the arbitrary. They valued liberty both as an end and as a means. They believed liberty to be the secret of happiness and courage to be the secret of liberty. They believed that freedom to think as you will and speak as you think are means indispensable to the discovery and spread of political truth; that without free speech and assembly discussion would be futile; that with them, discussion affords ordinarily adequate protection against the dissemination of noxious doctrine; that the greatest menace to freedom is an inert people; that public discussion is a political duty; and that this should be a fundamental principle of the American government. They recognized the risks to which all human institutions are subject. But they knew that order cannot be secured merely through fear of punishment for its infraction; that it is hazardous to discourage thought, hope and imagination; that fear breeds repression; that repression breeds hate; that hate menaces stable government; that the path of safety lies in the opportunity to discuss freely supposed grievances and proposed remedies; and that the fitting remedy for evil counsels is good ones. Believing in the power of reason as applied through public discussion, they eschewed silence coerced by law—the argument of force in its worst form. Recognizing the occasional tyrannies of governing majorities, they amended the Constitution so that free speech and assembly should be guaranteed.

How many of Emerson's premises do you find in the Brandeis view?

Each of these explanations has been used, to a greater or lesser extent, by the Supreme Court to justify the high value placed on freedom of speech in our constitutional scheme of government. Each may justify different notions of the breadth and depth of the First Amendment freedom and each may apply with peculiar force in particular contexts.

These fundamental justifications for protecting speech tend to divide into two main groups: those that stress the values to the individual and those that stress the values to the society of freedom of speech. The emphasis on value to the individual, contained in what are variously called the self-fulfillment or self-realization models, is on the importance of expression as a route to individual development and fulfillment.

a. For Individuals

A concept of "natural law" was actively discussed for a century before the Constitution was adopted. In attempting to reconcile government's role with individual rights, certain personal freedoms were seen as inviolable. They were "natural rights" of individuals, rights that official persons or bodies had no power to affect. Among these rights was freedom of expression.

This concept derived in large part from the 17th century English philosopher John Locke, who contended that government's purpose was to use its power to protect life, liberty and property, natural rights to which each individual was entitled. Locke's views influenced the language of the First Amendment with the notion of free speech as a natural right, and the Fifth Amendment ("No person shall . . . be deprived of life, liberty, or property, without due process of law. . . .").

Locke discussed the origin of society in terms of a social contract. He believed the pre-social status was one of freedom. Private property was recognized, but no security existed. To achieve security, people surrendered a certain amount of freedom to establish a government. But the government rested on the consent of the governed, who would control the government rather than vice versa. A government that encroached on an individual's rights should be abolished or changed.

Several commentators believe that even with this Lockean philosophy to draw on, the framers had no clear concept of the First Amendment's purpose. No matter what the framers might have had in mind, however, they could not have foreseen the many changes in media technology and society generally. Thus, more expansive views of freedom of communication became necessary.

b. For Society

Neither disputing nor relying upon the assertion that we as individuals profit from freedom of speech, the society-centered reasons offered for protection explain why we as a people are better for having First Amendment freedoms.

Marketplace of Ideas. The seminal view that freedom of expression enhances the social good came from John Milton's *Areopagitica* in 1644. Milton, an English poet and essayist, wanted a divorce and wrote an essay he hoped would lower the strict legal barriers prohibiting it. He was chastised for publishing without a license and wrote Areopagitica to induce Parliament to allow unlicensed printing. Milton argued that licensing was unworkable and an affront to those who had views to express. But more, he said, it was harmful to society, since people are better able to function as citizens if they are knowledgeable and exposed to different points of view. Attempting to assuage official fears that the Crown's views would be overwhelmed if unlicensed printing were allowed, Milton wrote: "And though all the winds of doctrine were let loose to play upon the earth, so Truth be in the field, we do injuriously by licensing and prohibiting to misdoubt her strength. Let her and Falsehood grapple; who ever knew Truth put to the worse, in a free and open encounter?"

English philosopher and economist John Stuart Mill, who wrote 200 years after Milton, believed more in full and free discussion than did Milton. Mill thought that society could function well only with such freedom. He saw freedom of thought, discussion and investigation as "goods in their own right" but, more importantly, thought that society benefits from an exchange of ideas. People could trade their false notions for true ones, but only if they could hear the true ones. Such open discussion would necessarily mean that false as well as true ideas would be expressed.

The concept of the marketplace of ideas, first enunciated by Milton, was recognized in American law by Justice Oliver Wendell Holmes. It was later developed by Mill, who was more skeptical about the ultimate emergence of truth in the marketplace. In Patterson v. Colorado, 205 U.S. 454, 462 (1907), Justice Holmes observed that the First Amendment prevents all "previous restraints upon publications," but allows "the subsequent punishment of such as may be deemed contrary to the public welfare. . . . The preliminary freedom extends to the false as well as to the true; the subsequent punishment may extend as well to the true as to the false." He took a broader view in Abrams v. United States, 250 U.S. 616 (1919). Abrams and others had been accused of publishing pamphlets that criticized Pres. Woodrow Wilson's sending of troops to help counter the Russian revolution. The pamphlets also advocated a strike against American munitions plants. A majority of the Supreme Court ruled that publishing such pamphlets during wartime was not protected by the First Amendment. In dissent, Justice Holmes, joined by Justice Brandeis, argued that the pamphlets did not attack the form of the United States government, and thus did not violate the sedition statute as charged.

The marketplace of ideas approach has been criticized from several sides. In a Marxist attack, American philosopher Herbert Marcuse disagreed with the basic premise of the marketplace notion, that rational beings engage in a free interchange of opinions and information. People are not rational because government and mass media manipulate them— each for its own purposes, he said. In an essay entitled "Repressive Tolerance" in *A Critique of Pure Tolerance* (1965), he started from the premise that "the people must be capable of deliberating and choosing on the basis of knowledge." He was appalled by the broadcaster's reporting of the momentous and the mundane in the same monotone: "It offends against humanity and truth by being calm where one should be enraged, by refraining from accusation where accusation is in the facts themselves."

Marcuse said the "concentration of economic and political power" allows "effective dissent" to be blocked where it could freely emerge, and the "monopolistic media" prejudge "right and wrong, true and false . . . wherever they affect the vital interest of the society." The situation was so dangerous, Marcuse believed, that he recommended "suspension of the right of free speech and free assembly" so that "spurious objectivity" is replaced by "intolerance against movements from the Right, and toleration of movements from the Left."

Another group adopted a quite different approach. In the mid–1940s, the Commission on Freedom of the Press was organized to study the press in America. Funded primarily by Time Inc. and Encyclopedia Britannica, Inc., and chaired by Robert M. Hutchins, the Commission was composed of philosophers, historians, law professors and others. No media professionals were included on the panel, but some were called to share their views with Commission members. The Commission found that press freedom was not seriously threatened in mid–20th century America. The press had, however, despite the enforcement of antitrust laws, become increasingly concentrated in the hands of fewer individuals. Media owners, in fact, were reasonably free from government interference, but the First Amendment had little direct application to most people.

One Commission member, Professor Chafee, stated that the press could not play its proper part in society in the "mere absence of governmental restrictions." Rather, "affirmative action by the government or others," would be needed. Chafee started with Justice Holmes' formulation, "The best test of truth is the power of the thought to get itself accepted in the competition of the market." *Abrams,* p. 17, *supra.* But how, Chafee asked, could views compete in a market constricted because of a lack of media outlets? He answered that "a free market requires regulation, just as a free market for goods needs law against monopoly. . . . The government can lay down the rules of the game which will promote rather than restrict free speech." Such laws might require "essential facilities accessible to all," methods to assure that communication channels remain open, and measures directed at particular communication industries "intended to promote freedom, improve content, or otherwise make them perform their proper function in a free society." Z. Chafee, 2 Government and Mass Communications 471 ff. (1947).

Later law professor Jerome A. Barron adopted the same approach. He said the marketplace is an antiquated and impractical concept because of changes in the media and society since 1791. It is difficult for a person to begin a broadcast service because of limits in spectrum allocation or to begin a newspaper because of the prohibitive cost. Barron found censorship by media because they limit the views they disseminate and permit few new or unpopular ideas to be heard widely. Barron concluded that those who do not control media should be able to express their views through the mass media. "At the very minimum," Barron wrote, "the creation of two remedies is essential—(1) a nondiscriminating right to purchase editorial advertisements in daily newspapers, and (2) a right of reply for public figures and public officers defamed in newspapers." J. Barron, Freedom of the Press for Whom? 6 (1973). See also, Barron, Access to the Press—A New First Amendment Right, 80 Harv.L.Rev. 1641 (1967).

Safety Valve. When a government permits freedom of expression, it not only allows society to be exposed to a wide range of ideas, it also brings about a stable and adaptable community, according to the late Professor Thomas Emerson. T. Emerson, The System of Freedom of Expression, 11–14 (1970). Substituting force for logic, which is what happens when freedom of expression is suppressed, makes it impossible to come to rational decisions. In addition, coercion is ineffective in changing thoughts and beliefs. Instead, stifling expression breeds discontent that focuses not on the issues being suppressed, but on the act of suppression itself.

Emerson argued that freedom of expression will not cause society to become fragmented, to divide into opposing camps. Rather, suppression of communication will do that. Freedom of speech and press will allow dissidents to express their ideas "in a release of energy, a lessening of frustration and a channeling of resistance into courses consistent with law and order."

Self-governance. A third reason that freedom of communication is valuable in a democratic society is that such a society is based on self-governance, on an informed citizenry that will intelligently elect its representatives. James Madison believed that the people, not the government, were sovereign, and that the main purpose of freedom of speech was to allow citizens to govern themselves in a free society.

In the late 1940s, Professor Alexander Meiklejohn agreed that self-governance was the most important concern of the First Amendment. He advocated distinguishing between two kinds of expression. Speech concerning the self-governing process was "political speech" and deserved absolute protection from governmental interference. Speech that was nonpolitical in character, "private speech," was protected only by the due process clause of the Fifth Amendment, which permits the government some leeway for regulation.

Meiklejohn drew this distinction between political and private speech because he believed the central purpose of the First Amendment is to give citizens the greatest opportunity to discuss and hear about society's problems, the very information one must have to function in a self-governing society.

Meiklejohn's emphasis on self-government might have suggested that the First Amendment would protect only what we conventionally regard as political speech. His vagueness on this point in his 1948 edition was criticized by Chafee, who was concerned about what types of speech were being relegated to the Fifth Amendment's protection. Chafee observed that "there are public aspects to practically every subject." If Meiklejohn intended this broad view of the First Amendment, then Chafee wondered how there could be any limitations in such traditionally regulated areas as obscenity and libel. If, however, Meiklejohn were to place scholarship and the arts in the category of private speech, Chafee would regard it as "shocking to deprive these vital matters of the protection of the inspiring words of the First Amendment." Book Review, 62 Harv.L.Rev. 891, 900 (1949).

3. THE FIRST AMENDMENT AND THE INSTITUTIONAL PRESS

"Congress shall make no law . . . abridging the freedom of speech, or of the press. . . ."

The lack of a broad consensus concerning the philosophical underpinnings of the majestic words of the First Amendment does not mean that the courts and legislatures of the United States are released from the obligation to obey the Amendment's dictates. To the contrary, our nation's lawmaking bodies have clearly acknowledged that the Amendment represents a constitutional bar to government action in numerous situations.

An appreciable and important fraction of these situations involves the institution of "the press," including the electronic press. This chapter sketches some of those elements of First Amendment doctrine that apply most directly to the press. Students interested in a more comprehensive exposition of First Amendment doctrine might consult M. Nimmer, Nimmer on Freedom of Speech (1984).

a. *Restriction on Government Power*

Liberty protected under the Fourteenth Amendment against encroachments of state governments is protected to the exact same extent that the First Amendment itself protects the freedoms of speech and press from the federal government. Lawyers and judges have developed the shorthand expression "incorporation" to express this idea. Because the First Amendment has been "incorporated" into the Fourteenth Amendment, its prohibitions are no less specific by virtue of such incorporation. This means that branches of the state governments are bound, to the same extent as the federal government, to respect the guarantees of the First Amendment.

Despite the considerable expansion of the field of operation of the First Amendment as a result of the incorporation doctrine, it is important to remember that the First Amendment is a bar only to abridgments by government. Private parties are free to "abridge" another's exercise of the speech and press clauses at will so long as they do not violate some other valid law in the process. For example, it is established that a right to distribute printed material is part and parcel of the First Amendment freedoms and the government is prohibited from interfering with such distribution. Lovell v. Griffin, 303 U.S. 444 (1938). On the other hand, private owners of properties may prohibit such distributions from taking place on their own property without running afoul of the

First Amendment. See PruneYard Shopping Center v. Robins, 447 U.S. 74 (1980).

b.   *The Protected Sphere*

Speech v. Conduct. More difficult than determining who is prohibited from interfering with protected expression is determining what forms of expressive activity fall within the protected category. Perhaps the most basic line between the protected and the unprotected is suggested by the distinction between "speech" and "conduct." Presumptively, at least, all oral and written communication falls within the protected sphere, and non-verbal conduct remains outside the domain of the First Amendment. Difficulties abound when verbal and non-verbal elements— "symbolic speech"—are mixed into a single expressive activity, such as labor picketing, protest marches or the wearing of armbands.

Consider, for example, United States v. O'Brien, 391 U.S. 367 (1968). *O'Brien* resulted from the burning, on the steps of the South Boston Courthouse, of Selective Service registration certificates by David Paul O'Brien and three companions during the Vietnam War. O'Brien did not deny burning his certificate; he told the jury he did so to influence others to adopt his antiwar beliefs. Appealing his conviction ultimately to the Supreme Court, O'Brien maintained that his burning of the certificate was "symbolic speech" protected by the First Amendment.

Chief Justice Warren, in the opinion for the Court, wrote:

> This Court has held that when "speech" and "nonspeech" elements are combined in the same course of conduct, a sufficiently important governmental interest in regulating the nonspeech element can justify incidental limitations on First Amendment freedoms. . . . [W]e think it clear that a governmental regulation is sufficiently justified if it is within the constitutional power of the government; if it furthers an important or substantial governmental interest; if the governmental interest is unrelated to the suppression of free expression; and if the incidental restriction on alleged First Amendment freedom is no greater than is essential to the furtherance of that interest.

Finding that the statute under which O'Brien was convicted met all of the requirements, the Court upheld O'Brien's conviction.

O'Brien is, of course, not a media case, but it has taken on particular importance for the electronic media because the requirements set forth in it have been used to determine the constitutionality of cable regulation in such cases as Home Box Office Inc. v. Federal Communications Commission (1977), Quincy Cable TV, Inc. v. Federal Communications Commission (1985) and Century Communications v. Federal Communications Commission (1987), all discussed in Chapter IX.

Another example of symbolic speech is found in Tinker v. Des Moines Independent Community School District, 393 U.S. 503 (1969), which established that public students' First Amendment rights, including the wearing of armbands, could be limited only if their exercise would cause material and substantial interference with school operations or a collision with the rights of others.

Protection for symbolic speech stirred public opinion in 1989 when the Supreme Court decided 5–4 that a Texas flag-desecration law was unconstitutional because of the First Amendment. Texas v. Johnson, 491 U.S. 397 (1989). The decision led to widespread calls for a Constitutional amendment and to the Federal Flag Protection Act of 1989, Congress's own attempt to protect the American flag from being burned or defaced. In two cases decided a year later, the Court, with the same 5–4 split, found the federal statute constitutionally flawed in the same way as the Texas statute because it suppressed expression. United States v. Eichman and United States v. Haggerty, 496 U.S. 310 (1990). Public opinion polls made clear that the First Amendment is not always popular; a New York Times/CBS News poll that year found that 83 percent of respondents thought flag burning should be against the law, and 59 percent would favor a constitutional amendment if it were the only way to make flag destruction illegal. New York Times, June 12, 1990, at p. B7. Critics said that making such an exception to the First Amendment would set a dangerous precedent.

Non-protected Speech. Though speech *generally* is a protected activity, the Supreme Court has long placed certain categories of words outside the First Amendment's protection. In 1942 the Court asserted, in Chaplinsky v. New Hampshire, 315 U.S. 568 (1942), that certain classes of expression might be subject to legal sanctions. Chaplinsky had been arrested for calling a town marshal a "God-damned racketeer and a damned Fascist." The Supreme Court characterized the expression as "fighting words . . . likely to cause violence." The words were not protected expression because they invited a violent response by the person to whom they were directed. The Court then observed that other types of speech, including obscenity and libel, were similarly outside the protection of the First Amendment. Many people presumed that "hate speech" was similarly unprotected, but the Court ruled in a 1992 case, R.A.V. v. City of St. Paul, Minn., 505 U.S. 377 (1992) that the First Amendment prohibits the government from "silencing speech on the basis of its content." A St. Paul ordinance made it a crime to engage in speech or behavior likely to arouse "anger or alarm" on the basis of "race, color, creed, religion or gender." A white teenager was accused of violating the law by burning a cross on the lawn of a black family's house. Justice Scalia, writing for a 5–member majority of the court, said "St. Paul has not singled out an especially offensive mode of expression. . . . It has not, for example, selected for prohibition only those 'fighting words' that communicate ideas in a threatening, as opposed to merely obnoxious manner." The other four justices found the St. Paul ordinance to be unconstitutional on the basis of overbreadth—thinking that there was too great a risk that it might deter speech or expression that deserved constitutional protection. Although "hate speech" (as we see from the St. Paul case) and some libels (as we shall see in Chapter XIII) are protected by the First Amendment, obscenity continues to remain outside of First Amendment protection.

Distribution. Freedom of speech and press have been held to imply more than the freedom only to speak and write. The First Amendment guarantees include the right to disseminate the words produced after creating them. In a milestone case, a city ordinance in Griffin, Ga., prescribed criminal penalties for distributing printed material without permission. The Court found the ordinance was overly broad because it included all "literature," making no distinction between that which the First Amendment does and does not protect. Also, the ordinance gave the city manager unbridled censorship powers since he was given no criteria for decision and was not obligated to explain why he refused permission to distribute. Lovell v. Griffin, 303 U.S. 444 (1938).

In 1988 the Supreme Court overturned portions of a newsrack ordinance in Lakewood, Ohio, that had given the mayor and an architectural review board unlimited discretion in denying permits for placement of newsracks on city property. A majority of the sitting justices held that distribution of newspapers is conduct related to expression and is therefore protected by the First Amendment. City of Lakewood v. Plain Dealer Publishing Co., 486 U.S. 750, 15 Med.L.Rptr. 1481 (1988).

In City of Cincinnati v. Discovery Network, Inc., 507 U.S. 410, 21 Med.L.Rptr. 1161 (1993), the Supreme Court held that a city ordinance prohibiting newsrack distribution of "commercial" publications (such as magazines listing real estate for sale) but allowing newsrack distribution of "non-commercial" publications (including newspapers) violated the First Amendment. The Court held that commercial publications could not be singled out to bear the entire burden of restricting the total number of newsracks in the interests of aesthetics and safety.

A federal court of appeals upheld an architectural commission's guideline banning of all "street furniture"—including newsracks—from Boston's Historic Beacon Hill District. The court held that the guideline was content neutral and that it did not violate the First Amendment because the commission's aesthetic concerns constitute a significant government interest, the guideline is narrowly tailored, and ample alternative channels exist for the distribution of the newspapers that challenged the guideline. Globe Newspaper Co. v. Beacon Hill Architectural Commission, 100 F.3d 175, 24 Med.L.Rptr. 2537 (1st Cir.1996).

Gathering. The "right to gather" information from willing private sources began to take shape in 1972 with two cases. In Kleindienst v. Mandel, 408 U.S. 753 (1972), American scholars sought to invite Mandel, a Belgian Marxist economist, to attend conferences and to speak at several American universities. Congress had barred visas for aliens who advocated "the economic, international and governmental doctrines of world communism or the establishment in the United States of a totalitarian dictatorship." After concluding that Mandel, as an alien, had no constitutional right of entry, the Court turned to the rights claimed by the scholars:

> The Government . . . suggests that the First Amendment is inapplicable because [the scholars] have free access to Mandel's ideas through his books and speeches, and because "technological developments," such as tapes or telephone hookups, readily supplant his physical presence. This argument overlooks what may be particular qualities inherent in sustained, face-to-face debate, discussion and questioning. . . . We are loath to hold on this record that existence of other alternatives extinguishes altogether any constitutional interest on the part of the [scholars] in this particular form of access.

The Court, however, concluded that this interest was overcome by the government's longstanding power to make rules for excluding aliens.

The second case to provide some indirect support for protection of gathering was Branzburg v. Hayes, 408 U.S. 665, 1 Med.L.Rptr. 2617 (1972). Although the Court held that the reporters had no First Amendment right to refuse to testify before a grand jury, the majority acknowledged that the Court was not suggesting "that news gathering does not qualify for First Amendment protection; without some protection for seeking out the news, freedom of the press could be eviscerated." The case is discussed in Chapter XVI.

Refusal to Speak. Most freedom of communication questions concern whether the government can prevent a person from, or punish a person for, speaking. In Chapter III we will see that another question is whether individuals can be forced to speak against their will. In the latter situation the broadcast media and the print media are treated quite differently.

c. Abridgment Defined

Determining whether the press is engaged in protected speech represents only half the question in evaluating whether a constitutional issue has been raised under the First Amendment. Courts must also determine whether an abridgment has taken place.

Prior Restraints. In the traditional view, prior restraints represented the quintessential, indeed exclusive, abridgments of speech. "Prior restraint" meant that rather than punishing the publisher by criminal or civil sanctions for what had been published, the government barred the publication from occurring in the first place. This is, of course, the essence of censorship. In English history the censor was an administrative official, who administered the licensing system. Recall the view of Blackstone, p. 12, *supra.*

Although it might have been argued that only administrative or executive branch behavior could constitute a prior restraint, it has become clear in this country that judicial orders that bar publications are also analyzed as prior restraints. Nonetheless, court orders imposing prior restraints are thought somewhat less objectionable than similar administrative actions because of a perception that administrators may cut procedural corners and otherwise be unfair in executing their obligations. Even so, some administrative prior restraints are permitted even today. The most obvious example is that the Supreme Court has permitted states to license motion pictures. Under such a system, it is a crime to exhibit a film that has not been approved in advance, even if the film is totally unobjectionable on any ground. This type of licensing system was upheld in Freedman v. Maryland, 380 U.S. 51, 1 Med.L.Rptr. 1126 (1965), so long as the administrative decision was subject to swift judicial review.

The deep-seated antagonism to prior restraint is seen in the Supreme Court's decision in Near v. Minnesota, 283 U.S. 697, 1 Med. L.Rptr. 1001 (1931), the first case in which the Court invalidated a state law because it violated the First and Fourteenth Amendments to the United States Constitution. More specifically, *Near* involved a Minnesota statute allowing officials to stop publication of "malicious, scandalous, and defamatory" newspapers and periodicals. Once stopped, publication could be resumed only on order of a judge, who would have to approve the content before allowing continued printing. The county attorney had brought an action to stop publication of a Minneapolis newspaper, *The Saturday Press*. The newspaper had accused certain government officials of being involved in bootlegging and gambling that it said were controlled by a "Jewish gangster."

The Supreme Court of the United States reversed the state court. Chief Justice Charles Evans Hughes, writing for the 5–4 majority, noted that Blackstone's observation that "[t]he liberty of the press . . . consists in laying no *previous* restraints upon publications . . ." was too broad. Although prior restraint is presumed to be unconstitutional, "the protection . . . is not absolutely unlimited." The Court then suggested some areas in which such restraints might be upheld:

> No one would question but that a government might prevent actual obstruction to its recruiting service or to the publication of sailing dates of transports or the number and location of troops. On similar grounds, the primary requirements of decency may be enforced against obscene publications. The security of the community life may be protected against incitements to acts of violence and the overthrow by force of orderly government. The constitutional guaranty of free speech does not "protect a man from an injunction against uttering words that may have all the effect of force." [ ]

Because the defendant's charges in the Near case did not come within any of these categories, prior restraint was impermissible.

The Court similarly struck down a Rhode Island system for reviewing publications for possible obscenity in Bantam Books, Inc. v. Sullivan, 372 U.S. 58, 1 Med.L.Rptr. 1116 (1963), a prior restraint on distribution of leaflets critical of a Chicago real estate agent in Organization for a

Better Austin v. Keefe, 402 U.S. 415, 1 Med.L.Rptr. 1021 (1971), and a restraint on publication of the "Pentagon Papers" in New York Times Co. v. United States, 403 U.S. 713, 1 Med.L.Rptr. 1031 (1971). In these decisions, the Court has said that "Any system of prior restraints of expression comes to this Court bearing a heavy presumption against its constitutional validity," and that the party seeking a restraint "carries a heavy burden of showing justification for the imposition of such a restraint."

A federal district judge in Wisconsin issued a preliminary injunction in 1979 restraining *The Progressive* magazine from publishing an article by Howard Morland about the H-bomb. Some people in communications law feared that the case could become the first Supreme Court case in which a prior restraint against the news media would be upheld, but the so-called "secret of the H-bomb" was published in other media before that ever happened, and the government withdrew its request for an injunction. The government might have gone ahead with criminal proceedings but did not. *The Progressive* published its article.

In 1980 Public Broadcasting Service broadcast a "documentary drama" portraying a love affair between a Saudi princess and a commoner, and their subsequent execution. The program also dwelt on some aspects of Saudi Arabian life that the Saudi government asserted were totally misrepresented. The program was patterned on a true story.

If the Saudi government had made a credible threat to cut off all oil shipments to the United States immediately upon the presentation of the program, and if the best evidence had been that such a cutoff would cripple the American economy, would the government have been able to obtain an injunction against the showing of the program? Is it crucial that no "secret" is involved?

A different aspect of the problem will be seen in Muir v. Alabama Educational Television Commission, discussed in Chapter VII.

In those rare instances in which prior restraints are imposed, they usually are reversed relatively promptly. As prominent media attorney Floyd Abrams has said, "The reasons for prior restraint always sounds pretty good, and the potential for damage to First Amendment rights always sound minimal [so judges may yield to requests for restraints], yet appellate courts have reversed consistently and quickly." In 1990 alone, there were several restraints, including a couple on electronic media, all eventually lifted. "Inside Edition" was temporarily restrained from broadcasting a videotape of a physician allegedly engaged in malpractice; the order was vacated by the court of appeals 11 days late. In re King World Productions, Inc., 898 F.2d 56, 17 Med.L.Rptr. 1531 (6th Cir.1990). Lifetime Cable was restrained from showing "Hilary in Hiding" about a custody battle on the grounds that irreparable harm would come to the child because of descriptions of sexual abuse; the order was vacated the same day. In re Lifetime Cable, 17 Med.L.Rptr. 1648 (D.C.Cir.1990).

That same year the issue of a prior restraint to protect a defendant's fair trial rights arose again in the case of former Panamanian leader Manuel Noriega, and the restraint was not so quickly overturned. Cable News Network (CNN) had obtained tape recordings of Noriega talking to members of his defense team. Normally, of course, attorney-client conversations are confidential. Fearing that Noriega's future trial could be prejudiced by CNN's playing of the tapes, the U.S. District Court for the Southern District of Florida issued a temporary restraining order barring their playing. The U.S. Court of Appeals for the Eleventh Circuit affirmed the ruling, and the Supreme Court of the United States, without a written opinion, refused to overrule the lower courts or to review the order. Cable News Network, Inc. v. Noriega, 498 U.S. 976, 18 Med.L.Rptr. 1358 (1990). Justices Thurgood Marshall and Sandra Day O'Connor dissented. The Supreme Court's action would not necessarily have precluded their considering the prior restraint later, but the trial court subsequently lifted the restraint and essentially ended the dispute.

CNN was subsequently convicted of criminal contempt of court as a result of its 1990 airing of Noriega's conversations with his attorneys. U.S. prosecutors had charged that CNN "knowingly and willfully" disobeyed an order by the judge not to air the tapes. Federal District Court Judge William Hoeveler convicted CNN and said CNN would be required to pay a "substantial fine" plus $85,000 in prosecution costs unless it broadcast an admission of error, in which case it would have to pay only the prosecution costs. CNN, in a statement approved by the judge, then announced that "it was in error in defying the order of the court and publishing the Noriega tape while appealing the judge's order." Broadcasting & Cable, April 4, 1994 at 57, and Entertainment Law Reporter, Jan. 1995 at 26.

Journalists subjected to restraining orders they believe to be unconstitutional have sometimes disobeyed those orders. The question has always been whether a subsequent finding that the restraining order was unconstitutional serves as a defense against a contempt citation for disobeying the order. In United States v. Dickinson, 465 F.2d 496 (5th Cir.1972), a federal judge ordered the media not to publish any testimony taken at a hearing for fear it might prejudice an upcoming state trial. Two reporters violated the order, were cited for criminal contempt and were fined $300 each. The court of appeals held the order unconstitutional but ruled that it had to be obeyed until overturned on appeal. The court held that such orders must be followed unless there is "a showing of 'transparent invalidity' or patent frivolity surrounding the order." The Supreme Court denied *certiorari*. 414 U.S. 979 (1973).

In the case titled In re Providence Journal Co., 820 F.2d 1342, 13 Med.L.Rptr. 1945 (1st Cir.1986), rehearing en banc 820 F.2d 1354, 14 Med.L.Rptr. 1029 (1st Cir.1987), a federal district court had held *The Providence Journal* and its executive editor in contempt of court for publishing truthful information obtained under the Freedom of Information Act while it was under a temporary restraining order (TRO) not to do so. The TRO was sought by a person who claimed the government had obtained the information in the first place by means that violated the person's constitutional right to privacy—and that its release was improper. The judge offered to decide the merits in the next day or two after the TRO was entered. The newspaper asked the judge to defer for another day, during which it published the information.

Although the judge later denied the preliminary injunction, he found the newspaper in contempt. The basis for requiring obedience to the TRO was that a court "ought to have time to determine legal issues presented to it, and has the right in the meantime to preserve the *status quo.*" The judge rejected the newspaper's argument that the plaintiff's claim was frivolous, and sentenced the newspaper to a fine of $100,000 and the executive editor to 18 months probation and 200 hours of public service.

The court of appeals reversed, holding that the district court's original restraining order was transparently invalid and that it constituted a presumptively unconstitutional prior restraint on pure speech by the press. The court held that the requisite heavy burden of proof necessary to justify such a restraint was not met and that the newspaper and editor should have been allowed to challenge its constitutionality at the contempt proceedings and that the order could not serve as the basis for a contempt citation.

A petition for rehearing *en banc* was granted, and the court added to, and modified, the panel opinion in a *per curiam* opinion holding that in such a case the publisher must make a good faith effort to seek emergency relief from the appellate court, and may proceed to publish and challenge the constitutionality of the order in the contempt proceedings only if timely access to the appellate court is not available or if timely decision is not forthcoming.

Although the Supreme Court of the United States granted *certiorari* in the case in 1987, it dismissed the case because of a procedural issue: the Court held that because the court-appointed special prosecutor had not obtained the solicitor general's authorization before filing for *certiorari,* he lacked authority to appear on behalf of the United States. 485 U.S. 693, 15 Med.L.Rptr. 1241 (1988).

Business Week magazine was subjected to a prior restraint in the fall of 1995 when a U.S. District Court judge in Ohio restrained publication of a story based on sealed documents related to a lawsuit between the Procter & Gamble Co. and Bankers Trust Co. Both Procter & Gamble and Bankers Trust had requested a restraining order when they learned that *Business Week* had the documents. A lawyer who worked for the law firm representing Bankers Trust but who was not working on the Procter & Gamble case and did not know the documents were sealed had provided copies of the documents to a *Business Week* reporter who had asked for them. Within a week of the trial judge's order, U.S. Supreme Court Justice John Paul Stevens was asked to stay the restraining order. He declined to do so, saying that he thought the "wiser course" was to give the district court and the court of appeals time to consider the merits of the First Amendment issue before it would be addressed by the Supreme Court. McGraw–Hill Companies, Inc. v. Procter & Gamble, 515 U.S. 1309, 23 Med.L.Rptr. 2247 (1995).

The U.S. Court of Appeals for the Sixth Circuit, in a 2–1 decision, called the injunction a "classic prior restraint," and held it to be unconstitutional. "Not only did the District Court fail to conduct any First Amendment inquiry before granting the two [temporary restraining orders], but it compounded the harm by holding hearings on issues that bore no relation to the right of Business Week to disseminate the information in its possession." Chief Judge Gilbert Merritt of the Sixth Circuit said the court was guided "by the holding of the First Circuit in [*Providence Journal,* p. 27, *supra*] that even a temporary restraint on pure speech is improper 'absent the most compelling circumstances.' . . . We can only conclude that, had the District Court not been rushed to judgment by both parties and had it engaged in the proper constitutional inquiry, the injunction would never have been issued." Procter & Gamble Co. v. Bankers Trust Co., 78 F.3d 219, 24 Med.L.Rptr. 1385 (6th Cir.1996).

Subsequent Sanctions. Though far less compelling from an historical point of view, it is quite clear that sanctions imposed after publication may be like prior restraints, in that they may prevent would-be speakers and writers from publishing protected speech. Such sanctions, whether they are penal in nature, such as imprisonment or fines, or civil damage awards or the denial of some privilege, generally raise precisely the same issues as prior restraints on publication. Recall Justice Holmes's comment in Patterson v. Colorado, p. 17, *supra*, that the First Amendment prevents all "previous restraints upon publications" but allows "the subsequent punishment of such as may be deemed contrary to the public welfare." Holmes' view that it was possible to make such a distinction so sharply has given way to a different view, as exemplified in a case involving *The Virginia Pilot.*

The *Virginia Pilot,* a newspaper published by Landmark Communications, Inc., was found guilty of a misdemeanor and fined $500 plus costs after it accurately reported that a named judge was under investigation by a state commission in a confidential proceeding. Chief Justice Burger delivered the opinion of the Court, reversing the decision of the Supreme Court of Virginia: "We conclude that the publication Virginia seeks to punish under its statute lies near the core of the First Amendment, and the Commonwealth's interests advanced by the imposition of criminal sanctions are insufficient to justify the actual and potential encroachments on freedom of speech and of the press which follow therefrom." Landmark Communications, Inc. v. Virginia, 435 U.S. 829, 3 Med.L.Rptr. 2153 (1978).

In Smith v. Daily Mail Publishing Co., 443 U.S. 97, 5 Med.L.Rptr. 1305 (1979), the Supreme Court was faced with a statute that made it a crime for a newspaper to publish a juvenile offender's name unless the paper had obtained the prior written approval of a court. The paper argued that the prior approval requirement acted in "operation and effect" like a licensing scheme. The Court decided the case in favor of the newspaper but avoided the question of whether the system had operated as a prior restraint:

> . . . [E]ven when a state attempts to punish publication after the event it must nevertheless demonstrate that its punitive action was necessary to further the state interests asserted [citing *Landmark*]. Since we conclude that this statute cannot satisfy the constitutional standards defined in *Landmark Communications, Inc.,* we need not decide whether, as argued by respondents, it operated as a prior restraint.

Neutral Regulation. The great proportion of government regulation of the press has never been considered to be abridgment so long as it is fairly applied, despite the considerable costs such regulation may exact from the press. Thus, for example, one may not operate a broadcasting station without obeying local building codes, the income tax laws and other tax statutes, the antitrust laws, the Occupational Safety and Health Act, or any of the myriad other bodies of general regulatory law administered by local, state and federal governments.

4. APPLYING THE FIRST AMENDMENT

An "abridgment" of protected speech is not, despite the apparently unqualified language of the First Amendment, necessarily unconstitutional.

a. *Balancing*

Most frequently, the Supreme Court has used a "balancing test" to determine the propriety of a restraint on freedom of expression. The test involves weighing two interests—the government's concern about protecting a particular interest, such as national security or individual reputation, and the individual's and society's interests in expression.

Professor Chafee, an early advocate of balancing, expressed the virtues of that approach in his Free Speech in the United States (1941) at 31 as follows:

> Or to put the matter another way, it is useless to define free speech by talk about rights. The agitator asserts his constitutional right to speak, the government asserts its constitutional right to wage war. The result is a deadlock. . . . To find the boundary line of any right, we must get behind rules of law to human facts. In our problem, we must regard the desires and needs of the individual human being who wants to speak and those of the great group of human beings among whom he speaks. That is, in technical language, there are individual interests and social interests, which must be balanced against each other, if they conflict, in order to determine which interest shall be sacrificed under the circumstances and

which shall be protected and become the foundation of a legal right. It must never be forgotten that the balancing cannot be properly done unless all the interests involved are adequately ascertained, and the great evil of all this talk about rights is that each side is so busy denying the official's claim to rights that it entirely overlooks the human desires and needs behind that claim.

Most freedom of expression cases are decided by balancing interests. The Supreme Court, without always explaining its approach, will use one of two variations of the balancing test. Focusing on the interests at stake in the individual case is commonly characterized as "ad hoc" balancing: the specific interests applicable to the facts of the particular case are considered crucial. The court attempts to identify the state's interest in limiting or preventing the speech in question and the would-be speaker's and society's interests in having the speech permitted.

At other times, a more general process, called "definitional" or "categorical" balancing, is used. Here the interests analyzed transcend the merits of a particular case. Rather than asking, for example, whether the value of speech in a particular case outweighs the arguments for proscribing it, the Court might generalize and consider the values of that category of speech, or that category of speaker, and develop a more general analysis. Recall *Chaplinsky,* p. 22, *supra.*

b. *Preferred Position*

A basic tenet of constitutional law calls upon courts to presume that enactments of legislative bodies are constitutional. If the legislation has a rational basis, courts will generally hold it constitutional. In United States v. Carolene Products Co., 304 U.S. 144 (1938), involving the validity of a federal economic regulation, Justice Stone, writing for the majority, restated this generally accepted view of deference to legislatures. But in one of the Court's most famous footnotes, footnote 4, Justice Stone wrote:

> There may be narrower scope for operation of the presumption of constitutionality when legislation appears on its face to be within a specific prohibition of the Constitution, such as those of the first ten amendments, which are deemed equally specific when held to be embraced within the Fourteenth. . . .

> It is unnecessary to consider now whether legislation which restricts those political processes which can ordinarily be expected to bring about repeal of undesirable legislation, is to be subjected to more exacting scrutiny under the general prohibitions of the Fourteenth Amendment than are most other types of legislation. . . .

Justice Stone was suggesting that legislation that inhibits political freedoms, such as freedom of communication, must survive more "exacting judicial scrutiny" than other legislative acts. Instead of having a presumption of constitutionality, such legislation might be presumed to inhibit a basic freedom and the government might have to show an overriding need for it, not simply a rational basis. As a result of some cases that built on this footnote, freedom of communication became a "preferred freedom," one that courts would not allow the legislature to restrict without a compelling state interest.

c. *Clear and Present Danger*

The balance between speech and anti-speech interests is struck in a wide variety of issues affecting mass media. In defamation, for example, speech interests are balanced against the individual's interest in reputation. In other cases, speech interests must be balanced against privacy interests, property interests, security interests, public safety and morals, and even countervailing speech interests, to name only a few. The balance struck in each situation differs as the countervailing interests vary in weight and as the value of the speech interest itself changes in various contexts.

One important example of the balancing process is the evolution of the "clear and present danger" test originally framed by Justice Oliver Wendell Holmes in such cases as *Abrams,* p. 17, *supra,* and Schenck v. United States, *infra*. These cases represent the struggle of the courts to accommodate both the federal government's interest in maintaining the integrity of its effort to wage war and the dissenters' free speech rights. The Espionage Act banned attempts to cause insubordination in the armed forces or to obstruct military recruiting or to conspire to achieve these results. Most of these cases, which confronted the Court from 1919 until the mid–1920s, involved radical speakers who opposed the war effort and criticized the political and economic structure of the country.

Based on his marketplace of ideas approach, Justice Holmes saw the clear and present danger test as being least intrusive on freedom of expression in a society in which absolute freedom was impractical. In Schenck v. United States, 249 U.S. 47 (1919), Justice Holmes said that expression could be punished when "the words used are used in such circumstances and are of such a nature as to create a clear and present danger that they will bring about the substantive evils that Congress has a right to prevent. It is a question of proximity and degree."

Schenck involved a prosecution under the Espionage Act for publishing a leaflet that interfered with recruiting by urging young men to violate the draft law. Justice Holmes, writing for the majority, found that the leaflet could be closely connected with violations of the Conscription Act (proximity) and that this was a serious danger to the country's security (degree).

In *Abrams,* p. 17, *supra,* the Supreme Court upheld convictions in a case involving pamphlets calling for a strike of munitions workers. And six years later the Court upheld a conviction under a New York criminal statute that barred advocating overthrow of the government by violence. Gitlow v. New York, 268 U.S. 652 (1925).

The curious case of Dennis v. United States, 341 U.S. 494 (1951), involved prosecution of 11 leading members of the Communist Party for conspiring to advocate the forcible overthrow of the government of the United States. Although a plurality of the Court recognized that the Holmes–Brandeis position had evolved to become a majority view, the plurality refused to apply it to this case. The plurality observed that each case confronting Justices Holmes and Brandeis involved "a comparatively isolated event, bearing little relation in their minds to any substantial threat to the safety of the community. . . . They were not confronted with any situation comparable to the instant one—the development of an apparatus designed and dedicated to the overthrow of the Government, in the context of world crisis after crisis."

The Court adopted the test framed by Judge Learned Hand in the lower court: "In each case [courts] must ask whether the gravity of the 'evil,' discounted by its improbability, justifies such invasion of free speech as is necessary to avoid the danger." That statement "takes into consideration those factors which we deem relevant, and relates their significances. More we cannot expect from words." The plurality found that the requisite danger existed.

The status of clear and present danger remained unclear until Brandenburg v. Ohio, 395 U.S. 444 (1969), involving prosecution of a Ku Klux Klan member for advocating racial and religious bigotry. The Court pointed out that its decisions had "fashioned the principle that the constitutional guarantees of free speech and free press do not permit a State to forbid or proscribe advocacy of the use of force or of law violation except where such advocacy is directed to inciting or producing imminent lawless action and is likely to incite or produce such action." Because the criminal syndicalism statute under which Ohio proceeded permitted punishment of advocacy with no requirement of a showing that imminent lawless action was likely to follow, the convictions could not stand.

Despite the extended period during which the clear and present danger test has been discussed in the Supreme Court, its importance and utility must not be overstated.

d.   The Literalist Interpretation of the First Amendment

Some have argued that the First Amendment allows no room for interpretation because its language is absolute: "Congress shall make no law . . . abridging the freedom of speech, or of the press. . . ." They have concluded that the federal government "is without any power whatever under the Constitution to put any type of burden on speech and expression of ideas of any kind." Ginzburg v. United States, 383 U.S. 463, 476, 1 Med.L.Rptr. 1409, 1414 (1966)(Black, J., dissenting). Justice Black strongly criticized the balancing approach to First Amendment questions because the test could be used to justify a judge's predilections, but he did not believe that action should be protected to the same extent as speech.

Justice Black's distinction between speech and action provided the escape hatch for his absolutist view. For instance, he would not have required states to allow public high school students to wear black arm bands to protest the Vietnam war. Recall Tinker v. Des Moines Independent Community School District, p. 21, *supra*, (Black, J., dissenting). He called the behavior "action," not speech, and thus not protected by the First Amendment.

In his book, *The System of Freedom of Expression* 17 (1970), Professor Thomas Emerson drew a similar distinction, believing, with Justice Black, that expression should be absolutely protected by the First Amendment.

Recall Meiklejohn, too, believed in an absolute approach to the First Amendment—but only for "political speech." As with Justice Black and Emerson, his distinction narrows the types of expression to be afforded absolute protection, leaving to the courts the problem of defining "political speech" and differentiating it from unprotected or less protected expression.

5. "OR OF THE PRESS"

Until this point we have used the terms "freedom of speech" and "freedom of the press" interchangeably. Some have argued, however, that the speech and press guarantees have independent and distinct significance. Are some types of activity protected under the press clause not protected under the speech clause? Or are some activities, though they constitute protected speech, outside the press guarantee?

The most prominent proponent of the theory that the press clause is of different scope than the speech clause was Justice Potter Stewart, who contended, in a speech at Yale Law School reprinted in 26 Hastings Law Journal 631 (1975), that the press clause, unlike the speech guarantee, was a *structural* provision of the Constitution. Stewart relied heavily on the notion that the institutional press has a special role in our constitutional scheme as an additional check on the power of government officials. He asserted that because of this special role the institutional press in certain situations had rights of access and immunities growing out of the press clause to which the general citizenry could not lay claim.

Chief Justice Burger rejected this analysis. Concurring in First National Bank of Boston v. Bellotti, 435 U.S. 765, 3 Med.L.Rptr. 2105 (1978), he contended that the press clause of the First Amendment does not give the "institutional press" a special status. The Chief Justice thought the framers did not contemplate special privileges for the press, and he foresaw difficulty in defining what was and was not included in the "institutional press" if it were to be accorded special status.

Regardless of how the issue of special protection is resolved, it is true as a practical matter that certain First Amendment issues arise in connection with the institutional press, while others are generally raised in the context of individual speech.

C. ADMINISTRATIVE LAW

Congress usually creates administrative agencies when the task at hand requires continuing supervision, extensive technical considerations, or the development of expert skills, or all of these. The thought is that a group devoting full attention to such a problem may do a better job than Congress might do in sporadic legislative forays into an area. In 1927 Congress did not have the ability or time or desire to unravel the mess that had developed on the airwaves. The basic decision for Congress, in retrospect, was whether to decree a system of private ownership for the airwaves and to allow the courts to unravel the matters through lawsuits invoking property law, to opt for outright public ownership or to create an administrative body to develop and enforce an allocation system that would bring order from the chaos. As we will see in Chapter II, Congress chose the last of these.

All agencies must function within the direction that the legislature gives them by statute. Here, Congress had no specific idea how the Federal Radio Commission and its successor, the Federal Communications Commission (FCC), should proceed. Instead, Congress provided in § 303 of the Communications Act of 1934 that "Except as otherwise provided in this Act, the Commission from time to time, as public convenience, interest, or necessity requires shall [have powers to assign bands of frequencies to the various classes of radio stations and assign individual frequencies; decide the times each station may operate; establish areas to be served by any station; regulate the apparatus used with respect to the sharpness of the transmissions; take steps to prevent interference; suspend licenses upon a showing that a licensee has violated any statute or regulation or transmitted obscene communications; make rules and regulations that are necessary to carry out the other provisions of the statute; and require licensees to keep records the FCC may deem desirable]."

Notice that all these powers are conditioned on a showing that "public convenience, interest, or necessity requires" the regulation. This is a vague standard, and, as we shall see, the FCC has rarely been barred from acting on the ground that Congress did not authorize the particular regulation.

Despite the wide authority Congress has given the FCC in the regulation of electronic media, Congress does from time to time pass new legislation affecting the electronic media in major ways. In the Telecommunications Act of 1996, Congress made numerous changes in the law that are reflected in many of the chapters of this book. Among other things, Congress moved to deregulate cable rates, let local and long-distance telephone companies and cable companies into one another's businesses, and let television companies own stations that reach up to 35 percent of television viewers. Much of the media attention to the new act was devoted to the provisions outlawing transmission of sexually explicit materials to minors on computer networks and requiring television set manufacturers to equip new sets with a "V chip" so parents can electronically lock out shows labeled as offensive. Some of these new provisions faced court challenges immediately on First Amendment and other grounds, so it remains to be seen if they will be implemented.

An administrative agency such as the FCC usually functions in a variety of ways. Within its statutory authorization it may issue rules or regulations that have the virtual effect of statutes. At other times, it may have to choose between two applicants for a broadcasting license in what resembles a judicial proceeding. At still other times, it performs executive branch functions, as when it seeks out broadcasters or ham operators who are violating their licenses by using excessive power or unauthorized frequencies.

This variety of regulatory patterns may not comport with traditional understandings about the separation of powers, but these multi-function agencies have been with us for so long that little concern is voiced about their structure. As we shall see, however, questions are continually raised about whether the agency followed the statutory requirements in performing its functions, whether it followed its own rules, whether its decision was arbitrary and capricious and whether its processes met constitutional requirements.

An administrative agency like the FCC makes public announcements of possible changes in rules, through published Notices of Proposed Rulemaking (NPRMs), and similar announcements of inquiries, through Notices of Inquiry (NOIs). The public in general—and in particular those affected by the rules or inquiries—then have opportunity to voice their opinions for or against the proposed changes. In this way, such an agency is behaving as a quasi-legislature, providing room for debate before acting.

The rules or regulations adopted by the agency are, of course, binding on the people or businesses under its regulatory jurisdiction, but Congress always has the authority to create or change statutes, thus in effect overruling the administrative agencies.

There are literally hundreds of administrative agencies. Only a few of these are important to the electronic mass media. We turn now to a brief look at those particular agencies.

1. THE FEDERAL COMMUNICATIONS COMMISSION

In 1927 Congress created a five-member Federal Radio Commission to rationalize the radio spectrum and make allocations. In 1934 the agency was expanded to seven members, given jurisdiction over telephone and telegraph communication as well, and renamed the Federal Communications Commission. In 1982 Congress voted to return to a five-member commission. Each member is appointed by the President for a five-year term subject to Senate confirmation. No more than three members may be from the same political party. The terms are staggered so that no more than one expires in any year. If a member resigns in the middle of a term, the new appointment is only for the unexpired portion of that term. One consequence is that many of those appointed do not have the independence of beginning with a five-year term. The Chairman, chosen by the President, is the chief executive officer and has major administrative responsibilities, including the setting of the agenda. A chart showing the organization of the Commission is presented in Appendix C and is also available at the Commission's web site at www.fcc.gov/fccorgchart.html.

The FCC has six Bureaus and 10 Staff Offices. The most important for our purposes is the Media Bureau, including the Audio Division that licenses commercial and noncommercial educational AM radio, FM, Low Power FM, FM Translator and FM Booster broadcast services as well as the Video Division that licenses commercial and noncommercial educational TV, Low Power TV, Class A TV, TV translators and TV Booster broadcast services.

Also within the Media Bureau is the Industry Analysis Division, which conducts and participates in proceedings regarding media ownership and the economic aspects of existing and proposed rules and policies. The Division reviews license transfers that implicate significant policy issues.

Separate from the Media Bureau is the Enforcement Bureau, which enforces the Communications Act, as well as the Commission's rules, orders and authorizations.

When there is a hearing, it is conducted by the Commission's Office of Administrative Law Judges (OALJ). Such a proceeding is much like a trial, with documents and sworn testimony being received in evidence and cross-examination of witnesses. An Administrative Law Judge (ALJ) is an independent employee of the Commission. ALJs were formerly called Hearing Examiners. Following such a hearing, the Presiding Administrative Law Judge (PALJ) writes and issues an Intial Opinion that may be appealed to the full Commission.

When a decision by the Commission results in subsequent litigation, the Commission's Office of General Counsel takes over. That office also serves as the chief legal advisor to the Commission and assists in its decision-making.

President George W. Bush appointed Michael K. Powell (son of Secretary of State Colin Powell) Chairman of the FCC in 2001.

One of Powell's biggest supporters was Rep. W. J. "Billy" Tauzin (R.La.), chairman of the House Commerce Committee's telecommunications subcommittee, a strong advocate for change at the FCC. Tauzin said, "The new marketplace requires a new FCC that's built around a model of competition and choice rather than regulation." The Washington Post, Jan. 24, 2001 at E1.

Powell promised to restructure the organization, not by slashing jobs, but trying to make it more efficient.

For a description of the FCC's organization, see the agency's web site at www.fcc.gov/aboutus.html.

2. THE FEDERAL TRADE COMMISSION

The Federal Trade Commission (FTC) was established by the Federal Trade Commission Act (FTCA) in 1914. The Commission was initially charged with prohibiting "unfair methods of competition in commerce." As originally conceived, this phrase was intended to allow the FTC to enforce antitrust laws, laws that courts had viewed with some hostility. The agency also concerns itself with the Clayton Act of 1914, which outlaws specific practices recognized as instruments of monopoly. Soon the FTC tried to regulate deceptive advertising as a form of "unfair competition." In 1938 Congress passed the Wheeler–Lea Amendments to the FTCA explicitly giving the FTC the authority to regulate unfair or deceptive advertising.

Overseeing advertising is just one FTC task—though it, along with enforcing the antitrust laws, are the most important for the media. The agency is composed of five commissioners, including the chairman, appointed by the President and confirmed by the Senate for five-year terms. It has an annual budget of about $191 million (compared with $231 *billion* spent on advertising annually). Its other responsibilities include laws concerning antitrust violations, warranties, granting of credit, and label laws.

As an administrative agency, acting quasi-judicially and quasi-legislatively, the Commission deals with trade practices on a continuing and corrective basis. The FTC has no authority to punish; its function is to "prevent," through cease-and-desist orders and other means, those practices condemned by the law of federal trade regulation. However, court-ordered civil penalties up to $11,000 may be obtained for each violation of a Commission order or trade regulation.

Cases before the Commission may originate through a complaint by a consumer or a competitor, the Congress or from federal, state or municipal agencies.

3. NATIONAL TELECOMMUNICATIONS AND INFORMATION ADMINISTRATION

The National Telecommunications and Information Administration (NTIA) was established in 1978 as part of the Commerce Department, and NTIA is headed by the Assistant Secretary for Communications and Information. The reorganization that established NTIA combined within the new unit the former Office of Telecommunications Policy, which had been part of the Executive Office of the President, and the Office of Telecommunications of the Commerce Department. There had been concern about excessive Presidential influence on the Office of Telecommunications Policy during the Nixon administration.

In essence, NTIA is the telecommunications policy research department of the government. It does long-term studies into the effects of and need for telecommunication regulation. NTIA also advises the President on telecommunications policy issues.

NTIA's role is to formulate policies to support the development and growth of telecommunications, information and related industries; to further the efficient development and use of telecommunications and information services; to provide policy and management for federal use of the electromagnetic spectrum; and to provide telecommunications facilities grants to public service users.

4. EQUAL EMPLOYMENT OPPORTUNITY COMMISSION

The Equal Employment Opportunity Commission (EEOC), as might be imagined, is charged with enforcing the equal employment opportunity laws. Issues of illegal discrimination have become increasingly important for the electronic media, which are obligated to bear them in mind in making hiring or promotion decisions.

The EEOC was created by the Civil Rights Act of 1964 in an attempt to eliminate discrimination based on race, color, religion, sex or national origin in hiring, promoting, firing, wages, testing, training, apprenticeship and all other conditions of employment.

The Commission is a major publisher of data on the employment status of minorities and women.

Although the EEOC has primary responsibility for equal employment opportunities, broadcasters have had to comply with additional equal employment requirements imposed by the FCC since 1969. Federal judges struck down two versions of FCC equal employment requirements the judges viewed as unconstitutional quotas. See Lutheran Church–Missouri Synod v. FCC, 141 F.3d 344, reh'g denied 154 F.3d 487 (D.C.Cir.1998) and MD/DC/DE Broadcasters Association v. Federal Communications Commission, 236 F.3d 13 (D.C.Cir.2001).

The FCC in November 2002 approved a third version of industry recruiting rules. The new rules, effective in 2003, require broad outreach efforts by stations and require owners to document those efforts in their public files and to post them on their web sites, if they have them. Outreach efforts would include participation in job fairs, scholarships and internships. The commission said it would conduct random audits for compliance and would review performance at midterm and at license-renewal time. Although stations are not obligated to collect demographic data on employees or interviewees, they must document sources of referrals and specifics about the nature and extent of their advertising for job vacancies.

Stations can be fined or can have their licenses revoked for noncompliance. Broadcasting and Cable, Nov. 11, 2002, p. 20.

5. NATIONAL LABOR RELATIONS BOARD

The National Labor Relations Board (NLRB) was created by the National Labor Relations Act (NLRA) of 1935 (Wagner Act), as amended by the acts of 1947 (Taft–Hartley Act), 1959 (Landrum–Griffin Act), and 1974.

The Board has two principal functions: preventing and remedying unfair labor practices by employers and labor organizations or their agents and conducting secret ballot elections among employees in appropriate collective-bargaining units to determine whether or not they desire to be represented by a labor organization.

The electronic media are heavily unionized today with most management decisions affected to at least some extent by the various union contracts in effect.

D. INTERNATIONAL REGULATION OF ELECTRONIC MEDIA

Radio and television signals obviously do not stop at international borders, so neighboring countries' telecommunications concerns overlap. This is true whether one is talking about Western Europe, where a country has several nearby neighbors, or the United States, where we share a long border with Canada and a shorter one with Mexico.

The concern is not a new one. Napoleon III called a conference in Paris in 1865 to take some collective action to deal with technical standards, codes and tariffs for telegraph. Out of that conference came the International Telegraph Union, which has been called "the first genuine international, intergovernmental organization to see the light of day." Delegates to the conference adopted the international Morse code and agreed on the interconnection of important cities, hours of reception for telegrams, and the obligation to deliver messages from abroad.

Today's International Telecommunications Union (ITU) is a direct descendant of the group formed in Paris, but its interests go far beyond the "electric telegraph." Much of the technology of today and tomorrow—communications satellites, sea cables, fiber optics, dynamic radio systems, mass data storage and processing facilities—has and will have international implications. The constitution, statutes, administrative rules and regulation and case law of any single country obviously cannot govern the international traffic of messages, and international agreements are of increasing importance.

A reflection of that is the growth of the ITU. With more than 156 member nations today, it is headquartered in Geneva. Among its varied activities are the registration and management of frequencies and the collection and dissemination of massive amounts of information concerning telecommunications throughout the world.

The ITU Convention, which sets forth its rules of procedure, permits world and regional administrative conferences. A World Administrative Radio Conference (WARC) may have the authority to revise most of the regulations or may have jurisdiction only in a limited area. Such conferences in Geneva in 1959 and 1979 and in Atlantic City in 1974 had broad jurisdiction. For example, in Geneva in 1979, delegates from 140 member countries met to work on 14,000 proposals that had been submitted to amend the Radio Regulations. More limited WARCs have dealt specifically with Broadcasting Satellites, Aeronautical Mobile communications, and Space Telecommunications. Similarly, World Radiocommunications Conferences (WRCs) have had participants from 140 countries and have dealt with satellite spectrum allocations and a number of new broadband global satellite systems. More than 1,000 delegates are expected at the ITU World Radiocommunication Conference (WRC–2003) scheduled for June 2003 in Geneva.

More than 160 nations have signed World Intellectual Property Organization (WIPO) treaties in the 1990s addressing issues of protecting copyrighted works in cyberspace. WIPO, a United Nations Organization, will be discussed in Chapter XIII.

Much more limited international implications are raised by Radio Marti and TV Marti (both named for Cuban patriot–writer Jose Marti), broadcasting facilities begun by the U.S. Government in the 1980s in an attempt to break what the Reagan administration considered the Cuban government's monopoly on news available to Cubans. The broadcasting is under the auspices of Voice of America, and the government of Fidel Castro has regularly jammed much of the broadcasting. Funding for Radio and TV Marti has been controversial.

Chapter II

THE SPECTRUM AND ITS UTILIZATION

A. THE NATURE OF THE SPECTRUM

The electromagnetic spectrum is a unique natural resource. Utilization does not use it up or wear it out. It does not require continual maintenance to remain usable. It is subject to pollution (interference), but once the interference is removed the pollution totally disappears. The value of the spectrum lies primarily in its use for conveying a wide variety of information at varying speeds over varying distances: in other words, for communication.

All electromagnetic radiation is a form of radiant energy, similar in many respects to heat, light or X-radiation. All of these types of radiation are considered by physicists to be waves resulting from the periodic oscillations of charged subatomic particles. All radiation has a measurable frequency, or rate of oscillation, which is measured in cycles per second, or hertz. One thousand cycles per second equals one kilocycle per second (1 kHz); 1,000 kilocycles per second equals one Megacycle per second (1 MHz); and 1,000 Megacycles per second equals one Gigacycle per second (1 GHz). The frequencies of electromagnetic radiation that comprise the radio spectrum span a wide range, from 10 kHz to 3,000,-000,000,000 cycles per second (3,000 GHz), all of which are nearly incomprehensibly rapid. Present technology allows use of the spectrum up to around 70 GHz. However, recent technological developments will soon allow the use of even higher frequencies.

The radio spectrum resource itself has three dimensions: space, time and frequency. Two spectrum users can transmit on the same frequency at the same time, if they are sufficiently separate physically; the physical separation necessary will depend on the power at which each signal is transmitted. They then occupy different parts of the spectrum in the spatial sense. Similarly, the spectrum can be divided in terms of frequency, dependent on the construction of the transmitting and receiving equipment; or in a temporal sense, dependent largely on the hours of use.

The spectrum is subject to the phenomenon of interference. One radio signal interferes with another to the extent that both have the same dimensions. That is, two signals of the same frequency that occupy the same physical space at the same time will interfere with each other (co-channel interference). Signals on adjacent channels may also interfere with each other. Interference usually obscures or destroys any information that either signal is carrying: the degree to which two signals occupy the same physical space depends on the intensity of the radiated power at a given point, which in turn depends on the construction of the transmitting equipment and antenna.

The spectrum is divided into numbered bands, extending from Very Low Frequencies (VLF) to Very, Ultra, Super and Extremely High Frequencies (EHF) and beyond. The lower frequencies of the radio spectrum are used for "point-to-point" communications and for navigational aids. AM radio is located in the range between 300 and 3,000 kHz, known as the Medium Frequency band (MF). FM radio and VHF television (channels 2–13) are in the Very High Frequency band (VHF), from 30 to 300 MHz. The Ultra High Frequency band, from 300 to 3,000 MHz, is the location of UHF television (channels 14–69). Still higher frequencies are used for microwave relays and communication satellites.

The effective limitations on use of the radio spectrum are defined by (1) the propagation characteristics of the various frequencies and (2) the level of interference. Low frequency radio waves are best suited to long distance communications. In the lowest frequency bands the radio waves propagate primarily along the ground or water and follow the curvature of the earth. The attenuation of these "ground waves" generally increases with frequency; VLF waves may be propagated for thousands of miles, which explains their value for point-to-point communication. Ground waves in the HF band below VHF can propagate no more than a few hundred miles and above that band they become unimportant. Sky wave propagation is important up to the start of the VHF band. These radio waves tend to depart from the earth's surface and are reflected by the ionosphere, an electrically charged region of the atmosphere 35 to 250 miles above the earth. The amount of reflection depends on the level of daily solar activity, the time of day, the season, geographical location, the length of the signal path and the angle at which the waves strike the ionosphere. The reflection of sky waves is much greater at night, when they may be transmitted over great distances. Above 30 MHz, radio waves tend to pierce the ionosphere rather than to be reflected, and line-of-sight transmission becomes increasingly necessary. As frequency increases above 30 MHz, surface objects absorb radiation at an increasing rate until at 1 GHz a clear unobstructed line of sight becomes necessary. In the very highest frequencies, the waves are subject to substantial absorption by water vapor and oxygen in the atmosphere and cannot be used for communication.

Interference constitutes the second major limitation on the use of the electromagnetic spectrum. As noted above, interference results when two signals attempt to occupy the same spectrum in all three of its dimensions. Even if two users wish to transmit on the same frequency, interference can be avoided by sufficient geographical separation between transmitters, limitations of the power radiated by each transmitter, limitations on antenna height, or separation of the signals in time. The first three techniques cause spatial differentiation; the last affects the temporal dimension.

Standard (AM) broadcasting propagates its waves by "amplitude modulation." The sound waves vary in power, producing variations in the height of the waves that are transmitted. The receiving unit decodes these height variations, reproducing the original sounds. AM transmissions occur in the MF band and thus have a long range primary service through ground waves, particularly near the lower end of the band. AM also can utilize sky waves to provide a secondary service at night.

FM broadcasting utilizes "frequency modulation" rather than "amplitude modulation." In this system the height of the wave is held constant, but the frequency of the waves transmitted is varied. This type of broadcasting provides higher-quality service with less interference than does AM, but it serves smaller areas, because the waves of the VHF band do not follow the surface of the earth and are not reflected by the ionosphere. This also means that FM service is unaffected by sky-wave interference at night.

Television utilizes separate signals for the visual and the sound components. The picture is transmitted by amplitude modulation and the sound by frequency modulation. Because the transmissions are either in the VHF or UHF bands, the range of the signal is short and television cannot utilize either long ground waves or sky waves.

B. ALLOCATION OF THE SPECTRUM

The method of dividing the spectrum resource among prospective users is enormously complex and highly controversial. The general term "allocation policy" includes three separate but not always distinct processes, each of which involves both technical and nontechnical considerations. The allocation process is the division of the spectrum into blocks of frequencies to be used by specified services or users. Thus, the television service is allocated certain frequencies in the VHF and UHF bands, microwave users are allocated certain frequencies in the UHF and SHF bands, and so on. The second process, allotment, involves the distribution of spectrum rights within allocated bands to users in various geographical areas. Assignment, the third process, denotes the choice among potential individual users of allocated and allotted channels or frequency bands. We usually refer to all three processes under the general label of "allocation policy."

Perhaps the most important objective consideration in formulating an allocation policy is the technical usability of the spectrum itself. Technical usability is dependent primarily on three factors: the propagation characteristics of each frequency range, interference problems and their resolution, and limitations imposed by the communications system itself, especially the transmitting and receiving equipment. In other words, it is dependent on the physics of radio waves, other users of the spectrum and the technical state of the electronics industry. Frequency characteristics themselves seldom pose significant problems, for although there are optimal frequency ranges for various services, these tend to be broad ranges. Consequently, there is usually considerable flexibility in the initial choice of a frequency for a given service except for whatever priority is given to those already utilizing the space.

Several forms of interference may present problems because interference can be caused by an overcrowded frequency, insufficient geographical separation or unduly strong power levels.

The third constraint on spectrum allocation involves the technology of the communications system used, especially the antenna system and the transmitting and receiving equipment. Any major change in receivers might create economic problems for the public and thus for the industry as a whole.

The problem of crowding in the broadcasting industry began early in the 1920s. The episode is recounted by Justice Frankfurter in his opinion for the Court in National Broadcasting Co. v. United States, 319 U.S. 190 (1943), a case to which we return later:

> Federal regulation of radio begins with the Wireless Ship Act of June 24, 1910, 36 Stat. 629, which forbade any steamer carrying or licensed to carry fifty or more persons to leave any American port unless equipped with efficient apparatus for radio communication, in charge of a skilled operator. The enforcement of this legislation was entrusted to the Secretary of Commerce and Labor, who was in charge of the administration of the marine navigation laws. But it was not until 1912 when the United States ratified the first international radio treaty, 37 Stat. 1565, that the need for general regulation of radio communication became urgent. In order to fulfill our obligations under the treaty, Congress enacted the Radio Act of August 13, 1912, 37 Stat. 302. This statute forbade the operation of radio apparatus without a license from the Secretary of Commerce and Labor; it also allocated certain frequencies for the use of the Government, and imposed restrictions upon the character of wave emissions, the transmission of distress signals and the like.
>
> The enforcement of the Radio Act of 1912 presented no serious problems prior to the World War. Questions of interference arose only rarely because there were more than enough frequencies for all the stations then in existence. The war accelerated the development of the art, however, and in 1921 the first standard broadcast stations were established. They grew rapidly in number, and by 1923 there were several hundred such stations throughout the country. The Act of 1912 had not set aside any particular frequencies for the use of private broadcast stations; consequently, the Secretary of Commerce selected two frequencies, 750 and 833 kilocycles, and licensed all stations to operate upon one or the other of these channels. The number of stations increased so rapidly, however, and the situation became so chaotic, that the Secretary, upon recommendation of the National Radio Conferences which met in Washington in 1923 and 1924, established a policy of assigning specified frequencies to particular stations. The entire radio spectrum was divided into numerous bands, each allocated to a particu-

lar kind of service. The frequencies ranging from 550 to 1500 kilocycles (96 channels in all, since the channels were separated from each other by 10 kilocycles) were assigned to the standard broadcast stations. But the problems created by the enormously rapid development of radio were far from solved. The increase in the number of channels was not enough to take care of the constantly growing number of stations. Since there were more stations than available frequencies, the Secretary of Commerce attempted to find room for everybody by limiting the power and the hours of operation of stations in order that several stations might use the same channel. The number of stations multiplied so rapidly, however, that by November, 1925, there were almost 600 stations in the country, and there were 175 applications for new stations. Every channel in the standard broadcast band was, by that time, already occupied by at least one station, and many by several. The new stations could be accommodated only by extending the standard broadcast band, at the expense of the other types of services, or by imposing still greater limitations upon time and power. The National Radio Conference which met in November, 1925, opposed both of these methods and called upon Congress to remedy the situation through legislation.

[During 1926 courts held that the Secretary of Commerce lacked the power to stem the tide, and his pleas for self-regulation went unheeded by the burgeoning new industry.]

From July, 1926, to February 23, 1927, when Congress enacted the Radio Act of 1927, 44 Stat. 1162, almost 200 new stations went on the air. These new stations used any frequencies they desired, regardless of the interference thereby caused to others. Existing stations changed to other frequencies and increased their power and hours of operation at will. The result was confusion and chaos. With everybody on the air, nobody could be heard.

1. THE FEDERAL COMMUNICATIONS COMMISSION

As we noted in Chapter I, the Radio Act of 1927 and the Communications Act of 1934 rejected the idea of a market system of spectrum allocation and of any property rights in the spectrum resource. The Federal Communications Commission has the sole power to allocate the radio spectrum, to establish general standards of operations and to license persons to use designated parts of the spectrum.

Many services must be placed, but some critics of Commission policies charge undue reliance on the bloc allocation concept, which calls for allocating discrete frequency bands to classes of users essentially without regard to geographical location and maintaining a relatively strict segregation among allocations. This can lead to such anomalous results as marine bands in Nebraska and forestry bands in New York City. These problems are exacerbated by the general administrative difficulty of changing an allocation once made: the start-up costs are so great and the capital investment is usually so heavy that there is a strong economic incentive not to move users from one frequency band to another. Thus, as new uses develop, they are allocated higher and higher frequencies, with little consideration of which frequencies are technically best suited for which services. For example, location of radio broadcasting in the AM band (535–1605 kHz) may be inefficient. Local broadcasting might be moved to the current FM band (88–108 MHZ), which is much better suited technically to local radio, and long distance broadcasting might be moved to frequencies below 500 kHz to take advantage of the long distance ground wave propagation characteristics at those frequencies.

Another claim is that area coverage by broadcasting stations would require less spectrum if the Commission were to drop its so-called "local station goal." High-power stations in major urban centers could serve the entire country in only one-third the spectrum space presently used. Yet local stations are important; they are outlets for local news and forums for local citizens to express their views, they serve local advertisers, and they provide such local services as weather reports (which might be critical in areas subject to flash flooding or sudden tornadoes or storms).

2. RADIO ALLOCATION

a. *AM Allocation*

AM broadcasting occupies slightly more than 1 MHZ of spectrum in the Medium Frequency band between 535 kHz and 1605 kHz. This is divided into 107 assignable channels each with a bandwidth of 10 kHz. AM stations are divided into four major classes. Class I "clear channel" stations are high-power stations designed to provide primary (groundwave) service to a metropolitan area and its environs and secondary nighttime (sky-wave) service to an extended rural area. Class II stations also operate on clear channels with primary service areas limited by interference from Class I stations. A Class II station must usually avoid causing interference within the normally protected service areas of Class I or other Class II stations. Class III stations are medium powered and are designed to provide service primarily to larger cities and contiguous rural areas. Class IV stations are low powered and operate on local channels to provide service to a city or town and contiguous areas.

The 1927 Act creating the Federal Radio Commission had charged the Commission to provide "fair, efficient, and equitable radio service" to all areas of the country. The Commission then proceeded by establishing general engineering constraints such as maximum interference standards, and by allocating each of the 107 frequencies to a class of stations. Within these general constraints, the Commission adopted a first-come-first-served approach. An applicant who could find a promising community could apply for a license to serve that community if it could find a channel that would satisfy the various general constraints. An applicant had to show that it would not interfere excessively with the signals of existing stations nor expose too many of its new listeners to interference beyond certain acceptable limits.

Clear Channels. As noted earlier, because of the sky-wave phenomenon, powerful AM stations can be received at great distances at night. In the 1940s, with an estimated 20 million persons uncovered by local radio service at night, the FCC created a group of 25 powerful stations operating at 50 kw. Each station shared its daytime channel frequency with other stations around the country. However, at sundown all the others left the air so that the channel was clear except for the powerful station, which could reach distant and remote areas of the country.

With the development of FM radio and a surge in interest in AM radio, some argued that the clear channel stations should have their protections reduced to allow more diversity. In response, the clear channel stations argued that their power should be increased to 750 kw so that they could provide additional service. The FCC faced the issue in 1961 but reached no conclusion. In a compromise, it ordered that 13 of the 25 frequencies be shared with one or two other stations, but left the remainder fully protected while it continued to consider the problem.

In 1980 the Commission acted decisively. The number of persons unserved by nighttime local radio was down to 4 million, and applicants were clamoring for space on the AM spectrum. The Commission decided to end the clear channel concept but to protect those stations from interference for a radius of 750 miles. This still permits them to reach larger areas than ordinary stations, but it also permits an additional 125 stations to broadcast at night.

The new stations are limited in power to 1 kw except in special cases. At the same time, the FCC explicitly refused to allow the clear channel stations to raise their power above 50 kw. (In the 1930s an experiment permitted a Cincinnati station to broadcast at 500 kw. The experiment was terminated, and a limit of 50 kw imposed for all stations.)

Similarly, in 1985 the Commission voted to allow full-time stations to use frequencies previously reserved for foreign clear channel stations. These channels were available as a result of new agreements negotiated with Canada, Mexico and the Bahamas. AM Broadcast Stations (Nighttime Operations on Canadian, Mexican and Bahamian Clear Channels), 101 F.C.C.2d 1, 58 R.R.2d 655 (1985).

Expanding the Band. A second way to increase the number of AM stations is to expand the part of the spectrum available for such broadcasting. This occurred in 1979, when the World Administrative Radio Conference decided to increase the AM band in the Western Hemisphere so that it will run from 525 to 1705 kHz.

Agreements reached at subsequent Regional Administrative Radio Conferences (RARC) limit stations in the new section of the band to 10 kw. The Commission has decided to use the expanded band to reduce congestion in the existing AM band. By allowing existing AM licensees to operate new stations in the expanded band, and then, after a transition period, shut down their old stations, the Commission hopes to reduce interference and improve signal quality. The FCC will limit the entire expanded band to these migrating AM stations. AM Improvement, 6 F.C.C.Rcd. 6273, 69 R.R.2d 1395 (1991).

Final assignment of the new channels has been delayed by various petitions for reconsideration. For example, in 1994, the FCC rejected a proposal by the the National Association for the Advancement of Colored People (NAACP), the League of United Latin American Citizens and the National Black Media Coalition. The groups asserted that "awarding 100% of the expanded band to incumbent broadcasters 'will have little or no impact on AM band interference,' whereas awarding some of the expanded band to minorities would substantially alleviate the 'gross underrepresentation' of minorities in the ownership of broadcast stations."

Their proposed solution was "a scheme whereby incumbent broadcasters migrating to the expanded band would be issued tax certificates for selling their existing band stations to minorities. The seller would retain its license for a station in the expanded band. As part of this proposal, the minority buyers would then be allowed to operate these existing band stations together with new expanded band stations to be awarded them for a five year transitional period." The FCC held to its earlier decision that reducing AM congestion had to be the top priority in awarding the expanded band licenses. AM Improvement, 8 F.C.C.Rcd. 3250 (1993).

A further delay was caused by errors in the AM Engineering Database which caused errors in the ranking of stations applying for migration to the new channels. After correcting the errors, the FCC issued a new allotment plan. AM Expanded Band (Allotment Plan), 12 F.C.C.Rcd. 3185 (1997). Still more challenges to the allotment plan and delays in clearing other services from that portion of the band continue to delay service.

b. *FM Allocation*

FM broadcasting, which began around 1940, is located in the VHF band. It occupies the frequencies between 88 and 108 MHZ, which are excellent for aural broadcast service and allow an effective range of 30 to 75 miles. That spectrum space is divided into 100 assignable channels, each 200 kHz wide. The lowest 20 channels are reserved for noncommercial educational stations; the remaining 80 are given over to commercial use. Commercial FM channels were originally divided into three classes: A, B and C. Class A channels were designed for use by low-power stations serving relatively small communities and the surrounding area. Class B channels were for medium-power stations intended to serve a sizable city or town or the principal city of an urbanized area. Class C channels were used by high-power stations serving a city and large surrounding areas. Commercial FM assignments are based on a Table of Assignments, in which communities are assigned a specific number of FM stations of specified power and on specific channels. Licenses are given only for stations within the communities listed in the Table of Assignments or within a 15 mile radius—unless an application to change the table is granted.

In the late 1970s the demand for FM licenses increased dramatically as FM outlets started to overcome the traditional dominance of AM stations. The superior quality of the FM signal and the availability of stereo were the keys to this change.

In an effort to meet the increased demand for FM stations, the FCC initiated a drop-in rulemaking allowing new FM stations to be started without interfering with present broadcasters. FM Broadcast Stations (Additional Commercial Allocations), 53 R.R.2d 1550 (1983). 47 C.F.R. § 73.202 (1983). This rulemaking created three new intermediary classes of commercial licenses: B1, C1 and C2. In addition, Class A licenses are now permitted on channels previously set aside for Class B and Class C licenses.

In 1984 the FCC approved a list of 689 locations, an initial step in the omnibus rulemaking process. Most of the new availabilities were Class A licenses in the southeast. These stations are now all on the air.

In 2000 the FCC adopted rules authorizing a new low-power FM service. Two new classes of stations were authorized, one with a power limit of 10 watts, the other with a power limit of 100 watts. Stations will be exclusively noncommercial. For the first two years, licenses will be awarded exclusively to local entities. Low Power FM, 15 F.C.C.Rcd. 2205. The NAB, claiming the likelihood that these new stations would cause interference with existing FM stations, opposed the creation of these new stations and lobbied Congress to prohibit the FCC from proceeding with its plans.

Although Congress declined to prohibit LPFM service, it did include in a 2000 appropriations bill a provision requiring the FCC to strengthen interference protection for existing full-power stations. The FCC subsequently modified the LPFM rules to comply. Creation of a Low Power Radio Service, 16 F.C.C.Rcd. 8026 (2001).

c. *Beneficiaries*

Who were the beneficiaries of these attempts to increase the number of broadcast outlets? In radio, daytime AM broadcasters argued forcefully that they deserved the opportunity to obtain fulltime outlets. Meanwhile, the Commission had long been concerned that minority groups were woefully underrepresented among the owners of broadcast licenses. Although minority ownership does not necessarily mean that a station's programming will take minority tastes into special account, the FCC believes that minority ownership itself is important—and that the other may follow. Other demonstrations of the FCC's concern about minorities in broadcasting are discussed elsewhere in this and later chapters.

In the FM drop-in rulemaking, *supra,* the Commission voted to give preference both to AM daytime broadcasters and to minority applicants. FM Broadcast Assignments, 101 F.C.C.2d 638, 57 R.R.2d 1607 (1985), reconsidered in part, 59 R.R.2d 1221, reconsideration denied, 2 F.C.C.Rcd. 481, 61 R.R.2d 1704 (1987). The preference was affirmed. National Black Media Coalition v. Federal Communications Commission, 822 F.2d 277 (2d Cir.1987).

In contrast, the Commission specifically rejected petitions requesting preference for minority and non-commercial applicants for the new stations authorized for either domestic or foreign clear channels, p. 47, *supra.* Deletion of AM Acceptance Criteria, 102 F.C.C.2d 548, 59 R.R.2d 521 (1985); AM Broadcast Stations (Nighttime Operations on Clear Channels), 3 F.C.C.Rcd. 3597, 64 R.R.2d 1475 (1988), recon. denied, AM Broadcast Stations (Nighttime Operations on Canadian, Mexican and Bahamian Clear Channels), 66 R.R.2d 1049 (1989).

In a separate action, the Commission temporarily froze all applications for new AM daytime stations and indicated it would seek through rulemaking procedure to make the freeze permanent. AM Daytime Applications (Temporary Freeze), 1 F.C.C.Rcd. 1264, 61 R.R.2d 1067 (1986). The Commission believed it could find ways to expand service for current daytimers but would be unable to help any new daytime stations. One method will be allowing AM daytimers to participate in the migration to the expanded band, pp. 48–49, *supra.* Note that in 1990, as part of its inquiry into improving AM radio, the Commission instituted a freeze on all AM broadcast applications. AM Improvement, 5 F.C.C.Rcd. 4381.

3. Television Allocation

The first licensing of television stations in this country occurred in 1941 and involved 18 channels. The first assignment plan was developed in 1945, based solely on the VHF channels. It involved the assignment of about 400 stations to 140 major market centers. Early comers quickly preempted the 100 choice assignments. In 1948, because of unexpected problems with tropospheric interference and concern that the 1945 assignment plan could cause problems, the Commission ordered a freeze on channel assignments.

The freeze ended with the issuance of the Sixth Report and Order on Television Allocations, 17 Fed.Reg. 3905, 1 R.R. 91:601 (1952), creating the Table of Assignments. The Commission rejected the idea of moving all television to the UHF band. Instead, 12 VHF channels were retained, and 70 new UHF channels were added, so that the Table provided for about 620 VHF and 1400 UHF stations. Television uses an enormous amount of spectrum compared to radio. One VHF channel uses six MHZ—six times more than the entire AM band.

The Commission generated the Table of Assignments from its hierarchy of priorities: (1) to provide at least one television service to every part of the United States; (2) to provide each community with at least one television station; (3) to provide a choice of at least two television services to all parts of the U.S.; (4) to provide each community with at least two television stations; and (5) to assign remaining channels to communities on the basis of population, geographical location and the number of television services already available to that community. Note the emphasis on "local" outlets. Is this a sound hierarchy?

In making these assignments the Commission decided to "intermix" VHF and UHF channels as a single service in the same markets. Many observers warned that the newer UHF channels could not survive, but the Commission apparently believed that the demand for VHF would overflow into the UHF band, and it also feared that failure to intermix would relegate UHF stations to markets overshadowed by VHF outlets in nearby metropolitan areas, or to remote rural areas. In any event, the Table of Assignments called for combined VHF and UHF channels in the following pattern: six to 10 for cities with population over 1 million; four to six for cities with 250,000 to 1,000,000; two to four for those with populations between 50,000 and 250,000; and one to two for communities under 50,000.

Because the Table tended to allot three VHF stations to most markets with only a few getting more than three, the three major networks could now program almost entirely through VHF affiliates. This gave them strong audience and advertiser support. Without adequate set penetration, UHF stations found it difficult if not impossible to secure advertising revenues and network affiliation. By the end of 1956, there were 395 VHF stations and 96 UHF stations on the air. By this time Dumont, a fourth network, had collapsed. By 1960 only 75 (15 percent) of the 575 commercial stations on the air were UHF, even though 70 percent of the total channel assignments were UHF.

The Commission recognized that intermixture was not working. In 1956, while considering broader solutions such as the transfer of all television to the UHF band, the Commission adopted deintermixture as an "interim" measure in several communities, making them all-UHF. In 1961 the Commission planned to deintermix eight more communities. This time, however, the opposition from established VHF stations was formidable. After a fierce battle, Congress entered the fray and enacted a compromise: the All Channel Receiver Act of 1962. The Act, which became § 303(s) of the Communications Act, authorized the Commission to order that all sets shipped in interstate commerce be capable of receiving both VHF and UHF signals. The VHF interests gave their support for the proposal in exchange for the Commission's indefinite suspension of deintermixture proposals. The Commission did require "all-channel" receivers and declared a moratorium on most pending deintermixture proposals. The Commission's regulation came too late for many of the UHF pioneers of the 1950s. (In 1971 the Commission began steps to require detent ("click") dialing on all UHF receivers.)

The continued underutilization of UHF spots led the FCC to begin to reallocate frequencies to competing uses of the airwaves. Channels 70 to 83 were reassigned for land mobile use. In some cities Channels 14 to 20 are being used by land mobile operators and are being shared elsewhere. By 1980, 63 percent of the television assignments were UHF. The vacancy rates were as follows: 61 of the 578 commercial VHFs; 266 of the 648 commercial UHFs; 23 of the 136 noncommercial VHFs; and 374 of the 570 noncommercial UHFs. In the top 100 markets, vacancies existed on 86 UHF channels but on no commercial VHF. In the top 200 markets, the comparable figures were 176 and six.

In addition to the intermixture problem, UHF stations are also more expensive to operate because it takes 10 times as much power for a UHF transmitter to reach the same area as a VHF transmitter. Because of the inferior wave-propagation qualities of UHF signals compared with VHF signals, UHF stations are permitted to operate at a power of 5,000 kw compared with 100 or 316 kw for VHF stations. However, the energy costs are so high that few UHF stations operate at maximum permitted power.

During 1979 the future of UHF suddenly brightened. Applicants sought stations that had gone begging since 1952, existing stations were sold at increasingly higher prices and major broadcast owners became interested in UHF for the first time. The change in climate was apparently due to a variety of independent factors coming into play at the same time. Viewers were finding "click" dialing or newer digital dialing systems more attractive; cable television was improving the reception of the UHF stations. Another temporary boost came from the introduction of Subscription Television (STV), an over-the-air pay television system in which viewers who wish to buy the service are supplied decoders that unscramble the signal being transmitted. Although little original programming was being provided, the prospect of uncut motion pictures without commercials was sufficiently attractive to make the venture appear profitable.

However, due to increasing cable penetration, piracy of signals and growing interest in Multi-channel Multipoint Distribution Service (MMDS, which will be discussed in Chapter X), STV ceased to be viable. By 1991 there were no STV stations in operation.

A few UHF stations became profitable as the result of developments in cable television. Because of changes in FCC rules governing cable systems, it became possible for a single television station, in effect, to become a network by supplying its programs by satellite to cable systems throughout the country. The operation of these "superstations" is described more extensively in the discussion of cable television in Chapters VIII and IX.

A more gradual improvement in the financial picture for UHF stations came from the increasing number of homes subscribing to cable television. When received through cable, UHF and VHF stations are of comparable quality. This is believed to be one of the major reasons for the development of the new broadcast networks such as Fox, which we will discuss later in this chapter.

At the conclusion of the Digital Television transition period, p. 58, *infra*, channels 63, 64, 68 and 69 will be reallocated to public safety use, while channels 60–62 and 65–67 will be reallocated to commercial use. The commercial channels may be used for fixed, land mobile or broadcast use and will be assigned by competitive bidding. Reallocation of Television Channels 60–69, the 746–806 Mhz band, 12 F.C.C.Rcd. 22953 (1998).

Low-Power Television. In 1982 the FCC approved the start of a new television service of perhaps as many as 4,000 low-power television (LPTV) stations throughout the country. These stations operate at a power sufficient to reach viewers within a radius of 10–15 miles. It is up to the applicant to find spots on the VHF and UHF bands in which such stations will not interfere with existing stations.

LPTV operators are permitted to join together by satellite to set up networks. Neither the duopoly nor the one-to-a-market rules, which we will discuss in Chapter XII, apply to LPTV. There is no limit set on the number of LPTV licenses one entity can have. Programming restrictions are also minimal. The FCC political access rules and § 315 of the Communications Act (see Chapter V) apply only to licensee-originated programming.

A lottery procedure for initial licensing of LPTV was approved by the Commission in March 1983. Selection from Among Competing Applications Using Random Selection or Lotteries Instead of Comparative Hearings, 48 Fed.Reg. 27,182 (1983). This procedure was necessitated by the great number of applications. Applications for LPTV licenses were frozen in September 1983 and the lottery disposed of competing applications at a rate of 250–350 each month. By 1987 the backlog was reduced to the point where the Commission was able to resume accepting applications. The first window produced more than 1,500 applications. (Under FCC procedures, a period of time—a "window"—is set during which applications for specified channels and locations will be accepted.) In 1988 a second window produced almost 1,000 more applications.

4. DIGITAL BROADCASTING

As discussed at p. 44, *supra*, television and radio signals use either amplitude or frequency modulation to transmit information. By interpreting differences in the frequency or amplitude of the signal broadcast receivers can reproduce the sound and pictures that are being transmitted. This method of measuring variations in a continuous signal is referred to as analog broadcasting.

There is, however, another way to convey information in broadcast signals. Digital broadcasting is a system whereby the information is represented by a sequence of discrete codes similar to those used by modern computers. Digital broadcasting offers a number of advantages compared to analog.

The first is an increase in quality. Because analog receivers interpret any variation in the signal as a change in the information, analog signals are highly susceptible to interference. In contrast, digital receivers interpret variations in signal as different information only when the variation is sufficient to actually change the code. A good example of this is the difference between vinyl records (analog) and compact discs (digital).

A second major advantage is compression. It is possible to remove redundant information from a digital signal prior to transmission. This information can then be restored by the receiving device. For example, with TV most of the picture does not change from one frame to the next. Instead of transmitting the entire picture with each frame, a digitally compressed signal would only carry information on those parts of the picture that changed while telling the receiver to keep the rest from the previous frame. The advantage of this is that more information can be transmitted in less bandwidth.

a.   *High Definition Television*

HDTV is television with approximately twice as many scan lines as the current United States standard of 525 lines. Coupled with a change in the aspect ratio (the ratio between the width and height of the picture) HDTV delivers vastly superior picture quality. It also uses a digital multi-speaker audio system. Proponents of the new service claim that it is equivalent in quality to 35 mm. film.

When first proposed in the early 1980s, HDTV raised a number of difficult questions. One of these was one often faced by the Commission in allocating spectrum for new services. Should the Commission determine the technical standards for such a service or leave it to the marketplace to decide? In the past the Commission has tried both approaches. For example, in 1953 the Commission chose the National Television System Committee (NTSC) standard for color television. Amendment of the Commission's Rules Governing Color Television Transmissions, 41 F.C.C. 658 (1953).

In contrast, in 1982 the FCC authorized AM radio stations to broadcast in stereo but refused to choose from among five incompatible systems. Licensees were free to use any of the five systems. AM Stereophonic Broadcasting, 51 R.R.2d 1 (1982). Six years later the FCC again refused to choose among the two remaining systems or to mandate that all AM stereo receivers be capable of decoding the signals produced by both systems. AM Stereophonic Broadcasting, 64 R.R.2d 516 (1988).

Section 214 of the Telecommunications Authorization Act of 1992 contained a requirement that the FCC adopt a single AM stereo standard within one year after the date of enactment of the Act. The Commission adopted the Motorola C–Quam system because it had become the *de facto* market standard. "[O]f the approximately 660 U.S. AM broadcasting stations that have converted to stereo operation, 591 use the Motorola [C–Quam] system, an additional 37 use the Harris C–Quam compatible system, and somewhat fewer than 20 employ the [incompatible] Kahn system." AM Radio Stereophonic Transmitting Equipment Standard, 8 F.C.C.Rcd. 8216, 74 R.R.2d 244 (1993).

What factors should influence the Commission's decision on whether or not to set a standard? In the case of AM stereo, is it relevant that as of 1993 less than 20 percent of U.S. AM stations broadcast in stereo? In the case of HDTV, the Commission ultimately decided to set a standard. In doing so, it then had to address a number of other key issues: Where in the spectrum would HDTV be located and how much spectrum space would be allocated for each station? Would HDTV signals have to be compatible with NTSC receivers? Who would be eligible for the new licenses?

In 1988 the Commission decided that Advanced Television (ATV), "any system that results in improved television audio and video quality, whether the methods employed improve the existing NTSC transmission system or constitute an entirely new system," should utilize existing broadcast allocations. Advanced Television Systems and Their Impact on the Existing Television Broadcast Service, 3 F.C.C.Rcd. 6520, 65 R.R.2d 295 (1988). According to the FCC, attempting to identify additional unused spectrum space with propagation characteristics appropriate for ATV would only delay the development of ATV.

The Commission also decided that ATV signals would be limited to 6 MHZ despite the fact that when first proposed, HDTV required a bandwidth greater than the 6 MHZ required by NTSC stations. The Commission also decided that "service must be continued to the public's existing NTSC receivers, at least during the transition period to ATV." Note that these restrictions apply only to terrestrial broadcasting. The Commission specifically declined to set any restrictions on ATV delivered by Direct Broadcast Satellite (DBS) or nonbroadcast media such as cable.

Two years later the Commission decided that simulcasting would be used to continue service to NTSC receivers during the transition to ATV. Advanced Television Systems, 5 F.C.C.Rcd. 5656, 68 R.R.2d 167 (1990).

In 1992 the Commission decided a number of additional issues. These included limiting initial eligibility for ATV licenses to existing TV licensees and adopting a two-year deadline for them to apply for ATV licenses (to be paired with their original licenses) and a three-year deadline for construction of ATV facilities, once assigned. In addition, once ATV becomes the prevalent medium, broadcasters will be forced to convert to ATV by surrendering one of each of their paired channels and ceasing to broadcast in NTSC. Advanced Television Systems, 7 F.C.C.Rcd. 3340, 70 R.R.2d 1102 (1992).

Meanwhile, six proposed ATV systems were tested. The most significant development was that five of the systems were digital, as opposed to analog systems. Before the FCC could choose an HDTV standard, the proponents of the five remaining proposed systems (the analog system proponent having withdrawn its proposal) decided to merge and develop a single HDTV standard.

The merged HDTV group, dubbed the "Grand Alliance," delivered a finished prototype for testing to the FCC's Advisory Committee on Advanced Television Service (ACATS) in 1994. Meanwhile, the FCC dropped consideration of the systems that had been proposed by the various members of the grand alliance prior to the merger agreement. ACATS adopted the Grand Alliance system in its 1995 recommendation to the FCC. With its adoption ATV was designated digital television (DTV).

Broadcasters, however, were indicating some concern over the FCC's plan. The same digital technology that allows HDTV to be compressed into 6 MHZ allows an improved NTSC signal. Even though it doesn't equal the quality of HDTV, it may be good enough to satisfy consumers. At the same time digital NTSC permits compressing several NTSC signals into a single 6 MHZ channel (multichannel NTSC). If broadcasters were to be locked into HDTV and consumers chose digital NTSC, the broadcasters would be at a serious competitive disadvantage with cable and other media that have the capability of transmitting both.

In 1995 the FCC issued a Notice of Proposed Rulemaking on digital broadcasting. The NPRM identified four primary goals: "[1] To preserve our nation's free, universal broadcasting service; [2] To foster an expeditious and orderly transition to digital technology which will allow the public to receive the benefits of digital television, including HDTV; [3] To eventually recover spectrum in contiguous blocks from coast-to-coast for new, as yet undefined services, to allow the public the full benefit of its spectrum; [4] To ensure that the spectrum will be used in a manner which best serves the public interest." Advanced Television Systems, 10 F.C.C.Rcd. 10540 (1995).

Congress established a framework for DTV licenses in the Telecommunications Act of 1996 by adding a new § 336, entitled Broadcast Spectrum Flexibility, to the Communications Act. 47 U.S.C.A. § 336. Licenses are limited to existing television licensees and allow licensees to offer ancillary or supplementary services over their ATV channel. Fees can be assessed only to the extent the licensee uses the ATV channel to deliver subscription services or services "for which the licensee directly or indirectly receives compensation from a third party in return for transmitting material furnished by such third party (other than commercial advertisements used to support broadcasting for which a subscription fee is not required)."

In 1997 the Commission adopted rules governing licensing, construction and operation of digital television stations. Licensees are allowed to determine their own mix of services, as long as they broadcast a minimum of one "free digital video programming service that is at least comparable in resolution to today's service and aired during the same time periods as today's analog service. The Commission will not require broadcasters to air 'high definition' programming or initially to simul-cast their analog programming on the digital channel."

This led to a major debate among broadcasters, the computer industry and others as to what form DTV should take. The debate revolves around two key elements of the DTV signal: the number of scan lines and whether progressive or interlaced scanning is used. Progressive scanning is when each scan line is transmitted in order, while interlaced scanning is when all the odd-numbered scan lines are transmitted in order and then the even-numbered lines are similarly transmitted.

Both of these variables affect the quality of the picture and the bandwidth required to transmit them. The three primary combinations being considered are 480 progressive (480P), 720 progressive (720P) and 1080 interlaced (1080I). The FCC considers the first of these a standard-definition signal and the other two high-definition signals. For broad-casters, the trade-off is between signal quality and number of signals they can broadcast. The issue for the computer industry is compatibility. Computer monitors are now almost uniformly progressive scan. If pro-gressive scan is used for DTV, it will make it easier for computers to also function as DTV sets.

Affiliates of the top 4 networks located in the top 10 markets were required to be on the air with a digital signal by May 1, 1999. Affiliates of those same networks located in markets 11–30, had to be on the air by Nov. 1, 1999. Other licensees were given more time, but the target date for ending NTSC service was set as 2006. Advanced Television Systems, 11 F.C.C.Rcd. 12809, 7 C.R. 863 (1997).

Under provisions added to the Communications Act in 1997, broad-casters will not be required to return analog spectrum by Dec. 31, 2006, if any of the following conditions exist:

1. One or more stations in a market affiliated with one of the four major networks are not broadcasting digital signals.

2. Fewer than 85 percent of the TV households in a market subscribe to a multichannel video service carrying at least one digital signal from each local television station.

3. Fewer than 85 percent of the TV households in a market have either a digital television set or an analog set with a digital to analog converter.

47 U.S.C.A. § 309(j)(14)(B).

How quickly consumers will embrace DTV is hard to predict. The first sets offered for sale were all extremely expensive, between $5 and $10 thousand dollars. Prices have dropped, but are still much higher than analog sets. Until more DTV service is available, there is limited incentive to purchase the sets, but at the same time, until more people have sets, there is little incentive to offer more DTV programming.

There are also equipment compatibility problems, especially with regard to cable. If cable systems can't or won't offer DTV service, will the two thirds of the population who receive their television service from cable systems be deterred from purchasing DTV sets? (We will discuss this further in Chapter IX.)

Furthermore, many stations are having difficulty installing DTV transmitters. Many transmitter towers are unable to bear the additional weight of DTV transmitters. The alternative—building new towers—presents several problems. First, they are expensive. Second, it is hard to find land for these towers. Finally, there are a limited number of companies qualified to erect these towers. As a result, many stations have not met the deadlines set by the FCC for offering service.

Finally, broadcasters are still unsure how to program DTV. Should they broadcast a single HDTV channel or multiple SDTV channels? Do they use any of this spectrum for ancillary services such as datacasting? Which format or formats (480P, 720P and/or 1080I) do they use?

With many stations having failed to meet the deadlines for commencing DTV service (May 1, 2002), there is a growing consensus that the deadline for returning analog channels (2006), will not be met. The small-market stations are finding it especially difficult to meet the deadlines because their conversion costs are the same as large-market stations, but their revenues and budgets are not.

In an attempt to hasten the transition to DTV, the FCC adopted rules requiring all televisions with a screen size of 13 inches or greater, and video recorders to have a digital tuner by 2007. The requirement will be phased in over a three-year period, starting with large screen (36 inches or greater) televisions. Review of the Commission's Rules and Policies Affecting the Conversion To Digital Television, 17 F.C.C.Rcd. 15,978 (2002).

In 2003 the Commission issued a further NPRM on DTV to review the unresolved issues involved in the transition including: "(1) whether the FCC should retain, revise, or remove the requirement that licensees simulcast a certain percentage of their analog channel on their DTV channel; (2) whether there are steps the FCC needs to take to assist noncommercial television stations in the transition; (3) whether there are labeling requirements for TV-related consumer equipment that would assist the transition and protect consumers; (4) whether and how the FCC should license multiple lower-powered transmitters, similar to cellular telephone systems, called distributed transmission systems; (5) whether broadcasters should be required to include Program System and Information Protocol ("PSIP") information within their digital signals to ensure the availability of certain functions; (6) whether the FCC should adopt digital V-chip requirements; and (7) what station identification requirements should apply to digital stations." 2003 WL 168409 (F.C.C.).

The FCC had also indicated that it might impose additional public interest obligations on digital television licensees such as children's programming requirements or free time for political candidates in return for the free spectrum broadcasters are receiving. However, a decision on this issue was left for further proceedings. Advanced Television Systems, 11 F.C.C.Rcd. 12809, 7 C.R. 863 (1997).

The decision on public interest obligations was postponed pending the submission of the report of the "Advisory Committee on the Public Interest Obligations of Digital Television Broadcasters." The Committee was composed of members of the commercial and noncommercial broadcasting industry, computer industries, producers, academic institutions, public interest organizations, and the advertising community. Executive Order 13038, 62 Fed.Reg. 12065 (Mar. 11, 1997).

The Committee issued its report in late 1998. It contained 10 recommendations:

1. Disclosure of Public Interest Activities by Broadcasters: Digital broadcasters should be required to make enhanced disclosures of their public interest programming and activities on a quarterly basis, using standardized checkoff forms that reduce administrative burdens and can be easily understood by the public.

2. Voluntary Standards of Conduct: The National Association of Broadcasters, acting as the representative of the broadcasting industry, should draft an updated voluntary Code of Conduct to highlight and reinforce the public interest commitments of broadcasters. [We will discuss this further in Chapter VI]

3. Minimum Public Interest Requirements: The FCC should adopt a set of minimum public interest requirements for digital television broadcasters in the areas of community outreach, accountability, public service announcements, public affairs programming, and closed captioning.

4. Improving Education Through Digital Broadcasting: Congress should create a trust fund to ensure enhanced and permanent funding for public broadcasting to help it fulfill its potential in the digital television environment and remove it from the vicissitudes of the political process. When spectrum now used for analog broadcasting is returned to the government, Congress should reserve the equivalent of 6 MHz of spectrum for each viewing community in order to establish channels devoted specifically to noncommercial educational programming. Congress should establish an orderly process for allocating the new channels as well as provide adequate funding from appropriate revenue sources. Broadcasters that choose to implement datacasting should transmit information on behalf of local schools, libraries, community-based nonprofit organizations, governmental bodies, and public safety institutions. This activity should count toward fulfillment of a digital broadcaster's public interest obligations. [We will discuss this further in Chapter VII.]

5. Multiplexing and the Public Interest: Digital television broadcasters who choose to multiplex, and in doing so reap enhanced economic benefits, should have the flexibility to choose between paying a fee, providing a multicasted channel for public interest

purposes, or making an in-kind contribution. Given the uncertainties of this still-hypothetical market, broadcasters should have a 2–year moratorium on any fees or contributions to allow for experimentation and innovation. Small-market broadcasters should be given an opportunity to appeal to the FCC for additional time. The moratorium should begin after the market penetration for digital television reaches a stipulated threshold.

6. Improving the Quality of Political Discourse: If Congress undertakes comprehensive campaign finance reform, broadcasters should commit firmly to do their part to reform the role of television in campaigns. This could include repeal of the "lowest unit rate" requirement in exchange for free airtime, a broadcast bank to distribute money or vouchers for airtime, and shorter time periods of selling political airtime, among other changes. In addition, the television broadcasting industry should voluntarily provide 5 minutes each night for candidate-centered discourse in the 30 days before an election. Finally, blanket bans on the sale of airtime to all State and local political candidates should be prohibited. [We will discuss this further in Chapter V.]

7. Disaster Warnings in the Digital Age: Broadcasters should work with appropriate emergency communications specialists and manufacturers to determine the most effective means to transmit disaster warning information. The means chosen should be minimally intrusive on bandwidth and not result in undue additional burdens or costs on broadcasters. Appropriate regulatory authorities should also work with manufacturers of digital television sets to make sure that they are modified to handle these kinds of transmissions.

8. Disability Access to Digital Programming: Broadcasters should take full advantage of new digital closed-captioning technologies to provide maximum choice and quality for Americans with disabilities, where doing so would not impose an undue burden on the broadcasters. These steps should include the gradual expansion of captioning on public service announcements, public affairs programming, and political programming; the allocation of sufficient audio bandwidth for the transmission and delivery of video description; disability access to ancillary and supplementary services; and collaboration between regulatory authorities and set manufacturers to ensure the most efficient, inexpensive, and innovative capabilities for disability access.

9. Diversity in Broadcasting: Diversity is an important value in broadcasting, whether it is in programming, political discourse, hiring, promotion, or business opportunities within the industry. The Advisory Committee recommends that broadcasters seize the opportunities inherent in digital television technology to substantially enhance the diversity available in the television marketplace. Serving diverse interests within a community is both good business and good public policy. [We will discuss this further in Chapter XII.]

10. New Approaches to Public Interest Obligations in the New Television Environment: Although the Advisory Committee makes no consensus recommendation about entirely new models for fulfilling public interest obligations, it believes that the Administration, the Congress, and the FCC should explore alternative approaches that allow for greater flexibility and efficiency while affirmatively serving public needs and interests.

In its 2003 NPRM reviewing unresolved issues regarding DTV, the FCC asked for further comments in the ongoing public interest obligations NPRM, as well as the Children's DTV Public Interest NPRM.

b. *Digital Audio Radio Service*

Proposals to use digital transmission for radio initially took a slightly different approach, satellite delivery. In 1995 the FCC allocated the 2310–2360 MHZ band for satellite digital audio radio services (DARS). The FCC listed several potential benefits of the new service. It "will provide continuous radio service of compact disk quality for all listeners and will offer an increased choice of over-the-air audio programming. Further, a satellite delivery system for DARS will make it possible to serve segments in the United States which are currently underserved and unserved. . . . [It] has the potential to provide new services to rural listeners, minority and ethnic groups, and audiences whose first language is not English. In addition, this new service will provide opportunities for domestic economic development and improve U.S. competitiveness in the world marketplace." However, broadcasters opposed DARS, arguing that it would have an adverse impact on local radio service. The Commission was not persuaded.

> While we believe that it is possible that competition from a new regional or national satellite radio service might diminish the financial ability of some terrestrial stations to provide local service, we are not prepared to deny the allocation of spectrum for future satellite DARS and the benefits that may accrue from the provision of such service to the public, on the basis of potential for economic harm to some stations.

Digital Audio Radio Services, 10 F.C.C.Rcd. 2310, 76 R.R.2d 1477 (1995).

Following a spectrum auction for DARS licenses, the FCC awarded licenses to two companies, American Mobile Radio Corporation and Satellite CD Radio Inc. American Mobile Radio Corporation, 13 F.C.C.Rcd. 8829, 9 C.R. 1162 (1997) and Satellite CD Radio Inc., 13 F.C.C.Rcd. 7971, 9 C.R. 1174 (1997). We will discuss satellite-delivered broadcast services further in Chapter X.

Existing radio licensees were finally given a chance to provide digital radio service when the FCC authorized interim, in-band, on-channel (IBOC) digital audio broadcasts on a voluntary basis. Using IBOC, AM and FM stations will be able to transmit both analog and digital signals on the same channel. As IBOC does not require the use of a second channel, the transition to digital service in radio is expected to be much easier than in television. The Commission deferred any decision on licensing and service rule changes to a future rulemaking proceeding. Digital Audio Broadcasting Systems and Their Impact on the Terrestrial Radio Broadcast Service, 17 F.C.C.Rcd. 19,990 (2002).

C. A NOTE ON THE ECONOMICS OF TELEVISION

The basic unit in the broadcasting system is the individual station that receives the license from the Federal Communications Commission. As of December 2002, 1719 full-power television stations (710 VHF and 1009 UHF) were operating in the United States. Of the operating stations, 1338 were commercial (583 VHF and 755 UHF), and the remainder were noncommercial. In addition, there were 591 LPTV stations (106 VHF and 485 UHF).

Because of multiple ownership limitations to be discussed in Chapter XII, the ownership of the commercial stations is widely distributed. Prior to the 1985 relaxation of the multiple ownership rules, there were several group owners whose holdings included the maximum five VHFs. Among these group owners were the three major networks. Each owned and operated one VHF in New York City, Los Angeles and Chicago. The fourth and fifth VHFs were located in six different cities. These 15 O & Os (owned and operated) were a major source of profit for the television networks. The O & Os realized 90 percent of their revenue from non-network sales because of their desirable frequencies in major cities.

As a result of changes in regulation and competition from newer technologies, especially cable, the basic structure of the television industry began to change in the 1980s. For example, with the relaxation of the multiple ownership rules, the networks acquired additional O & Os. Meanwhile, as previously discussed, increased cable penetration strengthened the mostly independent UHF stations. This in turn led to increased competition for programming. In addition, the three networks lost viewers both to the independents and to cable.

In the 1990s more radical changes occurred. Fox Television started a fourth network. Originally, Fox supplied prime-time programming for only two hours, two nights a week. Gradually, this was expanded to seven nights a week, as well as to non-prime-time programming.

During this time Fox executed a series of deals aimed at making it equal or superior to ABC, CBS and NBC. The first move was to outbid CBS for the television rights to the National Football League's National Football Conference games. This led some CBS affiliates to switch to Fox.

The significance of this, however, was dwarfed by Fox's next move. In 1994 Fox signed an affiliation agreement with New World Communications Group. New World's eight stations and four stations New World had agreed to buy from Argyle Television signed 10–year affiliation agreements with Fox. In return Fox purchased $250 million of New

World stock and loaned New World $250 million. The seven-year loan was interest free. The deal also granted New World the right to run some of its syndicated programming on Fox-owned stations.

Of these 12 stations, eight were CBS affiliates, three were ABC affiliates and one was an NBC affiliate. Of greater significance was the fact that all 12 of these stations were VHF, whereas the former Fox affiliates in these markets were UHF. Seven of the stations were located in the top 21 markets in the country. Broadcasting & Cable, May 30, 1994 at 6.

The Fox–New World deal had a domino effect as the other networks scrambled to find new affiliates in these markets. In addition, all four networks sought to lock up affiliates in other markets. Soon CBS announced a 10–year affiliation agreement with Group W for its five stations, all major market VHF stations. A year later Westinghouse, the parent Company of Group W, purchased CBS. We will discuss this deal in Chapter XII.

Two new networks debuted in 1995. The United Paramount Network (UPN) and the Warner Brothers Network (WB), each started by offering two hours of prime-time programming two nights a week. By 1999 WB had reached its current schedule of three hours on Sunday and two hours, Monday through Friday. UPN had reached its current schedule of two hours on Monday through Friday.

Still another network, Pax Net, was launched in 1998. It was promoted as a family-oriented network, with a prime-time schedule consisting primarily of reruns of such shows as "Highway to Heaven," "Touched by an Angel" and "Dr. Quinn, Medicine Woman." More original programming has been added, while keeping to the family-friendly theme.

The majority of the commercial stations are affiliated with one or more networks by contractual arrangements. Of the 1338 commercial stations, more than 200 are affiliated with each of the four major networks. Although unaffiliated VHFs used to exist in markets with more than three commercial VHFs, this is no longer the case with the advent of the new networks. Similarly, the number of affiliated UHF stations has grown dramatically. Group owners other than the networks may produce some programs for their group or may treat their stations as individual facilities with each one affiliated with a different network or no network.

The economic relationships of commercial television stations are complex. Although it would have been possible for stations to develop their own programming and sell time to advertisers or to have the advertisers prepare programming and place it on individual stations, the industry has developed differently. The most important feature from the outset has been the role of the networks. It would have been possible for a network to own no stations and to perform no function other than as a broker between individual stations and national advertisers with no involvement in programming, or it could have arranged for the distribution of programs, often simultaneously, over common carrier intercon-nections. Instead, networks emerged as group owners who each con-trolled stations in five of the largest cities in the country. These have been profitable in their own right and have formed a solid base of guaranteed viewers.

To make the brokering function simpler and to maximize the audiences they can deliver, networks seek affiliates in each of the 200–odd market areas. A station, owned individually or by a group, will seek affiliation. The station will be relieved from having to create or purchase much of its programming because the network will supply programs to the affiliates and the profit will be more than it could make by remaining independent. The affiliate will be able to sell advertising for some spots in and around the network programming. Moreover, the network may pay fees ("compensation") to affiliates depending upon how much net-work programming they carry in excess of about 20 hours per week. The result is that the station clears time for the most popular programs without charge in order to be able to sell the available commercial time for these features, and is persuaded to clear for the next tier of programs by receiving a fee. To obtain these advantages, the station turns its audience over to the network for the agreed-upon programming and gives up most of its independent efforts. Occasionally, the relationship is discontinued.

Reduced revenues due to declining shares of the audience have caused the major networks to consider reducing compensation to their affiliates. There are, however, several risks involved in doing so. First, the affiliates may find it more attractive to replace less successful network programming with syndicated programming. Second, the affili-ates may balk at renewing their affiliation agreements. For example, in 1992 CBS had to modify a proposed reduction in affiliate compensation under pressure from its affiliates. Broadcasting, July 6, 1992 at 3.

Continuing decreases in ratings and increases in programming costs have raised questions regarding the continued viability of the network model. As NBC President Robert Wright observed, "The network model is a suspicious model in this day and age. The idea of the network having to maintain a very high national rating and having only advertising to lay it off against—and having most of the profitability appear at the local stations—is just a flawed concept." In keeping with this view, NBC has proposed forming a joint venture with its affiliates and phasing out compensation payments over a 10–year period. "Nets, affils square off," Broadcasting and Cable, May 18, 1998 at 4.

However, it has been difficult to convince affiliates to give up compensation payments. Broadcasters are always be reluctant to give up a revenue stream they are accustomed to receiving. This reluctance can only be worse at a time when they are incurring the costs of implement-ing DTV.

Another sign of increasingly contentious network-affiliate relations was Fox Television's 1999 decision to reduce the affiliates' commercial

30–second availabilities in prime-time network programming from 90 to 70 per week. Fox stated the move was necessary due to the "ever widening imbalance in profits between" the network and its affiliates. Fox offered affiliates the option of buying those spots and an additional 15, but reserved the right to cancel the buy-back program if less than 75 percent of the affiliates elect to participate. Broadcasting & Cable, Apr. 12, 1999 at 14. Network-affiliate relations finally reached the breaking point in 2001 when a coalition of affiliates asked the FCC to investigate alleged network violations of the chain broadcasting rules. We will discuss this in greater detail in Chapter XII.

Program production is generally thought to fall into two categories: the production of news, documentaries and public affairs programs, and the production of entertainment programming. Although news programming has not always been remunerative and could be left to local stations, the fact that so much of the news is national or international has led the networks themselves to undertake much of the production responsibility for these programs. Although the networks could contract with independent producers for this programming, they have uniformly decided to develop their own news and public affairs organizations and to produce all of their own programs in this category. Moreover, some networks will not buy documentaries from independent producers. The probable explanation is that the networks want total editorial control over this sensitive area to protect their stations from complaints and charges that may arise.

The considerations in entertainment programming are obviously quite different. In the earlier days of television, advertisers developed their own programming, perhaps through independent producers, and bought time to present the program and related commercials. The network simply sold time and access to the O & Os and affiliates in a single deal. As television developed, networks became more aware of the importance of continuity throughout the evening's entertainment programming, so that one show would link with the next to produce the largest loyal audiences. This required considering what the other networks were programming. Advertiser-initiated programming could aim for demographically discrete groups but could not accommodate all these concerns. By now advertiser-prepared programs have virtually disappeared and network productions play a minor role due at least in part to the financial interest and syndication rules to be discussed in Chapter XII. The independent producer pattern has become dominant. This entails interdependence of independent producers, local stations, advertisers and the networks.

Independent stations must operate in a totally different pattern because they must provide all their own programs. Independents tend to exist in markets with a large number of stations and thus compete not only with each other but also with network affiliates. If one of the networks did not have an affiliate in a market, it would make sense for the network to obtain an affiliate to increase the audience it can provide advertisers, and for the station to become an affiliate because network programming is more popular than alternatives, and affiliates are generally much more profitable than independents. If the network alternative is unavailable, the independents produce some inexpensive local programming and purchase programming from syndicators, who negotiate with individual stations rather than networks. The stations generally bargain for exclusive local rights for a period of time. Some programs are prepared by producers specially for syndication, but others have previously run on networks ("off-network programs") and are now being offered to the independents—or to affiliates who want to fill open time. Occasionally, independents join together to form an impromptu network for simultaneous showing of a sporting event or other single feature, but that is unusual and is likely to involve a program that the networks have rejected.

Rerun syndications are generally preferred to original syndications because they are proven commodities. Station managers will be able to predict how successful a rerun of specific material will be in their viewing area. Also, off-network syndications may be less expensive because most of the original creative costs have been returned by the network runs, whereas a first-run syndication must return its costs all at once. To reduce this differential, first-run syndications were traditionally less expensive shows that did not compete with the types of off-network programs that are most commonly and successfully syndicated; first-run syndications moved out of the situation comedy-mystery-detective script situation into game shows and talk shows. Independent stations have "stripped" some of the syndicated programs by presenting them at the same viewing time five days each week. The original program may have been shown on the network once a week, but enough backlog has been developed so that a station using syndication programming may be able to show the program daily and thereby build a loyal audience on a day-by-day basis. This helps the independent's quest for advertising.

The success during the 1987–1988 season of "Star Trek: The Next Generation" led to an increase in the number of first-run syndicated shows that appear directly competitive with both off-network syndicated shows and current network programs. Also contributing to the increase in first-run syndication has been the growing need for programming. Whereas it used to be that the only market for syndicated programming was broadcast stations, now an ever increasing number of cable channels need programming also. It is becoming more and more common for off-net syndicated programming to end up on cable channels as opposed to broadcast stations.

Advertisers may deal at one of several levels. National advertisers may work through networks as well as in specific local markets through "national spot" advertising. Local advertisers will deal directly with local stations, both affiliates and independents. In all cases the rates are determined by the size and characteristics of the audience that can be delivered to the advertiser.

The following is from the FCC's decision to sunset the Prime Time Access Rule, which limits network affiliates' ability to carry network programming during prime time. As part of the decision the FCC summarized the state of the broadcast and video programming industries (as of 1995). We will return to the substance of this decision in Chapter XII.

REVIEW OF THE PRIME TIME ACCESS RULE, SECTION 73.658(k) OF THE COMMISSION'S RULES
Federal Communications Commission, 1995.
10 F.C.C.Rcd. 5672.

. . .

A.   The Structure of the Industry

5.   We begin by summarizing briefly how the market for the purchase and sale of television programs operates. Television stations obtain programming for delivery to their viewers in a variety of ways. First, stations that affiliate with a television network obtain an entire package or schedule of programming directly from their network. This network "feed" is delivered to affiliated stations via satellite. Affiliated stations then broadcast the network programming to their local audiences. Some of the network feed is comprised of programs produced in-house by the network, such as the nightly national news and some entertainment programming. Much of the network feed, however, consists of programs produced by independent program production companies, with the network acting as a broker between these suppliers and its affiliated stations.

6.   Affiliated television stations also program portions of the broadcast day independently of their network. They air locally originated programming, primarily local news, public affairs, and sports programming. They also obtain programming from suppliers called "syndicators," entities that sell programming to television stations, primarily on an individual basis. In contrast to a network feed which supplies a schedule of network programming pursuant to an agreement between the network and a station, a syndicator licenses programs for exhibition on a station-by-station, program-by-program basis.

7.   Each of the original three major networks, ABC, CBS, and NBC, has over two hundred affiliates nationwide. (Each of the networks also owns and operates a number of stations throughout the country.) They each reach 99 percent of U.S. television households. The Fox Broadcasting Company has developed as a fourth network, with over 150 affiliated stations (as well as a number of its own "owned and operated" stations). (Fox also has over 40 secondary broadcast affiliates throughout the country.)[6] The percentage of U.S. television households capable of receiving Fox network programming is 97 percent as of February 1995.

***

6. By "secondary," we mean that the affiliated station airs only part of the network schedule of programs or delays the broadcast of these programs to a different time period.

8. Recently, two new networks have been launched. The United Paramount Network ("UPN"), owned by subsidiaries of Chris–Craft Industries, Inc.,[8] began service on January 16, 1995, with 96 affiliates. UPN had 67 percent coverage through primary affiliates and an additional 16 percent coverage through secondary affiliations for a total coverage of 83 percent. A recent report indicates that UPN has added nine new affiliates—three primary and six secondary—to increase their audience reach to 86.5 percent, including coverage by primary affiliates of 73 percent. WB, affiliated with Warner Brothers (which, in turn, is owned by Time Warner), began broadcasting on January 11, 1995, with 47 affiliates and superstation WGN. WB has a national reach of 78 percent, with 18 percent of this reach achieved through cable delivery on WGN. . . .

9. There are now over 450 local commercial broadcast stations that are not affiliated with the ABC, CBS, or NBC networks. While these stations have traditionally been called "independent" stations, approximately 300 of these commercial stations are now affiliated with and obtain several hours of prime-time programming from the Fox, UPN, or WB networks. Approximately 150 of these stations are affiliated with Fox. Some of these stations have dual affiliations. In addition to airing this network programming, independent stations air some locally originated programming. Much of their programming, however, is obtained from program producers or syndicators. These programs include movies previously shown in theaters, television series previously aired on network affiliates (*i.e.,* off-network programs such as reruns of *The Cosby Show*), and series produced for first-run viewing on the independent stations (*e.g., Star Trek: The Next Generation*).

. . .

B. The Video Programming Production Market

32. . . . Entertainment series, news magazine shows, and game shows are examples of the programs sold by independent producers and syndicators of prime-time programs to network affiliates and independents. The list can be extended to include movies (whether for television, theatrical presentation, or cassette rental), sports programs, talk shows, news programming (local and national), musical variety, dramas, arts presentations, etc. Suppliers of these programs include not only those suppliers that actually are employed in a given year to produce programming for network prime time but also those producers willing and able to produce such programming in the event that market price increased above the competitive level. The list of suppliers will include television networks, independent syndicators, Hollywood movie studios, and international video producers. Buyers of such programming are not limited to television broadcasters but will include other purchasers of video pro-

---

8. Paramount Pictures Corporation, a subsidiary of Viacom, Inc., has provided funding and assistance in the launch of UPN. Paramount also holds a contingent ownership interest in UPN. [ ]

gramming such as cable networks and operators, direct broadcast satellite operators, videocassette distributors and, most recently, video programming affiliates of local telephone companies, which propose to offer video dialtone service. This market is "clearly national and perhaps international in scope, because television broadcasters obtain a large portion of their programs from national providers."

. . .

42. . . . Producers rely to a great extent on their ability to sell reruns of their programs—*i.e.*, off-network programs—to recoup their costs and to earn a profit. The license fee the networks pay for the right to air prime-time entertainment programs often does not cover the costs of producing these programs. According to the Coalition [to Enhance Diversity], in fact, the network license fee usually covers only 70 percent of the producer's costs, resulting in production deficits for network programming. . . .

. . .

49. . . . [F]our companies—Paramount, Warner Brothers, Fox, and King World—distribute over 95 percent of the first-run syndicated programming aired during [prime time]. The first three are major Hollywood studios that have been major suppliers of prime time programming. . . . [104] King World is a new entrant to the market since [1970], and in fact is the leading supplier of [prime time] first-run programming. But its two most popular programs—*Wheel of Fortune* and *Jeopardy*—got their start as *network* programs and then went into first-run syndication. . . .

. . .

57. . . . In 1994, 181 first-run syndicated programs were broadcast, and 18 of the 25 most popular syndicated programs were first-run. Satellite delivery is now available to non-network suppliers, reducing their distribution costs, previously a disadvantage compared to network distribution to affiliates. . . .

. . .

61. . . . Indeed, many independents already broadcast first-run programs in prime time opposite network broadcasts; among non-Fox independent stations in the top–50 markets, 39 percent of prime time hours were first-run syndication.

. . .

72. The number of independent television stations has grown by almost 450 percent since [1970], from 82 stations in 1970 to over 450 today. . . .

. . .

104. These three studios accounted for 17.5 percent of the entertainment series programs supplied to the three networks during the 1969–70 season. They accounted for 21.7 percent of such programming during the 1993–94 season. [   ]

108. . . . The emergence of the Fox network certainly can be said to have improved affiliate bargaining power by creating a viable affiliation alternative to ABC, CBS, and NBC. This is demonstrated by the flurry of recent affiliation switches. Since May 1994, 68 stations have changed network affiliation. Of these, 21 switched from one of the three original networks to the Fox network. This competition for affiliates has apparently resulted in greater affiliate compensation. . . .

. . .

Notes and Questions

1.   The television industry is in the middle of a period of great change. The power of the three major networks has greatly diminished. The three original major networks' share of the market declined from 90 percent in 1969 to 47 percent in 1997. By 2001, even with Fox Television included, the major networks combined ratings dropped below 50 percent. Also of concern to the networks was a significant overall increase in the median age of their viewers. The figures for each network were as follows: CBS–51.2, ABC–46.6, NBC–45, Fox–36, UPN–34.1, WB–29.1. Broadcasting & Cable, June 18, 2001. Independents, the other networks and various cable services have all contributed to this decline. The growth of the Internet (discussed in Chapter XI) has also been linked to this decline.

2.   Declining audiences have led to declining revenues. Profits for the four networks dropped 12 percent in 2001. This has again led the networks to propose reducing affiliate compensation and/or restructuring the affiliate-network business relationship. Further changes to the structure of the broadcast industry and video programming markets are expected. We will discuss these in Chapter XII.

3.   To keep matters in perspective, perhaps it is well to realize that television accounted for 33 percent of major mass media advertising expenditures in 2002. By comparison, newspapers carried 35 percent of the total, magazines 9 percent, radio 14 percent, and cable television 9 percent.

Chapter III

JUSTIFICATIONS FOR GOVERNMENT REGULATION

A. "PUBLIC INTEREST" AND GOVERNMENT REGULATION

We have just been considering the special nature of the spectrum and various actions that the FCC has taken to regulate the behavior of those who use part of the spectrum. We turn now to the legal question of what justifies the Commission in undertaking these forms of regulation, plus other types of regulation that we consider later. Although a few cases challenged this power early in the life of the FCC, the first major case to address the problem was National Broadcasting Co. v. United States, 319 U.S. 190 (1943).

After conducting a study of business practices and ownership patterns of radio networks in 1941, the Federal Communications Commission concluded that the major networks (NBC and CBS) exerted too much control over the broadcast industry through control over local station programming. To correct this situation, the Commission issued the Chain Broadcasting Regulations, which defined permissible relationships between networks and stations in terms of affiliation, network programming of affiliates' time and network ownership of stations. These regulations were aimed at dissuading individual licensees from entering contracts that gave the networks the power to exert such control over licensees. NBC challenged the Commission's authority to adopt regulations controlling licensee behavior not related to technical and engineering matters. We will return to the substance of these regulations in Chapter XII.

The first claim was that Congress had not authorized the FCC to adopt these regulations. Section 303 of the Act provided that the Commission "as public interest, convenience, or necessity requires, shall . . . have authority to make special regulations applicable to radio stations engaged in chain broadcasting." NBC argued that the "public interest" language was to be read as limited to technical and engineering aspects of broadcasting—and that these were not the basis for the FCC's regulations in this case.

The Court noted that several sections of the Act authorized the FCC in furtherance of the "public interest, convenience, or necessity" to do such things as "study new uses for radio, . . . and generally encourage the larger and more effective use of radio in the public interest" and to provide a "fair, efficient and equitable distribution [of licenses] among the states." Building from these several grants of power, the Court rejected NBC's claim:

The Act itself establishes that the Commission's powers are not limited to the engineering and technical aspects of regulation of radio communication. Yet we are asked to regard the Commission as a kind of traffic officer, policing the wave lengths to prevent stations from interfering with each other. But the Act does not restrict the Commission merely to supervision of the traffic. It puts upon the Commission the burden of determining the composition of that traffic. The facilities of radio are not large enough to accommodate all who wish to use them. Methods must be devised for choosing from among the many who apply. And since Congress itself could not do this, it committed the task to the Commission.

. . .

. . . The Commission's licensing function cannot be discharged, therefore, merely by finding that there are no technological objections to the granting of a license. If the criterion of "public interest" were limited to such matters, how could the Commission choose between two applicants for the same facilities, each of whom is financially and technically qualified to operate a station? Since the very inception of federal regulation by radio, comparative considerations as to the services to be rendered have governed the application of the standard of "public interest, convenience, or necessity." [   ]

. . .

These provisions, individually and in the aggregate, preclude the notion that the Commission is empowered to deal only with technical and engineering impediments to the "larger and more effective use of radio in the public interest." We cannot find in the Act any such restriction of the Commission's authority. Suppose, for example, that a community can, because of physical limitations, be assigned only two stations. That community might be deprived of effective service in any one of several ways. More powerful stations in nearby cities might blanket out the signals of local stations so that they could not be heard at all. The stations might interfere with each other so that neither could be clearly heard. One station might dominate the other with the power of its signal. But the community could be deprived of good radio service in ways less crude. One man, financially and technically qualified, might apply for and obtain the licenses of both stations and present a single service over the two stations, thus wasting a frequency otherwise available to the area. The language of the Act does not withdraw such a situation from the licensing and regulatory powers of the Commission, and there is no evidence that Congress did not mean its broad language to carry the authority it expresses.

The Court then considered NBC's claims that if Congress did authorize the FCC to do this, the statute was unconstitutional. The first argument was that the phrase "public interest" was too vague a standard for delegating functions to the FCC. The Court disagreed and relied on an earlier broadcasting case in which it had said that the phrase "is as concrete as the complicated factors for judgment in such a field of delegated authority permit." The phrase is not to be interpreted as giving the FCC "unlimited power." Next, the Court rejected NBC's First Amendment claim:

> We come, finally, to an appeal to the First Amendment. The Regulations, even if valid in all other respects, must fall because they abridge, say the appellants, their right of free speech. If that be so, it would follow that every person whose application for a license is denied by the Commission is thereby denied his constitutional right of free speech. Freedom of utterance is abridged to many who wish to use the limited facilities of radio. Unlike other modes of expression, it is subject to governmental regulation. Because it cannot be used by all, some who wish to use it must be denied. But Congress did not authorize the Commission to choose among applicants upon the basis of their political, economic or social views, or upon any other capricious basis. If it did, or if the Commission by these Regulations proposed a choice among applicants upon some such basis, the issue before us would be wholly different. The question here is simply whether the Commission, by announcing that it will refuse licenses to persons who engage in specified network practices (a basis for choice, which we hold is comprehended within the statutory criterion of "public interest"), is thereby denying such persons the constitutional right of free speech. The right of free speech does not include, however, the right to use the facilities of radio without a license. The licensing system established by Congress in the Communications Act of 1934 was a proper exercise of its power over commerce. The standard it provided for the licensing of stations was the "public interest, convenience, or necessity." Denial of a station license on that ground, if valid under the Act, is not a denial of free speech.

Notes and Questions

1. The origin of the phrase, "public interest, convenience and necessity," § 309(a), or "public convenience, interest or necessity," § 307(a), is unclear from legislative documents. A former chairman of the Commission, Newton Minow, suggested the origin in Equal Time 8–9 (1964): Sen. Clarence C. Dill, who had played a major part in the early legislation, told Minow that the drafters had reached an impasse in attempting to define a regulatory standard for this new, uncharted activity. A young lawyer who had been loaned to the Senate by the Interstate Commerce Commission proposed the words because they were used in other federal statutes.

Judge Henry Friendly, in *The Federal Administrative Agencies* 54–55 (1962), commented on the standard:

> The only guideline supplied by Congress in the Communications Act of 1934 was "public convenience, interest, or necessity." The

standard of public convenience and necessity introduced into the federal statute book by Transportation Act, 1920, conveyed a fair degree of meaning when the issue was whether new or duplicating railroad construction should be authorized or an existing line abandoned. It was to convey less when, as under the Motor Carrier Act of 1935, or the Civil Aeronautics Act of 1938, there would be the added issue of selecting the applicant to render a service found to be needed; but under those statutes there would usually be some demonstrable factors, such as, in air route cases, ability to render superior one-plane or one-carrier service because of junction of the new route with existing ones, lower costs due to other operations, or historical connection with the traffic, that ought to have enabled the agency to develop intelligible criteria for selection. The standard was almost drained of meaning under section 307 of the Communications Act, where the issue was almost never the need for broadcasting service but rather who should render it.

2. The Radio Commission's first obligation was to clear the airwaves to avoid destructive interference. It decided in 1928 that "as between two broadcasting stations with otherwise equal claims for privileges, the station which has the longest record of continuous service has the superior right." Great Lakes Broadcasting Co., 3 F.R.C.Ann.Rep. 32 (1929), modified on other grounds 37 F.2d 993 (D.C.Cir.1930), certiorari dismissed 281 U.S. 706 (1930). In that case, involving three competing stations, the Commission also stated, however, that if there was a "substantial disparity" in the services being offered by the stations, "the claim of priority must give way to the superior service." The Commission was soon evaluating service in terms of program content. In *Great Lakes*, the Commission contented itself with noting that stations using formats that appeal to only a "small portion" of the public were not serving the public interest because each member of the listening public is entitled to service from each station in the community.

3. In its early years the Radio Commission showed no hesitation in denying renewal of licenses because of the content of the speech uttered over the station. Section 29 of the 1927 Act, reenacted as § 326 of the 1934 Act, provided in relevant part:

> Nothing in this Act shall be understood or construed to give the licensing authority the power of censorship over the radio communications or signals transmitted by any radio station, and no regulation or condition shall be promulgated or fixed by the licensing authority which shall interfere with the right of free speech by means of radio communication.

In 1930 the Commission denied renewal of a license to KFKB on the ground that the station was being controlled and used by Dr. J.R. Brinkley to further his personal interest. Dr. Brinkley had three half-hour programs daily in which he answered anonymous inquiries on health and medicine and usually recommended several of his own tonics and prescriptions that were known to the public only by numerical designations. Druggists paid a fee to Dr. Brinkley for each sale they made.

In affirming the denial of renewal, KFKB Broadcasting Association v. Federal Radio Commission, 47 F.2d 670 (D.C.Cir.1931), the court rejected the station's argument that the Commission had censored in violation of § 29:

> This contention is without merit. There has been no attempt on the part of the commission to subject any part of appellant's broadcasting matter to scrutiny prior to its release. In considering the question whether the public interest, convenience, or necessity will be served by a renewal of appellant's license, the commission has merely exercised its undoubted right to take note of appellant's past conduct, which is not censorship.

In Trinity Methodist Church, South v. Federal Radio Commission, 62 F.2d 850 (D.C.Cir.1932), certiorari denied 288 U.S. 599 (1933), the controlling figure was the minister of the church, Dr. Shuler, who regularly defamed government institutions and officials, and attacked labor groups and various religions. The Commission's denial of renewal was affirmed. The court concluded that the broadcasts "without facts to sustain or to justify them" might fairly be found not to be within the public interest:

> If it be considered that one in possession of a permit to broadcast in interstate commerce may, without let or hindrance from any source, use these facilities, reaching out, as they do, from one corner of the country to the other, to obstruct the administration of justice, offend the religious susceptibilities of thousands, inspire political distrust and civic discord, or offend youth and innocence by the free use of words suggestive of sexual immorality, and be answerable for slander only at the instance of the one offended, then this great science, instead of a boon, will become a scourge and the nation a theater for the display of individual passions and the collusion of personal interests. This is neither censorship nor previous restraint, nor is it a whittling away of the rights guaranteed by the First Amendment, or an impairment of their free exercise. Appellant may continue to indulge his strictures upon the characters of men in public office. He may just as freely as ever criticize religious practices of which he does not approve. He may even indulge private malice or personal slander—subject, of course, to being required to answer for the abuse thereof—but he may not, as we think, demand, of right, the continued use of an instrumentality of commerce for such purposes, or any other, except in subordination to all reasonable rules and regulations Congress, acting through the Commission, may prescribe.

4.   The Supreme Court did not again consider the FCC's power until 26 years after *NBC*. Because this case, Red Lion v. Federal Communications Commission, 395 U.S. 367, 16 R.R.2d 2029, 1 Med.L.Rptr. 2053 (1969), affects everything else that follows, we consider it at the outset of our

exploration of broadcasting law. The case deals fairly closely with the personal attack part of the broader fairness doctrine. The case also refers to the "equal opportunities" rule (sometimes incorrectly called the "equal time" rule), which applies during election campaigns. Although we look at each of these doctrines in detail in Chapter V, including the FCC's 1987 decision eliminating much, if not all, of the fairness doctrine, we must introduce each one now so that *Red Lion* can be fully understood.

As part of the first Communications Act, Congress passed what is now § 315, which requires any broadcaster who sells or gives time for a candidate's use to treat all other candidates for the same office equally. This means, for example, that a broadcaster who sells a candidate for Congress 15 minutes of prime time, must be prepared to sell each opponent of that candidate 15 minutes of prime time at the same price.

The fairness doctrine, on the other hand, was not imposed by Congress. Developed by the Commission on its own in the 1940s, the doctrine had two separate parts. One part required the broadcaster to air issues that "are so critical or of such great public importance that it would be unreasonable for a licensee to ignore them completely." Much more attention had been paid to the second part of the doctrine—that if a broadcaster did cover a "controversial issue of public importance" it had to take steps to assure that important contrasting views were also presented. These views could be presented by the licensee itself or by speakers chosen by the licensee.

The personal attack aspect of the fairness doctrine emerged in decisions in which the FCC ordered stations that had broadcast programs attacking a person's character during a discussion of a controversial issue of public importance to inform the person and offer him time to present his side. The Red Lion case arose from such a situation.

While the Red Lion case was being litigated, the FCC decided to promulgate a formal rule to make the personal attack doctrine more precise and more readily enforceable. The personal attack rule applied when "during the presentation of views on a controversial issue of public importance, an attack is made upon the honesty, character, integrity, or like personal qualities of an identified person or group." Notice and an opportunity to respond were required.

At the same time the FCC decided to promulgate a formal political editorial rule providing that when a licensee editorially endorsed a candidate for political office, other candidates for the same office were to be advised of the endorsement and offered a reasonable opportunity to respond. The same opportunity was to be extended to any candidate who was attacked in an editorial.

As soon as these two formal rules were announced, the Radio Television News Directors Association (RTNDA) sued to declare the rules unconstitutional. The court of appeals agreed and held that the rules violated the First Amendment. The Supreme Court heard both cases together and decided them in the same opinion.

RED LION BROADCASTING CO. v. FEDERAL COMMUNICATIONS COMMISSION

Supreme Court of the United States, 1969.
395 U.S. 367, 89 S.Ct. 1794, 16 R.R.2d 2029, 1, 23 L.Ed.2d 371 Med.L.Rptr. 2053.

Mr. Justice White delivered the opinion of the Court.

The Federal Communications Commission has for many years imposed on radio and television broadcasters the requirement that discussion of public issues be presented on broadcast stations, and that each side of those issues must be given fair coverage. This is known as the fairness doctrine, which originated very early in the history of broadcasting and has maintained its present outlines for some time. It is an obligation whose content has been defined in a long series of FCC rulings in particular cases, and which is distinct from the statutory requirement of § 315 of the Communications Act that equal time be allotted all qualified candidates for public office. Two aspects of the fairness doctrine, relating to personal attacks in the context of controversial public issues and to political editorializing, were codified more precisely in the form of FCC regulations in 1967. The two cases before us now, which were decided separately below, challenge the constitutional and statutory bases of the doctrine and component rules. *Red Lion* involves the application of the fairness doctrine to a particular broadcast, and *RTNDA* arises as an action to review the FCC's 1967 promulgation of the personal attack and political editorializing regulations, which were laid down after the *Red Lion* litigation had begun.

I.

A.

The Red Lion Broadcasting Company is licensed to operate a Pennsylvania radio station, WGCB. On November 27, 1964, WGCB carried a 15–minute broadcast by the Reverend Billy James Hargis as part of a "Christian Crusade" series. A book by Fred J. Cook entitled "Goldwater—Extremist on the Right" was discussed by Hargis, who said that Cook had been fired by a newspaper for making false charges against city officials; that Cook had then worked for a Communist-affiliated publication; that he had defended Alger Hiss and attacked J. Edgar Hoover and the Central Intelligence Agency; and that he had now written a "book to smear and destroy Barry Goldwater." When Cook heard of the broadcast he concluded that he had been personally attacked and demanded free reply time, which the station refused. After an exchange of letters among Cook, Red Lion, and the FCC, the FCC declared that the Hargis broadcast constituted a personal attack on Cook; that Red Lion had failed to meet its obligation under the fairness doctrine as expressed in Times–Mirror Broadcasting Co., 24 P & F Radio Reg. 404 (1962), to send a tape, transcript, or summary of the broadcast to Cook and offer him reply time; and that the station must provide reply time whether or not Cook would pay for it. On review in the Court of Appeals for the District of Columbia Circuit, the FCC's position was upheld as constitutional and otherwise proper. [   ]

. . .

C.

Believing that the specific application of the fairness doctrine in *Red Lion,* and the promulgation of the regulations in *RTNDA,* are both authorized by Congress and enhance rather than abridge the freedoms of speech and press protected by the First Amendment, we hold them valid and constitutional, reversing the judgment, below in *RTNDA* and affirming the judgment below in *Red Lion.*

II.

The history of the emergence of the fairness doctrine and of the related legislation shows that the Commission's action in the *Red Lion* case did not exceed its authority, and that in adopting the new regulations the Commission was implementing congressional policy rather than embarking on a frolic of its own.

A.

Before 1927, the allocation of frequencies was left entirely to the private sector, and the result was chaos. It quickly became apparent that broadcast frequencies constituted a scarce resource whose use could be regulated and rationalized only by the Government. Without government control, the medium would be of little use because of the cacophony of competing voices, none of which could be clearly and predictably heard. Consequently, the Federal Radio Commission was established to allocate frequencies among competing applicants in a manner responsive to the public "convenience, interest, or necessity."

Very shortly thereafter the Commission expressed its view that the "public interest requires ample play for the free and fair competition of opposing views, and the commission believes that the principle applies to all discussions of issues of importance to the public." . . . After an extended period during which the licensee was obliged not only to cover and to cover fairly the views of others, but also to refrain from expressing his own personal views, Mayflower Broadcasting Corp., 8 F.C.C. 333 (1940), the latter limitation on the licensee was abandoned and the doctrine developed into its present form.

There is a twofold duty laid down by the FCC's decisions and described by the 1949 Report on Editorializing by Broadcast Licensees, 13 F.C.C. 1246 (1949). The broadcaster must give adequate coverage to public issues, [   ], and coverage must be fair in that it accurately reflects the opposing views. [   ] This must be done at the broadcaster's own expense if sponsorship is unavailable. [   ] Moreover, the duty must be met by programming obtained at the licensee's own initiative if available from no other source. . . .

When a personal attack has been made on a figure involved in a public issue, both the doctrine of cases such as *Red Lion* and *Times Mirror Broadcasting Co.,* 24 P & F Radio Reg. 404 (1962), and also the 1967 regulations at issue in *RTNDA* require that the individual attacked himself be offered an opportunity to respond. Likewise, where one candidate is endorsed in a political editorial, the other candidates must themselves be offered reply time to use personally or through a spokesman. These obligations differ from the general fairness requirement that issues be presented, and presented with coverage of competing views, in that the broadcaster does not have the option of presenting the attacked party's side himself or choosing a third party to represent that side. But insofar as there is an obligation of the broadcaster to see that both sides are presented, and insofar as that is an affirmative obligation, the personal attack doctrine and regulations do not differ from the preceding fairness doctrine. The simple fact that the attacked men or unendorsed candidates may respond themselves or through agents is not a critical distinction, and indeed, it is not unreasonable for the FCC to conclude that the objective of adequate presentation of all sides may best be served by allowing those most closely affected to make the response, rather than leaving the response in the hands of the station which has attacked their candidacies, endorsed their opponents, or carried a personal attack upon them.

B.

The statutory authority of the FCC to promulgate these regulations derives from the mandate to the "Commission from time to time, as public convenience, interest, or necessity requires" to promulgate "such rules and regulations and prescribe such restrictions and conditions . . . as may be necessary to carry out the provisions of this chapter. . . ." 47 U.S.C. § 303 and § 303(r). The Commission is specifically directed to consider the demands of the public interest in the course of granting licenses, 47 U.S.C. §§ 307(a), 309(a); renewing them, 47 U.S.C. § 307; and modifying them. Ibid. Moreover, the FCC has included among the conditions of the Red Lion license itself the requirement that operation of the station be carried out in the public interest, 47 U.S.C. § 309(h). This mandate to the FCC to assure that broadcasters operate in the public interest is a broad one, a power "not niggardly but expansive," National Broadcasting Co. v. United States, 319 U.S. 190, 219 (1943), whose validity we have long upheld. [   ] It is broad enough to encompass these regulations.

The fairness doctrine finds specific recognition in statutory form, is in part modeled on explicit statutory provisions relating to political candidates, and is approvingly reflected in legislative history.

In 1959 the Congress amended the statutory requirement of § 315 that equal time be accorded each political candidate to except certain appearances on news programs, but added that this constituted no exception *"from the obligation imposed upon them under this Act to operate in the public interest and to afford reasonable opportunity for their discussion of conflicting views on issues of public importance."* Act of September 14, 1959, § 1, 73 Stat. 557, amending 47 U.S.C. § 315(a) (emphasis added). This language makes it very plain that Congress, in 1959, announced that the phrase "public interest," which had been in the Act since 1927, imposed a duty on broadcasters to discuss both sides of controversial public issues. In other words, the amendment vindicated the FCC's general view that the fairness doctrine inhered in the public interest standard. Subsequent legislation declaring the intent of an earlier statute is entitled to great weight in statutory construction. And here this principle is given special force by the equally venerable principle that the construction of a statute by those charged with its execution should be followed unless there are compelling indications that it is wrong, especially when Congress has refused to alter the administrative construction. Here, the Congress has not just kept its silence by refusing to overturn the administrative construction, but has ratified it with positive legislation. Thirty years of consistent administrative construction left undisturbed by Congress until 1959, when that construction was expressly accepted, reinforce the natural conclusion that the public interest language of the Act authorized the Commission to require licensees to use their stations for discussion of public issues, and that the FCC is free to implement this requirement by reasonable rules and regulations which fall short of abridgment of the freedom of speech and press, and of the censorship proscribed by § 326 of the Act.

The objectives of § 315 themselves could readily be circumvented but for the complementary fairness doctrine ratified by § 315. The section applies only to campaign appearances by candidates, and not by family, friends, campaign managers, or other supporters. Without the fairness doctrine, then, a licensee could ban all campaign appearances by candidates themselves from the air and proceed to deliver over his station entirely to the supporters of one slate of candidates, to the exclusion of all others. In this way the broadcaster could have a far greater impact on the favored candidacy than he could by simply allowing a spot appearance by the candidate himself. It is the fairness doctrine as an aspect of the obligation to operate in the public interest, rather than § 315, which prohibits the broadcaster from taking such a step.

     . . .

In light of the fact that the "public interest" in broadcasting clearly encompasses the presentation of vigorous debate of controversial issues of importance and concern to the public; the fact that the FCC has rested upon that language from its very inception a doctrine that these issues must be discussed, and fairly; and the fact that Congress has acknowledged that the analogous provisions of § 315 are not preclusive in this area, and knowingly preserved the FCC's complementary efforts, we think the fairness doctrine and its component personal attack and political editorializing regulations are a legitimate exercise of congressionally delegated authority. . . .

III.

The broadcasters challenge the fairness doctrine and its specific manifestations in the personal attack and political editorial rules on conventional First Amendment grounds, alleging that the rules abridge their freedom of speech and press. Their contention is that the First Amendment protects their desire to use their allotted frequencies continuously to broadcast whatever they choose, and to exclude whomever they choose from ever using that frequency. No man may be prevented from saying or publishing what he thinks, or refusing in his speech or other utterances to give equal weight to the views of his opponents. This right, they say, applies equally to broadcasters.

A.

Although broadcasting is clearly a medium affected by a First Amendment interest, United States v. Paramount Pictures, Inc., 334 U.S. 131, 166 (1948), differences in the characteristics of new media justify differences in the First Amendment standards applied to them. [ ] For example, the ability of new technology to produce sounds more raucous than those of the human voice justifies restrictions on the sound level, and on the hours and places of use, of sound trucks so long as the restrictions are reasonable and applied without discrimination. [ ]

Just as the Government may limit the use of sound-amplifying equipment potentially so noisy that it drowns out civilized private speech, so may the Government limit the use of broadcast equipment. The right of free speech of a broadcaster, the user of a sound truck, or any other individual does not embrace a right to snuff out the free speech of others. Associated Press v. United States, 326 U.S. 1, 20 (1945).

When two people converse face to face, both should not speak at once if either is to be clearly understood. But the range of the human voice is so limited that there could be meaningful communications if half the people in the United States were talking and the other half listening. Just as clearly, half the people might publish and the other half read. But the reach of radio signals is incomparably greater than the range of the human voice and the problem of interference is a massive reality. The lack of know-how and equipment may keep many from the air but only a tiny fraction of those with resources and intelligence can hope to communicate by radio at the same time if intelligible communication is to be had, even if the entire radio spectrum is utilized in the present state of commercially acceptable technology.

It was this fact, and the chaos which ensued from permitting anyone to use any frequency at whatever power level he wished, which made necessary the enactment of the Radio Act of 1927 and the Communications Act of 1934, as the Court has noted at length before. National Broadcasting Co. v. United States, 319 U.S. 190, 210–214 (1943). It was this reality which at the very least necessitated first the division of the radio spectrum into portions reserved respectively for public broadcasting and for other important radio uses such as amateur operation, aircraft, police, defense, and navigation; and then the subdivision of each portion, and assignment of specific frequencies to individual users or groups of users. Beyond this, however, because the frequencies reserved for public broadcasting were limited in number, it was essential for the Government to tell some applicants that they could not broadcast at all because there was room for only a few.

Where there are substantially more individuals who want to broadcast than there are frequencies to allocate, it is idle to posit an unabridgeable First Amendment right to broadcast comparable to the right of every individual to speak, write, or publish. If 100 persons want broadcast licenses but there are only 10 frequencies to allocate, all of them may have the same "right" to a license; but if there is to be any effective communication by radio, only a few can be licensed and the rest must be barred from the airwaves. It would be strange if the First Amendment, aimed at protecting and furthering communications, prevented the Government from making radio communication possible by requiring licenses to broadcast and by limiting the number of licenses so as not to overcrowd the spectrum.

This has been the consistent view of the Court. Congress unquestionably has the power to grant and deny licenses and to eliminate existing stations. FRC v. Nelson Bros. Bond & Mortgage Co., 289 U.S. 266 (1933). No one has a First Amendment right to a license or to monopolize a radio frequency; to deny a station license because "the public interest" requires it "is not a denial of free speech." National Broadcasting Co. v. United States, 319 U.S. 190, 227 (1943).

By the same token, as far as the First Amendment is concerned those who are licensed stand no better than those to whom licenses are refused. A license permits broadcasting, but the licensee has no constitutional right to be the one who holds the license or to monopolize a radio frequency to the exclusion of his fellow citizens. There is nothing in the First Amendment which prevents the Government from requiring a licensee to share his frequency with others and to conduct himself as a proxy or fiduciary with obligations to present those views and voices which are representative of his community and which would otherwise, by necessity, be barred from the airwaves.

This is not to say that the First Amendment is irrelevant to public broadcasting. On the contrary, it has a major role to play as the Congress itself recognized in § 326, which forbids FCC interference with "the right of free speech by means of radio communication." Because of the scarcity of radio frequencies, the Government is permitted to put restraints on licensees in favor of others whose views should be expressed on this unique medium. But the people as a whole retain their interest in free speech by radio and their collective right to have the medium function consistently with the ends and purposes of the First Amendment. It is the right of the viewers and listeners, not the right of the broadcasters, which is paramount. See FCC v. Sanders Bros. Radio

Station, 309 U.S. 470, 475 (1940); FCC v. Allentown Broadcasting Corp., 349 U.S. 358, 361–362 (1955); 2 Z. Chafee, Government and Mass Communications 546 (1947). It is the purpose of the First Amendment to preserve an uninhibited marketplace of ideas in which truth will ultimately prevail, rather than to countenance monopolization of that market, whether it be by the Government itself or a private licensee. Associated Press v. United States, 326 U.S. 1, 20 (1945); New York Times Co. v. Sullivan, 376 U.S. 254, 270 (1964); Abrams v. United States, 250 U.S. 616, 630 (1919) (Holmes, J., dissenting). "[S]peech concerning public affairs is more than self-expression; it is the essence of self-government." Garrison v. Louisiana, 379 U.S. 64, 74–75 (1964). See Brennan, The Supreme Court and the Meiklejohn Interpretation of the First Amendment, 79 Harv.L.Rev. 1 (1965). It is the right of the public to receive suitable access to social, political, esthetic, moral, and other ideas and experiences which is crucial here. That right may not constitutionally be abridged either by Congress or by the FCC.

B.

Rather than confer frequency monopolies on a relatively small number of licensees, in a Nation of 200,000,000, the Government could surely have decreed that each frequency should be shared among all or some of those who wish to use it, each being assigned a portion of the broadcast day or the broadcast week. The ruling and regulations at issue here do not go quite so far. They assert that under specified circumstances, a licensee must offer to make available a reasonable amount of broadcast time to those who have a view different from that which has already been expressed on his station. The expression of a political endorsement, or of a personal attack while dealing with a controversial public issue, simply triggers this time sharing. As we have said, the First Amendment confers no right on licensees to prevent others from broadcasting on "their" frequencies and no right to an unconditional monopoly of a scarce resource which the Government has denied others the right to use.

In terms of constitutional principle, and as enforced sharing of a scarce resource, the personal attack and political editorial rules are indistinguishable from the equal-time provision of § 315, a specific enactment of Congress requiring stations to set aside reply time under specified circumstances and to which the fairness doctrine and these constituent regulations are important complements. That provision, which has been part of the law since 1927, Radio Act of 1927, § 18, 44 Stat. 1170, has been held valid by this Court as an obligation of the licensee relieving him of any power in any way to prevent or censor the broadcast, and thus, insulating him from liability for defamation. The constitutionality of the statute under the First Amendment was unquestioned. Farmers Educ. & Co–op. Union v. WDAY, 360 U.S. 525 (1959).

Nor can we say that it is inconsistent with the First Amendment goal of producing an informed public capable of conducting its own affairs to require a broadcaster to permit answers to personal attacks occurring in the course of discussing controversial issues, or to require that the political opponents of those endorsed by the station be given a chance to communicate with the public.[18] Otherwise, station owners and a few networks would have unfettered power to make time available only to the highest bidders, to communicate only their own views on public issues, people and candidates, and to permit on the air only those with whom they agreed. There is no sanctuary in the First Amendment for unlimited private censorship operating in a medium not open to all. "Freedom of the press from governmental interference under the First Amendment does not sanction repression of that freedom by private interests." Associated Press v. United States, 326 U.S. 1, 20 (1945).

C.

It is strenuously argued, however, that if political editorials or personal attacks will trigger an obligation in broadcasters to afford the opportunity for expression to speakers who need not pay for time and whose views are unpalatable to the licensees, then broadcasters will be irresistibly forced to self-censorship and their coverage of controversial public issues will be eliminated or at least rendered wholly ineffective. Such a result would indeed be a serious matter, for should licensees actually eliminate their coverage of controversial issues, the purposes of the doctrine would be stifled.

At this point, however, as the Federal Communications Commission has indicated, that possibility is at best speculative. The communications industry, and in particular the networks, have taken pains to present controversial issues in the past, and even now they do not assert that they intend to abandon their efforts in this regard. It would be better if the FCC's encouragement were never necessary to induce the broadcasters to meet their responsibility. And if experience with the administration of these doctrines indicates that they have the net effect of reducing rather than enhancing the volume and quality of coverage, there will be time enough to reconsider the constitutional implications. The fairness doctrine in the past has had no such overall effect.

That this will occur now seems unlikely, however, since if present licensees should suddenly prove timorous, the Commission is not powerless to insist that they give adequate and fair attention to public issues. It does not violate the First Amendment to treat licensees given the privilege of using scarce radio frequencies as proxies for the entire community, obligated to give suitable time and attention to matters of great public concern. To condition the granting or renewal of licenses on a willingness to present representative community views on controver-

---

18. The expression of views opposing those which broadcasters permit to be aired in the first place need not be confined solely to the broadcasters themselves as proxies. "Nor is it enough that he should hear the arguments of adversaries from his own teachers, presented as they state them, and accompanied by what they offer as refuta- tions. That is not the way to do justice to the arguments, or bring them into real contact with his own mind. He must be able to hear them from persons who actually believe them; who defend them in earnest, and do their very utmost for them." J. Mill, On Liberty 32 (R. McCallum ed. 1947).

sial issues is consistent with the ends and purposes of those constitutional provisions forbidding the abridgment of freedom of speech and freedom of the press. Congress need not stand idly by and permit those with licenses to ignore the problems which beset the people or to exclude from the airways anything but their own views of fundamental questions. The statute, long administrative practice, and cases are to this effect.

Licenses to broadcast do not confer ownership of designated frequencies, but only the temporary privilege of using them. 47 U.S.C. § 301. Unless renewed, they expire within three years. 47 U.S.C. § 307(d). The statute mandates the issuance of licenses if the "public convenience, interest, or necessity will be served thereby." 47 U.S.C. § 307(a). In applying this standard the Commission for 40 years has been choosing licensees based in part on their program proposals. In FRC v. Nelson Bros. Bond & Mortgage Co., 289 U.S. 266, 279 (1933), the Court noted that in "view of the limited number of available broadcasting frequencies the Congress has authorized allocation and licenses." In determining how best to allocate frequencies, the Federal Radio Commission considered the needs of competing communities and the programs offered by competing stations to meet those needs; moreover, if needs or programs shifted the Commission could alter its allocations to reflect those shifts. Id., at 285. . . .

D.

The litigants embellish their First Amendment arguments with the contention that the regulations are so vague that their duties are impossible to discern. Of this point it is enough to say that, judging the validity of the regulations on their face as they are presented here, we cannot conclude that the FCC has been left a free hand to vindicate its own idiosyncratic conception of the public interest or of the requirements of free speech. . . .

We need not and do not now ratify every past and future decision by the FCC with regard to programming. There is no question here of the Commission's refusal to permit the broadcaster to carry a particular program or to publish his own views; of a discriminatory refusal to require the licensee to broadcast certain views which have been denied access to the airwaves; of government censorship of a particular program contrary to § 326; or of the official government view dominating public broadcasting. Such questions would raise more serious First Amendment issues. But we do hold that the Congress and the Commission do not violate the First Amendment when they require a radio or television station to give reply time to answer personal attacks and political editorials.

E.

It is argued that even if at one time the lack of available frequencies for all who wished to use them justified the Government's choice of those who would best serve the public interest by acting as proxy for those who would present differing views, or by giving the latter access directly to broadcast facilities, this condition no longer prevails so that continuing control is not justified. To this there are several answers.

Scarcity is not entirely a thing of the past. Advances in technology, such as microwave transmission, have led to more efficient utilization of the frequency spectrum, but uses for that spectrum have also grown apace. Portions of the spectrum must be reserved for vital uses unconnected with human communication, such as radio-navigational aids used by aircraft and vessels. Conflicts have even emerged between such vital functions as defense preparedness and experimentation in methods of averting midair collisions through radio warning devices. "Land mobile services" such as police, ambulance, fire department, public utility, and other communications systems have been occupying an increasingly crowded portion of the frequency spectrum and there are, apart from the licensed amateur radio operators' equipment, 5,000,000 transmitters operated on the "citizens' band" which is also increasingly congested. Among the various uses for radio frequency space, including marine, aviation, amateur, military, and common carrier users, there are easily enough claimants to permit use of the whole with an even smaller allocation to broadcast radio and television uses than now exists.

Comparative hearings between competing applicants for broadcast spectrum space are by no means a thing of the past. The radio spectrum has become so congested that at times it has been necessary to suspend new applications. The very high frequency television spectrum is, in the country's major markets, almost entirely occupied, although space reserved for ultra high frequency television transmission, which is a relatively recent development as a commercially viable alternative, has not yet been completely filled.[25]

25. In a table prepared by the FCC on the basis of statistics current as of August 31, 1968, VHF and UHF channels allocated to and those available in the top 100 market areas for television are set forth:

Commercial

Market Areas	Channels Allocated		Channels On the Air, Authorized, or Applied for		Available Channels	
	VHF	UHF	VHF	UHF	VHF	UHF
Top 10	40	45	40	44	0	1
Top 50	157	163	157	136	0	27
Top 100	264	297	264	213	0	84

Noncommercial

Market Areas	Channels Allocated		Channels On the Air, Authorized, or Applied for		Available Channels	
	VHF	UHF	VHF	UHF	VHF	UHF
Top 10	7	17	7	16	0	1
Top 50	21	79	20	47	1	32
Top 100	35	138	34	69	1	69

1968 FCC Annual Report 132–135.

The rapidity with which technological advances succeed one another to create more efficient use of spectrum space on the one hand, and to create new uses for that space by ever growing numbers of people on the other, makes it unwise to speculate on the future allocation of that space. It is enough to say that the resource is one of considerable and growing importance whose scarcity impelled its regulation by an agency authorized by Congress. Nothing in this record, or in our own researches, convinces us that the resource is no longer one for which there are more immediate and potential uses than can be accommodated, and for which wise planning is essential. This does not mean, of course, that every possible wavelength must be occupied at every hour by some vital use in order to sustain the congressional judgment. The substantial capital investment required for many uses, in addition to the potentiality for confusion and interference inherent in any scheme for continuous kaleidoscopic reallocation of all available space may make this unfeasible. The allocation need not be made at such a breakneck pace that the objectives of the allocation are themselves imperiled.

Even where there are gaps in spectrum utilization, the fact remains that existing broadcasters have often attained their present position because of their initial government selection in competition with others before new technological advances opened new opportunities for further uses. Long experience in broadcasting, confirmed habits of listeners and viewers, network affiliation, and other advantages in program procurement give existing broadcasters a substantial advantage over new entrants, even where new entry is technologically possible. These advantages are the fruit of a preferred position conferred by the Government. Some present possibility for new entry by competing stations is not enough, in itself, to render unconstitutional the Government's effort to assure that a broadcaster's programming ranges widely enough to serve the public interest.

In view of the scarcity of broadcast frequencies, the Government's role in allocating those frequencies, and the legitimate claims of those unable without governmental assistance to gain access to those frequencies for expression of their views, we hold the regulations and ruling at issue here are both authorized by statute and constitutional.[28] The judgment of the Court of Appeals in *Red Lion* is affirmed and that in

28. We need not deal with the argument that even if there is no longer a technological scarcity of frequencies limiting the number of broadcasters, there nevertheless is an economic scarcity in the sense that the Commission could or does limit entry to the broadcasting market on economic grounds and license no more stations than the market will support. Hence, it is said, the fairness doctrine or its equivalent is essential to satisfy the claims of those excluded and of the public generally. A related argument, which we also put aside, is that quite apart from scarcity of frequencies, technological or economic, Congress does not abridge freedom of speech or press by legislation directly or indirectly multiplying the voices and views presented to the public through time sharing, fairness doctrines, or other devices which limit or dissipate the power of those who sit astride the channels of communication with the general public. Cf. Citizen Pub. Co. v. United States, 394 U.S. 131 (1969).

RTNDA reversed and the causes remanded for proceedings consistent with this opinion.

It is so ordered.

Not having heard oral argument in these cases, MR. JUSTICE DOUGLAS took no part in the Court's decision.

Notes and Questions

1. The Court states that the differences among the technical aspects of media warrant different regulatory treatment. Compare Jackson, J., concurring, in Kovacs v. Cooper, 336 U.S. 77, 97 (1949): "The moving picture screen, the radio, the newspaper, the handbill, the sound truck and the street corner orator have differing natures, values, abuses and dangers. Each, in my view, is a law unto itself."

2. The Court states that only a tiny fraction of those who want to broadcast are able to do so "even if the entire radio spectrum is utilized." Who decided how much of the spectrum to allocate to radio? Could a niggardly or inefficient allocation of radio space justify government exercise of its regulatory power? The notion of "scarcity" plays a major role in the Court's analysis. What does the term appear to mean in the opinion?

Consider whether scarcity is present in the following contexts: (a) all three radio outlets allocated to a community are being used; (b) of the five radio outlets allocated, three are being used; (c) all 40 radio outlets allocated to an urban area are being used; (d) seven of the 40 outlets are vacant.

3. Does Justice White's next-to-last paragraph suggest that the reality of scarcity in the past will be enough to justify continuing regulation even if it were determined that no scarcity exists today?

4. Justice White says that "It is the right of the viewers and listeners, not the right of the broadcasters, which is paramount. [ ] It is the purpose of the First Amendment to preserve an uninhibited marketplace of ideas in which truth will ultimately prevail, rather than to countenance monopolization of that market, whether it be by the Government itself or a private licensee." What philosophical strands are being brought together here?

When Justice White says that the "right" involved in the case belongs to "the public" and that this "right may not constitutionally be abridged either by Congress or by the FCC," is he suggesting that the absence of governmental control of broadcasters' programming would deny the public's constitutional right to "receive suitable access to social, political, esthetic, moral and other ideas and experiences?"

5. There is reason to believe that Fred Cook's demand for reply time was part of a broader effort to use the fairness doctrine to soften attacks on the Kennedy administration by right-wing political commentators. The plan was to monitor right-wing programs and then to demand

balance under the general fairness doctrine. F. Friendly, The Good Guys, The Bad Guys and the First Amendment (1976). If the result was that licensees cancelled several right-wing commentators, would that affect your reaction to the *Red Lion* decision? Did Cook misuse the doctrine?

6. By concentrating on the scarcity issue and declaring that the rights of the listeners were paramount, the Court seemed to be agreeing with scholars like law professor Jerome Barron, who argued that the development of mass media had reduced the "marketplace of ideas" to a romantic fantasy. Reasoning that increased concentration in media ownership had resulted in a marketplace failure, Barron contended that a government-created right of access to the media was not just allowed, but indeed required by the First Amendment.

Barron did not limit this to broadcasting, however. Due to economic as opposed to technological scarcity, the number of daily newspapers in this country had been reduced to the point where he felt the same arguments should apply. It was not very long before he had his chance to argue this point before the Supreme Court. Miami Herald Publishing Co. v. Tornillo, 418 U.S. 241, 1 Med.L.Rptr. 1898 (1974), involved a Florida right-of-reply statute which provided a political candidate attacked by a newspaper space to respond.

The Court unanimously ruled the statute unconstitutional under the First Amendment. The Court argued that requiring a newspaper to print replies interfered with the editorial discretion of the publisher and had a "chilling effect" on the publisher's First Amendment rights. "Faced with the penalties that would accrue to any newspaper that published news or commentary arguably within the reach of the right-of-access statute, editors might well conclude that the safe course is to avoid controversy. Therefore, under the operation of the Florida statute, political and electoral coverage would be blunted or reduced."

What was especially interesting about the case, however, was that there were no references to *Red Lion*. Are the two cases in any way contradictory? Is it relevant that there are approximately seven to eight times as many radio stations in this country as there are daily newspapers? Or that there are fewer than 40 cities in the entire country with more than one daily newspaper? Is there a difference between technological and economic scarcity?

7. Aside from the spectrum scarcity arguments, there are intrinsic differences between print and broadcast media. There is a physical limit to the number of words that can be uttered intelligibly over a broadcasting facility during a 24–hour day. Based on an estimate of about 200,000 words, using normal speaking patterns, one author suggests that a newspaper is the equivalent of between one and three 24–hour programs. But newspaper readers can at any time go directly to what interests them and skim or ignore the rest. In broadcasting, the choice is made for the listener by the broadcaster; the speed, content and se-

quence are fixed. Baxter, Regulation and Diversity in Communications Media, 64 Am.Econ.Rev. 392 (1974). Might such differences justify greater regulation of broadcasting?

On the other hand, broadcasting is an inelastic medium. In order to carry a response by the subject of a personal attack, the broadcaster must drop other programming. In contrast, a newspaper does have the option of adding pages. Does this mean that the chilling effect of forced access is greater for the broadcast media?

8. Other differences between the print and electronic media emphasize the greater impact of broadcasting in conveying certain types of information. The vivid telecasts during the Vietnam War are thought to have been a strong factor in the shift of public attitude against that war, beyond the potential of any verbal journalism. Another major difference is the role of sound in broadcasting, which makes it possible to use songs and jingles effectively in advertising. During the discussion of the broadcast advertising of cigarettes, one court observed:

> Written messages are not communicated unless they are read, and reading requires an affirmative act. Broadcast messages, in contrast, are "in the air." In an age of omnipresent radio, there scarcely breathes a citizen who does not know some part of a leading cigarette jingle by heart. Similarly, an ordinary habitual television watcher can *avoid* these commercials only by frequently leaving the room, changing the channel, or doing some other such affirmative act. It is difficult to calculate the subliminal impact of this pervasive propaganda, which may be heard even if not listened to, but it may reasonably be thought greater than the impact of the written word.

Banzhaf v. Federal Communications Commission, 405 F.2d 1082, 1100–01, 14 R.R.2d 2061, 1 Med.L.Rptr. 2037 (D.C.Cir.1968), certiorari denied 396 U.S. 842 (1969). Does this suggest an additional basis for regulating some aspects of broadcasting?

Does the *Banzhaf* view of broadcasting imply a "captive audience" comparable to the addressees of sound trucks in residential neighborhoods or political advertisements in mass transit vehicles? Is turning off the program like averting your eyes from offensive wording on someone's jacket? Is it relevant to this aspect of the discussion that most television sets and radios are in private homes? These questions are the focus of Federal Communications Commission v. Pacifica Foundation, which is discussed in Chapter VI.

9. The Supreme Court returned to the question of forced access once again in Columbia Broadcasting System, Inc. v. Democratic National Committee, 412 U.S. 94, 27 R.R.2d 907, 1 Med.L.Rptr. 1855 (1973). The Court decided that broadcasters were not obligated to accept paid advertisements from "responsible" individuals and groups. The majority relied upon *Red Lion*.

Justice Stewart, in a separate concurring opinion, stated, "I agreed with the Court in *Red Lion,* although with considerable doubt, because I thought that that much Government regulation of program content was within the outer limits of First Amendment tolerability."

In another concurring opinion, Justice Douglas stated of *Red Lion:* "I did not participate in that decision and, with all respect, would not support it. The Fairness Doctrine has no place in our First Amendment regime." He argued that the uniqueness of the spectrum was "due to engineering and technical problems. But the press in a realistic sense is likewise not available to all. Small or 'underground' papers appear and disappear; and the weekly is an established institution. But the daily papers now established are unique in the sense that it would be virtually impossible for a competitor to enter the field due to the financial exigencies of this era. The result is that in practical terms the newspapers and magazines, like TV and radio, are available only to a selected few."

10. The most recent extended discussion of the bases for regulating broadcasting occurred in Federal Communications Commission v. League of Women Voters of California. The three plaintiffs were the League, which wished to persuade public noncommercial educational broadcasters to take editorial positions; a listener who wished to hear such editorials; and a noncommercial broadcaster that wished to take editorial stands. The impediment was § 399 of the Public Broadcasting Act of 1967, as amended in 1981:

> No noncommercial educational broadcasting station which receives a grant from the Corporation for Public Broadcasting under subpart C of this part may engage in editorializing. No noncommercial educational broadcasting station may support or oppose any candidate for public office.

The case in fact centered on the first sentence of the section, which most of the justices thought severable from the second sentence. The core of the decision, centering on the nature of "public broadcasting," is reprinted in Chapter VII. Here we focus on the majority's background discussion of the bases for regulating broadcasting.

The issue arose in the context of determining the "appropriate standard of review." The trial court, whose judgment of unconstitutionality was on direct review, had held that § 399 could survive constitutional scrutiny only if it served a "compelling" governmental interest. The FCC argued that a less demanding standard was appropriate. It based this argument in part on the "special characteristic" of spectrum scarcity and in part on the unique role of noncommercial broadcasting in this country.

The response of the five-member majority follows.

FEDERAL COMMUNICATIONS COMMISSION v. LEAGUE
OF WOMEN VOTERS OF CALIFORNIA

Supreme Court of the United States, 1984.
468 U.S. 364, 104 S.Ct. 3106, 56 R.R.2d 547, 82 L.Ed.2d 278, 10 Med.L.Rptr. 1937.

[After setting forth the facts discussed in the introduction to this case, *supra,* and reviewing the history of noncommercial broadcasting, Justice Brennan addressed the appropriate standard of review in the following passage:]

JUSTICE BRENNAN delivered the opinion of the Court.

. . .

At first glance, of course, it would appear that the District Court applied the correct standard. Section 399 plainly operates to restrict the expression of editorial opinion on matters of public importance, and, as we have repeatedly explained, communication of this kind is entitled to the most exacting degree of First Amendment protection. [ ] Were a similar ban on editorializing applied in newspapers and magazines, we would not hesitate to strike it down as violative of the First Amendment. E.g., Mills v. Alabama, 384 U.S. 214 (1966). But, as the Government correctly notes, because broadcast regulation involves unique considerations, our cases have not followed precisely the same approach that we have applied to other media and have never gone so far as to demand that such regulations serve "compelling" governmental interests. At the same time, we think the Government's argument loses sight of concerns that are important in this area and thus misapprehends the essential meaning of our prior decisions concerning the reach of Congress' authority to regulate broadcast communication.

The fundamental principles that guide our evaluation of broadcast regulation are by now well established. First we have long recognized that Congress, acting pursuant to the Commerce Clause, has power to regulate the use of this scarce and valuable national resource. The distinctive feature of Congress' efforts in this area has been to ensure through the regulatory oversight of the FCC that only those who satisfy the "public interest, convenience and necessity" are granted a license to use radio and television broadcast frequencies. 47 U.S.C. § 309(a).[11]

Second, Congress may, in the exercise of this power, seek to assure that the public receives through this medium a balanced presentation of

11. [ ].
The prevailing rationale for broadcast regulation based on spectrum scarcity has come under increasing criticism in recent years. Critics, including the incumbent Chairman of the FCC, charge that with the advent of cable and satellite television technology, communities now have access to such a wide variety of stations that the scarcity doctrine is obsolete. See, e.g., Fowler & Brenner, A Marketplace Approach to Broadcast Regulation, 60 Tex.L.Rev. 207, 221–226 (1982). We are not prepared, however, to reconsider our long-standing approach without some signal from Congress or the FCC that technological developments have advanced so far that some revision of the system of broadcast regulation may be required.

information on issues of public importance that otherwise might not be addressed if control of the medium were left entirely in the hands of those who own and operate broadcasting stations. Although such governmental regulation has never been allowed with respect to the print media, [*Tornillo,* p. 90, *supra*], we have recognized that "differences in the characteristics of new media justify differences in the First Amendment standards applied to them." [*Red Lion,* p. 78, *supra*]. The fundamental distinguishing characteristic of the new medium of broadcasting that, in our view, has required some adjustment in First Amendment analysis is that "[b]roadcasting frequencies are a scarce resource [that] must be portioned out among applicants." Columbia Broadcasting System, Inc. v. Democratic National Committee, 412 U.S. 94, 101 (1973). Thus, our cases have taught that, given spectrum scarcity, those who are granted a license to broadcast must serve in a sense as fiduciaries for the public by presenting "those views and voices which are representative of his community and which would otherwise, by necessity, be barred from the airwaves." *Red Lion,* supra, at 389. As we observed in that case, because "[i]t is the purpose of the First Amendment to preserve an uninhibited marketplace of ideas in which truth will ultimately prevail, . . . the right of the public to receive suitable access to social, political, esthetic, moral and other ideas and experiences [through the medium of broadcasting] is crucial here [and it] may not constitutionally be abridged either by the Congress or the FCC." Id., at 390.

Finally, although the government's interest in ensuring balanced coverage of public issues is plainly both important and substantial, we have, at the same time, made clear that broadcasters are engaged in a vital and independent form of communicative activity. As a result, the First Amendment must inform and give shape to the manner in which Congress exercises its regulatory power in this area. Unlike common carriers, broadcasters are "entitled under the First Amendment to exercise 'the widest journalistic freedom consistent with their public [duties].'" Columbia Broadcasting System, Inc. v. FCC, 453 U.S. 367, 395 (1981) (quoting Columbia Broadcasting System, Inc. v. Democratic National Committee, supra, at 110). See also FCC v. Midwest Video Corp., 440 U.S. 689, 703 (1979). Indeed, if the public's interest in receiving a balanced presentation of views is to be fully served, we must necessarily rely in large part upon the editorial initiative and judgment of the broadcasters who bear the public trust. See Columbia Broadcasting System, Inc. v. Democratic National Committee, supra, at 124–127.

Our prior cases illustrate these principles. In *Red Lion,* for example, we upheld the FCC's "fairness doctrine"—which requires broadcasters to provide adequate coverage of public issues and to ensure that this coverage fairly and accurately reflects the opposing views—because the doctrine advanced the substantial governmental interest in ensuring balanced presentations of views in this limited medium and yet posed no threat that a "broadcaster [would be denied permission] to carry a particular program or to publish his own views." Id., at 396.[12] Similarly, in Columbia Broadcasting System, Inc. v. FCC, supra, the Court upheld the right of access for federal candidates imposed by § 312(a)(7) of the Communications Act both because that provision "makes a significant contribution to freedom of expression by enhancing the ability of candidates to present, and the public to receive, information necessary for the effective operation of the democratic process," id., at 396, and because it defined a sufficiently "*limited* right of 'reasonable' access" so that "the discretion of broadcasters to present their views on any issue or to carry any particular type of programming" was not impaired. Id., at 396–397 (emphasis in original). Finally, in Columbia Broadcasting System, Inc. v. Democratic National Committee, supra, the Court affirmed the FCC's refusal to require broadcast licensees to accept all paid political advertisements. Although it was argued that such a requirement would serve the public's First Amendment interest in receiving additional views on public issues, the Court rejected this approach, finding that such a requirement would tend to transform broadcasters into common carriers and would intrude unnecessarily upon the editorial discretion of broadcasters. 412 U.S., at 123–125. The FCC's ruling, therefore, helped to advance the important purposes of the Communications Act, grounded in the First Amendment, of preserving the right of broadcasters to exercise "the widest journalistic freedom consistent with [their] public obligations," and of guarding against "the risk of an enlargement of Government control over the broadcast discussion of public issues." 412 U.S., at 110, 127.[13]

12. We note that the FCC, observing that "[i]f any substantial possibility exists that the [fairness doctrine] rules have impeded, rather than furthered, First Amendment objectives, repeal may be warranted on that ground alone," has tentatively concluded that the rules, by effectively chilling speech, do not serve the public interest, and has therefore proposed to repeal them. Notice of Proposed Rulemaking In re Repeal or Modification of the Personal Attack and Political Editorial Rules, 48 Fed.Reg. 28295, 28298, 28301 (June 21, 1983). Of course, the Commission may, in the exercise of its discretion, decide to modify or abandon these rules, and we express no view on the legality of either course. As we recognized in *Red Lion,* however, were it to be shown by the Commission that the fairness doctrine "has the effect of reducing rather than enhancing" speech, we would then be forced to reconsider the constitutional basis of our decision in that case. 395 U.S., at 393.

13. This Court's decision in FCC v. Pacifica Foundation, 438 U.S. 726 (1978), upholding an exercise of the Commission's authority to regulate broadcasts containing "indecent" language as applied to a partic-

ular afternoon broadcast of a George Carlin monologue, is consistent with the approach taken in our other broadcast cases. There, the Court focused on certain physical characteristics of broadcasting—specifically, that the medium's uniquely pervasive presence renders impossible any prior warning for those listeners who may be offended by indecent language, and, second, that the ease with which children may gain access to the medium, especially during daytime hours, creates a substantial risk that they may be exposed to such offensive expression without parental supervision. Id., at 748–749. The governmental interest in reduction of those risks through Commission regulation of the timing and character of such "indecent broadcasting" was thought sufficiently substantial to outweigh the broadcaster's First Amendment interest in controlling the presentation of its programming. Id., at 750. In this case, by contrast, we are faced not with indecent expression, but rather with expression that is at the core of First Amendment protections, and no claim is made by the Government that the expression of editorial opinion by noncommercial stations will create a substantial "nuisance" of the kind addressed in FCC v. Pacifica Foundation.

Thus, although the broadcasting industry plainly operates under restraints not imposed upon other media, the thrust of these restrictions has generally been to secure the public's First Amendment interest in receiving a balanced presentation of views on diverse matters of public concern. As a result of these restrictions, of course, the absolute freedom to advocate one's own positions without also presenting opposing viewpoints—a freedom enjoyed, for example, by newspaper publishers and soapbox orators—is denied to broadcasters. But, as our cases attest, these restrictions have been upheld only when we were satisfied that the restriction is narrowly tailored to further a substantial governmental interest, such as ensuring adequate and balanced coverage of public issues. [ ] Making that judgment requires a critical examination of the interests of the public and broadcasters in light of the particular circumstances of each case. E.g., FCC v. Pacifica Foundation, supra.

[Justice Brennan then turned to a consideration of the specifics of this case. His discussion of this issue, and the opinions of the dissenting justices are reprinted in Chapter VII.]

Notes and Questions

1. Opponents of content regulation of broadcasting took footnotes 11 and 12 as a sign that the Court was willing to reconsider the First Amendment status of broadcasters. The *1985 Fairness Report,* to be discussed in Chapter V, was considered by many to be a specific response to these footnotes.

2. Just what are the limits set by *Red Lion*? Consider the following from Judge Starr's concurrence in Syracuse Peace Council v. Federal Communications Commission, 867 F.2d 654, 16 Med.L.Rptr. 1225 (D.C.Cir.1989), certiorari denied, 493 U.S. 1019 (1990). The case was an appeal of the FCC's determination that the fairness doctrine was unconstitutional and that it disserved the public interest. We will return to the case in Chapter V.

> . . . Although the parties agree that *Red Lion* is king, they strenuously disagree over the proper interpretation of that seminal decision. For its part, the FCC argues that the constitutional question turns on whether enforcement of the fairness doctrine
>
> > (1) chills speech and results in the net reduction of the presentation of controversial issues of public importance and
> >
> > (2) excessively infringes on the editorial discretion of broadcast journalists and involves unnecessary government intervention to the extent that it is no longer narrowly tailored to meet its objective.
>
> [ ] The FCC believes that regulatory intervention through the vehicle of the fairness doctrine is not "narrowly tailored" if the number (and distribution) of media outlets ensures public access to diverse viewpoints.

[ ] That is, if access to diverse viewpoints can be achieved without the fairness doctrine, then the doctrine is not "narrowly tailored" because it unnecessarily interferes with editorial decisions. Finally, the FCC interprets *Red Lion* to render the fairness doctrine unconstitutional if either of these tests (net reduction or not "narrowly tailored") is satisfied. [   ]

Petitioners' most vigorous attack is aimed at the proposition that the numerosity of media outlets and intrusive impact of the fairness doctrine may, without more, render the fairness doctrine unconstitutional. Petitioners contend that the relevant concern is the number of media outlets relative to the demand of broadcasters (expressed through license applications) for such outlets. More pertinently, petitioners direct our attention to the unique characteristic of broadcast regulation, namely the potential for interference occasioned by the fact that the broadcasters spectrum can physically accommodate only a finite number of users. The potential for signal interference among competing broadcasters, it is argued, necessitates an allocation system whereby regulatory authority assures to broadcasters exclusive use of their portions of the spectrum. As this system by its nature excludes some who wish to broadcast, the readmission of excluded speakers via the fairness doctrine is constitutionally permissible, petitioners maintain, as an adjunct to the licensing system.

To recap: as petitioners see it, the fairness doctrine is constitutionally permissible so long as *allocational scarcity* exists, namely, that demand for broadcast frequencies exceeds supply. [ ] The FCC, in contrast, asserts that the constitutionality of the doctrine depends on *numerical scarcity* in the sense that, without government intervention, the public is not provided with access to diverse viewpoints.

There is thus a rather pivotal difference in the perspectives vying for judicial approbation. As I see it, the FCC's position is much better founded; indeed, in my view, petitioners have fallen badly into error by misreading *Red Lion*. There is, to be sure, language in *Red Lion* with respect to the scarcity of the broadcast spectrum and the consequent tendency toward unrequited demand for frequencies. [ ] Under *Red Lion*, however, that sort of scarcity seems to constitute a necessary (rather than sufficient) condition of the fairness doctrine's legitimacy. That is, allocational scarcity accounts for the fundamental difference in First Amendment treatment of print and broadcast media. [   ] However, spectrum scarcity, without more, does not necessarily justify regulatory schemes which intrude into First Amendment territory. This point is made clear by the familiar cases in which the Court has upheld broadcast regulation on the ground that the regulation *furthered* substantial First Amendment interests, see *Red Lion,* [   ]; CBS, Inc. v. FCC, 453 U.S. 367, 396 (1981); and by [CBS v. DNC], where the Court held that the FCC need not require licensees to accept all paid political advertisements because such a requirement unduly impinged upon broadcasters' rights and produced little public benefit. In short, petitioners conflate the Supreme Court's choice of a standard for evaluating broadcast regulation with the Court's application of its chosen standard to the interests assertedly advanced by a particular regulatory regime.

3. A good example of the criticism leveled at the scarcity rationale can be found in Telecommunications Research and Action Center v. Federal Communications Commission, 801 F.2d 501, 61 R.R.2d 330, 13 Med. L.Rptr. 1881, rehearing denied 806 F.2d 1115, 61 R.R.2d 1342, 13 Med.L.Rptr. 1896 (D.C.Cir.1986), certiorari denied 482 U.S. 919 (1987). The case was an appeal of the Commission's refusal to apply the political broadcast rules to teletext and is discussed in Chapter X. The court acknowledged that it was bound by *Red Lion,* but questioned the Supreme Court's reliance on scarcity as a rationale for distinguishing between the broadcast and print media:

> . . . The basic difficulty in this entire area is that the line drawn between the print media and the broadcast media, resting as it does on the physical scarcity of the latter, is a distinction without a difference. Employing the scarcity concept as an analytic tool, particularly with respect of new and unforeseen technologies, inevitably leads to strained reasoning and artificial results.

> It is certainly true that broadcast frequencies are scarce but it is unclear why that fact justifies content regulation of broadcasting in a way that would be intolerable if applied to the editorial process of the print media. All economic goods are scarce, not least the newsprint, ink, delivery trucks, computers, and other resources that go into the production and dissemination of print journalism. Not everyone who wishes to publish a newspaper, or even a pamphlet, may do so. Since scarcity is a universal fact, it can hardly explain regulation in one context and not another. The attempt to use a universal fact as a distinguishing principle necessarily leads to analytical confusion.

> Neither is content regulation explained by the fact that broadcasters face the problem of interference, so that the government must define usable frequencies and protect those frequencies from encroachment. This governmental definition of frequencies is another instance of a universal fact that does not offer an explanatory principle for differing treatment. A publisher can deliver his newspapers only because government provides streets and regulates traffic on the streets by allocating rights of way. Yet no one would contend that the necessity for these governmental functions, which are certainly analogous to the government's function in allocating broadcast frequencies, could justify regulation of the content of a newspaper to ensure that it serves the needs of citizens.

> There may be ways to reconcile *Red Lion* and *Tornillo* but the "scarcity" of broadcast frequencies does not appear capable of doing

so. Perhaps the Supreme Court will one day revisit this area of the law and either eliminate the distinction between print and broadcast media, surely by pronouncing *Tornillo* applicable to both, or announce a constitutional distinction that is more usable than the present one.

How convincing is the court's critique? What constitutional distinction might the court find more usable than the scarcity rationale?

B. IS BROADCASTING "GOVERNMENT ACTION"?

The issues raised in *NBC, Red Lion* and *League of Women Voters* revolve around the broadcaster's claim that the First Amendment protects it from government regulation. Sometimes claims in the name of the First Amendment are made by private citizens against the media. In *Tornillo,* the citizen's claim failed. But when such a claim is made against broadcast media, a new element enters the picture. When government undertakes to provide a forum for discussion, or a street for parades, it must not discriminate among prospective users according to their views. Government must be neutral in such situations. If too many want to parade or use the forum, government might develop a lottery system or queuing system; but it could not prefer those views it liked. Some have argued that this analysis applies to broadcasters—that they are so closely related to, and regulated by, government that their actions are government action, and, thus, bound by the neutrality principle.

The Supreme Court avoided this question in *Columbia Broadcasting System, Inc.*, p. 91, *supra.* The DNC wanted to buy commercial time to urge financial support for the party. Another group Business Executives' Move for Peace (BEM) sought to buy time to oppose the war in Vietnam. The broadcasters refused to sell time to either group because the proposed commercials did not fit into the type of programming the broadcasters wanted to present. The DNC and BEM asked the FCC to order the broadcasters to take their commercials—at least as long as they were taking commercials from other sources. The FCC refused. The Supreme Court upheld the FCC's refusal.

The DNC–BEM claim that the broadcasters should be treated as government fragmented the Court badly. Three justices met it head on and rejected it. They were concerned that the "concept of journalistic independence could not co-exist with a reading of the challenged conduct of the licensee as government action" because a government medium could not exercise editorial judgment as to what content should be carried or excluded.

The three observed, however, that even if the First Amendment applied to this case, the groups were not entitled to access. Here, they relied on Meiklejohn's theme that the essential point was "not that everyone shall speak, but that everything worth saying shall be said." Congress and the Commission might reasonably conclude that the "allocation of journalistic priorities should be concentrated on the licensee rather than diffused among many. This policy gives the public some assurance that the broadcaster will be answerable if he fails to meet its legitimate needs. No such accountability attaches to the private individual."

Three other justices agreed that even if government action were involved in the case, there was no violation of the groups' rights under the First Amendment. They therefore refused to pass on the question of government involvement.

Justice Douglas, concurring, did not decide the question. He noted that if a licensee were to be considered a federal agency it would "within limits of its time be bound to disseminate all views." If a licensee was not considered a federal agency, "I fail to see how constitutionally we can treat TV and radio differently than we treat newspapers." He agreed that "The Commission has a duty to encourage a multitude of voices but only in a limited way, viz., by preventing monopolistic practices and by promoting technological developments that will open up new channels. But censorship or editing or the screening by Government of what licensees may broadcast goes against the grain of the First Amendment."

In dissent Justice Brennan, with whom Justice Marshall concurred, disagreed:

> Thus, given the confluence of these various indicia of "governmental action"—including the public nature of the airwaves, the governmentally created preferred status of broadcasters, the extensive Government regulation of broadcast programming, and the specific governmental approval of the challenged policy—I can only conclude that the Government "has so far insinuated itself into a position" of participation in this policy that the absolute refusal of broadcast licensees to sell air time to groups or individuals wishing to speak out on controversial issues of public importance must be subjected to the restraints of the First Amendment.

The dissenters then concluded that the absolute refusal did violate the First Amendment. "The retention of such *absolute* control in the hands of a few Government licensees is inimical to the First Amendment, for vigorous, free debate can be attained only when members of the public have *some* opportunity to take the initiative and editorial control into their own hands." The emergence of broadcasting as "the public's prime source of information," has "made the soapbox orator and the leafleteer virtually obsolete."

The case, however, indicates only that the Constitution does not create a right of access to broadcasting. It does not address the question of whether Congress might enact a statute requiring broadcasters as a condition of their licenses to give a certain period of time per day or week to members of the public. How might those who wish to speak be selected? Would such a statute be valid? Might the Commission issue a rule to the same effect? Even if such a statute or rule would be constitutional, would it be sound? What does this controversy say about the "agenda-setting" role of media?

In the DNC–BEM case, much of the majority's approach was based on the power to enforce the broadcaster's responsibility to program in the public interest because of the two prongs of the fairness doctrine. It is ironic that the fairness doctrine, resisted by the broadcasters in *Red Lion,* also shielded them from having to give unlimited access to their broadcasting facilities. As a broadcaster, which would you find a greater interference with your freedom—the fairness doctrine or a rule requiring you to give some persons or groups access to your facilities? This issue as it pertains to Public Broadcasting is discussed in Chapter VII in Muir v. Alabama Educational Television Commission.

Chapter IV

BROADCAST LICENSING

In this chapter we consider the substantive and procedural aspects of the licensing activities of the Federal Communications Commission. As we have seen, the Commission was charged with reducing interference on the airwaves, which eventually, in the name of the public interest, involved licensing. The current licensing system bears little resemblance to that which existed prior to the last decade. However, because the earlier system was central to the development of the overall system of broadcast regulation, we begin by examining how until recently this process functioned from the initial stage of awarding a vacant spot to the conditions for transferring a license. We will then discuss the major changes in the process that occurred in the last decade.

A. INITIAL LICENSING

1. THE ADMINISTRATIVE PROCESS AT WORK

First we must examine the process by which the Commission grants licenses to applicants. To seek a license for a broadcast frequency, an applicant first asks the Commission for a construction permit to build the facility. If the construction permit is granted, the license will then follow almost automatically if the facility is constructed on schedule.

The application is filed initially with the part of the FCC called the Mass Media Bureau. Its staff reviews the papers to identify any deficiency. If the case is a routine one, the Commissioners have authorized the staff of the Mass Media Bureau to issue the license. If, however, the application raises any fact questions or legal questions, then a more complex procedure is required.

Section 309(a) of the Communications Act provides that if after examining an application the Commission concludes that the "public interest, convenience, and necessity" will be served it shall grant the application. But subsection (e) provides that "if a substantial and material question of fact is presented or the Commission for any reason is unable to make the finding specified in [subsection (a)], it shall formally designate the application for hearing . . . and shall forthwith notify the applicant . . . of such action and the grounds and reasons therefor, specifying with particularity the matters and things in issue. . . ."

The "hearing" mentioned in the statute is conducted by a member of the FCC's staff called an Administrative Law Judge (ALJ) who functions much as a regular judge presiding over a trial—except that there is no jury and the issues to be explored at the hearing are prescribed, or designated, in advance by the Commission. For example, if the application seems to raise no problem except the question of whether the applicant is adequately financed for the initial period, the Commission will order the ALJ to conduct a hearing limited to that fact question.

Does the applicant have an adversary at the hearing? The answer is that if the Mass Media Bureau has raised a question about the applicant's answers, the Mass Media Bureau itself may take part in the hearing to oppose the applicant. If the fact dispute is resolved in favor of the applicant, and the rest of the application is proper, the ALJ may grant the permit. If the Mass Media Bureau thinks the ALJ has made a mistake, it may appeal within the agency—sometimes to a "review board" that serves as an appellate decision-making body and sometimes to the Commissioners themselves. By the same token, if the judge's ruling favors the Bureau, the unhappy applicant may appeal within the agency.

If the Commission eventually decides against issuing a license or a construction permit, the unhappy applicant may then appeal to the courts—usually to the United States Court of Appeals for the District of Columbia Circuit. In this situation, the adversary is the Commission itself, represented by its general counsel's staff. However the court of appeals may decide, the losing side may seek Supreme Court review by filing a petition for a writ of *certiorari*.

An indication of how the court views its role in reviewing broadcast licensing is found in Greater Boston Television Corp. v. Federal Communications Commission, 444 F.2d 841, 850–53, 20 R.R.2d 2052, 1 Med. L.Rptr. 2003 (D.C.Cir.1970), certiorari denied 403 U.S. 923 (1971), to which we return shortly for its substantive part (footnotes citing a wealth of authorities have been omitted):

> Assuming consistency with law and the legislative mandate, the agency has latitude not merely to find facts and make judgments, but also to select the policies deemed in the public interest. The function of the court is to assure that the agency has given reasoned consideration to all the material facts and issues. This calls for insistence that the agency articulate with reasonable clarity its reasons for decision, and identify the significance of the crucial facts, a course that tends to assure that the agency's policies effectuate general standards, applied without unreasonable discrimination. . . .

> Its supervisory function calls on the court to intervene not merely in case of procedural inadequacies or bypassing of the mandate in the legislative charter, but more broadly if the court becomes aware, especially from a combination of danger signals, that the agency has not really taken a "hard look" at the salient problems, and has not genuinely engaged in reasoned decision-making. If the agency has not shirked this fundamental task, however, the court exercises restraint and affirms the agency's action even though the court

would on its own account have made different findings or adopted different standards. Nor will the court upset a decision because of errors that are not material, there being room for the doctrine of harmless error. . . .

This posture of judicial self-restraint would apply to review of actions of administrative agencies generally.

This brief description assumes that it is possible for the Commission, or its Bureau, to deny an application for a vacant frequency or channel—even though no one else has applied for it. Although this may seem surprising, it does happen.

We might note now that the same hearing process may be required at other stages in the licensing process. When a licensee applies for a renewal, if claims are made that the licensee has misbehaved in some way or should not get the license renewed, any fact questions that need to be resolved will be explored at a similar hearing conducted by an ALJ.

In the interests of simplicity, the foregoing description of the administrative process assumes that when the FCC decides to grant or renew a license to an applicant who has no competitors that is the end of the process. If the applicant has beaten out challengers they can carry the fight into the courts. But if the applicant has no challenger and the Commission decides in its favor, the Bureau—even if it has disagreed with that result—cannot attack the decision of its agency.

Standing for Competitors. Other parties, however, do have a right to participate ("standing"). For example, existing licensees can object to the granting of a new license on the grounds that it will cause technical interference with existing stations. A more difficult question is raised when a competitor wishes to argue that there is not enough potential advertising revenue in the community to support an additional station. At one time the Commission's was receptive to such arguments, but it is no longer. See Policies Regarding Detrimental Effects of Proposed New Broadcasting Stations on Existing Stations, 4 F.C.C.Rcd. 2276, 66 R.R.2d 19 (1989).

Standing for Listeners. For many years the Commission firmly rejected all efforts of listeners or citizen groups to take a formal part in the licensing process. Formally stated, the FCC denied outsiders standing to participate.

In 1966, however, the court of appeals ordered that citizen groups be allowed to participate in these proceedings. In Office of Communication of United Church of Christ v. Federal Communications Commission, 359 F.2d 994, 7 R.R.2d 2001 (D.C.Cir.1966), the opinion by then Circuit Judge Warren Burger said in part:

> The argument that a broadcaster is not a public utility is beside the point. True it is not a public utility in the same sense as strictly regulated common carriers or purveyors of power, but neither is it a purely private enterprise like a newspaper or an automobile agency. A broadcaster has much in common with a newspaper publisher, but

he is not in the same category in terms of public obligations imposed by law. A broadcaster seeks and is granted the free and exclusive use of a limited and valuable part of the public domain; when he accepts that franchise it is burdened by enforceable public obligations. A newspaper can be operated at the whim or caprice of its owners; a broadcast station cannot. After nearly five decades of operation the broadcast industry does not seem to have grasped the simple fact that a broadcast license is a public trust subject to termination for breach of duty.

. . .

Public participation is especially important in a renewal proceeding, since the public will have been exposed for at least three years to the licensee's performance, as cannot be the case when the Commission considers an initial grant, unless the applicant has a prior record as a licensee. In a renewal proceeding, furthermore, public spokesmen, such as Appellants here, may be the only objectors. In a community served by only one outlet, the public interest focus is perhaps sharper and the need for airing complaints often greater than where, for example, several channels exist. Yet if there is only one outlet, there are no rivals at hand to assert the public interest, and reliance on opposing applicants to challenge the existing licensee for the channel would be fortuitous at best. Even when there are multiple competing stations in a locality, various factors may operate to inhibit the other broadcasters from opposing a renewal application. An imperfect rival may be thought a desirable rival, or there may be a "gentleman's agreement" of deference to a fellow broadcaster in the hope he will reciprocate on a propitious occasion.

He also noted that the fears of regulatory agencies that they will be flooded with applications have rarely been borne out.

In the period since this case, the feared flood has not developed, though citizen groups are playing a more active part in the regulatory processes of the Commission than before. Their most common legal action is the filing of a petition to deny a renewal application on the ground that the applicant has failed to meet the required level of public service.

Negotiation and Agreement. Another possibility is to negotiate. In order to avoid the expense of defending against petitions to deny renewals, broadcasters will sometimes enter into agreements with citizen groups that challenge their license applications or renewals. In return for withdrawal of the challenge, a broadcaster typically undertakes to make certain changes in its station's operation. The broadcaster may promise to change its employment policies, to support local production of broadcast programming, or to attempt to expand certain types of programming.

The Commission generally allows broadcasters to enter into the agreements if they maintain responsibility at all times for determining how best to serve the public interest. Agreements Between Broadcast Licensees and the Public, 57 F.C.C.2d 42 (1975). Does recognition of these private agreements serve the public interest? Does it allow a broadcaster to "buy off" citizen groups who may be in the best position to point out programming deficiencies? In 1988 the Commission examined these issues as part of a more general inquiry into abuses of the comparative renewal process. We will discuss this in more detail later in this chapter.

Unlicensed Stations. For years, the FCC has had difficulty with unlicensed or "pirate" radio stations. Operators of these low-power stations have argued that, as long as their stations do not interfere with licensed broadcasters, they have a First Amendment right to broadcast. In 1998 a federal district court ordered Stephen Dunifer to cease broadcasting. The court had four years previously refused to issue the requested order holding that the government had not shown that Dunifer's First Amendment claim would fail. The court subsequently concluded that Dunifer could not assert a constitutional claim because he had never sought an FCC broadcast license. At that time, the FCC had estimated that there were 112 pirate radio stations operating in the United States. United States v. Dunifer, 997 F.Supp. 1235 (1998).

2. INTRODUCTION TO BASIC QUALIFICATIONS

In the 1934 Act, Congress empowered the Federal Communications Commission to grant licenses to applicants for radio stations for periods of up to three years "if public convenience, interest, or necessity will be served thereby." § 307(a). Section 307(b) requires the Commission to make "such distribution of licenses, frequencies, hours of operation, and of power among the several states and communities as to provide a fair, efficient, and equitable distribution of radio service to each of the same."

As we have seen, the Commission responded by allocating a portion of the spectrum for standard (AM) radio service and then subdividing that space further by requiring very powerful stations to use certain frequencies and weaker stations to utilize others and some stations to leave the air at sundown. The Commission used its rulemaking powers to develop these allocations and then set engineering standards of separation and interference. The 1934 Act empowered the Commission to promulgate "such rules and regulations and prescribe such restrictions and conditions, not inconsistent with law, as may be necessary to carry out the provisions of this chapter." § 303(r). The Commission did not allocate the AM frequencies to particular cities. Instead, it left it to those interested in broadcasting to determine whether they could organize an AM broadcast facility in a given location that complied with the various allocation and interference rules. With FM and television, the Commission utilized rulemaking to allocate particular frequencies to particular cities. An applicant for one of these licenses must apply for the assigned frequency in the listed, or a nearby, community or must seek to change the frequency assignments through an amendment of the rules.

In addition to requiring proof that a grant will serve the "public convenience, interest, or necessity," § 307(a), the Act also requires that each applicant demonstrate that it meets basic "citizenship, character, and financial, technical, and other qualifications," § 308(b). An applicant who fails to satisfy any one of the following "basic qualifications" is ineligible to receive a license.

a. *Legal Qualifications.* An applicant for a license must comply with the specific requirements of the Communications Act and the Commission's rules. For example, there are restrictions on permitting aliens to hold radio and broadcast licenses. § 310(b). Prior revocation of an applicant's license by a federal court for an antitrust violation precludes grant of a new application. § 313. An application will be denied if its grant would result in violation of the Commission's multiple ownership or crossownership rules or its chain broadcasting regulations. (We will discuss these in Chapter XII.)

The limitation on foreign ownership became a major problem for Fox Television Stations (FTS), when its license for WNYW–TV came up for renewal. The Metropolitan Council of NAACP Branches filed a petition to deny alleging, among other things, that FTS was in violation of the rules governing foreign ownership and that FTS had deliberately concealed this violation from the FCC. The issue centered on the corporate structure of FTS and its parent company.

2. On May 23, 1994, FTS informed the Mass Media Bureau that The News Corporation Ltd. ("News Corp."), an Australian company, owns more than 99 percent of the corporate equity capital of FTS's parent company, Twentieth Holdings Corporation ("THC"), even though News Corp. owns only 24 percent of THC's voting stock. To determine whether the renewal application may be granted, we must therefore assess that ownership structure in light of Section 310(b)(4) of the Communications Act, which provides in pertinent part that: No broadcast . . . license shall be granted to or held by . . . any corporation directly or indirectly controlled by any other corporation of which . . . more than one-fourth of the capital stock is owned of record or voted by . . . any corporation organized under the laws of a foreign country . . . if the Commission finds that the public interest will be served by the refusal or revocation of such license. 47 U.S.C. § 310(b)(4). We must also decide whether the application should be designated for hearing based on other issues raised by Metro NAACP.

3. More specifically, this case presents the following issues: (1) whether News Corp.'s ownership of 99 percent of the capital contributed to THC exceeds Section 310(b)(4)'s benchmark of 25 percent of the "capital stock" of the company; (2) whether, if News Corp.'s interest is deemed to exceed the benchmark, FTS has intentionally concealed that fact or misrepresented its compliance with the stat-

ute in applications and other filings submitted to the Commission beginning in 1985; (3) whether News Corp. exercises de facto control over FTS or whether K. Rupert Murdoch, the Chairman of News Corp., controls FTS as the representative of News Corp.; and (4) if we find that FTS's alien ownership exceeds the benchmark, that FTS is under alien control, or that FTS has lacked candor, what remedial action, if any, is appropriate.

. . .

. . . For the reasons set forth below, we deny Metro NAACP's Petition to Deny, and grant FTS's renewal application conditioned upon FTS's election either (1) to submit information demonstrating that the level of FTS's foreign ownership is consistent with the public interest; or (2) to come into compliance with the foreign ownership benchmark of Section 310(b)(4).

6. We find that News Corp.'s ownership of THC's "capital stock" exceeds the 25 percent foreign ownership benchmark established in Section 310(b)(4). THC wholly owns the licensee, FTS. Although News Corp. owns only 24 percent of the total number of outstanding shares of THC stock, News Corp. contributed over 99 percent of the capital invested in THC and is entitled to virtually all of the economic incidents of THC's operation. In these circumstances, we conclude that the statute requires us to evaluate not only the number of shares of stock held by alien owners, but also the amount of equity capital contributed by such owners. Such an approach effectuates the statutory objective, and will enable the Commission to perform a bona fide analysis of alien ownership. . . .

7. Even though FTS exceeds the ownership benchmark, we do not conclude that FTS intentionally misrepresented or concealed that fact. Although there are some disputed issues as to subsidiary or "proximate" facts, the totality of the evidence before us does not present a substantial and material question of fact on the ultimate issue of whether FTS misrepresented the facts or lacked candor in its 1985 transfer application or any of its subsequent filings with this Commission. . . .

8. We recognize that our reported interpretations of Section 310(b)(4) at the time FTS filed its original application in 1985 did not clearly indicate that a foreign corporation's equity capital contributions were of decisional significance to the Commission in determining a corporate parent's compliance with the statutory benchmark. Thus, although the Commission had held that capital contributions were relevant in the limited partnership context, the totality of the circumstances leads us to conclude that FTS did not believe that it had a duty to disclose the amount of equity capital contributed to THC by foreign interests, and thus FTS did not intentionally conceal this information in an effort to deceive the Commission.

9.　We further find that Murdoch, by virtue of his controlling voting interest in THC, exercises de jure control over that company and its wholly-owned subsidiary, FTS. Moreover, the record shows that Murdoch was in charge of THC's day-to-day operations and dominated its corporate affairs. While FTS and THC are subsidiaries of News Corp. for financial reporting purposes, the totality of the evidence demonstrates that Murdoch, a United States citizen, nonetheless exercises de facto control over THC. We reject the contention that as a consequence of his position with News Corp., Murdoch is acting as a representative of alien interests.

10.　[T]he Commission holds that News Corp.'s 99 percent capital contribution to THC exceeds the 25 percent benchmark. A licensee is permitted to exceed the benchmark, however, where the Commission expressly finds that the "public interest" would be served. Absent such a public interest finding, FTS must comply with the benchmark.

The Commission gave FTS 45 days to either submit a "showing of why non-compliance with the Section 310(b)(4) benchmark is in the public interest," or a proposal as to how and when it would comply with the benchmark. Fox Television Stations, Inc., 10 F.C.C.Rcd. 8452, 77 R.R.2d 1043 (1995).

FTS altered its capital structure by exchanging News Corp.'s share of THC's paid-in capital for debt. However, this was not sufficient to bring FTS into compliance with the foreign ownership benchmark. Therefore, FTS also submitted data on the tax consequences of more extensive restructuring and arguments as to the public interest benefits of continued FTS ownership.

The Commission held that the public interest would not be served by subjecting FTS to the over $500 million in tax costs that would be incurred in bringing FTS into compliance with the benchmark. The Commission also noted that FTS had set up its original corporate structure in good faith reliance on published FCC decisions and that there was no evidence of foreign influence on FTS. Fox Television Stations, Inc., 11 F.C.C.Rcd. 5714, 78 R.R.2d 1294 (1995).

b.　*Technical Qualifications.* An applicant for a broadcast station must also comply with the Commission's standards for transmission. These standards include such issues as interference with existing or allocated stations and efficiency of operation, gains or losses of service to affected populations, structure, power and location of the antenna, coverage and quality of the signal in the areas to be served, and studio location and operating equipment utilized.

c.　*Financial Qualifications.* Although the applicant must show it has an adequate financial base to commence operations, it need not demonstrate that it can sustain operations indefinitely. The test applied by the Commission is that the applicant must have sufficient funds to operate a broadcast station for three months without advertising revenue. The Commission may also inquire into the applicant's estimates of the amounts that will be actually required to operate the station and the reliability of its proposed sources of funds, such as estimated advertising revenues. As part of its order establishing auctions for new broadcast licenses the Commission eliminated this requirement for those proceedings. Implementation of Section 309(j) of the Communications Act—Competitive Bidding for Commercial Broadcast and Instructional Television Fixed Service Licenses, 13 F.C.C.Rcd. 15920, 13 C.R. 279 (1998).

d. *Character Qualifications*. Until the mid–1980s character issues considered by the Commission included past criminal convictions of the applicant, trafficking in broadcast licenses, failure to keep the Commission informed of changes in the applicant's status and other situations that raised questions as to the integrity or reliability of the applicant in the broadcasting function. In 1986, in keeping with the move toward deregulation, the Commission narrowed the scope of character examinations. The Commission confined its interest to three areas: misconduct involving violations of the Act or Commission rules, misrepresentations or lack of candor before the Commission and fraudulent programming.

Other than those issues, the Commission would consider as relevant only criminal fraud convictions, adjudicated cases of broadcast-related antitrust or anticompetitive misconduct and felony convictions substantially related to operating as a broadcaster in a manner consistent with Commission rules and policies. Character Qualifications in Broadcast Licensing, 102 F.C.C.2d 1179, 59 R.R.2d 801 (1986). The policy statement was upheld on appeal. National Association for Better Broadcasting v. Federal Communications Commission, 830 F.2d 270, 63 R.R.2d 1501 (D.C.Cir.1987).

Several years later the Commission expanded the scope of character examinations to include any felony conviction, regardless of whether it was broadcast related or not. The FCC's rationale for this expansion was that "[b]ecause all felonies are serious crimes, any conviction provides an indication of an applicant's or licensee's propensity to obey the law." The FCC also expanded consideration of antitrust violations to cover all mass-media-related violations instead of just broadcast-related ones.

With regard to both felony convictions and antitrust violations the Commission will, however, continue to take into consideration mitigating factors such as "the willfulness of the misconduct, the frequency of the misconduct, the currentness of the misconduct, the seriousness of the misconduct, the nature of the participation (if any) of managers or owners, efforts made to remedy the wrong, overall record of compliance with FCC rules and policies, and rehabilitation." The Commission also reiterated its willingness to condition license grants on the outcome of allegations being adjudicated in courts or other agencies. Character Qualifications Policy, 5 F.C.C.Rcd. 3252, 67 R.R.2d 1107 (1990).

On reconsideration, the FCC clarified its position with regard to misdemeanor convictions. They do not have to be reported to the Commission, but in appropriate cases serious misdemeanor convictions may be considered in evaluating the character qualifications of an applicant. Character Qualifications Policy, 69 R.R.2d 278 (1991).

e. The final category of basic qualifications, "other," has been interpreted to refer primarily to character issues, but it may also overlap with public interest considerations.

3. SUBSTANTIVE CONSIDERATIONS

Assuming an applicant met the basic qualifications, such as citizenship and financial security, how did the Commission decide if granting the application will serve the "public interest, convenience and necessity"? In this section we will take an extensive look at the substantive considerations in the process, starting with the single applicant for the single vacancy.

As noted earlier, even though an applicant had met the basic qualifications and was the only applicant for the license, that applicant did not necessarily get the license. Given that the FCC was created in large part to reduce crowding and eliminate chaos, what role could it play when only one applicant sought an available spot? A first answer may be found in *NBC,* p. 72, *supra,* where the Court recognized that the FCC could act beyond its policeman's role and consider the public interest. Sometimes the public interest might be better served by leaving a vacancy that a good applicant might later fill rather than by taking the first comer.

But this, of course, required that the FCC be able to distinguish a "good" applicant from a lesser one. From the beginning the Commission confronted the tension between using criteria that directly address programming considerations and the concern that too close a look at proposed programming could amount to government control.

The Commission believed that the "entire listening public within the service area of a station, or of a group of stations in one community, is entitled to service from that station or stations." Specialized stations were entitled to little or no consideration. In the Commission's opinion, "the tastes, needs, and desires of all substantial groups among the listening public should be met, in some fair proportion by a well-rounded program, in which entertainment, consisting of music of both classical and lighter grades, religion, education and instruction, important public events, discussions of public questions, weather, market reports and news, and matters of interest to all members of the family find a place." Recognizing that communities differed and that other variables were relevant, the Commission did not erect a "rigid schedule."

In 1946 the Commission issued a report entitled Public Service Responsibility of Broadcast Licensees (known generally as the "Blue Book"). The Commission stressed that although licensees bore the primary responsibility for program service, the Commission would still play a part: "In issuing and in renewing the licenses of broadcast stations, the Commission proposes to give particular consideration to four program service factors relevant to the public interest." One category was the carrying of "sustaining" (unsponsored) programs during hours "when the public is awake and listening." This would provide balance by allowing the broadcast of certain types of programs that did not lend themselves to sponsorship, including experimental programs. Second, the Commission called for local live programs to encourage local self-expression. Third, the Commission expected "programs devoted to the discussion of public issues." Finally, the Commission, expressing concern about excessive advertising, announced that "in its application forms the Commission will request the applicant to state how much time he proposes to devote to advertising matter in any one hour."

In 1960 the Commission changed direction. In Report and Statement of Policy Re: Commission En Banc Programming Inquiry, 25 Fed.Reg. 7291, 20 R.R. 1901 (1960), the FCC asserted that "the principal ingredient of the licensee's obligation to operate his station in the public interest is the diligent, positive and continuing effort . . . to discover and fulfill the tastes, needs and desires of his service area, for broadcast service." Broadcasters were advised to meet this obligation in two ways: they were to consult with members of the listening public who could receive the station's signal and with a variety of community leaders. The distinction between sustaining and sponsored programs was explicitly abandoned.

In 1971 the Commission elaborated upon and clarified the applicant's obligation. The Primer on Ascertainment of Community Problems by Broadcast Applicants, 27 F.C.C.2d 650, 21 R.R.2d 1507 (1971), standardized the Commission's policy with respect to ascertainment of, and programming for, community needs. It placed specific ascertainment requirements upon all commercial applicants for new broadcast stations, modification of existing facilities and renewals. The Primer required that an applicant determine the economic, ethnic and social composition of the communities it proposed to serve and that principals or management-level employees consult with leaders from each significant community group. The applicant was also to consult with a random sample of members of the general public. Finally, the applicant had to set forth in its license application, program proposals designed to meet community problems identified. The ascertainment had to take place within six months of the application.

The courts readily accepted the Commission's emphasis on the importance of the ascertainment process. In Henry v. Federal Communications Commission, 302 F.2d 191 (D.C.Cir.), certiorari denied 371 U.S. 821 (1962), Suburban Broadcasters filed the sole application for a permit to construct the first commercial FM station in Elizabeth, N.J. Although Suburban was found legally, technically and financially qualified, the Commission found that Suburban had made no inquiry into the characteristics or programming needs of Elizabeth and was "totally without knowledge of the area." Suburban's program proposals for Elizabeth were identical to those submitted in its application for an AM station in Berwyn, Ill., and in the application of two of its principal stockholders for an FM station in Alameda, Calif. Although acknowledging the community's "presumptive need" for its first FM service, the Commission denied the permit, finding that a grant would not serve the public interest.

On appeal, the Commission's denial was upheld on the ground that an applicant could be required to "demonstrate an earnest interest in serving a local community by evidencing a familiarity with its particular needs and an effort to meet them."

In 1976 the FCC amended the ascertainment regulations to require interviews "within the following [19] institutions and elements commonly found in a community." The list included agriculture, business, charities, religion, and organizations of elderly, youth and women. "A licensee is permitted to show that one or more of these institutions or elements is not present in its community. At its option it may also utilize the 'other' category to interview leaders in its elements not found on the checklist." Other groups, particularly from the gay community, soon claimed that broadcasters were not using the "other" category to interview them, and asked to be added to the list of 19. The FCC rejected that approach because its studies did not indicate that gay (or handicapped) persons were significant elements in all or most communities. Instead, it declared that broadcasters must ascertain unlisted groups if the groups first bear the burden of getting in touch with the broadcasters to let them know of the group's needs and problems. Amendment of the Primers on Ascertainment of Community Problems, 76 F.C.C.2d 401, 47 R.R.2d 189 (1980).

The ascertainment process was designed to allow the FCC to consider proposed programming from the standpoint of the nature of the community rather than the Commission's own ideas of what is "good" programming. It was part of the Commission's continued emphasis on localism.

In 1981 the FCC adopted, 6–1, a set of proposals reducing the regulations affecting commercial radio licensees. Deregulation of Radio, 84 F.C.C.2d 968, 49 R.R.2d 1 (1981). The underlying rationale was that with over 8,000 radio stations on the air, the Commission could rely on competition in the market to provide appropriate service. Among the changes was the elimination of the formal ascertainment requirements. The Commission's order deleting formal ascertainment procedures for all radio broadcasters was upheld in Office of Communication of the United Church of Christ v. Federal Communications Commission, 707 F.2d 1413, 53 R.R.2d 1371 (D.C.Cir.1983).

In 1984 the Commission adopted a similar set of changes in the regulations for commercial television. Formal ascertainment was eliminated because, according to the Commission, the administrative costs outweighed the benefits. Deregulation of Commercial Television, 98 F.C.C.2d 1075, 56 R.R.2d 1005 (1984). We will return to the changes brought about by these proceedings in the section on renewals.

4. THE COMPARATIVE PROCEEDING

If two or more applicants file for use of the same or interfering facilities, the Commission must choose which applicant will receive the license. For many years, the Commission made its decision through a comparative hearing among all qualified applicants to determine which would best serve the public interest. An applicant in a comparative proceeding not only had to meet minimum qualifications but also to prevail when judged on the Commission's comparative criteria. These criteria, which involved considerations other than those applied in the non-comparative proceeding, evolved through adjudication rather than rulemaking.

After years of this process, the Commission issued a policy statement outlining the criteria to be used in comparative proceedings. Policy Statement on Comparative Broadcast Hearings, 1 F.C.C.2d 393, 5 R.R.2d 1901 (1965).

The Commission noted that choosing one from among several qualified applicants for a facility was one of its primary responsibilities. The process involved an extended hearing in which the various applicants were compared on a variety of subjects. The "subject does not lend itself to precise categorization or to the clear making of precedent. The various factors cannot be assigned absolute values." Moreover, the membership of the Commission is continually changing and each member has his or her own idea of what factors are important. Thus, the statement is not binding, and the Commission is not obligated to deal with all cases "as it has dealt with some that seem comparable." Nonetheless, it is "important to have a high degree of consistency of decision and of clarity in our basic policies." The statement was to "serve the purpose of clarity and consistency of decision, and the further purpose of eliminating from the hearing process time-consuming elements not substantially related to the public interest." The Commission declared that this statement "does not attempt to deal with the somewhat different problems raised where an applicant is contesting with a licensee seeking renewal of license." The Commission then turned to the merits and identified "two primary objectives": "best practicable service to the public" and "maximum diffusion of control of the media of mass communications."

The FCC then listed a series of comparative criteria to be used in determining which applicant would best serve those two primary objectives:

1. *Diversification of control of the media of mass communication.*—Diversification is a factor of primary significance since, as set forth above, it constitutes a primary objective in the licensing scheme.

2. *Full-time participation in station operation by owners.*—We consider this factor to be of substantial importance. It is inherently desirable that legal responsibility and day-to-day performance be

closely associated. In addition, there is a likelihood of greater sensitivity to an area's changing needs, and of programing designed to serve these needs, to the extent that the station's proprietors actively participate in the day-to-day operation of the station. This factor is thus important in securing the best practicable service. It also frequently complements the objective of diversification, since concentrations of control are necessarily achieved at the expense of integrated ownership.

. . .

3. *Proposed program service.—* . . . The importance of program service is obvious. The feasibility of making a comparative evaluation is not so obvious. Hearings take considerable time and precisely formulated program plans may have to be changed not only in details but in substance, to take account of new conditions obtaining at the time a successful applicant commences operation. Thus, minor differences among applicants are apt to prove to be of no significance.

. . .

4. *Past broadcast record.*—This factor includes past ownership interest and significant participation in a broadcast station by one with an ownership interest in the applicant. It is a factor of substantial importance upon the terms set forth below.

A past record within the bounds of average performance will be disregarded, since average future performance is expected. Thus, we are not interested in the fact of past ownership per se, and will not give a preference because one applicant has owned stations in the past and another has not.

We are interested in records which, because either unusually good or unusually poor, give some indication of unusual performance in the future. . . .

. . .

5. *Efficient use of frequency.*—In comparative cases where one of two or more competing applicants proposes an operation which, for one or more engineering reasons, would be more efficient, this fact can and should be considered in determining which of the applicants should be preferred. . . .

6. *Character.*—The Communications Act makes character a relevant consideration in the issuance of a license. See section 308(b), 47 U.S.C. § 308(b). Significant character deficiencies may warrant disqualification, and an issue will be designated where appropriate. Since substantial demerits may be appropriate in some cases where disqualification is not warranted, petitions to add an issue on conduct relating to character will be entertained. In the absence of a designated issue, character evidence will not be taken. Our intention here is not only to avoid unduly prolonging the hearing process, but also to avoid those situations where an appli-

cant converts the hearing into a search for his opponents' minor blemishes, no matter how remote in the past or how insignificant.

7. *Other factors.*—As we stated at the outset, our interest in the consistency and clarity of decision and in expedition of the hearing process is not intended to preclude the full examination of any relevant and substantial factor. We will thus favorably consider petitions to add issues when, but only when, they demonstrate that significant evidence will be adduced.

Although he concurred, Commissioner Robert E. Lee expressed serious reservations:

> Over the years I have participated in decisions in hundreds of "comparative proceedings" and candor compels me to say that our method of selection of the winning applicant has given me grave concern. I realize, of course, that where we have a number of qualified applicants in a consolidated proceeding for a single facility in a given community, it is necessary that we grant one and deny the others. The ultimate choice of the winner generally sustains the Commission's choice despite the recent rash of demands from the court. Thus, it would appear that we generally grant the "right" application. However, I am not so naive as to believe that granting the "right application" could not, in some cases, be one of several applications.
>
> . . .
>
> Historically, a prospective applicant hires a highly skilled communications attorney, well versed in the procedures of the Commission. This counsel has a long history of Commission decisions to guide him and he puts together an application that meets all of the so-called criteria. There then follows a tortuous and expensive hearing wherein each applicant attempts to tear down his adversaries on every conceivable front, while individually presenting that which he thinks the Commission would like to hear. The examiner then makes a reasoned decision which, at first blush, generally makes a lot of sense—but comes the oral argument and all of the losers concentrate their fire on the "potential" winner and the Commission must thereupon examine the claims and counterclaims, "weigh" the criteria and pick the winner which, if my recollection serves me correctly, is a different winner in about 50 percent of the cases.
>
> The real blow, however, comes later when the applicant that emerged as the winner on the basis of our "decisive" criteria sells the station to a multiple owner or someone else that could not possibly have prevailed over other qualified applicants under the criteria in an adversary proceeding. It may be that there is no better selection system than the one being followed. If so, it seems like a "hell of a way to run a railroad," and I hope these few comments may inspire the Commission to find that better system even if it requires changes in the Communications Act.

The *1965 Policy Statement* eliminated three specific criteria—staffing and related plans, likelihood of effectuation of proposals, and proposed studios and equipment—that had formerly been used for comparison.

In 1986 the Commission eliminated character as a comparative criterion. Recall it is still a basic qualification. Character Qualifications in Broadcast Licensing, 102 F.C.C.2d 1179, 59 R.R.2d 801 (1986).

Did choosing licensees on the basis of proposed programming violate either the First Amendment or § 326 of the Communications Act? How far could the Commission go in examining applicants' programming proposals? These questions were answered in Johnston Broadcasting Co. v. Federal Communications Commission, 175 F.2d 351, 359 (D.C.Cir. 1949):

> As to appellant's contention that the Commission's consideration of the proposed programs was a form of censorship, it is true that the Commission cannot choose on the basis of political, economic or social views of an applicant. But in a comparative consideration, it is well recognized that comparative service to the listening public is the vital element, and programs are the essence of that service. So, while the Commission cannot prescribe any type of program (except for prohibitions against obscenity, profanity, etc.) it can make a comparison on the basis of public interest and, therefore, of public service. Such a comparison of proposals is not a form of censorship within the meaning of the statute. . . .

When was a comparative hearing required? In Ashbacker Radio Corp. v. Federal Communications Commission, 326 U.S. 327 (1945), the Commission had held a hearing on an application for a construction permit while an application for license modification in a nearby community was pending. The grant of the construction permit precluded the license modification. The Court held that the second applicant was denied its § 309(e) right to a hearing by the granting of the first application. As a result, the *Ashbacker* doctrine requires that whenever mutually exclusive applications are pending, the Commission must hold a single comparative hearing on all of the applications before granting any of them.

Although the Commission has emphasized localism, there has always been an undercurrent of doubt. In the early 1960s, when the Commission appeared to favor not only local programs but also live presentations, Judge Friendly observed, "I wonder also whether the Commission is really wise enough to determine that live telecasts, so much stressed in the decisions, e.g., of local cooking lessons, are always 'better' than a tape of Shakespeare's Histories." Friendly, The Federal Administrative Agencies: The Need for Better Definition of Standards, 75 Harv.L.Rev. 1055, 1071 (1962). This concern was restated in a different context by a former chairman of the Commission:

> [T]he automatic preference accorded local applicants disregards the possibility that, depending on the facts of a particular case, a

competitor's proposed use of a professional employee-manager from outside the community might very well bring imagination, an appreciation of the role of journalism, and sensitivity to social issues far exceeding that of a particular local owner-manager.

Hyde, FCC Policies and Procedures Relating to Hearings on Broadcast Applications, 1975 Duke L.J. 253, 277.

In the mid–1970s, the Chairman of the House Communications Subcommittee estimated that local television averaged 80 percent nonlocal programming and "maybe that's the way the viewers want it." He was suggesting that Congress might reconsider the desirability of localism. See Broadcasting, Nov. 22, 1976 at 20.

Minority Ownership. In TV 9, Inc. v. Federal Communications Commission, 495 F.2d 929 (D.C.Cir.1973), rehearing en banc denied (1974), Comint Corp., Mid–Florida Television Corporation and six other applicants sought a construction permit for Channel 9 in Orlando, Fla. In making the award to Mid–Florida, the Commission rejected Comint's contention that it was entitled to special consideration because two of Comint's principals were local black residents and 25 percent of those to be served by Channel 9 were black. The Commission's position was that the Communications Act was "color blind" and did not permit considerations of color in the award of licenses. The court disagreed and ruled that the ownership interests and participation of the two black residents gave Comint an edge in providing "broader community representation and practicable service to the public by increasing diversity of content, especially of opinion and viewpoint." We will examine the issue of minority preferences in more detail in Chapter XII.

In 1978 the Commission began granting women a preference in comparative proceedings. In 1992 the court of appeals struck down a license award based in part on such a preference. Lamprecht v. Federal Communications Commission, 958 F.2d 382, 70 R.R.2d 658 (D.C.Cir. 1992). *Lamprecht* is discussed in more detail in Chapter XII.

Previously, the Commission had refused to grant preferences to women applicants in the lotteries being held to award LPTV licenses. Lottery Selection (Preference for Women), 10 F.C.C.2d 1401, 58 R.R.2d 1077 (1985), affirmed sub nom. Pappas v. Federal Communications Commission, 807 F.2d 1019, 61 R.R.2d 1398 (D.C.Cir.1986).

The "recent rash of remands from the court" referred to by Commissioner Lee was caused by the revelation in the late 1950s that an FCC Commissioner had been bribed to vote in certain ways in licensing proceedings. Because the outcomes of these comparative hearings were not readily predictable, it was relatively easy for a Commissioner to vote one way in a particular case without being embarrassed by previous votes he might have cast in other licensing cases. The incentive to offer bribes was due to the fact that a license is awarded without charging the applicant the value of the part of the spectrum being licensed. In addition, due in part to the fact that renewals were virtually automatic, television channels in large cities had acquired great value.

After the bribes came to light, the court of appeals remanded virtually every licensing decision the FCC had recently made for a second look by what was then an FCC with some new faces.

B. RENEWAL OF LICENSES

1. INTRODUCTION

The initial license period was limited to three years by § 307(d), and the Commission considered renewal applications from about one-third of all licensees each year. In 1981 Congress changed license terms to five years for television and seven years for radio. The 1996 Telecommunications Act extended the maximum license term to eight years for both radio and television. At the outset, as it sought to unclutter the AM spectrum, the Commission frequently denied renewals, but after the initial flurry, denials were rare unless the broadcaster's behavior fell far below par. With the large number of renewal applications now filed annually, the FCC staff cannot fully investigate the performance of each applicant. Instead, the Commission has relied increasingly on informal complaints from citizens or citizen groups, and on petitions to deny renewal that became possible after the United Church of Christ case, p. 104, *supra*. Section 307(d) authorized renewals only on the same terms as initial grants—public interest, convenience and necessity.

Traditionally, members of the public who wished to challenge a station's renewal could obtain a great deal of information from the licensee itself. Broadcast licensees were required to keep detailed program logs and show them to the public on request. Commercial TV licensees were also required to submit a composite week log. (The "composite week" referred to a practice by which the Commission each year identified one Sunday, one Monday, etc. from the prior year by which to judge whether licensees had honored their obligations. This avoided the necessity of considering an entire year's data at renewal time.)

In addition, broadcasters were required to place the results of their formal ascertainment in their public file—a collection of material available for inspection by anyone wishing to see it. Also in the public file are almost all applications filed with the FCC—including any accompanying documents, all written citizen agreements, ownership reports, network contracts, all documents relating to present or future ownership of the station, a manual on the public file prepared by the FCC, all requests for broadcast time by candidates for political office and the station's response, annual employment reports and a model EEO program, letters from the public pertaining to station operation, certification of pre-and post-filing announcements, and documents relating to sponsorship identification of political or public controversy programming.

In *Deregulation of Radio,* p. 113, *supra,* the Commission eliminated the requirement that commercial radio licensees keep program logs. Instead each radio station would have to list between five and 10 issues of public importance in its community that it had addressed in its programming. There was no requirement that this programming be produced locally. It was this failure to require local production that brought forth the sole dissent on the Commission.

A specialized station would be able to adhere to its special focus and allow other stations in the market to serve other needs. A classical music station need no longer present national or world news, but might emphasize artistic and cultural news and events. A station presenting black programming in an urban area, might no longer need to worry about presenting programs that would be of interest to other segments of the community. The FCC expected that the array of stations would, one way or another, meet the varied needs and interests of the community's audience.

As a result of the appellate court remand of *Deregulation of Radio,* the Commission changed the annual issues/programs list to a quarterly list and specified that a minimum of five issues must be listed.

When the revised issues/program list was challenged on appeal, the court rejected the revised list as inadequate to provide someone filing a petition to deny sufficient information to make a *prima facie* case. Office of Communication of United Church of Christ v. Federal Communications Commission, 779 F.2d 702, 59 R.R.2d 895 (D.C.Cir.1985). In 1986 the Commission revised the regulation to require a list of programs that have provided the station's most significant treatment of community issues during the preceding three-month period. Deregulation of Radio, 104 F.C.C.2d 505, 60 R.R.2d 789 (1986).

At the same time, in response to a petition for reconsideration, the Commission modified its order deregulating television to require the quarterly issues/program list, but otherwise affirmed its decision. Programming and Commercialization Policies (Reconsideration), 104 F.C.C.2d 357, 60 R.R.2d 526 (1986). Action for Children's Television (ACT) and Black Citizens for a Fair Media both filed appeals in *Deregulation of Television.* ACT's appeal centered on the elimination of commercial guidelines; Black Citizens for a Fair Media's appeal focused on the lack of program reporting requirements in renewal applications. In 1987 the court of appeals affirmed the Commission's actions with one exception. The court held that, given the previous special treatment accorded children's television by the Commission, it had presented inadequate justification for its elimination of commercial guidelines for children's television. We will discuss children's television in more detail in Chapter VI.

In 1981 the Commission drastically shortened and simplified the application forms that renewal applicants had to use. All commercial radio renewal applicants and 95 percent of the commercial television renewal applicants filled out short five-question forms. The other randomly chosen five percent had to complete longer forms similar to the old 21–page forms. This "postcard renewal" process was affirmed on appeal. The court of appeals rejected the contention that the duty to award renewals based on the public interest was violated by the absence of any questions concerning licensees' nonentertainment programming. "Although the FCC has deleted from the application many questions which previously supplied substantial information, we believe that it was not arbitrary or capricious for the Commission to conclude, in the exercise of its discretion, that it still has sufficient information to make the 'public interest' determination." Black Citizens for a Fair Media v. Federal Communications Commission, 719 F.2d 407, 54 R.R.2d 1151 (D.C.Cir.1983), certiorari denied 467 U.S. 1255 (1984).

In *Deregulation of Television, supra*, the Commission eliminated the requirement that 5 percent of commercial television renewal applicants fill out the longer renewal application forms. As a result, all commercial radio and television renewal applicants used the five-question short form.

However, concern over two specific aspects of television programming, children's programs and violence on television, both discussed in Chapter VI, have caused Congress to add requirements for television license renewal applications. In accordance with the Children's Television Act of 1990, licensees must include with their renewal application information on how they have served the "educational and informational needs of children." The 1996 Telecommunications Act added a requirement that each renewal applicant attach as an exhibit "a summary of written comments and suggestions received from the public . . . that comment on the applicant's programming, . . ., and that are characterized by the commentor as constituting violent programming." 47 U.S.C.A. § 308(d).

The FCC was generally reluctant to deny renewals except in egregious cases. The reason is the size of the penalty that denial of renewal inflicts on the licensee in a world in which VHF stations may be worth $500 million or more, and even radio stations may be worth tens of millions of dollars.

Penalties and Short Renewals. Before 1960 the Commission had few weapons for dealing with misbehavior, since Congress assumed that denial of renewal would suffice in most cases, with revocation during the term to handle the most serious violations. But the Commission came to view denial of renewal as too harsh for all but the most serious violations of rules or other misbehavior. In the 1960 amendments to the Communications Act, Congress explicitly authorized shorter renewals by amending § 307(d), but this could not be utilized until the end of the license period. To fill this gap, Congress responded with §§ 503(b) et seq. to provide the Commission with "an effective tool in dealing with violations in situations where revocation or suspension does not appear to be appropriate." Under § 503(b), the Commission can impose a fine, called a forfeiture, against a licensee who has violated a specific rule.

Responding to the Commission's repeated requests for the authority to levy heavier forfeitures—the maximum fine was $2,000 per violation—Congress amended § 503(b)(2) in late 1989. Broadcasters and cable operators may now be assessed forfeitures of $25,000 per violation for each day of a continuing violation up to a maximum of $250,000 for any single act or failure to act. The Commission quickly adopted the new higher limits. Forfeitures, 5 F.C.C.Rcd. 3708, 67 R.R.2d 1193 (1990).

The new forfeiture schedule was struck down in U.S. Telephone Association v. F.C.C., 28 F.3d 1232, 75 R.R.2d 748 (D.C.Cir.1994) on the grounds that the FCC had implemented it without subjecting it to public comment.

After issuing an NPRM, Forfeiture Policy Statement, 10 F.C.C.Rcd. 2945 (1995), and receiving public comment, the Commission adopted the same schedule with minor modifications. Forfeiture Proceedings, 62 Fed.Reg. 43474 (Aug. 14, 1997).

The added array of sanctions reduced the likelihood that the denial of renewal would be used for what the Commission perceived to be lesser transgressions of the rules. The Commission has in the past resorted extensively to the short-term renewal. The expectation is that if the licensee performs properly during that period it will then return to the regular renewal cycle. In addition to the probationary impact, a short renewal imposes burdens of legal expenses and administrative effort in preparing and defending the application.

Single instances of fraudulent behavior toward advertisers or conducting rigged contests, traditionally led to forfeitures or short-term renewals. Among the most common types of fraud are billing advertisers for commercials that were never actually broadcast and the practice of "double-billing." The latter involves cooperative advertising in which a national manufacturer promises to share advertising expenses with its local retailers. The retailer gets a discount for volume, but the station sends it two bills—one for the actual discounted amount due and a second based on a higher non-discounted rate to be forwarded to the national manufacturer as the basis for the sharing.

After many years of warning against the practice and punishing violators with forfeitures and other penalties, the Commission, in the 1970s, began to deny license renewals to violators. The courts upheld the FCC. See White Mountain Broadcasting Co., Inc. v. Federal Communications Commission, 598 F.2d 274, 45 R.R.2d 681 (D.C.Cir.1979), cert. denied, 444 U.S. 963 (1979)(upholding denial of renewal where the practice had continued for five and one-half years with full knowledge of the president and sole shareholder of licensee). In the 1980s, however, the Commission again changed its attitude toward enforcing these regulations. In 1986, as part of an ongoing attempt to reduce overly restrictive regulations as well as those that duplicate other federal or state law, the Commission eliminated the rules on fraudulent billing. Elimination of Unnecessary Broadcast Regulation (Business Practices), 59 R.R.2d

1500 (1986). We will return to these "regulatory underbrush" proceedings in Chapter VI.

2. Substantive Grounds for Nonrenewal

a. *Non-speech Considerations*

Just as the Commission may deny an uncontested application for a vacant channel, it may deny renewal when no other applicant seeks the spot and even when no complaint has been made. The Mass Media Bureau may argue against renewals when it believes that they would not serve the public interest.

Lying to the Commission may be the clearest basis for denying renewal. In its early years the FCC did not treat dishonesty toward the Commission with heavy sanctions. This led to more examples of such behavior. Finally the Commission denied the renewal of a station whose general manager, for 12 years, had concealed from the Commission the fact that a vice-president of a network secretly owned 24 percent of the station's stock. The station appealed on the grounds, among others, that the harsh treatment came without warning and that there was no indication that the FCC would not have renewed the station's application even if it had known the truth.

The Supreme Court upheld the denial of renewal. The fact that the FCC had previously dealt more mildly with similar cases did not prevent it from changing course without warning. Also, the "fact of concealment may be more significant than the facts concealed. The willingness to deceive a regulatory body may be disclosed by immaterial and useless deceptions as well as by material and persuasive ones." The fact that stockholders of a majority of the shares had no knowledge of the dishonesty did not bar the FCC from acting—"the fact that there are innocent stockholders cannot immunize the corporation from the consequences of such deception." Stockholders often suffer from the misdeeds of their chosen officers. Federal Communications Commission v. WOKO, Inc., 329 U.S. 223 (1946).

Sometimes the Commission has held that the manager's deceit is the licensee's responsibility because of its failure to exercise adequate control and supervision consistent with its responsibilities as a licensee. Renewal was denied and the court affirmed in such a case. Continental Broadcasting, Inc. v. Federal Communications Commission, 439 F.2d 580, 20 R.R.2d 2126 (D.C.Cir.), certiorari denied 403 U.S. 905 (1971).

Because the license is issued to the licensee, the licensee must meet the standards of the Communications Act and the FCC. Misbehavior of the officers may show that the licensee knew of the misbehavior or a serious failure to control the station. In an appropriate situation, either may justify denial of renewal. We will consider such a case, RKO v. Federal Communications Commission, later in this chapter.

However, in 1980 the Commission unanimously renewed the license of a Westinghouse broadcasting station despite claims that the licensee's parent corporation had engaged in criminal misrepresentations to federal agencies. Because the licensee was "virtually autonomous," the parent's misdeeds did not reflect on the licensee's qualifications. Westinghouse Broadcasting Co., 75 F.C.C.2d 736, 46 R.R.2d 1431 (1980).

In response to the Anti–Drug Abuse Act of 1988, the Commission announced a new ground for possible non-renewal or revocation. "[A]bsent extenuating or mitigating circumstances, the Commission intends promptly to take all appropriate steps, including initiation of license revocation proceedings, where information comes to our attention that FCC licensees or their principals have been convicted of drug trafficking." Drug Trafficking Policy, 4 F.C.C.Rcd. 7533, 66 R.R.2d 1617 (1989).

b. Speech Considerations

As you will recall, p. 119, *supra*, in its early days the Commission was not hesitant about denying renewals when it disapproved of the speech being uttered. The potential implications of that practice were not tested because the situation eased after the famous Mayflower Broadcasting Corp. case, 8 F.C.C. 333 (1940), in which the Commission renewed a license but appeared to criticize the licensee for editorializing: "A truly free radio cannot be used to advocate the causes of the licensee. . . . In brief, the broadcaster cannot be an advocate." The case apparently deterred controversial discussion and therefore reduced the need for the Commission to judge speech directly. The situation changed after the Commission's Report on Editorializing by Broadcast Licensees, 13 F.C.C. 1246, 1 R.R. pt. 3, § 91.21 (1949), which directed licensees to devote a reasonable portion of their broadcast time to the discussion of controversial issues of public importance and to encourage the presentation of various views on these questions. This has also affected renewal cases.

In one case, the FCC found that a disc jockey had been using vulgar and suggestive language. When the FCC began to investigate, the licensee denied all knowledge of the offending conduct. Because of the history of complaints, the Commission found that denial not credible, which raised a question about the licensee's character qualifications. After renewal was denied, the court affirmed but did so explicitly on the character ground, refusing to pass on whether the speech alone would have justified nonrenewal. Robinson v. Federal Communications Commission, 334 F.2d 534, 2 R.R.2d 2001 (D.C.Cir.), certiorari denied 379 U.S. 843 (1964).

In Walton Broadcasting, Inc., 78 F.C.C.2d 857, 47 R.R.2d 1233 (1980), the Commission denied renewal to a station that had tried to build upon the popularity of a new disc jockey by having him disappear and reporting that he had been kidnapped. Listeners jammed telephone lines to the police and the radio station. The licensee was an absentee owner who took no steps to rectify the matter until after the FCC began investigating. The renewal was denied because the licensee failed to exercise adequate control over the station's operations:

> The misconduct in this case, the hoax broadcast of news and the false announcement about the kidnapping or disappearance in a non-news context over a 4–day period, was designed to shock and alarm KIKX's listening public. The misconduct can be traced directly to the licensee's failure to require promotion formats be approved, its failure to transmit and emphasize the substance of its policies to its station manager, its failure to insure that the manager understood its policies, its failure to check to see if he transmitted the information to on-the-air personnel, and its failure to understand and inculcate the most elementary principle of public trusteeship.

The licensee was also found responsible for six technical violations of the logging rules and 12 engineering violations. Because the control was inadequate and the resulting misconduct was quite serious, the penalty of nonrenewal was justified.

Another kind of deception was attempted by a minister whose initial efforts to acquire a station for his seminary were challenged by groups who believed that his past record showed that he would not honor the fairness doctrine (see Chapter V) or his other obligations. The prospective licensee responded by promising to provide balanced programming. Within 10 days of obtaining the license, the licensee began drastically altering its format and groups complained that the licensee was not living up to its obligations. The Commission denied renewal on two grounds: alleged violations of the fairness doctrine and deception practiced on the Commission in obtaining the license. On appeal, the court affirmed, 2–1. Two judges agreed on the deception ground, but the dissenter found that ground "too narrow a ledge" for decision. He thought that the Commission had really denied renewal because of the speech uttered on the station, and he concluded that this was impermissible. Brandywine–Main Line Radio, Inc. v. Federal Communications Commission, 473 F.2d 16, 25 R.R.2d 2010, 1 Med.L.Rptr. 2067 (D.C.Cir. 1972), certiorari denied 412 U.S. 922 (1973), Douglas, J. dissenting.

In United Television Co., 55 F.C.C.2d 416, 34 R.R.2d 1465 (1975), the Commission denied renewal to a station accused of violating 18 U.S.C.A. § 1304 by broadcasting information concerning lotteries. This was done by ministers who "broadcast programs offering three-digit scripture citations in return for monetary donations." The licensee conceded that the language used in the broadcasts referred to numbers games. The Commission, rejecting the claim that freedom of religion was involved, stated that it had the power to determine whether asserted beliefs are "sincerely held" and whether the ministers were in "good faith." Because the numbered references were not part of any creed and "the representations of the ministers concerning financial blessings defy belief," the Commission concluded that no First Amendment problem was involved. There was no specific reference to the speech and press parts of the First Amendment. This behavior alone was held to warrant denial and to bar United from a comparative hearing. In addition to this misbehavior, the licensee was found to have engaged in false and misleading advertising as well as violations of technical rules.

United's appeal failed. United Broadcasting Co. v. Federal Communications Commission, 565 F.2d 699 (D.C.Cir.1977), certiorari denied 434 U.S. 1046 (1978). The court, however, refused to accept the speech ground. It noted that the FCC's order cited several independent reasons for nonrenewal, including technical violations: "In our view, the long history of persistent violations of those rules was a sufficient reason for disqualification. The Commission's decision is therefore affirmed on the basis of its discussion of this issue, and we reach no other question tendered by this appeal."

In Trustees of the University of Pennsylvania, 69 F.C.C.2d 1394, 44 R.R.2d 747 (1978), the Commission denied a renewal application from a university. Listeners had complained for some time that announcers on the station had frequently used obscenity and that entire programs had been obscene. The University took few steps to meet the problem until after the FCC began inquiries and ordered a hearing on the renewal application. The Commission denied renewal exclusively on the ground that the licensee had totally abdicated its control over the station's management. The Commission explicitly indicated that the ALJ had denied renewal because of lack of control "and it is that conclusion which we today affirm." The FCC refused to accept the argument that noncommercial licensees should not be held to the same level of accountability as commercial licensees. Finally, "corrective action taken by the licensee cannot mitigate its unsatisfactory performance . . . because remedial steps which were taken came only after months of critical deficiencies in supervision and control of the station and, moreover, they occurred after it became clear the station's license was in jeopardy."

A dissenting Commissioner argued for a short-term renewal on the ground that the FCC had been renewing university stations for years although it knew that they "were not as tightly controlled as commercially operated stations." He was distressed that the University and the community should suffer because of the actions of a "few immature, irresponsible students" who "should have been spanked long ago and the matter ended there."

The most dramatic nonrenewal on speech grounds involved the station in Jackson, Miss., that was the subject of the United Church of Christ case discussed at p. 104, *supra*. Strangely, the case did *not* involve a Commission decision not to renew. Groups claimed that the station had violated the fairness doctrine, had failed to air contrasting viewpoints on racial matters, had given blacks inadequate exposure, had generally been disrespectful to blacks, had discriminated against local Catholics and had given inadequate time to public affairs. Blacks constituted 45 percent of the population of the station's primary service area. The FCC gave the licensee a short renewal and ordered it to honor its obligations.

After the FCC had been ordered to allow the citizen groups to participate and to reconsider the case, it decided that the station deserved renewal because the allegations had not been proven.

On a second appeal, the court reversed on the ground that the FCC's decision was not supported by substantial evidence. The FCC's errors included placing the burden of proof on the citizen groups rather than on the renewal applicant and failing to accept uncontradicted testimony about the station's practices, including cutting off national programs that showed blacks in a favorable light or discussed racial issues. Sometimes the licensee falsely blamed technical difficulties for the interruptions in service. Office of Communication of United Church of Christ v. Federal Communications Commission, 425 F.2d 543, 16 R.R.2d 2095 (D.C.Cir.1969).

Rather than remand again, the court itself vacated the license and ordered the FCC to invite applications for the now vacant channel—and to provide for interim operation of the facility. Finally, the station was taken over by a different licensee.

Surely the most widescale nonrenewal occurred when the Commission refused to renew licenses for eight educational stations in Alabama as well as an application for a construction permit for a ninth. Alabama Educational Television Commission, 50 F.C.C.2d 461, 32 R.R.2d 539 (1975). The Commission found that "blacks rarely appeared on AETC programs; that no black instructors were employed in connection with locally-produced in-school programs; and that unexplained decisions or inconsistently applied policies caused the preemption of almost all black-oriented network programming." The Commission concluded that the "licensee followed a racially discriminatory policy in its overall programming practices and, by reason of its pervasive neglect of a black minority consisting of approximately 30 percent of the population of Alabama, its programming did not adequately meet the needs of the public it was licensed to serve." Although a station need not meet minority needs by special programming, the licensee "cannot with impunity ignore the problems of significant minorities in its service areas." Two dissenters argued that the improvements in the last few years should justify more lenient treatment. The majority used that improvement, which came only after the challenges to renewal, to waive its usual rule that an applicant who is denied renewal is ineligible to reapply for that same station. The state agency here was permitted to reapply but it did so on equal footing with the other applicants.

Generally, however, a licensee runs no risk of losing its license because of what it broadcasts so long as the content is not obscene or otherwise proscribed, as discussed in Chapter VI. The clearest judicial exposition of this view occurred when a petition to deny renewal was filed against a radio station that had broadcast several programs that "made offensive comments concerning persons of the Jewish faith, equating Judaism with Socialism and Socialism with Communism." The Commission granted renewal without a hearing. The court of appeals affirmed. Anti–Defamation League of B'Nai B'rith v. Federal Communications Commission, 403 F.2d 169, 14 R.R.2d 2051 (D.C.Cir.1968), certiorari denied 394 U.S. 930 (1969).

The court approvingly quoted from the Commission's opinion in the case:

> The Commission has long held that its function is not to judge the merit, wisdom or accuracy of any broadcast discussion or commentary but to insure that all viewpoints are given fair and equal opportunity for expression and that controverted allegations are balanced by the presentation of opposing viewpoints. Any other position would stifle discussion and destroy broadcasting as a medium of free speech. To require every licensee to defend his decision to present any controversial program that has been complained of in a license renewal hearing would cause most—if not all—licensees to refuse to broadcast any program that was potentially controversial or offensive to any substantial group. More often than not this would operate to deprive the public of the opportunity to hear unpopular or unorthodox views.

The court rejected the petitioner's main contention that "recurrent bigoted appeals to anti-Semitic prejudice" was a basis for denial of renewal. Here it quoted extensively from the opinion of a concurring Commissioner:

> It is not only impractical—and impossible in any ultimate sense—to separate an appeal to prejudice from an appeal to reason in this field, it is equally beyond the power or ability of authority to say what is religious or racial. There are centuries of bloody strife to prove that man cannot agree on what is or is not "religion."
>
> . . .
>
> Nevertheless these subjects will and must be discussed. But they cannot be freely discussed if there is to be an official ban on the utterance of "falsehood" or an "appeal to prejudice" as officially defined. All that the government can properly do, consistently with the right of free speech, is to demand that the opportunity be kept open for the presentation of all viewpoints. Yet this would be impossible under the rule espoused by the ADL. . . . If what the ADL calls "appeals to racial or religious prejudice" is to be classed with hard-core obscenity, then it has no right to be heard on the air, and the only views which are entitled to be broadcast on matters of concern to the ADL are those which the ADL holds or finds acceptable. This is irreconcilable with either the Fairness Doctrine or the right of free speech.
>
> Talk of "responsibility" of a broadcaster in this connection is simply a euphemism for self-censorship. It is an attempt to shift the onus of action against speech from the Commission to the broadcaster, but it seeks the same result—suppression of certain views and arguments. . . . Attempts to impose such schemes of self-censor-

ship have been found as unconstitutional as more direct censorship efforts by government. [   ]

Promise v. Performance. If the Commission "encourages" promises of certain types of programs, how should the Commission treat disparities between the promises and the actual performance? The Commission's general reluctance to deny renewals originally led it to overlook disparities. The subject is discussed extensively in Moline Television Corp., 31 F.C.C.2d 263, 22 R.R.2d 745 (1971), dealing with an assertion that an applicant obtained a station by lavish promises and failed to carry them out. The commission noted that it had "not awarded a preference to any applicant based on proposed programming. The door to a sorry episode has been firmly closed."

In West Coast Media, Inc., 79 F.C.C.2d 610, 47 R.R.2d 1709 (1980), a petition to deny renewal was filed against a San Diego FM station for failing to comply with its promises to the FCC. After a hearing, the FCC denied renewal. The Commission stressed that it had not set minimum program requirements to qualify for renewal. Instead, the licensee is obliged to comply substantially with its promises for future performance. "Insubstantial variations do not raise a question of the licensee's ability" to serve the public interest. Here the licensee fell far below its promises. In such cases "the Commission confines its review of programming performance to a determination of whether the licensee made reasonable and good faith efforts to effectuate its proposal. Moreover, the licensee must show that its programming has been appropriately responsive to community problems, needs and interests."

After reviewing the case, including the licensee's explanations for the substantial disparity, the Commission concluded that the record showed that the licensee failed to make "reasonable and good faith efforts to effectuate its proposal." This order was upheld in West Coast Media, Inc. (KDIG) v. Federal Communications Commission, 695 F.2d 617, 52 R.R.2d 1295 (D.C.Cir.1982), certiorari denied 464 U.S. 816 (1983).

3.   COMPARATIVE RENEWAL PROCEEDINGS

In the early years of regulation of each medium, except perhaps for AM, so many vacant frequencies existed that few applicants tried to oust incumbents. When such a challenge did occur, the Commission undertook the difficult comparison of the incumbent's actual performance and the challenger's proposed operation. In a major case involving renewal of the license of a Baltimore AM station, the Commission's analysis included some factors favoring the incumbent and others favoring the challenger. Hearst Radio, Inc. (WBAL), 15 F.C.C. 1149, 6 R.R. 994 (1951). Although the incumbent had not integrated ownership and management this did not matter because its actual performance was now available for review. Similarly, although the incumbent also controlled an FM station, a television station and a newspaper in Baltimore, it had not abused its power so this was not a serious problem. The Commission found little difference in programming despite the challenger's strong assertions to the contrary, and concluded:

> We have found that both of the applicants are legally, technically, and financially qualified and must therefore choose between them as their applications are mutually exclusive. We have discussed at some length why the criteria which we may sometimes consider as determining factors when one of the applicants is not operating the facilities sought and where the applicants have not proved their abilities, are not controlling factors in the light of the record of WBAL. The determining factor in our decision is the clear advantage of continuing the established and excellent service now furnished by WBAL and which we find to be in the public interest, when compared to the risks attendant on the execution of the proposed programming of Public Service Radio Corporation, excellent though the proposal may be.

This decision was thought to give renewal applicants such an advantage that prospective challengers began to seek entry by other means, such as buying an existing facility or seeking available, though less desirable, vacant frequencies. In its *1965 Policy Statement on Comparative Broadcast Hearings*, p. 114, *supra*, the Commission noted that it was not attempting to deal with "the somewhat different problems raised where an applicant is contesting with a licensee seeking renewal of a license." Yet, later that year, in a case in which two applicants were challenging the incumbent, the Commission stated that, on further consideration, it had "concluded that the policy statement should govern the introduction of evidence in this and similar proceedings where a renewal application is contested. . . . However, we wish to make it clear that the parties will be free to urge any arguments they may deem applicable concerning the relative weights to be afforded the evidence bearing on the various comparative factors." Seven (7) League Productions, Inc., 1 F.C.C.2d 1597 (1965).

Although the Commission might have developed a special set of standards governing renewal cases, it found it quite difficult to do so. This was not a serious problem so long as few applicants challenged renewal applicants. But in the 1960s and early 1970s, those who wished to get into broadcasting were faced with virtually no vacancies on the spectrum (except UHF) and greatly increasing prices for existing stations. Despite the warning of *Hearst,* applicants began increasingly to challenge incumbents. Whether because the incumbents were superior— or at least equal—or because the denial of renewal imposed a serious financial penalty, the Commission continued to favor renewal applicants.

The WHDH Case. However, in a complex case that dragged on 15 years, the Commission rendered a decision that shocked the broadcast industry. In 1954, four mutually exclusive applicants began a contest for Channel 5 in Boston. After hearings, the FCC selected WHDH, Inc., which was wholly owned by the *Boston Herald–Traveler* newspaper.

While the losers appealed, WHDH began broadcasting. During the appeals, it was learned WHDH's president, Robert Choate, had had private meetings with the FCC chairman in what was later described as a "meaningful and improper, albeit subtle, attempt to influence the Commission."* The FCC reopened the case in 1960, and WHDH again was selected—but given only a four-month license because of the misbehavior. Appeals were again taken. When WHDH filed for renewal, the FCC invited competing applications.

As a result of a new hearing in 1966, the FCC found WHDH's past record within the bounds of average performance and thus not entitled to special credit. On diversification grounds, WHDH fared badly because of its newspaper connection. In 1969 the FCC awarded BBI the license. When WHDH argued that it should benefit from the *Hearst* decision, the FCC responded that this was not an ordinary renewal case because of its "unique events and procedures." Even though WHDH had been operating for 12 years, all but four months of that had been on temporary licenses and its only permanent license had been very short because of the misbehavior.

On appeal, the court affirmed the FCC's grant of the license to BBI instead of WHDH. *Greater Boston Television Corp.*, p. 103, *supra*. If renewal criteria had been applied, the relationship between WHDH and the newspaper would not have been considered—and WHDH would have gotten the benefits of *Hearst* and might well have gotten the license. The court recognized that the FCC had put this case into a special category and had not treated WHDH as a renewal applicant, which it found entirely appropriate given the peculiar history of the case.

The court recognized that in ordinary cases renewal expectancies "are provided in order to promote security of tenure and to induce efforts and investments, furthering the public interest, that may not be devoted by a licensee without reasonable security." But that did not apply here.

Even before the court's decision in *Greater Boston,* the industry mobilized to overturn what it saw as a retreat from *Hearst*. The FCC sought to forestall Congressional action by adopting a Policy Statement on Comparative Hearings Involving Regular Renewal Applicants, 22 F.C.C.2d 424, 18 R.R.2d 1901 (1970). Briefly, that policy stated that in any hearing between an incumbent and a challenger, the incumbent would obtain a controlling preference by demonstrating substantial past performance without serious deficiencies. The FCC would never get to consider the merits of the challenger if the incumbent's record met the non-comparative renewal standard.

---

* Once a proceeding is underway, parties are generally prohibited from meeting with Commission personnel outside the presence of other parties to the proceeding. The rationale for the prohibition on "ex parte" contacts is that opponents would not have the opportunity to rebut statements made at these meetings because they would be unaware of them.

The new Policy Statement was challenged in Citizens Communications Center v. Federal Communications Commission, 447 F.2d 1201, 22 R.R.2d 2001 (D.C.Cir.1971). At issue was whether the Policy Statement violated § 309(e) of the Communications Act and the *Ashbacker* doctrine. Section 309(e) states in part, "If, in the case of any application to which subsection (a) of this section applies, . . . the Commission for any reason is unable to make the finding specified in such subsection, it shall formally designate the application for hearing on the ground or reasons then obtaining. . . . Any hearing subsequently held upon such application shall be a full hearing in which the applicant and all other parties in interest shall be permitted to participate. . . ."

The court of appeals decided that the Policy Statement did violate § 309(e) and the *Ashbacker* doctrine despite the Commission's inclusion of all competing applicants in the renewal proceeding:

> To circumvent the *Ashbacker* strictures, however, [the Commission] adds a new twist: the Policy Statement would limit the "comparative" hearing to a single issue—whether the incumbent licensee had rendered "substantial" past performance without serious deficiencies. If the examiner finds that the licensee has rendered such service, the "comparative" hearing is at an end and, barring successful appeal, the renewal application must be granted. Challenging applicants would thus receive no hearing at all on their own applications, contrary to the express provisions of Section 309(e) which requires a full hearing.

> In *Ashbacker* the Commission had promised the challenging applicant a hearing on his application after the rival application was granted. The Supreme Court in *Ashbacker* said that such a promise was "an empty thing." At least the Commission here must be given credit for honesty. It does not make any empty promises. It simply denies the competing applicants the "full hearing" promised them by Section 309(e) of the Act. Unless the renewal applicant's past performance is found to be insubstantial or marred by serious deficiencies, the competing applications get no hearing at all. The proposition that the 1970 Policy Statement violates Section 309(e), as interpreted in *Ashbacker,* is so obvious it need not be labored.

The court did not, however, rule that superior performance by a licensee should be ignored. "At the same time, *superior* performance should be a plus of major significance in renewal proceedings. Indeed, as *Ashbacker* recognizes, in a renewal proceeding, a new applicant is under a greater burden to 'make the comparative showing necessary to displace an established licensee.' "

Thus, some renewal expectancy was clearly allowed but its exact role in the renewal process still needed clarification. *Citizens Communications Committee* stated it could never reach the level of a controlling preference. But just how much weight should renewal expectancy be given and how good did the licensee's performance have to be to earn it?

During the early 1970s broadcasters sought legislation clarifying the position of licensees in the renewal process. Their reliance on the Commission had been shaken by their perception of the WHDH case, and the Commission's efforts to reassure them failed when the 1970 *Policy Statement* was upset. The pressure on Congress was aimed mainly toward obtaining a renewal standard that avoided the comparative treatment for an incumbent that had generally been acceptable during the prior period. In 1974 the broadcasters nearly succeeded. Different bills passed the House, 379–14, and the Senate, 69–2, but a conference was never held because the Chairman of the House Interstate Commerce Committee refused to name conferees. He was angry because he believed the broadcasters had reneged on a deal by maneuvering on the floor of each house to raise the term of the license to five years from the Committee's proposed four years. The concern about the length of the term was felt most strongly by smaller broadcasters who were hoping to avoid the paperwork and legal expenses that occurred every three years. These broadcasters were also not usually subject to challenges. The holders of licenses in the large urban areas cared more about the standards to be utilized in renewal cases and less about the length of the term. The result of the maneuvering was that neither group got anything at that time.

The Central Florida Case. Throughout the 1970s, the Commission continued to grant renewals except in cases of serious licensee misconduct. Although the Commission purported not to be, it appeared to be giving incumbent licensees a controlling preference for "superior" or even "substantial" service. One such case involved the application by Cowles Florida Broadcasting, Inc., for renewal of the license for its Daytona Beach, Fla., television station. The administrative law judge, in recommending renewal, characterized Cowles' performance as "thoroughly acceptable." The Commission granted renewal, 4–3; but the majority, after its own study of the record, concluded that the performance was "superior" and warranted renewal even though the challenger, Central Florida Enterprises, Inc., had gained advantages on several other issues, including diversification, integration and minority participation, as well as the incumbent's having moved its main studio location in violation of an FCC regulation. The majority also chose to disregard mail fraud allegations against other subsidiaries of Cowles' parent company.

One dissenter thought that the majority had distorted the record to find "superior" service. He thought it only "solid" and would have held that enough to justify renewal but felt constrained to dissent because the court of appeals had set a higher standard. Another dissenter followed much the same path and urged alternative licensing techniques such as lotteries and auctions.

In an order "clarifying" its earlier opinion, a majority of the Commission explained that its previous use of "superior" was not meant to suggest "exceptional when compared to other broadcast stations" in the area or elsewhere. Rather, the intention was to distinguish "between the two situations—one where the licensee has served the public interest but in the least permissible fashion still sufficient to be renewed in the absence of competing applications, and the other where the licensee has done so in a solid, favorable fashion." The licensee was said to be in the second group. The majority shifted from "superior" to "substantial."

The court of appeals reversed the renewal and remanded. Central Florida Enterprises, Inc. v. Federal Communications Commission, 598 F.2d 37, 44 R.R.2d 345 (D.C.Cir.1978). The court's final position (after an original opinion, an order amending that opinion, and a supplemental opinion denying a petition for rehearing) rejected the Commission's entire approach to comparative renewal proceedings—and found inadequacies in its dealings with specific issues. The Commission purported to be following its *1965 Policy Statement* in conducting a full hearing. The court observed:

> It found favorably to Central [the challenger] on each of diversification, integration, and minority participation, and adversely to Cowles on the studio move question. Then simply on the basis of a wholly noncomparative assessment of Cowles' past performance as "substantial," the Commission confirmed Cowles' "renewal expectancy." Even were we to agree (and we do not agree) with the Commission's trivialization of each of Central's advantages, we still would be unable to sustain its action here. The Commission nowhere even vaguely described how it aggregated its findings into the decisive balance; rather, we are told that the conclusion is based on "administrative 'feel.'" Such intuitional forms of decision-making, completely opaque to judicial review, fall somewhere on the distant side of arbitrary.

On remand the Commission again awarded the license to Cowles. In doing so, the Commission explained why renewal expectancy was in the public interest:

> The justification for a renewal expectancy is three-fold. (1) There is no guarantee that a challenger's paper proposals will, in fact, match the incumbent's proven performance. Thus, not only might replacing an incumbent be entirely gratuitous, but *it might even deprive the community of an acceptable service and replace it with an inferior one.* (2) Licensees should be encouraged through the likelihood of renewal to make investments *to ensure quality service. Comparative renewal proceedings cannot function as a "competitive spur" to licensees if their dedication to the community is not rewarded.* (3) Comparing incumbents and challengers as if they were both new applicants could lead to a haphazard restructuring of the broadcast industry especially considering the large number of group owners. *We cannot readily conclude that such a restructuring could serve the public interest.*

Cowles Broadcasting, Inc. (WESH–TV,) 86 F.C.C.2d 993, 49 R.R.2d 1138 (1981).

Central Florida appealed once more. This time the court of appeals affirmed, albeit somewhat reluctantly. Because the Commission had made detailed findings on each of the comparative criteria and only awarded the license to Cowles after weighing all of the factors, the court upheld the award. However, the court noted its concern:

> Finally, we must note that we are still troubled by the fact that the record remains that an incumbent *television* licensee has *never* been denied renewal in a comparative challenge. American television viewers will be reassured, although a trifle baffled, to learn that even the worst television stations—those which are, presumably, the ones picked out as vulnerable to a challenge—are so good that they never need replacing. We suspect that somewhere, sometime, somehow, some television licensee *should* fail in a comparative renewal challenge, but the FCC has never discovered such a licensee yet. As a court we cannot say that it must be Cowles here.

Central Florida Enterprises, Inc. v. Federal Communications Commission, 683 F.2d 503, 51 R.R.2d 1405 (D.C.Cir.1982), certiorari denied 460 U.S. 1084 (1983).

The court in *Central Florida II* had noted with some hope that the Commission had recently taken a radio station license away from the incumbent and awarded it to the challenger. Ironically, less than a year later, when the court was presented with the case, the court did not approve. Simon Geller had operated a one-man classical music FM station in Gloucester, Mass., since the early 1960s. In 1981 Grandebanke Corporation filed a competing application. The Commission held that because less than one percent of the station's programming was of a nonentertainment nature and the station broadcast no news, editorials, or locally produced programming, Geller was not entitled to the benefit of renewal expectancy. Simon Geller, 91 F.C.C.2d 1253, 52 R.R.2d 709 (1982).

On appeal, the FCC's action was vacated and the case remanded. The court began by characterizing it as "yet another meandering effort by the [FCC] to develop a paradigm for its license renewal hearings."

> For years this court has urged the FCC to put some bite into its comparative hearings. [citing *Central Florida I*] Indeed, we have too long hungered for just one instance in which the FCC properly denied an incumbent's renewal expectancy. Unfortunately, in the process of seeking to respond to this court's signals with regard to renewal expectancy, the FCC ignored its own precedents as to the other factors that must be considered in conducting a comparative analysis.

The court of appeals agreed that Geller was entitled to no renewal expectancy because his programming did not even attempt to respond to ascertained community needs and problems. The FCC then properly turned to the comparative criteria. Here, however, the court concluded that the FCC had improperly diminished the value of Geller's obvious advantages of diversification and integration of ownership and management because it tied each to its view of Geller's programming. The FCC thus failed to accord to Geller the importance it had usually attached to diversification and integration in prior cases. The case was remanded for further consideration. Geller v. Federal Communications Commission, 737 F.2d 74, 56 R.R.2d 435 (D.C.Cir.1984). On remand, the Commission granted Geller's application for renewal, Simon Geller, 102 F.C.C.2d 1443, 59 R.R.2d 579 (1985).

The courts and public interest groups were not the only ones to criticize the comparative renewal process. Broadcasters complained that challengers were using the system to extort money from existing broadcasters. In 1988 the Commission issued an NOI/NPRM aimed at reforming the comparative renewal process. Among the proposed changes were limits on the amount of money that challengers could receive in return for withdrawing applications and/or petitions to deny and stricter ownership and financial disclosure requirements. The Commission also proposed to clarify the comparative licensing criteria, questioned the heavy weight given diversification of media as a criterion, and requested comments on both the weight that should be accorded renewal expectancy and the bases for awarding it. Formulation of Policies and Rules Relating to Broadcast Renewal Applicants, Competing Applicants, and Other Participants to the Comparative Renewal Process and to the Prevention of Abuses of the Renewal Process, 3 F.C.C.Rcd. 6019 (1988).

In 1989 the FCC took some initial steps towards curbing abuse of the license renewal process. First, the Commission adopted a prohibition on "all payments to competing applicants (other than the incumbent licensee) for the withdrawal of an application prior to the Initial Decision stage of a comparative hearing. Thereafter, we will approve settlements that do not exceed the withdrawing party's legitimate and prudent expenses for filing and litigating the competing application."

The Commission reasoned that this would weed out weak applications filed for the purpose of extracting settlement payments. The cost of staying in until an initial decision would be too great for a non *bona fide* applicant. Further, an applicant that lost in the initial decision stage would have very little leverage, especially if the initial decision was in the incumbent's favor.

At the same time allowing recovery of legitimate and prudent expenses after the initial decision provides "an efficient way to resolve comparative licensing proceedings, preserve funds for service to the public, and allow us to conserve our limited administrative resources."

The Commission also placed a legitimate and prudent expense limitation on settlements of petitions to deny:

> 41. We believe that a legitimate and prudent expense limitation on settlement payments of petitions to deny strikes the appropriate balance between deterring abuse and not discouraging the filing of such petitions. By prohibiting payments in excess of legitimate and prudent expenses we are removing the profit motive for filing petitions to deny. This should help ensure that petitions are

filed for legitimate public interest purposes. By permitting recovery of legitimate and prudent expenses, we are preserving the petition to deny process as a monitoring and regulatory tool. It is more likely that individuals or public interest groups will perform their function of informing us of licensee deficiencies if they can maintain hope of recovery of the expenses they incur. To preserve the private attorney general function of petitions to deny, we believe we should provide for the possibility that a petitioner can be made economically whole.

The FCC also announced that it would review all future citizens' agreements—contracts in which licensees agree to "implement a nonfinancial reform such as a programming or an employment initiative" in return for the dismissal of a petition to deny. In determining whether an agreement furthers the public interest the Commission:

> . . . will presume that any agreement with a petitioner that calls for the *petitioner*, or any person or organization related to the petitioner, to carry out for a fee, any programming, employment or other "nonfinancial" initiative does not further the public interest and hence will be disapproved. As discussed above, this type of arrangement is particularly susceptible to abuse. In contrast, a licensee's agreement with a petitioner to make changes in operations or programming, either *by itself* or through *disinterested third parties* without further participation by the petitioner, will likely be approved. For example, we will regard an agreement to increase minority employment by using, for a fee, the services of *petitioner* or any person or organization related to petitioner, as presumptively contrary to the public interest, and it will likely be disapproved. In contrast, we will regard an agreement to increase the pool of minority applicants for employment by contracting with a third party, completely independent from petitioner, as consistent with the public interest, and it will likely be approved.

The Commission will allow these presumptions to be rebutted by clear and convincing evidence that they are incorrect as applied to a specific citizens' agreement. Broadcast Renewal Applicants (Abuses of Comparative Renewal Process), 4 F.C.C.Rcd. 4780, 66 R.R.2d 708 (1989).

Various petitions for reconsideration were denied, 5 F.C.C.Rcd. 3902, 67 R.R.2d 1515 (1990). At the same time, the Commission adopted similar rules governing petitions to deny and citizens' agreements for new stations, license modification, and transfer applications. Abuses of the Broadcast Licensing and Allotment Processes, 5 F.C.C.Rcd. 3911, 67 R.R.2d 1526 (1990).

C. TRANSFER OF LICENSES

In part because of the Commission's renewal policies, radio and television licenses acquired substantial value. When a licensee decides to leave broadcasting altogether or to switch services or locations at the end of a license period, the licensee has no opportunity to reap profit. To reap profits, the licensee must seek renewal and, during the term, sell the facilities and goodwill and assign the license to a prospective buyer. In some ways this "transfer" procedure resembles the sale of any business, but the Commission's rules substantially affect the transaction.

Section 310(d) of the Communications Act requires the Commission to pass on all transfers and find that "the public interest, convenience, and necessity will be served thereby." But it also provides that in deciding whether the public interest would be served by the transfer the Commission "may not consider whether the public interest . . . might be served by the transfer . . . to a person other than the proposed transferee or assignee." Why might Congress have imposed this limitation?

When a transferee applies for its first full term, should it be judged as an original applicant who must compete in a comparative hearing without any advantage of incumbency or as a renewal applicant? What are the justifications for each view?

Despite the possible objections to transfer applications, most are granted, usually with little or no delay. This kind of turnover suggests a problem for the Commission. If licenses acquire substantial value a tendency may develop to build up stations and then sell them at a profit. This might be viewed as undermining the "public interest" philosophy of the licensing process. On the other hand, the public may benefit from someone's building up a station, even though that person's motive is to sell it for a profit.

In 1962 the Commission adopted a rule prohibiting licensees from transferring a broadcast license during the first three years after acquisition unless a hardship waiver—usually upon a showing of financial loss—was granted. The rationale for this rule was a belief that it took three years for a licensee to learn the needs and interests of the community and institute programming responsive to those needs and interests. Frequent changes in ownership were viewed as disruptive and thus contrary to the public interest. Applications for Voluntary Assignments or Transfer of Control, 32 F.C.C. 689, 23 R.R. 1503 (1962).

Twenty years later the Commission reversed its position on this issue after concluding that a willing buyer was more likely to serve the public interest than an unwilling owner prohibited from selling the station. Although the three-year rule was abolished, a one-year limitation was instituted for licenses acquired through the comparative hearing process. Applications for Voluntary Assignments or Transfer of Control, 52 R.R.2d 1081 (1982). Subsequently the one-year rule was extended to licenses obtained through the minority ownership policy. We will discuss this policy in Chapter XI.

1. FORMAT CHANGES

Until 1970 the foregoing summary would have covered most of the major problems related to transfers, but then the question of format change arose, plaguing the courts and the Commission for a decade until the Supreme Court decided the issue. The problem arose when a prospective transferee of a radio license proposed to change the station's distinctive programming format.

FEDERAL COMMUNICATIONS COMMISSION
v. WNCN LISTENERS GUILD

Supreme Court of the United States, 1981.
450 U.S. 582, 101 S.Ct. 1266, 49 R.R.2d 271, 67 L.Ed.2d 521, 5 Med.L.Rptr. 1449.

Mr. Justice White delivered the opinion of the Court.

Sections 309(a) and 310(d) of the Communications Act of 1934, 48 Stat. 1064, as amended, 47 U.S.C. § 151 et seq. (Act), empower the Federal Communications Commission to grant an application for license transfer or renewal only if it determines that "the public interest, convenience, and necessity" will be served thereby. The issue before us is whether there are circumstances in which the Commission must review past or anticipated changes in a station's entertainment programming when it rules on an application for renewal or transfer of a radio broadcast license. The Commission's present position is that it may rely on market forces to promote diversity in entertainment programming and thus serve the public interest.

This issue arose when, pursuant to its informal rulemaking authority, the Commission issued a "Policy Statement" concluding that the public interest is best served by promoting diversity in entertainment formats through market forces and competition among broadcasters and that a change in entertainment programming is therefore not a material factor that should be considered by the Commission in ruling on an application for license renewal or transfer. Respondents, a number of citizens groups interested in fostering and preserving particular entertainment formats, petitioned for review in the Court of Appeals for the District of Columbia Circuit. That court held that the Commission's Policy Statement violated the Act. We reverse the decision of the Court of Appeals.

I

Beginning in 1970, in a series of cases involving license transfers, the Court of Appeals for the District of Columbia Circuit gradually developed a set of criteria for determining when the "public-interest" standard requires the Commission to hold a hearing to review proposed changes in entertainment. Noting that the aim of the Act is "to secure the maximum benefits of radio to all the people of the United States," [ ], the Court of Appeals ruled in 1974 that "preservation of a format [that] would otherwise disappear, although economically and technologically viable and preferred by a significant number of listeners, is generally in the public interest." [ ] It concluded that a change in format would not present "substantial and material questions of fact" requiring a hearing if (1) notice of the change had not precipitated "significant public grumbling"; (2) the segment of the population preferring the format was too small to be accommodated by available frequencies; (3) there was an adequate substitute in the service area for the format being abandoned; or (4) the format would be economically unfeasible even if the station were managed efficiently. The court rejected the Commission's position that the choice of entertainment formats should be left to the judgment of the licensee, stating that the Commission's interpretation of the public-interest standard was contrary to the Act.

In January 1976, the Commission responded to these decisions by undertaking an inquiry into its role in reviewing format changes. In particular, the Commission sought public comment on whether the public interest would be better served by Commission scrutiny of entertainment programming or by reliance on the competitive marketplace.

Following public notice and comment, the Commission issued a Policy Statement pursuant to its rulemaking authority under the Act. The Commission concluded in the Policy Statement that review of format changes was not compelled by the language or history of the Act, would not advance the welfare of the radio-listening public, would pose substantial administrative problems, and would deter innovation in radio programming. In support of its position, the Commission quoted from FCC v. Sanders Brothers Radio Station, 309 U.S. 470, 475 (1940): "Congress intended to leave competition in the business of broadcasting where it found it, to permit a licensee . . . to survive or succumb according to his ability to make his programs attractive to the public." The Commission also emphasized that a broadcaster is not a common carrier and therefore should not be subjected to a burden similar to the common carrier's obligation to continue to provide service if abandonment of that service would conflict with public convenience or necessity.

The Commission also concluded that practical considerations as well as statutory interpretation supported its reluctance to regulate changes in formats. Such regulation would require the Commission to categorize the formats of a station's prior and subsequent programming to determine whether a change in format had occurred; to determine whether the prior format was "unique"; and to weigh the public detriment resulting from the abandonment of a unique format against the public benefit resulting from that change. The Commission emphasized the difficulty of objectively evaluating the strength of listener preferences, of comparing the desire for diversity within a particular type of programming to the desire for a broader range of program formats and of assessing the financial feasibility of a unique format.

Finally, the Commission explained why it believed that market forces were the best available means of producing diversity in entertainment formats. First, in large markets, competition among broadcasters had already produced "an almost bewildering array of diversity" in entertainment formats. Second, format allocation by market forces accommodates listeners' desires for diversity within a given format and also produces a variety of formats. Third, the market is far more flexible than governmental regulation and responds more quickly to changing public tastes. Therefore, the Commission concluded that "the market is the allocation mechanism of preference for entertainment formats, and . . . Commission supervision in this area will not be conducive either to producing program diversity [or] satisfied radio listeners."

The Court of Appeals, sitting en banc, held that the Commission's policy was contrary to the Act as construed and applied in the court's prior format decisions. [ ] The court questioned whether the Commission had rationally and impartially re-examined its position and particularly criticized the Commission's failure to disclose a staff study on the effectiveness of market allocation of formats before it issued the Policy Statement. The court then responded to the Commission's criticisms of the format doctrine. First, although conceding that market forces generally lead to diversification of formats, it concluded that the market only imperfectly reflects listener preferences[23] and that the Commission is statutorily obligated to review format changes whenever there is "strong prima facie evidence that the market has in fact broken down." [ ] Second, the court stated that the administrative problems posed by the format doctrine were not insurmountable. Hearings would only be required in a small number of cases, and the Commission could cope with problems such as classifying radio format by adopting "a rational classification schema." [ ] Third, the court observed that the Commission had not demonstrated that the format doctrine would deter innovative programming. Finally, the court explained that it had not directed the Commission to engage in censorship or to impose common carrier obligations on licensees: *WEFM* did not authorize the Commission to interfere with licensee programming choices or to force retention of an existing format; it merely stated that the Commission had the power to consider a station's format in deciding whether license renewal or transfer would be consistent with the public interest. [ ]

Although conceding that it possessed neither the expertise nor the authority to make policy decisions in this area, the Court of Appeals asserted that the format doctrine was "law," not "policy," and was of the view that the Commission had not disproved the factual assumptions underlying the format doctrine. Accordingly, the court declared that the Policy Statement was "unavailing and of no force and effect." [ ]

II

Rejecting the Commission's reliance on market forces to develop diversity in programming as an unreasonable interpretation of the Act's public-interest standard, the Court of Appeals held that in certain circumstances the Commission is required to regard a change in entertainment format as a substantial and material fact in deciding whether a license renewal or transfer is in the public interest. With all due respect, however, we are unconvinced that the Court of Appeal's format doctrine

---

23. The court observed . . . that because broadcasters rely on advertising revenue they tend to serve persons with large discretionary incomes. [ ] The dissenting opinion noted that the Commission had not rejected this assumption. [ ]

is compelled by the Act and that the Commission's interpretation of the public-interest standard must therefore be set aside.

It is common ground that the Act does not define the term "public interest, convenience, and necessity." The Court has characterized the public-interest standard of the Act as "a supple instrument for the exercise of discretion by the expert body which Congress has charged to carry out its legislative policy." [   ] Although it was declared in National Broadcasting Co. v. United States, supra, that the goal of the Act is "to secure the maximum benefits of radio to all the people of the United States," [   ], it was also emphasized that Congress had granted the Commission broad discretion in determining how that goal could best be achieved. The Court accordingly declined to substitute its own views on the best method of encouraging effective use of the radio for the views of the Commission. [   ] Similarly, in FCC v. National Citizens Committee for Broadcasting, 436 U.S. 775 (1978), we deemed the policy of promoting the widest possible dissemination of information from diverse sources to be consistent with both the public-interest standard and the First Amendment, [   ], but emphasized the Commission's broad power to regulate in the public interest. We noted that the Act permits the Commission to promulgate "such rules and regulations, . . . not inconsistent with law, as may be necessary to carry out the provisions of [the Act]," and that this general rule-making authority permits the Commission to implement its view of the public-interest standard of the Act "so long as that view is based on consideration of permissible factors and is otherwise reasonable." [   ] Furthermore, we recognized that the Commission's decisions must sometimes rest on judgment and prediction rather than pure factual determinations. In such cases complete factual support for the Commission's ultimate conclusions is not required since " 'a forecast of the direction in which future public interest lies necessarily involves deductions based on the expert knowledge of the agency.' "

The Commission has provided a rational explanation for its conclusion that reliance on the market is the best method of promoting diversity in entertainment formats. . . . The Court of Appeals places great value on preserving diversity among formats, while the Commission emphasizes the value of intraformat as well as interformat diversity. Finally, the Court of Appeals is convinced that review of format changes would result in a broader range of formats, while the Commission believes that government intervention is likely to deter innovative programming.

        . . .

Our opinions have repeatedly emphasized that the Commission's judgment regarding how the public interest is best served is entitled to substantial judicial deference. [   ] Furthermore, diversity is not the only policy the Commission must consider in fulfilling its responsibilities under the Act. The Commission's implementation of the public-interest standard, when based on a rational weighing of competing policies, is not to be set aside by the Court of Appeals, for "the weighing of policies under the 'public interest' standard is a task that Congress has delegated to the Commission in the first instance." [   ] The Commission's position on review of format changes reflects a reasonable accommodation of the policy of promoting diversity in programming and the policy of avoiding unnecessary restrictions on licensee discretion. As we see it, the Commission's Policy Statement is in harmony with cases recognizing that the Act seeks to preserve journalistic discretion while promoting the interests of the listening public.

. . .

III

. . .

A major underpinning of its Policy Statement is the Commission's conviction, rooted in its experience, that renewal and transfer cases should not turn on the Commission's presuming to grasp, measure, and weigh the elusive and difficult factors involved in determining the acceptability of changes in entertainment format. To assess whether the elimination of a particular "unique" entertainment format would serve the public interest, the Commission would have to consider the benefit as well as the detriment that would result from the change. Necessarily, the Commission would take into consideration not only the number of listeners who favor the old and the new programming but also the intensity of their preferences. It would also consider the effect of the format change on diversity within formats as well as on diversity among formats. The Commission is convinced that its judgments in these respects would be subjective in large measure and would only approximately serve the public interest. It is also convinced that the market, although imperfect, would serve the public interest as well or better by responding quickly to changing preferences and by inviting experimentation with new types of programming. Those who would overturn the Commission's Policy Statement do not take adequate account of these considerations.

. . .

IV

Respondents contend that the Court of Appeals' judgment should be affirmed because, even if not violative of the Act, the Policy Statement conflicts with the First Amendment rights of listeners "to receive suitable access to social, political, esthetic, moral, and other ideas and experiences." [*Red Lion*, p. 78, *supra*]. *Red Lion* held that the Commission's "fairness doctrine" was consistent with the public-interest standard of the Communications Act and did not violate the First Amendment, but rather enhanced First Amendment values by promoting "the presentation of vigorous debate of controversial issues of importance and concern to the public." [   ] Although observing that the interests of the people as a whole were promoted by debate of public issues on the radio, we did not imply that the First Amendment grants individual listeners the right to have the Commission review the abandonment of their favorite entertainment programs. The Commission seeks to further the interests of the listening public as a whole by relying on market forces to promote diversity in radio entertainment formats and to satisfy the entertainment preferences of radio listeners. This policy does not conflict with the First Amendment.

Contrary to the judgment of the Court of Appeals, the Commission's Policy Statement is not inconsistent with the Act. It is also a constitutionally permissible means of implementing the public-interest standard of the Act. Accordingly, the judgment of the Court of Appeals is reversed, and the case is remanded for further proceedings consistent with this opinion.

So ordered.

[Justice Marshall joined by Justice Brennan dissented, arguing that the Commission's failure to include a waiver provision in the Policy Statement made it too inflexible:

> The Policy Statement completely forecloses any possibility that the Commission will reexamine the validity of its general policy on format changes as it applies to particular situations. Thus, even when it can be conclusively demonstrated that a particular radio market does not function in the manner predicted by the Commission, the Policy Statement indicates that the Commission will blindly assume that a proposed format change is in the "public interest." This result would occur even where reliance on the market to ensure format diversity is shown to be misplaced, and where it thus appears that action by the Commission is necessary to promote the public interest in diversity. This outcome is not consistent with the Commission's statutory responsibilities.

Justice Marshall argued that although the court of appeals might have gone too far in providing specific guidelines for handling unique formats, it was well within its authority when it held that the lack of any "safety valve" in the Policy Statement was a violation of the Commission's public interest obligations.]

Notes and Questions

1. *WNCN Listeners Guild,* like many of the cases involving the Commission, revolves around the problem of defining "public interest, convenience and necessity." Is a clear definition possible? If not, how much deference should the Commission be given in applying the standard?

2. In his dissent, Justice Marshall argued that it was not impossible for the Commission to define formats. He noted two suggestions by the court of appeals for dealing with this issue. One was to develop "a format taxonomy which, even if imprecise at the margins, would be sustainable so long as not irrational." Alternatively, the Commission could avoid defining formats altogether "by simply taking the existence

of significant and bona fide listener protest as sufficient evidence that the station's endangered programming has certain unique features for which there are no ready substitutes."

Are these two suggestions in any way contradictory? The first emphasizes treating the format as a whole, and the latter focuses on individual features within a format. What are the pros and cons of each approach?

3. The Policy Statement at issue in *WNCN Listeners Guild* dealt only with renewals and transfers. Assuming that the Commission should review at least some format changes, is it practical to do so only with regard to applications for transfer or renewal? Under these restrictions review of a format change might not be possible until years after the change takes place.

4. In 1985 a citizen group again tried to get the Commission to hold a hearing on a transfer involving a format change. The group alleged that because the station in question was simulcasting programming on its AM and FM stations 25 percent of the time and running similar formats the rest of the time, it was clear that competition in the marketplace was not producing diversity and therefore the Policy Statement should not apply. The Commission refused to hold a hearing, reaffirming its position of non-intervention in format controversies. WEAM Radio, Inc., 58 R.R.2d 141 (1985).

The court of appeals affirmed the Commission's decision not to hold a hearing. Citing *WNCN Listeners Guild,* the court held that the Commission can rely on the Policy Statement unless presented with persuasive evidence that the rationale of the Policy Statement is not applicable to the market in which the station in question is located. Committee to Save WEAM v. Federal Communications Commission, 808 F.2d 113, 61 R.R.2d 1444 (D.C.Cir.1986).

5. However, in another format case, a Commission decision to dismiss a petition to deny and grant renewal without a hearing was reversed by the court of appeals. The petition to deny was filed by Citizens for Jazz on WRVR, Inc. The court felt that there was sufficient evidence that the licensee, Viacom, Inc., misrepresented its programming intentions in its transfer application. Citizens for Jazz on WRVR, Inc. v. Federal Communications Commission, 775 F.2d 392, 59 R.R.2d 249 (D.C.Cir.1985).

2. The RKO Case

Perhaps the most complex and longest-running licensing controversy involved the stations owned by RKO General, Inc. Although most of the controversy was tied to renewal applications for the various stations, transfer applications were also involved. Overall, this long-running soap opera highlighted many issues raised by the licensing process.

The first RKO license to be challenged was that of KHJ, Channel 9, Los Angeles, in 1966. The examiner recommended denial of renewal and granting of the license to the challenger, Fidelity Television, Inc. He criticized KHJ's past programming, particularly its concentration on old films and its ignoring of community criticism of excessive violence in the movies. The Commission reversed the examiner and granted the renewal. In comparing the various factors, the Commission concluded that RKO's programming and community relations, though not "unusually good" or "superior," were also not "insubstantial" or "unusually poor." Thus, the "record must be deemed to be within the bounds of average performance expected of all licensees" and warranted neither a merit nor a demerit. After reviewing all the factors the Commission concluded that the two applicants were essentially equal and that the outcome rested on a decision that "credit must be given in a comparative renewal proceeding, when the applicants are otherwise equal, for the value to the public in the continuation of the existing service."

The challenger's appeal was rejected, Fidelity Television, Inc. v. Federal Communications Commission, 515 F.2d 684, 32 R.R.2d 1607, rehearing denied 1975 WL 3583, 34 R.R.2d 419 (D.C.Cir.), certiorari denied 423 U.S. 926 (1975). The court stressed that this was not a situation in which a "superior applicant is denied a license because to give it to him would work a 'forfeiture' of his opponent's investment." Rather, the incumbent's performance, was enough to "withstand the competition of a 'nothing' competitor."

While this case was progressing through the Commission and court of appeals, two other RKO General stations were challenged when they applied for license renewal. In 1969 two challengers, Community Broadcasting of Boston, Inc., and The Dudley Station Corp., filed applications for the license of WNAC–TV, Channel 7, Boston, and in 1974 Multi–State Communications, Inc. filed an application for the license of WOR–TV, Channel 9, New York City.

Among the issues that were raised in the WNAC–TV proceeding were allegations that RKO and its parent company, General Tire and Rubber Co., had engaged in anticompetitive practices and that RKO had violated the sponsorship identification requirements of § 317 during its broadcasts of the "Della Reese Show." (We will discuss sponsorship identification in Chapter VI.) In 1974 the ALJ awarded the license to RKO after concluding that RKO had not knowingly engaged in anticompetitive practices and that the violations that occurred with respect to the "Della Reese Show" were cause for a comparative demerit as opposed to disqualification.

In early 1975 the Securities and Exchange Commission started investigating General Tire with respect to illegal bribes of foreign public officials and illegal foreign bank accounts. Then, in late 1975, before the full FCC had heard oral argument on WNAC–TV's license renewal, Community filed a petition to reopen the record and enlarge the issues. The petition, accompanied by 640 pages of exhibits, alleged that General Tire had engaged in illegal and unethical conduct in both the United States and foreign countries and that RKO had violated the FCC's rules and "exhibited a lack of candor" by failing to disclose ongoing investigations into General Tire's conduct.

Meanwhile, the ongoing SEC investigation uncovered several examples of misconduct by General Tire. Finally, an SEC complaint was in early 1976, covering among others, all the misconduct detailed in the 1975 Community petition. On the same day, General Tire entered into a consent decree that prohibited "the concealment of any of the misconduct alleged in the SEC complaint including, inter alia, unlawful political contributions, unlawful payments to foreign government officials and the overbilling of affiliates and subsidiaries." The decree also set up a Special Review Committee to further investigate General Tire's conduct and file a report with the SEC and the court. Four days later, RKO advised the FCC of the SEC inquiry and the consent decree for the first time.

The next year, the Commission decided that any action should be delayed until the submission of the Review Committee's report. While the parties awaited the filing of the report, further issues surfaced. During the years 1972–1976, RKO had knowingly failed to properly complete the barter and trade portion of the financial report (form 324) that was required at that time.

When the Special Review Committee's report was finally filed in 1977, it confirmed most of Community's allegations. Among the Review Committee's findings were the following: "(a) General Tire and certain of its subsidiaries engaged in various schemes and practices that resulted in improper domestic political contributions; (b) Aerojet, an RKO subsidiary, gave gratuities to military and other government-connected personnel having dealings with Aerojet; (c) General Tire and its affiliates maintained and used improper secret and unrecorded funds designed to avoid foreign currency exchange and tax laws; (d) General Tire and its affiliates paid bribes to foreign agents and officials not only to do business in a country but also to keep competitors out; (e) through the use of secret bank accounts, General Tire systematically overbilled its foreign affiliates; and (f) RKO did not maintain adequate records concerning the amount or use of consideration resulting from its barter and trade transactions."

The next year, before the FCC had taken further action on the renewal application, Community and Dudley filed another petition seeking approval of the transfer of WNAC–TV's license to New England Television Corporation-formed by the merger of Community and Dudley-for $54 million. The sale was contingent on the FCC's granting RKO's renewal application. The petition was opposed by Fidelity Television, Inc. and Multi–State Communications, Inc., challengers for RKO's Los Angeles and New York television licenses respectively. Those proceedings had by this time been conditioned on the outcome of the Boston proceeding.

In 1980 the Commission denied the RKO application for renewal of the WNAC–TV license:

> In general the evidence is clear and convincing that RKO has engaged in a variety of misconduct which renders it unfit to be a

Commission licensee for Channel 7 in Boston. RKO has engaged in an improper reciprocal trades program that was anticompetitive, it has knowingly filed false financial statements with this Commission, and it has not been entirely honest and forthcoming in its dealings with the Commission in these proceedings. our concern here is heightened by the misconduct engaged in by RKO's parent, General Tire. General Tire not only controls RKO as a legal matter; the record also demonstrates that General Tire has exercised practical control over RKO operations in certain respects and has involved the broadcast operations in serious misconduct. It is that close legal and practical relationship that further taints RKO's qualifications. This record thus compels the conclusion that we cannot trust RKO to operate Channel 7 in the future in a manner consistent with the public interest.

The Commission also denied RKO's renewal applications for the Los Angeles and New York stations reasoning that RKO was equally unfit to hold those licenses. However, the Commission delayed any final action on the one other TV license and 12 radio licenses held by RKO.

Commissioners Lee and Quello filed separate dissents, each arguing that the punishment-potentially the loss of all 16 licenses-was gross overkill. Commissioner Lee entitled his dissent "Capital Punishment." Commissioner Washburn dissented separately on the grounds that there was insufficient connection between General Tire's conduct and the ability of RKO to operate its stations in the public interest to justify the penalty.

The court of appeals rejected all but one of the FCC's justifications for the license revocation. RKO v. Federal Communications Commission, 670 F.2d 215, 50 R.R.2d 821 (D.C.Cir.1981), certiorari denied, 457 U.S. 1119 (1982). The reciprocal trade practices had occurred 15 years earlier. First, those practices were viewed less critically at that time. Second, the court held that conduct that ceased 15 years earlier had minimal predictive value regarding the future conduct of the licensee.

With regard to the question of financial misrepresentations, the court found that there was insufficient evidence that the misrepresentations were "intentional and knowing." Finally, the FCC's use of General Tire's nonbroadcast misconduct was a departure from its policy of not giving significant weight to such misconduct by corporate entities.

Nevertheless, the court upheld the disqualification of RKO in the Boston proceeding on the basis of lack of candor:

> The Commission found that three instances demonstrated RKO's lack of candor before the agency during a period from 1975 to 1977. First, RKO failed to inform the FCC that there was a factual basis to the allegations first made against General Tire by Community in late 1975. [   ] Second, RKO failed to report the initiation of a formal SEC investigation of General Tire in February 1976. [   ] Finally, RKO failed to concede that it had inaccurately reported trade and barter revenues when pressed to do so by Community in

April 1977, despite the indication in General Tire's 1976 Annual Report that there might be some problems with these accounts. [   ]

A. *The Merits of the FCC's Finding*

The record fully supports the Commission's finding that RKO did not display full candor before the Commission during the period from late 1975 to July 1976. Uncontroverted documentary evidence shows that General Tire responded to the initial phase of the SEC's inquiry regarding overseas operations in May 1975. [   ] As the SEC investigation progressed, RKO's competitors began pressing the FCC to reopen the Boston proceeding, alleging facts that were similar or identical to the admissions later made by General Tire in the consent decree and its Special Report. RKO's first response was to seek an extension of time in which to respond, citing the need to consult with "persons who may have knowledge of the pertinent facts." [   ] More than a month later, in January 1976, RKO clearly decided to stonewall the opposition and the FCC. This seems the only explanation for RKO's decision to file a document opposing the suggestion that the Boston proceeding be reopened on the ground that "there is no factual or legal foundation for this pyramid of charges," that "the charges, as we show below, are groundless," and that other charges were "essentially unsupported."

. . .

Section 1.65 of the Commission's Rules requires applicants to inform the Commission within thirty days whenever "there has been a substantial change" regarding any matter that may be "of decisional significance in a Commission proceeding involving the pending application." 47 C.F.R. S 1.65 (1979). This requires that an applicant inform the Commission "of all facts, whether requested in [renewal] Form 303 or not, that may be of decisional significance so that the Commission can make a realistic decision based on *all* relevant factors." [   ] Unlike a private party haled into court, or a corporation such as General Tire facing an investigation by the SEC, RKO had an affirmative obligation to inform the Commission of the facts the FCC needed in order to license broadcasters in the public interest. As a licensing authority, the Commission is not expected to "play procedural games with those who come before it in order to ascertain the truth," [   ], and license applicants may not indulge in common-law pleading strategies of their own devise.

The court also rejected various defenses asserted by RKO. The lack of evidence that the Commission was in fact misled by RKO's failure to disclose was found irrelevant since it was the attempt to mislead that indicated a lack of fitness to hold the license. A claim that RKO's actions were on advice of counsel was dismissed since it was long settled that "advice of counsel cannot excuse a clear breach of duty by a licensee." Finally, the court turned to the issue of whether RKO was denied a hearing on the "lack of candor" issue. Given that the lack of candor was clearly proven by documents submitted by RKO in the renewal hearing itself, the court concluded that no purpose would be served by holding a separate hearing on that issue.

The court declined to extend its holding in the Boston proceeding to the other RKO licenses:

> RKO's lack of candor during the Boston proceeding justifies its disqualification there because the misconduct took place directly before the trier of fact and has bearing on its general character, but the same cannot be said of the Los Angeles and New York City proceedings. . . . The FCC could not have known, when it conditioned either of these proceedings as it did, that the Boston outcome would turn on a lack of candor issue that had not even been designated in the Boston proceeding. RKO's misconduct did not occur directly before the trier of fact in either the Los Angeles or New York City proceedings. Accordingly, these decisions must be remanded to the Commission for further consideration as it deems appropriate.

While the New York proceeding was pending, Congress amended the Communications Act (adding § 331) to require that the Commission renew the license of any VHF commercial licensee willing to relocate to a state with no VHF commercial television stations. After RKO notified the FCC in September, 1982, that it would move WOR–TV from New York City to Secaucus, N.J., its license was renewed. RKO General, Inc. (WOR–TV), 53 R.R.2d 469 (1983). In addition, RKO was granted a temporary waiver of the main studio rule, which permitted the use of the station's existing New York studio facilities while the Commission's renewal order was on appeal. Otherwise, RKO would have been required to expend large sums of money on studio construction in New Jersey during a period when the station's relocation was uncertain. RKO General, Inc., 54 R.R.2d 853 (1983). The grant of the five-year license to RKO without a hearing, pursuant to § 331, was unanimously affirmed in Multi–State Communications, Inc. v. Federal Communications Commission, 728 F.2d 1519, 55 R.R.2d 911 (D.C.Cir.1984), certiorari denied 469 U.S. 1017 (1984).

In addition to WOR and KHJ, RKO owned one other TV station and 12 radio stations. In 1983, acting under an order from the court of appeals, the Commission started accepting competing applications for the other 13 RKO stations. More than 160 applications were filed. Initially, no action on these applications was to be taken until the character issue in the KHJ case was decided. In 1985, however, the Commission decided to start comparative proceedings among the applicants.

In 1985 Westinghouse Broadcast and Cable (Group W) agreed to purchase KHJ–TV from RKO for $313 million. Technically, the proposal called for RKO to dismiss its application for renewal and sell KHJ's physical assets to Group W for $215 million. As a result of RKO's withdrawal of its application, Fidelity would be awarded the license.

Fidelity would then sell its stock to Group W for $95 million. Group W would also pay Fidelity's current liabilities, approximately $3.25 million.

When the deal had not been approved after more than a year, Westinghouse withdrew. The withdrawal caused a major uproar because, as an outgrowth of the proposed deal, the Commission had suggested a way to settle the proceedings involving the other RKO properties. The Commission requested that for each property interested parties enter into purchase negotiations with all the applicants. The hope was that all properties could be disposed of in this fashion, providing a quick end to all litigation while removing RKO from the broadcasting business. The various proceedings were suspended to allow for these negotiations.

After several months agreements appeared likely for only a minority of the properties. The suspensions in the various proceedings were therefore ended. Meanwhile, Disney Co. negotiated a deal for KHJ similar to the earlier Westinghouse proposal.

The ALJ then found RKO unfit to hold a license and stripped it of all its remaining licenses. The finding was based on RKO's conduct with regard to the barter and trade agreements between 1971–1975, especially its destruction of a 1974 internal audit and subsequent efforts to conceal that destruction and the circumstances surrounding it. The ALJ also found RKO Networks guilty of fraudulent practices that altered audience ratings reports and fraudulent billing:

> 512. If RKO had been able to establish that its dishonesty would not recur, its claims of equity, based on its programming and broadcast history, would take on meaning. But the Commission is obligated by the Communications Act to license only those persons or entities that are of good character. No case ever before decided by this Commission presents dishonesty comparable to RKO's. There is not a single case of fraudulent billing practices investigated and reviewed by this Commission which exhibits as many practices affecting as many advertisers over as many years. During the time consumed by this proceeding, RKO repeatedly misrepresented the truth and engaged in dishonest broadcasting activities. These findings lead to the conclusion that RKO cannot be trusted to act as a fiduciary of the public interest; RKO General, Inc. is unqualified to continue as a broadcast licensee.

RKO General, Inc. (KHJ–TV), 2 F.C.C.Rcd. 4807, 63 R.R.2d 866 (A.L.J. 1987).

In 1988 the Commission voted 2–1 to allow RKO to transfer its Los Angeles TV station and Memphis radio station. The settlement agreement called for Disney to pay $218,625,000 to RKO and $105,375,000 to Fidelity Television. The Commission declined to decide the issue of RKO's qualifications as a licensee. Instead, likening the transfers to its minority distress sale policy (to be discussed in Chapter XI), the Commission argued that approval would "further the public interest by helping to bring service to the public expeditiously by an unquestionably qualified licensee and will also preserve the Commission's objective of deterring licensee misconduct." The deterrence would come from limiting RKO's compensation to 75 percent of fair market value. The Commission also asserted that the public interest would be served by avoiding countless years of further regulation.

Commissioner Dennis dissented. Noting that the ALJ had found that "RKO had engaged in a pervasive, continuous pattern of deceit-even after the Boston license was revoked," she argued that a Commission determination as to RKO's qualifications was absolutely necessary. If RKO was unfit, it should lose its licenses without compensation. If it was fit, then it should be free to either keep its stations or sell them at fair market value. Dennis expressed concern that the decision "sends the wrong signal to station licensees-that the way to avoid license revocation is to prolong a proceeding until the Commission loses its will to litigate further." RKO General, Inc. (KHJ–TV), 3 F.C.C.Rcd. 5057, 65 R.R.2d 192 (1988).

The Commission subsequently approved similar settlement agreements for the other RKO stations. A settlement agreement for the last of the RKO stations was approved in early 1991. The terms were similar to the other RKO settlement agreements with RKO receiving significantly less than 75 percent of the station's fair market value. RKO General, Inc. (KFRC), 6 F.C.C.Rcd. 1816, 68 R.R.2d 1341 (1991).

In *Character Qualifications in Broadcast Licensing*, p. 110 *supra,* the commission adopted a rule prohibiting applicants and licensees from making any written "misrepresentation or willful material omission[s] bearing on any matter within the jurisdiction of the Commission." 47 C.F.R. § 73.1015. In *Character Qualifications Policy*, p. 110, *supra,* the FCC amended Part I of its rules in order to emphasize that this requirement applies to all FCC applicants, licensees and permittees, not just those involved in broadcasting. 47 C.F.R. § 1.17.

3. HOSTILE TAKEOVERS OF CORPORATIONS

Up until now we have been looking at cases where the incumbent licensee wishes to transfer the license. In the mid-'80s, the Commission found itself faced with a different sort of problem: hostile takeovers of corporations with broadcast properties. The leading example was Ted Turner's unsuccessful attempt in 1985 to take over CBS. How should the Commission treat cases like this?

What if existing shareholders wish to replace a corporation's board of directors? Does this constitute a transfer of control and, if so, is it the same as an attempt by outsiders to take over a corporation? The Commission faced this issue for the first time in Committee for Full Value of Storer Communications, Inc., 57 R.R.2d 1651 (1985). The Committee for Full Value of Storer Communications, Inc. was a group of dissident Storer stockholders who wished to sell all the assets of Storer and distribute the proceeds to the stockholders. Because the incumbent board of directors opposed this plan, the dissidents announced that they would stage a proxy contest to elect a board of directors that would implement their plan. The scheme raised several important questions for the Commission.

Under § 309(b) of the Communications Act, applications for a transfer of control of a broadcast licensee are subject to a public notice requirement and a 30–day waiting period. The purpose of these requirements is to give members of the public who feel that the proposed transfer is not in the public interest an opportunity to file a petition to deny. However, § 309(c) contains an exception to these requirements for cases where the transfer of control is not substantial. Thus, the Commission had to determine whether election of a new board of directors, absent any significant change in stock ownership, constitutes a transfer of control, and if so is it a substantial transfer of control.

The Mass Media Bureau concluded that ownership of the corporation resides in the stockholders, and thus there is no transfer of control, substantial or otherwise. The Commission disagreed, holding that electing a new board of directors is a transfer of control, but because the ultimate control of any corporation rests with the stockholders, the transfer of control is not a substantial one. The practical effect of this decision was that the Committee did have to file an application for transfer of control, but the application was not subject to the public notice and 30–day waiting period requirements.

The Commission's decision was affirmed on appeal. The court of appeals reasoned that the Commission had not abused its discretion in resolving a case with competing policy considerations. Although a change in directors might indeed result in a major change in the working control of the corporation, determining what constitutes a "substantial" change was a complex task best resolved by the Commission. Also, there was the danger that requiring public notice and a 30–day waiting period in any such proxy fight would allow incumbent boards of directors to use the Commission to insulate them from challenges since the added delay and cost that would occur might well discourage such challenges. Storer Communications, Inc. v. Federal Communications Commission, 763 F.2d 436, 58 R.R.2d 244 (D.C.Cir.1985).

Despite the favorable ruling, the Committee for Full Value of Storer Communications, Inc. was unable to elect a majority of the board of directors.

In 1986 the Commission affirmed its previous policies on proxy contests and tender offers. In most proxy contests, a short form application with certain additional information concerning the basic qualifications of the candidates for board of directors will be sufficient. In the case of hostile takeover attempts, a long form application will be required. Pending review of the long form application, a special temporary authorization (STA) will be issued to a trustee approved by the Commission. Tender Offers and Proxy Contests, 59 R.R.2d 1536 (1986).

The court of appeals rejected an appeal by the Office of Communication of the United Church of Christ, Action for Children's Television and the National Organization for Women, holding that the Commission's Policy Statement was not ripe for review. According to the court, there were too many ambiguities and unanswered questions in the Policy Statement. The court thought it was necessary to await the application of the Statement to a specific case. Office of Communication of United Church of Christ v. Federal Communications Commission, 826 F.2d 101, 63 R.R.2d 1065 (D.C.Cir.1987).

What if a licensee goes bankrupt? How will the station license be treated? Liens on station licenses are prohibited. However, a federal district court and a federal bankruptcy court have each concluded that the prohibition does not extend to liens on the proceeds of sales of broadcast stations. A bare lien on the proceeds does not interfere with the FCC's regulation of broadcast licensees. State Street Bank and Trust Co. v. Arrow Communications, Inc., 833 F.Supp. 41, 74 R.R.2d 166 (D.Mass.1993); In re Thomas Communications, Inc., 161 B.R. 621, 74 R.R.2d 1066 (Bkrtcy.S.D.W.Va.1993).

One difficult question for the Commission is determining when a *de facto,* as opposed to *de jure,* transfer of control has occurred. In CBS Management Changes (Transfer of Control Allegations), 2 F.C.C.Rcd. 2274, 62 R.R.2d 852 (1987), Fairness in Media alleged that there was an unauthorized *de facto* transfer of control to Loews Corp. and its chairman, Laurence A. Tisch. Loews had purchased almost 25 percent of CBS common stock and subsequently Tisch was appointed chief executive officer of CBS. Despite statements by Robert Preston Tisch, President of Loews, various CBS directors and others that Laurence Tisch intended to take control of CBS, the Commission determined that a *de facto* transfer of control had not taken place. The Commission noted that there was no evidence that Laurence Tisch had sufficient influence on the shareholders unassociated with Loews to constitute a *de facto* transfer of control. Also, some of Tisch's proposals to change CBS had been rejected by the board of directors, indicating that he did not control the board.

D. THE DEVELOPMENT OF THE CURRENT SYSTEM

After controlling comparative licensing proceedings for more than 25 years the *1965 Policy Statement* was called into question. The process began in Bechtel v. Federal Communications Commission, 957 F.2d 873, 70 R.R.2d 397 (D.C.Cir.1992), in which three parties were seeking a license. Bechtel was eliminated on the ground that the other two were proposing integration of ownership and management whereas Bechtel was proposing to hire a full-time manager. This overcame whatever advantages Bechtel might have had over the others.

On Bechtel's appeal from the grant to one of the other parties, the court vacated and remanded on the ground that the FCC had never come to grips with Bechtel's challenge to the significance being given to the integration factor. The Commission had simply followed its past practices without explanation. In passing, the court noted that Bechtel had challenged the other parties and the Commission to show a single case in the last 10 years "in which a licensee prevailed in a comparative hearing based upon its integration proposal and then actually constructed and operated the station in conformity with that proposal for a period substantially exceeding one year." According to the court, no example was produced.

In addition, the court cited one episode alleged by Bechtel in which an integrated applicant won a license and then within five months had contracted to sell it for $4 million to a group broadcaster.

On remand, the Commission concluded that the integration criterion was still valid. Bechtel had asserted that two rule changes adopted by the Commission since the integration criterion was first applied to comparative licensing proceedings had undermined its validity. The first of these two was the Commission's decision to exclude passive investors (e.g., limited partners and non-voting stockholders) from the calculation of the integration credit. Anax Broadcasting, Inc., 87 F.C.C.2d 483, 49 R.R.2d 1589 (1981). The second was the reduction of the required holding period for licenses obtained in a comparative proceeding from three years to one year. Transfer of Broadcast Facilities, 52 R.R.2d 1081 (1982). Bechtel alleged that the combination of these two rule changes had encouraged passive investors to seek out people who would propose to run a station fulltime, thus qualifying for 100 percent integration credit, and then, only one year after building the station, to sell it to a nonintegrated entity.

The FCC rejected this argument, claiming that it rigorously examined license proposals and denied integration credit to those it found unreliable or in bad faith. Furthermore, the Commission concluded that even the one-year holding period was a sufficient deterrent to the type of speculation Bechtel had argued was being encouraged. With regard to the challenge, *supra,* to cite successful examples of the application of the integration criterion, the Commission simply noted that Bechtel, not the Commission, had the burden of proof. Thus, the Commission concluded that it did not have to cite any examples. Anchor Broadcasting Limited Partnership, 7 F.C.C.Rcd. 4566, 70 R.R.2d 1569 (1992).

On reconsideration, the Commission ultimately adhered to its earlier approach and vigorously defended the integration criterion. Anchor Broadcasting Limited Partnership, 8 F.C.C.Rcd. 1674, 72 R.R.2d 98 (1993).

BECHTEL v. FEDERAL COMMUNICATIONS COMMISSION

United States Court of Appeals, District of Columbia Circuit, 1993.
10 F.3d 875, 22 Med.L.Rptr. 1097, 74 R.R.2d 348.

Before WILLIAMS, SENTELLE, and HENDERSON, CIRCUIT JUDGES.

WILLIAMS, CIRCUIT JUDGE:

In choosing among mutually exclusive applicants seeking to build and operate a new broadcasting station, the Federal Communications

Commission prefers applicants who promise that the station's owners will participate in its management. An applicant who lost because of this policy now attacks it as arbitrary and capricious.

The Commission's preference for the "integration" of ownership and management originated more than 45 years ago in a rather mild form. "Other significant factors being equal," declared one decision, "the Commission is inclined to prefer an applicant who intends to manage and operate the proposed station personally rather than to entrust its operations to employees." . . . The Commission recognized that integration was not necessarily the most reliable indicator of these things, and it put little weight on integration when it had other reasons to believe that an applicant would be responsible and responsive. [   ]

The powerful integration preference that now prevails dates back to a policy statement issued in 1965. See [*1965 Policy Statement*, p. 114, *supra*]. . . . Three decades later, this case squarely calls into question the validity of continued use of the integration preference.

. . .

II. THE STATUS OF POLICY STATEMENTS

Policy statements are exempt from the Administrative Procedure Act's notice-and-comment requirements, see 5 U.S.C. § 553(b), and hence may take effect without the rigors—and presumed advantages—of that process. The price to the agency is that the policy "is subject to complete attack before it is finally applied in future cases." [   ] Sooner or later the agency must meet its obligation to respond to criticisms. [   ]

This does not mean that policy statements have no effect. Although the agency must respond to challenges and be ready to consider "the underlying validity of the policy itself," [   ], it need not repeat itself incessantly. When a party attacks a policy on grounds that the agency already has dispatched in prior proceedings, the agency can simply refer to those proceedings if their reasoning remains applicable and adequately refutes the challenge. But the agency must always stand ready "to hear new argument" and "to reexamine the basic propositions" undergirding the policy. [   ]

III. THE COMMISSION'S DEFENSE
OF ITS INTEGRATION POLICY

. . . [T]he Commission attributes three basic advantages to integration, which can be described under the headings "incentives," "interest," and "information." First, owner-managers—because of their direct financial and legal stake in the station's performance—have better *incentives* than mere employee-managers, and hence stations run by integrated owners are more likely to respond to community needs and to comply with Commission rules. Second, integrated owners are more likely than absentee owners to have an active *interest* in the operation of their stations, and an interested owner tends to improve performance. Third, on-site owners are better positioned than absentee owners to gather relevant *information* about whether the station is fully satisfying community needs and complying with Commission rules. [ ] Finally, recognizing that the integration credit is by no means a perfect predictor of whether a licensee will serve "the public interest, convenience, and necessity" (the statutory standard for assessing applications), [ ], the Commission also urges that the integration preference has the advantage of objectivity.

A.   Some Common Problems

We will address the arguments one by one, but first we raise some points that apply equally to *all* the three claimed substantive advantages.

1.   Lack of Performance

Whatever the benefits of integration, they would last only if the Commission insisted on licensees maintaining the owner-manager relation or if successful licensees tended to adopt the integrated structure of their own free will. Neither appears to be the case.

Perhaps in recognition of integration's artificiality, the Commission has done little to ensure its continuation once the promise of integration has carried an applicant to victory. On the first anniversary of the commencement of program tests, people who have won their station in a comparative hearing must report any deviations from their integration proposals. [ ] But as long as they do not misrepresent their intentions in their applications, abandonment of those proposals apparently carries no consequences. [ ] After the first anniversary, moreover, no reports are required. Similarly, while successful applicants in comparative hearings generally cannot transfer or assign their stations during the first year of operations, [ ], thereafter a licensee who had won his station through his integration proposal could "turn around and sell it . . . without regard to the buyer's 'integration' or lack thereof." *Bechtel I*, 957 F.2d at 880.[2]

The Commission, while admitting that it has never actually addressed the issue, suggests that "an applicant proposing integration and having, at the time of the proposal, a present intention to sell the station after one year would not be entitled to integration credit." [ ] But denying integration credit to people who manifest a present intention to sell out quickly—or revoking the licenses of the handful who could after the fact be proved to have misrepresented their intentions—is not the same thing as guaranteeing permanent integration. Indeed, Bechtel has repeatedly challenged the Commission to identify a *single* instance in which an applicant who won his station on the basis of his integration proposal continued to operate the station as promised for an appreciable

---

2. Transfers are subject to Commission approval, but the Commission's inquiry is limited to whether the proposed transfer will serve "the public interest, convenience, and necessity;" the Communications Act bars the Commission from holding a com-parative hearing to assess whether transfer to another person might *better* serve the public interest. [ ] Since integration is not a threshold qualification, stations can readily be transferred to non-integrated owners.

period of time. Though such examples surely must exist, the Commission has failed to provide *one*. According to Bechtel, in fact, the Commission has never made any effort to determine "the actual length of time its 'integrated' license winners have owned and operated their broadcast stations." [ ]

The Commission has launched a rulemaking proceeding to consider boosting the one-year holding period for stations won in comparative hearings to three years after the start of operations, and perhaps making parallel changes in the reporting requirement. 8 F.C.C.Rcd. 5475 (1993). . . . But even if the Commission reaches (and adequately defends) a new conclusion in the pending rulemaking, a three-year holding period would still give it no reason to think that integration proposals will "be adhered to on a permanent basis," as the Commission contemplated in 1965. [ ]

Bechtel, who proposed to build a station that would serve 21% more people than the facility proposed by the applicant that won the Selbyville permit, argues that "the ephemeral period of initial ownership of a broadcast station . . . is vastly outweighed as a public interest factor by the lasting impact of a technical facility which provides greater coverage. . . ." [ ] Since the Commission does not know how long the typical successful applicant adheres to his integrated proposal, it can offer no real response to this argument.

2.   Lack of Evidence

The Commission's uncertainty about the practical effects of its integration policy is not limited to the question of how long integration persists. Despite its twenty-eight years of experience with the policy, the Commission has accumulated no evidence to indicate that it achieves even one of the benefits that the Commission attributes to it. As a result, the Commission ultimately rests its defense of the integration criterion on the deference that we owe to its "predictive judgments." [ ]

But as Bechtel protests, the relevant predictions have now had almost three decades to succeed or fail. There comes a time when reliance or unverified predictions begins to look a bit threadbare. "The Commission's necessarily wide latitude to make policy based upon predictive judgments deriving from its general expertise implies a correlative duty to valuate its policies over time to ascertain whether they work—that is, whether they actually produce the benefits the Commission originally predicted they would." *Bechtel I*, 957 F.2d at 881 (citation omitted).

What is more, the predictions at the root of the integration policy seems rather implausible. As Bechtel's counsel observed at oral argument, the fact that corporate America generally does not insist upon the integration of ownership and management casts doubt on the Commission's rosy speculations about the benefits of integration. Without adopting the Panglossian view that all economic arrangements that exist must necessarily be efficient, one should still be skeptical when regulatory agencies promote organizational forms that private enterprise would not otherwise adopt. . . .

Finally, it is worth noting that the "predictive judgments" at the root of the integration policy concern an area that the Commission has sometimes considered beyond its expertise. In scrutinizing integration proposals asserted by rival claimants to be illegitimate, purely formal, or otherwise inadequate, the Commission has disclaimed any "particular expertise in finance or business management" and accordingly expressed itself "reluctant to second-guess an applicant's business judgment—so long as it is, in fact, a good faith business decision." . . .

Of course the Commission may believe that the goals that Congress has directed it to pursue in the license allocation process—"the public interest, convenience, and necessity," 47 U.S.C. § 309 (a)—are in the end unmeasurable. Especially given the strictures of the First Amendment, that may be so. But the Commission seems not to have taken that position; it seems to believe that it is applying testable hypotheses. On that assumption, its failure over a 28–year period to generate a shred of supporting evidence is rather telling.

3.   Exclusion of Other Factors

Even if integration's claimed advantages were more plausible than we find them, they would not necessarily justify the extraordinary weight that the Commission assigns to integration. The Commission has identified "two primary objectives" for its comparative process: generating "a maximum diffusion of control of the media of mass communications" and securing "the best practicable service to the public." [   ] In the typical case, the integration criterion is "the most important element of best practicable service." In other words, the Commission generally deems an applicant's integration proposal more important than his past broadcast record, his proposed program service, or the efficiency of his proposed use of frequency.

Within the framework of the integration criterion, the Commission does take certain "qualitative" factors into account: an applicant's integration credit can be enhanced if the proposed owner-managers live in the station's service area, have participated in civic affairs, have broadcast experience, or belong to a minority group. But the "quantitative" portion of the integration credit tends to swamp the qualitative.

The Commission calculates the quantitative portion with a numerical precision that masks the fuzziness of the underlying facts (discussed below). It applies a formula . . . under which a proposed owner-manager's integration score is 10000 x (ownership share) x (hours per week/40)2. An applicant's overall quantitative score is the sum of the scores of each of its proposed owner-managers. Thus, applicants who get credit for full-time integration of all their owners receive the maximum score of 10,000. Because the formula squares the fraction representing the owner's proposed working portion of a 40–hour week, part-time management is discounted at a more-than-linear rate; a 100% owner who proposed to devote 30 hours a week to the station would get only 5625 points—(10000) x (¾)2. [   ]

Qualitative factors cannot overcome a "clear" quantitative advantage—which the Commission defines as a difference of at least 1250. [   ] An applicant whose proposed owner-manager knows nothing about either broadcasting or the community but promises to work a 40–hour week, for example, will handily win an integration preference over one whose proposed owner-manager is a veteran broadcaster who has spent his whole life in the station's community but proposes to work a 36–hour week at the station (scoring only 8100). [   ] All this occurs under a policy whose stated goal is to pick owners who are aware of and responsive to their communities' special needs.

Of course, comparative hearings turn on other issues when the applicants have similar integration proposals, and the integration preference itself can range from slight to substantial. But . . . [a]n applicant that secures a "clear" quantitative advantage in integration (the 1250) will normally win the station, as long as it meets the Commission's threshold criteria and does not own other media interests.

Given all the factors that affect a station's performance, the Commission faces a difficult task in justifying this remarkable system.

. . .

B. Incentives

1. Financial Incentives

The Commission asserts that stations perform better when managed by those with the "most direct financial interest" in the venture. [   ] The Commission has not defined exactly what it means by "financial interest." However the term is defined, though, the integration policy does not serve this goal.

For instance, in calculating integration credit, the Commission does not take the ownership interests of limited partners into account if all the limited partners are sufficiently insulated from influence over the partnership's affairs. Anax Broadcasting, Inc., 87 F.C.C. 2d 483 (1981). When an applicant is organized as a corporation rather than a partnership, the same is true for the interests of nonvoting shareholders. Accordingly, an applicant can get full integration credit even though the general partner or voting shareholder has only a small percentage of the equity in the firm, the rest of which is held by people who will have nothing to do with the station. . . . Because the Commission's method of measuring "ownership" focuses on voting power rather than profit share, the Commission does not insist that the proposed "owner-managers" stand to gain much if the station is especially profitable.

. . .

In short, whatever the benefits of ensuring that day-to-day management decisions are made by people whose money is directly on the line, the integration policy does not achieve them.

2. Legal Accountability

The Commission also considers it "inherently desirable" that day-to-day management decisions be made by people with "legal responsibility" for the station. [ ] But station employees can be held legally responsible for their acts even if they don't own the station. . . .

It may be true, as the Commission suggests, that station owners have the *most* legal accountability for the station. But to a large extent they have this accountability whether or not they work at the station. Stations are not insulated from the threat of license revocation, 47 U.S.C. § 312, or nonrenewal, *id.* § 307, merely because they are owned by absentee investors. Nor does absentee ownership protect stations from the forfeiture provisions of 47 U.S.C. § 503(b). Since absentee owners thus have strong incentives to ensure that their station complies with the relevant statutes and rules, the incremental contribution of the integration preference on this score appears trivial.

C. Interest

The Commission also asserts that integrated owners are more likely than absentee owners to have an active interest in the operation of their stations. . . .

At the outset, one might question the Commission's decision to stress an owner's interest in station operations over other factors, such as his skill or his experience. In most cases, broadcast experience merits at most a "qualitative" enhancement of an applicant's integration score. Yet even assuming that owner-manager integration is a perfect yardstick for the manager's interest, it is hard to see why a relatively modest differential (12.5%, or 1250 out of 10000) in "interest" should overwhelm a substantial difference in experience. . . .

In any event, the integration criterion simply measures one *form* in which owners may express their interest. . . . [E]xecutives routinely supervise a variety of firm activities, a few hours to each, without being the least bit apathetic about the performance of any. Likewise, no integration credit is awarded for proposals to spend less than 20 hours a week at a station, [   ], even though an owner who spends each morning at his station is far from passive or inaccessible.

Further, the very existence of the integration criterion weakens any correlation between a proposed owner's integration and his real interest in the station. It may well be that before the Commission began dispensing permits on the basis of integration proposals, only owners interested in broadcast operations would propose to work at the station. But now that applicants have every incentive to declare an intention to manage (and need honor that declaration for only a year at most), the empirical inference is severely weakened.

D. Information

According to the Commission, on-site owners have better sources of information than absentee owners. . . .

. . .

. . . But the Commission evidently does not take its own argument very seriously, for it insists that owner-managers spend at least 20 hours a week at the station in order to receive *any* integration credit. It is hard to see why picking up the week's influx [of mail] should take more than a few minutes, and, even, assuming an avalanche of mail and only semi-competent staff work, why mastering its content should take more than a few hours.

Familiarity with a community seems much more likely than station visitors or correspondence to make one aware of community needs. But even long-time local residence generates at most a "qualitative" enhancement of an applicant's integration credit.

E.   Objectivity.

Aside from the substantive advantages that the Commission attributes to integration, the Commission claims a procedural advantage. As a "structural" factor, it says, the integration criterion can be applied more consistently and objectively than other possible ways of assessing an applicant's likely responsiveness to community needs. [   ]

Any "objectivity" added by the integration criterion is unfortunately illusory. The Commission's scores for quantitative integration merely lend the policy a veneer of precision; every step towards the magic number is packed with subjective judgments, some generic, some ad hoc.

At a generic level, the Commission's weighting system, by which it *squares* the fraction representing the owner's proposed working portion of a 40–hour week, is simply a fancy way for the Commission to express its view that the value of integration fall off sharply when owner-managers work less than full-time. [   ] It has not a shred of data supporting the basic conjecture, let alone that the relationship is best captured by squaring the fraction rather than cubing it.

Similarly, the Commission's formula seems to assume that the importance of ownership share varies on a *linear* basis, disregarding issues of control that might seem critical. [The court noted that there would be no clear preference between a 45% owner and a 55% owner despite the fact that only the 55% owner would have a controlling interest. Yet an 88% owner would have a clear preference over a 75% owner, even though both would have a controlling interest.]

Applying the formula requires more subjective decisions. In calculating the hours to be worked by each applicant-owner, for example, the Commission usually takes the prospective owner's word at face value, even though it knows that the promise is likely made in large part to please the Commission, that the Commission will do little or nothing to enforce the promise therefore may quite possibly be bogus. . . . Further, many cases turn on whether a proposed job should be classified as part of station "management." . . .

So far as measuring ownership is concerned, the Commission's policy provides rich incentives for the adoption of firm structures that we

characterized in Bechtel I (quoting Bechtel) as "strange and unnatural."
[   ] After all, if a station can be acquired for legal fees and minor
engineering services, and can be sold a year later for several million
dollars, one would expect to see a good deal of ingenuity. In Bechtel I we
recited some of the startling arrangements manifested just in this case
itself:

> In our case, for example, best friends and co-owners of a station
> swear not to consult with each other; family members with valuable
> broadcast knowledge and experience agree not to assist the tyro
> station manager in the family; people with steady jobs and families
> in one city pledge to leave them and move permanently to another;
> and wealthy retirees promise to move and work in small summer
> towns in Delaware with which they have no former connection.

Id.

. . .

We are quite aware that the Commission's task is a difficult one. As
it is charged with handing out extremely valuable resources, the number
of parties lined up to win them inevitably will greatly exceed the supply.
Yet common sense, not to mention the First Amendment, counsel
against the Commission's trying to decide what America should see and
hear over the airwaves. Further, the ability to pick person's and firms
who will be "successful" at delivering any kind of services is a rare one,
however, success might be defined; that is why it commands generous
rewards in the market. . . . All these difficulties flow from the statutory
scheme itself.

All that said, the integration preference is peculiarly without foundation. While the Commission makes it a central focus of *allocation*, the
Commission takes no interest whatever in the matter when it comes *to
transfers* or even in the continuing conduct of the original licensee. The
Commission appears to have *no* evidence that the preferred structure
even survives among the winners, much less that it does so among
especially outstanding broadcasters. Because of applicants' incentive to
create a facade of integration, and the difficulty of identifying sound
business practices, even the preference's touted objectivity proves an
illusion. Though we owe substantial deference to the Commission's
expertise, we are forbidden to suspend our disbelief totally. We find the
integration policy arbitrary and capricious.

IV.   REMEDY

At times, the Commission has suggested that the pendency of a
rulemaking designed to reconsider the integration criterion permits the
Commission to continue applying the criterion in the meantime. [   ] If a
policy is arbitrary and capricious, however, the mere fact that the
Commission is reconsidering that policy does not authorize the Commission to continue making arbitrary and capricious policy. As Bechtel was
denied a license on the basis of an arbitrary and capricious policy, she is
entitled to a proceeding in which the Commission considers her applica-

tion (and any other application properly before it) under standards free of that policy.

. . .

The Commission's decision is reversed and the matter is remanded for further proceedings consistent with this opinion.

So ordered.

Notes and Questions

1. In January 1994 the Commission put a freeze on comparative licensing proceedings, new station applications, and requests for upgrades and major modifications pending the conclusion of its NPRM on this subject, n. 2, *infra*. Seven months later, the freeze was lifted for everything except mutually exclusive applications. Shortly thereafter, as a means of facilitating settlements, the Commission modified its order to suspend limits on settlement payments for 90 days. Public Notice, FCC Freezes Comparative Proceedings, 9 F.C.C.Rcd. 1055 (1994), modified, 9 F.C.C.Rcd. 6689 (1994), further modified, 10 F.C.C.R. 12182 (1995).

2. The Commission also responded to the remand in *Bechtel* by issuing a notice of proposed rulemaking aimed at reconsidering the entire 1965 statement. Reexamination of the Policy Statement on Comparative Broadcast Hearings, 7 F.C.C.Rcd. 2664 (1992). The Commission asked for comments on whether to retain each of the factors set out in that statement. It also suggested awarding a "finder's preference" for applicants who persuade the Commission to allot a new frequency, and for a "service continuity preference" designed "to enhance the public interest in the comparative process by encouraging comparative applicants to retain the stations they are attempting to secure through the comparative hearing for a certain period of time."

Because of uncertainty as to changes that might be made by a proposed telecommunications bill, the Commission delayed any action in this proceeding. However, the 1996 Telecommunications Act did not address initial licensing proceedings.

3. Could the revision of the *1965 Policy Statement* suggested by the FCC have adequately addressed the problem? Had Congress given the FCC a difficult, if not impossible, task? What alternatives might have been preferable?

Some critics suggested that the Commission emphasize one or two factors, such as diversity, and use these as the major bases for decision. Others suggested using more factors but giving each a preannounced weight, so that the result would be more predictable than it was.

Still another suggestion was to award the license to the winner of a lottery among equally qualified applicants. The theory of this approach was that sometimes there simply is no superior applicant and it is unrealistic, if not dishonest, to announce a single winner on the merits. The lottery idea could be applied to all applicants who met the basic tests and also had offered maximum diversification or some other added criteria.

In 1980 the FCC voted, 4–3, to order its staff to prepare a decision that would award the license by lottery to one of two applicants who were both judged superior to a third but equal to each other. Two dissenters complained that one applicant should win on the merits because of the full-time participation of a black woman who was a 5–percent owner. The third dissenter argued that the action was "an impermissible abdication of the Commission's statutory responsibilities and an improper denial of the hearing rights of the applicants." The FCC had an obligation to make "public-interest judgments" rather than use lotteries. Broadcasting, June 9, 1980 at 30. In 1981 the FCC abandoned the idea of a lottery, but shortly thereafter Congress amended § 309 of the Communications Act to authorize the use of lotteries.

In response to that amendment, the Commission developed lottery procedures for some licensing proceedings including LPTV. These procedures gave preferences (additional chances) for minority ownership and diversity. Then, in 1984, the Commission decided that even though the lottery statute did not authorize the use of lotteries to resolve ties in comparative proceedings, the general public interest standard gave the FCC the authority to adopt such a system. Thus, where the Commission found applicants who were "in true equipoise on comparative factors" it used a lottery to decide which applicant will be awarded the license. Lottery Selection Among Applicants, 57 R.R.2d 427 (1984). On appeal the court held that the order would not be ripe for review until the lottery procedure was actually used. National Latino Media Coalition v. Federal Communications Commission, 816 F.2d 785, 62 R.R.2d 1552 (D.C.Cir.1987).

4.   Still another approach would be to auction airwave licenses. This would also serve to increase government revenue. Most proposals dealt with new services or with those already being assigned by lottery. See, e.g., Auctions Urged for Airwaves, N.Y.Times (Natl), Mar. 18, 1993 at C1. There was some early indication that the Clinton Administration wanted to apply an auction approach to existing broadcast assignments when they came up for renewal—a position that would have raised enormous political problems for any auction proposal. There was increasing concern that the lottery approach had simply produced entities that specialized in making massive numbers of applications for a new service—and then selling the assignments that they won in the lottery.

Generally, see Auctioning Radio Spectrum Licenses (study of the Congressional Budget Office, March 1992).

5.   The attractiveness of the auction approach was increased by the success from a financial standpoint of auctions for Personal Communication Services (PCS) spectrum. Early, PCS auctions raised $20 billion. Pressure on both Congress and the President to balance the budget, also made auctions more attractive. The use of spectrum auction proceeds to

help balance the budget was a politically attractive alternative to raising taxes and/or cutting government services.

As the Commission struggled to devise a new comparative licensing scheme that would survive judicial scrutiny, Congress finally settled the issue. The 1997 budget bill, p. 58, *supra*, replaced comparative proceedings for analog channels with auctions. The bill provided existing applicants with a six-month period during which they could settle competing applications.

Procedures for the new auction process were announced in 1998, *Implementation of Section 309(j) of The Communications Act*, p. 110, *supra*. The process starts with a uniform filing window for mutually exclusive applications. All applicants who file a short form application during this time period are permitted to bid.

The Commission delegated to the Mass Media Bureau the authority to establish the bidding procedures, including upfront payments, minimum opening bids and/or reserve prices for each auction or group of auctions of broadcast service construction permits:

> With respect to the methodology to be employed in establishing each of these mechanisms, among the factors the Bureaus may consider are the type of service that will be offered, the amount of spectrum being auctioned, the degree of competition from incumbent providers, the size of the geographic service areas, potential advertising revenue, unalterable limitations due to physical phenomena (e.g., propagation losses), equipment design limitations, issues of interference with other spectrum bands, and any other relevant factors that could reasonably have an impact on valuation of the spectrum being auctioned.

Following the auction, the winning bidder files a long form application. A 15–day public comment period is opened, during which petitions to deny can be filed. If no petition to deny is filed or the FCC dismisses all petitions that are filed, the winning bidder pays the balance of the bid and be issued a construction permit.

Pursuant to § 309(j), those frozen applications that were not settled were scheduled for auction. Auctions were limited to applicants who filed prior to July 1, 1997, unless there was only one application for a given license, in which case competing applications were accepted.

Dissatisfaction with the Commission's renewal standards also grew during the '80s and '90s. The following quote from Judge Silberman's concurrence in a renewal case from 1990 typified the feelings of many:

> It appears to me that virtually all the factors upon which the FCC relies in awarding or renewing broadcast licenses are in a sense fictitious; they are not really predictive of programming substance. Nor is it apparent to me that it is possible to articulate a public interest in any particular kind of programming (such as "nonentertainment"). When I sit on these cases, therefore, I feel somewhat like Alice in Wonderland. We have no alternative as a reviewing

court, however, but to treat the FCC's elaboration of the public interest as if it made sense and therefore to insist on a consistent application of what we may really think are fanciful factors.

Quite obviously the FCC shrinks from the prospect of taking the license away from the incumbent, but in the absence of a system whereby a license holder pays the public for the license (as in an auction) it is hard to see how the FCC can justify the weight it places on incumbency in this case. The Commission appears to act as if incumbency and the renewal expectancy were a property interest—which it is not. Monroe Communications Corp. v. Federal Communications Commission, 900 F.2d 351, 67 R.R.2d 843, 17 Med.L.Rptr. 1703 (D.C.Cir.1990).

The question, of course, was whether a better system could be devised. Was it possible to compare incumbents and new applicants in a way that would accurately predict who would better serve the public interest? If not, should comparative renewals be eliminated as had been proposed in Congress in the early 1970s, p. 131, *supra*?

Congress eventually came to that conclusion. The 1996 Telecommunications Act mandates a non-comparative renewal process. Under this new procedure the Commission is directed to grant a renewal application if it finds:

(A) the station has served the public interest, convenience, and necessity;

(B) there have been no serious violations by the licensee of this Act or the rules and regulations of the Commission; and

(C) there have been no other violations by the licensee of this Act or the rules and regulations of the Commission which, taken together, would constitute a pattern of abuse.

The Commission is specifically prohibited from consideration of whether the public interest might be better served by awarding the license to someone other than the renewal applicant. If a renewal applicant fails to meet the criteria listed above, the Commission may decide to deny renewal. Then, and only then, are others permitted to apply for the license. 47 U.S.C.A § 309(k).

What will the effect of this new system be? Will licensees still have an adequate incentive to serve the public interest? Remember the FCC's justification for renewal expectancy, p. 134, *supra*. Will others still have an incentive to present to the FCC evidence of a licensee's wrongdoing or failure to serve the public interest?

Chapter V

LEGAL CONTROL OF BROADCAST
PROGRAMMING: POLITICAL
SPEECH

In this chapter and the next we will consider direct regulation of content but not necessarily prohibitions on speech. This chapter will focus on political speech, including news. The next chapter will cover content regulation of other types of speech, which the FCC and courts have tended to treat as lower in the hierarchy of First Amendment values.

We begin this chapter with Congressional legislation to provide access and fairness in the electoral process. No speech is prohibited. Rather, broadcasters are told that they must allow certain candidates to use the station's facilities. In addition, if a candidate for an office is allowed to use the facilities, all other candidates for that office must be allowed equal opportunities.

We then turn to doctrines developed by the Commission itself that require broadcasters who have allowed certain types of comments to be made over their facilities to expose their listeners to contrasting viewpoints on that subject.

In each case, consider whether the regulations, although not prohibitory, may nonetheless indirectly influence broadcasters to air or not to air certain types of content.

A. EQUAL OPPORTUNITIES AND ACCESS IN POLITICAL CAMPAIGNS

1. EQUAL OPPORTUNITIES—SECTION 315

In the Radio Act of 1927, § 18 provided:

> If any licensee shall permit any person who is a legally qualified candidate for any public office to use a broadcasting station, he shall afford equal opportunities to all other such candidates for that office in the use of such broadcasting station; . . . *Provided,* That such licensee shall have no power of censorship over the material broadcast under the provisions of this paragraph. No obligation is hereby imposed upon any licensee to allow the use of its station by any such candidate.

This became § 315 of the 1934 Act. Although the Commission has explicit rulemaking power to carry out the provisions of § 315(a), few rules have been promulgated. Most of the problems involve requests in the heat of an election campaign, and for this reason few decisions have been reviewed by the courts.

a.   General Application

One major limitation on the applicability of § 315 was defined in 1951, when it was held that the section did not apply to uses of a broadcast facility on behalf of a candidate unless the candidate appeared personally during the program. This meant that friends and campaign committees could purchase time without triggering § 315. Felix v. Westinghouse Radio Stations, 186 F.2d 1 (3d Cir.1950). This raised a separate set of problems discussed at p. 204, *infra*.

Section 315 applies only to "legally qualified" candidates for public office. According to § 73.1940(a) of the Commission's rules, a legally qualified candidate is one who:

> (i) has publicly announced his or her intention to run for nomination or office;

> (ii) is qualified under the applicable local, state or federal law to hold the office for which he or she is a candidate; and

> (iii) has met the qualifications set forth in either paragraphs (a)(2), (3), or (4) below.

In essence, these other subparagraphs require the candidate either to have qualified for a place on the ballot or to have made a public commitment to seeking election by the write-in method as well as a substantial showing of being a bona-fide candidate for the office. Ways of making a substantial showing include "making campaign speeches, distributing campaign literature, issuing press releases, maintaining a campaign committee, and establishing campaign headquarters (even though the headquarters in some instances might be the residence of the candidate or his campaign manager)." 47 C.F.R. § 73.1940(a)(1–5).

Another basic question regarding § 315 was resolved in Farmers Educational & Cooperative Union v. WDAY, Inc., 360 U.S. 525 (1959), when the Court unanimously held that a licensee was barred from censoring the comments of a speaker exercising rights under § 315. The Court also held, 5–4, that the section preempted state defamation law and created an absolute privilege that protected the licensee from liability for statements made by such a candidate. Are these rulings sound? Because of the way the litigation arose, neither party challenged the constitutionality of § 315. Note, however, that although the station is protected from liability for defamation, the person who utters the statements is subject to liability under the general rules of defamation. We will examine these rules in Chapter XIV.

Other content problems under § 315 are rare, but do arise. Among the candidates running in 1972 for the Democratic nomination for Senator from Georgia, one was broadcasting the following spot announcement:

I am J.B. Stoner. I am the only candidate for U.S. Senator who is for the white people. I am the only candidate who is against integration. All of the other candidates are race mixers, to one degree or another. I say we must repeal Gambrell's civil rights law. Gambrell's law takes jobs from us whites and gives those jobs to the niggers. The main reason why niggers want integration is because the niggers want our white women. I am for law and order with the knowledge that you cannot have law and order and niggers too. Vote white. This time vote your convictions by voting white racist J.B. Stoner into the run-off election for U.S. Senator. Thank you.

Several groups asked the Commission to rule that a licensee may, and has the responsibility to, withhold announcements under § 315 if they "pose an imminent and immediate threat to the safety and security of the public it serves." The groups alleged that the spot had created racial tension and that the Mayor of Atlanta had urged broadcasters not to air the advertisement. Letter to Lonnie King, 36 F.C.C.2d 635, 25 R.R.2d 54 (1972). The Commission refused to issue the requested order:

> The relief requested in your letter would amount to an advance approval by the Commission of licensee censorship of a candidate's remarks. By way of background, we note that Constitutional guarantees do not permit the proscription of even the advocacy of force or of law violation "except where such advocacy is directed to inciting or producing imminent lawless action and is likely to incite or produce such action." Brandenburg v. Ohio, 395 U.S. 444, 447 (1969). And a prior restraint bears a heavy presumption against its constitutional validity. Carroll v. President and Commissioners of Princess Anne, 393 U.S. 175, 181 (1968). While there may be situations where speech is "so interlaced with burgeoning violence that it is not protected," Carroll v. President and Commissioners of Princess Anne, 393 U.S. at 180 and while a similar approach might warrant overriding the no-censorship command of Section 315, we need not resolve that difficult issue here, for we conclude on the basis of the information before us that there is no factual basis for the relief you request. Despite your report of threats of bombing and violence, there does not appear to be that clear and present danger of imminent violence which might warrant interfering with speech which does not contain any direct incitement to violence. A contrary conclusion here would permit anyone to prevent a candidate from exercising his rights under Section 315 by threatening a violent reaction. In view of the precise commands of Sections 315 and 326, we are constrained to deny your requests.

The FCC has also received occasional complaints about political announcements that contain indecent language. The problem of indecent and obscene political announcements will be discussed in Chapter VI.

b.　*Exemptions*

During its early years the statute apparently caused few serious problems. The advent of television, however, changed matters dramatically. In 1956 the Commission issued two major rulings during the presidential campaign. In one it ruled that presentation of Pres. Dwight Eisenhower's appearance in a two-to-three minute appeal on behalf of the annual drive of the United Community Funds would be a "use" of the facility by a candidate that would trigger the equal opportunities provision. The section carried no exception for "public service" nor did it require the appearance to be "political." Columbia Broadcasting System (United Fund), 14 R.R. 524 (F.C.C.1956). One week before the election, President Eisenhower requested and received 15 minutes of free time from the three networks to discuss the sudden eruption of war in the Middle East. The Democrats' request for equal time was granted by the networks, although the FCC later indicated that § 315 did not apply. Columbia Broadcasting System (Suez Crisis), 14 R.R. 720 (F.C.C.1956).

This response to an incumbent, speaking as President rather than as candidate, was unusual for the Commission, which had interpreted "use" very broadly. It did so, again, in 1959 when a third-party candidate for mayor of Chicago, Lar Daly, requested equal time on the basis of two series of television clips of his opponents, incumbent Mayor Richard Daley and the Republican challenger. One group of clips showed the two major candidates filing their papers (46 seconds), Mayor Daley accepting the nomination (22 seconds) and a one-minute clip asking the Republican why he was running. A second group of clips included "nonpolitical" activities such as a 29–second clip of Mayor Daley on a March of Dimes appeal and 21 seconds of his greeting President Frondizi of Argentina at a Chicago airport. The Commission, in a long opinion, ruled that both groups required equal time. Columbia Broadcasting System, Inc. (Lar Daly), 26 F.C.C. 715 (1959). It relied on the words "use" and "all" in the statute and thought the issue of who initiated the appearance (such as the March of Dimes, asking the Mayor to appear) to be irrelevant. Although formal campaigning was the most obvious way of putting forward a candidacy, "of no less importance is the candidate's appearance as a public servant, as an incumbent office holder, or as a private citizen in a nonpolitical role." Such "appearances and uses of a nonpolitical nature may confer substantial benefits on a candidate who is favored."

Congressional response was swift—and negative. Hearings began within days after the decision, and the result was an amended version of § 315:

> Sec. 315. (a) If any licensee shall permit any person who is a legally qualified candidate for any public office to use a broadcasting station, he shall afford equal opportunities to all other such candidates for that office in the use of such broadcasting station: *Provided,* That such licensee shall have no power of censorship over the material broadcast under the provisions of this section. No obligation is hereby imposed upon any licensee to allow the use of its station by any such candidate.* Appearance by a legally qualified candidate on any—

---

* In 1971 Congress amended this sentence by adding "under this subsection" after the word "imposed." The reason for this is given when we consider § 312(a)(7) shortly.

(1) bona fide newscast,

(2) bona fide news interview,

(3) bona fide news documentary (if the appearance of the candidate is incidental to the presentation of the subject or subjects covered by the news documentary), or

(4) on-the-spot coverage of bona fide news events (including but not limited to political conventions and activities incidental thereto), shall not be deemed to be use of a broadcasting station within the meaning of this subsection. Nothing in the foregoing sentence shall be construed as relieving broadcasters, in connection with the presentation of newscasts, news interviews, news documentaries, and on-the-spot coverage of news events, from the obligation imposed upon them under this chapter to operate in the public interest and to afford reasonable opportunity for the discussion of conflicting views on issues of public importance.

Recall the significance of this episode to the Court in *Red Lion,* p. 78, *supra.*

In 1960 Congress suspended the operation of § 315 so that the stations could give time to national candidates without creating a § 315 obligation. This permitted the Kennedy–Nixon debates to be held without need to provide free time for the many minority candidates. There was no incumbent and no major third party candidate—two factors that made the debates politically possible.

Presidential election problems returned in 1964. First, the Commission ruled that coverage of an incumbent President's press conferences were not exempt under either § 315(a)(2) or (4). Nor were those of his main challenger. Columbia Broadcasting System (Presidential Press Conference), 3 R.R.2d 623 (F.C.C.1964). Then, two weeks before the election, the three networks granted Pres. Lyndon Johnson time to comment on two events that had just occurred: a sudden change of leadership was announced in Moscow, and China exploded a nuclear device. The Commission adhered to its 1956 ruling that this was not a "use." It also upheld a network claim that this program came within § 315(a)(4) as a bona fide news event. Republican National Committee (Dean Burch), 3 R.R.2d 647 (F.C.C.1964). An appeal of this ruling to the court of appeals led to an affirmance on a divided vote, 3–3, without opinion. A petition for *certiorari* was denied, Goldwater v. Federal Communications Commission, 379 U.S. 893 (1964), with Justice Goldberg, joined by Justice Black, dissenting with opinion. They argued that the case presented substantial questions and that the Commission seemed not to be consistent in its own decisions.

In 1968 Sen. Eugene McCarthy announced early that he was a candidate for the Democratic nomination for President against the incumbent, Lyndon Johnson. During a traditional year-end interview with television reporters, President Johnson criticized Senator McCarthy and made several political statements. McCarthy sought "equal time" but the Commission denied the request on the ground that the President had not announced that he was a candidate for re-election and thus did not come within the statute or the Commission's rules on who is a "legally qualified candidate" for office. Eugene McCarthy, 11 F.C.C.2d 511, 12 R.R.2d 106 (1968). On appeal, the Commission's position was affirmed. McCarthy v. Federal Communications Commission, 390 F.2d 471, 12 R.R.2d 2003 (D.C.Cir.1968). Shortly thereafter President Johnson abruptly announced that he would not seek reelection.

In 1972 the problems centered around the Democratic nomination. Just before the crucial California primary, CBS held a joint session of "Face the Nation," expanded from its regular half-hour to one hour, featuring Senators Hubert Humphrey and George McGovern, the two leading candidates in the primary and for the nomination. The network claimed that this was a bona fide news interview and thus exempt under § 315(a)(2) from time requests by other Democratic candidates. Similar programs on other networks raised similar questions. The Commission found the changes did not deprive the programs of their bona fide character as interviews, and perceived and intended its opinion to accord "with the remedial purpose of the 1959 amendments to accord leeway to licensee journalistic decisions." Hon. Sam Yorty and Hon. Shirley Chisholm, 35 F.C.C.2d 572, 24 R.R.2d 447 (1972). On Chisholm's appeal, the FCC's ruling was vacated. Chisholm v. Federal Communications Commission, 24 R.R.2d 2061 (D.C.Cir.1972). The court thought the program more a debate than an interview. On remand, the Commission begrudgingly complied and ordered the networks to grant Chisholm one half-hour of prime time before the election. 35 F.C.C.2d 579, 24 R.R.2d 720 (1972).

The FCC has granted general exemptions under (a)(2) to such programs as "Today," "Donahue" and "Good Morning America." In determining whether a show falls under the (a)(2) exemption "the Commission considers the following factors: (1) whether it is regularly scheduled; (2) how long it has been broadcast; (3) whether the broadcaster produces and controls the program; (4) whether the broadcaster's decisions on the format, content and participants are based on its reasonable, good faith journalistic judgment rather than on an intention to advance the candidacy of a particular person; and (5) whether the selection of persons to be interviewed and topics to be discussed are based on their newsworthiness." CBS Inc., 63 R.R.2d 483 (M.Med.Bur.1987).

The FCC Changes Course. Through the 1960s and 1970s, various proposals were made in Congress to amend or repeal § 315. Nothing came of any of them. But in 1975 the Commission responded dramatically to two petitions. It overruled its 1962 decisions that coverage of a debate did not come within the exemption for on-the-spot coverage of bona fide news events. The Commission said that it had misinterpreted legislative history when it required the appearance of the candidate to be incidental to the coverage of a separate news event. The Commission now concluded that in 1959 Congress intended to run the risks of political favoritism among broadcasters in an effort to allow broadcasters to "cover the political news to the fullest degree." Debates were exempt if controlled by someone other than the candidates or the broadcaster, and if judged to be bona fide news events under § 315(a)(4).

In a companion ruling, the Commission overruled its 1964 decision on press conference coverage. It decided that full coverage of a press conference by any incumbent or candidate would come within the exemption for on-the-spot coverage of a bona fide news event if it "may be considered newsworthy and subject to on-the-spot coverage." But the Commission refused to bring a press conference within the exemption for bona fide news interviews because the licensee did not "control" the format and the event was not "regularly scheduled." Petitions of Aspen Institute and CBS, Inc., 55 F.C.C.2d 697, 35 R.R.2d 49 (1975).

Appeals were taken against both parts of the Commission's 1975 rulings. The main contentions were that the Commission had not followed the Congressional mandate when it permitted the candidate to "become the event" under the (a)(4) exemption, and that the statute did not allow the Commission to uphold licensee decisions as long as they are in "good faith"—that it is for the Commission to make these judgments. By a vote of 2–1, the court affirmed both rulings, Chisholm v. Federal Communications Commission, 538 F.2d 349, 1 Med.L.Rptr. 2207 (D.C.Cir.1976). The opinions differed as to the significance of the complex legislative history, with the majority concluding that the Commission's interpretation was "reasonable." Rehearing *en banc* was denied. A petition for *certiorari* was denied 429 U.S. 890 (1976), White, J., dissenting.

Seizing on the Commission's rulings, the League of Women Voters set up "debates" between the two major Presidential candidates in 1976. They were held in auditoriums before invited audiences. The candidates were questioned by panelists selected by the League after consultation with the participants. Television was allowed to cover the events—but the League imposed restrictions against showing the audience or any audience reactions. Although the networks complained about the restrictions and about the way the panelists were selected, they did carry the programs live and in full.

Again in 1980 the League took steps to sponsor debates among the major candidates. It decided that John Anderson's showing in public opinion polls was sufficiently strong to warrant his inclusion in a three-way debate. When Pres. Jimmy Carter refused to participate in a debate with Anderson, the League went ahead anyway and staged an Anderson–Reagan debate. If networks decided to cover the event, as CBS and NBC did, the coverage would be exempt under (a)(4) because the networks and licensees were making the judgment it was a bona fide news event even without the President.

After Anderson's ratings fell to around 10 percent, the League invited Carter and Reagan to debate. Both accepted the invitation and held a single head-to-head debate a week before the election.

In 1980, just before the primaries began, President Carter, seeking renomination as Democratic candidate for President in a contest against Sen. Edward M. Kennedy, held a press conference that was carried live in prime time by the three commercial networks and the Public Broadcasting Service. Senator Kennedy, claiming that President Carter had used more than five minutes on that occasion to attack him and to misstate several of his positions, sought relief from the FCC.

In Kennedy for President Committee v. Federal Communications Commission, 636 F.2d 432, 47 R.R.2d 1537, 6 Med.L.Rptr. 1705 (D.C.Cir.1980)(*Kennedy I*), the Senator asked for equal opportunities under § 315 to respond to the "calculated and damaging statements" and to "provide contrasting viewpoints." The FCC denied the request. On appeal, the court affirmed.

The press conference was exempt under § 315(a)(4) so long as the broadcasters reasonably believed that the conference was a "bona fide news event." The Commission said, in a passage approved by the court, that an incumbent President "may well have an advantage over his opponent in attracting media coverage" but "absent strong evidence that broadcasters were not exercising their bona fide news judgment, the Commission will not interfere with such judgments." The Senator was free to hold a press conference the next day to rebut the charges. Indeed, generally, Senator Kennedy was getting substantial media coverage.

The court traced the history of the exemptions to § 315 and adhered to its decision in *Chisholm* upholding the Commission's new approach to § 315. "The only inquiry now in order is whether there was anything so peculiar about the February 13 presidential press conference as to remove it from the ambit of *Aspen* and *Chisholm*." The court found no reason to doubt the broadcasters' good faith. It also concluded that the actual content of the event could not control the question of exemption. Not only would the Commission and the courts have to make difficult judgments about content, context and impact, but also the goal of the exemptions would be defeated if broadcasters could not know until after an event whether it was exempt.

Senator Kennedy then argued that the First Amendment required that he be granted time to respond, even if the statute did not. The court rejected that contention on the basis of *CBS*, p. 91, *supra*:

> From its inception more than a half-century ago, federal regulation of broadcasting has largely entrusted protection of that public right to short-term station licensees functioning under Commission supervision, and with liberty as well as responsibility to determine who may get on the air and when. The history of this era portrays

Congress' consistent refusal to mandate access to the air waves on a non-selective basis and, contrariwise, its decision "to permit private broadcasting to develop with the widest journalistic experience consistent with its public obligations." [*CBS*] The Commission has honored that policy in a series of rulings establishing that a private right to utilize the broadcaster's facilities exists only when specially conferred. The net of these many years of legislative and administrative oversight of broadcasting is that "[o]nly when the interests of the public are found to outweigh the private journalistic interests of the broadcasters will government power be asserted within the framework of the Act."

The First Amendment permits Congress to enforce the public's primary interests by using broadcasters as public trustees, and *CBS* shows that no one has a constitutional right to broadcast his own views on any matter.

A similar First Amendment attack on the application of (a)(4) to candidate debates was rejected in Johnson v. Federal Communications Commission, 829 F.2d 157, 63 R.R.2d 1492, 14 Med.L.Rptr. 1711 (D.C.Cir.1987). Sonia Johnson, who was running for President in 1984 as the nominee of the Citizens Party, and her running mate, Richard Walton, argued that "by 1984 the televised presidential and vice-presidential debates had become so institutionalized as to be a prerequisite for election." Thus, "their exclusion from the 1984 debates [restricted] their access to the ballot and impinge[d] upon associational choices protected by the First Amendment." Treating the claim as a demand for broadcast access, the court of appeals found *Kennedy I* and *CBS v. DNC* controlling. "In the present case, we find the First Amendment interests of candidates, broadcasters and the public adequately served by the adjustments made in the Communications Act, and perceive no basis for disturbing the Commission's denial of petitioners' complaint."

In Petitions of Henry Geller et al., 95 F.C.C.2d 1236, 54 R.R.2d 1246 (1983), the FCC reversed long-standing administrative decisions by permitting broadcasters themselves to sponsor debates between political candidates without having to provide uninvited candidates with equal broadcasting opportunities. Such debates may still fall within the § 315(a)(4) exemption. The Commission concluded that its previous interpretations neither represented the outer bounds of its legislated authority under the statute nor met the overriding Congressional mandate to encourage broadcast coverage of electoral issues. Third-party sponsorship was not the *sine qua non* of impartiality. For example, the risks of favoritism in the news interview format [§ 315(a)(2)] were thought to be no different from those in the debate format and therefore disparate treatment was not justified. The League of Women Voters' argument that this approach creates too great a risk of favoritism was rejected. The risks inherent in broadcaster-sponsored debates were no greater than the *Chisholm* court had understood the 1959 amendments to be willing to accept.

The Commission also noted that in many cases a broadcaster may be "the ideal, and perhaps the only, entity interested in promoting a debate between candidates for a particular office, especially at the state or local level." Exempting broadcaster-sponsored debates would therefore increase the number of debates and ultimately benefit the public. Finally, a debate's exempt status "should not be contingent upon whether a broadcaster is the sponsoring or controlling entity—for such control generally would not affect the program's news value." The Commission also made clear that this new interpretation of § 315(a)(4) did not authorize licensees to favor or disfavor any candidate. The League's expedited appeal was rejected without opinion. League of Women Voters v. FCC, 731 F.2d 995 (D.C.Cir.1984).

A debate between Gov. Michael Dukakis of Massachusetts and Rep. Richard Gephardt (D.–Mo.) presented the Commission with a slightly different question. Could a candidate-sponsored, as opposed to a broadcaster-sponsored, debate be considered exempt under § 315(a)(4)? In extending the exemption to candidate-sponsored debates, the Commission reemphasized its position that the identity of the sponsor is not a factor in determining if an event is newsworthy. As long as the broadcaster retains ultimate control over the amount and type of coverage, an event can qualify for exemption (a)(4). WCVB–TV, 63 R.R.2d 665 (M.Med.Bur.1987).

In King Broadcasting Co., 6 F.C.C.Rcd. 4998, 69 R.R.2d 1017 (1991), the Commission broadened the concept of "on-the-spot coverage of bona fide news events" by ruling that the broadcast of two hour-long programs in which the two major party presidential candidates would be given back-to-back half-hour segments to present their messages qualified under § 315(a)(4). These programs "reasonably may be viewed as news 'events' subject to broadcast coverage" within the exemption. Neither candidacy would be promoted since the order of presentation was to be decided by coin toss for the first pair of programs and reversed for the second.

What if a "major" third candidate enters the race? In 1996 Ross Perot alleged several violations of § 315 by the television networks. First, he argued that the extensive coverage of the Republican and Democratic Conventions entitled him to free time. The Commission rejected his argument that the unique situation of a major third party candidate mandated a departure from the policy of exempting convention coverage under § 315(a)(4). The Commission also rejected his request for time based on the debates between Robert Dole and President Clinton, again finding the debates qualified under (a)(4). The Committee on Presidential Debates had excluded Perot from the debates.

Perot's final complaint involved a plan by Fox Television to present ten 60–second statements by each Presidential candidate as well as a longer statement the night before the election. This plan which was in response to complaints about the quality of information offered to the voters during election campaigns. The FCC had approved the plan as qualifying under (a)(4). Fox had decided to limit the program to candidates approved by the CPD for the Presidential debates. This complaint was also denied. Complaint of Ross Perot, 11 F.C.C.Rcd. 13109 (1996).

The "on the spot" language of § 315(a)(4) also has produced litigation. Groups afraid that an exempt program, such as a debate, might be recorded and replayed several times to the detriment of excluded candidates, have argued that the statute permits only one showing—and that it must be live. The FCC rejected this and allowed the broadcaster to tape the live event and to present it once during the next 24 hours. When that ruling was challenged, the court affirmed the Commission. The agency had authority to develop a balance between rigidly equal opportunities and the new freedom provided by the 1959 exemptions. There was no showing that the FCC had misconstrued the law, and it had fully explained what it was doing. Office of Communication of the United Church of Christ v. Federal Communications Commission, 590 F.2d 1062, 44 R.R.2d 261, 4 Med.L.Rptr. 1410 (D.C.Cir.1978).

The one-day rule was eliminated in *Henry Geller,* p. 176, *supra.* The reasonableness of a delayed broadcast will now be left to the broadcaster's good faith determination that the delay of more than one day after the occurrence of the exempt debate will better serve the community. Such delay, however, must be motivated by concerns of informing the public, and not in order to favor or disfavor any candidate.

The other subdivisions, (a)(1) and (a)(3), have given rise to fewer problems. In 1976 supporters of Ronald Reagan complained when a Miami television station broadcast six-minute interviews with Pres. Gerald Ford on five consecutive evening newscasts. The complaint asserted that the segments were from a single half-hour interview that had been broken up into five parts. The Commission held that even if the 30–minute interview would not have been exempt under § 315, inclusion of the segments within newscasts would not preclude "exempt status pursuant to § 315(a)(1) unless it has been shown that such a decision is clearly unreasonable or in bad faith." Even though this was broadcast during the last week of a primary campaign and might benefit President Ford, the complainants "have not shown that the licensee in deciding to air them, considered anything other than their newsworthiness." Citizens for Reagan, 58 F.C.C.2d 925, 36 R.R.2d 885 (1976). Does the statute's use of "bona fide" support the Commission's decision to leave the decision in the first instance with the licensee? If a program is exempt, that status is not lost simply because its timing may help one candidate more than another. The day before the Iowa caucus vote in 1980, President Carter was the guest on NBC's "Meet the Press," a program normally exempt under (a)(2) as a bona fide news interview program. One of his opponents argued that the program lost its exemption because of the impact just before the critical first voting of the 1980 primary process.

The FCC rejected the complaint. So long as the format remained the same and was controlled by the broadcaster, and the choice of guest was based on newsworthiness, the FCC would not intervene. The spirit of the *Aspen* decision was to leave judgments of newsworthiness to the professionals. In this case, because there was no showing that the incumbent's appearance would not be newsworthy, the timing was not controlling.

An ABC special entitled "Who is Ross Perot?," aired before Perot declared his presidential candidacy in 1992, was held to be a bona fide news interview exempt from the equal opportunities requirement. See Fulani v. Federal Communications Commission, 49 F.3d 904, 23 Med. L.Rptr. 1813 (2d Cir.1995). An independent candidate, Lenora Fulani, pointed out that although ABC characterized the program as part of its "Nightline" series, the special did not use that name, the regular host did not appear, and the program ran 70 minutes longer than the usual Nightline time period. Nevertheless, the court deferred to "the FCC's rational and reasonable finding" that the show met the requirements for exemption. The broadcast furthered Congress's goal of providing the public with full coverage of political news events, the court said.

c. *Nonpolitical Appearances*

For many years the Commission defined "use" as "any positive appearance by a candidate by voice or picture." Thus, in United Way of America, 35 R.R.2d 137 (F.C.C.1975), which was decided at about the same time as the Aspen–CBS petitions, the Commission, 4–3, adhered to its earlier rulings that an appearance by candidate Ford opening an annual charity fund drive came within § 315. Similarly, the Commission consistently held that appearances by television personalities or film stars after they had announced their candidacy for office constituted a "use" under § 315. In Adrien Weiss, 58 F.C.C.2d 342, 36 R.R.2d 292 (1976), the Broadcast Bureau ruled that the showing of old Ronald Reagan films on television would require the offering of equal opportunities to other Republican presidential aspirants. The Bureau relied heavily on the claim that nonpolitical uses can be very effective. The Commission refused to review the Bureau's decision, with two Commissioners concurring separately and two dissenting. These four all thought that common sense dictated exempting movies made before Reagan actively entered politics, but the two concurring Commissioners thought that any change should be made by Congress.

In 1992, as part of an extensive review of its political broadcasting rules, the Commission narrowed its definition to "non-exempt candidate appearances that are controlled, approved, or sponsored by the candidate (or the candidate's authorized committee) after the candidate becomes legally qualified." This effectively overruled *Adrien Weiss* but not *United Way of America*. Codification of the Commission's Political Programming Policies, 7 F.C.C.Rcd. 4611, 70 R.R.2d 1331 (1992).

However, in 1994 the FCC concluded that there might not have been sufficient evidence to support the narrowing of the definition of "use," and returned to its prior definition: "any 'positive' appearance of a candidate by voice or appearance." Political Programming Policies (Definition of "Use"), 9 F.C.C.Rcd. 651, 74 R.R.2d 611 (1994).

In Pat Paulsen, 33 F.C.C.2d 297, affirmed 33 F.C.C.2d 835, 23 R.R.2d 861 (1972), affirmed 491 F.2d 887, 29 R.R.2d 854 (9th Cir.1974), the Commission rejected a comedian's argument that applying § 315 would deprive him of due process and equal protection by forcing him to give up his livelihood in order to run for public office. Their interpretation was held permissible "to achieve the important and legitimate objectives of encouraging political discussion and preventing unfair and unequal use of the broadcast media."

In 1985 a California television reporter raised similar objections to § 315 as it applied to him. He also argued that § 315 violated the First Amendment. In the alternative he asked that the Commission rule that appearing on the air as a journalist would not trigger § 315. The Commission denied his requests. William H. Branch, 101 F.C.C.2d 901 (1985).

On appeal, the court relied heavily on *Kennedy I* in affirming the Commission's actions.

BRANCH v. FEDERAL COMMUNICATIONS COMMISSION

United States Court of Appeals, District of Columbia Circuit, 1987.
824 F.2d 37, 63 R.R.2d 826, 14 Med.L.Rptr. 1465.

Certiorari denied 485 U.S. 959, 108 S.Ct. 1220, 99 L.Ed.2d 421 (1988).

Before Bork and Starr, Circuit Judges, and McGowan, Senior Circuit Judge.

Bork, Circuit Judge:

. . .

Branch initially contends that the statute's "equal time" provisions do not apply to him because the statute exempts the television appearances of a newscaster candidate from their coverage. . . . Branch reads the statutory language to mean: the "equal opportunities" requirement applies only when there is a "use" of a broadcasting station; a candidate's appearance on a bona fide newscast does not constitute such a "use"; thus Branch's appearances on KOVR's bona fide news broadcasts are not subject to the "equal opportunities" requirement. The apparent simplicity of this argument, however, is misleading.

. . .

The legislative history of the 1959 amendments conclusively establishes three critical and overlapping points. First, Congress' central concern in taking action was to overrule the Commission's *Lar Daly* decision. . . .

Second, the purpose of overruling *Lar Daly* was to restore the understanding of the law that had prevailed previously. [   ] That understanding, as we have noted, required "equal opportunities" whenever any candidate appeared on the air, unless the candidate was the subject of "a routine news broadcast." . . .

Third, Congress objected to the imposition of "equal opportunities" obligations on any station that carried news coverage of a candidate, because it deterred the broadcast media from providing the public with full coverage of political news events, and many other news events as well. [ ] To the extent that Congress may have done more than reverse *Lar Daly*, by exempting broadcast coverage of news interviews and news documentaries in addition to newscasts and on-the-spot coverage of news events, it did so to protect a station's ability to exercise broad discretion in choosing which *newsworthy events* to present to the public. [ ]

Thus Congress' intent in enacting the amended section 315 is readily discernible. "Appearance by a legally qualified candidate," which is not "deemed to be use of a broadcasting station," is coverage of the candidate that is presented to the public as news. The "appearance" of the candidate is itself expected to be the newsworthy item that activates the exemption. "By modifying all four categories [not deemed to be 'use'] with the phrase 'bona fide,' Congress plainly emphasized its reliance on newsworthiness as the basis for an exemption." [ ]

The thrust of the language is brought out further in the third and fourth specific exemptions. The "news documentary" exemption applies only "if the appearance of the candidate is incidental to *the presentation of the subject or subjects covered by the news documentary*." [ ] This passage relates the candidate's appearance to the subjects covered in the program. If the candidate's appearance has nothing to do with the subjects that are being covered as news—whether because the candidate is a regular employee on all such programs or, to take another example, because the candidate is being offered a gratuitous appearance that realistically is unrelated to the news content of the program—then the exemption does not apply. Similarly, the fourth exemption for "on-the-spot coverage" of news applies only to "coverage of bona fide news events." [ ] Here again the focus is on a news *event* that is being covered, with the candidate's appearance expected to occur as part of the event *being covered*.

When a broadcaster's employees are being sent out to cover a news story involving other persons, therefore, the "bona fide news event" is the activity engaged in by those other persons, not the work done by the employees covering the event. The work done by the broadcaster's employees is not a part of the event, for the event would occur without them and they serve only to communicate it to the public. For example, when a broadcaster's employees are sent out to cover a fire, the fire is the "bona fide news" event and the reporter does not become a part of that event merely by reporting it. There is nothing at all "newsworthy" about the work being done by the broadcaster's own employees, regardless of whether any of those employees happens also to be a candidate for public office.

. . .

Moreover, Congress' objection to *Lar Daly* was that it discouraged wide broadcast coverage of political news events by restricting a station's ability to determine which news *events* to present to the public. Congress solved this problem by exempting any on-air appearance by a candidate who is the *subject* of news coverage. It is irrelevant to that problem whether a station has broad discretion to determine which of its employees will actually present the news on the air. . . . At all times, the focus was not on preserving anyone's "right" to appear on the air, but on preserving broadcasters' ability to present to the public certain kinds of news programs and news events.

In opposition to that consistent approach, Branch asks this court to read the phrase "[a]ppearance by a legally qualified candidate on any [news program]" as exempting from the "equal opportunities" rule all on-air work done by newscaster candidates. We cannot do so. As we have already noted, such a reading would be at odds with the law before *Lar Daly*, which Congress explicitly sought to restore through the 1959 amendments. In addition, this reading would raise a station's news employees to an elevated status not shared by any of its other employees: although the work done on the air by any other employee on any other program would not be exempt, *see, e.g., [Paulsen]*, the work done on the air by news employees would be. Yet this novel division was never endorsed, or even discussed by Congress.

. . .

IV.

We have determined that section 315 does not exempt newscaster candidates from the strictures of the "equal opportunities" rule. Branch challenges the statute, as so interpreted, on several constitutional grounds. . . .

A.

Branch's first objection is that the statute extinguishes his right to seek political office. That he has such a right is undeniable, though the Constitution and the Supreme Court's cases in the area do not pinpoint the precise grounds on which it rests. [ ] But whatever its source, the right is not implicated in this case. "In approaching candidate restrictions, it is essential to examine in a realistic light the extent and nature of their impact on voters." [ ] Here that impact is slight. The "equal opportunities" rule does not extinguish anyone's right to run for office. It simply provides that certain uses of a broadcast station by a candidate entitle other candidates for the same office to equal time. That the rule will affect some candidates favorably and others unfavorably is obvious. It may cause certain candidates to receive less time on the air than if the statute did not exist. But the Supreme Court has held that no individual has any right of access to the broadcast media. [*CBS v. DNC*]

The core of Branch's challenge on this point is that the statute imposes an undue burden on his ability to run for office because he cannot, during the time he is a candidate, do his normal work of reporting news on the air for station KOVR. But nobody has ever thought that a candidate has a right to run for office and at the same time to avoid all personal sacrifice. [ ] Even if the practicalities of campaigning for office are put to one side, many people find it necessary to choose between their jobs and their candidacies. The Hatch Act requires government employees to resign from work if they wish to run for certain political offices, [ ], and involves many more intrusive restrictions as well, yet the Supreme Court has upheld it against constitutional challenge. [ ] More recently, the Court upheld a Texas law that required certain public officials to resign from office if they wished to become candidates for certain other offices. [ ]

Indeed, the burdens Branch complains of are borne by all other radio and television personalities under section 315, though the exception he seeks would apply only to newscasters. In [*Paulsen*] those burdens were upheld against essentially the same objection made here.

. . . . Under established law, *Paulsen* was correct in finding the burdens imposed by section 315 justifiable as "both reasonable and necessary to achieve the important and legitimate objectives of encouraging political discussion and preventing unfair and unequal use of the broadcast media." *Id.* at 892.

B.

Branch's second constitutional objection to section 315 is that the "equal opportunities" rule violates the first amendment. He cites [*Miami Herald*], where the Supreme Court unanimously struck down a Florida law that gave political candidates a right to reply to criticisms and attacks published in newspapers. . . . The "equal opportunities" rule, in Branch's view, is identical to a right-of-reply statute in its impact.

The Supreme Court has expressly held, however, that the first amendment's protections for the press do not apply as powerfully to the broadcast media. In [*Red Lion*], the Court upheld the government's authority "to put restraints on licensees in favor of others whose views should be expressed on this unique medium." *Id.* at 390. What makes the broadcast medium unique, in the Court's view, is the scarcity of frequencies. *Id.* at 389–90.

While doubts have been expressed that the scarcity rationale is adequate to support differing degrees of first amendment protection for the print and electronic media, *see e.g.*, [*TRAC*]; [*Meredith*], it remains true nonetheless, that Branch's first amendment challenge is squarely foreclosed by *Red Lion*. . . . In the course of its opinion, the Court held that the statutory "equal opportunities" rule in section 315 and the Commission's own fairness doctrine rested on the same power to regulate "a scarce resource which the government has denied others the right to use." . . .

Nor can we adopt Branch's suggestion that this court would be justified in stepping away from *Red Lion*. The Supreme Court recently reaffirmed *Red Lion* and disavowed any intention "to reconsider our longstanding approach without some signal from Congress or the FCC that technological developments have advanced so far that some revision of the system of broadcast regulation may be required." [*League of Women Voters*] The Commission may now have sent just such a signal by issuing a report which concludes that section 315 is unconstitutional and should be abandoned. *See* [*1985 Fairness Report*]. But unless the Court itself were to overrule *Red Lion*, we remain bound by it.

C.

Branch's final constitutional challenge to section 315 is that it impermissibly limits the discretion of broadcast stations to select the particular people who will present the news on the air to the public. Branch thus attempts to press the third-party rights of broadcasters who are not parties to this case. . . .

. . .

Nonetheless, the third-party challenge Branch advances is rebutted by *Red Lion*. A burden on the ability to present a particular broadcaster on the air, which applies to all broadcasters irrespective of the content of the news they present, is a much less significant burden than rules requiring the transmission of replies to personal attacks and political editorials, which were upheld in *Red Lion*. The latter provisions apply directly to political speech, and weigh more heavily on some messages than on others, depending on the precise content of the message conveyed. In contrast, the burdens on broadcasters that Branch asserts here do not "impair the discretion of broadcasters to present their views on any issue or to carry any particular type of programming." Columbia Broadcasting System, Inc. v. Federal Communications Commission, 453 U.S. 367, 396–97 (1981). Moreover, we note again that there is no right of any particular individual to appear on television. *See, e.g.,* [*CBS v. DNC*].

The petition for review is therefore,

Denied.

[Judge Starr concurred on the ground that although he agreed with Branch's interpretation of the statute, the Congressional intent was, in his view, "insufficiently clear to overturn the Commission's contrary reading."]

d.   *Lowest Unit Rate*

In 1971, as part of legislation concerning election campaigning, Congress passed two statutes that affect broadcasting during political campaigns. One requires that candidates using broadcast facilities during the 45 days before a primary and the 60 days before a general election be charged rates not to exceed "the lowest unit charge of the

station for the same class and amount of time for the same period. . . ." At all other times, the rates charged candidates are not to
exceed "the charges made for comparable use of such station by other
users thereof." 47 U.S.C.A. § 315(b). The major difference between the
two quoted passages is that during the 45—and 60—day periods, the
candidate pays the rate that the highest-volume advertiser would pay for
that time. At other times, the candidate pays the rates charged to those
who advertise as little or as much as the candidate does.

The lowest unit rate provision has caused great confusion among
broadcasters. Most often a broadcaster will charge a candidate the lowest
commercial rate for the number of spots bought when the rule requires
giving the candidate all volume and frequency discounts offered to any
advertiser regardless of the number of spots purchased. However, this is
not necessarily the lowest overall spot rate because the rule applies only
to spots of the same class or type. Thus, a candidate buying prime time
spots does not get the benefit of non-prime-time rates. Barter and per-
inquiry spots are not applicable to the calculation of lowest unit rate.

Broadcasters are allowed to set certain conditions for political advertising—broadcast quality, prepayment, etc., but any discrimination in
the application of these conditions to different candidates is strictly
prohibited. For an example of the application of § 315(b), see Alpha
Broadcasting Corporation, 102 F.C.C.2d 18, 57 R.R.2d 469 (1984).

As the 1988 general election got underway, the Commission found it
necessary to address the application of § 315(b) to certain broadcast
sales practices. Lowest Unit Charge Requirements, 65 R.R.2d 85 (1988).
Causing the most concern were "the sale of commercial time on a
preemptible only basis and the sale of commercials on a weekly rotation
throughout dayparts rather than at a particular day and time." The
latter, often referred to as "run-of-schedule spots," are placed in whatever time slots are available after the higher-priced "fixed-time spots"
have been scheduled.

The FCC decided that preemptible spots—spots that can be
preempted by other spots for which a higher rate is paid—and run-of-
schedule spots each constitute a separate class of time for the purposes
of § 315(b). With regard to preemptible spots, included in the calculation
will be any "make good" spots that have aired in the same week as the
candidate's spots. A make good is a spot offered to an advertiser whose
original spot was preempted. Often make goods are sold at a lower rate
than the original spot.

In 1990 the Mass Media Bureau conducted an audit of 30 television
and radio stations to determine the level of compliance with the political
programming rules, particularly the lowest unit rate requirement. The
Bureau found that, "at sixteen of the twenty audited television stations
(80%), candidates paid more for broadcast time than commercial advertisers in virtually every daypart or program time period analyzed.
Indeed, candidates sometimes paid more than every commercial advertiser aired in the same dayparts. Candidates fared better on radio, paying

more than commercial advertisers at only four of the eight audited stations that sold time to candidates.''

The primary cause of the disparity was the fact that candidates tended to buy non-preemptible, fixed-time commercials. This assured that the candidates' commercials would not only run, but would do so at the exact times they wanted. In contrast, commercial advertisers tended to buy preemptible commercials. Because they were willing to risk that their commercials might be preempted if enough non-preemptible commercials were sold, they paid a lower rate. Technically, preemptible commercials are a different class of time, and thus, selling them at a lower rate is not a violation of the lowest unit rate requirement. However, the Bureau indicated a concern that candidates were not being given adequate information regarding the likelihood that a preemptible commercial would in fact be preempted and the availability of "make good" commercials in the event that preemptions did occur.

Based on its preliminary findings, the Bureau urged broadcasters to "disclose to candidates all rates and the availability of package options available to commercial advertisers. . . . This disclosure should specify all discount privileges, including every level of preemptibility, the approximate clearance potential of time purchased at current effective selling levels, and special package plans. The disclosure should also indicate the station's policies with respect to make goods and the availability of negotiating for time if that is the practice with commercial advertisers." Political Programming Audit, 68 R.R.2d 113 (M.M.Bur.1990).

The audit resulted in further questions from both candidates and broadcasters still seemingly confused over the exact requirements of the lowest unit rate provision of the Act. In *Codification of Commission's Political Programming Policies*, p. 179, *supra*, the FCC attempted to clear up this confusion. First, it imposed a full disclosure requirement with regard to advertising rates on licensees. At a minimum this disclosure must include:

> a) A description and definition of each class [of time] available to commercial advertisers which is complete enough to allow candidates to identify and understand what specific attributes differentiate each class;

> b) A complete description of the lowest unit charge and related privileges (such as priorities against preemption and make goods prior to specific deadlines) for each class of time offered to commercial advertisers;

> c) A description of the station's method of selling preemptible time based upon advertiser demand, commonly known as the "current selling level," with the stipulation that candidates will be able to purchase at these demand-generated rates in the same manner as commercial advertisers;

d) An approximation of the likelihood of preemption for each kind of preemptible time; and

e) An explanation of the station's sales practices, if any, that are based on audience delivery.

Licensees are also required to treat political candidates the same as their most-favored commercial advertiser, not only with regard to advertising rates but also to other sales practices including "make goods, preemption priorities and any other factors that enhance the value of a spot."

In addition, licensees are now permitted to create more than one class of preemptible time, as long as the classes are distinguished by some demonstrable benefit to the advertiser, e.g. different levels of protection against preemption. Similarly, licensees can now have separate non-preemptible and fixed position classes of time. (Fixed position guarantees an exact time for the spot; non-preemptible guarantees only that the spot will run sometime during a particular day or time period.) Stations may not, however, create special classes of time for candidates only.

Finally, stations that offer timely make goods to commercial advertisers for a specific class of time must offer similar make goods to political candidates. These make goods "must air before the election 'where the licensee would so treat its most-favored commercial advertiser where time is of the essence.'" Make goods must also be included in the calculation of lowest unit charge. Thus, where a make good is placed in a more valuable program or daypart, the cost of the make good must be included in the calculation of lowest unit charge for that program or daypart.

Another question raised during the 1990 elections involved jurisdiction over lowest-unit-rate disputes. Various Alabama and Georgia television stations had been sued for alleged violations of the lowest-unit-rate requirement. The cases had produced conflicting district court rulings on the question of whether the FCC has exclusive jurisdiction over lowest-unit-rate violations. The candidates had also filed complaints with the FCC.

The FCC issued a declaratory ruling preempting any state cause of action involving § 315(b). At the same time it outlined the procedures for bringing a lowest-unit-rate complaint. Complainants are required to file a short, plain statement of the claim sufficient to show that the complainant is entitled to the relief requested. The complaint must be served on the station. The station will then be given 10 days to answer. If the Media Bureau determines that a *prima facie* case has been made, the parties will be given the choice of either mediation or evaluation and disposition by the Bureau. Lowest Unit Charge Requirements (Preemption of State Jurisdiction), 6 F.C.C.Rcd. 7511, 70 R.R.2d 1 (1991). Two petitions for reconsideration were denied. 7 F.C.C.Rcd. 4123, 70 R.R.2d 1355 (1992). An appeal was dismissed on the ground that the Commission's declaratory ruling was not ripe for review. Miller v. Federal Communications Commission, 66 F.3d 1140 (11th Cir.1995).

2. REASONABLE ACCESS—SECTION 312(A)(7)

In 1971, at the same time it passed the lowest unit rate provision, Congress adopted § 312(a)(7), providing that the Commission may revoke a license:

> (7) for willful or repeated failure to allow reasonable access to or to permit purchase of reasonable amounts of time for the use of a broadcasting station by a legally qualified candidate for Federal elective office on behalf of his candidacy.

The legislative history indicates that one purpose of the overall legislation was to "give candidates for public office greater access to the media so that they may better explain their stand on the issues and thereby more fully and completely inform the voters."

It was only in 1980 that cases involving the section began to reach the courts.

The first case raised the questions of when the campaign had begun and how requests should be treated. The Carter–Mondale Committee asked each major network to sell it 30 minutes of prime time in December 1979 (just after the formal announcement that President Carter was seeking renomination), in order to show a documentary on President Carter's first term. CBS offered two five-minute segments, one of which would be in prime time. ABC indicated that it would make time available beginning in January 1980. NBC said that it was "too early in the political season for nationwide broadcast time to be made available for paid political purposes." The Committee complained to the FCC, which found the stations in violation of § 312(a)(7), by a vote of 4–3. The court of appeals affirmed.

CBS, INC. v. FEDERAL COMMUNICATIONS COMMISSION

Supreme Court of the United States, 1981.
453 U.S. 367, 101 S.Ct. 2813, 49 R.R.2d 1191, 69 L.Ed.2d 706, 7 Med.L.Rptr. 1563.

CHIEF JUSTICE BURGER delivered the opinion of the Court.

[The Court agreed with the FCC that the section had "created an affirmative, promptly enforceable right of reasonable access to the use of broadcast stations for individual candidates seeking federal elective office" rather than simply codifying prior policies that the FCC had developed under the general public interest standard. The Court relied on the specific language of the statute itself, the legislative history and what the Court found to be the FCC's consistent administrative interpretation of the language since the statute's enactment. Perhaps the "most telling evidence" of Congressional intent was the contemporaneous change in § 315 from a statement that "No obligation is imposed upon any licensee to allow the use of its station by" a candidate to the statement that no such obligation "is imposed under this subsection [§ 315(a)]."]

III

A

Although Congress provided in § 312(a)(7) for greater use of broadcasting stations by federal candidates, it did not give guidance on how the Commission should implement the statute's access requirement. Essentially, Congress adopted a "rule of reason" and charged the Commission with its enforcement. . . . The Commission has issued some general interpretative statements, but its standards implementing § 312(a)(7) have evolved principally on a case-by-case basis and are not embodied in formalized rules. . . .

Broadcasters are free to deny the sale of air time prior to the commencement of a campaign, but once a campaign has begun, they must give reasonable and good faith attention to access requests from "legally qualified" candidates for federal elective office. Such requests must be considered on an individualized basis, and broadcasters are required to tailor their responses to accommodate, as much as reasonably possible, a candidate's stated purposes in seeking air time. In responding to access requests, however, broadcasters may also give weight to such factors as the amount of time previously sold to the candidate, the disruptive impact on regular programming, and the likelihood of requests for time by rival candidates under the equal opportunities provision of § 315(a). These considerations may not be invoked as pretexts for denying access; to justify a negative response, broadcasters must cite a realistic danger of substantial program disruption—perhaps caused by insufficient notice to allow adjustments in the schedule—or of an excessive number of equal time requests. Further, in order to facilitate review by the Commission, broadcasters must explain their reasons for refusing time or making a more limited counteroffer. If broadcasters take the appropriate factors into account and act reasonably and in good faith, their decisions will be entitled to deference even if the Commission's analysis would have differed in the first instance. But if broadcasters adopt "across-the-board policies" and do not attempt to respond to the individualized situation of a particular candidate, the Commission is not compelled to sustain their denial of access. [ ] Petitioners argue that certain of these standards are contrary to the statutory objectives of § 312(a)(7).

(1)

The Commission has concluded that, as a threshold matter, it will independently determine whether a campaign has begun and the obligations imposed by § 312(a)(7) have attached. [ ] Petitioners assert that, in undertaking such a task, the Commission becomes improperly involved in the electoral process and seriously impairs broadcaster discretion.

However, petitioners fail to recognize that the Commission does not set the starting date for a campaign. Rather, on review of a complaint alleging denial of "reasonable access," it examines objective evidence to find whether the campaign has already commenced, "taking into account the position of the candidate *and the networks* as well as other factors." . . . Such a decision is not, and cannot be, purely one of editorial judgment.

. . .

(2)

Petitioners also challenge the Commission's requirement that broadcasters evaluate and respond to access requests on an individualized basis. In petitioners' view, the agency has attached inordinate significance to candidates' needs, thereby precluding fair assessment of broadcasters' concerns and prohibiting the adoption of uniform policies regarding requests for access.

While admonishing broadcasters not to " 'second guess' the 'political' wisdom or . . . effectiveness" of the particular format sought by a candidate, the Commission has clearly acknowledged that "the candidate's . . . request is by no means conclusive of the question of how much time, if any, is appropriate. Other . . . factors, such as the disruption or displacement of regular programming (particularly as affected by a reasonable probability of requests by other candidates), must be considered in the balance." [ ] Thus, the Commission mandates careful consideration of, not blind assent to, candidates' desires for air time.

Petitioners are correct that the Commission's standards proscribe blanket rules concerning access; each request must be examined on its own merits. While the adoption of uniform policies might well prove more convenient for broadcasters, such an approach would allow personal campaign strategies and the exigencies of the political process to be ignored. A broadcaster's "evenhanded" response of granting only time spots of a fixed duration to candidates may be "unreasonable" where a particular candidate desires less time for an advertisement or a longer format to discuss substantive issues. . . . § 312(a)(7) assures a right of reasonable access to *individual* candidates for federal elective office, and the Commission's requirement that their requests be considered on an *individualized* basis is consistent with that guarantee.

[The Court concluded that the Commission's actions were a "reasoned attempt to effectuate the statute's access requirement, giving broadcasters room to exercise their discretion but demanding that they act in good faith." These ground rules were sufficiently clear in late 1979 to permit the FCC to rule that the networks had violated the statute by failing to grant "reasonable access."]

IV

Finally, petitioners assert that § 312(a)(7) as implemented by the Commission violates the First Amendment rights of broadcasters by unduly circumscribing their editorial discretion. . . .

. . .

The First Amendment interests of candidates and voters, as well as broadcasters, are implicated by § 312(a)(7). We have recognized that "it is of particular importance that candidates have the . . . opportunity to make their views known so that the electorate may intelligently evaluate the candidates' personal qualities and their positions on vital public issues before choosing among them on election day." [Buckley v. Valeo]. [ ] Indeed, "speech concerning public affairs is . . . the essence of self-government." [Garrison v. Louisiana] The First Amendment "has its fullest and most urgent application precisely to the conduct of campaigns for public office." [Monitor Patriot Co. v. Roy] Section 312(a)(7) thus makes a significant contribution to freedom of expression by enhancing the ability of candidates to present, and the public to receive, information necessary for the effective operation of the democratic process.

Petitioners are correct that the Court has never approved a *general* right of access to the media. [ ] Nor do we do so today. Section 312(a)(7) creates a *limited* right to "reasonable" access that pertains only to legally qualified federal candidates and may be invoked by them only for the purpose of advancing their candidacies once a campaign has commenced. The Commission has stated that, in enforcing the statute, it will "provide leeway to broadcasters and not merely attempt *de novo* to determine the reasonableness of their judgments. . . ." If broadcasters have considered the relevant factors in good faith, the Commission will uphold their decisions. See 629 F.2d, at 25. Further, § 312(a)(7) does not impair the discretion of broadcasters to present their views on any issue or to carry any particular type of programming.

Section 312(a)(7) represents an effort by Congress to assure that an important resource—the airwaves—will be used in the public interest. We hold that the statutory right of access, as defined by the Commission and applied in these cases, properly balances the First Amendment rights of federal candidates, the public, and broadcasters.

The judgment of the Court of Appeals is

Affirmed.

[Justice White, joined by Justices Rehnquist and Stevens, dissented on the grounds that the decision negated "the long-standing statutory policy of deferring to editorial judgments that are not destructive of the goals of the Act." Justice White also argued that the Commission had misinterpreted § 312(a)(7). His reading of the legislative history led him to believe that Congress intended only "to codify what it conceived to be the pre-existing duty of the broadcasters to serve the public interest by presenting political broadcasts."]

JUSTICE STEVENS, dissenting.

. . . The approach the Federal Communications Commission has taken in this case, now adopted by the Court, creates an impermissible risk that the Commission's evaluation of a given refusal by a licensee will be biased—or will appear to be biased—by the character of the office

held by the candidate making the request.* Indeed, anyone who listened
to the campaign rhetoric that was broadcast in 1980 must wonder how
an impartial administrator could conclude that any presidential candidate was denied "reasonable access" to the electronic media. That
wonderment is not dispelled by anything said in the opinions for the
majority of the Commission in this case.

Notes and Questions

1. The relationship between § 312(a)(7) and § 315 was central to
Kennedy for President Committee v. Federal Communications Commission, 636 F.2d 417, 47 R.R.2d 1521, 6 Med.L.Rptr. 1722
(D.C.Cir.1980)(*Kennedy II*). On March 14, 1980, President Carter made a
30–minute speech in the afternoon and held a press conference from 9 to
9:30 p.m. The three major commercial networks carried both programs
live, except that ABC delayed the press conference for three hours.
Senator Kennedy charged that these programs saturated the public with
the President's views on the economy only four days before the Illinois
primary. He asked for free time to reply under § 312(a)(7). The networks denied the request, the Commission refused to order that time be
granted, and the court affirmed.

The court began by noting that Congress, in 1971, enacted
§ 312(a)(7) and § 315(b)(1), requiring lowest charges to candidates using
broadcast facilities, because Congress was concerned about the rising
cost of candidates' televised appearances:

> It was believed that the informational and educational aspects of
> political broadcasting would be greatly enhanced by ensuring that
> more time would be made available to candidates at lower rates.
> This expectably would encourage less dependence on thirty-to sixty-
> second "spots"—necessarily little more than slogans—in favor of
> longer, more illuminating presentations; it would also enable more
> candidates to afford the television appearances so instrumental to
> present-day electioneering.

The court concluded that the "most straightforward reading" of
§ 312(a)(7) "is that broadcasters may fulfill their obligation thereunder
either by allotting free time to a candidate *or* by selling the candidate
time at the rates prescribed by Section 315(b)." Considering the legislative history, the FCC's consistent administrative interpretations and the
apparent statutory scheme of the various provisions, the court concluded
that § 312(a)(7), although seeking to assure federal candidates access to
broadcasting, did not "confer the privilege of using the broadcaster's

---

* The possibility that Commission decisions under § 312(a)(7) may appear to be
biased is well illustrated by this case. In its
initial decision and its decision on the networks' petitions for reconsideration, the
Commission voted 4–3 in favor of the Carter–Mondale Presidential Committee. [   ]

In both instances, the four Democratic
Commissioners concluded that the networks had violated the statute by denying
the Committee's request for access; the
three Republican Commissioners disagreed.
[   ]

facilities without charge." The choice of giving or selling time is for the broadcaster:

> Should Section 312(a)(7) be construed as automatically entitling a candidate to responsive broadcast access whenever and for whatever reason his opponent has appeared on the air, Section 315(a)'s exemptions would soon become meaningless. Statutes are to be interpreted, if possible, to give operation to all of their parts, and to maintain them in harmonious working relationship.

Because Kennedy never claimed that he had not been given an opportunity to buy time, he could not invoke § 312(a)(7). Nor had he sought relief under § 315.

2. In 1981 the National Conservative Political Action Committee (NCPAC) petitioned the Commission for a ruling that an independent political action committee (PAC) had a right of reasonable access similar to that granted candidates for federal office by § 312(a)(7). The Broadcast Bureau rejected NCPAC's request, finding nothing in either the language of § 312(a)(7) or its legislative history that would support a right of access for anyone other than a candidate for federal office. The Commission upheld the Bureau's action, citing *CBS*, p. 91, *supra*. National Conservative Political Action Committee (NCPAC), 89 F.C.C.2d 626, 51 R.R.2d 233 (1982).

3. After *CBS*, the general rule for federal candidates is that broadcasters cannot establish across-the-board policies, but rather must consider the particular needs of each individual candidate. There is one exception to that, however. Stations may establish a policy of not selling any political advertisements during news programming. Commission Policy in Enforcing Section 312(a)(7), 68 F.C.C.2d 1079, 43 R.R.2d 1029 (1978). *In Codification of the Commission's Political Programming Policies*, p. 179, *supra*, the FCC decided to continue this policy. In addition, the Commission will now allow stations to treat news adjacencies (commercials aired immediately before or after a newscast) as a separate class of time for purposes of calculating lowest unit charge, p. 184, *supra*.

4. The National Association of Broadcasters filed a request for a declaratory ruling that would limit § 312(a)(7) to those increments of program time that "the station ordinarily sells to commercial advertisers or which it ordinarily programs." Opponents to the request argued that this would be contrary to the FCC policy requiring licensees to give individual consideration to each request. The Commission decided that broadcasters can only be required to supply the same lengths of program time that they have sold to a commercial advertiser or programmed within the previous year. National Association of Broadcasters, 9 F.C.C.Rcd. 5778, 76 R.R.2d 200 (1994). However, on reconsideration, the Commission reversed itself, holding that broadcasters must at least consider requests for unusual lengths of time. People for the American Way, 17 C.R. 186 (1999).

5. During the 1996 campaign, Ross Perot sought to purchase eight half-hour, prime-time slots from each of the four major networks, as well as a

show during prime-time the night before the election. Although each of the networks sold him some of the time requested, none of them granted the full request. Each network justified its action by noting the disruption to its schedule and the potential for other requests. The Commission denied Perot's § 312(a)(7) complaint, holding that the networks had given individual consideration to Perot's needs and balanced them against legitimate competing concerns. *Ross Perot*, p. 178, *supra*.

B. THE FAIRNESS DOCTRINE

1. IN GENERAL

Beginning in Chapter III with *Red Lion*, and at several points during the licensing discussion, we have had occasion to note the existence of, and to consider aspects of, the Commission-created fairness doctrine. As we shall discuss later in this chapter the Commission repealed the doctrine, at least in part, in 1987. However, because the doctrine was such a central part of the broadcast regulatory scheme for so many years, it is worth examining.

The Commission was concerned with fairness and the exposure of varying views since its earliest days. Indeed, the Radio Commission in 1928 indicated as much in a discussion of the implications of the limited spectrum. It observed that there was not room "for every school of thought, religious, political, social, and economic, each to have its separate broadcasting station, its mouthpiece in the ether." Such ideas "must find their way into the market of ideas by the existing public-service stations, and if they are of sufficient importance to the listening public, the microphone will undoubtedly be available. If it is not, a well-founded complaint will receive the careful consideration of the commission in its future action with reference to the station complained of." Great Lakes Broadcasting Co., 3 F.R.C.Ann.Rep. 32 (1929), modified on other grounds 37 F.2d 993 (D.C.Cir.1930), certiorari dismissed 281 U.S. 706 (1930).

The doctrine evolved through case law until it became the subject of a major report in 1949. The doctrine had two separate parts. One part required the broadcaster to air issues that "are so critical or of such great public importance that it would be unreasonable for a licensee to ignore them completely." Much more attention has been paid to the second part of the doctrine—that if broadcasters covered "controversial issues of public importance" they had to take steps to assure that important contrasting views are also presented. These views could be presented by the licensees themselves or by speakers chosen by the licensees.

In 1959, when § 315 was amended, p. 171, *supra*, many people interpreted the phrase, "nothing in the foregoing sentence shall be construed as relieving broadcasters . . . from the obligation under this chapter to operate in the public interest and to afford reasonable opportunity for the discussion of conflicting views on issues of public importance" as codifying the fairness doctrine in the Communications Act. This interpretation was the majority view until 1986, when the court of appeals held that the fairness doctrine was not codified in the Communications Act. *TRAC*, p. 98, *supra*. We will discuss the substance of this case—an appeal of the Commission's refusal to apply the fairness doctrine, as well as § 315 and § 312(a)(7), to teletext—in Chapter X.

a.   *The 1974 Fairness Report*

In 1974 the Commission conducted a major review of the fairness doctrine, and then issued a report explaining the operation of the doctrine. Fairness Report of 1974, 48 F.C.C.2d 1, 30 R.R.2d 1261 (1974), reconsideration 58 F.C.C.2d 691, 36 R.R.2d 1021 (1976). The Commission first restated its commitment to the goal of "uninhibited, robust, wide open" debate on public issues and the need to recognize that achievement of this goal must be compatible with the public interest in "the larger and more effective use of radio" § 303(g). This included the fact that "ours is a commercially-based broadcast system" and that the Commission's policies "should be consistent with the maintenance and growth of that system." The Commission then quoted a critical passage from its Report on Editorializing, 13 F.C.C. 1246, 1249 (1949), in which the fairness doctrine was formally announced:

> It is axiomatic that one of the most vital questions of mass communication in a democracy is the development of an informed public opinion through the public dissemination of news and ideas concerning the vital public issues of the day. . . . The Commission has consequently recognized the necessity for licensees to devote a reasonable percentage of their broadcast time to the presentation of news and programs devoted to the consideration and discussion of public issues of interest in the community served by the particular station. And we have recognized, with respect to such programs, the paramount right of the public in a free society to be informed and to have presented to it for acceptance or rejection the different attitudes and viewpoints concerning these vital and often controversial issues which are held by the various groups which make up the community. It is this right of the public to be informed, rather than any right on the part of the Government, any broadcast licensee or any individual member of the public to broadcast his own particular views on any matter, which is the foundation stone of the American system of broadcasting.

The *1974 Fairness Report* stressed that two basic duties were involved: "(1) the broadcaster must devote a reasonable percentage of time to coverage of public issues; and (2) his coverage of these issues must be fair in the sense that it provides an opportunity for the presentation of contrasting points of view." The Commission also noted that in 1970 it had described the two parts of the fairness doctrine "as the single most important requirement of operation in the public interest—the *sine qua non* for grant of a renewal of license." The Commission denied that imposition of these two duties could be inhibiting:

18.　In evaluating the possible inhibitory effect of the fairness doctrine, it is appropriate to consider the specifics of the doctrine and the procedures employed by the Commission in implementing it. When a licensee presents one side of a controversial issue, he is not required to provide a forum for opposing views on that same program or series of programs. He is simply expected to make provision for the opposing views in his *overall programming.* Further, there is no requirement that any precisely equal balance of views be achieved, and all matters concerning the particular opposing views to be presented and the appropriate spokesmen and format for their presentation are left to the licensee's discretion subject only to a standard of reasonableness and good faith.

19.　As a matter of general procedure, we do not monitor broadcasts for possible violations, but act on the basis of complaints received from interested citizens. These complaints are not forwarded to the licensee for his comments unless they present *prima facie* evidence of a violation. Allen C. Phelps, 21 F.C.C.2d 12 (1969). Thus, broadcasters are not burdened with the task of answering idle or capricious complaints. By way of illustration, the Commission received some 2,400 fairness complaints in fiscal 1973, only 94 of which were forwarded to licensees for their comments.

20.　While there may be occasional exceptions, we find it difficult to believe that these policies add significantly to the overall administrative burdens involved in operating a broadcast station. . . . The Supreme Court has made it clear and it should be reemphasized here that "if present licensees should suddenly prove timorous, the Commission is not powerless to insist that they give adequate and fair attention to public issues." Red Lion Broadcasting Co. v. FCC, 395 U.S. at 393.

As to the first duty imposed, the Commission noted:

We have, in the past, indicated that some issues are so critical or of such great public importance that it would be unreasonable for a licensee to ignore them completely. [　] But such statements on our part are the rare exception, not the rule, and we have no intention of becoming involved in the selection of issues to be discussed, nor do we expect a broadcaster to cover each and every important issue which may arise in his community.

26.　We wish to emphasize that the responsibility for the selection of program material is that of the individual licensee. That responsibility "can neither be delegated by the licensee to any network or other person or group, or be unduly fettered by contractual arrangements restricting the licensee in his free exercise of his independent judgments." Report on Editorializing, 13 FCC at 1248. We believe that stations, in carrying out this responsibility, should be alert to the opportunity to complement network offerings with local programming on these issues, or with syndicated programming.

The Commission then turned to the second, and more frequently litigated, aspect of the fairness doctrine. With regard to the question of what issues would trigger fairness doctrine obligations, the Commission stated that it would "rely heavily on the reasonable, good faith, judgments of our licensees" as to what was a "controversial issue of public importance." But licensees were told that the term did not include everything that was "newsworthy":

> The principal test of public importance, however, is . . . a subjective evaluation of the impact that the issue is likely to have on the community at large. If the issue involves a social or political choice, the licensee might well ask himself whether the outcome of that choice will have a significant impact on society or its institutions. It appears to us that these judgments can be made only on a case-by-case basis.
>
> 31. The question of whether an issue is "controversial" may be determined in a somewhat more objective manner. Here, it is highly relevant to measure the degree of attention paid to an issue by government officials, community leaders, and the media. The licensee should be able to tell, with a reasonable degree of objectivity, whether an issue is the subject of vigorous debate with substantial elements of the community in opposition to one another.

The FCC also refused to issue strict guidelines governing what would be deemed a "reasonable opportunity for contrasting points of view." Although licensees had to "make reasonable allowance[s] for presentations by genuine partisans who actually believe in what they are saying . . . there [were] a variety of spokesmen and formats which could reasonably be deemed to be appropriate."

Finally, the Commission stated that there were no mathematical formulas to be used in determining the reasonableness of the opportunities for contrasting points of view. "Indeed, we have long felt that the basic goal of creating an informed citizenry would be frustrated if for every controversial item or presentation on a newscast or other broadcast the licensee had to offer equal time to the other side. . . . Similarly, we do not believe that it would be appropriate for the Commission to establish any other mathematical ratio, such as 3 to 1 or 4 to 1, to be applied in all cases. We believe that such an approach is much too mechanical in nature and that in many cases our preconceived ratios would prove to be far from reasonable. In the case of a 10-second personal attack [explained below], for example, fairness may dictate that more time be afforded to answer the attack than was given the attack itself." See Public Media Center v. Federal Communications Commission, 587 F.2d 1322, 4 Med.L.Rptr. 1634 (D.C.Cir.1978) (considering time of day messages aired, how many new messages were aired as opposed to repetitions of earlier ones, lengths of messages, and comparison of ratios of total minutes on each side).

An important part of the second prong came from Cullman Broadcasting Co., 40 F.C.C.2d 576 (1963), holding that in situations under the doctrine broadcasters had to provide the forum for the expression of the contrasting views at their own expense if paid sponsorship could not be found.

Another portion addressed the question of fairness in news broadcasts. Based on the public interest standard, the Commission has a policy against "rigging, staging, or distorting" the news. Such a practice "is a most heinous act against the public interest—indeed, there is no act more harmful to the public's ability to handle its affairs." Hunger in America, 20 F.C.C.2d 143, 17 R.R.2d 674 (1969) (infant on camera said to be suffering from malnutrition but in fact suffered from another ailment). See also WBBM–TV, 18 F.C.C.2d 214 (1969) (allegations that pot party was staged for camera crew).

In Galloway v. Federal Communications Commission, 778 F.2d 16, 12 Med.L.Rptr. 1443 (D.C.Cir.1985), Dr. Galloway was identified on a "60 Minutes" program as being involved in a fraudulent accident insurance scheme. His effort to obtain administrative sanctions against CBS failed at the FCC on appeal. The Commission decided that it should ask only whether there had been "the deliberate portrayal of a 'significant event' which did not in fact occur but rather is 'acted out' at the behest of news personnel."

As the court understood the Commission, it was necessary that the "distortion or staging be deliberately intended to slant or mislead. It is not enough to dispute the accuracy of a news report." The complainant needs "extrinsic evidence" such as "written or oral instructions from station management, outtakes, or evidence of bribery." In addition, the "distortion must involve a significant event and not merely a minor or incidental aspect of the news report." The real criterion is whether the public is being "deceived about a matter of significance."

In one part, a person being asked whether it was possible to make a lot of money with this scheme answered in a qualified manner and concluded that "It's simply not worth it." On the actual program he was shown answering simply "yes." The "yes" had been taken from the person's answer to a completely different question. The court thought the decision not to include the subject's cautionary remarks was more a "matter of editorial discretion . . . than an act of deliberate distortion." Although the "substitution of an answer to another question may fairly be considered distortion *per se,* when it does affect the 'basic accuracy' of the answer it is not 'significant' enough to violate FCC rules."

When the complaint argued that the threshold requirements for a distortion complaint were virtually unattainable, the court replied that perhaps "the broad public interest standard would justify a stricter policy, but neither the language nor the legislative history of the statute demand it. Congress has shown concern with the danger of distortion in television news, but it has never enacted a more particular regulation of the practice. This court will not presume to do so."

In Gen. William Westmoreland's libel suit against CBS, the producer, in violation of internal CBS guidelines, gave only friendly interviewees some idea in advance of the questions they would be asked. One friendly interviewee was interviewed a second time so that he could "come across" better. The producer also may have photographed friendly witnesses from a distance, giving them a "halo" effect, while zooming "in tight" on unfriendly witnesses so that their images looked more like mug shots and they could be seen perspiring. Should government be involved in investigating these practices or in imposing sanctions for their occurrence?

The court of appeals affirmed the 1974 Fairness Report on all but two minor issues in National Citizens Committee for Broadcasting v. Federal Communications Commission, 567 F.2d 1095 (D.C.Cir.1977), certiorari denied 436 U.S. 926.

b.   *The Affirmative Duty to Raise Issues*

Although, the Commission always referred to the fairness doctrine as having two parts, virtually all the litigation and discussion have involved the second part: the requirement that a licensee who has presented one side of a controversial issue of public importance must present contrasting views.

In 1976, for the first time, the Commission applied the first part. A Congresswoman sent an 11–minute tape opposing strip mining to West Virginia radio stations to counter a presentation in favor of strip mining that had been distributed to many stations by the U.S. Chamber of Commerce. One station, WHAR, refused to play the tape because it had not presented the first program. Indeed, it had presented nothing on the issue except items on regular newscasts taken from the AP news service. Several persons and groups complained to the Commission contending that in this part of West Virginia at this time the question of strip mining was of primary importance. In its renewal application, WHAR had cited "development of new industry" and "air and water pollution" as issues of great concern to its listeners. In addition, bills on the subject were pending in Congress at the time, and local newspapers were extensively discussing the question. (Presentation of a five-minute tape by an outspoken foe of strip mining was held not to be relevant because he did not discuss the economic or ecological aspects of strip mining or the pending legislation.)

The Commission asserted that although a violation of the first part "would be an exceptional situation and would not counter our intention to stay out of decisions concerning the selection of specific programming matter," this was such a case and demonstrated an "unreasonable exercise" of discretion. The Commission quoted the passage from *Red Lion* that "if the present licensees should suddenly prove timorous, the Commission is not powerless to insist that they give adequate and fair attention to public issues." The lack of any prior request to program on this subject was irrelevant because "it is the station's obligation to make

an affirmative effort to program on issues of concern to its community."
The role of the AP news items was minimal because it was not even clear
which ones were aired. "Where, as in the present case, an issue has
significant and possibly unique impact on the licensee's service area, it
will not be sufficient for the licensee as an indication of compliance with
the fairness doctrine to show that it may have broadcast an unknown
amount of news touching on a general topic related to the issue cited in a
complaint." The station was ordered to tell the Commission within 20
days how it intended to meet its fairness obligations. Rep. Patsy Mink,
59 F.C.C.2d 987, 37 R.R.2d 744 (1976).

What is the difference between saying (1) a station has an obligation
to present programs on the need for good dental hygiene, even though
the subject may not be controversial, and (2) a station must present
programs on a controversial issue in the community? Are both covered
by the fairness doctrine?

What is the justification for requiring each station in a community
to present a range of views on controversial issues of public importance?
Why is it not enough if the spectrum as a whole provides contrasting
viewpoints? Is there more or less reason to require a station to raise
important subjects when other stations in the community are doing so?
Thus, in the strip mining case, should it matter that other broadcasters
are devoting extensive coverage to the subject? What has this obligation
to do with "fairness"?

c. *Entertainment Programming*

Occasionally entertainment programming raised problems under the
fairness doctrine. One typical example would be a story in which a
character considers whether to seek an abortion. See Diocesan Union of
Holy Name Societies, 41 F.C.C.2d 297, 29 R.R.2d 545 (1973)(involving a
pro-abortion theme). Must contrasting views be presented? If so, must it
be by other entertainment programming or will an interview program
suffice? What about implicit presentations, such as a series featuring a
happily married couple of different faiths? Must the licensee provide for
contrasting views against interfaith marriages?

d. *Commercials*

In the 1960s the Commission decided that advertisements for cigarettes required stations to present some programming on the dangers of
smoking. This ruling was upheld in Banzhaf v. Federal Communications
Commission, 405 F.2d 1082, 14 R.R.2d 2061, 1 Med.L.Rptr. 2037
(D.C.Cir.1968), certiorari denied 396 U.S. 842 (1969). Although the
licensee could decide how to meet this requirement, most licensees
presented material that had been prepared by the American Cancer
Society and similar organizations.

The Commission attempted to treat the cigarette case as unique.
Thus, when opponents of high-powered automobiles wanted the FCC to

require licensees to present contrasting views on the value of such cars, the FCC refused. On appeal, the court of appeals could not distinguish the cigarette situation from the high-powered car situation and ordered the FCC to be consistent. Friends of the Earth v. Federal Communications Commission, 449 F.2d 1164, 22 R.R.2d 2145 (D.C.Cir.1971).

The Commission, in an omitted portion of its *1974 Fairness Report*, rethought the question of applying the fairness doctrine to commercials. It finally decided to divide commercials into those that simply try to sell products and those that present a "meaningful statement which obviously addresses, and advocates a point of view on, a controversial issue of public importance." The latter, also called "editorial" or "advocacy" advertisements, gave rise to obligations under the fairness doctrine. If an advertisement was false or misleading, it might give rise to some action by the Federal Trade Commission or by competitors, but the fairness doctrine was not the appropriate way to handle commercials that do not address public issues.

This position was quickly challenged in the courts in a case involving a commercial for snowmobiles. Environmental groups complained that the commercials showed only one side of the controversial issue of the desirability of snowmobiles. The FCC rejected the complaint on the ground that, although the environmental effects of snowmobiles might involve a controversial issue of public importance, the commercials themselves were not devoted to an obvious or meaningful discussion of that issue.

The court of appeals affirmed. Public Interest Research Group v. Federal Communications Commission, 522 F.2d 1060, 34 R.R.2d 1375 (1st Cir.1975), certiorari denied 424 U.S. 965 (1976). The appellants argued that the FCC had no authority to retreat from its earlier rulings that selling commercials might invoke the fairness doctrine. The court disagreed. "In the absence of statutory or constitutional barriers, an agency may abandon earlier precedents and frame new policies." Congress had not frozen the fairness doctrine in any particular form. Nor was there any reason to require the FCC to apply the doctrine to all commercials or to none.

Finally, the appellants argued that the First Amendment itself required that the fairness doctrine be rigorously enforced so that the airwaves would be true public forums for the presentation of divergent views. The court rejected this argument. Although the *Red Lion* approach might be furthered by extending the fairness doctrine to all advertising, the court did "not view that question, in the short and long run, as so free from doubt that courts should impose an inflexible response as a matter of constitutional law. We believe that the first amendment permitted the Commission not only to experiment with full-scale application of the fairness doctrine to advertising but also to retreat from its experiment when it determined from experience that the extension was unworkable."

After the *Banzhaf* decision, Congress moved into the picture. In 1969 it adopted 15 U.S.C.A. § 1335: "After January 1, 1971, it shall be unlawful to advertise cigarettes on any medium of electronic communication subject to the jurisdiction of the Federal Communications Commission."

The statute was challenged by broadcasters—but not by cigarette manufacturers. It was upheld by a three-judge court in Capital Broadcasting Co. v. Mitchell, 333 F.Supp. 582 (D.D.C.1971), affirmed without opinion 405 U.S. 1000 (1972). The dissenting opinion in the lower court suggested that the cigarette manufacturers were not at all unhappy to be ordered to stop advertising on radio and television because it had become unprofitable.

The court rejected the argument that this amounted to censorship in violation of § 326 because licensees were still free to present pro-smoking messages—except to the extent that Congress had forbidden commercial messages. The Commission was leaving that decision to the licensees. Moreover, some aspects of anti-smoking messages might still be found to invoke the fairness doctrine—but health danger was not one of them. Also, it was permissible to consider at renewal time whether a licensee carried programs on the dangers of smoking—not because it was a controversial issue, but because one aspect of meeting the public interest is to warn about dangers to health and safety, even if they are obvious and non-controversial. What might the Commission do at renewal time if it found a licensee had presented several debates on cigarette smoking in which half the speakers argued that there was no health hazard in smoking? Is there a tension between saying that licensees are free to program pro-smoking material if they wish and that they will be judged at renewal time on how they have programmed on matters of health and safety?

2. Personal Attack Rules

As we saw in *Red Lion,* p. 78, *supra,* the personal attack part of the general fairness doctrine was crystallized into a rule, 47 C.F.R. § 73.123:

(a) When, during the presentation of views on a controversial issue of public importance, an attack is made upon the honesty, character, integrity or like personal qualities of an identified person or group, the licensee shall, within a reasonable time and in no event later than 1 week after the attack, transmit to the person or group attacked (1) notification of the date, time and identification of the broadcast; (2) a script or tape (or an accurate summary if a script or tape is not available) of the attack; and (3) an offer of a reasonable opportunity to respond over the licensee's facilities.

(b) The provisions of paragraph (a) of this section shall not be applicable (1) to attacks on foreign groups or foreign public figures; (2) to personal attacks which are made by legally qualified candidates, their authorized spokesmen, or those associated with them in the campaign, on other such candidates, their authorized spokes-men, or persons associated with the candidates in the campaign; and (3) to bona fide newscasts, bona fide news interviews, and on-the-spot coverage of a bona fide news event (including commentary or analysis contained in the foregoing programs, but the provisions of paragraph (a) of this section shall be applicable to editorials of the licensee).

The first point to note is that the episode had to occur "during the presentation of views on a controversial issue of public importance." This limitation meant that personal attacks unrelated to such a discussion did not invoke the rule—and presumably were left exclusively to defamation suits. Why was this distinction drawn?

Sometimes it was difficult to determine what constitutes "during the presentation of views on a controversial issue of public importance." In Straus Communications, Inc. v. Federal Communications Commission, 530 F.2d 1001, 35 R.R.2d 1649 (D.C.Cir.1976), a licensee's argument that time for reply was not justified because the attack did not take place during such a discussion was rejected by the Commission. On appeal, the court ruled that the Commission had used the wrong standard when stating that it "believed" that the comment was sufficiently related to an earlier discussion of a meat boycott to justify the conclusion that the personal attack occurred during a continuation of that discussion. The court concluded that the proper approach was for the Commission to judge "the objective reasonableness of the licensee's determination" that the meat boycott discussion had long since ended.

See also Polish American Congress v. Federal Communications Commission, 520 F.2d 1248, 34 R.R.2d 1359 (7th Cir.1975), certiorari denied 424 U.S. 927 (1976), in which the complainants had claimed that a skit of Polish jokes on television violated the personal attack part of the fairness doctrine. The Commission rejected the complaint. On appeal, the court stated that the order must be upheld "if the Commission properly determined that ABC's conclusion that the broadcast did not involve a controversial issue of public importance was not unreasonable or in bad faith." The court concluded that "the Commission was correct in ruling that ABC did not overstep its discretion in failing to find a controversial issue of public importance." This was true whether the issue was stated to be (1) whether "Polish Americans are inferior to other human beings in terms of intelligence, personal hygiene, etc." or (2) whether "promulgating" Polish jokes by broadcasting them is desirable. If the former, ABC could reasonably conclude that even if some people felt that way they had not generated enough support to raise a controversial issue of public importance. Even if they had, ABC could conclude that the skit presented did not constitute a "discussion" of this issue. If the issue was the latter, no controversy was shown.

The Commission also employed a narrow definition of what constituted a personal attack. In *Straus,* the FCC decided that calling a Congressman a coward did not constitute a personal attack. Similarly, the rule was held inapplicable to remarks reflecting on a journalist's personal competence. Reverend Lester Kinsolving, 41 R.R.2d 573 (1977).

3. FAIRNESS IN POLITICAL CAMPAIGNS

The fairness doctrine entered into political issues in two ways. The first involved the use of broadcasting by the party in power, particularly the President, between political campaigns. The courts took the view that when the President speaks on an issue of national concern, the party out of power had no automatic right to reply. The only exception occurred when the President delivered five uninterrupted speeches during a seven-month period about the war in Indochina. Because broadcast coverage of that dispute had otherwise been roughly in balance, the FCC decided that the networks were obligated to provide free time for a spokesman from the other side of the issue.

But that instance aside, the courts considered the speeches of a President just one factor to weigh in deciding whether the required rough balance in the presentation of contrasting views had been achieved. As usual, the FCC generally deferred to the views of the licensees, and the courts generally deferred to the views of the FCC. The subject is explored extensively in Democratic National Committee v. Federal Communications Commission, 481 F.2d 543 (D.C.Cir.1973)(unsuccessful attempt to obtain free reply time to counter President's speeches on economic policy).

The second role of the fairness doctrine in politics involved the campaign itself. Because § 315 was construed not to cover appearances by anyone other than candidates, and because the section also does not cover ballot propositions, many important political campaign broadcasts must be regulated under provisions much less precise than § 315. Not surprisingly, as television became increasingly important in election campaigns, questions not covered by § 315 arose more frequently.

a. Uses by Supporters

Turning first to a close parallel situation, what are the controlling principles when Candidate A's friends or campaign committee purchase time to further his candidacy or to attack B, his opponent? In its Letter to Nicholas Zapple, 23 F.C.C.2d 707, 19 R.R.2d 421 (1970), the Commission stated that the 1959 amendment to § 315 had explicitly recognized the operation of the fairness doctrine when the candidate's own appearance was exempted from § 315. The doctrine was thought equally applicable here. Moreover, when candidates are supported or their opponents attacked, although the licensee has the responsibility of identifying suitable speakers for opposing views, "barring unusual circumstances, it would not be reasonable for a licensee to refuse to sell time to spokesmen for or supporters of candidate B comparable to that previously bought on behalf of candidate A." But there was no obligation to provide B's supporters with free time. Although usually requiring that time be given away, if necessary, to get contrasting views before the public, the Commission thought this unsound in the political arena. To hold otherwise would require licensees, or other advertisers, to subsidize B's campaign. The rejection of subsidization meant that even if A's friends mounted a personal attack on B, B would not get free time. The Commission has adhered closely to the *Zapple* ruling, which is sometimes referred to as the "quasi equal opportunities" or "political party" corollary to the fairness doctrine.

In 1979 the Commission decided that Congress intended that "uses" under § 315 and *Zapple* were to be mutually exclusive of the fairness doctrine. The Commission concluded that licensees should not be responsible for "uses" because they have no control over them. As a result, the personal attack rule was rewritten to provide that it did not apply to personal attacks occurring during uses under § 315 or those occurring under *Zapple* situations.

More generally, the fairness doctrine was declared not to apply to issues raised during "uses." The Commission believed that issues raised during "uses" were likely to be of such public interest that other views would be aired in due course without the goad of the fairness doctrine. Personal Attacks and Applicability of the Fairness Doctrine to Section 315 "Uses," 78 F.C.C.2d 457, 45 R.R.2d 1635 (1979).

A new problem emerged in 1980 involving groups organized by friends of Ronald Reagan but not controlled by the candidate. These groups are not bound by spending limits that may bind the candidates themselves. When these groups began to buy time on broadcast stations, the Carter campaign committee complained to the FCC that the stations selling time to these "independent expenditure groups" should be required to make equal, and free, opportunities available to the Carter campaign (and presumably to all other campaigns). These should be free, the Carter committee asserted, because it and the Reagan campaign were each limited to $29.4 million for campaigning because they agreed to accept federal funds. As a result, they could not match both the money Reagan was spending and that being spent by the independent groups.

The FCC rejected the claim on the ground that friends of Carter could start comparable groups to match the expenditures being made by the Reagan groups. To allow the Carter campaign free time would put the Commission in the position of benefitting one of the candidates at the expense of the other, whose friends had been required to pay for his time.

In an effort to apply the *Zapple* ruling outside campaign periods, CBS and others asked the FCC to declare that "when a licensee sells broadcast time for political advertisements by a political party, independent political committee or other supporters of a candidate, whether during or outside a campaign period, the *Cullman* doctrine does not apply and thus, the licensee has no obligation to provide free time to opposing groups." The FCC refused on the ground that Congress had shown that § 315 was to apply only during campaign periods and that

Zapple was designed to supplement the statute only during the same periods. At other times, *Cullman* applied. CBS, Inc., 95 F.C.C.2d 1152 (1983). As a result, many licensees simply refused to sell time for these political advertisements. Remember that Political Action Committees have no right of access under § 312(a)(7), *National Conservative Political Action Committee,* p. 193, *supra.*

In *Kennedy II,* p. 192, *supra,* after rejecting the candidate's claims under § 312 and § 315, the court turned to the role of the fairness doctrine in political campaigns. The Broadcast Bureau and the Commission had found three fatal flaws in Sen. Edward M. Kennedy's reliance on the fairness doctrine in this case—and the court agreed. First, he had failed to define the particular controversial issue involved with sufficient specificity. Second, there was no showing that the networks had failed to present contrasting viewpoints on the national economy in their overall programming. The fairness doctrine "does not operate with the dissective focus of" § 315(a). "Intelligent assessment of the nature and caliber of a broadcaster's overall programming obviously cannot be confined to one program, or even to one day's presentations, so a failure to show some fairness deficiency on the whole is necessarily fatal."

Even if imbalance were established, the third flaw was that Senator Kennedy had no "individual right to broadcast his views on the current economic crisis." Kennedy did not show that he was "uniquely and singularly qualified to represent those who dispute the President's economic leadership or strategies."

The Commission's dismissal of a fairness complaint alleging unbalanced coverage of economic matters was upheld in DNC v. Federal Communications Commission, 717 F.2d 1471, 54 R.R.2d 941 (D.C.Cir. 1983). Disparities approximating three to one and four to one in favor of the pro-Administration economic view occurred on the networks. Compliance with fairness doctrine obligations was to be measured by a standard of good faith and reasonableness, not by reference to "rough approximations of equality." Since the disparities were not "glaring," and the audiences were not shown to be very different in size, the Commission's dismissal of the complaint was reasonable. Although the court cited data showing that fairness complainants prevail in roughly 1 in 1,000 cases, the court rejected Commission statements that fairness complaints will inevitably be futile.

b. *Political Editorials*

In a section of the personal attack rules, 47 C.F.R. § 73.123(c), the Commission covered political editorials:

> Where a licensee, in an editorial (i) endorses or (ii) opposes a legally qualified candidate or candidates, the licensee shall, within 24 hours after the editorial, transmit to respectively (i) the other qualified candidate or candidates for the same office or (ii) the candidate opposed in the editorial (1) notification of the date and the

time of the editorial; (2) a script or tape of the editorial; and (3) an offer of a reasonable opportunity for a candidate or a spokesman of the candidate to respond over the licensee's facilities: *Provided, however,* That where such editorials are broadcast within 72 hours prior to the day of the election, the licensee shall comply with the provisions of this paragraph sufficiently far in advance of the broadcast to enable the candidate or candidates to have a reasonable opportunity to prepare a response and to present it in a timely fashion.

Be sure to note that a single editorial on behalf of one candidate created an opportunity to respond for *each* opposing candidate. This was true regardless of the number of opposing candidates. Friends of Howard Miller, 72 F.C.C.2d 508, 45 R.R.2d 1142 (1979).

c. *Ballot Propositions*

In the *1974 Fairness Report*, the Commission reached the conclusion that such matters as referenda, initiative and recall propositions, bond proposals, and constitutional amendments were to be regulated under the fairness doctrine. The area was thought closer to general political discussion not involving elections than it was to the election of individuals to office. Thus, the *Cullman* doctrine requiring the licensee to present contrasting views, by the use of free time if necessary, was applicable. One argument against the *Cullman* doctrine was that some groups might spend their available money on non-broadcast media, wait for the other side to buy broadcast time, and then insist on free time under *Cullman* to counter their adversary. The Commission was not persuaded. First, this concern could always be raised against *Cullman*, but the Commission thought it most important that the public have access to contrasting views. On the tactical level, the Commission noted that the fairness doctrine did not guarantee equality of exposure of views nor who will be chosen as speakers. Those who relied solely on *Cullman* "have no assurance of obtaining equality by such means." Fairness Report, 48 F.C.C.2d 1, 33, 30 R.R.2d 1261, 1302 (1974).

4. THE ELIMINATION OF THE FAIRNESS DOCTRINE

As noted earlier, in 1987 the Commission eliminated the fairness doctrine. We now turn to the sequence of events that led to that decision, beginning with the *1985 Fairness Report*. Inquiry into Section 73.1910 of the Commission's Rules and Regulations Concerning the General Fairness Obligations of Broadcast Licensees, 102 F.C.C.2d 142, 58 R.R.2d 1137 (1985). In the report the Commission concluded that the doctrine was no longer justified. Although it did not question "the interest of the listening and viewing public in obtaining access to diverse and antagonistic sources of information," the FCC thought that the doctrine was neither a "necessary or appropriate means by which to effectuate this interest." The interest in "viewpoint diversity is fully served by the multiplicity of voices in the marketplace today." Moreover, "the intrusion by government into the content of programming occasioned by the enforcement of the doctrine unnecessarily restricts the journalistic freedom of broadcasters" and "actually inhibits the presentation of controversial issues of public importance to the detriment of the public and in degradation of the editorial prerogatives of broadcast journalists."

On the scarcity point, the FCC asserted that since *Red Lion* there had been a 48 percent increase in radio outlets and a 44 percent increase in television outlets. By 1984, 96 percent of television households received five or more signals. During that period the networks' share of the market had declined from 90 percent to 76 percent, and the number of independent television stations had risen from 90 to 214. Other electronic distribution systems, such as cable and multichannel multipoint distribution systems, had exploded. Finally, the FCC pointed to the continued availability of more than 1,700 daily newspapers and the increase in the number of periodicals from 6,960 in 1950 to 10,688 in 1982. The Commission concluded that "the dynamics of the information services marketplace overall insures that the public will be sufficiently exposed to controversial issues of public importance."

On the inhibition point, the Commission stressed that the fairness doctrine reduced the number of diverse views and the amount of controversial programming reaching the public. The reasoning began with the fact that enforcement of the first prong of the doctrine was virtually nonexistent. But the responsive programming requirement of the second prong came into play whenever a licensee undertook to present controversial programming even if beyond what was required under the first prong. The result was that broadcasters were being encouraged "to air only the minimal amount of controversial issue programming sufficient to comply with the first prong. By restricting the amount and type of controversial programming aired, a broadcaster minimizes the potentially substantial burdens associated with the second prong of the doctrine."

Broadcasters were burdened by being found in violation of the second prong because of the risks of being ordered to present programs without compensation or of having to defend against the charges and incurring legal expenses. The Commission cited the Spokane station that spent $20,000 in legal fees in successfully defending a fairness charge and NBC's expense of more than $100,000 in the "Pensions" case. The more remote risk of nonrenewal was an additional burden listed by the Commission.

The answer was not to enforce the first prong more rigorously because that "would increase the government's intrusion into the editorial decisionmaking process of broadcast journalists. It would enlarge the opportunity for governmental officials to abuse the doctrine for partisan political purposes."

The FCC also noted that it was inextricably involved in the "dangerous task of evaluating the merits of particular viewpoints" as it tried to distinguish statements that are "significant enough to warrant broadcast coverage" and those that "do not rise to the level of a major viewpoint of sufficient public importance that triggers responsive programming obligations."

If a responsive obligation was imposed, the Commission then had to consider the content offered by the licensee to show that it had met its obligation. In addition, the Commission noted how much of its staff time was needed to deal with inquiries and complaints related to the doctrine—6,787 hours in 1984. Finally, the Commission cited examples in which the fairness doctrine was misused by White House administrations intent upon gaining political advantage.

All of these costs were said to be unnecessary because of the recent increase in available information sources. To the argument that the doctrine was useful to provide broadcasters with a protection against outside pressures, the Commission responded that broadcasters were not asking for such protection and that print journalists did not need such protection.

Despite all the negative points made in the report, the Commission did not eliminate the doctrine. Instead, because of the "intense Congressional interest in the Fairness Doctrine" and uncertainty as to whether the doctrine was codified in § 315 of the Communications Act, the FCC deferred action until Congress had an opportunity to review the report—and announced that it would continue to enforce the doctrine.

However, during the 1980s a fairness complaint against Meredith Corporation's WTVH in Syracuse, N.Y., was working its way through the Commission and the court of appeals. Initially, the Commission found the station had violated the fairness doctrine in connection with a series of advertisements arguing that a nuclear power plant was a "sound investment for New York." The Commission refused to consider Meredith's arguments that the doctrine was unconstitutional.

The court of appeals reversed and remanded. Although regulatory agencies cannot invalidate acts of Congress, the Commission had not found that the doctrine was mandated by the Communications Act. Further, although an agency is not required to reconsider the merits of a rule each time it applies the rule, the Commission in this case had "undermined the legitimacy of its own Rule" by issuing the *1985 Fairness Report*. Meredith Corp. v. Federal Communications Commission, 809 F.2d 863, 62 R.R.2d 89, 13 Med.L.Rptr. 1993 (D.C.Cir.1987).

Before the Commission could reconsider its decision, a court of appeals in a different case determined that the doctrine was not mandated by the Communications Act. *TRAC*, p. 98, *supra*. Thus forced to reconsider the doctrine, itself, the Commission decided that the doctrine was unconstitutional and that it disserved the public interest. Syracuse Peace Council, 2 F.C.C.Rcd. 5043, 63 R.R.2d 541 (1987). The Commission's decision was appealed by the public interest group that had brought the original fairness complaint.

The court of appeals affirmed with each judge writing a separate opinion. *Syracuse Peace Council*, p. 96, *supra*. Although the Commission had asserted that its public interest and constitutional findings were "inextricably intertwined," Judge Williams found "that the Commission's public interest determination was an independent basis for its decision and was supported by the record." He therefore found it unnecessary to reach the constitutional issue.

With regard to the second prong of the fairness doctrine, Judge Williams noted that FCC's decision was a policy judgment to which the court owed great deference. Because the Commission's judgments were "almost entirely predictive . . . complete factual support for the Commission's ultimate conclusions [was] not required."

Turning to the Commission's elimination of the affirmative portion of the doctrine, Judge Williams rejected the FCC's argument that the doctrine was a unified whole—so that if one part fell so did the other. The Commission had not explained why the parts were not severable. However, he felt that the Commission had provided sufficient independent reasons for terminating the first prong:

> First, removal of the fairness doctrine's second requirement would reduce the need for the coverage requirement. With the chilling effects of the second requirement ended, the Commission expected that "coverage of controversial issues will be forthcoming naturally, without the need for continued enforcement of the first prong." . . .

> Second, it viewed the coverage requirement as in significant part duplicative of its independent requirement that broadcasters cover issues "of importance" to their communities. [ ] While the FCC acknowledged on reconsideration that the two programming requirements were not identical, it saw sufficient similarity to believe that the community issues rule would fill any material regulatory gap. [ ]

> Third, in its discussion of the fairness doctrine as a whole the Commission relied heavily on its view that government involvement in the editorial process was offensive. [ ] That judgment of course applies to the editorial decisions required for enforcement of the first prong, and the Commission made the point expressly: "[T]he doctrine requires the government to second-guess broadcasters' judgment on such sensitive and subjective matters as the 'controversiality' and 'public importance' of a particular issue. . . ." [ ] It also alluded to the offensive character of government first-prong decisions in distinguishing that part of the doctrine from the community issues requirement. . . .

Judge Wald concurred with the part of Judge Williams' opinion that upheld the FCC's decision to abrogate the second prong of the fairness doctrine as an exercise of its statutory authority to regulate in the public interest. She dissented, however, as to the elimination of the first prong.

First, she argued that the Commission had failed to provide adequate notice to the parties of its intent to consider that part of the doctrine. Remember that the original complaint against Meredith had only involved the second prong.

She also rejected the argument that the overlap between first prong obligations and the duty to cover issues of importance to the community justified the FCC's action. Although, there was a substantial overlap the two obligations were not duplicative. Specifically, a broadcaster could provide extensive coverage of community issues without covering any issues of a controversial nature.

> Moreover, I do not believe that the FCC's obligation to identify the costs of an unwanted regulation could be satisfied by a bare showing that the rule would impinge on broadcasters' editorial freedom. I believe it is still the law that, in the regulation of electronic media, "[i]t is the right of the viewers and listeners, not the right of the broadcasters, which is paramount." [*Red Lion*] . . .

> . . . [T]he Commission has made no effort whatsoever to explain how continued enforcement of the doctrine's first prong could induce broadcasters to alter their programming decisions in ways which would ultimately disserve the public interest.

Judge Starr agreed with Judge Williams that both parts of the FCC's decision should be affirmed. However, he did so on completely different grounds.

> . . . With all respect to the court's view enunciated today, I am convinced that the record in this case simply will not, fairly read, yield the conclusion that the agency has based the specific decision before us independently on non-constitutional grounds. There is, therefore, no proper basis for skirting the Commission's constitutional analysis (unless we were to conclude, as I do not, that the Commission erred in even considering that issue); in short, the constitutional justifications for the Commission's action must, alas, be considered.

Having concluded that the court was required to analyze the constitutional basis of the FCC's decision, Judge Starr found it necessary to address two questions. First, did the Commission apply the correct constitutional principles? As discussed previously, p. 96, *supra*, Judge Starr determined that the Commission had done so.

Second, were the FCC's factual determinations arbitrary and capricious? Here his analysis paralleled that of Judge Williams. There was reasonable support in the record for the Commission's findings, especially given the degree of deference required.

Turning to the first prong of the doctrine, Judge Starr also rejected the FCC's severability analysis. He also rejected the argument that the first prong was largely duplicative of the community issues requirement. He noted that previously the FCC had:

. . . loosened the issue-responsive obligation in part because of a distinct obligation imposed under Part One. [ ] In light of the admitted difference between the two regulatory standards, I am of the view that the Commission's "largely duplicative" rationale is inadequate.

Despite these deficiencies, I nonetheless agree that the Commission reasonably eliminated Part One in light of the FCC's findings that the explosive growth in media outlets, combined with the removal of the deterrent to controversial public issue programming imposed by Part Two of the doctrine, will adequately ensure availability of such programs. [ ] The reasonableness of the Commission's decision to eliminate Part One is reinforced by the (inevitably) predictive quality of the FCC's reasoning. It is in this sense that I agree with Judge Williams that the Commission is entitled to conclude that elimination of Part One would not create an impermissible regulatory gap. . . .

In a 1987 letter to Rep. John Dingell (D.–Mich.), then-FCC Chairman Dennis Patrick indicated that *Syracuse Peace Council* was limited to the facts of that case. Thus, technically, the Commission had not yet made a decision concerning enforcement of the personal attack and political editorial rules, the *Zapple* doctrine, or the application of the fairness doctrine to political campaigns and ballot issues.

Subsequently, the Commission decided that the rules on fairness in elections on ballot propositions had *not* survived the demise of the underlying doctrine. That repeal, in Arkansas AFL–CIO v. KARK–TV, 7 F.C.C.Rcd. 541, 70 R.R.2d 369 (1992) was affirmed, 2–1, in Arkansas AFL–CIO v. Federal Communications Commission, 980 F.2d 1190, 20 Med.L.Rptr. 2127, 71 R.R.2d 996 (8th Cir.1992).

The panel majority agreed with the result of the D. C. Circuit in the *TRAC* case, p. 98, *supra*, that the 1959 amendment to § 315 had not enacted the fairness doctrine into statute. It rejected the literal analysis of the *TRAC* court, but reached the same result on the basis of legislative history. It then agreed with *Syracuse Peace Council*, p. 96, *supra*, that the FCC was free to repeal its own creation if it wanted to do so. The dissenter thought the legislative history supported the view that the Congress had indeed affirmatively enacted the fairness doctrine—and that the FCC was without power to abandon it.

The Eighth Circuit voted to rehear the case *en banc* and withdrew the panel's judgment and opinion. The case took an unusual turn when the FCC, which had defended its action before the original panel, changed its position and argued that the case should be remanded so that the Commission could reconsider it in light of the court's statutory analysis. The reason for the change in posture may be explained by the fact that two Commissioners had left their positions but had not yet been replaced. Two of the remaining three Commissioners had dissented from the FCC's original decision. At this point, the court granted a motion for realignment of the parties, leaving KARK to argue that the FCC's original action be affirmed.

The court then affirmed, 7–5. Five judges, in an opinion written by Judge Beam, decided that the legislative history showed that the fairness doctrine was not codified, while five dissenting judges argued that the legislative history showed that the doctrine was codified. Judges Richard Arnold and Morris Arnold cast the deciding votes, in a concurring opinion authored by the former. He found the arguments for each point of view to be "very nearly evenly balanced." He therefore based his decision on his belief that technological developments since *Red Lion* might well cause it to be reconsidered. Because "[s]tatutes should be interpreted, if possible, to avoid doubts about their constitutionality," he construed the statute not to require the fairness doctrine. Judge Loken joined both the lead opinion and Judge Arnold's concurring opinion. Arkansas AFL–CIO v. Federal Communications Commission, 11 F.3d 1430, 74 R.R.2d 401, 22 Med.L.Rptr. 1001 (8th Cir.1993).

Even before the elimination of the fairness doctrine, the NAB had sought to have the personal attack and political editorial rules repealed. In response to the NAB's 1980 petition, the FCC issued an NPRM, Repeal or Modification of the Personal Attack and Political Editorial Rules, 48 Fed. Reg. 28295 (June 21, 1983). No action was taken for several years. Following the FCC's decision in *Syracuse Peace Council*, the NAB, RTNDA and others filed a Petition for Expedited Rulemaking in 1987. Again, no action was taken, even after a second petition was filed in 1990.

RTNDA filed a petition for writ of mandamus in the D.C. Circuit in 1996. The court of appeals denied the mandamus petition without prejudice, giving the Commission six months to make significant progress toward possible repeal or modification of the rules. In re Radio–Television News Directors Association, 1997 WL 150084 (D.C.Cir.1997). The Commission then issued an announcement of its inability to take action due to a 2–2 split on the issue. After RTNDA renewed its petition, the court of appeals ordered the Commission to take a formal vote. The order also required those Commissioners voting against repeal or substantial modification to supply a statement of their reasons. In re Radio–Television News Directors Association, 159 F.3d 636 (D.C.Cir.1998).

In June 1998, the Commission took the formal vote and found itself still deadlocked. Commissioners Powell and Furchtgott–Roth voted to repeal the rules and issued a statement detailing their reasons for doing so. Commissioners Ness and Tristani voted to retain the rules, while also issuing a statement. Chairman Kennard did not participate. Repeal or Modification of the Personal Attack and Political Editorial Rules, 13 F.C.C.Rcd. 21901, 12 C.R. 497 (1998).

Commissioners Powell and Furchtgott–Roth argued that *Syracuse Peace Council* compelled elimination of the rules. The failure to do so was, in their view, "arbitrary and capricious decisionmaking."

In contrast, Commissioners Ness and Tristani concluded that:

these two rules continue to serve as important components of a broadcaster's public interest obligations and complement the important objectives served by the equal opportunities requirements of Section 315(a) and the reasonable access provisions of Section 312(a)(7) of the Communications Act. In addition, these rules serve the public interest by helping to ensure that the same audience that heard the broadcast of an endorsement or personal attack be accessible to the individual concerned.

They did indicate a willingness to "streamline" the rules.

The court of appeals viewed the statement of Commissioners Ness and Tristani supporting retention of the rules to be the opinion of the agency. That statement was then found insufficient as a justification for retention because it assumed the underlying validity of the rules without offering any justification or evidence to support that position. The court was therefore unable to determine "whether [the rules] continue to serve the public interest [or] whether they burden First Amendment interests too severely." At the same time the court was unable to conclude that the FCC would not be able to justify the rules. Accordingly the case was remanded to the FCC for an explanation of why the rules should not be modified or repealed.

Less than 2 months before the 2000 Presidential Election, the FCC voted, 3–2, to suspend the rules for 60 days for the purpose of compiling a better record on which to review the rules. Commissioners Ness and Tristani were joined in this action by Chairman Kennard, who had until this time recused himself in the proceeding.

The majority directed broadcasters to present evidence of their claim that there would be more editorializing in the absence of the political editorial rule. Broadcasters were also instructed to collect information "regarding complaints concerning personal attacks that are received while the rule is suspended, and to compare the number and nature of the complaints made during the 60 days to a comparable period while the rule was in effect."

The majority also criticized the Commission's First Amendment analysis in *Syracuse Peace Council*, p. 96, *supra*, and asked broadcasters and other interested parties to comment on the effects of the repeal of the fairness doctrine.

Commissioners Powell and Furchtgott–Roth dissented, arguing that the suspension for 60 days was designed to prevent the court from taking action and ultimately to extend the rules while delaying court review. They also asserted that no useful information could be obtained during a 60–day suspension of the rules. Finally, Commissioner Powell asserted that the discussion of Syracuse Peace Council was not only unnecessary, but a transparent attempt "to preserve its authority to regulate broadcast speech content with less worry about First Amendment constraint." Repeal or Modification of the Personal Attack and Political Editorial Rules, 15 F.C.C.Rcd. 19973 (2000).

One week later the court of appeals acted decisively.

RADIO–TELEVISION NEWS DIRECTORS ASSOCIATION v. FEDERAL COMMUNICATIONS COMMISSION

United States Court of Appeals, District of Columbia Circuit, 2000.
229 F.3d 269, 28 Med.L.Rptr. 2465.

Before: EDWARDS, CHIEF JUDGE and ROGERS, CIRCUIT JUDGE.**

Opinion for the Court filed by CIRCUIT JUDGE ROGERS.

ROGERS, CIRCUIT JUDGE:

[The court began by recounting the procedural history of RTNDA's challenge to the rules including the FCC's order suspending the rules for 60 days.] In view of its Order, the Commission contends that the motion for mandamus is now moot. [ ] The matter is not so simple, however.

Neither the timing nor the substance of the Order responds to the court's remand order in 1999. From the silence of the Commission until October 4, 2000, and the statements of the two dissenting Commissioners, it can reasonably be inferred that until the court's order of July 24, 2000 . . . the Commission had taken no action to respond to the remand. Consistent with the decision of the court, the two Commissioners supporting the rules could have submitted a new justification with or without new data, or the Commission could have commenced a new proceeding to gather such data. The separate statement of Commissioner Powell indicates that the deadlock might not have persisted had some intermediary steps been proposed. On this record, the court can only conclude that its remand order for expeditious action was ignored.[6]

Be that as it may, the court is now confronted with the October 4th Order. Clearly, the Order is not responsive to the court's remand. The Commission still has not provided adequate justification for the rules, and in its Order provides no assurance that it will do so. The suspension of the rules for 60 days simply has the effect of further postponing a final decision by the Commission. Incredibly, the Order reinstates the rules before the Commission will have received any of the updated information that the Commission states it requires in order to evaluate the rules. *See* Order § 7. Thus, notwithstanding the Commission's continuing failure to provide adequate justification, as of December 3, 2000, petitioners would again be subject to the rules that they have contended since 1980 have serious consequences and that the court has acknowledged have some effect on speech and cause some interference with broadcasters' editorial judgments. The Order provides no assurance whatsoever that

---

** Judge Wald was originally a member of the panel.

6. *See also* § 402(h), which provides:

In the event that the court shall render a decision and enter an order reversing the order of the Commission, it shall remand the case to the Commission to carry out the judgment of the court and it shall be the duty of the Commission, in the absence of the proceedings to review such judgment, to *forthwith give effect thereto,* and unless otherwise ordered by the court, to do so upon the basis of the proceedings already had and the record upon which said appeal was heard and determined. 47 U.S.C.A. § 402(h)(West 1991)(emphasis added).

the Commission will proceed expeditiously once it receives the requested information. It follows that petitioners' *Motion for Mandamus* is not moot. [   ]

In other words, it is folly to suppose that the 60–day suspension and call to update the record cures anything. As petitioners point out in their *Reply to the FCC Response to the Emergency Motion,* the Commission updated the record four years ago and still did not provide an adequate justification for the rules. *See* id. at 2. Apparently the Commission views the presidential election period as a particularly good opportunity to gauge the effect of the rules. *See* Order § 7. The rules, once reinstated, will be effective year-round. Pretermitting whether the requirement of the First Amendment suggested by the Order is skewed, not only does the Order provide short notice for broadcasters to change their plans, but their conduct will in any event be affected by the fact that the rules will be reinstated on December 3, 2000. In short, the October 4th Order compounds the problems, affording no relief to petitioners and no assurance that final action is imminent, much less to be expeditiously accomplished. The petition to vacate the rules has been pending since 1980, and less stalwart petitioners might have abandoned their effort to obtain relief long ago. If these circumstances do not constitute agency action unreasonably delayed,[   ], it is difficult to imagine circumstances that would.

In these extraordinary circumstances, the court's decision is preordained and the mandamus will issue. [   ] The court has afforded repeated opportunities for the Commission to take final action. Despite its filings suggesting to the court that something would happen, the Commission, once again, has done nothing to cure the deficiencies of which it has been long aware. Of course, the Commission may institute a new rule-making proceeding to determine whether, consistent with constitutional constraints, the public interest requires the personal attack and political editorial rules. These are issues that the court has yet to decide. Nevertheless, extraordinary action by the court is warranted in this case, particularly in view of the fact that the six reasons proffered in support of the rules were all wanting. [   ] The Commission has delayed final action for two decades, to the detriment of petitioners. While it acknowledged the need for a prompt decision, the Commission failed to act for nine months. Finally, its response consists of an order that further postpones a final decision without any assurance of a final decision.

Accordingly, the court hereby recalls its mandate and issues a writ of mandamus directing the Commission immediately to repeal the personal attack and political editorial rules.

Notes and Questions

1. If a future FCC were to decide to reinstate the personal attack and political editorial rules, what evidence would the Commission need to present for the rules to pass constitutional muster?

2. Some broadcasters believed that then-Chairman William Kennard intended not only to reinstate the rules, but to bring back, in some form, the fairness doctrine. The results of the 2000 Presidential election ended this speculation as the change in administration led to a change in the composition of the Commission. With a 3–2 Republican majority and Commissioner Powell having been elevated to Chairman, any action in this area prior to a change in administration is extremely unlikely.

5. PROPOSED CHANGES FOR DTV

One of the recommendations of the Advisory Committee on the Public Interest Obligations of Digital Television Broadcasters, p. 60, *supra*, focused on political speech:

> (6a) If Congress undertakes comprehensive campaign finance reform, broadcasters should commit firmly to do their part to reform the role of television in campaigns. This could include repeal of the "lowest unit rate" requirement in exchange for free air time, a broadcast bank to distribute money or vouchers for airtime, and shorter time periods for selling political air time, among other changes.

> (6b) The television broadcasting industry should voluntarily provide 5 minutes each night for candidate-centered discourse in the thirty days before an election. (6c) Blanket bans on the sale of air time to all state and local political candidates should be prohibited.

The committee voiced great dissatisfaction with the current state of political campaigning, especially in the area of campaign finance. It argued that the high cost of campaigning, especially the cost of television commercials, serves as a barrier to entry for candidates. The committee also argued that the current political access rules are ineffective, if not in some cases counterproductive.

For example, the committee was especially critical of the lowest-unit-rate requirement:

> The so-called lowest unit rate, the mandated discount advertising rate for candidates, is a complex and cumbersome system that clearly does not work very well. It does not work for candidates, who are confused by the system, and whose time-buying practices often make the lowest unit rate meaningless or superfluous. It can be a bureaucratic nightmare for broadcasters, with extensive reporting requirements and frequent lawsuits from candidates convinced they are being cheated. In the digital age, lowest unit rate becomes even more cumbersome and costly.

The committee's proposal would eliminate lowest unit rate, in return for broadcasters providing some free time, perhaps one minute of free time for each two minutes of time bought at market rates. Other ways of addressing the cost problem included distributing vouchers for air-time (perhaps funded by fees for using digital spectrum for ancillary services) to candidates and a shortened time period during which broadcasters would be required to sell time to political candidates.

Recommendation 6(b) is aimed at what the committee argued is the decreasing quality of political discourse. The five-minute blocks would allow for more in-depth discussions of issues than current campaign advertisements contain. The committee also suggests giving broadcasters flexibility to choose the formats, races and candidates for these five-minute blocks so that they can find "creative ways to improve political discourse, provide opportunities for candidates to get messages across to voters and to enhance voter understanding without heavy monetary costs to broadcasters, regulation of the content of programming, or without it being a kind of programming that will cause viewers to turn away." This would require exempting them from § 315 obligations.

The final recommendation for political access is to prohibit blanket bans on sale of time to state and local candidates. This would not be as broad a rule as the reasonable access requirement for all federal candidates. Rather it would be a requirement that broadcasters sell to candidates in at least some state and local races. Broadcasters would be free to choose which races. As previously noted, p. 62, *supra*, the Commission has asked for further comment on these recommendations.

Chapter VI

LEGAL CONTROL OF BROADCAST PROGRAMMING: NONPOLITICAL SPEECH

In Chapter V we examined legal controls on broadcast programming that were concerned primarily with political speech. We now turn to other content regulation of broadcasting. Here the restrictions often take the form of direct bans on speech. As we examine each case, ask yourself whether these restrictions are more, or less, justifiable than those covered in the previous chapter.

A. DRUGS

YALE BROADCASTING CO. v. FEDERAL COMMUNICATIONS COMMISSION

United States Court of Appeals, District of Columbia Circuit, 1973. 478 F.2d 594.
Certiorari denied 414 U.S. 914, 94 S.Ct. 211, 38 L.Ed.2d 152 (1973).

Before DANAHER, SENIOR CIRCUIT JUDGE, and ROBINSON and WILKEY, CIRCUIT JUDGES.

WILKEY, CIRCUIT JUDGE:

The source of this controversy is a Notice issued by the Federal Communications Commission regarding "drug oriented" music allegedly played by some radio stations. This Notice and a subsequent Order, the stated purposes of which were to remind broadcasters of a pre-existing duty, required licensees to have knowledge of the content of their programming and on the basis of this knowledge to evaluate the desirability of broadcasting music dealing with drug use. Appellant, a radio station licensee, argues first that the Notice and the Order are an unconstitutional infringement of its First Amendment right to free speech. . . .

. . .

Despite all its attempts to assuage broadcasters' fears, the Commission realized that if an Order can be misunderstood, it will be misunderstood—at least by some licensees. To remove any excuse for misunderstanding, the Commission specified examples of how a broadcaster could obtain the requisite knowledge. A licensee could fulfill its obligation through (1) pre-screening by a responsible station employee, (2) monitoring selections while they were being played, or (3) considering and responding to complaints made by members of the public. The Order made clear that these procedures were merely suggestions, and were not to be regarded as either absolute requirements or the exclusive means for fulfilling a station's public interest obligation.

Having made clear our understanding of what the Commission has done, we now take up appellant's arguments seriatim.

III. AN UNCONSTITUTIONAL BURDEN ON FREEDOM OF SPEECH

Appellant's first argument is that the Commission's action imposes an unconstitutional burden on a broadcaster's freedom of speech. This contention rests primarily on the Supreme Court's opinion in Smith v. California,[12] in which a bookseller was convicted of possessing and selling obscene literature. The Supreme Court reversed the conviction. Although the State had a legitimate purpose in seeking to ban the distribution of obscene materials, it could not accomplish this goal by placing on the bookseller the procedural burden of examining every book in his store. To make a bookseller criminally liable for all the books sold would necessarily "tend to restrict the books he sells to those he has inspected; and thus the State will have imposed a restriction upon the distribution of constitutionally protected as well as obscene literature. . . ."

Appellant compares its own situation to that of the bookseller in *Smith* and argues that the Order imposes an unconstitutional burden on a broadcaster's freedom of speech. The two situations are easily distinguishable.

Most obviously, a radio station can only broadcast for a finite period of twenty-four hours each day; at any one time a bookstore may contain thousands of hours' worth of readable material. Even if the Commission had ordered that stations pre-screen all materials broadcast, the burden would not be nearly so great as the burden imposed on the bookseller in *Smith.* As it is, broadcasters are not even required to pre-screen their maximum twenty-four hours of daily programming. Broadcasters have specifically been told that they may gain "knowledge" of what they broadcast in other ways.

A more subtle but no less compelling answer to the appellant's argument rests upon *why* knowledge of drug oriented music is required by the Commission. In *Smith,* knowledge was imputed to the purveyor in order that a criminal sanction might be imposed and the dissemination halted. Here the goal is to assure the broadcaster has adequate knowledge. . . .

We say that the licensee must have *knowledge* of what it is broadcasting; the precise *understanding* which may be required of the licensee is only that which is reasonable. No radio licensee faces any realistic possibility of a penalty for misinterpreting the lyrics it has chosen or permitted to be broadcast. If the lyrics are completely obscure, the station is not put on notice that it is in fact broadcasting material which

---

12. 361 U.S. 147 (1959).

would encourage drug abuse. If the lyrics are meaningless, incoherent, the same conclusion follows. The argument of the appellant licensee, that so many of these lyrics are obscure and ambiguous, really is a circumstance available to some degree in his defense for permitting their broadcast, at least until their meaning is clarified. Some lyrics or sounds are virtually unintelligible. To the extent they are completely meaningless gibberish and approach the equivalent of machinery operating or the din of traffic, they, of course, do not communicate with respect to drugs or anything else, and are not within the ambit of the Commission's order. Speech is an expression of sound or visual symbols which is intelligible to some other human beings. At some point along the scale of human intelligibility the sounds produced may slide over from characteristics of free speech, which should be protected, to those of noise pollution, which the Commission has ample authority to abate.[15]

We not only think appellant's argument invalid, we express our astonishment that the licensee would argue that before the broadcast it has no knowledge, and cannot be required to have any knowledge, of material it puts over the airwaves. We can understand that the individual radio licensees would not be expected to know in advance the content or the quality of a network program, or a free flowing panel discussion of public issues, or other audience participation program, and certainly not a political broadcast. But with reference to the broadcast of that which is frequently termed "canned music," we think the Commission may require that the purveyors of this to the public make a reasonable effort to know what is in the "can." No producer of pork and beans is allowed to put out on a grocery shelf a can without knowing what is in it and standing back of both its content and quality. The Commission is not required to allow radio licensees, being freely granted the use of limited air channels, to spew out to the listening public canned music, whose content and quality before broadcast is totally unknown.

Supposedly a radio licensee is performing a public service—that is the raison d'etre of the license. If the licensee does not have specific knowledge of what it is broadcasting, how can it claim to be operating in the public interest? Far from constituting any threat to freedom of speech of the licensee, we conclude that for the Commission to have been less insistent on licensees discharging their obligations would have verged on an evasion of the Commission's own responsibilities.

By the expression of the above views we have no desire whatsoever to express a value judgment on different types of music, poetry, sound, instrumentation, etc., which may appeal to different classes of our most diverse public. "De gustibus non est disputandum." But what we are saying is that whatever the style, whatever the expression put out over the air by the radio station, for the licensee to claim that it has no responsibility to evaluate its product is for the radio station to abnegate completely what we had always considered its responsibility as a licensee. All in all, and quite unintentionally, the appellant-licensee in its free

15. Cf. Noise Control Act of 1972, Pub.L. No. 92–574, 86 Stat. (1972).

speech argument here has told us a great deal about quality in this particular medium of our culture.

. . .

For the reasons given above, the action of the Federal Communications Commission is

Affirmed.

Notes and Questions

1.   A motion for a rehearing *en banc* was denied over the objection of Chief Judge Bazelon, who commented that:

> . . . the Order restated its basic threat: "the broadcaster could jeopardize his license by failing to exercise licensee responsibility in this area." As we have recognized, "licensee responsibility" is a nebulous concept. It could be taken to mean—as the panel opinion takes it—only that "a broadcaster must 'know' what it is broadcasting." On the other hand, in light of the earlier Notice, and in light of the renewed warnings in the Order about the dangers of "drug-oriented" popular songs, broadcasters might have concluded that "responsibility" meant "prohibition."

> . . .

This case presents several other questions of considerable significance: Is the popular song a constitutionally protected form of speech?[23] Do the particular songs at which these directives were aimed have a demonstrable connection with illegal activities? If so, is the proper remedy to "discourage or eliminate" the playing of such songs? Can the FCC assert regulatory authority over material that could not constitutionally be regulated in the printed media?[25]

Clearly, the impact of the Commission's order is ripe for judicial review. And, on that review, it would be well to heed Lord Devlin's recent warning:

> If freedom of the press . . . [or freedom of speech] perishes, it will not be by a sudden death. . . . It will be a long time dying from a debilitating disease caused by a series of erosive measures, each of which, if examined singly, would have a good deal to be said for it.

23. Popular songs might be considered mere entertainment, or even noise pollution. Yale Broadcasting Co. v. FCC, at 598, 599. On the other hand, historians and sociologists have noted that the popular song has been an important medium of political, moral, and aesthetic expression in American life.

25. See Brandywine–Main Line Radio, Inc. v. FCC, 473 F.2d 16 (D.C.Cir. 1972)(Chief Judge Bazelon, dissenting)(ap-

plication of the Fairness Doctrine). Unlike the "Fairness Doctrine" cases, there can be no assertion here that the chilling effect is incidental to providing access to the media for viewpoints that would contribute to a fuller debate on public issues. The question is thus presented whether the rationale of the "Fairness Doctrine," or any other realities of the electronic media, warrant intrusion on broadcasters' free speech rights in this case.

2.   The Supreme Court denied *certiorari*, 414 U.S. 914 (1973). Justice Brennan would have granted the writ and set the case for argument. Justice Douglas dissented along the lines sketched by Chief Judge Bazelon. He noted that the Commission majority apparently had intended to ban drug-related lyrics from the air and that at a Congressional hearing the Chairman testified that if a licensee were playing songs that the Commission thought promoted the use of "hard drugs," "I know what I would do, I would probably vote to take the license away." Even though drug lyrics might not cause great concern if banned, "next year it may apply to comedy programs, and the following year to news broadcasts." He concluded that:

> The Government cannot, consistent with the First Amendment, require a broadcaster to censor its music any more than it can require a newspaper to censor the stories of its reporters. Under our system the Government is not to decide what messages, spoken or in music, are of the proper "social value" to reach the people.

3.   Could Congress ban pro-drug broadcasts—whether of songs or of normal speech? Are your views here consistent with your views about Congressional power to ban cigarette commercials, p. 202, *supra?*

4.   Could Congress ban pro-drug messages in the print media? What about pro-cigarette messages? For more than a decade, the American Medical Association has recommended extending the ban on cigarette commercials to all media. We will return to the issue of banning commercials for certain products later in this chapter.

5.   In response to a proposal by the Parents Music Resource Center, many record companies now place warning labels on records with lyrics that contain explicit sexual language, profanity or violence. What if the Commission were to ban the playing of records with warning labels? What if the Commission merely indicated a belief that playing records with those labels was against the public interest?

B.   OBSCENITY AND INDECENCY

Obscenity as a class of speech has long been viewed as unprotected by the First Amendment, even though the Supreme Court did not address the issue until 1957. In Roth v. United States, 354 U.S. 476 (1957), the Court held that even though it was "expression," obscenity was outside the protection of the First and Fourteenth Amendments.

The current definition of obscenity, the *Miller* standard, was handed down by the Supreme Court in Miller v. California, 413 U.S. 15, 1 Med.L.Rptr. 1441 (1973):

> (a) whether "the average person, applying contemporary community standards" would find that the work, taken as a whole, appeals to the prurient interest, [   ]; (b) whether the work depicts or describes, in a patently offensive way, sexual conduct specifically defined by the applicable state law; and (c) whether the work, taken as a whole, lacks serious literary, artistic, political, or scientific value.

In order for something to be declared obscene, all three parts of the test must be met.

Because obscenity is beyond the protection of the First Amendment, both state and federal government are free to regulate it. However, statutes that are not limited to material covered by the *Miller* standard are usually considered unconstitutionally overbroad. For example, in Erznoznik v. Jacksonville, 422 U.S. 205, 1 Med.L.Rptr. 1508 (1975), the Court struck down an ordinance forbidding the showing of nudity on drive-in theatre screens visible from the public streets. When its captive audience justification proved unsuccessful, the city also asserted that the ordinance was justified as a protection of children. This also failed because the restriction was "broader than permissible. The ordinance is not directed against sexually explicit nudity, nor is it otherwise limited. Rather, it sweepingly forbids display of films containing any uncovered buttocks or breasts, irrespective of contexts or pervasiveness. Thus, it would bar a film containing a picture of a baby's buttocks, the nude body of a war victim, or scenes from a culture in which nudity is indigenous. . . . Clearly all nudity cannot be deemed obscene even as to minors." In appropriately drafted statutes, it is possible to protect minors from obscenity even though such a statute could not apply to the general public. See Ginsberg v. New York, 390 U.S. 629, 1 Med.L.Rptr. 1424 (1968) for a discussion of the states' power to regulate minors' access to obscene material.

1. THE ORIGIN OF THE RULES ON INDECENCY

The subject of obscenity did not become a problem on radio and television until the 1960s. In the earlier years of these media, the licensees apparently had no practical reason to want to test the limits of permissible communication and were unsure what the Commission might legally do to licensees who stepped over the line.

In the 1934 Act, § 326, the prohibition on censorship, also contained a passage forbidding the use of obscene or indecent speech in broadcasting. In 1948 that ban was removed from § 326 and added to the general criminal law in 18 U.S.C.A. § 1464:

> Whoever utters any obscene, indecent, or profane language by means of radio communication shall be fined not more than $10,000 or imprisoned not more than two years, or both.

Several other sections empower the Commission to impose sanctions for violation of § 1464.

In 1964 the Commission considered renewal of stations belonging to the Pacifica Foundation. Five programs had provoked complaints: two poets reading their own works; one author reading from his novel; a recording of Edward Albee's "Zoo Story"; and a program "in which eight homosexuals discussed their attitudes and problems." All were broadcast late at night except one of the poetry readings. The Commission indicated that it was "not concerned with individual programs" but with whether there had been a pattern of programming inconsistent with the public interest. Although it found nothing to bar renewal, the Commission discussed the five programs, claiming it would be "useful" to the "industry and the public."

The Commission found three of the programs were well within the licensee's judgment under the public interest standard. The Commission recognized that provocative programming might offend some listeners. To rule such programs off the air, however, would mean that "only the wholly inoffensive, the bland, could gain access to the radio microphone or TV camera." The remedy for offended listeners was to turn off the program. The two poetry readings raised different questions. One did not measure up to the licensee's standards for presentation, but it had not been carefully screened because it had come from a reputable source. The other reading, involving 28 poems, was broadcast at 7:15 p.m. because the station's editor admitted he had been lulled by the poet's "rather flat, monotonous voice" and did not catch unidentified "offensive words" in the 19th poem. The errors were isolated and thus caused no renewal problem. Pacifica Foundation, 36 F.C.C. 147, 1 R.R.2d 747 (1964). For a history of Pacifica's struggle in 1964, including the fact that no broadcaster came to its defense, see Barton, The Lingering Legacy of Pacifica: Broadcasters' Freedom of Silence, 53 Journ.Q. 429 (1976).

Another episode involved a taped interview on a noncommercial FM station with Jerry Garcia, leader of the Grateful Dead. Garcia apparently used "various patently offensive words as adjectives, introductory expletives, and as substitutes for 'et cetera.' " The Commission imposed a forfeiture of $100 for "indecency" and apparently hoped for a court test of its powers. Eastern Educational Radio (WUHY–FM), 24 F.C.C.2d 408, 18 R.R.2d 860 (1970). The licensee paid the fine, and the case was over.

Next came charges of obscenity leveled at "topless radio," midday programs consisting of "call-in talk shows in which masters of ceremonies discuss intimate sexual topics with listeners, usually women." The format quickly became quite popular. The Commission responded to complaints by ordering its staff to tape several of the shows and to present a condensed tape of some of the most offensive comments. The next day, Chairman Burch spoke to the National Association of Broadcasters condemning the format. Two weeks later the Commission issued a Notice of Apparent Liability proposing a forfeiture of $2,000 against one licensee. Sonderling Broadcasting Corp. (WGLD–FM), 27 R.R.2d 285 (F.C.C.1973). The most troublesome language was apparently:

> Female Listener: . . . of course I had a few hangups at first about—in regard to this, but you know what we did—I have a craving for peanut butter all that [sic] time so I used to spread this on my husband's privates and after a while, I mean, I didn't even need the peanut butter anymore.
>
> Announcer: (Laughs) Peanut butter, huh?

> Listener: Right. Oh, we can try anything—you know—any, any of these women that have called and they have, you know, hangups about this, I mean they should try their favorite—you know like—uh. . . .
>
> Announcer: Whipped cream, marshmallow. . . .

In addition, the host's conversation with a complaining listener was thought to be suffused with "leering innuendo." The Commission thought this program ran afoul of both the "indecency" and "obscenity" standards of § 1464. On the other hand, the Commission disclaimed any intention to ban the discussion of sex entirely:

> We are emphatically not saying that sex *per se* is a forbidden subject on the broadcast medium. We are well aware that sex is a vital human relationship which has concerned humanity over the centuries, and that sex and obscenity are not the same thing. In this area as in others, we recognize the licensee's right to present provocative or unpopular programming which may offend some listeners, Pacifica Foundation, 36 F.C.C. 147, 149 (1964). Second, we note that we are not dealing with works of dramatic or literary art as we were in *Pacifica*. We are rather confronted with the talk or interview show where clearly the interviewer can readily moderate his handling of the subject matter so as to conform to the basic statutory standards which, as we point out, allow much leeway for provocative material. . . . The standards here are strictly defined by the law: The broadcaster must eschew the "obscene or indecent."

Again the Commission sought a test: "we welcome and urge judicial consideration of our action." Commissioner Johnson dissented on several grounds, including the view that the Commission had no duty to act in these cases and should leave the matter to possible prosecution by the Justice Department. Sonderling denied liability but paid the fine. Two citizen groups asked the Commission to reconsider on the grounds that listeners' rights to hear such programs had been disregarded by the Commission's action. The Commission reaffirmed its action. 41 F.C.C.2d 777, 27 R.R.2d 1508 (1973). It indicated that it had based its order "on the pervasive and intrusive nature of broadcast radio, even if children were left completely out of the picture." It went on, however, to point out that children were in the audience in these afternoon programs and there was some evidence that the program was not intended solely for adults. "The obvious intent of this reference to children was to convey the conclusion that this material was unlawful, and that it was even more clearly unlawful when presented to an audience which included children."

The citizen groups appealed but lost. Illinois Citizens Committee for Broadcasting v. Federal Communications Commission, 515 F.2d 397, 31 R.R.2d 1523 (D.C.Cir.1974). The court refused to allow the petitioners to make certain procedural arguments that it thought were open only to the licensee itself. On the merits:

The excerpts cited by the Commission contain repeated and explicit descriptions of the techniques of oral sex. And these are presented, not for educational and scientific purposes, but in a context that was fairly described by the FCC as "titillating and pandering." The principles of Ginzburg v. United States, 383 U.S. 463 (1966) are applicable, for commercial exploitation of interests in titillation is the broadcaster's sole end. It is not a material difference that here the tone is set by the continuity provided by the announcer rather than, as in *Ginzburg,* by the presentation of the material in advertising and sale to solicit an audience. We cannot ignore what the Commission took into account—that the announcer's response to a complaint by an offended listener and his presentation of advertising for auto insurance are suffused with leering innuendo. Moreover, and significantly, "Femme Forum" is broadcast from 10 a.m. to 3 p.m. during daytime hours when the radio audience may include children—perhaps home from school for lunch, or because of staggered school hours or illness. Given this combination of factors, we do not think that the FCC's evaluation of this material infringes upon rights protected by the First Amendment.

The FCC found Sonderling's broadcasts obscene. . . .

. . .

Petitioners object that the Commission's determination was based on a brief condensation of offensive material and did not take into account the broadcast as a whole, as would seem to be required by certain elements of both the *Memoirs* and the *Miller* tests. The Commission's approach is not inappropriate in evaluating a broadcasting program that is episodic in nature—a cluster of individual and typically disconnected commentaries, rather than an integrated presentation. It is commonplace for members of the radio audience to listen only to short snatches of a broadcast, and programs like "Femme Forum" are designed to attract such listeners.

We conclude that, where a radio call-in show during daytime hours broadcasts explicit discussions of ultimate sexual acts in a titillating context, the Commission does not unconstitutionally infringe upon the public's right to listening alternatives when it determines that the broadcast is obscene.

The court explicitly did not rely upon the Commission's argument that it had latitude to hold things "indecent" that are not obscene.

A motion for rehearing *en banc* was denied over the lengthy dissent of Chief Judge Bazelon, 515 F.2d at 407, 33 R.R.2d at 118 (1975). He was much concerned about the ability of the Commission, by "raised eyebrow" and the Chairman's speech, virtually to end a popular format. He saw this as "flagrant and illegal censorship."

INTRODUCTION TO THE PACIFICA CASE

Two points should be made before reading the following case. The first involves the notion of "nuisance" in law. Activities that may be socially desirable are often called nuisances if located in the wrong place. This might include a factory that emits smoke in an amount that would be acceptable in a factory district but is unacceptable in a residential district. The legal goal is to encourage the factory either to conform to the needs of its surroundings or to relocate to a factory area.

The second point involves a conflict within the Court about the legitimacy of regulations based on the content of the communication. In Police Department of Chicago v. Mosley, 408 U.S. 92 (1972), the Court invalidated an ordinance that barred picketing outside schools unless the picketing was related to a labor-management dispute concerning the school. "Once a forum is opened up to assembly or speaking by some groups, government may not prohibit others from assembling or speaking on the basis of what they intend to say."

In Young v. American Mini Theatres, Inc., 427 U.S. 50, 1 Med. L.Rptr. 1151 (1976), Detroit adopted a zoning ordinance requiring that theaters that specialized in showing sexually explicit movies had to be separated from one another by a minimum distance. The Court upheld the ordinance 5–4, but there was no majority opinion. Justice Stevens, for the plurality of four, said that the *Mosley* statement must be kept in context. Even though the First Amendment did not permit "total suppression of erotic materials that have some arguably artistic value, it is manifest that society's interest in protecting this type of expression is of a wholly different, and lesser, magnitude than the interest in untrammeled political debate. . . . [F]ew of us would march our sons and daughters off to war to preserve the citizen's right to see 'Specified Sexual Activities' exhibited in the theaters of our choice."

The plurality then concluded that the record supported the city council's conclusion that unfortunate effects followed from the clustering of such enterprises in one area.

Justice Powell provided the crucial fifth vote on the ground that this case involved "an example of innovative land-use regulation, implicating First Amendment concerns only incidentally and to a limited extent." The ordinance did not "restrict in any significant way the viewing of these movies by those who desire to see them."

The four dissenters considered the decision "a drastic departure from established principles of First Amendment law." These principles require that regulations concerning the time, place and manner of communicating "be content-neutral except in the limited context of a captive or juvenile audience."

As we will see, this conflict reappears in *Pacifica.*

FEDERAL COMMUNICATIONS COMMISSION v. PACIFICA FOUNDATION

Supreme Court of the United States, 1978.
438 U.S. 726, 98 S.Ct. 3026, 43 R.R.2d 493, 57 L.Ed.2d 1073, 3 Med.L.Rptr. 2553.

[George Carlin, a "satiric humorist," recorded a 12–minute monologue entitled "Filthy Words" before a live audience in a California theater. The theme was "the words you couldn't say on the public, ah, airwaves." Carlin then proposed a basic list: "The original seven words were shit, piss, fuck, cunt, cocksucker, motherfucker, and tits. Those are the ones that will curve your spine, grow hair on your hands and (laughter) maybe, even bring us, God help us, peace without honor (laughter) um, and a bourbon." Carlin then discussed "shit" and "fuck" at length, including the various phrases that use each word. The following passage gives some idea of the format:

> Now the word shit is okay for the man. At work you can say it like crazy. Mostly figuratively. Get that shit out of here, will ya? I don't want to see that shit anymore. I can't *cut* that shit, buddy. I've had that shit up to here. I think you're full of shit myself. (laughter) He don't know shit from Shinola. (laughter) You know that? (laughter) Always wondered how the Shinola people felt about that? (laughter) Hi, I'm the new man from Shinola. (laughter) Hi, how are ya? Nice to see ya. (laughter) How are ya? (laughter) Boy, I don't know, whether to shit or wind my watch. (laughter) Guess I'll shit on my watch. (laughter) Oh, *the* shit is going to hit *de* fan. (laughter) Built like a brick shit-house. (laughter) Up, he's up shit's creek. (laughter) He's had it. (laughter) He hit me, I'm sorry. (laughter) Hot shit, holy shit, tough shit, eat shit. (laughter) Shit-eating grin. Uh, whoever thought of that was ill. (murmur laughter) He had a shit-eating grin! He had a what? (laughter) Shit on a stick. (laughter) Shit in a handbag. I always like that.

One weekday afternoon at 2 p.m., Pacifica's FM station in New York City played the monologue during a discussion about society's attitude toward language. The station warned that the monologue included language that might offend some listeners. A man who apparently did not hear the warning heard the broadcast while driving with his 15–year-old son, and complained to the Commission. In response to an inquiry from the Commission, Pacifica responded that Carlin was a "significant social satirist" who "like Twain and Sahl before him, examines the language of ordinary people." Apparently, no one else complained about the broadcast.

The Commission ruled that Pacifica's action was subject to administrative sanction. Instead of imposing a formal sanction, it put the order in the file for possible use if subsequent complaints were received. The Commission asserted four reasons for treating broadcasting differently from other media: access by unsupervised children; because radio receivers are in the home, privacy interests are entitled to extra deference; unconsenting adults may tune in without a warning that offensive language is being used; and scarcity of spectrum space requires government to license in the public interest. Further facts are stated in the opinions.]

MR. JUSTICE STEVENS delivered the opinion of the Court (Parts I, II, III, and IV–C) and an opinion in which THE CHIEF JUSTICE and MR. JUSTICE REHNQUIST joined (Parts IV–A and IV–B).

This case requires that we decide whether the Federal Communications Commission has any power to regulate a radio broadcast that is indecent but not obscene.

. . .

. . . [T]he Commission found a power to regulate indecent broadcasting in two statutes: 18 U.S.C. § 1464, which forbids the use of "any obscene, indecent, or profane language by means of radio communications," and 47 U.S.C. § 303(g), which requires the Commission to "encourage the larger and more effective use of radio in the public interest."

The Commission characterized the language used in the Carlin monologue as "patently offensive," though not necessarily obscene, and expressed the opinion that it should be regulated by principles analogous to those found in the law of nuisance where the "law generally speaks to *channeling* behavior more than prohibiting it. . . . [T]he concept of 'indecent' is intimately connected with the exposure of children to language that describes, in terms patently offensive as measured by contemporary community standards for the broadcast medium, sexual or excretory activities and organs, at times of the day when there is a reasonable risk that children may be in the audience." 56 F.C.C.2d, at 98.[5]

. . . In summary, the Commission stated: "We therefore hold that the language as broadcast was indecent and prohibited by 18 U.S.C. 1464."

After the order issued, the Commission was asked to clarify its opinion by ruling that the broadcast of indecent words as part of a live newscast would not be prohibited. . . . The Commission noted that its "declaratory order was issued in a specific factual context," and declined to comment on various hypothetical situations presented by the petition.[7] . . .

The United States Court of Appeals for the District of Columbia reversed, with each of the three judges on the panel writing separately.

Having granted the Commission's petition for certiorari, 434 U.S. 1008, we must decide: (1) whether the scope of judicial review encompasses more than the Commission's determination that the monologue was indecent "as broadcast"; (2) whether the Commission's order was a form of censorship forbidden by § 326; (3) whether the broadcast was

---

5. Thus, the Commission suggested, if an offensive broadcast had literary, artistic, political, or scientific value, and were preceded by warnings, it might not be indecent in the late evening, but would be so during the day, when children are in the audience.

7. The Commission did, however, comment that:

" '[I]n some cases, public events likely to produce offensive speech are covered live, and there is no opportunity for journalistic editing.' Under these circumstances we believe that it would be inequitable for us to hold a licensee responsible for indecent language. . . . We trust that under such circumstances a licensee will exercise judgment, responsibility, and sensitivity to the community's needs, interests, and tastes."
[ ]

indecent within the meaning of § 1464; and (4) whether the order violates the First Amendment of the United States Constitution.

I

The general statements in the Commission's memorandum opinion do not change the character of its order. Its action was an adjudication. . . . The specific holding was carefully confined to the monologue "as broadcast."

. . . Accordingly, the focus of our review must be on the Commission's determination that the Carlin monologue was indecent as broadcast.

II

The relevant, statutory questions are whether the Commission's action is forbidden "censorship" within the meaning of 47 U.S.C. § 326 and whether speech that concededly is not obscene may be restricted as "indecent" under the authority of 18 U.S.C. § 1464. The questions are not unrelated, for the two statutory provisions have a common origin. . . .

The prohibition against censorship unequivocally denies the Commission any power to edit proposed broadcasts in advance and to excise material considered inappropriate for the airwaves. The prohibition, however, has never been construed to deny the Commission the power to review the content of completed broadcasts in the performance of its regulatory duties.[9]

During the period between the original enactment of the provision in 1927 and its re-enactment in the Communications Act of 1934, the courts and the Federal Radio Commission held that the section deprived the Commission of the power to subject "broadcasting matter to scrutiny prior to its release," but they concluded that the Commission's "undoubted right" to take note of past program content when considering a licensee's renewal application "is not censorship."

Not only did the Federal Radio Commission so construe the statute prior to 1934; its successor, the Federal Communications Commission, has consistently interpreted the provision in the same way ever since. [ ] And, until this case, the Court of Appeals for the District of Columbia has consistently agreed with this construction. . . .

Entirely apart from the fact that the subsequent review of program content is not the sort of censorship at which the statute was directed, its history makes it perfectly clear that it was not intended to limit the

---

9. Zechariah Chafee, defending the Commission's authority to take into account program service in granting licenses, interpreted the restriction on "censorship" narrowly: "This means, I feel sure, the sort of censorship which went on in the seventeenth century in England—the deletion of specific items and dictation as to what should go into particular programs." 2 Z. Chafee, Government and Mass Communications 641 (1947).

Commission's power to regulate the broadcast of obscene, indecent, or profane language. . . .

There is nothing in the legislative history to contradict this conclusion. . . .

We conclude, therefore, that § 326 does not limit the Commission's authority to impose sanctions on licensees who engage in obscene, indecent, or profane broadcasting.

III

The only other statutory question presented by this case is whether the afternoon broadcast of the "Filthy Words" monologue was indecent within the meaning of § 1464.[13] Even that question is narrowly confined by the arguments of the parties.

The Commission identified several words that referred to excretory or sexual activities or organs, stated that the repetitive, deliberate use of those words in an afternoon broadcast when children are in the audience was patently offensive, and held that the broadcast was indecent. Pacifica takes issue with the Commission's definition of indecency, but does not dispute the Commission's preliminary determination that each of the components of its definition was present. Specifically, Pacifica does not quarrel with the conclusion that this afternoon broadcast was patently offensive. Pacifica's claim that the broadcast was not indecent within the meaning of the statute rests entirely on the absence of prurient appeal.

The plain language of the statute does not support Pacifica's argument. The words "obscene, indecent, or profane" are written in the disjunctive, implying that each has a separate meaning. Prurient appeal is an element of the obscene, but the normal definition of "indecent" merely refers to nonconformance with accepted standards of morality.

Pacifica argues, however, that this Court has construed the term "indecent" in related statutes to mean "obscene" as that term was defined in Miller v. California, 413 U.S. 15 (1973). Pacifica relies most heavily on the construction this Court gave to 18 U.S.C. § 1461 in Hamling v. United States, 418 U.S. 87 (1974). See also United States v. Twelve 200–Foot Reels of Film, 413 U.S. 123, 130 n. 7 (1973)(18 U.S.C. § 1462) (dicta). . . .

The reasons supporting *Hamling*'s construction of § 1461 do not apply to § 1464. Although the history of the former revealed a primary concern with the prurient, the Commission has long interpreted § 1464 as encompassing more than the obscene. The former statute deals primarily with printed matter enclosed in sealed envelopes mailed from

---

13. In addition to § 1464, the Commission also relied on its power to regulate in the public interest under 47 U.S.C. § 303(g). We do not need to consider whether § 303 may have independent significance in a case such as this. The statutes authorizing civil penalties incorporate § 1464, a criminal statute. See 47 U.S.C. §§ 312(a)(6), 312(b)(2), and 503(b)(1)(E). But the validity of the civil sanctions is not linked to the validity of the criminal penalty. The legislative history of the provisions establishes their independence. . . .

one individual to another; the latter deals with the content of public broadcasts. It is unrealistic to assume that Congress intended to impose precisely the same limitations on the dissemination of patently offensive matter by such different means.[17]

Because neither our prior decisions nor the language or history of § 1464 supports the conclusion that prurient appeal is an essential component of indecent language, we reject Pacifica's construction of the statute. When that construction is put to one side, there is no basis for disagreeing with the Commission's conclusion that indecent language was used in this broadcast.

IV

Pacifica makes two constitutional attacks on the Commission's order. First, it argues that the Commission's construction of the statutory language broadly encompasses so much constitutionally protected speech that reversal is required even if Pacifica's broadcast of the "Filthy Words" monologue is not itself protected by the First Amendment. Second, Pacifica argues that inasmuch as the recording is not obscene, the Constitution forbids any abridgment of the right to broadcast it on the radio.

A

The first argument fails because our review is limited to the question whether the Commission has the authority to proscribe this particular broadcast. As the Commission itself has emphasized, its order was "issued in a specific factual context." 59 F.C.C.2d, at 893. That approach is appropriate for courts as well as the Commission when regulation of indecency is at stake, for indecency is largely a function of context—it cannot be adequately judged in the abstract.

The approach is also consistent with [*Red Lion*, p. 78, *supra*]. . . .

It is true that the Commission's order may lead some broadcasters to censor themselves. At most, however, the Commission's definition of indecency will deter only the broadcasting of patently offensive references to excretory and sexual organs and activities.[18] While some of these references may be protected, they surely lie at the periphery of First Amendment concern. Cf. Bates v. State Bar, 433 U.S. 350, 380–381

---

17. This conclusion is re-enforced by noting the different constitutional limits on Congress' power to regulate the two different subjects. Use of the postal power to regulate material that is not fraudulent or obscene raises "grave constitutional questions." Hannegan v. Esquire, Inc., 327 U.S. 146, 156 (1946). But it is well settled that the First Amendment has a special meaning in the broadcasting context. See, e.g., FCC v. National Citizens Committee for Broadcasting, 436 U.S. 775 (1978); Red Lion Broadcasting Co., Inc. v. FCC, 395 U.S. 367 (1969); Columbia Broadcasting System, Inc.

v. Democratic National Committee, 412 U.S. 94 (1973). For this reason, the presumption that Congress never intends to exceed constitutional limits, which supported *Hamling's* narrow reading of § 1461, does not support a comparable reading of § 1464.

18. A requirement that indecent language be avoided will have its primary effect on the form, rather than the content, of serious communication. There are few, if any, thoughts that cannot be expressed by the use of less offensive language.

(1977). [*Young,* p. 228]. The danger dismissed so summarily in *Red Lion,* in contrast, was that the broadcasters would respond to the vagueness of the regulations by refusing to present programs dealing with important social and political controversies. Invalidating any rule on the basis of its hypothetical application to situations not before the Court is "strong medicine" to be applied "sparingly and only as a last resort." Broadrick v. Oklahoma, 413 U.S. 601, 613 (1973). We decline to administer that medicine to preserve the vigor of patently offensive and excretory speech.

B

When the issue is narrowed to the facts of this case, the question is whether the First Amendment denies government any power to restrict the public broadcast of indecent language in any circumstances.[19] For if the government has any such power, this was an appropriate occasion for its exercise.

The words of the Carlin monologue are unquestionably "speech" within the meaning of the First Amendment. It is equally clear that the Commission's objections to the broadcast were based in part on its content. The order must therefore fall if, as Pacifica argues, the First Amendment prohibits all governmental regulation that depends on the content of speech. Our past cases demonstrate, however, that no such absolute rule is mandated by the Constitution.

The classic exposition of the proposition that both the content and the context of speech are critical elements of First Amendment analysis is Mr. Justice Holmes' statement for the Court in Schenck v. United States:

> "We admit that in many places and in ordinary times the defendants in saying all that was said in the circular would have been within their constitutional rights. But the character of every act depends upon the circumstances in which it is done. . . . The most stringent protection of free speech would not protect a man in falsely shouting fire in a theatre and causing a panic. It does not even protect a man from an injunction against uttering words that may have all the effect of force. . . . The question in every case is whether the words used are used in such circumstances and are of such a nature as to create a clear and present danger that they will bring about the substantive evils that Congress has a right to prevent." 249 U.S. 47, 52.

Other distinctions based on content have been approved in the years since *Schenck.* The government may forbid speech calculated to provoke

---

19. Pacifica's position would of course deprive the Commission of any power to regulate erotic telecasts unless they were obscene under Miller v. California, 413 U.S. 15 (1973). Anything that could be sold at a newsstand for private examination could be publicly displayed on television.

We are assured by Pacifica that the free play of market forces will discourage indecent programming. "Smut may," as Judge Leventhal put it, "drive itself from the market and confound Gresham," 556 F.2d at 35; the prosperity of those who traffic in pornographic literature and films would appear to justify his skepticism.

a fight. See Chaplinsky v. New Hampshire, 315 U.S. 568 (1942). It may pay heed to the " 'commonsense differences' between commercial speech and other varieties." Bates v. State Bar, 433 U.S. 350, 381 (1977). It may treat libels against private citizens more severely than libels against public officials. See Gertz v. Robert Welch, Inc., 418 U.S. 323 (1974). Obscenity may be wholly prohibited. [*Miller*]. And only two Terms ago we refused to hold that a "statutory classification is unconstitutional because it is based on the content of communication protected by the First Amendment." [*Young*].

The question in this case is whether a broadcast of patently offensive words dealing with sex and excretion may be regulated because of its content. Obscene materials have been denied the protection of the First Amendment because their content is so offensive to contemporary moral standards. Roth v. United States, 354 U.S. 476 (1957). But the fact that society may find speech offensive is not a sufficient reason for suppressing it. Indeed, if it is the speaker's opinion that gives offense, that consequence is a reason for according it constitutional protection. For it is a central tenet of the First Amendment that the government must remain neutral in the marketplace of ideas. If there were any reason to believe that the Commission's characterization of the Carlin monologue as offensive could be traced to its political content—or even to the fact that it satirized contemporary attitudes about four-letter words[22]—First Amendment protection might be required. But that is simply not this case. These words offend for the same reasons that obscenity offends.[23] Their place in the hierarchy of First Amendment values was aptly sketched by Mr. Justice Murphy when he said, "such utterances are no essential part of any exposition of ideas, and are of such slight social value as a step to truth that any benefit that may be derived from them is clearly outweighed by the social interest in order and morality." Chaplinsky v. New Hampshire, 315 U.S. 568, 572 (1942).

Although these words ordinarily lack literary, political, or scientific value, they are not entirely outside the protection of the First Amendment. Some uses of even the most offensive words are unquestionably protected. See, e.g., Hess v. Indiana, 414 U.S. 105 (1973). Indeed, we may assume, *arguendo*, that this monologue would be protected in other contexts. Nonetheless, the constitutional protection accorded to a communication containing such patently offensive sexual and excretory

22. The monologue does present a point of view; it attempts to show that the words it uses are "harmless" and that our attitudes toward them are "essentially silly." [ ] The Commission objects, not to this point of view, but to the way in which it is expressed. The belief that these words are harmless does not necessarily confer a First Amendment privilege to use them while proselytizing, just as the conviction that obscenity is harmless does not license one to communicate that conviction by the indiscriminate distribution of an obscene leaflet.

23. The Commission stated: "Obnoxious, gutter language describing these matters has the effect of debasing and brutalizing human beings by reducing them to their mere bodily functions. . . ." 56 F.C.C.2d, at 98. Our society has a tradition of performing certain bodily functions in private, and of severely limiting the public exposure or discussion of such matters. Verbal or physical acts exposing those intimacies are offensive irrespective of any message that may accompany the exposure.

language need not be the same in every context. It is a characteristic of speech such as this that both its capacity to offend and its "social value," to use Mr. Justice Murphy's term, vary with the circumstances. Words that are commonplace in one setting are shocking in another. To paraphrase Mr. Justice Harlan, one occasion's lyric is another's vulgarity. Cf. Cohen v. California, 403 U.S. 15, 25.

In this case it is undisputed that the content of Pacifica's broadcast was "vulgar," "offensive," and "shocking." Because content of that character is not entitled to absolute constitutional protection under all circumstances, we must consider its context in order to determine whether the Commission's action was constitutionally permissible.

C

We have long recognized that each medium of expression presents special First Amendment problems. Joseph Burstyn, Inc. v. Wilson, 343 U.S. 495, 502–503 (1952). And of all forms of communication, it is broadcasting that has received the most limited First Amendment protection. Thus, although other speakers cannot be licensed except under laws that carefully define and narrow official discretion, a broadcaster may be deprived of his license and his forum if the Commission decides that such an action would serve "the public interest, convenience, and necessity." Similarly, although the First Amendment protects newspaper publishers from being required to print the replies of those whom they criticize, Miami Herald Publishing Co. v. Tornillo, 418 U.S. 241, it affords no such protection to broadcasters; on the contrary, they must give free time to the victims of their criticism. Red Lion Broadcasting Co. v. FCC, 395 U.S. 367 (1969).

The reasons for these distinctions are complex, but two have relevance to the present case. First, the broadcast media have established a uniquely pervasive presence in the lives of all Americans. Patently offensive, indecent material presented over the airwaves confronts the citizen, not only in public, but also in the privacy of the home, where the individual's right to be let alone plainly outweighs the First Amendment rights of an intruder. Rowan v. U.S. Post Office Department, 397 U.S. 728 (1970). Because the broadcast audience is constantly tuning in and out, prior warnings cannot completely protect the listener or viewer from unexpected program content. To say that one may avoid further offense by turning off the radio when he hears indecent language is like saying that the remedy for an assault is to run away after the first blow. One may hang up on an indecent phone call, but that option does not give the caller a constitutional immunity or avoid a harm that has already taken place.[27]

Second, broadcasting is uniquely accessible to children, even those too young to read. Although Cohen's written message might have been

---

27. Outside the home, the balance between the offensive speaker and the unwilling audience may sometimes tip in favor of the speaker, requiring the offended listener to turn away. See Erznoznik v. Jacksonville, 422 U.S. 205 (1975).

incomprehensible to a first grader, Pacifica's broadcast could have enlarged a child's vocabulary in an instant. Other forms of offensive expression may be withheld from the young without restricting the expression at its source. Bookstores and motion picture theaters, for example, may be prohibited from making indecent material available to children. We held in Ginsberg v. New York, 390 U.S. 629 (1968), that the government's interest in the "well being of its youth" and in supporting "parents' claim to authority in their own household" justified the regulation of otherwise protected expression. *Id.*, at 640 and 639.[28] The ease with which children may obtain access to broadcast material, coupled with the concerns recognized in *Ginsberg*, amply justify special treatment of indecent broadcasting.

It is appropriate, in conclusion, to emphasize the narrowness of our holding. This case does not involve a two-way radio conversation between a cab driver and a dispatcher, or a telecast of an Elizabethan comedy. We have not decided that an occasional expletive in either setting would justify any sanction or, indeed, that this broadcast would justify a criminal prosecution. The Commission's decision rested entirely on a nuisance rationale under which context is all-important. The concept requires consideration of a host of variables. The time of day was emphasized by the Commission. The content of the program in which the language is used will also affect the composition of the audience,[29] and differences between radio, television, and perhaps closed-circuit transmissions, may also be relevant. As Mr. Justice Sutherland wrote, a "nuisance may be merely a right thing in the wrong place—like a pig in the parlor instead of the barnyard." Euclid v. Ambler Realty Co., 272 U.S. 365, 388 (1926). We simply hold that when the Commission finds that a pig has entered the parlor, the exercise of its regulatory power does not depend on proof that the pig is obscene.

The judgment of the Court of Appeals is reversed.

MR. JUSTICE POWELL, with whom MR. JUSTICE BLACKMUN joins, concurring.

I join Parts I, II, III, and IV(C) of Mr. Justice Stevens' opinion, and with its conclusion that the Commission's holding in this case does not violate the First Amendment. . . .

. . . Because I do not subscribe to all that is said in Part IV, however, I state my views separately.

---

28. The Commission's action does not by any means reduce adults to hearing only what is fit for children. Cf. Butler v. Michigan, 352 U.S. 380, 383 (1957). Adults who feel the need may purchase tapes and records or go to theatres and nightclubs to hear these words. In fact, the Commission has not unequivocally closed even broadcasting to speech of this sort; whether broadcast audiences in the late evening contain so few children that playing this monologue would be permissible is an issue neither the Commission nor this Court has decided.

29. Even a prime-time recitation of Chaucer's Miller's Tale would not be likely to command the attention of many children who are both old enough to understand and young enough to be adversely affected by passages such as "And prively he caughte hire by the queynte." G. Chaucer, *The Miller's Tale* 1.3276 (c. 1386).

I

It is conceded that the monologue at issue here is not obscene in the constitutional sense. See 56 F.C.C.2d 94, 98 (1975); Brief for Petitioner 18. Nor, in this context, does its language constitute "fighting words" within the meaning of Chaplinsky v. New Hampshire, 315 U.S. 568 (1942). Some of the words used have been held protected by the First Amendment in other cases and contexts. [   ] I do not think Carlin, consistently with the First Amendment, could be punished for delivering the same monologue to a live audience composed of adults who, knowing what to expect, chose to attend his performance. See Brown v. Oklahoma, 408 U.S. 914 (1972)(Powell, J., concurring in result). And I would assume that an adult could not constitutionally be prohibited from purchasing a recording or transcript of the monologue and playing or reading it in the privacy of his own home. Cf. Stanley v. Georgia, 394 U.S. 557 (1969).

But it also is true that the language employed is, to most people, vulgar and offensive. It was chosen specifically for this quality, and it was repeated over and over as a sort of verbal shock treatment. The Commission did not err in characterizing the narrow category of language used here as "patently offensive" to most people regardless of age.

The issue, however, is whether the Commission may impose civil sanctions on a licensee radio station for broadcasting the monologue at two o'clock in the afternoon. The Commission's primary concern was to prevent the broadcast from reaching the ears of unsupervised children who were likely to be in the audience at that hour. In essence, the Commission sought to "channel" the monologue to hours when the fewest unsupervised children would be exposed to it. See 56 F.C.C.2d at 98. In my view, this consideration provides strong support for the Commission's holding.

The Court has recognized society's right to "adopt more stringent controls on communicative materials available to youths than on those available to adults." Erznoznik v. City of Jacksonville, [   ]. This recognition stems in large part from the fact that "a child . . . is not possessed of that full capacity for individual choice which is the presupposition of First Amendment guarantees." Ginsberg v. New York, supra, at 649–650 (Stewart, J., concurring in result). Thus, children may not be able to protect themselves from speech which, although shocking to most adults, generally may be avoided by the unwilling through the exercise of choice. At the same time, such speech may have a deeper and more lasting negative effect on a child than an adult. For these reasons, society may prevent the general dissemination of such speech to children, leaving to parents the decision as to what speech of this kind their children shall hear and repeat:

> "[C]onstitutional interpretation has consistently recognized that the parents' claim to authority in their own household to direct the rearing of children is basic in the structure of our society. 'It is cardinal with us that the custody, care and nurture of the child

reside first in the parents, whose primary function and freedom include preparation for obligations the state can neither supply nor hinder.' Prince v. Massachusetts, [321 U.S. 158, 166 (1944)]. The legislature could properly conclude that parents and others, teachers for example, who have this primary responsibility for children's well-being are entitled to the support of laws designed to aid discharge of that responsibility." Ginsberg v. New York, supra, at 639.

The Commission properly held that the speech from which society may attempt to shield its children is not limited to that which appeals to the youthful prurient interest. The language involved in this case is as potentially degrading and harmful to children as representations of many erotic acts.

In most instances, the dissemination of this kind of speech to children may be limited without also limiting willing adults' access to it. Sellers of printed and recorded matter and exhibitors of motion pictures and live performances may be required to shut their doors to children, but such a requirement has no effect on adults' access. See Ginsberg v. New York, supra, at 634–635. The difficulty is that such a physical separation of the audience cannot be accomplished in the broadcast media. During most of the broadcast hours, both adults and unsupervised children are likely to be in the broadcast audience, and the broadcaster cannot reach willing adults without also reaching children. This, as the Court emphasizes, is one of the distinctions between the broadcast and other media to which we often have adverted as justifying a different treatment of the broadcast media for First Amendment purposes. [ ] In my view, the Commission was entitled to give substantial weight to this difference in reaching its decision in this case.

A second difference, not without relevance, is that broadcasting—unlike most other forms of communication—comes directly into the home, the one place where people ordinarily have the right not to be assaulted by uninvited and offensive sights and sounds. . . . The Commission also was entitled to give this factor appropriate weight in the circumstances of the instant case. This is not to say, however, that the Commission has an unrestricted license to decide what speech, protected in other media, may be banned from the airwaves in order to protect unwilling adults from momentary exposure to it in their homes.[2] Making the sensitive judgments required in these cases is not easy. But this responsibility has been reposed initially in the Commission, and its judgment is entitled to respect.

---

2. It is true that the radio listener quickly may tune out speech that is offensive to him. In addition, broadcasters may preface potentially offensive programs with warnings. But such warnings do not help the unsuspecting listener who tunes in at the middle of the program. In this respect, too, broadcasting appears to differ from books and records, which may carry warnings on their faces, and from motion pictures and live performances, which may carry warnings on their marquees.

II

As the foregoing demonstrates, my views are generally in accord with what is said in Part IV(C) of Mr. Justice Stevens' opinion. I therefore join that portion of his opinion. I do not join Part IV(B), however, because I do not subscribe to the theory that the Justices of this Court are free generally to decide on the basis of its content which speech protected by the First Amendment is most "valuable" and hence deserving of the most protection, and which is less "valuable" and hence deserving of less protection. Compare ante, at 15–19; [*Young*] (opinion of Stevens, J.), with *id.*, at 73 n. 1 (Powell, J., concurring).[3] In my view, the result in this case does not turn on whether Carlin's monologue, viewed as a whole, or the words that comprise it, have more or less "value" than a candidate's campaign speech. This is a judgment for each person to make, not one for judges to impose upon him.[4]

The result turns instead on the unique characteristics of the broadcast media, combined with society's right to protect its children from speech generally agreed to be inappropriate for their years, and with the interest of unwilling adults in not being assaulted by such offensive speech in their homes. Moreover, I doubt whether today's decision will prevent any adult who wishes to receive Carlin's message in Carlin's own words from doing so, and from making for himself a value judgment as to the merit of the message and words. . . .

Mr. Justice Brennan, with whom Mr. Justice Marshall joins, dissenting.

I agree with Mr. Justice Stewart that, under Hamling v. United States, 418 U.S. 87 (1974) and United States v. 12 200–ft. Reels of Film, 413 U.S. 123 (1973), the word "indecent" in 18 U.S.C. § 1464 must be construed to prohibit only obscene speech. . . .

I

For the second time in two years, see [*Young*], the Court refuses to embrace the notion, completely antithetical to basic First Amendment values, that the degree of protection the First Amendment affords protected speech varies with the social value ascribed to that speech by five Members of this Court. See opinion of Mr. Justice Powell. . . . Yet despite the Court's refusal to create a sliding scale of First Amendment protection calibrated to the Court's perception of the worth of a communication's content, and despite our unanimous agreement that the Carlin monologue is protected speech, a majority of the Court nevertheless finds that, on the facts of this case, the FCC is not constitutionally barred from imposing sanctions on Pacifica for its airing of the Carlin monologue. This majority apparently believes that the FCC's disapproval of

3. The Court has, however, created a limited exception to this rule in order to bring commercial speech within the protection of the First Amendment. See Ohralik v. Ohio State Bar Association, 436 U.S. 447 (1978).

4. For much the same reason, I also do not join IV(A). I had not thought that the application *vel non* of overbreadth analysis should depend on the Court's judgment as to the value of the protected speech that might be deterred. . . .

Pacifica's afternoon broadcast of Carlin's "Dirty Words" recording is a permissible time, place, and manner regulation. . . .

A

Without question, the privacy interests of an individual in his home are substantial and deserving of significant protection. In finding these interests sufficient to justify the content regulation of protected speech, however, the Court commits two errors. First, it misconceives the nature of the privacy interests involved where an individual voluntarily chooses to admit radio communications into his home. Second, it ignores the constitutionally protected interests of both those who wish to transmit and those who desire to receive broadcasts that many—including the FCC and this Court—might find offensive.

. . . I believe that an individual's actions in switching on and listening to communications transmitted over the public airways and directed to the public at-large do not implicate fundamental privacy interests, even when engaged within the home. Instead, because the radio is undeniably a public medium, these actions are more properly viewed as a decision to take part, if only as a listener, in an ongoing public discourse. See Note, Filthy Words, the FCC, and the First Amendment: Regulating Broadcast Obscenity, 61 Va.L.Rev. 579, 618 (1975). Although an individual's decision to allow public radio communications into his home undoubtedly does not abrogate all of his privacy interests, the residual privacy interests he retains vis-a-vis the communication he voluntarily admits into his home are surely no greater than those of the people present in the corridor of the Los Angeles courthouse in *Cohen* who bore witness to the words "Fuck the Draft" emblazoned across Cohen's jacket. Their privacy interests were held insufficient to justify punishing Cohen for his offensive communication.

Even if an individual who voluntarily opens his home to radio communications retains privacy interests of sufficient moment to justify a ban on protected speech if those interests are "invaded in an essentially intolerable manner," Cohen v. California, supra, at 21, the very fact that those interests are threatened only by a radio broadcast precludes any intolerable invasion of privacy; for unlike other intrusive modes of communication, such as sound trucks, "[t]he radio can be turned off," Lehman v. City of Shaker Heights, 418 U.S. 298, 302 (1974)—and with a minimum of effort. . . . Whatever the minimal discomfort suffered by a listener who inadvertently tunes into a program he finds offensive during the brief interval before he can simply extend his arm and switch stations or flick the "off" button, it is surely worth the candle to preserve the broadcaster's right to send, and the right of those interested to receive, a message entitled to full First Amendment protection. . . .

The Court's balance, of necessity, fails to accord proper weight to the interests of listeners who wish to hear broadcasts the FCC deems offensive. It permits majoritarian tastes completely to preclude a protected message from entering the homes of a receptive, unoffended minority.

No decision of this Court supports such a result. Where the individuals comprising the offended majority may freely choose to reject the material being offered, we have never found their privacy interest of such moment to warrant the suppression of speech on privacy grounds. . . .

B

Most parents will undoubtedly find understandable as well as commendable the Court's sympathy with the FCC's desire to prevent offensive broadcasts from reaching the ears of unsupervised children. Unfortunately, the facial appeal of this justification for radio censorship masks its constitutional insufficiency.

Because the Carlin monologue is obviously not an erotic appeal to the prurient interests of children, the Court, for the first time, allows the government to prevent minors from gaining access to materials that are not obscene, and are therefore protected, as to them. It thus ignores our recent admission that "[s]peech that is neither obscene as to youths nor subject to some other legitimate proscription cannot be suppressed solely to protect the young from ideas or images that a legislative body thinks unsuitable for them." [*Erznoznik*][3] The Court's refusal to follow its own pronouncements is especially lamentable since it has the anomalous subsidiary effect, at least in the radio context at issue here, of making completely unavailable to adults material which may not constitutionally be kept even from children. . . .

In concluding that the presence of children in the listening audience provides an adequate basis for the FCC to impose sanctions for Pacifica's broadcast of the Carlin monologue, the opinions of my Brother Powell and my Brother Stevens both stress the time-honored right of a parent to raise his child as he sees fit—a right this Court has consistently been vigilant to protect. See Wisconsin v. Yoder, 406 U.S. 205 (1972); Pierce v. Society of Sisters, 268 U.S. 510 (1925). Yet this principle supports a result directly contrary to that reached by the Court. *Yoder* and *Pierce* hold that parents, *not* the government, have the right to make certain decisions regarding the upbringing of their children. As surprising as it may be to the individual Members of the Court, some parents may actually find Mr. Carlin's unabashed attitude toward the seven "dirty words" healthy, and deem it desirable to expose their children to the manner in which Mr. Carlin defuses the taboo surrounding the words.

---

3. It may be that a narrowly drawn regulation prohibiting the use of offensive language on broadcasts directed specifically at younger children constitutes one of the "other legitimate proscription[s]" alluded to in *Erznoznik*. This is so both because of the difficulties inherent in adapting the *Miller* formulation to communications received by young children, and because such children are "not possessed of that full capacity for individual choice which is the presupposition of the First Amendment guarantees." Ginsberg v. New York, 390 U.S. 629, 649–650 (1968)(Stewart, J., concurring). I doubt, as my Brother Stevens suggests, ante, at 17 n. 20, that such a limited regulation amounts to a regulation of speech based on its content, since, by hypothesis, the only persons at whom the regulated communication is directed are incapable of evaluating its content. To the extent that such a regulation is viewed as a regulation based on content, it marks the outermost limits to which content regulation is permissible.

Such parents may constitute a minority of the American public, but the absence of great numbers willing to exercise the right to raise children in this fashion does not alter the right's nature or its existence. Only the Court's regrettable decision does that.[4]

C

As demonstrated above, neither of the factors relied on by both the opinion of my Brother Powell and the opinion of my Brother Stevens— the intrusive nature of radio and the presence of children in the listening audience—can, when taken on its own terms, support the FCC's disapproval of the Carlin monologue. These two asserted justifications are further plagued by a common failing: the lack of principled limits on their use as a basis for FCC censorship. No such limits come readily to mind, and neither of the opinions constituting the Court serve to clarify the extent to which the FCC may assert the privacy and children-in-the-audience rationales as justification for expunging from the airways protected communications the Commission finds offensive. . . .

. . . The opinions of both my Brother Powell and my Brother Stevens take the FCC at its word, and consequently do no more than permit the Commission to censor the afternoon broadcast of the "sort of verbal shock treatment," opinion of Mr. Justice Powell, involved here. To insure that the FCC's regulation of protected speech does not exceed these bounds, my Brother Powell is content to rely upon the judgment of the Commission while my Brother Stevens deems it prudent to rely on this Court's ability accurately to assess the worth of various kinds of speech.[6] For my own part, even accepting that this case is limited to its facts, I would place the responsibility and the right to weed worthless and offensive communications from the public airways where it belongs and where, until today, it resided: in a public free to choose those communications worthy of its attention from a marketplace unsullied by the censor's hand.

II

. . .

. . . The idea that the content of a message and its potential impact on any who might receive it can be divorced from the words that are the vehicle for its expression is transparently fallacious. A given word may have a unique capacity to capsule an idea, evoke an emotion, or conjure

---

4. The opinions of my Brothers Powell and Stevens rightly refrain from relying on the notion of "spectrum scarcity" to support their result. As Chief Judge Bazelon noted below, "although scarcity has justified *increasing* the diversity of speakers and speech, it has never been held to justify censorship." See Red Lion Broadcasting Co. v. FCC, 395 U.S. 367, 396 (1969).

6. Although ultimately dependent upon the outcome of review in this Court, the approach taken by my Brother Stevens would not appear to tolerate the FCC's suppression of any speech, such as political speech, falling within the core area of First Amendment concern. The same, however, cannot be said of the approach taken by my Brother Powell, which, on its face, permits the Commission to censor even political speech if it is sufficiently offensive to community standards. A result more contrary to rudimentary First Amendment principles is difficult to imagine.

up an image. Indeed, for those of us who place an appropriately high value on our cherished First Amendment rights, the word "censor" is such a word. Mr. Justice Harlan, speaking for the Court, recognized the truism that a speaker's choice of words cannot surgically be separated from the ideas he desires to express when he warned that "we cannot indulge the facile assumption that one can forbid particular words without also running a substantial risk of suppressing ideas in the process." Cohen v. California, 403 U.S., at 26. Moreover, even if an alternative phrasing may communicate a speaker's abstract ideas as effectively as those words he is forbidden to use, it is doubtful that the sterilized message will convey the emotion that is an essential part of so many communications.

. . .

The Court apparently believes that the FCC's actions here can be analogized to the zoning ordinances upheld in Young v. American Mini Theatres, supra. For two reasons, it is wrong. First, the zoning ordinances found to pass constitutional muster in *Young* had valid goals other than the channeling of protected speech. [ ] No such goals are present here. Second, . . . the ordinances do not restrict the access of distributors or exhibitors to the market or impair the viewing public's access to the regulated material. [ ] Again, this is not the situation here. Both those desiring to receive Carlin's message over the radio and those wishing to send it to them are prevented from doing so by the Commission's actions. Although, as my Brethren point out, Carlin's message may be disseminated or received by other means, this is of little consolation to those broadcasters and listeners who, for a host of reasons, not least among them financial, do not have access to, or cannot take advantage of, these other means.

. . .

III

It is quite evident that I find the Court's attempt to unstitch the warp and woof of First Amendment law in an effort to reshape its fabric to cover the patently wrong result the Court reaches in this case dangerous as well as lamentable. Yet there runs throughout the opinions of my Brothers Powell and Stevens another vein I find equally disturbing: a depressing inability to appreciate that in our land of cultural pluralism, there are many who think, act, and talk differently from the Members of this Court, and who do not share their fragile sensibilities. It is only an acute ethnocentric myopia that enables the Court to approve the censorship of communications solely because of the words they contain.

. . . The words that the Court and the Commission find so unpalatable may be the stuff of everyday conversations in some, if not many, of the innumerable subcultures that comprise this Nation. Academic research indicates that this is indeed the case. [ ] As one researcher concluded, "[w]ords generally considered obscene like 'bullshit' and 'fuck' are considered neither obscene nor derogatory in the [black] vernacular except in particular contextual situations and when used with certain intonations." [   ] Cf. Keefe v. Geanakos, 418 F.2d 359, 361 (1st Cir.1969) (finding the use of the word "motherfucker" commonplace among young radicals and protestors).

Today's decision will thus have its greatest impact on broadcasters desiring to reach, and listening audiences comprised of, persons who do not share the Court's view as to which words or expressions are acceptable and who, for a variety of reasons, including a conscious desire to flout majoritarian conventions, express themselves using words that may be regarded as offensive by those from different socio-economic backgrounds.[8]. . .

Mr. Justice Stewart, with whom Mr. Justice Brennan, Mr. Justice White, and Mr. Justice Marshall join, dissenting.

. . .

The statute pursuant to which the Commission acted, 18 U.S.C. § 1464, makes it a federal offense to utter "any obscene, indecent, or profane language by means of radio communication." The Commission held, and the Court today agrees, that "indecent" is a broader concept than "obscene" as the latter term was defined in Miller v. California, 413 U.S. 15, because language can be "indecent" although it has social, political, or artistic value and lacks prurient appeal. 56 F.C.C.2d, at 97–98. But this construction of § 1464, while perhaps plausible, is by no means compelled. To the contrary, I think that "indecent" should properly be read as meaning no more than "obscene." Since the Carlin monologue concededly was not "obscene," I believe that the Commission lacked statutory authority to ban it. Under this construction of the statute, it is unnecessary to address the difficult and important issue of the Commission's constitutional power to prohibit speech that would be constitutionally protected outside the context of electronic broadcasting.

. . .

Notes and Questions

1.   Is the "risk" of tuning in an offensive program on radio or television any greater than the risk of encountering offensive language on a person's clothing in a public place, as in Cohen v. California, 403 U.S. 15 (1971)? What about offensive films visible from the street while being shown at an outdoor movie theater, *Erznoznik*, p. 224, *supra*? If averting your eyes is an adequate remedy in these cases, why is turning off the radio or television set not adequate here? Is the fact that one may occur in the home relevant?

---

8. Under the approach taken by my Brother Powell, the availability of broadcasts *about* groups whose members comprise such audiences might also be affected. Both news broadcasts about activities involving these groups and public affairs broadcasts about their concerns are apt to contain interviews, statements, or remarks by group leaders and members which may contain offensive language to an extent my Brother Powell finds unacceptable.

2. It is easier to warn viewers that an adult, or possibly offensive, program is being presented when television is involved. In some countries, such programs carry a white dot in a corner of the picture so that a viewer can know the nature of the programming instantly. Would this solve our problems so far as television is concerned? Is there a similar technique that can be used for radio? Is it enough that certain stations become known as likely to present certain kinds of material offensive to some? What more could the licensee have done here to warn adult listeners?

3. It has long been agreed that Congress has preempted the matter of obscenity on radio and television—both of which are within "radio communication." Thus, a state may not impose its movie censorship scheme on films shown on television.

2. Development of the Current Rules

Following *Pacifica* the Commission's enforcement of the indecency provisions of § 1464 was essentially nonexistent. In the mid–1980s citizen groups put increasing pressure on the Commission actively to enforce § 1464.

Finally, in 1987 the Commission took action against three broadcast stations and one amateur radio operator. One station had broadcast excerpts from the play, "Jerker." The play was running in Los Angeles and had previously run in New York. Much of the play consists of telephone conversations between two homosexuals dying of AIDS in which they share their sexual fantasies. In an interview with the play's director that preceded the excerpts, the play was characterized as "blazingly erotic." The Commission rejected arguments by Pacifica that the excerpts should be considered in the context of the play's message—"the need to affirm life in the face of death." "Notwithstanding the licensee's assertion, we do not believe the context dilutes or ameliorates the patently offensive manner in which the sexual activity was described." Pacifica Foundation, Inc., 2 F.C.C.Rcd. 2698, 62 R.R.2d 1191 (1987). The Commission also referred the broadcast to the Justice Department for a possible obscenity prosecution. The Justice Department declined tc take any action.

A second station had aired a song that in the Commission's view "contained a number of patently offensive references to sexual organs and activities as measured by contemporary community standards for the broadcast medium." The Regents of the University of California, 2 F.C.C.Rcd. 2703, 62 R.R.2d 1199 (1987).

The complaint against the third station centered on "The Howard Stern Show." The show is an example of a radio format often referred to as "shock radio." Characterized by humor full of sexual innuendo and ridicule, it is considered offensive and tasteless by its opponents. At the same time, it is successful in the ratings. For example, Stern's show had moved from number 16 to three in the Philadelphia market. Infinity

Broadcasting Corp. of Pennsylvania, 2 F.C.C.Rcd. 2705, 62 R.R.2d 1202 (1987). Several stations toned down "shock radio" shows as a result of the Commission's actions.

Because the application of the indecency provisions of § 1464 in these cases represented a departure from previous Commission Policy, the stations were warned, but no further action was taken. At the same time, in a public notice, the Commission announced its intent to expand its enforcement of § 1464. New Indecency Enforcement Standards to be Applied to All Broadcast and Amateur Radio Licensees, 2 F.C.C.Rcd. 2726, 62 R.R.2d 1218 (1987).

Rather than limiting enforcement of § 1464 to the seven "dirty words" contained in the Carlin dialogue, the Commission announced it would "apply the *generic* definition of broadcast indecency advanced in *Pacifica,* which is: 'Language or material that depicts or describes, in terms patently offensive as measured by contemporary community standards for the broadcast medium, sexual or excretory activities or organs.' "

The Commission also announced a change in the times during which programming would be subject to the indecency provisions of § 1464. ". . . [I]ndecency will be actionable when there is a reasonable risk that children may be in the audience, but . . . this benchmark is not susceptible to a uniform standard. . . . [D]espite prior assumptions that children were not in the broadcasting audience at 10:00 p.m., recent evidence for the markets involved indicates that there is still a reasonable risk that children may be in the listening audience at [those] hours." Thus, as was the case in both the new Pacifica case and the Regents of the University of California case, programs after 10 p.m. could still be subject to the indecency provisions of § 1464 if there was evidence that children were in the audience.

In response to various Petitions for Clarification and Petitions for Reconsideration, including ones from the three broadcast licensees involved in the original decision, the Commission issued a further opinion and order on indecency. Infinity Broadcasting Corporation of Pennsylvania (Indecency Policy Reconsideration), 3 F.C.C.Rcd. 930, 64 R.R.2d 211 (1987). The FCC began by rejecting a request by Morality in Media that some "sexually explicit, yet non-obscene material" be absolutely prohibited. Such a prohibition would in the Commission's opinion be unconstitutional because the Supreme Court decision in *Pacifica* authorized only "the imposition of reasonable time, place and manner restrictions on the broadcast of indecent material in order to advance the government's interest in protecting children." In a footnote the Commission indicated that it would rely on parents to supervise their children after midnight, thus creating a "safe harbor" for broadcasts of indecent—but not obscene—programs. Although the footnote did not indicate when the "safe harbor" would end, the FCC's general counsel suggested at a press conference that 6 a.m. was the appropriate time. In a concurrence,

Commissioner Dennis suggested that the "safe harbor" start at the conclusion of prime time.

Next the Commission declined to define "patently offensive" or exempt material with "serious literary, artistic, political or scientific value."

14. "Patently offensive" is a phrase that must, of necessity, be construed with reference to specific facts. We cannot and will not attempt to provide petitioners with a comprehensive index or thesaurus of indecent words or pictorial depictions that will be considered patently offensive. There is no way to construct a definitive list that would be both comprehensive and not over-inclusive in the abstract, without reference to the specific context. All we hold here, therefore, is that, in the three cases before us, we properly found the material identified as indecent to be patently offensive.

15. Our approach here is consistent with that of the courts, which have likewise never attempted to identify with the degree of certainty requested by petitioners the complete and definitive range of material that falls within the generic, legal definitions of certain categories of speech. [The Commission cited obscenity law as a specific example where the term "patently offensive" had passed constitutional muster.]

. . .

17. The merit of a work is also one of the many variables that make up a work's "context," as the Court implicitly recognized in *Pacifica* when it contrasted the Carlin monologue to Elizabethan comedies and works of Chaucer. But merit is simply one of many variables, and it would give this particular variable undue importance if we were to single it out for greater weight or attention than we give other variables. We decline to do so in deciding the three cases before us. We must, therefore, reject an approach that would hold that if a work has merit, it is *per se* not indecent. At the same time, we must reject the notion that a work's "context" can be reviewed in a manner that artificially excludes merit from the host of variables that ordinarily comprise context. The ultimate determinative factor in our analysis, however, is whether the material, when examined in context, is patently offensive. . . .

After reviewing the three specific cases and concluding that the broadcasts in each case were indecent, the Commission did clarify the definition of the phrase, "contemporary community standards," as used in the definition of indecency. The standard is that of "an average broadcast viewer." Thus, the Commission will use a national standard for indecency as opposed to the local standard for obscenity prescribed by *Miller*.

Finally, the FCC turned to a request that it defer to the reasonable, good faith judgment of a licensees when determining whether they have violated § 1464:

. . . Although we acknowledge that the statute requires a broadcaster to make judgments as to whether certain material would violate the statute, the fact that the decision may not be an easy one cannot excuse the broadcaster from having to exercise its judgment, any more than it can excuse the Commission from exercising its enforcement responsibilities. We note, however, that it is standard procedure for the Commission, in deciding whether to impose a sanction for violation of the law and, if so, what those sanctions should be, to give weight to the reasonable determinations of licensees endeavoring to comply with the law. Because licensees demonstrating reasonable judgment have no cause to fear the imposition of unjustified sanctions, we reject the petitioners' contentions that the editorial decisions of broadcasters will be inappropriately chilled by continuation of this approach.

The Commission's decision was appealed by various trade organizations and public interest groups. They argued that the term "indecent" was unconstitutionally vague, that the Commission's channeling decision reduced adults to seeing and hearing material fit only for children, and that the channeling decision was arbitrary and capricious.

The appellate court rejected the first argument, holding that *Pacifica* precluded it from addressing the issue, because the Supreme Court had not found "indecent" unconstitutionally vague in that case. Action for Children's Television v. Federal Communications Commission, 852 F.2d 1332, 65 R.R.2d 45, 15 Med.L.Rptr. 1907 (D.C.Cir.1988)(*ACT I*).

The court also found that channeling *per se* did not violate the First Amendment rights of adults. Rather it was an attempt to balance four competing interests that had been identified by the Commission:

"(1) the government, which has a compelling interest in protecting children from indecent material; (2) parents, who are entitled to decide whether their children are exposed to such material if it is aired; (3) broadcasters, who are entitled to air such material at times of day when there is not a reasonable risk that children may be in the audience; and (4) adult listeners, who have a right to see and hear programming that is inappropriate for children but not obscene."

The court found, however, ". . . [T]he first two interests identified by the FCC coalesce; the government's role is to facilitate parental supervision of children's listening. . . . Thus, the FCC must endeavor to determine what channeling rule will most effectively promote parental— as distinguished from government—control."

Because the FCC had failed to present adequate evidence that its safe harbor period was a proper accommodation between the various competing interests, the court found that part of the Commission's decision arbitrary and capricious. One of the problems cited by the court was the FCC's reliance on ratings data for children 12–17, when it had previously indicated that age 12 was the upper limit for children who needed protection from exposure to indecent material. Also, the Commission had used ratings data for the total radio audience as opposed to the audiences for the shows at issue.

The court vacated the FCC's rulings in *Pacifica Foundation* and *Regents of the University of California*. However, the court affirmed the Commission's decision in *Infinity* because the programming at issue was broadcast between those early morning programs and the Carlin broadcast in the earlier Pacifica case, which was aired in the early afternoon.

Later that same year in an appropriations rider, Congress passed a requirement that the FCC enforce its anti-indecency policy 24 hours a day. The FCC complied with the requirement and passed the 24–hour–a–day ban. When the ban's effective date was stayed by the court of appeals, the Commission asked the court of appeals to remand the case involving the 24–hour ban to the Commission to give it a chance to build a record justifying the ban. Over the opposition of the media challengers, the court of appeals remanded the case to the Commission for a "full and fair" inquiry on the ban.

Both proponents and opponents of the 24–hour–a–day ban hoped that the Supreme Court might provide support for their position in a case involving "dial-a-porn," prerecorded pornographic messages available to telephone callers for a small per-call fee. Sable Communications of California, Inc. v. Federal Communications Commission, 492 U.S. 115, 16 Med.L.Rptr. 1961 (1989). In 1988 Congress had attempted to abolish dial-a-porn by making it a crime to provide obscene or indecent commercial telephone messages in interstate commerce. The Supreme Court unanimously held the statute unconstitutional insofar as it proscribed material that was not obscene:

> Sexual expression which is indecent but not obscene is protected by the First Amendment, and the government does not submit that the sale of such materials to adults could be criminalized solely because they are indecent. The government may, however, regulate the content of constitutionally protected speech in order to promote a compelling interest if it chooses the least restrictive means to further the articulated interest. We have recognized that there is a compelling interest in protecting the physical well-being of minors. This interest extends to shielding minors from the influence of literature that is not obscene by adult standards. [ ] The government may serve this legitimate interest, but to withstand constitutional scrutiny, "it must do so by narrowly drawn regulations designed to serve those interests without unnecessarily interfering with First Amendment freedoms." [ ]

The government argued that a total ban on dial-a-porn was the only effective way to prevent it from reaching minors, because enterprising youngsters would find some way to avoid lesser restrictions such as codes, scrambling procedures, or access by credit card only. The Court refused to defer to Congress's view on that point, noting that both the FCC and the court of appeals had concluded that the lesser restrictions would be "feasible and effective" in preventing access by children.

The Court in *Sable* did not make any specific reference to the pending dispute over broadcast indecency. In 1989, 17 media groups, relying heavily on *Sable* and the earlier decision of the court of appeals, filed briefs challenging the constitutionality of the 24–hour ban on indecent broadcast speech.

In 1990 the Commission unanimously adopted a report supporting a 24–hour–a–day ban on indecency for both radio and television. In its report the Commission argued that because children are part of the broadcast audience 24 hours a day, time channeling would be ineffective in promoting the government's interest in protecting children from indecent programming. The Commission also rejected the use of technological restrictions such as limiting indecency to the Second Audio Program (SAP) channel, which allows television sets equipped with a decoder to receive a different audio track for a program.

Given the ineffectiveness of less restrictive means of protecting children, the Commission concluded that the 24–hour ban would be a narrowly tailored way of serving a compelling government. Thus, according to the Commission, the ban was constitutional under the test adopted by the Supreme Court in *Sable*.

The Commission's action was reversed on appeal. Action for Children's Television v. Federal Communications Commission, 932 F.2d 1504, 69 R.R.2d 179, 18 Med.L.Rptr. 2153 (D.C.Cir.1991)(*ACT II*). The court found the reversal mandated by *ACT I*:

> Our holding in *ACT I* that the Commission must identify some reasonable period of time during which indecent material may be broadcast necessarily means that the Commission may not ban such broadcasts entirely. The fact that Congress itself mandated the total ban on broadcast indecency does not alter our view that, under *ACT I*, such a prohibition cannot withstand constitutional scrutiny. While "we do not ignore" Congress' apparent belief that a total ban on broadcast indecency is constitutional, it is ultimately the judiciary's task, particularly in the First Amendment context, to decide whether Congress has violated the constitution. [   ] . . .

> Nothing else in the intervening thirty-four months has reduced the precedential force *ACT I*. Indeed, the Supreme Court's decision in *Sable*, striking down a total ban on indecent commercial telephone messages, affirmed the protected status of indecent speech and reiterated the strict constitutional standard that government efforts to regulate the content of speech must satisfy. [   ]

The court's decision essentially placed the Commission in the position it had been in after *ACT I*, but prior to the appropriations rider. In other words the Commission was once again directed to initiate a proceeding to determine " 'the times at which indecent material may be broadcast,' to carefully review and address the specific concerns we raised in *ACT I*: among them, the appropriate definitions of 'children' and 'reasonable risk' for channeling purposes, the paucity of station-or program-specific audience data expressed as a percentage of the relevant age group population, and the scope of the government's interest in regulating indecent broadcasts."

A petition for *certiorari* was denied, 503 U.S. 913 (1992).

Before the Commission could initiate a proceeding, Congress intervened once more. The Public Telecommunications Act of 1992, Pub.Law 102–356, § 16(a), 106 Stat. 949, 954, included provisions requiring the FCC to promulgate regulations prohibiting the broadcasting of indecent programming between the hours of 6 a.m. and midnight. Public radio and television stations that go off the air before or at midnight would be permitted to broadcast indecency between 10 p.m. and midnight.

As soon as the FCC issued the new rules, broadcasters challenged them in the United States Court of Appeals for the District of Columbia. The complainants relied on the earlier decisions of the court and argued that nothing in this record met the fatal flaws that upset the earlier rules. The court agreed.

However, the D.C. Circuit voted to rehear the case *en banc* and withdrew the panel's judgment and opinion. 11 F.3d 170 (D.C.Cir.1993).

ACTION FOR CHILDREN'S TELEVISION v. FEDERAL COMMUNICATIONS COMMISSION (ACT III)

United States Court of Appeals, District of Columbia
Circuit, 1995. 58 F.3d 654, 78 R.R.2d 685.
Certiorari denied *sub nom.* Pacifica Foundation v. Federal Communications
Commission, 516 U.S. 1043, 116 S.Ct. 701, 133 L.Ed.2d 658 (1996).

Before EDWARDS, CHIEF JUDGE, and WALD, SILBERMAN, BUCKLEY, WILLIAMS, GINSBURG, SENTELLE, HENDERSON, RANDOLPH, ROGERS, and TATEL, CIRCUIT JUDGES.

BUCKLEY, CIRCUIT JUDGE:

We are asked to determine the constitutionality of section 16(a) of the Public Telecommunications Act of 1992, which seeks to shield minors from indecent radio and television programs by restricting the hours within which they may be broadcast. . . .

We find that the Government has a compelling interest in protecting children under the age of 18 from exposure to indecent broadcasts. We are also satisfied that, standing alone, the "channeling" of indecent broadcasts to the hours between midnight and 6:00 a.m. would not unduly burden the First Amendment. Because the distinction drawn by Congress between the two categories of broadcasters bears no apparent relationship to the compelling Government interests that section 16(a) is intended to serve, however, we find the more restrictive limitation unconstitutional. Accordingly, we grant the petitions for review and remand the cases to the Federal Communications Commission with instructions to revise its regulations to permit the broadcasting of indecent material between the hours of 10:00 p.m. and 6:00 a.m.

. . .

II. DISCUSSION

. . .

At the outset, we dismiss petitioners' vagueness challenge as meritless. The FCC's definition of indecency in the new regulations is identical to the one at issue in *ACT II*, where we stated that "the Supreme Court's decision in Pacifica dispelled any vagueness concerns attending the [Commission's] definition," as did our holding in *ACT I*. 932 F.2d at 1508. Petitioners fail to provide any convincing reasons why we should ignore this precedent.

We now proceed to petitioners' remaining constitutional arguments.

A. The First Amendment Challenge

It is common ground that "[s]exual expression which is indecent but not obscene is protected by the First Amendment." [*Sable*, p. 250, *supra*]. The Government may, however, regulate the content of constitutionally protected speech in order to promote a compelling interest if it chooses the least restrictive means to further the articulated interest. *Id*. Thus, a restriction on indecent speech will survive First Amendment scrutiny if the "Government's ends are compelling [and its] means [are] carefully tailored to achieve those ends." *Id*.

[The court then reviewed the pervasiveness and accessibility-to-children rationales originally advanced in *Pacifica*, p. 228, *supra*, for treating broadcasting differently than other media.]

1. The compelling Government interests

In examining the Government's interests in protecting children from broadcast indecency, it is important to understand that hard-core pornography may be deemed indecent rather than obscene if it is "not patently offensive" under the relevant contemporary community standards. The Second Circuit, for example, has found that the "detailed portrayals of genitalia, sexual intercourse, fellatio, and masturbation" contained in a grab bag of pornographic materials (which included such notorious films as "Deep Throat") are not obscene in light of the community standards prevailing in New York City. [ ] Therefore, as Justice Scalia has observed, "[t]he more narrow the understanding of what is 'obscene,' and hence the more pornographic what is embraced within the residual category of 'indecency,' the more reasonable it becomes to insist upon greater assurance of insulation from minors." Sable, 492 U.S. at 132 (Scalia, J., concurring).

The Commission identifies three compelling Government interests as justifying the regulation of broadcast indecency: support for parental supervision of children, a concern for children's well-being, and the protection of the home against intrusion by offensive broadcasts. Because we find the first two sufficient to support such regulation, we will not address the third.

Petitioners do not contest that the Government has a compelling interest in supporting parental supervision of what children see and hear on the public airwaves. . . .

Although petitioners disagree, we believe the Government's own interest in the well-being of minors provides an independent justification for the regulation of broadcast indecency. The Supreme Court has described that interest as follows:

> It is evident beyond the need for elaboration that a State's interest in safeguarding the physical and psychological well-being of a minor is compelling. A democratic society rests, for its continuance, upon the healthy, well-rounded growth of young people into full maturity as citizens. Accordingly, we have sustained legislation aimed at protecting the physical and emotional well-being of youth even when the laws have operated in the sensitive area of constitutionally protected rights.

New York v. Ferber, 458 U.S. 747, 756–57 (1982)(internal quotation marks and citations omitted); [   ]

While conceding that the Government has an interest in the well-being of children, petitioners argue that because "no causal nexus has been established between broadcast indecency and any physical or psychological harm to minors," [   ], that interest is "too insubstantial to justify suppressing indecent material at times when parents are available to supervise their children." [   ] That statement begs two questions: The first is how effective parental supervision can actually be expected to be even when parent and child are under the same roof; the second, whether the Government's interest in the well-being of our youth is limited to protecting them from clinically measurable injury.

As Action for Children's Television argued in an earlier FCC proceeding, "parents, no matter how attentive, sincere or knowledgeable, are not in a position to really exercise effective control" over what their children see on television. In re Action for Children's Television, 50 F.C.C.2d 17, 26 (1974). [The court then cited as confirmation several studies showing approximately half of all teenagers have televisions in their bedrooms and usually watch television alone or with friends. Eighty percent of all children have radios in their bedrooms.]

With respect to the second question begged by petitioners, the Supreme Court has never suggested that a scientific demonstration of psychological harm is required in order to establish the constitutionality of measures protecting minors from exposure to indecent speech. . . .

Finally, we think it significant that the Supreme Court has recognized that the Government's interest in protecting children extends beyond shielding them from physical and psychological harm. The statute that the Court found constitutional in *Ginsberg* sought to protect children from exposure to materials that would "impair[   ] [their] ethical and moral development." 390 U.S. at 641 (emphasis added). Furthermore, although the Court doubted that this legislative finding "expresse[d] an accepted scientific fact," *id.*, it concluded that the legislature could properly support the judgment of parents and others, teachers for example, who have [the] primary responsibility for children's well-being . . . [by] . . . assessing sex-related material harmful to minors according to prevailing standards in the adult community as a whole with respect to what is suitable material for minors. *Id.* at 639 (internal quotation marks omitted).

The Court noted, in the context of obscenity, that [i]f we accept the well nigh universal belief that good books, plays, and art lift the spirit, improve the mind, enrich the human personality, and develop character, can we then say that a . . . legislature may not act on the corollary assumption that commerce in obscene books, or public exhibitions focused on obscene conduct, have a tendency to exert a corrupting and debasing impact leading to antisocial behavior. . . . The sum of experience . . . affords an ample basis for legislatures to conclude that a sensitive, key relationship of human existence, central to family life, community welfare, and the development of human personality, can be debased and distorted by crass commercial exploitation of sex. Paris Adult Theatre I v. Slaton, 413 U.S. 49, 63 (1973). Congress does not need the testimony of psychiatrists and social scientists in order to take note of the coarsening of impressionable minds that can result from a persistent exposure to sexually explicit material just this side of legal obscenity. . . .

We are not unaware that the vast majority of States impose restrictions on the access of minors to material that is not obscene by adult standards. . . . In light of Supreme Court precedent and the social consensus reflected in state laws, we conclude that the Government has an independent and compelling interest in preventing minors from being exposed to indecent broadcasts. See *Sable*, 492 U.S. at 126 (Government's compelling interest in well-being of minors extends "to shielding [them] from the influence of literature that is not obscene by adult standards").

Petitioners argue, nevertheless, that the Government's interest in supporting parental supervision of children and its independent interest in shielding them from the influence of indecent broadcasts are in irreconcilable conflict. The basic premise of this argument appears to be that the latter interest potentially undermines the objective of facilitating parental supervision for those parents who wish their children to see or hear indecent material.

The Supreme Court has not followed this reasoning. Rather, it treats the Government interest in supporting parental authority and its "independent interest in the well-being of its youth," [ ], as complementary objectives mutually supporting limitations on children's access to material that is not obscene for adults. [ ] And while it is true that the decision in *Ginsberg* "denie[d] to children free access to books . . . to which many parents may wish their children to have uninhibited access," id. at 674 (Fortas, J., dissenting), as Justice Brennan pointed out in writing for the majority, "the prohibition against sales to minors [did] not bar parents who so desire[d] from purchasing the [material] for their children." *Id.* at 639; see also *Pacifica*, 438 U.S. at 749–50; *id.* at 769–70 (Brennan, J., dissenting).

Today, of course, parents who wish to expose their children to the most graphic depictions of sexual acts will have no difficulty in doing so through the use of subscription and pay-per-view cable channels, de-layed-access viewing using VCR equipment, and the rental or purchase of readily available audio and video cassettes. Thus the goal of support-ing "parents' claim to authority in their own household to direct the rearing of their children," *id.*, is fully consistent with the Government's own interest in shielding minors from being exposed to indecent speech by persons other than a parent. Society "may prevent the general dissemination of such speech to children, leaving to parents the decision as to what speech of this kind their children shall hear and repeat." *Pacifica*, 438 U.S. at 758 (Powell, J., concurring in part and concurring in the judgment).

    . . .

2. Least restrictive means

The Government may regulate the content of constitutionally pro-tected speech in order to promote a compelling interest if it chooses the least restrictive means to further the articulated interest. . . . [B]ut to withstand constitutional scrutiny, it must do so by narrowly drawn regulations designed to serve those interests without unnecessarily inter-fering with First Amendment freedoms. *Sable*, 492 U.S. at 126 (internal quotation marks omitted). . . .

a. Definition of "children"

Petitioners concede that it is appropriate to protect young children from exposure to indecent broadcasts. They remind us, however, that in *ACT I* we found it "troubling [that] the FCC ventures no explanation why it takes teens aged 12–17 to be the relevant age group for channel-ing purposes" in light of the fact that in an earlier legislative proposal, "the Commission would have required broadcasters to minimize the risk of exposing to indecent material children under age 12," 852 F.2d at 1341–42 (emphasis in original), and that in ACT II we directed the Commission on remand to address the question of the appropriate definition of "children." 932 F.2d at 1510.

Although, in *ACT II*, we made no mention of the fact, in its 1990 Report, the FCC defined "children" to include "children ages 17 and under." 5 F.C.C.R. at 5301. The agency offered three reasons in support of its definition: Other federal statutes designed to protect children from indecent speech use the same standard (citing 47 U.S.C.A. § 223(b)(3)(Supp. II 1990)(forbidding indecent telephone communica-tions to persons under 18)); most States have laws penalizing persons who disseminate sexually explicit materials to children ages 17 and under; and several Supreme Court decisions have sustained the constitutionality of statutes protecting children ages 17 and under. [   ]

We find these reasons persuasive. . . . In light of Supreme Court precedent and the broad national consensus that children under the age of 18 need to be protected from exposure to sexually explicit materials, the Commission was fully justified in concluding that the Government interest extends to minors of all ages.

b. The midnight to 6:00 a.m. "safe harbor"

Although, for the reasons set forth in Part II. B. below, we will require the Commission to allow the broadcast of indecent material between 10:00 p.m. and 6:00 a.m., we will address the propriety of section 16(a)'s midnight to 6:00 a.m. safe harbor. We do so for two reasons: First, in addressing the "narrowly tailored" issue, the parties have focused their arguments on the evidence offered by the Commission in support of the section's 6:00 a.m. to midnight ban on indecent programming. Second, the principles we bring to bear in our analysis of the midnight to 6:00 a.m. safe harbor apply with equal force to the more lenient one that the Commission must adopt as a result of today's opinion. Although fewer children will be protected by the expanded safe harbor, that fact will not affect its constitutionality. If the 6:00 a.m. to midnight ban on indecent programming is permissible to protect minors who listen to the radio or view television as late as midnight, the reduction of the ban by two hours will remain narrowly tailored to serve this more modest goal.

In *Pacifica*, the Supreme Court found that it was constitutionally permissible for the Government to place restrictions on the broadcast of indecent speech in order to protect the well-being of our youth. 438 U.S. at 749–51. We have since acknowledged that such restrictions may take the form of channeling provided "that the Commission . . . identify some reasonable period of time during which indecent material may be broadcast. . . ." *ACT II*, 932 F.2d at 1509. The question, then, is what period will serve the compelling governmental interests without unduly infringing on the adult population's right to see and hear indecent material. We now review the Government's attempt to strike that balance.

The Supreme Court has stated that "a government body seeking to sustain a restriction on . . . speech must demonstrate that the harms it recites are real and that its restriction will in fact alleviate them to a material degree." [   ]; see also Turner Broadcasting System, Inc. v. FCC, 114 S.Ct. 2445, 2470 (1994)(same). . . .

. . .

It is apparent, then, that of the approximately 20.2 million teenagers and 36.3 million children under 12 in the United States, [   ], a significant percentage watch broadcast television or listen to radio from as early as 6:00 a.m. to as late as 11:30 p.m.; and in the case of teenagers, even later. We conclude that there is a reasonable risk that large numbers of children would be exposed to any indecent material broadcast between 6:00 a.m. and midnight.

. . .

The remaining question, then, is whether Congress, in enacting section 16(a), and the Commission, in promulgating the regulations, have taken into account the First Amendment rights of the very large numbers of adults who wish to view or listen to indecent broadcasts. We believe they have. The data indicate that significant numbers of adults view or listen to programs broadcast after midnight. . . . [Of the estimated 181 million adult listeners], . . . approximately 6 percent . . . listen to the radio between 10:00 p.m. and 11:00 p.m. while 4 percent of them do so between midnight and 1:00 a.m. *Id.*

While the numbers of adults watching television and listening to radio after midnight are admittedly small, they are not insignificant. Furthermore, as we have noted above, adults have alternative means of satisfying their interest in indecent material at other hours in ways that pose no risk to minors. We therefore believe that a midnight to 6:00 a.m. safe harbor takes adequate account of adults' First Amendment rights.

Petitioners argue, nevertheless, that delaying the safe harbor until midnight will have a chilling effect on the airing of programs during the evening "prime time" hours that are of special interest to adults. They cite, as examples, news and documentary programs and dramas that deal with such sensitive contemporary problems as sexual harassment and the AIDS epidemic and assert that a broadcaster might choose to refrain from presenting relevant material rather than risk the consequences of being charged with airing broadcast indecency. Whatever chilling effects may be said to inhere in the regulation of indecent speech, these have existed ever since the Supreme Court first upheld the FCC's enforcement of section 1464 of the Radio Act. The enactment of section 16(a) does not add to such anxieties; to the contrary, the purpose of channeling, which we mandated in *ACT I* and reaffirmed in *ACT II*, 852 F.2d at 1343–44; 932 F.2d at 1509, and which Congress has now codified, is to provide a period in which radio and television stations may let down their hair without worrying whether they have stepped over any line other than that which separates protected speech from obscenity. Thus, section 16(a) has ameliorated rather than aggravated whatever chilling effect may be inherent in section 1464.

. . .

In this case, determining the parameters of a safe harbor involves a balancing of irreconcilable interests. It is, of course, the ultimate prerogative of the judiciary to determine whether an act of Congress is consistent with the Constitution. Nevertheless, we believe that deciding where along the bell curves of declining adult and child audiences it is most reasonable to permit indecent broadcasts is the kind of judgment that is better left to Congress, so long as there is evidence to support the legislative judgment. Extending the safe harbor for broadcast indecency to an earlier hour involves "a difference only in degree, not a less restrictive alternative in kind." [　] It follows, then, that in a case of this kind, which involves restrictions in degree, there may be a range of safe harbors, each of which will satisfy the "narrowly tailored" requirement of the First Amendment. We are dealing with questions of judgment; and here, we defer to Congress's determination of where to draw the line.

. . .

Recognizing the Government's compelling interest in protecting children from indecent broadcasts, Congress channeled indecent broadcasts to the hours between midnight and 6:00 a.m. in the hope of minimizing children's exposure to such material. Given the substantially smaller number of children in the audience after midnight, we find that section 16(a) reduces children's exposure to broadcast indecency to a significant degree. We also find that this restriction does not unnecessarily interfere with the ability of adults to watch or listen to such materials both because substantial numbers of them are active after midnight and because adults have so many alternative ways of satisfying their tastes at other times. Although the restrictions burden the rights of many adults, it seems entirely appropriate that the marginal convenience of some adults be made to yield to the imperative needs of the young. We thus conclude that, standing alone, the midnight to 6:00 a.m. safe harbor is narrowly tailored to serve the Government's compelling interest in the well-being of our youth.

B.　The Public Broadcaster Exception

. . .

Congress has provided no explanation for the special treatment accorded [public] stations other than the following: "In order to accommodate public television and radio stations that go off the air at or before 12 midnight, the FCC's enforcement authority would extend [to] the hour of 10 o'clock p.m. for those stations." [　] The Commission has done little better. . . . In its brief, the Commission justifies the disparate treatment accorded public and commercial broadcasters who sign off the air at midnight by suggesting that the latter may be able to finance the extension of their broadcasting day through the sale of advertising time. The agency also argues that allowing these public stations to begin broadcasting indecent material at 10:00 p.m. despite the significantly larger number of children in the radio and television audiences represents a reasonable trade-off because it serves the "substantial" (as opposed to "compelling") governmental interest in accommodating the free speech rights of those stations. The Commission does not address the phenomenon of "children's grazing" that it used so effectively in arguing against the relevance of program-specific statistics.

. . .

Whatever Congress's reasons for creating it, the preferential safe harbor has the effect of undermining both the argument for prohibiting the broadcasting of indecent speech before that hour and the constitutional viability of the more restrictive safe harbor that appears to have been Congress's principal objective in enacting section 16(a). . . .

. . .

Congress has failed to explain what, if any, relationship the disparate treatment accorded certain public stations bears to the compelling Government interest—or to any other legislative value—that Congress sought to advance when it enacted section 16(a). . . .

C.   Our Decisions in *ACT I* and *ACT II*

Petitioners maintain that our holdings in *ACT I* and *ACT II* preclude our finding that section 16(a) is narrowly tailored to achieve the Government's compelling interest as defined by them. While we have addressed their principal arguments above—and have done so in a manner that we believe to be consistent with our holdings in those two cases—we point to certain essential differences between this case and those with which we dealt in *ACT I* and *ACT II*.

Act I involved an assessment of the constitutionality of channeling decisions that had been made by the FCC on its own initiative; here we are dealing with an act of Congress which, as the Supreme Court has pointed out, enjoys a "presumption of constitutionality" that is not to be equated with "the presumption of regularity afforded an agency in fulfilling its statutory mandate." . . . It is true, of course, that in *Act II* we vacated a total ban on indecent broadcasts that Congress had attached to an appropriations bill. In doing so, we stated that our holding in *Act I* necessarily means that the Commission may not ban such broadcasts entirely. The fact that Congress itself mandated the total ban on broadcast indecency does not alter our view that, under *Act I*, such a prohibition cannot withstand constitutional scrutiny. 932 F.2d at 1509. . . .

While our holdings in this case are generally consistent with those in our two earlier decisions, we acknowledge that there are significant differences in our approach to certain of the issues. To the degree that the analyses in those earlier cases disagree with that contained in today's decision, they are, of course, superseded.

III.   CONCLUSION

"If there is a bedrock principle underlying the First Amendment, it is that the government may not prohibit the expression of an idea simply because society finds the idea itself offensive or disagreeable." [ ] The Constitution, however, permits restrictions on speech where necessary in order to serve a compelling public interest, provided that they are narrowly tailored. We hold that section 16(a) serves such an interest. But because Congress imposed different restrictions on each of two categories of broadcasters while failing to explain how this disparate treatment advanced its goal of protecting young minds from the corrupting influences of indecent speech, we must set aside the more restrictive one. Accordingly, we remand this case to the Federal Communications Commission with instructions to limit its ban on the broadcasting of indecent programs to the period from 6:00 a.m. to 10:00 p.m.

It is so ordered.

EDWARDS, CHIEF JUDGE, dissenting:

In this case, the majority upholds as constitutional a total ban of "indecent" speech on broadcast television and radio between the hours of 6 a.m. and midnight. The majority readily acknowledges that indecent speech (as distinguished from obscene speech) is fully protected by the Constitution, and that the Government may not regulate such speech based on its content except when it chooses the least restrictive means to effectively promote an articulated compelling interest. In this case, the Government fails to satisfy the acknowledged constitutional strictures.

. . .

Because the statutory ban imposed by section 16(a) is not the least restrictive means to further compelling state interests, the majority decision must rest primarily on a perceived distinction between the First Amendment rights of broadcast media and cable (and all other non-broadcast) media. The majority appears to recognize that section 16(a) could not withstand constitutional scrutiny if applied against cable television operators; nonetheless, the majority finds this irrelevant because it believes that "there can be no doubt that the traditional broadcast media are properly subject to more regulation than is generally permissible under the First Amendment." This is the heart of the case, plain and simple.

Respectfully, I find the majority's position flawed. First, because I believe it is no longer responsible for courts to provide lesser First Amendment protection to broadcasting based on its alleged "unique attributes," I would scrutinize section 16(a) in the same manner that courts scrutinize speech restrictions of cable media.

Second, I find it incomprehensible that the majority can so easily reject the "public broadcaster exception" to section 16(a), [ ], and yet be blind to the utterly irrational distinction that Congress has created between broadcast and cable operators. No one disputes that cable exhibits more and worse indecency than does broadcast. And cable television is certainly pervasive in our country. Today, a majority of television households have cable, and over the last two decades, the percentage of television households with cable has increased every year. However, the Government does not even attempt to regulate cable with the same heavy regulatory hand it applies to the broadcast media. There is no ban between 6 a.m. and midnight imposed on cable. Rather, the Government relies on viewer subscription and individual discretion instead of regulating commercial cable. Viewers may receive commercial cable, with all of its indecent material, to be seen by adults and children at any time, subject only to the viewing discretion of the cable subscriber. "Furthermore, many subscribers purchase cable service to get improved [broadcast] television reception, and a number of basic cable subscriptions are packaged to include channels that offer some indecent programming; so these subscribers will get indecent programming whether they want it or not." [Alliance For Community Media v. Federal

Communications Commission, 56 F.3d 105 (D.C.Cir.1995)] (Edwards, C.J., dissenting). In other words, the Government assumes that this scheme, which relies on personal subscription and individual discretion, fosters parental choice and protects children without unduly infringing on the free speech rights of cable operators and the adult audience.

If exposure to "indecency" really is harmful to children, then one wonders how to explain congressional schemes that impose iron-clad bans of indecency on broadcasters, while simultaneously allowing a virtual free hand for the real culprits—cable operators. And the greatest irony of all is that the majority holds that section 16(a) is constitutional in part because, in allowing parents to subscribe to cable television as they see fit, Congress has facilitated parental supervision of children. In other words, Congress may ban indecency on broadcast television because parents can easily purchase all the smut they please on cable! I find this rationale perplexing.

At bottom, I dissent for three reasons: First, the Government's asserted interests in facilitating parental supervision and protecting children from indecency are irreconcilably in conflict in this case. Second, the Commission offers no evidence that indecent broadcasting harms children. And although it is an easy assumption to make—that indecent broadcasting is harmful to minors—Supreme Court doctrine suggests that the Government must provide some evidence of harm before enacting speech-restrictive regulations. Finally, the Government has made no attempt to search out the least speech-restrictive means to promote the interests that have been asserted. For these reasons, section 16(a) should be struck down as unconstitutional.

I. FIRST AMENDMENT PROTECTIONS FOR THE BROADCAST MEDIA

[Judge Edwards first recounted the rationales for giving broadcasting more limited First Amendment protection than other media. He then argued that the scarcity rationale no longer has any validity. "Today, however, the nation enjoys a proliferation of broadcast stations, and should the country decide to increase the number of channels, it need only devote more resources toward the development of the electromagnetic spectrum."]

B. Accessibility to Children and Pervasiveness

The two additional rationales offered by the plurality opinion in *Pacifica*, attempting to distinguish broadcasting from other media, also fail to justify limited First Amendment protection of broadcast. The plurality found that "broadcasting is uniquely accessible to children, even those too young to read." *Pacifica*, 438 U.S. at 749.[23] This charac-

---

23. In Joseph Burstyn, the Court faced a similar argument, "that motion pictures possess a greater capacity for evil, particularly among the youth of a community, than other modes of expression." 343 U.S. at 502. The Court responded that, "[e]ven if one were to accept this hypothesis, it does not follow that motion pictures should be disqualified from First Amendment protection. If there be capacity for evil it may be relevant in determining the permissible scope of community control, but it does not

teristic, however, fails to distinguish broadcast from cable; and, notably, the rationale is absent from the Court's *TBS* opinion.

The plurality in *Pacifica* added another rationale which really has two components. The opinion reasoned that "the broadcast media have established a uniquely pervasive presence in the lives of all Americans. . . . [The] material presented over the airwaves confronts the citizen, not only in public, but also in the privacy of the home."[24] *Id.* at 748. Again, the pervasiveness of its programming hardly distinguishes broadcast from cable. As noted above, cable is pervasive: a majority of television households have cable today, and this percentage has increased every year over the last two decades. [ ] The intrusiveness rationale, that the material confronts the citizen in the privacy of his or her home, likewise, does not distinguish broadcast from cable, nor account for the divergent First Amendment treatment of the two media. . . .

It is relevant that *Pacifica* was a plurality opinion which provided a very limited holding. See 438 U.S. at 750 ("It is appropriate . . . to emphasize the narrowness of our holding. . . . The Commission's decision rested entirely on a nuisance rationale under which context is all-important."). . . . But beyond the narrowness of the Court's decision, it seems clear now that Pacifica is a flawed decision, at least when one considers it in light of enlightened economic theory, technological advancements, and subsequent case law. The critical underpinnings of the decision are no longer present. Thus, there is no reason to uphold a distinction between broadcast and cable media pursuant to a bifurcated First Amendment analysis.[25]

II. FULL FIRST AMENDMENT PROTECTION OF BROADCAST

Because no reasonable basis can be found to distinguish broadcast from cable in terms of the First Amendment protection the two media should receive, I would review section 16(a) and the Enforcement Order under the stricter level of scrutiny courts apply to content-based regulations of cable. . . .

In this case, the majority views the broadcast media as disfavored in the application of First Amendment rights, relying principally on Pacifica; however, my colleagues nonetheless agree that section 16(a) reflects a

---

authorize substantially unbridled censorship such as we have here." *Id.*

24. The plurality opinion added: Because the broadcast audience is constantly tuning in and out, prior warnings cannot completely protect the listener or viewer from unexpected program content. . . . This elaboration on the intrusiveness rationale, of course, does not distinguish broadcast from cable.

25. Zechariah Chafee provides a historical view of the Court's wavering toleration of speech-restrictive regulations on different media: Newspapers, books, pamphlets, and large meetings were for many centuries the only means of public discussion, so that the need for their protection has long been generally realized. On the other hand, when additional methods for spreading facts and ideas were introduced or greatly improved by modern inventions, writers and judges had not got into the habit of being solicitous about guarding their freedom. And so we have tolerated censorship of the mails, the importation of foreign books, the stage, the motion picture, and the radio. Zechariah Chafee, FREE SPEECH IN THE UNITED STATES 381 (1942).

content-based regulation that is subject to exacting scrutiny. . . . In my view, there is no way that section 16(a) can survive exacting scrutiny.

. . .

B. Compelling Interests

. . .

As I discussed in the panel decision, Action for Children's Television v. FCC, 11 F.3d 170, 183–86 (D.C.Cir.1993)(Edwards, J., concurring), one of the most significant problems with the Government's defense of its regulations is that its first two asserted interests, at least as the FCC appears to define their scope here, are irreconcilably in conflict. The Commission cannot simultaneously seek to facilitate parental supervision over their children's exposure to indecent programming and at the same time protect all children from indecent speech by imposing a flat ban on indecent programming from the hours of 6 a.m. to midnight. Simply put, among the myriad of American parents, not every parent will decide, as the Commission has, that the best way to raise its child is to have the Government shield children under eighteen from indecent broadcasts. Furthermore, not every parent will agree with the Commission's definition of indecency, nor whether it is appropriate in some contexts, nor at what age their own children may be exposed to such programming. In asserting both interests—facilitating parental supervision and protecting children from indecent broadcast—the Government must assume not only that parents agree with the Commission, but that parents supervise their children in some uniform manner. Surely, this is not the case. When acting consciously, some parents may prohibit their children from any exposure to indecent material; some may impose a modified prohibition depending upon the content of the programming and the child's maturity; still others may view or listen to indecent material with their children, either to criticize, endorse, or remain neutral about what they see or hear. A complete ban on indecent broadcasts does not facilitate the variety of American parents in supervising their children's exposure to broadcasting.

The Commission maintains that these two interests bolster and reinforce each other. . . . But here, the Commission assumes that parents are unavailable or inept at the task of parenting, and essentially establishes itself as the final arbiter of what broadcast American children may see and hear. In so doing, the Government tramples heedlessly on parents' rights to rear their children as they see fit and to inculcate them with their own moral values.[29] Courts generally do not take these moves lightly. We have long recognized the rights of parents to raise their children in the manner they see fit. . . . When the Government does intervene in the rearing of children contrary to parents' prefer-

---

29. At one point in its brief, the Commission attempts to narrow its interest in facilitating parents by claiming that it "aids parents who choose not to expose their children to indecent material." [   ] This does not absolve the Government from tram-

pling on the rights of parents. The only difference, is that in so phrasing its interest, the Commission only clarifies the parents on whom it tramples: those parents who do not agree with the Commission about how best to raise their children.

ences, it is usually in response to some significant breakdown within the family unit or in the complete absence of parental caretaking. Society protects children who are abused, neglected, or abandoned, because the harm is clear and such actions are contrary to civilized notions of parenting. The Government does not generally tell parents what speech their children should and should not hear absent some showing of harm to their children.

In other contexts, these two interests—facilitating parental supervision and protecting children from indecency—may have worked in tandem. For example, in *Pacifica*, a father's complaint that his son heard an indecent monologue prompted the FCC to enforce sanctions. *Pacifica*, 438 U.S. at 729–33. In that case, facilitating parental control and protecting the well-being of minors might have simultaneously converged; the parent agreed with the Commission (or vice versa). In *Ginsberg*, the statute only prohibited selling obscene magazines to minors; it did not prohibit the selling of obscene magazines to everyone. 390 U.S. at 634–35. Again, this statute may be viewed as facilitating parental control while simultaneously protecting children from indecency. . . . The instant case, however, differs . . .; this ban removes indecent speech from the broadcast airwaves beyond the reach of adults and parents, essentially mandating the Commission's desired result. Once it becomes clear that, in this context, these two interests conflict, it is then important to determine which compelling interest takes precedence.

The FCC asserts that its primary interest is in facilitating parental supervision. [   ] The Commission is wise to assert its interest in facilitating parents as its primary interest, for this surely offers a firmer base for permissible regulation. As the Supreme Court stated in *Ginsberg*, [i]t is cardinal with us that the custody, care and nurture of the child reside first in the parents, whose primary function and freedom include preparation for obligations the state can neither supply nor hinder. 390 U.S. at 639 [   ].

However, if facilitating parental supervision means allowing parents to run the household in the manner they choose, then the FCC has preempted, not facilitated, parental control in enforcing section 16(a). While the Government's interest in protecting the well-being of children is undoubtedly compelling, when it conflicts with parental preferences and arguably treads on First Amendment rights, case law requires the Government to show some evidence of harm. It is easy to assume that there must be ill effects from exposing children, and especially young ones, to indecent material, but Supreme Court doctrine suggests that we must check our assumptions. And with respect to exposure to broadcast indecency and the impact on children, we have yet to unearth any ill effects.

The Supreme Court has not established what is required in terms of a showing of harm from exposure to indecency. Although harm was not at issue in Pacifica, one can read the plurality opinion there as assuming that the indecent monologue harmed children. Recent Supreme Court case law, however, suggests that more is required. In *TBS*, [t]he Court was clear about the burdens on the Government: "It must demonstrate that the recited harms are real, not merely conjectural, and that the regulation will in fact alleviate these harms in a direct and material way." *Id.* [ ] While the Court in *TBS* noted that Congress's predictive judgments are entitled to substantial deference, and that Congress is not required to make a record of the type an agency must make, it stressed that Congress's judgments are not insulated from "meaningful judicial review." 114 S.Ct. at 2471 (plurality). "On the contrary," the Court stated "we have stressed in First Amendment cases that the deference afforded to legislative findings does 'not foreclose our independent judgment of the facts bearing on an issue of constitutional law.'" *Id.* (quoting *Sable*, 492 U.S. at 129).

. . .

In contending that the Government must protect children's well being, the Commission makes two arguments: first, it asserts that it may assume that indecent broadcast material harms children as a matter of law, citing *Pacifica* and *Ginsberg*; and, second, it suggests that the congressional sponsors considered evidence of the negative effects of television on young viewers. [ ] The Commission's reliance on *Pacifica* does not help its case; the question of harm was not before that Court, and, as discussed earlier, the interest in the protection of children was not necessarily at odds with the interest in facilitating parental supervision in that case. Contrary to the Commission's assertion, the Court in *Ginsberg* did not presume harm as a matter of law. Rather, the Court struggled with the question of whether the legislature had shown evidence of a causal link between "obscenity" and "impairing the ethical and moral development" of youth. 390 U.S. at 641–42. Under rationality review, the Court found that it could not state that the statute's regulation of obscenity had "no rational relation to the objective of safeguarding such minors from harm." *Id.* at 643. In this case, the court is not reviewing regulations that deal with obscenity, nor is the court operating under rationality review.

The congressional sponsors do not offer any evidence of a link between exposure to indecency and harm to children. Five out of the eight articles cited address materials involving violence, not indecency, and the remaining three discuss sexual materials but do not account for any harm. There simply is no evidence that indecent broadcasts harm children, the absence of which stands in striking contrast, to the wealth of research conducted on the harmful effects of televised violence. . . . Accordingly, the only interest the Commission asserts which is indeed compelling in this context is facilitating parental supervision.

C. Least Restrictive Means

It would be hard to object to some sort of regulation of indecency in broadcast as well as other media were it narrowly tailored to facilitate parental supervision of children's exposure to indecent material. . . .

Although unlikely, it is conceivable that such a ban on indecent programming could be the least restrictive means of facilitating parental control. For example, the Government might show that significant numbers of unsupervised children were watching or listening to programs containing indecency during the hours of the ban, that parents wished to limit what their children saw or heard, and that other means of controlling such exposure was considered and found to be ineffective. In this case, the Government offers no data on actual parental supervision, parental preferences, or on the effectiveness of parental supervision at different hours of the day and night. The Commission presents no program-specific data of what children watch, despite the existence of this data. . . . Without this kind of data, the Commission's decision to ban indecent broadcasting during the extensive period here in question is not narrowly tailored to serve the asserted interest of facilitating parental supervision.

More telling perhaps than the lack of data on parental supervision and the programming children watch, is the lack of any consideration of other less speech-restrictive means in the Enforcement Order. The Commission simply asserted: the broadcast indecency channeling program . . . most effectively serves the compelling interest of protecting children from exposure to indecent broadcast material without intruding excessively on the rights of those entitled to present or receive such material. We therefore believe that the means chosen is the least restrictive available for the broadcast medium and that other alternatives cannot effectively further this interest. [ ] To what other alternatives is the Commission referring? Absent from the Commission's decision is any discussion of an alternative method. And yet, at oral argument, counsel for the FCC assured the court that blocking technology, in which a chip placed in television sets prevents certain shows from being transmitted, is available. [ ] This device actually facilitates parental supervision in allowing parents to choose what programs or stations to block; and it is undoubtedly less speech-restrictive since parents assume control.[35]. . . The Commission's Enforcement Order shows no consideration of alternatives when they clearly exist. Therefore, the Commission's ban on indecent broadcast cannot be seen as the least restrictive means to facilitate parental control.

In summary, the Government's ban on indecent speech is not the least restrictive means available to further the Commission's primary compelling interest of facilitating parental supervision of their children's exposure to indecent programming.[36] The Commission has failed to show

---

35. Counsel for the FCC noted that "[t]his [technology] really hasn't been pushed here," suggesting that the reason was expense (but citing no evidence to support the suggestion). Tr. of Oral Argument at 62. While the cost may or may not in fact be prohibitive, the Commission at a minimum should have considered less speech-restrictive options like this one.

36. The majority finds that a 6 a.m. to midnight ban is the least restrictive means to further compelling interests and then goes on to find that a 6 a.m. to 10 p.m. ban is also the least restrictive means. While a 6 a.m. to 10 p.m. ban is certainly less speech restrictive than a 6 a.m. to midnight ban, it seems absurd to suggest that they are both the least restrictive means. As the majority

that its secondary interest, protecting children from exposure to indecent broadcast, is compelling when it conflicts with the rights of parents to rear their children in the way they see fit and when it is advanced with no evidence of harm. In applying the same level of scrutiny to regulations of broadcast as we do to regulations of cable and other media, it seems clear that section 16(a) and the Enforcement Order violate the First Amendment.

III. CONCLUSION

The Constitution prohibits the Government from infringing on the free speech rights of its citizens without showing that a content-based regulation is the least restrictive means to further compelling interests. The Government's ban on indecent speech fails to pass exacting scrutiny. I would vacate the FCC's Enforcement Order and hold section 16(a) of the Public Telecommunications Act of 1992 unconstitutional.

WALD, CIRCUIT JUDGE, with whom ROGERS AND TATEL, CIRCUIT JUDGES, join, dissenting:

"At the heart of the First Amendment lies the principle that each person should decide for him or herself the ideas and beliefs deserving of expression, consideration, and adherence. Our political system and cultural life rest upon this ideal." Turner Broadcasting System, Inc. v. FCC, 114 S.Ct. 2445, 2458 (1994). Very often this principle is not such an easy one to live up to or to live with. But presumptively, expression that many or even most of us find deeply reprehensible may not be, on that basis alone, proscribed. In R.A.V. v. City of St. Paul, 112 S.Ct. 2538, 2550 (1992), for instance, the Court held that racist fighting words could not be penalized on the basis of the hatred they expressed. Thus, whatever our collective interests in a "meritorious polity" and the moral development of the "people [who] govern it," Majority Opinion ("Maj. op.") at 17, governmental enforcement of those interests is radically constrained by the First Amendment's guarantee of freedom of expression.

This principle of free speech admits of limited exceptions, one of which is the permissibility of some government regulation of broadcast indecency. In FCC v. Pacifica Foundation, 438 U.S. 726, 729, 750–51 (1978), for example, the Supreme Court concluded that the Federal Communications Commission could constitutionally penalize the daytime broadcast of a dialogue containing the repeated use of "filthy words." . . .

Because indecent speech is fully within the ambit of First Amendment protection, the permissibility of government regulation of indecency depends crucially on the distinction between banning and channelling speech. . . .

Because the channelling of indecency effectuates a very delicate balance between the uncontestable First Amendment rights of adult

itself notes, "the preferential safe harbor has the effect of undermining . . . the constitutional viability of the more restrictive safe harbor that appears to have been Congress's principal objective in enacting section 16(a)."

viewers and the interests of parents (or society) in protecting immature children from indecent material—interests I discuss at greater length below—the design of the channelling is of utmost constitutional import. This the majority recognizes, in theory if not in fact: "The question, then, is what period will serve the compelling governmental interests without unduly infringing on the adult population's right to see and hear indecent material." [   ]

. . .

It is in implementing this balance that I part decisively with the majority. Any time-based ban on the airing of indecency intrudes substantially into the rights of adult viewers and listeners and places the government in the extraordinarily sensitive role of censor. By now, at least in the posture of the current case, it is probably too late to revisit our conclusion that the chill brought about by the Commission's open-textured definition of indecency is insufficiently great to invalidate the regulation. See Action for Children's Television v. FCC, 852 F.2d 1332, 1338–40 (D.C.Cir.1988)("ACT I"). Even a cursory glance at the Commission's enforcement policy to date, however, suggests that that chill is quite substantial, heightening the need for a meaningful safe harbor.[1]

Because the Commission insists that indecency determinations must be made on a case-by-case basis and depend upon a multi-faceted consideration of the context of allegedly indecent material, broadcasters have next-to-no guidance in making complex judgment calls. Even an all clear signal in one case cannot be relied upon by broadcasters "unless both the substance of the material they aired and the context in which it was aired were substantially similar." Sagittarius Broadcasting Corp., Notice of Apparent Liability, 7 F.C.C.R. 6873, 6874 (1992). Thus, conscientious broadcasters and radio and television hosts seeking to steer clear of indecency face the herculean task of predicting on the basis of a series of hazy case-by-case determinations by the Commission which side of the line their program will fall on. When, for instance, radio station hosts read over the air from a Playboy Magazine interview of Jessica Hahn about her alleged rape by the Reverend Jim Bakker, they did not regard the material as indecent because it involved matters of obvious public concern. The Commission, however, issued a notice of apparent liability for a forfeiture of $2,000, explaining that, "while the newsworthy nature of broadcast material and its presentation in a serious, newsworthy manner would be relevant contextual considerations in an indecency determination, they are not, in themselves, dispositive factors." KSD–FM, Notice of Apparent Liability, 6 F.C.C.R. 3689, 3689 (1990). News-

---

1. In light of the Commission's dramatically expanding enforcement policy—from the period extending several years beyond Pacifica in which the Commission only enforced the regulation against broadcasts substantially similar to the "filthy words" monologue penalized in that case to the current, ever-increasing reach of Commission enforcement—I am at a loss to understand the majority's conclusion that "[w]hatever chilling effects may be said to inhere in the regulation . . . have existed ever since the Supreme Court first upheld the FCC's enforcement of section 1464 of the Radio Act." [   ] As broadcasters learn of the Commission's more aggressive stance, their prophylactic measures are bound to increase.

worthiness, the Commission explained, is "simply one of many variables"; no single feature renders a work per se not indecent. *Id*. Although
in reading the interview, the hosts had said that the account made them
"sick," that it described rape rather than consensual sex, and that they
regretted their earlier jokes about the incident, the Commission concluded, without elaboration, that the presentation was "pandering." *Id*. at
3689–90. As this one case exemplifies so well, in enforcing the indecency
regulations the Commission takes upon itself a delicate and inevitably
subjective role of drawing fine lines between "serious" and "pandering"
presentations. And even a "serious" presentation of newsworthy material is emphatically not shielded from liability. This incident and the
Commission's discussion of it suggests that enforcement of its indecency
regulation involves both government-and self-censorship of much material that presents far harder choices than the glaring examples of smut
emphasized to such rhetorical effect by the majority. [   ]

Because of this potential for significant incursion into the First
Amendment rights of adult viewers and listeners during the hours of the
day and evening when the ban is in effect, it is particularly important
that the channelling "balance" struck by the government preserve a
meaningful place on the spectrum for adult rights to hear and view
controversial or graphic nonobscene material—that airing of such material not be restricted to a safe harbor that is in reality a ship's graveyard.
Thus, I cannot agree with the majority that determining the perimeter of
the safe harbor can be relegated to the category of discretionary line-
drawing akin to the distance from polls at which electioneering is
allowed and so largely shielded from judicial review. [   ] God or the
Devil (pick your figure of speech) is in the details. Because the safe
harbor constitutes the exclusive repository for the substantial First
Amendment rights of adults, its boundaries are of "constitutional dimension." [   ] For that reason, it cannot be beyond the competence of this
court to ensure that the safe harbor ensures meaningful as opposed to
pro forma accommodation of adult rights.

On the basis of the information given us by the Commission and
that was before Congress, it is impossible to conclude that the midnight
to 6 a.m. safe harbor strikes a constitutionally acceptable balance. . . .
Without a clear exposition of the scope of the government's interest, we
cannot know whether its means are tailored to be the least restrictive
available. [   ] ("the extent of the restriction on protected speech [must
be] in reasonable proportion to the interests served"). Yet, in the record
before Congress, there is as little evidence regarding the magnitude of
psychological or moral harm, if any, to children and teenagers who see
and hear indecency as there is that such exposure even occurs inside the
current safe harbor. In the six years that the safe harbor has been
operating from 8 p.m. to 6 a.m., and the prior years in which it covered
10 p.m. to 6 a.m., the government has adduced no concrete evidence of
real or even potential harm suffered by the exposure of children to
indecent material. We have not a scintilla of evidence as to how many
allegedly indecent programs have been either aired or seen or heard by

children inside or outside the safe harbor. Thus, even if the government were allowed to presume harm from mere exposure to indecency, surely it cannot progressively constrict the safe harbor in the absence of any indication that the presumed harm is even occurring under the existing regime.

Even if the government were acting on a tabula rasa, rather than on the basis of years of experience with a less restrictive ban, its delineation of the midnight to 6 a.m. safe harbor would be unjustifiable. . . .

The majority is right: the government's primary if not exclusive interest is in "shielding minors from being exposed to indecent speech by persons other than a parent." Given the significant First Amendment rights of adults at stake, moreover, the government has a constitutional responsibility to key its response to the presumed harm from indecency to facilitating parental control, rather than to government censorship per se. When most parents are presumably able to supervise their children, adult viewers should have access to the speech to which they are entitled. [ ]

Because the government can pursue whatever legitimate interests it has in protecting children by facilitating parental control, I do not believe that it can impose a valid ban during any hours it pleases solely because some children are in the audience. Nor do I believe that we can throw up our hands at the assumed impossibility of parental supervision simply because large numbers of children have television sets in their own room. Either or both of these excuses would justify a 24–hour ban as easily as the current 18–hour ban. Reasoning along these lines totally ignores the adult First Amendment interest that the majority purportedly recognizes and, effectively, gives the government unharnessed power to censor.

. . . Though it may be entirely logical for the government to assist parents by purging the airwaves of indecency during certain hours when parental supervision typically is at a low ebb, the government should be put to the task of demonstrating that the banned hours are based on a showing that these are the times of preponderant children viewing and the times when parents are otherwise absorbed in work in or out of the home. . . .

In constructing a safe harbor the government needs to give more careful consideration to those hours in the evening when parental control could reasonably be relied upon in lieu of censorship to protect children. . . .

Despite the majority's valiant effort to extract evidence for the government's position from the sparse record before us, the pickings are too slim for constitutional legitimacy. [ ] There is no evidence at all of psychological harm from exposure to indecent programs aired inside the current safe harbor. There is no evidence either that parents cannot supervise their children in those safe harbor hours or that "grazing" is leading to any significant viewing of indecency. Finally, the imminence of "V-chip" technology to enable parental control of all violence-and indecency-viewing suggests that a draconian ban from 6 a.m. to midnight is decidedly premature.

In spite of this evidentiary black hole, we have a broadside ban on vaguely defined indecency during all hours when most working people are awake, with a small bow to prior judicial rulings that a complete ban is unconstitutional, but no attempt to fashion an accommodation between the First Amendment and family values. The net effect of the majority's decision is a gratuitous grant of power allowing casual and lightly reviewed administrative decisionmaking about fundamental liberties. I respectfully dissent.

Notes and Questions

1. The Telecommunications Act of 1996 requires new television sets to have a chip capable of selectively blocking shows based on codes contained in the program signal—the "V-chip" referred to by Judge Wald. We will discuss this in greater detail later in this chapter. What effect should this have on the constitutionality of channeling indecency to a safe harbor period?

2. In a separate case, various broadcasters had challenged the constitutionality of the FCC's procedures for imposing forfeitures for the broadcast of indecent material. The basic claim was based on the long period of time that usually elapses between the allegedly indecent material being broadcast and final disposition of the case—anywhere from two to seven years. As the court noted, the uncertainty caused by these long delays is exacerbated by other factors:

> . . . First, a broadcaster claiming that a forfeiture is unconstitutional runs the risk of incurring an increased forfeiture for any subsequent indecency violation, [ ], and the possibility that the Commission will invoke the ultimate sanction, revocation of the broadcaster's license. See 47 U.S.C. §§ 307–309. Second, individual Commissioners have taken an active public role in criticizing broadcasters for airing indecent material and have let it be known that sanctions for such activity are likely to increase. Furthermore, the Commission will not, as a matter of policy, issue a declaratory ruling on whether a proposed broadcast is indecent. Thus, the only official guidance about the Commission's standards of decency available to a broadcaster is what can be gleaned from published [Notices of Apparent Liability] and forfeiture orders.

The constitutional claim was "that by forcing broadcasters to comply with the Commission's unreviewed determinations of indecency the scheme operates as a system of 'informal censorship' similar to the one held unconstitutional in *Bantam Books, Inc. v. Sullivan,* 372 U.S. 58, 83 S.Ct. 631, 9 L.Ed.2d 584 (1963)."

The court of appeals, although troubled by the FCC's procedures, found them constitutional. The court, in an opinion by Judge Ginsburg, distinguished *Bantam Books* because, "[u]nlike the Rhode Island Commission, which sought to regulate materials that could not be proscribed as obscene, 372 U.S. at 62 n. 4, 83 S.Ct. at 635 n. 4, so far as this record shows the FCC is not enforcing the statutory ban on indecency against material that is not indecent."

Judge Edwards concurred with reservations. He believed that decision was technically correct, but expressed the same concerns with indecency law in general that he voiced in *ACT III*, p. 252 *supra*, and *Alliance for Community Media*, to be discussed in Chapter IX.

Judge Tatel dissented, arguing that the court had not adequately distinguished *Bantam Books*:

> Like the Rhode Island Commission to Encourage Morality in Youth, the FCC censors speech, buttressing its informal powers through coercion and intimidation. The Rhode Island Commission warned that it would refer violators to the Attorney General, [ ]; the FCC threatens to increase fines, revoke licenses, and prevent acquisition of additional stations, [ ]. While judicial review is possible in both schemes—a criminal obscenity prosecution in Bantam Books and civil enforcement of FCC forfeiture orders here—in neither case are the parties practically able to obtain judicial review within any reasonable time frame.

Most troubling to Judge Tatel was the FCC's long-running battle with Infinity Broadcasting and, more specifically, Howard Stern.

> The Commission's treatment of Infinity Broadcasting Corporation demonstrates the leverage the agency has over broadcasters, as well as its use of unreviewed indecency determinations to impose stiff monetary penalties. The Commission notified Infinity and one of its subsidiaries that it intended to levy a $200,000 forfeiture on each of three stations that broadcast the same allegedly indecent program. [ ] It based this unusually large fine on "the apparent pattern of indecent broadcasting exhibited by Infinity over a substantial period since our initial indecency warning." [ ] The Commission warned that any future failures to comply with its indecency regulations would produce additional sanctions, including possible revocation of Infinity's broadcast licenses. [ ] Commissioner Quello made this threat explicit: "We could, for example, say 'enough is enough' and set all, or some, of Infinity's licenses for hearing to determine whether Infinity possesses the character to continue to hold them or whether they should be revoked. At this time—and I underline, at this time—I am not persuaded to take this step." [ ] Because of Infinity's alleged indecent programming, the Commission also seriously considered blocking its proposed acquisition of additional stations, but ultimately allowed the acquisition to go through at least in part, according to one Commissioner, because Infinity bowed to the Commission's threats and promised not to broadcast the program containing the allegedly indecent material on the newly acquired stations. [ ] In a subsequent Notice of Apparent Liability to Infinity regarding material aired in a different segment of the

same program, the Commission acknowledged the extent to which the licensee had caved in to Commission pressure, noting with approval Infinity's efforts to conform to the FCC's view of indecency by rigorously reviewing and modifying programs, as well as by instituting a multiple "delay" mechanism and requiring management-level personnel to monitor continuously the programs as they aired. [ ] But again, the Commission warned that "any future infractions [of the indecency regulations] would place Infinity's continuing fitness as a Commission licensee in question." [ ]

Action for Children's Television v. Federal Communications Commission, 59 F.3d 1249, 78 R.R.2d 922 (D.C.Cir.1995)(*ACT IV*). A petition for *certiorari* was denied. 516 U.S. 1072 (1996).

3. Shortly after the *en banc* decision in *ACT III*, Infinity Broadcasting negotiated a settlement with the FCC concerning the numerous indecency complaints that had been filed. Infinity agreed to pay $1.7 million in two installments starting with a $1 million payment. Infinity also pledged to a program to educate on-air personnel regarding FCC indecency actions. Sagitarrius Broadcasting Corp. (Settlement Agreement), 10 F.C.C.Rcd. 12245 (1995).

4. Pursuant to a 1994 settlement agreement with Evergreen Media Corporation, in 2001 the Commission issued a Policy Statement intended to provide additional guidance to the indecency rules. The statement began with a history of indecency regulation, followed by a summary of the FCC's analytical approach to indecency complaints.

Indecency findings involve at least two fundamental determinations. First, the material alleged to be indecent must fall within the subject matter scope of our indecency definition—that is, the material must describe or depict sexual or excretory organs or activities. [ ]

Second, the broadcast must be *patently offensive* as measured by contemporary community standards for the broadcast medium. In applying the "community standards for the broadcast medium" criterion, the Commission has stated:

The determination as to whether certain programming is patently offensive is not a local one and does not encompass any particular geographic area. Rather, the standard is that of an average broadcast viewer or listener and not the sensibilities of any individual complainant.

[ ]

In determining whether material is patently offensive, the *full context* in which the material appeared is critically important. It is not sufficient, for example, to know that explicit sexual terms or descriptions were used, just as it is not sufficient to know only that no such terms or descriptions were used. Explicit language in the context of a *bona fide* newscast might not be patently offensive, while sexual innuendo that persists and is sufficiently clear to make the sexual meaning inescapable might be. Moreover, contextual determinations are necessarily highly fact-specific, making it difficult to catalog comprehensively all of the possible contextual factors that might exacerbate or mitigate the patent offensiveness of particular material. An analysis of Commission case law reveals that various factors have been consistently considered relevant in indecency determinations. . . .

The principal factors that have proved significant in our decisions to date are: (1) the *explicitness or graphic nature* of the description or depiction of sexual or excretory organs or activities; (2) whether the material *dwells on or repeats at length* descriptions of sexual or excretory organs or activities; (3) *whether the material appears to pander or is used to titillate*, or *whether the material appears to have been presented for its shock value*. In assessing all of the factors, and particularly the third factor, the overall context of the broadcast in which the disputed material appeared is critical. Each indecency case presents its own particular mix of these, and possibly other, factors, which must be balanced to ultimately determine whether the material is patently offensive and therefore indecent. No single factor generally provides the basis for an indecency finding.

The Commission then gave a series of specific examples of both successful and unsuccessful indecency complaints to illustrate each of the principle factors. This was followed by a description of the actual enforcement process, including the minimum requirements for an indecency complaint to be considered: "(1) a full or partial tape or transcript or significant excerpts of the program; (2) the date and time of the broadcast; and (3) the call sign of the station involved."

Commissioner Tristani dissented, arguing in part that "the Statement perpetuates the myth that broadcast indecency standards are too vague and compliance so difficult that a Policy Statement is necessary to provide further guidance [and that the] Statement diverts this Agency's attention and resources away from the ongoing problem of lax enforcement, which is a pressing concern of America's citizens." She also expressed a concern that the Policy Statement would become "a 'how-to' manual for those licensees who wish to tread the line drawn by our cases. It likely may lead to responses to future enforcement actions that cite the Statement as establishing false safe Harbors." Industry Guidance on the Commission's Case Law Interpreting 18 U.S.C. §§ 1464 and Enforcement Policies Regarding Broadcast Indecency, 16 F.C.C.Rcd. 7999 (2001).

In contrast, many broadcasters argued that the statement did not adequately define indecency and that the standards were still too vague. Which side has the better of this argument?

5. Soon after the Policy Statement was issued, a notice of apparent liability for broadcast indecency issued to a Colorado radio station caused new controversy. The station had played an edited version of "The Real

Slim Shady" by Eminem a total of 408 times during the spring and summer of 2000. The version the station played was a " 'radio edit' version that omitted certain offensive language through the use of a muting device or overdubbed sound effect." The Enforcement Bureau, found the edited version to be indecent and set the forfeiture at $7,000.

The lyrics cited by the Enforcement Bureau were as follows:

Feminist women love Eminem

(Eminem's vocal turntable sound effect: "sicka sicka sicka") Slim Shady, I'm sick of him

Look at him, walking around grabbin' his you know what, flippin' the you know who

"Yeah, but he's so cute, though"

Yeah, probably got a couple of screws up in my head loose

But the worse is what's going on in your parents' bedroom

Sometimes I want to get on TV and just let loose, but can't

But it's cool for Tom Green to hump a dead moose:

"My bum is on your lips

My bum is on your lips"

And if I'm lucky you might just give it a little kiss

And that's the message we deliver to little kids

And expect them not to know what a woman's BLEEP is

Of course, they're gonna know what intercourse is

by the time they hit fourth grade

They got the Discovery Channel, don't they?

"We ain't nothin' but mammals"

Well, some of us cannibals

*   *   *   *   *   *   *

It's funny cause at the rate I'm goin'

When I'm 30 I'll be the only person in the nursing home flirting

Pinching nurses' asses when I'm BLEEP or jerkin'

Said I'm jerkin' but this whole bag of Viagra isn't workin'

FCC officials denied charges that the agency was increasing indecency enforcement efforts, but some broadcast attorneys disagreed, saying that the number of indecency investigations was increasing. Broadcasting & Cable, June 11, 2001 at 54. The station challenged the fine and the FCC rescinded it. Citadel Broadcasting Company, 17 F.C.C.Rcd. 483 (202).

3. Application to News and Politics

In a clarification sought by the Radio Television News Directors Association (RTNDA), after the initial ruling in *Pacifica*, p. 228, *supra*, the Commission announced that its decision was not meant to impinge on the coverage of news events in which offensive speech is sometimes uttered without a chance for editing: "Under these circumstances we believe that it would be inequitable for us to hold a licensee responsible for indecent language." Pacifica Foundation, 59 F.C.C.2d 892, 36 R.R.2d 1008 (1976). What if there is time for editing the dialogue but to do so would change the impact of the event? Can this be handled by an announcer who says, "At this point the speaker launched into a stream of obscenities"?

Vice President Nelson Rockefeller once used a finger gesture generally considered "obscene" when replying in kind to a heckler during a campaign rally. Most newspapers ran the photograph, but some did not. Would the decision be different for television stations? Are the considerations different for the 6 p.m. and the 11 p.m. news? Does the fact that it was in the course of a live news event make a difference?

That same year, a primary election for governor was held in Georgia. J. B. Stoner, a legally qualified candidate, speaking under § 315, made broadcast messages using the word "nigger." Black groups asked the Commission to bar such language as indecent under the *Pacifica* principle. The Broadcast Bureau rejected the request. First, it ruled that the word was not "language that describes in the broadcast medium, sexual or excretory activities and organs, at times of the day when there is reasonable risk that children may be in the audience," quoting the Commission's language in *Pacifica*. Also, the Commission had already announced that "we intend strictly to observe the narrowness of the Pacifica holding." Even if the Commission were to find the word obscene or indecent, under § 315 the candidate could not be prevented from using the word during his "use" of the licensee's facilities. Julian Bond, 69 F.C.C.2d 943, 43 R.R.2d 1015 (Bd.Bur.1978).

During the 1980 Presidential campaign, one radio commercial began as follows: A man says "Bullshit!" After a woman says "What?," the man's voice replies: "Carter, Reagan, and Anderson. It's all Bullshit! Bullshit!" Then the party's candidate says "Too bad people have to use such strong language, but isn't that what you think too? That's why we started an entirely new political party, the Citizens Party." The FCC, which received many complaints and inquiries, responded that the precedents were quite clear that no censorship was possible—at least unless a candidate created a clear and present danger of riot or violence.

The campaign director said that for six months the media had been covering only the three major candidates "despite the fact that they have little to say of substance about the problems of the nation." He observed that "It's a sad commentary on the media that we received more attention as a result of using that word than we've received in the last six months combined."

In 1983 *Hustler* magazine publisher Larry Flynt was reported to be intending to use clips from X-rated films in television ads supporting his presidential candidacy. This caused Sen. Jeremiah Denton (R–Ala.) to introduce legislation to allow broadcasters to refuse to air pornographic political announcements despite the no-censorship provision of § 315. Subsequently the FCC indicated that it would not apply the no-censorship provision to obscene or indecent political announcements. The issue never arose as Flynt chose not to run.

During the election campaign of 1992, some federal candidates sought to present advertisements purporting to depict dead fetuses. Broadcasters sought to channel them to later evening hours on the ground of indecency or at least to disassociate their stations from the advertisements. The technical claim of indecency was based on the assertion that the advertisements presented excretory functions.

DANIEL BECKER v. FEDERAL COMMUNICATIONS COMMISSION

United States Court of Appeals, District of Columbia Circuit, 1996.
95 F.3d 75.

Before SILBERMAN and ROGERS, CIRCUIT JUDGES, and BUCKLEY,* SENIOR CIRCUIT JUDGE.

BUCKLEY, SENIOR CIRCUIT JUDGE:

These consolidated cases arise from the efforts of a candidate for federal office to air political advertisements portraying images of aborted fetuses during time periods of his selection. Petitioners Washington Area Citizens Coalition Interested in Viewers' Constitutional Rights ("WAC–CI") and the candidate, Daniel Becker, seek review of a Federal Communications Commission order permitting a broadcast licensee to restrict the broadcast of campaign advertisements that may be "harmful to children" to times of the day when children are less likely to be in the viewing audience. Petitioners claim that the ruling violates §§ 312(a)(7) and 315(a) of the Communications Act of 1934 ("Act"). We agree.

. . .

The 1992 election season witnessed the advent of political advertisements depicting the aftermath of abortions. See Lilli Levi, The FCC, Indecency, and Anti–Abortion Political Advertising, III Vill. Sports & Ent. L.J. 85, 86–88 (1996) ("Anti–Abortion Political Advertising"). In that year, Daniel Becker was a qualified candidate for election to the United States House of Representatives from Georgia's Ninth Congressional District. At 7:58 p.m. on July 19, Station WAGA–TV, which was then licensed to Gillett Communications of Atlanta, Inc. ("Gillett"), aired, at Mr. Becker's request, a campaign advertisement that included

---

* At the time of oral argument, Judge Buckley was a circuit judge in active ser-   vice. He assumed senior status on September 1, 1996.

photographs of aborted fetuses. WAGA–TV received numerous complaints from viewers who saw the advertisement.

Anticipating that Mr. Becker would wish to broadcast similar materials later in the campaign, Gillett filed a petition with the Commission requesting a declaratory ruling on the following question: Whether a licensee may channel a use by a legally-qualified federal candidate to a safe harbor when children are not generally present in the audience if the licensee determines in good faith that the proposed use is indecent or otherwise unsuitable for children. [   ] This was followed by a petition by [a law firm that sought a declaratory ruling that broadcasters may decline political advertisements] that "present [   ] graphic depictions of aborted fetuses or any other similar graphic depictions of excised or bloody fetal tissue, where there is, in the good-faith judgment of the licensee, a reasonable risk that children may be in the audience. . . ."

After viewing a tape of Mr. Becker's July 1992 advertisement, and in response to the two petitions, the FCC's Mass Media Bureau ("Bureau") [found the advertisement was not indecent and rejected the requested relief].

In October 1992, Mr. Becker again sought to purchase air time from WAGA–TV. He wished to broadcast a 30–minute political program entitled "Abortion in America: The Real Story" on November 1 between 4:00 p.m. and 5:00 p.m., following a televised professional football game. WAGA–TV refused to air the program at the time requested, claiming that the advertisement would violate the indecency provision of 18 U.S.C. § 1464. It stated that it would carry the program only within the safe harbor hours of midnight to 6:00 a.m. Mr. Becker filed a complaint with the FCC on October 27, 1992.

Faced with Mr. Becker's complaint and [the law firms'] application for review, the FCC issued a Request for Comments [on how to handle the situation and in the interim the Bureau concluded that § 312(a)(7) did not require the licensee to honor the time request in this case].

[In] 1994, the FCC issued the Memorandum Opinion and Order that is the subject of this appeal. . . . In it, the FCC concluded (1) that Mr. Becker's initial advertisement was not indecent, (2) that there was evidence in the record "indicating that the graphic political advertisements at issue can be psychologically damaging to children," (3) that "nothing in 312(a)(7) precludes a broadcaster's exercise of some discretion with respect to placement of political advertisements so as to protect children," and (4) that channeling would not violate the no-censorship provision of section 315(a). [   ]

WACCI and Mr. Becker petition the court for review of this FCC order. WAGA License, Inc., has intervened on behalf of the FCC.

II. ANALYSIS

. . .

A. Section 312(a)(7)

. . .

Petitioners argue that the Declaratory Ruling deviates from [the FCC's] policy guidelines because there is nothing in them that would allow broadcasters to take the content of a political advertisement into account in determining what constitutes "reasonable access"; nor do they permit a licensee to deny a candidate access to adult audiences of his choice merely because significant numbers of children may also be watching television. Mr. Becker also objects to the ruling on the basis that it gives broadcasters a standardless discretion to determine whether an advertisement "may be harmful to children." For its part, the FCC contends that the ruling is consistent with both its past policies and the language and purpose of section 312(a)(7). Emphasizing its past practice of deferring to a broadcaster's reasonable and good faith discretion in making reasonable access decisions, the FCC argues that there is no basis for the position that it may never be appropriate for a broadcaster to take the graphic nature of abortion images into consideration when deciding at what hour to broadcast a particular advertisement.

We believe that petitioners have the better part of the argument. As we explain below, by permitting a licensee to channel political advertisements that it believes may harm children, the Declaratory Ruling frustrates what the Commission itself has identified as Congress's primary purpose in enacting section 312(a)(7); namely, to ensure "candidates access to the time periods with the greatest audience potential. . . ." Licensee Responsibility, 47 F.C.C.2d at 517; see also Section 312(a)(7) Policy, 68 F.C.C.2d at 1090. The FCC claims, nevertheless, that its order is consistent with this policy, citing the following passage from Declaratory Ruling: If licensees do channel, . . . they are expected to provide access to times with as broad an audience potential as is consistent with the federal candidate's right to reasonable access. This is consistent with our general policy under Section 312(a)(7) that licensees should afford access to federal candidates in prime time, when access to voters is greatest. 9 F.C.C.R. at 7647. We are unpersuaded.

The problem with this statement is that it is not possible, on the one hand, to channel a political advertisement to a time when there is little risk "that large numbers of children may be in the audience," id., and, on the other, to assure the candidate of "as broad an audience potential as is consistent with [his] right of reasonable access." Id. We recently concluded, on the basis of an FCC study issued in 1993, that "there is a reasonable risk that large numbers of children would be exposed to any . . . material broadcast between 6:00 a.m. and midnight." [*ACT III*, p. 252, *supra*]. It is apparent, then, that a licensee will not be able to channel the advertisement to a time "when access to voters is greatest" without exposing it to substantial numbers of children.

We are faced, then, with competing interests—the licensee's desire to spare children the sight of images that are not indecent but may nevertheless prove harmful, and the interest of a political candidate in exercising his statutory right of "access to the time periods with the greatest audience potential." Licensee Responsibility, 47 F.C.C.2d at 517. The Commission has made it clear that when these two interests are in conflict, the licensee is free to decide in favor of the children. [ ]

Finally, while it is possible to visualize accommodations at the margin in which a political message is broadcast during school hours or the late, late evening when significantly fewer children are watching television, any such accommodation is apt to deprive a candidate of particular categories of adult viewers whom he may be especially anxious to reach. It is common knowledge that campaign strategists rely on survey research to target specific voting groups with television advertisements. See generally Dan Koeppel, The High–Tech Election (of 1992), Brandweek 18, Mar. 2, 1992. We can surmise, for example, that early shift factory workers whom a candidate wishes to reach are not apt to stay up beyond their normal bedtimes just to see his political advertisements. Thus, the ruling creates a situation where a candidate's ability to reach his target audience may be limited and his "personal campaign strategies . . . ignored." See CBS, Inc., 453 U.S. at 389.

The FCC points out that it has previously acknowledged that " 'there may be circumstances when a licensee might reasonably refuse broadcast time to political candidates during certain parts of the broadcast day.' " [ ] The FCC has never defined those circumstances; but in describing the circumstances that a licensee is entitled to take into consideration in refusing candidates' access to particular time frames, the Commission's concerns have focused on making sure that the exercise by candidates of their rights under the section would not "disrupt a station's broadcast schedule." Section 312(a)(7) Policy, 68 F.C.C.2d at 1090; cf. CBS, Inc., 453 U.S. at 387 (to justify a denial of access, "broadcasters must cite a realistic danger of substantial program disruption . . . or of an excessive number of equal time requests"). Thus, the FCC has advised that a licensee may take into account its "broader programming and business commitments, including the multiplicity of candidates in a particular race, the program disruption that will be caused by political advertising, and the amount of time already sold to a candidate in a particular race." 1991 Policy Statement, 7 F.C.C.R. at 681–82; see also Section 312(a)(7) Policy, 68 F.C.C.2d at 1090. None of these circumstances is remotely concerned with the content of a campaign advertisement, and we can see no connection between a licensee's right to protect his programming from disruption and a licensee's asserted right to shield children from the sight of disturbing images.

The Commission states, quite correctly, that in applying section 312(a)(7), it has always "rel[ied] upon the reasonable good faith judgments of licensees to determine what constitutes reasonable access." 1991 Policy Statement, 7 F.C.C.R. at 679; see also Section 312(a)(7) Policy, 68 F.C.C.2d at 1089. The Supreme Court has cautioned, however, that "endowing licensees with a 'blank check' to determine what constitutes 'reasonable access' would eviscerate § 312(a)(7)." CBS, Inc., 453 U.S. at 390 n. 12. We believe that the standardless discretion that the FCC has granted broadcasters to channel political messages will do just that. While the Declaratory Ruling emphasizes that broadcasters may not channel an advertisement "out of disagreement with the candidate's political position," and that "[t]he licensee's discretion should relate to the nature of the graphic imagery in question and not to any political position the candidate espouses," 9 F.C.C.R. at 7647–48, the Commission now allows licensees to channel images based entirely on a subjective judgment that a particular advertisement might prove harmful to children. All that it asks is that that judgment be "reasonable" and made in good faith.

These are slippery standards, and it is of small solace to a losing candidate that an appellate court might eventually find that the Commission's approval of a licensee's channeling decision was an abuse of discretion or contrary to law. Moreover, the acceptance of a subjective standard renders it impossible to determine whether it was the advertisement's message rather than its images that the licensee found too shocking for tender minds.

In many instances, of course, it will be impossible to separate the message from the image, when the point of the political advertisement is to call attention to the perceived horrors of a particular issue. Indeed, this was the apparent purpose of many of the candidates who ran abortion advertisements similar to Mr. Becker's. See Anti–Abortion Political Advertising, III Vill. Sports & Ent. L.J. at 89 n.11 (discussing candidates who felt the advertisements were "a necessary offense," in order to "show that it's a life or death issue"). And the political uses of television for shock effect is not limited to abortion. See id. at 95 ("Other subjects that could easily lead to shocking and graphic visual treatment include the death penalty, gun control, rape, euthanasia and animal rights.")

Finally, in arguing that a licensee has the authority under the Act to channel material that might harm the young, the Commission points to Congress's "concern with protecting children from the adverse effects of televised material," [   ], and contends that "the public interest standard of the [Communications] Act clearly contemplates that appropriate measures may be taken to protect the well-being of children, as reflected in" other provisions of the Act. [   ]

. . . . [T]he Commission offers no evidence that Congress intended to subordinate a candidate's right of reasonable access to a licensee's assessment of the public interest. To the contrary, it seems to us that the right of access accorded candidates by sections 312(a)(7) and 315(a) overrides the programming discretion that is otherwise allowed licensees by the Act, except in those circumstances already specified in the Commission's policy guidelines.

B.   Section 315(a)

. . .

The FCC has recognized that the "[c]ase law interpreting [section 315(a)] has uniformly barred licensees from exercising any power of censorship over the content of political broadcasts whether they are 'first' uses or responses to first uses." Hammond for Governor Committee, 69 F.C.C.2d 946, 947 (Broadcast Bur.1978). In its Declaratory Ruling, the FCC stated: We are not granting licensees the ability to delete political statements. We are simply recognizing that a licensee may, consistent with its public interest obligations, channel political advertisements containing graphic abortion imagery to times when, although consistent with its obligation to provide reasonable access, the likelihood that children will be in the audience is diminished. This added measure of licensee discretion does not constitute "censorship" as that term is used in the Communications Act. 9 F.C.C.R. at 7649.

According to the FCC, that ruling is consistent with section 315(a)'s no censorship provision because the Commission was careful to emphasize broadcasters' continuing obligation to air, in full, political advertisements with graphic abortion images should they choose to channel them to times when there were not large numbers of children in the viewing audience. The Commission also insists that the ruling does not allow licensees to dictate what issues a candidate may address in its advertisement or to "exercise their discretion in a manner that has the practical effect of censorship" by, for example, airing the advertisement during a period of "minimal viewership," such as 2:00 a.m. to 6:00 a.m. [ ] The FCC further argues that, in any event, the competing public interest in protecting the welfare of children outweighs "the minimal intrusion on a candidate's unfettered ability to present his message at the particular time preferred by the candidate." [ ]

For their part, petitioners assert that the ruling compromises section 315(a)'s no censorship provision in two ways: First, by granting licensees the content-based discretion to refuse to broadcast particular advertisements during a particular period, it enables them not only to discriminate against a candidate on the basis of speech, but to inhibit the manner in which he is able to discuss public issues. Second, by enabling the licensee to determine when an advertisement that "may be harmful to children" will air, the ruling deprives the candidate of the ability to convey his message when and how he sees fit by presenting him with the choice of either changing its content or accepting a time slot that deprives him of his preferred audience.

The FCC has never defined censorship in the context of section 315(a), although it has provided guidance in the form of lists of acts that constitute censorship and of those that do not—neither of which refers to channeling. See Political Primer 1984, 100 F.C.C.2d at 1510–13. The Supreme Court, however, has stated that [t]he term censorship, . . . as commonly understood, connotes any examination of thought or expression in order to prevent publication of "objectionable" material. We find no clear expression of legislative intent, nor any other convincing reason to indicate Congress meant to give "censorship" a narrower meaning in § 315. [*WDAY*, p. 169, *supra*]. In [*WDAY*] the Court held that section 315(a) prohibited a broadcaster from removing defamatory statements from the advertisements of a legally qualified candidate. From the

Court's discussion, we may discern two guiding principles: First, the basic purpose of section 315(a) is to permit the "full and unrestricted discussion of political issues by legally qualified candidates." Id. at 529. Second, the section reflects Congress's "deep hostility to censorship either by the Commission or by a licensee." Id. at 528.

Although the Court was discussing a case in which a licensee sought to excise certain references in a political advertisement, we believe that these principles apply with equal force to this case because of the leverage that the threat of channeling provides a licensee in the heat of a political election. As the Court observed in *WDAY, Inc.*, [b]ecause of the time limitation inherent in a political campaign, erroneous decisions by a station could not be corrected by the courts promptly enough to permit the candidate to bring improperly excluded material before the public. It follows from all this that allowing censorship . . . would almost inevitably force a candidate to avoid controversial issues during political debates . . . and hence restrict the coverage of consideration relevant to intelligent political decision. We . . . are unwilling to assume [ ] that Congress intended any such result. 360 U.S. at 530–31. [ ]

Not only does the power to channel confer on a licensee the power to discriminate between candidates, it can force one of them to back away from what he considers to be the most effective way of presenting his position on a controversial issue lest he be deprived of the audience he is most anxious to reach. This self-censorship must surely frustrate the "full and unrestricted discussion of political issues" envisioned by Congress.

The rationale behind *WDAY, Inc.* requires us to agree with petitioners that "censorship" encompasses more than the refusal to run a candidate's advertisement or the deletion of material contained in it.

. . . We further believe that the actions here constituted censorship, within the Supreme Court's definition in *WDAY, Inc.* . . . in violation of Section 315(a) of the Act. Id. at 495. . . .

. . .

Finally, section 315(a) not only prohibits censorship, it also requires that candidates be given "equal opportunities" to use a broadcaster's facilities. To satisfy this requirement, a broadcaster must "make available periods of approximately equal audience potential to competing candidates to the extent that this is possible." Political Primer 1984, 100 F.C.C.2d at 1505. The FCC claims that the Declaratory Ruling does not involve the equal opportunity provision because there was no equal opportunity request before it. Because the equal opportunity requirements "forbid any kind of discrimination by a station between competing candidates," however, channeling clearly implicates the equal opportunity provision of section 315(a).

This is so because if a station channels one candidate's message but allows his opponent to broadcast his messages in prime time, the first candidate will have been denied the equal opportunity guaranteed by this section. On the other hand, if the station relegates the opponent's advertisements to the broadcasting Siberia to which the first candidate was assigned, it would be violating the opponent's right of reasonable access under section 312(a)(7). We agree with petitioners that these provisions may not be read to create such a tension.

We conclude from the above that permitting the content-based channeling of political advertisements thwarts the objectives of both section 312(a)(7) and section 315(a) by restricting candidates' ability to "fully and completely inform the voters," CBS, Inc., 453 U.S. at 379 (internal quotation marks and citation omitted), and by inhibiting the "full and unrestricted discussion of political issues by legally qualified candidates," WDAY, Inc., 360 U.S. at 529. . . .

. . .

III. CONCLUSION

The Commission's Declaratory Ruling violates the "reasonable access" requirement of section 312(a)(7) by permitting content-based channeling of non-indecent political advertisements, thus denying qualified candidates the access to the broadcast media envisioned by Congress. The ruling also permits licensees to review political advertisements and to discriminate against candidates on the basis of their content, in violation of both the "no censorship" and "equal opportunities" provisions of section 315(a). Therefore, we grant the petitions for review and vacate the ruling.

So ordered.

Notes and Questions

1. Recall the Barry Commoner ad discussed at p. 277, *supra*. Could it be channeled to the safe harbor time period?

2. If a political ad can be channeled, how should the § 312(a)(7) and § 315 conflicts be addressed?

C. SAFETY—VIOLENCE AND PANIC

The 1980s saw an increase in lawsuits asserting that mass media are legally liable for personal injuries that can be traced in one way or another to a broadcast. These cases, which have not yet produced definitive results, raise some of the most hotly disputed questions in all of media liability. The examples that follow suggest the range of situations that might give rise to controversy. The cases tend to fall into two main categories—those in which the content of the program has an immediate impact on the recipient and those in which the recipient engages in conduct that hurts third parties. Both types of cases raise questions about tort law and the First Amendment.

The most extensive suit raising this question arose out of a television drama entitled "Born Innocent."

OLIVIA N. v. NATIONAL BROADCASTING CO.

California Court of Appeal, First District, 1981.
126 Cal.App.3d 488, 178 Cal.Rptr. 888, 7 Med.L.Rptr. 2359.

Before: CALDECOTT, P.J., CHRISTIAN and POCHE, JJ.

CHRISTIAN, J.:

Olivia N. appeals from a judgment of nonsuit terminating her action against the National Broadcasting Company and the Chronicle Broadcasting Company. Appellant sought damages for physical and emotional injury inflicted by assailants who had seen a television broadcast of a film drama.

[The case was originally dismissed before trial, but the appellate court held that improper procedure below had deprived the plaintiff of her right to a jury trial. After a jury was empaneled on the remand and plaintiff had made an opening statement, the trial judge dismissed the case on the ground that the only basis for recovery would be a showing that NBC intended that violence follow its presentation of the drama. Since plaintiff did not make that claim, the case was dismissed.]

At 8 p.m. on September 10, 1974, NBC telecast nationwide, and Chronicle Broadcasting Company broadcast locally, a film entitled "Born Innocent."

> The subject matter of the television film was the harmful effect of a state-run home upon an adolescent girl who had become a ward of the state. In one scene of the film, the young girl enters the community bathroom of the facility to take a shower. She is then shown taking off her clothes and stepping into the shower, where she bathes for a few moments. Suddenly, the water stops and a look of fear comes across her face. Four adolescent girls are standing across from her in the shower room. One of the girls is carrying a "plumber's helper," waving it suggestively by her side. The four girls violently attack the younger girl, wrestling her to the floor. The young girl is shown naked from the waist up, struggling as the older girls force her legs apart. Then the television film shows the girl with the plumber's helper making intense thrusting motions with the handle of the plunger until one of the four says "That's enough." The young girl is left sobbing and naked on the floor. [ ]

It is alleged that on September 14, 1974, appellant, aged 9, was attacked and forcibly "artificially raped" with a bottle by minors at a San Francisco beach. [ ] The assailants had viewed and discussed the "artificial rape" scene in "Born Innocent," and the film allegedly caused the assailants to decide to commit a similar act on appellant. Appellant offered to show that NBC had knowledge of studies on child violence and should have known that susceptible persons might imitate the crime enacted in the film. Appellants alleged that "Born Innocent" was particularly likely to cause imitation and that NBC televised the film without proper warning in an effort to obtain the largest possible viewing audience. Appellant alleged that as a proximate result of respondents' telecast, she suffered physical and psychological damage.

Appellant contends that where there is negligence liability could constitutionally be imposed despite the absence of proof of incitement as defined in Brandenburg v. Ohio, 395 U.S. 444, 447 (1969). Appellant argues in the alternative that a different definition of "incitement" should be applied to the present circumstances.

"Analysis of this appeal commences with recognition of the overriding constitutional principle that material communicated by the public media, including fictional material such as the television drama here at issue, is generally to be accorded protection under the First Amendment to the Constitution of the United States. [   ]" First Amendment rights are accorded a preferred place in our democratic society. [   ] First Amendment protection extends to a communication, to its source and to its recipients. [   ] "[A]bove all else, the First Amendment means that government has no power to restrict expression because of its message, its ideas, its subject matter, or its content." . . .

. . .

The electronic media are also entitled to First Amendment protection. . . .

Appellant does not seek to impose a prior restraint on speech; rather, she asserts civil liability premised on traditional negligence actions for a television broadcast is obvious. "The fear of damage awards . . . may be markedly more inhibiting than the fear of prosecution under a criminal statute." New York Times Co. v. Sullivan, 376 U.S. 254, 277 (1964). Realistically, television networks would become significantly more inhibited in the selection of controversial materials if liability were to be imposed on a simple negligence theory. "[T]he pall of fear and timidity imposed upon those who would give voice to public criticism is an atmosphere in which the First Amendment cannot survive." New York Times v. Sullivan [   ]. . . .

Although the First Amendment is not absolute, the television broadcast of "Born Innocent" does not, on the basis of the opening statement of appellant's attorney, fall within the scope of unprotected speech. Appellant concedes that the film did not constitute an "incitement" within the meaning of [Brandenburg]. Notwithstanding the pervasive effect of the broadcasting media (see FCC v. Pacifica Foundation (1978) 438 U.S. 726, 748; Note, The Future of Content Regulation in Broadcasting (1981) 69 Cal.L.Rev. 555, 580–581) and the unique access afforded children [Pacifica], the effect of the imposition of liability could reduce the U.S. adult population to viewing only what is fit for children. [   ] Incitement is the proper test here. [   ] In areas outside of obscenity the United States Supreme Court has "consistently held that the fact that protected speech may be offensive to some does not justify its suppression. See, e.g., Cohen v. California, 403 U.S. 15 (1971)." [   ] . . . The television broadcast which is the subject of this action concededly did not fulfill the incitement requirements of *Brandenburg*. Thus it is constitutionally protected.

Appellant would distinguish between the fictional presentation of "Born Innocent" and news programs and documentaries. But that distinction is too blurred to protect adequately First Amendment values. "Everyone is familiar with instances of propaganda through fiction. What is one man's amusement, teaches another's doctrine." [ ] If a negligence theory is recognized, a television network or local station could be liable when a child imitates activities portrayed in a news program or documentary. Thus, the distinction urged by appellant cannot be accepted. [ ] . . . "Among free men, the deterrents ordinarily to be applied to prevent crime are education and punishment for violations of the law, not abridgment of the rights of free speech. . . ." [ ] The trial court's determination that the First Amendment bars appellant's claim where no incitement is alleged must be upheld.

[*Pacifica* was held inapplicable to anything other than regulation of indecency.]

Notes and Questions

1. Is there any possible showing that should entitle plaintiff to a judgment against NBC? What if the plaintiff could show that NBC officials had been warned by psychologists that the program was likely to provoke imitation? Is it significant that there was only one reported case of imitation? What if plaintiff could show only that the attackers heard about the program from friends but that none of them saw it? Is it relevant that the show was presented at 8 p.m.?

2. Is there a difference between the "Born Innocent" program and a news broadcast that reports the details of a recent case of torture in the city—which is then imitated by persons unknown?

3. *Direct Harm.* During a 1979 broadcast of "The Tonight Show," a Hollywood stunt man showed how to stage a hanging that appeared real but was not. A few hours after the program, a 14–year–old boy was found hanging in front of his television set, which was on, and tuned to the local outlet that had carried that show. The plaintiff's attorney alleged that "the entire tenor of the scene was such as to challenge a teenaged boy to imitate the hanging." The trial judge dismissed the complaint in 1980.

The dismissal was affirmed in DeFilippo v. National Broadcasting Co., 446 A.2d 1036, 8 Med.L.Rptr. 1872 (R.I.1982). The court concluded that "incitement" was required and that it could not be shown here. Plaintiff was apparently the only viewer who tried the stunt and those on the program had warned viewers that this was not something to try at home. To permit recovery here "would invariably lead to self-censorship by broadcasters in order to remove any matter that may be emulated and lead to a law suit."

4. *Indirect Harm. Olivia N.* is only one of a number of cases in which a victim has claimed that a broadcast caused listeners or viewers to engage in conduct that led to plaintiff's injury.

In one such case later relied on by the plaintiff in *Olivia N.*, a radio station catering to teenagers broadcast clues as to the whereabouts of a disc jockey and offered a cash prize to the first listener to reach him. Two teenagers reached the correct location but were not the first to arrive. While following the disc jockey to his next stop, the two drivers vied for position on the freeway and thereby caused a fatal accident. The court held that the station owed the decedent a duty of care and had violated it. Weirum v. RKO General, Inc., 15 Cal.3d 40, 123 Cal.Rptr. 468, 539 P.2d 36 (1975). Without relying on the fact that the contest was a boost for the station, the court easily rejected the station's First Amendment claim as "clearly without merit. The issue here is civil accountability for the foreseeable results of a broadcast which created an undue risk of harm to decedent. The First Amendment does not sanction the infliction of physical injury merely because achieved by word, rather than act." Is this sound? The court in *Olivia N.* distinguished *Weirum* on the ground that the station in that case actively encouraged the conduct leading to the accident. No such encouragement was present in "Born Innocent."

5. *The Zamora Case.* In Florida, 15–year–old Ronald Zamora was convicted of murdering his 83–year–old neighbor and was sentenced to a long prison term. He sued all three networks claiming that between the ages of 5 and 15 he had become involuntarily addicted to, and "completely subliminally intoxicated" by, extensive viewing of television violence. He claimed that the networks had "impermissibly stimulated, incited and instigated" him to duplicate the atrocities he viewed on television. He alleged further that he had developed a sociopathic personality, had become desensitized to violent behavior and had become a danger to himself and others. The trial judge dismissed the complaint. Zamora v. Columbia Broadcasting System, 480 F.Supp. 199 (S.D.Fla.1979).

The judge refused to impose any tort obligation on the networks because he concluded that courts lack "the legal and institutional capacity to identify isolated depictions of violence, let alone the ability to set the standard for media dissemination of items containing 'violence' in one form or the other. Airway dissemination is, and to some extent should be, regulated but not on the basis or by the [tort] procedure suggested by the plaintiffs."

To the extent plaintiff was arguing for the regulation of programming that would adversely affect "susceptible" viewers, the judge indicated that the "imposition of such a generally undefined and undefinable duty would be an unconstitutional exercise by this Court in any event." Plaintiffs "would place broadcasters in jeopardy for televising Hamlet, Julius Caesar, Grimm's Fairy Tales; more contemporary offerings such as All Quiet On The Western Front, and even The Holocaust, and indeed would render John Wayne a risk not acceptable by any but the boldest broadcasters."

The judge observed, however, that "One day, medical or other sciences with or without the cooperation of programmers may convince the F.C.C. or the Courts that the delicate balance of First Amendment rights should be altered to permit some additional limitations in programming." But this case did not present such an occasion.

The judge implied that the plaintiff's approach in the "Born Innocent" case was stronger because of its claim that a specific program stimulated the harmful conduct. Is that a sound distinction? Note that the *Zamora* suit involves direct harm because the viewer is the one claiming that his life has been ruined by the programming. There is no reason, however, to think that the judge would have been any more receptive to a suit by the heirs of the dead neighbor against the networks.

6. Is the plaintiff's case stronger in general if more recipients are affected? If half the viewers faint in front of their screens after viewing a particularly gory shot of a murder victim presented during a news program, is the case any different from one in which a few "susceptible" viewers faint? Is there any reason to distinguish the cases in which direct harm occurs from those in which indirect harm occurs? Can you imagine a case in which the "average" viewer would be induced to engage in antisocial behavior that harmed others?

7. *Mass Hysteria*. Another substantive problem involves programs that frighten the listening public. At 11 p.m. on Oct. 30, 1974, a radio station in Rhode Island presented a contemporary version of the famous H.G. Wells's "War of the Worlds," that had been presented on the same night in 1938. A meteorite was reported to have fallen in a sparsely populated community killing several people; later "black-eyed, V-shaped mouthed, glistening creatures dripping saliva" were reported to have emerged from what turned out to be a capsule, and other landings were reported. What steps would you expect the licensee to take before presenting such a program—or is it inappropriate to present such material at any time? Telephone calls from frightened, and later from angry, listeners flooded the station, police and other public service departments.

The licensee had taken several steps before the program to inform state public safety officials in the listening area of the station. The state police in turn sent notices to all their stations in the area alerting them to the program. Approximately once an hour from noon until 10 p.m. the licensee broadcast the following promotional announcement: "Tonight at 11 p.m., WPRO invites you to listen to a spoof of the 1930s a special Halloween classic presentation. . . ." The last was made about an hour before the program. Three announcements were made during the program—after 47, 48 and 56 minutes. The reason for the timing was said to be that the first 30 to 35 minutes of the show involved what appeared to be a meteor crashing in a remote spot and the arrival of creatures was not reported until 30 minutes into the program.

The Commission told the licensee that it had not met its responsibility to operate in a manner consistent with the public interest. The warnings were inadequate because "it is a well known fact that the radio audience is constantly changing. The only way to assure adequately that the public would not be alarmed in this case would be an introductory statement repeated at frequent intervals throughout the program." One Commissioner dissented because intrusion into presentations of drama should be made with "utmost caution" and the licensee's precautions "were not in my opinion unreasonable." Capital Cities Communications, Inc., 54 F.C.C.2d 1035, 34 R.R.2d 1016 (1975).

Would the Commission's suggestions impinge on the dramatic effect sought by the licensee? Is that relevant? Can you think of other ways to meet the Commission's concern? Recall the greater ease of warning an unwilling audience about possibly offensive programs over television as opposed to radio. Is that distinction applicable here?

8. During the Persian Gulf War, a St. Louis disk jockey played an old Civil Defense alert, causing listeners to believe a nuclear attack was in progress. The disk jockey was suspended, and the station issued an apology. Broadcasting, Feb. 4, 1991 at 29. The licensee was subsequently fined $25,000. Letter to KSHE–FM, 6 F.C.C.Rcd. 2289, 69 R.R.2d 155 (1991).

9. After the St. Louis incident, as well as incidents in Pasadena and Providence the Commission issued an NPRM seeking comments on a new hoax rule. The Pasadena case involved a radio station airing a call from a man who supposedly had killed his girlfriend. A police investigation of the "murder" ensued and the hoax was only exposed when viewers of a "Unsolved Mysteries" (NBC) story on the "crime" notified police of the similarities between the caller and a disc jockey who had subsequently been hired by the station.

In the Providence hoax, a station's news director announced that the station's morning man had been shot just outside the station. The news director then refused to disclose the hoax even when ordered to by the station's general manager. The news director and morning man were both fired. Broadcasting, July 29, 1991 at 68.

In 1992, after receiving comments, the Commission decided to issue a rule rather than rely on a policy. In part the rule approach was chosen because it permitted the Commission to use the forfeiture provisions of § 503(b) rather than simply the non-monetary sanctions available under a policy approach. The Commission issued the following rule:

> No licensee or permittee of any broadcast station shall broadcast false information concerning a crime or a catastrophe if (a) the licensee knows this information is false, (b) it is foreseeable that broadcast of the information will cause substantial public harm, and (c) broadcast of the information does in fact directly cause substantial public harm. Any programming accompanied by a disclaimer will be presumed not to pose foreseeable harm if the disclaimer clearly

characterizes the program as a fiction and is presented in a way that is reasonable under the circumstances.

FOOTNOTE 1. For purposes of this rule, "public harm" must begin immediately, and cause direct and actual damage to property or to the health or safety of the general public, or diversion of law enforcement or other public health and safety authorities from their duties. The public harm will be deemed foreseeable if the licensee could expect with a significant degree of certainty that public harm would occur. A "crime" is any act or omission that makes the offender subject to criminal punishment by law. A "catastrophe" is a disaster or imminent disaster involving a violent or sudden event affecting the public.

The disclaimer feature was prompted by concern over broadcasts of acknowledged fiction. In comments, the Commission observed that a disclaimer would be presumptively reasonable if it came at the beginning and at the end of the program and at intervals during the program no longer than 15 minutes apart. Broadcast Hoaxes, 7 F.C.C.Rcd. 4106, 70 R.R.2d 1383 (1992).

D. CHILDREN'S PROGRAMMING

Over the years, groups have expressed special concern about programs aimed at children. Some have been concerned primarily with commercials and others have been concerned about the content of the programs themselves. Still others have been concerned that there is too little children's programming. All of these concerns and conflicts became more heated in the late 1970s. As we consider each situation, note the different approaches being considered. Sometimes it is prohibiting certain content; sometimes it involves mandatory programming; and sometimes it is conditional in the sense that a broadcaster who presents one kind of content may be obligated to present other types of programs. Also note that occasionally the FCC invokes the aid of private groups such as the National Association of Broadcasters (NAB) to alter a practice within the industry.

1. PROGRAM CONTENT

Most of the concern about the impact of television on children has stressed the role of violence and sexual innuendo. Although some groups have been concerned about these matters as far as adults are concerned, more seem concerned about their impact on children. Under Butler v. Michigan, 352 U.S. 380 (1957), it is unlawful for government to impose a complete ban on printed matter that is legally protected as to adults, simply to keep the material from children. Might that rule be different with television or radio? Does *Pacifica* suggest differences?

a. *Government Action*

Although the Surgeon General has issued reports on the relationship between violence and television, and other academic studies have addressed the same issue primarily in connection with children, the Commission has never attempted to regulate the area in any substantive way. It has been asked several times but each time has refused.

In 1972, for example, the Commission was asked to analogize the area to cigarette smoking because of the actions of the Surgeon General in the two areas. George Corey, 37 F.C.C.2d 641, 25 R.R.2d 437 (1972). The complainant sought to have three Boston stations carry a public service notice at appropriate times: "Warning: Viewing of violent television programming by children can be hazardous to their mental health and well being." The Commission rejected the request on two grounds. First, it stated any action should come by rule rather than moving against a few stations. Second, the Commission rejected the contention that the fairness doctrine was applicable to violent programming. The cigarette episode was discussed:

> However, it could not reasonably or logically be concluded that the mere viewing of a person smoking a cigarette during a movie being broadcast on television constitutes a discussion of a controversial issue of public importance thus raising a fairness doctrine obligation. Similarly, we cannot agree that the broadcast of violent episodes during entertainment programs necessarily constitutes the presentation of one side of a controversial issue of public importance. It is simply not an appropriate application of the fairness doctrine to say that an entertainment program—whether it be Shakespeare or an action-adventure show—raises a controversial issue if it contains a violent scene and has a significant audience of children. Were we to adopt your construction that the depiction of a violent scene is a discussion of one side of a controversial issue of public importance, the number of controversial issues presented on entertainment shows would be virtually endless (e.g., a scene with a high-powered car; or one showing a person taking an alcoholic drink or cigarette; depicting women in a soft, feminine, or light romantic role). Finally, we note that there are marked differences in the conclusiveness of the hazard established in this area as against cigarette smoking. [   ]

> The real thrust of your complaint would appear to be not fairness in the discussion of controversial issues but the elimination of violent TV children's programming because of its effect on children. That issue is being considered particularly by appropriate Congressional committees and agencies such as HEW. [   ] It is a difficult, complex, and sensitive matter. But whatever its resolution, there is no basis for the action along the line proposed by you.

In its Report on the Broadcast of Violent, Indecent, and Obscene Material, 51 F.C.C.2d 418, 32 R.R.2d 1367 (1975), the Commission explained to Congress that the violence area was unlike the obscenity area because of the totally different statutory framework involved. In the absence of any prohibitions on violence in programming, "industry self-regulation is preferable to the adoption of rigid governmental standards." The Commission took this position for two reasons. First, it feared the constitutional questions that would emerge from such an intrusion into program content. Second, the judgments concerning the suitability of certain programming for children are "highly subjective." A speech by Chairman Wiley was quoted to the effect that slapstick comedy, an episode in Peter Pan when Captain Hook is eaten by a crocodile, and the poisoning of Snow White by the witch, all raise judgmental questions for which there is no objective standard.

b. Private Action

The NAB is a private voluntary organization whose membership includes the four major networks, well over half the television stations in the country and some 3,000 radio broadcasters. The NAB promulgated codes and standards that members had to follow if they wished to retain membership. The codes addressed such matters as how many minutes of commercials were appropriate in an hour; what types of commercials should not be accepted; what material should not be shown on the screen; and how subjects such as suicide or astrology or religion should be treated.

A broadcaster that adhered to the code could display the NAB seal. The NAB maintained a staff that advised members about the propriety of their behavior under the codes.

In 1975 the result of the interaction of the network officials, the FCC chairman and the NAB was the promulgation of the "family viewing policy" as an amendment to the NAB's Television Code. Under the policy, programs of a violent or sexually-oriented nature were wholly barred from the time slots before 9 p.m. (8 p.m. Central Time). This required moving some programs that had been popular in earlier prime-time slots and also involved decisions about which programs were affected in the first place. The entire story of the development and early enforcement of the family viewing policy is traced at length in G. Cowan, *See No Evil: The Backstage Battle over Sex and Violence on Television* (1979). The policy was challenged in court as being the result of illegal government pressure. Writers Guild of America West, Inc. v. American Broadcasting Co., Inc., 609 F.2d 355 (9th Cir.1979), certiorari denied 449 U.S. 824 (1980). After years of litigation complicated by jurisdictional issues, all parties in the case agreed to a settlement in 1984. The Family Viewing Policy had not been enforced for years.

c. The V–Chip

Rep. Edward Markey (R.–Mass.) had long been a strong proponent of "requiring sets sold in the U.S. to incorporate technology to block channels or programs that parents deem too violent for their children." He was finally successful in getting this V-chip requirement passed as part of Title V(b) of the Telecommunications Act of 1996 which adds § 551 to the Communications Act (47 U.S.C.A. § 551). We will return to Title V, The Communications Decency Act (CDA), in Chapters IX and XI.

Section 551 starts with Congressional findings that television influences children's perception of acceptable values and behavior, that the average child watches 25 hours of television a week, that there is a correlation between watching violent programming and violent behavior, and that children are negatively affected by the pervasive and casual treatment of sexual material on television. These findings are followed by the conclusion that:

> (8) There is a compelling governmental interest in empowering parents to limit the negative influences of video programming that is harmful to children.

> (9) Providing parents with timely information about the nature of upcoming video programming and with the technological tools that allow them easily to block violent, sexual, or other programming that they believe harmful to their children is a nonintrusive and narrowly tailored means of achieving that governmental interest. (47 U.S.C.A. § 551(a)(8)–(9)).

To accomplish this the Act requires television manufacturers to include in all sets 13 inches or greater a device that enables viewers to block all programs with a common rating.

The Act also required the FCC to establish an advisory committee "composed of parents, television broadcasters, television programming producers, cable operators, appropriate public interest groups and other interested individuals from the private sector" to recommend guidelines and procedures "for the identification and rating of video programming that contains sexual, violent, or other indecent material about which parents should be informed before it is displayed to children." In addition the FCC was to issue rules requiring video distributors to transmit ratings for any program that has been rated.

The advisory committee was to be appointed one year after the Act was enacted. However, if the Commission determined that video programming distributors had adopted voluntary rating rules acceptable to the Commission and agreed to transmit these ratings, then the provisions concerning the advisory committee would not take effect.

The Act also created a technology fund to encourage development of blocking technology and the availability of this technology to low-income parents. 47 U.S.C.A. § 552.

The V-chip provisions are quite controversial. Supporters like Rep. Markey have hailed them as a great victory for parents and their right to raise their children as they see fit. Opponents view them as a serious infringement of First Amendment rights and/or unworkable.

In terms of the effectiveness of the V-chip several questions arose. Was it possible to rate hundreds of thousands of hours of television programming a year? Was it possible to develop a ratings system sophisticated enough to be suitable for children of all different ages and parents with differing views of what is appropriate, while at the same time being simple enough for parents to use? Similarly, could a device be designed that is easy enough for parents to program and yet too difficult for children to bypass?

The First Amendment questions revolve around the potential chilling effect on programmers and broadcasters. A show that is likely to be blocked in a substantial number of homes may attract fewer advertisers or lower rates. This, it is argued could reduce programming to that fit for children.

After initially threatening to challenge the constitutionality of the V-chip requirements, broadcasters announced that they would cooperate by developing a rating system similar to that of the Motion Picture Association of America. The new ratings system drew extensive criticism from public interest groups. The primary complaint was the lack of specific information on violence, nudity and language. Widespread dissatisfaction with the system among citizen groups and Congress led to a new ratings system.

6. According to the Industry, the *TV Parental Guidelines* are designed so that "category and program-specific content indicators will provide parents with information that will help them make informed decisions about what their children should watch on television." The *TV Parental Guidelines* describe a voluntary rating system consisting of six descriptive labels designed to indicate the appropriateness of television programming to children according to age and/or maturity; content indicators concerning sexual situations, violence, language or dialogue; transmission of the ratings information over line 21 of the Vertical Blanking Interval ("VBI"); display of on-screen rating icons and indicators; and the establishment of an Oversight Monitoring Board.

7. The Industry states that the *TV Parental Guidelines* will apply to all television programming except for news, sports, and unedited MPAA rated movies on premium cable channels. The *TV Parental Guidelines* (labels and content indicators, and respective meanings) are:

For programs designed solely for children:

TV-Y (All Children—*This program is designed to be appropriate for all children*). Whether animated or live-action, the themes and elements in this program are specifically designed for a very young audience, including children from ages 2–6. This program is not expected to frighten younger children.

TV-Y7 (Directed to Older Children—*This program is designed for children age 7 and above*). It may be more appropriate for children who have acquired the developmental skills needed to distinguish between make-believe and reality. Themes and elements in this program may include mild fantasy or comedic violence, or may frighten children under the age of 7. Therefore, parents may wish to consider the suitability of this program for their very young children. Note: For those programs where fantasy violence may be more intense or more combative than other programs in this category, such programs will be designated **TV-Y7–FV**.

For programs designed for the entire audience, the general categories are:

TV-G (General Audience—*Most parents would find this program suitable for all ages*). Although this rating does not signify a program designed specifically for children, most parents may let younger children watch this program unattended. It contains little or no violence, no strong language and little or no sexual dialogue or situations.

TV-PG (Parental Guidance Suggested—*This program contains material that parents may find unsuitable for younger children*). Many parents may want to watch it with their younger children. The theme itself may call for parental guidance and/or the program contains one or more of the following: moderate violence (V), some sexual situations (S), infrequent coarse language (L), or some suggestive dialogue (D).

TV–14 (Parents Strongly Cautioned—*This program contains some material that many parents would find unsuitable for children under 14 years of age*). Parents are strongly urged to exercise greater care in monitoring this program and are cautioned against letting children under the age of 14 watch unattended. This program contains one or more of the following: intense violence (V), intense sexual situations (S), strong coarse language (L), or intensely suggestive dialogue (D).

TV-MA (Mature Audience Only—*This program is specifically designed to be viewed by adults and therefore may be unsuitable for children under 17*). This program contains one or more of the following: graphic violence (V), explicit sexual activity (S), or crude indecent language (L).

8. As proposed by the Industry, rating icons and associated content symbols appear for 15 seconds at the beginning of all rated programming and through the use of a display button on a remote control device thereafter. Under the *TV Parental Guidelines*, the rating guidelines will typically be applied to television programs by broadcast and cable networks and producers, while television stations retain the right to substitute the rating they deem appropriate for their audience. The Industry notes that cable networks and television stations will provide rating information to newspapers and publishers of printed and electronic program guides, and will re-

quest that these publishers include the appropriate information in their guides.

Implementation of Section 551 of the Telecommunications Act of 1996, 13 F.C.C.Rcd. 8232, 11 C.R. 934 (1998).

Not everyone adopted the new guidelines. NBC continued to use the original age-only ratings and Black Entertainment Television (BET) did not use any ratings at all.

In accordance with the provisions of the Telecommunications Act of 1996, the Commission had to accept the voluntary system or appoint a commission to develop another one:

29.   We do not believe that the statute requires that every video programming distributor nationwide agree to transmit the ratings. Such a reading would mean, for example, that the failure of a single small television station to transmit the ratings would cause the entire system to fail. On the other hand, we believe that participation must be sufficiently ubiquitous to achieve Congress' goals in enacting Section 551, including the goal of permitting parents "to *easily* block violent, sexual or other programming that they believe harmful to their children." The more video programming distributors that do not participate, and the larger the audience reach of the distributors that do not participate, the more difficulty parents will have blocking the programming they consider inappropriate. We stress that we are not forcing any video programming distributor to transmit ratings, or suggesting that they transmit a particular ratings scheme. Under 551(e), we are required to determine whether, as a factual matter, video programming distributors have voluntarily agreed to transmit the Industry proposal. If we find that they have not, the 1996 Act provides that the Commission shall prescribe "on the basis of recommendations from an advisory committee established by the Commission . . . guidelines and recommended procedures for the identification and rating of video programming that contains sexual, violent, or other indecent material about which parents should be informed before it is displayed to children."

30.   The decisions of individual parties, such as NBC and BET, not to participate in the current Industry proposal can make it more difficult for parents who wish to use content indicators to block programming using the *TV Parental Guidelines*. In the case of BET, which will transmit no ratings at all, parents may be required to use a separate date/time/channel blocking mechanism to block programming (assuming that their television set provides such a feature). As for NBC, a major network, parents will not be able to block programming based upon the different content indicators within each age-based category. Under the *TV Parental Guidelines*, for instance, a parent who was primarily concerned about exposing his or her child to television violence could establish a more restrictive standard for the violent programming that would be allowed to enter the home than for sexual situations or strong language. This will not be

possible under the NBC approach. Nonetheless, parents will be able to block programming based on age categories.

31. Based on the record, we conclude that Congress' goals will be achieved to a sufficient degree to warrant a finding that video programming distributors have voluntarily agreed to broadcast the Industry ratings system. To our knowledge, the only national video programming distributors that have elected not to participate are BET and NBC. Given this near-unanimity, we believe that the *TV Parental Guidelines* will provide parents with a useful and easy-to-use tool to block programming that they consider harmful to their children.

Implementation of Section 551 of the Telecommunications Act of 1996, *supra*.

There is still the possibility that someone (most likely a broadcaster or programmer) will challenge the V-chip requirement on First Amendment grounds. If so, how should a court rule?

2. Too Few Programs for Children

There has long been concern that too few programs are written expressly for children. Although the prime time access rule (discussed in Chapter XII) was motivated in part by hopes that this type of programming would result, the rule had no such effect. Following a petition in 1970 from Action for Children's Television (ACT) to require children's programming, the FCC spent much of the 1970s trying to decide how to react. In 1974 it issued a Policy Statement asking licensees to "make a meaningful effort" to increase overall programming for children; to air "a reasonable amount" of programming designed to educate and inform children, not simply to entertain them; to address the needs of both preschool and school-age children; and to air these programs on weekdays as well as weekends.

Three years later the Commission declined to require the networks to provide instructional programs to educate children about television advertising. The Commission was concerned about the impact of the First Amendment and § 326 on an order requiring programs with certain content. The issue was not so critical that, under the first part of the fairness doctrine, a licensee who ignored the issue would be acting unreasonably. Finally, because commercials being shown did not meaningfully discuss the issue, it did not come within the second part of the fairness doctrine. Council on Children, Media and Merchandising, 65 F.C.C.2d 421, 40 R.R.2d 1718 (1977).

The Commission concluded in 1979 that, over a five-year period, the amount of children's programming per station had increased less than one hour per week (from 10.5 to 11.3 hours) and that this was totally accounted for by new programming from independent stations. Network affiliates had not increased their programming at all. No significant increase in education or informational programs was detected. Few licensees sought to develop age-specific programs for children. Finally, although only 8 percent of children's television viewing occurred on weekends, almost half the programs for children were presented on weekends.

The staff concluded that "the small numbers of children and their limited appeal to advertisers, combined with the small outlets in most markets, create incentives for the commercial television system to neglect the specific needs of the child audience." Age-specific programming would be even less attractive to broadcasters because of the further splitting of an already small market.

In Children's Television Programming and Advertising Practices, 75 F.C.C.2d 138 (1979), the FCC announced a proposed rulemaking in which it listed five options. These were to rescind the *1974 Policy Statement* and rely on program sources other than commercial broadcasting; to maintain or modify the policy statement; to institute mandatory programming requirements; to develop renewal guidelines; or to increase the number of video outlets.

The Commission completed the proceeding in 1983. Mandatory children's programming obligations for television stations were rejected. The FCC found that the amount of children's programming available was substantial with a lot of variety. It noted that establishment of quotas might be impermissible content-based regulation and would create difficult definitional problems. Such quotas would also preclude the establishment of experimental children's services and efforts at specialization. Although no quotas were created, each licensee has the obligation to consider the needs of all significant elements of the community. A licensee at renewal time must demonstrate the attention devoted to the needs of children in its viewing audience, but may consider the alternative program sources available to children in its area. Children's Television Programming, 55 R.R.2d 199 (1984). On appeal, the D.C. Circuit affirmed the Commission's position that alternatives such as public broadcasting and cable could be considered in assessing the need for children's programming. "To be sure, Congress did not intend noncommercial broadcasting to 'relieve commercial broadcasters of their responsibilities to present public affairs and public service programs, and in general to program their stations in the public interest,' [   ]. But that does not mean that the Commission must require commercial broadcasters to pursue those responsibilities in disregard of the fact that some gaps in the public interest may have been filled by that source while other needs remain entirely unmet." The court did not read the Commission's Order as relieving broadcasters of the obligation, under the public interest standard, to present age-specific programming. Action for Children's Television v. Federal Communications Commission, 756 F.2d 899, 57 R.R.2d 1406, 11 Med.L.Rptr. 2080 (D.C.Cir.1985).

An effort by citizen groups to deny license renewals to television stations that had no regularly scheduled children's programming failed in Washington Association for Television and Children v. Federal Communications Commission, 712 F.2d 677, 54 R.R.2d 293 (D.C.Cir.1983). The Commission's policy statement did not require regular scheduling, and the Commission did not have to prefer a station that presented regularly scheduled cartoons to one that presented educational specials. We will return to the question of mandating children's programming in our discussion of the Children's Television Act of 1990, p. 303, *infra.*

3. COMMERCIALS IN CHILDREN'S PROGRAMS

Efforts to eliminate all sponsorship of children's programs have been rejected by the Commission. The court of appeals affirmed on the ground that the FCC's refusal to adopt the ban "was a reasoned exercise of its broad discretion." The Commission had taken some steps, such as ordering a clear separation between programming and advertising on children's programs and prohibiting "host selling"—program hosts, personalities or characters endorsing products—and this could not be held insufficient as a matter of law. Action for Children's Television v. Federal Communications Commission, 564 F.2d 458, 40 R.R.2d 1577, 2 Med.L.Rptr. 2120 (D.C.Cir.1977).

The Commission had, however, established commercial guidelines limiting the amount of advertising that could be broadcast during children's shows. These guidelines were eliminated as part of *Deregulation of Television,* p. 113, *supra.* In *Action For Children's Television, supra,* the court of appeals held that the Commission provided inadequate justification for the elimination of the children's commercialization guidelines.

Another innovative attempt to address the question of commercials in children's programming occurred when Public Advocates, Inc., and ACT petitioned the Commission to require television licensees and cable companies to insert an inaudible electronic signal at the beginning and end of every advertisement aimed at children. The signal would allow parents to attach a device to their television sets which would blank out the advertisements. After a rulemaking proceeding, the Commission decided against such a requirement. The obvious effect of such a requirement would be to reduce the value of the advertising that in turn would diminish the economic base for children's programming. In essence it would be a milder form of the ban on advertising aimed at children that the Commission had rejected several years earlier. Children's Advertising Detector Signal, 100 F.C.C.2d 163, 57 R.R.2d 935 (1985). Is advertising the only effective way to finance children's programming?

In 1983 ACT and the National Association for Better Broadcasting (NABB) filed complaints against various licensees alleging violations of the Commission policy against "program length commercials." These complaints focused on a new marketing strategy for children's television, basing shows on toys that were already on the market. Among the shows at issue were "He–Man and the Masters of the Universe," "G.I. Joe: A Real American Hero," and "Pac–Man."

According to ACT and NABB, these shows were created for the sole purpose of selling the toys that were featured in the show. As further evidence of this allegation, ACT cited an arrangement offered by Telepictures Corporation whereby broadcasters could receive a share of the profits derived from the sale of "Thunder Cats" toys in return for carrying the "Thunder Cats" cartoon show.

The Commission rejected the complaints. "[O]nly when the program segment is 'so interwoven with, and in essence auxiliary to the sponsor's advertising . . . to the point that the entire program constitutes a single, commercial promotion for the sponsor's products or services' " will an entire program be considered a commercial. Because the toys featured in the shows were not being advertised during those shows, the Commission did not find an interweaving of commercials and program content sufficient to constitute a program length commercial.

> The fact that programming may serve commercial goals, however, in and of itself, is not controlling. If the existence of commercial rewards from associated products were the criteria for imposing restrictions upon children's programming, then no program-related product licensing would be possible and even popular educational programs such as "Sesame Street" and critically acclaimed commercial television programs like those in the "Peanuts" series would have to be eliminated from broadcast station schedules. We see no sensible or administratively practical method of making distinctions among programs based on the subjective intentions of the program producers or on the product licensing/program production sequence. Considering that ACT's, NABB's, and the Commission's primary intention is to prevent harm to children, we must consider what, if any, possible harm might result from product-based programming. There is, however, no evidence before us to demonstrate that exposure to programming based on products harms the child audience. Action for Children's Television, 58 R.R.2d 61 (F.C.C.1985).

In a related proceeding, the Commission rejected ACT's petition for rule making pertaining to profit-sharing arrangements in the broadcasting of children's programming. ACT asserted that profit-sharing arrangements such as that offered by Telepictures for "Thunder Cats" would induce licensees to select programs for financial as opposed to public interest reasons. The Commission concluded that such a danger was extremely speculative and did not warrant an NOI or NPRM, but stressed that licensees should not allow profit sharing or product tie-ins to detract from the " 'bedrock obligation of every broadcaster to be responsive to the needs and interests of its community, including the specialized needs of children in that community.' " Commissioner Rivera dissented, believing that profit sharing and product tie-ins raised enough questions to justify further study. Children's Programming (Profit–Sharing Arrangements), 100 F.C.C.2d 709, 58 R.R.2d 90 (1985).

NABB appealed the Commission's decision as it applied to NABB's complaint against KCOP–TV in Los Angeles. NABB argued that because

"He–Man and the Masters of the Universe" was provided to the station on a barter basis whereby the station furnished only two minutes of non-prime time for each show, the show was being obtained for "token payment." According to NABB this meant that under § 317 of the Communications Act the station had to identify the show's distributors as sponsors of the program. The Commission had rejected NABB's argument by ruling that § 317 applies only when a broadcast is "so interwoven with, and in essence auxiliary to the sponsor's advertising . . . to the point that the entire program constitutes a single commercial promotion for the sponsor's products or services." The court of appeals overruled the Commission, holding that § 317 is not limited to purely commercial broadcasts. National Association for Better Broadcasting v. Federal Communications Commission, 830 F.2d 270, 63 R.R.2d 1501 (D.C.Cir.1987).

Still another controversy over product tie-ins erupted when several companies announced plans for interactive children's television shows. By transmitting inaudible signals the shows will cause specially designed toys to react. ACT filed a petition with the Commission asking that the toys be declared against the public interest.

In response to these various petitions and remands, the FCC issued a combined NOI/NPRM. Revision of Programming and Commercialization Policies, Ascertainment Requirements, and Program Log Requirements for Commercial Television Stations, 2 F.C.C.Rcd. 7463 (1987). In the NOI/NPRM the Commission asked for comments pertaining to commercialization guidelines for children's shows as well as definitions of what constitutes commercial matter. It also asked for comments on the new toys designed to interact with specific children's shows.

Although this specific NOI/NPRM did not request comments on the sponsorship identification questions raised by barter deals for children's shows, the Commission indicated in a footnote that as a result of the remand in *NABB,* it would address those issues in the near future. Subsequently the FCC asked parties to the case to file comments.

4. THE CHILDREN'S TELEVISION ACT OF 1990

Before these proceedings could be completed, Congress passed a children's television bill. The Children's Television Act of 1990, Pub.L. 101–437, addressed both the programs available to children and advertising during those programs. The Act requires the FCC to include service to children as a factor in television renewal decision. It also limits commercial television stations to 12 minutes of commercial matter per hour during children's programming on weekdays and 10.5 commercial minutes per hour on weekends.

The Act directed the FCC to complete a proceeding implementing these requirements within 6 months. The three primary issues addressed by the proceeding were the standards to be used in setting commercial limits for children's programming, guidelines for evaluating at renewal time broadcasters' service to children, and the definition of program-length commercials.

IN THE MATTER OF POLICIES AND RULES CONCERNING CHILDREN'S TELEVISION PROGRAMMING

Federal Communications Commission, 1991.
6 F.C.C.Rcd. 2111, 68 R.R.2d 1615.

[For the purposes of implementing the commercial limits set forth in the Act, the Commission defined children's programming as "programs originally produced and broadcast primarily for an audience of children 12 years old and under." Commercial matter was defined as "air time sold for the purposes of selling a product," but the FCC added a number of clarifications:]

5. By requiring that air time be "sold," we mean that the advertiser must give some valuable consideration either directly or indirectly to the broadcaster or cablecaster as an inducement for airing the material. Without such a qualification, it would be difficult to distinguish mention of logos or brand name a writer or producer used to advance creative objectives. We also clarify that although our proposed definition only referred to air time sold "for purposes of selling a product," commercial matter also encompasses advertising for services.

6. We also find that the scope of Section 317 of the Communications Act, 47 USC § 317, which governs when the sponsors of broadcast material must be identified, is not coterminous with the scope of commercial matter. In particular we hold that material is not necessarily "commercial matter" for purposes of the Children's Television Act simply because Section 317 requires a sponsorship identification. . . . For example, nonprofit organizations purchasing air time for a public service message must identify themselves as sponsors under Section 317, even though such a message is not commercial material.

7. We accordingly find that the bare sponsorship identification announcement required under Section 317 and our implementing rules, where such material is not otherwise commercial in nature, will not be deemed commercial matter under our definition here. Thus, public service messages sponsored by nonprofit organizations that promote not-for-profit activities will not be considered commercial matter for purposes of applying the commercial limits. Similarly, air time sold for purposes of presenting educational and informational material, including "spot" announcements, with the only sponsorship mention a "sponsored by," is not commercial matter. The addition of product mentions or advertising to such an identification announcement, however, would constitute commercial matter. Moreover, where a station or cable operator promotes one of its upcoming programs and mentions that program's sponsor, even though not required to do so under Section 317, the mention of the sponsor will constitute commercial matter for purposes of determining whether the commercial limits have been exceeded. In such a case, the mention of the sponsor is not required under the Rule and is

thus clearly intended to promote the sponsor. Thus, if such a station or cable operator's promo (1) mentions that the upcoming program is "brought to you by" a sponsor, or (2) promotes a product or service related to the program or program sponsor, or (3) mentions a prize furnished by the program sponsor, the mention of the sponsor or the sponsor's product or services, not being required under our sponsorship identification rules, will be considered commercial matter. Promotions of upcoming programs which do not contain such sponsor-related mentions will not be deemed commercial matter.

[The Commission decided that it would count commercial minutes by the hour as opposed to by the program. Where a half-hour of children's programming is both preceded and followed by adult programming, the FCC applies the limits on a proportionate basis. The limits are not applied to children's programming segments less than a half hour in length.

Commercial limits also apply to cable operators with regard to local origination channels and cable network programs. They do not, however, apply to retransmissions of broadcast channels or access channels. (These distinctions are discussed in more detail in Chapters VIII and IX).]

III. Programming Renewal Review Requirements

14. The Children's Television Act requires that, in reviewing television license renewal applications, we consider whether the licensee has served "the educational and informational needs of children through the licensee's overall programming, including programming specifically designed to serve such needs." . . . In light of the legislative intent, we will implement this programming provision by reviewing a licensee's renewal application to determine whether, over the course of its license term, it has served the educational and informational needs of children in its overall programming, including programming specifically designed to serve such needs.

A. *Age Range of "Children"*

15. The Act does not define "children" for purposes of the educational and informational programming renewal review requirement. . . . After reviewing the variety of positions taken in the record, we find that the different policies underlying the Act's programming provision necessitate a broader conception of "children" than we used for commercial limits. While it is primarily younger children who need protection from commercial matter that they do not fully comprehend, older as well as younger children have unique needs and can benefit from programming directed to them. Teenagers are undergoing a transition to adulthood. They are still very influenced by adult role models and peers, including those portrayed on television. They are generally inexperienced and yet face many crucial decisions concerning sex, drugs, and their own identities. To fully comply with the Act's directive that licensees demonstrate responsiveness to the needs of the child audience, we believe that we

must interpret the programming renewal review requirement to apply to programs originally produced and broadcast for an audience of children 16 years of age and under.

. . .

18.　The *Notice* asked whether the Act requires broadcasters to target particular segments of the child audience. The legislative history, we find, permits but does not require such targeting to satisfy our renewal review. Imposing such a requirement would contravene the legislative intent to afford broadcasters maximum flexibility in determining the "mix" of programming they will present to meet children's special needs. Requiring each broadcaster to serve all age groups in order to pass our renewal review would probably result in less expensive and lower quality programming, possibly engendering what INTV describes as "sameness and mediocrity." We thus decline to adopt suggestions that broadcasters program to all ages or to each subset of children within the under 16 range. Stations may select the age groups they can most effectively serve.

B.　Standard

1.　Programming

19.　Although we stated the desire to avoid any *de facto* system of "precensorship" and to leave it to licensees to interpret the meaning of educational and informational programming, the *Notice* asked those commenters desiring a delineation of the Act's programming renewal review requirement to address what definition of "educational and informational" programming we might use. The *Notice* specifically referred to a description by Senator Inouye, as programming which furthers a child's intellectual, emotional and social development. After further reflection, we believe that a general definition of "educational and informational" programming for children would provide needed guidance to the industry as well as to Commission staff administering the statute, and would give licensees sufficient flexibility to exercise their discretion in serving children's needs. We also encourage licensees to use the assessment criteria proposed in the *Notice* in determining how to meet the educational and informational needs of children in their communities.

. . .

21.　We believe that a definition based on Senator Inouye's view, described above, or based on McGannon's formulation—content that serves children's cognitive/intellectual or social/emotional needs—is closer to the spirit of the Act and to our desire to stimulate, and not dictate, programming responsive to children's needs. Thus, programming that furthers the positive development of the child in any respect, including the child's cognitive/intellectual or emotional/social needs, can contribute to satisfying the licensee's obligation to serve the educational and informational needs of children.

22.   The *Notice* proposed to require each licensee to assess the needs of children given (1) the circumstances within the community, (2) other programming on the station, (3) programming aired on other broadcast stations within the community, and (4) other programs for children available in the broadcaster's community of license. Licensees would then air programs intended to meet "the educational and informational needs of children" responding to this assessment. In order to avoid unnecessary burdens, we are not requiring use of the proposed assessment criteria. We do, however, adopt them as permissive guidelines for exercise of licensee discretion in applying this definition. These factors can serve to make licensees' decisionmaking process more objective and may make it easier for licensees to justify programming decisions that are questioned. We therefore encourage their use. We are concerned with licensee responsiveness to children's needs, not with the precise methodology they use to assess those needs. We thus do not adopt proposals for structured assessment procedures. Licensees will retain reasonable discretion to determine the manner in which they assess the educational and informational needs of children in their communities, provided that they are able to demonstrate the methodology they have used.

. . .

24.   The Act imposes no quantitative standards and the legislative history suggests that Congress meant that no minimum amount criterion be imposed. Given this strong legislative directive direction, and the latitude afforded broadcasters in fulfilling the programming requirement, we believe that the amount of "specifically designed" programming necessary to comply with the Act's requirement is likely to vary according to other circumstances, including but not limited to, type of programming aired and other nonbroadcast efforts made by the station. We thus decline to establish any minimum programming requirement for licensees for renewal review independent of that established in the Act.

25.   At the request of numerous parties, we clarify that short segment programming, including vignettes and PSAs, may qualify as specifically designed educational and informational programming for children. Such material is well suited to children's short attention spans and can often be locally produced with acceptable production quality. It thus may be a particularly appropriate way for a local broadcaster to respond to specific children's concerns. Whether or not short segment programming fully satisfies the requirement to air programming "specifically designed" to meet children's needs depends on the entire context of the licensee's programming and nonbroadcast efforts directed at children. We also clarify that qualifying programming need not be locally produced and need not be live action, as opposed to animation. We can see no reason in the statute's purpose or legislative history for these restrictions. As the legislative history also indicates, general audience programming can contribute, as part of the licensee's overall programming, to serving children's needs pursuant to the Act. It does not by definition, however, satisfy the additional requirement that licensees air some programming

"specifically designed" to serve the educational and informational needs of children.

. . .

2. Nonbroadcast efforts

27.　Section 103(b) of the Act permits the Commission, in evaluating compliance with the broadcaster's obligation to demonstrate at renewal time that it served the educational and informational needs of children, to consider "in addition" to its programming (1) "any special nonbroadcast efforts . . . which enhance the educational and informational value" of programming meeting such needs and (2) any "special efforts" to produce or support programming broadcast by another station in the licensee's market that is specifically designed to meet such needs. . . .

28.　For nonbroadcast efforts to contribute to satisfying the Act's programming renewal review requirement, they must enhance the "educational and informational value" to children of television programming broadcast either by the licensee or by another station in the community. Thus, however, praiseworthy, community outreach efforts unrelated to television programming will not qualify. Similarly, we do not believe that support for children's radio programming, as some urge, although a very laudable objective, qualifies under Section 103(b)(2) as support for another licensee's programming. . . . For efforts to be credited toward satisfying the Act's programming renewal review requirements, they must somehow enhance or support educational and informational television programming for children.

29.　If a station produces or buys children's programs broadcast on another station, so as to qualify under Section 103(b)(2) of the Act, we hold that both stations may rely on such programming in their renewal applications. The extent of support, measured in both time and money, given to another station's programming will determine the weight afforded it. . . .

. . .

V. Program–Length Children's Commercials

A. Definition

40.　We find that the definition of program-length children's commercial proposed in the *Notice*—a program associated with a product in which commercials for that product aired—strikes the best balance between the important interests involved. This definition protects children from the confusion and deception the intermixture of related program and commercial material may inflict upon them, and still preserves the creative freedom and practical revenue sources that make children's programming possible. For the reasons given below, we adopt this definition.

41.　ACT maintains . . . that the Commission should establish a rebuttable presumption that if there is less than a two-year time span between the introduction of a television program and a related product or *vice versa*, this is *prima facie* evidence that the show is a program-length commercial. We do not find that this is a viable definition. We agree with numerous commenters that it would jeopardize highly acclaimed children's shows such as Sesame Street and Disney programs that have products associated with them. As CTW, the producer of Sesame Street, states, a program's relationship to products is not necessarily indicative of commercial content. According to CTW, ACT's proposal would inhibit the simultaneous introduction of any new CTW program series and associated products, such as books, magazines, games and computer software whose purpose is to extend the educational benefits of the series. We fear that such a definition would stifle creativity by restricting the sources that writers could draw upon for characters, would limit revenues from merchandising which are an important source of production funding, and would ignore the educational role toys or other related products can play in child development.

    . . .

44. The definition of children's program-length commercial that we are now adopting—a program associated with a product, in which commercials for that product are aired—is clear, easy to understand and apply, and narrowly tailored. It directly addresses a fundamental regulatory concern, that children who have difficulty enough distinguishing program content from unrelated commercial matter, not be all the more confused by a show that interweaves program content and commercial matter. Removal of related commercial matter should help alleviate this confusion. Our definition also would cover programs in which a product or service is advertised within the body of the program and not separated from program content as children's commercials are required to be. Contrary to ACT's view, we find that our definition clarifies the manner in which our traditional definition of program-length commercial applies to children's programs. We have previously so held. Given the First Amendment context of this issue, our approach is a restrained one. Should abuses occur, however, we will not hesitate to revisit this issue. We also note that our definition harmonizes with, and codifies to some degree, existing policies with respect to host-selling and adequate separation of commercial from program material in children's programs.[147]

45. In addition, a program will be considered a program-length commercial if a product associated with the program appears in commercial spots not separated from the start or close of the program by at least 60 seconds of unrelated material. It is reasonably likely that a young viewer will tune in immediately before or stay tuned immediately after a

---

147. Our policy against "host-selling" prohibits the use of program talent to deliver commercials. Action for Children's Television, 50 FCC2d 1, 8, 16–17 (1974). The policy applies to endorsements or selling by animated cartoon characters as well as "live" program hosts. [ ] "Host-selling" is a special application of our more general policy with respect to separation of commercial and program material. The separation policy is an attempt to aid children in distinguishing advertising from program material. It requires that broadcasters separate the two types of content by use of special measures such as "bumpers" (*e.g.*, "And now its time for a commercial break." "And now back to the [title of the program]"). Action for Children's Television, 50 FCC2d at 14–16. . . .

program, and that in such circumstances an adjacent spot would have the same effect as if the spot were included in the program itself. We do not find record evidence justifying extending this Rule beyond 60 seconds, or further expanding our host-selling policy, as ACT requests. In light of the short attention spans of children, particularly younger children most likely to confuse program and commercial material, we believe that a 60–second separation is adequate.

. . .

Notes and Questions

1. In an omitted portion of *Children's Television Programming*, the FCC denied ACT's petition regarding interactive children's programs, p. 303, *supra*, on the ground that there was no evidence that any interactive toys were currently for sale.

2. On the question of serving the educational needs of children, Congress and the FCC became concerned that broadcasters were seeking to meet the renewal review by listing programs as educational that did not "belong" in that category. In committee hearings, House Telecommunications Subcommittee Chairman Edward Markey relied on a private group's report showing that some stations were listing programs such as "The Jetsons," "The Flintstones" and "Yo Yogi!" as programs designed to meet children's educational needs. As to "Yo Yogi!," for example, a station reported "Snag learns that he can capture the bank-robber cockroach more successfully by using his head, rather than his muscles." For "Bucky O'Hare": "Good-doer Bucky fights off the evil toads from aboard his ship. Issues of social consciousness and responsibility are central themes of the program." Broadcasting, Oct. 5, 1992 at 40.

At about the same time, the FCC began taking steps to strengthen the rules by issuing an NOI raising doubts about whether to allow 30–second and 60–second programs to count as educational and by seeking comments on whether broadcasters could count existing shows that were intended primarily as entertainment. Policies and Rules Concerning Children's Television Programming, 58 Fed.Reg. 14367, R.R.2d Curr. Serv. 53:77 (1993).

3. Responding to pressure from the President, some members of Congress, and lobbyists, the FCC issued a regulation in 1996 that requires television stations to show three hours of children's educational programming each week. The regulation also provides, however, that stations that do not broadcast the three hours per week of regularly scheduled "core" educational programming will have the opportunity to demonstrate to the F.C.C. that they have shown enough specials, short programs, or public service announcements to meet their obligations to children under the 1990 Act. The 1996 regulations attempt to ensure that stations broadcast truly educational programs when children are likely to watch them. Before the regulations, stations were able to evade these requirements either by counting questionable shows such as "The

Jetsons" as educational or by broadcasting educational shows at 5:30 or 6 in the morning. The new regulations require that educational programs must be broadcast between 7 a.m. and 10 p.m. and provide for a stricter definition of "educational programming." 61 Fed. Reg. 43981 (Aug. 27, 1996). See also Lawrie Mifflin, U.S. Mandates Time on Television, N.Y.Times, Aug. 9, 1996 at A1. In the excerpts that follow, the FCC spells out its requirements and its justifications.

IN THE MATTER OF POLICIES AND RULES CONCERNING CHILDREN'S TELEVISION PROGRAMMING

Federal Communications Commission, 1996.
11 F.C.C.Rcd. 10660, 3 C.R. 1385.

1. In this Order, we take action to strengthen our enforcement of the Children's Television Act of 1990 ("CTA"), which requires the Commission, in its review of each television broadcast license renewal application, to "consider the extent to which the licensee . . . has served the educational and informational needs of children through the licensee's overall programming, including programming specifically designed to serve such needs." . . .

2. As explained in greater detail below, we conclude that our initial regulations implementing the CTA have not been fully effective in prompting broadcasters "to increase the amount of educational and informational broadcast television programming available to children." Our review of the record in this proceeding reveals several problems. First, because of their imprecision in defining the scope of a broadcaster's obligation under the Children's Television Act, our rules have led to a variation in the level and nature of broadcaster's compliance efforts that is incompatible with the intent of the CTA. . . . Second, some broadcasters are claiming to have satisfied their statutory obligations with shows that, by any reasonable benchmark, cannot be said to be "specifically designed" to educate and inform children within the meaning of the CTA. Third, parents and others frequently lack timely access to information about the availability of programming in their communities specifically designed to educate and inform children. . . .

9. Congress has recognized that television can benefit society by helping to educate and inform our children. In enacting the CTA, Congress cited research demonstrating that television programs designed to teach children specific skills are effective. For example, children who watch "Mr. Rogers' Neighborhood" and "Sesame Street" have been shown to learn task persistence, imaginative play, and letter and number skills. . . .

. . .

29. . . . [I]n enacting the CTA, Congress found that market forces were not sufficient to ensure that commercial stations would provide children's educational and information programming. . . .

[In the following paragraphs the Commission observed that broadcast revenues "depend on the size and the socio-demographic characteristics of the audience reached by the broadcaster's programming" and that broadcasters have "a reduced economic incentive to promote children's programming because children's television audiences are smaller than general audiences." They have "even less economic incentive to provide educational programs for children" because the audience is relatively small as is the potential advertising revenue. When broadcasters have aired children's programs they have often done so very early in the morning because they lose few adults in that time period. Few children's programs were found during prime time.]

33.   Furthermore, in the broadcasting marketplace it may be difficult for a small number of parents and others with strong demands for children's educational programming. . . . Therefore, broadcasters will have little incentive to provide such programming because the small audiences and small resulting advertising revenues means that there will be a substantial cost to them (the so-called "opportunity cost") of forgoing larger revenues from other types of programs not shown.

34.   The combination of all these market forces consequently can create economic disincentives for commercial broadcasters with respect to educational programming. Broadcasters who desire to provide substantial children's educational programming may face economic pressure not to do so because airing a substantial amount of educational programming may place that broadcaster at a competitive disadvantage compared to those who do very little. These and the other factors described above tend to lead to an underprovision of children's educational and informational television programming, as Congress found in the CTA. . . .

. . .

44.   Conclusion. We conclude, on the basis of the studies before us that while some broadcasters are providing educational and informational programming as Congress intended, some are not. Congress was dissatisfied with commercial broadcasters' performance in 1990 when, according to NAB, commercial broadcasters were devoting an average of two hours per week of airtime to educational programming. . . . Yet it appears that, six years after the enactment of the CTA, at least some broadcasters are providing less than that amount. Given the Commission's duty to treat similarly situated broadcasters in a similar manner, by approving the performance under the CTA of broadcasters providing very little educational programming we would signal that all broadcasters may provide a minimal amount of such programming. . . . Thus unless we modify our approach to implementing the CTA, broadcasters will be able to provide extremely little educational programming for children. That would be contrary to Congress' intent in enacting the CTA. . . .

. . .

III. PUBLIC INFORMATION INITIATIVES

52. . . . We believe the on-air identification of core programs would greatly assist parents in planning their children's viewing and improve the children's programming marketplace at minimal cost to stations. Accordingly, we will require broadcasters to provide on-air identification of core programs, in a manner and form that is at the sole discretion of the licensee, at the beginning of the program. Just as we require stations to provide on air station identification and sponsor identification, we believe the public would be served by requiring broadcasters to identify programs specifically designed to educate and inform children on the air. . . .

53. Some commentators speculated that on-air identifiers could deter children from watching educational programs. No commenter, however, presented evidence that such an effect will occur. We will revisit our decision to require on-air identification if, after some experience, parties present us with evidence that they in fact have a deterrent effect. In the meantime, broadcasters will have full discretion to design their identifiers to minimize or avoid any such effect. . . .

. . .

IV. DEFINITION OF PROGRAMMING "SPECIFICALLY DESIGNED" TO SERVE CHILDREN'S EDUCATIONAL AND INFORMATIONAL NEEDS . . .

84. . . . We believe that, to qualify as core programming, a show must have serving the educational and informational needs of children ages 16 and under as a significant purpose. The "significant purpose" standard appropriately acknowledges the point advanced by broadcasters and others to be successful, and thus, to serve children's needs as mandated by the CTA, educational and informational programming must also be entertaining and attractive to children. Accordingly, . . . we will require that core programming be specifically designed to meet the educational and informational needs of children ages 16 and under and have educating and informing children as a significant purpose. . . .

. . .

93. . . . We are persuaded that we should . . . require that the educational and informational objective of core programming be specified in writing. Requiring a statement of educational and informational purpose will ensure that broadcasters devote attention to the educational and informational goals of core programming and how those goals may be achieved. A written statement of educational and information purpose should also assist licensees to distinguish programs specifically designed to serve children's educational and informational needs from programs whose primary purpose is to entertain children. . . .

. . .

95. We will also require licensees to indicate a specific target age group for core programs. . . . Requiring licensees to specify the age

group a core program is intended to encourage them to consider whether the content of the program is suited to the interests, knowledge, vocabulary, and other abilities of that group. . . . We decline, however, to identify particular age ranges of children to which core programs may be directed. . . .

96.   In addition, we decline to require broadcasters to serve particular segments of the child audience. [Although the economic risks identified above might lead to more programs for older children as they merge into the adult group, the Commission thought it] undesirable to require broadcasters to serve particular segments of the child audience, in part because we did not have adequate data showing that in fact younger age groups are underserved relative to other children. We requested that those commenters who disagreed with this view submit data relevant to whether there was a shortage of educational programming targeted to certain age groups. . . . However, none of these parties submitted data demonstrating that a particular age group was underserved relative to other groups. . . .

. . .

99.   . . . After considering the evidence, we will limit the hours within which programming may qualify as core to a narrower time frame than that proposed in the NPRM. To qualify as core, a program must air between the hours of 7:00 a.m. and 10:00 p.m. In specifying this time period, our intention is to encourage broadcasters to air educational programming at times the maximum number of child viewers will be watching. . . . In other words, at 6:00 a.m. on weekdays, 1.3 million children are watching television. By 7:00 a.m., the number of children watching television is 5.1 million. Data also show that roughly as many (i.e., very few) young children are watching television at 6:00 a.m. as are watching at midnight. [Similar results were found for weekends.]

. . .

105.   . . . We continue to believe that qualifying core programming should be regularly scheduled, particularly in view of our emphasis on improving the flow of information to parents through published program guides and other means to enable them to select educational and informational programs for their children. Programming that is aired on a regular basis is more easily anticipated and located by viewers, and can build loyalty that will improve its chance for commercial success. . . . Furthermore, to count as regularly scheduled programming, such programs must be scheduled to air at least once a week. . . .

. . .

110.   . . . We believe that core programming should be at least 30 minutes in length. . . . [Such programs] are more likely than shorter programming to be regularly scheduled and to be listed in program guides, and thus are easier for parents to identify for their child's viewing. In addition, programs that are 30 minutes or longer allow more time for educational and informational material to be presented, and a

number of commenters stated that shows of this length can be particularly beneficial to children. . . .

. . .

V. PROCESSING GUIDELINE

. . .

120. . . . [U]nder this guideline, the Mass Media Bureau will be authorized to approve the Children's Television Act portions of a broadcaster's renewal application where the broadcaster has aired three hours per week (averaged over a six-month period) of educational and informational programming that has as a significant purpose serving the educational and informational needs of children ages 16 and under. A broadcaster can demonstrate that it has aired three hours per week of such programming in either of two ways: (A) By checking a box on its renewal application and providing supporting information indicating that it has aired three hours per week of regularly scheduled, weekly shows that are 30 minutes or longer and that otherwise meet the definition of "core programming" as described in Section IV, supra, or (B) By showing that it has aired a package of different types of educational and informational programming that, while containing somewhat less than three hours per week of core programming, demonstrates a level of commitment to educating and informing children that is at least equivalent to airing three hours per week of core programming. . . .

. . .

135. Broadcasters that do not fall within Category A or B will have their renewal applications referred to the full Commission. Licensees referred to the Commission should be on notice by this order that they will not necessarily be found to have complied with the Children's Television Act. Given the modest nature of the guideline described in Categories A and B, we expect few broadcasters will fail to meet this benchmark. However, even if a licensee did not meet the guideline for staff approval, it will have an opportunity to make a showing before the Commission that it has satisfied its Children's Television Act obligations in other ways. . . .

. . .

VII. FIRST AMENDMENT ISSUES

. . .

147. . . . The First Amendment arguments raised by opponents of our proposed CTA regulations essentially fall into two categories—arguments that attack the CTA obligation and arguments that attack the quantification of the CTA obligation. To the extent that some commenters argue that the CTA is unconstitutional, Congress itself addressed that issue. It specifically concluded that "it is well within the First Amendment strictures to require the FCC to consider, during the

license renewal process, whether a television licensee has provided information specifically designed to serve the educational and informational needs of children in the context of its overall programming." As the Senate Report noted, broadcasters, in exchange for "the free and exclusive use of a valuable part of the public domain," can be expected to serve as a public fiduciary, obliged to serve the needs and interests of their viewers. That obligation includes the obligation to serve the needs of children. Even more specifically, as the FCC, the courts, and Congress have concluded, a broadcaster's public interest obligation properly includes an obligation to serve the educational and informational needs of children. The question in this proceeding is not whether the Commission should give effect to the CTA, but how it should do so. . . .

. . .

149. The course we adopt today—defining what qualifies as programming "specifically designed" to serve the educational needs of children and giving broadcasters clear but nonmandatory guidance on how to guarantee compliance—is a constitutional means of giving effect to the CTA's programming requirement. "It does not violate the First Amendment to treat licensees given the privilege of using scarce radio frequencies as proxies for the entire community, obligated to give suitable time and attention to matters of great public concern." [*Red Lion*, p. 78, *supra*.] Congress's authority to order "suitable time and attention to matters of great public concern" includes the authority to require broadcasters to air programming specifically designed to further the educational needs of children. The airwaves belong to the public, not to any individual broadcaster. As the Supreme Court observed in CBS, Inc. v. FCC, "a licensed broadcaster is 'granted the free and exclusive use of a limited and valuable part of the public domain; when he accepts that franchise it is burdened by enforceable public obligations.'" The fact that Congress elected to retain public ownership of the broadcast spectrum and to lease it for free to private licensees for limited periods carries significant First Amendment consequences.

. . .

152. Our new regulations, like the CTA itself, impose reasonable, viewpoint-neutral conditions on a broadcaster's free use of the public airwaves. They do not censor or foreclose speech of any kind. They do not tell licensees what topics they must address. . . .

153. The CTA and our regulations directly advance the government's substantial, and indeed compelling, interest in the education of America's children. As Congress recognized, "[i]t is difficult to think of an interest more substantial than the promotion of the welfare of children who watch so much television and rely upon it for so much of the information they receive." In other contexts, the courts and commentators have recognized the government's "compelling" interest in "safeguarding the physical and psychological well being" of minors.

154. A recent case, [*ACT III*, p. 252, *supra*], . . . concluded that a legislature may regulate the exposure of children to indecent material on

the corollary assumption that indecent material may "exert a corrupting and debasing impact." If Congress and the Commission may rely on this corollary to ban broadcast of certain material during specified hours, even under standards of strict scrutiny, it should follow that the Commission's adoption of less restrictive measures to encourage the airing of material beneficial to children is consistent with the First Amendment. . . . The framers of the First Amendment understood that "the greatest menace to freedom is an inert people," as Justice Branders wrote. It is entirely consistent with the First Amendment to ask trustees of the public airwaves to pursue reasonable, viewpoint-neutral measures designed to increase the likelihood that children will grow into adults capable of fully participating in our deliberative democracy.

155. Such a requirement also is supported by [*Pacifica*, p. 228, *supra*]. In that case the Court recognized that "broadcasting is uniquely accessible to children" and that the broadcast media have established a uniquely pervasive presence in the lives of all Americans. Both of these factors support Congress's decision to require broadcasters to serve the educational needs of children. . . .

156. The measures we adopt today to advance the Nation's interest in the intellectual development of our children are sustainable under the *Pacifica* analysis as they are significantly less burdensome than the measure upheld [in *Pacifica*]. . . . The measures we adopt today do not ban programming of any type, they simply notify broadcasters that compliance with the CTA can be achieved with, on average, less than half an hour a day of programming expressing any viewpoint on any topic that broadcasters desire.

157. For those reasons, our implementing rules are constitutional under the traditional First Amendment standard. But even if evaluated under a heightened standard, our rules would pass muster because the interest advanced is compelling and our regulations are narrowly tailored. . . . Specifically, the processing guideline that we adopt today . . . provides a means by which a broadcaster can be certain that our staff will be in a position to process its renewal application without further review of the broadcaster's CTA efforts. . . .

[Although the unanimous order was issued by the Commission, several commissioners wrote concurring opinions. Chairman Hundt called this the "most important vote for children and education ever cast at the Commission." Commissioner Quello feared "future First Amendment incursions." He would have preferred that "core" programs need not be regularly scheduled and need not be at least 30 minutes long. He was particularly concerned about the implications of what could be justified by the last sentence of paragraph 154. Commissioner Ness emphasized the importance of children's television. Commissioner Chong thought that the concept of "core" programs was too restrictive and that quantification of any public interest obligation was inappropriate.]

Notes and Questions

1. How burdensome on broadcasters is the Order?

2. What are the strongest bases for First Amendment challenges to the Order? What is the best justification for the Order?

3. Is the continued survival of *Red Lion* essential to the Commission's effort?

4. Does the processing guideline assuage concern about the rigidity of the three-hour requirement?

E. MISCELLANEOUS CONSTRAINTS

1. LOTTERIES

Another specific substantive limitation on nonpolitical speech has been 18 U.S.C.A. § 1304, prohibiting broadcast of "any advertisement of or information concerning any lottery. . . ." What is the basis for this statute? As with the specific obscenity statute, the Commission has taken the view that it has responsibility for enforcement. This has been bolstered by the provisions in the Communications Act that provide for revocation of license and for forfeitures against those who violate § 1304: §§ 312(a)(6), 312(b), 503(b)(1)(E). Remember the United Television case discussed in Chapter IV.

A lottery is defined as anything containing three elements: chance, consideration and a prize. If all three are present, the broadcaster cannot air any information either as an advertisement or public service announcement concerning the lottery, and even news coverage is limited to situations where the lottery is truly newsworthy.

For many years it was irrelevant whether the beneficiary of the lottery was a commercial enterprise or a non-profit one. This was changed by the Charity Games Advertising Clarification Act of 1988, which expanded the exceptions to § 1304. The Commission also amended its rules to conform to these changes. Broadcasters may now advertise lotteries "if they are conducted by: (a) not-for-profit organizations; (b) governmental organizations; or (c) commercial entities, provided the lottery is clearly occasional and ancillary to the primary business of the commercial organization." Broadcast of Lottery Information (Charity Games), 67 R.R.2d 996 (1990). However, state law has not been preempted, leaving states free to restrict or prohibit lottery advertising. Thus, in many states the restrictions on broadcasters have effectively remained unchanged.

What constitutes chance as opposed to skill is up to the interpretation of the Commission. Guessing the number of beans in a jar has been held to be chance, but betting on horse races is viewed as skill. A golf tournament would be viewed as skill, but a hole-in-one contest would be chance. The distinction is supposed to be whether some difference in ability significantly improves a contestant's chances of winning. Where elements of both chance and skill are present—for example, a tie among all those who correctly answer contest questions is broken by a coin flip—then, assuming there is consideration and a prize, the contest is a lottery.

Consideration exists when an entrant must provide something of value to enter the contest. The most obvious examples of consideration are entry fees or purchase requirements. Sometimes, however, a significant expenditure of effort will be viewed as "shoe-leather" consideration. Thus, having to visit an automobile showroom is not consideration, but being required to take a test drive is. Similarly, having to be present at a drawing is not consideration as long as the drawing is held at a previously announced time. If, however, one must be present for a long period of time, then it is consideration.

The most common method of circumventing this lottery element is to allow people who have not provided consideration also to enter the contest. This is why so many giveaways advertise no purchase necessary or allow contestants to submit facsimiles of proofs of purchase. However, in order to avoid having the contest declared a lottery, those who do not provide consideration must have an equal chance of winning. Sometimes the question of what constitutes an equal chance presents a difficult problem. For example, in contests where people have to match the insides of soft drink bottle caps, the Commission has determined that a non-purchaser who sends in a self-addressed, stamped envelope must receive six bottle caps because people usually buy soft drinks in six-packs.

If the consideration does not go to the promoter, it is not a lottery. Thus, in the soft drink example above, the postage required to obtain the caps does not constitute consideration because the money goes to the Post Office, not the soft drink company. Similarly, a broadcaster could hold a contest inside a county fair without the admission fee constituting consideration, as long as the broadcaster did not receive any of the admissions proceeds.

The easiest element of a lottery to ascertain is the prize. If any contestant receives a benefit as a result of entering the contest, then there is a prize. Prizes usually take the form of money, merchandise, services or discounts.

When states began running their own lotteries, new questions arose concerning the ban on lottery information. After an early case that somewhat limited the scope of § 1304, New York State Broadcasters Association v. United States, 414 F.2d 990 (2d Cir.1969), the issue came to a head in New Jersey. During three consecutive news broadcasts each Thursday, the day of the drawing in the state lottery, a licensee wanted to announce: "The winning state lottery number drawn today is. . . ." The Commission in a declaratory ruling concluded that such a statement would violate § 1304, even though it was presented as a news item. A main argument was that this was "news" only to those who held tickets.

Experience had shown that the lottery's telephone lines were greatly overloaded on Thursdays as people called to learn the winning number. On a typical Thursday, there were 2,750,000 ticket-holders. On appeal, the court, sitting *en banc*, unanimously reversed the Commission's ban on such broadcasts. New Jersey State Lottery Commission v. United States, 491 F.2d 219 (3d Cir.1974). The court concluded that the Commission had misconstrued § 1304 by interpreting it to ban "news." Although the information here was of transitory value, the court noted that on Thursdays more people in New Jersey care about this information than care about any given stock market quotation. Thus, the size of the interested group could not be the test of news. Broadcasters should be free to decide what is news and what news will serve the public unless their decision is beyond the realm of reason. The court was also influenced by the no-censorship language of § 326, which reinforced its view that § 1304 should be limited to advertising and information meant to make a particular lottery more attractive to participants.

The government's petition for *certiorari* was granted to resolve the apparent conflict between the decisions of the Second and Third Circuits. After argument, but before decision, Congress passed a statute providing that § 1304 shall not apply to "an advertisement, list of prizes, or information concerning a lottery conducted by a State acting under the authority of State law . . . broadcast by a radio or television station licensed to a location in that State or an adjacent State which conducts such a lottery." 18 U.S.C.A. § 1307(a)(2). On the government's motion, the Court, over a dissent by Justice Douglas, vacated the judgment of the Third Circuit and remanded for its consideration of whether the case had become moot. United States v. New Jersey State Lottery Commission, 420 U.S. 371 (1975).

On remand, the court noted that states adjacent to New Jersey (and to intervenor New Hampshire) did not have state lotteries, so that broadcasters in those states were not permitted by § 1307 to broadcast information about the New Jersey (or New Hampshire) lottery. The concern about limited dissemination of "news" still existed and the case was not moot. The court reaffirmed its earlier decision rejecting the Commission's interpretation of § 1304. The result is reported in New Jersey State Lottery Commission v. United States, 519 F.2d 1398 (3d Cir.1975). The opinion is reported in 519 F.2d 1398, 34 R.R.2d 825 (1975).

We will discuss further developments regarding restrictions on lottery information later in this chapter.

Under the Charity Games Advertising Clarification Act of 1988, p. 318, *supra*, the adjacent states restriction was eliminated for states that have state-run lotteries. Regardless of whether a state has a state-run lottery, it does not apply to lotteries run by other government organizations or by non-profit or commercial organizations.

The only other significant case in this area involved whether so-called "give-away" programs on radio and television ran afoul of § 1304 as lotteries. The Supreme Court construed the statute narrowly and held that requiring contestants to listen to the program did not constitute a "valuable consideration." Thus, the Commission had no basis for prohibiting the programs. Federal Communications Commission v. American Broadcasting Co., 347 U.S. 284 (1954).

2. CONTESTS

The stations themselves, however, are permitted to run their own contests so long as they are not fraudulent, are not broadcast only during rating periods to increase the figures ("hypoing"), and do not disturb public safety. The Commission has rejected an effort to ban contests that involve no skill, such as those in which listeners tune in to know how much money is in the jackpot in case they are telephoned. The complaint was that this type of contest "bribed" listeners and tended to force other stations to compete by imitation rather than by making improvements in programming. The Commission refused to act, because it was not convinced that the problem required attention or that it was empowered to deal with such a situation. Broadcast of Station Contests, 37 R.R.2d 260 (F.C.C.1976). Does this kind of situation warrant action? Under what authority?

Although contests are not prohibited, they are subject to strict standards of honesty. 47 C.F.R. § 73.1216 provides:

> A licensee that broadcasts or advertises information about a contest it conducts shall fully and accurately disclose the material terms of the contest, and shall conduct the contest substantially as announced or advertised. No contest description shall be false, misleading, or deceptive with respect to any material terms.

When determining whether or not a contest is deceptive, the Commission is not limited to considering the promotional announcements as a complete package but can also look at individual announcements or even misleading phrases. For example, referring to a prize as a "$479 cash prize jackpot" when it consisted of $30 in cash and $449 in noncash prizes was held deceptive even though other promotional announcements made it clear that the jackpot was not all cash. Musical Heights, Inc., 40 R.R.2d 1016 (F.C.C.1977).

Note that the § 73.1216 requires that disclosure be full as well as accurate. Omission of relevant details can be viewed as seriously as deceptive statements. This applies to both the rules of the contest and the prizes to be awarded. Any ambiguity is decided against the licensee. Consider the following promotional announcement:

> THIS SOUND COULD MEAN 4 DAYS AND 3 NIGHTS FOR YOU AND YOUR COMPANION IN YOUR CHOICE OF *LAS VEGAS, SAN JUAN, FT. LAUDERDALE OR ACAPULCO, MEXICO. SECRET SOUNDS* ARE COMING THIS FRIDAY TO 99 WIBZ. EACH DAY FOR FIFTEEN DAYS WIBZ WILL BROADCAST A *SECRET SOUND* . . . LISTEN EACH DAY AND IDENTIFY

EACH SOUND, THEN ON MAY 7TH SEND IN A LIST OF THE *SECRET SOUNDS* AS YOU HAVE IDENTIFIED THEM. WE WILL SELECT THE 25 ENTRIES THAT COME THE CLOSEST TO BEING CORRECT THEN THOSE 25 PEOPLE WILL RECEIVE *4* DAYS AND *3* NIGHTS IN YOUR CHOICE OF *LAS VEGAS, SAN JUAN, FT. LAUDERDALE OR ACAPULCO. SECRET SOUNDS* STARTS THIS FRIDAY ON *WIBZ.* THE SOUNDS WILL BE BROADCAST NUMEROUS TIMES DURING THE DAY WITH A DIFFERENT SOUND EACH DAY FOR 15 DAYS. IT'S EASY . . . SIMPLY LISTEN AND WIN ON *WIBZ 99—STILL THE BEST ROCK!* (SORRY ONLY THOSE OVER 23 YEARS OF AGE ELIGIBLE.)

The Commission held that the above announcement was deceptive and misleading because it created the impression that transportation was included when in fact it was not. An official admonishment was placed in the station's files for consideration with the next renewal application. Randy Jay Broadcasting Co., 39 R.R.2d 937 (1977).

Often, where there has been deception as to the prizes to be awarded, stations have been required to provide the promised prizes. More serious violations—a "find the disc jockey" contest where the disc jockey was in another part of the country, a contest requiring winners to call during a specified time period when the phone was left off the hook, or a treasure hunt where the treasure was not hidden until the last day of the contest—have led to forfeitures and revocations.

In 1966 the Commission issued a Policy Statement entitled "Contests and Promotions Which Adversely Affect the Public Interest." 2 F.C.C.2d 464, 6 R.R.2d 671 (1966). Among the specific examples cited as contests that "adversely affect the public interest" were the following.

A contest which resulted in a vast accumulation of scrap metal in a certain location, blocking access to nearby commercial establishments.

A contest which led listeners to choose names at random from the telephone directory and to call the persons listed at all hours of the day and night causing great annoyance and effectively blocking use of their telephones for normal purposes.

Contests which, by requiring the participants to travel to a specified place in a very short time, have caused traffic violations and endangered life.

The broadcast of "scare" announcements or headlines which either are untrue or are worded in such a way as to mislead and frighten the public; e.g., a sudden announcement delivered in a tone of excitement to the effect that "amoebas" were invading a certain city, implying that the amoebas were dangerous creatures.

In 1985, as part of its ongoing attempt to remove "regulatory underbrush," the Commission rescinded the *1966 Policy Statement.* "[M]ost important by far in our conclusion to delete the policy is that it is simply unwarranted and unnecessary—the raison d'etre of this 'underbrush' proceeding. While the stated purposes for the policy of public safety, etc. are important, the examples cited therefor and the resultant policy constitute regulatory overkill. To issue a Public Notice cautioning all broadcast licensees against engaging in such an obvious hoax as 'amoebas' invading a city is simply an overreaction." The Commission concluded that alternative remedies were adequate to protect the public interest in these areas. These alternative remedies include civil suits (remember *Weirum,* p. 289, *supra*) and criminal statutes prohibiting disturbing the peace, maintaining a public nuisance, and making harassing phone calls. The Commission did note, however, that despite the elimination of the *1966 Policy Statement*, a broadcast of something similar to "War of the Worlds" without adequate cautionary language would still be a violation of the general duty to program in the public interest. Unnecessary Broadcast Regulation, 57 R.R.2d 939 (1985).

Broadcasts of Telephone Conversations. Some of the most common promotional contests involve telephoning a viewer or listener and broadcasting the conversation. Section 73.1206 of the Commission's rules sets strict guidelines for broadcasting phone conversations. if the conversation is live, the party answering the phone must give consent *before* the licensee can start to broadcast it. If the conversation is to be recorded for later broadcast, consent must be given before the recording can start. In response to broadcasters' complaints that this rule destroys all spontaneity, the Commission reexamined the rule and concluded that the loss of spontaneity was outweighed by the substantial privacy interests protected by the notice requirements. Broadcast of Telephone Conversations, 65 R.R.2d 444 (1988). Broadcasting telephone conversations may also raise invasion of privacy questions. We will discuss these issues in Chapter XV.

3.   PAYOLA AND PLUGOLA

Perhaps the biggest scandal ever to occur in broadcasting was the quiz show scandal of the late 1950s. At that time big money quiz shows such as "The $64,000 Question," "Tic Tac Dough" and "Twenty One" constituted one of the most popular forms of prime-time programming. However, in 1959 the nation was shocked when Charles Van Doren, a popular contestant and leading money winner on "Twenty One," testified before a House subcommittee that the shows were fixed. At approximately the same time, evidence surfaced that many disc jockeys and program directors were accepting bribes to play specific records on their stations. The latter practice became known as "payola."

Congressional and Commission reaction was swift. Section 317 of the Communications Act was amended, and two new sections, 508 and 509, were added to the Communications Act.

Section 317

(a)(1) All matter broadcast by any radio station for which any money, service or other valuable consideration is directly or indirectly paid, or promised to or charged or accepted by, the station so broadcasting, from any person, shall, at the time the same is so broadcast, be announced as paid for or furnished, as the case may be, by such person: *Provided,* That "service or other valuable consideration" shall not include any service or property furnished without charge or at a nominal charge for use on, or in connection with, a broadcast unless it is so furnished in consideration for an identification in a broadcast of any person, product, service, trademark, or brand name beyond an identification which is reasonably related to the use of such service or property on the broadcast.

Section 508 requires employees, program producers and program suppliers to notify broadcasters of any payments given or received for the purpose of inducing the inclusion of specific material in broadcast programming.

Section 509

(a) It shall be unlawful for any person, with intent to deceive the listening or viewing public—

(1) To supply to any contestant in a purportedly bona fide contest of intellectual knowledge or intellectual skill any special and secret assistance whereby the outcome of such contest will be in whole or in part prearranged or predetermined.

(2) By means of persuasion, bribery, intimidation, or otherwise, to induce or cause any contestant in a purportedly bona fide contest of intellectual knowledge or intellectual skill to refrain in any manner from using or displaying his knowledge or skill in such contest, whereby the outcome thereof will be in whole or in part prearranged or predetermined.

After the passage of these new provisions, the Commission issued notices that they would be strictly enforced.

Technically, payola is accepting or receiving money or other valuable consideration for the inclusion of material in a broadcast *without* disclosing that fact to the audience, while plugola is promoting goods or services in which someone responsible for selecting the material broadcast has a financial interest. The Commission has adopted several rules governing payola and plugola. In essence, these rules are aimed at preventing the public from being deceived as to the commercial nature of sponsored material. We will return to the most important of these rules, the sponsorship identification requirement, shortly.

The structure of the radio industry has changed dramatically since the original payola scandal. In the late 1950s, most radio programming was done by the individual stations. Now many stations have their music programmed by syndicated programmers who supply the music on record or tape as well as directions as to the order of play. Syndicators have even more control of programming with the hundreds of stations that are carrying satellite-delivered programming. How can the Commission control potential payola problems with these syndicators?

In 1980, after lengthy proceedings, the Commission concluded that plugola was best handled on a case-by-case basis and that "it would be difficult to frame a rule that covered the important elements of this complex subject without either going too far in regulating licensees or leaving important loopholes in the effectiveness of the rule." The Commission also noted that relatively few plugola complaints had been filed in the the late 1970s. Plugola Practices, 46 R.R.2d 1421 (F.C.C.1980).

However, after four people were indicted in early 1988 for payola, the Commission issued a reminder to broadcast licensees that payola could result not only in criminal charges, but in administrative sanctions against the stations involved. The Commission then attempted to clarify the licensees' obligations in this area:

> Both Section 317(c) of the Act and § 73.1212(b) of the Commission's Rules require that each licensee "exercise reasonable diligence to obtain from its employees, and from other persons with whom it deals" information to enable the licensee to comply with the sponsorship identification requirements of Section 317 of the Act. The "reasonable diligence" standard can require a higher duty of care by stations whose formats or other circumstances make them more susceptible to payola. Thus, for example, we would expect stations that report to record charting services to demonstrate greater diligence to prevent improper conduct by its principals and employees than would a station with an all-news format. It may fall short of "reasonable diligence" if the licensee of such a reporting station does nothing more than require its employees to execute affidavits stating that they will not violate laws and regulations prohibiting payola.

The Commission also indicated a willingness to give informal opinions to licensees concerning specific practices or situations. Payola and Undisclosed Promotion, 64 R.R.2d 1338 (1988).

4.   ADVERTISING AND COMMERCIAL PRACTICES

Broadcasters are of course subject to advertising regulation aimed at the mass media in general. However, as we saw in our discussion of cigarette advertising, p. 200, *supra*, broadcast advertising is also subject to special restrictions not applicable to other media.

a.   *Sponsorship Identification*

One such restriction is the sponsorship identification requirement that is part of the measures taken in response to the payola scandal. The Commission has interpreted § 317 to require that every advertisement must contain material specifying that it was paid for, and by whom. 47 C.F.R. § 73.1212. This information is obvious in most cases—a commercial for a specific brand of automobile is assumed to have been purchased by the manufacturer or dealers association promoted in the commercial. But it does restrict one specific form of advertising, "teasers." A teaser is an advertisement that withholds specific information to arouse the public's interest, e.g., "On August 2, automotive history will be made." Obviously, ads of this nature violate the sponsorship identification rules.

b. *Commercial Speech Doctrine*

Traditionally, special restrictions on broadcast advertising were not seen as raising serious constitutional problems. Although the special status of broadcasting contributed to the lack of constitutional protection, the primary reason was that commercial speech was viewed as outside the protection of the First Amendment. However, as a result of a series of Supreme Court decisions during the past 25 years, commercial speech now enjoys considerable First Amendment protection.

Thus far, the effect of these changes in the commercial speech doctrine on broadcast advertising restrictions has not yet been fully determined. In addition, to the inevitable reliance on *Red Lion* and the scarcity rationale, several arguments for allowing more extensive restrictions on the broadcast media have been advanced. Relying on *Pacifica,* advocates of regulation argue that the greater impact of broadcasting, its unique accessibility to children and its intrusion into the home all mandate less constitutional protection for broadcast advertising. Others contend that the restricted format of broadcast advertising—30– or 60– second commercials—makes it inherently deceptive and misleading.

During the past 30 years, there has been increasing pressure for a ban on alcoholic beverages on electronic media similar to the cigarette advertising ban. Due to the changes in the commercial speech doctrine, the constitutionality of such a ban is in doubt. The test that would have to be applied to any such restriction originated in Central Hudson Gas & Electric Corp. v. Public Service Commission of New York, 447 U.S. 557 (1980).

> In commercial speech cases, then, a four-part analysis has developed. At the outset, we must determine whether the expression is protected by the First Amendment. For commercial speech to come within that provision, it at least must concern lawful activity and not be misleading. Next, we ask whether the asserted governmental interest is substantial. If both inquiries yield positive answers, we must determine whether the regulation directly advances the governmental interest asserted, and whether it is not more extensive than is necessary to serve that interest.

The likelihood of a ban on alcoholic beverage advertising being found constitutional increased dramatically as a result of a 1986 Supreme Court decision. The case involved a selective ban on casino advertising in Puerto Rico.

In 1948 Puerto Rico legalized certain forms of casino gambling in an effort to encourage tourism. Although local residents were not banned from using the casinos, the legislature provided that casinos were not to advertise to the local public. Over the years, the focus of the regulation became one of identifying the primary audience of the advertisement in question. This meant that casinos might advertise within Puerto Rico if their primary audience was tourists rather than residents. In Posadas de Puerto Rico Associates v. Tourism Company of Puerto Rico, 478 U.S. 328, 13 Med.L.Rptr. 1033 (1986), the Court, 5–4, rejected a casino's facial challenge to the statute and the regulations.

For the majority, Justice Rehnquist began by noting that the case involved "pure commercial speech which does 'no more than propose a commercial transaction.'" He then applied the four-part test of *Central Hudson*. First, the regulation concerned a lawful activity and was not misleading or fraudulent. Second, the "reduction of demand for casino gambling by the residents of Puerto Rico" was a "substantial" government interest. Third, the regulation "directly advanced" the government's asserted interest:

> The Puerto Rico Legislature obviously believed . . . that advertising of casino gambling aimed at the residents of Puerto Rico would serve to increase the demand for the product advertised. We think the legislature's belief is a reasonable one. . . .

The Court rejected the casino's argument that the regulation was underinclusive because other types of gambling could be advertised to residents. The restrictions do in fact directly advance the government's interest in this case. Furthermore, the legislature's concern might have been casino gambling rather than horse racing, cockfighting and the lottery, which might "have been traditionally part of the Puerto Rican's roots."

Fourth, the restrictions were "no more extensive than necessary to serve the government's interest." The casino argued that the First Amendment required the government to reduce demand for casino gambling "not by suppressing commercial speech that might *encourage* such gambling, but by promulgating additional speech designed to *discourage* it." The Court disagreed:

> We think it is up to the legislature to decide whether or not such a "counterspeech" policy would be as effective in reducing the demand for casino gambling as a restriction on advertising. The legislature could conclude, as it apparently did here, that residents of Puerto Rico are already aware of the risks of casino gambling, yet would nevertheless be induced by widespread advertising to engage in such potentially harmful conduct. Cf. Capital Broadcasting Co. v. Mitchell, 333 F.Supp. 582, 585 (D.D.C.1971)(three-judge court)("Congress has convincing evidence that the Labelling Act of 1965 had not materially reduced the incidence of smoking") affirmed 405 U.S. 1000 (1972); Dunagin v. City of Oxford, Miss., 718 F.2d 738, 751 (5th Cir.1983)(en banc)(". . . The state's concern is

not that the public is unaware of the dangers of alcohol. . . . The concern instead is that advertising will unduly promote alcohol despite known dangers"), cert. denied 467 U.S. 1259 (1984).

This led the Court to conclude that the *Central Hudson* test had been met and that the lower courts had properly rejected the First Amendment claim.

The casino argued that cases like Bigelow v. Virginia, 421 U.S. 809, 1 Med.L.Rptr. 1919 (1975), dictated protection here. The Court disagreed. In *Bigelow,* the underlying activity (abortion) itself was protected. Here, though, the legislature "surely could have prohibited casino gambling" by residents altogether.

Finally, the casino argued that once the government chose to legalize casino gambling for residents, the First Amendment barred it from using restrictions on advertising to reduce demand for the activity. The Court disagreed:

> In our view, [the casino] has the argument backwards. . . . [I]t is precisely *because* the government could have enacted a wholesale prohibition of the underlying conduct that it is permissible for the government to take the less intrusive step of allowing the conduct, but reducing the demand through restrictions on advertising. It would surely be a Pyrrhic victory for casino owners . . . to gain recognition of a First Amendment right . . . only to thereby force the legislature into banning casino gambling by residents altogether. It would just as surely be a strange constitutional doctrine which would concede to the legislature the authority to totally ban a product or activity, but deny to the legislature the authority to forbid the stimulation of demand for the product or activity through advertising. . . . Legislative regulation of products or activities deemed harmful, such as cigarettes, alcoholic beverages, and prostitution, has varied from outright prohibition on the one hand, [   ], to legalization of the product or activity with restrictions on stimulation of its demand on the other hand, [   ]. To rule out the latter intermediate kind of response would require more than we find in the First Amendment.

Justice Brennan, joined by Justices Marshall and Blackmun, dissented. None of the differences between commercial and other speech "justify protecting commercial speech less extensively where, as here, the government seeks to manipulate behavior by depriving citizens of truthful information concerning lawful activities." Regulation of speech based on "fear that recipients will act on the information provided, . . . should be subject to strict judicial scrutiny." The majority improperly used the "relaxed standards" normally applied to commercial speech in its First Amendment analysis. It was incumbent on the government to "*prove* that the interests it seeks to further are real and substantial." Here there was no showing that "serious harmful effects" would result if local residents gambled in casinos.

Even if a substantial government interest had been shown, Justice Brennan found no showing that the advertising regulation would meet concerns about corruption or organized crime. Finally, he objected that Puerto Rico could "seek directly to address the specific harms" by monitoring casino operations to guard against the influences of crime, by vigorously enforcing its criminal laws to combat crime and prostitution, by putting limits on the size of the bets, or by promulgating additional speech. Contrary to the majority's view, it is not "up to the legislature" to decide whether the government's interest can be met by less intrusive means:

> Rather, it is incumbent upon the government to *prove* that more limited means are not sufficient to protect its interests, and for a *court* to decide whether or not the government has sustained this burden. [ ] In this case, nothing suggests that the Puerto Rico Legislature ever considered the efficacy of measures other than suppressing protected expression. More importantly, there has been no showing that alternative measures would inadequately safeguard the Commonwealth's interest in controlling the harmful effects allegedly associated with casino gambling. Under these circumstances, Puerto Rico's ban on advertising clearly violates the First Amendment.

Justice Brennan also rejected the majority's argument that banning speech was "less intrusive" than banning the activity itself. Once Puerto Rico made it legal for residents to gamble in casinos, the decision to ban truthful speech about that activity raised "serious" First Amendment questions. "I do not agree that a ban on casino advertising is 'less intrusive' than an outright prohibition of such activity. . . . [T]he 'constitutional doctrine' which bans Puerto Rico from banning advertisements concerning lawful casino gambling is not so strange a restraint—it is called the First Amendment."

Justice Stevens also dissented, joined by Justices Marshall and Blackmun. His focus was on the operation of the Puerto Rico regulatory scheme which he found to discriminate between publications and to involve aspects of prior restraint.

In Board of Trustees v. Fox, 492 U.S. 469 (1989), the Court held that the fourth prong of the *Central Hudson* analysis does not require that the regulation be the least restrictive means of effectively protecting the state's interest. In an opinion by Justice Scalia, the Court acknowledged that it had frequently said commercial speech restrictions could be no more extensive than "necessary" to serve the state's substantial interests, and that strictly speaking, such regulations are not "necessary" if less restrictive means are available. Indeed, in *Central Hudson* itself, the Court said "if the governmental interest could be served as well by a more limited restriction on commercial speech, the excessive restrictions cannot survive."

But Justice Scalia said "the reason of the matter requires something short of a least-restrictive-means standard." Otherwise, he said, restrictions on commercial speech would be even harder to justify than time-place-and-manner restrictions on core political speech, which need only be "tailored":

> What our decisions require is a " 'fit' between the legislature's ends and the means chosen to accomplish those ends," [ ]—a fit that is not necessarily perfect, but reasonable; that represents not necessarily the single best disposition but one whose scope is "in proportion to the interest served," [ ], that employs not necessarily the least restrictive means but, as we have put it in the other contexts discussed above, a means narrowly tailored to achieve the desired objective. Within those bounds we leave it to governmental decision-makers to judge what manner of regulation may best be employed.

> We reject the contention that the test we have described is overly permissive. It is far different, of course, from the "rational basis" test used for Fourteenth Amendment equal protection analysis. [ ] There it suffices if the law could be thought to further a legitimate governmental goal, without reference to whether it does so at inordinate cost. Here we require the government goal to be substantial, and the cost to be carefully calculated. Moreover, since the State bears the burden of justifying its restrictions, [ ], it must affirmatively establish the reasonable fit we require. By declining to impose, in addition, a least-restrictive-means requirement, we take account of the difficulty of establishing with precision the point at which restrictions become more extensive than their objective requires, and provide the legislative and executive branches needed leeway in a field (commercial speech) "traditionally subject to governmental regulation." [ ] Far from eroding the essential protections of the First Amendment, we think this disposition strengthens them. "To require a parity of constitutional protection for commercial and noncommercial speech alike could invite dilution, simply by a leveling process, of the force of the Amendment's guarantees with respect to the latter kind of speech."

The case involved a regulation of the State University of New York prohibiting commercial solicitations, such as "Tupperware parties" in dormitories. The Court remanded the case to determine whether the regulation had been applied in a manner that restricted noncommercial as well as commercial speech, and if not, whether it was overbroad nonetheless because of its potential applicability to noncommercial speech.

Justice Blackmun, joined by Justices Brennan and Marshall, dissented. They would have held the regulation overbroad on its face and therefore would not have reached the least-restrictive-means issue.

In the *Central Hudson* case the Commission "acknowledged that the ban is not a perfect vehicle for conserving energy." After *Fox* that admission obviously is not fatal to the Commission's case. Would the Court defer to the Commission's determination that the restriction was a reasonable though imperfect way of dampening unnecessary growth in energy consumption?

In United States v. Edge Broadcasting Co., a North Carolina radio station sought a declaratory judgment that it was permitted to carry advertising about the Virginia lottery. The station was located three miles from the border between the two states, and the station claimed that more than 90 percent of its listeners were in Virginia. Under 18 U.S.C. § 1304 broadcasting advertisements for a lottery is a crime. Section 1307 provides some exceptions—the closest of which is (a)(2), which exempts broadcasts by a station licensed to a location in the state holding the lottery or licensed to an adjacent state which itself conducts a lottery.

Recall from our discussion of 18 U.S.C.A. § 1304, p. 320, *supra*, that stations can only broadcast lottery advertisements for a state-run lottery conducted in an adjacent state if the state to which they are licensed conducts a lottery. Because North Carolina did not conduct a lottery, Edge was not permitted to carry advertisements for the Virginia lottery.

The district court declared the statutory ban on carrying such advertising to be unconstitutional. It construed the statute as applying only to commercial speech—and not to news reports about the Virginia lottery. Even so, it found the statute unconstitutionally restrictive. 732 F.Supp. 633, 17 Med.L.Rptr. 1649 (E.D.Va.1990).

The court of appeals affirmed, 2–1. 956 F.2d 263, 20 Med.L.Rptr. 1904 (4th Cir.1992). The majority accepted as substantial the government's federalism justification for the ban—the interest in permitting a non-lottery state to discourage gambling. Applying the four-prong test of *Central Hudson*, p. 326, *supra*, the majority held that the government failed the third prong—the requirement that the restriction be effective and direct. On the facts of this case, the station was so near Virginia that its North Carolina listeners got most of their news and information from Virginia media—all of which were permitted to, and did, carry lottery information: "Simply put, the North Carolina residents which the statutes purport to protect already are exposed to numerous Virginia Lottery advertisements through telecast, broadcast and print media."

The dissenter thought it a mistake to hold that simply because the 2 percent of North Carolinians who were exposed to the station's signal receive other information about the lottery, Congress cannot minimize the volume of that information. "Congress has the undoubted right to enact the legislation which it did. The fact that the legislation does not uniformly succeed in all instances is no reason to hold it unconstitutional." He was also concerned that, because radio waves cross states lines, the majority's decision, if "carried to its logical conclusion, as it will be, [ ], will serve to completely invalidate the statutes involved."

The Supreme Court reversed.

UNITED STATES v. EDGE BROADCASTING COMPANY

Supreme Court of the United States, 1993.

509 U.S. 418, 113 S.Ct. 2696, 73 R.R.2d 168, 125 L.Ed.2d 345, 21 Med.L.Rptr. 1577.

JUSTICE WHITE delivered the opinion of the Court, except as to Part III–D.

In this case we must decide whether federal statutes that prohibit the broadcast of lottery advertising by a broadcaster licensed to a State that does not allow lotteries, while allowing such broadcasting by a broadcaster licensed to a State that sponsors a lottery, are, as applied to respondent, consistent with the First Amendment.

. . .

II

The Government argues first that gambling implicates no constitutionally protected right, but rather falls within a category of activities normally considered to be "vices," and that the greater power to prohibit gambling necessarily includes the lesser power to ban its advertisement; it argues that we therefore need not proceed with a *Central Hudson* analysis. The Court of Appeals did not address this issue and neither do we, for the statutes are not unconstitutional under the standards of *Central Hudson* applied by the courts below.

III

. . .

In *Central Hudson*, we set out the general scheme for assessing government restrictions on commercial speech. [ ] Like the courts below, we assume that Edge, if allowed to, would air non-misleading advertisements about the Virginia lottery, a legal activity. As to the second *Central Hudson* factor, we are quite sure that the Government has a substantial interest in supporting the policy of nonlottery States, as well as not interfering with the policy of States that permit lotteries. As in [*Posadas*, p. 327, *supra*], the activity underlying the relevant advertising—gambling—implicates no constitutionally protected right; rather, it falls into a category of "vice" activity that could be, and frequently has been banned altogether. As will later be discussed, we also agree that the statutes are no broader than necessary to advance the Government's interest and hence the fourth part of the *Central Hudson* test is satisfied.

The Court of Appeals, however, affirmed the District Court's holding that the statutes were invalid because, as applied to Edge, they failed to advance directly the governmental interest supporting them. According to the Court of Appeals, whose judgment we are reviewing, this was because the 127,000 people who reside in Edge's nine county listening area in North Carolina receive most of their radio, newspaper, and television communications from Virginia-based media. These North Carolina residents who might listen to Edge "are inundated with Virginia's lottery advertisements" and hence, the court stated, prohibiting Edge from advertising Virginia's lottery "is ineffective in shielding North Carolina residents from lottery information." This "ineffective or remote measure to support North Carolina's desire to support North Carolina's desire to discourage gambling cannot justify infringement upon commercial free speech." [ ] In our judgment, the courts below erred in that respect.

A

The third *Central Hudson* factor asks whether the "regulation directly advances the governmental interest asserted." *Central Hudson*, [ ]. It is readily apparent that this question cannot be answered by limiting the inquiry to whether the governmental interest is directly advanced as applied to a single person or entity. Even if there were no advancement as applied in that manner—in this case, as applied to Edge—there would remain the matter of the regulation's general application to others—in this case, to all other radio and television stations in North Carolina and countrywide. The courts below thus asked the wrong question in ruling on the third *Central Hudson* factor. This is not to say that the validity of the statute's application to Edge is an irrelevant inquiry, but that issue properly should be dealt with under the fourth factor of the *Central Hudson* test. . . .

We have no doubt that the statutes directly advanced the governmental interest at stake in this case. . . . Instead of favoring either the lottery or the nonlottery State, Congress opted to support the antigambling policy of a State like North Carolina by forbidding stations in such a State from airing lottery advertising. At the same time it sought not to unduly interfere with the policy of a lottery sponsoring State such as Virginia. Virginia could advertise its lottery through radio and television stations licensed to Virginia locations, even if their signals reached deep into North Carolina. Congress surely knew that stations in one State could often be heard in another but expressly prevented each and every North Carolina station, including Edge, from carrying lottery ads. Congress plainly made the commonsense judgment that each North Carolina station would have an audience in that State, even if its signal reached elsewhere and that enforcing the statutory restriction would insulate each station's listeners from lottery ads and hence advance the governmental purpose of supporting North Carolina's laws against gambling. This congressional policy of balancing the interests of lottery and nonlottery States is the substantial governmental interest that satisfies *Central Hudson*, the interest which the courts below did not fully appreciate. It is also the interest that is directly served by applying the statutory restriction to all stations in North Carolina; and this would plainly be the case even if, as applied to Edge, there were only marginal advancement of that interest.

B

Left unresolved, of course, is the validity of applying the statutory restriction to Edge, an issue that we now address under the fourth *Central Hudson* factor, *i.e.*, whether the regulation is more extensive than is necessary to serve the governmental interest. . . .

We have no doubt that the fit in this case was a reasonable one. Although Edge was licensed to serve the Elizabeth City area, it chose to broadcast from a more northerly position, which allowed its signal to reach into the Hampton Roads, Virginia, metropolitan area. Allowing it to carry lottery ads reaching over 90% of its listeners, all in Virginia, would surely enhance its revenues. But just as surely, because Edge's signals with lottery ads would be heard in the nine counties in North Carolina that its broadcasts reached, this would be in derogation of the substantial federal interest in supporting North Carolina's laws making lotteries illegal. In this posture, to prevent Virginia's lottery policy from dictating what stations in a neighboring State may air, it is reasonable to require Edge to comply with the restriction against carrying lottery advertising. In other words, applying the restriction to a broadcaster such as Edge directly advances the governmental interest in enforcing the restriction in nonlottery States, while not interfering with the policy of lottery States like Virginia. We think this would be the case even if it were true, which it is not, that applying the general statutory restriction to Edge, in isolation, would no more than marginally insulate the North Carolinians in the North Carolina counties served by Edge from hearing lottery ads.

In Ward v. Rock Against Racism, 491 U.S. 781 (1989), we dealt with a time, place, or manner restriction that required the city to control the sound level of musical concerts in a city park, concerts that were fully protected by the First Amendment. We held there that the requirement of narrow tailoring was met if "the . . . regulation promotes a substantial government interest that would be achieved less effectively absent the regulation," provided that it did not burden substantially more speech than necessary to further the government's legitimate interests. *Id.*, at 799. In the course of upholding the restriction, we went on to say that "the validity of the regulation depends on the relation it bears to the overall problem the government's interest in an individual case." *Id.*, at 801.

The *Ward* holding is applicable here for we have observed that the validity of time, place, or manner restrictions is determined under standards very similar to those applicable in the commercial speech than is applied to fully protected speech. [*Fox*, p. 329, *supra*]. *Ward* thus teaches us that we judge the validity of the restriction in this case by the relation it bears to the general problem of accommodating the policies of both lottery and nonlottery States, not by the extent to which it furthers the Government's interest in an individual case.

This is consistent with the approach we have taken in the commercial speech context. . . .

. . .

C

We also believe that the courts below were wrong in holding that, as applied to Edge itself, the restriction at issue was ineffective and gave only remote support to the Government's interest.

As we understand it, both the Court of Appeals and the District Court recognized that Edge's potential North Carolina audience was the 127,000 residents of nine North Carolina counties, that enough of them regularly or from time to time listen to Edge to account for 11% of all radio listening in those counties, and that while listening to Edge they heard no lottery advertisements. It could hardly be denied, and neither court below purported to deny, that these facts, standing alone, would clearly show that applying the statutory restriction to Edge would directly serve the statutory purpose of supporting North Carolina's antigambling policy by excluding invitations to gamble from 11% of the radio listening time in the nine county area. Without more, this result could hardly be called either "ineffective," "remote," or "conditional," [ ]. . . . Otherwise, any North Carolina radio station with 127,000 or fewer potential listeners would be permitted to carry lottery ads because of its marginal significance in serving the State's interest.

Of course, both courts below pointed out, and rested their judgment on the fact, the 127,000 people in North Carolina who might listen to Edge also listened to Virginia radio stations and television stations that regularly carried lottery ads. Virginia newspapers carrying such material also were available to them. This exposure, the courts below thought, was sufficiently pervasive to prevent the restriction on Edge from furnishing any more than ineffective or remote support for the statutory purpose. We disagree with the conclusion because, in light of the facts relied on, it represents too limited a view of what amounts to direct advancement of the governmental interest that is present in this case.

Even if all the residents of Edge's North Carolina service area listen to lottery ads from Virginia stations, it would still be true that 11% of radio listening time in that area would remain free of such material. If Edge is allowed to advertise the Virginia lottery, the percentage of listening time carrying such material would increase from 38% to 49%. We do not think that *Central Hudson* compels us to consider this sequence to be without significance.

. . .

Moreover, to the extent that courts below assumed that §§ 1304 and 1307 would have to effectively shield North Carolina residents from information about lotteries to advance their purpose, they were mistaken. As the Government asserts, the statutes were not "adopt[ed] . . . to keep North Carolina residents ignorant of the Virginia Lottery for ignorance's sake," but to accommodate nonlottery States' interest in discouraging public participation in lotteries, even as they accommodate the countervailing interests of lottery States. [ ] Within the bounds of the general protection provided by the Constitution to commercial speech, we allow room for legislative judgments. [ ] Here, as in [*Posadas*], the Government obviously legislated on the premise that the advertising of gambling serves to increase the demand for the advertised product. [ ] Congress clearly was entitled to determine that broadcast of promotional advertising of lotteries undermines North Carolina's policy against gambling, even if the North Carolina audience is not wholly unaware of the lottery's existence. Congress has, for example, altogether banned the broadcast advertising of cigarettes, even though it could hardly have believed that this regulation would keep the public wholly ignorant of cigarettes. . . .

Thus, even if it were proper to conduct a *Central Hudson* analysis of the statutes only as applied to Edge, we would not agree with the courts below that the restriction at issue here, which prevents Edge from broadcasting lottery advertising to its sizable radio audience in North Carolina, is rendered ineffective by the fact that Virginia radio and television programs can be heard in North Carolina. In our view, the restriction, even as applied only to Edge, directly advances the governmental interest within the meaning of *Central Hudson*.

D

Nor need we be blind to the practical effect of adopting respondent's view of the level of particularity of analysis appropriate to decide its case. Assuming for the sake of argument that Edge had a valid claim that the statutes violated *Central Hudson* only as applied to it, the piecemeal approach it advocates would act to vitiate the Government's ability generally to accommodate States with differing policies. Edge has chosen to transmit from a location near the border between two jurisdictions with different rules, and rests its case on the spillover from the jurisdiction across the border. Were we to adopt Edge's approach, we would treat a station that is close to the line as if it were on the other side of it effectively extending the legal regime of Virginia inside North Carolina. One result of holding for Edge on this basis might well be that additional North Carolina communities, farther from the Virginia border, would receive broadcast lottery advertising from Edge. Broadcasters licensed to these communities, as well as other broadcasters serving Elizabeth City, would then be able to complain that lottery advertising from Edge and other similar broadcasters renders the federal statute ineffective as applied to them. Because the approach Edge advocates has no logical stopping point once state boundaries are ignored, this process might be repeated until the policy of supporting North Carolina's ban on lotteries would be seriously eroded. We are unwilling to start down that road.

IV

Because the statutes challenged here regulate commercial speech in a manner that does not violate the First Amendment, the judgment of the Court of Appeals is

Reversed.

JUSTICE SOUTER, with whom JUSTICE KENNEDY joins, concurring in part:

I agree with the Court that the restriction at issue here is constitutional, under our decision in [*Central Hudson*], even if that restriction is judged "as applied to Edge itself." [ ] I accordingly believe it is unnecessary to decide whether the restriction might appropriately be reviewed at a more lenient level of generality, and I take no position on that question.

JUSTICE STEVENS, with whom JUSTICE BLACKMUN joins, dissenting:

Three months ago this Court reaffirmed that the proponents of a restriction on commercial speech bear the burden of demonstrating a "reasonable fit" between the legislature's goals and the means chosen to effectuate those goals. [ ] While the " 'fit' " between means and ends need not be perfect, an infringement on constitutionally protected speech must be " 'in proportion to the interest served.' " [ ] In my opinion, the Federal Government's selective ban on lottery advertising unquestionably flunks that test; for the means chosen by the Government, a ban on speech imposed for the purpose of manipulating public behavior, is in no way proportionate to the Federal Government's asserted interest in protecting the antilottery policies of nonlottery States. Accordingly, I respectfully dissent.

As the Court acknowledges, the United States does not assert a general interest in restricting state-run lotteries. Indeed, it could not, as it has affirmatively removed restrictions on use of the airwaves and mails for the promotion of such lotteries. [ ] Rather, the federal interest in this case is entirely derivative. By tying the right to broadcast advertising regarding a state-run lottery to whether the State in which the broadcaster is located itself sponsors a lottery, Congress sought to support nonlottery States in their efforts to "discourag[e] public participation in lotteries." [ ]

Even assuming that nonlottery States desire such assistance from the Federal Government—an assumption that must be made without any supporting evidence—I would hold that suppressing truthful advertising regarding a neighboring State's lottery, an activity which is, of course, perfectly legal, is a patently unconstitutional means of effectuating the Government's asserted interest in protecting the policies of nonlottery States. Indeed, I had thought that we had so held almost two decades ago.

In [*Bigelow*, p. 328, *supra*], this Court recognized that a State had a legitimate interest in protecting the welfare of its citizens as they ventured outside the State's borders. [ ] We flatly rejected the notion, however, that a State could effectuate that interest by suppressing truthful, nonmisleading information regarding a legal activity in another State. We held that a State "may not, under the guise of exercising internal police powers, bar a citizen of another State from disseminating information about an activity that is legal in that State." [ ] To be sure, the advertising in *Bigelow* related to abortion, a constitutionally protected right, and the Court in [*Posadas*], relied on that fact in dismissing the force of our holding in that case, [   ]. But even a casual reading of *Bigelow* demonstrates that the case cannot fairly be read so narrowly. The fact that the information in the advertisement related to abortion was only one factor informing the Court's determination that there were substantial First Amendment interests at stake in the State's attempt to suppress truthful advertising about a legal activity in another State:

> Viewed in its entirety, the advertisement conveyed information of potential value to a diverse audience—not only to readers possibly in need of the services offered, but also to those with a general curiosity about, or genuine interest in, the subject matter or the law of another State and its development, and to readers seeking reform in Virginia. The mere existence of the [organization advertising abortion-related services] in New York City, with the possibility of its being typical of other organizations there, and the availability of the services offered, were not unnewsworthy. Also the activity advertised pertained to constitutional interests. [   ]

Bigelow is not about a woman's constitutionally protected right to terminate a pregnancy. It is about paternalism, and informational protectionism. It is about one State's interference with its citizens' fundamental constitutional right to travel in a state of enlightenment, not governmental-induced ignorance. [   ] I would reaffirm this basic First Amendment principle. In seeking to assist nonlottery States in their efforts to shield their citizens from the perceived dangers emanating from a neighboring State's lottery, the Federal Government has not regulated the content of such advertisements, to ensure that they are not misleading, nor has it provided for the distribution of more speech, such as warnings or educational information about gambling. Rather, the United States has selected the most intrusive, and dangerous, form of regulation possible—a ban on truthful information regarding a lawful activity imposed for the purpose of manipulating, through ignorance, the consumer choices of some of its citizens. Unless justified by a truly substantial governmental interest, this extreme, and extremely paternalistic, measure surely cannot withstand scrutiny under the First Amendment.

No such interest is asserted in this case. With barely a whisper of analysis, the Court concludes that a State's interest in discouraging lottery participation by its citizens is surely "substantial"—a necessary prerequisite to sustain a restriction on commercial speech, [   ]—because gambling "falls into a category of 'vice' activity that could be, and frequently has been, banned altogether," [   ].

I disagree. While a State may indeed have *an interest* in discouraging its citizens from participating in state-run lotteries, it does not necessarily follow that its interest is "substantial" enough to justify an infringement on constitutionally protected speech, especially one as draconian as the regulation at issue in this case. In my view, the sea change in public attitudes toward state-run lotteries that this country has witnessed in recent years undermines any claim that a State's interest in discouraging its citizens from participating in state-run lotteries is so substantial as to outweigh respondent's First Amendment right to distribute, and the public's right to receive, truthful, nonmisleading information about a perfectly legal activity conducted in a neighboring State.

. . . The Federal Government and the States simply do not have an overriding or "substantial" interest in seeking to discourage what virtually the entire country is embracing, and certainly not an interest that can justify a restriction on constitutionally protected speech as sweeping as the one the Court today sustains.

I respectfully dissent.

Notes and Questions

1. In Valley Broadcasting Co. v. United States, 820 F.Supp. 519, (D.Nev.1993), two radio broadcasters in Nevada sought to carry advertising for private gambling activities over the air. The FCC concluded that they were unable to do so under § 1304 (which was interpreted to cover casino gambling as a "lottery") and accompanying rules because Utah residents made up 4 percent of the audience of one station and Californians made up 19 percent of the audience of the other. Since neither state permitted private casino gambling, the FCC asserted a federalism interest in protecting the efforts of these states to stay free of such advertising. In a decision rendered before the Supreme Court decided *Edge Broadcasting*, the district judge issued a declaratory judgment that the statute and accompanying regulations were unconstitutional infringements on commercial speech. The judge found that the regulation only remotely advanced the federalism interest because it was difficult to accept the idea that the broadcasts "pose any real danger to the public policies" of the two states. Moreover, the judge concluded that the remedy was not a narrowly tailored solution, citing the state-lottery exception provided in § 1307 as an accommodation that would be appropriate for casino gambling as well as traditional state lotteries.

2. In contrast, a constitutional challenge to § 1304's prohibition of broadcasting advertisements for casino gambling by a group of broadcasters in the New Orleans metropolitan area was initially unsuccessful. In Greater New Orleans Broadcasting Association v. United States, 69 F.3d 1296, 77 R.R.2d 1352, 24 Media L. Rep. 1146 (5th Cir.1995), the court of appeals affirmed a lower court finding that § 1304 is constitutional as applied to casino gambling advertising. In applying the *Central Hudson* test, the appellate court relied heavily on *Posadas*, p. 327, *supra*, finding the broadcasters' arguments to be essentially the same ones that were used unsuccessfully by the casino operators in *Posadas*. The court also rejected the broadcasters' contention that *Edge Broadcasting* mandated a different result.

3. Cases such as *Posadas* and *Edge* led many to believe that the Supreme Court was willing to permit more regulation of commercial

speech about "vices," such as liquor and gambling, than other types of commercial speech. Another line of cases suggested that First Amendment protection for liquor advertising was reduced by the Twenty-first Amendment. That Amendment, ending nationwide Prohibition, gave the states power to prohibit sale or use of alcoholic beverages, and the Court had said this created a presumption of validity favoring state regulation against a First Amendment challenge. California v. LaRue, 409 U.S. 109 (1972).

The Court disavowed both of these theories in 44 Liquormart, Inc. v. Rhode Island, 517 U.S. 484, 24 Med.L.Rptr. 1673 (1996), striking down a state prohibition against price advertising of liquor. The Court unanimously rejected the idea that the states have special powers to regulate speech about liquor, all the justices agreeing that the Twenty-first Amendment does not qualify or limit rights under the First Amendment. Eight justices rejected the *Posadas* argument. Justice Stevens, joined by Justices Thomas, Kennedy, and Ginsburg, said *Posadas* "erroneously performed the First Amendment analysis."

> Although we do not dispute the proposition that greater powers include lesser ones, we fail to see how that syllogism requires the conclusion that the State's power to regulate commercial activity is "greater" than its power to ban truthful, nonmisleading commercial speech. Contrary to the assumption made in *Posadas*, we think it quite clear that banning speech may sometimes prove far more intrusive than banning conduct. As a venerable proverb teaches, it may prove more injurious to prevent people from teaching others how to fish than to prevent fish from being sold.
>
> . . . In short, we reject the assumption that words are necessarily less vital to freedom than actions, or that logic somehow proves that the power to prohibit an activity is necessarily "greater" than the power to suppress speech about it.
>
> As a matter of First Amendment doctrine, the *Posadas* syllogism is even less defensible. The text of the First Amendment makes clear that the Constitution presumes that attempts to regulate speech are more dangerous than attempts to regulate conduct. That presumption accords with the essential role that the free flow of information plays in a democratic society. As a result, the First Amendment directs that government may not suppress speech as easily as it may suppress conduct, and that speech restrictions cannot be treated as simply another means that the government may use to achieve its ends.

Justice O'Connor, joined by Justices Souter and Breyer and Chief Justice Rehnquist, did not repudiate the logic of *Posadas*, but noted that since that decision the Court has subjected speech regulations to closer scrutiny than *Posadas* would require. "The closer look that we have required since *Posadas* comports better with the purpose of the analysis set out in *Central Hudson*."

Justice Scalia did not express a view on the validity of *Posadas*.

The major disagreement within the Court in *44 Liquormart* was about the use of the *Central Hudson* test itself. Justices Stevens, Kennedy and Ginsburg argued that a complete ban on truthful, nonmisleading commercial speech requires stricter scrutiny than the familiar *Central Hudson* analysis provides.

The mere fact that messages propose commercial transactions does not in and of itself dictate the constitutional analysis that we should apply to decisions to suppress them. [   ]

When a State regulates commercial messages to protect consumers from misleading, deceptive, or aggressive sales practices, or requires the disclosure of beneficial consumer information, the purpose of its regulation is consistent with the reasons for according constitutional protection to commercial speech and therefore justifies less than strict review. However, when a state entirely prohibits the dissemination of truthful, nonmisleading commercial messages for reasons unrelated to the preservation of a fair bargaining process, there is far less reason to depart from the rigorous review that the First Amendment generally demands.

They viewed the ban on liquor price advertising as a regulation arising not from a need for consumer protection but from "the offensive assumption that the public will respond 'irrationally' to the truth," and therefore should be reviewed with "special care."

Justice Thomas proposed to go even further:

In cases such as this, in which the government's asserted interested is to keep legal users of a product or service ignorant in order to manipulate their choices in the marketplace, the balancing test adopted in [*Central Hudson*] should not be applied, in my view. Rather, such an "interest" is *per se* illegitimate and can no more justify regulation of "commercial" speech than it can justify regulation of "noncommercial" speech.

Justice Scalia said he shared Justice Thomas's discomfort with the *Central Hudson* test and Justice Stevens's aversion to paternalistic regulations designed to keep truthful information from consumers. But he said the briefs and arguments in the case did not give the Court "the wherewithal to declare *Central Hudson* wrong—or at least the wherewithal to say what ought to replace it," and therefore he merely concurred in the judgment that the regulation was invalid under *Central Hudson*, as did Justices O'Connor, Souter, and Breyer, and Chief Justice Rehnquist.

After the decision in *44 Liquormart*, the Court granted *certiorari* in *Greater New Orleans*, vacated the judgment and remanded "for further consideration in light of" *44 Liquormart*, 519 U.S. 801 (1996).

4. The appeal of *Valley Broadcasting* was decided after *44 Liquormart*. The court of appeals accepted the government's first claim, that "discouraging public participation in such games of chance overall is a

substantial interest." The second concern, helping states like Utah and California protect their antigambling environment was also substantial.

The court then asked whether § 1304 would directly advance those interests. Relying on the outcome in *44 Liquormart*, the court sensed that it would be harder for the government to prevail now than before that case. However, "common sense suggests that advertising increases participation; indeed, were this not so, it is unlikely that casinos would advertise." Still, the numerous exceptions in the statute led the court to reject the government's case. Among these were provisions that permitted ads for state-run lotteries, not-for-profit lotteries, and any gaming conducted by "Indian Tribes pursuant to the Indian Gaming Regulatory Act." Because other provisions of federal law undermine the alleged goals of § 1304, "there is little chance that [§ 1304] can directly and materially advance its aim." Valley Broadcasting Co. v. United States, 107 F.3d 1328, 25 Med.L.Rptr. 1363 (9th Cir.1997). The Supreme Court denied *certiorari*, 522 U.S. 1115 (1998).

5.   The Fifth Circuit, however, upheld § 1304 on remand, 2–1. Greater New Orleans Broadcasting Association v. United States, 149 F.3d 334, 26 Med.L.Rptr. 2107, 13 C.R. 452 (1998).

Judge Jones began the majority opinion by noting the recent history of the commercial speech doctrine:

> What seemed a fairly straightforward analysis when this panel first considered the constitutionality of the federal statute prohibiting the broadcast of radio and television advertisements for casino gambling, 18 U.S.C. § 1304, has dissolved into a welter of confusion following 44 Liquormart. On one hand, in 1993, the Supreme Court upheld a companion provision that bans some broadcast advertising of state-sponsored lotteries, and five Justices approved the following statement:
>
> > In response to the appearance of state-sponsored lotteries, Congress might have continued to ban all radio or television lottery advertisements, even by stations in States that have legalized lotteries.
>
> [*Edge Broadcasting*]. On the other hand, after *44 Liquormart* was decided, the Ninth Circuit felt obliged to hold unconstitutional the provision at issue in this case, which bans radio and television advertisements for privately-run casino gambling. Has *Edge* lost its edge in the succeeding five years? Or on the contrary, has the rule of *Edge*, become a constitutional mandate? Such that Congress can now ban broadcast advertisements for gambling only in states that prohibit such gambling? Finally, has the Supreme Court gone over the edge in constitutionalizing speech protection for socially harmful activities? The following discussion will suggest that the Supreme Court's jurisprudence has become as complex and difficult to rationalize as the statutory advertising regulations the Court has condemned.

After summarizing the court's original decision in this case, Judge Jones turned to what changes in the analysis were mandated by *44 Liquormart*. She rejected the argument that the third prong of *Central Hudson* had been changed, but concluded that the fourth prong now requires greater scrutiny than before.

Applying this revised version of 44 Liquormart to § 1304, Judge Jones found the ban constitutional. She specifically rejected the Ninth Circuit's conclusion that the numerous exceptions to § 1304 are inconsistent with the government's asserted interest and therefore, that the statute does not directly advance that interest.

> . . . The government may legitimately distinguish among certain kinds of gambling for advertising purposes, determining that the social impact of activities such as state-run lotteries, Indian and charitable gambling include social benefits as well as costs and that these other activities often have dramatically different geographic scope. That the broadcast advertising ban in § 1304 directly advances the government's policies must be evident from the casinos' vigorous pursuit of litigation to overturn it. See [*Posadas*, p. 327, *supra*], [　]. There is also no doubt that the prohibition on broadcast advertising reinforces the policy of states, such as Texas, which do not permit casino gambling. Further, as previously noted, the Supreme Court rejected in *Edge* the contention that permitting other forms of media to advertise certain types of gambling undercuts the government's policy interests. See [*Edge Broadcasting*]. . . .

Turning to the fourth prong of *Central Hudson*, Judge Jones concluded that even under the more demanding level of scrutiny mandated by *44 Liquormart*, the statute was still narrowly tailored to serve the government's interests, "reducing public participation in commercial gambling and in back-stopping the policies of anti-gambling states." She relied heavily on *Edge Broadcasting* in making this finding.

> The federal government's policy toward legalized gambling is consciously ambivalent. What began as a prohibition on all interstate lottery advertising has been successively, but gingerly modified to respect varying state policies and the federal government's encouragement of Indian commercial gambling. The remaining advertising limits reflect congressional recognition that gambling has historically been considered a vice; that it may be an addictive activity; that the consequences of compulsive gambling addiction affect children, the family, and society; and that organized crime is often involved in legalized gambling.

> In both *Edge* and *Posadas*, federal and territorial governmental decisions to discourage certain types of gambling, while couched in ambivalence similar to that contained in § 1304, were nevertheless regarded as justifiable. Moreover, in *Edge*, the restriction on broadcasting by a non-lottery-state station was upheld despite the fact that over ninety percent of the station's listeners lived in a state where the lottery is legal. The Court was persuaded that controlling

access to broadcast lottery advertising by thousands of local North Carolina households furthered North Carolina's anti-lottery policy. See [*Edge Broadcasting*].

A direct inference from *Edge* would therefore be that if the federal government may pursue a cautious policy toward the promotion of commercial gambling, then it may use one means at its disposal—a restriction on broadcast advertising—to control demand for the activity. . . .

. . . § 1304 cannot be considered broader than necessary to control participation in casino gambling. First, there is no blanket ban on advertising. The ban is more analogous to a time, place and manner restriction. Other media remain available, such as newspapers, magazines and billboards, and indeed broadcast advertising of casinos, without reference to gambling, is permitted. Section 1304 simply targets the powerful sensory appeal of gambling conveyed by television and radio, which are also the most intrusive advertising media, and the most readily available to children. Second, regulation of promotional advertising directly influences consumer demand, as compared with the indirect market effect criticized in *44 Liquormart*. Moreover, the efficacy of non-advertising-related means of discouraging casino gambling is purely hypothetical, as such measures would have to compete with the message of social approbation that would simultaneously be conveyed by unbridled broadcast advertising. Section 1304, in short, is tailored to fit the statutory purpose of controlling demand and does not unduly burden speech.

The government also defends the nationwide prohibition of this advertising as necessary to enforce the policies of non-casino-gambling states like Texas. The broadcasters view this restriction as overbroad and assert that only an *Edge*-like compromise, whereby broadcasters in pro-gambling states could advertise their casinos while non-gambling-state broadcasters could not do so, is constitutionally mandated by the narrow tailoring test. . . . But *44 Liquormart* does not provide any basis for reaching such results, and the broadcasters have identified no non-speech-related alternatives to § 1304 as a means of assisting anti-gambling states. If § 1304 can be upheld on the basis of protecting the non-gambling states, then it is reasonable for the broadcast ban to be nationwide in effect. . . .

. . .

Moreover, if this remand opinion is wrong, and § 1304 is invalidated, there will be no federal protection for non-casino-gambling states, and their citizens will be subject to the influence of broadcast advertising for privately owned casinos. This is not a neutral position; it is one that effectively awards federal sanction to an activity that is again coming to be viewed with moral and utilitarian suspicion. Historically, state and local government policies toward legalized gambling have oscillated between prohibition and regulated legalization, as the social problems gambling stimulates have risen and fallen. What is needed is legislative flexibility, so that the people's representatives can respond to the varying consequences of legalized gambling. If court decisions decree unbridled advertising of "truthful, non-misleading speech" however, the legislature's flexibility will be impaired. In the case of gambling, the consequences may be stark: whatever is legal may be advertised; only a prohibition of gambling will justify a ban on advertising. More disturbing, whatever gambling is legal anywhere may be advertised everywhere. No local prohibition of gambling will be meaningful, and communities will be less capable of insulating themselves and their children from the deleterious influence of gambling. Doctrinal rigidity in this type of case would seem to be the enemy of federalism, of flexible representative government, and of peoples' right to make choices to protect their community and their children. *Central Hudson*, as applied after *44 Liquormart*, does not totally foreclose such flexibility.

Judge Spolitz, who had dissented from the original decision, agreed with Judge Jones that the Supreme Court's recent commercial decisions failed to provide lower courts the "guidance a coherent, dispositive framework would have provided for evaluating these claims." Nevertheless, he concluded that *44 Liquormart* only strengthened his position that § 1304 violates the First Amendment.

A close reading of *44 Liquormart* discloses, however, that a majority of the Court felt strongly that truthful commercial speech about lawful services should enjoy greater first amendment protections than that previously afforded. It appears manifest that the Court will no longer defer to "legislative judgment," grant "broad discretion" for "paternalistic purposes," accept the "greater-includes-the-lesser" reasoning, or defer to the "vice" exception. Read together, the opinions in *44 Liquormart* teach that the government must use direct methods of controlling disfavored behavior. This, combined with the heavy burden of proof that is now placed on the government, substantially undercuts the validity of laws, such as the statute at issue here, which restrict nondeceptive commercial information.

Judge Spolitz also agreed with the Ninth Circuit's conclusion that the numerous exceptions to § 1304 prevent it from directly advancing the government's interest.

The Supreme Court granted *certiorari*.

GREATER NEW ORLEANS BROADCASTING ASSOCIATION, INC. v. UNITED STATES

Supreme Court of the United States, 1999.
527 U.S. 173, 119 S.Ct. 1923, 144 L.Ed.2d 161, 27 Med.L.Rptr. 1769.

JUSTICE STEVENS delivered the opinion of the Court.

Federal law prohibits some, but by no means all, broadcast advertising of lotteries and casino gambling. In [*Edge Broadcasting*, p. 332, *supra*], we upheld the constitutionality of 18 U.S.C. § 1304 as applied to broadcast advertising of Virginia's lottery by a radio station located in North Carolina, where no such lottery was authorized.

Today we hold that § 1304 may not be applied to advertisements of private casino gambling that are broadcast by radio or television stations located in Louisiana, where such gambling is legal.

[The Court began by reviewing the history of lottery advertising regulation, noting that "unlike the uniform federal antigambling policy that prevailed in 1934 when 18 U.S.C. § 1304 was enacted, federal statutes now accommodate both pro-gambling and antigambling segments of the national polity." This was followed by the procedural history of this case and a restatement of the *Central Hudson* test.]

IV

All parties to this case agree that the messages petitioners wish to broadcast constitute commercial speech, and that these broadcasts would satisfy the first part of the *Central Hudson* test: Their content is not misleading and concerns lawful activities, *i.e.,* private casino gambling in Louisiana and Mississippi. As well, the proposed commercial messages would convey information—whether taken favorably or unfavorably by the audience—about an activity that is the subject of intense public debate in many communities. In addition, petitioners' broadcasts presumably would disseminate accurate information as to the operation of market competitors, such as pay-out ratios, which can benefit listeners by informing their consumption choices and fostering price competition. Thus, even if the broadcasters' interest in conveying these messages is entirely pecuniary, the interests of, and benefit to, the audience may be broader. [　]

The second part of the *Central Hudson* test asks whether the asserted governmental interest served by the speech restriction is substantial. The Solicitor General identifies two such interests: (1) reducing the social costs associated with "gambling" or "casino gambling," and (2) assisting States that "restrict gambling" or "prohibit casino gambling" within their own borders. Underlying Congress' statutory scheme, the Solicitor General contends, is the judgment that gambling contributes to corruption and organized crime; underwrites bribery, narcotics trafficking, and other illegal conduct; imposes a regressive tax on the poor; and "offers a false but sometimes irresistible hope of financial advancement." [　] With respect to casino gambling, the Solicitor General states that many of the associated social costs stem from "pathological" or "compulsive" gambling by approximately 3 million Americans, whose behavior is primarily associated with "continuous play" games, such as slot machines. He also observes that compulsive gambling has grown along with the expansion of legalized gambling nationwide, leading to billions of dollars in economic costs; injury and loss to these gamblers as well as their families, communities, and government; and street, white-collar, and organized crime. [　]

We can accept the characterization of these two interests as "substantial," but that conclusion is by no means self-evident. No one seriously doubts that the Federal Government may assert a legitimate and substantial interest in alleviating the societal ills recited above, or in assisting like-minded States to do the same. Cf. [*Edge Broadcasting*]. But in the judgment of both the Congress and many state legislatures, the social costs that support the suppression of gambling are offset, and sometimes outweighed, by countervailing policy considerations, primarily in the form of economic benefits. Despite its awareness of the potential social costs, Congress has not only sanctioned casino gambling for Indian tribes through tribal-state compacts, but has enacted other statutes that reflect approval of state legislation that authorizes a host of public and private gambling activities. See, *e.g.,* 18 U.S.C. §§ 1307, 1953(b); 25 U.S.C. §§ 2701–2702, 2710(d); 28 U.S.C. § 3704(a). That Congress has generally exempted state-run lotteries and casinos from federal gambling legislation reflects a decision to defer to, and even promote, differing gambling policies in different States. Indeed, in *Edge* we identified the federal interest furthered by § 1304's partial broadcast ban as the "congressional policy of balancing the interests of lottery and nonlottery States." 509 U.S., at 428. Whatever its character in 1934 when § 1304 was adopted, the federal policy of discouraging gambling in general, and casino gambling in particular, is now decidedly equivocal.

Of course, it is not our function to weigh the policy arguments on either side of the nationwide debate over whether and to what extent casino and other forms of gambling should be legalized. Moreover, enacted congressional policy and "governmental interests" are not necessarily equivalents for purposes of commercial speech analysis. [   ] But we cannot ignore Congress' unwillingness to adopt a single national policy that consistently endorses either interest asserted by the Solicitor General. [   ] Even though the Government has identified substantial interests, when we consider both their quality and the information sought to be suppressed, the crosscurrents in the scope and application of § 1304 become more difficult for the Government to defend.

V

The third part of the *Central Hudson* test asks whether the speech restriction directly and materially advances the asserted governmental interest. "This burden is not satisfied by mere speculation or conjecture; rather, a governmental body seeking to sustain a restriction on commercial speech must demonstrate that the harms it recites are real and that its restriction will in fact alleviate them to a material degree." [   ] Consequently, "the regulation may not be sustained if it provides only ineffective or remote support for the government's purpose." *Central Hudson*, [p. 326, *supra*]. We have observed that "this requirement is critical; otherwise, 'a State could with ease restrict commercial speech in the service of other objectives that could not themselves justify a burden on commercial expression.'" [   ]

The fourth part of the test complements the direct-advancement inquiry of the third, asking whether the speech restriction is not more extensive than necessary to serve the interests that support it. . . . .

As applied to petitioners' case, § 1304 cannot satisfy these standards. With regard to the first asserted interest—alleviating the social costs of casino gambling by limiting demand—the Government contends that its broadcasting restrictions directly advance that interest because "promotional" broadcast advertising concerning casino gambling increases demand for such gambling, which in turn increases the amount of casino gambling that produces those social costs. Additionally, the Government believes that compulsive gamblers are especially susceptible to the pervasiveness and potency of broadcast advertising. [ ] Assuming the accuracy of this causal chain, it does not necessarily follow that the Government's speech ban has directly and materially furthered the asserted interest. While it is no doubt fair to assume that more advertising would have some impact on overall demand for gambling, it is also reasonable to assume that much of that advertising would merely channel gamblers to one casino rather than another. More important, any measure of the effectiveness of the Government's attempt to minimize the social costs of gambling cannot ignore Congress' simultaneous encouragement of tribal casino gambling, which may well be growing at a rate exceeding any increase in gambling or compulsive gambling that private casino advertising could produce. [ ] And, as the Court of Appeals recognized, the Government fails to "connect casino gambling and compulsive gambling with broadcast advertising for casinos"—let alone broadcast advertising for non-Indian commercial casinos. [ ]

We need not resolve the question whether any lack of evidence in the record fails to satisfy the standard of proof under *Central Hudson*, however, because the flaw in the Government's case is more fundamental: The operation of § 1304 and its attendant regulatory regime is so pierced by exemptions and inconsistencies that the Government cannot hope to exonerate it. [ ] Under current law, a broadcaster may not carry advertising about privately operated commercial casino gambling, regardless of the location of the station or the casino. 18 U.S.C. § 1304; 47 CFR 73.1211(a) (1998). On the other hand, advertisements for tribal casino gambling authorized by state compacts—whether operated by the tribe or by a private party pursuant to a management contract—are subject to no such broadcast ban, even if the broadcaster is located in or broadcasts to a jurisdiction with the strictest of antigambling policies. 25 U.S.C. § 2720. Government-operated, nonprofit, and "occasional and ancillary" commercial casinos are likewise exempt. 18 U.S.C. § 1307(a)(2).

The FCC's interpretation and application of §§ 1304 and 1307 underscore the statute's infirmity. Attempting to enforce the underlying purposes and policy of the statute, the FCC has permitted broadcasters to tempt viewers with claims of "Vegas-style excitement" at a commercial "casino," if "casino" is part of the establishment's proper name and the advertisement can be taken to refer to the casino's amenities, rather than directly promote its gaming aspects. While we can hardly fault the FCC in view of the statute's focus on the suppression of certain types of information, the agency's practice is squarely at odds with the governmental interests asserted in this case.

From what we can gather, the Government is committed to prohibiting accurate product information, not commercial enticements of all kinds, and then only when conveyed over certain forms of media and for certain types of gambling—indeed, for only certain brands of *casino* gambling—and despite the fact that messages about the availability of such gambling are being conveyed over the airwaves by other speakers.

Even putting aside the broadcast exemptions for arguably distinguishable sorts of gambling that might also give rise to social costs about which the Federal Government is concerned—such as state lotteries and parimutuel betting on horse and dog races, § 1307(a)(1)(B); 28 U.S.C. § 3704(a)—the Government presents no convincing reason for pegging its speech ban to the identity of the owners or operators of the advertised casinos. The Government cites revenue needs of States and tribes that conduct casino gambling, and notes that net revenues generated by the tribal casinos are dedicated to the welfare of the tribes and their members. [ ] Yet the Government admits that tribal casinos offer precisely the same types of gambling as private casinos. Further, the Solicitor General does not maintain that government-operated casino gaming is any different, that States cannot derive revenue from taxing private casinos, or that any one class of casino operators is likely to advertise in a meaningfully distinct manner than the others. . . .

Ironically, the most significant difference identified by the Government between tribal and other classes of casino gambling is that the former are "heavily regulated." [ ] If such direct regulation provides a basis for believing that the social costs of gambling in tribal casinos are sufficiently mitigated to make their advertising tolerable, one would have thought that Congress might have at least experimented with comparable regulation before abridging the speech rights of federally *un*regulated casinos. While Congress' failure to institute such direct regulation of private casino gambling does not necessarily compromise the constitutionality of § 1304, it does undermine the asserted justifications for the restriction before us. [ ]

There surely are practical and nonspeech-related forms of regulation—including a prohibition or supervision of gambling on credit; limitations on the use of cash machines on casino premises; controls on admissions; pot or betting limits; location restrictions; and licensing requirements—that could more directly and effectively alleviate some of the social costs of casino gambling.

. . .

Given the special federal interest in protecting the welfare of Native Americans, see California v. Cabazon Band of Mission Indians, 480 U.S. 202, 216–217, 107 S.Ct. 1083, 94 L.Ed.2d 244 (1987), we recognize that there may be valid reasons for imposing commercial regulations on non-

Indian businesses that differ from those imposed on tribal enterprises. It does not follow, however, that those differences also justify abridging non-Indians' freedom of speech more severely than the freedom of their tribal competitors. For the power to prohibit or to regulate particular conduct does not necessarily include the power to prohibit or regulate speech about that conduct. *44 Liquormart*, [p. 340, *supra*]; [   ]. It is well settled that the First Amendment mandates closer scrutiny of government restrictions on speech than of its regulation of commerce alone. *Fox*, [p. 329, *supra*]. And to the extent that the purpose and operation of federal law distinguishes among information about tribal, governmental, and private casinos based on the identity of their owners or operators, the Government presents no sound reason why such lines bear any meaningful relationship to the particular interest asserted: minimizing casino gambling and its social costs by way of a (partial) broadcast ban. [ ] Even under the degree of scrutiny that we have applied in commercial speech cases, decisions that select among speakers conveying virtually identical messages are in serious tension with the principles undergirding the First Amendment. [   ]

The second interest asserted by the Government—the derivative goal of "assisting" States with policies that disfavor private casinos— adds little to its case. We cannot see how this broadcast restraint, ambivalent as it is, might directly and adequately further any *state* interest in dampening consumer demand for casino gambling if it cannot achieve the same goal with respect to the similar *federal* interest.

Furthermore, even assuming that the state policies on which the Federal Government seeks to embellish are more coherent and pressing than their federal counterpart, § 1304 sacrifices an intolerable amount of truthful speech about lawful conduct when compared to all of the policies at stake and the social ills that one could reasonably hope such a ban to eliminate. The Government argues that petitioners' speech about private casino gambling should be prohibited in Louisiana because, "under appropriate conditions," [ ], citizens in neighboring States like Arkansas and Texas (which hosts tribal but not private commercial casino gambling) might hear it and make rash or costly decisions. To be sure, in order to achieve a broader objective such regulations may incidentally, even deliberately, restrict a certain amount of speech not thought to contribute significantly to the dangers with which the Government is concerned. See *Fox*, [ ]; cf. *Edge*, [ ]. But Congress' choice here was neither a rough approximation of efficacy, nor a reasonable accommodation of competing State and private interests. Rather, the regulation distinguishes among the indistinct, permitting a variety of speech that poses the same risks the Government purports to fear, while banning messages unlikely to cause any harm at all. Considering the manner in which § 1304 and its exceptions operate and the scope of the speech it proscribes, the Government's second asserted interest provides no more convincing basis for upholding the regulation than the first.

VI

Accordingly, respondents cannot overcome the presumption that the speaker and the audience, not the Government, should be left to assess the value of accurate and nonmisleading information about lawful conduct. [   ] Had the Federal Government adopted a more coherent policy, or accommodated the rights of speakers in States that have legalized the underlying conduct, see *Edge*, [   ], this might be a different case. But under current federal law, as applied to petitioners and the messages that they wish to convey, the broadcast prohibition in 18 U.S.C. § 1304 and 47 CFR § 73.1211 (1998) violates the First Amendment. The judgment of the Court of Appeals is therefore

Reversed.

CHIEF JUSTICE REHNQUIST, concurring.

Title 18 U.S.C. § 1304 regulates broadcast advertising of lotteries and casino gambling. I agree with the Court that "[t]he operation of § 1304 and its attendant regulatory regime is so pierced by exemptions and inconsistencies," *ante,* [   ], that it violates the First Amendment. But, as the Court observes:

> "There surely are practical and non-speech-related forms of regulation—including a prohibition or supervision of gambling on credit; limitations on the use of cash machines on casino premises; controls on admissions; pot or betting limits; location restrictions; and licensing requirements—that could more directly and effectively alleviate some of the social costs of casino gambling." *Ante,* [   ]

Were Congress to undertake substantive regulation of the gambling industry, rather than simply the manner in which it may broadcast advertisements, "exemptions and inconsistencies" such as those in § 1304 might well prove constitutionally tolerable. "The problem of legislative classification is a perennial one, admitting of no doctrinaire definition. Evils in the same field may be of different dimensions and proportions, requiring different remedies. Or so the legislature may think. Or the reform may take one step at a time, addressing itself to the phase of the problem which seems most acute to the legislative mind. The legislature may select one phase of one field and apply a remedy there, neglecting the others." [   ]

But when Congress regulates commercial speech, the *Central Hudson* test imposes a more demanding standard of review. I agree with the Court that that standard has not been met here and I join its opinion.

JUSTICE THOMAS, concurring in the judgment.

I continue to adhere to my view that "[i]n cases such as this, in which the government's asserted interest is to keep legal users of a product or service ignorant in order to manipulate their choices in the marketplace," the *Central Hudson* test should not be applied because "such an 'interest' is *per se* illegitimate and can no more justify regulation of 'commercial speech' than it can justify regulation of 'noncommercial' speech." 44 Liquormart, Inc. v. Rhode Island, 517 U.S. 484, 518,

116 S.Ct. 1495, 134 L.Ed.2d 711 (1996) (concurring in part and concurring in the judgment). Accordingly, I concur only in the judgment.

Notes and Questions

1. Although the Court indicated the ruling was that the statute was unconstitutional as applied to the Louisiana broadcasters, rather than on its face, the FCC indicated it would cease enforcing the regulation.

2. What if the rule were rewritten to apply only to states where casino gambling is illegal? Would it then pass constitutional muster?

c. The NAB Codes

As we have seen, indirect regulation of the content of broadcast programs was possible through the NAB Codes. The adherence was even greater because of the membership of the three original major networks. Because they abided by the Television Code, even affiliates that did not themselves belong would be carrying only material acceptable under the Code whenever they carried network programming.

Among the provisions of the code were several restrictions on advertising. Advertising of products such as hard liquor and contraceptives were prohibited. Limits on the total number of advertising minutes per hour were part of the code as was a ban on single 30–second advertisements for two or more unrelated products ("split 30s"). In 1979 the Justice Department brought an action against the NAB charging that certain of the commercial time restrictions violated the antitrust laws. In 1982 Judge Greene declared the prohibition against split 30s to be an antitrust violation. As a result the NAB negotiated a consent decree with the Justice Department that prohibited the NAB from adopting any rule respecting the quantity, placement, or format of advertising or other nonprogram material. In addition, although not as a requirement of the settlement, the NAB cancelled the advertising standards of the Television and Radio Codes and dissolved the Code Boards of Directors. Broadcasting and Government, Jan. 1, 1985 at 138–139.

In 1983 Alberto–Culver filed an action against the NAB, CBS, Inc., and several group owners alleging that they were still conspiring to prevent the broadcast of multiple product ads. Alberto–Culver negotiated a settlement with each of the broadcasters named in the case, and the suit was dismissed.

The Advisory Committee on the Public Interest Obligations of Digital Television Broadcasters, p. 60, *supra*, has recommended creation of a new code:

> A new industry statement of principles updating the 1952 Code would have many virtues. The most significant one is that it would enable the broadcasting industry to identify the high standards of public service that most stations follow and that represent the ideals and historic traditions of the industry. A new set of standards can

help counteract short-term pressures that have been exacerbated by the incredibly competitive landscape broadcasters now face, particularly when compared to the first 30–some years of the television era. Those competitive pressures can lead to less attention to public issues and community concerns. A renewed statement of principles can make salient and keep fresh general aspirations that can easily be lost in the hectic atmosphere and pressures of day-to-day operations.

To ensure that broadcasters fulfill their obligations as public trustees, we endorse self-regulation by knowledgeable industry people. This could serve as an effective tool to minimize government regulation. To that end, we recommend that the National Association of Broad-casters, acting as the representative of the broadcasting industry, draft a new set of principles or statement of standards. The Advisory Committee hopes that the NAB will develop and recommend self-regulatory standards to and for the industry. The standards should be drafted and implemented by the NAB and the industry, preferably with input from community and public interest leaders, without pressure, interference, or direct or indirect enforcement by the government. The public, the marketplace, and the court of public opinion can then judge their efficacy.

d. *Commercial Practices*

The Commission has long taken an interest in the commercial practices of broadcast licensees. Recall the White Mountain Broadcasting case where renewal was denied for "double billing." In 1985, as part of another "regulatory underbrush" proceeding, the Commission eliminated many of these rules and issued an NPRM proposing deletion of others. Among the regulations deleted were those covering distortion of audience ratings, selection of sports announcers, conflicts of interest, promotion of nonbroadcast business of a station, concert promotion announcements, and false, misleading or deceptive advertisements. As in the other "underbrush" proceedings, the Commission argued that the policies eliminated "either relate to areas which often are not within this Commission's area of expertise and where either alternate remedies exist to deter the activity addressed by the particular policy or where marketplace forces will correct the particular abuse." Unnecessary Broadcast Regulation, 57 R.R.2d 913 (1985). The court of appeals rejected a petition for review of the Commission's order. Telecommunications Research and Action Center v. Federal Communications Commission, 800 F.2d 1181, 61 R.R.2d 61 (D.C.Cir.1986).

The regulations proposed for deletion in that proceeding were subsequently eliminated. They applied to fraudulent billing practices, network clipping and joint sales practices. Unnecessary Broadcast Regulation, 59 R.R.2d 1500 (1986).

In addition, the Commission no longer hears complaints regarding distortion of a station's ratings or inaccurate signal coverage maps. It did state that the filing of a misleading coverage map would imply unacceptable character and could place a station's renewal at risk. Unnecessary Broadcast Regulation (Advertising Misrepresentations), 54 R.R.2d 705 (F.C.C.1983).

Although the Commission has for the most part ceased to regulate commercial practices, they can still give rise to civil actions. In 2000 CBS was sued for its innovative use of virtual insertion technology. This technology allows substituting or adding images into video footage. Specifically, CBS was able to replace building signage with the CBS logo in its coverage of the Times Square New Year's Eve celebration. OTS Signs, a billboard company that owned many of the billboards that were replaced in the TV coverage, has sued CBS for unfair competition, deceptive trade practices and trespass. OTS argued that the value of that signage was based in part on its visibility during the New Year's Eve coverage and that CBS was appropriating its product without compensation.

The issues raised by the suit could extend far beyond this specific situation. Using virtual insertion technology, ads, signs even products can be "placed" in any video programming. For example, an identifiable can of beer could be put on Marlon Brando's desk in "The Godfather?" To what extent should broadcasters be permitted to do this? Does the type of programming make a difference? For example, what if the same can of beer were to be placed on the President's desk during news coverage?

5.   Other Constraints

a.   Sports Blackouts

In 1973 Congress passed a statute to resolve the clamor raised by the refusal of professional football teams to permit televising of a home game that was being televised to other parts of the country (47 U.S.C.A. § 331). It provided that professional sports telecasts could not be barred if all the tickets had been sold 72 hours before game time, and spelled out the conditions under which the rights to telecast could be made available. The statute expired by its own terms in 1975. A permanent anti-blackout statute was blocked in 1976, but the National Football League agreed to follow the expired statute.

b.   Other Underbrush

We considered some of the policies eliminated in the regulatory underbrush proceedings earlier in this chapter. Policies aimed at discouraging liquor advertisements in dry areas, restrictions on broadcasts of foreign language programs, broadcast of astrology information, music format service agreements, repetitious broadcasts, call-in polls, private interest broadcasts, the use of sirens and sound effects, and rules regarding harassing and threatening phone calls resulting from broadcasts were all eliminated. Unnecessary Broadcast Regulation, 54 R.R.2d 1043 (F.C.C.1983). The FCC also eliminated restrictions on horse racing programming and advertising. Unnecessary Broadcast Regulation, 56 R.R.2d 976 (F.C.C.1984).

Chapter VII

NONCOMMERCIAL BROADCASTING

A. DEVELOPMENT OF PUBLIC BROADCASTING

Virtually all of our attention so far has been devoted to commercial broadcasting. Most of the litigation and regulation has involved commercial broadcasters, and, in terms of viewers, commercial broadcasting is the preeminent part of the picture. But it is not the only part. AM broadcasting developed too early for the Commission to be able to consider reserving spots for noncommercial educational stations. In allocating FM and television, however, the Commission was able to plan in advance and reserved certain spots for educational broadcasters. These are usually operated by academic institutions, by governmental groups, or by groups organized by private citizens. Although an academic institution may operate a station only in a community where it operates a bona fide fulltime school, a private or governmental organization may qualify for a station in any community as long as it demonstrates an educational goal and a commitment to the advancement of an educational program. A station run by a sectarian academic institution may be eligible for a reserved educational spot in the community in which the school is located. If an organization's central purpose is religious, it is not eligible for a reserved channel. We will return to the issue of religious broadcasting later in this chapter.

Although many of the Commission's rules apply equally to commercial and noncommercial licensees, there are some differences. For example, the duopoly and multiple ownership rules are not applicable to noncommercial licensees. In 1988 the Commission amended its public file requirements for non-commercial licensees to conform them to the requirements for commercial licensees. Issues–Programs List for Public Broadcasting Licensees, 3 F.C.C.Rcd. 1032, 64 R.R.2d 667 (1988).

The comparative licensing criteria for the commercial portion of the spectrum were not used for the portion reserved for noncommercial stations. Instead, applicants were evaluated as to "the extent to which each of the proposed operations will be 'integrated into the overall operations and objectives' of the respective applicants." Noncommercial applicants for commercial portions of the spectrum were subject to the comparative criteria used for commercial stations.

As part of the NPRM on comparative criteria issued after *Bechtel*, p. 155, *supra*, the Commission proposed eliminating this "vague standard" and replacing it with a modified version of the point system proposed for commercial stations.

Concerned that its inclusion in the broader licensing NPRM was inhibiting a full range of comments on this particular issue, the FCC later issued a separate NPRM on comparative criteria for new or open noncommercial licenses. Comparative Standards for New Noncommercial Educational Applicants, 10 F.C.C.Rcd. 2877 (1995).

The 1997 Balanced Budget Act, p. 58, *supra*, granted the Commission authority to use a lottery to award licenses for noncommercial stations, while explicitly prohibiting auctions for these licenses. In response, the FCC issued an NPRM proposing a lottery system similar to that used for LPTV licenses, p. 54, *supra*, but also requesting comment on the alternative of a point system. Reexamination of the Comparative Standards for Noncommercial Educational Applicants, 13 F.C.C.Rcd. 21167 (1998). A petition for reconsideration was denied. 17 F.C.C.Rcd. 13132 (2002).

The requirement of different systems for commercial and noncommercial licensing (auctions and lotteries) each of which is prohibited for the other presents another problem. When a noncommercial applicant competes against a commercial applicant for a license in the unreserved portion of the band, how should the FCC determine who gets the license?

The Commission decided to continue using its comparative system for noncommercial licenses in the reserved portion of the spectrum, but to require participation in the auction process for noncommercial entities applying for licenses in the unreserved portion. Reexamination of the Comparative Standards for Noncommercial Educational Applicants, 15 F.C.C.Rcd 7386 (2000).

On appeal, the portion of the order mandating participation in the auction process for licenses in the unreserved spectrum was vacated. The majority held that the plain language of the Balanced Budget Act of 1997 prohibits requiring noncommercial entities to participate in a competitive bidding process. In a concurrence, Judge Randolph argued that the provision in question was "a mess," noting that at oral argument the Commission's lawyers were as baffled as he was regarding the meaning of some of it. However, he rejected the Commission's justification for including noncommercial applicants in the auction process, "that some conflict existed between the general rule embodied in § 309(j)(1), requiring auctions, and the exception in § 309(j)(2)." He argued that an exception cannot *conflict* with a general rule and the Commission's reliance on an erroneous argument required vacating that portion of the order. National Public Radio v. Federal Communications Commission, 254 F.3d 226 (D.C.Cir.2001).

The development of public broadcasting and several questions it raises are considered in the following case.

ACCURACY IN MEDIA, INC. v. FEDERAL COMMUNICATIONS COMMISSION

United States Court of Appeals, District of Columbia Circuit, 1975.
521 F.2d 288, 35 R.R.2d 241.

Certiorari denied 425 U.S. 934, 96 S.Ct. 1664, 48 L.Ed.2d 175 (1976).

Before BAZELON, CHIEF JUDGE, LEVENTHAL, CIRCUIT JUDGE and WEIGEL, UNITED STATES DISTRICT JUDGE for the Northern District of California.

BAZELON, CHIEF JUDGE.

Accuracy in Media, Inc. (AIM) filed two complaints with the FCC against the Public Broadcasting Service (PBS) concerning two programs distributed by PBS to its member stations. AIM alleged that the programs, dealing with sex education and the American system of criminal justice, were not a balanced or objective presentation of each subject and requested the FCC to order PBS to rectify the situation. The legal basis for AIM's complaints was the Fairness Doctrine and 47 U.S.C. § 396(g)(1)(A)(1970). On its initial hearing of the matter, the FCC concluded that the PBS had not violated the Fairness Doctrine and invited comments from interested parties on its authority to enforce whatever standard of program regulation was contained in § 396(g)(1)(A). AIM does not seek the review of the Commission's decision on the Fairness Doctrine issue.

Section 396(g)(1)(A) is part of the Public Broadcasting Act of 1967, an act which created the Corporation for Public Broadcasting (CPB) and authorized it to fund various programming activities of local, non-commercial broadcasting licensees. Section 396(g)(1)(A) qualifies that authorization in the following language:

> In order to achieve the objectives and to carry out the purposes of this subpart, as set out in subsection (a) of this section, the Corporation is authorized to—
>
> > (A) facilitate the full development of educational broadcasting in which programs of high quality, obtained from diverse sources, will be made available to noncommercial educational television or radio broadcast stations, with strict adherence to objectivity and balance in all programs or series of programs of a controversial nature. . . .

AIM contends that since the above-mentioned PBS programs were funded by the CPB, pursuant to this authorization, the programs must contain "strict adherence to authorization and balance," a requirement AIM contends is more stringent than the standard of balance and fairness in overall programming contained in the Fairness Doctrine. AIM alleges that the two relevant programs did not meet this more stringent standard of objectivity and balance.

After consideration of the comments received on the matter, invited in its preliminary decision discussed above, the Commission concluded that it had no jurisdiction to enforce the mandate of § 396(g)(1)(A) against CPB. . . .

I. THE ORGANIZATION OF PUBLIC BROADCASTING IN THE UNITED STATES

Resolution of the issues raised by AIM's petition requires an understanding of the operation of the public broadcasting system. There are three tiers to this operation, each reflecting a different scheme of governmental regulation. The basic level is comprised of the local, noncommercial broadcasting stations that are licensed by the FCC and, with a few exceptions, subject to the same regulations as commercial licenses. Through the efforts of former Commissioner Frieda Hennock, the FCC has reserved exclusive space in its allocation of frequencies for such noncommercial broadcasters. Other than this specific reservation, noncommercial licensees are still subject to the same renewal process and potential challenges as their commercial counterparts.

Such was the state of the public broadcasting system until the passage of the Educational Television Facilities Act in 1962. The Act added the element of government funding to public broadcasting by establishing a grant program for noncommercial facilities. This second level of the system was reorganized and expanded by the Public Broadcasting Act of 1967 which created the Corporation for Public Broadcasting (CPB). The Corporation, the product of a study made by the Carnegie Commission on Educational Television, was established as a funding mechanism for virtually all activities of noncommercial broadcasting. In setting up this nonprofit, private corporation, the Act specifically prohibited CPB from engaging in any form of "communication by wire or radio."

The third level of the public broadcasting system was added in 1970 when CPB and a group of noncommercial licensees formed the Public Broadcasting Service (PBS) and National Public Radio. The Public Broadcasting Service operates as the distributive arm of the public television system. As a nonprofit membership corporation, it distributes national programming to approximately 150 educational licensees via common carrier facilities. This interconnection service is funded by the Corporation (CPB) under a contract with PBS; in addition, much of the programming carried by PBS is either wholly or partially funded by CPB. National Public Radio provides similar services for noncommercial radio. In 1974, CPB and the member licensees of PBS agreed upon a station program cooperative plan[14] to insure local control and origination

---

14. The Station Program Cooperative (SPC) is a unique concept in program selection and financing for public television stations. Though the idea of public broadcasting as a "fourth network" had been proposed at various times, the 1974 plan reversed this trend toward centralization. Under the SPC, certain programming will be produced only if the individual local sta- tions decide together to fund the production. The local licensees will be financed through the CPB and other sources; the funding of specific programs will be by a 4 to 5 ratio (station funds to national cooperative funds). The aim of this cooperative is to reinforce the existing licensee responsibility for programming discretion. Through this plan the local stations will eventually

of noncommercial broadcasting funded by CPB. Though PBS is the national coordinator under this scheme, it is not a "network" in the commercial broadcasting sense, and does not engage in "communication by wire or radio," except to the extent that it contracts for interconnection services.

II. FCC JURISDICTION OVER THE CORPORATION FOR PUBLIC BROADCASTING

With the structure of the public broadcasting system in view, we turn to AIM's contention that the FCC should enforce the mandate of § 396(g)(1)(A) against the CPB. Since the Section is clearly directed to the Corporation and its programming activities, we have no doubt that the Corporation must respect the mandate of the Section. However, we conclude that nothing in the language and legislative history of the Federal Communications Act or the Public Broadcasting Act of 1967 authorizes the FCC to enforce that mandate against the CPB.

Section 398 of the Communications Act expresses the clear intent of Congress that there shall be no direct jurisdiction of the FCC over the Corporation. That section states that nothing in the 1962 or 1967 Acts "shall be deemed (1) to amend any other provision of, or requirement under this Act; or (2) to authorize any department, agency, officer, or employee of the United States to exercise any direction, supervision or control over educational television or radio broadcasting, or over the Corporation or any of its grantees or contractors. . . ." Since the FCC is obviously an "agency . . . of the United States" and since any enforcement of § 396(g)(1)(A) would necessarily entail "supervision" of the Corporation, the plain words of subsection (2) preclude FCC jurisdiction. . . .

Congress desired to establish a program funding agency which would be free from governmental influence or control in its operations. Yet, the lawmakers feared that such complete autonomy might lead to biases and abuses of its own. The unique position of the Corporation is the synthesis of these competing influences. Reference to the legislative history of the 1967 Act shows a deep concern that governmental regulation or control over the Corporation might turn the CPB into a Government spokesman. Congress thus sought to insulate CPB by removing its "programming activity from governmental supervision." . . .

. . .

AIM maintains that this view of FCC jurisdiction to enforce § 396(g)(1)(A) renders the section nugatory and hence ignores the Congressional sentiment that biases and abuses within the public broadcasting system should be controlled. We do not view our holding on the FCC's jurisdiction as having that effect. Rather, we take notice of the carefully balanced framework designed by Congress for the control of CPB activities.

assume the responsibility for support of the cooperative and the Corporation will

concentrate on new programming development. [   ]

The Corporation was established as nonprofit and non-political in nature and is prohibited from owning or operating "any television or radio broadcast station, system or network, community antenna system, or interconnection, or production facility." Numerous statutory safeguards were created to insure against partisan abuses.[28] Ultimately, Congress may show its disapproval of any activity of the Corporation through the appropriation process.[29] This supervision of CPB through its funding is buttressed by an annual reporting requirement.[30] Through these statutory requirements and control over the "purse-strings," Congress reserved for itself the oversight responsibility for the Corporation.

A further element of this carefully balanced framework of regulation is the accountability of the local noncommercial licensees under established FCC practice, including the Fairness Doctrine in particular. This existing system of accountability was clearly recognized in the 1967 legislative debates as a crucial check on the power of the CPB. . . .

. . .

The framework of regulation of the Corporation for Public Broadcasting we have described—maximum freedom from interference with programming coupled with existing public accountability requirements—is sensitive to the delicate constitutional balance between First Amendment rights of the broadcast journalist and the concerns of the viewing public struck in Columbia Broadcasting System, Inc. v. Democratic National Committee, 412 U.S. 94 (1973). There the Supreme Court warned that "only when the interests of the public are found to outweigh the private journalistic interests of the broadcasters" will governmental interference with broadcast journalism be allowed. The Court on the basis of this rule rejected a right of access to broadcast air time greater than that mandated by the Fairness Doctrine as constituting too great a "risk of an enlargement of Governmental control over the content of broadcast discussion of public issues."

It is certainly arguable that FCC application of the standard—whatever that standard may be—of § 396(g)(1)(A) could "risk [an] enlargement of Government control over the content of broadcast discussion of public issues" in the following two ways: whereas the existing Fairness Doctrine requires only that the presentation of a controversial issue of public importance be balanced in *overall* programming, § 396(g)(1)(A) might be argued to require balance of controversial issues within each individual program. Administration of such a standard would certainly require a more active role by the FCC in oversight of

28. Other statutory checks on the Corporation include: restricting the Board membership to no more than eight out of fifteen members from the same political party, § 396(c)(1). The composition of the Board was an important issue during debate and the decision to make the Board bipartisan was a significant addition to the original Carnegie Commission proposal. The Act also requires that the CPB's accounts be audited annually by an independent accountant, § 396(*l*)(1)(A), and *may* be audited by the General Accounting Office, § 396(*l*)(2)(A).

29. Section 396(k) assures that most of the CPB's operating budget be derived through the Congressional appropriation process.

30. 47 U.S.C. § 396(i)(1970).

programming. Furthermore, whereas the FCC has at present carefully avoided anything but the most limited inquiry into the factual accuracy of programming, § 396(g)(1)(A) by use of the term "objective" could be read to expand that inquiry and thereby expand FCC oversight of programming. Both of these potential enlargements of government control of programming, whether directed against the CPB, PBS or individual noncommercial licensees, threaten to upset the constitutional balance struck in *CBS*. We will not presume that Congress meant to thrust upon us the substantial constitutional questions such a result would raise. We thus construe § 396(g)(1)(A) and the scheme of regulation for public broadcasting as a whole to avoid such questions.

. . . We hold today only that the FCC has no function in this scheme of accountability established by § 396(g)(1)(A) and the 1967 Act in general other than that assigned to it by the Fairness Doctrine. Therefore, we deny the petition for review and affirm the Commission's decision rejecting jurisdiction over the Corporation for Public Broadcasting.

So ordered.

Notes and Questions

1. What is the difference between the fairness doctrine and AIM's reading of § 396(g)(1)(A)? Why does the court think that one would call for more Commission intervention in programming than the other?

2. The court suggests that PBS, although thought of by many as a another network, does not properly fit such a description. Why not?

3. Despite the ruling in the AIM case, the Commission retains several controls over public noncommercial broadcasters. The primary power is to be found in the licensing process. Recall the denial of renewal to the eight Alabama stations, p. 127, *supra*. A fundamental dispute over the proper role of educational stations emerged when WNET in New York was challenged on its application for renewal: Commissioner Hooks dissented from the approval on the ground that the station was programming for a small elite minority and essentially neglecting the needs of larger groups in the community that would benefit from language, vocational and remedial programs. Elite programming is defended on the ground that the noncommercial stations do not get enough money from public sources and must solicit funds from their communities. It is thought that a station that presents culturally high-level programs for the wealthier segments of the community will have better success at raising the funds necessary to keep the station going. Is this a problem? How might the situation be changed?

4. Concern about adequate funding for public broadcasting has increased because of continuing decreases in federal funding. In 1981 Congress created the Temporary Commission on Alternative Financing for Public Telecommunications (TCAF). Chaired by Commissioner Quello of the FCC, TCAF was directed as part of its investigation of

alternative funding to oversee an 18–month experiment allowing some public broadcasters to sell advertising. Nine public television stations participated in the experiment. Although the advertising experiment generated significant income for the participants, it was not extended.

TCAF recommended to Congress that advertising not be allowed but that enhanced underwriting (allowing identification of contributors to include product identifications and slogans) be given explicit approval. What are the risks of allowing advertising on noncommercial stations? What other funding mechanisms should be considered? Congress did not include any provision for further advertising experiments in the latest CPB funding authorization.

5. In keeping with these recommendations and the Public Broadcasting Amendments Act of 1981, the Commission reconsidered its 1982 ruling prohibiting the inclusion of brand names in donor acknowledgements. "[D]onor acknowledgements utilized by public broadcasters may include (1) logograms or slogans which identify and do *not* promote, (2) location, (3) value neutral descriptions of a product line or service, (4) brand and trade names and product or service listings." Noncommercial Educational Broadcasting Stations, 97 F.C.C.2d 255, 55 R.R.2d 1190 (1984).

6. A 1995 CPB report to Congress stated that CPB "is committed to concrete measures that will address overlapping signals and duplication of service." CPB proposed limiting its federal grants to one public television station per market. This would encourage mergers between stations in the same market. Broadcasting & Cable, May 22, 1995 at 46.

7. A new potential funding source was suggested by the Advisory Committee on the Public Interest Obligations of Digital Television Broadcasters, p. 60, *supra*:

> Improving Education Through Digital Broadcasting: Congress should create a trust fund to ensure enhanced and permanent funding for public broadcasting to help it fulfill its potential in the digital television environment and remove it from the vicissitudes of the political process. When spectrum now used for analog broadcasting is returned to the government, Congress should reserve the equivalent of 6 MHz of spectrum for each viewing community in order to establish channels devoted specifically to noncommercial educational programming. Congress should establish an orderly process for allocating the new channels as well as provide adequate funding from appropriate revenue sources. Broadcasters that choose to implement datacasting should transmit information on behalf of local schools, libraries, community-based nonprofit organizations, governmental bodies, and public safety institutions. This activity should count toward fulfillment of a digital broadcaster's public interest obligations.

The committee expressed concern that Public Broadcasting will not have sufficient funds for the conversion to digital. The committee envisions a trust fund sufficient to cover not only the conversion costs, but also ongoing operating expenses. This would permit the elimination of enhanced underwriting announcements. The committee report also argued for an increased emphasis on educational programming through additional public broadcasting channels and through datacast services.

8. Section 399(b) required public broadcasters to make and retain for 60 days (to allow inspection by government or public) audio tapes for all programs "in which any issue of public importance is discussed." It was declared unconstitutional in an *en banc* decision, 5–4. Community–Service Broadcasting of Mid–America, Inc. v. Federal Communications Commission, 593 F.2d 1102, 43 R.R.2d 1675, 4 Med.L.Rptr. 1257 (D.C.Cir.1978). The majority relied on equal protection grounds—that no similar burden was imposed on commercial broadcasters. Several members of the majority also expressed varying degrees of certainty that such a provision imposed on all broadcasters would violate the First Amendment. The dissenters thought that the statutory requirement of "objectivity and balance" justified the special obligation of § 399(b).

9. The Public Telecommunications Act of 1992, p. 252, *supra,* imposed a requirement on the CPB Board of Directors to provide a reasonable opportunity for members of the public to comment on the "quality, diversity, creativity, excellence, innovation, objectivity, and balance of public broadcasting services, including all public broadcasting programming of a controversial nature." Based on this information the directors must take such steps in awarding programming grants as are necessary to facilitate objectivity and balance in programming of a controversial nature.

B. CONTENT REGULATION OF PUBLIC BROADCASTING

One of the more troublesome questions in the 1967 Act involved § 399's restrictions on editorializing, p. 92, *supra*. What arguments might be made against such a provision? What arguments to sustain it?

In 1982 a district judge declared unconstitutional the ban on editorializing by stations accepting CPB grants. The Supreme Court, 5–4, affirmed.

FEDERAL COMMUNICATIONS COMMISSION v. LEAGUE
OF WOMEN VOTERS OF CALIFORNIA

Supreme Court of the United States, 1984.
468 U.S. 364, 104 S.Ct. 3106, 82 L.Ed.2d 278, 10 Med.L.Rptr. 1937.

Justice Brennan delivered the opinion of the Court.

[The background of the case and an excerpt from an earlier part of Justice Brennan's opinion appear at page 93, *supra*.]

III

We turn now to consider whether the restraint imposed by § 399 satisfies the requirements established by our prior cases for permissible broadcast regulation. Before assessing the government's proffered justifications for the statute, however, two central features of the ban against editorializing must be examined, since they help to illuminate the importance of the First Amendment interests at stake in this case.

A

First, the restriction imposed by § 399 is specifically directed at a form of speech—namely, the expression of editorial opinion—that lies at the heart of First Amendment protection. In construing the reach of the statute, the FCC has explained that "although the use of noncommercial educational broadcast facilities by licensees, their management or those speaking on their behalf for the propagation of the licensee's own views on public issues is not permitted, such prohibition should not be construed to inhibit any *other* presentations on controversial issues of public importance." As we recently reiterated in NAACP v. Claiborne Hardware Co., 458 U.S. 886 (1982), "expression on public issues 'has always rested on the highest rung of the hierarchy of First Amendment values.'" Id., at 913 (quoting Carey v. Brown, 447 U.S. 455, 467 (1980)). And we have emphasized that:

> "The freedom of speech and of the press guaranteed by the Constitution embraces at least the liberty to discuss publicly and truthfully all matters of public concern without previous restraint or fear of subsequent punishment. . . . Freedom of discussion, if it would fulfill its historic function in this nation, must embrace all issues about which information is needed or appropriate to enable the members of society to cope with the exigencies of their period." Thornhill v. Alabama, 310 U.S. 88, 101–102 (1940).

The editorial has traditionally played precisely this role by informing and arousing the public, and by criticizing and cajoling those who hold government office in order to help launch new solutions to the problems of the time. Preserving the free expression of editorial opinion, therefore, is part and parcel of "our profound national commitment . . . that debate on public issues should be uninhibited, robust, and wide-open." New York Times v. Sullivan, 376 U.S. 254, 270 (1964). As we recognized in Mills v. Alabama, supra, the special place of the editorial in our First Amendment jurisprudence simply reflects the fact that the press, of which the broadcasting industry is indisputably a part, United States v. Paramount Pictures, Inc., 334 U.S. 131, 166 (1948), carries out a historic, dual responsibility in our society of reporting information and of bringing critical judgment to bear on public affairs. Indeed, the pivotal importance of editorializing as a means of satisfying the public's interest in receiving a wide variety of ideas and views through the medium of broadcasting has long been recognized by the FCC; the Commission has for the past 35 years actively encouraged commercial broadcast licensees to include editorials on public affairs in their programming. Because § 399 appears to restrict precisely that form of speech which the Framers of the Bill of Rights were most anxious to protect—speech that is "indispensable to the discovery and spread of political truth"—we must be especially careful in weighing the interests that are asserted in support of this restriction and in assessing the precision with which the ban is crafted. Whitney v. California, 274 U.S. 357, 375 (1927) (Brandeis, J., concurring).

Second, the scope of § 399's ban is defined solely on the basis of the content of the suppressed speech. A wide variety of non-editorial speech "by licensees, their management or those speaking on their behalf," In re Complaint of Accuracy in Media, Inc., [　], 45 F.C.C.2d, at 302, is plainly not prohibited by § 399. Examples of such permissible forms of speech include daily announcements of the station's program schedule or over-the-air appeals for contributions from listeners. Consequently, in order to determine whether a particular statement by station management constitutes an "editorial" proscribed by § 399, enforcement authorities must necessarily examine the content of the message that is conveyed to determine whether the views expressed concern "controversial issues of public importance." Ibid.

As Justice Stevens observed in Consolidated Edison Co. v. Public Service Commission, 447 U.S. 530 (1980), however, "[a] regulation of speech that is motivated by nothing more than a desire to curtail expression of a particular point of view on controversial issues of general interest is the purest example of a 'law . . . abridging the freedom of speech, or of the press.' A regulation that denies a group of persons the right to address a selected audience on 'controversial issues of public policy' is plainly such a regulation." Id., at 546 (concurring opinion); accord id., at 537–540 (majority opinion). Section 399 is just such a regulation, for it singles out noncommercial broadcasters and denies them the right to address their chosen audience on matters of public importance. . . .

B

In seeking to defend the prohibition on editorializing imposed by § 399, the Government urges that the statute was aimed at preventing two principal threats to the overall success of the Public Broadcasting Act of 1967. According to this argument, the ban was necessary, first, to protect noncommercial educational broadcasting stations from being coerced, as a result of federal financing, into becoming vehicles for government propagandizing or the objects of governmental influence; and, second, to keep these stations from becoming convenient targets for capture by private interest groups wishing to express their own partisan viewpoints.[16] By seeking to safeguard the public's right to a balanced presentation of public issues through the prevention of either governmental or private bias, these objectives are, of course, broadly consistent

---

16. The Government also contends that § 399 is intended to prevent the use of taxpayer monies to promote private views with which taxpayers may disagree. This argument is readily answered by our decision in Buckley v. Valeo, 424 U.S. 1, 90–93 (1976)(per curiam). As we explained in that case, virtually every congressional appropriation will to some extent involve a use of public money as to which some taxpayers may object. Id., at 91–92. Nevertheless, this does not mean that those taxpayers have a constitutionally protected right to enjoin such expenditures. Nor can this interest be invoked to justify a congressional decision to suppress speech.

with the goals identified in our earlier broadcast regulation cases. But, in sharp contrast to the restrictions upheld in *Red Lion* or in Columbia Broadcasting System, Inc. v. FCC, which left room for editorial discretion and simply required broadcast editors to grant others access to the microphone, § 399 directly prohibits the broadcaster from speaking out on public issues even in a balanced and fair manner. The Government insists, however, that the hazards posed in the "special" circumstances of noncommercial educational broadcasting are so great that § 399 is an indispensable means of preserving the public's First Amendment interests. We disagree.

(1)

When Congress first decided to provide financial support for the expansion and development of noncommercial educational stations, all concerned agreed that this step posed some risk that these traditionally independent stations might be pressured into becoming forums devoted solely to programming and views that were acceptable to the Federal government. That Congress was alert to these dangers cannot be doubted. It sought through the Public Broadcasting Act to fashion a system that would provide local stations with sufficient funds to foster their growth and development while preserving their tradition of autonomy and community-orientation. . . .

The intended role of § 399 in achieving these purposes, however, is not as clear. The provision finds no antecedent in the Carnegie Report, which generally provided the model for most other aspects of the Act. It was not part of the Administration's original legislative proposal. And it was not included in the original version of the Act passed by the Senate. The provision found its way into the Act only as a result of an amendment in the House. Indeed, it appears that, as the House Committee Report frankly admits, § 399 was added not because Congress thought it was essential to preserving the autonomy and vitality of local stations, but rather "out of an abundance of caution." H.R.Rep. No. 572, 90th Cong., 1st Sess. 20 (1967). [ ][18]

More importantly, an examination of both the overall legislative scheme established by the 1967 Act and the character of public broadcasting demonstrates that the interest asserted by the Government is not substantially advanced by § 399. First, to the extent that federal financial support creates a risk that stations will lose their independence through the bewitching power of governmental largesse, the elaborate

---

18. Of course, as the Government points out, Congress has consistently retained the basic proscription on editorializing in § 399, despite periodic reconsiderations and modifications of the Act in 1973, 1978, and 1981. Brief for the United States 25–27; see also n. 7, supra. A reviewing court may not easily set aside such a considered congressional judgment. At the same time, "[d]eference to a legislative finding cannot limit judicial inquiry when First Amendment rights are at stake. . . . Were it otherwise, the scope of freedom of speech and of the press would be subject to legislative definition and the function of the First Amendment as a check on legislative power would be nullified." Landmark Communications, Inc. v. Virginia, 435 U.S. 829, 843–844 (1978).

structure established by the Public Broadcasting Act already operates to insulate local stations from governmental interference. Congress not only mandated that the new Corporation for Public Broadcasting would have a private, bipartisan structure, see §§ 396(c)–(f), but also imposed a variety of important limitations on its powers. The Corporation was prohibited from owning or operating any station, § 396(g)(3), it was required to adhere strictly to a standard of "objectivity and balance" in disbursing federal funds to local stations, § 396(g)(1)(A), and it was prohibited from contributing to or otherwise supporting any candidate for office, § 396(f)(3).

The Act also established a second layer of protections which serve to protect the stations from governmental coercion and interference. Thus, in addition to requiring the Corporation to operate so as to "assure the maximum freedom [of local stations] from interference with or control of program content or other activities," § 396(g)(1)(D), the Act expressly forbids "any department, agency, officer, or employee of the United States [from] exercis[ing] any direction, supervision, or control over educational television or radio broadcasting, or over the Corporation or any of its grantees or contractors . . .," § 398(a). . . . The principal thrust of the amendments, therefore, has been to assure long-term appropriations for the Corporation and, more importantly, to insist that it pass specified portions of these funds directly through to local stations to give them greater autonomy in defining the uses to which those funds should be put. Thus, in sharp contrast to § 399, the unifying theme of these various statutory provisions is that they substantially reduce the risk of governmental interference with the editorial judgments of local stations without restricting those stations' ability to speak on matters of public concern.[19]

Even if these statutory protections were thought insufficient to the task, however, suppressing the particular category of speech restricted by § 399 is simply not likely, given the character of the public broadcasting system, to reduce substantially the risk that the Federal Government will seek to influence or put pressure on local stations. An underlying supposition of the Government's argument in this regard is that individual noncommercial stations are likely to speak so forcefully on particular issues that Congress, the ultimate source of the stations' Federal funding, will be tempted to retaliate against these individual stations by

---

19. Furthermore, the risk that federal coercion or influence will be brought to bear against local stations as a result of federal financing is considerably attenuated by the fact that CPB grants account for only a portion of total public broadcasting income. CPB, Public Broadcasting Income: Fiscal Year 1982, at Table 2 (Final Report, Dec. 1983)(noting that federal funds account for 23.4% of total income for all public broadcasting stations). The vast majority of financial support comes from state and local governments, as well as a variety of private sources, including foundations, businesses, and individual contributions; indeed, as the CPB recently noted, "[t]he diversity of support in America for public broadcasting is remarkable," CPB, 1982 Annual Report 2 (1982). Given this diversity of funding sources and the decentralized manner in which funds are secured, the threat that improper federal influence will be exerted over local stations is not so pressing as to require the total suppression of editorial speech by these stations.

restricting appropriations for all of public broadcasting. But, as the District Court recognized, the character of public broadcasting suggests that such a risk is speculative at best. There are literally hundreds of public radio and television stations in communities scattered throughout the United States and its territories, see CPB, 1983–84 Public Broadcasting Directory 20–50, 66–86 (Sept. 1983). Given that central fact, it seems reasonable to infer that the editorial voices of these stations will prove to be as distinctive, varied, and idiosyncratic as the various communities they represent. More importantly, the editorial focus of any particular station can fairly be expected to focus largely on issues affecting only its community.[20] Accordingly, absent some showing by the Government to the contrary, the risk that local editorializing will place all of public broadcasting in jeopardy is not sufficiently pressing to warrant § 399's broad suppression of speech.

Indeed, what is far more likely than local station editorials to pose the kinds of dangers hypothesized by the Government are the wide variety of programs addressing controversial issues produced, often with substantial CPB funding, for national distribution to local stations. . . .

Furthermore, the manifest imprecision of the ban imposed by § 399 reveals that its proscription is not sufficiently tailored to the harms it seeks to prevent to justify its substantial interference with broadcasters' speech. Section 399 includes within its grip a potentially infinite variety of speech, most of which would not be related in any way to governmental affairs, political candidacies or elections. Indeed, the breadth of editorial commentary is as wide as human imagination permits. But the Government never explains how, say, an editorial by local station management urging improvements in a town's parks or museums will so infuriate Congress or other Federal officials that the future of public broadcasting will be imperiled unless such editorials are suppressed. Nor is it explained how the suppression of editorials alone serves to reduce the risk of governmental retaliation and interference when it is clear that station management is fully able to broadcast controversial views so long as such views are not labelled as its own. [　]

The Government appears to recognize these flaws in § 399, because it focuses instead on the suggestion that the source of governmental influence may well be state and local governments, many of which have established public broadcasting commissions that own and operate local noncommercial educational stations.[22] The ban on editorializing is all the more necessary with respect to these stations, the argument runs, because the management of such stations will be especially likely to

---

20. This likelihood is enhanced with respect to public stations because they are required to establish community advisory boards which must reasonably reflect the "diverse needs and interests of the communities served by such station[s]." § 396(k)(9)(A). . . .

22. As the Government points out in its Brief, at least two-thirds of the public television broadcasting stations in operation are licensed to (a) state public broadcasting authorities or commissions, in which commission members are often appointed by the governor with the advice and consent of the state legislature, (b) state universities or educational commissions, or (c) local school boards or municipal authorities. [　]

broadcast only editorials that are favorable to the state or local authorities that hold the purse strings. The Government's argument, however, proves too much. First, § 399's ban applies to the many private noncommercial community organizations that own and operate stations that are not controlled in any way by state or local government. Second, the legislative history of the Public Broadcasting Act clearly indicates that Congress was concerned with "assur[ing] complete freedom from any *Federal Government influence.*" [ ] Consistently with this concern, Congress refused to create any federally owned stations and it expressly forbid the CPB to own or operate any television or radio stations, § 396(g)(3). By contrast, although Congress was clearly aware in 1967 that many noncommercial educational stations were owned by state and local governments, it did not hesitate to extend Federal assistance to such stations, it imposed no special requirements to restrict state or local control over these stations, and, indeed, it ensured through the structure of the Act that these stations would be as insulated from Federal interference as the wholly private stations.

Finally, although the Government certainly has a substantial interest in ensuring that the audiences of noncommercial stations will not be led to think that the broadcaster's editorials reflect the official view of the government, this interest can be fully satisfied by less restrictive means that are readily available. To address this important concern, Congress could simply require public broadcasting stations to broadcast a disclaimer every time they editorialize which would state that the editorial represents only the view of the station's management and does not in any way represent the views of the Federal Government or any of the station's other sources of funding. Such a disclaimer—similar to those often used in commercial and noncommercial programming of a controversial nature—would effectively and directly communicate to the audience that the editorial reflected only the views of the station rather than those of the government. . . .

In sum, § 399's broad ban on all editorializing by every station that receives CPB funds far exceeds what is necessary to protect against the risk of governmental interference or to prevent the public from assuming that editorials by public broadcasting stations represent the official view of government. The regulation impermissibly sweeps within its prohibition a wide range of speech by wholly private stations on topics that do not take a directly partisan stand or that have nothing whatever to do with federal, state, or local government.

(2)

Assuming that the Government's second asserted interest in preventing noncommercial stations from becoming a "privileged outlet for the political and ideological opinions of station owners and management," Brief at 34, is legitimate, the substantiality of this asserted interest is dubious. The patent over-and underinclusiveness of § 399's ban "undermines the likelihood of a genuine [governmental] interest" in preventing private groups from propagating their own views via public broadcasting. First National Bank of Boston v. Bellotti, supra, 435 U.S., at 793. If it is true, as the government contends, that noncommercial stations remain free, despite § 399, to broadcast a wide variety of controversial views through their power to control program selection, to select which persons will be interviewed, and to determine how news reports will be presented, Brief at 41, then it seems doubtful that § 399 can fairly be said to advance any genuinely substantial governmental interest in keeping controversial or partisan opinions from being aired by noncommercial stations. . . .

In short, § 399 does not prevent the use of noncommercial stations for the presentation of partisan views on controversial matters; instead, it merely bars a station from specifically communicating such views on its own behalf or on behalf of its management. If the vigorous expression of controversial opinions is, as the Government assures us, affirmatively encouraged by the Act, and if local licensees are permitted under the Act to exercise editorial control over the selection of programs, controversial or otherwise, that are aired on their stations, then § 399 accomplishes only one thing—the suppression of editorial speech by station management. It does virtually nothing, however, to reduce the risk that public stations will serve solely as outlets for expression of narrow partisan views. What we said in Columbia Broadcasting System, Inc. v. Democratic National Committee, supra, applies, therefore, with equal force here: the "sacrifice [of] First Amendment protections for so speculative a gain is not warranted. . . ." 412 U.S., at 127.

Finally, the public's interest in preventing public broadcasting from becoming forums for lopsided presentations of narrow partisan positions is already secured by a variety of other regulatory means that intrude far less drastically upon the "journalistic freedom" of noncommercial broadcasters. [ ] The requirements of the FCC's fairness doctrine, for instance, which apply to commercial and noncommercial stations alike, ensure that such editorializing would maintain a reasonably balanced and fair presentation of controversial issues. Thus, even if the management of a noncommercial educational station were inclined to seek to further only its own partisan views when editorializing, it simply could not do so. . . . Since the breadth of § 399 extends so far beyond what is necessary to accomplish the goals identified by the Government, it fails to satisfy the First Amendment standards that we have applied to this area.

We therefore hold that even if some of the hazards at which § 399 was aimed are sufficiently substantial, the restriction is not crafted with sufficient precision to remedy those dangers that may exist to justify the significant abridgement of speech worked by the provision's broad ban on editorializing. The statute is not narrowly tailored to address any of the government's suggested goals. Moreover, the public's "paramount right" to be fully and broadly informed on matters of public importance through the medium of noncommercial educational broadcasting is not well served by the restriction, for its effect is plainly to diminish rather than augment "the volume and quality of coverage" of controversial issues. *Red Lion,* supra, at 393. Nor do we see any reason to deny noncommercial broadcasters the right to address matters of public concern on the basis of merely speculative fears of adverse public or governmental reactions to such speech.

IV

Although the Government did not present the argument in any form to the District Court, it now seeks belatedly to justify § 399 on the basis of Congress' Spending Power. Relying upon our recent decision in Regan v. Taxation With Representation, 461 U.S. 540 (1983), the Government argues that by prohibiting noncommercial educational stations that receive CPB grants from editorializing, Congress has, in the proper exercise of its Spending Power, simply determined that it "will not subsidize public broadcasting station editorials." Brief of the United States 42. In *Taxation With Representation,* the Court found that Congress could, in the exercise of its Spending Power, reasonably refuse to subsidize the lobbying activities of tax-exempt charitable organizations by prohibiting such organizations from using tax-deductible contributions to support their lobbying efforts. . . .

　. . .

Of course, if Congress were to adopt a revised version of § 399 that permitted noncommercial educational broadcasting stations to establish "affiliate" organizations which could then use the station's facilities to editorialize with non-federal funds, such a statutory mechanism would plainly be valid under the reasoning of *Taxation With Representation.* Under such a statute, public broadcasting stations would be free, in the same way that the charitable organization in *Taxation With Representation* was free, to make known its views on matters of public importance through its non-federally funded, editorializing affiliate without losing federal grants for its non-editorializing broadcast activities. [ ] But in the absence of such authority, we must reject the Government's contention that our decision in *Taxation With Representation* is controlling here.

V

In conclusion, we emphasize that our disposition of this case rests upon a narrow proposition. We do not hold that the Congress or the FCC are without power to regulate the content, timing, or character of speech by noncommercial educational broadcasting stations. Rather, we hold only that the specific interests sought to be advanced by § 399's ban on editorializing are either not sufficiently substantial or are not served in a sufficiently limited manner to justify the substantial abridgement of important journalistic freedoms which the First Amendment jealously protects. Accordingly, the judgment of the District Court is affirmed.

JUSTICE REHNQUIST, with whom THE CHIEF JUSTICE and JUSTICE WHITE join, dissenting.

All but three paragraphs of the Court's lengthy opinion in this case are devoted to the development of a scenario in which the government appears as the "Big Bad Wolf" and appellee Pacifica as "Little Red Riding Hood." In the Court's scenario the Big Bad Wolf cruelly forbids Little Red Riding Hood from taking to her grandmother some of the food that she is carrying in her basket. Only three paragraphs are used to delineate a truer picture of the litigants, wherein it appears that some of the food in the basket was given to Little Red Riding Hood by the Big Bad Wolf himself, and that the Big Bad Wolf had told Little Red Riding Hood in advance that if she accepted his food she would have to abide by his conditions. Congress in enacting § 399 of the Public Broadcasting Act, 47 U.S.C. (Supp. V) § 399, has simply determined that public funds shall not be used to subsidize noncommercial, educational broadcasting stations which engage in "editorializing" or which support or oppose any political candidate. I do not believe that anything in the First Amendment to the United States Constitution prevents Congress from choosing to spend public monies in that manner. Perhaps a more appropriate analogy than that of Little Red Riding Hood and the Big Bad Wolf is that of Faust and Mephistopheles; Pacifica, well aware of § 399's condition on its receipt of public money, nonetheless accepted the public money and now seeks to avoid the conditions which Congress legitimately has attached to receipt of that funding.

. . .

The Court's three-paragraph discussion of why § 399, repeatedly reexamined and retained by Congress, violates the First Amendment is to me utterly unpersuasive. Congress has rationally determined that the bulk of the taxpayers whose monies provide the funds for grants by the CPB would prefer not to see the management of local educational stations promulgate its own private views on the air at taxpayer expense. Accordingly Congress simply has decided not to subsidize stations which engage in that activity.

. . .

This is not to say that the government may attach *any* condition to its largess; it is only to say that when the government is simply exercising its power to allocate its own public funds, we need only find that the condition imposed has a rational relationship to Congress' purpose in providing the subsidy and that it is not primarily "aimed at the suppression of dangerous ideas." Cammarano v. United States, 358 U.S. 498, 513 (1959), quoting Speiser v. Randall, 357 U.S. 513, 519 (1958). In this case Congress' prohibition is directly related to its purpose in providing subsidies for public broadcasting, and is plainly rational for Congress to have determined that taxpayer monies should not be used to subsidize management's views or to pay for management's exercise of partisan politics. Indeed, it is entirely rational for Congress to have wished to avoid the appearance of government sponsorship of a particular view or a particular political candidate. Furthermore, Congress' prohibition is strictly neutral. In no sense can it be said that

Congress has prohibited only editorial views of one particular ideological bent. Nor has it prevented public stations from airing programs, documentaries, interviews, etc. dealing with controversial subjects, so long as management itself does not expressly endorse a particular viewpoint. And Congress has not prevented station management from communicating its own views on those subjects through any medium other than subsidized public broadcasting.

For the foregoing reasons I find this case entirely different from the so-called "unconstitutional condition" cases, wherein the Court has stated that the government "may not deny a benefit to a person on a basis that infringes his constitutionally protected interests—especially his interest in freedom of speech." Perry v. Sindermann, 408 U.S. 593, 597 (1972). In those cases the suppressed speech was not content-neutral in the same sense as here, and in those cases, there is at best only a strained argument that the legislative purpose of the condition imposed was to avoid *subsidizing* the prohibited speech. Speiser v. Randall, supra, is illustrative of the difference. In that case California's decision to deny its property tax exemption to veterans who would not declare that they would not work to overthrow the government was plainly directed at suppressing what California regarded as speech of a dangerous content. And the condition imposed was so unrelated to the benefit to be conferred that it is difficult to argue that California's property tax exemption actually subsidized the dangerous speech.

Here, in my view, Congress has rationally concluded that the bulk of taxpayers whose monies provide the funds for grants by the CPB would prefer not to see the management of public stations engage in editorializing or the endorsing or opposing of political candidates. Because Congress' decision to enact § 399 is a rational exercise of its spending powers and strictly neutral, I would hold that nothing in the First Amendment makes it unconstitutional. Accordingly, I would reverse the judgment of the District Court.

Justice White: Believing that the editorializing and candidate endorsement proscription stand or fall together and being confident that Congress may condition use of its funds on abstaining from political endorsements, I join Justice Rehnquist's dissenting opinion.

Justice Stevens, dissenting.

The court jester who mocks the King must choose his words with great care. An artist is likely to paint a flattering portrait of his patron. The child who wants a new toy does not preface his request with a comment on how fat his mother is. Newspaper publishers have been known to listen to their advertising managers. Elected officials may remember how their elections were financed. By enacting the statutory provision that the Court invalidates today, a sophisticated group of legislators expressed a concern about the potential impact of government funds on pervasive and powerful organs of mass communication. One need not have heard the raucous voice of Adolph Hitler over Radio Berlin to appreciate the importance of that concern.

As Justice White correctly notes, the statutory prohibitions against editorializing and candidate endorsements rest on the same foundation. In my opinion that foundation is far stronger than merely "a rational basis" and it is not weakened by the fact that it is buttressed by other provisions that are also designed to avoid the insidious evils of government propaganda favoring particular points of view. The quality of the interest in maintaining government neutrality in the free market of ideas—of avoiding subtle forms of censorship and propaganda—outweigh the impact on expression that results from this statute. Indeed, by simply terminating or reducing funding, Congress could curtail much more expression with no risk whatever of a constitutional transgression.

. . .

Although appellees originally challenged the validity of the entire statute, in their amended complaint they limited their attack to the prohibition against editorializing. In its analysis of the case, the Court assumes that the ban on political endorsements is severable from the first section and that it may be constitutional.[3] In view of the fact that the major difference between [the restrictions on editorializing and] the ban on political endorsements is based on the content of the speech, it is apparent that the entire rationale of the Court's opinion rests on the premise that it may be permissible to predicate a statutory restriction on candidate endorsements on the difference between the content of that kind of speech and the content of other expressions of editorial opinion.

The Court does not tell us whether speech that endorses political candidates is more or less worthy of protection than other forms of editorializing, but it does iterate and reiterate the point that "the expression of editorial opinion" is a special kind of communication that "is entitled to the most exacting degree of First Amendment protection." [ ].[4]

Neither the fact that the statute regulates only one kind of speech, nor the fact that editorial opinion has traditionally been an important kind of speech, is sufficient to identify the character or the significance of the statute's impact on speech. Three additional points are relevant. First, the statute does not prohibit Pacifica from expressing its opinion through any avenue except the radio stations for which it receives federal financial support. It eliminates the subsidized channel of communication as a forum for Pacifica itself, and thereby deprives Pacifica of an

3. The Court actually raises the wrong severability issue. The serious question in this regard is whether the entire public funding scheme is severable from the prohibition on editorializing and political endorsements. The legislative history of the statute indicates the strength of the congressional aversion to these practices. . . .

4. Thus, once again the Court embraces the obvious proposition that some speech is more worthy of protection than other speech—that the right to express editorial opinion may be worth fighting to preserve even though the right to hear less worthy speech may not—a proposition that several members of today's majority could only interpret "as an aberration" in Young v. American Mini Theatres, 427 U.S. 50, 87 (1976)(dissenting opinion)("The fact that the 'offensive' speech here may not address 'important' topics—'ideas of social and political significance,' in the Court's terminology, *ante*, does not mean that it is less worthy of constitutional protection." Ibid.)

advantage it would otherwise have over other speakers, but it does not exclude Pacifica from the marketplace for ideas. Second, the statute does not curtail the expression of opinion by individual commentators who participate in Pacifica's programs. Third, and of greatest significance for me, the statutory restriction is completely neutral in its operation—it prohibits all editorials without any distinction being drawn concerning the subject matter or the point of view that might be expressed.[5]

II

The statute does not violate the fundamental principle that the citizen's right to speak may not be conditioned upon the sovereign's agreement with what the speaker intends to say. On the contrary, the statute was enacted in order to protect that very principle—to avoid the risk that some speakers will be rewarded or penalized for saying things that appeal to—or are offensive to—the sovereign.[7] The interests the statute is designed to protect are interests that underlie the First Amendment itself.

In my judgment the interest in keeping the Federal Government out of the propaganda arena is of overriding importance. That interest is of special importance in the field of electronic communication, not only because that medium is so powerful and persuasive, but also because it is the one form of communication that is licensed by the Federal Government.[8] When the government already has great potential power over the electronic media, it is surely legitimate to enact statutory safeguards to

5. Section 399's ban on editorializing is a content based restriction on speech, but not in the sense that the majority implies. The majority speaks of "editorial opinion" as if it were some sort of special species of opinion, limited to issues of public importance. The majority confuses the typical content of editorials with the meaning of editorial itself. An editorial is, of course, a statement of the *management's* opinion on any topic imaginable. The Court asserts that what the statute "forecloses is the expression of editorial opinion on 'controversial issues of public importance.' " The statute is not so limited. The content which is prohibited is that the station is not permitted to state its opinion with respect to any matter. In short, it may not be an on-the-air advocate if it accepts government funds for its broadcasts. The prohibition on editorializing is not directed at any particular message a station might wish to convey. . . .

Paradoxically, section 399 is later attacked by the majority as essentially being under-inclusive because it does not prohibit "controversial" national programming that is often aired with substantial federal funding. . . . Next, § 399's ban on editorializing is attacked by the majority on over-inclusive grounds—because it is content-neutral—since it prohibits a "potentially infinite variety of speech, most of which would not be related in any way to governmental affairs, political candidacies or elections." . . .

7. . . .

Moreover, the statute will also protect the listener's interest in not having his tax payments used to finance the advocacy of causes he opposes. The majority gives extremely short shrift to the Government's interest in minimizing the use of taxpayer monies to promote private views with which the taxpayers may disagree. The Court briefly observes that the taxpayers do not have a constitutionally protected right to enjoin such expenditures and then leaps to the conclusion that given the fact that the funding scheme itself is not unconstitutional, this interest cannot be used to support the statute at issue. The conclusion manifestly does not follow from the premise, and this interest is plainly legitimate and significant.

8. We have consistently adhered to the following guiding principles applicable to First Amendment claims in the area of broadcasting, and they bear repeating at some length: [quoting from *Red Lion*].

make sure that it does not cross the threshold that separates neutral regulation from the subsidy of partisan opinion.

The Court does not question the validity of the basic interests served by § 399. Instead, it suggests that the statute does not substantially serve those interests because the Public Broadcasting Act operates in many other respects to insulate local stations from governmental interference. In my view, that is an indication of nothing more than the strength of the governmental interest involved here—Congress enacted many safeguards because the evil to be avoided was so grave. Organs of official propaganda are antithetical to this nation's heritage and Congress understandably acted with great caution in this area. It is no answer to say that the other statutory provisions "substantially reduce the risk of government interference with the editorial judgments of the local stations without restricting the stations' ability to speak out on matters of public concern." [ ] The other safeguards protect the stations from interference with judgments that they will necessarily make in selecting programming, but those judgments are relatively amorphous. No safeguard is foolproof; and the fact that funds are dispensed according to largely "objective" criteria certainly is no guarantee. Individuals must always make judgments in allocating funds, and pressure can be exerted in subtle ways as well as through outright fund-cutoffs.

Members of Congress, not members of the Judiciary, live in the world of politics. When they conclude that there is a real danger of political considerations influencing the dispensing of this money and that this provision is necessary to insulate grantees from political pressures in addition to the other safeguards, that judgment is entitled to our respect.

The magnitude of the present danger that the statute is designed to avoid is admittedly a matter about which reasonable judges may disagree.[10] Moreover, I would agree that the risk would be greater if other statutory safeguards were removed. It remains true, however, that Congress has the power to prevent the use of public funds to subsidize the expression of partisan points of view, or to suppress the propagation of dissenting opinions. No matter how great or how small the immediate risk may be, there surely is more than a theoretical possibility that future grantees might be influenced by the ever present tie of the political purse strings, even if those strings are never actually pulled.

. . .

III

The Court describes the scope of § 399's ban as being "defined solely on the basis of the content of the suppressed speech," [ ], at 18,

---

10. The majority argues that the Government's concededly substantial interest in ensuring that audiences of educational stations will not perceive the station to be a government propaganda organ can be fully satisfied by requiring such stations to broadcast a disclaimer each time they editorialize stating that the editorial "does not in any way represent the views of the Federal Government. . . ." [ ] This solution would be laughable were it not so Orwellian: the answer to the fact that there is a real danger that the editorials are really government propaganda is for the government to require the station to tell the audience that it is not propaganda at all!

and analogizes this case to the regulation of speech we condemned in Consolidated Edison Co. v. Public Serv. Comm'n, 447 U.S. 530 (1980). This description reveals how the Court manipulates labels without perceiving the critical differences behind the two cases.

In *Consolidated Edison* the class of speakers that was affected by New York's prohibition consisted of regulated public utilities that had been expressing their opinion on the issue of nuclear power by means of written statements inserted in their customers' monthly bills. Although the scope of the prohibition was phrased in general terms and applied to a select group of speakers, it was obviously directed at spokesmen for a particular point of view. The justification for the restriction was phrased in terms of the potential offensiveness of the utilities' messages to their audiences. It was a classic case of a viewpoint-based prohibition.

In this case, however, although the regulation applies only to a defined class of noncommercial broadcast licensees, it is common ground that these licensees represent heterogenous points of view.[12] There is simply no sensible basis for considering this regulation a viewpoint restriction—or, to use the Court's favorite phrase, to condemn it as "content-based"—because it applies equally to station owners of all shades of opinion. Moreover, the justification for the prohibition is not based on the "offensiveness" of the messages in the sense that that term was used in *Consolidated Edison*. Here, it is true that taxpayers might find it offensive if their tax monies were being used to subsidize the expression of editorial opinion with which they disagree, but it is the fact of the subsidy—not just the expression of the opinion—that legitimates this justification. Furthermore, and of greater importance, the principal justification for this prohibition is the overriding interest in forestalling the creation of propaganda organs for the Government.

I respectfully dissent.

Notes and Questions

1. How realistic are the fears of the dissenting justices? President Nixon once vetoed the CPB budget because of dissatisfaction with CPB programming. Are noncommercial licensees likely to be influenced by the "power of the purse?" If, indeed, prohibitions on specific forms of speech are unconstitutional, how can noncommercial licensees be insulated from government control?

2. In response to a complaint by Sen. James F. Buckley (R.-N.Y.), the Commission held that § 312(a)(7) was equally applicable to commercial and noncommercial stations. However, only those noncommercial stations using channels specifically reserved for noncommercial broadcasting are prohibited from charging for the time they must make available. Senator James F. Buckley, 63 F.C.C.2d 952, 38 R.R.2d 1255 (1976).

---

12. That does not necessarily mean, however, "that the editorial voices of these stations will prove to be as distinctive, varied, and idiosyncratic as the various communities they represent," [ ], given the potential effects of government funding, [ ].

3.   From a First Amendment perspective, the crucial difference between commercial and noncommercial broadcasting involves the question of the licensee's ability to control content and to reject programming. In *League of Women Voters*, the Court was faced with the problem of indirect control of PBS stations through the CPB funding mechanism. Consider, however, that more than 140 PBS stations are under some form of government ownership. What effect should that have on the ability of those licensees to control content and reject programming? Consider the following case.

MUIR v. ALABAMA EDUCATIONAL TELEVISION COMMISSION

United States Court of Appeals, Fifth Circuit, en banc, 1982.688
F.2d 1033, 52 R.R.2d 935, 8 Med.L.Rptr. 2305.
Certiorari denied 460 U.S. 1023, 103 S.Ct. 1274, 75 L.Ed.2d 495 (1983).

[In this case, decided by the old Fifth Circuit before it was split, 22 judges participated in the decision. Judge Hill's opinion, referred to by all as the majority opinion, has the implicit support of 10 judges. Judge Garwood states that he concurs in the majority opinion and then adds some thoughts of his own. Judge Rubin and the three judges who join him say that they join only the result reached by the majority because they reach their conclusion on a different basis. Yet, they join in the views expressed by Judge Garwood (who says that he joins the majority opinion). That makes 15. However, subsequent cases have held that Judge Rubin's opinion, as opposed to Judge Hill's, is the majority opinion. See e.g., Schneider v. Indian River Community College Foundation, Inc., 875 F.2d 1537 (11th Cir.1989). The seven dissenters write three opinions. Judge Garwood's opinion is placed earlier in the sequence to make matters easier to understand. The opinions in this case offer enough food for thought to match the size of the bench.]

Before BROWN, CHARLES CLARK, RONEY, GEE, TJOFLAT, HILL, FAY, RUBIN, VANCE, KRAVITCH, FRANK M. JOHNSON, HENDERSON, REAVLEY, POLITZ, HATCHETT, ANDERSON, RANDALL, TATE, SAM D. JOHNSON, THOMAS A. CLARK, WILLIAMS and GARWOOD, CIRCUIT JUDGES.

JAMES C. HILL, CIRCUIT JUDGE:

I. *Introduction*

The two appeals before this Court on consolidated rehearing raise the important and novel question of whether individual viewers of public television stations, licensed by the Federal Communications Commission to state instrumentalities, have a First Amendment right to compel the licensees to broadcast a previously scheduled program which the licensees have decided to cancel. For the reasons below we find that the viewers do not have such a right.

Both cases before us concern the decisions of the licensees not to broadcast the program "Death of a Princess." In Muir v. Alabama Educational Television Commission, 656 F.2d 1012 (5th Cir.1981), the District Court for the Northern District of Alabama denied the plaintiff viewers' motion for a preliminary injunction requiring the defendant licensee, Alabama Educational Television Commission (AETC), to broadcast the program. The district court found (1) that the likelihood of success on the merits criterion for an injunction had not been shown; (2) that the First Amendment protects the right of broadcasters, private and public, to make programming decisions free of interference; and (3) that viewers have no First Amendment right of access to the Alabama educational television network sufficient to compel the showing of "Death of a Princess." The court granted summary judgment for AETC.

In Barnstone v. University of Houston, 514 F.Supp. 670 (S.D.Tex. 1980), the District Court for the Southern District of Texas reached a different conclusion and granted the injunction requested by the plaintiff viewers and ordered the defendant licensee, University of Houston, to broadcast the program. The court held that KUHT–TV, the television station operated by the university, was a public forum and as such it could not deny access to speakers—here, the producers of "Death of a Princess"—who wished to be heard in the public forum, unless its reasons for doing so could withstand the rigorous scrutiny to which "prior restraints" are traditionally subjected.

On appeal a panel of this court affirmed the District Court's decision in *Muir*. The panel held that the plaintiffs had no constitutional right to compel the broadcast of "Death of a Princess," and that AETC's refusal to broadcast the program was a legitimate exercise of its statutory authority as a broadcast licensee and was protected by the First Amendment. In *Barnstone* another panel of this court found that the decision in *Muir* required that the panel reverse the judgment of the District Court for the Southern District of Texas and dissolve the injunctive relief which had been granted the plaintiffs.

We directed both cases be consolidated and reheard en banc. We now affirm the judgment of the District Court for the Northern District of Alabama in *Muir* and reverse the judgment of the District Court for the Southern District of Texas in *Barnstone*.

II. *Factual Background*

The *Muir* case arose when AETC decided not to broadcast "Death of a Princess," which had been scheduled for broadcast on May 12, 1980 at 8:00 p.m. The program, one of thirteen in the series "World," is a dramatization of the investigation by the program's director, producer, and co-author into the motivations and circumstances which were said to have led to the July 1977 execution for adultery of a Saudi Arabian princess and her commoner lover.

AETC, organized under Ala.Code 1975, § 16–7–1, is responsible for "making the benefits of educational television available to and promoting its use by inhabitants of Alabama" and has "the duty of controlling and supervising the use of channels reserved by the Federal Communications Commission to Alabama for noncommercial, educational use." Ala.Code 1975, § 16–7–5. AETC operates a statewide network of nine noncommercial, educational television stations licensed by the Federal Communications Commission under the Communications Act of 1934 (47 U.S.C. §§ 151, et seq.). AETC is funded through state legislative appropriations from the Special Education Trust Fund, matching federal grants through the Corporation for Public Broadcasting (CPB), and private contributions.

AETC is a member of the Public Broadcasting Service (PBS), a non-profit corporation distributing public, non-commercial television programs to its members by satellite. AETC is also a member of the Station Program Cooperative (SPC), a program funding and acquisition mechanism operated by PBS. Membership in SPC entitles licensees to participate in the selection and funding of national public television programs distributed by PBS. Only those licensees who contribute to a program's cost have a right to broadcast it. Those who contribute are free to broadcast or not to broadcast the program.

PBS's acquisition of the program series "World" was funded by 144 public television licensees, including AETC, through the SPC. During the week prior to the scheduled broadcast of "Death of a Princess" AETC received numerous communications from Alabama residents protesting the showing of the program. The protests expressed fear for the personal safety and well-being of Alabama citizens working in the Middle East if the program was shown. On May 10 AETC announced its decision not to broadcast the film as scheduled.

Appellants Muir, Buttram, and Faircloth, residents of Alabama who had planned to watch "Death of a Princess," brought this action on May 12, 1980 under the First and Fourteenth Amendments and 42 U.S.C. § 1983, seeking to compel AETC to broadcast the film, and preliminary and permanent injunctions against AETC's making "political" decisions on programming. The *Barnstone* case arose in a factual context similar to that of *Muir*. The University of Houston is a co-educational institution of higher learning funded and operated by the State of Texas. See Tex.Educ.Code Ann. §§ 111.01 et seq. The university funds and operates KUHT–TV, a public television station licensed to the university by the F.C.C. As a member of the SPC, KUHT–TV contributed to the funding of the "World" program series. KUHT–TV scheduled "Death of a Princess" for broadcast on May 12, 1980 at 8:00 p.m.

On May 1, 1980 KUHT–TV announced that it had decided not to broadcast the program. This decision was made by Dr. Patrick J. Nicholson, University of Houston Vice–President for Public Information and University Relations. Dr. Nicholson had never previously made a programming decision such as this, though as the university official charged with the responsibility of operating KUHT–TV he had the power to do so. In a press release announcing the cancellation Dr. Nicholson gave the basis of his decision as "strong and understandable objections by the government of Saudi Arabia at a time when mounting crisis in the Middle East, our long friendship with the Saudi government and U.S. national interest all point to the need to avoid exacerbating the situation." Dr. Nicholson also expressed a belief that the program was not balanced in a "responsible manner."[5]

Upon learning of Dr. Nicholson's decision, on May 8, 1980, plaintiff Barnstone brought a suit to require KUHT–TV to air "Death of a Princess." Ms. Barnstone argued that as a subscriber to and regular viewer of KUHT–TV her First and Fourteenth Amendment rights were violated by the decision to cancel the program.

III. *The First Amendment Does Not Prohibit Governmental Expression*

The central argument advanced by the plaintiffs on appeal is that their First Amendment rights were violated when the defendants, as state actors, denied the plaintiffs an opportunity to view "Death of a Princess" on the public television stations operated by the defendants. We are thus called upon to determine whether the First Amendment rights of viewers impose limits on the programming discretion of public television stations licensed to state instrumentalities.

The First Amendment operates to protect private expression from infringement by government. Such protection applies both to the right to speak and the right to hear and is operative in a variety of contexts. The amendment prohibits government from controlling or penalizing expression which has been singled out by government because of the expression's viewpoint. The First Amendment also prohibits government from taking certain actions which impermissibly constrict the flow of information or ideas.

The plaintiffs emphasize that the protection of the First Amendment extends only to private expression and not to governmental expression. They assert that the amendment serves only to confer duties on government—not rights. While this argument of the plaintiffs may be essentially correct it in no way resolves the issue before us. To find that the government is without First Amendment protection is not to find that the government is prohibited from speaking or that private individuals have the right to limit or control the expression of government. Even without First Amendment protection government may "participate in the marketplace of ideas," and "contribute its own views to those of other speakers." Community–Service Broadcasting v. F.C.C., 593 F.2d 1102, 1110 n. 17 (D.C.Cir.1978). As Justice Stewart aptly noted in Columbia Broadcasting System, Inc. v. Democratic National Committee, 412 U.S. 94, 139, n. 7 (1973)(Stewart, J., concurring) (hereinafter CBS),

5. In addition to the reasons cited in the press release, the District Court, upon consideration of Dr. Nicholson's testimony, found four other reasons why the cancellation decision may have been made. First, Dr. Nicholson testified that he considered the program to be "in bad taste." Second, Dr. Nicholson expressed concern that some members of the public might believe that the "docu-drama" was a true documentary. Third, Dr. Nicholson testified that the University of Houston had previously entered into a contract with the Saudi Arabian royal family to instruct a particular princess. Finally, Dr. Nicholson testified that he had been in charge of fund raising activities for the university from 1957–1978 and that a significant percentage of the university's private contributions came from major oil companies and from individuals in oil related companies.

"[g]overnment is not restrained by the First Amendment from controlling its own expression . . . '[t]he purpose of the First Amendment is to protect the private expression and nothing in the guarantee precludes the government from controlling its own expression or that of its agents.' "[12]

Our essential task thus does not center on determining whether AETC and the University of Houston are vested with a First Amendment right to make the programming decisions which they make regarding "Death of a Princess." In the absence of a violation of constitutional right inhering in the plaintiffs, AETC and the University of Houston are free to make whatever programming decisions they choose, consistent with statutory and regulatory requirements. The fundamental question before us is whether in making the programming decisions at issue here, the defendants violated the First Amendment rights of the plaintiffs.

IV. *The Regulatory Framework Enacted by Congress*

Our inquiry into the constitutional issue at hand is aided by a brief review of the broadcast legislation enacted by Congress. . . .

. . .

The picture which emerges from the regulatory scheme adopted by Congress is one which clearly shows broadcast licensees endowed with the privilege and responsibility of exercising free programming control of their broadcasts, yet also charged with the obligation of making programming decisions which protect the legitimate interests of the public. The right to the free exercise of programming discretion is, for private licensees, not only statutorily conferred but also constitutionally protected. *CBS.* Under the existing statutes public licensees such as AETC and the University of Houston possess the same rights and obligations to make free programming decisions as their private counterparts; however, as state instrumentalities, these public licensees are without the protection of the First Amendment. This lack of constitutional protection implies only that government could possibly impose restrictions on these licensees which it could not impose on private licensees. The lack of First Amendment protection does not result in the lessening of any of the statutory rights and duties held by the public licensees. It also does not result in individual viewers gaining any greater right to influence the programming discretion of the public licensees.

V. *KUHT–TV and AETC Are Not Public Forums*

It is clear that Congress did not deem it necessary for viewers to be accorded a right of access to television broadcast stations in order for the

---

12. Government expression, being unprotected by the First Amendment, may be subject to legislative limitation which would be impermissible if sought to be applied to private expression. Yet there is nothing to suggest that, absent such limitation, government is restrained from speaking any more than are the citizens. Freedom of expression is the norm in our society, for government (if not restrained) and for the people. Freedom of speech is not good government because it is in the First Amendment; it is in the First Amendment because it is good government.

public's First Amendment interests in this medium to be fully realized. Indeed it is clear that Congress concluded that the First Amendment rights of public television viewers are adequately protected under a system where the broadcast licensee has sole programming discretion but is under an obligation to serve the public interest. In spite of this Congressional scheme the District Court in *Barnstone* found that KUHT–TV was a public forum because it was operated by the government for public communication of views on issues of political and social significance. The court held that as a public forum the station could not deny access to speakers who wished to be heard in the forum, unless the requirements for prior restraint were satisfied. 514 F.Supp. at 689–91.

The plaintiffs now urge that we affirm the District Court's ruling that public television stations are public forums. The plaintiffs, unlike the District Court, however, do not argue for a public right of access to the stations. Instead the plaintiffs contend that as public forums the stations are prohibited by the First Amendment from making programming decisions motivated by hostility to the communicative impact of a program's message and stemming from a specific viewpoint of the broadcaster.

We find both the holding of the District Court and the argument of the plaintiffs to be incorrect. The Supreme Court has recently rejected the theory adopted by the District Court that because a government facility is "specifically used for the communication of information and ideas" it is *ipso facto* a public forum. United States Postal Service v. Council of Greenburgh Civic Ass'ns, 453 U.S. 114 (1981).[22] A facility is a public forum only if it is designed to provide a general public right of access to its use, or if such public access has historically existed and is not incompatible with the facility's primary activity.

. . .

In the cases in which a public facility has been deemed a public forum the speakers have been found to have a right of access because they were attempting to use the facility in a manner fully consistent with the "pattern of usual activity" and "the general invitation extended." The pattern of usual activity for public television stations is the statutorily mandated practice of the broadcast licensee exercising sole programming authority. The general invitation extended to the public is not to schedule programs, but to watch or decline to watch what is offered.[25] It is thus clear that the public television stations involved in the cases before us are not public forums. The plaintiffs have no right of access to compel the broadcast of any particular program.

22. The Court in *United States Postal Service* ruled that mailboxes are not public forums.

25. Similarly producers of television programs are extended no invitation to air their programs on the public television stations. Producers are, of course, free to submit their programs to the stations with a request that they be broadcast, but they have no right to compel the broadcast. The decision whether to broadcast a program remains entirely with the licensee. The District Court for the Southern District of Texas thus erred in finding that the producers of "Death of a Princess" had a right of access to station KUHT–TV to broadcast the film.

Our holding today is consistent with the Supreme Court's ruling in *CBS* that television stations operated by private broadcast licensees provide no public right of access. . . .

The plaintiffs stress that they do not argue for the creation of a public right of access to public television stations. They contend that, even without a public right of access, the stations are public forums and as such cannot make programming decisions based on communicative impact of a program. We find this contention to be untenable. It is the right of public access which is the essential characteristic of a public forum and the basis which allows a speaker to challenge the state's regulation of the forum. The gravamen of a speaker's public forum complaint is the invalid and discriminatory denial of his right of access to the forum. If a speaker does not have a right of access to a facility, that facility by definition is not a "public forum" and the speaker is without grounds for challenge under the public forum doctrine.

VI.　*The Decision to Cancel Death of a Princess Was Not Governmental Censorship*

The plaintiffs argue that even if we decline to characterize KUHT–TV and AETC as public forums we should nonetheless find that the defendants violated the plaintiffs' First Amendment rights by "censoring" "Death of a Princess." The plaintiffs contend that censorship, in violation of the First Amendment, occurs when state officials in charge of state operated public television stations decide to cancel a scheduled program because of the officials' opposition to the program's political content.

There is no question that "the First Amendment means that government has no power to restrict expression because of its message, its ideas, its subject matter, or its content. . . . The essence of this forbidden censorship is content control." Police Dept. of Chicago v. Mosley, 408 U.S. 92, 95–96 (1972). . . .

We are not convinced that editorial decisions of public television stations owned and operated by the state must, or should, be viewed in the same manner and subjected to the same restrictions as state regulatory activity affecting speech in other areas. Standard First Amendment doctrine condemns content control by governmental bodies where the government sponsors and financially supports certain facilities through the use of which others are allowed to communicate and to exercise their own right of expression. Government is allowed to impose restrictions only as to "time, place, or manner" in the use of such public access facilities—public forums. As we observed earlier, however, the First Amendment does not prohibit the government, itself, from speaking, nor require the government to speak. Similarly, the First Amendment does not preclude the government from exercising editorial control over its own medium of expression. [　]

The plaintiffs concede that state officials operating public television stations can exercise some editorial discretion. They contend, however, that in exercising this discretion the officials must be "carefully neutral as to which speakers or viewpoints are to prevail in the marketplace of ideas." The plaintiffs further contend that if the officials restrict a program due to the political content of the program then the restriction is presumptively unconstitutional. The plaintiffs suggest that we adopt the evidentiary standard established by the Supreme Court in Mt. Healthy City School Dist. v. Doyle, 429 U.S. 274 (1977). Under this standard the initial burden would be on the plaintiffs to show that unconstitutional motivations were a "substantial" or "motivating" factor in the defendants' decisions to cancel "Death of a Princess." Once this burden is met by the plaintiffs the duty shifts to the defendants to show that the decisions would have been the same if the improper factor had not been considered.

The plaintiffs' analysis fails to recognize a number of essential differences between typical state regulation of private expressive activity and the exercise of editorial discretion by state officials responsible for the operation of public television stations. When state officials operate a public television station they must necessarily make discriminating choices. As the Supreme Court pointed out in CBS, 412 U.S. at 124, "[f]or better or worse, editing is what editors are for; and editing is selection and choice of material." In exercising their editorial discretion state officials will unavoidably make programming decisions which can be characterized as "politically motivated." All television broadcast licensees are required, under the public interest standard, to cover political events and to provide news and public affairs programs dealing with the political, social, economic and other issues which concern their community. [   ] The licensees are thus required to make the inherently subjective determination that their programming decisions are responsive to the needs, problems and interests of the residents of the area they serve. Red Lion, 395 U.S. at 380. A general proscription against political programming decisions would clearly be contrary to the licensees' statutory obligations, and would render virtually every programming decision subject to judicial challenge.

The plaintiffs seek to draw a distinction between a decision not to show a program and a decision to cancel a previously scheduled program. They suggest that while it is a proper exercise of editorial discretion for a licensee initially to decide not to schedule a program, it is constitutionally improper for the licensee to decide to cancel a scheduled program because of its political content. In support of their view the plaintiffs cited decisions holding that school officials may be free initially to decide which books to place in their school libraries but that a decision to remove any particular book may be subject to constitutional challenge. We are not persuaded, however, that the distinction urged upon us is valid or that the school library cases are applicable.

The decision to cancel a scheduled program is no less editorial in nature than an initial decision to schedule the program. [   ] Both decisions require the licensee to determine what will best serve the public interest, and, as we noted earlier, such a determination is inherently subjective and involves judgments which could be termed "political."

School libraries are distinguishable from broadcast stations in a number of important ways. There are limited hours in a day for broadcasting, and broadcast licensees are constantly required to make sensitive choices between available programs. Cf. Board of Education v. Pico, 457 U.S. 853, 875, n. 1, (1982)("The school's finite resources—as well as the limited number of hours in the day—require that educational officials make sensitive choices between subjects to be offered. . . .")(Blackmun, J., concurring in part). The maintenance of one volume on a library shelf does not (absent space limitations) preempt another. In broadcast, only one transmission of information, entertainment, or other message can occur at any one time. A library constantly and simultaneously proffers a myriad of written materials. As discussed in Part IV, hereinabove, the Congress has undertaken its careful analysis and balancing of conflicting interests involved in broadcasting and in public broadcasting, and the judicial branch should pay careful attention. [ ] There have been no comparable deliberations or enactments by that branch with respect to libraries. More specifically, there is no counterpart, vis-a-vis libraries, to the Federal Communications Commission's "Fairness Doctrine." When a television broadcaster finds that it has scheduled a program espousing one view, it may have unwittingly encumbered its limited broadcast hours with a requirement that equal time be devoted to other viewpoints which might touch upon an issue of limited interest in its viewing area. But the maintenance of one volume espousing one side of an issue does not invoke government regulation requiring that shelf space be made available for all other views. Finally, a school would be expected to furnish only one library for its student population. The residents of a state may expect a choice of a number of television stations, often with the publicly owned facility attracting the smallest number of viewers.

The right to cancel a program is, furthermore, far more integral a part of the operation of a television station than the decision to remove a book from a school library. Libraries typically have at least the opportunity to review a book before acquiring it, therefore, there may be "few legitimate reasons why a book, once acquired, should be removed from a library not filled to capacity." [ ] In comparison, television stations frequently do not have the chance to see a program until after the station's schedule has been printed, and there are numerous legitimate reasons why a station may decide to cancel a program it has initially scheduled. Indeed FCC regulations specifically require that licensees retain the power to reject any program which the licensee has already contracted for if the licensee determines that the program is "unsatisfactory or unsuitable or contrary to the public interest." 47 C.F.R. § 73.658.

We conclude that the defendants' editorial decisions to cancel "Death of a Princess" cannot be properly characterized as "censorship." Had the states of Alabama and Texas sought to prohibit the exhibition of the film by another party then indeed a question of censorship would have arisen. Such is not the case before us. The states have not sought to forbid or curtail the right of any person to show or view the film. In fact plaintiff Barnstone has already viewed the film at an exhibition at Rice University in Houston. The state officials in charge of AETC and KUHT–TV have simply exercised their statutorily mandated discretion and decided not to show a particular program at a particular time. There is a clear distinction between a state's exercise of editorial discretion over its own expression and a state's prohibition or suppression of the speech of another.

VII. *The Plaintiffs Can Seek Remedial Relief From the FCC*

Our holding that the defendants did not violate the plaintiffs' First Amendment rights does not preclude the plaintiffs from challenging the propriety of the defendants' programming decision with the FCC. Our decision is limited to the constitutional issue presented. We offer no opinion as to whether or not the actions of AETC and the University of Houston comport with their statutory and regulatory obligation.

. . .

VIII. *Conclusion*

The decisions of AETC and the University of Houston to cancel "Death of a Princess" did not violate the First Amendment rights of the plaintiffs. The plaintiffs have no constitutional right to compel the broadcast of the program. Accordingly, we find that the District Court for the Northern District of Alabama properly awarded summary judgment to AETC. We also find that the District Court for the Southern District of Texas erred in issuing its order requiring KUHT–TV to broadcast the program.

. . .

GARWOOD, CIRCUIT JUDGE, concurring.

I concur in the majority opinion, and append these remarks only to point up two additional interrelated matters I believe significant.

First, plaintiffs are not attacking governmental "public" broadcasting as such. Nor do they seek to require its operation to be on a pure "open forum" basis—like an empty stage available to all comers—where each citizen can cause the broadcast of his or her program of choice, with their inevitable selectivity determined by completely content neutral factors such as lot, or first come first served or the like. Rather, plaintiffs seek to become a *part* of governmental "public" broadcasting essentially as it is, except they want it to broadcast this particular program of their choice. However, there is simply no way for them—together with all others who might wish to assert similar rights for their favorite "dramatization"—to become a part of *such* "conventional" (as distinguished from pure "open forum") governmental broadcasting *except* on the basis of governmental selection of the individual programs.

As the majority opinion convincingly demonstrates, in television broadcasting not only is selection inevitable, but it is likewise inevitable that in numerous instances it will be largely based on factors that are not content neutral and on considerations that involve sympathy for or hostility to the program's "message" on the part of the party having the power of selection. This is *not* to say that program selection influenced by "message" sympathy or hostility on the part of governmental television stations is a desirable phenomenon, or even one which is wholly consistent with the values underlying the First Amendment. But such a characteristic is part and parcel of the operation of the conventional (not pure "open forum") governmental television stations of which plaintiffs seek to avail themselves. They are not entitled to have a special exception made in their favor so that for this particular program *they* are entitled to make the selection and require that these conventionally operated governmental stations broadcast it.

. . .

In the second place, plaintiffs do not assert that the stations in question have, on the basis of their agreement or disagreement with the different points of view involved or for similar "political" type reasons, structured their programming so that it constitutes a one-sided or slanted presentation of any matter of public concern, importance or controversy, whether relevant to the "message" of plaintiffs' desired program or otherwise.[3] So far as any such matters are concerned, plaintiffs' complaint is made essentially in a vacuum—they claim that merely because on one particular occasion a "political" type decision was made *not* to air one specific program plaintiffs wished to see, they therefore have a right to a court order directing these conventionally operated government stations to promptly air this precise program. We have rejected this claim. This is not to say, however, that no private citizen has a right to question the programming of governmental "public" television stations under any circumstances, or that the remedy of complaint to the F.C.C. will always be adequate.

A private citizen has no constitutional right to force a conventionally operated governmental "public" television station to enter with its broadcasting a particular propaganda war by showing a specific program selected by the citizen. Whether it is proper for such a governmental station to enter that kind of a war at all, or whether if it does so it may nevertheless present only one side while refusing, for reasons of a "political" nature, to broadcast any competing view, are questions of a different nature that are not now before us.

RUBIN, CIRCUIT JUDGE, with whom POLITZ, RANDALL and WILLIAMS, CIRCUIT JUDGES, join, specially concurring.

---

3. And plaintiffs do not contend their particular (or some similar) program must be shown to fairly balance the presentation on this subject matter which the stations have improperly slanted by showing some other program or programs.

While I join in the result reached by the majority, I reach my conclusion on a different basis. Therefore, I join in the views expressed by Judge Garwood and add:

The sensitive and important issues in these cases cannot be resolved simply by attempting to decide whether a television station operated by a state agency is, or is not, a public forum. That term is but a label, developed to describe a location the use of which is open to the public. It does not express a definition but a conclusion. . . .

The issue directly presented can be stated simply: whether an individual viewer has a right to compel a television station operated by a state agency to broadcast a single program previously scheduled by an employee of the agency that a higher-ranking state official has decided, because of its content, to cancel. This pretermits the factual questions whether the program was canceled for what the dissent calls "legitimate reasons" and whether the official's objection to the content of the program and to its political implications was in either of these cases the sole reason for canceling "Death of a Princess" or merely the decisive one. Although these are not unimportant inquiries, they do not focus on the crucial issue: how does the first amendment control state action when the state is operating a television station?

Determination of the constitutional limitations that result because a television licensee is a state agency rather than a private agency must take into account not only the rights of viewers but a number of other considerations. The license is federally bestowed. The state agency licensee has both a statutory duty to comply with the rules and regulations governing the use of its license and, like other licensees, the statutory right to determine the way in which it shall fulfill that duty. Those state employees who are charged with operation of the station, whether high or low in the managerial hierarchy, may have some right to free expression, which may be stronger if, for example, they function in an academic environment devoted to freedom of inquiry. Those who want access to the medium in order not to view and listen but to disseminate a message must also be considered. Viewers also have an interest in the content of programs, not only because of their "right to see" but also because the state agency is financed at least in part by viewers as taxpayers.

These interests are all entitled to consideration and some or all of them may be accorded constitutional protection. . . .

Even the fact that the state is engaged in television broadcasting does not fully define the constitutional limitations on its actions, for such broadcasting might be designed to serve differing purposes. Licensing is not destiny. That the state is the licensee does not predetermine the station's function. The state may elect the station's mission, so long as this mission is consistent with the station's license and the Constitution. The prerogatives of managers, editors, and programmers, the rights of access of those who seek exposure, and the rights of viewers, as well as the prerogatives of the licensee itself as a state agency, are at least in part determined by this mission.

All, or in other instances a part, of a station's programs might be devoted to providing a medium for the communication of competing views. Some channels on cable television networks and some viewer or listener call-in programs on television and radio stations are of this kind. Some television stations are devoted entirely to educational purposes, designed solely for pedagogy. Others may be operated to furnish a varied menu of entertainment having greater cultural and educational value than the programs available on commercial stations. While the record is not clear, it appears that the two stations involved in these cases were of this sort. Neither station has been shown to have been a magazine of the air, a forum for all views, or a dispassionate communicator on issues of the day. Each appears to serve instead a diet that differs from commercial television primarily in appeal to a somewhat more sophisticated audience, the absence of commercials, and efforts to raise funds from viewers.

The function of a state agency operating an informational medium is significant in determining first amendment restrictions on its actions. State agencies publish alumni bulletins, newsletters devoted to better farming practices, and law reviews; they operate or subsidize art museums and theater companies and student newspapers. The federal government operates the Voice of America and Radio Free Europe and Radio Liberty, publishes "journals, magazines, periodicals, and similar publications" that are "necessary in the transaction of the public business," including newspapers for branches of the Armed Forces, and pays the salaries of many federal officials who, like the President's Press Secretary, communicate with the public through the media. The first amendment does not dictate that what will be said or performed or published or broadcast in these activities will be entirely content-neutral. In those activities that, like television broadcasting to the general public, depend in part on audience interest, appraisal of audience interest and suitability for publication or broadcast inevitably involves judgment of content.

If the state is conducting an activity that functions as a marketplace of ideas, the Constitution requires content neutrality. Thus, a state university may not override editorial freedom for student newspapers. If, however, the state's activity is devoted to a specific function rather than general news dissemination or free exposition of ideas, the state may regulate content in order to prevent hampering the primary function of the activity, just as it may to some degree restrict the content of material distributed or displayed on military establishments, in prisons, on public buses, or in public hospitals.

All of the opinions in Board of Educ. v. Pico, 457 U.S. 853 (1982) recognize such a distinction either implicitly or expressly.[18]. . .

---

18. Seven justices filed opinions in *Pico*. The Court divided four-four on the constitutional issue of the extent to which the first amendment limits the discretion of a school board to remove books from a school library. Justice White concurred in the judgment of the Court but did not reach this issue. [   ]

. . .

While the Mobile and Houston television stations are operated by state agencies, neither station is designed to function as a marketplace of ideas, a medium open to all who have a message, whatever its nature. The staff of each station had made an initial programming decision based in part on their assessment of the content of "Death of a Princess." Had the initial decision been not to use the program, the argument might have been made that this too was censorship and violated the potential viewers' right to see. If a decision is initially made at one level to use a program and is then reversed at a higher level, the content assessment involved is more apparent, but it is not necessarily converted thereby from legitimate programming into forbidden censorship.

Judicial reassessment of the propriety of a programming decision made in operating a television station involves not only interference with station management but also reevaluation of all the content-quality-audience reaction factors that enter into a decision to use or not to use a program by a medium that cannot possibly, by its very nature, accommodate everything that every viewer might desire. With deference to the dicta observations made in the *Pico* plurality opinion, our reexamination of such a decision cannot logically be confined to occasions when higher officials overrule subordinates. If it is forbidden censorship for the higher official to cancel a program, it is equally censorship for the lower officials to decide initially to reject a program.

The Constitution is categoric but it does not command the theoretical. The state's discretion is confined by the functions it may perform as a broadcast licensee, and the purpose to which it has dedicated its license. Moreover, these cases involve only one program, not a licensee policy or practice of, for example, favoring only one political party, or of broadcasting racially or religiously discriminatory views. Neither complaint even alleges that either station has a policy of curtailing access to ideas. Each seeks only to compel the defendant station to show a single program. Judicial intervention might be required if these or other licensees should adopt or follow policies or practices that transgress constitutional rights. But, one call, even if it is ill-advised, does not constitute a policy or practice, and judicial intervention does not appear required or warranted for a single programming decision.

For these reasons, although I cannot agree with all of the majority opinion, particularly its discussion of the application of the public forum doctrine, I concur in the result.

KRAVITCH, CIRCUIT JUDGE, dissenting:

I agree with the analysis in Judge Johnson's thorough and well-reasoned dissent, with one exception: his statement that the government's decision to withdraw a program becomes presumptively unconstitutional once a plaintiff has shown that the decision was made because of the program's "substantive content." In my view, in addition to "substantive content," there must be shown an improper motivation, an intent to "restrict[ ] access to the political ideas or social perspectives discussed. . . ." Board of Education v. Pico, 457 U.S. 853, 879 (1982) (Blackmun, J., concurring). In this regard I agree with Judge Reavley. I do not join Judge Reavley's dissent, however, because his standard suggests that intent to suppress must be the *sole* factor before the withdrawal violates the First Amendment. The *Pico* plurality explicitly stated that an improper motive is a "decisive factor" and makes the withdrawal unconstitutional if it is a "substantial factor." Id. at __ & n. 22 (plurality opinion of Brennan, J., Marshall, J., and Stevens, J.). The improper motivation need not be the only factor in the withdrawal decision. For these reasons I write separately.

FRANK M. JOHNSON, JR., CIRCUIT JUDGE, with whom HATCHETT, ANDERSON, TATE and THOMAS A. CLARK, CIRCUIT JUDGES, join, dissenting.

I dissent because I am convinced that the majority has committed a serious error in applying the law to these cases. The clearly defined issue in these appeals is whether the executive officers of a state operated public television station may cancel a previously scheduled program because it presents a point of view disagreeable to the religious and political regime of a foreign country. The majority opinion permitting cancellation on these grounds flies completely in the face of the First Amendment and our tradition of vigilance against governmental censorship of political and religious expression.

. . .

The majority of the Court . . . has affirmed *Muir* and reversed *Barnstone* in an opinion which grants state authorities unlimited discretion to regulate the content of public television within their control. Because state law and FCC licensing grant defendants full broadcasting authority over these stations in their respective areas, the majority's decision confers unrestricted control over a monopoly market. [ ] By finding no other restriction on state operated television than that imposed by federal regulation, the Court has elevated "the Communications Act above the Constitution." [ ] Moreover, the Court has abdicated its duty in an area in which the plaintiffs have no comparable remedy.

The freedom of expression protected by the First Amendment encompasses the rights of both speakers and listeners. . . . The proper inquiry for this Court, then, should not be whether the Communications Act grants state broadcasters editorial discretion, but whether the action of state officials in these cases abridged free expression protected by the First Amendment. [ ]

Our system of constitutional protection clearly reflects the free discussion of public issues on the basis of the political, religious, or ideological content of the message. Freedom of expression concerning public issues "is at the heart of the First Amendment's protection." [ ] Self-government suffers when those in power suppress competing views on public issues. [ ] As a result, federal courts have consistently struck down content-based restrictions on the discussion of public issues. [ ]

. . .

The majority opinion completely ignores the critical issue in these cases by concluding that "[t]he state officials in charge of AETC and KUHT–TV have simply exercised their statutorily mandated discretion and decided not to show a particular program at a particular time." The very simple answer to that position is that FCC regulation is designed neither to preempt judicial scrutiny nor to redress state censorship as alleged in these cases.

Federal regulation of the broadcast media, for the most part, reflects the government's attempt to balance the allocation of a scarce resource with the First Amendment interests of private broadcasters and the public. [ ] The fact that state operated television stations are entitled to exercise editorial discretion, however, does not absolve them of their First Amendment responsibilities. "The First Amendment protects the press *from* governmental interference; it confers no analogous protection *on* the Government." CBS, Inc. v. FCC, 395 U.S. at 390 (First Amendment protects against governmental monopolization of the free marketplace of ideas). The majority commits fundamental error when it permits state broadcasters to ride on the coattails of their private counterparts. Even when the majority admits that state broadcasters "are without the protection of the First Amendment," it offers no principled reason why this "implies only that government could possibly impose restrictions on these licensees which it could not impose on private licensees."

In addition, while it is true that the FCC hears complaints similar to those raised in these cases, it is also true that the FCC routinely denies relief. A brief review of the cases cited by the majority reveals that the FCC steadfastly refuses to depart from its "longstanding policy of deferring to licensee discretion." . . .

Complaints regarding individual cancellation decisions are regularly denied. [ ]

Thus it is clear that the majority's deference to the FCC in these cases that present important constitutional questions amounts to nothing more than ". . . a promise to the ear . . ." which will most certainly be broken "to the hope." [ ] Relying on the system of FCC regulation, the majority has granted state broadcasters immunity from constitutional scrutiny. . . . Because the FCC does not distinguish between private and public broadcasters in its regulation of the airwaves, [ ], it provides no protection from the kind of state censorship alleged in these cases.

The concurring opinions of Judges Rubin and Garwood erroneously suggest that official censorship may only be found when the state operates a medium which is "content neutral," [ ], or which is a "public forum." [ ] In all other cases, the concurrences suppose, the state must be given unbridled authority to discriminate among different viewpoints, even if the state chooses to suppress a particular point of view solely on the basis of the political content of the message. Otherwise, the opinions caution, any citizen would have the "right" to force the state operated televisions in this case to broadcast any program of his choosing.

These suppositions erroneously ignore the proper considerations a Court may give the editorial process.

In the recent case of Board of Educ. v. Pico, 457 U.S. 853 (1982), both the plurality and Justice Blackmun recognized the presence of enforceable First Amendment rights, even within the context of a highly discretionary state function. As Justice Blackmun wrote, concurring: "In my view, we strike a proper balance here by holding that school officials may not remove books for the *purpose* of restricting access to the political ideas or social perspectives discussed in them, when that action is motivated simply by the officials' disapproval of the ideas involved." Id. at 899–80, (Blackmun, J., concurring). Unlike Judges Hill and Rubin, I find allegations of censorship in the context of state operated television broadcasting entitled to much greater scrutiny than similar allegations involving school board regulation of students' reading material. Public television stations "provide educational, cultural, and discussion programs which serve the general community." [ ] AETC is specifically charged with the duty "of making the benefits of educational television available to and promoting its use by inhabitants of Alabama. . . ." Ala.Code 1975, § 16–7–5. Viewed in the context of these stations' purposes and the framework of existing regulation, the editorial discretion of a state broadcaster is more circumscribed than that of a school board member. Moreover, the facts of both *Muir* and *Barnstone* reveal dramatic departures from established editorial practice in direct response to the urgings or implied threats of a foreign government.

Finally, the concurring opinions would appear to recognize official censorship by state television broadcasters when that censorship is conducted as a "policy or practice" of the state. Neither opinion, however, advances a principled distinction between censorship which is a "policy or practice" and that which is an individual overt act of suppression. It is clear to me that the First Amendment does not prohibit censorship only when it reaches the level of state "policy." To do so would be to allow the state to abrogate the fundamental concept of individual civil liberty. [ ]

It is the judiciary which is the ultimate arbiter of the fundamental rights involved in these cases. Courts may not abdicate their duty by reference to a system of administrative regulation, or because they would prefer that the plaintiffs take their complaints elsewhere. We must review the allegations of state censorship in the context of television broadcasting according to applicable legal standards. The standard for evaluating the allegations of abridgment in these cases must be that which was articulated in Mt. Healthy City School Dist. v. Doyle, 429 U.S. 274, 287 (1977). Once the plaintiff demonstrates that the government has silenced a message because of its substantive content, the government's decision becomes presumptively unconstitutional. The government should then be allowed to demonstrate that it would have taken the same action on the basis of legitimate reasons. Finally, the plaintiff should be given a full opportunity to refute the government's assertion.

. . .

REAVLEY, CIRCUIT JUDGE, dissenting:

I cannot join the majority or concurring opinions for the reason that each of these television stations does far more than transmit expressions of the state. Our desire to free non-profit public broadcasting from judicial interference is no justification for pretending that the state is not relaying messages into the idea marketplace. I must conclude that the state encounters the First Amendment requirement of neutrality for reasons generally discussed in my original panel concurrence. Barnstone v. University of Houston, KUHT–TV, 660 F.2d 137, 138 (5th Cir.1981).

On the other hand, I would not go so far as Judge Johnson does to make the state's decision presumptively unconstitutional whenever a program is not shown "because of its substantive content." State operated television stations should be given more latitude, even to choose on the basis of substantive content, in their program selection. They should be entitled to pursue excellence, to build viewing audiences, to respond to what viewers want, and to consider the effect of their programs upon that audience. Bona fide programming decisions would not, for me, violate First Amendment neutrality. Only if the decision to show or not to show were based upon viewpoint alone, in juxtaposition to the personal viewpoint of the programming authority or state superiors, entirely aside from any opinion as to program value or effect, would I regard neutrality abused and court action justifiable.

Notes and Questions

1.   Judge Garwood points out that the plaintiffs did not "attack governmental 'public' broadcasting as such." Are there any grounds for such an attack? What are the justifications for allowing government organizations, such as AETC or the University of Houston, to be broadcast licensees?

2.   Given the difficulty of finding alternative funding and the difficulty of insulating recipients of government funding from interference—either direct or indirect—in their programming policies, what changes should be made in the public broadcasting scheme?

3.   Because many of these stations are run by state and local governments, which also provide some of the financing, an additional set of problems has emerged with regard to the power of the state to impose restrictions more stringent than those imposed by Congress. In State v. University of Maine, 266 A.2d 863 (Me.1970), the state-run educational television system was partially financed from state funds. A statute ordered that no facilities "supported in whole or in part by state funds shall be used directly or indirectly for the promotion, advertisement or

advancement of any political candidate . . . or for the purpose of advocating or opposing any specific program, existing or proposed, of governmental action which shall include, but shall not be limited to, constitutional amendments, tax referendums or bond issues."

The court concluded that the limitations ran counter to federal demands that a licensee operating in the public interest may not flatly ban all such programming. The role of state funding gave the state no added power in this area. Although the state "has a valid surviving power to protect its citizens in matters involving their health and safety or to protect them from fraud and deception, it has no such valid interest in protecting them from the dissemination of ideas as to which they may be called upon to make an informed choice."

4. Both the majority in *League of Women Voters* and Judge Hill in *Muir* relied in part on the protection against one-sided programming afforded by the fairness doctrine. How much protection against pro-government bias can necessarily be expected from the FCC when its members are political appointees? Now that the doctrine has been eliminated, does the analysis change? Are there stronger arguments for retaining it with respect to noncommercial broadcasting?

5. Should the analysis be any different where election coverage is concerned?

ARKANSAS EDUCATIONAL TELEVISION
COMMISSION v. FORBES

Supreme Court of the United States, 1998.
523 U.S. 666, 118 S.Ct. 1633, 140 L.Ed.2d 875, 26 Med.L.Rptr. 1673, 11 C.R. 1421.

JUSTICE KENNEDY delivered the opinion of the Court.

A state-owned public television broadcaster sponsored a candidate debate from which it excluded an independent candidate with little popular support. The issue before us is whether, by reason of its state ownership, the station had a constitutional obligation to allow every candidate access to the debate. We conclude that, unlike most other public television programs, the candidate debate was subject to constitutional constraints applicable to nonpublic fora under our forum precedents. Even so, the broadcaster's decision to exclude the candidate was a reasonable, viewpoint-neutral exercise of journalistic discretion.

I

Petitioner, the Arkansas Educational Television Commission (AETC), is an Arkansas state agency owning and operating a network of five noncommercial television stations (Arkansas Educational Television Network or AETN). The eight members of AETC are appointed by the Governor for 8–year terms and are removable only for good cause. [ ] AETC members are barred from holding any other state or federal office, with the exception of teaching positions. [ ] To insulate its programming decisions from political pressure, AETC employs an Executive

Director and professional staff who exercise broad editorial discretion in planning the network's programming.

AETC has also adopted the Statement of Principles of Editorial Integrity in Public Broadcasting, which counsel adherence to "generally accepted broadcasting industry standards, so that the programming service is free from pressure from political or financial supporters."

In the spring of 1992, AETC staff began planning a series of debates between candidates for federal office in the November 1992 elections. AETC decided to televise a total of five debates, scheduling one for the Senate election and one for each of the four congressional elections in Arkansas. Working in close consultation with Bill Simmons, Arkansas Bureau Chief for the Associated Press, AETC staff developed a debate format allowing about 53 minutes during each 1–hour debate for questions to and answers by the candidates. Given the time constraint, the staff and Simmons "decided to limit participation in the debates to the major party candidates or any other candidate who had strong popular support." [   ]

On June 17, 1992, AETC invited the Republican and Democratic candidates for Arkansas' Third Congressional District to participate in the AETC debate for that seat. Two months later, after obtaining the 2,000 signatures required by Arkansas law, [   ], respondent Ralph Forbes was certified as an independent candidate qualified to appear on the ballot for the seat. Forbes was a perennial candidate who had sought, without success, a number of elected offices in Arkansas. On August 24, 1992, he wrote to AETC requesting permission to participate in the debate for his district, scheduled for October 22, 1992. On September 4, AETC Executive Director Susan Howarth denied Forbes' request, explaining that AETC had "made a bona fide journalistic judgement that our viewers would be best served by limiting the debate" to the candidates already invited. [   ]

On October 19, 1992, Forbes filed suit against AETC, seeking injunctive and declaratory relief as well as damages. Forbes claimed he was entitled to participate in the debate under both the First Amendment and 47 U.S.C. § 315, which affords political candidates a limited right of access to television air time. [After Forbes lost a request for an injunction mandating his participation, a trial was held at which the jury expressly found that the decision to exclude Forbes "had not been influenced by political pressure or disagreement with his views." The district court held for AETC. On appeal, the court of appeals reversed.]

II

Forbes has long since abandoned his statutory claims under 47 U.S C. § 315, and so the issue is whether his exclusion from the debate was consistent with the First Amendment. The Court of Appeals held it was not, applying our public forum precedents. Appearing as *amicus curiae* in support of petitioners, the Solicitor General argues that our forum precedents should be of little relevance in the context of television broadcasting. At the outset, then, it is instructive to ask whether public forum principles apply to the case at all.

Having first arisen in the context of streets and parks, the public forum doctrine should not be extended in a mechanical way to the very different context of public television broadcasting. In the case of streets and parks, the open access and viewpoint neutrality commanded by the doctrine is "compatible with the intended purpose of the property." [   ] So too was the requirement of viewpoint neutrality compatible with the university's funding of student publications in [   ]. In the case of television broadcasting, however, broad rights of access for outside speakers would be antithetical, as a general rule, to the discretion that stations and their editorial staff must exercise to fulfill their journalistic purpose and statutory obligations.

Congress has rejected the argument that "broadcast facilities should be open on a nonselective basis to all persons wishing to talk about public issues." [CBS v. DNC, p. 91, *supra*]. Instead, television broadcasters enjoy the "widest journalistic freedom" consistent with their public responsibilities. [   ] Among the broadcaster's responsibilities is the duty to schedule programming that serves the "public interest, convenience, and necessity." 47 U.S.C. § 309(a). Public and private broadcasters alike are not only permitted, but indeed required, to exercise substantial editorial discretion in the selection and presentation of their programming.

As a general rule, the nature of editorial discretion counsels against subjecting broadcasters to claims of viewpoint discrimination. Programming decisions would be particularly vulnerable to claims of this type because even principled exclusions rooted in sound journalistic judgment can often be characterized as viewpoint-based. To comply with their obligation to air programming that serves the public interest, broadcasters must often choose among speakers expressing different viewpoints. "That editors—newspaper or broadcast—can and do abuse this power is beyond doubt," [CBS v. DNC]; but "[c]alculated risks of abuse are taken in order to preserve higher values." [*Id.*] Much like a university selecting a commencement speaker, a public institution selecting speakers for a lecture series, or a public school prescribing its curriculum, a broadcaster by its nature will facilitate the expression of some viewpoints instead of others. Were the judiciary to require, and so to define and approve, pre-established criteria for access, it would risk implicating the courts in judgments that should be left to the exercise of journalistic discretion.

When a public broadcaster exercises editorial discretion in the selection and presentation of its programming, it engages in speech activity. [   ] Although programming decisions often involve the compilation of the speech of third parties, the decisions nonetheless constitute communicative acts. [   ]

Claims of access under our public forum precedents could obstruct the legitimate purposes of television broadcasters. Were the doctrine given sweeping application in this context, courts "would be required to oversee far more of the day-to-day operations of broadcasters' conduct, deciding such questions as whether a particular individual or group has had sufficient opportunity to present its viewpoint and whether a particular viewpoint has already been sufficiently aired." [CBS v. DNC] "The result would be a further erosion of the journalistic discretion of broadcasters," transferring "control over the treatment of public issues from the licensees who are accountable for broadcast performance to private individuals" who bring suit under our forum precedents. [*Id.*] In effect, we would "exchange 'public trustee' broadcasting, with all its limitations, for a system of self-appointed editorial commentators." [*Id.*]

In the absence of any congressional command to "[r]egimen[t] broadcasters' in this manner," [*Id.*], we are disinclined to do so through doctrines of our own design. This is not to say the First Amendment would bar the legislative imposition of neutral rules for access to public broadcasting. Instead, we say that, in most cases, the First Amendment of its own force does not compel public broadcasters to allow third parties access to their programming.

Although public broadcasting as a general matter does not lend itself to scrutiny under the forum doctrine, candidate debates present the narrow exception to the rule. For two reasons, a candidate debate like the one at issue here is different from other programming. First, unlike AETC's other broadcasts, the debate was by design a forum for political speech by the candidates. Consistent with the long tradition of candidate debates, the implicit representation of the broadcaster was that the views expressed were those of the candidates, not its own. The very purpose of the debate was to allow the candidates to express their views with minimal intrusion by the broadcaster. In this respect the debate differed even from a political talk show, whose host can express partisan views and then limit the discussion to those ideas.

Second, in our tradition, candidate debates are of exceptional significance in the electoral process. "[I]t is of particular importance that candidates have the opportunity to make their views known so that the electorate may intelligently evaluate the candidates' personal qualities and their positions on vital public issues before choosing among them on election day." CBS, Inc. v. FCC, [p. 188, *supra*] Deliberation on the positions and qualifications of candidates is integral to our system of government, and electoral speech may have its most profound and widespread impact when it is disseminated through televised debates. A majority of the population cites television as its primary source of election information, and debates are regarded as the "only occasion during a campaign when the attention of a large portion of the American public is focused on the election, as well as the only campaign information format which potentially offers sufficient time to explore issues and policies in depth in a neutral forum." [   ]

As we later discuss, in many cases it is not feasible for the broadcaster to allow unlimited access to a candidate debate. Yet the requirement of neutrality remains; a broadcaster cannot grant or deny access to a candidate debate on the basis of whether it agrees with a candidate's views. Viewpoint discrimination in this context would present not a "[c]alculated ris[k]," [CBS v. DNC], but an inevitability of skewing the electoral dialogue.

The special characteristics of candidate debates support the conclusion that the AETC debate was a forum of some type. The question of what type must be answered by reference to our public forum precedents, to which we now turn.

III

Forbes argues, and the Court of Appeals held, that the debate was a public forum to which he had a First Amendment right of access. Under our precedents, however, the debate was a nonpublic forum, from which AETC could exclude Forbes in the reasonable, viewpoint-neutral exercise of its journalistic discretion.

A

For our purposes, it will suffice to employ the categories of speech fora already established and discussed in our cases. "[T]he Court [has] identified three types of fora: the traditional public forum, the public forum created by government designation, and the nonpublic forum." Cornelius v. NAACP Legal Defense & Ed. Fund, Inc., 473 U. S. 788, 802 (1985). Traditional public fora are defined by the objective characteristics of the property, such as whether, "by long tradition or by government fiat," the property has been "devoted to assembly and debate." [ ] The government can exclude a speaker from a traditional public forum "only when the exclusion is necessary to serve a compelling state interest and the exclusion is narrowly drawn to achieve that interest." [ ]

Designated public fora, in contrast, are created by purposeful governmental action. "The government does not create a [designated] public forum by inaction or by permitting limited discourse, but only by intentionally opening a nontraditional public forum for public discourse." [ ] Hence "the Court has looked to the policy and practice of the government to ascertain whether it intended to designate a place not traditionally open to assembly and debate as a public forum." [ ] If the government excludes a speaker who falls within the class to which a designated public forum is made generally available, its action is subject to strict scrutiny. [ ]

Other government properties are either nonpublic fora or not fora at all. [ ] The government can restrict access to a nonpublic forum "as long as the restrictions are reasonable and [are] not an effort to suppress expression merely because public officials oppose the speaker's view." [ ]

In summary, traditional public fora are open for expressive activity regardless of the government's intent. The objective characteristics of these properties require the government to accommodate private speakers. The government is free to open additional properties for expressive use by the general public or by a particular class of speakers, thereby creating designated public fora. Where the property is not a traditional public forum and the government has not chosen to create a designated public forum, the property is either a nonpublic forum or not a forum at all.

B

The parties agree the AETC debate was not a traditional public forum. The Court has rejected the view that traditional public forum status extends beyond its historic confines, [   ]; and even had a more expansive conception of traditional public fora been adopted, see [   ], the almost unfettered access of a traditional public forum would be incompatible with the programming dictates a television broadcaster must follow. [   ] The issue, then, is whether the debate was a designated public forum or a nonpublic forum.

Under our precedents, the AETC debate was not a designated public forum. To create a forum of this type, the government must intend to make the property "generally available," Widmar v. Vincent, 454 U. S. 263, 264 (1981), to a class of speakers. Accord, *Cornelius*, [   ]. . . .

A designated public forum is not created when the government allows selective access for individual speakers rather than general access for a class of speakers. . . .

. . .

These cases illustrate the distinction between "general access," [   ], which indicates the property is a designated public forum, and "selective access," [   ], which indicates the property is a nonpublic forum. On one hand, the government creates a designated public forum when it makes its property generally available to a certain class of speakers, as the university made its facilities generally available to student groups in [*Widmar*]. On the other hand, the government does not create a designated public forum when it does no more than reserve eligibility for access to the forum to a particular class of speakers, whose members must then, as individuals, "obtain permission," [   ], to use it. For instance, the Federal Government did not create a designated public forum in *Cornelius* when it reserved eligibility for participation in the CFC drive to charitable agencies, and then made individual, non-ministerial judgments as to which of the eligible agencies would participate. [   ]

The *Cornelius* distinction between general and selective access furthers First Amendment interests. By recognizing the distinction, we encourage the government to open its property to some expressive activity in cases where, if faced with an all-or-nothing choice, it might not open the property at all. That this distinction turns on governmental intent does not render it unprotective of speech. Rather, it reflects the reality that, with the exception of traditional public fora, the government retains the choice of whether to designate its property as a forum for specified classes of speakers.

Here, the debate did not have an open-microphone format. Contrary to the assertion of the Court of Appeals, AETC did not make its debate generally available to candidates for Arkansas' Third Congressional District seat. Instead, just as the Federal Government in *Cornelius* reserved eligibility for participation in the CFC program to certain classes of voluntary agencies, AETC reserved eligibility for participation in the debate to candidates for the Third Congressional District seat (as opposed to some other seat). At that point, just as the Government in Cornelius made agency-by-agency determinations as to which of the eligible agencies would participate in the CFC, AETC made candidate-by-candidate determinations as to which of the eligible candidates would participate in the debate. "Such selective access, unsupported by evidence of a purposeful designation for public use, does not create a public forum." [　] Thus the debate was a nonpublic forum.

In addition to being a misapplication of our precedents, the Court of Appeals' holding would result in less speech, not more. In ruling that the debate was a public forum open to all ballot-qualified candidates, [　], the Court of Appeals would place a severe burden upon public broadcasters who air candidates' views. In each of the 1988, 1992, and 1996 Presidential elections, for example, no fewer than 22 candidates appeared on the ballot in at least one State. [　] In the 1996 congressional elections, it was common for 6 to 11 candidates to qualify for the ballot for a particular seat. [　] In the 1993 New Jersey gubernatorial election, to illustrate further, sample ballot mailings included the written statements of 19 candidates. [　] On logistical grounds alone, a public television editor might, with reason, decide that the inclusion of all ballot-qualified candidates would "actually undermine the educational value and quality of debates." [　]

Were it faced with the prospect of cacophony, on the one hand, and First Amendment liability, on the other, a public television broadcaster might choose not to air candidates' views at all. A broadcaster might decide " 'the safe course is to avoid controversy,' . . . and by so doing diminish the free flow of information and ideas." [　] In this circumstance, a "[g]overnment-enforced right of access inescapably 'dampens the vigor and limits the variety of public debate.' " [　]

These concerns are more than speculative. As a direct result of the Court of Appeals' decision in this case, the Nebraska Educational Television Network canceled a scheduled debate between candidates in Nebraska's 1996 United States Senate race. [　] A First Amendment jurisprudence yielding these results does not promote speech but represses it.

C

The debate's status as a nonpublic forum, however, did not give AETC unfettered power to exclude any candidate it wished. As Justice O'Connor has observed, nonpublic forum status "does not mean that the government can restrict speech in whatever way it likes." [　] To be consistent with the First Amendment, the exclusion of a speaker from a nonpublic forum must not be based on the speaker's viewpoint and must otherwise be reasonable in light of the purpose of the property. [   ]

In this case, the jury found Forbes' exclusion was not based on "objections or opposition to his views." [   ] The record provides ample support for this finding, demonstrating as well that AETC's decision to exclude him was reasonable.

AETC Executive Director Susan Howarth testified Forbes' views had "absolutely" no role in the decision to exclude him from the debate. [   ] She further testified Forbes was excluded because (1) "the Arkansas voters did not consider him a serious candidate"; (2) "the news organizations also did not consider him a serious candidate"; (3) "the Associated Press and a national election result reporting service did not plan to run his name in results on election night"; (4) Forbes "apparently had little, if any, financial support, failing to report campaign finances to the Secretary of State's office or to the Federal Election Commission"; and (5) "there [was] no 'Forbes for Congress' campaign headquarters other than his house." [   ] Forbes himself described his campaign organization as "bedlam" and the media coverage of his campaign as "zilch." [   ] It is, in short, beyond dispute that Forbes was excluded not because of his viewpoint but because he had generated no appreciable public interest. [   ]

There is no substance to Forbes' suggestion that he was excluded because his views were unpopular or out of the mainstream. His own objective lack of support, not his platform, was the criterion. Indeed, the very premise of Forbes' contention is mistaken. A candidate with unconventional views might well enjoy broad support by virtue of a compelling personality or an exemplary campaign organization. By the same token, a candidate with a traditional platform might enjoy little support due to an inept campaign or any number of other reasons.

Nor did AETC exclude Forbes in an attempted manipulation of the political process. The evidence provided powerful support for the jury's express finding that AETC's exclusion of Forbes was not the result of "political pressure from anyone inside or outside [AETC]." [   ] here is no serious argument that AETC did not act in good faith in this case. AETC excluded Forbes because the voters lacked interest in his candidacy, not because AETC itself did.

The broadcaster's decision to exclude Forbes was a reasonable, viewpoint-neutral exercise of journalistic discretion consistent with the First Amendment. The judgment of the Court of Appeals is

Reversed.

JUSTICE STEVENS, with whom JUSTICE SOUTER and JUSTICE GINSBURG join, dissenting.

The Court has decided that a state-owned television network has no "constitutional obligation to allow every candidate access to" political debates that it sponsors. [   ] I do not challenge that decision. The judgment of the Court of Appeals should nevertheless be affirmed. . . .

The ad hoc decision of the staff of the Arkansas Educational Television Commission (AETC) raises precisely the concerns addressed by "the many decisions of this Court over the last 30 years, holding that a law subjecting the exercise of First Amendment freedoms to the prior restraint of a license, without narrow, objective, and definite standards to guide the licensing authority, is unconstitutional." Shuttlesworth v. Birmingham, 394 U. S. 147, 150–151 (1969).

In its discussion of the facts, the Court barely mentions the standardless character of the decision to exclude Forbes from the debate. In its discussion of the law, the Court understates the constitutional importance of the distinction between state ownership and private ownership of broadcast facilities. . . .

I

Two months before Forbes was officially certified as an independent candidate qualified to appear on the ballot under Arkansas law, the AETC staff had already concluded that he "should not be invited" to participate in the televised debates because he was "not a serious candidate as determined by the voters of Arkansas." He had, however, been a serious contender for the Republican nomination for Lieutenant Governor in 1986 and again in 1990. Although he was defeated in a runoff election, in the three-way primary race conducted in 1990—just two years before the AETC staff decision—he had received 46.88% of the statewide vote and had carried 15 of the 16 counties within the Third Congressional District by absolute majorities. Nevertheless, the staff concluded that Forbes did not have "strong popular support." [ ]

Given the fact that the Republican winner in the Third Congressional District race in 1992 received only 50.22% of the vote and the Democrat received 47.20%, it would have been necessary for Forbes, who had made a strong showing in recent Republican primaries, to divert only a handful of votes from the Republican candidate to cause his defeat. Thus, even though the AETC staff may have correctly concluded that Forbes was "not a serious candidate," their decision to exclude him from the debate may have determined the outcome of the election in the Third District.

If a comparable decision were made today by a privately owned network, it would be subject to scrutiny under the Federal Election Campaign Act unless the network used "pre-established objective criteria to determine which candidates may participate in [the] debate." [ ] No such criteria governed AETC's refusal to permit Forbes to participate in the debate. Indeed, whether that refusal was based on a judgment about "newsworthiness"—as AETC has argued in this Court—or a judgment about "political viability"—as it argued in the Court of Appeals—the facts in the record presumably would have provided an adequate basis either for a decision to include Forbes in the Third District debate or a decision to exclude him, and might even have required a cancellation of two of the other debates.

The apparent flexibility of AETC's purported standard suggests the extent to which the staff had nearly limitless discretion to exclude Forbes from the debate based on ad hoc justifications. Thus, the Court of Appeals correctly concluded that the staff's appraisal of "political viability" was "so subjective, so arguable, so susceptible of variation in individual opinion, as to provide no secure basis for the exercise of governmental power consistent with the First Amendment." [   ]

II

AETC is a state agency whose actions "are fairly attributable to the State and subject to the Fourteenth Amendment, unlike the actions of privately owned broadcast licensees." [   ] The AETC staff members therefore "were not ordinary journalists: they were employees of government." [   ] The Court implicitly acknowledges these facts by subjecting the decision to exclude Forbes to constitutional analysis. Yet the Court seriously underestimates the importance of the difference between private and public ownership of broadcast facilities, despite the fact that Congress and this Court have repeatedly recognized that difference.

In [CBS v. DNC], the Court held that a licensee is neither a common carrier, [   ], nor a public forum that must accommodate " 'the right of every individual to speak, write, or publish,' " [   ] Speaking for a plurality, Chief Justice Burger expressed the opinion that the First Amendment imposes no constraint on the private network's journalistic freedom. He supported that view by noting that when Congress confronted the advent of radio in the 1920's, it "was faced with a fundamental choice between total Government ownership and control of the new medium—the choice of most other countries—or some other alternative." [   ] Congress chose a system of private broadcasters licensed and regulated by the Government, partly because of our traditional respect for private enterprise, but more importantly because public ownership created unacceptable risks of governmental censorship and use of the media for propaganda. "Congress appears to have concluded . . . that of these two choices—private or official censorship—Government censorship would be the most pervasive, the most self-serving, the most difficult to restrain and hence the one most to be avoided." [   ]

While noncommercial, educational stations generally have exercised the same journalistic independence as commercial networks, in 1981 Congress enacted a statute forbidding stations that received a federal subsidy from engaging in "editorializing." Relying primarily on cases involving the rights of commercial entities, a bare majority of this Court held the restriction invalid. [*League of Women Voters*, p. 93, *supra*]. Responding to the dissenting view that "the interest in keeping the Federal Government out of the propaganda arena" justified the restriction, [   ], the majority emphasized the broad coverage of the statute and concluded that it "impermissibly sweeps within its prohibition a wide range of speech by wholly private stations on topics that . . . have nothing whatever to do with federal, state, or local government." [   ] The Court noted that Congress had considered and rejected a ban that would have applied only to stations operated by state or local governmental entities, and reserved decision on the constitutionality of such a limited ban. [ ]

The League of Women Voters case implicated the right of "wholly private stations" to express their own views on a wide range of topics that "have nothing whatever to do with . . . government." [ ] The case before us today involves only the right of a state-owned network to regulate speech that plays a central role in democratic government. Because AETC is owned by the State, deference to its interest in making *ad hoc* decisions about the political content of its programs necessarily increases the risk of government censorship and propaganda in a way that protection of privately owned broadcasters does not.

III

. . .

. . . The dispositive issue in this case, then, is not whether AETC created a designated public forum or a nonpublic forum, as the Court concludes, but whether AETC defined the contours of the debate forum with sufficient specificity to justify the exclusion of a ballot-qualified candidate.

AETC asks that we reject Forbes' constitutional claim on the basis of entirely subjective, ad hoc judgments about the dimensions of its forum. The First Amendment demands more, however, when a state government effectively wields the power to eliminate a political candidate from all consideration by the voters. All stations must act as editors, see ante, at 5–6, and when state-owned stations participate in the broadcasting arena, their editorial decisions may impact the constitutional interests of individual speakers. A state-owned broadcaster need not plan, sponsor, and conduct political debates, however. When it chooses to do so, the First Amendment imposes important limitations on its control over access to the debate forum.

AETC's control was comparable to that of a local government official authorized to issue permits to use public facilities for expressive activities. In cases concerning access to a traditional public forum, we have found an analogy between the power to issue permits and the censorial power to impose a prior restraint on speech. Thus, in our review of an ordinance requiring a permit to participate in a parade on city streets, we explained that the ordinance, as written, "fell squarely within the ambit of the many decisions of this Court over the last 30 years, holding that a law subjecting the exercise of First Amendment freedoms to the prior restraint of a license, without narrow, objective, and definite standards to guide the licensing authority, is unconstitutional." [*Shuttlesworth*].

We recently reaffirmed this approach when considering the constitutionality of an assembly and parade ordinance that authorized a county official to exercise discretion in setting the amount of the permit fee. In Forsyth County v. Nationalist Movement, 505 U.S. 123 (1992), relying on *Shuttlesworth* and similar cases, we described the breadth of the administrator's discretion thusly:

> There are no articulated standards either in the ordinance or in the county's established practice. The administrator is not required to rely on any objective factors. He need not provide any explanation for his decision, and that decision is unreviewable. Nothing in the law or its application prevents the official from encouraging some views and discouraging others through the arbitrary application of fees. The First Amendment prohibits the vesting of such unbridled discretion in a government official. [   ]

Perhaps the discretion of the AETC staff in controlling access to the 1992 candidate debates was not quite as unbridled as that of the Forsyth County administrator. Nevertheless, it was surely broad enough to raise the concerns that controlled our decision in that case. No written criteria cabined the discretion of the AETC staff. Their subjective judgment about a candidate's 'viability' or 'newsworthiness' allowed them wide latitude either to permit or to exclude a third participant in any debate.

Moreover, in exercising that judgment they were free to rely on factors that arguably should favor inclusion as justifications for exclusion. Thus, the fact that Forbes had little financial support was considered as evidence of his lack of viability when that factor might have provided an independent reason for allowing him to share a free forum with wealthier candidates.

The televised debate forum at issue in this case may not squarely fit within our public forum analysis, but its importance cannot be denied. Given the special character of political speech, particularly during campaigns for elected office, the debate forum implicates constitutional concerns of the highest order, as the majority acknowledges. [   ] Indeed, the planning and management of political debates by state-owned broadcasters raise serious constitutional concerns that are seldom replicated when state-owned television networks engage in other types of programming. . . . Surely the Constitution demands at least as much from the Government when it takes action that necessarily impacts democratic elections as when local officials issue parade permits.

The reasons that support the need for narrow, objective, and definite standards to guide licensing decisions apply directly to the wholly subjective access decisions made by the staff of AETC. The importance of avoiding arbitrary or viewpoint-based exclusions from political debates militates strongly in favor of requiring the controlling state agency to use (and adhere to) pre-established, objective criteria to determine who among qualified candidates may participate. When the demand for speaking facilities exceeds supply, the State must "ration or allocate the scarce resources on some acceptable neutral principle." [   ] A constitutional duty to use objective standards—i.e., "neutral principles"—for determining whether and when to adjust a debate format would impose only a modest requirement that would fall far short of a duty to grant every multiple-party request. Such standards would also have the benefit of providing the public with some assurance that state-owned broadcasters cannot select debate participants on arbitrary grounds.

Like the Court, I do not endorse the view of the Court of Appeals that all candidates who qualify for a position on the ballot are necessarily entitled to access to any state-sponsored debate. I am convinced, however, that the constitutional imperatives that motivated our decisions in cases like *Shuttlesworth* command that access to political debates planned and managed by state-owned entities be governed by pre-established, objective criteria. Requiring government employees to set out objective criteria by which they choose which candidates will benefit from the significant media exposure that results from state-sponsored political debates would alleviate some of the risk inherent in allowing government agencies—rather than private entities—to stage candidate debates.

Accordingly, I would affirm the judgment of the Court of Appeals.

Notes and Questions

1. Do the dissent's facts about the political role of Forbes in Arkansas undercut the majority's reasoning? AETC's reasoning?

2. Was AETC's decision "a reasonable viewpoint-neutral exercise of journalistic discretion" as stated by the majority? Did AETC have "nearly limitless discretion to exclude Forbes from the debate based on ad hoc justifications" as charged by the dissent? Might both be accurate?

3. The majority expresses concern that were "the judiciary to require, and so to define and approve, pre-established criteria for access, it would risk implicating the courts in judgments that should be left to the exercise of journalistic discretion." What is the dissent's response? Who has the better of it?

4. How close is the analogy between AETC here and the police chief or mayor who authorizes marches or sets permit fees? Does the majority's emphasis on the structure and operation of AETC differentiate the two? Do the two events—political campaigns and marches—lend themselves equally to the "pre-established objective criteria" that the dissent would require?

5. If the dissent's written guidelines existed, would "newsworthiness" or "public viability" be sufficiently specific? Is there an important difference between these two terms? Would the guidelines have to say in advance whether lack of money for a campaign was a reason for—or against—inclusion? If so, which should it be?

6. The majority offers the possibility that Congress might impose "neutral rules for access to public broadcasting." Would that be a good idea after this case? What might they look like? Is there a difference between access for candidates and access for those who espouse ideas?

7. The court of appeals had distinguished *Forbes* in Marcus v. Iowa Public Television, 97 F.3d 1137 (8th Cir.1996). In *Marcus*, Iowa Public

Television, a state actor, scheduled a series of "co-appearances by the major candidates seeking to represent Iowa's five congressional districts in the Iowa delegation in Washington, D.C." All of the major candidates were either Democrats or Republicans, and IPTV refused to allow other candidates to participate in the joint appearances. Some of the excluded candidates sought an injunction requiring IPTV to allow all qualified candidates to participate in the scheduled programming. The district court found that although the programs constituted a limited public forum, exclusion of plaintiffs did not violate their First Amendment rights because IPTV's policies were narrowly tailored to promote the station's compelling interest in limiting its reporting to newsworthy events.

The Eighth Circuit affirmed. The court first found that the balance of harms weighed against issuing an injunction because interference with the editorial discretion of IPTV would constitute "a significant injury to the editorial integrity of IPTV." Moreover, the court noted that IPTV had declared it would cancel the scheduled joint appearances rather than allow other candidates to participate in order to maintain its "journalistic integrity and its credibility with its viewers." Finally, the court distinguished *Forbes*, noting that there is an important distinction between a decision not to allow participation based on a determination that a candidate is not viable and a decision not to allow participation because a candidate is not newsworthy:

> [*Forbes*] cannot be read to mandate the inclusion of every candidate on the ballot for any debate sponsored by a public television station. Nor does [*Forbes*] suggest that public television station administrators, because they are government actors, have no discretion whatsoever in making broadcast determinations. Rather, [*Forbes*] held that there was no compelling interest in excluding candidates from a debate based on the viability of the candidate. Unlike "viability," which is ultimately for the voters to decide, "newsworthiness" is peculiarly a decision within the domain of journalists.

Noting that "there are clearly objective elements of newsworthiness," the court accepted the district court's decision that IPTV had properly determined that none of the plaintiffs were newsworthy based on the "feeble efforts in their campaigns to generate public support for their candidacies." One judge dissented, arguing that *Forbes* clearly controlled the outcome of the case:

> In my view, there can be no realistic argument advanced that a subjective opinion by a government employee that a candidate is or is not "newsworthy" is different from a subjective conclusion that he or she is not "politically viable." The inquiry involves two peas from the same analytical pod. *Forbes* requires us to grant the emergency injunction requested in this case.

C. RELIGIOUS BROADCASTING

As noted earlier, religious institutions may be eligible for reserved educational channels. The test used by the Commission to decide whether an institution is eligible for a reserved spot is "whether the primary thrust is educational, albeit with a religious aspect to the educational activity. Recognizing that some overlap in purposes is, or can be, involved, we look to the application as a whole to determine which is the essential purpose and which is incidental." Bible Moravian Church, Inc., 28 F.C.C.2d 1, 21 R.R.2d 492 (1971)(rejecting an application for a reserved educational spot).

Religious institutions that do not meet the educational qualifications are able to apply for other spots as noncommercial licensees. In such instances, the rules applicable to other broadcasters are applicable to religious broadcasters as well. In addition, the Commission will apply the 'fair break' doctrine by inquiring as to "whether the applicant, whatever his own views, is likely to give a 'fair break' to others who do not share them." Noe v. Federal Communications Commission, 260 F.2d 739, 742 (D.C.Cir.1958). The Commission has made one major exception to its general rules in allowing a religious broadcaster to consider an applicant's religion for employment, but only to "those persons hired to espouse a particular religious philosophy over the air."

In its early days of reallocating frequencies, when there were no spots reserved for educational broadcasting, the Radio Commission had occasion to consider the value of a station emphasizing religious programming. It decided that such programming was usually aimed at too narrow a base of listeners and this "discriminated against" the rest of the listeners. "In rare cases it is possible to combine a general public-service station and a high-class religious station in a division of time which will approximate a well-rounded program. In other cases religious stations must accept part time on inferior channels or daylight assignments. . . ." Great Lakes Broadcasting Co., 3 F.R.C.Ann.Rep. 32 (1929), modified on other grounds 37 F.2d 993 (D.C.Cir.1930), certiorari dismissed 281 U.S. 706 (1930). As the spectrum expanded, religious broadcasting gained a more secure footing.

Some have argued that religious programming provides too narrow a base to justify the allocation of a license. An effort to persuade the Commission of this failed in 1975. Multiple and Religious Ownership of Educational Stations, 54 F.C.C.2d 941, 34 R.R.2d 1217 (1975). Two persons requested a "freeze" on all grants of reserved educational FM and television channels to religious institutions pending a study of their value. The Commission thought this would violate its obligation of "neutrality" toward sectarian applicants. The Commission concluded that no new policies were needed and decided to continue ad hoc enforcement of its existing policies such as the fairness doctrine and "the principle that a broadcast station may not be used solely to promote the personal or partisan objectives of the broadcaster."

Chapter VIII

STRUCTURAL REGULATION
OF CABLE TELEVISION

Our discussion until this point has been addressed solely to broadcasting. Some programs reached the public through radios and others through television sets. In this chapter and the next three we will examine other forms of communication that do not necessarily involve broadcasting—though the end product can emerge through the television set. It is important to recognize at the outset that although broadcasting and the television set have been joined, new technology permits the television set to be used for communications that have not been broadcast. The most obvious example is the use of DVD players, which permit the owner of a television set to buy or rent a DVD at a store and play it on a television set at home—all without any use of the spectrum. That activity much more closely resembles the showing of movies at home than anything else.

A. DEVELOPMENT

Cable television, the first of the "new" communication technologies, involves the transmission of electrical signals over wires to television sets in homes or elsewhere. The technique involves a studio, called the "head-end," and either coaxial or fiber optic cables that physically connect the head-end with every television set in the system. The cable is capable of carrying such a wide range of electrical signals that it can simultaneously carry signals sufficient for 55 or more television channels. (As the signals are carried along the cable they become weaker and must be amplified along the way.)

Some cable systems, using the video compression technology that is a byproduct of HDTV development, p. 55, *supra,* now offer more than hundreds of channels. As more systems are converted from analog to digital, the number of systems with 150 or more channels should increase dramatically. Annual Assessment of the Status of Competition in the Market for the Delivery of Video Programming, 17 F.C.C.Rcd. 26901 (2002).

It is possible to transmit certain signals in scrambled forms that require decoders, but others can be received by all users. It is also possible to run a system in which the users are able to send signals back to the head-end: voting on a question asked on a program, ordering merchandise or telling a quarterback what plays to call in a semiprofessional football game.

The programming sent out from the head-end can come from many sources. System owners might send out a variety of motion pictures they have bought or rented; they might send camera crews out to cover local high school football games; they might present live programs from their own studios; they might carry programs prepared by others specially for cable that they receive by wire or by satellite; or they might seek to transmit over their systems the signals and programs broadcast by television stations. This last source of programming raises serious questions of the relationship between cable and over-the-air television. So long as the cable system carries only programming from other sources, cable television is simply another competitor of broadcasting, along with movies, phonograph records, books and other communications sources. In fact, however, cable has been intimately involved with broadcasting since its inception—and that has produced substantial conflict.

Cable transmission was first used in the 1950s to provide television reception in remote locations that otherwise would have received none. For example, a community in the mountains of West Virginia could construct an antenna on high ground to receive the signals of nearby television stations and transmit them through cable to households in the community. Such systems were called CATV for "community antenna television." Because cable was the only means of bringing television service to these remote areas, television broadcasters welcomed the additional viewers.

It was soon realized, however, that cable could do more than merely provide television service to remote areas. In 1961 a cable operator began serving San Diego, a city already served by three VHF network affiliates. The cable operator erected an antenna capable of picking up signals from Los Angeles, 100 miles away. In addition to the three networks received locally, cable offered four independent stations that served Los Angeles with sports, old motion pictures and reruns of network shows. The San Diego experience demonstrated that the three channels offered by over-the-air signals were not enough to satisfy an ordinary audience and that viewers were willing to pay for more diversified programming through importation of distant signals. In effect, cable television service filled in the uneven pattern of FCC station allocation. Because cable offered a service alternative to that offered by local, over-the-air stations, television broadcasters began to view cable transmission as a competitive threat.

The spread of color television also provided a new impetus to cable development. VHF signals tend to bounce off large obstacles rather than bend around them. Hence a tall building can act like a weak transmitter, rebroadcasting the television signal at the same frequency as the station from which the signal originates. The result is interference, barely noticeable on a black-and-white set, but more pronounced on a color set. Cable provides the residents of large cities something that an over-the-air television signal cannot—a high-quality color picture. Thus, cable television invaded large cities, despite the presence of a full complement of VHF signals.

Finally, cable began to originate programming not available to viewers of network or independent television. Cable systems offered entertainment programming, sports events and special programs designed to meet the interests of discrete groups. Communication satellites made nationwide distribution of this programming economically feasible. The discovery that viewers were willing to pay a few dollars more per month for programming not available on over-the-air television led to the development of pay-cable service.

Pay cable involves the cable distribution of non-broadcast programming for which the subscriber is charged an additional program or channel fee beyond the regular monthly fee for over-the-air television channels, access and local origination channels, and advertiser-supported cable programming services. The systems for distributing pay cable vary technically. The simplest method is to distribute the programming on one or more channels of a cable television system in garbled form. System subscribers who wish to receive the additional programming are supplied with a device that converts the programming transmission so that it can be understood. It is technically possible, but more expensive, to use systems that permit a separate charge to be made for each program viewed. These either require the subscriber to purchase a ticket for each program in advance, which when inserted into a decoding device in the subscriber's home provides access to the programming, or to utilize the return communications capacity of a cable system or a telephone connection to activate a central computer facility that releases the programming through the subscriber's decoding device (an addressable converter) and performs the billing functions.

For many years, most cable systems have utilized a fee structure known as "tiering." A relatively low monthly fee gives the subscriber access to the local over-the-air television stations as well as any community access or local origination channels. Access channels carry programming produced by citizens or community groups, and local origination consists of local news, sports and public affairs programming produced by the cable operator. Sometimes advertiser-supported services such as the Entertainment and Sports Programming Network (ESPN), the Cable News Network (CNN) and over-the-air signals imported from other parts of the country are included. This level of service is known as "basic."

An additional monthly fee gives the subscriber access to other specialized programming services ranging from children's programs to adult entertainment. These services are usually bundled together in groups called "tiers." Thus, the subscriber sometimes had to take several unwanted program services to obtain one desired service. Usually a higher tier includes all the programming available in lower tiers. As will be discussed later in this chapter, mandatory purchase of tiers has been phased out due to requirements enacted in the Cable Competition and Consumer Protection Act of 1992.

The range of programming available via cable has grown greatly. One of the first major developments was the emergence of the so-called "superstation"—an independent television station that makes its programs available to cable systems throughout the country, via satellite transmission.

The most famous superstation was Turner Broadcasting's Channel 17 in Atlanta (WTBS), which has access to 200 live sporting events each year. The cable systems made the programs available as part of their basic monthly charge to attract subscribers.

Channel 17 prospered by increased charges for advertising on its programs that were reaching up to 30 million more viewers than previously. In addition, Turner began substituting national commercials for local commercials in the feed he sends Southern Satellite Systems, Inc., the company that distributes Channel 17 nationally. Thus, there were two versions of Channel 17. One was broadcast in Atlanta; the other was distributed to cable systems throughout the country. An estimated 40 percent of the local commercials were replaced. We will discuss the copyright implications of this practice in Chapter IX. Program suppliers increased charges to Channel 17 because the program was reaching a much larger audience than it did before, and cable distribution could result in reduced licensing fees or even preclude sales to local stations in cities receiving the cable program.

In 1998 TBS ceased to be a superstation. It now sends a totally separate signal to cable systems. The reason for the change is that it enables cable operators to insert local commercials making it more attractive to them. As long as TBS was a retransmission of a broadcast channel, inserting any local material was prohibited by the terms of the compulsory copyright license, which we will discuss in Chapter IX.

Other superstations followed, but they lagged behind the Atlanta enterprise, which had a two-year head start. Some, using wires or microwaves instead of satellites, became regional stations.

Around the same time, video programmers began to use satellites to deliver original programming services directly to cable operators. Among the services now available are programming directed to racial and religious groups, all-news and all-sports channels, live coverage of Congress, children's programming, movie and entertainment channels, adult movies and cultural programming.

This decade has brought another wave of new cable channels. Many of these are new services produced by existing cable programmers. For example, Viacom owns MTV, MTV2, Nickelodeon, Nick at Night, TV Land, BET, VH1, TNN, CMT, Noggin, Showtime, The Movie Channel and Flix, and is part owner of Comedy Central and Sundance Channel. We will discuss the increasing concentration of ownership of cable channels in Chapter XII.

Thus, cable has provided a variety of services. It began as a way of bringing to a community programming that would have been available but for geographical barriers. Then it imported programs from communities beyond the reach of normal reception. Later it became a service for those who wished to improve reception of their local signals. These features have been combined with each other as well as with the origination of new programming on cable—and this origination may be local or part of a network that programs specially for cable subscribers.

By late–2002 cable systems had been installed in 73.5 million (68.9 percent) of the nation's 105 million television homes. Systems varied in size from a few hundred homes to some in larger cities with hundreds of thousands of subscribers. The largest multiple system operators (MSOs) owned hundreds of systems. Pay cable reached 51.6 million of these subscribers. The pay systems ranged from Home Box Office, with 26 million subscribers, to specialized services with only a few thousand subscribers.

A relatively new development is the provision of cable programming by telephone companies. (Until recently it was assumed that telcos would have to rewire existing systems by using fiber optic cable before beginning a video service because they were considered essential to transmit moving images. As we will discuss shortly, this may not be true.) The impetus occurred when telephone companies were cleared to offer services ranging from video programming to electronic yellow pages. The FCC then recommended that statutory bars against telcos offering video services where they provided local phone service be lifted. Telephone Company–Cable Television Cross–Ownership Rules, 7 F.C.C.Rcd. 5781, 71 R.R.2d 70 (1992). We will discuss cases challenging the constitutionality of this restriction in Chapter XII.

B. JURISDICTION

1. FCC Jurisdiction

When the first CATV systems emerged in the late 1950s, rural television stations became concerned about their local dominance. Their requests that the FCC assume jurisdiction over the activities of these new enterprises were rejected on the ground that the problem was trivial and no different from a request for protection against motion picture theaters or publishers, who also compete with broadcasting.

In 1962, however, the FCC changed direction and began to deny cable systems permission to carry broadcast signals that might adversely affect local television. The Commission had two main concerns. First, it believed that if cable systems were allowed to import distant signals, this would fragment the audience available to local stations, erode their revenue bases, affect their programming and perhaps cause the stations to leave the air—to the public's detriment.

The second concern was that a cable system's use of retransmitted broadcast programming, for which the cable system had paid nothing, gave it an unfair competitive advantage over local television stations because the latter had to pay considerable sums to those who held the copyrights on particular programs. We will discuss the relationship between copyright law and cable regulation in Chapter IX.

These two concerns—for fragmentation and program costs—led the FCC to embark on a series of regulations designed to keep cable systems subservient to over-the-air broadcasting. Recall that this was the period of weak UHF stations, for whom audience fragmentation might well have been fatal.

One of the restrictions imposed was a ban on importing distant signals (those from outside the market area) into a top–100 market unless the cable system could prove that the importation would not hurt UHF development in that market. This restriction resulted in the first court challenge to the FCC's authority to regulate cable. United States v. Southwestern Cable Co., 392 U.S. 157 (1968). The Commission relied on § 2(a) of the Communications Act: "The provisions of this Act shall apply to all interstate and foreign communication by wire or radio. . . ." 47 U.S.C.A. § 152(a). Southwestern argued that "§ 152(a) does not independently confer regulatory authority upon the Commission, but instead merely prescribes the forms of communication to which the Act's other provisions may separately be made applicable." Because there were no specific cable provisions in the Act, Southwestern contended the Commission had no authority to regulate cable.

The Court rejected that argument as an overly restrictive reading of the Act. Relying on *National Broadcasting Co.,* p. 72, *supra,* the Court held that Congress had delegated "not niggardly but expansive powers" over electronic media to the Commission and that a broad reading of the Act was required:

> Moreover, the Commission has reasonably concluded that regulatory authority over CATV is imperative if it is to perform with appropriate effectiveness certain of its other responsibilities. Congress has imposed upon the Commission the "obligation of providing a widely dispersed radio and television service," with a "fair, efficient, and equitable distribution" of service among the "several States and communities." 47 U.S.C. § 307(b). . . . The Commission has concluded, and Congress has agreed, that these obligations require for their satisfaction the creation of a system of local broadcasting stations, such that "all communities of appreciable size [will] have at least one television station as an outlet for local self-expression." In turn the Commission has held that an appropriate system of local broadcasting may be created only if two subsidiary goals are realized. First, significantly wider use must be made of the available ultra-high-frequency channels. Second, communities must be encouraged "to launch sound and adequate programs to utilize the television channels now reserved for educational purposes." These subsidiary goals have received the endorsement of Congress.

> The Commission has reasonably found that the achievement of each of these purposes is "placed in jeopardy by the unregulated explosive growth of CATV." [ ] Although CATV may in some circumstances make possible "the realization of some of the [Commission's] most important goals," [ ], its importation of distant

signals into the service areas of local stations may also "destroy or seriously degrade the service offered by a television broadcaster," [ ], and thus ultimately deprive the public of the various benefits of a system of local broadcasting stations. In particular, the Commission feared that CATV might, by dividing the available audiences and revenues, significantly magnify the characteristically serious financial difficulties of UHF and educational television broadcasters. The Commission acknowledged that it could not predict with certainty the consequences of unregulated CATV, but reasoned that its statutory responsibilities demand that it "plan in advance of foreseeable events, instead of waiting to react to them." [ ] We are aware that these consequences have been variously estimated, but must conclude that there is substantial evidence that the Commission cannot "discharge its overall responsibilities without authority over this important aspect of television service." [ ]

The Commission has been charged with broad responsibilities for the orderly development of an appropriate system of local television broadcasting. The significance of its efforts can scarcely be exaggerated, for broadcasting is demonstrably a principal source of information and entertainment for a great part of the Nation's population. The Commission has reasonably found that the successful performance of these duties demands prompt and efficacious regulation of community antenna television systems. We have elsewhere held that we may not, "in the absence of compelling evidence that such was Congress' intention . . . prohibit administrative action imperative for the achievement of an agency's ultimate purposes." [ ] There is no such evidence here, and we therefore hold that the Commission's authority over "all interstate . . . communication by wire or radio" permits the regulation of CATV systems.

There is no need here to determine in detail the limits of the Commission's authority to regulate CATV. It is enough to emphasize that the authority which we recognize today under § 152(a) is restricted to that reasonably ancillary to the effective performance of the Commission's various responsibilities for the regulation of television broadcasting. The Commission may, for these purposes, issue "such rules and regulations and prescribe such restrictions and conditions, not inconsistent with law," as "public convenience, interest, or necessity requires." 47 U.S.C. § 303(r). We express no views as to the Commission's authority, if any, to regulate CATV under any other circumstances or for any other purposes.

Although *Southwestern Cable* established that the Commission did have jurisdiction over cable, it left unanswered the boundaries of that jurisdiction. The next challenge arose from the promulgation in the late 1960s of rules requiring larger cable systems to originate a certain amount of programming from their own resources. This requirement was upheld, 5–4, by the Supreme Court in United States v. Midwest Video Corp. (*Midwest Video I*), 406 U.S. 649 (1972), on the ground that the regulation was "reasonably ancillary" to the FCC's obligations to regulate over-the-air television. Because cable operators had become enmeshed with television broadcasting, the FCC could require them to engage in the functional equivalent of broadcasting. Chief Justice Burger concurred but noted that the FCC's regulations "strain[ed] the outer limits of even the open-ended and pervasive jurisdiction that has evolved by decisions of the Commission and the Courts." Ironically, less than two years later, the FCC eliminated the origination requirement because it concluded that quality local programming could not be obtained by government mandate.

Instead, the Commission issued rules requiring new cable systems to allocate four of their 20 channels to public, educational, local government (PEG) and leased access. The systems had to make equipment available for studio use by the public and could not control who might use the facilities or what they might say. Charges for use of the facilities were controlled. The court of appeals invalidated the regulations. Once again the Court was asked to define the limits of the Commission's jurisdiction.

This time the Court held, 6–3, that the Commission had exceeded its authority. Section 3(h) of the Communications Act (17 U.S.C.A. § 153(h)) prohibits the Commission from treating broadcasters as common carriers. The access-channel requirements "plainly impose common-carrier obligations on cable operators." The Court concluded that, given Congress' express disapproval of common-carrier status for broadcasters, imposing such status on cable could not be construed as "reasonably ancillary to the effective performance of [the FCC's] various responsibilities for the regulation of television broadcasting." Federal Communications Commission v. Midwest Video Corporation (*Midwest Video II*), 440 U.S. 689, 45 R.R.2d 581, 4 Med.L.Rptr. 2345 (1979).

The mandatory access rules had also been challenged on First Amendment grounds. The Court chose not to address that issue at that time. We will return to it in Chapter IX.

2. PREEMPTION

Cable, unlike broadcasting, is regulated by both state and federal government. State and local jurisdiction was originally based primarily on the cable operator's use of the city streets and other rights of way. As we have seen, federal jurisdiction grew out of the FCC's jurisdiction over broadcasting. Gradually a conflict arose over where the line between state and federal jurisdiction should be drawn.

The majority of cable operators preferred to have state and local jurisdiction restricted as much as possible. They believed that some cities were making impossible demands in return for their franchises and imposing heavy burdens on the cable operators once the franchises were awarded. There were also serious fears that franchise renewal in cable would not carry the same renewal expectancy that was present in broadcasting (discussed in Chapter IV).

At the same time the FCC was gradually asserting the right to preempt more and more state and local regulation. As these issues reached the courts, the Commission's position was generally being upheld. In 1984, in a case in which it was not directly involved, the Commission received strong support for its asserted right to preempt.

CAPITAL CITIES CABLE, INC. v. CRISP

Supreme Court of the United States, 1984.

467 U.S. 691, 104 S.Ct. 2694, 56 R.R.2d 263, 81 L.Ed.2d 580, 10 Med.L.Rptr. 1873.

[In 1980 the Oklahoma Attorney General decided that the state's ban on the advertising of alcoholic beverages applied to advertisements carried by out-of-state broadcast stations when retransmitted by Oklahoma cable television systems. Because the definition of alcoholic beverages did not include beer, and there was little, if any, electronic media advertising of hard liquors, the statute was only applied to electronic media advertising of wine. Capital Cities Cable filed a suit seeking a declaratory judgment that application of the law violated the Supremacy Clause and First Amendment to the Federal Constitution. The district court found the ban a violation of the First Amendment, but the decision was reversed by the court of appeals.]

JUSTICE BRENNAN delivered the opinion of the Court.

The question presented in this case is whether Oklahoma may require cable television operators in that State to delete all advertisements for alcoholic beverages contained in the out-of-state signals that they retransmit by cable to their subscribers. Petitioners contend that Oklahoma's requirement abridges their rights under the First and Fourteenth Amendments and is pre-empted by federal law. Because we conclude that this state regulation is pre-empted, we reverse the judgment of the Court of Appeals for the Tenth Circuit and do not reach the First Amendment question.

. . .

II

Petitioners and the FCC contend that the federal regulatory scheme for cable television systems administered by the Commission is intended to pre-empt any state regulation of the signals carried by cable system operators. Respondent apparently concedes that enforcement of the Oklahoma statute in this case conflicts with federal law, but argues that because the State's advertising ban was adopted pursuant to the broad powers to regulate the transportation and importation of intoxicating liquor reserved to the States by the Twenty-first Amendment, the statute should prevail notwithstanding the conflict with federal law.

. . .

. . . Under the Supremacy Clause, U.S. Const., Art. VI, cl. 2, the enforcement of a state regulation may be pre-empted by federal law in several circumstances: first, when Congress, in enacting a federal statute, has expressed a clear intent to pre-empt state law, [ ]; second, when it is clear despite the absence of explicit pre-emptive language, that Congress has intended, by legislating comprehensively, to occupy an entire field of regulation and has thereby "left no room for the States to supplement" federal law, [ ]; and, finally, when compliance with both state and federal law is impossible, [ ], or when the state law "stands as an obstacle to the accomplishment and execution of the full purposes and objectives of Congress." [ ]

And as we made clear in Fidelity Federal Savings and Loan Ass'n v. de la Cuesta, 458 U.S. 141 (1982):

> "Federal regulations have no less pre-emptive effect than federal statutes. Where Congress has directed an administrator to exercise his discretion, his judgments are subject to judicial review only to determine whether he has exceeded his authority or acted arbitrarily. When the administrator promulgates regulations intended to pre-empt state law, the court's inquiry is similarly limited: 'If [h]is choice represents a reasonable accommodation of conflicting policies that were committed to the agency's care by the statute, we should not disturb it unless it appears from the statute or its legislative history that the accommodation is not one that Congress would have sanctioned.'" [ ]

The power delegated to the FCC plainly comprises authority to regulate the signals carried by cable television systems. In United States v. Southwestern Cable Co., 392 U.S. 157 (1968), the Court found that the Commission had been given "broad responsibilities" to regulate all aspects of interstate communication by wire or radio by virtue of § 2(a) of the Communications Act of 1934, 47 U.S.C. § 152(a), and that this comprehensive authority included to regulate cable communications systems. [ ] We have since explained that the Commission's authority extends to all regulatory actions "necessary to ensure the achievement of the Commission's statutory responsibilities." FCC v. Midwest Video Corp., 440 U.S. 689, 706 (1979). Accord, United States v. Midwest Video Corp., 406 U.S. 649, 665–667 (1972). Therefore, if the FCC has resolved to pre-empt an area of cable television regulation and if this determination "represents a reasonable accommodation of conflicting policies" that are within the agency's domain, [ ], we must conclude that all conflicting state regulations have been precluded.

A

In contrast to commercial television broadcasters, which transmit video signals to their audience free of charge and derive their income principally from advertising revenues, cable television systems generally operate on the basis of a wholly different entrepreneurial principle. In return for service fees paid by subscribers, cable operators provide their customers with a variety of broadcast and nonbroadcast signals obtained from several sources. . . . Over the past twenty years, pursuant to its delegated authority under the Communications Act, the FCC has unambiguously expressed its intent to pre-empt any state or local regulation of this entire array of signals carried by cable television systems.

The Commission began its regulation of cable communication in the 1960s. At that time, it was chiefly concerned that unlimited importation of distant broadcast signals into the service areas of local television broadcasting stations might, through competition, "destroy or seriously degrade the service offered by a television broadcaster," and thereby cause a significant reduction in service to households not served by cable systems. . . .

. . . In marking the boundaries of its jurisdiction, the FCC determined that, in contrast to its regulatory scheme for television broadcasting stations, it would not adopt a system of direct federal licensing for cable systems. Instead, the Commission announced a program of "deliberately structured dualism" in which state and local authorities were given responsibility for granting franchises to cable operators within their communities and for overseeing such local incidents of cable operations as delineating franchise areas, regulating the construction of cable facilities, and maintaining rights of way. [ ] At the same time, the Commission retained exclusive jurisdiction over all operational aspects of cable communication, including signal carriage and technical standards. . . . The Commission has also made clear that its exclusive jurisdiction extends to cable systems' carriage of specialized, non-broadcast signals. . . .

Although the FCC has recently relaxed its regulation of importation of distant broadcast signals to permit greater access to this source of programming for cable subscribers, it has by no means forsaken its regulatory power in this area. [ ] Indeed, the Commission's decision to allow unfettered importation of distant broadcast signals rested on its conclusion that "the benefits to existing and potential cable households from permitting the carriage of additional signals are substantial. Millions of households may be afforded not only increased viewing options, but also access to a diversity of services from cable television that presently is unavailable in their communities." 79 F.C.C.2d, at 746. [ ] . . . Clearly, the full accomplishment of such objectives would be jeopardized if state and local authorities were now permitted to restrict the ability of cable operators to provide these diverse services to their subscribers.

Accordingly, to the extent it has been invoked to control the distant broadcast and nonbroadcast signals imported by cable operators, the Oklahoma advertising ban plainly reaches beyond the regulatory authority reserved to local authorities by the Commission's rules, and trespasses into the exclusive domain of the FCC. To be sure, Oklahoma may, under current Commission rules, regulate such local aspects of cable systems as franchisee selection and construction oversight, [ ], but, by requiring cable television operators to delete commercial advertising contained in signals carried pursuant to federal authority, the State has clearly exceeded that limited jurisdiction and interfered with a regulatory area that the Commission has explicitly pre-empted.

B

Quite apart from this generalized federal pre-emption of state regulation of cable signal carriage, the Oklahoma advertising ban plainly conflicts with specific federal regulations. These conflicts arise in three principal ways. First, the FCC's so-called "must-carry" rules require certain cable television operators to transmit the broadcast signals of any local television broadcasting station that is located within a specified 35–mile zone of the cable operator or that is "significantly viewed" in the community served by the operator. [ ] These "must-carry" rules require many Oklahoma cable operators, including petitioners, to carry signals from broadcast stations located in nearby states such as Missouri and Kansas. [ ] In addition, under Commission regulations, the local broadcast signals that cable operators are required to carry must be carried "in full, without deletion or alteration of any portion. . . ." [ ] Because, in the Commission's view, enforcement of these non-deletion rules serves to "prevent a loss of revenues to local broadcasters sufficient to result in reduced service to the public," they have been applied to commercial advertisements as well as to regular programming. [ ] Consequently, those Oklahoma cable operators required to carry out-of-state broadcast signals in full, including any wine commercials, are subject to criminal prosecution under Oklahoma law as a result of their compliance with federal regulations.

Second, current FCC rulings permit, and indeed encourage, cable television operators to import out-of-state television broadcast signals and retransmit those signals to their subscribers. [ ] For Oklahoma cable operators, this source of cable programming includes signals from television broadcasting stations located in Kansas, Missouri and Texas, as well as the signals from so-called "superstations" in Atlanta and Chicago. [ ] It is undisputed that many of these distant broadcast signals retransmitted by petitioners contain wine commercials that are lawful under federal law and in the states where the programming originates. Nor is it disputed that cable operators who carry such signals are barred by Commission regulations from deleting or altering any portion of those signals, including commercial advertising. [ ] Under Oklahoma's advertising ban, however, these cable operators must either delete the wine commercials or face criminal prosecution. Since the Oklahoma law, by requiring deletion of a portion of these out-of-state signals, compels conduct that federal law forbids, the State ban clearly "stands as an obstacle to the accomplishment and execution of the full purposes and objectives" of the federal regulatory scheme. [ ]

Finally, enforcement of the state advertising ban against Oklahoma cable operators will affect a third source of cable programming over which the Commission has asserted exclusive jurisdiction. Aside from relaying local television broadcasting in accordance with the "must-carry" rules, and distant broadcast signals, cable operators also transmit specialized nonbroadcast cable services to their subscribers. This source of programming . . . includes such advertiser-supported national cable programming as the Cable News Network (CNN) and the Entertainment and Sports Programming Network (ESPN). Although the Commission's "must-carry" and non-deletion rules do not apply to such nonbroadcast cable services, the FCC, as noted earlier, [   ], has explicitly stated that state regulation of these services is completely precluded by federal law.

Petitioners generally receive such signals by antenna, microwave receiver, or by satellite dish and retransmit them by wire to their subscribers. But unlike local television broadcasting stations that transmit only one signal and receive notification from their networks concerning advertisements, cable operators simultaneously receive and channel to their subscribers a variety of signals from many sources without any advance notice about the timing or content of commercial advertisements carried on those signals. [   ] As the record of this case indicates, developing the capacity to monitor each signal and delete every wine commercial before it is retransmitted would be a prohibitively burdensome task. [   ] . . . Accordingly, if the state advertising ban is enforced, Oklahoma cable operators will be compelled either to abandon altogether their carriage of both distant broadcast signals and specialized nonbroadcast cable services or run the risk of criminal prosecution. As a consequence, the public may well be deprived of the wide variety of programming options that cable systems make possible.

Such a result is wholly at odds with the regulatory goals contemplated by the FCC. Consistent with its congressionally defined charter to "make available, so far as possible, to all the people of the United States a rapid, efficient, Nation-wide and world-wide wire and radio communication service . . .," 47 U.S.C. § 151, the FCC has sought to ensure that "the benefits of cable communications become a reality on a nationwide basis." [   ] With that end in mind, the Commission has determined that only federal pre-emption of state and local regulation can assure cable systems the breathing space necessary to expand vigorously and provide a diverse range of program offerings to potential cable subscribers in all parts of the country. While that judgment may not enjoy universal support, it plainly represents a reasonable accommodation of the competing policies committed to the FCC's care and we see no reason to disturb the agency's judgment. And, as we have repeatedly explained, when federal officials determine, as the FCC has here, that restrictive regulation of a particular area is not in the public interest, "States are not permitted to use their police power to enact such a regulation." [   ]

C

Although the FCC has taken the lead in formulating communications policy with respect to cable television, Congress has considered the impact of this new technology, and has, through the Copyright Revision Act of 1976, 90 Stat. 2541, 17 U.S.C. § 101 et seq., acted to facilitate the cable industry's ability to distribute broadcast programming on a national basis. Prior to the 1976 revision, the Court has determined that the retransmission of distant broadcast signals by cable systems did not subject cable operators to copyright infringement liability because such retransmissions were not "performances" within the meaning of the 1909 Copyright Act. [ ] In revising the Copyright Act, however, Congress concluded that cable operators should be required to pay royalties to the owners of copyrighted programs retransmitted by their systems on pain of liability for copyright infringement. At the same time, Congress recognized that "it would be impractical and unduly burdensome to require every cable system to negotiate [appropriate royalty payments] with every copyright owner" in order to secure consent for such retransmission. [ ] Section 111 of the 1976 Act codifies the solution devised by Congress. It establishes a program of compulsory copyright licensing that permits cable systems to retransmit distant broadcast signals without securing permission from the copyright owner and, in turn, requires each system to pay royalty fees to a central royalty fund based on a percentage of its gross revenues. To take advantage of this compulsory licensing scheme, a cable operator must satisfy certain reporting requirements, § 111(d)(1) and (2)(A), pay specified royalty fees to a central fund administered by the Register of Copyrights, § 111(d)(2)(B)–(D), and (3), and refrain from deleting or altering commercial advertising on the broadcast signals it transmits, § 111(c)(3). Failure to comply with these conditions results in forfeiture of the protections of the compulsory licensing system.

In devising this system, Congress has clearly sought to further the important public purpose framed in the Copyright Clause, U.S. Const., Art. I, § 8, of rewarding the creators of copyrighted works, and of "promoting broad public availability of literature, music, and the other arts," [ ]. Compulsory licensing not only protects the commercial value of copyrighted works but also enhances the ability of cable systems to retransmit such programs carried on distant broadcast signals, thereby allowing the public to benefit by the wider dissemination of works carried on television broadcast signals. By requiring cable operators to delete commercial advertisements for wine, however, the Oklahoma ban forces these operators to lose the protections of compulsory licensing. Of course, it is possible for cable systems to comply with the Oklahoma ban by simply abandoning their importation of the distant broadcast signals covered by the Copyright Act. But such a loss of viewing options would plainly thwart the policy identified by both Congress and the FCC of facilitating and encouraging the importation of distant broadcast signals.

III

[Oklahoma argued that even if normal pre-emption analysis invalidated the ban, it was valid because of the Twenty-first Amendment. "States enjoy broad power under § 2 of the Twenty-first Amendment to regulate the importation and use of intoxicating liquor within their borders." The Court decided that the state interest in regulating liquor was outweighed by the substantial "federal objective of ensuring widespread availability of diverse cable services throughout the United

States." In reaching this conclusion the Court was heavily influenced by the extremely limited approach that Oklahoma had taken to further its asserted interest. Oklahoma had only banned electronic media advertising of wine. There was no direct regulation of consumption or even a ban on other alcoholic beverage advertising.]

IV

We conclude that the application of Oklahoma's alcoholic beverage advertising ban to out-of-state signals carried by cable operators in that State is pre-empted by federal law and that the Twenty-first Amendment does not save the regulation from pre-emption. The judgment of the Court of Appeals is

Reversed.

Notes and Questions

1. How does the balance between state and federal regulation set out here differ from the balance established in broadcast regulation? Why have these differences developed? Is either model preferable to the other?

2. By deciding the case on preemption grounds, the Court avoided having to address the First Amendment question concerning regulation of alcoholic beverage advertising. Recall our discussion of this issue in Chapter VI.

3. TITLE VI OF THE COMMUNICATIONS ACT

The FCC's increasingly aggressive policy of preemption had already led the National League of Cities (NLC) to pursue legislative relief. However, lengthy negotiations between NLC and the National Cable Television Association (NCTA) had not produced a compromise satisfactory to both constituencies. Perhaps given new impetus by Court decisions such as *Crisp,* a compromise bill was drafted and presented to Congress with the backing of both groups. This bill was enacted into law as the Cable Communications Policy Act of 1984.

One of the provisions of the Cable Act amended § 2 of the Communications Act of 1934 to include within the FCC's jurisdiction "cable service to all persons engaged within the United States in providing such service, and to the facilities of cable operators which relate to such service, as provided in Title VI." 47 U.S.C.A. § 152. Thus, the Commission no longer had to derive its jurisdiction over cable from its jurisdiction over broadcasting, and courts no longer had to determine whether a Commission rule was reasonably ancillary to its jurisdiction over broadcasting.

The 1984 Act also added Title VI, "Cable Communications," to the Communications Act. Title VI contains the specific provisions governing cable. 47 U.S.C.A. §§ 521–559.

The 1984 Act did not eliminate jurisdictional disputes between the Commission and local authorities. For example, in 1985 the Commission promulgated rules establishing technical standards for cable signal quality and preempting local cable authorities from imposing standards of their own. Technical and Operational Requirements of Part 76 Cable Television, 102 F.C.C.2d 1372, 59 R.R.2d 569 (1985). The Commission's standards applied only to "cable channels devoted to delivering standard broadcast television service," Class I channels, but the preemption of local standards applied to all cable service.

On appeal, the court upheld the preemption of Class I channels, but found that in preempting standards for all other cable service without imposing any standards of its own, the Commission was in apparent conflict with § 626 of the Cable Act. One of the factors a franchisor is required to consider in a renewal proceeding is "the quality of the operator's service, including signal quality. . . ." 47 U.S.C.A. § 546(c)(1)(B):

> The Cable Act thus requires franchisors to consider the quality of a cable operator's signal when considering his renewal application. And a franchisor's determination that the operator's signal quality has been inadequate must be the product of reasoned decision-making. Petitioner argues that franchising authorities cannot evaluate reasonably a cable operator's signal quality without referring to objective technical standards; otherwise franchising authorities and cable operators alike would be cast into an endless series of subjective disputes over whether the Section 626 renewal criterion of "signal quality" has been satisfied. We agree.

The court, finding the failure to consider the apparent conflict to be arbitrary and capricious, vacated the preemption of technical standards for non-Class I channels. City of New York v. Federal Communications Commission, 814 F.2d 720, 62 R.R.2d 914 (D.C.Cir.1987).

The various petitioners that had brought the original action sought *certiorari* with regard to the Class I channels ruling. The Supreme Court granted *certiorari* and affirmed the lower court ruling. The Court relied heavily on § 624 of the Cable Act. "In [§ 624], Congress specified that the local franchising authority could regulate 'services, facilities, and equipment' in certain respects, and could enforce those requirements, but § 624(e) of the Act grants the Commission the power to 'establish technical standards relating to the facilities and equipment of cable systems which a franchising authority may require in the franchise.'" The Court concluded that there was nothing to indicate that the Commission's decision was contrary to what Congress intended. City of New York v. Federal Communications Commission, 486 U.S. 57, 64 R.R.2d 1423 (1988).

In response to the remand on Class II, III and IV signals, the Commission developed signal quality standards for Class II, III and IV signals. Cable Television Technical and Operational Requirements, 7 F.C.C.Rcd. 2021 (1992).

In 1992 Congress overrode President Bush's veto and enacted the Cable Television Consumer Protection and Competition Act of 1992. The 1992 Act required the Commission to "prescribe regulations which establish minimum technical standards relating to cable systems' technical operation and signal quality." In addition, franchising authorities were permitted to include the FCC's technical standards as requirements of franchise agreements and those that wished to impose more stringent standards than the Commission's were authorized to apply to the Commission for a waiver. The latter two provisions were, however, repealed by the Telecommunications Act of 1996. Subsequently, the FCC concluded that its 1992 order met the requirements of the 1992 Act. Cable Television Technical and Operational Requirements, 7 F.C.C.Rcd. 8676 (1992). We will discuss other aspects of the 1992 Act and 1996 Act throughout this and Chapters 9–10 and 12.

C. FRANCHISING

Cable systems operate under franchise authority granted by a municipality, though state agencies also may grant permission to operate. See, e.g., Clear Television Cable Corp. v. Board of Public Utility Commissioners, 85 N.J. 30, 424 A.2d 1151 (1981). A franchise gives the cable operator access to city streets and other rights-of-way within a defined area for specific periods of time. Prior to 1992 franchises were usually awarded after competitive bidding by several companies in response to a request for proposals outlining the requirements of the franchising authority. In practice they were almost always exclusive. After a franchise is awarded, a franchise agreement is signed specifying services the system must provide, construction schedules and franchise fees. Prior to 1984 many also specified fees the operators could charge subscribers.

For a while the competition among cable operators for city franchises was incredibly intense. At the height of the franchising process, operators were willing to promise almost anything to obtain a franchise. For example, in 1981 Denver attracted bids from three firms, one offering a 215–channel system including a 107–channel home network. The three offered basic home services for monthly fees ranging from nothing to $3.95.

Unfortunately, once they had obtained the franchises, many of these operators discovered that cable was not necessarily the gold mine they had anticipated. Some of these operators asked the cities to renegotiate the franchise agreements, eliminating some of the promised services. Others sold the franchises. One company that found itself in that position, Warner Amex Cable Communications, ended up building a 56–channel system in Milwaukee in lieu of the 108–channel system originally agreed upon. Broadcasting, Oct. 29, 1984 at 10.

From the 1970s into the early 1980s, when franchising competition was at its peak, cities were able to demand far more than large numbers of channels. Access channels, studios, mobile vans, financial contributions to access foundations and free wiring of public buildings were commonly sought—and offered. In many cities, cable companies ended up providing benefits totally unrelated to cable service. These benefits ranged from building new libraries to planting trees along the roads.

A slightly more subtle approach to winning the franchise competition was a practice known as "rent-a-citizen." Prominent local citizens were given shares in the local subsidiary of a company seeking the franchise. If the company was granted the franchise, these shares suddenly acquired great value. Obviously, this meant that these prominent citizens would exert all their influence towards having that company awarded the franchise.

In addition, the cable company would try to persuade the city that these citizens would provide local ownership, thus guaranteeing that the cable company would always be looking out for the city's best interests. The reality was that these citizens never had a controlling interest in even the local subsidiary. Their influence was minimal. Furthermore, the arrangement between the company and the local stockholders almost always included a buy-back arrangement providing that after a few years the local citizens would sell the stock back to the company for a healthy profit.

Spurred on by cable industry hype and franchising fever, the cities kept increasing the cost of obtaining franchises. Gradually, the FCC increased its limitations on state and municipal regulation of cable. Among the more important restrictions imposed by the Commission were a prohibition of rate regulation of premium services and a ceiling on franchise fees. Further restrictions were under consideration when the Cable Communications Policy Act of 1984 was enacted.

Although the 1984 Act left franchising still the province of state and local governments, it placed certain restrictions on the franchising process. The most important of these is a prohibition on regulating cable service as a common carrier. Franchising authorities are also prohibited from specifying video programming or other information services in requests for proposals. 47 U.S.C.A. § 544.

In addition, franchising authorities cannot charge more than five percent of gross revenues as a franchise fee. In the case of franchises in existence at the time the 1984 Act was enacted, money used to support community access channels is not covered by the five percent limit. 47 U.S.C.A. § 542. The Commission eliminated its rule limiting franchise fees to three percent (five percent with a waiver).

One of the great fears of cable operators was non-renewal. Specific guidelines for franchise renewal were set out in great detail in the 1984 Act. A denial of renewal must be based on a finding that the operator failed to comply substantially with the existing franchise agreement; that the quality of the operator's service was unreasonable in light of community needs; that the operator lacks necessary technical, financial or legal ability to fulfill the promises made in its proposal; or that the operator's proposal is not reasonable in terms of meeting the future needs of the community. This created what is in effect a strong renewal expectancy. 47 U.S.C.A. § 546.

During this period, there were no serious challenges to the cities' authority to extract everything possible from the cable companies by running what was, in essence, an auction, with the franchise going to the highest bidder. Probably, most companies were loath to start fights with the cities for fear of being denied the franchises. As a result, serious questions remained unanswered. What is the connection between a city's control of public rights-of-way and authority over cable programming? Is awarding a franchise based in part on programming promises a violation of the First Amendment? If there was room for more than one company's cables, did awarding an exclusive franchise violate the First Amendment?

These issues were raised in a suit against the city of Los Angeles. The case arose when Preferred Communications requested a cable franchise after refusing to participate in the city's competitive franchising process. When denied the franchise, Preferred sued, alleging the franchising process violated the First Amendment. The suit was dismissed for failure to state a claim upon which relief could be granted, and Preferred appealed. [Note: When a suit is dismissed for failure to state a claim upon which relief can be granted, it means that even if every fact in dispute is assumed to be in the plaintiff's favor, the plaintiff would still lose the case. Thus, the issue on appeal is not should the plaintiff have won the case, but rather, has the plaintiff at least indicated a chance of winning the case. If the plaintiff wins the appeal, the case will then proceed further.]

The court of appeals framed the issue in the case as follows:

> Can the City, consistent with the First Amendment, limit access by means of an auction process to a given region of the City to a single cable television company, when the public utility facilities and other public property in that region necessary to the installation and operation of a cable television system are physically capable of accommodating more than one system?

The court, in a sweeping opinion, concluded that the city could not. Preferred Communications, Inc. v. City of Los Angeles, 754 F.2d 1396, 57 R.R.2d 1339 (9th Cir.1985).

The Supreme Court affirmed, but on narrower grounds. Although the Court agreed that operating a cable system clearly involved First Amendment activities, it was unwilling to make a decision on the exact application of the First Amendment to cable without additional factual information:

> But this case is different from a case between private litigants for two reasons: first, it is an action of a municipal corporation taken pursuant to a city ordinance that is challenged here, and, second, the ordinance is challenged on colorable First Amendment grounds. The City has adduced essentially factual arguments to justify the

restrictions on cable franchising imposed by its ordinance, but the factual assertions of the City are disputed at least in part by the respondent. We are unwilling to decide the legal questions posed by the parties without a more thoroughly developed record of proceedings in which the parties have an opportunity to prove those disputed factual assertions upon which they rely.

The case was remanded for trial. City of Los Angeles v. Preferred Communications, Inc., 476 U.S. 488, 106 S.Ct. 2034, 60 R.R.2d 792, 90 L.Ed.2d 480, 12 Med.L.Rptr. 2244 (1986).

The case raised more questions than it answered. What relevant facts might be developed on remand—and how might they help clarify the legal issues? Might some standard between the current newspaper standard and the current broadcasting standard be a useful resolution of the issue? If so, what should that standard be?

Preferred had been expected to resolve a number of cases involving constitutional challenges to the cable franchising process. The Supreme Court's refusal to set a specific First Amendment standard for cable meant that the lower courts had to proceed with little guidance. The results were inconsistent as can be seen from the following cases.

In Central Telecommunications, Inc. v. TCI Cablevision, Inc., 800 F.2d 711 (8th Cir.1986) the court held:

> [T]he evidence reveals that the City's cable television market is currently a natural monopoly which, under present technology, offers room for only one operator at a time. Thus, we hold that the City could properly offer a de facto exclusive franchise in order to create competition for its cable television market.

TCI had asserted a First Amendment defense to allegations that it had engaged in illegal monopolistic practices aimed at keeping exclusive control of the local cable market. In essence, TCI argued that exclusive franchises were unconstitutional and therefore Central Telecommunications had not been deprived of any protectable interest by TCI's conduct. The Supreme Court denied *certiorari*. 480 U.S. 910 (1987).

Similarly, a district court judge rejected Erie Telecommunications, Inc.'s First Amendment attack on the franchise-fee and access-channel provisions of its franchise agreement with the City of Erie. According to the judge, "In its effort to preserve an uninhibited marketplace of ideas, government is entrusted with protecting the First Amendment rights of cable television viewers." Erie Telecommunications, Inc. v. City of Erie, 659 F.Supp. 580, 62 R.R.2d 1467 (W.D.Pa.1987).

On appeal, the court never reached the First Amendment issue. As part of the franchise agreement, Erie Telecommunications had executed a Mutual Release and Covenant in which it had agreed to release the city from any and all claims related to the franchise agreement. The court held that this precluded the cable company's raising any challenges to the agreement. Erie Telecommunications, Inc. v. City of Erie, Pennsylvania, 853 F.2d 1084, 65 R.R.2d 1 (3d Cir.1988).

However, in Century Federal, Inc. v. City of Palo Alto, California, 648 F.Supp. 1465, 61 R.R.2d 1348 (N.D.Cal.1986), the court ruled that a franchising process under which the cities of Palo Alto, Menlo Park and Atherton intended to grant only one franchise was unconstitutional on its face. In reaching this conclusion, the court applied the *O'Brien* test, p. 21, *supra*.

The court found that four of the five "substantial" interests asserted by the cities to support its grant of a *de facto* exclusive franchise were based on the idea that cable is a natural monopoly. "Essentially, the Cities argue that if there is a reasonable probability that their service area will economically support only one CTV operator, then they should be able to choose, at the outset, that operator who will provide the highest quality service and use the offer of an exclusive franchise as a plum to bargain for certain concessions, e.g., access channels, that they might not be able to acquire if an operator knew that it would have to compete with other cable providers." The court found that rationale unacceptable as an asserted government interest under *O'Brien*. "The paternalistic role in the First Amendment that the Cities envision for government is simply inconsistent with the purpose and goals of the First Amendment."

The cities' final asserted interest, minimizing disruption of the public domain, was not found to be furthered by the franchising process. The court reasoned that if multiple cable systems were installed simultaneously, there would be no more disruption of the public domain than if a single system were installed.

The court took care to point out that it was not holding that cities "necessarily have to open their cable facilities to all comers regardless of size, shape, quality or qualifications." It was holding only that the cities had not offered evidence of a substantial government interest that justified granting a *de facto* exclusive franchise.

Later, in further proceedings in the same case, the court held also that the cities' universal service and state-of-the-art technology requirements were unconstitutional. In striking down the universal service requirement, the court noted that freedom of speech necessarily implies " 'a concomitant freedom *not* to speak publicly, one which serves the same ultimate end as freedom of speech in its affirmative aspect.' [*Pacific Gas*]." Requiring service to an entire community as a prerequisite to serving any part of the community infringed that right not to speak.

Turning to the cities' requirement for state-of-the-art technology, the court applied the *O'Brien* test. The cities' assertion that the important government interest served by the regulation was preventing disruption of the public domain for system improvements was dismissed as overly speculative. Century Federal, Inc. v. City of Palo Alto, California, 710 F.Supp. 1552, 63 R.R.2d 1736 (N.D.Cal.1987).

In still a third proceeding in the case, the court also struck down the franchise fee, performance bond requirement and security fund requirement mandated by the franchising process. The court emphasized that other similar users of the public rights of way such as Pacific Bell and Pacific Gas and Electric were not subject to the same fees and requirements. Thus, under Minneapolis Star & Tribune Co. v. Minnesota Commissioner of Revenue, 460 U.S. 575, 9 Med.L.Rptr. 1369 (1983) (involving a state tax on newsprint and ink used in publications of a certain circulation value), "the government had an unusually heavy burden of justification." The court found that the city had not met that burden. Century Federal, Inc. v. City of Palo Alto, California, 710 F.Supp. 1559, 65 R.R.2d 875 (N.D.Cal.1988).

Similarly, in Group W Cable, Inc. v. Santa Cruz, 669 F.Supp. 954, 63 R.R.2d 1656 (N.D.Cal.1987), Group W successfully challenged Santa Cruz's refusal to renew its franchise. Applying *O'Brien*, the court held that the city's grant of an exclusive franchise to a competing company violated the First Amendment. Relying on *Miami Herald,* p. 90, *supra*, the court also struck down franchising provisions requiring state-of-the-art technology.

In 1990 in the *Preferred* remand, the district court ruled on a number of motions for summary judgment by both parties. In making the rulings the court divided the various franchise requirement into two categories: restrictions imposing an incidental burden on speech, which are subject to the *O'Brien* test, and restrictions "intended to curtail expression," which are subject to the highest level of judicial scrutiny. The court defined this to mean that the government had to show that the challenged regulation "is a precisely drawn means of serving a compelling state interest."

The court held that the limit of one cable operator in any franchise area was an incidental burden. Nevertheless, it was unconstitutional as a matter of law because the one operator requirement was too restrictive a method of achieving the city's substantial interests in minimizing disruption and visual blight.

A requirement of participation of local individuals and/or groups in the ownership and operation of the cable system was held non-incidental "as it, at the very least, indirectly bans speech by favoring speakers 'responsive to the needs of the South Central area residents' over others." The court then found the government's interest in localism compelling, and thus the requirement was held constitutional.

The court also found unconstitutional the city's use of overall character as a factor in awarding a cable franchise. Because the character inquiry was not limited to past criminal or civil liability, but in fact included consideration of whether the applicant had ever "initiated litigation against a franchising authority or ha[d] a franchising authority instigated litigation against it," the court found the requirement a non-incidental burden on speech. The requirement was not narrowly tailored to serve the city's asserted interest in protecting its citizens from fraud because it allowed the city to take into account whether the applicant had ever brought "legitimate challenges to franchise ordinances invoking first amendment rights."

The state-of-the-art-technology requirement was also found a non-incidental burden on speech after the city asserted as one of its purposes "promoting universal availability of educational opportunities." The promotion of certain forms of speech over others, here educational speech, made the requirement non-incidental. Because the city failed to support its conclusion that this requirement would promote its interests with empirical evidence, the court found that they were not compelling interests.

The court also found provisions allowing the city to purchase the franchise at below-market value and to require continued service after the expiration or revocation of the franchise unconstitutional under *O'Brien*. Again applying *O'Brien*, it upheld provisions prohibiting transfer of the franchise without the city's consent and requiring universal service. Finally, it struck down a five-year franchise term because the city failed to offer evidence why such a short franchise term was needed. Preferred Communications, Inc. v. City of Los Angeles, 67 R.R.2d 366 (C.D.Cal.1990).

A few months later, the court issued still another series of rulings on motions for summary judgment. Among the more important of these were the following: The five-percent franchise fee was held to be an incidental burden on speech. The court further held that the fee furthered the substantial government interest "in receiving compensation from private individuals who benefit from the commercial exploitation of that property" in a narrowly tailored fashion. Thus, under *O'Brien*, the fee requirement was constitutional.

However, the Court found the city's requirement of a $10,000 filing fee, a $500 good faith deposit and a $60,000 processing fee (this last fee to be paid only by the winning applicant) to be unconstitutional. The city had justified these fees as necessary to cover the costs of the franchising process. Because the fees were calculated to cover the original franchising process, some of which had subsequently been declared unconstitutional, the city was, in effect, requiring the applicants to pay for the expenses of an unconstitutional review process.

Finally, a requirement that the cable franchisee create a cable advisory board, every aspect of which would be subject to the city's approval, was found unconstitutional. The city justified the board as a means of furthering localism. Finding that the board constituted a direct burden on speech, the court held that, to be constitutional, it had to be a precisely drawn means of furthering the compelling localism interests. Because there was nothing in the requirement limiting the board's role to advising the cable company on local interests, the requirement, in the court's opinion, was not precisely drawn and, thus, unconstitutional. Preferred Communications, Inc. v. City of Los Angeles, 68 R.R.2d 121 (C.D.Cal.1990).

The court of appeals affirmed the holding that the city's granting of a *de facto* monopoly cable franchise was unconstitutional. As far as the lower court's other holdings were concerned, the court of appeals held that it was premature to review them. The case was remanded with instructions to the district court that "if the city failed to offer another franchise for bidding within due course, the district court shall order the city to do so." Preferred Communications, Inc. v. City of Los Angeles, 13 F.3d 1327, 74 R.R.2d 508 (9th Cir.1994). A petition for *certiorari* was denied, 512 U.S. 1235 (1994).

One problem raised by holdings such as that in *Century Federal* is the effect on existing franchisees who have complied with, universal service and state-of-the-art technology requirements in return for exclusive franchises. Suddenly, a second company is allowed to cable only the most lucrative sections of a city without the expense of many of the original franchise requirements. Not only is the first company deprived of the exclusive franchise it bargained for, but the second company has a major competitive edge. In Sacramento, after a district court decision prohibiting an exclusive franchise, the city granted additional franchises, which do not contain universal service requirements. The original franchisee filed suit claiming that the grant of these additional franchises violated its franchise agreement. The case was settled out of court.

The 1992 Act included some changes in the rules governing the franchising process. First, exclusive franchises are prohibited. 47 U.S.C.A. § 541(a)(1). However, this prohibition does not apply retroactively. James Cable Partners, L.P. v. City of Jamestown, 43 F.3d 277 (6th Cir.1995). In holding the law prospective only, the court stated its disagreement with Cox Cable Communications, Inc. v. United States, 992 F.2d 1178 (11th Cir.1993) and instead stressed the intervening Landgraf v. USI Film Products, 511 U.S. 244 (1994), in which the Court had stated:

> It will frequently be true . . . that retroactive application of a new statute would vindicate its purpose more fully. That consideration, however, is not sufficient to rebut the presumption against retroactivity. Statutes are seldom crafted to pursue a single goal, and compromises necessary to their enactment may require adopting means other than those that would most effectively pursue the main goal.

The 1992 Act requires franchisees to submit specific written notices to invoke renewal proceedings. Franchising authorities must commence renewal proceedings within six months of receiving this written notice. Submission of a renewal notice does not preclude a franchise authority from revoking a franchise for cause during the renewal process. 47 U.S.C.A. § 546.

The 1992 Act also prohibited transfers of cable systems within 36 months of acquisition or initial construction. The Commission was permitted to waive this requirement "in the cases of default, foreclosure, or other financial distress." 47 U.S.C.A. § 537. Note the similarity between this provision and the FCC's original antitrafficking rules governing broadcast license transfers, p. 138, *supra*. This provision was repealed by the 1996 Telecommunications Act.

Finally, the 1992 Act added a provision limiting law suits against franchising authorities or other governmental bodies arising out of the regulation of cable service to injunctive or declaratory relief. Essentially this provision protects franchising authorities and other governmental bodies from any liability for monetary damages. 47 U.S.C.A. § 555.

Renewal. The cable franchises granted in the 1970s started coming due for renewal in the 1990s. One of the first contested cases to emerge was Union CATV, Inc. v. City of Sturgis, 107 F.3d 434 (6th Cir.1997). The city, pursuant to the 1992 Cable Act, adopted a report that identified the future cable-related needs and interests of the city. These included wiring a local school and a five-year renewal term. Union, the incumbent, submitted a proposal that sought a 20–year renewal and argued against the need to wire the school. After the city denied renewal, Union went to court. Under the statute, a proposal for renewal must be granted if it is "reasonable to meet the future cable-related community needs and interests, taking into account the cost of meeting such needs and interests." The trial judge's grant of the city's motion for summary judgment was affirmed on appeal.

Because Union had not even arguably satisfied the two needs noted, the city argued that Union must fail. In a ruling of first impression, the court decided that the courts were permitted to exercise limited review of the city's determination of its needs and interests. That is, the cable operator must be permitted to demonstrate that "its proposal is 'reasonable' despite its failure to meet certain identified community needs and interests. When a proposal does not satisfy an identified need, the court must decide whether the operator has established that the cost of meeting that need so outweighs the value of the need that the proposal is nonetheless reasonable." This is not to be a *de novo* review because it would be "inappropriate for a federal court to second-guess the city in its identification of such needs and interests." The degree of deference was to be "comparable to that owed a jury."

In reviewing the proposal itself, the court concluded that Union had failed to show that the cost of satisfying either of the two needs warranted overruling the city's choice of needs or the city's determination that Union had not met them.

D. RATE REGULATION

The 1984 Act allowed regulation only of rates for basic cable service, and then only in the absence of effective competition. This provision was viewed as a major victory for cable operators, who had long argued that rate regulation was unnecessary due to competition from other communication technologies. Opponents of the provision contended that cable was effectively a monopoly and, thus, cable rates were not subject to adequate pressure from competition.

The Commission initially defined effective competition as the availability of three or more off-the-air television signals in the market. The Commission rejected the suggestion of some parties that the availability of the three major networks be part of the definition. Cable Communications Act Rules, 58 R.R.2d 1 (1985).

The court of appeals held that the standard for measuring signal availability was insufficiently justified and remanded that issue for further proceedings. American Civil Liberties Union v. Federal Communications Commission, 823 F.2d 1554, 63 R.R.2d 730 (D.C.Cir.1987), certiorari denied 485 U.S. 959 (1988).

On remand, the Commission modified the definition of effective competition. A cable system was subject to effective competition only if three or more off-air signals were available in all geographic areas served by that system. The three signals did not have to be the same ones for all parts of the cable system's service area. A presumption of availability was created if the station's predicted coverage met a certain minimum standard or the station was "significantly viewed" in that community. However, the presumption could be rebutted by actual engineering data. Cable Communications Policy Act Rules (Signal Availability Standard), 3 F.C.C.Rcd. 2617, 64 R.R.2d 1276 (1988).

Three years later, the Commission revisited this area and concluded that in at least some cases cable rates had increased unreasonably. Under the three-signal definition of effective competition, less than four percent of all cable systems were subject to rate regulation. The FCC decided, therefore, to change the definition once again. Under the new definition a cable system was subject to effective competition if (1) six unduplicated over-the air broadcast signals were available in the entire cable community or (2) an independently owned, competing multichannel video service was available to at least 50 percent of the homes and subscribed to by at least 10 percent of the homes passed by the cable system. Effective Competition, 6 F.C.C.Rcd. 4545, 69 R.R.2d 671 (1991).

One of the driving forces behind the 1992 Cable Act was a perception that cable rates had increased to unreasonable levels. Even after the Commission narrowed its definition of effective competition, only a small percentage of cable systems were subject to rate regulation and even then the only rates regulated were those for basic cable service. The 1992 Act made several major changes in the area of rate regulation. As was the case prior to the 1992 Act, rate regulation is precluded for cable systems subject to effective competition. However, the 1992 Act set out the following requirements for effective competition. Either "fewer than 30 percent of the households in the franchise area subscribe to the cable service of a cable system," or the franchise area must be served by at least two "unaffiliated multichannel video programmers" offering comparable video programming to at least half of the households in that area and at least 15 percent of the households in the franchise area must subscribe to programming services offered by "multichannel video programming distributors other than the largest multichannel video programming distributors," or at least 50 percent of the households in the area must be served by a multichannel video programming distributor operated by the franchising authority for that area.

The following excerpt from Time Warner Entertainment v. Federal Communications Commission, 56 F.3d 151, 78 R.R.2d 1 (D.C.Cir.1995), certiorari denied, 516 U.S. 1112, 116 S.Ct. 911, 133 L.Ed.2d 842 (1996). Explains the rate regulation structure set by the 1992 Act.

> The Act divides the cable services of a system that is subject to rate regulation into three categories: (1) the basic service tier; (2) cable programming service; and (3) video programming offered on a per channel or per program basis, which alone is not subject to rate regulation. 47 U.S.C. §§ 543(a)(1), (l)(2). The basic service tier includes local broadcast channels; those non-commercial public, educational, and government-access channels that the cable system is required by its franchise to carry; and such additional channels as the cable operator may in its discretion include in this tier. 47 U.S.C. § 543(b)(7). The Act provides that a cable subscriber must purchase the basic service tier in order to gain access to other service tiers, 47 U.S.C. § 543(b)(7), and instructs the Commission to establish regulations that "ensure that the rates for the basic service tier are reasonable" and are "designed to achieve the goal of protecting subscribers . . . from rates . . . that exceed the rates that would be charged for the basic service tier if such cable system were subject to effective competition." 47 U.S.C. § 543(b)(1). Each local franchising authority that has been certified by the FCC may enforce the FCC's basic service tier rate regulations within its franchise area. 47 U.S.C. §§ 543(a)(2)-(6).

> Cable programming service includes all cable channels that are neither part of the cable system's basic tier offering nor offered on a per channel or per program basis. 47 U.S.C. § 543(l)(2). The Act charges the Commission (rather than local franchising authorities) with enforcement of the rate regulations for cable programming service, 47 U.S.C. § 543(a)(2)(B); the Commission must establish criteria to identify and create procedures for lowering any "unreasonable" rate for cable programming service. 47 U.S.C. § 543(c)(1). FCC review of rates for cable programming service is triggered on a case-by-case basis when a subscriber, franchising authority, or other relevant State or local governmental entity files a complaint. 47 U.S.C. §§ 543(c)(1)(B), (c)(3).

The Commission created further incentives for cable operators to add new channels in Implementation of Sections of the Cable Television Consumer Protection and Competition Act of 1992: Rate Regulation, Sixth Order on Reconsideration, Fifth Report and Order and Seventh Notice of Proposed Rulemaking, 10 F.C.C.Rcd. 1226, 76 R.R.2d 859 (1994). Operators are allowed to increase rates by a fixed amount per month per channel as an alternative to a percentage mark-up. This is intended to be an incentive to add inexpensive or cost-free channels.

Operators can also add "new product tiers" beyond the currently existing basic and non-basic tiers for which they can charge any rate providing existing service is not fundamentally changed and subscribers affirmatively request a new tier.

When thousands of rate complaints were filed, the Commission was faced with a huge backlog. To quickly reduce this backlog the FCC decided to attempt reaching comprehensive settlements with each of the major MSOs. The first of these "social contracts" was negotiated with Continental Cablevision.

The Commission gave three reasons for negotiating this agreement: "(1) assuring fair and reasonable rates for Continental's cable service customers; (2) improving Continental's cable service by substantially upgrading the channel capacity and technical reliability of its United States cable systems; and (3) reducing the administrative burden and costs of regulation for local governments, the Federal Communications Commission ('Commission'), and Continental." Social Contract for Continental Cablevision, 10 F.C.C.Rcd. 5668 (1995).

The following are the major provisions of this agreement as summarized by the Commission:

> The resolution of 148 cost-of-service cases and 229 benchmark cases . . . filed between September 1, 1993 and the Publication Date.

> As part of the resolution of these cost-of-service and benchmark cases, Continental will make in-kind refunds to its affected customers totalling approximately $9.5 million.

> The rates for BST cost-of-service cases resolved pursuant to this Contract will be reduced as necessary from their current levels, which Continental submitted under cost-of-service principles, to levels calculated pursuant to Commission Form 1200. Future BST increases for these franchises will be based solely on inflation and external cost increases, as permitted by 47 C.F.R. § 76.922(d), including all subsequent clarifications and amendments.

> [Local Franchising Authorities (LFAs)] will have the ability to "opt out" of BST cost-of-service Refunds and elect to resolve any amounts owed to customers with Continental pursuant to Commission rules. Also, BST benchmark cases currently pending before LFAs will be resolved by Continental and the LFAs pursuant to Commission rules.

> Continental will convert its existing BSTs in all franchises into "Lifeline Basic" tiers so that customers who only can afford or who only want the most basic local programming may purchase it for a low monthly fee. To accomplish this, Continental will reduce its BST rates for all *regulated* franchises to 15% below the rates required by Commission Form 1200 and will reduce its BST rates for all *unregulated* franchises to 15% below Current Rates.

Continental will forego its right to use cost-of-service justifications to support any future rate increases in any franchises covered by this Contract during the period that the Contract remains in effect.

On a going-forward basis, Continental's BST and CPST rates for all subscribers will be limited by the Commission's rules for inflation and external cost adjustments and by the "Going–Forward" rules. In order to fund the six-year capital spending program required as part of this Contract, Continental will be permitted to conduct a second round of "Going–Forward" channel additions over the three-year period from 1998–2000.

Continental will be permitted to migrate up to four existing CPST services on each system to a single "Migrated Product Tier" ("MPT"), provided the tier is offered without a buy-through requirement of any tier other than the BST. Initially, the MPT will be capped at current CPST levels for the migrated channels on the tier, and increases will be based on inflation and external costs, pursuant to Commission rules. However, there will be no limitation on the number of new channels that Continental may add to this tier at the price of $.20 per channel plus license fees. After January 1, 1997, Continental may convert the MPT into a New Product Tier ("NPT"), provided the tier is offered without a buy-through requirement of any tier other than the BST.

Continental agrees to spend at least $1.35 billion from 1995 through 2000 to rebuild and upgrade its domestic cable facilities. This represents an annual investment that is 120% of Continental's average annual capital expenditures from 1990 through 1994.

This Contract or any settlement contained herein does not constitute an admission by Continental of any violation of, or failure to conform to, any law, rule, or policy.

After soliciting comments on this proposal, the FCC decided to finalize the contract. Social Contract for Continental Cablevision, 11 F.C.C.Rcd. 299, 1 C.R.2d 895 (1995). Similar contracts with Time Warner, Cox Communications and Times–Mirror were negotiated. Social Contract for Time Warner Cable, 11 F.C.C.Rcd. 2788, 1 C.R. 1170 (1995); Cox Communications, Inc. and Times–Mirror Cable Television, Inc., 11 F.C.C.Rcd. 1972, 2 C.R. 294 (1995).

Even with the increase in the benchmark rate from 10 to 17 percent, rate regulation did not seem to have the desired effect on cable rates. Thus, less than four years after passing the 1992 Act, Congress changed course dramatically. The 1996 Telecommunications Act terminated CPST rate regulation as of March 31, 1999. 47 U.S.C.A. § 543(c)(4). In addition, the Commission was only required to respond to CPST rate complaints filed by franchising authorities. Previously, a complaint by even one subscriber required the FCC review.

The 1996 Act also changed the definition of effective competition. Remember that systems facing effective competition are not subject to either BST or CPST rate regulation. The following alternative was added to the definition:

> (D) a local exchange carrier or its affiliate (or any multichannel video programming distributor using the facilities of such carrier or its affiliate) offers video programming services directly to subscribers by any means (other than direct-to-home satellite services) in the franchise area of an unaffiliated cable operator which is providing cable service in that franchise area, but only if the video programming services so offered in that area are comparable to the video programming services provided by the unaffiliated cable operator in that area. 47 U.S.C.A. § 543 (1)(1)(D).

This section was necessitated by the 1996 Act's provisions permitting phone companies to offer cable service. We will discuss this in more detail in Chapter XII. Note that "by any means" includes a phone company delivering programming by cable, MMDS (discussed in Chapter X) and OVS (discussed in Chapter XII).

The 1996 Act also made several other changes regarding rate regulation. Small cable operators, defined as serving less than one percent of all subscribers in the country and not affiliated with any company that has gross annual revenues in excess of $250 million, are not subject to CPST rate regulation in franchise areas with 50,000 or fewer subscribers. Those that offered only BST as of Dec. 31, 1994, are not subject to any rate regulation.

Multiple dwelling units are no longer subject to the uniform pricing requirement unless the prices are shown to be "predatory." Programming offered on a per-channel or per-programming basis is also exempted from the uniform pricing requirement.

A new question facing the Commission is how digital television, p. 55, *supra*, will affect rate regulation. Specifically, to what tier would these channels be assigned? This could be very complicated because a single DTV channel could be used to broadcast multiple programs simultaneously. If some were subscription services and some were not, how would that decision be made?

In Carriage of Digital Television Broadcast Signals, 16 F.C.C.Rcd. 2598 (2001), discussed more extensively in the next chapter, the Commission addressed some of these questions. Digital broadcast signals must be available on the BST and subject to rate regulation under the jurisdiction of the local franchising authority. Cable systems subject to effective competition are not rate regulated and may place the digital signals on whatever tiers they wish.

The Commission also asked for further comment on how to treat systems offering an analog version a DTV channel on the BST, while offering the digital version on a separate tier:

We believe that it would facilitate the digital transition to permit cable operators that are carrying a broadcast station's analog signal on the basic tier to carry that broadcast station's digital signal on a digital tier pursuant to retransmission consent. We seek comment on permitting such carriage and whether it would encourage more cable operators to voluntarily carry a broadcaster's digital signal. . . . We also seek comment on limiting this approach to those situations in which the digital programming is a simulcast of the analog programming available on the basic tier.

E. MISCELLANEOUS RESTRICTIONS

1. CUSTOMER SERVICE STANDARDS

One of the most common complaints about cable television has been in the area of customer service. The 1992 Act gives franchising authorities the right to establish and enforce customer service requirements. Furthermore, the FCC was directed to established standards for customer service requirements. These standards had to include: "(1) cable system office hours and telephone availability; (2) installations, outages, and service calls; and (3) communications between the cable operator and the subscriber (including standards governing bills and refunds)." 47 U.S.C.A. § 552.

Pursuant to this section of the Act, the FCC adopted an extensive set of customer service standards. Cable Television Customer Service Standards, 72 R.R.2d 477 (1993). Local franchise authorities must determine the manner in which these standards, which became effective July 1, 1993, are to be enforced. At least 90 days prior to beginning enforcement, a franchising authority must give a cable operator written notification of its intent to do so.

> To the extent that existing franchise agreements may prohibit franchise authority enforcement of customer service standards, such provisions are preempted by the Federal statute. A franchise authority that chooses to enforce the FCC standards . . . may unilaterally modify the franchise agreement to the extent necessary or desirable to implement local enforcement of the FCC's customer service requirements. Of course, franchise authorities may also enforce service requirements either pursuant to the terms of an existing franchise agreement which provide for effective enforcement; with the consent of the affected cable operator; pursuant to applicable State or municipal consumer protection or consumer service law or regulation; or pursuant to the franchising process.

Under normal operating conditions, the following service requirements must be met at least 95 percent of the time.

A. Standard installations will be performed within seven business days after an order has been placed. . . .

B. Excluding conditions beyond the control of the operator, the cable operator will begin working on "service interruptions" promptly and in no event later than 24 hours after the interruption becomes known. The cable operator must begin actions to correct other service problems the next business day after notification of the service problem.

C. The "appointment window" alternatives for installations, service calls, and other installation activities will be either a specific time or, at maximum, a four hour time block during normal business hours. . . .

D. An operator may not cancel an appointment with a customer after the close of business on the business day prior to the scheduled appointment.

E. If a cable operator representative is running late for an appointment with a customer and will not be able to keep the appointment as scheduled, the customer will be contacted. . . .

Normal operating conditions includes "those service conditions which are within the control of the cable operator." A service interruption is defined as the "loss of picture or sound on one or more channels."

Cable operators are also required to "maintain a local, toll-free or collect call telephone access line which will be available 24 hours a day, seven days a week." Outside of normal business hours the line can be answered by a service or answering machine. "Under normal operating conditions, telephone answer time by a customer representative, including wait time, shall not exceed 30 seconds from when the connection is made. If the call needs to be transferred, transfer time shall not exceed 30 seconds. . . . Under normal operating conditions, the caller will receive a busy signal less than three percent of the time."

"Normal business hours" means "those hours during which most similar business in the community are open to serve customers." It must include "evening hours at least one night per week and/or some weekend hours."

Finally, cable operators must provide written information on products, services, prices, options, installation, maintenance, channel positions, and billing and complaint procedures, at the time of installation, annually and upon request. Cable operators must also provide 30–days-advance notice of changes in any of the above.

2. EQUIPMENT COMPATIBILITY

Many cable systems use scrambling or encryption systems and devices such as converter boxes and remote control devices that effectively disable advanced features built into television receivers and videocassette recorders. For example, when a cable system uses a converter box to decode some or all channels, channel selection must be made through the converter. Whatever channel is selected will be delivered to the television and/or VCR on a single specified channel (usually either channel three or four). Because the channel selection uses the converter's tuner as opposed to the television or VCR's tuner, features that utilize those tuners are rendered unusable. Among these are the ability to watch one channel while recording another or to record two consecutive programs that appear on different channels.

The 1992 Act required the Commission to submit to Congress a report on "means of assuring compatibility between televisions and video cassette recorders and cable systems, consistent with the need to prevent theft of cable service," and then to promulgate regulations to assure such compatibility.

In 1994 the Commission issued regulations designed to "assure improved compatibility between existing cable system and consumer TV equipment." They require cable operators to:

1) refrain from scrambling program signals carried on the basic tier of service.

2) offer subscribers supplemental equipment to enable them to use the special features and functions of their TV equipment with cable service; this includes providing subscribers the option of having simultaneous access to all signals that do not need to be processed by a set-top device;

3) provide a consumer education program to inform subscribers of potential compatibility problems; this includes notice that remote controls and supplemental equipment compatible with the set-top devices used by the cable system are available from third-party vendors and;

4) allow set-top devices that incorporate remote control capability to be operated with subscriber-owned remote controls or otherwise take no action that would prevent the use of such remote controls, including changing the infrared codes used to operate the remote control capabilities of the set-top devices they employ so as to adversely affect the operation of consumer-purchased remote controls.

To achieve "more effective compatibility through new cable and consumer equipment," the rules require "cable ready" consumer TV equipment and cable systems to use a standard channel plan. Cable System–Consumer Equipment Compatibility, 9 F.C.C.Rcd. 1981, 75 R.R.2d 152 (1994).

The FCC also concluded that use of a standard interface connector, or "Decoder Interface," in "consumer TV equipment and associated component descrambler/decoder devices to be provided by cable systems" will increase compatibility and eliminate the need for a set-top box. However, noting that the cable and consumer electronics industries were close to agreement on a Decoder Interface standard, the FCC decided not to impose one at that time.

Here, once again, Congress changed direction in the 1996 Telecommunications Act, relying more on competition and less on regulation. The Commission is now required, in prescribing regulations ensuring equipment compatibility, to consider "the need to maximize open competition in the market for all features, functions, protocols, and other product and service options of converter boxes and other cable converters unrelated to the descrambling or decryption of cable television signals." 47 U.S.C.A. § 624(A)(c)(1)(A). Congress also added a finding that "compatibility among televisions, video cassette recorders, and cable systems can be assured with narrow technical standards that mandate a minimum degree of common design and operation, leaving all features, functions, protocols, and other product and service options for selection through open competition in the market." 47 U.S.C.A. § 624(A)(a)(4). How do the rules already issued by the Commission comport with these new requirements?

The development of DTV is raising an entire new set of compatibility issues. Although the cable industry is moving to digital set-top boxes, many systems have yet to make the conversion. In addition, not all digital set-top boxes are compatible with DTV. Some won't work with any form of DTV. Others will work with some forms but not others.

Because digital television sets are in the early stages of design and manufacture, and because there are no FCC standards for DTV sets, it is not even clear what capabilities digital set-top boxes would need. How much signal processing the boxes will have to perform will affect not only the design but the cost. The FCC has asked for public comment on these issues. Carriage of the Transmissions of Digital Television Broadcast Stations, 13 F.C.C.Rcd. 15092 (1998).

Section 629 of the 1996 Act was designed to allow a competitive market for set-top boxes to develop by directing the Commission to issue regulations "to assure the commercial availability, to consumers of multichannel video programming . . . of converter boxes, interactive communications equipment, and other equipment used by consumers to access multichannel video programming . . . from manufacturers, retailers, and other vendors not affiliated with any multichannel video programming distributor." At the same time Congress directed that these regulations should not "jeopardize security of multichannel video programming . . ., or impede the legal rights of a provider of such services to prevent theft of service."

Pursuant to § 629, the FCC adopted regulations requiring cable companies to separate set-top boxes into two components. "One part would contain the operational and functional components such as the tuner, the remote control circuitry, the power supply, and any other non-access control features. A second part would contain the access control features." The former could be sold at retail, while the latter stay within the exclusive control of the cable operators.

In addition, the Commission ordered cable operators to cease providing integrated boxes (ones containing both components) as of January 1,

2005. Operators would, however, be permitted to offer operational and control boxes in competition with retail stores. The majority argued that integrated boxes, which no other seller could offer, would give cable operators an unfair advantage and prevent the open market contemplated by the statute from developing. Commissioner Powell dissented on this point. He thought "that efficiencies might well accompany the integration of security and ancillary functions in a single device, and that the Commission's ban might 'den[y] a cost effective choice for consumers.'"

On reconsideration, noting the cable industry was rapidly moving from analog to digital delivery, the FCC limited the regulations to digital and hybrid (single devices capable of converting both analog and digital singles) set-top boxes. The revised regulations were affirmed on appeal. General Instrument Corporation v. Federal Communications Commission, 213 F.3d 724, 20 C.R. 870 (D.C.Cir.2000).

In *Carriage of Digital Television Broadcast Signals*, p. 445, *supra*, the Commission addressed the effect of DTV on set-top box rules:

77. In the [*NPRM*], we observed that the Act mandates that all commercial television signals shall be provided to every subscriber of a cable system and be viewable on all television receivers of subscribers that are connected by the cable operator or for which the cable operator provides a connection. In general, most cable subscribers are able to view analog broadcast stations on analog cable-ready television sets. In the case of the new digital television service, the Commission has recently adopted labeling requirements for digital television receivers. Based on an industry agreement on technical standards, any receiver labeled as "Digital Cable Ready" will be "capable of receiving analog basic, digital basic, and digital premium cable television programming by direct connection to a cable system providing digital programming. . . . A security card (or POD) provided by the cable operator is required to view encrypted programming." . . . In the case of digital television receivers that do not meet the digital cable ready criteria, a subscriber may need a set top box to view broadcast digital signals delivered via cable.

. . .

79. We will not require a cable operator to provide subscribers with a set top box capable of processing digital signals for display on analog sets. We recognize that if we were to impose such a requirement, all subscribers would be forced to pay for equipment that converts digital programming that may be identical in content to the analog programming to which they already have access without a set top box. The result would be that subscribers without the capability of viewing digital signals and who will receive duplicate analog programming when the Commission's simulcasting requirements commence in 2003, would be required to pay for a converter box to receive duplicate digital signals. We do not believe that this result is what Congress intended in enacting section 614(b)(7).

Chapter IX

CONTENT REGULATION OF CABLE TELEVISION

Because of the early view that cable television was merely an enhancement of broadcast television, many of the same restrictions on content that were developed for broadcasting are applicable to cable. At the same time there are very few cases involving these restrictions.

Many of the political access rules have also been applied to origination cablecasting. The equal opportunities provision applicable to cable is essentially identical to that which governs broadcasting. There is also an equivalent lowest-unit-rate provision. 47 C.F.R. § 76.205.

There were also regulations applying the fairness doctrine, including the personal attack and political editorial rules, to origination cablecasting. 47 C.F.R. § 76.209. In 1983 the Commission instituted proceedings aimed at eliminating the fairness doctrine for cable. However, no action was ever taken in these proceedings.

One political access provision that is not applicable to cable is the reasonable access requirement of § 312(a)(7). In its 1991 political access NPRM, p. 179, *supra*, the FCC proposed extending that requirement to cable. In its final order, however, the Commission concluded that Congress never intended § 312(a)(7) to apply to cable.

Because the cable operators are not responsible under these rules for secondary transmissions or mandated access channels, and because many of the premium cable channels do not carry any political programming, there have been no real tests of the application of the rules. Also contributing to the lack of cases is the limited size of the audience for many cable programs.

Among the restrictions on nonpolitical speech are a prohibition on cablecasting lottery information and a requirement for sponsorship identification. These provisions mirror the broadcasting rules. Also, the ban on cigarette advertising applies to cable.

In addition to these, however, there are other content rules that are either peculiar to cable or have developed in a fashion markedly different than the broadcast versions. We turn now to these.

A. COPYRIGHT PROBLEMS

One of the major factors that has influenced the Commission in its decisions governing signal carriage has been the application of copyright law to the retransmission of broadcast signals by cable operators. The question has always been whether or not cable operators should have to compensate either the broadcasters or the program producers for retransmission and, if so, how the compensation should be determined.

The issue first reached the Supreme Court in Fortnightly Corp. v. United Artists Television, Inc., 392 U.S. 390, 13 R.R.2d 2061 (1968). The case involved a West Virginia cable operator who was retransmitting the signals of five broadcast television stations. The stations were all located between 50 and 85 miles from the cable system. Fortnightly provided no other service.

United Artists, which owned the copyright to various shows that were aired over the five broadcast stations, claimed that the retransmission constituted infringement of its copyrights. The Court held that retransmission was not a "performance," and thus, there was no infringement. The Court was unable to find a real distinction between a viewer's antenna system and the cable company's equipment. Both were designed to improve reception of the broadcast signals.

When cable systems started using microwaves to import signals from around the country, there was some question whether this would change the copyright issue. The Supreme Court decided that the fact that there was no way a non-cable subscriber could receive these signals using existing technology did not make a difference. "When a television broadcaster transmits a program, it has made public for simultaneous viewing and hearing the contents of that program. The privilege of receiving the broadcast electronic signals and of converting them into the sights and sounds of the program inheres in all members of the public who have the means of doing so. The reception and rechanneling of these signals for simultaneous viewing is essentially a viewer function, irrespective of the distance between the broadcast station and the ultimate viewer." Teleprompter Corporation v. Columbia Broadcasting System, Inc., 415 U.S. 394, 29 R.R.2d 1011 (1974).

These copyright rulings greatly increased the importance to local broadcasters of the FCC signal carriage rules. The increased coverage afforded the imported signals was of minimal value to them, because their local advertisers had little or no interest in reaching consumers in other parts of the country. Meanwhile, the imported signals fragmented the local audiences, reducing the number of viewers they could offer to local advertisers.

There also was an apparent inequity in the system. Broadcasters had to pay royalties or license fees for much of their programming. Cable operators were paying nothing to distribute the exact same programming and were collecting a fee for doing so. The Copyright Act of 1976 attempted to remedy this seemingly unfair situation.

In the 1976 copyright statute, retransmission of broadcast signals by cable systems is defined as copyright infringement. However, the simultaneous retransmission, "secondary transmission," of broadcast signals is governed by a complex compulsory licensing scheme. Section 111 provides, in effect, that cablecasters need pay no royalties for programs on "local" (or "must-carry") stations that they are required to carry. (We will discuss the must-carry rules later in this chapter.) Cablecasters are permitted to carry the copyrighted programs of "distant" (or "may-carry") stations without the owner's consent in return for the payment of a compulsory royalty fee. This fee is fixed by statute and depends on the size of the cable system and whether the distant station is commercial or educational.

The Act represented a compromise between the interests of broadcasters and cable operators. Although cable operators now had to pay for the right to retransmit broadcast programming, broadcasters were still unable to withhold the right to carry the programming.

Because of this inability to refuse transmission consent, certain stations found themselves unwilling superstations. As previously noted, the added audience resulting from the cable distribution is of little value to the broadcaster. The only way to benefit is to sell to national advertisers as opposed to local or regional advertisers. Meanwhile, there are several disadvantages to being a superstation, although Turner, for one, found them outweighed by the advantages. Program acquisition costs increase as a result of the increased audience. In addition, certain sports programming is unavailable because the importation of that programming into other areas of the country would violate agreements between the syndicator and the league or conference. For example, WTBS was unable to carry baseball playoff games involving the Atlanta Braves, even though the station that carries a team during the regular season is normally entitled to carry that team's playoff games. Importation of the games on WTBS into other markets would have conflicted with an agreement between the networks and professional baseball giving the networks exclusivity outside the markets of the teams participating in the playoffs.

A second controversy involves distribution of the royalties collected each year. Demands from the various claimants, such as program producers and syndicators, sports leagues, music groups, broadcast licensees themselves, and others, greatly exceed 100 percent. In 1980 the Copyright Royalty Tribunal (CRT) allocated the 1978 revenues, giving 75 percent to program producers and syndicators, and 3.25 percent to commercial television broadcasters. This means that total copyright payments to all commercial television for programs carried during 1978 by cable systems amounted to $476,000.

The enactment of the Copyright Act of 1976 was soon followed by a change in the Commission's attitude toward cable. In 1980 the FCC repealed the distant signal limitations, p. 417, *supra*, and syndicated program exclusivity rule. We will discuss the syndicated exclusivity rule in Chapter XI. The Commission argued that there was no real evidence that repeal of the rules would seriously harm broadcasters. Furthermore, the new copyright act now provided compensation for the retransmission of those programs. Finally, with regard to syndicated program exclusivity, the viewers' interest in "time-diversity"—seeing programs when they wanted—was more compelling than the local station's interest in the exclusive programming. Deletion of the old rule would not reduce the supply of programs for television. The deletion of the rules was upheld in

Malrite T.V. of New York v. Federal Communications Commission, 652 F.2d 1140 (2d Cir.1981), certiorari denied 454 U.S. 1143 (1982).

As a result of the FCC's repeal of the distant signal rules, the Tribunal raised the rates cable operators had to pay for distant signals. Large cable systems became liable for a compulsory license fee of 3.75 percent of their basic revenues for each distant signal added since June 24, 1981, the date on which the repeal of the distant signal rules became effective. This increase was upheld in National Cable Television Association, Inc. v. Copyright Royalty Tribunal, 724 F.2d 176, 55 R.R.2d 387 (D.C.Cir.1983). In response, some cable operators dropped distant signals to reduce their copyright liability. Superstations were the major casualties.

Because of these changes, fee distribution also became more complicated. There were now three funds at stake: the basic royalties, the 3.75 percent fund which contains the fees for distant signals added after June 24, 1981, and the syndex fund which contains a surcharge adopted as a result of the repeal of the syndicated program exclusivity rules.

However, broadcasters continued to receive a very small portion of the fees. For example, when the CRT issued distributed the approximately $100 million in 1984 cable television royalties, the NAB received 5 percent of the "basic" fund and the "3.75" fund, but only 0.7 percent of the "syndex" fund. The distribution of the 1985 funds was settled with the claimants' receiving the same percentages as were awarded in 1984.

As a result of the FCC's adoption of new syndication exclusivity rules, p. 777, *infra*, the CRT drastically reduced the application of the syndex surcharge. Essentially, it applies only to retransmission of stations that were covered by the old rules but not the new ones.

Broadcasters continued to maintain that cable's contribution to the fund was tiny when compared with the fact that commercial television broadcasters spend some 35 percent of their budgets on program acquisition. Cable operators claimed the fees were prohibitive. Meanwhile, the FCC asserted that any economic problem for the broadcasters derived from the Copyright Act or the Tribunal's allocation—and relief had to come from those sources.

For years, the compulsory license and royalty provision was under attack in Congress. The decisions in *Quincy Cable* and *Century Communications* (to be discussed later in this chapter) only intensified the pressure. The problem was that the 1976 Act did not contemplate the changes in FCC rules that permitted the growth of superstations and increased carriage of distant signals. The result was that an increasing amount of cable programming was coming from distant sources, leaving the program suppliers with less control over geographical distribution of their products. Complaints were also heard from major sports leagues because, for example, an Atlanta baseball game could be shown on a Boston area cable system at the same time another game was being played in Boston. In 1985 the Atlanta Braves and New York Yankees agreed to pay the other major league teams a special annual fee based on the subscriber base of the superstations that carry their games. The other teams whose games were carried by superstations followed suit.

The National Basketball Association tried a different approach to this problem by limiting to 20 the number of games allowed on a local signal received by more than five percent of the cable subscribers located outside the team's local market. Superstation WGN, which had already contracted to carry more than 20 games, successfully sued the NBA, claiming the rule was an unreasonable restraint of trade in violation of antitrust law. Chicago Professional Sports Limited Partnership v. National Basketball Association, 961 F.2d 667 (7th Cir.), certiorari denied 506 U.S. 954 (1992).

Broadcasters continued to argue that the compulsory license should be abolished and replaced by a negotiated agreement between the cable system and the originating broadcaster (who, under contract, would need the consent of the copyright owner). This need not lead to individual negotiations—the matter could be handled the way song writers grant licenses and collect royalties, through such groups as ASCAP and BMI that grant bulk licenses for a fee and then distribute the proceeds according to a formula.

When the must-carry rules were first struck down in *Quincy Cable*, discussed later in this chapter, the Commission suggested that Congress consider eliminating the compulsory license for cable retransmission. In conjunction with that suggestion, the Commission issued a Notice of Inquiry aimed at developing a record on the effects of the compulsory license. Compulsory Copyright License for Cable Retransmission, 2 F.C.C.Rcd. 2387 (1987).

Following the inquiry, the Commission voted to recommend to Congress that the compulsory copyright license for cable retransmission of broadcast signals be eliminated. Chairman Dennis Patrick and Patricia Diaz Dennis voted to recommend elimination for both local and distant signals, while James Quello dissented with regard to local signals. Recall that at this time the Commission was operating with only three members. Compulsory Copyright License for Cable Retransmission, 4 F.C.C.Rcd. 6711, 66 R.R.2d 1259 (1989).

Although efforts to abolish the compulsory license have been unsuccessful, broadcasters scored a partial victory with the retransmission consent option for local signals contained in the 1992 Cable Act. We will address that option in conjunction with our discussion of the must-carry rules.

The Unaltered Transmission Requirement. One of the requirements for coverage by the compulsory copyright license for secondary transmissions is that the signal be transmitted unaltered. In 1985 the court of appeals upheld a ruling that Ted Turner's practice of substituting national commercials for local ones, p. 415, *supra*, did not cause Southern Satellite Systems, Inc. (SSS) to forfeit the compulsory license. The court held that Turner's microwave feed to SSS, which already contained the national commercials, was a primary transmission. Because SSS transmitted this signal unaltered, it was covered by the compulsory license. Hubbard Broadcasting, Inc. v. Southern Satellite Systems, Inc., 777 F.2d 393, 59 R.R.2d 392 (8th Cir.1985), certiorari denied 479 U.S. 1005 (1986).

B. MUST–CARRY RULES

As discussed in the previous chapter, all of the major challenges to the Commission's jurisdiction over cable prior to the 1984 Cable Act resulted from the Commission's various signal carriage rules. Each of these rules was designed to protect local broadcasting from cable competition. The rules were divided into two categories: rules limiting the programming cable systems could carry (the "may-carry" rules) and rules requiring cable systems to carry local broadcasters' signals (the "must-carry" rules). Although both were designed to prevent cable from unfairly competing with broadcasting, the must-carry rules arguably, at least, are content-based rules. We will therefore discuss them in this chapter, while leaving the discussion of the may-carry rules to Chapter XI.

One of the earliest signal carriage rules, the must-carry rules originally required cable systems to retransmit the signal of any local television station or "significantly viewed" station that requested carriage. Cable systems were allowed to request a waiver of the rule where it created hardship, but the process was a slow one, and few waivers were granted. The rules imposed a special hardship on the smaller systems as most of the channels could be occupied by must-carry channels. Because of overlapping signals, some systems were forced to carry several affiliates of the same network or similarly duplicative stations to the exclusion of other non-duplicative services.

The purpose was to protect local broadcasters, especially UHF stations, whose picture quality was noticeably inferior to that provided by cable. There was also concern that people would remove their television antennas upon subscribing to cable, or at the least fail to maintain them, putting broadcasters not carried by the cable system at a great competitive disadvantage.

After the compulsory license scheme was enacted in the Copyright Act of 1976, many believed that it was a trade-off for the must-carry rules. Although the legislative history on this issue is inconclusive, many cable operators were reluctant to challenge the must-carry rules for fear of losing the compulsory license.

However, in 1980 Turner Broadcasting System (TBS) petitioned the Commission to institute rulemaking proceedings to delete the must-carry rules. TBS argued that the rules violated the First Amendment rights of cable operators and furthermore, that, at the least, extensive changes in the broadcast and cable industries since the promulgation of the rules required a re-examination of the rules. The Commission denied the TBS petition.

Meanwhile, the FCC ordered Quincy Cable Television, Inc., operator of a cable system in Quincy, Wash., to carry the signals of various Spokane, Wash., television stations and fined it $5,000 for failing to do so. Quincy Cable's appeal of the order and the fine was consolidated with TBS's appeal.

In Quincy Cable TV, Inc. v. Federal Communications Commission, 768 F.2d 1434, 58 R.R.2d 977 (D.C.Cir.1985), the court concluded that the must-carry rules, as drafted, violated the First Amendment.

The court thought that the Commission's rules created "undifferentiated protectionism." The Commission had failed in its attempt to strike a balance between the competing interests of controlling a new technology that allegedly threatened long-established values, such as serving community needs through a locally-oriented press, and the regulatory throttling of the number and variety of outlets for free expression. Because the rules failed under the *O'Brien* test, p. 21, *supra*, the court found it unnecessary to determine if a higher level of scrutiny was required.

Under pressure from Congress, the Commission drafted a new set of must-carry rules. A First Amendment challenge to the revised rules quickly followed. Century Communications Corporation v. Federal Communications Commission, 835 F.2d 292, 64 R.R.2d 113 (D.C.Cir.1987).

Along with the new rules the FCC had asserted a new rationale for them. The new rationale was based on an inexpensive piece of equipment called an A–B switch. Using this device a viewer can switch back and forth between a TV antenna and a cable feed, by merely flipping the switch. The Commission argued that, because of the long history of must carry and the lack of information about A–B switches, it would take five years for viewers to become acclimated to these devises. The must-carry rules were therefore necessary for this five-year transition period.

The rules themselves were less sweeping than the original ones struck down in *Quincy*.

> . . . [The Commission] set forth limits on how many channels a cable carrier must devote to must-carry: carriers with 20 channels or less were not required to carry any must-carry stations; carriers with between 21 and 26 stations could be required to carry up to 7 channels of must-carry stations; and carriers with 27 or more channels could be required to devote up to 25% of their system to must-carry signals. [ ] It also limited the pool of potential must-carry channels to those satisfying a "viewing standard" generally demonstrating a minimum viewership of the channel in question. . . . The Commission also authorized cable operators to refuse to carry more than one station affiliated with the same commercial network. [ ] Finally, the Commission limited the number of non-commercial stations required to be carried, stating that when the

cable system had fewer than 54 channels and an eligible noncommercial station or translator existed, the cable operator must devote at least one channel to a noncommercial station; and that when the cable system had 54 or more stations, it must devote two must-carry channels to such endeavors.

The court of appeals again found it unnecessary to decide which level of First Amendment scrutiny was appropriate because the new rules also failed under the more relaxed *O'Brien* test. The court found that the FCC failed to offer sufficient evidence that absent must-carry rules cable systems would cease to carry large numbers of broadcast stations. Furthermore, even if this were true, there was no evidence to support the assertion that it would take five years for viewers to learn about A–B switches.

At this point the FCC chose not to attempt yet again to draft must-carry rules that would pass constitutional muster. Broadcasters then focused their lobbying efforts on Congress. These efforts were rewarded in the 1992 Cable Act.

The 1992 Act has two separate must-carry provisions. Section 614 sets out the must-carry rules for commercial television stations, while § 615 sets out the must-carry rules for noncommercial television stations. Under § 614 cable systems with 300 or fewer subscribers are exempt. Other cable systems with 12 or fewer channels must carry a minimum of three local broadcast signals. Systems with more than 12 channels must carry all local broadcast stations up to a maximum of one third of the total number of the system's channels. If the number of local commercial television stations exceeds the maximum number of must-carry signals, the cable operator is permitted to choose which stations will be carried subject to the following restrictions. First, no low-power station can be carried unless all local commercial stations are carried. Second, if a cable operator chooses to carry a broadcast network affiliate, the operator must carry the affiliate of that network that is closest to the principal headend of the cable system.

Notwithstanding these requirements, systems are not required to carry local commercial television stations that substantially duplicate the programming of another local commercial television station carried by the system.

The must-carry status of stations whose programming is predominately sales presentations or program-length commercials was left open pending a Commission determination of whether such stations are serving the public interest, convenience and necessity. The FCC subsequently ruled that such stations do serve the public interest, convenience and necessity, and designated them as local commercial stations for must-carry purposes. Home Shopping Station Issues, 8 F.C.C.Rcd. 5321 (1993).

Section 615 sets out the carriage requirements for qualified noncommercial educational television stations. Cable systems with 12 or fewer channels must carry one local noncommercial educational television station. Stations with 13 to 36 channels must carry all local noncommercial educational television stations up to a maximum of three. Systems with more than 36 channels must carry all local noncommercial educational television stations. In the event that there are no local noncommercial educational television stations, a cable system must import one noncommercial educational television station. These must carry requirements do not apply to stations whose signal is considered a distant signal for copyright purposes unless the station pays any increase in copyright costs attributable to the carriage of that station. 47 U.S.C.A. § 535.

The 1992 Act also created a new alternative to must carry that permits a commercial television station to waive its must-carry right in return for the right to require the station's consent before a cable system can carry its signal. In essence this requires each station to determine the value of its signal to nearby cable systems. The assumption was that the more attractive stations would choose retransmission consent in order to force cable systems to pay for the right to carry them. Lower-rated stations would be likely to opt for must carry. Every three years stations have the right to change their status. 47 U.S.C.A. § 325. We will discuss retransmission consent in greater detail later in this chapter.

In addition, every station carried under the provisions of § 614, must be carried on either the channel number on which the station is broadcast, "the channel on which it was carried on July 19, 1985, or on the channel on which it was carried on January 1, 1992, at the election of the station." Stations can be carried on other channels only with their consent. The Commission has been given the authority to resolve any channel positioning disputes. 47 U.S.C.A. § 534.

Not surprisingly, cable groups immediately challenged the new must-carry provisions.

TURNER BROADCASTING SYSTEM, INC. v. FEDERAL COMMUNICATIONS COMMISSION

Supreme Court of the United States, 1997.
520 U.S. 180, 117 S.Ct. 1174, 137 L.Ed.2d 369, 25 Med.L.Rptr. 1449.

JUSTICE KENNEDY delivered the opinion of the Court, except as to a portion of Part II–A–1.

. . .

I

. . . Soon after Congress enacted the [*1992 Cable Act*], appellants brought suit against the United States and the Federal Communications Commission (both referred to here as the Government) in the United States District Court for the District of Columbia, challenging the constitutionality of the must-carry provisions under the First Amendment. The three-judge District Court, in a divided opinion, granted summary judgment for the Government and intervenor-defendants. A majority of the court sustained the must-carry provisions under the intermediate standard of scrutiny set forth in [*O'Brien*, p. __, *supra*], concluding the must-carry provisions were content-neutral "industry-specific antitrust and fair trade" legislation narrowly tailored to preserve local broadcasting beset by monopoly power in most cable systems, growing concentration in the cable industry, and concomitant risks of programming decisions driven by anticompetitive policies. 819 F.Supp. 32, 40, 45–47 (DC 1993).

On appeal, we agreed with the District Court that must-carry does not "distinguish favored speech from disfavored speech on the basis of the ideas or views expressed," [ ], but is a content-neutral regulation designed "to prevent cable operators from exploiting their economic power to the detriment of broadcasters," and "to ensure that all Americans, especially those unable to subscribe to cable, have access to free television programming—whatever its content." [ ] We held that, under the intermediate level of scrutiny applicable to content-neutral regulations, must-carry would be sustained if it were shown to further an important or substantial governmental interest unrelated to the suppression of free speech, provided the incidental restrictions did not "burden substantially more speech than is necessary to further" those interests. [ ] Although we "ha[d] no difficulty concluding" the interests must-carry was designed to serve were important in the abstract, [ ], a four-Justice plurality concluded genuine issues of material fact remained regarding whether "the economic health of local broadcasting is in genuine jeopardy and need of the protections afforded by must-carry," and whether must-carry " 'burden[s] substantially more speech than is necessary to further the government's legitimate interests.' " [ ] Justice Stevens would have found the statute valid on the record then before us; he agreed to remand the case to ensure a judgment of the Court, and the case was returned to the District Court for further proceedings. [ ]

The District Court oversaw another 18 months of factual development on remand "yielding a record of tens of thousands of pages" of evidence, Turner Broadcasting v. FCC, 910 F.Supp. 734, 755 (DC 1995), comprised of materials acquired during Congress' three years of pre-enactment hearings, see *Turner*, [ ], as well as additional expert submissions, sworn declarations and testimony, and industry documents obtained on remand. Upon consideration of the expanded record, a divided panel of the District Court again granted summary judgment to appellees. [ ] The majority determined "Congress drew reasonable inferences" from substantial evidence before it to conclude that "in the absence of must-carry rules, 'significant' numbers of broadcast stations would be refused carriage." [ ] The court found Congress drew on studies and anecdotal evidence indicating "cable operators had already dropped, refused to carry, or adversely repositioned significant numbers of local broadcasters," and suggesting that in the vast majority of cases the broadcasters were not restored to carriage in their prior position. *Ibid*. Noting evidence in the record before Congress and the testimony of experts on remand, *id.*, at 743, the court decided the noncarriage problem would grow worse without must-carry because cable operators had refrained from dropping broadcast stations during Congress' investigation and the pendency of this litigation, [   ], and possessed increasing incentives to use their growing economic power to capture broadcasters' advertising revenues and promote affiliated cable programmers. [   ] The court concluded "substantial evidence before Congress" supported the predictive judgment that a local broadcaster denied carriage "would suffer financial harm and possible ruin." [   ] It cited evidence that adverse carriage actions decrease broadcasters' revenues by reducing audience levels, [   ], and evidence that the invalidation of the FCC's prior must-carry regulations had contributed to declining growth in the broadcast industry. [   ]

The court held must-carry to be narrowly tailored to promote the Government's legitimate interests. . . . Judge Jackson would have preferred a trial to summary judgment, but concurred in the judgment of the court. [   ]

Judge Williams dissented. His review of the record, and particularly evidence concerning growth in the number of broadcasters, industry advertising revenues, and per-station profits during the period without must-carry, led him to conclude the broadcast industry as a whole would not be " 'seriously jeopardized' " in the absence of must-carry. [   ] Judge Williams acknowledged the Government had a legitimate interest in preventing anticompetitive behavior, and accepted that cable operators have incentives to discriminate against broadcasters in favor of their own vertically integrated cable programming. [   ] He would have granted summary judgment for appellants nonetheless on the ground must-carry is not narrowly tailored. In his view, must-carry constitutes a significant (though "diminish[ing]," [   ]) burden on cable operators' and programmers' rights, [   ], and the Cable Act's must-carry provisions suppress more speech than necessary because "less-restrictive" alternatives exist to accomplish the Government's legitimate objectives. [   ]

This direct appeal followed. See 47 U.S.C. § 555(c)(1); 28 U.S.C. § 1253. We noted probable jurisdiction, 516 U.S. ___ (1996), and we now affirm.

II

We begin where the plurality ended in [*Turner I*], applying the standards for intermediate scrutiny enunciated in *O'Brien*. A content-neutral regulation will be sustained under the First Amendment if it advances important governmental interests unrelated to the suppression of free speech and does not burden substantially more speech than necessary to further those interests. *O'Brien*, [   ]. As noted in [*Turner I*], must-carry was designed to serve "three interrelated interests: (1) preserving the benefits of free, over-the-air local broadcast television, (2) promoting the widespread dissemination of information from a multiplicity of sources, and (3) promoting fair competition in the market for television programming." [   ] We decided then, and now reaffirm, that each of those is an important governmental interest. We have been most explicit in holding that " 'protecting noncable households from loss of regular television broadcasting service due to competition from cable systems' is an important federal interest." [ ] (quoting [*Capital Cities Cable*, p. 420, *supra*]). Forty percent of American households continue to rely on over-the-air signals for television programming. Despite the growing importance of cable television and alternative technologies, " 'broadcasting is demonstrably a principal source of information and entertainment for a great part of the Nation's population.' " [*Turner I*] (quoting [*Southwestern Cable Co.*, p. 417, *supra*]). We have identified a corresponding "governmental purpose of the highest order" in ensuring public access to "a multiplicity of information sources," [ ] And it is undisputed the Government has an interest in "eliminating restraints on fair competition . . ., even when the individuals or entities subject to particular regulations are engaged in expressive activity protected by the First Amendment." [ ]

On remand, and again before this Court, both sides have advanced new interpretations of these interests in an attempt to recast them in forms "more readily proven." 910 F.Supp., at 759 (Williams, J., dissenting). The Government downplays the importance of showing a risk to the broadcast industry as a whole and suggests the loss of even a few broadcast stations "is a matter of critical importance." [ ] Taking the opposite approach, appellants argue Congress' interest in preserving broadcasting is not implicated unless it is shown the industry as a whole would fail without must-carry, [ ], and suggest Congress' legitimate interest in "assuring that the public has access to a multiplicity of information sources," [*Turner I*], extends only as far as preserving "a minimum amount of television broadcast service." [ ]

These alternative formulations are inconsistent with Congress' stated interests in enacting must-carry. The congressional findings do not reflect concern that, absent must-carry, "a few voices," [ ], would be lost from the television marketplace. In explicit factual findings, Congress expressed clear concern that the "marked shift in market share from broadcast television to cable television services," Cable Act § 2(a)(13), note following 47 U.S.C. § 521, resulting from increasing market penetration by cable services, as well as the expanding horizontal concentration and vertical integration of cable operators, combined to give cable systems the incentive and ability to delete, reposition, or decline carriage to local broadcasters in an attempt to favor affiliated cable programmers. §§ 2a(2)-(5), (15). Congress predicted that "absent the reimposition of [must-carry], additional local broadcast signals will be deleted, repositioned, or not carried" (§ 2(a)(15); see also § 2(a)(8)(D)), with the end result that "the economic viability of free local broadcast television and its ability to originate quality local programming will be seriously jeopardized." § 2(a)(16).

At the same time, Congress was under no illusion that there would be a complete disappearance of broadcast television nationwide in the absence of must-carry. Congress recognized broadcast programming (and network programming in particular) "remains the most popular programming on cable systems," § 2(a)(19). Indeed, reflecting the popularity and strength of some broadcasters, Congress included in the Cable Act a provision permitting broadcasters to charge cable systems for carriage of the broadcasters' signals. See § 6, codified at 47 U.S.C. § 325. Congress was concerned not that broadcast television would disappear in its entirety without must-carry, but that without it, "significant numbers of broadcast stations will be refused carriage on cable systems," and those "broadcast stations denied carriage will either deteriorate to a substantial degree or fail altogether." . . .

Nor do the congressional findings support appellants' suggestion that legitimate legislative goals would be satisfied by the preservation of a rump broadcasting industry providing a minimum of broadcast service to Americans without cable. We have noted that " 'it has long been a basic tenet of national communications policy that the widest possible dissemination of information from diverse and antagonistic sources is essential to the welfare of the public.' " [*Turner I*] " '[I]ncreasing the number of outlets for community self-expression' " represents a " 'long-established regulatory goa[l] in the field of television broadcasting.' " [*Midwest Video I*, p. 418, *supra*]. Consistent with this objective, the Cable Act's findings reflect a concern that congressional action was necessary to prevent "a reduction in the number of media voices available to consumers." § 2(a)(4). Congress identified a specific interest in "ensuring [the] continuation" of "the local origination of [broadcast] programming," § 2(a)(10), an interest consistent with its larger purpose of promoting multiple types of media, § 2(a)(6), and found must-carry necessary "to serve the goals" of the original Communications Act of 1934 of "providing a fair, efficient, and equitable distribution of broadcast services" (§ 2(a)(9)). In short, Congress enacted must-carry to "preserve the existing structure of the Nation's broadcast television medium while permitting the concomitant expansion and development of cable television." [   ]

Although Congress set no definite number of broadcast stations sufficient for these purposes, the Cable Act's requirement that all cable operators with more than 12 channels set aside one-third of their channel capacity for local broadcasters, § 4, 47 U.S.C. § 534(b)(1)(B), refutes the notion that Congress contemplated preserving only a bare minimum of stations. Congress' evident interest in "preserv[ing] the existing structure," [   ], of the broadcast industry discloses a purpose to prevent any significant reduction in the multiplicity of broadcast programming sources available to noncable households. . . . It is for Congress to decide how much local broadcast television should be preserved for noncable households, and the validity of its determination" 'does not turn on a judge's agreement with the responsible decisionmaker concerning' . . . the degree to which [the Government's] interests should be promoted." [   ]

The dissent proceeds on the assumption that must-carry is designed solely to be (and can only be justified as) a measure to protect broadcasters from cable operators' anticompetitive behavior. [ ] Federal policy, however, has long favored preserving a multiplicity of broadcast outlets regardless of whether the conduct that threatens it is motivated by anticompetitive animus or rises to the level of an antitrust violation. See [*Capital Cities Cable*]; [*Midwest Video I*], (FCC regulations "were . . . avowedly designed to guard broadcast services from being undermined by unregulated [cable] growth"); [*NBC*, p. 72, *supra*] (" 'While many of the network practices raise serious questions under the antitrust laws, . . . [i]t is not [the FCC's] function to apply the antitrust laws as such' ") (quoting FCC Report on Chain Broadcasting Regulations (1941)). Broadcast television is an important source of information to many Americans. Though it is but one of many means for communication, by tradition and use for decades now it has been an essential part of the national discourse on subjects across the whole broad spectrum of speech, thought, and expression. [ ] Congress has an independent interest in preserving a multiplicity of broadcasters to ensure that all households have access to information and entertainment on an equal footing with those who subscribe to cable.

A

On our earlier review, we were constrained by the state of the record to assessing the importance of the Government's asserted interests when "viewed in the abstract," [*Turner I*]. The expanded record now permits us to consider whether the must-carry provisions were designed to address a real harm, and whether those provisions will alleviate it in a material way. [ ] We turn first to the harm or risk which prompted Congress to act. The Government's assertion that "the economic health of local broadcasting is in genuine jeopardy and in need of the protections afforded by must-carry," [ ], rests on two component propositions: First, "significant numbers of broadcast stations will be refused carriage on cable systems" absent must-carry, [ ]. Second, "the broadcast stations denied carriage will either deteriorate to a substantial degree or fail altogether." [ ]

In reviewing the constitutionality of a statute, "courts must accord substantial deference to the predictive judgments of Congress." [ ] Our sole obligation is "to assure that, in formulating its judgments, Congress has drawn reasonable inferences based on substantial evidence." [ ] As noted in the first appeal, substantiality is to be measured in this context by a standard more deferential than we accord to judgments of an administrative agency. . . . This principle has special significance in cases, like this one, involving congressional judgments concerning regulatory schemes of inherent complexity and assessments about the likely interaction of industries undergoing rapid economic and technological change. Though different in degree, the deference to Congress is in one respect akin to deference owed to administrative agencies because of their expertise. . . . Even in the realm of First Amendment questions where Congress must base its conclusions upon substantial evidence, deference must be accorded to its findings as to the harm to be avoided and to the remedial measures adopted for that end, lest we infringe on traditional legislative authority to make predictive judgments when enacting nationwide regulatory policy.

1

We have no difficulty in finding a substantial basis to support Congress' conclusion that a real threat justified enactment of the must-carry provisions. We examine first the evidence before Congress and then the further evidence presented to the District Court on remand to supplement the congressional determination.

As to the evidence before Congress, there was specific support for its conclusion that cable operators had considerable and growing market power over local video programming markets. Cable served at least 60 percent of American households in 1992, see Cable Act § 2(a)(3), and evidence indicated cable market penetration was projected to grow beyond 70 percent. [ ] As Congress noted (§ 2(a)(2)), cable operators possess a local monopoly over cable households. Only one percent of communities are served by more than one cable system, [ ]. Even in communities with two or more cable systems, in the typical case each system has a local monopoly over its subscribers. [ ] Cable operators thus exercise "control over most (if not all) of the television programming that is channeled into the subscriber's home . . . [and] can thus silence the voice of competing speakers with a mere flick of the switch." [*Turner I*]

[The Court cited evidence that both horizontal and vertical integration in the cable industry was increasing.] Congress concluded that "vertical integration gives cable operators the incentive and ability to favor their affiliated programming services" (§ 2(a)(5));. . . .

. . .

The reasonableness of Congress' conclusion was borne out by the evidence on remand, which also reflected cable industry favoritism for integrated programmers. [ ]

In addition, evidence before Congress, supplemented on remand, indicated that cable systems would have incentives to drop local broadcasters in favor of other programmers less likely to compete with them for audience and advertisers. Independent local broadcasters tend to be the closest substitutes for cable programs, because their programming tends to be similar, [ ], and because both primarily target the same type of advertiser: those interested in cheaper (and more frequent) ad spots than are typically available on network affiliates. [ ] The ability of broadcast stations to compete for advertising is greatly increased by cable carriage, which increases viewership substantially. [ ] With expanded viewership, broadcast presents a more competitive medium for television advertising. Empirical studies indicate that cable-carried broadcasters so enhance competition for advertising that even modest increases in the numbers of broadcast stations carried on cable are correlated with significant decreases in advertising revenue to cable systems. [ ] Thus, operators stand to benefit by dropping broadcast stations. [ ]

Cable systems also have more systemic reasons for seeking to disadvantage broadcast stations: Simply stated, cable has little interest in assisting, through carriage, a competing medium of communication. . . . Evidence adduced on remand indicated cable systems have little incentive to carry, and a significant incentive to drop, broadcast stations that will only be strengthened by access to the 60% of the television market that cable typically controls. [ ] Congress could therefore reasonably conclude that cable systems would drop broadcasters in favor of programmers—even unaffiliated ones—less likely to compete with them for audience and advertisers. The cap on carriage of affiliates included in the Cable Act, 47 U.S.C. § 533(f)(1)(B); (47 CFR § 76.504) (1995), and relied on by the dissent, [ ], is of limited utility in protecting broadcasters.

The dissent contends Congress could not reasonably conclude cable systems would engage in such predation because cable operators, whose primary source of revenue is subscriptions, would not risk dropping a widely viewed broadcast station in order to capture advertising revenues. [ ] However, if viewers are faced with the choice of sacrificing a handful of broadcast stations to gain access to dozens of cable channels (plus network affiliates), it is likely they would still subscribe to cable even if they would prefer the dropped television stations to the cable programming that replaced them. Substantial evidence introduced on remand bears this out: With the exception of a handful of very popular broadcast stations (typically network affiliates), a cable system's choice between carrying a cable programmer or broadcast station has little or no effect on cable subscriptions, and subscribership thus typically does not bear on carriage decisions. [ ]

It was more than a theoretical possibility in 1992 that cable operators would take actions adverse to local broadcasters; indeed, significant numbers of broadcasters had already been dropped. The record before Congress contained extensive anecdotal evidence about scores of adverse carriage decisions against broadcast stations. [ ] Congress considered an FCC-sponsored study detailing cable system carriage practices in the wake of decisions by the United States Court of Appeals for the District of Columbia Circuit striking down prior must-carry regulations. See [Quincy Cable, p. 453, supra]; [Century Communications, p. 453, supra]. It indicated that in 1988, 280 out of 912 responding broadcast stations had been dropped or denied carriage in 1,533 instances. [ ] Even assuming that every station dropped or denied coverage responded to the survey, it would indicate that nearly a quarter (21 percent) of the approximately 1,356 broadcast stations then in existence, id., at 40, had been denied carriage. The same study reported 869 of 4,303 reporting cable systems had denied carriage to 704 broadcast stations in 1,820 instances, [ ], and 279 of those stations had qualified for carriage under the prior must-carry rules. [ ] A contemporaneous study of public television stations indicated that in the vast majority of cases, dropped stations were not restored to the cable service. [　]

Substantial evidence demonstrated that absent must-carry the already "serious," [　], problem of noncarriage would grow worse because "additional local broadcast signals will be deleted, repositioned, or not carried," § 2(a)(15). The record included anecdotal evidence showing the cable industry was acting with restraint in dropping broadcast stations in an effort to discourage reregulation. [　] There was also substantial evidence that advertising revenue would be of increasing importance to cable operators as subscribership growth began to flatten, providing a steady, increasing incentive to deny carriage to local broadcasters in an effort to capture their advertising revenue. . . .

Additional evidence developed on remand supports the reasonableness of Congress' predictive judgment. Approximately 11 percent of local broadcasters were not carried on the typical cable system in 1989. [　] The figure had grown to even more significant proportions by 1992. According to one of appellants' own experts, between 19 and 31 percent of all local broadcast stations, including network affiliates, were not carried by the typical cable system. [ ] Based on the same data, another expert concluded that 47 percent of local independent commercial stations, and 36 percent of noncommercial stations, were not carried by the typical cable system. The rate of noncarriage was even higher for new stations. [　] Appellees introduced evidence drawn from an empirical study concluding the 1988 FCC survey substantially underestimated the actual number of drops, [　], and the noncarriage problem grew steadily worse during the period without must-carry. By the time the Cable Act was passed, 1,261 broadcast stations had been dropped for at least one year, in a total of 7,945 incidents. [　]

The dissent cites evidence indicating that many dropped broadcasters were stations few viewers watch, [　], and it suggests that must-carry thwarts noncable viewers' preferences. [　] Undoubtedly, viewers without cable—the immediate, though not sole, beneficiaries of efforts to preserve broadcast television—would have a strong preference for carriage of any broadcast program over any cable program, for the simple reason that it helps to preserve a medium to which they have access. The methodological flaws in the cited evidence are of concern. [　] Even aside from that, the evidence overlooks that the broadcasters added by must-carry had ratings greater than or equal to the cable programs they replaced. [　] (Indeed, in the vast majority of cases, cable systems were able to fulfill their must-carry obligations using spare channels, and did not displace cable programmers.) [　] On average, even the lowest-rated station added pursuant to must-carry had ratings better than or equal to at least nine basic cable program services carried on the system. [　] If cable systems refused to carry certain local broadcast stations because of their subscribers' preferences for the cable services carried in their place, one would expect that all cable programming services would have ratings exceeding those of broadcasters not carried. That is simply not the case.

[The Court noted that evidence on remand indicated that the trend towards greater horizontal and vertical concentration had continued since the passage of the must-carry rules.]

This is not a case in which we are called upon to give our best judgment as to the likely economic consequences of certain financial arrangements or business structures, or to assess competing economic theories and predictive judgments, as we would in a case arising, say, under the antitrust laws. "Statutes frequently require courts to make policy judgments. The Sherman Act, for example, requires courts to delve deeply into the theory of economic organization." [   ] The issue before us is whether, given conflicting views of the probable development of the television industry, Congress had substantial evidence for making the judgment that it did. We need not put our imprimatur on Congress' economic theory in order to validate the reasonableness of its judgment.

2

The harm Congress feared was that stations dropped or denied carriage would be at a "serious risk of financial difficulty," 512 U.S., at 667, and would "deteriorate to a substantial degree or fail altogether." [   ] Congress had before it substantial evidence to support its conclusion. Congress was advised the viability of a broadcast station depends to a material extent on its ability to secure cable carriage. [   ] One broadcast industry executive explained it this way: "Simply put, a television station's audience size directly translates into revenue—large audiences attract larger revenues, through the sale of advertising time. If a station is not carried on cable, and thereby loses a substantial portion of its audience, it will lose revenue. With less revenue, the station can not serve its community as well. The station will have less money to invest in equipment and programming. The attractiveness of its programming will lessen, as will its audience. Revenues will continue to decline, and the cycle will repeat." [   ] Empirical research in the record before Congress confirmed the " 'direct correlation [between] size in audience and station [advertising] revenues,' " [   ], and that viewership was in turn heavily dependent on cable carriage. [   ]

Considerable evidence, consisting of statements compiled from dozens of broadcasters who testified before Congress and the FCC, confirmed that broadcast stations had fallen into bankruptcy, [   ], curtailed their broadcast operations, [   ], and suffered serious reductions in operating revenues as a result of adverse carriage decisions by cable systems. [   ] The record also reflected substantial evidence that stations without cable carriage encountered severe difficulties obtaining financing for operations, reflecting the financial markets' judgment that the prospects are poor for broadcasters unable to secure carriage. [   ] Evidence before Congress suggested the potential adverse impact of losing carriage was increasing as the growth of clustering gave MSO's centralized control over more local markets. [   ] Congress thus had ample basis to conclude that attaining cable carriage would be of increasing importance to ensuring a station's viability. We hold Congress could conclude from the substantial body of evidence before it that "absent legislative action, the free local off-air broadcast system is endangered." [   ]

The evidence assembled on remand confirms the reasonableness of the congressional judgment. . . .

To be sure, the record also contains evidence to support a contrary conclusion. Appellants (and the dissent in the District Court) make much of the fact that the number of broadcast stations and their advertising revenue continued to grow during the period without must-carry, albeit at a diminished rate. Evidence introduced on remand indicated that only 31 broadcast stations actually went dark during the period without must-carry (one of which failed after a tornado destroyed its transmitter), and during the same period some 263 new stations signed on the air. [   ] New evidence appellants produced on remand indicates the average cable system voluntarily carried local broadcast stations accounting for about 97 percent of television ratings in noncable households. [   ] Appellants, as well as the dissent in the District Court, contend that in light of such evidence, it is clear "the must-carry law is not necessary to assure the economic viability of the broadcast system as a whole." [   ]

This assertion misapprehends the relevant inquiry. The question is not whether Congress, as an objective matter, was correct to determine must-carry is necessary to prevent a substantial number of broadcast stations from losing cable carriage and suffering significant financial hardship. Rather, the question is whether the legislative conclusion was reasonable and supported by substantial evidence in the record before Congress. [*Turner I*]. In making that determination, we are not to "reweigh the evidence *de novo*, or to replace Congress' factual predictions with our own." [   ] Rather, we are simply to determine if the standard is satisfied. If it is, summary judgment for defendants-appellees is appropriate regardless of whether the evidence is in conflict. . . .

Although evidence of continuing growth in broadcast could have supported the opposite conclusion, a reasonable interpretation is that expansion in the cable industry was causing harm to broadcasting. Growth continued, but the rate of growth fell to a considerable extent during the period without must-carry (from 4.5 percent in 1986 to 1.7 percent by 1992), and appeared to be tapering off further. [   ] Broadcast advertising revenues declined in real terms by 11 percent between 1986 and 1991, during a period in which cable's real advertising revenues nearly doubled. [   ] While these phenomena could be thought to stem from factors quite separate from the increasing market power of cable (for example, a recession in 1990–1992), it was for Congress to determine the better explanation. . . . A fundamental principle of legislation is that Congress is under no obligation to wait until the entire harm occurs but may act to prevent it. . . .

    . . .

We think it apparent must-carry serves the Government's interests "in a direct and effective way." [   ] Must-carry ensures that a number of local broadcasters retain cable carriage, with the concomitant audience access and advertising revenues needed to support a multiplicity of stations. Appellants contend that even were this so, must-carry is broader than necessary to accomplish its goals. We turn to this question.

B

The second portion of the *O'Brien* inquiry concerns the fit between the asserted interests and the means chosen to advance them. Content-neutral regulations do not pose the same "inherent dangers to free expression," [*Turner I*], that content-based regulations do, and thus are subject to a less rigorous analysis, which affords the Government latitude in designing a regulatory solution. [ ] Under intermediate scrutiny, the Government may employ the means of its choosing " 'so long as the . . . regulation promotes a substantial governmental interest that would be achieved less effectively absent the regulation,' " and does not " 'burden substantially more speech than is necessary to further' " that interest. [*Turner I*].

The must-carry provisions have the potential to interfere with protected speech in two ways. First, the provisions restrain cable operators' editorial discretion in creating programming packages by "reduc[ing] the number of channels over which [they] exercise unfettered control." [*Turner I*]. Second, the rules "render it more difficult for cable programmers to compete for carriage on the limited channels remaining." *Ibid*.

Appellants say the burden of must-carry is great, but the evidence adduced on remand indicates the actual effects are modest. Significant evidence indicates the vast majority of cable operators have not been affected in a significant manner by must-carry. Cable operators have been able to satisfy their must-carry obligations 87 percent of the time using previously unused channel capacity, [ ]; 94.5 percent of the 11,628 cable systems nationwide have not had to drop any programming in order to fulfill their must-carry obligations; the remaining 5.5 percent have had to drop an average of only 1.22 services from their programming, [ ]; and cable operators nationwide carry 99.8 percent of the programming they carried before enactment of must-carry. [ ] Appellees note that only 1.18 percent of the approximately 500,000 cable channels nationwide is devoted to channels added because of must-carry, [ ]; weighted for subscribership, the figure is 2.4 percent. . . .

We do not understand appellants to dispute in any fundamental way the accuracy of those figures, only their significance. [ ] They note national averages fail to account for greater crowding on certain (especially urban) cable systems, [ ], and contend that half of all cable systems, serving two-thirds of all cable subscribers, have no available capacity, [ ]. Appellants argue that the rate of growth in cable programming outstrips cable operators' creation of new channel space, that the rate of cable growth is lower than claimed, [ ], and that must-carry infringes First Amendment rights now irrespective of future growth. [ ]

Finally, they say that regardless of the percentage of channels occupied, must-carry still represents "thousands of real and individual infringements of speech." [　]

While the parties' evidence is susceptible of varying interpretations, a few definite conclusions can be drawn about the burdens of must-carry. It is undisputed that broadcast stations gained carriage on 5,880 channels as a result of must-carry. While broadcast stations occupy another 30,006 cable channels nationwide, this carriage does not represent a significant First Amendment harm to either system operators or cable programmers because those stations were carried voluntarily before 1992, and even appellants represent, [　], that the vast majority of those channels would continue to be carried in the absence of any legal obligation to do so. [　] The 5,880 channels occupied by added broadcasters represent the actual burden of the regulatory scheme. Appellants concede most of those stations would be dropped in the absence of must-carry, [　], so the figure approximates the benefits of must-carry as well.

Because the burden imposed by must-carry is congruent to the benefits it affords, we conclude must-carry is narrowly tailored to preserve a multiplicity of broadcast stations for the 40 percent of American households without cable. [　] Congress took steps to confine the breadth and burden of the regulatory scheme. For example, the more popular stations (which appellants concede would be carried anyway) will likely opt to be paid for cable carriage under the "retransmission consent" provision of the Cable Act; those stations will nonetheless be counted towards systems' must-carry obligations. Congress exempted systems of 12 or fewer channels, and limited the must-carry obligation of larger systems to one-third of capacity, 47 U.S.C. § 534(b)(1); see also §§ 535(b)(2)–(3); allowed cable operators discretion in choosing which competing and qualified signals would be carried, § 534(b)(2); and permitted operators to carry public stations on unused public, educational, and governmental channels in some circumstances, § 535(d).

Appellants say the must-carry provisions are overbroad because they require carriage in some instances when the Government's interests are not implicated: the must-carry rules prohibit a cable system operator from dropping a broadcaster "even if the operator has no anticompetitive motives, and even if the broadcaster that would have to be dropped . . . would survive without cable access." [　] We are not persuaded that either possibility is so prevalent that must-carry is substantially overbroad. . . . Broadcasters with stronger finances tend, however, to be popular ones that ordinarily seek payment from cable systems for transmission, so their reliance on must-carry should be minimal. It appears, for example, that no more than a few hundred of the 500,000 cable channels nationwide are occupied by network affiliates opting for must-carry [　], a number insufficient to render must-carry "substantially broader than necessary to achieve the government's interest." [　] Even on the doubtful assumption that a narrower but still practicable must-carry rule could be drafted to exclude all instances in which the Government's interests are not implicated, our cases establish that content-neutral regulations are not "invalid simply because there is some imaginable alternative that might be less burdensome on speech." [ ]

Appellants posit a number of alternatives in an effort to demonstrate a less-restrictive means to achieve the Government's aims. . . . Our precedents establish that when evaluating a content-neutral regulation which incidentally burdens speech, we will not invalidate the preferred remedial scheme because some alternative solution is marginally less intrusive on a speaker's First Amendment interests. "So long as the means chosen are not substantially broader than necessary to achieve the government's interest, . . . the regulation will not be invalid simply because a court concludes that the government's interest could be adequately served by some less-speech-restrictive alternative." [ ] It is well established a regulation's validity "does not turn on a judge's agreement with the responsible decisionmaker concerning the most appropriate method for promoting significant government interests." [ ]

. . .

III

Judgments about how competing economic interests are to be reconciled in the complex and fast-changing field of television are for Congress to make. Those judgments "cannot be ignored or undervalued simply because [appellants] cas[t] [their] claims under the umbrella of the First Amendment." [CBS v. DNC, p. 91, *supra*], 412 U.S., at 103. Appellants' challenges to must-carry reflect little more than disagreement over the level of protection broadcast stations are to be afforded and how protection is to be attained. We cannot displace Congress' judgment respecting content-neutral regulations with our own, so long as its policy is grounded on reasonable factual findings supported by evidence that is substantial for a legislative determination. Those requirements were met in this case, and in these circumstances the First Amendment requires nothing more. The judgment of the District Court is affirmed.

It is so ordered.

Justice Stevens, concurring.

As Justice Kennedy clearly explains, the policy judgments made by Congress in the enactment of legislation that is intended to forestall the abuse of monopoly power are entitled to substantial deference. [ ] That is true even when the attempt to protect an economic market imposes burdens on communication. [ ] If this statute regulated the content of speech rather than the structure of the market, our task would be quite different. [ ] Though I write to emphasize this important point, I fully concur in the Court's thorough opinion.

Justice Breyer, concurring in part.

I join the opinion of the Court except insofar as Part II–A–1 relies on an anticompetitive rationale. I agree with the majority that the statute must be "sustained under the First Amendment if it advances important governmental interests unrelated to the suppression of free speech and does not burden substantially more speech than necessary to further those interests." [　] I also agree that the statute satisfies this standard. My conclusion rests, however, not upon the principal opinion's analysis of the statute's efforts to "promot[e] fair competition," [　], but rather upon its discussion of the statute's other objectives, namely " '(1) preserving the benefits of free, over-the-air local broadcast television,' " and " '(2) promoting the widespread dissemination of information from a multiplicity of sources.' " [　] Whether or not the statute does or does not sensibly compensate for some significant market defect, it undoubtedly seeks to provide over-the-air viewers who lack cable with a rich mix of over-the-air programming by guaranteeing the over-the-air stations that provide such programming with the extra dollars that an additional cable audience will generate. I believe that this purpose—to assure the over-the-air public "access to a multiplicity of information sources," [　]—provides sufficient basis for rejecting appellants' First Amendment claim.

I do not deny that the compulsory carriage that creates the "guarantee" extracts a serious First Amendment price. It interferes with the protected interests of the cable operators to choose their own programming; it prevents displaced cable program providers from obtaining an audience; and it will sometimes prevent some cable viewers from watching what, in its absence, would have been their preferred set of programs. [　] This "price" amounts to a "suppression of speech."

But there are important First Amendment interests on the other side as well. The statute's basic noneconomic purpose is to prevent too precipitous a decline in the quality and quantity of programming choice for an evershrinking non-cable-subscribing segment of the public. [　] This purpose reflects what "has long been a basic tenet of national communications policy," namely that "the widest possible dissemination of information from diverse and antagonistic sources is essential to the welfare of the public." [*Turner I*]. That policy, in turn, seeks to facilitate the public discussion and informed deliberation, which, as Justice Brandeis pointed out many years ago, democratic government presupposes and the First Amendment seeks to achieve. [　] Indeed, [*Turner I*] rested in part upon the proposition that "assuring that the public has access to a multiplicity of information sources is a governmental purpose of the highest order, for it promotes values central to the First Amendment." [　]

With important First Amendment interests on both sides of the equation, the key question becomes one of proper fit. That question, in my view, requires a reviewing court to determine both whether there are significantly less restrictive ways to achieve Congress' over-the-air programming objectives, and also to decide whether the statute, in its effort to achieve those objectives, strikes a reasonable balance between potentially speech-restricting and speech-enhancing consequences. [　] The majority's opinion analyzes and evaluates those consequences, and I agree with its conclusions in respect to both of these matters. [   ]

In particular, I note (and agree) that a cable system, physically dependent upon the availability of space along city streets, at present (perhaps less in the future) typically faces little competition, that it therefore constitutes a kind of bottleneck that controls the range of viewer choice (whether or not it uses any consequent economic power for economically predatory purposes), and that some degree—at least a limited degree—of governmental intervention and control through regulation can prove appropriate when justified under *O'Brien* (at least when not "content based"). [   ] I also agree that, without the statute, cable systems would likely carry significantly fewer over-the-air stations, [   ], that station revenues would therefore decline, [ ], and that the quality of over-the-air programming on such stations would almost inevitably suffer, [   ]. I agree further that the burden the statute imposes upon the cable system, potential cable programmers, and cable viewers, is limited and will diminish as typical cable system capacity grows over time.

Finally, I believe that Congress could reasonably conclude that the statute will help the typical over-the-air viewer (by maintaining an expanded range of choice) more than it will hurt the typical cable subscriber (by restricting cable slots otherwise available for preferred programming). The latter's cable choices are many and varied, and the range of choice is rapidly increasing. The former's over-the-air choice is more restricted; and, as cable becomes more popular, it may well become still more restricted insofar as the over-the-air market shrinks and thereby, by itself, becomes less profitable. In these circumstances, I do not believe the First Amendment dictates a result that favors the cable viewers' interests.

These and other similar factors discussed by the majority, lead me to agree that the statute survives "intermediate scrutiny," whether or not the statute is properly tailored to Congress' purely economic objectives.

JUSTICE O'CONNOR, with whom JUSTICE SCALIA, JUSTICE THOMAS, and JUSTICE GINSBURG join, dissenting.

In sustaining the must-carry provisions of the [*1992 Cable Act*], against a First Amendment challenge by cable system operators and cable programmers, the Court errs in two crucial respects. First, the Court disregards one of the principal defenses of the statute urged by appellees on remand: that it serves a substantial interest in preserving "diverse," "quality" programming that is "responsive" to the needs of the local community. The course of this litigation on remand and the proffered defense strongly reinforce my view that the Court adopted the wrong analytic framework in the prior phase of this case. See [*Turner I*] (O'Connor, J., concurring in part and dissenting in part). Second, the Court misapplies the "intermediate scrutiny" framework it adopts. Although we owe deference to Congress' predictive judgments and its evaluation of complex economic questions, we have an independent duty to identify with care the Government interests supporting the scheme, to inquire into the reasonableness of congressional findings regarding its necessity, and to examine the fit between its goals and its consequences. [ ] The Court fails to discharge its duty here.

I

I did not join those portions of the principal opinion in [*Turner I*] holding that the must-carry provisions of the Cable Act are content neutral and therefore subject to intermediate First Amendment scrutiny. [ ] The Court there referred to the "unusually detailed statutory findings" accompanying the Act, in which Congress recognized the importance of preserving sources of local news, public affairs, and educational programming. [ ] Nevertheless, the Court minimized the significance of these findings, suggesting that they merely reflected Congress' view of the "intrinsic value" of broadcast programming generally, rather than a congressional preference for programming with local, educational, or informational content. [ ]

In [*Turner I*], the Court drew upon Senate and House reports to identify three "interests" that the must-carry provisions were designed to serve: "(1) preserving the benefits of free, over-the-air local broadcast television, (2) promoting the widespread dissemination of information from a multiplicity of sources, and (3) promoting fair competition in the market for television programming." [ ] The Court reiterates these interests here, [ ], but neither the principal opinion nor the partial concurrence ever explains the relationship between them with any clarity.

Much of the principal opinion treats the must-carry provisions as a species of antitrust regulation enacted by Congress in response to a perceived threat that cable system operators would otherwise engage in various forms of anticompetitive conduct resulting in harm to broadcasters. [ ] The Court recognizes that appellees cannot show an anticompetitive threat to broadcast television simply by demonstrating that "a few" broadcast stations would be forced off the air in the absence of must-carry. [ ] No party has ever questioned that adverse carriage decisions by cable operators will threaten some broadcasters in some markets. The notion that Congress premised the must-carry provisions upon a far graver threat to the structure of the local broadcast system than the loss of "a few" stations runs through virtually every passage in the principal [*Turner I*] opinion that discusses the Government interests the provisions were designed to serve. [ ] Ostensibly adopting this framework, the Court now asks whether Congress could reasonably have thought the must-carry regime necessary to prevent a "significant reduction in the multiplicity of broadcast programming sources available to noncable households." [ ]

I fully agree that promoting fair competition is a legitimate and substantial Government goal. But the Court nowhere examines whether the breadth of the must-carry provisions comports with a goal of preventing anticompetitive harms. Instead, in the course of its inquiry into whether the must-carry provisions are "narrowly tailored," the principal opinion simply assumes that most adverse carriage decisions are anti-competitively motivated, and that must-carry is therefore a measured response to a problem of anticompetitive behavior. [ ] We ordinarily do not substitute unstated and untested assumptions for our independent evaluation of the facts bearing upon an issue of constitutional law. [ ]

Perhaps because of the difficulty of defending the must-carry provisions as a measured response to anticompetitive behavior, the Court asserts an "independent" interest in preserving a "multiplicity" of broadcast programming sources. [ ] In doing so, the Court posits existence of "conduct that threatens" the availability of broadcast television outlets, quite apart from anticompetitive conduct. [ ] We are left to wonder what precisely that conduct might be. Moreover, when separated from anticompetitive conduct, this interest in preserving a "multiplicity of broadcast programming sources" becomes poorly defined. Neither the principal opinion nor the partial concurrence offers any guidance on what might constitute a "significant reduction" in the availability of broadcast programming. The proper analysis, in my view, necessarily turns on the present distribution of broadcast stations among the local broadcast markets that make up the national broadcast "system." Whether cable poses a "significant" threat to a local broadcast market depends first on how many broadcast stations in that market will, in the absence of must-carry, remain available to viewers in noncable households. It also depends on whether viewers actually watch the stations that are dropped or denied carriage. The Court provides some raw data on adverse carriage decisions, but it never connects that data to markets and viewership. Instead, the Court proceeds from the assumptions that adverse carriage decisions nationwide will affect broadcast markets in proportion to their size; and that all broadcast programming is watched by viewers. Neither assumption is logical or has any factual basis in the record.

Appellees bear the burden of demonstrating that the provisions of the Cable Act restricting expressive activity survive constitutional scrutiny. See [Turner I]. As discussed below, the must-carry provisions cannot be justified as a narrowly tailored means of addressing anticompetitive behavior. [ ] As a result, the Court's inquiry into whether must-carry would prevent a "significant reduction in the multiplicity of broadcast programming sources" collapses into an analysis of an ill-defined and generalized interest in maintaining broadcast stations, wherever they might be threatened and whatever their viewership. Neither the principal opinion nor the partial concurrence ever explains what kind of conduct, apart from anticompetitive conduct, threatens the "multiplicity" of broadcast programming sources. Indeed, the only justification advanced by the parties for furthering this interest is heavily content based. It is undisputed that the broadcast stations protected by must-carry are the "marginal" stations within a given market, [   ]; the record on remand reveals that any broader threat to the broadcast system was entirely mythical. Pressed to explain the importance of preserving noncable viewers' access to "vulnerable" broadcast stations, appellees empha-size that the must-carry rules are necessary to ensure that broadcast stations maintain "diverse," "quality" programming that is "respon-sive" to the needs of the local community. [ ] Must-carry is thus justified as a way of preserving viewers' access to a Spanish or Chinese language station or of preventing an independent station from adopting a home-shopping format. [ ] Undoubtedly, such goals are reasonable and important, and the stations in question may well be worthwhile targets of Government subsidies. But appellees' characterization of must-carry as a means of protecting these stations, like the Court's explicit concern for promoting " 'community self-expression' " and the " 'local origination of broadcast programming,' " [ ], reveals a content-based preference for broadcast programming. This justification of the regulatory scheme is, in my view, wholly at odds with the [*Turner I*] Court's premise that must-carry is a means of preserving "access to free television programming—whatever its content," 512 U.S., at 649 (em-phasis added).

I do not read Justice Breyer's opinion—which analyzes the must-carry rules in part as a "speech-enhancing" measure designed to ensure a "rich mix" of over-the-air programming, [ ]—to treat the content of over-the-air programming as irrelevant to whether the Government's interest in promoting it is an important one. The net result appears to be that five Justices of this Court do not view must-carry as a narrowly tailored means of serving a substantial governmental interest in prevent-ing anticompetitive behavior; and that five Justices of this Court do see the significance of the content of over-the-air programming to the Government's and appellees' efforts to defend the law. Under these circumstances, the must-carry provisions should be subject to strict scrutiny, which they surely fail.

II

The principal opinion goes to great lengths to avoid acknowledging that preferences for "quality," "diverse," and "responsive" local pro-gramming underlie the must-carry scheme, although the partial concur-rence's reliance on such preferences is explicit. [ ] I take the principal opinion at its word and evaluate the claim that the threat of anticompet-itive behavior by cable operators supplies a content-neutral basis for sustaining the statute. It does not.

The [*Turner I*] Court remanded the case for a determination wheth-er the must-carry provisions satisfy intermediate scrutiny under [*O'Brien*]. . . . The [*Turner I*] plurality found that genuine issues of material fact remained as to both parts of the *O'Brien* analysis. On whether must-carry furthers a substantial governmental interest, the [*Turner I*] Court remanded the case to test two essential and unproven propositions: "(1) that unless cable operators are compelled to carry broadcast stations, significant numbers of broadcast stations will be refused carriage on cable systems; and (2) that the broadcast stations denied carriage will either deteriorate to a substantial degree or fail altogether." [   ] As for whether must-carry restricts no more speech than essential to further Congress' asserted purpose, the [*Turner I*] plurality found evidence lacking on the extent of the burden that the must-carry provisions would place on cable operators and cable programmers. [   ]

The District Court resolved this case on cross-motions for summary judgment. As the Court recognizes, [   ], the fact that the evidence before Congress might have been in conflict will not necessarily preclude summary judgment upholding the must-carry scheme. The question, rather, is what the undisputed facts show about the reasonableness of Congress' conclusions. We are not, however, at liberty to substitute speculation for evidence or to ignore factual disputes that call the reasonableness of Congress' findings into question. The evidence on remand demonstrates that appellants, not appellees, are entitled to summary judgment.

A

The principal opinion devotes substantial discussion to the structure of the cable industry, [   ], a matter that was uncontroversial in [*Turner I*]. [   ] As of 1992, cable already served 60 percent of American households. I agree with the observation that Congress could reasonably predict an increase in cable penetration of the local video programming market. . . .

What was not resolved in *Turner* was whether "reasonable inferences based on substantial evidence," [   ], supported Congress' judgment that the must-carry provisions were necessary "to prevent cable operators from exploiting their economic power to the detriment of broadcasters," [   ]. Because I remain convinced that the statute is not a measured response to congressional concerns about monopoly power, [   ], in my view the principal opinion's discussion on this point is irrelevant. But even if it were relevant, it is incorrect.

1

The [*Turner I*] plurality recognized that Congress' interest in curtailing anticompetitive behavior is substantial "in the abstract." [   ] The principal opinion now concludes that substantial evidence supports the congressional judgment that cable operators have incentives to engage in significant anticompetitive behavior. It appears to accept two related arguments on this point: first, that vertically integrated cable operators prefer programming produced by their affiliated cable programming networks to broadcast programming, [   ]; and second, that potential advertising revenues supply cable system operators, whether affiliated with programmers or not, with incentives to prefer cable programming to broadcast programming. [   ]

To support the first proposition, the principal opinion states that "[e]xtensive testimony" before Congress showed that in fact operators do have incentives to favor vertically integrated programmers. . . .

[A]ccepting as reasonable Congress' conclusion that cable operators have incentives to favor affiliated programmers, Congress has already limited the number of channels on a cable system that can be occupied by affiliated programmers. 47 U.S.C. § 533(f)(1)(B); 47 CFR § 76.504 (1995). Once a cable system operator reaches that cap, it can no longer bump a broadcaster in favor of an affiliated programmer. If Congress were concerned that broadcasters favored too many affiliated programmers, it could simply adjust the cap. Must-carry simply cannot be justified as a response to the allegedly "substantial" problem of vertical integration.

The second argument, that the quest for advertising revenue will supply cable operators with incentives to drop local broadcasters, takes two forms. First, some cable programmers offer blank slots within a program into which a cable operator can insert advertisements; appellees argue that "[t]he opportunity to sell such advertising gives cable programmers an additional value to operators above broadcast stations. . . ." [ ] But that "additional value" arises only because the must-carry provisions require cable operators to carry broadcast signals without alteration. 47 U.S.C. § 534(b)(3). . . . [T]he Government cannot have "a 'substantial interest' in remedying a competitive distortion that arises entirely out of a detail in its own purportedly remedial legislation." [ ] Second, appellees claim that since cable operators compete directly with broadcasters for some advertising revenue, operators will profit if they can drive broadcasters out of the market and capture their advertising revenue. Even if the record before Congress included substantial evidence that "advertising revenue would be of increasing importance to cable operators as subscribership growth began to flatten," [ ], it does not necessarily follow that Congress could reasonably find that the quest for advertising revenues supplies cable operators with incentives to engage in predatory behavior, or that must-carry is a reasonable response to such incentives. There is no dispute that a cable system depends primarily upon its subscriber base for revenue. A cable operator is therefore unlikely to drop a widely viewed station in order to capture advertising revenues—which, according to the figures of appellees' expert, account for between one and five percent of the total revenues of most large cable systems. [ ] In doing so, it would risk losing subscribers. Nevertheless, appellees contend that cable operators will drop some broadcast stations in spite of, and not because of, viewer preferences. The principal opinion suggests that viewers are likely to subscribe to cable even though they prefer certain over-the-air programming to cable programming, because they would be willing to trade access to their preferred channel for access to dozens of cable channels. [ ] Even assuming that, at the margin, advertising revenues would drive cable systems to drop some stations—invariably described as "vulnerable" or "smaller" independents, [ ]; [ ]—the strategy's success would depend upon the additional untested premise that the advertising revenues freed by dropping a broadcast station will flow to cable operators rather than to other broadcasters.

2

Under the standard articulated by the [*Turner I*] plurality, the conclusion that must-carry serves a substantial governmental interest depends upon the "essential propositio[n]" that, without must-carry, "significant numbers of broadcast stations will be refused carriage on cable systems." [ ] In analyzing whether this undefined standard is satisfied, the Court focuses almost exclusively on raw numbers of stations denied carriage or "repositioned"—that is, shifted out of their traditional channel positions.

The Court begins its discussion of evidence of adverse carriage decisions with the 1988 study sponsored by the Federal Communications Commission. [ ] But in [*Turner I*], the plurality criticized this very study, noting that it did not indicate the time frame within which carriage denials occurred or whether the stations were later restored to their positions. . . .

In canvassing the additional evidence offered on remand, the Court focuses on the suggestion of one of appellees' experts that the 1988 FCC survey underestimated the number of drops of broadcast stations in the non-must-carry era. The data do not indicate which of these stations would now qualify for mandatory carriage. . . . [Many] of [the] drops existing as of mid–1992 remained uncured as of mid–1994, fully 19 months after the present must-carry rules went into effect. [ ] The Court discounts the importance of whether dropped stations now qualify for mandatory carriage, on the ground that requiring any such showing places an "improper burden" on the Legislative Branch. [ ] It seems obvious, however, that if the must-carry rules will not reverse those adverse carriage decisions on which appellees rely to illustrate the Government "interest" supporting the rules, then a significant question remains as to whether the rules in fact serve the articulated interest. Without some further analysis, I do not see how the Court can, in the course of its independent scrutiny on a question of constitutional law, deem Congress' judgment "reasonable."

In any event, the larger problem with the Court's approach is that neither the FCC study nor the additional evidence on remand canvassed by the Court, [ ], says anything about the broadcast markets in which adverse carriage decisions take place. The Court accepts Congress' stated concern about preserving the availability of a "multiplicity" of broadcast stations, but apparently thinks it sufficient to evaluate that concern in the abstract, without considering how much local service is already available in a given broadcast market. . . .

Nor can we evaluate whether must-carry is necessary to serve an interest in preserving broadcast stations without examining the value of the stations protected by the must-carry scheme to viewers in noncable households. By disregarding the distribution and viewership of stations not carried on cable, the Court upholds the must-carry provisions without addressing the interests of the over-the-air television viewers that Congress purportedly seeks to protect. [ ] . . . The only analysis in the record of the relationship between carriage and noncable viewership favors the appellants. A 1991 study by Federal Trade Commission staff concluded that most cable systems voluntarily carried broadcast stations with any reportable ratings in noncable households and that most instances of noncarriage involved "relatively remote (and duplicated) network stations, or local stations that few viewers watch." [   ]

. . . The Court suggests that it is appropriate to disregard the low noncable viewership of stations denied carriage, because in some instances cable viewers preferred the dropped broadcast channels to the cable channels that replaced them. [   ] The viewership statistics in question, as well as their significance, are sharply disputed, but they are also irrelevant. The issue is whether the Government can demonstrate a substantial interest in forced carriage of certain broadcast stations, for the benefit of viewers who lack access to cable. That inquiry is not advanced by an analysis of relative cable household viewership of broadcast and cable programming. When appellees are pressed to explain the Government's "substantial interest" in preserving noncable viewers' access to "vulnerable" or "marginal" stations with "relatively small" audiences, it becomes evident that the interest has nothing to do with anticompetitive behavior, but has everything to do with content—preserving "quality" local programming that is "responsive" to community needs. [   ] Indeed, Justice Breyer expressly declines to accept the anticompetitive rationale for the must-carry rules embraced by the principal opinion, and instead explicitly relies on a need to preserve a "rich mix" of "quality" programming. [   ]

3

I turn now to the evidence of harm to broadcasters denied carriage or repositioned. The Court remanded for a determination whether broadcast stations denied carriage would be at " 'serious risk of financial difficulty' " and would " 'deteriorate to a substantial degree or fail altogether.' " [   ] The [*Turner I*] plurality noted that there was no evidence that "local broadcast stations have fallen into bankruptcy, turned in their broadcast licenses, curtailed their broadcast operations, or suffered a serious reduction in operating revenues" because of adverse carriage decisions. [   ] The record on remand does not permit the conclusion, at the summary judgment stage, that Congress could reasonably have predicted serious harm to a significant number of stations in the absence of must-carry.

The purported link between an adverse carriage decision and severe harm to a station depends on yet another untested premise. Even accepting the conclusion that a cable system operator has a monopoly over cable services to the home, [ ], it does not necessarily follow that the operator also has a monopoly over all video services to cabled households. Cable subscribers using an input selector switch and an antenna can receive broadcast signals. Widespread use of such switches would completely eliminate any cable system "monopoly" over sources of video input. [   ] Growing use of direct-broadcast satellite television also tends to undercut the notion that cable operators have an inevitable monopoly over video services entering cable households. [   ]

In the Cable Act, Congress rejected the wisdom of any "substantial societal investment" in developing input selector switch technology. § 2(a)(18). In defending this choice, the Court purports to identify "substantial evidence of technological shortcomings" that prevent widespread, efficient use of such devices. But nearly all of the "data" in question are drawn from sources predating the enactment of must-carry by roughly six years. [   ] The Court notes the importance of deferring to congressional judgments about the "interaction of industries undergoing rapid economic and technological change." [   ] But this principle does not require wholesale deference to judgments about rapidly changing technologies that are based on unquestionably outdated information.

The Court concludes that the evidence on remand meets the threshold of harm established in [*Turner I*]. The Court begins with the "[c]onsiderable evidence" that broadcast stations denied carriage have fallen into bankruptcy. [   ] The analysis, however, does not focus on features of the market in which these stations were located or on the size of the audience they commanded. The "considerable evidence" relied on by the Court consists of repeated references to the bankruptcies of the same 23 commercial independent stations—apparently, new stations. [   ] Because the must-carry provisions have never been justified as a means of enhancing broadcast television, I do not understand the relevance of this evidence, or of the evidence concerning the difficulties encountered by new stations seeking financing. [   ]

. . .

Moreover, unlike other aspects of the record on remand, the station-specific accounts cited by the Court do permit an evaluation of trends in the various broadcast markets, or "areas of dominant influence," in which carriage denials allegedly caused harm. The Court does not conduct this sort of analysis. Were it to do so, the Court would have to recognize that all but one of the commercial broadcast stations cited as claiming a curtailment in operations or a decline in revenue was broadcasting within an area of dominant influence that experienced net growth, or at least no net reduction, in the number of commercial broadcast stations operating during the non-must-carry era. . . .

In sum, appellees are not entitled to summary judgment on whether Congress could conclude, based on reasonable inferences drawn from substantial evidence, that " 'absent legislative action, the free local off-air broadcast system is endangered.' " [   ] . . . The principal opinion disavows a need to closely scrutinize the logic of the regulatory scheme at issue on the ground that it "need not put [its] imprimatur on Congress' economic theory in order to validate the reasonableness of its judgment." [   ] That approach trivializes the First Amendment issue at stake in this case. A highly dubious economic theory has been advanced as the "substantial interest" supporting a First Amendment burden on cable operators and cable programmers. In finding that must-carry serves a substantial interest, the principal opinion necessarily accepts that theory. The partial concurrence does not, but neither does it articulate what threat to the availability of a "multiplicity" of broadcast stations would exist in a perfectly competitive market.

B

I turn now to the second portion of the *O'Brien* inquiry, which concerns the fit between the Government's asserted interests and the means chosen to advance them. The Court observes that "broadcast stations gained carriage on 5,880 channels as a result of must-carry," and recognizes that this forced carriage imposes a burden on cable system operators and cable programmers. [ ] But the Court also concludes that the other 30,006 cable channels occupied by broadcast stations are irrelevant to measuring the burden of the must-carry scheme. The must-carry rules prevent operators from dropping these broadcast stations should other more desirable cable programming become available, even though operators have carried these stations voluntarily in the past. The must-carry requirements thus burden an operator's First Amendment freedom to exercise unfettered control over a number of channels in its system, whether or not the operator's present choice is aligned with that of the Government.

Even assuming that the Court is correct that the 5,880 channels occupied by added broadcasters "represent the actual burden of the regulatory scheme," [ ], the Court's leap to the conclusion that must-carry "is narrowly tailored to preserve a multiplicity of broadcast stations," [   ], is nothing short of astounding. The Court's logic is circular. Surmising that most of the 5,880 channels added by the regulatory scheme would be dropped in its absence, the Court concludes that the figure also approximates the "benefit" of must-carry. Finding the scheme's burden "congruent" to the benefit it affords, the Court declares the statute narrowly tailored. The Court achieves this result, however, only by equating the effect of the statute—requiring cable operators to add 5,880 stations—with the governmental interest sought to be served. . . . Positing the effect of a statute as the governmental interest "can sidestep judicial review of almost any statute, because it makes all statutes look narrowly tailored." [   ] Without a sense whether most adverse carriage decisions are anticompetitively motivated, it is improper to conclude that the statute is narrowly tailored simply because it prevents some adverse carriage decisions. [   ]

In my view, the statute is not narrowly tailored to serve a substantial interest in preventing anticompetitive conduct. I do not understand Justice Breyer to disagree with this conclusion. [   ] Congress has commandeered up to one third of each cable system's channel capacity for the benefit of local broadcasters, without any regard for whether doing so advances the statute's alleged goals. To the extent that Congress was concerned that anticompetitive impulses would lead vertically integrated operators to prefer those programmers in which the operators have an ownership stake, the Cable Act is overbroad, since it does not impose its requirements solely on such operators. An integrated cable operator cannot satisfy its must-carry obligations by allocating a channel to an unaffiliated cable programmer. And must-carry blocks an operator's access to up to one third of the channels on the system, even if its affiliated programmer provides programming for only a single channel. The Court rejects this logic, finding the possibility that the must-carry regime would require reversal of a benign carriage decision not "so prevalent that must-carry is substantially overbroad." [   ] The principal opinion reasons that "cable systems serving 70 percent of subscribers are vertically integrated with cable programmers, so anticompetitive motives may be implicated in a majority of systems' decisions not to carry broadcasters." [   ] It is unclear whether the principal opinion means that anticompetitive motives may be implicated in a majority of decisions, or in decisions by a majority of systems. In either case, the principal opinion's conclusion is wholly speculative. We do not know which of these vertically integrated systems are affiliated with one cable programmer and which are affiliated with five cable programmers. Moreover, Congress has placed limits upon the number of channels that can be used for affiliated programming. 47 U.S.C. § 533(f)(1)(B). The principal opinion does not suggest why these limits are inadequate or explain why, once a system reaches the limit, its remaining carriage decisions would also be anticompetitively motivated. Even if the channel limits are insufficient, the principal opinion does not explain why requiring carriage of broadcast stations on one third of the system's channels is a measured response to the problem.

Finally, I note my disagreement with the Court's suggestion that the availability of less-speech-restrictive alternatives is never relevant to *O'Brien*'s narrow tailoring inquiry. [   ] The [*Turner I*] Court remanded this case in part because a plurality concluded that "judicial findings concerning the availability and efficacy of constitutionally acceptable less restrictive means of achieving the Government's asserted interests" were lacking in the original record. [   ] The Court's present position on this issue is puzzling.

Our cases suggest only that we have not interpreted the narrow tailoring inquiry to "require elimination of all less restrictive alternatives." [   ] Put another way, we have refrained from imposing a least-restrictive-means requirement in cases involving intermediate First Amendment scrutiny. [   ] It is one thing to say that a regulation need not be the least-speech-restrictive means of serving an important governmental objective. It is quite another to suggest, as I read the majority to do here, that the availability of less-speech-restrictive alternatives cannot establish or confirm that a regulation is substantially broader than necessary to achieve the Government's goals. . . .

As shown above, [   ], in this case it is plain without reference to any alternatives that the must-carry scheme is "substantially broader than necessary," [   ], to serve the only governmental interest that the principal opinion fully explains—preventing unfair competition. If Congress truly sought to address anticompetitive behavior by cable system operators, it passed the wrong law. [   ] Nevertheless, the availability of less restrictive alternatives—a leased-access regime and subsidies—reinforces my conclusion that the must-carry provisions are overbroad.

Consider first appellants' proposed leased-access scheme, under which a cable system operator would be required to make a specified proportion of the system's channels available to broadcasters and independent cable programmers alike at regulated rates. Leased access would directly address both vertical integration and predatory behavior, by placing broadcasters and cable programmers on a level playing field for access to cable. The principal opinion never explicitly identifies any threat to the availability of broadcast television to noncable households other than anticompetitive conduct, nor does Justice Breyer's partial concurrence. Accordingly, to the extent that leased access would address problems of anticompetitive behavior, I fail to understand why it would not achieve the goal of "ensuring that significant programming remains available" for noncable households. [   ] The Court observes that a leased access regime would, like must-carry, "reduce the number of cable channels under cable systems' control in the same manner as must-carry." [   ] No leased access scheme is currently before the Court, and I intimate no view on whether leased access, like must-carry, imposes unacceptable burdens on cable operators' free speech interests. It is important to note, however, that the Court's observation that a leased access scheme may, like must-carry, impose First Amendment burdens does not dispose of the narrow tailoring inquiry in this case. As noted, a leased access regime would respond directly to problems of vertical integration and problems of predatory behavior. Must-carry quite clearly does not respond to the problem of vertical integration. [   ] In addition, the must-carry scheme burdens the rights of cable programmers and cable operators; there is no suggestion here that leased access would burden cable programmers in the same way as must-carry does. In both of these respects, leased access is a more narrowly tailored guard against anticompetitive behavior. Finally, if, as the Court suggests, Congress were concerned that a leased access scheme would impose a burden on "small broadcasters" forced to pay for access, subsidies would eliminate the problem.

Subsidies would not, of course, eliminate anticompetitive behavior by cable system operators—a problem that Congress could address directly or through a leased-access scheme. Appellees defend the must-carry provisions, however, not only as a means of preventing anticompetitive behavior, but also as a means of protecting "marginal" or "vulnerable" stations, even if they are not threatened by anticompetitive behavior. The principal opinion chooses not to acknowledge this interest explicitly, although Justice Breyer does. Even if this interest were content neutral—which it is not—subsidies would address it directly. The Court adopts appellees' position that subsidies would serve a "very different purpose than must-carry. Must-carry is intended not to guarantee the financial health of all broadcasters, but to ensure a base number of broadcasters survive to provide service to noncable households." [ ] To the extent that Justice Breyer sees must-carry as a "speech-enhancing" measure designed to guarantee over-the-air broadcasters "extra dollars," [ ], it is unclear why subsidies would not fully serve that interest. In any event, I take appellees' concern to be that subsidies, unlike must-carry, would save some broadcasters that would not survive even with cable carriage. There is a straightforward solution to this problem. If the Government is indeed worried that imprecision in allocation of subsidies would prop up stations that would not survive even with cable carriage, then it could tie subsidies to a percentage of stations' advertising revenues (or, for public stations, member contributions), determined by stations' access to viewers. . . . The Court also suggests that a subsidy scheme would involve the Government in making "content-based determinations about programming." [ ] Even if that is so, it does not distinguish subsidies from the must-carry provisions. In light of the principal opinion's steadfast adherence to the position that a preference for "diverse" or local-content broadcasting is not a content-based preference, the argument is ironic indeed.

. . .

IV

In sustaining the must-carry provisions of the Cable Act, the Court ignores the main justification of the statute urged by appellees and subjects restrictions on expressive activity to an inappropriately lenient level of scrutiny. The principal opinion then misapplies the analytic framework it chooses, exhibiting an extraordinary and unwarranted deference for congressional judgments, a profound fear of delving into complex economic matters, and a willingness to substitute untested assumptions for evidence. In light of gaps in logic and evidence, it is improper to conclude, at the summary judgment stage, that the must-carry scheme serves a significant governmental interest "in a direct and effective way." [ ] Moreover, because the undisputed facts demonstrate that the must-carry scheme is plainly not narrowly tailored to serving the only governmental interest the principal opinion fully explains and embraces—preventing anticompetitive behavior—appellants are entitled to summary judgment in their favor.

Justice Breyer disavows the principal opinion's position on anticompetitive behavior, and instead treats the must-carry rules as a "speech-enhancing" measure designed to ensure access to "quality" programming for noncable households. Neither the principal opinion nor the partial concurrence explains the nature of the alleged threat to the availability of a "multiplicity of broadcast programming sources," if that threat does not arise from cable operators' anticompetitive conduct. Such an approach makes it impossible to discern whether Congress was addressing a problem that is "real, not merely conjectural," and whether must-carry addresses the problem in a "direct and material way." [*Turner I*].

I therefore respectfully dissent, and would reverse the judgment below.

Notes and Questions

1. Compare each opinion with the others in its treatment of the questions of deference to Congress and in the determination of the level of scrutiny to be applied.

2. Compare each opinion's view of the role of "local" broadcasters and of "local" programming.

3. If compression of signals and the era of 500–channel cable systems come into being, what impact will that have on the controversy over the must-carry provisions?

4. As discussed in Chapter VIII, the 1996 Telecommunications Act has eliminated the prohibition on RBOCs' providing cable service in their local service. What impact should that have on the controversy over the must-carry provisions? What is the relevance of Congress' finding that where such competition exists, rate regulation is no longer needed?

5. New cable channels continue to be launched. As of mid–2002, there were 308 national cable networks. Assessment of the Status of Competition in Markets for the Delivery of Video Programming, p. 412, *supra*. What effect will the continuing increase in programming services have on the must-carry controversy?

6. *Retransmission Consent*. In a separate proceeding, a district court found constitutional a number of provisions of the 1992 Cable Act, including retransmission consent, rate regulation and mandatory carriage of PEG channels. Judge Jackson applied the same reasoning he used in *Turner*. Because the 1992 act was, in his opinion, primarily economic regulation, he held that the *O'Brien* test was the appropriate level of scrutiny. Most of the challenged provisions were, in his view, content-neutral regulations aimed at increasing diversity or, in the case of rate regulation, "to keep rates affordable to the public." Daniels Cablevision, Inc. v. United States, 819 F.Supp. 32, 72 R.R.2d 366, 21 Med.L.Rptr. 1993 (D.D.C.1993). This part of the decision was upheld on appeal. Time Warner v. Federal Communications Commission, 56 F.3d 151, 78 R.R.2d 1 (D.C.Cir.1995) cert. denied, 516 U.S. 1112 (1996).

There had been much discussion about whether cable systems would be willing to pay for retransmission consent and the impact on both the stations and the cable system if the cable system refused to go that route. As the deadline approached for television stations to choose between must carry and retransmission consent, both cable MSOs and TV group owners were engaged in public posturing regarding what the MSOs were willing to give and the TV station owners would be willing to accept in return for retransmission consent. For example, Time Warner announced that it would not pay one cent to broadcasters, while Capital Cities/ABC announced that it would be seeking cash compensation. Broadcasting & Cable, June 7, 1993 at 6.

However, less than two months later, Capital Cities/ABC and Hearst started signing deals with cable systems whereby, in return for retransmission consent for Capital Cities/ABC and Hearst TV stations, the cable companies agreed to pay for and carry ESPN2, a new cable channel owned by Capital Cities/ABC and Hearst.

Fox entered into similar deals trading retransmission consent for its affiliates for carriage of its new cable channel. These deals required cable channels to pay 25 cents per subscriber to Fox. In turn, Fox broadcast affiliates could choose between a seven and one half cent cut or a five cent cut plus an ownership interest in the new cable channel. Broadcasting & Cable, July 12, 1993 at 16.

After months of insisting on cash compensation for retransmission consent, CBS ended up granting retransmission consent for one year without obtaining anything in return. Broadcasting & Cable, Oct. 4, 1993 at 6.

A new round of retransmission consent negotiations took place during 1996. Most of the major broadcast group owners renewed their agreements exchanging carriage of their cable channels for retransmission consent. In addition to the channels mentioned above some major channels that were the subject of retransmission consent agreements are NBC's America's Talking, Scripps Howard's Home & Garden Television and the TV Food Network owned by Tribune Broadcasting and the Providence Journal Co.

7. In 1998 the FCC issued a Notice of Proposed Rulemaking addressing the effect of DTV, p. 55, *supra*, on the must-carry rules and retransmission consent. Carriage of the Transmissions of Digital Television Broadcast Stations, 13 FCC Rcd. 15092 (1998). Three years later, the Commission announced its initial action. The decision illustrates the complexity of applying old law to new technology, a problem we return to in the next chapter.

CARRIAGE OF DIGITAL TELEVISION BROADCAST SIGNALS

Federal Communications Commission, 2001.
11 F.C.C.Rcd. 2598.

By the Commission: Commissioners Ness and Furchtgott–Roth approving in part, dissenting in part, and issuing separate statements; Commissioner Powell issuing a statement; Commissioner Tristani dissenting and issuing a statement.

I. INTRODUCTION

. . .

3. On this point, we tentatively conclude that, based on the existing record evidence, a dual carriage requirement appears to burden cable operators' First Amendment interests substantially more than is necessary to further the government's substantial interests of preserving the

benefits of free over-the-air local broadcast television; promoting the widespread dissemination of information from a multiplicity of sources; and promoting fair competition in the market for television programming. However, in order to ensure that we have a sufficient body of evidence before us in which to evaluate this issue fully, so that we can ultimately resolve the issue of mandatory dual carriage, we find it necessary to issue a *Further Notice of Proposed Rulemaking* addressing several critical questions at the center of the carriage debate including, *inter alia*: (1) whether a cable operator will have the channel capacity to carry the digital television signal of a station, in addition to the analog signal of that same station, and without displacing other programming or services; (2) whether market forces, through retransmission consent, will provide cable subscribers access to digital television signals and television stations' access to carriage on cable systems; and (3) how the resolution of the carriage issues would impact the digital transition process. The responses to these and other inquiries will help determine the answer to the dual carriage issue. In the *Further Notice*, we also raise questions concerning the applicability of the rules and policies we adopt herein to satellite carriers under the Satellite Home Viewer Improvement Act of 1999 ("SHVIA"). These and other matters will be addressed in the second phase of this proceeding.

4.   At the outset, we recognize a number of statutory and public policy goals inherent in Section 614 and 615, and other parts of the Act. These include: (1) maximizing incentives for inter-industry negotiation; (2) minimizing disruption to cable subscribers as well as the cable industry; (3) promoting efficiency and innovation in new technologies and services; (4) advancing multichannel video competition; (5) maximizing the introduction of digital broadcast television; and (6) maintaining the strength and competitiveness of broadcast television. Our goal is to facilitate an efficient market-oriented structure that implements the Act in a manner that, to the extent possible, permits private agreements to resolve issues. Based on the importance of cable television in the video programming marketplace, we believe that the cooperation and participation by the cable industry during the transition period would further the successful introduction of digital broadcast television.

II. BACKGROUND

. . .

7.   In a recent Memorandum Opinion and Order regarding band-clearing of the 700 MHz spectrum ("*700 MHz Order*"), the Commission reiterated that cable carriage can play an important role as an alternative distribution channel during the transition period by providing continued service to viewers who would otherwise be deprived of broadcast service. Although the Commission stated that it would be considering the scope and manner of cable carriage of digital broadcast signals in this proceeding, it discussed the cable industry's carriage obligations for future digital television signals in the *700 MHz Order*. First, the Commission clarified that cable systems are ultimately obligated to accord

carriage rights to local broadcasters' digital signals. Specifically, the Commission stated that existing analog stations that return their analog spectrum allocation and convert to digital are entitled to mandatory carriage for their digital signals consistent with applicable statutory and regulatory provisions. The Commission also stated that to facilitate the continuing availability during the transition of the analog signal of a broadcaster who is party to a voluntary band clearing agreement with new 700 MHz licensees, such a broadcaster could, in this context and at its own expense, provide its broadcast digital signal in an analog format for carriage on cable systems. Specifically, the Commission stated that, in these circumstances, nothing prohibits the cable system from providing such signals in an analog format to subscribers, in addition to or in place of the broadcast digital signal, pursuant to an agreement with the broadcaster.

III. CARRIAGE DURING THE DTV TRANSITION

8. The statutory provision triggering this rulemaking is found in Section 614(b)(4)(b) of the Act. This section requires that:

> At such time as the Commission prescribes modifications of the standards for television broadcast signals, the Commission shall initiate a proceeding to establish any changes in the signal carriage requirements of cable television systems necessary to ensure cable carriage of such broadcast signals of local commercial television stations which have been changed to conform with such modified standards.

9. In the *Notice*, we recognized that, as a policy matter, the most difficult carriage issues arise during the transition because there will exist, for a temporary period, approximately twice as many television broadcast signals as are now on the air. We noted that toward the end of the transition period, there would be an increasing redundancy of basic content between the analog and digital signals as the Commission's simulcasting requirements are phased in. We recognized that, to the extent that the Commission imposes a dual carriage requirement, cable operators could be required to carry double the amount of television signals, that will eventually carry identical content, while having to drop various and varied cable programming services where channel capacity is limited. We sought comment on several carriage options that address the needs of the broadcasters and the concerns of the cable operators as well as the timing of mandatory digital broadcast signal carriage rules. These proposals included a range of approaches from "immediate" or dual carriage, in which cable systems would be required to carry both analog and digital commercial television signals up to the one-third capacity limit; the "either-or" proposal, in which broadcasters could choose must carry for either their analog or digital signals during the transition years; and the "no must carry proposal," under which digital signals would not have mandatory carriage rights during the transition period, but only when the transition is over.

10.   The broadcast industry generally urges the Commission to impose a dual carriage requirement during the transition period to ensure that viewers have continued access to all available local television programming. In contrast, NCTA and other cable industry participants contend that digital must carry will "dictate technological outcomes before the market is ready." Time Warner argues that if cable operators were required to carry digital broadcast signals during the transition, an operator's channel line-up would consist of blank screens because most consumers will not have digital television receivers or converters allowing them to display digital signals on their analog sets. Cable programmers oppose a dual carriage requirement because they fear being dropped or being unable to gain carriage due to the addition of digital television signals to a cable operators' channel line-up.

11.   There was support for the "either-or" proposal, particularly from the public interest community. The United Church of Christ and other consumer advocates, filing jointly ("UCC"), believe that this middle-ground proposal, as it applies to commercial television stations, is the "most market friendly and statute friendly" solution. They state that as penetration of digital receivers increases, compatibility between digital television receivers and cable equipment improves, and broadcasters finalize business plans for their new digital signal, each broadcaster can decide which of its signals it would prefer to be carried. UCC believes this option will help speed the transition to digital, preserve local broadcasting, and avoid duplicative signals that reduce diversity.

12.   After reviewing the extensive comments on the central issue of dual carriage during the transition period, we find it is unjustified for the Commission to act at this time in light of the constitutional questions the subject presents, including the related issues of economic impact. We need further information on a range of issues, including cable system channel capacity and digital retransmission consent agreements to build a substantial record upon which to develop the best policy for the various entities impacted in this area. Notwithstanding our decision to obtain further comment on these matters, it is important to clarify that broadcast stations operating only with digital signals are entitled to mandatory carriage under the Act. We find that the burden on a cable operator to carry such stations is *de minimis*, with regard to new digital-only stations, and is essentially a trade-off in the case of a station substituting its digital signal in the place of its analog signal. To implement this clarification, we amend Section 76.5, the definition of television broadcast station, and specifically include the digital television Table of Allotments found at Section 73.622 of the Commission's rules.

A.   Commercial Television Stations

13.   Section 614(a) of the Communications Act of 1934, as amended, provides:

> Carriage Obligations.—Each cable operator shall carry, on the cable system of that operator, the signals of local commercial television

stations and qualified low power stations as provided by this section. Carriage of additional broadcast television signals on such system shall be at the discretion of such operator, subject to section 325(b).

This section requires carriage for local commercial stations subject to the other provisions of Section 614. This section does not distinguish between analog and digital signals and supports the argument that digital signals are entitled to mandatory carriage.

. . .

B. Noncommercial Television Stations

17. The importance of ensuring that noncommercial educational stations are accessible to the viewing public is consistently emphasized in the Act itself and its legislative history. Indeed, the Act mandates that cable operators devote additional channel capacity for the carriage of noncommercial educational television stations ("NCEs"). Congress found "a substantial governmental and First Amendment interest in ensuring that cable subscribers have access to local noncommercial stations."

18. As stated above, Section 614(b)(4)(B) requires the Commission to initiate a proceeding to establish any changes in the signal carriage requirements of cable television systems that are necessary "to ensure cable carriage of such broadcast signals of local commercial television stations. . . ." (emphasis added). In the *Notice* we asked how, if at all, carriage rights for digital noncommercial educational stations are affected given that they are not explicitly discussed in this section.

. . .

19. We believe that the government's interest in ensuring the availability of local noncommercial educational television on cable systems is manifest. Section 615(a) states that "[E]ach cable operator of a cable system shall carry the signals of qualified noncommercial educational television stations in accordance with the provisions of this section." Section 615(a) does not distinguish between digital and analog signals with regard to the 'signals' that must be carried. The Act does not contain any words or provisions specifically excluding the carriage of NCE digital television signals. The legislative history of the Act is also void of any language suggesting that Congress intended to deny mandatory carriage to digital NCE station signals. In addition, there is an implication in Section 336 and its legislative history that Congress intended the Commission to address all must carry issues in the Section 614(b)(4)(B) proceeding, including those relating to noncommercial educational stations covered by Section 615. Section 336 applies only to advanced (digital) television services; it has no application in the analog context. Section 336(b)(3) specifies that ancillary and supplementary services have no mandatory carriage rights under Section 614 or 615, which necessarily contemplates some consideration of must carry under Section 615 for noncommercial educational stations. The legislative history of the conference agreement for this section states: "With respect

to (b)(3), the conferees do not intend this paragraph to confer must carry status on advanced [digital] television or other video services offered on designated frequencies. Under the 1992 Cable Act, that issue is to be the subject of a Commission proceeding under section 614(b)(4)(B) of the Communications Act.'' The most logical inference is that Congress contemplated that the Commission would address the issue of must carry for digital signals in the proceeding authorized by Section 614(b)(4)(B), which would cover both local commercial and noncommercial television stations.

20.   We therefore find that the digital signals of NCE stations are to be treated like their commercial counterparts for cable carriage purposes. Thus, NCE stations that broadcast only in digital are entitled to immediate carriage by cable systems, subject to the parameters set forth in Section 615 of the Act and the relevant Commission orders. And, like our decision with regard to commercial television stations, we decline to address the dual carriage issue for NCE stations in this phase of the proceeding.

. . .

IV.   RETRANSMISSION CONSENT ISSUES

. . .

25.   The *Notice* raised numerous issues related to retransmission consent that can be resolved in this *Report and Order*. The issues are as follows: (1) whether separate retransmission consent/must carry elections are permitted for the analog and digital signals of a broadcast station; (2) whether the timing of the election cycle must be modified; (3) whether a broadcaster may agree to partial carriage of its digital signal; (4) whether the digital replacement signals for analog superstations should be treated as new signals for purposes of the retransmission consent provisions or should have the same status as the ones they replace; (5) whether to extend the prohibition on analog exclusive retransmission consent agreements to the digital context; (6) whether the Commission should prohibit analog-digital signal tying arrangements; and (7) the status of NCE stations under Section 325.

26.   **Separate Analog and Digital Carriage Agreements**. . . .

27.   With regard to those stations that simultaneously broadcast analog and digital television signals, we conclude that a broadcaster is permitted to treat the two differently for carriage purposes. That is, a television station may choose must carry or retransmission consent for its analog signal and retransmission consent for its digital signal. This policy permits the same broadcaster to negotiate a retransmission consent agreement for some or all of its digital signal, if that is what it desires. Our decision here is intended to further the digital transition because we believe cable operators would be more willing to carry certain streams of digital content or ancillary or supplementary data if it is offered by a particular television station, even if that station chose must carry for its

analog signal. We believe this scenario would be precluded if we were to prohibit a station from making such a selection.

28.   We also find that DTV-only stations may choose either retransmission consent or mandatory carriage like their analog counterparts. The retransmission consent rules and regulations contained in Section 76.64 would likewise apply to digital broadcast television signals.

29.   **Modification of the Election Cycle** In the *Notice*, we indicated that the Act requires local commercial television stations to elect either must carry or retransmission consent on a triennial basis. We noted that new television stations can make their initial election anytime between 60 days prior to commencing broadcast and 30 days after commencing broadcast with the initial election taking effect 90 days after it is made. . . . We believe that the Commission's existing new station rules should be used in the digital carriage context. The existing requirements are non-controversial and both cable operators and broadcasters are well accustomed to their use. Thus, for television stations broadcasting only a digital signal, the current rules applicable to new analog signals would apply. Our holding here would also apply to new digital-only noncommercial television signals, even though they are not specifically covered by Section 76.64 of the Commission's rules.

30.   **Retransmission Consent Agreements for Partial Digital Signal Carriage**. . . .

31.   We conclude that for purposes of promoting the transition and encouraging voluntary cable carriage of broadcast digital signals when a television station chooses retransmission consent, the broadcaster and cable operator may negotiate for partial carriage of a local digital television signal.[82] We believe that this policy, which applies to digital-only television stations and television stations with both analog and digital signals, will benefit both parties and help to accomplish the Congressional goal of transitioning to digital television. In this instance, the broadcaster gains access to cable subscribers for some part of its signal, and the cable operator can conserve channel capacity and carry that programming which it believes subscribers will want. We note that this policy is a departure from the Commission's analog carriage rules that require a cable operator to carry local television signals in their entirety. In interpreting the statute in 1994, the Commission noted that the statutory language would appear to permit broadcasters to negotiate with cable operators for retransmission consent for any part of their signal. The Commission found that some negotiated partial carriage was clearly permitted based upon the language in Section 325 but concluded that, as a matter of policy, the statutory provisions should be read in concert to require carriage of "must-carry qualified stations" in their entirety even in the context of retransmission consent. We adopt a different approach here because the statute gives the Commission flexi-

---

82. "Partial" carriage may be considered in any number of ways, including   hours, bits or programming streams.

bility to devise new rules for digital carriage when necessary. We believe that in the case of digital signal carriage, the provisions should be read to permit the parties to freely negotiate for partial carriage in the context of retransmission consent. The goal of facilitating the transition to digital signals is furthered by this interpretation because cable operators are likely to negotiate retransmission consent agreements with more stations if carriage of something less than the full complement of a broadcaster's digital signal is permitted. This outcome may accelerate the digital transition in many markets. In arriving at this determination, we considered that prohibiting partial carriage in the context of retransmission consent would not only discourage voluntary carriage of programming subject to mandatory carriage, but would also be likely to preclude the carriage of desirable programming streams or data services that are not subject to mandatory carriage. . . . We conclude that permitting partial carriage in the context of retransmission consent is appropriate at least for the duration of the transition. When the transition is completed or substantially underway, we can consider whether partial carriage continues to be necessary to facilitate carriage of digital signals over the long term.

32. **Retransmission Consent Exemption for Superstations.** Section 325(b)(2)(D) exempts cable operators from the obligation to obtain retransmission consent from superstations whose "signals" were available by a satellite or common carrier on May 1, 1991. This provision's legislative history states that an exemption from retransmission consent was necessary "to avoid sudden disruption to established relationships" between superstations and satellite carriers. United Video has explained that the exemption permits it to continue to uplink superstations signals and transmit them to cable operators and other facilities-based multichannel video providers. We will treat the digital signals of superstations the same as their analog signals for retransmission consent purposes. If the analog signal was exempt from Section 325, it follows that the station's digital signal is also exempt. We believe that maintaining the status quo and tracking the Act's original intent will permit video program distributors to continue to uplink superstation signals and provide them to cable operators and their subscribers. This policy may speed the transition, and the purchase of digital television equipment, because cable operators may transmit digital superstations into markets where a full array of digital television services may be lacking.

33. **Prohibition on Exclusive Agreements.** In the *Must Carry Order*, we specifically prohibited exclusive retransmission consent agreements between television broadcast stations and cable operators. Congress recently codified the Commission's exclusive retransmission consent prohibition as one of the many amendments to Section 325 under the SHVIA. The Act now states that a broadcaster cannot enter into an exclusive retransmission consent arrangement with any MVPD until 2006. We have recently implemented the statutory ban on exclusive arrangements. Consistent with the new provision and rule, we apply the current prohibition on exclusive retransmission

consent agreements to negotiations involving the carriage of digital television broadcast signals until January 1, 2006.

. . .

36. **NCE Stations.** Section 325 of the Act expressly states that NCE stations do not have retransmission consent rights. As such, an NCE station cannot withhold its signal from being carried by any MVPD. An NCE station, however, is free to negotiate with cable systems and other MVPDs for voluntary carriage. In the digital context, an NCE station may multiplex its digital signal and air several video programming streams at once. In this regard, we note that an NCE station, because it is not covered by Section 325, may enter into an exclusive digital carriage arrangement for any service it may offer or any programming stream that is not subject to a mandatory carriage requirement under Section 615 and our findings herein. Against this backdrop, we expect cable operators and other MVPDs to participate in discussions with NCE stations concerning the voluntary carriage of their digital broadcast signals.

V. DIGITAL BROADCAST SIGNAL CARRIAGE REQUIREMENTS

A. Channel Capacity

37. **Definition.** Section 614(b)(1)(B) provides that a cable operator, with more than 12 usable activated channels, shall not have to devote more than "one-third of the aggregate number of usable activated channels" for the carriage of commercial television stations. Despite this language, there is some dispute as to how the terms "usable activated channels" and "cable system capacity" should be defined in the digital context. We requested comment on the definition of "usable activated channels" for digital television carriage purposes. We noted that many cable operators now have, or soon will have, the technical ability to fit several programming services into one 6 MHz cable channel. Thus, we asked how advances in signal compression technology should affect the definition of channel capacity. We also asked whether the one-third channel capacity requirement for digital broadcast television carriage purposes means one-third of a cable operator's digital channel capacity or one-third of all 6 MHz blocks, including both the analog and digital channels.

. . .

39. Under the Act, a cable operator must make available for signal carriage purposes up to one-third of its usable activated channels. Because of the development of digital signal processing and signal compression technologies, the number of video services carried on a cable system is no longer a simple calculation and may change dynamically over time depending on the amount of motion in the video content, the amount of compression that takes place, and whether the service in question is carried in a standard or high definition digital format. We

have taken these developments into consideration in revising the channel capacity determination.

40.   The channel capacity calculation can be made by taking the total usable activated channel capacity of the system in megahertz and dividing it by three.[111] One third of this capacity, defined in megahertz, is the limit on the amount of system spectrum that a cable operator must make available for commercial broadcast signal carriage purposes. Carriage requests would then have to be accommodated to the extent of this limit in whatever format and by whatever technique is appropriate and is otherwise consistent with the rules. We believe, out of the options presented in the *Notice*, this is the easiest for the operator to calculate. While a calculation based on programming or bits may be possible, both are more difficult than the megahertz method to quantify cable capacity for purposes of the one-third statutory cap. In a digital environment, as cable operators reallocate spectrum from analog to digital, the digital programming and bit carrying capacity of the cable system changes.[112] Therefore, neither programming nor bits provide a constant that can easily be applied to determine channel capacity. In contrast, the number of megahertz employed by a cable system stays constant and does not vary as the allocation of spectrum from analog to digital progresses.

41.   To determine the one-third cap for broadcast signal carriage purposes, the first step is to determine the number of "usable activated channels" on the cable system. "Activated channels" would continue to be defined . . . as those channels engineered at the headend of a cable system for the provision of services generally available to residential subscribers of the cable system, regardless of whether such services actually are provided, including any channel designated for public, educational or governmental use. "Usable activated channels," would continue to be defined . . . as those activated channels of a cable system, except those channels whose use for the distribution of broadcast signals would conflict with technical and safety regulations. Thus, this calculation includes but is not limited to the cable spectrum used for internet service, pay-per-view and video-on-demand, and telephony. Next, the number of usable activated channels is expressed in megahertz and then divided by three to determine the one third cap. For example, if a cable

---

111.   Megahertz ("MHz") is a unit of frequency denoting one million Hertz or one million cycles per second and is closely tied to bandwidth. The telecommunications bandwidth is typically measured in Hertz for analog communications. For example, an analog NTSC television channel occupies a bandwidth of 6 MHz. In digital communications, bandwidth is typically measured in bits per second identified by a specific method of encoding. For example, an HDTV channel encoded in 8 VSB, would occupy a digital bandwidth of about 19.4 megabits per second ("mbps") which, in turn, would require a 6 MHz bandwidth. In digital cable operations, where a 64 QAM encoding tech-

nique is used, that same 6 MHz bandwidth can provide up to 27 mbps of digital bandwidth. That would mean a 6 MHz bandwidth in such a cable system can carry a 19.4 mbps HDTV channel and still be able to provide other video or data services with the remaining 7.6 megabits in that same 6 MHz bandwidth. *See also Newton's Telecom Dictionary*, 11th ed., July 1996.

112.   The concept of bits and bit rates is applicable to digital programming signals, but not to analog programming signals. Thus, there is no way to express the part of a cable system's capacity attributable to analog programming in terms of bits.

system's downstream operation begins at 54 MHz and continues through 550 MHz, but 50 MHz is unactivated, the total amount of usable channels on a system-wide basis is 446 MHz (i.e. 550 MHz–54 MHz–50 MHz). One-third of this figure, approximately 149 MHz in this example, is the maximum amount of megahertz to be used for the carriage of local commercial television signals for such a system. A cable operator must provide each local television station that is entitled to mandatory carriage with a sufficient amount of capacity to carry its primary digital video signal. The amount of capacity devoted to carriage purposes for each television station will change as an operator upgrades to a digital cable standard.[115]

42. **Carriage Priority.** In the *Notice*, we recognized that when the one-third capacity limit has been reached, Section 614(b)(2) provides that "the cable operator shall have discretion in selecting which such stations shall be carried on its cable system." . . . We find that the Act provides a cable operator with discretion to choose which signals it will carry if it has met its carriage quota. Thus, a cable operator should be able to select which signals to carry above the one-third limit. Under the existing carriage structure, all local commercial television signals that are carried, whether they have chosen retransmission consent or must carry, are counted as part of the one-third cap calculation. This policy of counting retransmission consent stations will continue to apply in the digital carriage context.

43. **NCE Stations.** We recognize that the carriage of NCE stations is not included in the one-third statutory cap. Instead, a cable operator's carriage obligations are based on the number of channels on a particular cable system. . . . We see no reason to depart from the existing rules regarding NCE carriage. As such, cable systems with the capacity to carry 36 or more channels will be required to carry 3 or more qualified NCE stations, subject to the other provisions of the Act and our rules.

B. Signal Quality

44. Section 614(h) of the Act specifies that, to qualify for carriage, stations must deliver a good quality signal to the principal headend of the cable system. For local commercial television stations, this is defined as a signal level of–45dBm for UHF signals and–49dBm for VHF signals. The Act delegated to the Commission the authority to establish good quality signal criteria for low power television stations and for qualified local noncommercial educational television stations. We held that the commercial television station definition of good quality signal be applied in the same manner to noncommercial and LPTV television stations under the UHF/VHF paradigm.

45. In the *Notice*, we asked whether the signal quality standards established for analog signals are relevant for digital signals or whether

---

115. For example, a cable operator with an analog-based cable system would devote 6 MHz of bandwidth to the carriage of a high definition television signal, but a cable operator using the 64 QAM digital format may only have to devote 4 MHz to the carriage of that same high definition signal.

new parameters for good signal quality should be established. . . . We note that in adopting the digital television transmission standard, the Commission recognized the differences between analog and digital television signals. The analog NTSC transmission standard is engineered so that even when a station's signal strength slowly decreases, a television set is still able to display the video and audio components, albeit at a degraded level. On the other hand, under the DTV transmission standard, as the station's signal level decreases, the digital television set continues to display a good picture, but then may abruptly turn blue when the signal strength drops below a certain threshold.[131] Against this backdrop, we believe it is necessary to develop a new reception standard aptly suited to the new digital technology used to transmit digital television signals.

46. We conclude that the signal level necessary to provide a good quality digital television signal at a cable system's principal headend is–61 dBm. . . . We believe that when a signal level of–61 dBm is delivered to the cable system headend, the signal will be of sufficient strength that the cable operator can deliver a good quality picture to its subscribers. A television station that does not agree to be responsible for the costs of delivering to the cable system a signal of good quality, under the revised standard, is not eligible for carriage.

C. Content of Signals Subject to Mandatory Carriage

47. We now address the specific content of a digital television signal that is subject to the mandatory carriage obligation. We note that analog broadcast stations generally have one video broadcast product. That is, only a single program is broadcast at a time and that program is the main feature of the broadcast. Only a relatively minor amount of communications capacity is available apart from that program transmission. Some capacity is available in the vertical blanking interval ("VBI") for the transmission of communications that are separate from, but related to, the principal video output or are unrelated to that content. The related content is typically closed captioning and program rating information. The unrelated content would be typified by videotext or data-type communications.

48. Digital television stations will operate on a much more flexible basis. The system described in the ATSC DTV Standard includes discrete subsystem descriptions, or "layers," for video source coding and compression, audio source coding and compression, service multiplex and transport, and RF/transmission. In addition to being able to broadcast one, and under some circumstances two, high definition digital television programs, the standard allows for multiple streams, or "multicasting,"

---

131. This is known as the "cliff effect." That is, if a signal is received, a good quality picture can be constructed at the television receiver; however, once the signal falls below a minimum signal level threshold, no picture can be reconstructed or displayed by the television receiver. There are, however, certain receiver implementation schemes which allow the receiver to display and hold the last picture received before the signal fell below the threshold.

of standard definition digital television programming at a visual quality better than the current NTSC analog standard. Multiple programming streams may be broadcast at the same time or with a variety of data streams accompanying the main video content. These data streams may be either associated with the video content in some manner or completely separate from it.

49. A critical component of digital broadcast television is the program and system information protocol ("PSIP"). This is the standard protocol for transmission of the relevant data tables, describing system information and event descriptions, contained within digital packets carried in the digital broadcast transport stream multiplex. System information allows navigation of, and access to, each of the channels within the transport stream, whereas event descriptions give the user content information for browsing and selection. PSIP is composed of four main tables: (1) system time table; (2) ratings region table; (3) master guide table; and (4) virtual channel table. The latter table is of particular importance in the carriage context because it contains a list of all the channels that are or will be on-line, plus their attributes. Among the attributes are the channel name, navigation identifiers, and stream components and types. PSIP allows the broadcaster to customize information to guide viewers to channel numbers they are familiar with.

50. **Primary Video.** In the analog context it is clear that a cable operator subject to a mandatory carriage obligation is not required to carry all of the communications output of a television broadcast station. Three provisions of the Act provide the main focus of the arguments regarding this question in the context of digital broadcast signal carriage. First, Section 614(b)(3) of the Act entitled "Content to be Carried," states that a cable operator shall carry in its entirety the "primary video" of the station. Second, it requires carriage of the "accompanying audio" and "line 21 closed caption transmission" of each station. Third, the operator must carry "to the extent technically feasible, program-related material carried in the vertical blanking interval or on subcarriers." The statute is specific that "Retransmission of other material in the vertical blanking interval or other nonprogram-related material (including teletext and other subscription and advertiser-supported information services) shall be at the discretion of the cable operator." Section 614 is applicable to the carriage of commercial stations. Largely parallel provisions are contained in Section 615 relating to the carriage of noncommercial stations. In addition to the provisions that are not specific to digital television broadcasting, Section 336(b)(3) of the Act which has specific applicability to "advanced television services" provides that "no ancillary or supplementary service shall have any right to carriage under section 614 or 615."

51. In the *Notice*, we asked how we should define "primary video" if a broadcaster chooses to broadcast multiple standard definition digital television streams, or a mixture of high definition and standard definition digital television streams, as is permitted under the rules. We sought input on which video programming services provided by a licen-

see should be considered primary and should be entitled to carriage if the primary video includes less than all of the streams of programming broadcast. We asked whether the definition should be flexible, allowing the broadcaster to choose which transmissions it considers being primary.

. . .

53. We recognize that the terms 'primary video' as used in sections 614(b)(3) and 615(g)(1) are susceptible to different interpretations. Because the terms are not expressly defined in the Act, to determine the meaning, we analyze the terms 'primary video' within their statutory context, consider the legislative history, and examine the technological developments at the time the must carry provisions were enacted.

54. The term primary video, as found in Sections 614 and 615 of the Act, suggests that there is some video that is primary and some that is not. In this instance, we rely on the canon of statutory construction that effect must be given to every word of a statute and that no part of a provision will be read as superfluous. Here, we must give effect to the word "primary." The dictionary definitions of "primary" are "First or highest in rank, quality, or importance" and "Being or standing first in a list, series, or sequence." Based on the plain words of the Act, we conclude that, to the extent a television station is broadcasting more than a single video stream at a time, only one of such streams of each television station is considered "primary." The choice as to which, among several possible video programming streams, should be considered primary is a decision left to the broadcaster.

. . .

57. Based on the record currently before us, we conclude that "primary video" means a single programming stream and other program-related content. With the advent of digital television, broadcast stations now have the opportunity to include in their video service a panoply of program-related content. Indeed, far more video content is possible broadcasting a digital signal than broadcasting in an analog format. For example, a digital television broadcast of a sporting event could include multiple camera angles from which the viewer may select. The statute contemplates and our rules require that cable operators provide mandatory carriage for this program-related content. In contrast, if a digital broadcaster elects to divide its digital spectrum into several separate, independent and unrelated programming streams, only one of these streams is considered primary and entitled to mandatory carriage. The broadcaster must elect which programming stream is its primary video, and the cable operator is required to provide mandatory carriage to only such designated stream. While we do not believe that Congress specifically contemplated programming of the type described above (i.e., data or video that is separate from but associated with the primary video) in drafting Section 614(b)(3), the policies underlying this Section are consistent with our conclusion here in the context of digital signal carriage. Based on the language in 614(b)(3), Congress was concerned that manda-

tory carriage be limited to the broadcaster's primary program stream but also include related content as described here. In the FNPRM we seek comment on the appropriate parameters for "program-related" in the digital context.

58. **Ancillary and Supplementary Services**. Section 336 of the Act provides that "no ancillary or supplementary service shall have any right to carriage under section 614 or 615." Neither the Act nor the legislative history define the terms 'ancillary or supplementary.' Section 614(b)(3) of the Act requires cable operators to carry "to the extent technically feasible, program-related material carried in the vertical blanking interval or subcarriers" but states that "[r]etransmission of other material in the vertical blanking interval or other nonprogram-related material (including teletext and other subscription and advertiser-supported information services) shall be at the discretion of the cable operator." . . .

59. With respect to the definition of ancillary and supplementary services, the Commission's *DTV Fifth Report and Order* states that ancillary and supplementary services include "any service provided on the digital channel other than free, over-the-air services." Section 73.624(c) of the Commission's rules specifies that "any video broadcast signal provided at no direct charge to viewers shall not be considered ancillary or supplementary." While not defining the class exhaustively, Section 73.624(c) indicates that ancillary and supplementary services include, but are not limited to, "computer software distribution, data transmissions, teletext, interactive materials, aural messages, paging services, audio signals, [and] subscription video [video programming for which the broadcaster charges a fee]. . . ." Section 73.646 of the Commission's rules states that telecommunications services provided on the vertical blanking interval ("VBI") or in the visual signal, in either analog or digital mode, are ancillary. Based on the foregoing, we find that the services specified in Sections 73.624(c) and 73.646 are ancillary or supplementary in the context of digital cable carriage and are not entitled to mandatory carriage.

60. In addition, we believe there may be certain services associated with broadcast digital video programming, while not ancillary or supplementary, would still not entitled to mandatory carriage because they are not program related. Currently, in addition to a broadcaster's primary analog video programming, Section 614(b)(3) requires cable operators to carry "to the extent technically feasible, program-related material carried in the vertical blanking interval or on subcarriers . . ." However, "[r]etransmission of other material in the vertical blanking interval or other nonprogram-related material (including teletext and other subscription and advertiser-supported information services) shall be at the discretion of the cable operator." In the analog context, we have specified certain factors for determining what material carried in the VBI is sufficiently program-related as to qualify for must carry rights. Due to the technical differences between digital and analog transmission, *e.g.*, there is no VBI in a digital signal, the foregoing concepts cannot transfer directly into a digital environment. What is anticipated is that a televi-

sion station will provide internet-based services, such as e-commerce applications, to the public. While this type of business plan promises to enhance a television station's digital presence, the carriage of internet offerings by a cable operator likely would not be required under the must carry provisions unless the broadcaster can demonstrate that such material should be considered program-related.

61.   In this vein, we note that there are certain over-the-air digital services sufficiently related to the broadcaster's primary digital video programming that are entitled to carriage. These include, but are not limited to, closed captioning information, program ratings data for use in conjunction with the V-chip functions of receivers, Source Identification Codes ("SID Codes") used by Nielsen Media Research in the preparation of program ratings, and the channel mapping and tuning protocols that are part of PSIP. These services provide useful information to viewers, broadcasters, and/or cable operators, and are intended for use in direct conjunction with the programming.[170] In general, we will continue to use the same factors enumerated in *WGN*, that are used in the analog context to determine what material is considered program-related.[171] The *WGN* court set out a three-part test for making a determination. First, the broadcaster must intend for the information in the VBI to be seen by the same viewers who are watching the video signal. Second, the VBI information must be available during the same interval of time as the video signal. Third, the VBI information must be an integral part of the program. The court in *WGN* held that if the information in the VBI is intended to be seen by the viewers who are watching the video signal, during the same interval of time as the video signal, and as an integral part of the program on the video signal, then the VBI and the video signal must both be carried if one is to be carried.

62.   As noted, digital signals do not contain a VBI. The Commission's rule in Section 76.56(e) describes what cable systems may carry in the VBI. This subsection is revised to revise the reference to VBI to take account of digital technology.

63.   **Program Guides**. We sought comment on the status of advanced programming retrieval systems and other digital channel selection devices that filter and prioritize video programs for viewers. . . .

64.   We find that the carriage of program guide information is a matter to be addressed under Sections 614(b)(3) and 615(g)(1) of the Act. As

---

170. We note that independent of the "program related" and "ancillary or supplementary" concepts, cable operators are required to pass through closed captioning data contained in analog and digital video programming. 47 C.F.R. §§ 76.606, 79.1(c). We further note that while the Commission has refrained from promulgating regulations requiring delivery of the codes necessary for operation of the "V-chip," it has done so based upon the voluntary assumption of this responsibility by video program

distributors. *In the Matter of Technical Requirements to Enable Blocking of Video Programming based on Program Ratings, Report and Order*, 13 FCC Rcd 11248, 11259 (1998).

171. 693 F.2d at 624–25. The Commission declined to further define "program-related," apart from the WGN analysis, noting that carriage of information in the VBI was rapidly evolving. *Must Carry Order*, 8 FCC Rcd at 2986.

stated earlier, all program-related broadcast material found in the analog signal's VBI must be carried, unless it is technically infeasible for the operator to do so. In the digital television context, there is no VBI for EPG information to be carried on, rather, the EPG data would be part of the PSIP. In this circumstance, we find that program guide data that are not specifically linked to the video content of the digital signal being shown cannot be considered program-related, and, therefore, are not subject to a carriage requirement.

. . .

D. Duplicative Signals

66.   Section 614(b)(5) of the Communications Act provides that "a cable operator shall not be required to carry the signal of any local commercial television station that substantially duplicates the signal of another local television station which is carried on the cable system, or to carry the signals of more than one local commercial television station affiliated with a particular broadcast network . . ." A parallel rule applies to the carriage of NCE station signals.[192] Congress enacted these provisions to preserve a cable operator's editorial discretion while ensuring that the public has access to a diversity of local television signals.

. . .

68.   We recognize that reaching a conclusion on this matter is complicated by our requirements for the digital transition. The Commission established a staged implementation schedule for the introduction of digital television in the rules governing the transition. In the early stages of the transition, broadcasters have flexibility in selecting the digital programming they offer. The Commission refrained from imposing simulcasting requirements during this phase in order to afford broadcasters the freedom to experiment with program and service offerings. Thus, for example, a broadcaster's initial digital programming may be entirely original, it may simply duplicate a certain amount of its analog programming, or it may combine original digital content with analog content. Beginning April 1, 2003, the rules mandate an increasing level of duplication of program content between the analog and digital signals, eventually reaching a 100% simulcasting requirement which continues until a broadcaster's analog channel is terminated and returned to the Commission.

69.   We will not revise the duplication definitions and requirements at this time. More information is needed on the digital programming currently made available by broadcasters before we act in this regard. . . .

E. Material Degradation

70.   Section 614(b)(4)(A) of the Act discusses the cable operator's treatment and processing of analog broadcast station signals and provides

---

192. *Id.* These simulcasting requirements are intended to minimize viewer disruption as the content of the analog signal is slowly replicated on the digital signal.

that the signals of local commercial television stations shall be carried without material degradation. The *Notice* asked to what extent this provision precludes cable operators from altering the digital format of digital broadcast television signals when the transmission is processed at the system headend or in customer premises equipment. Under the Act, the Commission's carriage standards must ensure that, "to the extent technically feasible, the quality of signal processing and carriage provided by a cable system for the carriage of local commercial television stations will be no less than that provided by the system for carriage of any other type of signal." To address this provision, the *Notice* sought comment on whether the Act requires an operator to carry all local commercial television stations that broadcast in a 1080I high definition format if it carries a cable programming service such as HBO in the 1080I HDTV format.

71. We note that the Advanced Television Systems Committee ("ATSC") DTV Standard adopted by the Commission was recommended by the Advisory Committee on Advanced Television Service ("ACATS") and developed by the Grand Alliance. It provides for 19.4 megabits per second ("mbps") for each 6 MHz channel over-the-air. The Commission neither adopted a single standard for high definition television nor imposed a HDTV requirement on broadcasters. Rather, the Commission drew the distinction between standard definition ("SDTV") and high definition ("HDTV") in the digital context. The electronics industry and ATSC define high definition television as having a vertical display resolution of 720p, 1080I, or higher; an aspect ratio capable of displaying a 16:9 image at the minimum resolution level; and receiving and reproducing Dolby digital audio.[204] In contrast, standard definition digital

---

204. ATSC Restates Definitions for HDTV and SDTV Transmission Standards, Press Release (Feb. 20, 1998) at www.atsc.org/Presshtml/PR_Def.html. The Executive Committee of the Advanced Television Systems Committee has approved for release the following statement regarding the identification of the HDTV and SDTV transmission formats within the ATSC Digital Television Standard: "There are six video formats in the ATSC DTV standard which are High Definition. They are the the 1080 line by 1920 pixel formats at all picture rates (24, 30 and 60 pictures per second), and the 720 line by 1280 pixel formats at these same picture rates. All of these formats have a 16:9 aspect ratio." ; *DTV Fifth Further Notice of Proposed Rule Making*, 11 FCC Rcd. 6235, 6237 (1996) ("DTV Fifth FNPRM") (Noting that 720–line and 1080–line formats represent high-resolution video). Both high-resolution formats use a picture aspect ratio of 16 units horizontally by 9 units vertically. The choices of 1280 pixels per line for the 720–line format and

1920 pixels per line for the 1080–line format result in square pixels for both formats, based on the 16:9 aspect ratio. "I" designates "interlaced" scanning and "P" designates "progressive" scanning. Progressive scanning lines are presented in succession from the top of the picture to the bottom, with a complete image sent in each frame as is commonly found in computer displays today. For interlaced scanning, which also is used in NTSC (analog) television, odd and even numbered lines of the picture are sent consecutively, as two separate fields. These two fields are superimposed to create one frame, or complete picture, at the receiver. The interlace picture rates can be 24, 30 or 60 fields per second. *Id.* at 11 FCC Rcd at 6237–38. *See also* CEA Expands Definitions for DTV Products, www.digitalbroadcasting.com, September 6, 2000 (Definitions, which now allow for DTV to be defined in the 4:3 aspect ratio standard, are expected to be incorporated into new products in time for holiday buying season).

displays resolution lower than high definition, requires no specific ratio, and produces "usable" audio and picture.

72. . . . From our perspective, the issue of material degradation is about the picture quality the consumer receives and is capable of perceiving and not about the number of bits transmitted by the broadcaster if the difference is not really perceptible to the viewer. Such an interpretation is consistent with the language of the Act, which applies to *material* degradation, not merely technical changes in the signals.[209] Moreover, as discussed above, the Act prohibits mandatory carriage for ancillary or supplementary services and our rules provide that material that is not program-related is not subject to the mandatory carriage requirement. If such bitstream material that is not subject to mandatory carriage is subtracted from the entire 6 MHz over-the-air digital signal, by necessity there will be fewer than 19.4 mbps to be carried on the cable system. Moreover, whenever a digital signal is remodulated for carriage on a cable system, fewer bits are needed than to transmit the signal over the air.[212] Thus, it is inappropriate to use 19.4 mbps, or any specific number of bits, to denote what constitutes a degraded signal. The number of bits appropriate for mandatory carriage will vary based on the programming and service choices of each broadcaster.

73. With regard to defining picture quality for digital carriage purposes, . . . [s]ection 614(b)(4)(A) requires that cable operators shall provide the same "quality of signal processing and carriage" for broadcasters' signals as they provide for any other type of signal. Consequently, in the context of mandatory carriage of digital broadcast signals, a cable operator may not provide a digital broadcast signal in a lesser format or lower resolution than that afforded to any digital programmer (e.g., non-broadcast cable programming, other broadcast digital program, etc.) carried on the cable system, provided, however, that a broadcast signal delivered in HDTV must be carried in HDTV.[216] This result also

209. 47 U.S.C. § 534(b)(4)(A). This interpretation is also consistent with the Act's general mandate of ensuring that cable operators do not favor their own cable programming video services over those video services provided by broadcasters.

212. A broadcaster's over-the-air HDTV signal, for example, requires 19.4 mbps, which accounts for both the programming or data, as well as an overhead data stream that includes error correction. When a cable system carries this HDTV signal using QAM modulation, it removes the broadcaster's overhead data stream and replaces it with the overheada stream appropriate for the specific cable system. Generally the resulting bit rate is somewhat less than 19.4. This reduction in bit rate does not affect picture quality and is not considered material degradation.

216. We recognize that it may be especially burdensome for small systems with

limited channel capacity (such as systems with fewer than 330 MHz) to carry a HDTV signal if they are not otherwise providing any HDTV programming. In this regard, we note that mandatory carriage is limited to one-third of the cable system's capacity, as defined *infra*. We also recognize that carriage of a HDTV signal using 8 VSB pass-through may require the allocation of more than 6 MHz of bandwidth due to the difference in channel alignments between broadcast over-the-air transmission and cable carriage. An 8–VSB pass-through of a broadcast station may straddle two cable channels and result in the loss of additional channels in the system (i.e., the cable operator is not able to use these additional channels to carry other programming). Therefore, if a small system, which is not otherwise carrying any HDTV signals, is required to carry a broadcast signal in HDTV such that it straddles two channels in this way, it may include all of its lost

protects the interests of cable subscribers by focussing on the comparable resolution of the picture, as visible to a consumer, rather than the number of lines or bits transmitted, which may not make a viewable difference on a consumer's equipment.

74.   We also find that for purposes of supporting the ultimate conversion to digital signals and facilitating the return of the analog spectrum, a television station may demand that one of its HDTV or SDTV television signals be carried on the cable system for delivery to subscribers in an analog format. We do not believe the conversion of a digital signal to an analog format under these specific and temporary circumstances is precluded by the nondegradation requirement in sections 614(b)(4)(A) and 615(g)(2). Many cable subscribers do not yet have television sets capable of receiving or displaying digital signals in their fully advanced format. Thus, if we were to mandate digital-to-digital transmission at this stage of the transition period, cable subscribers would be unable to properly receive the signals. Obviously this was not the intended goal of the nondegradation requirement in sections 614(b)(4)(A) and 615(g)(2). Allowing digital-to-analog conversion for a limited time during a critical stage of the transition period will further the digital transition because a television station would be more willing to return its analog spectrum to the government, and convert to digital service, knowing that cable subscribers without digital equipment may still be able to view the relevant programming. We recognize, that permitting digital-to-analog conversion will not provide an impetus for cable subscribers to purchase digital television sets, but will allow new digital stations and stations that return their analog spectrum to continue to reach cable subscribers who have only analog receivers while commencing over-the-air service to attract and reach non-cable viewers who purchase digital television sets. With these points in mind, we will allow a television station to provide one of its digital signals to cable systems in an analog format only during the early stages of the transition period. We will revisit this policy after 2003 to ensure that this policy is fostering the conversion to digital television service and to determine when equipment is available so that broadcast signals can be delivered and carried in digital format.[217] As the transition moves forward, television broadcast stations will be required to deliver their signals in digital format and cable operators will be required to carry them in digital format, as discussed above.

. . .

76.   **Digital Modulation Techniques.** We are mindful that digital television signals are transmitted in the 8 VSB[219] digital broadcast

spectrum when calculating its one-third capacity.

217. We understand that for some time the technology has been available to manufacture cable boxes that can either deliver a digital signal to the subscriber's digital equipment or downconvert the signal to be displayed on analog equipment. [   ] Apparently there is not as yet sufficient demand to produce these boxes for retail purchase or for rental from the cable operator. We will monitor the market's progress to ensure that our permission for analog conversion at the headend does not interfere with the marketplace availability of such boxes.

219. VSB is a form of amplitude modulation in which one sideband of the main modulated signal and a small part of the

modulation technique while operators will use either 64 or 256 QAM[220] as the cable digital modulation technique. Both 64 and 256 QAM likely will provide cable operators with a greater degree of operating efficiency than does 8 VSB, and also permits the carriage of a higher data rate, with less bits devoted to error correction, when compared with the digital broadcast system. Therefore, we will permit cable operators to remodulate digital broadcast signals from 8 VSB to 64 or 256 QAM.[221] We will not require cable operators to pass through 8 VSB. Notwithstanding this conclusion, we believe that cable pass-through of a digital broadcast signal without alteration is an option for allowing the first purchasers of digital television sets to receive digital signals from their cable systems. Under this scenario, the 8 VSB signal could pass through the cable system and the cable set-top box without change and connect to the digital television set, or the cable could bypass the set-top box and be connected to a cable coaxial connection on the digital television receiver. We believe that pass-through is an option for operators of certain cable systems[222] that wish to offer subscribers digital broadcast channels, but recognize in the long term, that pass-through is not an effective solution for the majority of cable systems.

. . .

G. Channel Location

81. Section 614(b)(6) generally provides that commercial television stations carried pursuant to the mandatory carriage provision are entitled to be carried on a cable system on the same channel number on which the station broadcasts over-the-air. Under Section 615(g)(5) noncommercial television stations generally have the same right. The Act also permits commercial and noncommercial television stations to negotiate a mutually beneficial channel position with the cable operator. In seeking comment on the applicability of these types of requirements in the digital context, we noted that station licensees received new digital broadcast frequency assignments and channel numbers that are different

---

other sideband of the same signal are transmitted. The 8 VSB standard has been optimized for terrestrial broadcast television delivery where transmission errors and data loss are likely. The current analog television standard also uses VSB.

220. Quadrature amplitude modulation, or QAM, is a complex modulation technique, using variations in both signal phase and amplitude. We note that 256 QAM has a 38 Mpbs data rate while 64 QAM has a 27 Mbps data rate.

221. The ATSC standards on which the 8 VSB digital television broadcasting system is based, involved the participation of the cable industry. It was anticipated in the ATSC process that non-broadcast digital video program providers would be using a 16 VSB modulation system. Although ca-

ble operators are now using QAM, rather than VSB, it was clearly contemplated throughout the process that the cable industry and the broadcasting industry would not be using the same modulation technique. . . . For purposes of Section 76.630 of our rules, we clarify that we do not consider the utilization of QAM modulation by a cable operator in the provision of digital cable television service to involve scrambling, encryption or similar technologies of the type referenced therein. *See* 47 C.F.R. § 76.630.

222. This may be applicable to cable systems that will not be providing any digital cable programming or systems not wanting to incur the additional expense of 8 VSB to either 64 or 256 QAM conversion at the headend or in the set-top box.

from their analog channel numbers. We pointed out that the advent of advanced programming retrieval systems and other channel selection devices may alleviate the need for specific channel positioning requirements. In this regard, the ATSC established channel identification protocols, or PSIPs,[240] that link the digital channel number with that assigned to the analog channel.

. . .

83.　In the digital environment it is generally anticipated that broadcast signals will be identified and tuned to through the PSIP information process rather than by identification with the specific frequency on which the station is broadcasting. Given the new digital table of allotments, we find that there is no need to implement channel positioning requirements for digital television signals of the same type currently applicable to analog signals. Rather, as the majority of commenters have suggested, we find that the channel mapping protocols contained in the PSIP identification stream adequately address location issues consistent with Congress's concerns about nondiscriminatory treatment of television stations by cable operators. We believe this technology-based solution will resolve broadcaster concerns. PSIP assures that cable subscribers are able to locate a desired digital broadcast signal and ensures that digital television stations are able to fairly compete with cable programming services in the digital environment. . . .

. . .

VII.　FURTHER NOTICE OF PROPOSED RULEMAKING

112.　As noted above, after reviewing the comments submitted in this proceeding, we arrive at the tentative conclusion that, based on the current record, a dual carriage requirement may burden cable operators' First Amendment interests more than is necessary to further the important governmental interests they would promote. However, we seek to gather substantial evidence on this matter so that we may evaluate the issues on a complete and full record. Accordingly, we request further information on a number of matters, including, but not limited to: (1) the need for dual carriage for a successful transition to digital television and return of the analog spectrum; (2) cable system channel capacity; and (3) digital retransmission consent. Much has changed since we first opened this docket in July of 1998, and it is necessary to update the record to reflect events pertinent to the carriage issues being debated. In addition, we ask whether cable operators should be allowed to increase

---

240.　*See Program and System Information Protocol for Terrestrial Broadcast and Cable*, ATSC Document A/65 (Dec. 23, 1997) ("For broadcasters with existing NTSC licenses, the major channel number for the existing NTSC channels, as well as the Digital TV channels, controlled by the broadcaster, shall be set to the current NTSC RF channel number. [ ] Assume a broadcaster who has an NTSC broadcast license for RF channel 13 is assigned RF channel 39 for Digital ATSC broadcast. That broadcaster will use major channel number 13 for identification of the analog NTSC channel on RF channel 13, as well as the digital channels it is controlling on RF channel 39.")

subscriber rates for each 6 MHz of capacity devoted to the carriage of digital broadcast signals.

113. To date in this proceeding, we have received comments arguing that the statute requires dual carriage or that the statute forbids it. It is our view, having deliberated extensively on this question, that neither of these views prevail. Based on the record currently before us, we believe that the statute neither compels dual carriage; nor prohibits it. It is precisely the ambiguity of the statute that has driven this policy debate. In order to weigh the constitutional questions inherent in a statutory construction that would permit dual carriage, we believe it is appropriate and necessary to more fully develop the record in this regard. Because any decision requiring dual carriage would likely be subject to a constitutional challenge, and because an administrative agency can consider potential constitutional infirmities in deciding between possible interpretations of a statute, we are compelled to further develop the record on the impact dual carriage would have on broadcast stations, cable operators and cable programmers, as well as consumers. We believe that more evidence is necessary because the Supreme Court sustained the Act's analog broadcast signal carriage requirements against a First Amendment challenge principally because Congress and the broadcasting industry built a substantial record of the harm to television stations in the absence of mandatory analog carriage rules. . . .

114. We also recognize that the intermediate scrutiny factors established in *U.S. v. O'Brien* and applied in the *Turner* cases, for determining whether a content-neutral rule or regulation violates the Constitution, must also be satisfied here. . . .

115. In the case of dual carriage, we believe that the record is insufficient to demonstrate the degree of harm broadcasters will suffer without the carriage of both signals. In addition, we must carefully consider the burden such a requirement would impose on the cable operator. We seek information on digital retransmission consent agreements to determine the degree to which cable operators are carrying digital signals on a voluntary basis. If broadcasters are being carried by agreement, then they may not be harmed in the absence of a digital carriage requirement. In addition, First Amendment precedent requires that we tailor the carriage requirement to avoid burdening more speech than necessary. In this regard, the impact of mandatory carriage on cable systems was relevant in *Turner*. We therefore seek substantive information to determine cable system channel capacity.

. . .

A. Digital Television Transition and Mandatory Carriage

117. Both Congress and the Commission have worked to develop a digital television transition that accounts for the needs of the broadcast industry, while recognizing the government's interest in the prompt return of the analog broadcast spectrum. The Commission's stated expectation when the DTV rules were adopted was that analog television

broadcasting would cease no later than the end of 2006. With passage of the *Balanced Budget Act of 1997*, Congress codified the December 31, 2006 analog television termination date, but also adopted certain exceptions to it. The *Notice* in this proceeding discussed must carry rules for possible application during a temporary transitional period prior to the cessation of analog broadcasting. Because of the nature of the exceptions set forth in the *Balanced Budget Act of 1997*, questions have arisen as to how long the transition period might last either with or without a dual carriage requirement. Some have expressed doubt that the return of the analog broadcast spectrum will be completed by the end of 2006, regardless of whether there is a digital carriage requirement. Others have argued that dual carriage is necessary to enable broadcasters to meet the statutory tests and complete the transition on time. None of the participants in this proceeding, however, have provided a concise plan for how and when the transition will be completed. As such, a number of questions concerning the transition have arisen. For example, under what circumstances and statutory interpretations will the statutory criteria for the auction of recaptured broadcast television spectrum be satisfied? Will the analog television license be returned when 85% or more of the television households in a market *either* subscribe to an MVPD that carries all of the digital broadcast stations in the market *or* have a DTV receiver or digital downconverter to receive the digital signal over the air? Or is there a different interpretation of the statutory exceptions? Will the spectrum be returned if some of the MVPD subscribers are unable to receive and view the DTV programming notwithstanding that it is carried by the MVPD because they do not have a digital receiver or converter? How does the growth of competitive noncable MVPD's change the analysis? Alternatively, would the analog licenses be returned in a market in which 85% of the television households had a DTV receiver or digital-to-analog converter, but only 30% subscribed to a MVPD that carried all of the digital television stations in the market?

118.   Understanding how the affected parties expect to complete the transition, and exactly how the law applies, substantially affects the Commission's policy approach to the digital television transition as well as to the overall issue of cable carriage. A mandatory dual carriage requirement, for example, would place a more significant and lasting burden on a cable operator's constitutional rights if in fact there will be a substantially extended transition to a digital-only environment. We seek comment on these transition issues and ask for more specific comment on when the analog spectrum is likely to be returned under both mandatory and non-mandatory dual carriage scenarios. We also seek comment on whether and how the dual carriage burden on cable operators may be lessened by using a transitional approach limiting dual carriage to a specified period of time. For example, in this regard, how would a three year limit on dual carriage affect the constitutional question?

119. There are several other issues concerning the rollout of digital broadcast television that still remain. For example, a number of digital television licensees in markets 11–30, that were required to begin digital broadcasting on November 1, 1999 have asked for extensions of time to build out their facilities. Such petitions assert that these extensions may have been necessary because local zoning requirements have hindered the construction of digital broadcast towers or because there are construction and equipment delays. Whatever the case may be, it is difficult to proceed with the dual carriage question if it remains unclear how and when digital signals will become available in any particular market. Because an operator is only required to carry broadcast signals up to one-third of its channel capacity, to rule on the dual carriage issue now may result in on-air digital signals being carried, at the expense of those yet-to-air digital signals that may not be carried because the operator's one-third cap has been met and the operator is reluctant to disrupt viewers by changing signals carried. In this regard, we ask whether we should wait for all or a more significant number of broadcasters to build out their facilities before considering a dual carriage rule to avoid this potential disruption.

120. We also note that there appears to be a limited amount of original digital programming being broadcast. This calls into question the practicality of imposing a dual carriage rule at this time. Cable subscribers would not immediately benefit from a dual carriage rule if there is little to view but duplicative material. In addition, there is a risk that if carriage were mandated, cable subscribers would lose existing cable programming services that would be replaced on the channel line-up by digital television signals with less programming. It is difficult to decide definitional issues, such as what would be considered a "duplicative signal" without more information. We ask broadcasters to describe what part of their planned digital programming streams will be devoted to simulcast of their analog programming and what parts are, or will be used, for other programming. We ask broadcasters to provide us with information on the exact amount of digital programming, on a weekly basis, being aired in a high definition format and the exact amount of original digital programming. We also seek comment on the number of hours, in an average day, that a broadcaster currently airs digital television, and specifically high definition digital programming.

121. We also seek further comment on issues relevant to the carriage of digital signals by small operators. As described in the Order, above, the SCBA expressed concern that allowing broadcasters to tie analog and digital retransmission consent could have a negative financial effect on small cable operators. The current record does not contain adequate evidence on this point. We specifically request information on small cable operators' equipment costs to deliver digital signals to subscribers and experiences thus far with retransmission consent negotiations involving both analog and digital signals.

122. **Program-related.** In addition, as discussed above, cable operators are required to carry "program-related" material as part of the

broadcaster's primary video. We seek comment on the proper scope of program-related in the digital context. As we note in the Order above, we believe that digital television offers the ability to enhance video programming in a number of ways. For example, a digital television broadcast of a sporting event could include multiple camera angles from which the viewer may select. In addition, a digital broadcast could enable viewers to select other embedded information such as sports statistics to complement a sports broadcast or detailed financial information to complement a financial news broadcast. We seek comment on whether such information or interactive enhancements like playing along with a game or chatting during a TV program should qualify as "program related." What are broadcasters' plans in this regard? What are the technical requirements for broadcasting, receiving and viewing this programming material? Would they be viewed on a screen simultaneously or is it necessary to change channels or select a different view on the same screen? What is the proper relationship between "program-related" and "ancillary or supplementary" in terms of the statutory objectives? To what extent, if any, is "program-related" limited by ancillary or supplementary? We also note that the statutory language that describes "program-related" in the context of NCE stations differs in some respects from the language regarding program-related content for commercial stations. Specifically, Section 615(g)(1), establishing the content of NCE stations to be carried by cable operators, tracks the language of Section 614(b)(3)(A), the provision for commercial broadcasters, except that the NCE provision goes on to include in the definition of "program related" material: "that may be necessary for receipt of programming by handicapped persons or for educational or language purposes." In light of the foregoing, we seek comment on how to define "program related" material for NCE stations. How, if at all, should it differ from "program-related" in the context of commercial stations? For example, some commenters have argued that if an NCE station multicasts programming for "educational" purposes the cable operator should carry all such program streams. We seek comment on whether these "educational" program streams should qualify as "program related" in the context of must carry, particularly in light of the language in 615(g)(1) noted above.

B. Channel Capacity

123. In the *Notice*, we sought quantified estimates and forecasts of available usable channel capacity. We asked whether there were differences in channel capacity that are based on franchise requirements, patterns of ownership, geographic location, or other factors. We also inquired about the average number of channels dedicated to various categories of programming, such as pay-per-view, leased access, local and non-local broadcast channels, and others that would assist us in understanding the degree to which capacity is, and will be, available over the next several years. . . .

. . .

125. We first reiterate the questions we posed in the *Notice*, as summarized in paragraph 121, above. . . . We specifically seek comment on the number of cable systems nationwide, on a percentage basis, that are now, or soon will be, upgraded to 750 MHz. With regard to these kinds of systems, we ask how many channels are now, or soon will be available for video programming. We seek comment on whether it is possible for 750 MHz systems to be channel-locked and have no capacity to carry additional digital broadcast signals. We seek comment on cable industry plans to build systems of greater capacity in the future.

126. We also seek comment on techniques that conserve or recapture cable channel capacity. Data on this matter is important because it may belie the cable industry's claim that there is, or will be, no channel capacity to add more programming. [The Commission then gave examples of hardware or software that might increase a cable system's capacity by as much as 40 percent.]

. . .

[Each of the Commissioners issued a separate statement. Commissioner Ness emphasized the importance of gathering more information relevant to the definition of program related. She also dissented from the tentative conclusion that "industry has failed to meet its constitutional burden."

Finally, Ness noted the complications that could result from the Commission's definition of "primary video."

> A single-stream interpretation of "primary video" could have the odd result of requiring broadcasters and cable operators to continuously examine broadcasters' content to determine whether the signal is primary video, program related, or something else. For example, if a broadcaster in a tri-state area offers a main news program, and then breaks away to three video streams to cover local news in each state, would the entire news program be primary video, would the breakout streams be program related, or neither? A cable operator would have to draw these conclusions. In contrast, a definition of "primary video" that includes all free, non-subscription video programming streams would be easier to administer.

Thus, while supporting the FCC's definition, based on the current record, she indicated a willingness to "entertain on reconsideration new or refined support for a statutory construction that justifies the carriage of multiplexed free video programming."

Commissioner Furchtgott–Roth dissented from the decision to delay a final decision on dual-carriage, arguing that there was a sufficient record to make that decision and that any benefits gained by further investigation would be outweighed by the continued uncertainty the delay would cause for both the broadcast and cable industries.

Commissioner Powell agreed with Commissioner Ness that the definition of "primary video" would cause problems, but asserted that it was compelled by the statute. Finally, Commissioner Tristani dissented from both the definition of "primary video" and the decision to delay a final definition of "program related."]

Notes and Questions

1. The NAB filed a petition asking the FCC to reconsider the portion of the order declining to mandate carriage of both analog and digital stations during the transition period. Meanwhile, NCTA filed a petition asking the Commission to reconsider mandating carriage in analog form, if requested, of those DTV stations not affiliated with an analog station. Broadcasting & Cable, April 30, 2001 at 11.

2. The disagreement over the definition of "primary video" is based on the technological changes that occurred subsequent to the 1992 Cable Act. As the rate of technological change continues to increase, how can problems of this type be minimized? For example, should more authority be delegated to agencies such as the FCC?

C. ACCESS CHANNELS

The elimination of the Commission's access channel requirements in *Midwest Video II,* p. 419, *supra,* did not eliminate mandatory access channels. Filling the vacuum were state and municipal requirements. Most cities demanded access channels and studios as a prerequisite for obtaining a cable franchise. Often these demands were more extensive than the FCC's had been.

In the Cable Communications Policy Act of 1984, Congress provided express authorization for access channel requirements. Section 611 states that access channels for public, educational and governmental use ("PEG channels") can be required as part of a franchise proposal or a proposal for renewal. 47 U.S.C.A. § 531. Furthermore, a federal requirement to set aside some channels for commercial use by persons unaffiliated with the operator is imposed on all systems with 36 or more activated channels. The number of channels that must be set aside varies according to the size of the system. 47 U.S.C.A. § 532.

The 1992 Cable Act gives the FCC authority to establish "maximum reasonable rates" that a cable operator can charge for leased access channels. 47 U.S.C.A. § 532. In addition, the Act gives cable operators the right to use up to one third of any leased access channels required under § 612 (47 U.S.C.A. § 532) of the Communications Act for "the provision of programming from a qualified minority programming source or from any qualified educational programming source." The Act defines qualified minority programming source as "a programming source which devotes substantially all of its programming to coverage of minority viewpoints, or to programming directed at members of minority groups, and which is over 50 percent minority-owned." A qualified educational programming source is defined as "a programming source which devotes substantially all of its programming to educational or instructional programming that promotes public understanding of mathematics, the sciences, the humanities, and the arts and has a documented annual expenditure on programming exceeding $15,000,000." 47 U.S.C.A. § 532(i).

The Court in *Midwest Video II* chose not to address the question of whether mandatory access channels violate the First Amendment. Thus, when a host of constitutional challenges to access channel and local origination franchise requirements were filed in conjunction with the franchising cases discussed at p. 430, *supra*, the lower courts had no guidance. The result was a series of inconsistent decisions. Some examples follow.

In the *Preferred* remand, p. 433, *supra*, mandatory PEG access channels were held a non-incidental burden on speech. The city asserted two compelling interests in access channels: "(1) to protect the First Amendment interests of various parties by promoting the availability of diverse sources of information over a cable system; and (2) providing groups and individuals historically excluded from the electronic media with access to the medium of cable communications."

Although these were held to be compelling interests, the requirement was still found unconstitutional. The reason was that the city failed to explain why eight channels were necessary to achieve these interests.

Similarly, in *Century Federal*, p. 435, *supra*, the court, citing *Tornillo* and *Pacific Gas,* found the access channels to be an impermissible intrusion into the editorial functions of the cable operator.

However, in Chicago Cable Communications v. Chicago Cable Commission, 879 F.2d 1540, 66 R.R.2d 1222 (7th Cir.1989), certiorari denied 493 U.S. 1044 (1990), the Commission fined a group of three cable franchisees for failing to honor the local origination clause of the franchises. That clause required 4½ hours per week of local programming geared to Chicago. The violation was said to have occurred when the group presented local programming that had been prepared by a suburban affiliate even though the group said that it selected programs that it believed would be interesting to its Chicago customers.

Among other defenses, the group contended that the First Amendment prevented the content control inherent in the clause and its enforcement. The district court enforced the fine, and the court of appeals affirmed. The court adhered to an earlier cable decision in which it said that "there are enough differences between cable television and the non-television media to allow more government regulation of the former." The court chose to apply the *O'Brien* test.

The court concluded that the government had met its burdens of establishing the elements of the *O'Brien* test. Promotion of "community self-expression can increase direct communications between residents by featuring topics of local concern. Encouragement of 'localism' certainly qualifies as an important or substantial interest." The court approvingly quoted the district court's statement that the "important qualities of localism (community pride, cultural diversity, *etc.*) may not be furthered enough simply by the availability of local broadcast television stations for retransmission over cable systems, but may require original cable programming specifically concerning the locality and directed at that locality's residents." An additional interest fostered by the requirement was providing jobs for residents: "Production of programming in the City provides career opportunities as well as potential internships for students studying communications at local schools." These were enough to satisfy *O'Brien*'s second prong.

As to the congruence between means and ends, the court relied on Supreme Court language to the effect that "so long as the neutral regulation promotes a substantial government interest that would be achieved less effectively absent the regulation," an incidental burden on speech is permissible. Here on the one hand was a requirement of only 4½ hours per week with no requirement of any specific kind of programming. "As long as the particular episode is geared to Chicago—be it sports, politics, news, weather, entertainment, *etc.*—[the group] has full discretion over what it may desire to transmit. This restriction on [the group's] control in meeting the minimal [local origination] requirements does not divest it of discretion, for, as in *Midwest Video*, the cable operator here still retains the ultimate decision" over which programs to present.

On the other hand, cable "is an economically scarce medium. Unlike the traditional forms of print media, a cable programmer enjoys a virtual monopoly over its area, without the threat of an alternative provider. As a result the government, which serves as the representative of the cable customers, is duty-bound to recognize the effects of 'medium scarcity' by ensuring that the few programmers who are granted a franchise make optimum use of it. [　] With this in mind, it is within the City's rights, arguably its responsibilities, to proffer some requirements guaranteeing that the cable customers are, to the extent possible, accorded a range of programming from the franchisee, since the cable viewing public has no other channel to which to turn."

The interlocking ownership of various media organizations led to a test of municipal power over cable access channels in New York City. The franchisee, Time Warner, decided to carry MSNBC rather than the Fox News Channel. Mayor Giuliani sought to force Time Warner to let Fox (which would eliminate commercials) use one of the city-run, noncommercial PEG channels on the Time Warner system. The mayor argued that Fox's inability to reach the New York audience might cause Fox to fail and would cost hundreds of jobs in New York City, where Fox was headquartered. Others argued that Giuliani was acting to help the owner of Fox, Rupert Murdoch, a political ally of Giuliani's, to fight Time Warner's rejection of its news channel.

The cable operator sought a preliminary injunction to prevent the city from carrying Fox News on its PEG channels even without commercials. A federal district judge granted the injunction, ruling that the city's efforts violated the statute's limitations on the use of PEG channels. Further, the city was interfering with Time Warner's First Amendment rights to decide what programs to carry on its channels. The judge also concluded that the action had been taken to "reward a friend and to further a particular viewpoint." It was not that Time Warner had any right to control the PEG channels; rather it was that Time Warner was being forced to carry a program on its system that it did not want to carry, and that did not fit into a category over which it was declared to have no control, such as must-carry stations or leased access. Time Warner Cable of New York City v. City of New York, 943 F.Supp. 1357 (S.D.N.Y.1996).

The case was subsequently settled. Time Warner added Fox News to systems (including New York City) serving 3 million subscribers. Carriage will be extended to systems serving an additional 5 million subscribers by 2001. In return, Fox agreed to pay fees of up to $10 per subscriber. Fox also agreed not to oppose Time Warner's plan to convert superstation TBS to a cable network (discussed at p. 415, *supra*). Broadcasting & Cable, July 28, 1997 at 14.

The conflict over access channels has another side—produced by the requirement that the cable operator not censor any access material. More than 1,200 of the nation's 8,000 systems offer some form of public access, and an estimated 40,000 hours of public access programming is produced each week. In cities in which access channels exist, they may be opposed by citizens who are offended by what is presented. Some examples from two channels fully devoted to public access in Austin, Texas, are reported in Schwartz, Austin Gets an Eyeful: Sacrilege and the Klan, *Channels*, Mar./Apr. 1985, at 42–43: (a) in front of a crucifix "a man in a Charles Manson mask dances and chants incoherently about sex and religion"; (b) a Ku Klux Klan leader interviews a man who had been imprisoned for fire-bombing school buses during Detroit's busing controversy; and (c) a Halloween program in which a slimy monster comes out of a nearby lake and kills everything in its path. Some groups wanted to end access, particularly because of the Klan programs.

Operators of the public access channels are permitted to schedule programs. The Austin channels, for example, extended their hours. One result was that the group that put the Manson program on was moved from 10:30 p.m. to 1 a.m. In San Francisco, the operators scheduled a Klan program for 3:30 p.m. on Tuesdays and sandwiched it between programs produced by Chinese for Affirmative Action, the Anti–Defamation League, and Jewish Community Relations. San Francisco Chronicle, Dec. 29, 1986, at A6.

Apart from the suits by cable operators seeking to be free of the access requirement, suits began to come from the other direction. In Kansas City, Mo., the Klan failed to get on the access channel. The city had insisted that the franchisee provide an access channel. When the Klan requested access, the operator refused because the show was not locally produced. The Missouri Klan then offered to provide a program featuring interviews with local advocates of white supremacy. The operator agreed to air the show. Before the Klan members could be trained in using the equipment and producing the show, the city council passed legislation converting the channel to a community programming channel under operator control. The operator offered the Klan a guest appearance on a hosted half-hour talk show. The Klan rejected the offer because it had no control over the program. The operator refused to permit the Klan to air its own program.

The ACLU brought suit. One claim was that the city council's action was intended "to suppress the 'racialist' viewpoint" of the Klan. A second argument was that the city, by granting only one cable franchise, had incurred a constitutional obligation to require the operator to provide an access channel. In 1989, the city council reinstated the access channel, and the case was dropped.

D. INDECENCY

Initially, indecency was rarely a problem on the public access channels. "Shows containing nudity are usually more expensive to film and are often shown on other channels, known as leased-access channels, where time is sold for a fee of about $100 a half-hour and commercials are allowed." N.Y. Times, April 13, 1987, at 19. More recently, however, the controversy over indecency on broadcast television, p. 223, *supra*, has extended to cable programming, including both public access channels and leased access channels.

Most of the early controversy surrounding restrictions on cable programming involved state and local attempts to ban indecent programs or nudity. The key question was whether *Pacifica*, p. 228, *supra*, or *Erznoznik*, p. 224, *supra*, should control. Generally, the courts held that *Pacifica* was limited to broadcast television. For example, the court of appeals struck down the section of a Miami ordinance that prohibited cable distribution of indecent material on the grounds that it was overbroad. The court distinguished *Pacifica*, reasoning that an affirmative action, subscribing, was necessary to receive cable television. In a reference to Justice Stevens' "pig in the parlor" analogy in *Pacifica*, the court wryly observed, "[i]t seems to us, however, that if an individual voluntarily opens his door and allows a pig into his parlor, he is in less of a position to squeal." Cruz v. Ferre, 755 F.2d 1415, 57 R.R.2d 1452 (11th Cir.1985).

A similar Utah statute was struck down on similar grounds. Community Television of Utah, Inc. v. Wilkinson, 611 F.Supp. 1099, 11 Med.L.Rptr. 2217 (D.Utah 1985). The Cable Television Programming Decency Act authorized the filing of nuisance actions against anyone who continuously and knowingly distributed indecent material over cable television. Material was defined as indecent if it was "presented in a patently offensive way for the time, place and manner, and context in which the material is presented." The court held that the statute was unconstitutionally vague and overbroad.

The decision was upheld on appeal. The court adopted the lower court's reasoning without adding any of its own. One judge specially concurred to indicate that he felt *Pacifica* should be the standard used in evaluating cable indecency statutes. However, he found the Utah Cable Television Programming Decency Act unconstitutionally vague and over-broad under even the more relaxed *Pacifica* standard. Jones v. Wilkinson, 800 F.2d 989, 61 R.R.2d 1, 13 Med.L.Rptr. 1913 (10th Cir.1986). The Supreme Court summarily affirmed without opinion. 480 U.S. 926 (1987).

The 1984 Cable Act included a provision that anyone who "transmits over any cable system any matter which is obscene or otherwise unprotected by the Constitution of the United States shall be fined not more than $10,000 or imprisoned not more than two years." 47 U.S.C.A. § 559. Could someone be prosecuted for indecent programming under this statute? As a result of this provision, the Commission eliminated its regulation banning obscene or indecent cable programming. Cable Communications Act Rules, 58 R.R.2d 1 (1985).

The 1984 Act also added a requirement that cable operators must, upon request, sell or lease lock-out devices to subscribers. 47 U.S.C.A. § 544(2)(a).

The 1992 Act contained a provision permitting cable operators to "enforce prospectively a written and published policy of prohibiting programming that the cable operator reasonably believes describes or depicts sexual or excretory activities or organs in a patently offensive manner as measured by contemporary community standards." 47 U.S.C.A. § 532. In accordance with this provision, the Commission promulgated regulations requiring cable operators to place all indecent programming intended for carriage on leased access channels on a single leased access channel. These regulations also required cable operators to block this channel absent a written request for access from the subscriber. Furthermore, under these regulations, cable programmers were required to identify indecent programming to cable operators. Cable Access Channels (Indecent Programming), 8 F.C.C.Rcd. 998, 71 R.R.2d 1177 (1993). The FCC also promulgated regulations enabling cable operators to prohibit obscene or sexually explicit material on PEG channels. Cable Access Channels (Indecent Programming), 8 F.C.C.Rcd. 2638, 72 R.R.2d 274 (1993).

The court of appeals struck down both regulations, finding that they violated the First Amendment. Alliance for Community Media v. Federal Communications Commission, 10 F.3d 812, 22 Med.L.Rep. 1033 (D.C.Cir. 1993) and Action for Children's Television v. Federal Communications Commission, 11 F.3d 170, 21 Med.L.Rep. 2289 (D.C.Cir.1993).

The D.C. Circuit, sitting *en banc*, reversed the panel decision in Alliance for Community Media v. Federal Communications Commission, 56 F.3d 105 (D.C.Cir.1995) (en banc). The majority held that the 1992 Cable Act merely permitted cable operators to ban indecent programs on leased channels, leaving them free to decide for themselves whether to do so, and therefore such a ban did not constitute state action. The court rejected the challengers' argument that the real purpose of the act was to impose procedural and financial burdens on cable operators who permitted indecent programs.

The court agreed that there was state action in the portion of the statute directing cable operators to segregate indecent programming on a channel that is to be blocked unless the subscriber requests access in writing. But the majority said this did not violate the First Amendment because it furthered a compelling state interest in shielding children from indecent programming while only minimally burdening adults who wish to watch it. The opinion said *Pacifica*, p. 228, *supra*, was the appropriate authority, rather than *Sable*, p. 250, *supra*, because leased access channels automatically come into all subscribers' homes. Four dissenting judges thought the blocking provision was unconstitutional and three thought other provisions of the statute were also unconstitutional.

The Supreme Court granted *certiorari* and, in a highly fractured opinion, found constitutional, 7–2, the section of the 1992 Act that permits cable operators to prohibit indecent programming transmitted over leased access channels (§ 10(a)), but struck down, 6–3, the provision that required cable operators to segregate and block indecent programming if they broadcasted it (§ 10(b)) and, 5–4, the provision that permitted cable operators to prohibit indecent programming on public access channels (§ 10(c)). Denver Area Educational Telecommunications Consortium, Inc. v. Federal Communications Commission, 518 U.S. 727 (1996).

Section 10(a). In a cautious opinion, Justice Breyer, writing for four justices, found § 10(a) to be a narrowly tailored response to the problem of protecting children from indecent programming:

> We can decide this case . . . by closely scrutinizing § 10(a) to assure that it properly addresses an extremely important problem, without imposing, in light of the relevant interests, an unnecessarily great restriction on speech. The importance of the interest at stake here— protecting children from exposure to patently offensive depictions of sex; the accommodation of the interests of programmers in maintaining access channels and of cable operators in editing the contents of their channels; the similarity of the problem and its solution to those at issue in *Pacifica* [ ]; and the operators to make editorial decisions, lead us to conclude that § 10(a) is a sufficiently tailored response to an extraordinarily important problem.

Justice Thomas, writing for three justices, agreed that § 10(a) was constitutional, arguing that the leased access provisions infringe upon the speech rights of cable operators and that § 10(a) simply returned some degree of editorial discretion to cable operators:

> It is one thing to compel an operator to carry leased and public access speech, in apparent violation of Tornillo, but it is another thing altogether to say that the First Amendment forbids Congress

to give back part of the operators' editorial discretion, which all recognize as fundamentally protected, in favor of a broader access right. It is no answer to say that leased and public access are content neutral and that §§ 10(a) and (c) are not, for that does not change the fundamental fact, which petitioners never address, that it is the operators' journalistic freedom that is infringed, whether the challenged restrictions be content neutral or content based.

Justice Kennedy, writing for himself and Justice Ginsburg, would have found § 10(a) unconstitutional. He argued that laws requiring cable operators to provide leased access are the "practical equivalent of making them common carriers, analogous in this respect to telephone companies." Finding that laws, like § 10(a), which preclude a common carrier from transmitting protected speech, are subject to strict scrutiny, Justice Kennedy would have struck the law because it was not narrowly tailored to protect children from indecent programming, because operators may still choose to allow indecent programming and because, if they do choose to prohibit the programming, adults as well as children will be deprived of it.

Section 10(b). Justice Breyer delivered the opinion of the Court striking down § 10(b), holding that the "segregate and block" requirements were overly restrictive, means (such as scrambling laws and lockboxes) are currently available to restrict children's access to indecent programming. Justice Thomas, writing for the three dissenters argued that § 10(b) was a narrowly tailored method of protecting children, and he rejected the majority's lockbox analysis on the grounds that, unlike the blocking law, "a subscriber armed with only a lockbox must carefully monitor all leased access programming and constantly reprogram the lockbox to keep out the undesired program."

Section 10(c). Writing for three justices, Justice Breyer found that § 10(c) was unconstitutional. He emphasized four differences between §§ 10(c) and 10(a). First, unlike § 10(a), § 10(c) did not restore editorial rights back to cable operators because operators have traditionally reserved channel capacity for PEG channels on their own initiative. Second, unlike leased access channels, public access channels are subject to complex supervisory systems that can independently disapprove particular programming. Third, the existence of these systems aimed at encouraging programming considered valuable by the community suggests that a cable operator's veto would be less likely to achieve the objective of protecting children and would be more likely to prevent programming that is not indecent. Fourth, examination of legislative history suggests that the public programming control systems currently in place would "avoid, minimize, or eliminate" any child-related problems concerning indecent programming.

Based on these differences, Justice Breyer concluded that the law "would not significantly restore editorial rights of cable operators, but would greatly increase the risk that certain categories of programming (say, borderline offensive programs) will not appear. At the same time, given present supervisory mechanisms, the need for this particular provision, aimed directly at public access channels, is not obvious. . . . [W]e conclude that the Government cannot sustain its burden of showing that § 10(c) is necessary to protect children or that it is appropriately tailored to secure that end."

Justice Kennedy, joined by Justice Ginsburg, provided the fourth and fifth votes to strike § 10(c), but they found the law unconstitutional on other grounds. Justice Kennedy argued that public access channels are public forums: "Required by the franchise authority as a condition of the franchise and open to all comers, they are designated public forum of unlimited character. . . . They provide groups and individuals who generally have not had access to the electronic media with the opportunity to become sources of information in the electronic marketplace of ideas." As a content-based speech restriction in a public forum, § 10(c) was subject to strict scrutiny, and Justice Kennedy concluded that it failed this searching inquiry for the same reasons that he thought § 10(a) failed it. The justices who would have upheld § 10(c) relied on the same arguments that led them to vote to uphold § 10(a).

The 1992 Cable Act also contained a provision requiring cable operators to give at least 30 days' notice to subscribers of any free previews of "premium channels" offering movies rated X, NC–17, or R by the Motion Picture Association of America. In *Daniels Cablevision*, p. 483, *supra*, the court found this provision unconstitutional. Because the requirement was content-based, it had to be a narrowly tailored means of accomplishing a compelling interest. Because not all R–, NC–17–and X-rated movies are indecent, the court found the restriction overbroad.

On appeal, the court upheld the 30–day notice requirement, *Time Warner*, p. 483, *supra*. It first noted that it was unclear whether the provision is a restriction on speech at all, since it does not prohibit cable operators from running any program they wish. The court noted that the government has a substantial interest in facilitating parents' ability to control the programming coming into their homes. Advance notice of previews furthers this interest by providing parents with information about future programming. The court rejected the district court's argument that lockboxes would constitute a less intrusive and equally effective method of protecting children, noting that parents cannot effectively use lockboxes unless they know in advance what programming will be carried by each channel.

The 1996 Telecommunications Act added several new provisions dealing with obscene or indecent cable programming. The penalty for transmitting obscene programming is now a fine of up to $100,000, up to two years imprisonment or both. 47 U.S.C.A. § 559. Cable operators are permitted to refuse to transmit any public access or leased access program or portion thereof that contains obscenity, indecency or nudity. 47 U.S.C.A. § 531(e); 47 U.S.C.A. § 532(c)(2).

Still another provision requires all multichannel video distributors to scramble both the audio and video portions of any "sexually explicit adult programming or other programming that is indecent on any channel of its service primarily dedicated to sexually-oriented programming" to prevent non-subscribers from receiving such channels. Until a distributor is able to fully scramble such channels, transmission of this programming must be channeled away from hours when a significant number of children are likely to view it (as determined by the FCC). 47 U.S.C.A. § 561.

Prior to the effective date of this provision, Playboy Entertainment Group, Inc., obtained a temporary restraining order prohibiting the FCC from enforcing it. The court found that Playboy had demonstrated a serious likelihood of prevailing on the merits of its First Amendment challenge because there appear to be less restrictive means of accomplishing the government's objective of protecting minors from indecent programming. The court specifically cited lock boxes as one such alternative. Playboy was also likely to suffer irreparable harm because many cable systems were incapable of implementing the required scrambling by the effective date of the provision and thus would have had to restrict the carriage of Playboy's cable programming to late night hours. Playboy Entertainment Group, Inc. v. United States, 918 F.Supp. 813, 3 C.R. 51, 24 Med.L.Rptr. 1522 (D.Del.1996). Playboy was quoted as stating it did not object to the scrambling but that it did object to the fact that the ban does not apply to other cable channels that "occasionally run similar fare." Broadcasting & Cable, Mar. 11, 1996 at 16.

When the case came before the three-judge district court, the temporary restraining order was dissolved on the ground that the plaintiffs were unlikely to prevail on any of their three theories: free speech, equal protection, and vagueness. 945 F.Supp. 772 (D.Del.1996). The Supreme Court summarily affirmed the dissolution of the temporary restraining order, 520 U.S. 1141 (1997).

Subsequently, the district court ruled that the Playboy Channel can be carried 24 hours-a-day, even though it is not fully scrambled—the audio can still be heard and the video is occasionally clear. The court found that a system allowing individual homes to block the signal was a less restrictive means of accomplishing the government's objective.

The case was appealed directly to the Supreme Court, pursuant to the statute.

UNITED STATES v. PLAYBOY ENTERTAINMENT GROUP, INC.

Supreme Court of the United States, 2000.
529 U.S. 803, 120 S.Ct. 1878, 146 L.Ed.2d 865, 20 C.R. 551, 28 Med.L.Rptr. 1801.

JUSTICE KENNEDY delivered the opinion of the Court.

. . .

Appellee Playboy Entertainment Group, Inc., challenged the statute as unnecessarily restrictive content-based legislation violative of the First Amendment. After a trial, a three-judge District Court concluded that a regime in which viewers could order signal blocking on a household-by-household basis presented an effective, less restrictive alternative to § 505. 30 F.Supp.2d 702, 719 (D.Del.1998). Finding no error in this conclusion, we affirm.

I

Playboy Entertainment Group owns and prepares programs for adult television networks, including Playboy Television and Spice. Playboy transmits its programming to cable television operators, who retransmit it to their subscribers, either through monthly subscriptions to premium channels or on a so-called "pay-per-view" basis. Cable operators transmit Playboy's signal, like other premium channel signals, in scrambled form. The operators then provide paying subscribers with an "addressable converter," a box placed on the home television set. The converter permits the viewer to see and hear the descrambled signal. It is conceded that almost all of Playboy's programming consists of sexually explicit material as defined by the statute.

The statute was enacted because not all scrambling technology is perfect. Analog cable television systems may use either "RF" or "baseband" scrambling systems, which may not prevent signal bleed, so discernible pictures may appear from time to time on the scrambled screen. Furthermore, the listener might hear the audio portion of the program.

These imperfections are not inevitable. The problem is that at present it appears not to be economical to convert simpler RF or baseband scrambling systems to alternative scrambling technologies on a systemwide scale. Digital technology may one day provide another solution, as it presents no bleed problem at all. Indeed, digital systems are projected to become the technology of choice, which would eliminate the signal bleed problem. Digital technology is not yet in widespread use, however. With imperfect scrambling, viewers who have not paid to receive Playboy's channels may happen across discernible images of a sexually explicit nature. How many viewers, how discernible the scene or sound, and how often this may occur are at issue in this case.

. . .

When the statute became operative, most cable operators had "no practical choice but to curtail [the targeted] programming during the [regulated] sixteen hours or risk the penalties imposed . . . if any audio or video signal bleed occur[red] during [those] times." [ ] The majority of operators—"in one survey, 69%"—complied with § 505 by time channeling the targeted programmers. Ibid. Since "30 to 50% of all adult programming is viewed by households prior to 10 p.m.," the result was a significant restriction of communication, with a corresponding reduction in Playboy's revenues. [ ]

In March 1998, the District Court held a full trial and concluded that § 505 violates the First Amendment. [ ] The District Court observed that § 505 imposed a content-based restriction on speech. Id., at

714–715. It agreed that the interests the statute advanced were compelling but concluded the Government might further those interests in less restrictive ways. [ ] One plausible, less restrictive alternative could be found in another section of the Act: § 504, which requires a cable operator, "[u]pon request by a cable service subscriber . . . without charge, [to] fully scramble or otherwise fully block" any channel the subscriber does not wish to receive. 110 Stat. 136, 47 U.S.C. § 560 (1994 ed., Supp. III). As long as subscribers knew about this opportunity, the court reasoned, § 504 would provide as much protection against unwanted programming as would § 505. [ ] At the same time, § 504 was content neutral and would be less restrictive of Playboy's First Amendment rights. [ ]

The court described what "adequate notice" would include, suggesting

"[operators] should communicate to their subscribers the information that certain channels broadcast sexually-oriented programming; that signal bleed . . . may appear; that children may view signal bleed without their parents' knowledge or permission; that channel blocking devices . . . are available free of charge . . .; and that a request for a free device . . . can be made by a telephone call to the [operator]." [ ]

The means of providing this notice could include

"inserts in monthly billing statements, barker channels (preview channels of programming coming up on Pay–Per–View), and on-air advertisement on channels other than the one broadcasting the sexually explicit programming." [ ]

The court added that this notice could be "conveyed on a regular basis, at reasonable intervals," and could include notice of changes in channel alignments. [ ]

The District Court concluded that § 504 so supplemented would be an effective, less restrictive alternative to § 505, and consequently declared § 505 unconstitutional and enjoined its enforcement. [ ] The court also required Playboy to insist on these notice provisions in its contracts with cable operators. [ ]

. . .

II

Two essential points should be understood concerning the speech at issue here. First, we shall assume that many adults themselves would find the material highly offensive; and when we consider the further circumstance that the material comes unwanted into homes where children might see or hear it against parental wishes or consent, there are legitimate reasons for regulating it. Second, all parties bring the case to us on the premise that Playboy's programming has First Amendment protection. As this case has been litigated, it is not alleged to be obscene; adults have a constitutional right to view it; the Government disclaims any interest in preventing children from seeing or hearing it with the consent of their parents; and Playboy has concomitant rights under the First Amendment to transmit it. These points are undisputed.

The speech in question is defined by its content; and the statute which seeks to restrict it is content based. Section 505 applies only to channels primarily dedicated to "sexually explicit adult programming or other programming that is indecent." The statute is unconcerned with signal bleed from any other channels. See 945 F.Supp., at 785 ("[Section 505] does not apply when signal bleed occurs on other premium channel networks, like HBO or the Disney Channel"). The overriding justification for the regulation is concern for the effect of the subject matter on young viewers. Section 505 is not " 'justified without reference to the content of the regulated speech.' " [   ] It "focuses *only* on the content of the speech and the direct impact that speech has on its listeners." [   ] This is the essence of content-based regulation.

Not only does § 505 single out particular programming content for regulation, it also singles out particular programmers. The speech in question was not thought by Congress to be so harmful that all channels were subject to restriction. Instead, the statutory disability applies only to channels "primarily dedicated to sexually-oriented programming." 47 U.S.C. § 561(a) (1994 ed., Supp. III). One sponsor of the measure even identified appellee by name. See 141 Cong. Rec. 15587 (1995) (statement of Sen. Feinstein) (noting the statute would apply to channels "such as the Playboy and Spice channels"). Laws designed or intended to suppress or restrict the expression of specific speakers contradict basic First Amendment principles. Section 505 limited Playboy's market as a penalty for its programming choice, though other channels capable of transmitting like material are altogether exempt.

The effect of the federal statute on the protected speech is now apparent. It is evident that the only reasonable way for a substantial number of cable operators to comply with the letter of § 505 is to time channel, which silences the protected speech for two-thirds of the day in every home in a cable service area, regardless of the presence or likely presence of children or of the wishes of the viewers. According to the District Court, "30 to 50% of all adult programming is viewed by households prior to 10 p.m.," when the safe-harbor period begins. [   ] To prohibit this much speech is a significant restriction of communication between speakers and willing adult listeners, communication which enjoys First Amendment protection. It is of no moment that the statute does not impose a complete prohibition. The distinction between laws burdening and laws banning speech is but a matter of degree. The Government's content-based burdens must satisfy the same rigorous scrutiny as its content-based bans.

Since § 505 is a content-based speech restriction, it can stand only if it satisfies strict scrutiny. [*Sable*, p. 250, *supra*.] If a statute regulates speech based on its content, it must be narrowly tailored to promote a compelling Government interest. *Ibid.* If a less restrictive alternative would serve the Government's purpose, the legislature must use that alternative. [ACLU v.] Reno, 521 U.S., at 874, 117 S.Ct. 2329 ("[The CDA's Internet indecency provisions'] burden on adult speech is unacceptable if less restrictive alternatives would be at least as effective in achieving the legitimate purpose that the statute was enacted to serve"); [*Sable*] ("The Government may . . . regulate the content of constitutionally protected speech in order to promote a compelling interest if it chooses the least restrictive means to further the articulated interest"). To do otherwise would be to restrict speech without an adequate justification, a course the First Amendment does not permit.

Our precedents teach these principles. Where the designed benefit of a content-based speech restriction is to shield the sensibilities of listeners, the general rule is that the right of expression prevails, even where no less restrictive alternative exists. . . . Here, of course, we consider images transmitted to some homes where they are not wanted and where parents often are not present to give immediate guidance. Cable television, like broadcast media, presents unique problems, which inform our assessment of the interests at stake, and which may justify restrictions that would be unacceptable in other contexts. See [*DAETC*, p. 517, *supra*]; [*Pacifica*, p. 228, *supra*]. No one suggests the Government must be indifferent to unwanted, indecent speech that comes into the home without parental consent. The speech here, all agree, is protected speech; and the question is what standard the Government must meet in order to restrict it. As we consider a content-based regulation, the answer should be clear: The standard is strict scrutiny. This case involves speech alone; and even where speech is indecent and enters the home, the objective of shielding children does not suffice to support a blanket ban if the protection can be 1887 accomplished by a less restrictive alternative.

In [*Sable*], for instance, the feasibility of a technological approach to controlling minors' access to "dial-a-porn" messages required invalidation of a complete statutory ban on the medium. . . .

Our zoning cases, on the other hand, are irrelevant to the question here. [ ] We have made clear that the lesser scrutiny afforded regulations targeting the secondary effects of crime or declining property values has no application to content-based regulations targeting the primary effects of protected speech. [ ] The statute now before us burdens speech because of its content; it must receive strict scrutiny.

There is, moreover, a key difference between cable television and the broadcasting media, which is the point on which this case turns: Cable systems have the capacity to block unwanted channels on a household-by-household basis. The option to block reduces the likelihood, so concerning to the Court in *Pacifica*, [ ], that traditional First Amendment scrutiny would deprive the Government of all authority to address this sort of problem. The corollary, of course, is that targeted blocking enables the Government to support parental authority without affecting the First Amendment interests of speakers and willing listeners—listeners for whom, if the speech is unpopular or indecent, the privacy of their own homes may be the optimal place of receipt. Simply put, targeted blocking is less restrictive than banning, and the Government cannot ban speech if targeted blocking is a feasible and effective means of furthering its compelling interests. This is not to say that the absence of an effective blocking mechanism will in all cases suffice to support a law restricting the speech in question; but if a less restrictive means is available for the Government to achieve its goals, the Government must use it.

III

The District Court concluded that a less restrictive alternative is available: § 504, with adequate publicity. 30 F.Supp.2d, at 719–720. No one disputes that § 504, which requires cable operators to block undesired channels at individual households upon request, is narrowly tailored to the Government's goal of supporting parents who want those channels blocked. The question is whether § 504 can be effective.

When a plausible, less restrictive alternative is offered to a content-based speech restriction, it is the Government's obligation to prove that the alternative will be ineffective to achieve its goals. The Government has not met that burden here.

In support of its position, the Government cites empirical evidence showing that § 504, as promulgated and implemented before trial, generated few requests for household-by-household blocking. Between March 1996 and May 1997, while the Government was enjoined from enforcing § 505, § 504 remained in operation. A survey of cable operators determined that fewer than 0.5% of cable subscribers requested full blocking during that time. Id., at 712. The uncomfortable fact is that § 504 was the sole blocking regulation in effect for over a year; and the public greeted it with a collective yawn.

The District Court was correct to direct its attention to the import of this tepid response. Placing the burden of proof upon the Government, the District Court examined whether § 504 was capable of serving as an effective, less restrictive means of reaching the Government's goals. Id., at 715, 718–719. It concluded that § 504, if publicized in an adequate manner, could be. Id., at 719–720.

The District Court employed the proper approach. When the Government restricts speech, the Government bears the burden of proving the constitutionality of its actions. [   ] When the Government seeks to restrict speech based on its content, the usual presumption of constitutionality afforded congressional enactments is reversed. "Content-based regulations are presumptively invalid," [   ] and the Government bears the burden to rebut that presumption.

. . .

When a student first encounters our free speech jurisprudence, he or she might think it is influenced by the philosophy that one idea is as good as any other, and that in art and literature objective standards of style, taste, decorum, beauty, and esthetics are deemed by the Constitution to be inappropriate, indeed unattainable. Quite the opposite is true. The Constitution no more enforces a relativistic philosophy or moral nihilism than it does any other point of view. The Constitution exists precisely so that opinions and judgments, including esthetic and moral judgments about art and literature, can be formed, tested, and expressed. What the Constitution says is that these judgments are for the individual to make, not for the Government to decree, even with the mandate or approval of a majority. Technology expands the capacity to choose; and it denies the potential of this revolution if we assume the Government is best positioned to make these choices for us.

It is rare that a regulation restricting speech because of its content will ever be permissible. Indeed, were we to give the Government the benefit of the doubt when it attempted to restrict speech, we would risk leaving regulations in place that sought to shape our unique personalities or to silence dissenting ideas. When First Amendment compliance is the point to be proved, the risk of non-persuasion—operative in all trials—must rest with the Government, not with the citizen. [   ]

With this burden in mind, the District Court explored three explanations for the lack of individual blocking requests. [   ] First, individual blocking might not be an effective alternative, due to technological or other limitations. Second, although an adequately advertised blocking provision might have been effective, § 504 as written did not require sufficient notice to make it so. Third, the actual signal bleed problem might be far less of a concern than the Government at first had supposed. [   ]

To sustain its statute, the Government was required to show that the first was the right answer. According to the District Court, however, the first and third possibilities were "equally consistent" with the record before it. [   ] As for the second, the record was "not clear" as to whether enough notice had been issued to give § 504 a fighting chance. [   ] The case, then, was at best a draw. Unless the District Court's findings are clearly erroneous, the tie goes to free expression.

The District Court began with the problem of signal bleed itself, concluding "the Government has not convinced us that [signal bleed] is a pervasive problem." [   ] The District Court's thorough discussion exposes a central weakness in the Government's proof: There is little hard evidence of how widespread or how serious the problem of signal bleed is. Indeed, there is no proof as to how likely any child is to view a discernible explicit image, and no proof of the duration of the bleed or the quality of the pictures or sound. To say that millions of children are subject to a risk of viewing signal bleed is one thing; to avoid articulating the true nature and extent of the risk is quite another. Under § 505, sanctionable signal bleed can include instances as fleeting as an image appearing on a screen for just a few seconds. The First Amendment requires a more careful assessment and characterization of an evil in order to justify a regulation as sweeping as this. Although the parties have taken the additional step of lodging with the Court an assortment of videotapes, some of which show quite explicit bleeding and some of which show television static or snow, there is no attempt at explanation or context; there is no discussion, for instance, of the extent to which any particular tape is representative of what appears on screens nationwide.

The Government relied at trial on anecdotal evidence to support its regulation, which the District Court summarized as follows:

"The Government presented evidence of two city councilors, eighteen individuals, one United States Senator, and the officials of one city who complained either to their [cable operator], to their local Congressman, or to the FCC about viewing signal bleed on television. In each instance, the local [cable operator] offered to, or did in fact, rectify the situation for free (with the exception of 1 individual), with varying degrees of rapidity. Included in the complaints was the additional concern that other parents might not be aware that their children are exposed to this problem. In addition, the Government presented evidence of a child exposed to signal bleed at a friend's house. Cindy Omlin set the lockout feature on her remote control to prevent her child from tuning to adult channels, but her eleven year old son was nevertheless exposed to signal bleed when he attended a slumber party at a friend's house.

"The Government has presented evidence of only a handful of isolated incidents over the 16 years since 1982 when Playboy started broadcasting. The Government has not presented any survey-type evidence on the magnitude of the 'problem.' " Id., at 709 (footnote and record citations omitted).

Spurred by the District Court's express request for more specific evidence of the problem, [   ], the Government also presented an expert's spreadsheet estimate that 39 million homes with 29.5 million children had the potential to be exposed to signal bleed, [   ]. The Government made no attempt to confirm the accuracy of its estimate through surveys or other field tests, however. Accordingly, the District Court discounted the figures and made this finding: "[T]he Government presented no evidence on the number of households actually exposed to signal bleed and thus has not quantified the actual extent of the problem of signal bleed." [   ] The finding is not clearly erroneous; indeed it is all but required.

Once § 505 went into effect, of course, a significant percentage of cable operators felt it necessary to time channel their sexually explicit programmers. [   ] This is an indication that scrambling technology is not yet perfected. That is not to say, however, that scrambling is completely ineffective. Different cable systems use different scrambling systems, which vary in their dependability. "The severity of the problem varies from time to time and place to place, depending on the weather, the quality of the equipment, its installation, and maintenance." [   ] At even the good end of the spectrum a system might bleed to an extent sufficient to trigger the time-channeling requirement for a cautious cable operator. (The statute requires the signal to be *"fully* block[ed]." 47 U.S.C. § 561(a) (1994 ed., Supp. III) (emphasis added).) A rational cable operator, faced with the possibility of sanctions for intermittent bleeding, could well choose to time channel even if the bleeding is too momentary to pose any concern to most households. To affirm that the Government failed to prove the existence of a problem, while at the same time observing that the statute imposes a severe burden on speech, is consistent with the analysis our cases require. Here, there is no probative evidence in the record which differentiates among the extent of bleed at individual households and no evidence which otherwise quantifies the signal bleed problem.

In addition, market-based solutions such as programmable televisions, VCR's, and mapping systems (which display a blue screen when tuned to a scrambled signal) may eliminate signal bleed at the consumer end of the cable. [ ] Playboy made the point at trial that the Government's estimate failed to account for these factors. [ ] Without some sort of field survey, it is impossible to know how widespread the problem in fact is, and the only indicator in the record is a handful of complaints. [ ] If the number of children transfixed by even flickering pornographic television images in fact reached into the millions we, like the District Court, would have expected to be directed to more than a handful of complaints.

    . . .

Nor did the District Court err in its second conclusion. The Government also failed to prove § 504 with adequate notice would be an ineffective alternative to § 505. Once again, the District Court invited the Government to produce its proof. [ ] Once again, the Government fell short. See 30 F.Supp.2d, at 719 ("[The Government's argument that § 504 is ineffective] is premised on adequate notice to subscribers. It is not clear, however, from the record that notices of the provisions of § 504 have been adequate"). There is no evidence that a well-promoted voluntary blocking provision would not be capable at least of informing parents about signal bleed (if they are not yet aware of it) and about their rights to have the bleed blocked (if they consider it a problem and have not yet controlled it themselves).

The Government finds at least two problems with the conclusion of the three-judge District Court. First, the Government takes issue with the District Court's reliance, without proof, on a "hypothetical, enhanced version of Section 504." [ ] It was not the District Court's obligation, however, to predict the extent to which an improved notice scheme would improve § 504. It was for the Government, presented with a plausible, less restrictive alternative, to prove the alternative to be ineffective, and § 505 to be the least restrictive available means. Indeed, to the extent the District Court erred, it was only in attempting to implement the less restrictive alternative through judicial decree by requiring Playboy to provide for expanded notice in its cable service contracts. The appropriate remedy was not to repair the statute, it was to enjoin the speech restriction. Given the existence of a less restrictive means, if the Legislature wished to improve its statute, perhaps in the process giving careful consideration to other alternatives, it then could do so.

The Government also contends a publicized § 504 will be just as restrictive as § 505, on the theory that the cost of installing blocking devices will outstrip the revenues from distributing Playboy's programming and lead to its cancellation. [   ] This conclusion rests on the assumption that a sufficient percentage of households, informed of the potential for signal bleed, would consider it enough of a problem to order blocking devices—an assumption for which there is no support in the record. [   ] It should be noted, furthermore, that Playboy is willing to incur the costs of an effective § 504. One might infer that Playboy believes an advertised § 504 will be ineffective for its object, or one might infer the company believes the signal bleed problem is not widespread. In the absence of proof, it is not for the Court to assume the former.

It is no response that voluntary blocking requires a consumer to take action, or may be inconvenient, or may not go perfectly every time. A court should not assume a plausible, less restrictive alternative would be ineffective; and a court should not presume parents, given full information, will fail to act. If unresponsive operators are a concern, moreover, a notice statute could give cable operators ample incentive, through fines or other penalties for noncompliance, to respond to blocking requests in prompt and efficient fashion.

Having adduced no evidence in the District Court showing that an adequately advertised § 504 would not be effective to aid desirous parents in keeping signal bleed out of their own households, the Government can now cite nothing in the record to support the point. The Government instead takes quite a different approach. After only an offhand suggestion that the success of a well-communicated § 504 is "highly unlikely," the Government sets the point aside, arguing instead that society's independent interests will be unserved if parents fail to act on that information. [   ]

Even upon the assumption that the Government has an interest in substituting itself for informed and empowered parents, its interest is not sufficiently compelling to justify this widespread restriction on speech. The Government's argument stems from the idea that parents do not know their children are viewing the material on a scale or frequency to cause concern, or if so, that parents do not want to take affirmative steps to block it and their decisions are to be superseded. The assumptions have not been established; and in any event the assumptions apply only in a regime where the option of blocking has not been explained. The whole point of a publicized § 504 would be to advise parents that indecent material may be shown and to afford them an opportunity to block it at all times, even when they are not at home and even after 10 p.m. Time channeling does not offer this assistance. The regulatory alternative of a publicized § 504, which has the real possibility of promoting more open disclosure and the choice of an effective blocking system, would provide parents the information needed to engage in active supervision. The Government has not shown that this alternative, a regime of added communication and support, would be insufficient to secure its objective, or that any overriding harm justifies its intervention.

There can be little doubt, of course, that under a voluntary blocking regime, even with adequate notice, some children will be exposed to signal bleed; and we need not discount the possibility that a graphic image could have a negative impact on a young child. It must be remembered, however, that children will be exposed to signal bleed under time channeling as well. Time channeling, unlike blocking, does not eliminate signal bleed around the clock. Just as adolescents may be unsupervised outside of their own households, it is hardly unknown for them to be unsupervised in front of the television set after 10 p.m. The record is silent as to the comparative effectiveness of the two alternatives.

* * *

Basic speech principles are at stake in this case. When the purpose and design of a statute is to regulate speech by reason of its content, special consideration or latitude is not accorded to the Government merely because the law can somehow be described as a burden rather than outright suppression. We cannot be influenced, moreover, by the perception that the regulation in question is not a major one because the speech is not very important. The history of the law of free expression is one of vindication in cases involving speech that many citizens may find shabby, offensive, or even ugly. It follows that all content-based restrictions on speech must give us more than a moment's pause. If television broadcasts can expose children to the real risk of harmful exposure to indecent materials, even in their own home and without parental consent, there is a problem the Government can address. It must do so, however, in a way consistent with First Amendment principles. Here the Government has not met the burden the First Amendment imposes.

The Government has failed to show that § 505 is the least restrictive means for addressing a real problem; and the District Court did not err in holding the statute violative of the First Amendment. In light of our ruling, it is unnecessary to address the second question presented: whether the District Court was divested of jurisdiction to consider the Government's postjudgment motions after the Government filed a notice of appeal in this Court. The judgment of the District Court is affirmed.

It is so ordered.

. . .

JUSTICE BREYER, with whom THE CHIEF JUSTICE, JUSTICE O'CONNOR, and JUSTICE SCALIA join, dissenting.

This case involves the application, not the elucidation, of First Amendment principles. . . .

The basic, applicable First Amendment principles are not at issue. The Court must examine the statute before us with great care to determine whether its speech-related restrictions are justified by a "compelling interest," namely an interest in limiting children's access to sexually explicit material. In doing so, it recognizes that the legislature must respect adults' viewing freedom by "narrowly tailoring" the statute so that it restricts no more speech than necessary, and choosing instead any alternative that would further the compelling interest in a "less restrictive" but "at least as effective" way. [   ]

. . .

I

At the outset, I would describe the statutory scheme somewhat differently than does the majority. I would emphasize three background points. First, the statutory scheme reflects more than a congressional effort to control incomplete scrambling. Previously, federal law had left cable operators free to decide whether, when, and how to transmit adult channels. Most channel operators on their own had decided not to send adult channels into a subscriber's home except on request. But the operators then implemented that decision with inexpensive technology. Through signal "bleeding," the scrambling technology (either inadvertently or by way of enticement) allowed non subscribers to see and hear what was going on. That is why Congress decided to act.

. . .

The statute is carefully tailored to respect viewer preferences. It regulates transmissions by creating two "default rules" applicable unless the subscriber decides otherwise. Section 504 requires a cable operator to "fully scramble" any channel (whether or not it broadcasts adult programming) *if* a subscriber asks *not* to receive it. Section 505 requires a cable operator to "fully scramble" every adult channel *unless* a subscriber asks to receive it. Taken together, the two provisions create a scheme that permits subscribers to choose to see what they want. But each law creates a different "default" assumption about silent subscribers. Section 504 assumes a silent subscriber wants to see the ordinary (non adult) channels that the cable operator includes in the paid-for bundle sent into the home. Section 505 assumes that a silent subscriber does not want to receive adult channels. Consequently, a subscriber wishing to view an adult channel must "opt in," and specifically request that channel. See § 505. A subscriber wishing not to view any other channel (sent into the home) must "opt out." See § 504.

The scheme addresses signal bleed but only indirectly. From the statute's perspective signal "bleeding"—*i.e.,* a failure to fully "rearrange the content of the signal . . . so that the programming cannot be viewed or heard in an understandable manner," § 505(c),—amounts to transmission into a home. Hence "bleeding" violates the statute whenever a clear transmission of an unrequested adult channel would violate the statute.

Second, the majority's characterization of this statutory scheme as "prohibit[ing] . . . speech" is an exaggeration. [   ] Rather, the statute places a *burden* on adult channel speech by requiring the relevant cable operator either to use better scrambling technology, or, if that technology is too expensive, to broadcast only between 10 p.m. and 6 a.m. Laws that burden speech, say, by making speech less profitable, may create serious First Amendment issues, but they are not the equivalent of an absolute ban on speech itself. [   ] Thus, this Court has upheld laws that do not ban the access of adults to sexually explicit speech, but burden that access through geographical or temporal zoning. [   ] This Court has also recognized that material the First Amendment guarantees adults the right to see may not be suitable for children. And it has consequently held that legislatures maintain a limited power to protect children by restricting access to, but not banning, adult material. [   ] The difference—between imposing a burden and enacting a ban—can matter even when strict First Amendment rules are at issue.

Third, this case concerns only the regulation of commercial actors who broadcast "virtually 100% sexually explicit" material. [   ] The channels do not broadcast more than trivial amounts of more serious material such as birth control information, artistic images, or the visual equivalents of classical or serious literature. This case therefore does not present the kind of narrow tailoring concerns seen in other cases. [   ]

With this background in mind, the reader will better understand my basic disagreement with each of the Court's two conclusions.

II

The majority first concludes that the Government failed to prove the seriousness of the problem—receipt of adult channels by children whose parents did not request their broadcast. [   ] This claim is flat-out wrong. For one thing, the parties concede that basic RF scrambling does not scramble the audio portion of the program. [   ] For another, Playboy itself conducted a survey of cable operators who were asked: "Is your system in full compliance with Section 505 (no discernible audio or video bleed)?" To this question, 75% of cable operators answered "no." [   ] Further, the Government's expert took the number of homes subscribing to Playboy or Spice, multiplied by the fraction of cable households with children and the average number of children per household, and found 29 million children are potentially exposed to audio and video bleed from adult programming. [   ] Even discounting by 25% for systems that might be considered in full compliance, this left 22 million children in homes with faulty scrambling systems. . . .

I would add to this empirical evidence the majority's own statement that "*most* cable operators had 'no practical choice but to curtail'" adult programming by switching to nighttime only transmission of adult channels. [   ] *If signal bleed is not a significant empirical problem, then why, in light of the cost of its cure, must so many cable operators switch to night time hours?* There is no realistic answer to this question. I do not think it realistic to imagine that signal bleed occurs just enough to make cable operators skittish, without also significantly exposing children to these images. [   ]

If, as the majority suggests, the signal bleed problem is not significant, then there is also no significant burden on speech created by § 505. The majority cannot have this evidence both ways. And if, given this logical difficulty and the quantity of empirical evidence, the majority still believes that the Government has not proved its case, then it imposes a burden upon the Government beyond that suggested in any other First Amendment case of which I am aware.

III

The majority's second claim—that the Government failed to demonstrate the absence of a "less restrictive alternative"—presents a closer question. The specific question is whether § 504's "opt-out" amounts to a "less restrictive," but *similarly* practical and *effective,* way to accomplish § 505's child-protecting objective. . . . [A] "less restrictive alternative" must be "at least as effective in achieving the legitimate purpose that the statute was enacted to serve." [   ]

The words I have just emphasized, "similarly" and "effective," are critical. In an appropriate case they ask a judge not to apply First Amendment rules mechanically, but to decide whether, in light of the benefits and potential alternatives, the statute works speech-related harm (here to adult speech) out of proportion to the benefits that the statute seeks to provide (here, child protection).

These words imply a degree of leeway, however small, for the legislature when it chooses among possible alternatives in light of predicted comparative effects. Without some such empirical leeway, the undoubted ability of lawyers and judges to imagine *some* kind of slightly less drastic or restrictive an approach would make it impossible to write laws that deal with the harm that called the statute into being. As Justice Blackmun pointed out, a "judge would be unimaginative indeed if he could not come up with something a little less 'drastic' or a little less 'restrictive' in almost any situation, and thereby enable himself to vote to strike legislation down." [   ] Used without a sense of the practical choices that face legislatures, "the test merely announces an inevitable [negative] result, and the test is no test at all." [ ]

   . . .

I turn then to the major point of disagreement. Unlike the majority, I believe the record makes clear that § 504's opt-out is not a similarly effective alternative. Section 504 (opt-out) and § 505 (opt-in) work differently in order to achieve very different legislative objectives. Section 504 gives parents the power to tell cable operators to keep any channel out of their home. Section 505 does more. Unless parents explicitly consent, it inhibits the transmission of adult cable channels to children whose parents may be unaware of what they are watching, whose parents cannot easily supervise television viewing habits, whose parents do not know of their § 504 "opt-out" rights, or whose parents are simply unavailable at critical times. In this respect, § 505 serves the same interests as the laws that deny children access to adult cabarets or X-rated movies. [   ] These laws, and § 505, all act in the absence of direct parental supervision.

This legislative objective is perfectly legitimate. Where over 28 million school age children have both parents or their only parent in the work force, where at least 5 million children are left alone at home without supervision each week, and where children may spend afternoons and evenings watching television outside of the home with friends, § 505 offers independent protection for a large number of families. [   ] I could not disagree more when the majority implies that the Government's independent interest in offering such protection—preventing, say, an 8–year-old child from watching virulent pornography without parental consent—might not be "compelling." [   ] No previous case in which the protection of children was at issue has suggested any such thing. Indeed, they all say precisely the opposite. [   ] They make clear that Government has a compelling interest in helping parents by preventing minors from accessing sexually explicit materials in the absence of parental supervision. [   ]

By definition, § 504 does *nothing at all* to further the compelling interest I have just described. How then is it a similarly effective § 505 alternative?

The record, moreover, sets forth empirical evidence showing that the two laws are not equivalent with respect to the Government's objectives. As the majority observes, during the 14 months the Government was enjoined from enforcing § 505, "fewer than 0.5% of cable subscribers requested full blocking" under § 504. [   ] The majority describes this public reaction as "a collective yawn," [   ], adding that the Government failed to prove that the "yawn" reflected anything other than the lack of a serious signal bleed problem or a lack of notice which better information about § 504 might cure. The record excludes the first possibility—at least in respect to exposure, as discussed above. [   ] And I doubt that the public, though it may well consider the viewing habits of *adults* a matter of personal choice, would "yawn" when the exposure in question concerns young children, the absence of parental consent, and the sexually explicit material here at issue. [   ]

Neither is the record neutral in respect to the curative power of better notice. Section 504's opt-out right works only when parents (1) become aware of their § 504 rights, (2) discover that their children are watching sexually-explicit signal "bleed," (3) reach their cable operator and ask that it block the sending of its signal to their home, (4) await installation of an individual blocking device, and, perhaps (5) (where the block fails or the channel number changes) make a new request. Better notice of § 504 rights does little to help parents discover their children's viewing habits (step two). And it does nothing at all in respect to steps three through five. Yet the record contains considerable evidence that those problems matter, *i.e.,* evidence of endlessly delayed phone call responses, faulty installations, blocking failures, and other mishaps, leaving those steps as significant § 504 obstacles. [   ]

. . .

Even if better notice did adequately inform viewers of their § 504 rights, exercise of those rights by more than 6% of the subscriber base would itself raise Playboy's costs to the point that Playboy would be forced off the air entirely, [   ]—a consequence that would not seem to further anyone's interest in free speech. The majority, resting on its own earlier conclusion that signal bleed is not widespread, denies any likelihood that more than 6% of viewers would need § 504. But that earlier conclusion is unsound. [   ] The majority also relies on the fact that Playboy, presumably aware of its own economic interests, "is willing to incur the costs of an effective § 504." [ ] Yet that denial, as the majority admits, may simply reflect Playboy's knowledge that § 504, even with better notice, will not work. Section 504 is not a similarly effective alternative to § 505 (in respect to the Government's interest in protecting children), unless more than a minimal number of viewers actually use it; yet the economic evidence shows that if more than 6% do so, Playboy's programming would be totally eliminated. The majority provides no answer to this argument in its opinion—and this evidence is sufficient in and of itself to dispose of this case.

Of course, it is logically *possible* that "better notice" will bring about near perfect parental knowledge (of what children watch and § 504 opt-out rights), that cable operators will respond rapidly to blocking requests, and that still 94% of all informed parents will decided not to have adult channels blocked for free. But the *probability* that this remote *possibility* will occur is neither a "draw" nor a "tie." [   ] And that fact is sufficient for the Government to have met its burden of proof.

All these considerations show that § 504's opt-out, even with the Court's plan for "better notice," is *not* similarly effective in achieving the legitimate goals that the statute was enacted to serve.

IV

Section 505 raises the cost of adult channel broadcasting. In doing so, it restricts, but does not ban adult speech. Adults may continue to watch adult channels, though less conveniently, by watching at night, recording programs with a VCR, or by subscribing to digital cable with better blocking systems. [ ] The Government's justification for imposing this restriction—limiting the access of children to channels that broadcast virtually 100% "sexually explicit" material—is "compelling." The record shows no similarly effective, less restrictive alternative. Consequently § 505's restriction, viewed in light of the proposed alternative, is proportionate to need. That is to say, it restricts speech no more than necessary to further that compelling need. Taken together, these considerations lead to the conclusion that § 505 is lawful.

. . .

I respectfully dissent.

Notes and Questions

1. What is the fundamental disagreement between the majority and dissenting opinions?

2. How does this case differ from *ACT III*, p. 252, *supra*? More specifically, how does the targeted blocking available to cable subscribers differ from the v-chip which is now mandated for all new television sets?

Chapter X

NEW COMMUNICATIONS TECHNOLOGIES

As we discussed in Chapter VIII, at one time cable was seen as the ultimate communications technology. At the height of the franchising battles, operators were promising that cable would provide everything to everybody. Not only were those promises unfulfilled, but cable is no longer even the "new" technology. A proliferation of new delivery systems such as multipoint distribution service (MDS), direct broadcast satellites (DBS), satellite master antenna television (SMATV) and the Internet are fighting for their share of the communications marketplace.

As each of these services has developed, new regulatory questions have arisen. Does the FCC have jurisdiction and, if so, what regulatory framework can the Commission use? The FCC does not have complete freedom in developing regulatory frameworks for new technologies. Rather, the Commission must work within the context of the Communications Act. Originally, the Act provided two basic models for regulation. One is the "broadcast" model we studied in Chapters II–VII. The second is the "common-carrier" model to be discussed below. If a communications technology did not fit either of these models, the authority of the Commission to regulate it was questionable. This was a major issue in the regulation of cable. In *Midwest Video I,* p. 418, *supra,* the Commission's jurisdiction over cable was upheld as being ancillary to its jurisdiction over broadcasting. However, the exact limits of this jurisdiction were never clear, a problem that was solved by the Cable Communications Policy Act of 1984.

Common carriers are regulated under Title II of the Communications Act. The key element of common carrier regulation is that the "content is separated from the conduit." In other words, unlike broadcasters, common carriers have no editorial discretion. Instead, they must provide, in a non-discriminatory manner, the facilities for transmission of the customer's message. National Association of Regulatory Utility Commissioners v. Federal Communications Commission (NARUC I), 525 F.2d 630 (D.C.Cir.), certiorari denied 425 U.S. 992 (1976). Telephone and telegraph companies are examples of common carriers.

There are a number of other important distinctions between broadcasters and common carriers. The federal government has preempted state regulation of broadcasting. In contrast, common carriers are regulated on both the state and federal levels. Interstate service is regulated by the Federal Communications Commission, while intrastate service is regulated by state agencies.

Sometimes, however, the Commission will decide to preempt the states and regulate a service on a strictly federal basis. When the

Commission decides to preempt state regulation, it does not necessarily imply that the Commission will choose to regulate to the same extent. Instead, the FCC may choose to "preempt and forbear." This means that the Commission will eliminate the state regulations without substituting any of its own because the Commission believes as a matter of policy that no regulation is the proper regulation for that area.

The regulations most commonly subject to preemption are entry requirements and rate regulation. When a common carrier wishes to provide a service, the carrier is usually required to demonstrate a need for the service. Some states require that, in addition to showing need, an applicant demonstrate that current carriers are either unable to or unwilling to provide the additional needed service. These requirements can effectively bar any new entrants into a given type of service.

Because common carriers often enjoy either a natural or government-created monopoly, they are usually subject to rate regulation by either the FCC or appropriate state agencies. Rate regulation is usually eliminated when there is a finding of sufficient effective competition in the services provided.

Traditionally, the Commission assigned services to the two regulatory models based on the method of transmission. Thus, STV was under the broadcast model while for many years Multipoint Distribution Service (MDS) was a common carrier, because STV was transmitted through the broadcast portion of the spectrum, but MDS utilizes the microwave portion, which was viewed as a point-to-point medium. This led to seemingly anomalous results. For example, STV operators leasing their facilities to a movie service were subject to different regulations than MDS operators leasing their facilities to the same movie service. In fact, a third regulatory scheme obtained when the same movie service was carried over cable. Although many of these anomalies still exist, the Commission has started to take a new approach, imposing regulations based on the service provided as opposed to the method of transmission. In some cases, for example MDS, the Commission is now leaving the initial choice of regulatory model up to the licensee. In other words, licensees can decide for themselves which regulatory model would be most appropriate for the type of service they wish to offer.

Congress has now taken that approach in the 1996 Telecommunications Act. For example, as will be discussed in Chapter XII, phone companies can deliver video programming as common carriers, cable companies or a hybrid called "open video systems" (OVS).

Still another major concern for the Commission is that it not favor one service or technology over another. This attempt at regulatory neutrality has come to be called the "level playing field." As we will see, a level playing field can be very difficult to create. Nevertheless, it is an important issue as most of the regulatory battles involving new communications technologies are grounded firmly in economics. Although the rhetoric may concentrate on the public interest or even the First

Amendment, the real issue in almost every case is which service will gain some competitive advantage.

Obviously, the flood of new communications technologies has presented the FCC with serious problems as it tries to fit them into the traditional regulatory models. Let us now turn to some of these technologies and examine how the Commission attempted to resolve these problems.

A. MULTIPOINT DISTRIBUTION SERVICE (MDS)

MDS transmits microwave signals over super-high frequencies within a range of about 25 miles. The signal is received by a small microwave antenna, usually located on a rooftop. The signal can then be converted to a broadcast frequency and shown on a vacant VHF channel. Originally, MDS was intended to be used to transmit data. However, some operators found that a more profitable use was distribution of video programming to hotels and other multi-unit buildings. As the cost of converters and antenna systems dropped, it became feasible to distribute programming to even single-family dwellings. For example, in urban areas in which cable was not available, MDS was often used to distribute HBO programming.

In an early decision, the Commission preempted state and local regulation that serves to hinder the development of MDS. Orth–O–Vision, Inc., 69 F.C.C.2d 657, 44 R.R.2d 329 (1978), recon., 82 F.C.C.2d 178, 48 R.R.2d 503 (1980), affirmed sub nom. New York State Commission on Cable Television v. Federal Communications Commission, 669 F.2d 58, 50 R.R.2d 1201 (2d Cir.1982). In essence, the case preempted state and local government attempts to impose entry restrictions.

In 1983 the FCC reallocated eight of the 28 instructional television fixed service (ITFS) microwave channels to MDS, making multichannel multipoint distribution service (MMDS) available. ITFS (MDS Reallocation), 54 R.R.2d 107 (1983). MMDS operators may also obtain extra channel capacity by leasing an ITFS operator's excess capacity. MMDS is often referred to as wireless cable.

The Commission decided to use a lottery system to award licenses for the ITFS channels reallocated to MDS. In 1985 the Court of Appeals for the District of Columbia Circuit ordered the FCC either to postpone the MDS lottery scheduled for that time until rulemaking on women's preferences was completed or to protect women applicants until the rulemaking was completed. The Commission postponed the lottery. The next month the Commission voted to give women no preference in MDS lotteries and rescheduled the lottery. The Commission's decision was affirmed in *Pappas*, p. 118, *supra*.

When a huge backlog of applications developed, the FCC instituted a freeze on applications. Concerned that as soon as the freeze was lifted a similar backlog would develop, the FCC decided to change the manner in which MMDS licenses would be awarded. Under this new licensing plan, the FCC allotted:

> through a simultaneous multiple round bidding process, one MDS authorization for each of the 487 Basic Trading Areas (BTAs) and six additional BTA-like geographic areas. A BTA authorization holder will be able to construct facilities to provide wireless cable service over any usable MDS channels within the BTA, and will have preferred rights to the available ITFS frequencies and ITFS lease agreements within the BTA. A channel is usable if the proposed station design is in compliance with the Commission's interference standards.

> 3. Under the new rules, the signals of a BTA authorization holder cannot interfere with those of any other BTA authorization holder. Recognizing, however, that BTA lines do not always track desired service areas, the rules permit BTA authorization holders to negotiate interference protection rights. In addition, the rules we adopt require BTA authorization holders to honor the protected service areas of incumbent MDS operators within their BTAs. In a companion order, also adopted today, the Commission expanded the protected service areas of existing MDS stations. These various licensees and applicants that are authorized or proposed on or before June 15, 1995, including those stations that are subsequently modified, renewed or reinstated, are referred to . . . as . . . "incumbents." In order to facilitate the development of successful wireless cable systems, the rules permit BTA authorization holders to assign or transfer their entire BTAs, or partitioned portions of it, to incumbents or other parties. (Unserved areas may be included as long as the assignment or transfer takes place within the five-year build-out period that the rules impose.) Because the BTA authorization holder may be an incumbent, the rules permit the aggregation of existing and new MDS and ITFS channels within a BTA.

Pending applications filed prior to the freeze were decided under the old lottery system. Multipoint Distribution Service, 10 F.C.C.Rcd. 9589, 78 R.R.2d 856 (1995).

In 1998 the FCC authorized "MDS/ITFS licensees to construct digital two-way systems that could provide high-speed, high-capacity broadband service, including two-way Internet service via cellularized communication systems." Amendment of Parts 21 and 74 to Enable Multipoint Distribution Service and Instructional Television Fixed Service Licensees to Engage in Fixed Two–Way Transmissions, 13 F.C.C.Rcd. 19112 (1998), *recon.*, 14 F.C.C.Rcd. 12764 (1999), *further recon.*, 15 F.C.C.Rcd. 14566 (2000). This led to Sprint and Worldcom each investing more than $2 billion in acquiring MDS licenses and an additional $1 billion in new system construction. An initial filing window was opened in 2000, followed a year later by a rolling "one-day filing window process, which permits licensees to apply for authorizations on a first-come first-served basis." By late 2002, approximately 1600 applications had been filed.

In 2001 the Commission added a mobile application to the 2.5–2.69 Ghz band. The intent was to provide further flexibility for the use of this spectrum, including applications such as third-generation wireless phone service ("3G").

For many years MDS was regulated as a common carrier because, as we previously discussed, it was viewed by the Commission as a point-to-point service. Finally, in 1987 the Commission changed its regulations to permit MDS operators to choose the regulatory model to be used for them based on the service provided. 47 C.F.R. § 21.900–.908. The reason for the change was the Commission's recognition that MDS was often being used to deliver broadcast-type services. This was especially true of MMDS.

The maximum number of channels that an analog MMDS system can transmit is 33. As a result, analog MMDS has not been a viable competitor for cable. The advent of digital MMDS systems, with much higher channel capacities, p. 540, *supra*, led to predictions that it would result in more serious competition. However, this has not happened. The total number of MMDS subscribers remains approximately 700,000 and most companies are focusing on data transmission as opposed to video services.

B. DIRECT BROADCAST SATELLITES (DBS)

DBS is a system of broadcasting directly from studio to home via satellite. The technology involves the usual transmission to a satellite and the return to earth, where the signal is collected by a receiving dish from 18 inches to three feet in diameter placed on the roof of the home of the subscriber.

The first communications satellites were not suitable for DBS because their relatively weak signals could only be received by very large, expensive dishes. By the late 1970s, however, the technology had improved to the point where a commercial DBS system appeared feasible. It was now possible to build higher-powered satellites, which would allow the use of small, inexpensive dishes for home reception.

At the 1979 World Administrative Radio Conference (WARC–79) the 12 GHz band was allocated to DBS. Decisions on specific orbital locations and frequency assignments were left for the 1983 Regional Administrative Radio Conference (RARC–83). In the interim the Commission opened proceedings on domestic DBS service. As a result of those proceedings, the Commission decided to adopt interim DBS regulations pending the outcome of RARC–83. These interim DBS regulations authorizing domestic DBS service were adopted in July 1982. Three months later the Commission granted Satellite Television Corporation's (STC) application to construct an experimental DBS system offering subscription television service to the Eastern portion of the United States. Both the Interim DBS Regulations and the grant of STC's application were appealed.

NATIONAL ASSOCIATION OF BROADCASTERS v.
FEDERAL COMMUNICATIONS COMMISSION

United States Court of Appeals, District of Columbia Circuit, 1984.
740 F.2d 1190, 57 R.R.2d 1105.

Before TAMM, MIKVA and DAVIS, CIRCUIT JUDGES.

MIKVA, CIRCUIT JUDGE:

Of the technological innovations currently revolutionizing the communications field, the most recent, and potentially the most significant, is direct broadcast satellite service (DBS). DBS involves the transmission of signals from the earth to highpowered, geostationary satellites which then beam television signals directly to individual homes equipped to receive them. Use of satellites massively extends the range of a broadcast's voice by freeing it from the atmospheric limitations that traditionally limit terrestrial broadcasters to narrow broadcast areas; a single DBS signal will eventually be capable of reaching the entire continental United States. For this reason and others, DBS promises several significant advantages over existing television technology: high-quality service to individuals in rural or remote areas where conventional broadcasting is inefficient; the addition of many more channels even in urban areas already receiving several television signals; "narrowcasting" of programs to specialized tastes through the ability to aggregate small, widely dispersed audiences; the development of higher quality visual and audio signals through use of high-definition-television signals; and television transmission of non-entertainment programming, such as medical data and educational information.

The regulatory approach to DBS taken by the Federal Communications Commission . . . is as novel as the technology with which it is concerned. In essence, the Commission has chosen to deregulate DBS even before the service is born. . . . We find that, on the whole, the FCC has done a commendable job in assuring that regulation in the communications field not impede new technologies that offer substantial public benefits. . . . We also find, however, that in its zeal to promote this new technology, the FCC gave short shrift to certain of its statutory obligations, and we therefore vacate part of the Interim DBS regulations; in addition, our approval of other parts is qualified by several guidelines to which the Commission must hew in its continuing oversight of this nascent technology.

. . .

Analysis

I. *The FCC's Power to Approve Non–Local Broadcast Service*

DBS technology is inherently unsuitable for the provision of traditional local broadcast service. The satellites involved cannot presently be located with the requisite precision nor economically equipped with a sufficiently large antenna to provide a spot beam capable of covering only a traditional size local community. [ ] Moreover, many of the benefits of DBS—including narrowcasting and provision of service to less densely populated areas—could not practically be realized by a "local" DBS system. . . .

Petitioner NAB argues that the FCC does not have the power to approve a technology that will sever broadcast services from their traditional link to a particular community. NAB seeks to rest this Luddite argument on section 307(b) of the [Communications Act], which provides:

> the Commission shall make such *distribution of licenses . . . among the several States and communities* as to provide a fair, efficient, and equitable distribution of radio service to each of the same.

47 U.S.C. § 307(b)(emphasis added). NAB reads this provision to require that broadcast licenses indeed *be* "distributed" among the "States" and "communities;" NAB thus concludes that the Act mandates a system of *local* broadcast licensing and service with which STC's authorization, and DBS in general, is "fundamentally irreconcilable."

We do not think it necessary to ascribe to the framers of the Act an intent so shortsighted as to preclude new technology that offers the promise of substantial public benefit. The plain language of the Act does not compel such impracticable consequences. . . . The ultimate touchstone for the FCC is . . . the distribution of service, rather than of licenses or of stations; the constituency to be served is people, not municipalities. Moreover, the Commission also has an obligation to "encourage the larger and more effective use of radio in the public interest." 47 U.S.C. § 303(g). . . . Just as we have held that the Act does not bestow a vested right on any particular *licensee* to retention of its license, [ ], so too we now hold that the Act does not entrench any particular *system* of broadcasting: existing systems, like existing licensees, have no entitlement that permits them to deflect competitive pressure from innovative and effective technology.

In so holding we do not denigrate the importance of local programming to a national broadcasting system that is designed to serve the public interest. [ ] We need not define the outer limits of the Commission's authority to make this country's broadcasting system a regional or national one, however, for two reasons. First, the *DBS Order* does not by its terms eliminate local programming. Second, the Commission explicitly found that DBS will merely supplement the existing local broadcast system, rather than replace it, [ ], and we find no error in that finding. We therefore need not decide how far the Commission may go toward the elimination of local programming to hold that not *every* communications service approved by the Commission need be tied to a local community.

. . .

II. *Applicability to DBS of Broadcast Restrictions*

The most innovative of the steps taken by the FCC with respect to DBS was the Commission's decision, in the service of a "flexible regulatory approach" designed to stimulate DBS technology, not to apply to DBS the major regulatory restrictions traditionally imposed on broadcasters. Central to this approach was the Commission's refusal to extend the broadcast restrictions of Title III of the [Communications Act] to all DBS systems.

. . .

Among the statutory restraints that broadcasters currently face are section 312(a)(7), which requires that qualified candidates for federal office be provided reasonable access to broadcast facilities, and section 315, which provides that, if one political candidate is allowed to use a station, other qualified candidates must be given an equal opportunity to respond. Because DBS is likely to be a particularly attractive medium at least for presidential candidates, the question of how these broadcast restraints apply to DBS is of great moment.

The *DBS Order* established the following classificatory scheme for purposes of applying the Act's broadcasting rules. Those DBS applicants which propose to provide service (whether in the form of free or pay-TV) direct to homes and to "retain[ ] control over the content of the transmissions" will be treated as broadcasters. A DBS satellite owner can choose instead to operate as a common carrier, in which case satellite transmission services would have to be offered indiscriminately to the public pursuant to tariff under the provisions of Title II of the Act; a satellite owner who chooses the common carrier option will not be treated as a broadcaster. Also not treated as a broadcaster under the *DBS Order* are those who lease satellite space from a DBS common carrier and who use the leased channels to distribute programming via satellite to individual homes. These lessees, who neither own nor operate a DBS satellite, are referred to as "customer-programmers" of DBS common carriers, and it is they who control the content of the programming transmitted by a DBS common carrier.

. . .

We recognize the Commission's authority to approve services on an experimental basis in an effort to gather important market data to be used in the completion of a regulatory framework. [ ] Moreover, as other parts of this opinion will confirm, that discretion is particularly capacious when the Commission is dealing with new technologies unforeseen at the time the Communications Act was passed. But that discretion is not boundless: the Commission has no authority to experiment with its statutory obligations. We conclude that the Commission has engaged in precisely such forbidden statutory experimentation in exempting from Title III the customer-programmers of DBS common carriers.

Section 3(*o*) of the Communications Act defines "broadcasting" as "the dissemination of radio communications intended to be received by the public, directly or by the intermediary of relay stations." 47 U.S.C. § 153(*o*). We have previously held that the test for whether a particular activity constitutes broadcasting is whether there is "an intent for *public* distribution" and whether the programming is "of interest to the *general* . . . audience." . . .

When DBS systems transmit signals directly to homes with the intent that those signals be received by the public, such transmissions rather clearly fit the definition of broadcasting; radio communications are being disseminated with the intent that they be received by the public. That remains true even if a common carrier satellite leases its channels to a customer-programmer who does not own any transmission facilities; in such an arrangement, someone—either the lessee or the satellite owner—is broadcasting. Despite the argument of some intervenors and the suggestion of the government . . ., it also remains true regardless of whether a DBS system is advertiser or subscriber funded. . . . While the FCC may be coming increasingly to the view that subscription services are not "broadcasting", [   ], a view not yet passed upon by the courts, the *DBS Order* must rise or fall upon the FCC's articulated policies at the time of the order. And as the *Order* itself recognizes, these policies did not distinguish free-TV from pay-TV for purposes of defining "broadcasting." [   ] The FCC therefore cannot justify its exemption of some DBS systems from broadcast restrictions by pointing to the fact that those systems are subscriber rather than advertiser funded. [   ]

The irrationality of the Commission's view of the statute, which makes ownership the touchstone of broadcasting, is illustrated by the following example. If a DBS owner broadcasts programming directly to homes, it is subject to regulation as a broadcaster; if that owner sends its programs via leased channels on another satellite, the very same programming will be immune from broadcast regulation. Through a general system of cross-leasing, all DBS systems could therefore escape Title III. Nothing in the statutory definition allows the Commission to elevate form over function in this way nor suggests that the definition of broadcasting turns on whether the provider of the service leases satellite facilities from a common carrier or owns the satellite outright. . . .

. . .

Very real practical consequences could therefore follow from the FCC's exemption of common carrier DBS lessees from broadcast restrictions—consequences at odds with the basic objectives of the Communications Act. Under the *DBS Order,* a federal candidate who wanted access to a DBS system that was operated as a common carrier could not force either the satellite owner or its channel lessees to provide that access, for both would be immune from the Act's broadcast restraints; the candidate would instead have to rely on his or her purchasing power, as well as on the whim of the channel programmer, to receive access and an opportunity to respond to opponents. It was to avoid this very result, in which a speaker "who could afford the cost" could purchase enough time on a broadcast station operated as a common carrier to dominate American thought and American politics without any regulatory restraints, that Congress imposed restraints such as the equal opportunity rule upon broadcasters. [   ]

We therefore reject the central rationale upon which the Commission relied to exempt customer-programmers of DBS common carriers from the statutory constraints under which broadcasters must operate: the fact that Congress did not in 1934 contemplate DBS does not give the Commission a blank check to regulate DBS in any way it deems fit. . . .

The Commission's other rationales for its treatment of customer-programmers provide even less persuasive reasons for the Commission's departure from the statute's plain language. The claim that imposition of Title III obligations on channel lessees "merely would serve to duplicate the more pervasive" common carrier obligations of Title II, [   ], is clearly wrong, as Title II merely requires a carrier to accept all applicants for service on a non-discriminatory basis and thus offers no surrogate for Title III requirements such as reasonable access or equal opportunity. A common carrier *cannot* guarantee political candidates reasonable access to airtime or an equal opportunity to respond to opponents, for the sine qua non of a common carrier is the obligation to accept applicants on a non-content oriented basis. [The court also rejected an analogy to MDS. When the Commission decided not to apply broadcast regulations to MDS, it had not contemplated MDS being used to supply subscription television. Since the time the Commission had authorized the use of MDS for subscription television, no court had passed on the validity of exempting MDS programmer-customers from broadcast regulations.]

. . .

A final reason for exempting DBS customer-programmers from broadcast regulation, a reason not directly invoked by the FCC but raised by intervenors in the companion case, [   ], must also be rejected. These intervenors argue that the Commission never regulates *programmers* but only station *licensees*; examples of non-regulated programmers are said to be television networks, which provide programming over the facilities of affiliated broadcast stations, subscription television programmers, who perform similar functions on stations of television licensees, and pay television programmers such as Home Box Office, whose services are carried via satellites to cable television systems. However, the Commission previously *has* applied broadcast restraints to programmers and has been upheld in doing so. Columbia Broadcasting System, Inc. v. FCC, 629 F.2d 1, 26 (D.C.Cir.1980) (affirming Commission's authority to apply reasonable access requirements of Section 312(a)(7) to major broadcast networks) [affirmed by the Supreme Court]. The reason the FCC does not *ordinarily* regulate programmers is a simple one: the

Commission applies the statute directly to the entities responsible for program selection and transmission—the broadcast licensees. This approach is consistent with the Act's philosophy, for where a programmer operates through a broadcast licensee who must comply with the statute's broadcast restrictions, as is the case with STV programmers, the networks, and cable, the Act's objectives are met. But when both the customer-programmer *and* the common-carrier through which the former's signals are carried are immunized from broadcast regulation, as they are in the *DBS Order,* the statutory scheme is completely negated.

To avoid this result, we vacate that part of the *DBS Order* that exempts customer-programmers of DBS common carriers from the statutory requirements imposed on broadcasters. . . .

We also do not suggest that all uses of DBS constitute broadcasting; activity that would provide non-general interest, point-to-point service, where the format is of interest to only a narrow class of subscribers and does not implicate the broadcasting objectives of the Act, need not be regulated as broadcasting. . . .

. . .

III. *The FCC's Refusal to Apply its Ownership Restrictions to DBS*

In addition to refusing to impose statutory broadcast restrictions on customer-programmers of DBS common carrier, the FCC also declined to apply to DBS Commission regulations that seek to assure that control of the media is lodged in diverse hands. . . .

The interim DBS rules temporarily suspend for DBS both the multiple channel and the cross-ownership rules. . . .

The refusal to apply the cross-ownership rules to DBS is not at issue in this case. However, petitioner NAB argues that it was arbitrary and capricious for the FCC to relax temporarily the multiple-channel rule for DBS while leaving that same rule in place for terrestrial licensees.

At least at this early stage in the development of DBS, we reject that argument: DBS and traditional television broadcasting are not sufficiently similar in their technology, marketability, capitalization requirements, or other relevant factors that identical regulatory treatment of the two is required. Unlike conventional television systems, DBS systems are extraordinarily capital intensive and have high fixed costs; one applicant estimated that preoperational and first year expenditures alone would be $600 million. [   ] Weighing in against these costs are significant risks which the FCC has found to be associated with the new technology: (i) a lengthy delay (approaching five years) between issuance of a construction permit and initiation of service; (ii) reliance on unproven and developing technology; (iii) an uncertain and rapidly changing marketplace; (iv) operational and marketing problems associated with the provision of service and distribution of home receiving equipment over vast geographic areas. [   ]

These differences led several potential applicants to comment that no "responsible business organization" would enter the DBS field "without control over the programming of more than one channel." [   ] Such multiple-channel control allows counter programming, in which a satellite owner can offer movies on one channel, for example, sports on another, and cultural and children's programs on the third—thereby potentially attracting substantially more viewers than would be possible were only a single channel available. Based on the comments of some applicants that the ability to counterprogram was necessary to justify investment in DBS, the FCC concluded that, at least for the time being, it was unwise to impose ownership restrictions comparable to those existing in other areas. However, the FCC expressly reserved the right to impose ownership restrictions if actual operational experience with DBS systems demonstrated the need for increased regulatory intervention.

. . .

In this case, we conclude that the Commission acted within its discretion in suspending the multiple-channel restrictions. . . .

. . .

CONCLUSION

When technology as novel as DBS confronts a statute as broadly drafted as the Communications Act of 1934, the administering agency has substantial leeway in its efforts to harmonize the two. We conclude that, on the whole, the Commission has exercised this leeway in a reasonable manner. We therefore vacate only that portion of the *DBS Order* that makes broadcast restrictions inapplicable to some DBS systems and, with the caveats noted above, affirm the rest of that Order. We also affirm in its entirety the *STC Decision*.

It is so ordered.

Notes and Questions

1.   Subsequent to the court of appeals decision, STC attempted to find a partner to help finance its DBS operation. When none of the negotiations proved successful, STC abandoned its DBS plans entirely.

2.   At RARC–83, orbital slots and frequencies were awarded. A frequency band from 12.2 to 12.7 GHz was set aside for DBS. Meanwhile, further questions of satellite use and allocation were negotiated at the 1985 World Administrative Radio Conference, which has become known as Space–WARC, p. 40, *supra*.

3.   The first DBS system began operating in 1983, utilizing medium-power communications satellites. United Satellite Communications, Inc. (USCI) began five-channel service to central Indiana. The consumer response was far less than USCI had envisioned, and the service was discontinued in 1985.

The advent of high-power satellites, which only require 18–inch receiving dishes, and digital compression techniques, which allow more channels to be transmitted by each transponder, led to new DBS services. In 1994 Hughes Aircraft began its 150–channel DirecTv service. Also starting at about the same time was Hubbard Broadcasting's USSB, offering 24 channels. To receive either or both of these services, a subscriber has to purchase an 18–inch home dish and receiving equipment priced at approximately $300. In addition subscribers have to pay a monthly fee. A third high-power service, Echostar, began 40–channel service in 1996.

New applicants for DBS licenses now face a different set of rules Mutually exclusive applications are resolved by competitive bidding. Revision of Rules and Policies for the Direct Broadcast Satellite Service, 11 F.C.C.Rcd. 1297 (1995). The first set of channels auctioned under this procedure were purchased by MCI for $682 million. MCI Telecommunications Corp., 11 F.C.C.Rcd. 16275, 5 C.R. 673 (1995). We will discuss recent consolidation in the DBS industry in Chapter XII.

4. By mid–2002 DirecTv had more than 10 million subscribers and Echostar had more than 7 million. From June 2001 to June 2002, DBS' share of the multi-channel video market increased from 18 percent to 20.3 percent. Assessment of the Status of Competition in Markets for the Delivery of Video Programming, p. 412, *supra*.

5. Given the court's opinion in *NAB*, would the Commission's exemption of MDS customer-programmers from broadcast regulation be able to withstand a legal challenge? What distinctions between the new MMDS subscription television systems and DBS might allow a different result?

6. Concerned that the decision in *NAB* would indeed apply to other common carrier services, including MMDS, the Commission decided to reexamine its method of classifying STV and other subscription video programming services. In Subscription Video, 2 F.C.C.Rcd. 1001, 62 R.R.2d 389 (1987), the FCC changed from a content-based approach to service classification, known as the *"Functional Music* test," to an intent-based approach.

The Commission based the change on the language of the Communications Act of 1934. "The [Act] defines 'broadcasting' as the 'dissemination of radio communications intended to be received by the public, directly or by the intermediary of relay stations.' 47 U.S.C.A. § 153(o). Thus, the words of the statute clearly indicate that broadcast classification turns on the *intent* of the purveyor of radio communications that its service be received by the public."

Arguing that the intent of subscription service purveyors is to limit access to their signals, the Commission concluded that subscription services could not be classified as broadcasting. The Commission cited the need for special reception equipment and/or decoders to receive the service and the private contractual relationship between purveyors of subscription programming and their audiences as "indicia of an intent that the communications service not be received by the public."

By reclassifying subscription services as non-broadcast services, the Commission removed them from the application of various broadcast rules, including § 315, § 312(a)(7), the fairness doctrine and the FCC's broadcast equal opportunity rules.

The court of appeals upheld the FCC's action, 2–1. The majority found that the Communication Act definition of "broadcasting" was sufficiently ambiguous as to allow the Commission's interpretation. Nor did the apparent inconsistency between the Commission's decision and the court's decision in *NAB* make the decision arbitrary and capricious. The FCC had conducted a properly noticed rulemaking and supplied a reasoned explanation for the change in its approach. National Association for Better Broadcasting v. Federal Communications Commission, 849 F.2d 665, 64 R.R.2d 1570 (D.C.Cir.1988).

Chief Judge Wald dissented, arguing that the legislative history of the Act made it clear that services such as the ones at issue were intended to be treated as "broadcasting." She quoted former Commissioner Rivera: "It looks like broadcasting, smells like broadcasting, tastes like broadcasting, has all the benefits of broadcasting, but it's not regulated like broadcasting?" Many of her concerns echoed those of the court in *NAB*. For example, the absence of reasonable access and equal opportunities in her view invited unfair political propagandizing.

7.   Responding to a requirement of the 1992 Cable Act, the Commission has begun steps to order DBS programmers to meet the obligations of the election provisions of §§ 315 and 312(a)(7). 8 F.C.C.Rcd. 1589 (1993). Initially, a requirement that DBS set aside 4–7 percent of its transmission capacity for non-commercial educational and informational channels was struck down in *Daniels Cablevision*, p. 483, *supra*. The court was unable to find any significant government interest served by that requirement. Thus, it was unnecessary to decide whether the provision was content-based because it failed even the *O'Brien* test, p. 21, *supra*.

The court of appeals reversed and upheld the set-aside provision. The court rejected the argument that it should apply strict scrutiny to the provision because, as in the case of radio, there is a limit on the number of speakers who can use the DBS medium.

The court cited *Red Lion* for the proposition that "[w]here there are substantially more individuals who want to broadcast than there are frequencies to allocate, it is idle to posit an unabridgeable First Amendment right to broadcast comparable to the right of every individual to speak, write, or publish" and noted that the demand for DBS access far exceeds the available supply. Applying a "relaxed means of promoting the public interest in diversified mass communications," the court upheld the set-aside provision, observing that the set-aside provision "represents nothing more than a new application of a well-settled government policy of ensuring public access to noncommercial programming." Time Warner v. Federal Communications Commission, 93 F.3d 957 (D.C.Cir.1996).

A motion for rehearing *en banc* was denied on the ground that "a majority of the [10] judges of the court in regular active service did not vote in favor" although five of the eight voting judges voted for that rehearing and wrote an opinion dissenting from the denial on the DBS issue. 105 F.3d 723 (D.C.Cir.1997). The five asserted their "genuine uncertainty about the correct outcome" but thought the panel opinion's use of *Red Lion* was "fatally defective." DBS "is not subject to anything remotely approaching the 'scarcity' that the Court found" in *Red Lion*. The opinion sketched the nature and availability of DBS extensively. It also noted that the "scarcity" rationale of Red Lion had been extensively criticized and that, although the decision "is not in such poor shape that an intermediate court of appeals could properly announce its death, we can think twice before extending it to another medium."

The five judges asserted that if the DBS rules could be sustained "it would only be on the theory that the government is entitled to more leeway in setting the terms on which it supplies 'property' to private parties for speech purposes (or for purposes that include speech)," citing Rust v. Sullivan, 500 U.S. 173 (1991). Even so, the opinion noted dangers in relying on ownership to condition licenses: "We would see rather serious First Amendment problems if the government used its power of eminent domain to become the only lawful supplier of newsprint and then sold the newsprint only to licensed persons, issuing the licenses only to persons that promised to use the newsprint for papers satisfying government-defined rules of content."

8. Probably the biggest competitive disadvantage DBS has had vis-a-vis cable has been its inability to deliver local broadcast channels due both to a regulatory prohibition and capacity problems. The Satellite Home Viewer Improvement Act of 1999 (SHVIA), partially alleviated, but did not eliminate, the problem. Pub. Law 106–113, 113 Stat. 1501, 1501A–526 to 1501A–545 (Nov. 29, 1999).

Under the Act, DBS operators were permitted to retransmit local stations into their own markets, a practice known as local-into-local, on a selective basis without obtaining retransmission consent during the first six months following enactment of the SVHIA. From the expiration of the six-month period until Jan. 1, 2002, carriage on a selective basis was permitted, but retransmission consent had to be obtained. Now carriage of one local station gives all other stations in that market the option of retransmission consent or must-carry status.

Pursuant to the SHVIA, the FCC adopted specific must-carry regulations. For the most part, these regulations mirror those applicable to cable. Differences include a longer time period between election of retransmission consent/must-carry status and its taking effect, and replacement of the channel number requirements with one mandating that all local stations be on contiguous channels. Local broadcast stations are also prohibited from signing exclusive retransmission consent deals with a single satellite carrier. Implementation of the Satellite Home Viewer Improvement Act of 1999, 15 F.C.C.Rcd. 5445 (2000).

Shortly after passage of the Act, both DirecTV and Echostar began offering local-into-local in some markets. In each case only some channels (usually affiliates of the four major networks and a national PBS feed) were available. This selective approach was necessitated by capacity problems. Carrying all the local channels would reduce the number of markets where local channels could be offered.

Meanwhile, DBS operators filed multiple suits challenging the must-carry provisions of the SHVIA. One federal district court upheld the act, relying heavily on *Turner II*, p. 455, *supra*. Applying intermediate scrutiny, the court found the act furthered the important governmental interest of preserving free local broadcast television and was narrowly tailored to serve that interest. Satellite Broadcasting & Communications Association of America v. Federal Communications Commission, 146 F.Supp.2d 803 (E.D.Va.2001). 275 F.3d 337 (4th Cir.2001), certiorari denied, 122 S.Ct. 2588 (2002). The court's ruling was upheld on appeal. As a result, DBS companies now must offer all local channels in any market where they offer a local broadcast package.

At the same time, the FCC sought comment on the application of "network non-duplication, syndicated program exclusivity, and sports blackout rules to the carriage of digital television signals by satellite carriers."

9. DBS companies are now facing the possibility of having to share their spectrum with a land-based service offered by Northpoint Technology. In late 2000, the FCC authorized Northpoint to use the 12.2 to 12.7 GHz portion of the spectrum to transmit video programming and data to subscribers' homes. However, shortly thereafter, Congress passed a bill prohibiting the FCC from issuing licenses for the service prior to conducting independent tests to ensure any land-based services won't cause interference problems for satellite services. Broadcasting & Cable, March 26, 2001 at 44.

The independent tests, conducted by Mitre Corp. indicated that there would not be an interference problem caused by the spectrum sharing. The FCC then decided to divide the country into hundreds of geographical areas, similar to those used for MMDS, and auction licenses for these areas. The Commission refused to grant Northpoint (now known as Broadwave) any special consideration despite its role in developing terrestrial DBS. The auction is scheduled for mid–2003. Amendment of Parts 2 and 25 of the Commission's Rules to Permit Operations of NGSO FSS Systems Co-frequency with GSO and Terrestrial Systems in the Ku-band Frequency Range, 2003 WL 1873391 (F.C.C.). Broadwave is challenging the FCC's decision.

The land-based companies will have one distinct technological advantage over the satellite carriers in that they could carry local TV channels without any capacity problems.

10. The growth of DBS has almost eliminated one competitor in the MVPD marketplace. In 1979 the Commission decided to eliminate a licensing requirement for receive-only satellite dishes. Regulation of

Domestic Receive–Only Satellite Earth Stations, 74 F.C.C.2d 205, 46 R.R.2d 698 (1979). Over the next few years, the cost of receive-only satellite dishes dropped from more than $10,000 to under $1,000. As a result of this deregulation and sudden affordability, a rapidly increasing number of people have bought dishes for their homes. The dishes give them access to the hundreds of video signals being transmitted by communications satellites. Among these signals are many of the cable programming services and programming fed by the broadcast networks to their affiliates. In addition, a lot of unedited video, e.g. news feeds, can be picked up by the dishes.

The dishes became controversial because the dish owners were paying nothing for the programming. The cable programming companies argued that the dish owners were pirates, stealing the signals. The dish owners and their trade association, Society of Private and Commercial Earth Stations (SPACE), claimed that they were willing to pay for the service, but the programming companies refused to sell to them. From a legal standpoint, it was unclear whether § 605 of the Communications Act, which prohibited unauthorized reception of some signal transmissions, applied to home satellite dishes.

A compromise solution to the controversy was included in the Cable Communications Policy Act of 1984. Section 605, now redesignated § 705, of the Communications Act was amended to authorize receipt of any non-encrypted signal for private viewing, unless a system for marketing the programming service for private viewing has been established.

Many cable programming services began scrambling their signals to prevent any unauthorized reception. In 1986, acting upon requests from Congress and NTIA, the Commission announced an NOI to examine the issues raised by scrambling as well as the question of Commission authority to set standards for scrambling and regulate rates for satellite programming.

After gathering extensive comments, the Commission concluded that "government intervention into the home satellite dish marketplace, whether by the Commission or through legislation, is neither necessary or wise." Scrambling of Satellite Television Signals, 2 F.C.C.Rcd. 1669, 62 R.R.2d 687 (1987). This conclusion was based on the finding that scrambling served a legitimate public interest—"to protect programmers from commercial theft and to allow them to recover compensation from all who view their copyrighted product." The Commission also found that marketplace forces were creating a *de facto* technical standard for encryption equipment and that competitive distribution and marketing systems appeared to be developing.

Although the HSD market continued its success into the early '90s, eventually, the lower cost of DBS equipment and the ability to get hundreds of channels with a fixed dish has now reduced HSD to a fringe player in the MVPD business. As of mid–2002, there were approximately 700 thousand HSD customers, 300 thousand fewer than the year before.

C. SATELLITE MASTER ANTENNA TELEVISION (SMATV)

SMATV involves setting up one or more earth stations on a large building or complex and distributing by wire or cable the various programming received. The distinction between SMATV and cable television is that no city streets or rights of way are used. This prevents cities from subjecting SMATV operators to a franchising process. It also limits SMATV systems to large apartments and hotels where enough subscribers can be reached without crossing city streets.

In some ways SMATV resembles MMDS in that multiple channels are distributed to receiving systems most of which are set up on rooftops. However, there are some distinctions. SMATV uses large, expensive earth stations to receive the programming directly from satellites, whereas MMDS receives the satellite feeds at some central location and then redistributes them by microwave to the customer. Because the more expensive satellite receiving equipment must be located at each building served by SMATV, it is only viable for large buildings. In contrast, a single earth station facility allows MMDS to serve all buildings in an approximately 25–mile radius. Because the equipment needed at a customer's location is relatively inexpensive, a small microwave antenna and a converter, MMDS can economically serve single-family homes.

However, SMATV does have some advantages over MMDS. An SMATV system can offer essentially unlimited channels because the transmission from central facility to actual customers is through wires. MMDS is limited to the number of separate microwave channels available. Recall that until 1983 that limit was essentially a single channel.

SMATV's freedom from franchising requirements has long concerned cable operators, who argue that it gives SMATV an unfair competitive advantage. Cable companies must compete through a long and expensive process and often are required to pay franchise fees and make expensive concessions for the right to do business, but SMATV operators can just set up a dish and start delivering service. Furthermore, cable companies are required to offer service to everyone within their franchise areas. SMATV operators are free to choose their customers.

To counter this perceived inequity, cable operators tried to persuade state and local governments to regulate SMATV by imposing strict entry requirements similar to those applied to cable television. In 1983 Earth Satellite Communications, Inc., (ESCOM) was enjoined from constructing an SMATV system in East Orange, N.J., for failure to comply with the New Jersey Cable Television Act. ESCOM responded by filing a petition with the FCC asking it to preempt state and local entry regulation of SMATV. The Commission acted favorably on the ESCOM petition. The FCC's action was then appealed by the New York State Commission on Cable Television.

NEW YORK STATE COMMISSION ON CABLE TELEVISION
v. FEDERAL COMMUNICATIONS COMMISSION

United States Court of Appeals, District of Columbia Circuit, 1984.
749 F.2d 804, 57 R.R.2d 363.

Before TAMM, WILKEY, and EDWARDS, CIRCUIT JUDGES.

TAMM, CIRCUIT JUDGE. . . .

. . .

II.

. . .

B. *The Commission's Authority*

. . .

In its preemption order the Commission based its authority over SMATV upon the federal interest in "the unfettered development of interstate transmission of satellite signals." [   ] This development would be frustrated, the Commission found, if each state could impose its own entry restrictions upon systems that were part of the national satellite network. [   ] The Commission chose not to impose entry restrictions of its own, believing that open entry policies in the satellite field would create a more diverse and competitive telecommunications environment. [   ]

Petitioners do not challenge the general authority of the Commission to preempt state and local regulation of cable television in appropriate circumstances. Rather, they contend that, in this particular instance, because the Commission has failed to show that preemption is necessary "to ensure the achievement of the Commission's statutory responsibilities," FCC v. Midwest Video Corp., 440 U.S. 689, 706 (1979), it has acted beyond its authority. To support this contention, petitioners advance two closely related arguments. First, they contend that preemption of state and local regulation of SMATV is a reversal of well-established policy and therefore "presumptively" contrary to the achievement of the Commission's statutory responsibilities. Second, petitioners contend that the policies underlying the Communications Act cannot be advanced by the Commission's determination to allow SMATV to enter the telecommunications marketplace unregulated. We reject both of these arguments and conclude that the Commission's action is not only consistent with prior Commission policy, but also a " 'reasonable accommodation of conflicting policies' that are within the agency's domain." [   ]

1. The Allocation of Regulatory Responsibilities Between the Commission and State and Local Governments

During the past 12 years, the Commission has given local jurisdictions significant control over the franchising of traditional cable systems. Petitioners contend that the Commission's refusal to give state and local governments the same authority over SMATV as they have over traditional cable is a reversal of well-established policy. Careful review of Commission precedent, however, reveals that the petitioners' argument ignores the critical distinction the Commission has made between cable television systems that use public rights-of-way and systems, like SMATV, that are operated solely on private property.

The Commission recognized in 1972 that direct federal licensing of the thousands of cable systems operating in large and small communities throughout the country would place "an unmanageable burden on the Commission." . . . The Commission therefore created a "deliberately structured dualism" whereby local government would be responsible for selecting franchises, pursuant to minimum standards established by the Commission, while the Commission retained exclusive authority over all operational aspects of cable communication, including technical standards and signal carriage. [   ]

. . . Although the Commission recognized that "the essentially local service offered by cable television, at least in its formative stages, could best be developed through local participation and enforcement," it cautioned that "the developing duplicative and burdensome overregulation of cable television" was of increasing concern. [   ]

Following a comprehensive study of the effect of dual regulation upon the cable industry, the Commission in 1975 recognized the need for clarification of local governments' regulatory responsibilities. . . . The Commission made explicit its intention to preempt local regulation whenever necessary "to assure the orderly development of this new technology into the national communications structure." [   ]

Under this dual regulatory framework, the Commission has consistently retained exclusive authority over these elements of cable television that do not involve the use of public rights-of-way. The Commission has retained exclusive authority over the licensing of the satellites that transmit SMATV signals, [ ], and the earth stations that receive the satellite signals. [   ] The Commission has preempted regulation of pay television programming services and rates, [   ], and the carriage of television broadcast signals. [   ] As the Supreme Court stated in its unanimous *Crisp* decision, "[o]ver the past twenty years, pursuant to its delegated authority under the Communications Act, the FCC has unambiguously expressed its intent to preempt any state or local regulation of this entire array of signals carried by cable television systems." [   ]

A case similar to this appeal, Orth–O–Vision, Inc., 69 F.C.C.2d 657 (1978), recon., 82 F.C.C.2d 178 (1980), affirmed sub nom. New York State Commission on Cable Television v. FCC, 669 F.2d 58 (2d Cir.1982), clearly demonstrates the Commission's willingness to preempt state regulation of systems that do not involve the use of public rights-of-way. . . .

. . .

In affirming the Commission's preemption, the Second Circuit found that by denying franchises, municipalities could curtail the development of MDS. [   ] Since the Commission's policy of advancing the development of MDS was within its statutory authority, the Commission properly preempted conflicting state entry regulation. [   ]

. . . The Commission's preemption of a cable system, which, like the system involved in this appeal, does not use public rights-of-way, plainly refutes petitioners' contention that the Commission has arbitrarily reversed well-established policy.

2.   Commission Reliance on Market Forces to Regulate SMATV

In a general challenge to the Commission's decision not to impose entry regulations upon SMATV, petitioners contend that the Commission has failed to show that its open entry policy is necessary for the achievement of its statutory responsibilities. Franchise cable television and SMATV have flourished under local regulation, they claim, and no federal interest would be promoted by allowing SMATV to compete unregulated with traditional cable.

Although the Commission does not have unbridled discretion to use the marketplace to regulate an industry under its control, "the public interest touchstone of the Communications Act, beyond question, permits the FCC to allow the marketplace to substitute for direct Commission regulation in appropriate circumstances." [   ] Indeed, the Commission has increasingly come to rely upon market forces to regulate the entry and operation of new cable television systems. [   ]

Petitioners advance no credible argument to show that the market is an inappropriate tool for the Commission to choose in this instance to effectuate its statutory mandate. Competition, petitioner NYSCCT argues, will have a grave impact upon the existing cable franchises. The Commission's determination that SMATV should be allowed to serve residents of multi-unit dwellings cannot be challenged as contrary to the purposes of the Communications Act merely because some harm will be visited upon existing and developed franchises. Measuring the public interest standard of the Communications Act with sole reference to the impact Commission action would have upon a developed technology ensures a regulatory regime frozen into maintaining the status quo. We cannot read into the Communications Act a congressional intent to so prevent innovative technologies from conferring substantial benefits upon the viewing public. We therefore conclude that the Commission's present reliance on market forces to regulate the entry of SMATV into the cable television marketplace is consistent with its statutory mandate.

. . .

C.   *The Reasonableness of the Commission's Exercise of Authority*

Having established the preemption of state regulation of SMATV is within the Commission's statutory authority, we now consider whether in exercising its authority the Commission acted arbitrarily or capriciously. [   ] As this court recently stated in Wold Communications, Inc. v. FCC, 735 F.2d 1465, 1476 (D.C.Cir.1984), the proper inquiry under the arbitrary and capricious standard is "whether a reasonable person, considering the matter on the agency's table, could arrive at the judgment the agency made." [   ] Our discussion of the Commission's authority forecloses extensive inquiry into the rationality of its decision. A finding that the Commission has the power to preempt state regulation means that preemption is necessary for the full accomplishment of lawful Commission objectives. Establishing this logical relationship between the action taken—preemption—and the Commission policy involves, at least to a certain extent, the determination that the Commission has not acted arbitrarily or capriciously. Furthermore, the nature of this preemption action obviates extensive analysis of the facts upon which the determination was reached: the parties do not so much dispute the factual circumstances surrounding the cable industry as the kind of regulation that should or should not be imposed upon the existing and emerging cable systems. Yet, if the Commission has chosen rationally among competing policies, we cannot reverse because we would have chosen other means of effectuating the congressional mandate. . . .

Petitioner NYSCCT claims that there is inadequate evidence in the record to justify the Commission's conclusion that state and local regulations actually impede the growth of SMATV. The petitioner's comments to the Commission, however, betray the weakness of its contention. The petitioner argued that "[t]he principal evil of allowing private cable to exist outside the regulatory scheme for cable is the impact upon territorial cable television." [   ] Since the dominant theme of the petitioner's opposition to the preemption order is the alleged need to stifle SMATV development, the Commission rationally determined that federal preemption was necessary to effectuate its policy of enhancing the diversity of cable programming. [   ]

Petitioners contend with only slightly more force that the Commission acted arbitrarily by failing to consider the impact preemption and deregulation would have upon the traditional cable industry. Petitioner NYSCCT estimated that the unregulated entry of SMATV into the New York City marketplace would cost franchise cable systems between $348 million and $793 million over the lifetime of the franchises. To replace the revenue lost from those subscribers who would choose SMATV, the franchise systems would have to increase the rates of their remaining subscribers from $7.00 to $11.00 per month.

The Commission found NYSCCT's analysis unpersuasive for several reasons. First, the Commission stated that it is "not an economic guarantor of competitive communications technologies which may offer similar services to subscribers." [   ] Second, the Commission noted that NYSCCT's arguments had been raised and answered in the Orth–O–Vision proceedings. Finally, the Commission predicted that, in states such as New York where cable franchises have mandatory access to multi-unit dwellings, franchise cable and SMATV could co-exist or at least compete for the same subscribers. [   ]

The Commission's response, while terse, was reasonably commensurate with the persuasive force of the petitioner's argument. Petitioner's "economic analysis" purports to document the degree of SMATV penetration into the cable television marketplace. Instead of doing so, it simply assumes that SMATV will replace franchise cable in every apartment of every multi-unit dwelling. Moreover, the data provided by the petitioner, viewed in the most positive light, merely show what the Commission already recognizes: the unregulated entry of SMATV into the cable television marketplace will have a competitive impact upon franchise cable. Petitioner's argument does not relate to the Commission's evaluation of the *facts*; it merely involves a recharacterization of the petitioner's basic quarrel with the Commission's *policy* of allowing SMATV to compete with franchise cable. We have already determined that the Commission has the statutory authority to adopt the policy of preventing local governments from enforcing entry regulations that have the purpose or the effect of restricting SMATV's competitive position. Evidence purporting to document the degree of SMATV penetration into the cable television marketplace does nothing to undermine the rationality of this decision. [   ]

. . .

For the foregoing reasons, the Commission's order is affirmed.

Notes and Questions

1. The Commission's stated rationale for preempting state and local regulation of SMATV was to prevent such regulation from inhibiting the development of SMATV service to the public. Could it be argued, however, that the Commission's action served to give SMATV an unfair regulatory advantage over cable television? Which is more important, regulatory parity or service to the public? Would it make a difference if, as a result of SMATV competition, some cable systems failed, leaving many people with no service at all?

2. A controversy over treating certain SMATV systems as though they were cable systems has been resolved by the 1996 Telecommunications Act. The FCC had ruled that "wholly private" SMATVs did not need a franchise but that "external, quasi-private" SMATVs did need a franchise. Analyzing the case in equal protection terms, the court was "unable to imagine *any* basis" for the distinction. The FCC was ordered to explain it. The court deferred facing First Amendment questions until it is confronted with an as-applied claim, rather than the facial challenge in this case. Beach Communications, Inc. v. Federal Communications Commission, 959 F.2d 975, 70 R.R.2d 773 (D.C.Cir.1992).

The Supreme Court unanimously reversed. Applying a rational-basis review, the Court held that those seeking to overturn § 602(7) had the "burden to negate every conceivable basis that might support it. Since a legislature need not articulate its reasons for enacting a statute, it is entirely irrelevant for constitutional purposes whether the legislature was actually motivated by the conceived reason for the challenged distinction."

The Court identified two possible bases for the provisions § 602(7). The first was "that common ownership was indicative of systems for which the costs of regulation would outweigh the benefits to consumers." The second was that there would be a significant risk of SMATV operators exercising monopoly power. The Court reasoned that the first SMATV operator to install a dish "on one building in a block of separately owned buildings" would have a significant advantage over other operators seeking to serve those other buildings. The first operator, having installed a dish, could wire the rest of the block for the cost of the cable, whereas other operators would also have to pay to install a dish. "Thus, the first operator could charge rates well above his cost and still undercut the competition."

Justice Stevens concurred, but on different grounds. He argued that the standard of review applied by the majority was excessively deferential to Congress. In his opinion the standard should be "whether the classification is rationally related to 'a legitimate purpose that we may *reasonably presume* to have motivated an impartial legislature.'" Applying this standard he found that the exception distinguished between property owners using an improvement (the satellite dish) on their property and property owners using the improvement "to distribute signals to subscribers on *other people's property*." Thus, Congress could be presumed to be "motivated by an interest in allowing property owners to exercise freedom in the use of their own property." Federal Communications Commission v. Beach Communications, 508 U.S. 307, 73 R.R.2d 1, 21 Med.L.Rptr. 1466 (1993).

Congress reacted to the decision by including a provision in the 1996 Act altering the definition of cable system specifically to exclude "a facility that serves subscribers without using any public right-of-way." 47 U.S.C.A. § 522(7)(B).

3. A novel approach by a SMATV operator has allowed it to connect 12 different buildings without obtaining a cable franchise. Entertainment Connections, Inc. (ECI) uses Ameritech Supertrunking Video Service to distribute programming from its headend at one of its buildings to the other 11. The Commission concluded that ECI qualified for the private cable exemption of § 602(7)(B):

> which provides that "a facility that serves subscribers without using any public rights of way" does not constitute a cable system under Section 602(7). That ECI's signal moves across public rights-of-way to reach its subscribers does not by itself render ECI the operator of a cable system. The issue is whether the transport by Ameritech of ECI's signal constitutes a use of such rights-of-way by ECI as contemplated by Section 602(7)(B). It is Ameritech, not ECI, that uses the rights-of-way, as the Commission and courts have interpret-

ed the term, whether for installations, repair or maintenance of its facilities. Ameritech does not have unfettered use of public rights-of-way and must comply with a range of safety, convenience, and other requirements. The public safety and convenience and management of public rights-of-way, provide a key premise for the cable franchise requirement. Because Ameritech possesses the authority to operate in the right-of-way and to transmit ECI's, or other video distributors', signals, we conclude that the underlying premise tying the franchise requirement to the use of public rights-of-way is not present in ECI's circumstances, and that requiring ECI to obtain a franchise would be needlessly duplicative. . . . We cannot conclude that ECI's mere interaction with Ameritech's authorized facilities in the public right-of-way is the type of use to which Congress spoke in defining what constitutes a cable system.

The Commission also concluded that this decision was consistent with Congressional intent evidenced by its amendment of the Communication Act following the Court's decision in *Beach*. Entertainment Connections, Inc., 13 F.C.C.Rcd. 14277, 12 C.R. 800 (1998).

4. There are hundreds of SMATV providers in the U.S. with 3–55 thousand customers each. As of mid–2002 the total number of SMATV subscribers was approximately 1.6 million, virtually the same as the previous year.

5. Compare DBS, MMDS and SMATV. Are they sufficiently dissimilar as to require different regulatory approaches? If so, what differences justify that conclusion?

D. ELECTRONIC PUBLISHING

Electronic publishing puts pages of information, both text and images, on television sets or other display tubes. This information can be distributed as part of a television broadcast signal or cable television signal or as a separate data stream distributed through the spectrum, cable or telephone lines.

Teletext is a one-way system with signals flowing only from the computer to the screen. It operates by sending a continuous cycle of information to home television screens during the regular vertical blanking interval (VBI) of a television signal (the black horizontal line that appears when the vertical hold is not properly adjusted). A user chooses the desired "page" of information from a published index, and instructs the receiver terminal to "grab" the page as it goes by. When the user is finished, the page is released from the screen. Teletext can be delivered by either broadcasting or cable.

When the Commission authorized teletext service in 1983, several important questions had to be answered. Teletext Transmission, 53 R.R.2d 1309 (1983). Again, it was necessary to determine an appropriate regulatory model. As in the SCA proceeding, the Commission opted to place the onus on the licensee to decide this based on the nature of the service to be provided.

The Commission also decided that, even in the case of broadcast-related services, teletext would be exempt from content restrictions such as § 315 and the fairness doctrine. In response to petitions for reconsideration filed by various parties, the Commission reaffirmed its position, Teletext Transmission (Reconsideration), 57 R.R.2d 842 (1985):

> 14. . . . First, we dispute the contrary implications of some petitioners and reaffirm our intention to pursue continued enforcement of these content-related broadcast laws, policies and rules until and unless they are altered by ourselves or other competent authority. This, however, in no way alters or diminishes our authority and responsibility to interpret and apply these as necessary when novel questions and circumstances arise. This is particularly true as in this situation where new services are being authorized that could not be, or were not, contemplated when Congress passed related statutory provisions nor when this Commission enacted rules and policies designed to give force to these provisions. Our attention is further focused in this area where the changing nature of the industry due both to competitive and technological flux requires us to give primary concern to the First Amendment implications of our actions. . . .

> 15. . . . In this context we view our decision here as no way inconsistent with the court's views in NAB v. FCC, 740 F.2d 1190 (D.C.Cir.1984), for the reasons detailed below. We consider teletext clearly as an ancillary service not strictly related to the traditional broadcast mode of mass communication. First, the very definition of teletext confined the service to traditional print and textual data transmission. [   ] Thus, although these data will be transmitted at some point through the use of the electromagnetic spectrum, its primary and overriding feature will be its historical and cultural connection to the print media, especially books, magazines and newspapers. Users of this medium will not be listening or viewing teletext in any traditional broadcasting sense, but instead will be *reading* it, and thus be able to skip, scan and select the desired material in ways that are incomparable to anything in the history of broadcasting and broadcast regulation. In this light, we believe that the content regulations created for traditional broadcast operations are simply out of place in this new print-related textual data transmission medium. . . .

The Commission continued the analogy to print media by noting that modern newspapers are often written and edited in one location and then transmitted by satellite to other locations for printing. Relying on *Miami Herald*, p. 90, *supra*, the Commission concluded that application of content restrictions to teletext would serve "neither the letter nor the purpose of the First Amendment."

The Commission's decision was appealed by the Telecommunications Research and Action Center and the Media Access Project. As we discussed in Chapter V, the most significant aspect of the decision was the court of appeals' determination that the fairness doctrine was not codified by the 1959 amendments to § 315 of the Communications Act. However, the opinion also illustrates the difficulty of determining how much latitude the Commission has in developing regulatory frameworks for new technologies.

TELECOMMUNICATIONS RESEARCH AND ACTION CENTER v. FEDERAL COMMUNICATIONS COMMISSION

United States Court of Appeals, District of Columbia Circuit, 1986. 801 F.2d 501, 61 R.R.2d 330, 13 Med.L.Rptr. 1881. Rehearing denied 806 F.2d 1115, 61 R.R.2d 1342, 13 Med.L.Rptr. 1896. Certiorari denied 482 U.S. 919, 107 S.Ct. 3196, 96 L.Ed.2d 684 (1987).

Before: BORK, SCALIA, and MACKINNON, CIRCUIT JUDGES.

BORK, CIRCUIT JUDGE:

Petitioners challenge the Federal Communications Commission's decision not to apply three forms of political broadcast regulation to a new technology, teletext. Teletext provides a means of transmitting textual and graphic material to the television screens of home viewers.

. . .

The case before us presents the question whether the Commission erred in determining that these three political broadcast provisions do not apply to teletext. Because we find that the Commission acted reasonably with respect to section 312(a)(7) and the fairness doctrine, but erroneously held section 315 not to apply to teletext, we affirm in part and reverse in part, and remand to the Commission for further proceedings.

I.

The technologically novel element of teletext service is its utilization of an otherwise unused portion of the television broadcast signal. Television signals are not continuous but are sent in pulses. The human eye retains the image from one pulse to the next so that the picture is perceived as uninterrupted. The time between the pulses of regular television broadcasting ("main signal" transmission) is known as the "vertical blanking interval," and can be used for pulses that constitute teletext transmission. As treated by the Commission in the docket now before us, "teletext" refers exclusively to such over-the-air transmissions, and not to transmission of text and graphics by way of cable or telephone. Main signal operators now control and operate teletext, though the FCC has authorized the operation of teletext "on a franchise basis" or through the "leas[ing] of space to multiple users." [ ] The Commission, however, admonished licensees "that they remain responsible for all broadcast related teletext provided via the station's facilities, whether produced in-house or obtained from outside sources." [   ]

To receive teletext, the viewer must have a device to decode the signal carrying the textual information and graphics. Currently, viewers may purchase teletext decoders in retail stores selling television sets. In the future, at least some television manufacturers will build decoding equipment into selected television models. Broadcasters of teletext thus have no control over who obtains the ability to decode teletext signals.

. . .

On November 27, 1981, the FCC released a Notice of Proposed Rulemaking to explore possible authorization for television stations to operate teletext systems. [   ] The Commission announced its goal "to provide a regulatory environment that is conducive to the emergence and implementation of new technology and new uses of the [broadcast] spectrum." [   ] The Commission added that "[i]n the case of teletext, the available evidence appears to indicate that the forces of competition and the open market are well suited to obtaining the kinds and amounts of service that are most desirable in terms of the public interest." [   ] The Notice therefore proposed that "teletext . . . be treated as an anciallary [sic] service" and that "[s]tations . . . not be required to observe service guidelines or other performance standards." [   ]

In its *Report and Order,* [   ], the Commission addressed the applicability of political broadcast requirements to teletext and concluded that "as a matter of law, . . . sections [312(a)(7) and 315] need not be applied to teletext service," and that applying these provisions would be "both unnecessary and unwise as a matter of policy." [   ] Moreover, the Commission "conclude[d] that the Fairness Doctrine should not be applied to teletext services." [   ] Thus the *Report and Order* sought to adopt an approach of non-regulation of teletext under any of the political broadcasting provisions administered by the FCC.

The Commission noted that section 312(a)(7) guarantees federal candidates only " 'reasonable access' " to "a broadcasting station" and considered what access would be "reasonable" when dealing with "variant broadcast services" such as teletext. . . . [T]he FCC suggested that by providing a candidate access to the broad television audience attracted to the station's regular broadcast operation a licensee satisfied its section 312(a)(7) duties even if the broadcaster at the same time denied access to the more limited audience viewing the "ancillary or subsidiary" teletext service. [   ]

In contrast, the Commission found section 315 wholly inapposite to teletext. Noting that a broadcast "use" triggered section 315's substantive obligations, that a "use" required "a personal appearance by a legally qualified candidate by voice or picture," and that the textual and graphics nature of teletext made it "inherently not a medium by which a candidate [could] make a personal appearance," the Commission held that teletext could not trigger the requirements of section 315. [   ] The Commission also reasoned that teletext differed from "traditional broadcast programming" because it does not have the powerful audiovisual capabilities of main-channel broadcasting, and therefore, does not pose the danger of "abuse" of these powerful sound and image "uses" that Congress envisioned in enacting section 315. [   ]

The Commission reserved its most elaborate analysis for the fairness doctrine. It began with the contention that the fairness doctrine is a Commission-made policy, and that Congress did not codify the fairness doctrine when it added language recognizing that policy in the course of a 1959 amendment to section 315. [   ] Thus, the 1959 amendment does not compel extension of the fairness doctrine to "new services . . . which did not even exist" at the time, and applications of the doctrine to serve the public interest rests in the Commission's "sound judgment and discretion." [   ]

The Commission then determined that it should not apply the fairness doctrine to teletext, "primarily [because of] a recognition that teletext's unique blending of the print medium with radio technology fundamentally distinguishes it from traditional broadcast programming." [   ] Noting that "scarcity" of broadcasting frequencies provided the first amendment justification of the fairness doctrine's application to traditional broadcast media, the Commission posited an "[i]mplicit . . . assumption that . . . power to communicate ideas through sound and visual images . . . is significantly different from traditional avenues of communication because of the immediacy of the medium." [   ] In other words, because scarcity inheres in all provisions of goods and services, including the provision of information through print media, the lessened first amendment protection of broadcast regulation must also rely upon the powerful character of traditional broadcasting. Because teletext "more closely resembles . . . other print communication media such as newspapers and magazines," the Commission found the "scarcity" rationale, as reinterpreted, insufficient to justify regulating teletext.

The Commission also reasoned that teletext, as a print medium in an "arena of competition . . . includ[ing] all other sources of print material," would not encounter the same degree of scarcity, in the usual sense, as the sound and visual images of regular programming. [   ] Thus, the Commission felt it constitutionally suspect to apply the fairness doctrine to teletext. And, in light of its obligation to "encourage, not frustrate, the [   ] development" of new services like teletext, the FCC decided, therefore, to heed concerns of commenters that teletext services might not prove "viable if . . . burdened by Fairness Doctrine obligations" and to exempt teletext from the fairness doctrine. [   ]

. . .

II.

In the Commission's view the regulation of teletext's "unique blend of the print medium with radio technology" raises first amendment problems not associated with the regulation of traditional broadcasting. Thus, the argument goes, existing Supreme Court precedent upholding political content regulation of traditional broadcasting does not necessarily justify the application of such regulation to the new medium of teletext. While not concluding that this application to a "print medium" like teletext would violate the first amendment, the Commission suggested that its application of that regulation would be sufficiently suspect to justify not imputing to Congress an intent to apply "section 315 and similar statutory provisions, and . . . associated rules and policies, to the teletext medium." [   ] To appreciate the Commission's argument, a brief discussion of the case law will be useful.

[The court then reviewed *Red Lion* and the Supreme Court's reliance on the "scarcity rationale" to uphold the constitutionality of political broadcast regulation.]

The Commission believes, however, that the regulation of teletext falls not within the permissive approach of *Red Lion,* but rather within the strict first amendment rule applied to content regulation of the print media. [*Tornillo*] . . . If the Commission's view is correct, and *Tornillo* rather than *Red Lion* applies to teletext, that service is entitled to greater first amendment protections than ordinary broadcasting and it would be proper, at a minimum, to construe political broadcasting provisions narrowly to avoid constitutionally suspect results.

The Commission has offered two grounds for its view that *Tornillo* rather than *Red Lion* is pertinent. Both reasons relate to the textual nature of teletext service. First, the Commission read an "immediacy" component into the scarcity doctrine:

> Implicit in the "scarcity rationale . . . is an assumption that broadcasters, through their access to the radio spectrum, possess a power to communicate ideas through sound and visual images in a manner that is significantly different from traditional avenues of communication because of the immediacy of the medium."

[   ] Second, the Commission held that the print nature of teletext "more closely resembles, and will largely compete with, other print communication media such as newspapers and magazines." [   ] Under this analysis, scarcity of alternative first amendment resources does not exist with respect to teletext. We address these points in turn.

With respect to the first argument, the deficiencies of the scarcity rationale as a basis for depriving broadcasting of full first amendment protection, has led some to think that it is the immediacy and the power of broadcasting that causes its differential treatment. Whether or not that is true, we are unwilling to endorse an argument that makes the very effectiveness of speech the justification for according it less first amendment protection. More important, the Supreme Court's articulation of the scarcity doctrine contains no hint of any immediacy rationale. The Court based its reasoning on the physical scarcity of broadcasting frequencies, which, it thought, permitted attaching fiduciary duties to the receipt of a license to use a frequency. This "immediacy" distinction cannot, therefore, be employed to affect the ability of the Commission to regulate public affairs broadcasting on teletext to ensure "the right of the public to receive suitable access to social, political, esthetic, moral, and other ideas and experiences." *Red Lion,* [ ].

The Commission's second distinction—that a textual medium is not scarce insofar as it competes with other "print media"—also fails to dislodge the hold of *Red Lion.* The dispositive fact is that teletext is transmitted over broadcast frequencies that the Supreme Court has ruled scarce and this makes teletext's content regulable. . . .

. . .

. . . [N]either we nor the Commission are free to seek new rationales to remedy the inadequacy of the [scarcity] doctrine in this area. The attempt to do that has led the Commission to find "implicit" considerations in the law that are not really there. The Supreme Court has drawn a first amendment distinction between broadcast and print media on a premise of the physical scarcity of broadcast frequencies. Teletext, whatever its similarities to print media, uses broadcast frequencies, and that, given *Red Lion,* would seem to be that.

The Commission, therefore, cannot on first amendment grounds refuse to apply to teletext such regulation as is constitutionally permissible when applied to other, more traditional, broadcast media. We now turn to the consideration of the particular regulation at issue in this case.

III.

Section 312(a)(7) states that "[t]he Commission may revoke any station license or construction permit . . . for willful or repeated failure to allow reasonable access to or to permit purchase of reasonable amounts of time for the use of a broadcasting station by a legally qualified candidate for Federal elective office on behalf of his candidacy." 47 U.S.C. § 312(a)(7) (1982). The question here is the rationality of the Commission's decision about the applicability of this provision to teletext.

At the outset, we state what we understand the Commission's decision to be. In introducing its legal analysis, the Commission stated: "As discussed below, we have concluded that, as a matter of law, . . . sections [312(a)(7) and 315] need not be applied to teletext service." [ ] The Commission stated that "the statutory requirement of affording reasonable access is adequately satisfied by permitting federal candidates access to a licensee's regular broadcast operation; it does not require access to ancillary or subsidiary service offerings like teletext." The *Report and Order's* analysis of section 312(a)(7) concluded by stating that the Commission "perceive[d] no legal requirement that licensees grant federal candidates access to their teletext offerings." [ ] Finally, in rejecting reconsideration of this issue in its *Memorandum Opinion and Order,* the FCC asserted: "Guided as we are in such matters by a reasonableness standard, we find that a broadcaster could satisfy the 'reasonable access' rights of a candidate without use of teletext." [ ] We find it clear, therefore, that the Commission believes that a broadcaster cannot be deemed to have acted unreasonably under the statute on the ground that he or she adopts a policy refusing to permit any access to teletext. We now turn to our analysis of the Commission's conclusion on this point.

The scope of review in this case is quite narrow. In Columbia Broadcasting System, Inc. v. FCC, 453 U.S. 367, 386 (1981) ("CBS"), the Supreme Court stated that, in enacting section 312(a)(7), Congress "[e]ssentially . . . adopted a 'rule of reason' and charged the Commission with its enforcement." The Court also asserted that Congress "did not give guidance on how the Commission should implement the statute's access requirement." *Id.* . . . Thus, we approach the question of the agency's construction of section 312(a)(7) with significant "judicial deference," *CBS,* 453 U.S. at 390, and we must uphold that construction if it is a "reasonable" one. [ ] We now examine whether the "Commission's action represents a reasoned attempt to effectuate the statute's access requirement." *CBS,* 453 U.S. at 390.

   . . .

Contrary to Petitioners' assertions, there is, we believe no conflict between the Commission's section 312(a)(7) policy, as approved by the Supreme Court in *CBS,* and the decision made in the teletext docket. When the Supreme Court approved the Commission's policy of proscribing "blanket rules" or "uniform policies" concerning access, this meant only that broadcasters could not adopt policies that would effectively nullify the statute's rule of reason approach to granting access to federal candidates. This does not, and could not, suggest, however, that no rules may be applied in the determination of what access is reasonable under the statute. Reasonableness does not mean that an impressionistic judgment must be made in every case. . . . In the context of section 312(a)(7), Congress has empowered the Commission to establish rules and regulations to guide broadcasters in their determination of what access is reasonable, *see CBS,* 453 U.S. at 386 (citing 47 U.S.C. § 303(r)), and, while the Commission has principally developed standards on a case-by-case basis, it has also identified some of the extreme cases in which the reasonableness or unreasonableness of a practice is clear.

The Court in fact approved the use of per se rules by assenting to the Commission's policy limiting the applicability of section 312(a)(7) to the period after a campaign commences, a limitation nowhere found in the statute. . . . In the teletext decision, that is all the Commission did; it merely adopted a rule of per se reasonableness as to a minor portion of the station's operations because it believed the reasonableness of that exclusion to be clear.

   . . .

Nor do we think that the Supreme Court's approving description of Commission policy "requir[ing] [broadcasters] to tailor their responses to accommodate, as much as reasonably possible, a candidate's stated purpose in seeking air time," *CBS,* [ ], detracts from our conclusion. Petitioners argue that permitting licensees to refuse access to teletext allows broadcasters to ignore a candidate's desire both to provide "the public with detailed campaign information" and to discuss a complex set of campaign issues, and that this relieves the broadcaster of the need for the individualized tailoring of his or her response to the candidate's request. [   ] Implicit in the Commission's decision that a broadcaster need not provide access to teletext, however, is the conclusion that such purposes as discussion of complex issues may be satisfied by resort to the main channel. We cannot say that the Commission's conclusion is irrational. Complex campaign issues have been treated for years in television broadcasting, well before teletext, and we do not see, nor have petitioners directed us to, any evidence that carries the petitioners' burden of showing that main channel access cannot be tailored to satisfy, as much as reasonably possible, a candidate's desire for air time for such purposes. Accordingly, we affirm the Commission's decision with respect to section 312(a)(7).

IV.

. . .

. . . Even applying the considerable deference we owe the agency, however, we are unable to conclude that the agency's construction of the statute is a rational one, for it is plainly at odds with the language and intent of [§ 315]. *See CBS,* [   ]. We believe that the agency erred in concluding that the teletext does not constitute "traditional broadcast services" within the contemplation of the statute and that teletext is incapable of a "use" as that statutory term has evolved.

In section 153(*o*) of the Communications Act of 1934, Congress defined the term "broadcasting" to mean "dissemination of radio communications intended to be received by the public." 4 U.S.C. § 153(*o*) (1982). The Commission appears to have suggested that teletext transmissions are neither "radio communications" nor "intended to be received by the public." First, the Commission argued that the print nature of teletext differentiates it from more traditional types of electromagnetic transmissions, and that Congress, therefore, could not have intended to cover such a service under section 315. Second, the Commission distinguished teletext from "traditional broadcasting" in that teletext is an "ancillary" service. We address these points in turn.

The Commission's attempt to distinguish teletext from traditional broadcasting because of teletext's textual and graphic nature conflicts with the plain intent of Congress. The proper starting place for statutory interpretation is with "the language employed by Congress." [   ] On this question it is also the terminal point, for the definition of "radio communication" unmistakably includes such transmissions as teletext. In section 153(b) of the Act, Congress defined "radio communication" as

> the transmission by radio of *writing, signs, signals, pictures,* and sounds *of all kinds,* including all instrumentalities, facilities, apparatus, and services (among other things, the receipt, forwarding, and delivery of communications) incidental to such transmission.

47 U.S.C. § 153(b) (1982) (emphasis added). The text could hardly be clearer. Teletext falls squarely within this definition. Teletext involves "print and textual transmission" and that is plainly covered.

The Commission's attempt to distinguish teletext from the "traditional broadcast mode of mass communication" by calling it an "ancillary" service, [ ], departs without explanation from well-established precedent. Teletext and main channel broadcasting are merely different time intervals within the broadcast spectrum. Teletext is "ancillary" to main channel broadcasting only in the sense that it will probably not attract nearly as many viewers. But the Commission has explicitly held that the "number of actual or potential viewers is not significant" in determining whether some constitutes "broadcasting." [   ] What matters is "an intent for *public* distribution." Functional Music, Inc. v. FCC, 274 F.2d 543, 548 (D.C.Cir.1958) (emphasis in original), *cert. denied,* 361 U.S. 813 (1959). Under the *Functional Music* test, recently reaffirmed by this court in [*National Association of Broadcasters*, p. 542, *supra*], an intent for public distribution exists when the licensee's "programming can be, and is, of interest to the *general* . . . audience." [   ] The Commission has made no attempt to distinguish or repudiate this test, and no one disputes that teletext can and does carry programming, including news, sports, weather, and information about community events, of interest to a general audience. Given our conclusion about "radio communication," it is obvious that teletext service meets the statutory definition of "broadcasting" and that the Commission therefore erred in deciding that obligations applicable to "broadcasting stations" do not apply to teletext.

We reach a similar conclusion with respect to the Commission's efforts to establish as a matter of law that a candidate cannot "use" teletext within the meaning of section 315. In a careful analysis of the legislative history, Judge Maris concluded that Congress clearly intended section 315 to apply "only to the personal use of [transmission] facilities by the candidates themselves." [   ] The Commission has accordingly defined a "use" as follows:

> In the case of *spots,* if a candidate makes any appearance in which he is identified or identifiable by voice or picture, even if it is only to identify sponsorship of the spot, the whole announcement will be considered a use. In the case of a *program,* the entire program is a use if "the candidate's personal appearance(s) is substantial in length, integrally involved in the program, and indeed the focus of the program, and where the program is under the control and direction of the candidate."

1978 Political Broadcasting Primer, 69 F.C.C.2d at 2245 (emphasis in original). If, as the Commission urges in support of its conclusion that teletext is exempt from section 315, the teletext services were utterly incapable of a "use" thus defined, we might still doubt the rationality of a conclusion that one could not "use" teletext under section 315. Defining a "use" as a personal appearance by "voice or picture" suggests an approach under which the Commission defines "use" according to the qualities of the medium being used. In the case of traditional broadcasting, that "use" took on an audio-visual character consistent with that of the medium. Given the textual nature of teletext, it appears to be an unexplained departure from the Commission's past practice for it not to redefine "use" to account for the nature of the new medium. Such a redefinition would allow for "use" of teletext broadcasting when there was transmission of personal statements, reprints of speeches, policy papers by the candidate, and the like. These represent clear examples of a candidate's making a personal use of the teletext broadcasting medium and appear to fall within the meaning of section 315. At a minimum, the Commission would have to address whether the existence of personal "textual uses" of teletext might necessarily follow from the Commission's previous treatment of "uses" and then either redefine "use" to include such a situation or explain why it feels it can reasonably do so under the statutory scheme.

We also have a more particular objection to the Commission's reasoning. The Commission asserted that a "use" was not possible because teletext could not reproduce a "voice or picture" of a candidate. In this, the Commission ignored the fact that teletext is capable of high-resolution graphics and can transmit a recognizable image of a candidate using that capability. The transmission of a "drawing or other pictorial representation" of a candidate, if "identified or identifiable," will satisfy "the requirement for an appearance by voice or picture of a candidate." Carter/Mondale Reelection Committee, Inc., 80 F.C.C.2d 285, 286 (Broadcast Bureau 1980). Thus, even under the current definition, teletext cannot be found utterly incapable of a "use" under section 315. Because the Commission did not acknowledge or in any way deal with this inconsistent precedent, its ruling cannot be deemed the product of reasoned decisionmaking.

Accordingly, we reverse the Commission's decision with respect to section 315 and remand for further proceedings consistent with this opinion. We now turn to an examination of the Commission's treatment of the fairness doctrine.

V.

Because the fairness doctrine derives from the mandate to serve the public interest, the Commission is not bound to adhere to a view of the fairness doctrine that covers teletext. "An agency's view of what is in the public interest may change, either with or without a change in circumstances." *Greater Boston Corp. v. FCC*, [   ]. To the extent that the Commission's exemption of teletext amounts to a change in its view of what the public interest requires, however, the Commission has an obligation to acknowledge and justify that change in order to satisfy the demands of reasoned decisionmaking. . . .

The Commission has offered two justifications for its refusal to apply the fairness doctrine to teletext. First, the Commission relies on its theory about the textual nature of teletext and the first amendment implications flowing from this distinction between teletext and other, more traditional modes of broadcasting. . . .

The second justification is more substantial. The Commission decided, and petitioners have not disputed, that the burdens of applying the fairness doctrine might well impede the development of the new technology and that "the likelihood of licensees' embarking upon . . . endeavors [like teletext] will be substantially affected" by the agency's policy. [ ] Accordingly, the Commission explicitly concluded that "the public interest is better served by not subjecting teletext to Fairness Doctrine obligations." [ ]

We believe the Commission acted rationally in so concluding. Petitioners have not challenged the Commission's assertions about the negative impact the application of the fairness doctrine would have upon the development of teletext. Moreover, the Commission's view that encouragement of new technologies is not only rational, but is explicit in the Communications Act of 1934. *See* 47 U.S.C. § 303(g)(1982). In effect, the Commission posited an absence of fairness doctrine burdens and made predictions about the marginal encouragement to the development of teletext and the marginal diminution, if any, in the presentation of opposing viewpoints on controversial matters of public importance. In weighing the public interest implications of the two marginal effects, the Commission concluded that the balance favored forbearance from applying the fairness doctrine, and, absent a showing, not even attempted here, that this conclusion was arbitrary and capricious, we cannot disturb the Commission's decision on this point. Accordingly, with respect to the fairness doctrine, we affirm the decision of the Commission.

To summarize: we reverse and remand the Commission's decision for further proceedings consistent with this opinion as it concerns section 315 of the Communications Act of 1934, and we affirm the Commission's decision with respect to section 312(a)(7) and the fairness doctrine.

It is so ordered.

MacKINNON, CIRCUIT JUDGE, concurring in part and dissenting in part:

. . . I would thus allow reasonable access to teletext by legally qualified candidates for federal elected office on behalf of their candidacies. I would also hold that the fairness doctrine is applicable. . . . In my opinion this would not impede the development of teletext.

Notes and Questions

1. As previously noted, in *Subscription Video,* p. 549, *supra,* the Commission subsequently substituted an intent-based approach to service classification for the *Functional Music* test and redefined subscription programming services as nonbroadcast services. However, the FCC specifically declined to redefine subscription teletext in a similar fashion.

2. At the time of the Commission's original authorization of teletext service, the most controversial part of the ruling was the decision to allow cable systems to remove the teletext portion of the signal from any broadcast transmissions they carried. The importance of the Commission's failure to mandate carriage of teletext was reduced, however, by the *Quincy Cable* and *Century Communications* decisions.

Despite the Commission's ruling, cable operators are not free to remove all teletext from the (VBI) of secondary transmissions of broadcast signals. In WGN Continental Broadcasting Co. v. United Video, Inc., 693 F.2d 622, the court of appeals held that under some circumstances, stripping teletext constitutes a copyright violation. According to the court, main-channel programming and program-related teletext constitute a single, copyrighted work. Deletion of the teletext not only is infringement, but it removes the signal from the protection of the compulsory license normally applicable to secondary transmissions.

The extent of the protection afforded teletext providers by *WGN* is difficult to determine. It is not at all clear what constitutes program-related teletext. Closed-captioning and subtitles are obviously program-related material, as is provision of more detailed information concerning the subject of the main-channel programming, e.g., where to buy an advertised product. What about announcements of upcoming programs? The court thought they were also program-related material.

A second problem with *WGN* is its holding that deletion constitutes infringement. This relatively novel holding was based on a single case, Gilliam v. American Broadcasting Companies, Inc., 538 F.2d 14 (2d Cir.1976), and the facts in that case were markedly different. *Gilliam* involved a complaint by the British comedy group, Monty Python, that during a broadcast, ABC deleted material from one of their movies in a way that seriously damaged the artistic value of the movie.

Due in part to the limited success of teletext, *WGN* has yet to be tested further in the courts.

Chapter XI

THE INTERNET

Although some people have been using computers to send and receive information for many years, there was a dramatic increase in the use of computer bulletin board systems (BBSs), on-line services and the Internet in the 1990s. Together these are referred to by such terms as, "cyberspace," "the information superhighway," and the "national (or global) information infrastructure (NII or GII)." With this growth have come a number of difficult legal and regulatory questions.

A. DEVELOPMENT

Computer Bulletin Boards have been around the longest. Typically BBSs are computers accessible by telephone. They can either be open to the general public or limited to subscribers. Those with access can either download material from the BBS computer to their computers or post material from their computers to the BBS computer. This material can be anything that is capable of being stored on a computer. This includes text, still pictures, movies, videos and software. Most bulletin boards are devoted to specific subjects or types of material. In some cases the system operator (sysop) may screen what is posted on the board.

On-line services are an extension of the BBS concept. These services provide telephone access on a regional or national basis. They also provide a number of different databases including news, sports, weather, travel information and movie, art and restaurant reviews, as well as other services such as shopping, games, and electronic mail.

Despite their growth, the on-line services are now being eclipsed by the explosive growth of the Internet, especially that portion of it known as the World Wide Web. The beginnings of the Internet can be traced back to the late 1960s when the Defense Department's Advanced Research Projects Agency (ARPA) provided funding for the ARPANET, a network designed to connect computers at various universities. Within a few years 20 computers had been connected.

In the mid–1970s, specific computer protocols were developed allowing different computer networks utilizing a transmission method called packet-switching to interconnect. These protocols were the Transmission Control Protocol (TCP) and Internet Protocol (IP). Over the next decade various research Local Area Networks and workstations were connected to ARPANET, creating what became the Internet.

Starting in the mid–1980s, the National Science Foundation began funding the development of a number of regional computer networks, as well as an upgraded national network connection capable of carrying data at much higher speeds.

As a result the Internet now connects academic, government, research, commercial and international networks. It includes 150 countries, more than 4.85 million host computers and up to 65 million or more users, although the latter figure is open to debate. There is no way currently to get an accurate measurement.

The Internet is used for a wide variety of services including transferring files, Fax, E–Mail, remote computer use, mailing lists and bulletin board services, interactive information delivery services, interactive multiuser services, indexing services and long distance telephone.

The 1990s saw two major developments involving the Internet. The first was the change from a government-funded network to a commercial network. This opened the Internet up to commercial uses.

The second was the World Wide Web. The Web is based on a set of protocols developed at CERN, a physics laboratory in Geneva, Switzerland. There are three basic features, the first of which is a unique electronic address known as a URL (Uniform Resource Locator), which is assigned to every "Web Page," or document. The second is HTTP (Hypertext Transport Protocol), which sets standards for the transfer of text, audio and video files across the Internet. The third is HTML (Hypertext Markup Language), which allows automatic transfer from one point in a Web document to any other point within that document or any other document by simply clicking a computer mouse on highlighted text.

With the development of the Web and "web browser" software, such as Mosaic, Netscape and Microsoft's Internet Explorer, it has become possible for people with minimal technical expertise to search the Web and view or download text, pictures, and videos from computers located all over the world. It is even becoming possible to transmit and receive real-time audio and video, and carry on conversations.

1. Background

As we noted at the outset, the Internet is a vast, interactive medium consisting of a decentralized network of computers around the world. The Internet presents low entry barriers to anyone who wishes to provide or distribute information. Unlike television, cable, radio, newspapers, magazines or books, the Internet provides an opportunity for those with access to it to communicate with a worldwide audience at little cost. At least 400 million people use the Internet worldwide, and approximately 143 million Americans were using the Internet as of September 2001. Nat'l Telecomm. & Info. Admin., *A Nation Online: How Americans Are Expanding Their Use of the Internet* (February 2002), *available at http://www.ntia.doc.gov/ntiahome/dn/.*

. . .

Users may find content on the Web using engines that search for requested keywords. In response to a keyword request, a search engine will display a list of Web sites that may contain relevant content and provide links to those sites. Search engines and directories often return a limited number of sites in their search results (e.g., the Google search engine will return only 2,000 sites in response to a search, even if it has found, for example, 530,000 sites in its index that meet the search criteria).

A user may also access content on the Web by typing a URL (Uniform Resource Locator) into the address line of the browser. A URL is an address that points to some resource located on a Web server that is accessible over the Internet. This resource may be a Web site, a Web page, an image, a sound or video file, or other resource. A URL can be either a numeric Internet Protocol or "IP" address, or an alphanumeric "domain name" address. Every Web server connected to the Internet is assigned an IP address. A typical IP address looks like "13.1.64.14." Typing the URL *"http://13.1.64.14 /"* into a browser will bring the user to the Web server that corresponds to that address. For convenience, most Web servers have alphanumeric domain name addresses in addition to IP addresses. For example, typing in *"http:// www.paed.uscourts.gov"* will bring the user to the same Web server as typing in *"http://204.170.64.143."*

Every time a user attempts to access material located on a Web server by entering a domain name address into a Web browser, a request is made to a Domain Name Server, which is a directory of domain names and IP addresses, to "resolve," or translate, the domain name address into an IP address. That IP address is then used to locate the Web server from which content is being requested. A Web site may be accessed by using either its domain name address or its IP address.

A domain name address typically consists of several parts. For example, the alphanumeric URL *http://www.paed.uscourts.gov/documents/opinions* can be broken down into three parts. The first part is the transfer protocol the computer will use in accessing the content (e.g., "http" for Hypertext Transfer Protocol); next is the name of the host server on which the information is stored (e.g., *www.paed.uscourts.gov*); and then the name of the particular file or directory on that server (e.g., */documents/opinions*).

. . .

There are a number of Web hosting companies that maintain Web sites for other businesses and individuals, which can lead to vast amounts of diverse content being located at the same IP address. Hosting services are offered either for a fee, or in some cases, for free, allowing any individual with Internet access to create a Web site. Some hosting services are provided through the process of "IP-based hosting," where each domain name is assigned a unique IP number. For example, *www.baseball.com* might map to the IP address "10.3.5.9" and *www. XXX.com* might map to the IP address "10.0.42.5." Other hosting services are provided through the process of "name-based hosting," where multiple domain name addresses are mapped to a single IP address. If the hosting company were using this method, both *www.baseball.com* and *www.XXX.com* could map to a single IP address, e.g., "10.3.5.9." As a result of the "name-based hosting" process, up to tens of thousands of pages with heterogeneous content may share a single IP address.

2. The Indexable Web, the "Deep Web"; Their Size and Rates of Growth and Change

The universe of content on the Web that could be indexed, in theory, by standard search engines is known as the "publicly indexable Web." The publicly indexable Web is limited to those pages that are accessible by following a link from another Web page that is recognized by a search engine. This limitation exists because online indexing techniques used by popular search engines and directories such as Yahoo, Lycos and AltaVista, are based on "spidering" technology, which finds sites to index by following links from site to site in a continuous search for new content. If a Web page or site is not linked by others, then spidering will not discover that page or site.

Furthermore, many larger Web sites contain instructions, through software, that prevent spiders from investigating that site, and therefore the contents of such sites also cannot be indexed using spidering technology. Because of the vast size and decentralized structure of the Web, no search engine or directory indexes all of the content on the publicly indexable Web. We credit current estimates that no more than 50% of the content currently on the publicly indexable Web has been indexed by all search engines and directories combined. No currently available method or combination of methods for collecting URLs can collect the addresses of all URLs on the Web.

The portion of the Web that is not theoretically indexable through the use of "spidering" technology, because other Web pages do not link to it, is called the "Deep Web." Such sites or pages can still be made publicly accessible without being made publicly indexable by, for example, using individual or mass emailings (also known as "spam") to distribute the URL to potential readers or customers, or by using types of Web links that cannot be found by spiders but can be seen and used by readers. "Spamming" is a common method of distributing to potential customers links to sexually explicit content that is not indexable.

Because the Web is decentralized, it is impossible to say exactly how large it is. A 2000 study estimated a total of 7.1 million unique Web sites, which at the Web's historical rate of growth, would have increased to 11 million unique sites as of September 2001. Estimates of the total number of Web pages vary, but a figure of 2 billion is a reasonable estimate of the number of Web pages that can be reached, in theory, by standard search engines. We need not make a specific finding as to a figure, for by any measure the Web is extremely vast, and it is constantly growing. The indexable Web is growing at a rate of approximately 1.5 million pages per day. The size of the un-indexable Web, or the "Deep Web," while impossible to determine precisely, is estimated to be two to ten times that of the publicly indexable Web.

In addition to growing rapidly, Web pages and sites are constantly being removed, or changing their content. Web sites or pages can change content without changing their domain name addresses or IP addresses. Individual Web pages have an average life span of approximately 90 days.

3. The Amount of Sexually Explicit Material on the Web

There is a vast amount of sexually explicit material available via the Internet and the Web. Sexually explicit material on the Internet is easy to access using any public search engine, such as, for example, Google or AltaVista. Although much of the sexually explicit material available on the Web is posted on commercial sites that require viewers to pay in order to gain access to the site, a large number of sexually explicit sites may be accessed for free and without providing any registration information. Most importantly, some Web sites that contain sexually explicit content have innocuous domain names and therefore can be reached accidentally. A commonly cited example is *http://www.whitehouse.com*. Other innocent-sounding URLs that retrieve graphic, sexually explicit depictions include *http://www.boys.com,* *http://www.girls.com,* *http://www.coffeebeansupply.com,* and *http://www.BookstoreUSA.com*. Moreover, commercial Web sites that contain sexually explicit material often use a technique of attaching pop-up windows to their sites, which open new windows advertising other sexually explicit sites without any prompting by the user. This technique makes it difficult for a user quickly to exit all of the pages containing sexually explicit material, whether he or she initially accessed such material intentionally or not.

The percentage of Web pages on the indexed Web containing sexually explicit content is relatively small. Recent estimates indicate that no more than 1–2% of the content on the Web is pornographic or sexually explicit. However, the absolute number of Web sites offering free sexually explicit material is extremely large, approximately 100,000 sites.

B. THE COMMUNICATIONS DECENCY ACT

Concern over children's access to obscene and indecent material via computer led Congress to pass, as part of the 1996 Telecommunications Act, the Communications Decency Act. The Act authorized criminal penalties for anyone who in interstate or foreign communications knowingly:

> (A) uses an interactive computer service to send to a specific person or persons under 18 years of age, or

> (B) uses any interactive computer service to display in a manner available to a person under 18 years of age, any comment,

request, suggestion, proposal, image, or other communication that, in context, depicts or describes, in terms patently offensive as measured by contemporary community standards, sexual or excretory activities or organs, regardless of whether the user of such service placed the call or initiated the communication. . . .

The same applied to anyone who "knowingly permits any telecommunications facility under such person's control to be used for" such activities. Taking good faith measures (either by using blocking technology or requiring adult verification measures such as passwords or credit cards) to restrict minors from access to these communications was a defense. The FCC is authorized to describe "reasonable, effective, and appropriate measures" for people using this defense. 47 U.S.C.A. § 223. These provisions were immediately challenged by numerous citizens' groups and electronic publishers.

A preliminary injunction prohibiting enforcement of the provisions applicable to indecent communications was issued by a three-judge district court panel which unanimously found that the plaintiffs were likely to prevail on their arguments that those provisions are unconstitutional on their face. One unusual aspect of the decision was the inclusion of 123 paragraphs of findings of fact regarding the Internet. ACLU v. Reno, 929 F.Supp. 824 (E.D.Pa.1996).

JANET RENO v. AMERICAN CIVIL LIBERTIES UNION

Supreme Court of the United States, 1997.

521 U.S. 844, 117 S.Ct. 2329, 138 L.Ed.2d 874, 25 Media L. Rep. 1833, 8 C.R. 352.

JUSTICE STEVENS delivered the opinion of the Court.

At issue is the constitutionality of two statutory provisions enacted to protect minors from "indecent" and "patently offensive" communications on the Internet. Notwithstanding the legitimacy and importance of the congressional goal of protecting children from harmful materials, we agree with the three-judge District Court that the statute abridges "the freedom of speech" protected by the First Amendment.

I

The District Court made extensive findings of fact, most of which were based on a detailed stipulation prepared by the parties. See 929 F.Supp. 824, 830–849 (E.D.Pa.1996). The findings describe the character and the dimensions of the Internet, the availability of sexually explicit material in that medium, and the problems confronting age verification for recipients of Internet communications. Because those findings provide the underpinnings for the legal issues, we begin with a summary of the undisputed facts.

The Internet

. . .

The Internet has experienced "extraordinary growth." The number of "host" computers—those that store information and relay communications—increased from about 300 in 1981 to approximately 9,400,000 by the time of the trial in 1996. Roughly 60% of these hosts are located in the United States. About 40 million people used the Internet at the time of trial, a number that is expected to mushroom to 200 million by 1999.

Individuals can obtain access to the Internet from many different sources, generally hosts themselves or entities with a host affiliation. Most colleges and universities provide access for their students and faculty; many corporations provide their employees with access through an office network; many communities and local libraries provide free access; and an increasing number of storefront "computer coffee shops" provide access for a small hourly fee. Several major national "online services" such as America Online, CompuServe, the Microsoft Network, and Prodigy offer access to their own extensive proprietary networks as well as a link to the much larger resources of the Internet. These commercial online services had almost 12 million individual subscribers at the time of trial.

Anyone with access to the Internet may take advantage of a wide variety of communication and information retrieval methods. These methods are constantly evolving and difficult to categorize precisely. But, as presently constituted, those most relevant to this case are electronic mail ("e-mail"), automatic mailing list services ("mail exploders," sometimes referred to as "listservs"), "newsgroups," "chat rooms," and the "World Wide Web." All of these methods can be used to transmit text; most can transmit sound, pictures, and moving video images. Taken together, these tools constitute a unique medium—known to its users as "cyberspace"—located in no particular geographical location but available to anyone, anywhere in the world, with access to the Internet.

E-mail enables an individual to send an electronic message—generally akin to a note or letter—to another individual or to a group of addressees. The message is generally stored electronically, sometimes waiting for the recipient to check her "mailbox" and sometimes making its receipt known through some type of prompt. A mail exploder is a sort of e-mail group. Subscribers can send messages to a common e-mail address, which then forwards the message to the group's other subscribers. Newsgroups also serve groups of regular participants, but these postings may be read by others as well. There are thousands of such groups, each serving to foster an exchange of information or opinion on a particular topic running the gamut from, say, the music of Wagner to Balkan politics to AIDS prevention to the Chicago Bulls. About 100,000 new messages are posted every day. In most newsgroups, postings are automatically purged at regular intervals. In addition to posting a message that can be read later, two or more individuals wishing to communicate more immediately can enter a chat room to engage in real-time dialogue—in other words, by typing messages to one another that appear almost immediately on the others' computer screens. The District Court found that at any given time "tens of thousands of users are engaging in conversations on a huge range of subjects." It is "no exaggeration to conclude that the content on the Internet is as diverse as human thought.''

The best known category of communication over the Internet is the World Wide Web, which allows users to search for and retrieve information stored in remote computers, as well as, in some cases, to communicate back to designated sites. In concrete terms, the Web consists of a vast number of documents stored in different computers all over the world. Some of these documents are simply files containing information. However, more elaborate documents, commonly known as Web "pages," are also prevalent. Each has its own address—"rather like a telephone number." Web pages frequently contain information and sometimes allow the viewer to communicate with the page's (or "site's") author. They generally also contain "links" to other documents created by that site's author or to other (generally) related sites. Typically, the links are either blue or underlined text—sometimes images.

Navigating the Web is relatively straightforward. A user may either type the address of a known page or enter one or more keywords into a commercial "search engine" in an effort to locate sites on a subject of interest. A particular Web page may contain the information sought by the "surfer," or, through its links, it may be an avenue to other documents located anywhere on the Internet. Users generally explore a given Web page, or move to another, by clicking a computer "mouse" on one of the page's icons or links. Access to most Web pages is freely available, but some allow access only to those who have purchased the right from a commercial provider. The Web is thus comparable, from the readers' viewpoint, to both a vast library including millions of readily available and indexed publications and a sprawling mall offering goods and services.

From the publishers' point of view, it constitutes a vast platform from which to address and hear from a world-wide audience of millions of readers, viewers, researchers, and buyers. Any person or organization with a computer connected to the Internet can "publish" information. Publishers include government agencies, educational institutions, commercial entities, advocacy groups, and individuals. Publishers may either make their material available to the entire pool of Internet users, or confine access to a selected group, such as those willing to pay for the privilege. "No single organization controls any membership in the Web, nor is there any centralized point from which individual Web sites or services can be blocked from the Web."

Sexually Explicit Material

Sexually explicit material on the Internet includes text, pictures, and chat and "extends from the modestly titillating to the hardest-core." These files are created, named, and posted in the same manner as material that is not sexually explicit, and may be accessed either deliberately or unintentionally during the course of an imprecise search. "Once a provider posts its content on the Internet, it cannot prevent that content from entering any community." Thus, for example, "when the

UCR/California Museum of Photography posts to its Web site nudes by Edward Weston and Robert Mapplethorpe to announce that its new exhibit will travel to Baltimore and New York City, those images are available not only in Los Angeles, Baltimore, and New York City, but also in Cincinnati, Mobile, or Beijing—wherever Internet users live. Similarly, the safer sex instructions that Critical Path posts to its Web site, written in street language so that the teenage receiver can understand them, are available not just in Philadelphia, but also in Provo and Prague."

Some of the communications over the Internet that originate in foreign countries are also sexually explicit.

Though such material is widely available, users seldom encounter such content accidentally. "A document's title or a description of the document will usually appear before the document itself . . . and in many cases the user will receive detailed information about a site's content before he or she need take the step to access the document. Almost all sexually explicit images are preceded by warnings as to the content." For that reason, the "odds are slim" that a user would enter a sexually explicit site by accident. Unlike communications received by radio or television, "the receipt of information on the Internet requires a series of affirmative steps more deliberate and directed than merely turning a dial. A child requires some sophistication and some ability to read to retrieve material and thereby to use the Internet unattended."

Systems have been developed to help parents control the material that may be available on a home computer with Internet access. A system may either limit a computer's access to an approved list of sources that have been identified as containing no adult material, it may block designated inappropriate sites, or it may attempt to block messages containing identifiable objectionable features. "Although parental control software currently can screen for certain suggestive words or for known sexually explicit sites, it cannot now screen for sexually explicit images." Nevertheless, the evidence indicates that "a reasonably effective method by which parents can prevent their children from accessing sexually explicit and other material which parents may believe is inappropriate for their children will soon be available."

Age Verification

The problem of age verification differs for different uses of the Internet. The District Court categorically determined that there "is no effective way to determine the identity or the age of a user who is accessing material through e-mail, mail exploders, newsgroups or chat rooms." The Government offered no evidence that there was a reliable way to screen recipients and participants in such fora for age. Moreover, even if it were technologically feasible to block minors' access to newsgroups and chat rooms containing discussions of art, politics or other subjects that potentially elicit "indecent" or "patently offensive" contributions, it would not be possible to block their access to that material and "still allow them access to the remaining content, even if the overwhelming majority of that content was not indecent."

Technology exists by which an operator of a Web site may condition access on the verification of requested information such as a credit card number or an adult password. Credit card verification is only feasible, however, either in connection with a commercial transaction in which the card is used, or by payment to a verification agency. Using credit card possession as a surrogate for proof of age would impose costs on non-commercial Web sites that would require many of them to shut down. For that reason, at the time of the trial, credit card verification was "effectively unavailable to a substantial number of Internet content providers." [ ] Moreover, the imposition of such a requirement "would completely bar adults who do not have a credit card and lack the resources to obtain one from accessing any blocked material."

Commercial pornographic sites that charge their users for access have assigned them passwords as a method of age verification. The record does not contain any evidence concerning the reliability of these technologies. Even if passwords are effective for commercial purveyors of indecent material, the District Court found that an adult password requirement would impose significant burdens on noncommercial sites, both because they would discourage users from accessing their sites and because the cost of creating and maintaining such screening systems would be "beyond their reach."[23]

In sum, the District Court found: "Even if credit card verification or adult password verification were implemented, the Government presented no testimony as to how such systems could ensure that the user of the password or credit card is in fact over 18. The burdens imposed by credit card verification and adult password verification systems make them effectively unavailable to a substantial number of Internet content providers." [ ]

II

The Telecommunications Act of 1996, Pub.L. 104–104, 110 Stat. 56, was an unusually important legislative enactment. As stated on the first of its 103 pages, its primary purpose was to reduce regulation and encourage "the rapid deployment of new telecommunications technologies." The major components of the statute have nothing to do with the Internet; they were designed to promote competition in the local telephone service market, the multichannel video market, and the market for over-the-air broadcasting. The Act includes seven Titles, six of which are the product of extensive committee hearings and the subject of discussion in Reports prepared by Committees of the Senate and the House of Representatives. By contrast, Title V—known as the "Commu-

---

23. [ ]: "At least some, if not almost all, non-commercial organizations, such as the ACLU, Stop Prisoner Rape or Critical Path AIDS Project, regard charging listeners to access their speech as contrary to their goals of making their materials available to a wide audience free of charge. . . ."

nications Decency Act of 1996" (CDA)—contains provisions that were either added in executive committee after the hearings were concluded or as amendments offered during floor debate on the legislation. An amendment offered in the Senate was the source of the two statutory provisions challenged in this case. They are informally described as the "indecent transmission" provision and the "patently offensive display" provision.

The first, 47 U.S.C.A. § 223(a) (Supp.1997), prohibits the knowing transmission of obscene or indecent messages to any recipient under 18 years of age. . . .

. . .

The second provision, § 223(d), prohibits the knowing sending or displaying of patently offensive messages in a manner that is available to a person under 18 years of age. . . .

The breadth of these prohibitions is qualified by two affirmative defenses. See § 223(e)(5). One covers those who take "good faith, reasonable, effective, and appropriate actions" to restrict access by minors to the prohibited communications. § 223(e)(5)(A). The other covers those who restrict access to covered material by requiring certain designated forms of age proof, such as a verified credit card or an adult identification number or code. § 223(e)(5)(B).

III

On February 8, 1996, immediately after the President signed the statute, 20 plaintiffs filed suit against the Attorney General of the United States and the Department of Justice challenging the constitutionality of §§ 223(a)(1) and 223(d). . . . After an evidentiary hearing, that Court entered a preliminary injunction against enforcement of both of the challenged provisions. Each of the three judges wrote a separate opinion, but their judgment was unanimous.

Chief Judge Sloviter doubted the strength of the Government's interest in regulating "the vast range of online material covered or potentially covered by the CDA," but acknowledged that the interest was "compelling" with respect to some of that material. 929 F.Supp., at 853. She concluded, nonetheless, that the statute "sweeps more broadly than necessary and thereby chills the expression of adults" and that the terms "patently offensive" and "indecent" were "inherently vague." *Id.*, at 854. She also determined that the affirmative defenses were not "technologically or economically feasible for most providers," specifically considering and rejecting an argument that providers could avoid liability by "tagging" their material in a manner that would allow potential readers to screen out unwanted transmissions. *Id.*, at 856. Chief Judge Sloviter also rejected the Government's suggestion that the scope of the statute could be narrowed by construing it to apply only to commercial pornographers. *Id.*, at 854–855.

Judge Buckwalter concluded that the word "indecent" in § 223(a)(1)(B) and the terms "patently offensive" and "in context" in § 223(d)(1) were so vague that criminal enforcement of either section would violate the "fundamental constitutional principle" of "simple fairness," *id.*, at 861, and the specific protections of the First and Fifth Amendments, *id.*, at 858. He found no statutory basis for the Government's argument that the challenged provisions would be applied only to "pornographic" materials, noting that, unlike obscenity, "indecency has not been defined to exclude works of serious literary, artistic, political or scientific value." *Id.*, at 863. Moreover, the Government's claim that the work must be considered patently offensive "in context" was itself vague because the relevant context might "refer to, among other things, the nature of the communication as a whole, the time of day it was conveyed, the medium used, the identity of the speaker, or whether or not it is accompanied by appropriate warnings." *Id.*, at 864. He believed that the unique nature of the Internet aggravated the vagueness of the statute. *Id.*, at 865, n. 9.

Judge Dalzell's review of "the special attributes of Internet communication" disclosed by the evidence convinced him that the First Amendment denies Congress the power to regulate the content of protected speech on the Internet. *Id.*, at 867. His opinion explained at length why he believed the Act would abridge significant protected speech, particularly by noncommercial speakers, while "[p]erversely, commercial pornographers would remain relatively unaffected." *Id.*, at 879. He construed our cases as requiring a "medium-specific" approach to the analysis of the regulation of mass communication, *id.*, at 873, and concluded that the Internet—as "the most participatory form of mass speech yet developed," id., at 883—is entitled to "the highest protection from governmental intrusion," *ibid.*[30]

The judgment of the District Court enjoins the Government from enforcing the prohibitions in § 223(a)(1)(B) insofar as they relate to "indecent" communications, but expressly preserves the Government's right to investigate and prosecute the obscenity or child pornography activities prohibited therein. The injunction against enforcement of §§ 223(d)(1) and (2) is unqualified because those provisions contain no separate reference to obscenity or child pornography.

---

30. See also 929 F.Supp., at 877: "Four related characteristics of Internet communication have a transcendent importance to our shared holding that the CDA is unconstitutional on its face. We explain these characteristics in our Findings of fact above, and I only rehearse them briefly here. First, the Internet presents very low barriers to entry. Second, these barriers to entry are identical for both speakers and listeners. Third, as a result of these low barriers, astoundingly diverse content is available on the Internet. Fourth, the Internet provides significant access to all who wish to speak in the medium, and even creates a relative parity among speakers." According to Judge Dalzell, these characteristics and the rest of the District Court's findings "lead to the conclusion that Congress may not regulate indecency on the Internet at all." *Ibid.* Because appellees do not press this argument before this Court, we do not consider it. Appellees also do not dispute that the Government generally has a compelling interest in protecting minors from "indecent" and "patently offensive" speech.

. . .

IV

In arguing for reversal, the Government contends that the CDA is plainly constitutional under three of our prior decisions: (1) [*Ginsberg*, p. ___, *supra*]; (2) [*Pacifica*, p. ___, *supra*]; and (3) Renton v. Playtime Theatres, Inc., 475 U.S. 41, 106 S.Ct. 925, 89 L.Ed.2d 29 (1986). A close look at these cases, however, raises—rather than relieves—doubts concerning the constitutionality of the CDA.

In *Ginsberg*, we upheld the constitutionality of a New York statute that prohibited selling to minors under 17 years of age material that was considered obscene as to them even if not obscene as to adults. We rejected the defendant's broad submission that "the scope of the constitutional freedom of expression secured to a citizen to read or see material concerned with sex cannot be made to depend on whether the citizen is an adult or a minor." 390 U.S., at 636, 88 S.Ct., at 1279. In rejecting that contention, we relied not only on the State's independent interest in the well-being of its youth, but also on our consistent recognition of the principle that "the parents'claim to authority in their own household to direct the rearing of their children is basic in the structure of our society."

In four important respects, the statute upheld in *Ginsberg* was narrower than the CDA. First, we noted in *Ginsberg* that "the prohibition against sales to minors does not bar parents who so desire from purchasing the magazines for their children." [ ] Under the CDA, by contrast, neither the parents' consent—nor even their participation—in the communication would avoid the application of the statute.[32] Second, the New York statute applied only to commercial transactions, [ ], whereas the CDA contains no such limitation. Third, the New York statute cabined its definition of material that is harmful to minors with the requirement that it be "utterly without redeeming social importance for minors." [ ] The CDA fails to provide us with any definition of the term "indecent" as used in § 223(a)(1) and, importantly, omits any requirement that the "patently offensive" material covered by § 223(d) lack serious literary, artistic, political, or scientific value. Fourth, the New York statute defined a minor as a person under the age of 17, whereas the CDA, in applying to all those under 18 years, includes an additional year of those nearest majority.

. . .

As with the New York statute at issue in *Ginsberg*, there are significant differences between the order upheld in *Pacifica* and the CDA. First, the order in *Pacifica*, issued by an agency that had been regulating radio stations for decades, targeted a specific broadcast that

---

32. Given the likelihood that many E-mail transmissions from an adult to a minor are conversations between family members, it is therefore incorrect for the dissent to suggest that the provisions of the CDA, even in this narrow area, "are no different from the law we sustained in Ginsberg." [ ]

represented a rather dramatic departure from traditional program content in order to designate when—rather than whether—it would be permissible to air such a program in that particular medium. The CDA's broad categorical prohibitions are not limited to particular times and are not dependent on any evaluation by an agency familiar with the unique characteristics of the Internet. Second, unlike the CDA, the Commission's declaratory order was not punitive; we expressly refused to decide whether the indecent broadcast "would justify a criminal prosecution." [ ] Finally, the Commission's order applied to a medium which as a matter of history had "received the most limited First Amendment protection," [ ], in large part because warnings could not adequately protect the listener from unexpected program content. The Internet, however, has no comparable history. Moreover, the District Court found that the risk of encountering indecent material by accident is remote because a series of affirmative steps is required to access specific material.

In *Renton*, we upheld a zoning ordinance that kept adult movie theatres out of residential neighborhoods. The ordinance was aimed, not at the content of the films shown in the theaters, but rather at the "secondary effects"—such as crime and deteriorating property values—that these theaters fostered: " 'It is th[e] secondary effect which these zoning ordinances attempt to avoid, not the dissemination of "offensive" speech.' " [ ] According to the Government, the CDA is constitutional because it constitutes a sort of "cyberzoning" on the Internet. But the CDA applies broadly to the entire universe of cyberspace. And the purpose of the CDA is to protect children from the primary effects of "indecent" and "patently offensive" speech, rather than any "secondary" effect of such speech. Thus, the CDA is a content-based blanket restriction on speech, and, as such, cannot be "properly analyzed as a form of time, place, and manner regulation." [ ]

These precedents, then, surely do not require us to uphold the CDA and are fully consistent with the application of the most stringent review of its provisions.

V

. . . [S]ome of our cases have recognized special justifications for regulation of the broadcast media that are not applicable to other speakers, see [*Red Lion*, p. ___, *supra*]; [*Pacifica*]. In these cases, the Court relied on the history of extensive government regulation of the broadcast medium, [ ]; the scarcity of available frequencies at its inception, see, e.g., [*Turner I*, p. ___, *supra*]; and its "invasive" nature, see [*Sable*, p. ___, *supra*].

Those factors are not present in cyberspace. Neither before nor after the enactment of the CDA have the vast democratic fora of the Internet been subject to the type of government supervision and regulation that has attended the broadcast industry. Moreover, the Internet is not as "invasive" as radio or television. The District Court specifically found that "[c]ommunications over the Internet do not 'invade' an individual's home or appear on one's computer screen unbidden. Users seldom encounter content 'by accident.' " [ ] It also found that "[a]lmost all sexually explicit images are preceded by warnings as to the content," and cited testimony that " 'odds are slim' that a user would come across a sexually explicit sight by accident." [ ].

We distinguished *Pacifica* in *Sable*, [ ], on just this basis. . . . We agreed that "there is a compelling interest in protecting the physical and psychological well-being of minors" which extended to shielding them from indecent messages that are not obscene by adult standards, [ ], but distinguished our "emphatically narrow holding" in *Pacifica* because it did not involve a complete ban and because it involved a different medium of communication, [ ]. We explained that "the dial-it medium requires the listener to take affirmative steps to receive the communication." [ ] "Placing a telephone call," we continued, "is not the same as turning on a radio and being taken by surprise by an indecent message." [ ]

Finally, unlike the conditions that prevailed when Congress first authorized regulation of the broadcast spectrum, the Internet can hardly be considered a "scarce" expressive commodity. It provides relatively unlimited, low-cost capacity for communication of all kinds. The Government estimates that "[a]s many as 40 million people use the Internet today, and that figure is expected to grow to 200 million by 1999." This dynamic, multifaceted category of communication includes not only traditional print and news services, but also audio, video, and still images, as well as interactive, real-time dialogue. Through the use of chat rooms, any person with a phone line can become a town crier with a voice that resonates farther than it could from any soapbox. Through the use of Web pages, mail exploders, and newsgroups, the same individual can become a pamphleteer. As the District Court found, "the content on the Internet is as diverse as human thought." [ ] We agree with its conclusion that our cases provide no basis for qualifying the level of First Amendment scrutiny that should be applied to this medium.

VI

Regardless of whether the CDA is so vague that it violates the Fifth Amendment, the many ambiguities concerning the scope of its coverage render it problematic for purposes of the First Amendment. For instance, each of the two parts of the CDA uses a different linguistic form. The first uses the word "indecent," 47 U.S.C.A. § 223(a) (Supp.1997), while the second speaks of material that "in context, depicts or describes, in terms patently offensive as measured by contemporary community standards, sexual or excretory activities or organs," § 223(d). Given the absence of a definition of either term,[35] this difference in

---

35. "Indecent" does not benefit from any textual embellishment at all. "Patently offensive" is qualified only to the extent that it involves "sexual or excretory activities or organs" taken "in context" and

language will provoke uncertainty among speakers about how the two standards relate to each other and just what they mean.[37] Could a speaker confidently assume that a serious discussion about birth control practices, homosexuality, the First Amendment issues raised by the Appendix to our *Pacifica* opinion, or the consequences of prison rape would not violate the CDA? This uncertainty undermines the likelihood that the CDA has been carefully tailored to the congressional goal of protecting minors from potentially harmful materials.

The vagueness of the CDA is a matter of special concern for two reasons. First, the CDA is a content-based regulation of speech. The vagueness of such a regulation raises special First Amendment concerns because of its obvious chilling effect on free speech. [   ] Second, the CDA is a criminal statute. In addition to the opprobrium and stigma of a criminal conviction, the CDA threatens violators with penalties including up to two years in prison for each act of violation. The severity of criminal sanctions may well cause speakers to remain silent rather than communicate even arguably unlawful words, ideas, and images. [   ] As a practical matter, this increased deterrent effect, coupled with the "risk of discriminatory enforcement" of vague regulations, poses greater First Amendment concerns than those implicated by the civil regulation reviewed in [*Denver*, p. ___, *supra*].

The Government argues that the statute is no more vague than the obscenity standard this Court established in [*Miller*, p. ___, *supra*]. But that is not so. . . . Because the CDA's "patently offensive" standard (and, we assume arguendo, its synonymous "indecent" standard) is one part of the three-prong *Miller* test, the Government reasons, it cannot be unconstitutionally vague.

The Government's assertion is incorrect as a matter of fact. The second prong of the *Miller* test—the purportedly analogous standard—contains a critical requirement that is omitted from the CDA: that the proscribed material be "specifically defined by the applicable state law." This requirement reduces the vagueness inherent in the open-ended term "patently offensive" as used in the CDA. Moreover, the *Miller* definition is limited to "sexual conduct," whereas the CDA extends also to include (1) "excretory activities" as well as (2) "organs" of both a sexual and excretory nature.

The Government's reasoning is also flawed. Just because a definition including three limitations is not vague, it does not follow that one

"measured by contemporary community standards."

37. The statute does not indicate whether the "patently offensive" and "indecent" determinations should be made with respect to minors or the population as a whole. The Government asserts that the appropriate standard is "what is suitable material for minors." [   ] But the Conferees expressly rejected amendments that

would have imposed such a "harmful to minors" standard. See S. Conf. Rep. No. 104–230, p. 189 (1996) (S.Conf.Rep.), 142 Cong. Rec. H1145, H1165–1166 (Feb. 1, 1996). The Conferees also rejected amendments that would have limited the proscribed materials to those lacking redeeming value. See S. Conf. Rep., at 189, 142 Cong. Rec. H1165–1166 (Feb. 1, 1996).

of those limitations, standing by itself, is not vague.[38] Each of *Miller*'s additional two prongs—(1) that, taken as a whole, the material appeal to the "prurient" interest, and (2) that it "lac[k] serious literary, artistic, political, or scientific value"—critically limits the uncertain sweep of the obscenity definition. The second requirement is particularly important because, unlike the "patently offensive" and "prurient interest" criteria, it is not judged by contemporary community standards. [ ] This "societal value" requirement, absent in the CDA, allows appellate courts to impose some limitations and regularity on the definition by setting, as a matter of law, a national floor for socially redeeming value. The Government's contention that courts will be able to give such legal limitations to the CDA's standards is belied by *Miller*'s own rationale for having juries determine whether material is "patently offensive" according to community standards: that such questions are essentially ones of fact.

In contrast to *Miller* and our other previous cases, the CDA thus presents a greater threat of censoring speech that, in fact, falls outside the statute's scope. Given the vague contours of the coverage of the statute, it unquestionably silences some speakers whose messages would be entitled to constitutional protection. That danger provides further reason for insisting that the statute not be overly broad. The CDA's burden on protected speech cannot be justified if it could be avoided by a more carefully drafted statute.

VII

We are persuaded that the CDA lacks the precision that the First Amendment requires when a statute regulates the content of speech. In order to deny minors access to potentially harmful speech, the CDA effectively suppresses a large amount of speech that adults have a constitutional right to receive and to address to one another. That burden on adult speech is unacceptable if less restrictive alternatives would be at least as effective in achieving the legitimate purpose that the statute was enacted to serve.

. . .

It is true that we have repeatedly recognized the governmental interest in protecting children from harmful materials. See *Ginsberg*, [ ]; *Pacifica*, [ ]. But that interest does not justify an unnecessarily broad suppression of speech addressed to adults. As we have explained, the Government may not "reduc[e] the adult population . . . to . . . only what is fit for children." *Denver*, [ ] (internal quotation marks omitted) (quoting *Sable*, [ ]). "[R]egardless of the strength of the government's interest" in protecting children, "[t]he level of discourse reaching a mailbox simply cannot be limited to that which would be suitable for a sandbox." [ ]

---

38. Even though the word "trunk," standing alone, might refer to luggage, a swimming suit, the base of a tree, or the long nose of an animal, its meaning is clear when it is one prong of a three-part description of a species of gray animals.

The District Court was correct to conclude that the CDA effectively resembles the ban on "dial-a-porn" invalidated in *Sable,* [   ]. In *Sable,* [   ], this Court rejected the argument that we should defer to the congressional judgment that nothing less than a total ban would be effective in preventing enterprising youngsters from gaining access to indecent communications. *Sable* thus made clear that the mere fact that a statutory regulation of speech was enacted for the important purpose of protecting children from exposure to sexually explicit material does not foreclose inquiry into its validity. As we pointed out last Term, that inquiry embodies an "over-arching commitment" to make sure that Congress has designed its statute to accomplish its purpose "without imposing an unnecessarily great restriction on speech." *Denver,* [   ].

In arguing that the CDA does not so diminish adult communication, the Government relies on the incorrect factual premise that prohibiting a transmission whenever it is known that one of its recipients is a minor would not interfere with adult-to-adult communication. The findings of the District Court make clear that this premise is untenable. Given the size of the potential audience for most messages, in the absence of a viable age verification process, the sender must be charged with knowing that one or more minors will likely view it. Knowledge that, for instance, one or more members of a 100–person chat group will be minor—and therefore that it would be a crime to send the group an indecent message—would surely burden communication among adults.

The District Court found that at the time of trial existing technology did not include any effective method for a sender to prevent minors from obtaining access to its communications on the Internet without also denying access to adults. The Court found no effective way to determine the age of a user who is accessing material through e-mail, mail exploders, newsgroups, or chat rooms. [   ] As a practical matter, the Court also found that it would be prohibitively expensive for noncommercial— as well as some commercial—speakers who have Web sites to verify that their users are adults. [   ] These limitations must inevitably curtail a significant amount of adult communication on the Internet. By contrast, the District Court found that "[d]espite its limitations, currently available user-based software suggests that a reasonably effective method by which parents can prevent their children from accessing sexually explicit and other material which parents may believe is inappropriate for their children will soon be widely available." [   ] (emphases added).

The breadth of the CDA's coverage is wholly unprecedented. Unlike the regulations upheld in Ginsberg and Pacifica, the scope of the CDA is not limited to commercial speech or commercial entities. Its open-ended prohibitions embrace all nonprofit entities and individuals posting indecent messages or displaying them on their own computers in the presence of minors. The general, undefined terms "indecent" and "patently offensive" cover large amounts of nonpornographic material with serious educational or other value.[44] Moreover, the "community standards"

44. Transmitting obscenity and child pornography, whether via the Internet or

criterion as applied to the Internet means that any communication available to a nation-wide audience will be judged by the standards of the community most likely to be offended by the message. The regulated subject matter includes any of the seven "dirty words" used in the Pacifica monologue, the use of which the Government's expert acknowledged could constitute a felony. See Olsen Test., Tr. Vol. V, 53:16–54:10. It may also extend to discussions about prison rape or safe sexual practices, artistic images that include nude subjects, and arguably the card catalogue of the Carnegie Library.

For the purposes of our decision, we need neither accept nor reject the Government's submission that the First Amendment does not forbid a blanket prohibition on all "indecent" and "patently offensive" messages communicated to a 17–year-old—no matter how much value the message may contain and regardless of parental approval. It is at least clear that the strength of the Government's interest in protecting minors is not equally strong throughout the coverage of this broad statute. Under the CDA, a parent allowing her 17–year-old to use the family computer to obtain information on the Internet that she, in her parental judgment, deems appropriate could face a lengthy prison term. See 47 U.S.C.A. § 223(a)(2) (Supp.1997). Similarly, a parent who sent his 17–year-old college freshman information on birth control via e-mail could be incarcerated even though neither he, his child, nor anyone in their home community, found the material "indecent" or "patently offensive," if the college town's community thought otherwise.

The breadth of this content-based restriction of speech imposes an especially heavy burden on the Government to explain why a less restrictive provision would not be as effective as the CDA. It has not done so. The arguments in this Court have referred to possible alternatives such as requiring that indecent material be "tagged" in a way that facilitates parental control of material coming into their homes, making exceptions for messages with artistic or educational value, providing some tolerance for parental choice, and regulating some portions of the Internet—such as commercial web sites—differently than others, such as chat rooms. Particularly in the light of the absence of any detailed findings by the Congress, or even hearings addressing the special problems of the CDA, we are persuaded that the CDA is not narrowly tailored if that requirement has any meaning at all.

VIII

. . .

The Government first contends that, even though the CDA effectively censors discourse on many of the Internet's modalities—such as chat groups, newsgroups, and mail exploders—it is nonetheless constitutional because it provides a "reasonable opportunity" for speakers to engage in

---

other means, is already illegal under federal law for both adults and juveniles. See 18 U.S.C. §§ 1464–1465 (criminalizing obsceni- ty); § 2251 (criminalizing child pornography). . . .

the restricted speech on the World Wide Web. [ ] This argument is unpersuasive because the CDA regulates speech on the basis of its content. A "time, place, and manner" analysis is therefore inapplicable. [ ] It is thus immaterial whether such speech would be feasible on the Web (which, as the Government's own expert acknowledged, would cost up to $10,000 if the speaker's interests were not accommodated by an existing Web site, not including costs for database management and age verification). The Government's position is equivalent to arguing that a statute could ban leaflets on certain subjects as long as individuals are free to publish books. . . .

The Government also asserts that the "knowledge" requirement of both §§ 223(a) and (d), especially when coupled with the "specific child" element found in § 223(d), saves the CDA from overbreadth. Because both sections prohibit the dissemination of indecent messages only to persons known to be under 18, the Government argues, it does not require transmitters to "refrain from communicating indecent material to adults; they need only refrain from disseminating such materials to persons they know to be under 18." [   ]

This argument ignores the fact that most Internet fora—including chat rooms, newsgroups, mail exploders, and the Web—are open to all comers. The Government's assertion that the knowledge requirement somehow protects the communications of adults is therefore untenable. Even the strongest reading of the "specific person" requirement of § 223(d) cannot save the statute. It would confer broad powers of censorship, in the form of a "heckler's veto," upon any opponent of indecent speech who might simply log on and inform the would-be discoursers that his 17–year-old child—a "specific person . . . under 18 years of age," 47 U.S.C.A. § 223(d)(1)(A) (Supp.1997)—would be present.

Finally, we find no textual support for the Government's submission that material having scientific, educational, or other redeeming social value will necessarily fall outside the CDA's "patently offensive" and "indecent" prohibitions. See also n. 37, supra.

IX

The Government's three remaining arguments focus on the defenses provided in s 223(e)(5). First, relying on the "good faith, reasonable, effective, and appropriate actions" provision, the Government suggests that "tagging" provides a defense that saves the constitutionality of the Act. The suggestion assumes that transmitters may encode their indecent communications in a way that would indicate their contents, thus permitting recipients to block their reception with appropriate software. It is the requirement that the good faith action must be "effective" that makes this defense illusory. The Government recognizes that its proposed screening software does not currently exist. Even if it did, there is no way to know whether a potential recipient will actually block the encoded material. Without the impossible knowledge that every guardian in America is screening for the "tag," the transmitter could not reasonably rely on its action to be "effective."

For its second and third arguments concerning defenses—which we can consider together—the Government relies on the latter half of § 223(e)(5), which applies when the transmitter has restricted access by requiring use of a verified credit card or adult identification. Such verification is not only technologically available but actually is used by commercial providers of sexually explicit material. These providers, therefore, would be protected by the defense. Under the findings of the District Court, however, it is not economically feasible for most noncommercial speakers to employ such verification. Accordingly, this defense would not significantly narrow the statute's burden on noncommercial speech. Even with respect to the commercial pornographers that would be protected by the defense, the Government failed to adduce any evidence that these verification techniques actually preclude minors from posing as adults.[47] Given that the risk of criminal sanctions "hovers over each content provider, like the proverbial sword of Damocles," the District Court correctly refused to rely on unproven future technology to save the statute. The Government thus failed to prove that the proffered defense would significantly reduce the heavy burden on adult speech produced by the prohibition on offensive displays.

We agree with the District Court's conclusion that the CDA places an unacceptably heavy burden on protected speech, and that the defenses do not constitute the sort of "narrow tailoring" that will save an otherwise patently invalid unconstitutional provision. In *Sable*, [ ], we remarked that the speech restriction at issue there amounted to " 'burn[ing] the house to roast the pig.' " The CDA, casting a far darker shadow over free speech, threatens to torch a large segment of the Internet community.

X

At oral argument, the Government relied heavily on its ultimate fallback position: If this Court should conclude that the CDA is insufficiently tailored, it urged, we should save the statute's constitutionality by honoring the severability clause, see 47 U.S.C. § 608, and construing nonseverable terms narrowly. In only one respect is this argument acceptable.

A severability clause requires textual provisions that can be severed. We will follow § 608's guidance by leaving constitutional textual elements of the statute intact in the one place where they are, in fact, severable. . . . As set forth by the statute, the restriction of "obscene" material [in § 223(a)] enjoys a textual manifestation separate from that for "indecent" material, which we have held unconstitutional. Therefore, we will sever the term "or indecent" from the statute, leaving the rest of

---

47. Thus, ironically, this defense may significantly protect commercial purveyors of obscene postings while providing little (or no) benefit for transmitters of indecent messages that have significant social or artistic value.

§ 223(a) standing. In no other respect, however, can § 223(a) or § 223(d) be saved by such a textual surgery.

The Government also draws on an additional, less traditional aspect of the CDA's severability clause, 47 U.S.C., § 608, which asks any reviewing court that holds the statute facially unconstitutional not to invalidate the CDA in application to "other persons or circumstances" that might be constitutionally permissible. It further invokes this Court's admonition that, absent "countervailing considerations," a statute should "be declared invalid to the extent it reaches too far, but otherwise left intact." [ ] There are two flaws in this argument.

First, the statute that grants our jurisdiction for this expedited review, 47 U.S.C.A. § 561 (Supp.1997), limits that jurisdictional grant to actions challenging the CDA "on its face." Consistent with § 561, the plaintiffs who brought this suit and the three-judge panel that decided it treated it as a facial challenge. We have no authority, in this particular posture, to convert this litigation into an "as-applied" challenge. . . .

Second, . . . [i]n considering a facial challenge, this Court may impose a limiting construction on a statute only if it is "readily susceptible" to such a construction. [ ] See also [*Erznoznik*, p. ___, *supra*] ("readily subject" to narrowing construction). The open-ended character of the CDA provides no guidance whatever for limiting its coverage.

. . .

XI

In this Court, though not in the District Court, the Government asserts that—in addition to its interest in protecting children—its "[e]qually significant" interest in fostering the growth of the Internet provides an independent basis for upholding the constitutionality of the CDA. [ ] The Government apparently assumes that the unregulated availability of "indecent" and "patently offensive" material on the Internet is driving countless citizens away from the medium because of the risk of exposing themselves or their children to harmful material.

We find this argument singularly unpersuasive. The dramatic expansion of this new marketplace of ideas contradicts the factual basis of this contention. The record demonstrates that the growth of the Internet has been and continues to be phenomenal. As a matter of constitutional tradition, in the absence of evidence to the contrary, we presume that governmental regulation of the content of speech is more likely to interfere with the free exchange of ideas than to encourage it. The interest in encouraging freedom of expression in a democratic society outweighs any theoretical but unproven benefit of censorship.

For the foregoing reasons, the judgment of the district court is affirmed.

It is so ordered.

JUSTICE O'CONNOR, with whom THE CHIEF JUSTICE joins, concurring in the judgment in part and dissenting in part.

I write separately to explain why I view the Communications Decency Act of 1996(CDA) as little more than an attempt by Congress to create "adult zones" on the Internet. Our precedent indicates that the creation of such zones can be constitutionally sound. Despite the soundness of its purpose, however, portions of the CDA are unconstitutional because they stray from the blueprint our prior cases have developed for constructing a "zoning law" that passes constitutional muster.

Appellees bring a facial challenge to three provisions of the CDA. The first, which the Court describes as the "indecency transmission" provision, makes it a crime to knowingly transmit an obscene or indecent message or image to a person the sender knows is under 18 years old. 47 U.S.C.A. § 223(a)(1)(B) (May 1996 Supp.). What the Court classifies as a single " 'patently offensive display' " provision, [ ], is in reality two separate provisions. The first of these makes it a crime to knowingly send a patently offensive message or image to a specific person under the age of 18 ("specific person" provision). § 223(d)(1)(A). The second criminalizes the display of patently offensive messages or images "in a[ny] manner available" to minors ("display" provision). § 223(d)(1)(B). None of these provisions purports to keep indecent (or patently offensive) material away from adults, who have a First Amendment right to obtain this speech. [*Sable*] ("Sexual expression which is indecent but not obscene is protected by the First Amendment"). Thus, the undeniable purpose of the CDA is to segregate indecent material on the Internet into certain areas that minors cannot access. [ ]

The creation of "adult zones" is by no means a novel concept. States have long denied minors access to certain establishments frequented by adults. States have also denied minors access to speech deemed to be "harmful to minors." . . .

I

Our cases make clear that a "zoning" law is valid only if adults are still able to obtain the regulated speech. If they cannot, the law does more than simply keep children away from speech they have no right to obtain—it interferes with the rights of adults to obtain constitutionally protected speech and effectively "reduce[s] the adult population . . . to reading only what is fit for children." [*Butler*, p. ___, *supra*]. The First Amendment does not tolerate such interference. [ ]; [*Sable*]; [ ]. If the law does not unduly restrict adults' access to constitutionally protected speech, however, it may be valid. In [*Ginsberg*], for example, the Court sustained a New York law that barred store owners from selling pornographic magazines to minors in part because adults could still buy those magazines.

The Court in *Ginsberg* concluded that the New York law created a constitutionally adequate adult zone simply because, on its face, it denied access only to minors. The Court did not question—and therefore necessarily assumed—that an adult zone, once created, would succeed in preserving adults' access while denying minors' access to the regulated speech. Before today, there was no reason to question this assumption, for the Court has previously only considered laws that operated in the physical world, a world that with two characteristics that make it possible to create "adult zones": geography and identity. See Lessig, Reading the Constitution in Cyberspace, 45 Emory L.J. 869, 886 (1996). A minor can see an adult dance show only if he enters an establishment that provides such entertainment. And should he attempt to do so, the minor will not be able to conceal completely his identity (or, consequently, his age). Thus, the twin characteristics of geography and identity enable the establishment's proprietor to prevent children from entering the establishment, but to let adults inside.

The electronic world is fundamentally different. Because it is no more than the interconnection of electronic pathways, cyberspace allows speakers and listeners to mask their identities. Cyberspace undeniably reflects some form of geography; chat rooms and Web sites, for example, exist at fixed "locations" on the Internet. Since users can transmit and receive messages on the Internet without revealing anything about their identities or ages, see Lessig, supra, at 901, however, it is not currently possible to exclude persons from accessing certain messages on the basis of their identity.

Cyberspace differs from the physical world in another basic way: Cyberspace is malleable. Thus, it is possible to construct barriers in cyberspace and use them to screen for identity, making cyberspace more like the physical world and, consequently, more amenable to zoning laws. This transformation of cyberspace is already underway. Lessig, supra, at 888–889. Id., at 887 (cyberspace "is moving . . . from a relatively unzoned place to a universe that is extraordinarily well zoned"). Internet speakers (users who post material on the Internet) have begun to zone cyberspace itself through the use of "gateway" technology. Such technology requires Internet users to enter information about themselves—perhaps an adult identification number or a credit card number—before they can access certain areas of cyberspace, 929 F.Supp. 824, 845 (E.D.Pa.1996), much like a bouncer checks a person's driver's license before admitting him to a nightclub. Internet users who access information have not attempted to zone cyberspace itself, but have tried to limit their own power to access information in cyberspace, much as a parent controls what her children watch on television by installing a lock box. This user-based zoning is accomplished through the use of screening software (such as Cyber Patrol or SurfWatch) or browsers with screening capabilities, both of which search addresses and text for keywords that are associated with "adult" sites and, if the user wishes, blocks access to such sites. Id., at 839–842. The Platform for Internet Content Selection (PICS) project is designed to facilitate user-based zoning by encouraging Internet speakers to rate the content of their speech using codes recognized by all screening programs. Id., at 838–839.

Despite this progress, the transformation of cyberspace is not complete. Although gateway technology has been available on the World Wide Web for some time now, [ ], it is not available to all Web speakers,

[ ], and is just now becoming technologically feasible for chat rooms and USENET newsgroups, [ ]. Gateway technology is not ubiquitous in cyberspace, and because without it "there is no means of age verification," cyberspace still remains largely unzoned—and unzoneable. [ ] User-based zoning is also in its infancy. For it to be effective, (i) an agreed-upon code (or "tag") would have to exist; (ii) screening software or browsers with screening capabilities would have to be able to recognize the "tag"; and (iii) those programs would have to be widely available—and widely used—by Internet users. At present, none of these conditions is true. . . .

Although the prospects for the eventual zoning of the Internet appear promising, I agree with the Court that we must evaluate the constitutionality of the CDA as it applies to the Internet as it exists today. [ ] Given the present state of cyberspace, I agree with the Court that the "display" provision cannot pass muster. Until gateway technology is available throughout cyberspace, and it is not in 1997, a speaker cannot be reasonably assured that the speech he displays will reach only adults because it is impossible to confine speech to an "adult zone." Thus, the only way for a speaker to avoid liability under the CDA is to refrain completely from using indecent speech. . . .

The "indecency transmission" and "specific person" provisions present a closer issue, for they are not unconstitutional in all of their applications. As discussed above, the "indecency transmission" provision makes it a crime to transmit knowingly an indecent message to a person the sender knows is under 18 years of age. 47 U.S.C.A. § 223(a)(1)(B) (May 1996 Supp.). The "specific person" provision proscribes the same conduct, although it does not as explicitly require the sender to know that the intended recipient of his indecent message is a minor. § 223(d)(1)(A). Appellant urges the Court to construe the provision to impose such a knowledge requirement, [ ], and I would do so. [ ]

So construed, both provisions are constitutional as applied to a conversation involving only an adult and one or more minors—e.g., when an adult speaker sends an e-mail knowing the addressee is a minor, or when an adult and minor converse by themselves or with other minors in a chat room. In this context, these provisions are no different from the law we sustained in *Ginsberg*. Restricting what the adult may say to the minors in no way restricts the adult's ability to communicate with other adults. He is not prevented from speaking indecently to other adults in a chat room (because there are no other adults participating in the conversation) and he remains free to send indecent e-mails to other adults. The relevant universe contains only one adult, and the adult in that universe has the power to refrain from using indecent speech and consequently to keep all such speech within the room in an "adult" zone.

The analogy to *Ginsberg* breaks down, however, when more than one adult is a party to the conversation. If a minor enters a chat room otherwise occupied by adults, the CDA effectively requires the adults in the room to stop using indecent speech. If they did not, they could be prosecuted under the "indecency transmission" and "specific person" provisions for any indecent statements they make to the group, since they would be transmitting an indecent message to specific persons, one of whom is a minor. [   ] The CDA is therefore akin to a law that makes it a crime for a bookstore owner to sell pornographic magazines to anyone once a minor enters his store. Even assuming such a law might be constitutional in the physical world as a reasonable alternative to excluding minors completely from the store, the absence of any means of excluding minors from chat rooms in cyberspace restricts the rights of adults to engage in indecent speech in those rooms. The "indecency transmission" and "specific person" provisions share this defect.

But these two provisions do not infringe on adults' speech in all situations. And as discussed below, I do not find that the provisions are overbroad in the sense that they restrict minors' access to a substantial amount of speech that minors have the right to read and view. Accordingly, the CDA can be applied constitutionally in some situations. Normally, this fact would require the Court to reject a direct facial challenge. [   ] Appellees' claim arises under the First Amendment, however, and they argue that the CDA is facially invalid because it is "substantially overbroad"—that is, it "sweeps too broadly . . . [and] penaliz[es] a substantial amount of speech that is constitutionally protected," [   ]. I agree with the Court that the provisions are overbroad in that they cover any and all communications between adults and minors, regardless of how many adults might be part of the audience to the communication.

This conclusion does not end the matter, however. Where, as here, "the parties challenging the statute are those who desire to engage in protected speech that the overbroad statute purports to punish . . . [t]he statute may forthwith be declared invalid to the extent that it reaches too far, but otherwise left intact." [   ] There is no question that Congress intended to prohibit certain communications between one adult and one or more minors. . . . There is also no question that Congress would have enacted a narrower version of these provisions had it known a broader version would be declared unconstitutional. . . . I would therefore sustain the "indecency transmission" and "specific person" provisions to the extent they apply to the transmission of Internet communications where the party initiating the communication knows that all of the recipients are minors.

II

Whether the CDA substantially interferes with the First Amendment rights of minors, and thereby runs afoul of the second characteristic of valid zoning laws, presents a closer question. In *Ginsberg*, the New York law we sustained prohibited the sale to minors of magazines that were "harmful to minors." Under that law, a magazine was "harmful to minors" only if it was obscene as to minors. [   ] Noting that obscene speech is not protected by the First Amendment, [   ], and that New York was constitutionally free to adjust the definition of obscenity for minors, [ ], the Court concluded that the law did not "invad[e] the area of freedom of expression constitutionally secured to minors." [ ] New York therefore did not infringe upon the First Amendment rights of minors. Cf. [*Erznoznik*] (striking down city ordinance that banned nudity that was not "obscene even as to minors").

The Court neither "accept[s] nor reject[s]" the argument that the CDA is facially overbroad because it substantially interferes with the First Amendment rights of minors. [ ] I would reject it. *Ginsberg* established that minors may constitutionally be denied access to material that is obscene as to minors. As *Ginsberg* explained, material is obscene as to minors if it (i) is "patently offensive to prevailing standards in the adult community as a whole with respect to what is suitable . . . for minors"; (ii) appeals to the prurient interest of minors; and (iii) is "utterly without redeeming social importance for minors." [ ] Because the CDA denies minors the right to obtain material that is "patently offensive"—even if it has some redeeming value for minors and even if it does not appeal to their prurient interests—Congress' rejection of the *Ginsberg* "harmful to minors" standard means that the CDA could ban some speech that is "indecent" (i.e., "patently offensive") but that is not obscene as to minors.

I do not deny this possibility, but to prevail in a facial challenge, it is not enough for a plaintiff to show "some" overbreadth. Our cases require a proof of "real" and "substantial" overbreadth, [ ], and appellees have not carried their burden in this case. In my view, the universe of speech constitutionally protected as to minors but banned by the CDA—i.e., the universe of material that is "patently offensive," but which nonetheless has some redeeming value for minors or does not appeal to their prurient interest—is a very small one. . . . While discussions about prison rape or nude art, see ibid., may have some redeeming education value for adults, they do not necessarily have any such value for minors, and under *Ginsberg*, minors only have a First Amendment right to obtain patently offensive material that has "redeeming social importance *for minors*," [ ] (emphasis added). There is also no evidence in the record to support the contention that "many [e]-mail transmissions from an adult to a minor are conversations between family members," [ ], and no support for the legal proposition that such speech is absolutely immune from regulation. Accordingly, in my view, the CDA does not burden a substantial amount of minors' constitutionally protected speech.

Thus, the constitutionality of the CDA as a zoning law hinges on the extent to which it substantially interferes with the First Amendment rights of adults. Because the rights of adults are infringed only by the "display" provision and by the "indecency transmission" and "specific person" provisions as applied to communications involving more than one adult, I would invalidate the CDA only to that extent. Insofar as the "indecency transmission" and "specific person" provisions prohibit the use of indecent speech in communications between an adult and one or more minors, however, they can and should be sustained. The Court reaches a contrary conclusion, and from that holding that I respectfully dissent.

Notes and Questions

1. The publisher of an electronic newspaper, *American Reporter*, had also filed a successful request for an injunction against enforcement of the "indecency transmission" and "patently offensive display" sections of the CDA. Shea v. Reno, 930 F.Supp. 916, 3 C.R. 1344 (S.D.N.Y.1996). The Supreme Court affirmed without opinion, 521 U.S. 1113 (1997).

2. How appropriate is Justice O'Connor's zoning analogy? How accurate and inexpensive would gateway technology or blocking software have to be, before she would find the challenged provisions of the CDA constitutional?

3. Congress included another attempt to restrict online indecency in the 1998 Budget Act, p. ___, *supra*. The Child Online Protection Act (COPA) added § 231 to the Communications Act:

> (1) PROHIBITED CONDUCT.—Whoever knowingly and with knowledge of the character of the material, in interstate or foreign commerce by means of the World Wide Web, makes any communication for commercial purposes that is available to any minor and that includes any material that is harmful to minors shall be fined not more than $50,000, imprisoned not more than 6 months, or both.

> (2) INTENTIONAL VIOLATIONS.—In addition to the penalties under paragraph (1), whoever intentionally violates such paragraph shall be subject to a fine of not more than $50,000 for each violation. For purposes of this paragraph, each day of violation shall constitute a separate violation.

> (3) CIVIL PENALTY.—In addition to the penalties under paragraphs (1) and (2), whoever violates paragraph (1) shall be subject to a civil penalty of not more than $50,000 for each violation. For purposes of this paragraph, each day of violation shall constitute a separate violation.

> c) AFFIRMATIVE DEFENSE.—

>> (1) DEFENSE.—It is an affirmative defense to prosecution under this section that the defendant, in good faith, has restricted access by minors to material that is harmful to minors–

>>> (A) by requiring use of a credit card, debit account, adult access code, or adult personal identification number;

>>> (B) by accepting a digital certificate that verifies age; or

>>> (C) by any other reasonable measures that are feasible under available technology.

> (e)(2)(A). A person will be deemed to be "engaged in the business" if the person who makes a communication, or offers to make a communication, by means of the World Wide Web, that includes any

material that is harmful to minors, devotes time, attention, or labor to such activities, as a regular course of such person's trade or business, with the objective of earning a profit as a result of such activities (although it is not necessary that the person make a profit or that the making or offering to make such communications be the person's sole or principal business or source of income). A person may be considered to be engaged in the business of making, by means of the World Wide Web, communications for commercial purposes that include material that is harmful to minors, only if the person knowingly causes the material that is harmful to minors to be posted on the World Wide Web or knowingly solicits such material to be posted on the World Wide Web.

"Harmful to minors" was defined as:

any communication, picture, image, graphic image file, article, recording, writing, or other matter of any kind that is obscene or that—

> (A) the average person, applying contemporary community standards, would find, taking the material as a whole and with respect to minors, is designed to appeal to, or is designed to pander to, the prurient interest;

> (B) depicts, describes, or represents, in a manner patently offensive with respect to minors, an actual or simulated sexual act or sexual contact, an actual or simulated normal or perverted sexual act, or a lewd exhibition of the genitals or postpubescent female breast; and

> (C) taken as a whole, lacks serious literary, artistic, political, or scientific value for minors.

47 U.S.C.A. § 231(e)(6).

For the purposes of COPA, children are defined as under 17 years of age. 47 U.S.C.A. § 231(e)(7).

COPA was immediately challenged by a coalition led by the ACLU. Applying strict scrutiny, the court found that the protection of children was a compelling government interest. The court then turned to the question of whether COPA was the least restrictive means:

> Here, this Court's finding that minors may be able to gain access to harmful to minors materials on foreign Web sites, noncommercial sites, and online via protocols other than http demonstrates the problems this statute has with efficaciously meeting its goal. Moreover, there is some indication in the record that minors may be able to legitimately possess a credit or debit card and access harmful to minors materials despite the screening mechanisms provided in the affirmative defenses. See *Reno I*, [p. ___, *supra*], (noting that "[e]ven with respect to the commercial pornographers that would be protected by the defense[s] [provided in the CDA], the Government failed to adduce any evidence that these verification techniques actually preclude minors from posing as adults"). These

factors reduce the benefit that will be realized by the implementation of COPA in preventing minors from accessing such materials online.

On the record to date, it is not apparent to this Court that the defendant can meet its burden to prove that COPA is the least restrictive means available to achieve the goal of restricting the access of minors to this material. Of course, the final determination must await trial on the merits. The plaintiffs suggest that an example of a more efficacious and less restrictive means to shield minors from harmful materials is to rely upon filtering and blocking technology. Evidence was presented that blocking and filtering software is not perfect, in that it is possible that some appropriate sites for minors will be blocked while inappropriate sites may slip through the cracks. However, there was also evidence that such software blocks certain sources of content that COPA does not cover, such as foreign sites and content on other protocols. [   ] The record before the Court reveals that blocking or filtering technology may be at least as successful as COPA would be in restricting minors' access to harmful material online without imposing the burden on constitutionally protected speech that COPA imposes on adult users or Web site operators. Such a factual conclusion is at least some evidence that COPA does not employ the least restrictive means.

Beyond the debate over the relative efficacy of COPA compared to blocking and filtering technology, plaintiffs point to other aspects of COPA which Congress could have made less restrictive. Notably, the sweeping category of forms of content that are prohibited—"*any communication*, picture, image, graphic image file, article, recording, *writing*, or *other matter of any kind*" (emphasis added)—could have been less restrictive of speech on the Web and more narrowly tailored to Congress' goal of shielding minors from pornographic teasers if the prohibited forms of content had included, for instance, only pictures, images, or graphic image files, which are typically employed by adult entertainment Web sites as "teasers." In addition, perhaps the goals of Congress could be served without the imposition of possibly excessive and serious criminal penalties, including imprisonment and hefty fines, for communicating speech that is protected as to adults or without exposing speakers to prosecution and placing the burden of establishing an affirmative defense on them instead of incorporating the substance of the affirmative defenses in the elements of the crime.

Finding that the plaintiffs had established a likelihood of irreparable harm and of prevailing on the merits, the court granted a preliminary injunction against enforcement of COPA, albeit reluctantly:

The protection of children from access to harmful to minors materials on the Web, the compelling interest sought to be furthered by Congress in COPA, particularly resonates with the Court. This

Court and many parents and grandparents would like to see the efforts of Congress to protect children from harmful materials on the Internet to ultimately succeed and the will of the majority of citizens in this country to be realized through the enforcement of an act of Congress. However, the Court is acutely cognizant of its charge under the law of this country not to protect the majoritarian will at the expense of stifling the rights embodied in the Constitution. . . .

. . .

Despite the Court's personal regret that this preliminary injunction will delay once again the careful protection of our children, I without hesitation acknowledge the duty imposed on the Court and the greater good such duty serves. Indeed, perhaps we do the minors of this country harm if First Amendment protections, which they will with age inherit fully, are chipped away in the name of their protection.

ACLU v. Reno, 31 F.Supp. 473 (E.D.Pa.1999).

The court of appeals affirmed, but on a single ground.

We base our particular determination of COPA's likely unconstitutionality, however, on COPA's reliance on "contemporary community standards" in the context of the electronic medium of the Web to identify material that is harmful to minors. The overbreadth of COPA's definition of "harmful to minors" applying a "contemporary community standards" clause—although virtually ignored by the parties and the amicus in their respective briefs but raised by us at oral argument—so concerns us that we are persuaded that this aspect of COPA, without reference to its other provisions, must lead inexorably to a holding of a likelihood of unconstitutionality of the entire COPA statute. Hence we base our opinion entirely on the basis of the likely unconstitutionality of this clause, even though the District Court relied on numerous other grounds.

Because there is no way to limit access to web sites based on the geographic locale of each Internet user, every web publisher would be forced to comply with the most restrictive locale's community standards. The court found this to be an impermissible burden on speech. Having determined that the law would likely be found unconstitutional on this ground, the court of appeals affirmed the grant of the injunction without considering the other grounds on which the lower court relied. American Civil Liberties Union v. Reno, 217 F.3d 162, 28 Med.L.Rptr. 1897 (2000). The case was appealed to the Supreme Court.

JOHN ASHCROFT v. AMERICAN CIVIL LIBERTIES UNION

Supreme Court of the United States, 2002.
535 U.S. 564, 122 S.Ct. 1700, 152 L.Ed.2d 771, 30 Med.L.Rptr. 1801.

Justice Thomas announced the judgment of the Court and delivered the opinion of the Court with respect to Parts I, II, and IV, an opinion with respect to Parts III–A, III–C, and III–D, in which THE CHIEF JUSTICE and Justice SCALIA join, and an opinion with respect to Part III–B, in which THE CHIEF JUSTICS, Justice O'CONNOR, and Justice SCALIA join.

This case presents the narrow question whether the Child Online Protection Act's (COPA or Act) use of "community standards" to identify "material that is harmful to minors" violates the First Amendment. We hold that this aspect of COPA does not render the statute facially unconstitutional.

I

. . .

After our decision in *Reno v. American Civil Liberties Union,* Congress explored other avenues for restricting minors' access to pornographic material on the Internet. In particular, Congress passed and the President signed into law the Child Online Protection Act, 112 Stat. 2681–736 (codified in 47 U.S.C. § 231 (1994 ed., Supp. V)). COPA prohibits any person from "knowingly and with knowledge of the character of the material, in interstate or foreign commerce by means of the World Wide Web, mak[ing] any communication for commercial purposes that is available to any minor and that includes any material that is harmful to minors." 47 U.S.C. § 231(a)(1).

Apparently responding to our objections to the breadth of the CDA's coverage, Congress limited the scope of COPA's coverage in at least three ways. First, while the CDA applied to communications over the Internet as a whole, including, for example, e-mail messages, COPA applies only to material displayed on the World Wide Web. Second, unlike the CDA, COPA covers only communications made "for commercial purposes." [ ] And third, while the CDA prohibited "indecent" and "patently offensive" communications, COPA restricts only the narrower category of "material that is harmful to minors." [ ]

Drawing on the three-part test for obscenity set forth in *Miller v. California,* 413 U.S. 15, 93 S.Ct. 2607, 37 L.Ed.2d 419 (1973), COPA defines "material that is harmful to minors" as

any communication, picture, image, graphic image file, article, recording, writing, or other matter of any kind that is obscene or that–

(A) the average person, applying contemporary community standards, would find, taking the material as a whole and with respect to minors, is designed to appeal to, or is designed to pander to, the prurient interest;

(B) depicts, describes, or represents, in a manner patently offensive with respect to minors, an actual or simulated sexual act or sexual contact, an actual or simulated normal or perverted sexual act, or a lewd exhibition of the genitals or post-pubescent female breast; and

(C) taken as a whole, lacks serious literary, artistic, political, or scientific value for minors. 47 U.S.C. § 231(e)(6).

Like the CDA, COPA also provides affirmative defenses to those subject to prosecution under the statute. An individual may qualify for a defense if he, "in good faith, has restricted access by minors to material that is harmful to minors—(A) by requiring the use of a credit card, debit account, adult access code, or adult personal identification number; (B) by accepting a digital certificate that verifies age; or (C) by any other reasonable measures that are feasible under available technology." § 231(c)(1). Persons violating COPA are subject to both civil and criminal sanctions. A civil penalty of up to $50,000 may be imposed for each violation of the statute. Criminal penalties consist of up to six months in prison and/or a maximum fine of $50,000. An additional fine of $50,000 may be imposed for any intentional violation of the statute. § 231(a).

. . .

III

The Court of Appeals, however, concluded that this Court's prior community standards jurisprudence "has no applicability to the Internet and the Web" because "Web publishers are currently without the ability to control the geographic scope of the recipients of their communications." [   ] We therefore must decide whether this technological limitation renders COPA's reliance on community standards constitutionally infirm.

A

In addressing this question, the parties first dispute the nature of the community standards that jurors will be instructed to apply when assessing, in prosecutions under COPA, whether works appeal to the prurient interest of minors and are patently offensive with respect to minors. Respondents contend that jurors will evaluate material using "local community standards," [   ], while petitioner maintains that jurors will not consider the community standards of any particular geographic area, but rather will be "instructed to consider the standards of the adult community as a whole, without geographic specification." [   ]

In the context of this case, which involves a facial challenge to a statute that has never been enforced, we do not think it prudent to engage in speculation as to whether certain hypothetical jury instructions would or would not be consistent with COPA, and deciding this case does not require us to do so. It is sufficient to note that community standards need not be defined by reference to a precise geographic area. [   ] Absent geographic specification, a juror applying community standards will inevitably draw upon personal "knowledge of the community or vicinage from which he comes." [   ] . . .

B

Because juries would apply different standards across the country, and Web publishers currently lack the ability to limit access to their sites on a geographic basis, the Court of Appeals feared that COPA's "community standards" component would effectively force all speakers on the Web to abide by the "most puritan" community's standards. [   ] And such a requirement, the Court of Appeals concluded, "imposes an overreaching burden and restriction on constitutionally protected speech." [   ]

In evaluating the constitutionality of the CDA, this Court expressed a similar concern over that statute's use of community standards to identify patently offensive material on the Internet. We noted that "the 'community standards' criterion as applied to the Internet means that any communication available to a nationwide audience will be judged by the standards of the community most likely to be offended by the message." [*Reno*, p. ___, *supra.*] The Court of Appeals below relied heavily on this observation, stating that it was "not persuaded that the Supreme Court's concern with respect to the 'community standards' criterion has been sufficiently remedied by Congress in COPA." [   ]

The CDA's use of community standards to identify patently offensive material, however, was particularly problematic in light of that statute's unprecedented breadth and vagueness. The statute covered communications depicting or describing "sexual or excretory activities or organs" that were "patently offensive as measured by contemporary community standards"—a standard somewhat similar to the second prong of *Miller*'s three-prong test. But the CDA did not include any limiting terms resembling *Miller*'s additional two prongs. . . . The tremendous breadth of the CDA magnified the impact caused by differences in community standards across the country, restricting Web publishers from openly displaying a significant amount of material that would have constituted protected speech in some communities across the country but run afoul of community standards in others.

COPA, by contrast, does not appear to suffer from the same flaw because it applies to significantly less material than did the CDA and defines the harmful-to-minors material restricted by the statute in a manner parallel to the *Miller* definition of obscenity. [   ] To fall within the scope of COPA, works must not only "depic[t], describ[e], or represen[t], in a manner patently offensive with respect to minors," particular sexual acts or parts of the anatomy,[8] they must also be designed to appeal to the prurient interest of minors and "taken as a whole, lac[k] serious literary, artistic, political, or scientific value for minors." 47 U.S.C. § 231(e)(6).

These additional two restrictions substantially limit the amount of material covered by the statute. Material appeals to the prurient interest, for instance, only if it is in some sense erotic. Cf. *Erznoznik v. Jacksonville,* 422 U.S. 205, 213, and n. 10, 95 S.Ct. 2268, 45 L.Ed.2d 125

---

8. While the CDA allowed juries to find material to be patently offensive so long as it depicted or described "sexual or excretory activities or organs," COPA specifically delineates the sexual activities and anatomical features, the depictions of which may be found to be patently offensive: "an actual or simulated sexual act or sexual contact, an actual or simulated normal or perverted sexual act, or a lewd exhibition of the genitals or post-pubescent female breast." 47 U.S.C. § 231(e)(6)(B).

(1975). Of even more significance, however, is COPA's exclusion of material with serious value for minors. See 47 U.S.C. § 231(e)(6)(C). In *Reno,* we emphasized that the serious value "requirement is particularly important because, unlike the 'patently offensive' and 'prurient interest' criteria, it is not judged by contemporary community standards." 521 U.S., at 873, 117 S.Ct. 2329 (citing *Pope v. Illinois,* 481 U.S. 497, 500, 107 S.Ct. 1918, 95 L.Ed.2d 439 (1987)). This is because "the value of [a] work [does not] vary from community to community based on the degree of local acceptance it has won." *Id.,* at 500, 107 S.Ct. 1918. Rather, the relevant question is "whether a reasonable person would find . . . value in the material, taken as a whole." *Id.,* at 501, 107 S.Ct. 1918. Thus, the serious value requirement "allows appellate courts to impose some limitations and regularity on the definition by setting, *as a matter of law,* a national floor for socially redeeming value." *Reno, supra,* at 873, 117 S.Ct. 2329 (emphasis added), a safeguard nowhere present in the CDA.

C

When the scope of an obscenity statute's coverage is sufficiently narrowed by a "serious value" prong and a "prurient interest" prong, we have held that requiring a speaker disseminating material to a national audience to observe varying community standards does not violate the First Amendment. In *Hamling v. United States,* 418 U.S. 87, 94 S.Ct. 2887, 41 L.Ed.2d 590 (1974), this Court considered the constitutionality of applying community standards to the determination of whether material is obscene under 18 U.S.C. § 1461, the federal statute prohibiting the mailing of obscene material. . . .

. . .

Fifteen years later, *Hamling*'s holding was reaffirmed in [*Sable,* P. ___, *supra*]. *Sable* addressed the constitutionality of 47 U.S.C. § 223(b) (1982 ed., Supp. V), a statutory provision prohibiting the use of telephones to make obscene or indecent communications for commercial purposes. The petitioner in that case, a "dial-a-porn" operator, challenged, in part, that portion of the statute banning obscene phone messages. Like respondents here, the "dial-a-porn" operator argued that reliance on community standards to identify obscene material impermissibly compelled "message senders . . . to tailor all their messages to the least tolerant community." 492 U.S., at 124, 109 S.Ct. 2829. Relying on *Hamling,* however, this Court once again rebuffed this attack on the use of community standards in a federal statute of national scope: "There is no constitutional barrier under *Miller* to prohibiting communications that are obscene in some communities under local standards even though they are not obscene in others. *If Sable's audience is comprised of different communities with different local standards, Sable ultimately bears the burden of complying with the prohibition on obscene messages.*" 492 U.S., at 125–126, 109 S.Ct. 2829 (emphasis added).

The Court of Appeals below concluded that *Hamling* and *Sable* "are easily distinguished from the present case" because in both of those cases "the defendants had the ability to control the distribution of controversial material with respect to the geographic communities into which they released it" whereas "Web publishers have no such comparable control." 217 F.3d, at 175–176. In neither *Hamling* nor *Sable,* however, was the speaker's ability to target the release of material into particular geographic areas integral to the legal analysis. . . .

While Justice KENNEDY and Justice STEVENS question the applicability of this Court's community standards jurisprudence to the Internet, we do not believe that the medium's "unique characteristics" justify adopting a different approach than that set forth in *Hamling* and *Sable.* [ ] (KENNEDY, J., concurring in judgment). If a publisher chooses to send its material into a particular community, this Court's jurisprudence teaches that it is the publisher's responsibility to abide by that community's standards. The publisher's burden does not change simply because it decides to distribute its material to every community in the Nation. [ ] Nor does it change because the publisher may wish to speak only to those in a "community where avant garde culture is the norm," [ ] (KENNEDY, J., concurring in judgment), but nonetheless utilizes a medium that transmits its speech from coast to coast. If a publisher wishes for its material to be judged only by the standards of particular communities, then it need only take the simple step of utilizing a medium that enables it to target the release of its material into those communities.

Respondents offer no other grounds upon which to distinguish this case from *Hamling* and *Sable.* While those cases involved obscenity rather than material that is harmful to minors, we have no reason to believe that the practical effect of varying community standards under COPA, given the statute's definition of "material that is harmful to minors," is significantly greater than the practical effect of varying community standards under federal obscenity statutes. It is noteworthy, for example, that respondents fail to point out even a single exhibit in the record as to which coverage under COPA would depend upon which community in the country evaluated the material. As a result, if we were to hold COPA unconstitutional *because of* its use of community standards, federal obscenity statutes would likely also be unconstitutional as applied to the Web, a result in substantial tension with our prior suggestion that the application of the CDA to obscene speech was constitutional. See [*Reno*].

D

Respondents argue that COPA is "unconstitutionally overbroad" because it will require Web publishers to shield some material behind age verification screens that could be displayed openly in many communities across the Nation if Web speakers were able to limit access to their sites on a geographic basis. Brief for Respondents 33–34. "[T]o prevail in a facial challenge," however, "it is not enough for a plaintiff to show 'some' overbreadth." *Reno, supra,* at 896, 117 S.Ct. 2329 (O'CONNOR, J., concurring in judgment in part and dissenting in part). Rather, "the overbreadth of a statute must not only be real, but substantial as well."

Broadrick v. Oklahoma, 413 U.S. 601, 615, 93 S.Ct. 2908, 37 L.Ed.2d 830 (1973). At this stage of the litigation, respondents have failed to satisfy this burden, at least solely as a result of COPA's reliance on community standards. Because Congress has narrowed the range of content restricted by COPA in a manner analogous to *Miller*'s definition of obscenity, we conclude, consistent with our holdings in *Hamling* and *Sable,* that any variance caused by the statute's reliance on community standards is not substantial enough to violate the First Amendment.

IV

The scope of our decision today is quite limited. We hold only that COPA's reliance on community standards to identify "material that is harmful to minors" does not *by itself* render the statute substantially overbroad for purposes of the First Amendment. We do not express any view as to whether COPA suffers from substantial overbreadth for other reasons, whether the statute is unconstitutionally vague, or whether the District Court correctly concluded that the statute likely will not survive strict scrutiny analysis once adjudication of the case is completed below. While respondents urge us to resolve these questions at this time, prudence dictates allowing the Court of Appeals to first examine these difficult issues.

Petitioner does not ask us to vacate the preliminary injunction entered by the District Court, and in any event, we could not do so without addressing matters yet to be considered by the Court of Appeals. As a result, the Government remains enjoined from enforcing COPA absent further action by the Court of Appeals or the District Court.

For the foregoing reasons, we vacate the judgment of the Court of Appeals and remand the case for further proceedings.

It is so ordered.

Justice O'CONNOR, concurring in part and concurring in the judgment.

I agree with the plurality that even if obscenity on the Internet is defined in terms of local community standards, respondents have not shown that the Child Online Protection Act (COPA) is overbroad solely on the basis of the variation in the standards of different communities. [   ] Like Justice BREYER, however, [   ] (opinion concurring in part and concurring in judgment), I write separately to express my views on the constitutionality and desirability of adopting a national standard for obscenity for regulation of the Internet.

The plurality's opinion argues that, even under local community standards, the variation between the most and least restrictive communities is not so great with respect to the narrow category of speech covered by COPA as to, alone, render the statute substantially overbroad. [   ] I agree, given respondents' failure to provide examples of materials that lack literary, artistic, political, and scientific value for minors, which would nonetheless result in variation among communities judging the other elements of the test. Respondents' examples of material for which community standards would vary include such things as the appropriateness of sex education and the desirability of adoption by same-sex couples. [ ] Material addressing the latter topic, however, seems highly unlikely to be seen to appeal to the prurient interest in any community, and educational material like the former must, on any objective inquiry, [ ], have scientific value for minors.

But respondents' failure to prove substantial overbreadth on a facial challenge in this case still leaves open the possibility that the use of local community standards will cause problems for regulation of obscenity on the Internet, for adults as well as children, in future cases. In an as-applied challenge, for instance, individual litigants may still dispute that the standards of a community more restrictive than theirs should apply to them. And in future facial challenges to regulation of obscenity on the Internet, litigants may make a more convincing case for substantial overbreadth. Where adult speech is concerned, for instance, there may in fact be a greater degree of disagreement about what is patently offensive or appeals to the prurient interest.

Nor do I think such future cases can be resolved by application of the approach we took in [*Hamling*], and [*Sable*]. I agree with Justice KENNEDY that, given Internet speakers' inability to control the geographic location of their audience, expecting them to bear the burden of controlling the recipients of their speech, as we did in *Hamling* and *Sable,* may be entirely too much to ask, and would potentially suppress an inordinate amount of expression. [ ] For these reasons, adoption of a national standard is necessary in my view for any reasonable regulation of Internet obscenity.

  . . .

While I would prefer that the Court resolve the issue before it by explicitly adopting a national standard for defining obscenity on the Internet, given respondents' failure to demonstrate substantial over-breadth due solely to the variation between local communities, I join Parts I, II, III–B, and IV of Justice THOMAS' opinion and the judgment.

[Justice BREYER, argued that both the legislative history and the principle that the "Court will first ascertain whether a construction of the statute is fairly possible by which [a constitutional] question may be avoided," justified construing "community standard" to mean a national, adult standard.]

Justice KENNEDY, with whom Justice SOUTER and Justice GINSBURG join, concurring in the judgment.

I

If a law restricts substantially more speech than is justified, it may be subject to a facial challenge. [ ] There is a very real likelihood that the Child Online Protection Act (COPA or Act) is overbroad and cannot survive such a challenge. Indeed, content-based regulations like this one are presumptively invalid abridgements of the freedom of speech. [ ]

Yet COPA is a major federal statute, enacted in the wake of our previous determination that its predecessor violated the First Amendment. See [*Reno*]. Congress and the President were aware of our decision, and we should assume that in seeking to comply with it they have given careful consideration to the constitutionality of the new enactment. For these reasons, even if this facial challenge appears to have considerable merit, the Judiciary must proceed with caution and identify overbreadth with care before invalidating the Act.

In this case, the District Court issued a preliminary injunction against enforcement of COPA, finding it too broad across several dimensions. The Court of Appeals affirmed, but on a different ground. COPA defines "material that is harmful to minors" by reference to "contemporary community standards," 47 U.S.C. § 231(e)(6) (1994 ed., Supp. V); and on the theory that these vary from place to place, the Court of Appeals held that the definition dooms the statute "without reference to its other provisions." [ ] The Court of Appeals found it unnecessary to construe the rest of the Act or address the District Court's reasoning.

This single, broad proposition, stated and applied at such a high level of generality, cannot suffice to sustain the Court of Appeals' ruling. To observe only that community standards vary across the country is to ignore the antecedent question: community standards as to what? Whether the national variation in community standards produces overbreadth requiring invalidation of COPA, [ ], depends on the breadth of COPA's coverage and on what community standards are being invoked. Only by identifying the universe of speech burdened by COPA is it possible to discern whether national variation in community standards renders the speech restriction overbroad. In short, the ground on which the Court of Appeals relied cannot be separated from those that it overlooked.

. . .

II

. . . The nub of the problem is, as the Court has said, that "the 'community standards' criterion as applied to the Internet means that any communication available to a nationwide audience will be judged by the standards of the community most likely to be offended by the message." *Reno,* 521 U.S., at 877–878, 117 S.Ct. 2329. If material might be considered harmful to minors in any community in the United States, then the material is covered by COPA, at least when viewed in that place. This observation was the linchpin of the Court of Appeals' analysis, and we must now consider whether it alone suffices to support the holding below.

The quoted sentence from *Reno* was not casual dicta; rather, it was one rationale for the holding of the case. In *Reno,* the Court found "[t]he breadth of [COPA's predecessor] . . . wholly unprecedented," [ ], in part because of variation in community standards. The Court also relied on that variation to assess the strength of the Government's interest, which it found "not equally strong throughout the coverage of this broad statute." . . . Variation in community standards rendered the statute broader than the scope of the Government's own expressed compelling interest.

It is true, as Justice THOMAS points out, *ante,* at 1710–1712, that requiring a speaker addressing a national audience to meet varying community standards does not always violate the First Amendment. See [*Hamling*] (obscene mailings); [*Sable*] (obscene phone messages). These cases, however, are of limited utility in analyzing the one before us, because each mode of expression has its own unique characteristics, and each "must be assessed for First Amendment purposes by standards suited to it." [ ] Indeed, when Congress purports to abridge the freedom of a new medium, we must be particularly attentive to its distinct attributes, for "differences in the characteristics of new media justify . . . differences in the First Amendment standards applied to them." [*Red Lion*, p. __, *supra*] The economics and the technology of each medium affect both the burden of a speech restriction and the Government's interest in maintaining it.

In this case the District Court found as a fact that "[o]nce a provider posts its content on the Internet and chooses to make it available to all, it generally cannot prevent that content from entering any geographic community." [ ] By contrast, in upholding a ban on obscene phone messages, we emphasized that the speaker could "hire operators to determine the source of the calls or engag[e] with the telephone company to arrange for the screening and blocking of out-of-area calls or fin[d] another means for providing messages compatible with community standards." [*Sable*]. And if we did not make the same point in *Hamling*, that is likely because it is so obvious that mailing lends itself to geographic restriction. (The Court has had no occasion to consider whether venue would be proper in "every hamlet into which [obscene mailings] may wander," [*Hamling*] (dissenting opinion), for the petitioners in *Hamling* did not challenge the statute as overbroad on its face.) A publisher who uses the mails can choose the location of his audience.

The economics and technology of Internet communication differ in important ways from those of telephones and mail. Paradoxically, as the District Court found, it is easy and cheap to reach a worldwide audience on the Internet, [ ], but expensive if not impossible to reach a geographic subset, *id.,* at 484. A Web publisher in a community where avant garde culture is the norm may have no desire to reach a national market; he may wish only to speak to his neighbors; nevertheless, if an eavesdropper in a more traditional, rural community chooses to listen in, there is nothing the publisher can do. As a practical matter, COPA makes the eavesdropper the arbiter of propriety on the Web. And it is no answer to say that the speaker should "take the simple step of utilizing a [different] medium." [   ] (principal opinion of THOMAS, J.). "Our prior decisions have voiced particular concern with laws that foreclose an entire medium of expression . . . . [T]he danger they pose to the freedom of speech is readily apparent—by eliminating a common means of speaking, such measures can suppress too much speech." [   ]

. . .

In any event, we need not decide whether the statute invokes local or national community standards to conclude that vacatur and remand are in order. If the statute does incorporate some concept of national community standards, the actual standard applied is bound to vary by community nevertheless, as the Attorney General concedes. [   ]

For this reason the Court of Appeals was correct to focus on COPA's incorporation of varying community standards; and it may have been correct as well to conclude that in practical effect COPA imposes the most puritanical community standard on the entire country. . . . In striking down COPA's predecessor, the *Reno* Court identified this precise problem, and if the *Hamling* and *Sable* Courts did not find the problem fatal, that is because those cases involved quite different media. The national variation in community standards constitutes a particular burden on Internet speech.

III

The question that remains is whether this observation *"by it-self"* suffices to enjoin the Act. See *ante,* at 1713. I agree with the Court that it does not. *Ibid*. We cannot know whether variation in community standards renders the Act substantially overbroad without first assessing the extent of the speech covered and the variations in community standards with respect to that speech.

First, the breadth of the Act itself will dictate the degree of overbreadth caused by varying community standards. . . .

Second, community standards may have different degrees of variation depending on the question posed to the community. Defining the scope of the Act, therefore, is not relevant merely to the absolute number of Web pages covered, as Justice STEVENS suggests, [   ] (dissenting opinion); it is also relevant to the proportion of overbreadth, "judged in relation to the statute's plainly legitimate sweep." [   ] Because this issue was "virtually ignored by the parties and the amicus" in the Court of Appeals, [   ], we have no information on the question. Instead, speculation meets speculation. On the one hand, the Court of Appeals found "no evidence to suggest that adults *everywhere* in America would share the same standards for determining what is harmful to minors." [   ] On the other hand, Justice THOMAS finds "no reason to believe that the practical effect of varying community standards under COPA . . . is significantly greater than the practical effect of varying standards under federal obscenity statutes." [   ] When a key issue has "no evidence" on one side and "no reason to believe" the other, it is a good indication that we should vacate for further consideration.

. . .

As I have explained, however, any problem caused by variation in community standards cannot be evaluated in a vacuum. In order to discern whether the variation creates substantial overbreadth, it is necessary to know what speech COPA regulates and what community standards it invokes.

It is crucial, for example, to know how limiting is the Act's limitation to "communication for commercial purposes." 47 U.S.C. § 231(e)(2)(A). . . .

So COPA is narrower across this dimension than its predecessor; but how much narrower is a matter of debate. In the District Court, the Attorney General contended that the Act applied only to professional panderers, but the court rejected that contention, finding "nothing in the text of the COPA . . . that limits its applicability to so-called commercial pornographers only." [ ] Indeed, the plain text of the Act does not limit its scope to pornography that is offered for sale; it seems to apply even to speech provided for free, so long as the speaker merely hopes to profit as an indirect result. The statute might be susceptible of some limiting construction here, but again the Court of Appeals did not address itself to this question. The answer affects the breadth of the Act and hence the significance of any variation in community standards.

Likewise, it is essential to answer the vexing question of what it means to evaluate Internet material "as a whole," 47 U.S.C. §§ 231(e)(6)(A), (C), when everything on the Web is connected to everything else. As a general matter, "[t]he artistic merit of a work does not depend on the presence of a single explicit scene . . . .[T]he First Amendment requires that redeeming value be judged by considering the work as a whole. Where the scene is part of the narrative, the work itself does not for this reason become obscene, even though the scene in isolation might be offensive." *Ashcroft v. Free Speech Coalition,* 535 U.S. 234, 122 S.Ct. 1389, 1393, 152 L.Ed.2d 403 (2002). COPA appears to respect this principle by requiring that the material be judged "as a whole," both as to its prurient appeal, § 231(e)(6)(A), and as to its social value, § 231(e)(6)(C). It is unclear, however, what constitutes the denominator—that is, the material to be taken as a whole—in the context of the World Wide Web. See 31 F.Supp.2d, at 483 ("Although information on the Web is contained in individual computers, the fact that each of these computers is connected to the Internet through World Wide Web protocols allows all of the information to become part of a single body of knowledge"); [ ] ("From a user's perspective, [the World Wide Web] may appear to be a single, integrated system"). Several of the respondents operate extensive Web sites, some of which include only a small amount of material that might run afoul of the Act. The Attorney General contended that these respondents had nothing to fear from COPA, but the District Court disagreed, noting that the Act prohibits communication that "includes" any material harmful to minors. § 231(a)(1). In the District Court's view, "it logically follows that [COPA] would apply to any Web site that contains only some harmful to minors material." [ ] The denominator question is of crucial significance to the coverage of the Act.

Another issue is worthy of mention, because it too may inform whether the variation in community standards renders the Act substantially overbroad. . . . COPA does not address venue in explicit terms, so prosecution may be proper "in any district in which [an] offense was begun, continued, or completed." 18 U.S.C. § 3237(a). The Act's prohibition includes an interstate commerce element, 47 U.S.C. § 231(a)(1), and "[a]ny offense involving . . . interstate . . . commerce . . . may be inquired of and prosecuted in any district from, through, or into which such commerce . . . moves." 18 U.S.C. § 3237(a). In the context of COPA, it seems likely that venue would be proper where the material originates or where it is viewed. Whether it may be said that a Web site moves "through" other venues in between is less certain. And since, as discussed above, juries will inevitably apply their own community standards, the choice of venue may be determinative of the choice of standard. The more venues the Government has to choose from, the more speech will be chilled by variation across communities.

IV

In summary, the breadth of the Act depends on the issues discussed above, and the significance of varying community standards depends, in turn, on the breadth of the Act. The Court of Appeals was correct to focus on the national variation in community standards, which can constitute a substantial burden on Internet communication; and its ultimate conclusion may prove correct. There may be grave doubts that COPA is consistent with the First Amendment; but we should not make that determination with so many questions unanswered. The Court of Appeals should undertake a comprehensive analysis in the first instance.

Justice STEVENS, dissenting.

Appeals to prurient interests are commonplace on the Internet, as in older media. Many of those appeals lack serious value for minors as well as adults. Some are offensive to certain viewers but welcomed by others. For decades, our cases have recognized that the standards for judging their acceptability vary from viewer to viewer and from community to community. Those cases developed the requirement that communications should be protected if they do not violate contemporary community standards. In its original form, the community standard provided a shield for communications that are offensive only to the least tolerant members of society. Thus, the Court "has emphasized on more than one occasion that a principal concern in requiring that a judgment be made on the basis of 'contemporary community standards' is to assure that the material is judged neither on the basis of each juror's personal opinion, nor by its effect on a particularly sensitive or insensitive person or group." [Hamling] In the context of the Internet, however, community standards become a sword, rather than a shield. If a prurient appeal is offensive in a puritan village, it may be a crime to post it on the World Wide Web.

The Child Online Protection Act (COPA) restricts access by adults as well as children to materials that are "harmful to minors." . . .

. . .

COPA not only restricts speech that is made available to the general public, it also covers a medium in which speech cannot be segregated to avoid communities where it is likely to be considered harmful to minors. The Internet presents a unique forum for communication because information, once posted, is accessible everywhere on the network at once. The speaker cannot control access based on the location of the listener, nor can it choose the pathways through which its speech is transmitted. By approving the use of community standards in this context, Justice THOMAS endorses a construction of COPA that has "the intolerable consequence of denying some sections of the country access to material, there deemed acceptable, which in others might be considered offensive to prevailing community standards of decency." [   ]

If the material were forwarded through the mails, as in *Hamling,* or over the telephone, as in *Sable,* the sender could avoid destinations with the most restrictive standards. . . . Given the undisputed fact that a provider who posts material on the Internet cannot prevent it from entering any geographic community, see *ante,* at 1708, n. 6 (opinion of THOMAS, J.), a law that criminalizes a particular communication in just a handful of destinations effectively prohibits transmission of that message to all of the 176.5 million Americans that have access to the Internet, [   ] (opinion of THOMAS, J.). In light of this fundamental difference in technologies, the rules applicable to the mass mailing of an obscene montage or to obscene dial-a-porn should not be used to judge the legality of messages on the World Wide Web.

. . .

Justice THOMAS points to several other provisions in COPA to argue that any overbreadth will be rendered insubstantial by the rest of the statute. [   ] These provisions afford little reassurance, however, as they only marginally limit the sweep of the statute. It is true that, in addition to COPA's "appeals to the prurient interest of minors" prong, the material must be "patently offensive with respect to minors" and it must lack "serious literary, artistic, political, or scientific value for minors." 47 U.S.C. § 231(e)(6). Nonetheless, the "patently offensive" prong is judged according to contemporary community standards as well, [   ] (opinion of THOMAS, J.). Whatever disparity exists between various communities' assessment of the content that appeals to the prurient interest of minors will surely be matched by their differing opinions as to whether descriptions of sexual acts or depictions of nudity are patently offensive with respect to minors. . . .

Petitioner's argument that the "serious value" prong minimizes the statute's overbreadth is also unpersuasive. Although we have recognized that the serious value determination in obscenity cases should be based on an objective, reasonable person standard, [　], this criterion is inadequate to cure COPA's overbreadth because COPA adds an important qualifying phrase to the standard [*Miller*] formulation of the serious value prong. The question for the jury is not whether a reasonable person would conclude that the materials have serious value; instead, the jury must determine whether the materials have serious value *for minors*. Congress reasonably concluded that a substantial number of works, which have serious value for adults, do not have serious value for minors. . . . Thus, even though the serious value prong limits the total amount of speech covered by the statute, it remains true that there is a significant amount of protected speech within the category of materials that have no serious value for minors. That speech is effectively prohibited whenever the least tolerant communities find it harmful to minors. While the objective nature of the inquiry may eliminate any worry that the serious value determination will be made by the least tolerant community, it does not change the fact that, within the subset of images deemed to have no serious value for minors, the decision whether minors and adults throughout the country will have access to that speech will still be made by the most restrictive community.

Justice KENNEDY makes a similar misstep, [　] (opinion concurring in judgment), when he ties the overbreadth inquiry to questions about the scope of the other provisions of the statute. According to his view, we cannot determine whether the statute is substantially overbroad based on its use of community standards without first determining how much of the speech on the Internet is saved by the other restrictions in the statute. But this represents a fundamental misconception of our overbreadth doctrine. As Justice White explained in [　], "the overbreadth of a statute must not only be real, but substantial as well, *judged in relation to the statute's plainly legitimate sweep.*" (Emphasis added.) Regardless of how the Court of Appeals interprets the "commercial purposes" or "as a whole" provisions on remand, the question we must answer is whether the statute restricts a substantial amount of protected speech relative to its legitimate sweep by virtue of the fact that it uses community standards. These other provisions may reduce the absolute number of Web pages covered by the statute, but even the narrowest version of the statute abridges a substantial amount of protected speech that many communities would not find harmful to minors. Because Web speakers cannot limit access to those specific communities, the statute is substantially overbroad regardless of how its other provisions are construed.

. . .

In the context of most other media, using community standards to differentiate between permissible and impermissible speech has two virtues. As mentioned above, community standards originally served as a shield to protect speakers from the least tolerant members of society. By aggregating values at the community level, the *Miller* test eliminated the outliers at both ends of the spectrum and provided some predictability as to what constitutes obscene speech. But community standards also serve as a shield to protect audience members, by allowing people to self-sort based on their preferences. Those who abhor and those who tolerate sexually explicit speech can seek out like-minded people and settle in communities that share their views on what is acceptable for themselves and their children. This sorting mechanism, however, does not exist in cyberspace; the audience cannot self-segregate. As a result, in the context of the Internet this shield also becomes a sword, because the community that wishes to live without certain material not only rids itself, but the entire Internet of the offending speech.

In sum, I would affirm the judgment of the Court of Appeals and therefore respectfully dissent.

Notes and Questions

1. On remand the court of appeals again affirmed the district court decision, this time relying on the grounds used by the district court. Specifically, the court of appeals found that the statute failed strict scrutiny because it was neither narrowly tailored or the least restrictive means of achieving the compelling government interest in protecting children. The court also found the statute substantially overbroad. 2003 WL 755083 (3rd Cir.)

2. One major problem with regulating on-line obscenity and indecency is the question of community standards. If someone in one state obtains material from a computer located in another, which state's standards apply? What if the computer from which the material is being download-ed is in a different country, as opposed to merely a different state?

In United States v. Thomas, a couple who operated an adult bulletin board in California was prosecuted in Tennessee for violating 18 U.S.C.A. §§ 1462 and 1465, federal obscenity laws, based in part on material downloaded by a United States Postal Inspector in Tennessee. They were convicted based on the obscenity standards of Tennessee. The convictions were upheld on appeal. 74 F.3d 701, 24 Med.L.Rptr. 1321 (6th Cir.1996), certiorari den., 519 U.S. 820 (1996).

The court relied heavily on the fact that access to the bulletin board required applying for membership and paying a fee. Because the inspec-tor's application listed a home address and phone number located in Tennessee, the court reasoned that the defendants knew that their materials would be downloaded in Tennessee. It was therefore not unreasonable to subject them to the standards of Tennessee.

What if access to a bulletin board does not require membership, but can be accessed by anyone? Is it still reasonable to subject the system operator (sysop) to the standards of any jurisdiction where the material is downloaded? Is there an affirmative obligation to limit access?

The case also illustrates several other broader issues related to computer transmissions, including jurisdiction, venue and the applica-tion of statutes written prior to the advent of this form of communication. Mr. and Mrs. Thomas were extradited to Tennessee and tried there. Venue was based on the same reasoning that permitted the application of Tennessee obscenity standards.

The court also rejected a defense argument that § 1465 did not apply to the downloading of obscene pictures by computer because it did not specifically refer to computer transmissions. The court construed the statute to include computer transmissions because it was Congress' clear intent "to legislate comprehensively the interstate distribution of obscene materials." Subsequently, as part of the CDA, Congress amended the federal obscenity laws to include computer transmissions.

3. A journalist who sent and received child pornography over the Internet was convicted of violating the Protection of Children Against Sexual Exploitation Act despite his claim that it was in connection with a free-lance article on people trafficking in child pornography. The court rejected his assertion that the First Amendment protected his activities. His conviction was upheld on appeal. United States v. Matthews, 209 F.3d 338, 28 Med.L.Rptr. 1673 (2000).

4. Challenges to The Child Pornography Prevention Act, which includes computer-generated or "virtual" child pornography within its list of prohibited images met with mixed success in the courts. Two courts upheld the constitutionality of the Act, United States v. Acheson, 195 F.3d 645 (11th Cir.1999) and United States v. Hilton, 167 F.3d 61 (1st Cir.), certiorari denied, 528 U.S. 844 (1999). However, in a third case, the court of appeals found the provisions covering virtual child pornography unconstitutionally vague and overbroad. Free Speech Coalition v. Reno, 198 F.3d 1083 (9th Cir.1999).

The Supreme Court granted *certiorari* and struck down those provisions that covered material that was not produced with images of actual children as overbroad. Thus, material using adults who appeared to be children, as well as computer-generated material cannot be restricted unless it is obscene under *Miller*, p. ___, *supra*. However, actual images of children or morphed images that result from combining a child's with another are still subject to the Act. Ashcroft v. Free Speech Coalition, 535 U.S. 234, 122 S.Ct. 1389, 152 L.Ed.2d 403, 30 Med.L.Rptr. 1673 (2002).

5. Some public libraries, concerned that children will use library computers to access indecent or obscene materials on the Internet, have installed blocking software. Does this present a First Amendment problem? If the library only installs it on computers used by minors, as opposed to all the library computers, or gives adults a password allowing them to override the blocking software, does it change your answer? Is it relevant that some blocking software will screen for other categories such as violence, profanity and hate speech? What if the software is not 100 percent accurate? For example, these programs have blocked access to sites of the Heritage Foundation, the M.I.T. free-speech society, the U.S. Central Intelligence Agency, a banned-books archive and the National Organization for Women and to Reuters articles about AIDS. One

such program even blocked the White House Web Site—it blocked anything containing the word *couples*. "Censor's Sensibility," Time, Aug. 11, 1997.

A federal district court struck down a county library's restrictions on Internet access. At issue was the installation of blocking software on all computers with Internet access. "If a patron [was] blocked from accessing a site that she fe[lt] should not be blocked under the Policy, she [could] request that defendant unblock the site by filing an official, written request with the librarian stating her name, the site she want[ed] unblocked, and the reason why she want[ed]access the site." The librarian would then decide whether or not to unblock the site.

The court found that this was content regulation of a limited public forum and applied strict scrutiny. Because the plaintiffs hadn't challenged the asserted government interests, the court assumed that "minimizing access to illegal pornography and avoidance of creation of a sexually hostile environment" were compelling government interests. However, there having been only one complaint regarding use of the library computers to access pornography, the court held that the restriction was not necessary to prevent an actual as opposed to conjectured harm.

The court further found that there were numerous less restrictive ways to further the government interests including privacy screens on computer monitors, casual monitoring by library staff, installation of the software on only some computers and restricting minors to those computers, and permitting adults to turn off the filtering software. Mainstream Loudoun v. Board of Trustees of The Loudoun County Library, 24 F.Supp.2d 552 (E.D.Va.1998). The trustees chose not to appeal.

However, the mother of a 12–year old boy who accessed pornography using a library computer has sued the City of Livermore, Cal., seeking an injunction requiring installation of filtering software on library computers. The request was denied. An appeal was filed. See http://www.aclu.org/news/n011499.html.

6. In early 2001, Congress passed the Children's Internet Protection Act (CIPA), disqualifying any school or library with Internet Access from receiving discounted Internet access, Internet services, and internal connection services under 47 U.S.C. § 254(h) unless it can certify that appropriate Internet safety measures have been installed. Pub. L. No. 106–554 (*l*). Pursuant to CIPA, the FCC adopted regulations governing eligibility for these discounts:

> In order to receive discounts for Internet access and internal connections services under the universal service support mechanism, school and library authorities must certify that they are enforcing a policy of Internet safety that includes measures to block or filter Internet access for both minors and adults to certain visual depictions. These include visual depictions that are (1) obscene, or (2) child pornography, or, with respect to use of computers with Internet access by minors, (3) harmful to minors. An authorized person

may disable the blocking or filtering measure during any use by an adult to enable access for bona fide research or other lawful purpose.

A school administrative authority must certify that its policy of Internet safety includes monitoring the online activities of minors.

In order to receive discounts, school and library authorities must also certify that they have adopted and implemented an Internet safety policy addressing (i) access by minors to inappropriate matter on the Internet and World Wide Web; (ii) the safety and security of minors when using electronic mail, chat rooms, and other forms of direct electronic communications; (iii) unauthorized access, including so-called "hacking," and other unlawful activities by minors online; (iv) unauthorized disclosure, use, and dissemination of personal information regarding minors; and (v) measures designed to restrict minors' access to materials harmful to minors.

Federal–State Joint Board on Universal Service, 16 F.C.C.Rcd. 8182 (2001).

CIPA was challenged in a federal district court, under the name, Multnomah Library v. U.S.

AMERICAN LIBRARY ASSOCIATION, INC. v. UNITED STATES

United States District Court E.D. Pennsylvania, 2002.
201 F.Supp.2d 401.

Before: BECKER, Chief Circuit Judge, FULLAM and BARTLE, District Judges.

OPINION OF THE COURT

EDWARD R. BECKER, Chief Circuit Judge.

I. Preliminary Statement

This case challenges an act of Congress that makes the use of filtering software by public libraries a condition of the receipt of federal funding . . . Approximately 10% of the Americans who use the Internet access it at public libraries. And approximately 95% of all public libraries in the United States provide public access to the Internet.

    . . .

II. Findings of Fact

    . . .

C. The Internet

    . . .

b. Methods for Regulating Internet Use

The methods that public libraries use to regulate Internet use vary greatly. They can be organized into four categories: (1) channeling patrons' Internet use; (2) separating patrons so that they will not see what other patrons are viewing; (3) placing Internet terminals in public view and having librarians observe patrons to make sure that they are complying with the library's Internet use policy; and (4) using Internet filtering software.

. . .

E.   Internet Filtering Technology

1.   What Is Filtering Software, Who Makes It, and What Does It Do?

Commercially available products that can be configured to block or filter access to certain material on the Internet are among the "technology protection measures" that may be used to attempt to comply with CIPA. There are numerous filtering software products available commercially. Three network-based filtering products—SurfControl's Cyber Patrol, N2H2's Bess/i2100, and Secure Computing's SmartFilter—currently have the lion's share of the public library market. The parties in this case deposed representatives from these three companies. Websense, another network-based blocking product, is also currently used in the public library market, and was discussed at trial.

Filtering software may be installed either on an individual computer or on a computer network. Network-based filtering software products are designed for use on a network of computers and funnel requests for Internet content through a centralized network device. Of the various commercially available blocking products, network-based products are the ones generally marketed to institutions, such as public libraries, that provide Internet access through multiple terminals.

Filtering programs function in a fairly simple way. When an Internet user requests access to a certain Web site or page, either by entering a domain name or IP address into a Web browser, or by clicking on a link, the filtering software checks that domain name or IP address against a previously compiled "control list" that may contain up to hundreds of thousands of URLs. The three companies deposed in this case have control lists containing between 200,000 and 600,000 URLs. These lists determine which URLs will be blocked.

. . .

[N]o category definition used by filtering software companies is identical to CIPA's definitions of visual depictions that are obscene, child pornography, or harmful to minors. And category definitions and categorization decisions are made without reference to local community standards. Moreover, there is no judicial involvement in the creation of filtering software companies' category definitions and no judicial determination is made before these companies categorize a Web page or site.

. . .

3.   The Inherent Tradeoff Between Overblocking and Underblocking

There is an inherent tradeoff between any filter's rate of overblocking (which information scientists also call "precision") and its rate of underblocking (which is also referred to as "recall"). The rate of over-blocking or precision is measured by the proportion of the things a classification system assigns to a certain category that are appropriately classified. The plaintiffs' expert, Dr. Nunberg, provided the hypothetical example of a classification system that is asked to pick out pictures of dogs from a database consisting of 1000 pictures of animals, of which 80 were actually dogs. If it returned 100 hits, of which 80 were in fact pictures of dogs, and the remaining 20 were pictures of cats, horses, and deer, we would say that the system identified dog pictures with a precision of 80%. This would be analogous to a filter that overblocked at a rate of 20%.

. . .

4. Attempts to Quantify Filtering Programs' Rates of Over-and Underblocking

The government presented three studies, two from expert witnesses, and one from a librarian fact witness who conducted a study using Internet use logs from his own library, that attempt to quantify the over-and underblocking rates of five different filtering programs. The plaintiffs presented one expert witness who attempted to quantify the rates of over-and underblocking for various programs. Each of these attempts to quantify rates of over-and underblocking suffers from various methodological flaws.

. . .

7. Conclusion: The Effectiveness of Filtering Programs

Public libraries have adopted a variety of means of dealing with problems created by the provision of Internet access. The large amount of sexually explicit speech that is freely available on the Internet has, to varying degrees, led to patron complaints about such matters as unsought exposure to offensive material, incidents of staff and patron harassment by individuals viewing sexually explicit content on the Internet, and the use of library computers to access illegal material, such as child pornography. In some libraries, youthful library patrons have persistently attempted to use the Internet to access hardcore pornography.

Those public libraries that have responded to these problems by using software filters have found such filters to provide a relatively effective means of preventing patrons from accessing sexually explicit material on the Internet. Nonetheless, out of the entire universe of speech on the Internet falling within the filtering products' category definitions, the filters will incorrectly fail to block a substantial amount of speech. Thus, software filters have not completely eliminated the problems that public libraries have sought to address by using the filters, as evidenced by frequent instances of underblocking. Nor is there any quantitative evidence of the relative effectiveness of filters and the alternatives to filters that are also intended to prevent patrons from accessing illegal content on the Internet.

Even more importantly (for this case), although software filters provide a relatively cheap and effective, albeit imperfect, means for public libraries to prevent patrons from accessing speech that falls within the filters' category definitions, we find that commercially available filtering programs erroneously block a huge amount of speech that is protected by the First Amendment. Any currently available filtering product that is reasonably effective in preventing users from accessing content within the filter's category definitions will necessarily block countless thousands of Web pages, the content of which does not match the filtering company's category definitions, much less the legal definitions of obscenity, child pornography, or harmful to minors. Even Finnell, an expert witness for the defendants, found that between 6% and 15% of the blocked Web sites in the public libraries that he analyzed did not contain content that meets even the filtering products' own definitions of sexually explicit content, let alone CIPA's definitions.

. . .

No presently conceivable technology can make the judgments necessary to determine whether a visual depiction fits the legal definitions of obscenity, child pornography, or harmful to minors. Given the state of the art in filtering and image recognition technology, and the rapidly changing and expanding nature of the Web, we find that filtering products' shortcomings will not be solved through a technical solution in the foreseeable future. In sum, filtering products are currently unable to block only visual depictions that are obscene, child pornography, or harmful to minors (or, only content matching a filtering product's category definitions) while simultaneously allowing access to all protected speech (or, all content not matching the blocking product's category definitions). Any software filter that is reasonably effective in blocking access to Web pages that fall within its category definitions will necessarily erroneously block a substantial number of Web pages that do not fall within its category definitions.

III. Analytic Framework for the Opinion: The Centrality of *Dole* and the Role of the Facial Challenge

Both the plaintiffs and the government agree that, because this case involves a challenge to the constitutionality of the conditions that Congress has set on state actors' receipt of federal funds, the Supreme Court's decision in *South Dakota v. Dole,* 483 U.S. 203, 107 S.Ct. 2793, 97 L.Ed.2d 171 (1987), supplies the proper threshold analytic framework. The constitutional source of Congress's spending power is Article I, § 8, cl. 1, which provides that "Congress shall have Power . . . to pay the Debts and provide for the common Defence and general Welfare of the United States." In *Dole,* the Court upheld the constitutionality of a federal statute requiring the withholding of federal highway funds from any state with a drinking age below 21. [   ] In sustaining the provision's constitutionality, *Dole* articulated four general constitutional limitations on Congress's exercise of the spending power.

First, "the exercise of the spending power must be in pursuit of 'the general welfare.' " *Id.* at 207, 107 S.Ct. 2793. Second, any conditions that Congress sets on states' receipt of federal funds must be sufficiently clear to enable recipients "to exercise their choice knowingly, cognizant of the consequences of their participation." *Id.* (internal quotation marks and citation omitted). Third, the conditions on the receipt of federal funds must bear some relation to the purpose of the funding program. *Id.* And finally, "other constitutional provisions may provide an independent bar to the conditional grant of federal funds." *Id.* at 208, 107 S.Ct. 2793. In particular, the spending power "may not be used to induce the States to engage in activities that would themselves be unconstitutional. Thus, for example, a grant of federal funds conditioned on invidiously discriminatory state action or the infliction of cruel and unusual punishment would be an illegitimate exercise of the Congress'broad spending power." *Id.* at 210, 107 S.Ct. 2793.

Plaintiffs do not contend that CIPA runs afoul of the first three limitations. However, they do allege that CIPA is unconstitutional under the fourth prong of *Dole* because it will induce public libraries to violate the First Amendment. Plaintiffs therefore submit that the First Amendment "provide[s] an independent bar to the conditional grant of federal funds" created by CIPA. *Id.* at 208, 107 S.Ct. 2793. More specifically, they argue that by conditioning public libraries' receipt of federal funds on the use of software filters, CIPA will induce public libraries to violate the First Amendment rights of Internet content-providers to disseminate constitutionally protected speech to library patrons via the Internet, and the correlative First Amendment rights of public library patrons to receive constitutionally protected speech on the Internet.

The government concedes that under the *Dole* framework, CIPA is facially invalid if its conditions will induce public libraries to violate the First Amendment. The government and the plaintiffs disagree, however, on the meaning of *Dole's* "inducement" requirement in the context of a First Amendment facial challenge to the conditions that Congress places on state actors' receipt of federal funds. The government contends that because plaintiffs are bringing a facial challenge, they must show that under no circumstances is it possible for a public library to comply with CIPA's conditions without violating the First Amendment. The plaintiffs respond that even if it is possible for some public libraries to comply with CIPA without violating the First Amendment, CIPA is facially invalid if it "will result in the impermissible suppression of a substantial amount of protected speech."

Because it was clear in *Dole* that the states could comply with the challenged conditions that Congress attached to the receipt of federal funds without violating the Constitution, the *Dole* Court did not have occasion to explain fully what it means for Congress to use the spending power to "induce [recipients] to engage in activities that would them-

selves be unconstitutional." *Dole,* 483 U.S. at 210, 107 S.Ct. 2793; *see id.*
at 211, 107 S.Ct. 2793 ("Were South Dakota to succumb to the blandish-
ments offered by Congress and raise its drinking age to 21, the State's
action in so doing would not violate the constitutional rights of anyone."). Although the proposition that Congress may not pay state actors
to violate citizens' First Amendment rights is unexceptionable when
stated in the abstract, it is unclear what exactly a litigant must establish
to facially invalidate an exercise of Congress's spending power on this
ground.

In general, it is well-established that a court may sustain a facial
challenge to a statute only if the plaintiff demonstrates that the statute
admits of no constitutional application. [   ]

First Amendment overbreadth doctrine creates a limited exception
to this rule by permitting facial invalidation of a statute that burdens a
substantial amount of protected speech, even if the statute may be
constitutionally applied in particular circumstances. "The Constitution
gives significant protection from overbroad laws that chill speech within
the First Amendment's vast and privileged sphere. Under this principle,
[a law] is unconstitutional on its face if it prohibits a substantial amount
of protected expression." [*Ashcroft,* p. ___, *supra*] ; [   ]. This more
liberal test of a statute's facial validity under the First Amendment
stems from the recognition that where a statute's reach contemplates a
number of both constitutional and unconstitutional applications, the
law's sanctions may deter individuals from challenging the law's validity
by engaging in constitutionally protected speech that may nonetheless be
proscribed by the law. . . .

. . .

The Court's unconstitutional conditions cases, . . . , are not strictly
controlling, since they do not require a showing that recipients who
comply with the conditions attached to federal funding will, as state
actors, violate others' constitutional rights, as is the case under the
fourth prong of *Dole.* However, they are highly instructive.

The Supreme Court's pronouncements in the unconstitutional conditions cases on what is necessary for a plaintiff to mount a successful
First Amendment facial challenge to an exercise of Congress's spending
power have not produced a seamless web. . . .

Against this background, it is unclear to us whether, to succeed in
facially invalidating CIPA on the grounds that it will "induce the States
to engage in activities that would themselves be unconstitutional," *Dole,*
483 U.S. at 210, 107 S.Ct. 2793, plaintiffs must show that it is impossible
for public libraries to comply with CIPA's conditions without violating
the First Amendment, or rather simply that CIPA will effectively restrict
library patrons' access to substantial amounts of constitutionally protected speech, therefore causing many libraries to violate the First Amendment. However, we need not resolve this issue. Rather, we may assume
without deciding, for purposes of this case, that a facial challenge to
CIPA requires plaintiffs to show that any public library that complies

with CIPA's conditions will necessarily violate the First Amendment and, as explained in detail below, we believe that CIPA's constitutionality fails even under this more restrictive test of facial validity urged on us by the government. Because of the inherent limitations in filtering technology, public libraries can never comply with CIPA without blocking access to a substantial amount of speech that is both constitutionally protected and fails to meet even the filtering companies' own blocking criteria. We turn first to the governing legal principles to be applied to the facts in order to determine whether the First Amendment permits a library to use the filtering technology mandated by CIPA.

IV. Level of Scrutiny Applicable to Content-based Restrictions on Internet Access in Public Libraries

In analyzing the constitutionality of a public library's use of Internet filtering software, we must first identify the appropriate level of scrutiny to apply to this restriction on patrons' access to speech. While plaintiffs argue that a public library's use of such filters is subject to strict scrutiny, the government maintains that the applicable standard is rational basis review. . . .

Software filters, by definition, block access to speech on the basis of its content, and content-based restrictions on speech are generally subject to strict scrutiny. *See Playboy,* 529 U.S. at 813, 120 S.Ct. 1878 ("[A] content-based speech restriction . . . can stand only if it satisfies strict scrutiny."). Strict scrutiny does not necessarily apply to content-based restrictions on speech, however, where the restrictions apply only to speech on government property, such as public libraries. "[I]t is . . . well settled that the government need not permit all forms of speech on property that it owns and controls." [   ] We perforce turn to a discussion of public forum doctrine.

A. Overview of Public Forum Doctrine

The government's power to restrict speech on its own property is not unlimited. Rather, under public forum doctrine, the extent to which the First Amendment permits the government to restrict speech on its own property depends on the character of the forum that the government has created. [   ]

The Supreme Court has identified three types of fora for purposes of identifying the level of First Amendment scrutiny applicable to content-based restrictions on speech on government property: traditional public fora, designated public fora, and nonpublic fora. Traditional public fora include sidewalks, squares, and public parks:

> [S]treets and parks . . . have immemorially been held in trust for the use of the public and, time out of mind, have been used for purposes of assembly, communicating thoughts between citizens, and discussing public questions. Such use of the streets and public places has, from ancient times, been a part of the privileges, immunities, rights, and liberties of citizens.

[ ]

A second category of fora, known as designated (or limited) public fora, "consists of public property which the State has opened for use by the public as a place for expressive activity." [ ] Whereas any content-based restriction on the use of traditional public fora is subject to strict scrutiny, the state is generally permitted, as long as it does not discriminate on the basis of viewpoint, to limit a designated public forum to certain speakers or the discussion of certain subjects. [ ] Once it has defined the limits of a designated public forum, however, "[r]egulation of such property is subject to the same limitations as that governing a traditional public forum." [ ] Examples of designated fora include university meeting facilities,[ ], school board meetings, [ ], and municipal theaters, [ ].

The third category, nonpublic fora, consists of all remaining public property. "Limitations on expressive activity conducted on this last category of property must survive only a much more limited review. The challenged regulation need only be reasonable, as long as the regulation is not an effort to suppress the speaker's activity due to disagreement with the speaker's view." [   ]

B. Contours of the Relevant Forum: the Library's Collection as a Whole or the Provision of Internet Access?

To apply public forum doctrine to this case, we must first determine whether the appropriate forum for analysis is the library's collection as a whole, which includes both print and electronic resources, or the library's provision of Internet access. . . .

. . .

In this case, the patron plaintiffs are not asserting a First Amendment right to compel public libraries to acquire certain books or magazines for their print collections. Nor are the Web site plaintiffs claiming a First Amendment right to compel public libraries to carry print materials that they publish. Rather, the right at issue in this case is the specific right of library patrons to access information on the Internet, and the specific right of Web publishers to provide library patrons with information via the Internet. Thus, the relevant forum for analysis is not the library's entire collection, which includes both print and electronic media, such as the Internet, but rather the specific forum created when the library provides its patrons with Internet access.

Although a public library's provision of Internet access does not resemble the conventional notion of a forum as a well-defined physical space, the same First Amendment standards apply. [   ]

C. Content-based Restrictions in Designated Public Fora

Unlike nonpublic fora such as airport terminals, [   ], military bases, [   ], jail grounds, [   ], the federal workplace, [   ], and public transit vehicles, [ ], the purpose of a public library in general, and the provision of Internet access within a public library in particular, is "for use by the public . . . for expressive activity," [   ], namely, the dissemination and receipt by the public of a wide range of information. We are satisfied that when the government provides Internet access in a public library, it has created a designated public forum. [   ]

Relying on those cases that have recognized that government has leeway, under the First Amendment, to limit use of a designated public forum to narrowly specified purposes, and that content-based restrictions on speech that are consistent with those purposes are subject only to rational basis review, the government argues for application of rational basis review to public libraries' decisions about which content to make available to their patrons via the Internet. [   ]

. . .

Plaintiffs respond that the government's ability to restrict the content of speech in a designated public forum by restricting the purpose of the designated public forum that it creates is not unlimited. . . .

Although we agree with plaintiffs that the First Amendment imposes some limits on the state's ability to adopt content-based restrictions in defining the purpose of a public forum, precisely what those limits are is unclear, and presents a difficult problem in First Amendment jurisprudence. The Supreme Court's "cases have not yet determined . . . that government's decision to dedicate a public forum to one type of content or another is necessarily subject to the highest level of scrutiny. Must a local government, for example, show a compelling state interest if it builds a band shell in the park and dedicates it solely to classical music (but not to jazz)? The answer is not obvious." [   ]

We believe, however, that certain principles emerge from the Supreme Court's jurisprudence on this question. In particular, and perhaps somewhat counterintuitively, the more narrow the range of speech that the government chooses to subsidize (whether directly, through government grants or other funding, or indirectly, through the creation of a public forum) the more deference the First Amendment accords the government in drawing content-based distinctions.

At one extreme lies the government's decision to fund a particular message that the government seeks to disseminate. In this context, content-based restrictions on the speech that government chooses to subsidize are clearly subject to at most rational basis review, and even viewpoint discrimination is permissible. For example, "[w]hen Congress established a National Endowment for Democracy to encourage other countries to adopt democratic principles, 22 U.S.C. § 4411(b), it was not constitutionally required to fund a program to encourage competing lines of political philosophy such as communism and fascism." [   ]

. . .

The more broadly the government facilitates private speech, however, the less deference the First Amendment accords to the government's content-based restrictions on the speech that it facilitates. Thus, where the government creates a designated public forum to facilitate private speech representing a diverse range of viewpoints, the government's decision selectively to single out particular viewpoints for exclusion is subject to strict scrutiny. [   ]

Similarly, although the government may create a designated public forum limited to speech on a particular topic, if the government opens the forum to members of the general public to speak on that topic while selectively singling out for exclusion particular speakers on the basis of the content of their speech, that restriction is subject to strict scrutiny. For instance, in [   ], the Court held that where a school board opens its meetings for public participation, it may not, consistent with the First Amendment, prohibit teachers other than union representatives from speaking on the subject of pending collective-bargaining negotiations. [   ]

Finally, content-based restrictions on speech in a designated public forum are most clearly subject to strict scrutiny when the government opens a forum for virtually unrestricted use by the general public for speech on a virtually unrestricted range of topics, while selectively excluding particular speech whose content it disfavors. Thus, in [   ], the Court held that a local government violated the First Amendment when it denied a group seeking to perform the rock musical "Hair" access to a general-purpose municipal theater open for the public at large to use for performances. *See also* [*DAETC*, p. ___, *supra*] (Kennedy, J., concurring in the judgment) (suggesting that strict scrutiny would not apply to a local government's decision to "build[   ] a band shell in the park and dedicate[   ] it solely to classical music (but not jazz)," but would apply to "the Government's creation of a band shell in which all types of music might be performed except for rap music").

Similarly, in *FCC v. League of Women Voters of Cal.,* 468 U.S. 364, 104 S.Ct. 3106, 82 L.Ed.2d 278 (1984), the Court subjected to heightened scrutiny a federal program that funded a wide range of public broadcasting stations that disseminated speech on a wide range of subjects, where the federal program singled out for exclusion speech whose content amounted to editorializing. . . .

In sum, the more widely the state opens a forum for members of the public to speak on a variety of subjects and viewpoints, the more vulnerable is the state's decision selectively to exclude certain speech on the basis of its disfavored content, as such exclusions distort the marketplace of ideas that the state has created in establishing the forum. [   ]

Thus, we believe that where the state designates a forum for expressive activity and opens the forum for speech by the public at large on a wide range of topics, strict scrutiny applies to restrictions that single out for exclusion from the forum particular speech whose content is disfavored. "Laws designed or intended to suppress or restrict the expression of *specific* speakers contradict basic First Amendment principles." [*Playboy*, p. ___, *supra*]; [   ].

. . .

D. Reasons for Applying Strict Scrutiny

1. Selective Exclusion From a "Vast Democratic Forum"

Applying these principles to public libraries, we agree with the government that generally the First Amendment subjects libraries' content-based decisions about which print materials to acquire for their collections to only rational review. In making these decisions, public libraries are generally free to adopt collection development criteria that reflect not simply patrons' demand for certain material, but also the library's evaluation of the material's quality. [   ] Thus, a public library's decision to use the last $100 of its budget to purchase the complete works of Shakespeare even though more of its patrons would prefer the library to use the same amount to purchase the complete works of John Grisham, is not, in our view, subject to strict scrutiny. [   ]

Nonetheless, we disagree with the government's argument that public libraries' use of Internet filters is no different, for First Amendment purposes, from the editorial discretion that they exercise when they choose to acquire certain books on the basis of librarians' evaluation of their quality. The central difference, in our view, is that by providing patrons with even filtered Internet access, the library permits patrons to receive speech on a virtually unlimited number of topics, from a virtually unlimited number of speakers, without attempting to restrict patrons' access to speech that the library, in the exercise of its professional judgment, determines to be particularly valuable. [   ]

In those cases upholding the government's exercise of editorial discretion in selecting certain speech for subsidization or inclusion in a state-created forum, the state actor exercising the editorial discretion has at least reviewed the content of the speech that the forum facilitates. . . .

This exercise of editorial discretion is evident in a library's decision to acquire certain books for its collection. . . .

In contrast, in providing patrons with even filtered Internet access, a public library invites patrons to access speech whose content has never been reviewed and recommended as particularly valuable by either a librarian or a third party to whom the library has delegated collection development decisions. Although several of the government's librarian witnesses who testified at trial purport to apply the same standards that govern the library's acquisition of print materials to the library's provision of Internet access to patrons, when public libraries provide their patrons with Internet access, they intentionally open their doors to vast amounts of speech that clearly lacks sufficient quality to ever be considered for the library's print collection. Unless a library allows access to only those sites that have been preselected as having particular value, a method that, as noted above, was tried and rejected by the Westerville Ohio Public Library, [   ], even a library that uses software filters has opened its Internet collection "for indiscriminate use by the general public." [   ]

. . .

In providing its patrons with Internet access, a public library creates a forum for the facilitation of speech, almost none of which either the library's collection development staff or even the filtering companies have ever reviewed. Although filtering companies review a portion of the Web in classifying particular sites, the portion of the Web that the filtering companies actually review is quite small in relation to the Web as a whole. The filtering companies' harvesting process, described in our findings of fact, is intended to identify only a small fraction of Web sites for the filtering companies to review. Put simply, the state cannot be said to be exercising editorial discretion permitted under the First Amendment when it indiscriminately facilitates private speech whose content it makes no effort to examine. [   ]

While the First Amendment permits the government to exercise editorial discretion in singling out particularly favored speech for subsidization or inclusion in a state-created forum, we believe that where the state provides access to a "vast democratic forum[   ]," [*Reno*], open to any member of the public to speak on subjects "as diverse as human thought," [   ], and then selectively excludes from the forum certain speech on the basis of its content, such exclusions are subject to strict scrutiny. These exclusions risk fundamentally distorting the unique marketplace of ideas that public libraries create when they open their collections, via the Internet, to the speech of millions of individuals around the world on a virtually limitless number of subjects.[25]

. . .

2. Analogy to Traditional Public Fora

Application of strict scrutiny to public libraries' use of software filters, in our view, finds further support in the extent to which public libraries' provision of Internet access promotes First Amendment values in an analogous manner to traditional public fora, such as sidewalks and

---

25. In distinguishing restrictions on public libraries' print collections from restrictions on the provision of Internet access, we do not rely on the rationale adopted in *Mainstream Loudoun v. Board of Trustees of the Loudoun County Library,* 2 F.Supp.2d 783 (E.D.Va.1998). The *Loudoun* Court reasoned that a library's decision to block certain Web sites fundamentally differs from its decision to carry certain books but not others, in that unlike the money and shelf space consumed by the library's provision of print materials, "no appreciable expenditure of library time or resources is required to make a particular Internet publication available" once the library has acquired Internet access. *Id.* at 793–94.

We disagree. Nearly every librarian who testified at trial stated that patrons' demand for Internet access exceeds the library's supply of Internet terminals. Under such circumstances, every time library patrons visit a Web site, they deny other patrons waiting to use the terminal access to other Web sites. Just as the scarcity of a library's budget and shelf space constrains a library's ability to provide its patrons with unrestricted access to print materials, the scarcity of time at Internet terminals constrains libraries' ability to provide patrons with unrestricted Internet access:

The same budget concerns constraining the number of books that libraries can offer also limits the number of terminals, Internet accounts, and speed of access links that can be purchased, and thus the number of Web pages that patrons can view. This is clear to anyone who has been denied access to a Website because no terminal was unoccupied.

parks, in which content-based restrictions on speech are always subject to strict scrutiny. . . .

We acknowledge that the provision of Internet access in a public library does not enjoy the historical pedigree of streets, sidewalks, and parks as a vehicle of free expression. Nonetheless, we believe that it shares many of the characteristics of these traditional public fora that uniquely promote First Amendment values and accordingly warrant application of strict scrutiny to any content-based restriction on speech in these fora. Regulation of speech in streets, sidewalks, and parks is subject to the highest scrutiny not simply by virtue of history and tradition, but also because the speech-facilitating character of sidewalks and parks makes them distinctly deserving of First Amendment protection. Many of these same speech-promoting features of the traditional public forum appear in public libraries' provision of Internet access.

First, public libraries, like sidewalks and parks, are generally open to any member of the public who wishes to receive the speech that these fora facilitate, subject only to narrow limitations. [ ] Moreover, like traditional public fora, public libraries are funded by taxpayers and therefore do not charge members of the public each time they use the forum. The only direct cost to library patrons who wish to receive information, whether via the Internet or the library's print collection, is the time spent reading.

By providing Internet access to millions of Americans to whom such access would otherwise be unavailable, public libraries play a critical role in bridging the digital divide separating those with access to new information technologies from those that lack access. [ ] Public libraries that provide Internet access greatly expand the educational opportunities for millions of Americans who, as explained in the margin, would otherwise be deprived of the benefits of this new medium.[26]

Just as important as the openness of a forum to listeners is its openness to speakers. Parks and sidewalks are paradigmatic loci of First Amendment values in large part because they permit speakers to communicate with a wide audience at low cost. One can address members of the public in a park for little more than the cost of a soapbox, and one can distribute handbills on the sidewalk for little more than the cost of a pen, paper, and some photocopies. [ ]

Similarly, given the existence of message boards and free Web hosting services, a speaker can, via the Internet, address the public, including patrons of public libraries, for little more than the cost of

---

26. We have found that approximately 14.3 million Americans access the Internet at a public library, and Internet access at public libraries is more often used by those with lower incomes than those with higher incomes. We found that about 20.3% of Internet users with household family income of less than $15,000 per year use public libraries for Internet access, and ap- proximately 70% of libraries serving communities with poverty levels in excess of 40% receive E-rate discounts. The widespread availability of Internet access in public libraries is due, in part, to the availability of public funding, including state and local funding and the federal funding programs regulated by CIPA.

Internet access. As the Supreme Court explained in [*Reno*], "the Internet can hardly be considered a 'scarce' expressive commodity. It provides relatively unlimited, low-cost capacity for communication of all kinds." [ ] Although the cost of a home computer and Internet access considerably exceeds the cost of a soapbox or a few hundred photocopies, speakers wishing to avail themselves of the Internet may gain free access in schools, workplaces, or the public library. . . .

While public libraries' provision of Internet access shares many of the speech-promoting qualities of traditional public fora, it also facilitates speech in ways that traditional public fora cannot. In particular, whereas the architecture of real space limits the audience of a pamphleteer or soapbox orator to people within the speaker's immediate vicinity, the Internet renders the geography of speaker and listener irrelevant:

Through the use of chat rooms, any person with a phone line can become a town crier with a voice that resonates farther than it could from any soapbox. Through the use of Web pages, mail exploders, and newsgroups, the same individual can become a pamphleteer.

[*Reno*]. By providing patrons with Internet access, public libraries in effect open their doors to an unlimited number of potential speakers around the world, inviting the speech of any member of the public who wishes to communicate with library patrons via the Internet.

. . .

In short, public libraries, by providing their patrons with access to the Internet, have created a public forum that provides any member of the public free access to information from millions of speakers around the world. The unique speech-enhancing character of Internet use in public libraries derives from the openness of the public library to any member of the public seeking to receive information, and the openness of the Internet to any member of the public who wishes to speak. In particular, speakers on the Internet enjoy low barriers to entry and the ability to reach a mass audience, unhindered by the constraints of geography. Moreover, just as the development of new media "presents unique problems, which inform our assessment of the interests at stake, and which may justify restrictions that would be unacceptable in other contexts," [*Playboy*], the development of new media, such as the Internet, also presents unique possibilities for promoting First Amendment values, which also inform our assessment of the interests at stake, and which we believe, in the context of the provision of Internet access in public libraries, justify the application of heightened scrutiny to content-based restrictions that might be subject to only rational review in other contexts, such as the development of the library's print collection. *Cf. id.* at 818, 120 S.Ct. 1878 ("Technology expands the capacity to choose; and it denies the potential of this revolution if we assume the Government is best positioned to make these choices for us.").

A faithful translation of First Amendment values from the context of traditional public fora such as sidewalks and parks to the distinctly non-traditional public forum of Internet access in public libraries requires, in our view, that content-based restrictions on Internet access in public libraries be subject to the same exacting standards of First Amendment scrutiny as content-based restrictions on speech in traditional public fora such as sidewalks, town squares, and parks . . . .

In providing patrons with even filtered Internet access, a public library is not exercising editorial discretion in selecting only speech of particular quality for inclusion in its collection, as it may do when it decides to acquire print materials. By providing its patrons with Internet access, public libraries create a forum in which any member of the public may receive speech from anyone around the world who wishes to disseminate information over the Internet. Within this "vast democratic forum[ ]," [*Reno*], which facilitates speech that is "as diverse as human thought," [ ], software filters single out for exclusion particular speech on the basis of its disfavored content. We hold that these content-based restrictions on patrons' access to speech are subject to strict scrutiny.

V. Application of Strict Scrutiny

. . .

The application of strict scrutiny to a public library's use of filtering products thus requires three distinct inquiries. First, we must identify those compelling government interests that the use of filtering software promotes. It is then necessary to analyze whether the use of software filters is narrowly tailored to further those interests. Finally, we must determine whether less restrictive alternatives exist that would promote the state interest.

A. State Interests

We begin by identifying those legitimate state interests that a public library's use of software filters promotes.

1. Preventing the Dissemination of Obscenity, Child Pornography, and Material Harmful to Minors

[The court concluded that the state's in preventing the dissemination of obscenity and child pornography, and in preventing minors from being exposed to material harmful to their well-being was compelling.]

2. Protecting the Unwilling Viewer

. . .

Although neither the Supreme Court nor the Third Circuit has recognized a compelling state interest in shielding the sensibilities of unwilling viewers, beyond laws intended to preserve the privacy of individuals' homes or to protect captive audiences, we do not read the case law as categorically foreclosing recognition, in the public library setting, of the state's interest in protecting unwilling viewers. *See* [*Pacifica*, p. ___, supra] ("Outside the home, the balance between the offensive speaker and the unwilling audience may *sometimes* tip in favor of the speaker, requiring the offended listener to turn away.") (emphasis added). Under certain circumstances, therefore a public library might have a compelling interest in protecting library patrons and staff from unwilling exposure to sexually explicit speech that, although not obscene, is patently offensive.

3. Preventing Unlawful or Inappropriate Conduct

Several of the librarians proffered by the government testified that unfiltered Internet access had led to occurrences of criminal or otherwise inappropriate conduct by library patrons, such as public masturbation, and harassment of library staff and patrons, sometimes rising to the level of physical assault. . . .

Aside from a public library's interest in preventing patrons from using the library's Internet terminals to receive obscenity or child pornography, which constitutes criminal conduct, we are constrained to reject any compelling state interest in regulating patrons' conduct as a justification for content-based restrictions on patrons' Internet access. "[T]he Court's First Amendment cases draw vital distinctions between words and deeds, between ideas and conduct." [*Ashcroft*]. First Amendment jurisprudence makes clear that speech may not be restricted on the ground that restricting speech will reduce crime or other undesirable behavior that the speech is thought to cause, subject to only a narrow exception for speech that "is directed to inciting or producing imminent lawless action and is likely to incite or produce such action." [*Brandenburg*, p. ___, *supra*].

. . .

4. Summary

In sum, we reject a public library's interest in preventing unlawful or otherwise inappropriate patron conduct as a basis for restricting patrons' access to speech on the Internet. The proper method for a library to deter unlawful or inappropriate patron conduct, such as harassment or assault of other patrons, is to impose sanctions on such conduct, such as either removing the patron from the library, revoking the patron's library privileges, or, in the appropriate case, calling the police. We believe, however, that the state interests in preventing the dissemination of obscenity, child pornography, or in the case of minors, material harmful to minors, and in protecting library patrons from being unwillingly exposed to offensive, sexually explicit material, could all justify, for First Amendment purposes, a public library's use of Internet filters, provided that use of such filters is narrowly tailored to further those interests, and that no less restrictive means of promoting those interests exist. Accordingly, we turn to the narrow tailoring question.

B. Narrow Tailoring

. . .

The commercially available filters on which evidence was presented at trial all block many thousands of Web pages that are clearly not harmful to minors, and many thousands more pages that, while possibly harmful to minors, are neither obscene nor child pornography. [   ] Even the defendants' own expert, after analyzing filtering products' performance in public libraries, concluded that of the blocked Web pages to which library patrons sought access, between 6% and 15% contained no content that meets even the filtering products' own definitions of sexually explicit content, let alone the legal definitions of obscenity or child pornography, which none of the filtering companies that were studied use as the basis for their blocking decisions. Moreover, in light of the flaws in these studies, discussed in detail in our findings of fact above, these percentages significantly underestimate the amount of speech that filters erroneously block, and at best provide a rough lower bound on the filters' rates of overblocking. Given the substantial amount of constitutionally protected speech blocked by the filters studied, we conclude that use of such filters is not narrowly tailored with respect to the government's interest in preventing the dissemination of obscenity, child pornography, and material harmful to minors.

To be sure, the quantitative estimates of the rates of overblocking apply only to those four commercially available filters analyzed by plaintiffs' and defendants' expert witnesses. Nonetheless, given the inherent limitations in the current state of the art of automated classification systems, and the limits of human review in relation to the size, rate of growth, and rate of change of the Web, there is a tradeoff between underblocking and overblocking that is inherent in *any* filtering technology, as our findings of fact have demonstrated. We credit the testimony of plaintiffs' expert witness, Dr. Geoffrey Nunberg, that no software exists that can automatically distinguish visual depictions that are obscene, child pornography, or harmful to minors, from those that are not. Nor can software, through keyword analysis or more sophisticated techniques, consistently distinguish web pages that contain such content from web pages that do not.

In light of the absence of any automated method of classifying Web pages, filtering companies are left with the Sisyphean task of using human review to identify, from among the approximately two billion web pages that exist, the 1.5 million new pages that are created daily, and the many thousands of pages whose content changes from day to day, those particular web pages to be blocked. To cope with the Web's extraordinary size, rate of growth, and rate of change, filtering companies that rely solely on human review to block access to material falling within their category definitions must use a variety of techniques that will necessarily introduce substantial amounts of overblocking. These techniques include blocking every page of a Web site that contains only some content falling within the filtering companies' category definitions, blocking every Web site that shares an IP-address with a Web site whose content falls within the category definitions, blocking "loophole sites," such as anonymizers, cache sites, and translation sites, and allocating staff resources to reviewing content of uncategorized pages rather than re-reviewing pages, domain names, or IP-addresses that have been already categorized to determine whether their content has changed. While a filtering company could choose not to use these techniques, due to the overblocking errors they introduce, if a filtering company does not use such techniques, its filter will be ineffective at blocking access to speech that falls within its category definitions.

. . .

This finding is supported by the government's failure to produce evidence of any filtering technology that avoids overblocking a substantial amount of protected speech. Where, as here, strict scrutiny applies to a content-based restriction on speech, the burden rests with the government to show that the restriction is narrowly tailored to serve a compelling government interest. *See* [*Playboy*]; [ ]. Thus, it is the government's burden, in this case, to show the existence of a filtering technology that both blocks enough speech to qualify as a technology protection measure, for purposes of CIPA, and avoids overblocking a substantial amount of constitutionally protected speech.

Here, the government has failed to meet its burden. . . .

Where, as here, strict scrutiny applies, the government may not justify restrictions on constitutionally *protected* speech on the ground that such restrictions are necessary in order for the government effectively to suppress the dissemination of constitutionally *unprotected* speech, such as obscenity and child pornography. "The argument . . . that protected speech may be banned as a means to ban unprotected speech . . . . turns the First Amendment upside down. The Government may not suppress lawful speech as the means to suppress unlawful speech." [*Ashcroft*].

Thus, in *Ashcroft,* the Supreme Court rejected the government's argument that a statute criminalizing the distribution of constitutionally protected "virtual" child pornography, produced through computer imaging technology without the use of real children, was necessary to further the state's interest in prosecuting the dissemination of constitutionally unprotected child pornography produced using real children, since "the possibility of producing images by using computer imaging makes it very difficult for [the government] to prosecute those who produce pornography using real children." [*Ashcroft*]. By the same token, even if the use of filters is effective in preventing patrons from receiving constitutionally unprotected speech, the government's interest in preventing the dissemination of such speech cannot justify the use of the technology protection measures mandated by CIPA, which necessarily block substantial amounts of constitutionally protected speech.

. . .

For the same reason that a public library's use of software filters is not narrowly tailored to further the library's interest in preventing its computers from being used to disseminate visual depictions that are obscene, child pornography, and harmful to minors, a public library's use of software filters is not narrowly tailored to further the library's interest in protecting patrons from being unwillingly exposed to offensive, sexually explicit material. As discussed in our findings of fact, the filters required by CIPA block substantial numbers of Web sites that even the most puritanical public library patron would not find offensive, such as *http://federo.com,* a Web site that promotes federalism in Uganda, which N2H2 blocked as "Adults Only, Pornography," and *http://www.vvm.com/bond/home.htm,* a site for aspiring dentists, which was blocked by Cyberpatrol as "Adult/Sexually Explicit." We list many more such examples in our findings of fact, *see supra,* and find that such erroneously blocked sites number in at least the thousands.

Although we have found large amounts of overblocking, even if only a small percentage of sites blocked are erroneously blocked, either with respect to the state's interest in preventing adults from viewing material that is obscene or child pornography and in preventing minors from viewing material that is harmful to minors, or with respect to the state's interest in preventing library patrons generally from being unwillingly exposed to offensive, sexually explicit material, this imprecision is fatal under the First Amendment. [   ]

While the First Amendment does not demand perfection when the government restricts speech in order to advance a compelling interest, the substantial amounts of erroneous blocking inherent in the technology protection measures mandated by CIPA are more than simply *de minimis* instances of human error. [   ] Where the government draws content-based restrictions on speech in order to advance a compelling government interest, the First Amendment demands the precision of a scalpel, not a sledgehammer. We believe that a public library's use of the technology protection measures mandated by CIPA is not narrowly tailored to further the governmental interests at stake.

Although the strength of different libraries' interests in blocking certain forms of speech may vary from library to library, depending on the frequency and severity of problems experienced by each particular library, we conclude, based on our findings of fact, that any public library's use of a filtering product mandated by CIPA will necessarily fail to be narrowly tailored to address the library's legitimate interests. Because it is impossible for a public library to comply with CIPA without blocking substantial amounts of speech whose suppression serves no legitimate state interest, we therefore hold that CIPA is facially invalid, even under the more stringent standard of facial invalidity urged on us by the government, which would require upholding CIPA if it is possible for just a single library to comply with CIPA's conditions without violating the First Amendment. *See supra* Part III.

C. Less Restrictive Alternatives

The constitutional infirmity of a public library's use of software filters is evidenced not only by the absence of narrow tailoring, but also by the existence of less restrictive alternatives that further the government's legitimate interests. *See [Playboy]* ("If a less restrictive alternative would serve the Government's purpose, the legislature must use that alternative."); [*Sable*, p. ___, *supra*, ("The Government may . . . regulate the content of constitutionally protected speech in order to promote a compelling interest if it chooses the least restrictive means to further the articulated interest.")].

As is the case with the narrow tailoring requirement, the government bears the burden of proof in showing the ineffectiveness of less restrictive alternatives. . . .

We find that there are plausible, less restrictive alternatives to the use of software filters that would serve the government's interest in preventing the dissemination of obscenity and child pornography to library patrons. In particular, public libraries can adopt Internet use policies that make clear to patrons that the library's Internet terminals may not be used to access illegal content. Libraries can ensure that their patrons are aware of such policies by posting them in prominent places in the library, requiring patrons to sign forms agreeing to comply with the policy before the library issues library cards to patrons, and by presenting patrons, when they log on to one of the library's Internet terminals, with a screen that requires the user to agree to comply with the library's policy before allowing the user access to the Internet.

Libraries can detect violations of their Internet use policies either through direct observation or through review of the library's Internet use logs. In some cases, library staff or patrons may directly observe a patron accessing obscenity and child pornography. Libraries' Internet use logs, however, also provide libraries with a means of detecting violations of their Internet use policies. These logs, which can be kept regardless whether a library uses filtering software, record the URL of every Web page accessed by patrons. Although ordinarily the logs do not link particular URLs with particular patrons, it is possible, using access logs, to identify the patron who viewed the Web page corresponding to a particular URL, if library staff discover in the access logs the URL of a Web page containing obscenity or child pornography. . . .

Once a violation of a library's Internet use policy is detected through the methods described above, a library may either issue the patron a warning, revoke the patron's Internet privileges, or notify law enforcement, if the library believes that the patron violated either state obscenity laws or child pornography laws. Although these methods of detecting use of library computers to access illegal content are not perfect, and a library, out of respect for patrons' privacy, may choose not to adopt such policies, the government has failed to show that such methods are substantially less effective at preventing patrons from accessing obscenity and child pornography than software filters. As detailed in our findings of fact, the underblocking that results from the size, rate of change, and rate of growth of the Internet significantly impairs the software filters from preventing patrons from accessing obscenity and child pornography. Unless software filters are themselves perfectly effective at preventing patrons from accessing obscenity and child pornography, "[i]t is no response that [a less restrictive alternative] . . . may not go perfectly every time." [*Playboy*],; *cf.* [*DAETC*] ("No provision . . . short of an absolute ban, can offer certain protection against assault by a determined child.").

. . .

We acknowledge that some library staff will be uncomfortable using the "tap-on-the-shoulder" method of enforcing the library's policy against using Internet terminals to access obscenity and child pornography. The Greenville County Library, for example, experienced high turnover among library staff when staff were required to enforce the library's Internet use policy through the tap-on-the-shoulder technique. Given filters' inevitable underblocking, however, even a library that uses filtering will have to resort to a tap-on-the-shoulder method of enforcement, where library staff observes a patron openly violating the library's Internet use policy, by, for example, accessing material that is obviously child pornography but that the filtering software failed to block. Moreover, a library employee's degree of comfort in using the tap-on-the-shoulder method will vary from employee to employee, and there is no evidence that it is impossible or prohibitively costly for public libraries to hire at least some employees who are comfortable enforcing the library's Internet use policy.

We also acknowledge that use of a tap on the shoulder delegates to librarians substantial discretion to determine which Web sites a patron may view. Nonetheless, we do not believe that this putative "prior restraint" problem can be avoided through the use of software filters, for they effectively delegate to the filtering company the same unfettered discretion to determine which Web sites a patron may view. Moreover, as noted above, violations of a public library's Internet use policy may be detected not only by direct observation, but also by reviewing the library's Internet use logs after the fact, which alleviates the need for library staff to directly confront patrons while they are viewing obscenity or child pornography.

Similar less restrictive alternatives exist for preventing minors from accessing material harmful to minors. First, libraries may use the tap-on-the-shoulder method when minors are observed using the Internet to access material that is harmful to minors. Requiring minors to use specific terminals, for example in a children's room, that are in direct view of library staff will increase the likelihood that library staff will detect minors' use of the Internet to access material harmful to minors. Alternatively, public libraries could require minors to use blocking software only if they are unaccompanied by a parent, or only if their parent consents in advance to their child's unfiltered use of the Internet. "A court should not assume that a plausible, less restrictive alternative would be ineffective; and a court should not presume parents, given full information, will fail to act." [*Playboy*].

. . .

Finally, there are other less restrictive alternatives to filtering software that further public libraries' interest in preventing patrons from unwillingly being exposed to patently offensive, sexually explicit content on the Internet. To the extent that public libraries are concerned with protecting patrons from accidentally encountering such material while using the Internet, public libraries can provide patrons with guidance in finding the material they want and avoiding unwanted material. Some public libraries also offer patrons the option of using filtering software, if they so desire. [   ]

With respect to protecting library patrons from sexually explicit content viewed by other patrons, public libraries have used a variety of less restrictive methods. One alternative is simply to segregate filtered from unfiltered terminals, and to place unfiltered terminals outside of patrons' sight-lines and areas of heavy traffic. . . .

Alternatively, libraries can use privacy screens or recessed monitors to prevent patrons from unwillingly being exposed to material viewed by other patrons. We acknowledge that privacy screens and recessed monitors suffer from imperfections as alternatives to filtering. Both impose costs on the library, particularly recessed monitors, which, according to the government's library witnesses, are expensive. Moreover, some libraries have experienced problems with patrons attempting to remove the privacy screens. Privacy screens and recessed monitors also make it difficult for more than one person to work at the same terminal.

These problems, however, are not insurmountable. While there is no doubt that privacy screens and recessed terminals impose additional costs on libraries, the government has failed to show that the cost of privacy screens or recessed terminals is substantially greater than the cost of filtering software and the resources needed to maintain such software. Nor has the government shown that the cost of these alternatives is so high as to make their use prohibitive. With respect to the problem of patrons removing privacy screens, we find, based on the successful use of privacy screens by the Fort Vancouver Regional Library and the Multnomah County Public Library, that it is possible for public libraries to prevent patrons from removing the screens. Although privacy screens may make it difficult for patrons to work at the same terminal side by side with other patrons or with library staff, a library could provide filtered access at terminals that lack privacy screens, when patrons wish to use a terminal with others. Alternatively, a library can reserve terminals outside of patrons' sight lines for groups of patrons who wish unfiltered access.

We therefore conclude that the government has failed to show that the less restrictive alternatives discussed above are ineffective at furthering the government's interest either in preventing patrons from using library computers to access visual depictions that are obscene, child pornography, or in the case of minors, harmful to minors, or in preventing library patrons from being unwillingly exposed to patently offensive, sexually explicit speech.

D. Do CIPA's Disabling Provisions Cure the Defect?

The Government argues that even if the use of software filters mandated by CIPA blocks a substantial amount of speech whose suppression serves no legitimate state interest, and therefore fails strict scrutiny's narrow tailoring requirement, CIPA's disabling provisions cure any lack of narrow tailoring inherent in filtering technology. The disabling provision applicable to libraries receiving LSTA grants states that "[a]n administrator, supervisor, or other authority may disable a technology protection measure . . . to enable access for bona fide research or other lawful purposes." CIPA § 1712(a)(2) (codified at 20 U.S.C. § 9134(f)(3)). CIPA's disabling provision with respect to libraries receiving E-rate discounts similarly states that "[a]n administrator, supervisor, or other person authorized by the certifying authority . . . may disable the technology protection measure concerned, during use by an adult, to enable access for bona fide research or other lawful purpose." CIPA § 1721(b) (codified at 47 U.S.C. § 254(h)(6)(D)).

. . .

At bottom, however, we need not definitively construe CIPA's disabling provisions, since it suffices in this case to assume without deciding that the disabling provisions permit libraries to allow a patron access to any speech that is constitutionally protected with respect to that patron. Although this interpretation raises fewer constitutional problems than a narrower interpretation, this interpretation of the disabling provisions nonetheless fails to cure CIPA's lack of narrow tailoring. Even if the disabling provisions permit public libraries to allow patrons to access speech that is constitutionally protected yet erroneously blocked by the software filters, the requirement that library patrons ask a state actor's permission to access disfavored content violates the First Amendment.

The Supreme Court has made clear that content-based restrictions that require recipients to identify themselves before being granted access to disfavored speech are subject to no less scrutiny than outright bans on access to such speech. . . .

. . . By requiring library patrons affirmatively to request permission to access certain speech singled out on the basis of its content, CIPA will deter patrons from requesting that a library disable filters to allow the patron to access speech that is constitutionally protected, yet sensitive in nature. As we explain above, we find that library patrons will be reluctant and hence unlikely to ask permission to access, for example, erroneously blocked Web sites containing information about sexually transmitted diseases, sexual identity, certain medical conditions, and a variety of other topics. As discussed in our findings of fact, software filters block access to a wide range of constitutionally protected speech, including Web sites containing information that individuals are likely to wish to access anonymously.

. . .

To be sure, the government demonstrated that it is possible for libraries to permit patrons to request anonymously that a particular Web site be unblocked. In particular, the Tacoma Public Library has configured its computers to present patrons with the option, each time the software filter blocks their access to a Web page, of sending an anonymous email to library staff requesting that the page be unblocked. Moreover, a library staff member periodically scans logs of URLs blocked by the filters, in an effort to identify erroneously blocked sites, which the library will subsequently unblock. Although a public library's ability to permit anonymous unblocking requests addresses the deterrent effect of requiring patrons to identify themselves before gaining access to a particular Web site, we believe that it fails adequately to address the overblocking problem.

In particular, even allowing anonymous requests for unblocking burdens patrons' access to speech, since such requests cannot immediately be acted on. Although the Tacoma Public Library, for example, attempts to review requests for unblocking within 24 hours, requests sometimes are not reviewed for several days. And delays are inevitable in libraries with branches that lack the staff necessary immediately to review patron unblocking requests. Because many Internet users "surf" the Web, visiting hundreds of Web sites in a single session and spending only a short period of time viewing many of the sites, the requirement that a patron take the time to affirmatively request access to a blocked Web site and then wait several days until the site is unblocked will, as a practical matter, impose a significant burden on library patrons' use of the Internet. Indeed, a patron's time spent requesting access to an erroneously blocked Web site and checking to determine whether access was eventually granted is likely to exceed the amount of time the patron would have actually spent viewing the site, had the site not been erroneously blocked. This delay is especially burdensome in view of many libraries' practice of limiting their patrons to a half hour or an hour of Internet use per day, given the scarcity of terminal time in relation to patron demand.

The burden of requiring library patrons to ask permission to view Web sites whose content is disfavored resembles the burden that the Supreme Court found unacceptable in [*Denver*], which invalidated a federal law requiring cable systems operators to block subscribers' access to channels containing sexually explicit programming, unless subscribers requested unblocking in advance. The Court reasoned that "[t]hese restrictions will prevent programmers from broadcasting to viewers who select programs day by day (or, through 'surfing,' minute by minute). . . ." [*DAETC*]. . . .

. . .

Even if CIPA's disabling provisions could be perfectly implemented by library staff every time patrons request access to an erroneously blocked Web site, we hold that the content-based burden that the library's use of software filters places on patrons' access to speech suffers from the same constitutional deficiencies as a complete ban on patrons' access to speech that was erroneously blocked by filters, since patrons will often be deterred from asking the library to unblock a site and patron requests cannot be immediately reviewed. We therefore hold that CIPA's disabling provisions fail to cure CIPA's lack of narrow tailoring.

VI. Conclusion; Severability

. . .

In view of the severe limitations of filtering technology and the existence of these less restrictive alternatives, we conclude that it is not possible for a public library to comply with CIPA without blocking a very substantial amount of constitutionally protected speech, in violation of the First Amendment. Because this conclusion derives from the inherent limits of the filtering technology mandated by CIPA, it holds for any library that complies with CIPA's conditions. Hence, even under the stricter standard of facial invalidity proposed by the government, which would require us to uphold CIPA if only a single library can comply with CIPA's conditions without violating the First Amendment, we conclude that CIPA is facially invalid, since it will induce public libraries, as state actors, to violate the First Amendment. . . .

Having determined that CIPA violates the First Amendment, we would usually be required to determine whether CIPA is severable from the remainder of the statutes governing LSTA and E-rate funding. Neither party, however, has advanced the argument that CIPA is not severable from the remainder the Library Services and Technology Act and Communications Act of 1934 (the two statutes governing LSTA and E-rate funding, respectively), and at all events, we think that CIPA is severable.

. . .

For the foregoing reasons, we will enter a final judgment declaring Sections 1712(a)(2) and 1721(b) of the Children's Internet Protection Act, codified at 20 U.S.C. § 9134(f) and 47 U.S.C. § 254(h)(6), respectively, to be facially invalid under the First Amendment and permanently enjoining the defendants from enforcing those provisions.

ORDER

AND NOW, this 31st day of May, 2002, based on the foregoing findings of fact and conclusions of law, it is hereby ORDERED that:

(1) judgment is entered in favor of the plaintiffs and against the defendants, declaring that §§ 1712(a)(2) and 1721(b) of the Children's Internet Protection Act, 20 U.S.C. § 9134(f) and 47 U.S.C. § 254(h)(6), are facially invalid under the First Amendment to the United States Constitution; and

(2) the United States, Michael Powell, in his official capacity as Chairman of the Federal Communications Commission, the Federal Communi-

cations Commission, Beverly Sheppard, in her official capacity as Acting Director of the Institute of Museum and Library Services, and the Institute of Museum and Library Services are permanently enjoined from withholding federal funds from any public library for failure to comply with §§ 1712(a)(2) and 1721(b) of the Children's Internet Protection Act, 20 U.S.C. § 9134(f) and 47 U.S.C. § 254(h)(6).

Notes and Questions

1. The Supreme Court noted probable jurisdiction. The case was argued in early 2003.

2. Another legal problem faced by libraries that provide unfiltered access to the Internet can be found in an EEOC decision involving the Minneapolis Public Library. In a probable cause hearing, acting on complaints filed by several librarians, an ALJ held that such access created a "sexually hostile work environment." A settlement could not be reached leading the librarians to file a civil suit in early 2003. The case is entitled Cynthia L. Smith v. Minneapolis Public Library.

3. What is the proper balance between all the competing interests involved in library Internet access?

C. SAFETY AND VIOLENCE

An unusual case raising questions regarding the application of the First Amendment to cyberspace resulted from a story written by Jake Baker, an undergraduate at the University of Michigan. The story, a fictional account of the rape, torture and murder of a woman given the same name as one of Baker's classmates, was posted to the Internet newsgroup, alt.sex.stories. Newsgroups are a series of electronic bulletin boards, organized by subject matter, that are publicly available through the Internet.

Baker was arrested and charged with violating 18 U.S.C.A. § 875(c), which provides:

> Whoever transmits in interstate or foreign commerce any communication containing any threat to kidnap any person or any threat to injure the person of another, shall be fined under this title or imprisoned not more than five years, or both.

The original charge was based on the story, as well as certain e-mail messages to a man named Arthur Gonda who lived in Ontario, Canada. Although Gonda was also charged, he was never found. As the court later noted, "Gonda's identity is entirely unknown; 'he' could be a ten year old girl, an eighty year old man, or a committee in a retirement community playing the role of Gonda gathered around a computer."

For the first month after his arrest, Baker was held without bail. He was also expelled by the University of Michigan. Subsequently, the original charge was dropped and five new counts of violating 18 U.S.C.A.

§ 875(c) were brought. These new charges were based solely on the e-mail messages.

The new charges were dismissed. The judge held that under the First Amendment "only unequivocal, unconditional and specific expressions of intention immediately to inflict injury may be punished." Given the lack of specificity in the messages, as well as the unknown identity of Gonda, he found the factual evidence insufficient as a matter of law. He was also extremely critical of the government's actions in the case:

> . . . The government's enthusiastic beginning petered out to a salvage effort once it recognized that the communication which so much alarmed the University of Michigan officials was only a rather savage and tasteless piece of fiction. Why the government became involved in the matter is not really explained in the record.
>
> Baker is being prosecuted under 18 U.S.C. § 875(c) for his use of words, implicating fundamental First Amendment concerns. Baker's words were transmitted by means of the Internet, a relatively new communications medium that is itself currently the subject of much media attention. The Internet makes it possible with unprecedented ease to achieve world-wide distribution of material, like Baker's story, posted to its public areas. When used in such a fashion, the Internet may be likened to a newspaper with unlimited distribution and no locatable printing press—and with no supervising editorial control. But Baker's e-mail messages, on which the superseding indictment is based, were not publicly published but privately sent to Gonda. While new technology such as the Internet may complicate analysis and may sometimes require new or modified laws, it does not in this instance qualitatively change the analysis under the statute or under the First Amendment. Whatever Baker's faults, and he is to be faulted, he did not violate 18 U.S.C. § 875(c). . . . What the Court said at the conclusion of oral argument bears repeating: "[T]he Court is very skeptical, and about the best thing the government's got going for it at this moment is the sincerity of purpose exhibited by [the Assistant United States Attorneys prosecuting the case]. I am not sure that sincerity of purpose is either synonymous with a good case under the law, or even the exercise of good judgment."

United States v. Baker, 890 F.Supp. 1375, 23 Med.L.Rptr. 2025 (E.D.Mich.1995). The dismissal was upheld on appeal. 104 F.3d 1492 (6th Cir.1997).

In 1997 Planned Parenthood, along with some doctors and a clinic, filed suit against the creators of The Nuremberg Files, an antiabortion website, http://www.christiangallery.com. The plaintiffs claimed the site, which listed doctors who perform abortions, was in violation of the 1994 Clinic Entrances Act. Noting that the site listed detailed personal information about the doctors and their families, and that murdered doctors appeared on the list crossed out, plaintiffs argued the list was an attempt to incite people to murder the doctors listed. The defendants argued the site was protected by the First Amendment. "Abortion Foes' Internet Site on Trial," Washington Post, Jan. 15, 1999 at A03.

A jury found for the plaintiffs and awarded them $107 million. A key issue on appeal was the judge's instructions to the jury. He told the jurors that a finding of intent to cause violence was unnecessary as long as a " 'reasonable person' could consider the harsh words and graphics to be threats." Washington Post, Feb. 3, 1999 at A01.

The court of appeals reversed holding that ACLA's material was protected speech. The court found that it did not fall within the "true threats" exception. Planned Parenthood of the Columbia/Willamette, Inc. v. American Coalition of Life Activists. 244 F.3d 1007 (9th Cir.2001). A rehearing en banc was then granted.

PLANNED PARENTHOOD OF THE COLUMBIA/WILLAMETTE, INC. v. AMERICAN COALITION OF LIFE ACTIVISTS

United States Court of Appeals, Ninth Circuit, 2002.
290 F.3d 1058.

Opinion by Judge RYMER; Dissent by Judge REINHARDT; Dissent by Judge KOZINSKI; Dissent by Judge BERZON.

RYMER, Circuit Judge.

For the first time we construe what the Freedom of Access to Clinics Entrances Act (FACE), 18 U.S.C. § 248, means by "threat of force." FACE gives aggrieved persons a right of action against whoever by "threat of force . . . intentionally . . . intimidates . . . any person because that person is or has been . . . providing reproductive health services." 18 U.S.C. § 248(a)(1) and (c)(1)(A). This requires that we define "threat of force" in a way that comports with the First Amendment, and it raises the question whether the conduct that occurred here falls within the category of unprotected speech.

. . .

We reheard the case en banc because these issues are obviously important. We now conclude that it was proper for the district court to adopt our long-standing law on "true threats" to define a "threat" for purposes of FACE. FACE itself requires that the threat of force be made with the intent to intimidate. Thus, the jury must have found that ACLA made statements to intimidate the physicians, reasonably foreseeing that physicians would interpret the statements as a serious expression of ACLA's intent to harm them because they provided reproductive health services. Construing the facts in the light most favorable to physicians, the verdict is supported by substantial evidence. ACLA was aware that a "wanted"-type poster would likely be interpreted as a serious threat of death or bodily harm by a doctor in the reproductive health services community who was identified on one, given the previous pattern of "WANTED" posters identifying a specific physician followed by that physician's murder. The same is true of the posting about these physicians on that part of the "Nuremberg Files" where lines were drawn through the names of doctors who provided abortion services and who had been killed or wounded. We are independently satisfied that to this limited extent, ACLA's conduct amounted to a true threat and is not protected speech.

As we see no reversible error on liability or in the equitable relief that was granted, we affirm. However, we remand for consideration of whether the punitive damages award comports with due process.

I

. . .

II

Before turning to the merits, we must consider the standard of review because ACLA contends that in a free speech case it is de novo. Relying on [*Bose Corp.*, p. ___, *supra*], ACLA submits that we must first determine for ourselves whether its speech is classic protected speech or is a "true threat" by reviewing the entire record.

Physicians assert that the standard of review for which ACLA contends comes from libel cases, but that threat cases are different; the more searching review of the record incumbent upon courts in libel cases, they urge, is inapposite to threat cases. They also point out that we have decided all of our threats cases without engaging in de novo review of the factual record. [ ]

We do not entirely agree with either side. It is true that our threats cases have been decided without conducting a de novo review of the factual record, but the issue was not squarely presented in any of those cases. For this reason, we cannot take it as definitively resolved.

. . .

It is not easy to discern a rule from these cases that can easily be applied in a threats case where, by definition, a true threat is constitutionally unprotected. Indeed, FACE on its face requires that "threat of force" be defined and applied consistent with the First Amendment. Perhaps this explains why we have treated threat cases differently, explicitly holding that the question of whether there is a true threat is for the jury.

We conclude that the proper definition of a "threat" for purposes of FACE is a question of law that we review *de novo*. If it were clear that neither the Deadly Dozen nor the Crist poster, or the Nuremberg Files, was a threat as properly defined, the case should not have gone to the jury and summary judgment should have been granted in ACLA's favor. If there were material facts in dispute or it was not clear that the posters were protected expression instead of true threats, the question whether the posters and the Files amount to a "threat of force" for purposes of the statute was for the trier of fact. Assuming that the district court correctly defined "threat" and properly instructed the jury on the elements of liability pursuant to the statute, our review is for substantial evidence supporting the historical facts (including credibility determinations) and the elements of statutory liability (including intent). We review the district court's findings with respect to injunctive relief for clear error and its conclusions of law *de novo*. However, while we normally review the scope of injunctive relief for abuse of discretion, we will scrutinize the relief granted in this case to determine whether the challenged provisions of the injunction burden no more speech than necessary to achieve its goals. [ ]

Given that the verdict for physicians and the injunctive relief granted in their favor restrict speech, we review the record independently in order to satisfy ourselves that the posters and the Files constitute a "true threat" such that they lack First Amendment protection. We will consider the undisputed facts as true, and construe the historical facts, the findings on the statutory elements, and all credibility determinations in favor of the prevailing party. In this way we give appropriate deference to the trier of fact, here both the jury and the district judge, yet assure that evidence of the core constitutional fact—a true threat—falls within the unprotected category and is narrowly enough bounded as a matter of constitutional law.

III

ACLA argues that the First Amendment requires reversal because liability was based on political speech that constituted neither an incitement to imminent lawless action nor a true threat. It suggests that the key question for us to consider is whether these posters can be considered "true threats" when, in fact, the posters on their face contain no explicitly threatening language. Further, ACLA submits that classic political speech cannot be converted into non-protected speech by a context of violence that includes the independent action of others.

Physicians counter that this threats case must be analyzed under the settled threats law of this circuit. Following precedent, it was proper for the jury to take context into account. They point out that the district court limited evidence of anti-abortion violence to evidence tending to show knowledge of a particular defendant, and maintain that the objective standard on which the jury was instructed comports both with Ninth Circuit law and congressional intent. As the First Amendment does not protect true threats of force, physicians conclude, ACLA's speech was not protected.

A

We start with the statute under which this action arises. Section 248(c)(1)(A) gives a private right of action to any person aggrieved by reason of the conduct prohibited by subsection (a). Subsection (a)(1) provides:

(a) . . . Whoever—

(1) by force or threat of force or by physical obstruction, intentionally injures, intimidates or interferes with or attempts to injure,

intimidate or interfere with any person because that person is or has been, or in order to intimidate such person or any other person or any class of persons from, obtaining or providing reproductive health services . . . shall be subject to the . . . civil remedies provided in subsection (c). . . . 18 U.S.C. § 248(a)(1). The statute also provides that "[n]othing in this section shall be construed . . . to prohibit any expressive conduct (including peaceful picketing or other peaceful demonstration) protected from legal prohibition by the First Amendment to the Constitution." 18 U.S.C. § 248(d)(1).

FACE does not define "threat," although it does provide that "[t]he term 'intimidate' means to place a person in reasonable apprehension of bodily harm to him—or herself or to another." 18 U.S.C. § 248(e)(3). Thus, the first task is to define "threat" for purposes of the Act. This requires a definition that comports with the First Amendment, that is, a "true threat."

The Supreme Court has provided benchmarks, but no definition.

[*Brandenburg*, p. ___, *supra*] makes it clear that the First Amendment protects speech that advocates violence, so long as the speech is not directed to inciting or producing imminent lawless action and is not likely to incite or produce such action. [   ] If ACLA had merely endorsed or encouraged the violent actions of others, its speech would be protected.

However, while advocating violence is protected, threatening a person with violence is not. In *Watts v. United States,* 394 U.S. 705, 89 S.Ct. 1399, 22 L.Ed.2d 664 (1969), the Court explicitly distinguished between political hyperbole, which is protected, and true threats, which are not. Considering how to construe a statute which prohibited "knowingly and willfully . . . (making) any threat to take the life of or to inflict bodily harm upon the President," the Court admonished that any statute which criminalizes a form of pure speech "must be interpreted with the commands of the First Amendment clearly in mind. What is a threat must be distinguished from what is constitutionally protected speech." *Id.* at 705, 707, 89 S.Ct. 1399. In that case, an 18–year old war protester told a discussion group of other young people at a public rally on the Washington Monument grounds: "They always holler at us to get an education. And now I have already received my draft classification as 1–A and I have got to report for my physical this Monday coming. I am not going. If they ever make me carry a rifle the first man I want to get in my sights is L.B.J." [   ] His audience laughed. Taken in context, and given the conditional nature of the statement and the reaction of the listeners, the Court concluded that the speech could not be interpreted other than as "a kind of very crude offensive method of stating a political opposition to the President." [   ] Accordingly, it ordered judgment entered for Watts.

ACLA's position is that the posters, including the Nuremberg Files, are protected political speech under *Watts,* and cannot lose this character by context. But this is not correct. The Court itself considered context and determined that Watts's statement was political hyperbole instead of a true threat because of context. [ ] Beyond this, ACLA points out that the posters contain no language that is a threat. We agree that this is literally true. Therefore, ACLA submits, this case is really an incitement case in disguise. So viewed, the posters are protected speech under *Brandenburg* and [NAACP v. Claiborne Hardware Co., 458 U.S. 886, 102 S.Ct. 3409, 73 L.Ed.2d 1215 (1982)], which ACLA suggests is the closest analogue. We disagree that *Claiborne* is closely analogous.

In March 1966 black citizens in Claiborne County made a list of demands for racial equality and integration. Unsatisfied by the response, several hundred black persons at a meeting of the local National Association for the Advancement of Colored People (NAACP) voted to place a boycott on white merchants in the area. The boycott continued until October 1969. During this period, stores were watched and the names of persons who violated the boycott were read at meetings of the NAACP at the First Baptist Church, and published in a local paper called "Black Times." These persons were branded as traitors to the black cause, were called demeaning names, and were socially ostracized. A few incidents of violence occurred. Birdshot was fired at the houses of two boycott violators; a brick was thrown through a windshield; and a flower garden was damaged. None of the victims ceased trading with white merchants. Six other incidents of arguably unlawful conduct occurred. White business owners brought suit against the NAACP and Charles Evers, its field secretary, along with other individuals who had participated in the boycott, for violating Mississippi state laws on malicious interference with a business, antitrust, and illegal boycott. Plaintiffs pursued several theories of liability: participating in management of the boycott; serving as an "enforcer" or monitor; committing or threatening acts of violence, which showed that the perpetrator wanted the boycott to succeed by coercion when it could not succeed by persuasion; and as to Evers, threatening violence against boycott breakers, and as to the NAACP because he was its field secretary when he committed tortious and constitutionally unprotected acts. Damages for business losses during the boycott and injunctive relief were awarded.

The Court held that there could be no recovery based on intimidation by threats of social ostracism, because offensive and coercive speech is protected by the First Amendment. "The use of speeches, marches, and threats of social ostracism cannot provide the basis for a damages award. But violent conduct is beyond the pale of constitutional protection." 458 U.S. at 933, 102 S.Ct. 3409. There was some evidence of violence, but the violence was not pervasive.... Accordingly, the Court made clear that only losses proximately caused by unlawful conduct could be recovered. Further, civil liability could not be imposed consistent with the First Amendment solely on account of an individual's association with others who have committed acts of violence; he must have incited or authorized them himself.

For the same reasons the Court held that liability could not be imposed on Evers for his participation in the boycott itself, or for his threats of vilification or ostracism. However, the merchants also sought damages from Evers for his speeches. He gave one in April 1966, and two others in April 1969. In the first, he told his audience that they would be watched and that blacks who traded with white merchants would be answerable to him; he also said that any "uncle toms" who broke the boycott would "have their necks broken" by their own people. In his April 19, 1969 speech, Evers stated that boycott violators would be "disciplined" by their own people and warned that the Sheriff could not sleep with boycott violators at night. And on April 21, Evers gave another speech to several hundred people calling for a total boycott of white-owned businesses and saying: "If we catch any of you going in any of them racist stores, we're gonna break your damn neck." The Court concluded that the "emotionally charged rhetoric" of Evers's speeches was within the bounds of *Brandenburg*. It was not followed by violence, and there was no evidence—apart from the speeches themselves—that Evers authorized, ratified, or directly threatened violence. "If there were other evidence of his authorization of wrongful conduct, the references to discipline in the speeches could be used to corroborate that evidence." *Claiborne,* 458 U.S. at 929, 102 S.Ct. 3409. As there was not, the findings were constitutionally inadequate to support the damages judgment against him and, in turn, the NAACP.

Claiborne, of course, did not arise under a threats statute. The Court had no need to consider whether Evers's statements were true threats of force within the meaning of a threats statute; it held only that his speeches did not incite illegal activity, thus could not have caused business losses and could not be the basis for liability to white merchants. As the opinion points out, there was no context to give the speeches (including the expression "break your neck") the implication of authorizing or directly threatening unlawful conduct. To the extent there was any intimidating overtone, Evers's rhetoric was extemporaneous, surrounded by statements supporting non-violent action, and primarily of the social ostracism sort. No specific individuals were targeted. For all that appears, "the break your neck" comments were hyperbolic vernacular. Certainly there was no history that Evers or anyone else associated with the NAACP had broken anyone's neck who did not participate in, or opposed, this boycott or any others. Nor is there any indication that Evers's listeners took his statement that boycott breakers' "necks would be broken" as a serious threat that *their* necks would be broken; they kept on shopping at boycotted stores.

Thus, *Watts* was the only Supreme Court case that discussed the First Amendment in relation to true threats before we first confronted the issue. Apart from holding that Watts's crack about L.B.J. was not a true threat, the Court set out no standard for determining when a statement is a true threat that is unprotected speech under the First Amendment. Shortly after *Watts* was rendered, we had to decide in *Roy v. United States,* 416 F.2d 874 (9th Cir.1969), whether a Marine Corps private made a true threat for purposes of 18 U.S.C. § 871 against the President, who was coming to his base the next day, by saying: "I am

going to get him." We adopted a "reasonable speaker" test. As it has
come to be articulated, the test is:

> Whether a particular statement may properly be considered to be a
> threat is governed by an objective standard—whether a reasonable
> person would foresee that the statement would be interpreted by
> those to whom the maker communicates the statement as a serious
> expression of intent to harm or assault.

[　]

. . .

Under our cases, a threat is "an expression of an intention to inflict
evil, injury, or damage on another." [　] "Alleged threats should be
considered in light of their entire factual context, including the surrounding events and reaction of the listeners." [　] " 'The fact that a
threat is subtle does not make it less of a threat.' " [　] A true threat,
that is one "where a reasonable person would foresee that the listener
will believe he will be subjected to physical violence upon his person, is
unprotected by the first amendment." [　]

It is not necessary that the defendant intend to, or be able to carry
out his threat; the only intent requirement for a true threat is that the
defendant intentionally or knowingly communicate the threat. [　] Nevertheless, we are urged to adopt a subjective intent requirement for
FACE. In particular, amicus ACLU Foundation of Oregon, Inc., advocates a subjective intent component to "require evidence, albeit circum-
stantial or inferential in many cases, that the speaker actually *intended*
to induce fear, intimidation, or terror; namely, that the speaker intended
to threaten. If a person did not intend to threaten or intimidate (*i.e.,* did
not intend that his or her statement be understood as a threat), then the
speech should not be considered to be a 'true threat,' unprotected by the
First Amendment." However, this much is subsumed within the statutory standard of FACE itself, which requires that the threat of force be
made with the intent to intimidate. The "requirement of intent to
intimidate serves to insulate the statute from unconstitutional application to protected speech." [　] No reason appears to engraft another
intent requirement onto the statute, because whether or not the maker
of the threat has an actual intention to carry it out, "an apparently
serious threat may cause the mischief or evil toward which the statute
was in part directed." [　]

The dissents would change the test, either to require that the
speaker actually intend to carry out the threat or be in control of those
who will, or to make it inapplicable when the speech is public rather
than private. However, for years our test has focused on what *a reasonable speaker* would foresee the *listener's* reaction to be under the
circumstances, and that is where we believe it should remain. [　]
Threats are outside the First Amendment to "protect[　] individuals
from the fear of violence, from the disruption that fear engenders, and
from the possibility that the threatened violence will occur." [　] This
purpose is not served by hinging constitutionality on the speaker's

subjective intent or capacity to do (or not to do) harm. Rather, these factors go to how reasonably foreseeable it is to a speaker that the listener will seriously take his communication as an intent to inflict bodily harm. This suffices to distinguish a "true threat" from speech that is merely frightening. Thus, no reasonable speaker would foresee that a patient would take the statement "You have cancer and will die within six months," or that a pedestrian would take a warning "Get out of the way of that bus," as a serious expression of intent *to inflict* bodily harm; the harm is going to happen anyway.

Neither do we agree that threatening speech made in public is entitled to heightened constitutional protection just because it is communicated publicly rather than privately. [T]hreats are unprotected by the First Amendment "however communicated." [   ]

Therefore, we hold that "threat of force" in FACE means what our settled threats law says a true threat is: a statement which, in the entire context and under all the circumstances, a reasonable person would foresee would be interpreted by those to whom the statement is communicated as a serious expression of intent to inflict bodily harm upon that person. So defined, a threatening statement that violates FACE is unprotected under the First Amendment.

B

Although ACLA does not believe we should reach this point, if we do it submits that no claim was made out even under "true threats" cases. First, it argues that other threats cases were criminal actions against someone who made a real threat directly to others, not political speech as is the case here. It contrasts what it calls "a threat plus context" . . . with the absence of a direct threat in this case. However, our cases do not require that the maker of the threat personally cause physical harm to the listener. . . . No case to our knowledge has imposed such a requirement, and we decline to now. It is the making of the threat with intent to intimidate—not the implementation of it—that violates FACE.

 . . .

ACLA also maintains that "context" means the direct circumstances surrounding delivery of the threat, or evidence sufficient to resolve ambiguity in the words of the statement—not two weeks of testimony as occurred here in the district court. Otherwise, ACLA submits, FACE is facially invalid. However, none of our cases has limited "context" to explaining ambiguous words, or to delivery. We, and so far as we can tell, other circuits as well, consider the whole factual context and "all of the circumstances," [   ], in order to determine whether a statement is a true threat.

 . . .

Nor does consideration of context amount to viewpoint discrimination, as ACLA contends. ACLA's theory appears to be that because the posters did not contain any threat on their face, the views of abortion foes are chilled more than the views of abortion-right proponents because of the random acts of violence committed by some people against abortion providers. However, FACE itself is viewpoint neutral. [ ] Moreover, ACLA could not be liable under FACE unless *it* made a true threat *with the intent to intimidate* physicians. Thus it is making a threat to intimidate that makes ACLA's conduct unlawful, not its viewpoint.

Because of context, we conclude that the Crist and Deadly Dozen posters are not just a political statement. Even if the Gunn poster, which was the first "WANTED" poster, was a purely political message when originally issued, and even if the Britton poster were too, by the time of the Crist poster, the poster format itself had acquired currency as a death threat for abortion providers. Gunn was killed after his poster was released; Britton was killed after his poster was released; and Patterson was killed after his poster was released. Knowing this, and knowing the fear generated among those in the reproductive health services community who were singled out for identification on a "wanted"-type poster, ACLA deliberately identified Crist on a "GUILTY" poster and intentionally put the names of Hern and the Newhalls on the Deadly Dozen "GUILTY" poster to intimidate them. This goes well beyond the political message (regardless of what one thinks of it) that abortionists are killers who deserve death too.

The Nuremberg Files are somewhat different. Although they name individuals, they name hundreds of them. The avowed intent is "collecting dossiers on abortionists in anticipation that one day we may be able to hold them on trial for crimes against humanity." The web page states: "One of the great tragedies of the Nuremberg trials of Nazis after WWII was that complete information and documented evidence had not been collected so many war criminals went free or were only found guilty of minor crimes. We do not want the same thing to happen when the day comes to charge abortionists with their crimes. We anticipate the day when these people will be charged in PERFECTLY LEGAL COURTS once the tide of this nation's opinion turns against child-killing (as it surely will)." However offensive or disturbing this might be to those listed in the Files, being offensive and provocative is protected under the First Amendment. But, in two critical respects, the Files go further. In addition to listing judges, politicians and law enforcement personnel, the Files separately categorize "Abortionists" and list the names of individuals who provide abortion services, including, specifically, Crist, Hern, and both Newhalls. Also, names of abortion providers who have been murdered because of their activities are lined through in black, while names of those who have been wounded are highlighted in grey. As a result, we cannot say that it is clear as a matter of law that listing Crist, Hern, and the Newhalls on *both* the Nuremberg Files *and* the GUILTY posters is purely protected, political expression.

Accordingly, whether the Crist Poster, the Deadly Dozen poster, and the identification of Crist, Hern, Dr. Elizabeth Newhall and Dr. James

Newhall in the Nuremberg Files as well as on "wanted"-type posters, constituted true threats was properly for the jury to decide.

. . .

F

Having concluded that "threat of force" was properly defined and that no trial error requires reversal, we consider whether the core constitutional fact—a true threat—exists such that the Crist and Deadly Dozen Posters, and the Nuremberg Files as to Crist, Hern, and the Newhalls, are without First Amendment protection. The task in this case does not seem dramatically different from determining that the issue should have gone to the jury and that the jury was properly instructed under FACE. Nevertheless, we review the evidence on true threats independently.

The true threats analysis turns on the poster pattern. Neither the Crist poster nor the Deadly Dozen poster contains any language that is overtly threatening. Both differ from prior posters in that the prior posters were captioned "WANTED" while these are captioned "GUILTY." The text also differs somewhat, but differences in caption or words are immaterial because the language itself is not what is threatening. Rather, it is use of the "wanted"-type format in the context of the poster pattern—poster followed by murder—that constitutes the threat. Because of the pattern, a "wanted"-type poster naming a specific doctor who provides abortions was perceived by physicians, who are providers of reproductive health services, as a serious threat of death or bodily harm. After a "WANTED" poster on Dr. David Gunn appeared, he was shot and killed. After a "WANTED" poster on Dr. George Patterson appeared, he was shot and killed. After a "WANTED" poster on Dr. John Britton appeared, he was shot and killed. None of these "WANTED" posters contained threatening language, either. Neither did they identify who would pull the trigger. But knowing this pattern, knowing that unlawful action had followed "WANTED" posters on Gunn, Patterson and Britton, and knowing that "wanted"-type posters were intimidating and caused fear of serious harm to those named on them, ACLA published a "GUILTY" poster in essentially the same format on Dr. Crist and a Deadly Dozen "GUILTY" poster in similar format naming Dr. Hern, Dr. Elizabeth Newhall and Dr. James Newhall because they perform abortions. Physicians could well believe that ACLA would make good on the threat. One of the other doctors on the Deadly Dozen poster had in fact been shot before the poster was published. This is not political hyperbole. Nor is it merely "vituperative, abusive, and inexact." [ ] In the context of the poster pattern, the posters were precise in their meaning to those in the relevant community of reproductive health service providers. They were a true threat.

. . .

As a direct result of having a "GUILTY" poster out on them, physicians wore bullet-proof vests and took other extraordinary security measures to protect themselves and their families. ACLA had every reason to foresee that its expression of intent to harm (the "GUILTY" poster identifying Crist, Hern, Elizabeth Newhall and James Newhall by name and putting them in the File that tracks hits and misses) would elicit this reaction. Physicians' fear did not simply happen; ACLA intended to intimidate them from doing what they do.

This is the point of the statute and is conduct that we are satisfied lacks any protection under the First Amendment.

Violence is not a protected value. Nor is a *true threat* of violence *with intent to intimidate*. ACLA may have been staking out a position for debate when it merely advocated violence as in Bray's *A Time to Kill,* or applauded it, as in the Defense Action petitions. Likewise, when it created the Nuremberg Files in the abstract, because the First Amendment does not preclude calling people demeaning or inflammatory names, or threatening social ostracism or vilification to advocate a political position. [ ] But, after being on "wanted"-type posters, Dr. Gunn, Dr. Patterson, and Dr. Britton can no longer participate in the debate. By replicating the poster pattern that preceded the elimination of Gunn, Patterson and Britton, and by putting Crist, Hern, and the Newhalls in an abortionists' File that scores fatalities, ACLA was not staking out a position of debate but of threatened demise. This turns the First Amendment on its head.

Like "fighting words," true threats are proscribable. We therefore conclude that the judgment of liability in physicians' favor is constitutionally permissible.

IV

ACLA submits that the damage award must be reversed or limited to the compensatory damages because the punitive award amounts to judgment without notice, [ ]. . . . Although our review is de novo, the district court should be given the opportunity to evaluate the punitive damages award and to make findings with respect to its propriety. Therefore, we vacate the award of punitive damages and remand for the district court to consider in the first instance whether the award is appropriate . . . .

V

After trial, the district court found that each defendant used intimidation as a means of interfering with the provision of reproductive health services and acted with malice and with specific intent in threatening physicians. It found that physicians remain threatened by ACLA's threats, and have no adequate remedy at law. . . . Accordingly, it permanently enjoined each of the defendants, their agents, and all persons in active concert with any of them who receive actual notice, from threatening, with the specific intent to do so, Crist, Hern, Dr. Elizabeth Newhall, Dr. James Newhall, PPCW and PFWHC in violation of FACE; publishing, republishing, reproducing or distributing the Deadly Dozen Poster, or the Crist poster, or their equivalent, with specific intent to threaten physicians, PPCW or PFWHC; and from providing additional material concerning Crist, Hern, either Newhall, PPCW or PFWHC to the Nuremberg Files or any mirror web site with a specific intent to threaten, as well as from publishing the personally identifying information about them in the Nuremberg Files with a specific intent to threaten. The court also ordered ACLA to turn over possession of materials that are not in compliance with the injunction.

ACLA complains principally about the restraint on possessing the posters. . . . However, the posters in this case are quite different from a book; the "wanted"—type posters themselves—not their ideological content—are the tool for threatening physicians. In this sense the posters' status is more like conduct than speech. *Cf.* [*O'Brien*, p. ___, *supra*] (explaining distinction between speech and conduct, and holding that expressive aspect of conduct does not exempt it from warranted regulation). The First Amendment interest in retaining possession of the threatening posters is *de minimis,* while ACLA's continued possession of them constitutes part of the threat. The court heard all the evidence, which included testimony that some defendants obstructed justice and ignored injunctions. Accordingly, we cannot say that the turn-over order was broader than necessary to assure that this particular threat will not be used again.

. . .

CONCLUSION

A "threat of force" for purposes of FACE is properly defined in accordance with our long-standing test on "true threats," as "whether a reasonable person would foresee that the statement would be interpreted by those to whom the maker communicates the statement as a serious expression of intent to harm or assault." This, coupled with the statute's requirement of intent to intimidate, comports with the First Amendment.

We have reviewed the record and are satisfied that use of the Crist Poster, the Deadly Dozen Poster, and the individual plaintiffs' listing in the Nuremberg Files constitute a true threat. In three prior incidents, a "wanted"-type poster identifying a specific doctor who provided abortion services was circulated, and the doctor named on the poster was killed. ACLA and physicians knew of this, and both understood the significance of the particular posters specifically identifying each of them. ACLA realized that "wanted" or "guilty" posters had a threatening meaning that physicians would take seriously. In conjunction with the "guilty" posters, being listed on a Nuremberg Files scorecard for abortion providers impliedly threatened physicians with being next on a hit list. To this extent only, the Files are also a true threat. However, the Nuremberg Files are protected speech.

There is substantial evidence that these posters were prepared and disseminated to intimidate physicians from providing reproductive health services. Thus, ACLA was appropriately found liable for a true threat to intimidate under FACE.

Holding ACLA accountable for this conduct does not impinge on legitimate protest or advocacy. Restraining it from continuing to threaten these physicians burdens speech no more than necessary.

Therefore, we affirm the judgment in all respects but for punitive damages, as to which we remand.

AFFIRMED IN PART; VACATED AND REMANDED IN PART.

REINHARDT, Circuit Judge, with whom KOZINSKI, KLEINFELD, and BERZON, Circuit Judges, join, dissenting:

I concur fully in both Judge Kozinski's and Judge Berzon's dissents. The differences between the majority and dissenting opinions with respect to the First Amendment are clear. I write separately to emphasize one point: the majority rejects the concept that speech made in a political forum on issues of public concern warrants heightened scrutiny. [ ] This rejection, if allowed to stand, would significantly weaken the First Amendment protections we now enjoy. It is a fundamental tenet of First Amendment jurisprudence that political speech in a public arena is different from purely private speech directed at an individual. [ ] Political speech, ugly or frightening as it may sometimes be, lies at the heart of our democratic process. Private threats delivered one-on-one do not. The majority's unwillingness to recognize the difference is extremely troublesome. For this reason alone, I would be compelled to dissent.

KOZINSKI, Circuit Judge, with whom Circuit Judges REINHARDT, O'SCANNLAIN, KLEINFELD and BERZON join, dissenting:

The majority writes a lengthy opinion in a vain effort to justify a crushing monetary judgment and a strict injunction against speech protected by the First Amendment. The apparent thoroughness of the opinion, addressing a variety of issues that are not in serious dispute, masks the fact that the majority utterly fails to apply its own definition of a threat, and affirms the verdict and injunction when the evidence in the record does not support a finding that defendants threatened plaintiffs.

After meticulously canvassing the caselaw, the majority correctly distills the following definition of a true threat: "a statement which, in the entire context and under all the circumstances, a reasonable person would foresee would be interpreted by those to whom the statement is communicated as *a serious expression of intent to inflict bodily harm upon that person.*" [ ] The emphasized language is crucial, because it is not illegal—and cannot be made so-merely to say things that would frighten or intimidate the listener. For example, when a doctor says, "You have cancer and will die within six months," it is not a threat, even though you almost certainly will be frightened. Similarly, "Get out of the way of that bus" is not a threat, even though it is said in order to scare you into changing your behavior. By contrast, "If you don't stop performing abortions, I'll kill you" is a true threat and surely illegal.

The difference between a true threat and protected expression is this: A true threat warns of violence or other harm that the speaker controls. Thus, when a doctor tells a patient, "Stop smoking or you'll die of lung cancer," that is not a threat because the doctor obviously can't cause the harm to come about. Similarly, "If you walk in that neighborhood late at night, you're going to get mugged" is not a threat, unless it is clear that the speaker himself (or one of his associates) will be doing the mugging.

In this case, none of the statements on which liability was premised were overtly threatening. On the contrary, the two posters and the web page, by their explicit terms, foreswore the use of violence and advocated lawful means of persuading plaintiffs to stop performing abortions or punishing them for continuing to do so. Nevertheless, because context matters, the statements could reasonably be interpreted as an effort to intimidate plaintiffs into ceasing their abortion-related activities. If that were enough to strip the speech of First Amendment protection, there would be nothing left to decide. But the Supreme Court has told us that "[s]peech does not lose its protected character . . . simply because it may embarrass others *or coerce them into action*." [*Claiborne*] (emphasis added). In other words, some forms of intimidation enjoy constitutional protection.

. . . [S]tatements that are intimidating, even coercive, are protected by the First Amendment, so long as the speaker does not threaten that he, or someone acting in concert with him, will resort to violence if the warning is not heeded.

The majority recognizes that this is the standard it must apply, yet when it undertakes the critical task of canvassing the record for evidence that defendants made a true threat—a task the majority acknowledges we must perform *de novo*, [   ], its opinion fails to come up with any proof that defendants communicated an intent to inflict bodily harm upon plaintiffs.

Buried deep within the long opinion is a single paragraph that cites evidence supporting the finding that the two wanted posters prepared by defendants constituted a true threat. [   ] The majority does not point to any statement by defendants that they intended to inflict bodily harm on plaintiffs, nor is there any evidence that defendants took any steps whatsoever to plan or carry out physical violence against anyone. Rather, the majority relies on the fact that "the poster format itself had acquired currency as a death threat for abortion providers. Gunn was killed after his poster was released; Britton was killed after his poster was released; and Patterson was killed after his poster was released." [   ] But neither Dr. Gunn nor Dr. Patterson was killed by anyone connected with the posters bearing their names. [   ] In fact, Dr. Patterson's murder may have been unrelated to abortion: He was killed in what may have been a robbery attempt five months after his poster was issued; the crime is unsolved and plaintiffs' counsel conceded that no evidence ties his murderer to any anti-abortion group. [   ]

The record reveals one instance where an individual—Paul Hill, who is not a defendant in this case—participated in the preparation of the poster depicting a physician, Dr. Britton, and then murdered him some seven months later. All others who helped to make that poster, as well as those who prepared the other posters, did not resort to violence. And for years, hundreds of other posters circulated, condemning particular doctors with no violence ensuing. [ ] There is therefore no pattern showing that people who prepare wanted-type posters then engage in physical violence. To the extent the posters indicate a pattern, it is that almost all people engaged in poster-making were non-violent.

The majority tries to fill this gaping hole in the record by noting that defendants "kn[ew] the fear generated among those in the reproductive health services community who were singled out for identification on a 'wanted'-type poster." [ ] But a statement does not become a true threat because it instills fear in the listener; as noted above, many statements generate fear in the listener, yet are not true threats and therefore may not be punished or enjoined consistent with the First Amendment. [ ] In order for the statement to be a threat, it must send the message that the speakers themselves—or individuals acting in concert with them—will engage in physical violence. The majority's own definition of true threat makes this clear. Yet the opinion points to no evidence that defendants who prepared the posters would have been understood by a reasonable listener as saying that *they* will cause the harm.

. . .

Even assuming that one could somehow distill a true threat from the posters themselves, the majority opinion is still fatally defective . . .: Where the speaker is engaged in public political speech, the public statements themselves cannot be the sole proof that they were true threats, unless the speech directly threatens actual injury to identifiable individuals. Absent such an unmistakable, specific threat, there must be evidence *aside from the political statements themselves* showing that the public speaker would himself or in conspiracy with others inflict unlawful harm. [ ] The majority cites not a scintilla of evidence—other than the posters themselves—that plaintiffs or someone associated with them would carry out the threatened harm.

Given this lack of evidence, the posters can be viewed, at most, as a call to arms for *other* abortion protesters to harm plaintiffs. However, the Supreme Court made it clear that under *Brandenburg,* encouragement or even advocacy of violence is protected by the First Amendment: "[M]ere *advocacy* of the use of force or violence does not remove speech from the protection of the First Amendment." *Claiborne Hardware,* 458 U.S. at 927, 102 S.Ct. 3409 (citing *Brandenburg,* 395 U.S. at 447) (emphasis in the original). *Claiborne Hardware* in fact goes much farther; it cautions that where liability is premised on "politically motivated" activities, we must "examine critically the basis on which liability was imposed." *Id.* at 915, 102 S.Ct. 3409. As the Court explained, "Since respondents would impose liability on the basis of a public address—which predominantly contained highly charged political rhetoric lying at the core of the First Amendment—we approach this suggested basis for liability with extreme care." [   ] This is precisely what the majority does *not* do; were it to do so, it would have no choice but to reverse.

The activities for which the district court held defendants liable were unquestionably of a political nature. There is no allegation that any of the posters in this case disclosed private information improperly obtained. We must therefore assume that the information in the posters was obtained from public sources. All defendants did was reproduce this public information in a format designed to convey a political viewpoint and to achieve political goals. . . . The Nuremberg Files website is clearly an expression of a political point of view. The posters and the website are designed both to rally political support for the views espoused by defendants, and to intimidate plaintiffs and others like them into desisting abortion-related activities. This political agenda may not be to the liking of many people—political dissidents are often unpopular—but the speech, including the intimidating message, does not constitute a direct threat because there is no evidence other than the speech itself that the speakers intend to resort to physical violence if their threat is not heeded.

In determining whether the record here supports a finding of true threats, not only the reasoning but also the facts of *Claiborne Hardware* are highly relevant. *Claiborne Hardware* arose out of a seven-year effort (1966 to 1972) to obtain racial justice in Claiborne County, Mississippi. *Claiborne Hardware*, 458 U.S. at 898, 102 S.Ct. 3409. The campaign employed a variety of tactics, one among them being the boycotting of white merchants. *Id.* at 900, 102 S.Ct. 3409. The boycott and other concerted activities were organized by the NAACP, in the person of its Mississippi field secretary Charles Evers, as well as by other black organizations and leaders. *Id.* at 898–900, 102 S.Ct. 3409.

In order to persuade or coerce recalcitrant blacks to join the boycott, the organizers resorted to a variety of enforcement mechanisms. These included the posting of store watchers outside the boycotted stores. These watchers, also known as "Black Hats" or "Deacons," would "identif[y] those who traded with the merchants." *Id.* at 903, 102 S.Ct. 3409. The names were collected and "read aloud at meetings at the First Baptist Church and published in a local black newspaper." *Id.* at 909, 102 S.Ct. 3409. Evers made several speeches containing threats-including those of physical violence-against the boycott violators. *Id.* at 900 n. 28, 902, 926–27, 102 S.Ct. 3409. In addition, a number of violent acts—including shots fired at individuals' homes—were committed against the boycott breakers. *Id.* at 904–06, 102 S.Ct. 3409.

The lawsuit that culminated in the *Claiborne Hardware* opinion was brought against scores of individuals and several organizations, including the NAACP. The state trial court found defendants liable in damages and entered "a broad permanent injunction," which prohibited the defendants from engaging in virtually all activities associated with the boycott, including picketing and using store watchers. *Id.* at 893, 102 S.Ct. 3409. The Mississippi Supreme Court affirmed, finding liability based on a variety of state law theories, some of which had as their gravamen the use of force or threat of force by those engaged in the boycott. *Id.* at 894–95, 102 S.Ct. 3409.

The United States Supreme Court began its opinion in *Claiborne Hardware* by noting that "[t]he term 'concerted action' encompasses unlawful conspiracies and constitutionally protected assemblies" and that "certain joint activities have a 'chameleon-like' character." *Id.* at 888, 102 S.Ct. 3409. The Claiborne County boycott, the Court noted, "had such a character; it included elements of criminality and elements of majesty." *Id.* The Court concluded that the state courts had erred in ascribing to all boycott organizers illegal acts—including violence and threats of violence—of some of the activists. The fact that certain activists engaged in such unlawful conduct, the Court held, could not be attributed to the other boycott organizers, unless it could be shown that the latter had personally committed or authorized the unlawful acts. *Id.* at 932–34, 102 S.Ct. 3409.

In the portion of *Claiborne Hardware* that is most relevant to our case, *id.* at 927–32, 102 S.Ct. 3409, the Court dealt with the liability of the NAACP as a result of certain speeches made by Charles Evers. In these speeches, Evers seemed to threaten physical violence against blacks who refused to abide by the boycott, saying that:

- the boycott organizers knew the identity of those members of the black community who violated the boycott, *id.* at 900 n. 28, 102 S.Ct. 3409;

- discipline would be taken against the violators, *id.* at 902, 927, 102 S.Ct. 3409;

- "[i]f we catch any of you going in any of them racist stores, we're gonna break your damn neck," *id.* at 902, 102 S.Ct. 3409;

- "the Sheriff could not sleep with boycott violators at night" in order to protect them, *id.;*

- "blacks who traded with white merchants would be *answerable to him,*" *id.* at 900 n. 28, 102 S.Ct. 3409 (emphasis in the original).

These statements, the Supreme Court recognized, "might have been understood as inviting an unlawful form of discipline or, at least, *as intending to createa fear of violence whether or not improper discipline was specifically intended.*" *Id.* at 927, 102 S.Ct. 3409 (emphasis added). Noting that such statements might not be constitutionally protected, the Court proceeded to consider various exceptions to the rule that speech may not be prohibited or punished.

The Court concluded that the statements in question were not "fighting words" under the rule of *Chaplinsky v. New Hampshire,* 315 U.S. 568, 572–73, 62 S.Ct. 766, 86 L.Ed. 1031 (1942); nor were they likely to cause an immediate panic, under the rule of *Schenck v. United*

States, 249 U.S. 47, 52, 39 S.Ct. 247, 63 L.Ed. 470 (1919) ("The most stringent protection of free speech would not protect a man in falsely shouting fire in a theater and causing a panic."). *Id.* at 927, 102 S.Ct. 3409. Nor was the speech in question an incitement under *Brandenburg v. Ohio,* 395 U.S. 444, 89 S.Ct. 1827, 23 L.Ed.2d 430 (1969), because it resulted in no immediate harm to anyone. *Id.* at 927–28, 102 S.Ct. 3409. The Court also cited, and found inapplicable, its one case that had held "true threats" were not constitutionally protected, *Watts v. United States,* 394 U.S. 705, 705, 89 S.Ct. 1399, 22 L.Ed.2d 664 (1969). *Id.* at 928 n. 71, 102 S.Ct. 3409. The mere fact that the statements could be understood "as intending to create a fear of violence," *id.* at 927, 102 S.Ct. 3409, was insufficient to make them "true threats" under *Watts.*

The Court then considered the theory that the speeches themselves—which suggested violence against boycott violators—might constitute authorization or encouragement of unlawful activity, but flatly rejected it. *Id.* at 929, 102 S.Ct. 3409. The Court noted that the statements were part of the "emotionally charged rhetoric of Charles Evers' speeches," and therefore could not be viewed as authorizing lawless action, even if they literally did so: "Strong and effective extemporaneous rhetoric cannot be nicely channeled in purely dulcet phrases. An advocate must be free to stimulate his audience with spontaneous and emotional appeals for unity and action in a common cause. When such appeals do not incite lawless action, they must be regarded as protected speech." *Id.* at 928, 102 S.Ct. 3409. Absent "evidence—apart from the speeches themselves—that Evers authorized ... violence" against the boycott breakers, neither he nor the NAACP could be held liable for, or enjoined from, speaking. *Id.* at 929, 102 S.Ct. 3409. In other words, even when public speech sounds menacing, even when it *expressly* calls for violence, it cannot form the basis of liability unless it amounts to incitement or directly threatens actual injury to particular individuals.

While set in a different time and place, and involving a very different political cause, *Claiborne Hardware* bears remarkable similarities to our case:

- Like *Claiborne Hardware,* this case involves a concerted effort by a variety of groups and individuals in pursuit of a common political cause. Some of the activities were lawful, others were not. In both cases, there was evidence that the various players communicated with each other and, at times, engaged in concerted action. The Supreme Court, however, held that mere association with groups or individuals who pursue unlawful conduct is an insufficient basis for the imposition of liability, unless it is shown that the defendants actually participated in or authorized the illegal conduct.

- Both here and in *Claiborne Hardware,* there were instances of actual violence that followed heated rhetoric. The Court made clear, however, that unless the violence follows *promptly* after the speeches, thus meeting the stringent *Brandenburg* standard for incitement, no liability could be imposed on account of the speech.

• The statements on which liability was premised in both cases were made during the course of political rallies and had a coercive effect on the intended targets. Yet the Supreme Court held in *Claiborne Hardware* that coercion alone could not serve as the basis for liability, because it had not been shown-by evidence aside from the political speeches themselves-that defendants or their agents were involved in or authorized actual violence.

• In *Claiborne Hardware,* the boycott organizers gathered facts— the identity of those who violated the boycott—and publicized them to the community by way of speeches and a newspaper. As in our case, this ostentatious gathering of information, and publication thereof, were intended to put pressure on those whose names were publicized, and perhaps put them in fear that they will become objects of violence by members of the community. Yet the Supreme Court held that this could not form the basis for liability.

To the extent *Claiborne Hardware* differs from our case, the difference makes ours a far weaker case for the imposition of liability. To begin with, Charles Evers's speeches in *Claiborne Hardware* explicitly threatened physical violence. Referring to the boycott violators, Evers repeatedly went so far as to say that "we," presumably including himself, would "break your damn neck." 458 U.S. at 902, 102 S.Ct. 3409. In our case, the defendants never called for violence at all, and certainly said nothing suggesting that they personally would be involved in any violence against the plaintiffs.

Another difference between the two cases is that the record in *Claiborne Hardware* showed a concerted action between the boycott organizers, all of whom operated within close physical proximity in a small Mississippi county. By contrast, there is virtually no evidence that defendants had engaged in any concerted action with any of the other individuals who prepared "wanted" posters in the past.

The most striking difference between the two cases is that one of Evers's speeches in *Claiborne Hardware,* which expressly threatened violence against the boycott violators, was in fact followed by violence; he then made additional speeches, again referring to violence against boycott breakers. 458 U.S. at 900, 102 S.Ct. 3409 (April 1966 speech), at 902, 102 S.Ct. 3409 (April 1969 speeches). By contrast, the record here contains *no* evidence that violence was committed against any doctor after his name appeared on defendants' posters or web page.

The opinion's effort to distinguish *Claiborne Hardware* does not bear scrutiny. The majority claims that in *Claiborne Hardware,* "there was no context to give the speeches (including the expression 'break your neck') the implication of ... directly threatening unlawful conduct." Maj. op. at 1073. As explained above, the majority is quite wrong on this point, *see* pp. 1063 *supra,* but it doesn't matter anyway: Evers's statements were threatening on their face. Not only did he speak of breaking necks and inflicting "discipline," he used the first person plural "we" to indicate that he himself and those associated with him would be doing the neck-breaking, 458 U.S. at 902, 102 S.Ct. 3409, and he said that "blacks who traded with white merchants would be *answerable to him*," *id*. at 900 n. 28, 102 S.Ct. 3409 (emphasis in the original).

It is possible—as the majority suggests—that Evers's statements were "hyperbolic vernacular," Maj. op. at 1073, [FN10] but the trier of fact in that case found otherwise. The Supreme Court nevertheless held that the statements ought to be treated as hyperbole because of their political content. By any measure, the statements in our case are far less threatening on their face, yet the majority chooses to defer to the jury's determination that they were true threats.

The majority also relies on the fact that the posters here "were publicly distributed, but personally targeted." Maj. op. at 1085. But the threats in *Claiborne Hardware* were also individually targeted. Store watchers carefully noted the names of blacks who entered the boycotted stores, and those names were published in a newspaper and read out loud at the First Baptist Church, where Evers delivered his speeches. 458 U.S. at 903–04, 102 S.Ct. 3409. When speaking of broken necks and other discipline, Evers was quite obviously referring to those individuals who had been identified as defying the boycott; in fact, he stated explicitly that he knew their identity and that they would be answerable to him. *Id*. at 900 n. 28, 102 S.Ct. 3409. The majority's opinion simply cannot be squared with *Claiborne Hardware*.

Claiborne Hardware ultimately stands for the proposition that those who would punish or deter protected speech must make a very substantial showing that the speech stands outside the umbrella of the First Amendment. This message was reinforced recently by the Supreme Court in [*Ashcroft, p. ___, supra*], where the government sought to prohibit simulated child pornography without satisfying the stringent requirements of [*Miller, p. ___, supra*]. The Court rejected this effort, even though the government had earnestly argued that suppression of the speech would advance vital legitimate governmental interests, such as avoiding the exploitation of real children and punishing producers of real child pornography. *See id*. at 1402–04; *see also id*. at 1406–07 (Thomas, J., concurring in the judgment); *id*. at 1407–09 (O'Connor, J., concurring in the judgment in part and dissenting in part); *id*. at 1411–12 (Rehnquist, C.J., dissenting). The Court held that the connection between the protected speech and the harms in question is simply too "contingent and indirect" to warrant suppression. *Id*. at 1401–02; *see also id*. at 1403–04 ("The Government has shown no more than a remote connection between speech that might encourage thoughts or impulses and any resulting child abuse."). As Judge Berzon notes in her inspired dissent, defendants' speech, on its face, is political speech on an issue that is at the cutting edge of moral and political debate in our society, *see* Berzon Dissent at 1101–02, and political speech lies far closer to the core of the First Amendment than does simulated child pornography. "The right to think is the beginning of freedom, and speech must be protected from the government because speech is the beginning of thought." *Free Speech Coalition*, 122 S.Ct. at 1403–04. If political speech is to be deterred or punished, the rationale of *Free Speech Coalition* requires a far more robust and direct connection to unlawful conduct than these plaintiffs have offered or the majority has managed to demonstrate. The evidence that, despite their explicitly non-threatening language, the Deadly Dozen poster and the Nuremberg Files website were true threats is too "contingent and indirect" to satisfy the standard of *Free Speech Coalition.*

. . .

We have recognized that statements communicated directly to the target are much more likely to be true threats than those, as here, communicated as part of a public protest. Our case law also instructs that, in deciding whether the coercive speech is protected, it makes a big difference whether it is contained in a private communication-a face-to-face confrontation, a telephone call, a dead fish wrapped in newspaper— or is made during the course of public discourse. The reason for this distinction is obvious: Private speech is aimed only at its target. Public speech, by contrast, seeks to move public opinion and to encourage those of like mind. Coercive speech that is part of public discourse enjoys far greater protection than identical speech made in a purely private context.

. . .

Finally, a word about the remedy. The majority affirms a crushing liability verdict, including the award of punitive damages, in addition to the injunction. An injunction against political speech is bad enough, but the liability verdict will have a far more chilling effect. Defendants will be destroyed financially by a huge debt that is almost certainly not dischargeable in bankruptcy; it will haunt them for the rest of their lives and prevent them from ever again becoming financially self-sufficient. The Supreme Court long ago recognized that the fear of financial ruin can have a seriously chilling effect on all manner of speech, and will surely cause other speakers to hesitate, lest they find themselves at the mercy of a local jury. *See N.Y. Times Co. v. Sullivan,* 376 U.S. 254, 277– 79, 84 S.Ct. 710, 11 L.Ed.2d 686 (1964). The lesson of what a local jury has done to defendants here will not be lost on others who would engage in heated political rhetoric in a wide variety of causes.

In that regard, a retrospective liability verdict is far more damaging than an injunction; the latter at least gives notice of what is prohibited and what is not. The fear of liability for damages, and especially punitive damages, puts the speaker at risk as to what a jury might later decide is a true threat, and how vindictive it might feel towards the speaker and his cause. In this case, defendants said nothing remotely threatening, yet they find themselves crucified financially. Who knows what other neutral statements a jury might imbue with a menacing meaning based on the activities of unrelated parties. In such circumstances, it is especially important for an appellate court to perform its constitutional function of reviewing the record to ensure that the speech in question clearly falls into one of the narrow categories that is unprotected by the First Amendment. The majority fails to do this.

While today it is abortion protesters who are singled out for punitive treatment, the precedent set by this court—the broad and uncritical deference to the judgment of a jury—will haunt dissidents of all political stripes for many years to come. Because this is contrary to the principles of the First Amendment as explicated by the Supreme Court . . . , I respectfully dissent.

BERZON, Circuit Judge, with whom REINHARDT, KOZINSKI, and KLEINFELD, Circuit Judges, join, and O'SCANNLAIN, Circuit Judge, joins as to Part III only, dissenting:

This case is proof positive that hard cases make bad law, and that when the case is *very* hard—meaning that competing legal and moral imperatives pull with impressive strength in opposite directions—there is the distinct danger of making *very* bad law.

The majority opinion in this case suitably struggles with the difficult First Amendment issues before us concerning whether the posters and website at issue are or are not First Amendment protected speech. The legal standard the majority applies, however, is, in my view, insufficiently cognizant of underlying First Amendment values, for reasons that are largely explained in Judge Kozinski's dissent, and for additional reasons that I develop below.

Moreover, the majority, in an offhand way, also decides two evidentiary issues that, I can say with some confidence, would not be decided so summarily, and would probably not be decided in the same way, were this a less wrenching case on its facts. Keeping one's eyes on the broader picture is not always easy when people's lives—in this case the lives of medical professionals—are being severely disrupted because they are performing constitutionally protected activities in a perfectly lawful manner at the behest of people who want their services and are entitled to have them. As judges, though, we need to recognize that we are *not* writing for this day and place only, and that rulings that appear peripheral in the present context will take on great significance as applied in another.

I

The First Amendment and True Threats

1. *Clarifying the issue:* The reason this is a hard First Amendment case becomes somewhat obscured in all the factual detail and quotation of precedent that we as judges engage in. The essential problem—one that, as far as I am aware, is unique in the plethora of "threat" cases and perhaps more generally in First Amendment jurisprudence—is that the speech for which the defendants are being held liable in damages and are enjoined from reiterating in the future is, on its face, clearly, indubitably, and quintessentially the kind of communication that is fully protected by the First Amendment.

The point is not simply that the two posters and the Nuremberg files contain no *explicit* threats that take them outside the free speech umbrella. We are not talking simply about ambiguous or implicit threats that depend on context for their meaning, such as the Ryder trucks in *United States v. Hart,* 212 F.3d 1067 (8th Cir.2000). Rather, the pivotal issue for me is that what the communications in this case *do* contain has all the attributes that numerous cases and commentators have identified as core factors underlying the special protection accorded communication under our Constitution.

The posters and website are all public presentations on a matter of current moral and political importance; they provide information to the public on that matter and propose a—peaceful, legal—course of action; and they were presented with explicit reference to great moral and political controversies of the past. Cases that are a virtual First Amendment "greatest hits" establish that these kinds of expressions—those that provide information to the public (particularly when directed at publicly-available media), publish opinions on matters of public controversy, and urge others to action—are the kinds of speech central to our speech-protective regime, and remain so even when the message conveyed is, in substance, form, or both, anathema to some or all of the intended audience. [　]

.　.　.

2. *An analogy:* Stated in those terms, the issue bears a close resemblance to that faced by the courts with regard to First Amendment limitations on defamation actions, beginning with *New York Times Co. v. Sullivan.* Like "true threats," false speech has long been understood as a category of communication that contains few of the attributes that trigger constitutional speech protection and so great a likelihood of harming others that we refer to the speech as being beyond the protection of the First Amendment. [　] Like "true threats," false, defamatory speech can severely disrupt peoples' lives, both by affecting them emotionally (as does apprehension of danger) and by impairing their social ties, their professional activities, and their ability to earn a living (as does the perceived need to protect oneself from physical harm).

The Supreme Court since the 1960s has developed a set of discrete principles designed *not* to provide false speech with constitutional protection, but to erect, on an ascending scale depending upon the perceived value of the particular kind of speech to the common dialogue that the First Amendment is designed to foster, doctrinal protections within defamation law that minimize self-censorship of truthful speech. Those protections are based upon realistic assessment of the vagaries of litigation and the fear of crippling damages liability.

.　.　.

Our problem here is similar. Any "true threats" within the three communications at issue were encased in documents and public events that promoted—at least for those listeners not "in the know"—precisely the kind of "debate on public issues [that] should be uninhibited, robust, and wide-open, and that . . . may well include vehement, caustic, and sometimes unpleasantly sharp attacks. . . ." *New York Times,* 376 U.S. at 270, 84 S.Ct. 710. True, the targeted medical professionals and clinics were not public officials, but they were engaged in activities that the defendants, rightly or wrongly, regarded as both morally reprehensible and a matter for eventual governmental proscription through the political process (presumably through a constitutional amendment). Moreover, as both the majority and Judge Kozinski recognize, the posters and website remained core First Amendment speech even though—quite aside from any coded threat of physical harm—they exposed the targeted plaintiffs to other, nonviolent but still extremely disturbing, interference with their daily lives (in the form of unwanted public exposure and inflammatory rhetoric directed at them, their families, and their customers, both at home and at work) and even if they induced fear in the plaintiffs that people *unconnected with the defendants* might harm them.

Under these circumstances, the question for me becomes devising standards that, like the constitutional defamation standards that vary with the strength of the protection of the communication, rely not on an unitary "true threats" standard, as does the majority, but on considerations that lessen the danger of mistaken court verdicts and resulting self-censorship to a greater or lesser degree depending upon the nature of the speech in question and the role of speech of that nature in the scheme of the First Amendment.

3. *Some constitutional parameters:* Judge Kozinski, in his dissent, makes one important suggestion toward this end with which, for all the reasons already canvassed, I fully agree: He suggests that "statements communicated directly to the target are much more likely to be true threats than those, as here, communicated as part of a public protest." [ ] As a first cut at separating out the kinds of allegedly threatening communications that are central to First Amendment values and therefore must be tested by particularly stringent criteria before they can be prohibited, these two criteria—the public nature of the presentation and content addressing a public issue (which can include matters of social or economic as well as political import for the individuals involved, [   ].

        . . .

        . . . The criteria the Second Circuit [has] suggested to police the dividing line were that "the threat on its face and in the circumstances in which it is made is so unequivocal, unconditional, immediate and specific as to the person threatened, as to convey a gravity of purpose and imminent prospect of execution." . . .

[These] criteria for adjudging the protection accorded alleged threats uttered in the course of public communications on public issues seem appropriate to me . . . with one exception, an addition, and some explication:

First, the exception: I would not include the imminence or immediacy of the threatened action as a prerequisite to finding a true threat delivered as part of a public speech, if all of the other factors were present. The immediacy requirement calls to mind the standard the Supreme Court erected for proscription of inciting speech in *Brandenburg*. But as the majority can be read to recognize and as Judge Kozinski well explains, the separate constitutional category of unprotected speech for threats does not include statements that induce fear of violence by third parties.

Where there is no threat, explicit or implicit, that the speaker or someone under his or her control intends to harm someone, a statement inducing fear of physical harm must be either (1) a prediction or warning of injury, or (2) an inducement or encouragement of someone else to cause the injury. The former is, as Judge Kozinski suggests, clearly entitled to protection under the First Amendment as either informative or persuasive speech. The latter kind of statement may or may not be protected. Whether it is or not must be governed by the strict inducement standard of *Brandenburg* if the more than fifty years of contentious development of the protection of advocacy of illegal action is not to be for naught. [   ]

One can, however, justify a somewhat different standard for judging the constitutionality of a restriction upon threats than for a restriction upon inducement of violence or other illegal action. There is a difference for speech-protective purposes between a statement that one oneself intends to do something and a statement encouraging or advocating that someone else do it. The latter will result in harmful action only if someone else is persuaded by the advocacy. If there is adequate time for that person to reflect, any harm will be due to another's considered act. The speech itself, in that circumstance, does not create the injury, although it may make it more likely. The Supreme Court has essentially decided that free expression would be too greatly burdened by anticipatory squelching of advocacy which can work harm only indirectly if at all. [   ]

A true threat, in contrast, implies a firmness of purpose by the person speaking, not mediated through anyone else's rational or emotional reaction to the speech. Threatening speech thereby works directly the harms of apprehension and disruption, whether the apparent resolve proves bluster or not and whether the injury is threatened to be immediate or delayed. Further, the social costs of a threat can be heightened rather than dissipated if the threatened injury is promised for some fairly ascertainable time in the future—the "specific" prong—for then the apprehension and disruption directly caused by the threat will continue for a longer rather than a shorter period. So, while I would police vigorously the line between inducement and threats—as the jury instructions in this case did, although the majority opinion is less clear on this point—I would, where true threats are alleged, not require a finding of immediacy of the threatened harm.

Second, the addition: Although this court's cases on threats have not generally set any state of mind requirements, I would add to the *Kelner* requirements for proscribable threats in the public protest context the additional consideration whether the defendant subjectively intended the specific victims to understand the communication as an unequivocal threat that the speaker or his agents or coconspirators would physically harm them. Especially where the plaintiffs in such circumstances are relying *only* on surrounding context and are doing so to overcome the literal import of the words spoken, impairment of free public debate on public issues through self-censorship is a distinct possibility unless there is convincing proof that the literal meaning of the words was not what the defendants intended to convey.

The subjective intent requirement for alleged threats delivered in the course of public protest comports with Supreme Court precedent, both directly and by analogy. . . . [I]n *Brandenburg,* the Court held that in an incitement case, the plaintiff or the government must not only prove that a statement "is likely to incite or produce" imminent lawless action, but must also prove that the statement "is directed to inciting or producing" such action. [ ] This latter requirement is a subjective intent prerequisite, as it turns the speaker's liability in an incitement case on how the speaker intends others to understands his words. [ ]

With regard to this subjective intent requirement, there is no meaningful distinction between incitement cases and threat cases such as this one—that is, cases involving public protest speech, especially where the alleged threat, on its face, consisted entirely of advocacy. The First Amendment protects advocacy statements that are likely to produce imminent violent action, so long as the statements are not directed at producing such action. To do otherwise would be to endanger the First Amendment protection accorded advocacy of political change by holding speakers responsible for an impact they did not intend.

Similarly, a purely objective standard for judging the protection accorded such speech would chill speakers from engaging in facially protected public protest speech that some might think, in context, will be understood as a true threat although not intended as such. Unsure of whether their rough and tumble protected speech would be interpreted by a reasonable person as a threat, speakers will silence themselves rather than risk liability. Even though the Supreme Court has stated that protected political speech "is often vituperative, abusive, and inexact," speakers wishing to take advantage of these protected rhetorical means may be fearful of doing so under the majority's purely objective approach. [ ]

. . .

Third, the explication: "Unequivocal" cannot mean literal: Ryder trucks, in the United States in the 1990s, and burning crosses, in the United States in the twentieth and twenty-first centuries, have unambiguous meanings that the individuals targeted will be hurt (at least unless they do what the perpetrator of the threat wants them to do, whether it be stop performing abortions or move out of town). Instead, "unequivocal" means to me unambiguous, given the context. As such, the requirement is essentially a heightened burden of proof, requiring that a threatening meaning be clearly and convincingly apparent. And in determining whether that proof standard has been met, I would continue to apply the objective standard the majority embraces, based on our cases, in determining whether the speech in fact communicates an intent to harm specific individuals.

This case, I repeat, is uniquely difficult because to perceive a threat, one must *disregard* the actual language used and rely on context to *negate* the ordinary meaning of the communication. Further, the actual language is, in its own right, core First Amendment speech, speech that to a naive reader communicates protected information and ideas. So the crux of the plaintiffs' cause of action (once one accepts that only statements that evince an intention by the speaker or his or her agents to carry out the threat can be actionable) is really an assertion that the defendants were using Aesopian language or could be understood as doing so, and that the context in which the speech must be viewed provides the necessary evidence of the defendants' true, albeit coded, meaning.[11]

The first set of contextual evidence involves the poster/murder/poster/murder pattern the majority principally relies upon. Had the murders—or any murders, or any serious violence—been committed by the defendants and had the plaintiffs known that, the inference from the poster/murder pattern that the publication by them of posters similar to those previously followed by a murder might be a strong one. The inference would be stronger had the defendants also put out the earlier posters and had the plaintiffs known that. Neither is the case.

Plaintiffs' main submission to fill this gap was extensive evidence concerning the defendants' opinions condoning the use of violence against medical professionals who perform abortions, including general statements to that effect and particular statements concerning the people who murdered the doctors depicted on the previous posters, stating that their actions were justified and that they should be acquitted. Plaintiffs' closing argument, for example, went on for pages and pages about defendants' meetings and writings concerning the "justifiability of the use of force."

This evidence is certainly of some pertinence as to what the defendants may have intended to do. It is more likely that someone who believes in violence would intentionally threaten to commit it. It is also pertinent to what persons in the plaintiffs' position-that is, persons involved in the abortion controversy and alert to the division of opinion within it—would likely understand concerning defendants' communication. Individuals who believe in violence are not only more likely to *threaten* to commit it but also actually to commit it, and so defendants' views might well influence plaintiffs' perception of their speech. And since the defendants would know that, defendants' *public* statements approving the use of violence against doctors who perform abortion are

11. The term "Aesopian language" developed in Tsarist Russia to refer to language that, like Aesop's fables, disguises the true meaning of speech by the use of metaphors, symbols and analogies, in order to avoid censorship.

relevant to whether reasonable speakers in defendants' position would expect their communications to be understood as threats.

At the same time, heavy reliance on evidence of this kind raises profound First Amendment issues of its own. One can not read plaintiffs' closing argument in this case without fearing that the jury was being encouraged to hold the defendants liable for their abstract advocacy of violence rather than for the alleged coded threats in the posters and website, the instructions to the jury to the contrary notwithstanding. And while advocacy evidence may make both an intent to threaten and a perception that there was a threat more likely, that is not unequivocally so. People do not always practice what they preach, as the stringent incitement standard recognizes. If we are serious about protecting advocacy of positions such as defendants' sanctioning of violence, as we are constrained to be, then permitting that protected speech to be the determinative "context" for holding other facially protected, public protest speech—the posters and website in this case—to be a "true threat" seems to me simply unacceptable under the First Amendment.

Finally, I note that the approach I've outlined here fully comports with *Claiborne Hardware*. *Claiborne Hardware* applied an "extreme care" standard in determining "liability on the basis of a public address-which predominantly contained highly charged political rhetoric." 458 U.S. at 926–927, 102 S.Ct. 3409. It went on to note that "[i]n the passionate atmosphere in which the speeches were delivered, they *might* have been understood as inviting an unlawful form of discipline or, at least, as intending to create a fear of violence whether or not improper discipline was specifically intended." *Id.* at 927, 102 S.Ct. 3409 (emphasis added). After reviewing the actual words used in context, however, the Court concluded that "Evers' addresses did not exceed the bounds of protected speech." *Id.* at 929, 102 S.Ct. 3409. As I read the opinion, it held, essentially, that the supposed threats were not on their face unequivocal and were not made unequivocal by any contextual factors. So here.

I would therefore hold that under the special rules I would apply to public protest speech such as that in this case, plaintiffs' judgment cannot stand because, after a proper review of the record, we would have to conclude that there was no unequivocal, unconditional and specific threat.

II

. . .

III

. . .

IV.

Conclusion

As waves of fervent protest movements have ebbed and flowed, the courts have been called upon to delineate and enforce the line between protected speech and communications that are both of little or no value as information, expression of opinion or persuasion of others, and are of considerable harm to others. This judicial task has never been an easy one, as it can require—as here—recognizing the right of protesting groups to question deeply held societal notions of what is morally, politically, economically, or socially correct and what is not. The defendants here pose a special challenge, as they vehemently condone the view that murdering abortion providers—individuals who are providing medical services protected by the Constitution—is morally justified.

But the defendants have not murdered anyone, and for all the reasons I have discussed, neither their advocacy of doing so nor the posters and website they published crossed the line into unprotected speech. If we are not willing to provide stringent First Amendment protection and a fair trial to those with whom we as a society disagree as well as those with whom we agree—as the Supreme Court did when it struck down the conviction of members of the Ku Klux Klan for their racist, violence—condoning speech in *Brandenburg*—the First Amendment will become a dead letter. Moreover, the next protest group—which may be a new civil rights movement or another group eventually vindicated by acceptance of their goals by society at large—will (unless we cease fulfilling our obligation as judges to be evenhanded) be censored according to the rules applied to the last. I do not believe that the defendants' speech here, on this record and given two major erroneous evidentiary rulings, crossed the line into unprotected speech. I therefore dissent.

Notes and Questions

1. The Supreme Court granted *certiorari*, ___ S.Ct. ___ (2002).

2. Is there any qualitative or quantitative difference between Charles Ever's speech at a public rally and ACLA's publication on the Internet?

3. Would it matter if someone reading ACLA's material proceeded to murder a doctor listed on the site?

D. ACCESS

One of the more controversial issues surrounding the Internet involves the practice of "spamming"—indiscriminately sending e-mail (usually commercial solicitations) to large numbers of people. Cyber Promotions is a company whose primary business is sending commercial e-mails. After numerous complaints from its subscribers, who in fact ended up paying to receive these e-mails, whether they wanted to or not, America Online (AOL) took various actions to discourage the internet service providers (ISPs) used by Cyber Promotions from continuing to give the company access to the Internet for the purpose of sending e-mail to AOL subscribers. As a result, some ISPs ceased to do business with Cyber Promotions.

Cyber Promotions filed a series of complaints against AOL seeking to require AOL to give Cyber Promotions access to AOL's subscribers. Among the company's arguments was a claim that AOL was violating its First Amendment rights:

Cyber argues, however, that "by providing Internet e-mail and acting as the sole conduit to its members' Internet e-mail boxes, AOL has opened up that part of its network and as such, has sufficiently devoted this domain for public use. This dedication of AOL's Internet e-mail accessway performs a public function in that it is open to the public, free of charge to any user, where public discourse, conversations and commercial transactions can and do take place."
[ ] Cyber therefore contends that AOL's Internet e-mail accessway is similar to the company town in Marsh v. Alabama, 326 U.S. 501 (1946), which the Supreme Court found performed a public function and therefore was a state actor.

The court rejected the First Amendment argument, noting that AOL was not performing any municipal functions. Furthermore, there were numerous alternative avenues of access to AOL subscribers, including setting up a website, which AOL subscribers could access if they so wished. AOL has now taken steps to block Cyber Promotions from continuing to send e-mail messages (which had numbered in the millions) to AOL subscribers. Cyber Promotions, Inc. v. American Online, 948 F.Supp. 436, 24 Med.L.Rptr. 2505 (E.D.Pa.1996).

A different question is presented when the government attempts to limit spamming. Several states have passed anti-spamming statutes. These statutes vary in their approaches to the problem. For example, the California statute gives ISPs the right to develop and enforce their own anti-spamming policies. Cal. Bus. & Prof. Code § 17538.45 (West 1998). Others authorize civil suits when specific guidelines are not followed. For example, the Nevada statute establishes civil liability for commercial e-mail messages unless the following conditions are met:

(a) [the sender] has a preexisting business or personal relationship with the recipient; the recipient has expressly consented to receive the item of e-mail from the person; or (c) the advertisement is readily identifiable as promotional or contains a statement providing that is an advertisement, and clearly and conspicuously provides (1) the legal name, complete street address and e-mail address of the sender and (2) a notice providing that the recipient may decline to receive additional e-mail and procedures for opting out.

Nev. Rev. Stat., §§ 41.730, 41.735 (1998).

Still a third approach is to place specific restrictions on spam. For example, Washington prohibits commercial e-mail messages, originated in Washington or sent to a Washington resident that misrepresent any identifying information (sender, point of origin, transmission path, etc.) or contain false or misleading information in the subject line. Wash. Rev. Code §§ 19.190.005–.030 (1998).

Early challenges to these laws have been unsuccessful. See State v. Heckel, 143 Wash.2d 824, 24 P.3d 404 (2001); Ferguson v. Friendfinder, 94 Cal.App.4th 1255, 115 Cal.Rptr.2d 258 (2002). In both cases the trial court's finding that the statute violated the dormant Commerce Clause was reversed on appeal.

E. ENCRYPTION

A major controversy raised by the Internet's global nature involves encryption software. The government has long restricted the export of encryption software claiming that it presents a threat to national security. However, encryption is now viewed as essential to the security of international electronic commerce. In addition, many see encryption as necessary to protect individual privacy from both government and private intrusion.

PETER D. JUNGER v. WILLIAM DALEY

United States Court of Appeals, Sixth Circuit, 2000.
209 F.3d 481, 28 Med.L.Rptr. 1609.

Before MARTIN, CHIEF JUDGE; CLAY, CIRCUIT JUDGE; WEBER, DISTRICT JUDGE.*

BOYCE F. MARTIN, JR., CHIEF JUDGE.

. . .

ENCRYPTION AND SOFTWARE BACKGROUND

Encryption is the process of converting a message from its original form ("plaintext") into a scrambled form ("ciphertext"). Most encryption today uses an algorithm, a mathematical transformation from plaintext to ciphertext, and a key that acts as a password. Generally, the security of the message depends on the strength of both the algorithm and the key.

Encryption has long been a tool in the conduct of military and foreign affairs. Encryption has many civil applications, including protecting communication and data sent over the Internet. As technology has progressed, the methods of encryption have changed from purely mechanical processes, such as the Enigma machines of Nazi Germany, to modern electronic processes. Today, messages can be encrypted through dedicated electronic hardware and also through general-purpose computers with the aid of encryption software.

For a general-purpose computer to encrypt data, it must use encryption software that instructs the computer's circuitry to execute the encoding process. Encryption software, like all computer software, can be in one of two forms: object code or source code. Object code represents

---

* The Honorable Herman J. Weber, United States District Judge for the Southern District of Ohio, sitting by designation.

computer instructions as a sequence of binary digits (0s and 1s) that can be directly executed by a computer's microprocessor. Source code represents the same instructions in a specialized programming language, such as BASIC, C, or Java. Individuals familiar with a particular computer programming language can read and understand source code. Source code, however, must be converted into object code before a computer will execute the software's instructions. This conversion is conducted by compiler software. . . .

REGULATORY BACKGROUND

The Export Administration Regulations create a comprehensive licensing scheme to control the export of nonmilitary technology, software, and commodities. In 1996, the President transferred export jurisdiction over nonmilitary encryption items from the State Department to the Commerce Department's Bureau of Export Administration.

The Regulations are structured around the Commodity Control List, which lists items subject to export control. . . .

Encryption software, including both source code and object code, is regulated under Export Control Classification Number 5D002 for national security reasons. [ ] In addition, encryption technology and encryption hardware are regulated for national security reasons under different Classification Numbers. Generally, the Regulations require a license for the export of all encryption items to all foreign destinations, except Canada. See 65 Fed.Reg. 2492, 2499 (to be codified at 15 C.F.R. § 742.15(a)). Although the regulations provide some exceptions, most encryption software in electronic form remains subject to the license requirements for export. Encryption software in printed form, however, is not subject to the Regulations. See 15 C.F.R. § 734.3(b)(2).

The Regulations define "export" as the "actual shipment or transmission of items subject to the EAR out of the United States." Id. § 734.2(b)(1). For encryption software, the definition of "export" also includes publication of the software on the Internet, unless steps are taken to restrict foreign access to the Internet site. See 65 Fed.Reg. 2492, 2496 (to be codified at 15 C.F.R. § 734.2(b)(9)(ii)).

FACTUAL BACKGROUND

Peter Junger is a professor at the Case Western University School of Law. Junger maintains sites on the World Wide Web that include information about courses that he teaches, including a computers and the law course. Junger wishes to post on his web site encryption source code that he has written to demonstrate how computers work. Such a posting is defined as an export under the Regulations.

On June 12, 1997, Junger submitted three applications to the Commerce Department, requesting determinations of commodity classifications for encryption software programs and other items. On July 4, the Export Administration told Junger that Classification Number 5D002 covered four of the five software programs he had submitted. Although it found that four programs were subject to the Regulations, the Export Administration found that the first chapter of Junger's textbook, Computers and the Law, was an allowable unlicensed export. Though deciding that the printed book chapter containing encryption code could be exported, the Export Administration stated that export of the book in electronic form would require a license if the text contained 5D002 software. Since receiving the classification determination, Junger has not applied for a license to export his classified encryption source code.

Junger filed this action to make a facial challenge to the Regulations on First Amendment grounds, seeking declaratory and injunctive relief that would permit him to engage in the unrestricted distribution of encryption software through his web site. Junger claims that encryption source code is protected speech. The district court granted summary judgment in favor of the defendants, holding that encryption source code is not protected under the First Amendment, that the Regulations are permissible content-neutral regulations, and that the Regulations are not subject to facial challenge on prior restraint grounds.

We review the grant of summary judgment de novo. [ ]

The issue of whether or not the First Amendment protects encryption source code is a difficult one because source code has both an expressive feature and a functional feature. The United States does not dispute that it is possible to use encryption source code to represent and convey information and ideas about cryptography and that encryption source code can be used by programmers and scholars for such informational purposes. Much like a mathematical or scientific formula, one can describe the function and design of encryption software by a prose explanation; however, for individuals fluent in a computer programming language, source code is the most efficient and precise means by which to communicate ideas about cryptography.

The district court concluded that the functional characteristics of source code overshadow its simultaneously expressive nature. The fact that a medium of expression has a functional capacity should not preclude constitutional protection. Rather, the appropriate consideration of the medium's functional capacity is in the analysis of permitted government regulation.

The Supreme Court has explained that "all ideas having even the slightest redeeming social importance," including those concerning "the advancement of truth, science, morality, and arts" have the full protection of the First Amendment. [ ] This protection is not reserved for purely expressive communication. The Supreme Court has recognized First Amendment protection for symbolic conduct, such as draft-card burning, that has both functional and expressive features. See [*O'Brien*, p. ___, *supra*].

The Supreme Court has expressed the versatile scope of the First Amendment by labeling as "unquestionably shielded" the artwork of Jackson Pollack, the music of Arnold Schoenberg, or the Jabberwocky verse of Lewis Carroll. [ ] Though unquestionably expressive, these things identified by the Court are not traditional speech. Particularly, a musical score cannot be read by the majority of the public but can be used as a means of communication among musicians. Likewise, computer source code, though unintelligible to many, is the preferred method of communication among computer programmers.

(1) Because computer source code is an expressive means for the exchange of information and ideas about computer programming, we hold that it is protected by the First Amendment.

(2) The functional capabilities of source code, and particularly those of encryption source code, should be considered when analyzing the governmental interest in regulating the exchange of this form of speech. Under intermediate scrutiny, the regulation of speech is valid, in part, if "it furthers an important or substantial governmental interest." [*O'Brien*] In [*Turner*, p. ___, *supra*], the Supreme Court noted that although an asserted governmental interest may be important, when the government defends restrictions on speech "it must do more than simply 'posit the existence of the disease sought to be cured.' "Id. [ ] The government "must demonstrate that the recited harms are real, not merely conjectural, and that the regulation will in fact alleviate these harms in a direct and material way." Id. We recognize that national security interests can outweigh the interests of protected speech and require the regulation of speech. In the present case, the record does not resolve whether the exercise of presidential power in furtherance of national security interests should overrule the interests in allowing the free exchange of encryption source code.

Before any level of judicial scrutiny can be applied to the Regulations, Junger must be in a position to bring a facial challenge to these regulations. In light of the recent amendments to the Export Administration Regulations, the district court should examine the new regulations to determine if Junger can bring a facial challenge.

For the foregoing reasons, we REVERSE the district court and REMAND the case to the district court for consideration of Junger's constitutional challenge to the amended regulations.

Notes and Questions

1. In a similar case, a mathematician challenged the export rules. The district court found them unconstitutional. The appellate court affirmed, Bernstein v. United States Department of Justice, 176 F.3d 1132 (9th Cir.1999). However, a petition for rehearing has been granted and the circuit court opinion withdrawn.

2. One complicating factor in these cases is the constantly changing technology. For example, the court notes that it would take 27–41 years to break a 56–bit encryption system by brute force. Within a month of the decision's being issued, a group of researchers, sponsored by the Electronic Frontier Foundation, decoded a message encrypted in the 56–bit version of the government's Data Encryption Standard (DES) code in

less than three days. The group used a home-made supercomputer built for $250,000. "U.S. Data Code is Unscrambled in 56 Hours," New York Times, July 17, 1998 at D–1.

We will address other issues relating to interactive computer communications in Chapters XIII–XVI.

Chapter XII

MEDIA CONCENTRATION

As we saw when considering the NBC case, the Commission has long been concerned about excessive concentration of control over the process of deciding what programs to present. There are several ways to attack the problem. One, utilized in that case, is to prevent the networks from imposing their power on the licensees. Another is to order licensees to obtain their programs from non-network sources for certain periods of the day. Still another, which gets at this problem indirectly but also attacks other problems, is to attempt to diversify the ownership of broadcast facilities.

As the new communications media gained reach and power, the Commission had similar concerns regarding concentration with and across the various industries. These concerns led the FCC to extend these methods of limiting concentration of control beyond the broadcast industry. In this chapter we consider these various media concentration rules.

The Commission has used its rulemaking powers primarily to handle technical and engineering matters, which can be addressed in quantitative terms—and which are more likely to lend themselves to uniform treatment without the need for exceptions.

The Commission has also used rulemaking to achieve diversity of control—again perhaps because the material lends itself to quantitative expression, such as how many stations a person should be allowed to control in a particular area. It is important to realize, however, that even though the Commission may choose to adopt specific rules to meet a problem, it must always consider requests for waivers of that rule if the public interest would be furthered by the waiver. The 1934 Act grants the Commission powers to act in the public interest, and, although a rule may operate in the public interest most of the time, some exceptions may be in the public interest.

In 1980, for example, a radio station licensee in Alaska sought a license for a vacant television channel in the same community. A rule barred the same licensee from controlling radio and VHF stations in the same community. The community had three vacant VHF frequencies. If the FCC adhered to its rule, the community might not get any television service for several years. The Commission granted a waiver of its rule to meet the needs of the situation.

Note, however, that the Commission might be able to argue in some situations that the overriding public interest may be better served by rigorous adherence to a firm rule that all know will be followed, than by granting waivers that seriously undercut the thrust of a vitally important main rule.

A. LOCAL CONCENTRATION

1. DUOPOLY

Local concentration of control of mass media facilities has been a problem for the Commission at least since 1938, when it received an application for a standard broadcasting station in Flint, Mich., from applicants who already controlled another corporation that operated a standard broadcasting station in the same area. Although there were no rival applicants, the Commission refused to grant the second facility without a compelling showing that the public interest would be served in such a situation.

This was the beginning of the so-called "duopoly" rule, which the Commission formalized in a general rule that it would not grant a license to any applicant who already held a similar facility or license so located that the service areas of the two would overlap.

In the 1960s the Commission returned to this subject and recognized that the dwindling number of American newspapers made the impact of individual broadcasting stations "significantly greater." This reinforced the need for diversity in the broadcast media and led the Commission to announce that it would never again grant a duopoly.

During this period, however, the Commission was granting to the same applicant one AM, one FM and one television station in the same locality because this was not a duplication of facilities in the same service area. In 1970 the Commission moved to the next step and proposed the "one-to-a-customer" rule. Rules Relating to Multiple Ownership, 22 F.C.C.2d 306, 18 R.R.2d 1735 (1970). Under this rule licensees would be limited to one broadcast station in any given market, regardless of the type of broadcast service involved. The Commission viewed this as a logical extension of its earlier diversification rules:

> 21. Application of the principles set forth above dictates that one person should not be licensed to operate more than one broadcast station in the same place, and serving substantially the same public, unless some other relevant public interest consideration is found to outweigh the importance of diversifying control. It is elementary that the number of frequencies available for licensing is limited. In any particular area there may be many voices that would like to be heard, but not all can be licensed. A proper objective is the maximum diversity of ownership that technology permits in each area. We are of the view that 60 different licensees are more desirable than 50, and even that 51 are more desirable than 50. In a rapidly changing social climate, communication of ideas is vital. If a city has 60 frequencies available but they are licensed to only 50 different licensees, the number of sources for ideas is not maximized. It might be the 51st licensee that would become the communi-

cation channel for a solution to a severe social crisis. No one can say that present licensees are broadcasting everything worthwhile that can be communicated. We see no existing public interest reason for being wedded to our present policy that permits a licensee to acquire more than one station in the same area.

The Commission rejected an argument "that the good profit position of a multiple owner in the same market results in more in-depth informational programs being broadcast and thus, in more meaningful diversity. We do not doubt that some multiple owners may have a greater capacity to so program, but the record does not demonstrate that they generally do so. The citations and honors for exceptional programming appear to be continually awarded to a very few licensees—perhaps a dozen or so multiple owners out of a total of hundreds of such owners."

The Commission was persuaded, however, that UHF stations presented a special problem in that they were still weak competitively and few would go on the air unless affiliated with an established radio station. Therefore, the Commission refused to adopt a firm rule against radio-UHF combinations but again indicated that it would review those on a case-by-case basis. Finally, the Commission announced that the rules would be prospective only and no divestitures would be required, due to the large number of existing combinations and a sense that ordering divestiture for such a large group might very well create instability.

The rules as originally adopted would have banned not only VHF-radio combinations, but also AM–FM combinations, even though traditionally FM had been weak as a competitive force, and indeed the Commission during the 1950s had encouraged AM stations to acquire FM stations. On reconsideration the Commission decided that although FM stations were becoming more powerful competitors and increasingly profitable, most AM–FM combinations might still be "economically and/or technically interdependent." Concerned that the rules as originally adopted might hinder the development of FM service, the FCC modified them to permit the formation of new AM–FM combinations. Multiple Ownership of Standard, FM and TV Broadcast Stations, 28 F.C.C.2d 662, 21 R.R.2d 1551 (1971). Thus, only VHF-radio combinations were banned by the new rules.

In 1988 the FCC modified the duopoly rule to allow greater overlap between commonly-owned AM or between commonly-owned FM stations. The change reduced the minimum spacing required between such stations. The FCC also announced that it would be inclined to grant waivers of the one-to-a-market rule in those top 25 markets that have at least 30 broadcast voices.

A few years later, the FCC announced a further relaxation of the duopoly rules for radio. Arguing that the marked increase in competition had produced an extremely fragmented radio marketplace in which radio licensees would experience increasingly severe economic and financial stress, the Commission concluded that increased economies of scale were necessary for these licensees. The FCC decided to allow owners to own more stations in any single market. The exact number depended on the total number of stations in the market. The Commission also imposed a cap of 25 percent on the combined audience share of all stations owned by the one licensee as of the filing date of the application to acquire a new station. Radio Multiple Ownership Rules, 7 F.C.C.Rcd. 2755, 70 R.R.2d 903 (1992).

The relaxation of the duopoly rules, as well as changes in the multiple ownership rules, discussed later in this chapter, produced an extremely negative reaction by Congress. In response to this, the Commission modified the new duopoly rules. Licensees in markets with fewer than 15 radio stations were permitted to own up to three stations as long as the number owned was less than 50 percent of the total number of stations in the market. In markets with 15 or more stations, licensees were permitted to own up to four stations. No more than two could be in the same service. In addition, the Commission imposed an audience share cap of 25 percent. Radio Multiple Ownership Rules, Recon., 7 F.C.C.Rcd. 6387, 71 R.R.2d 227 (1992).

However, in the Telecommunications Act of 1996, Congress directed the FCC to further relax the duopoly rules for radio. Licensees in markets with 45 or more commercial radio stations can "own, operate, or control up to 8 stations, not more than 5 of which are in the same service." In markets with between 30 and 44 stations, the limit is seven stations, "not more than 4 of which are in the same service." In markets with between 15 and 29 stations, the limit is six stations, of which not more than four are in the same service. In markets with 14 or fewer stations, the limit is five stations, with not more than three in the same service, "except that a party may not own, operate, or control more than 50 percent of the stations in such market." 47 C.F.R. § 73.3555.

There is also an exception to these limits which allows the Commission to waive them where it finds that doing so "will result in an increase in the number of radio broadcast stations in operation."

The 1996 Act also directed the Commission to "conduct a rulemaking proceeding to determine whether to retain, modify, or eliminate" the duopoly rules for television. Finally, the FCC was required to extend its one-to-a-market waiver policy, p. __, *supra*, to the top 50 markets.

The 1997 budget bill, p. __, *supra*, modified the duopoly rule to allow any TV station in a city with 400,000 or more people as of the 1990 Census to keep its digital channel and bid on one of the returned analog channels.

2. THE NEWSPAPER–BROADCAST CROSSOWNERSHIP RULES

When the Commission adopted its one-to-a-customer rules, it also proposed the adoption of another set of rules that would proscribe common ownership of newspapers and broadcast facilities serving the same area and require divestiture of prohibited combinations. Although the Commission had flirted with such a regulation in the early 1940s, it had abandoned the attempt. The basis for the Commission movement in 1970 was an awareness that 94 television stations were affiliated through common control with newspapers in the same cities in which they were located. In addition, of course, "some newspapers own television stations in other cities, which also serve the city in which the newspaper is located." The Commission thought this situation was very similar to the joint ownership of two television stations in the same community, something the Commission has never permitted. "The functions of newspapers and television stations as journalists are so similar that their joint ownership is, in this respect, essentially the same as the joint ownership of two television stations." After extensive consideration, the Commission adopted rules in 1975 that prohibit granting a license for a television or radio station to any applicant who already controls, owns or operates a daily newspaper serving part of the same area.

FEDERAL COMMUNICATIONS COMMISSION v. NATIONAL CITIZENS COMMITTEE FOR BROADCASTING

Supreme Court of the United States, 1978.
436 U.S. 775, 98 S.Ct. 2096, 43 R.R.2d 152, 56 L.Ed.2d 697, 3 Med.L.Rptr. 2409.

MR. JUSTICE MARSHALL delivered the opinion of the Court.

. . .

I

A

. . .

In setting its licensing policies, the Commission has long acted on the theory that diversification of mass media ownership serves the public interest by promoting diversity of program and service viewpoints, as well as by preventing undue concentration of economic power. See, *e.g., Multiple Ownership of Standard, FM and Television Broadcast Stations,* 45 F.C.C. 1476, 1476–1477 (1964). . . .

. . .

Diversification of ownership has not been the sole consideration thought relevant to the public interest, however. The Commission's other, and sometimes conflicting, goal has been to ensure "the best practicable service to the public." [ ] To achieve this goal, the Commission has weighed factors such as the anticipated contribution of the owner to station operations, the proposed program service, and the past broadcast record of the applicant—in addition to diversification of ownership—in making initial comparative licensing decisions. [ ] Moreover, the Commission has given considerable weight to a policy of avoiding undue disruption of existing service. As a result, newspaper owners in many instances have been able to acquire broadcast licenses for stations serving the same communities as their newspapers, and the Commission has repeatedly renewed such licenses on findings that continuation of the service offered by the common owner would serve the public interest. [   ]

B

Against this background, the Commission began the instant rule-making proceeding in 1970 to consider the need for a more restrictive policy toward newspaper ownership of radio and television broadcast stations. [   ] Citing studies showing the dominant role of television stations and daily newspapers as sources of local news and other information, [   ], the notice of rulemaking proposed adoption of regulations that would eliminate all newspaper-broadcast combinations serving the same market, by prospectively banning formation or transfer of such combinations and requiring dissolution of all existing combinations within five years, [   ]. The Commission suggested that the proposed regulations would serve "the purpose of promoting competition among the mass media involved, and maximizing diversification of service sources and viewpoints." [   ] At the same time, however, the Commission expressed "substantial concern" about the disruption of service that might result from divestiture of existing combinations. [   ] . . .

        . . .

        . . . While recognizing the pioneering contributions of newspaper owners to the broadcast industry, the Commission concluded that changed circumstances made it possible, and necessary, for all new licensing of broadcast stations to "be expected to add to local diversity." [   ] In reaching this conclusion, the Commission did not find that existing co-located newspaper-broadcast combinations had not served the public interest, or that such combinations necessarily "spea[k] with one voice" or are harmful to competition. [   ] In the Commission's view, the conflicting studies submitted by the parties concerning the effects of newspaper ownership on competition and station performance were inconclusive, and no pattern of specific abuses by existing cross-owners was demonstrated. [   ] The prospective rules were justified, instead, by reference to the Commission's policy of promoting diversification of ownership: Increases of diversification of ownership would possibly result in enhanced diversity of viewpoints, and, given the absence of persuasive countervailing considerations, "even a small gain in diversity" was "worth pursuing." [   ]

With respect to the proposed across-the-board divestiture requirement, however, the Commission concluded that "a mere hoped-for gain in diversity" was not a sufficient justification, [   ]. Characterizing the divestiture issues as "the most difficult" presented in the proceeding, the Order explained that the proposed rules, while correctly recognizing the central importance of diversity considerations, "may have given too little weight to the consequences which could be expected to attend a focus on the abstract goal alone." [   ] Forced dissolution would promote diversity, but it would also cause "disruption for the industry and hardship for individual owners," "resulting in losses or diminution of service to the public." [   ]

The Commission concluded that in light of these countervailing considerations divestiture was warranted only in "the most egregious cases," which it identified as those in which a newspaper-broadcast combination has an "effective monopoly" in the local "marketplace of ideas as well as economically." [   ] The Commission recognized that any standards for defining which combinations fell within that category would necessarily be arbitrary to some degree, but "[a] choice had to be made." [   ] It thus decided to require divestiture only where there was common ownership of the sole daily newspaper published in a community and either (1) the sole broadcast station providing that entire community with a clear signal, or (2) the sole television station encompassing the entire community with a clear signal. [   ]

The Order identified 8 television-newspaper and 10 radio-newspaper combinations meeting the divestiture criteria. [   ] Waivers of the divestiture requirement were granted *sua sponte* to 1 television and 1 radio combination, leaving a total of 16 stations subject to divestiture. The Commission explained that waiver requests would be entertained in the latter cases, but, absent waiver, either the newspaper or the broadcast station would have to be divested by January 1, 1980, [   ].

. . .

C

. . .

. . . [T]he Court of Appeals affirmed the prospective ban on new licensing of co-located newspaper-broadcast combinations, but vacated the limited divestiture rules, and ordered the Commission to adopt regulations requiring dissolution of all existing combinations that did not qualify for a waiver under the procedure outlined in the order. [The court concluded that the Commission had no rational basis for banning prospective combinations while grandfathering most existing combinations. The court was also unable to find a rational basis for distinguishing between the 16 egregious cases that had to be divested and the remaining grandfathered combinations. The Commission, NAB, ANPA and some of the cross-owners who had been grandfathered under the Commission's order petitioned the Supreme Court for review.]

II

. . .

A

Section 303(r) of the Communications Act, [   ], provides that "the Commission from time to time, as public convenience, interest, or necessity requires, shall . . . [m]ake such rules and regulations and prescribe such restrictions and conditions, not inconsistent with law, as may be necessary to carry out the provisions of [the Act]." [   ] As the Court of Appeals recognized, [   ], it is now well established that this general rulemaking authority supplies a statutory basis for the Commission to enact regulations codifying its view of the public interest licensing standard, so long as that view is based on consideration of permissible factors and is otherwise reasonable. If a license applicant does not qualify under standards set forth in such regulations, and does not proffer sufficient grounds for waiver or change of those standards, the Commission may deny the application without further inquiry. [   ]

This Court has specifically upheld this rulemaking authority in the context of regulations based on the Commission's policy of promoting diversification of ownership. In United States v. Storer Broadcasting Co., [   ], we sustained the portion of the Commission's multiple ownership rules placing limitations on the total number of stations in each broadcast service a person may own or control. [   ] And in [*NBC,* p. ___, *supra*], we affirmed regulations that, *inter alia,* prohibited broadcast networks from owning more than one AM radio station in the same community, and from owning " 'any standard broadcast station in any locality where the existing standard broadcast stations are so few or of such unequal desirability . . . that competition would be substantially restrained by such licensing.' " [   ]

Petitioner NAB attempts to distinguish these cases on the ground that they involved efforts to increase diversification within the boundaries of the broadcasting industry itself, whereas the instant regulations are concerned with diversification of ownership in the mass communications media as a whole. NAB contends that, since the Act confers jurisdiction on the Commission only to regulate "communication by wire or radio," 47 U.S.C. § 152(a), it is impermissible for the Commission to use its licensing authority with respect to broadcasting to promote diversity in an overall communications market which includes, but is not limited to, the broadcasting industry.

This argument undersells the Commission's power to regulate broadcasting in the "public interest." In making initial licensing decisions between competing applicants, the Commission has long given "primary significance" to "diversification of control of the media of mass communications," and has denied licenses to newspaper owners on the basis of this policy in appropriate cases. [   ] As we have discussed on several occasions, [   ], the physical scarcity of broadcast frequencies, as well as problems of interference between broadcast signals, led Congress to delegate broad authority to the Commission to allocate broadcast licenses in the "public interest." And "[t]he avowed aim of the Communications Act of 1934 was to secure the maximum benefits of radio to all the people of the United States." [   ] It was not inconsistent with the statutory scheme, therefore, for the Commission to conclude that the maximum benefit to the "public interest" would follow from allocation of broadcast licenses so as to promote diversification of the mass media as a whole.

Our past decisions have recognized, moreover, that the First Amendment and antitrust values underlying the Commission's diversification policy may properly be considered by the Commission in determining where the public interest lies. "[T]he 'public interest' standard necessarily invites reference to First Amendment principles," Columbia Broadcasting System, Inc. v. Democratic National Committee, 412 U.S. 94, 122 (1973), and, in particular, to the First Amendment goal of achieving "the widest possible dissemination of information from diverse and antagonistic sources," Associated Press v. United States, supra, 326 U.S., at 20. See Red Lion Broadcasting Co. v. FCC, supra, at 385, 390. See also United States v. Midwest Video Corp., 406 U.S. 649, 667–669, and n. 27 (1972) (plurality opinion). And, while the Commission does not have power to enforce the antitrust laws as such, it is permitted to take antitrust policies into account in making licensing decisions pursuant to the public interest standard. See, e.g., United States v. Radio Corp. of America, 358 U.S. 334, 351 (1959); National Broadcasting Co. v. United States, supra, at 222–224. . . .

(2)

It is thus clear that the regulations at issue are based on permissible public interest goals and, so long as the regulations are not an unreasonable means for seeking to achieve these goals, they fall within the general rulemaking authority recognized in the *Storer Broadcasting* and *National Broadcasting* cases. Petitioner ANPA contends that the prospective rules are unreasonable in two respects: first, the rulemaking record did not conclusively establish that prohibiting common ownership of co-located newspapers and broadcast stations would in fact lead to increases in the diversity of viewpoints among local communications media; and second, the regulations were based on the diversification factor to the exclusion of other service factors considered in the past by the Commission in making initial licensing decisions regarding newspaper owners, [   ]. With respect to the first point we agree with the Court of Appeals that, notwithstanding the inconclusiveness of the rulemaking record, the Commission acted rationally in finding that diversification of ownership would enhance the possibility of achieving greater diversity of viewpoints. As the Court of Appeals observed, "[d]iversity and its effects are . . . elusive concepts, not easily defined let alone measured without making qualitative judgments objectionable on both policy and First Amendment grounds." [   ] Moreover, evidence of specific abuses by common owners is difficult to compile; "the possible benefits of competition do not lend themselves to specific forecast." [   ] In these circumstances, the Commission was entitled to rely on its judgment, based on experience, that "it is unrealistic to expect true diversity from a commonly owned station-newspaper combination. The divergency of their viewpoints cannot be expected to be the same as if they were antagonistically run." [   ]

As to the Commission's decision to give controlling weight to its diversification goal in shaping the prospective rules, the Order makes clear that this change in policy was a reasonable administrative response to changed circumstances in the broadcasting industry. [ ] The Order explained that, although newspaper owners had previously been allowed, and even encouraged to acquire licenses for co-located broadcast stations because of the shortage of qualified license applicants, a sufficient number of qualified and experienced applicants other than newspaper owners was now readily available. In addition, the number of channels open for new licensing had diminished substantially. It had thus become both feasible and more urgent for the Commission to take steps to increase diversification of ownership, and a change in the Commission's policy toward new licensing offered the possibility of increasing diversity without causing any disruption of existing service. In light of these considerations, the Commission clearly did not take an irrational view of the public interest when it decided to impose a prospective ban on new licensing of co-located newspaper-broadcast combinations.

B

Petitioners NAB and ANPA also argue that the regulations, though designed to further the First Amendment goal of achieving "the widest possible dissemination of information from diverse and antagonistic sources," Associated Press v. United States, supra, 326 U.S. at 20, nevertheless violate the First Amendment rights of newspaper owners. We cannot agree, for this argument ignores the fundamental proposition that there is no "unabridgeable First Amendment right to broadcast comparable to the right of every individual to speak, write, or publish." Red Lion Broadcasting Co. v. FCC, supra, 395 U.S. at 388.

. . .

In the instant case, far from seeking to limit the flow of information, the Commission has acted, in the Court of Appeals' words, "to enhance the diversity of information heard by the public without ongoing government surveillance of the content of speech." [ ] The regulations are a reasonable means of promoting the public interest in diversified mass communications; thus they do not violate the First Amendment rights of those who will be denied broadcast licenses pursuant to them. Being forced to "choose among applicants for the same facilities," the Commission has chosen on a "sensible basis," one designed to further, rather than contravene, "the system of freedom of expression." T. Emerson, The System of Freedom of Expression 663 (1970).

III

After upholding the prospective aspect of the Commission's regulations, the Court of Appeals concluded that the Commission's decision to limit divestiture to 16 "egregious cases" of "effective monopoly" was arbitrary and capricious within the meaning of the Administrative Procedure Act (APA), § 10(e), 5 U.S.C. § 706(2)(A). We agree with the Court of Appeals that regulations promulgated after informal rulemaking . . . may be invalidated by a reviewing court under the "arbitrary or capricious" standard if they are not rational and based on consideration of the relevant factors. [   ] Although this review "is to be searching and careful, [t]he court is not empowered to substitute its judgment for that of the agency." [   ]

In the view of the Court of Appeals, the Commission lacked a rational basis, first, for treating existing newspaper-broadcast combinations more leniently than combinations that might seek licenses in the future; and, second, even assuming a distinction between existing and new combinations had been justified, for requiring divestiture in the "egregious cases" while allowing all other existing combinations to continue in operation. We believe that the limited divestiture requirement reflects a rational weighing of competing policies, and we therefore reinstate the portion of the Commission's order that was invalidated by the Court of Appeals.

A

(1)

The Commission was well aware that separating existing newspaper-broadcast combinations would promote diversification of ownership. It concluded, however, that ordering widespread divestiture would not result in "the best practicable service to the American public," [   ], a goal that the Commission has always taken into account and that has been specifically approved by this Court, FCC v. Sanders Bros. Radio Station, 309 U.S. 470, 475 (1940); [   ]. In particular, the Commission expressed concern that divestiture would cause "disruption for the industry" and "hardship to individual owners," both of which would result in harm to the public interest. Order, at 1078. Especially in light of the fact that the number of co-located newspaper-broadcast combinations was already on the decline as a result of the prospective rules, the Commission decided that across-the-board divestiture was not warranted. [ ]

The Order identified several specific respects in which the public interest would or might be harmed if a sweeping divestiture requirement were imposed: the stability and continuity of meritorious service provided by the newspaper owners as a group would be lost; owners who had provided meritorious service would unfairly be denied the opportunity to continue in operation; "economic dislocations" might prevent new owners from obtaining sufficient working capital to maintain the quality of local programming; and local ownership of broadcast stations would probably decrease. [   ] We cannot say that the Commission acted irrationally in concluding that these public interest harms outweighed the potential gains that would follow from increasing diversification of ownership.

In the past, the Commission has consistently acted on the theory that preserving continuity of meritorious service furthers the public interest, both in its direct consequence of bringing proven broadcast service to the public, and in its indirect consequence of rewarding—and avoiding losses to—licensees who have invested the money and effort necessary to produce quality performance. Thus, although a broadcast license must be renewed every three years, and the licensee must satisfy the Commission that renewal will serve the public interest, both the Commission and the courts have recognized that a licensee who has given meritorious service has a "legitimate renewal expectanc[y]" and should not be destroyed absent good cause. [ ] Accordingly, while diversification of ownership is a relevant factor in the context of license renewal as well as initial licensing, the Commission has long considered the past performance of the incumbent as the most important factor in deciding whether to grant license renewal and thereby to allow the existing owner to continue in operation. Even where an incumbent is challenged by a competing applicant who offers greater potential in terms of diversification, the Commission's general practice has been to go with the "proven product" and grant renewal if the incumbent has rendered meritorious service. [ ] In the instant proceeding, the Commission specifically noted that the existing newspaper-broadcast cross-owners as a group had a "long record of service" from the outset. [ ] Notwithstanding the Commission's diversification policy, all were granted initial licenses upon findings that the public interest would be served thereby, and those that had been in existence for more than three years had also had their licenses renewed on the ground that the public interest would be furthered. The Commission noted, moreover, that in terms of percentage of time devoted to several categories of local programming, these stations had displayed "an undramatic but nonetheless statistically significant superiority" over other television stations. [ ] An across-the-board divestiture requirement would result in loss of the services of these superior licensees, and—whether divestiture caused actual losses to existing owners, or just denial of reasonably anticipated gains—the result would be that future licensees would be discouraged from investing the resources necessary to produce quality service.

At the same time, there was no guarantee that the licensees who replaced the existing cross-owners would be able to provide the same level of service or demonstrate the same longterm commitment to broadcasting. And even if the new owners were able in the long run to provide similar or better service, the Commission found that divestiture would cause serious disruption in the transition period. Thus, the Commission observed that new owners "would lack the long knowledge of the community and would have to begin raw," and—because of high interest rates—might not be able to obtain sufficient working capital to maintain the quality of local programming. [ ]

The Commission's fear that local ownership would decline was grounded in a rational prediction, based on its knowledge of the broadcasting industry and supported by comments in the record, [ ], that many of the existing newspaper-broadcast combinations owned by local interests would respond to the divestiture requirement by trading stations with out-of-town owners. It is undisputed that roughly 75% of the existing co-located newspaper-television combinations are locally owned, [ ], and these owners' knowledge of their local communities and concern for local affairs, built over a period of years, would be lost if they were replaced with outside interests. Local ownership in and of itself has been recognized to be a factor of some—if relatively slight—significance even in the context of initial licensing decisions. [ ] It was not unreasonable, therefore, for the Commission to consider it as one of several factors militating against divestiture of combinations that have been in existence for many years.

In light of these countervailing considerations, we cannot agree with the Court of Appeals that it was arbitrary and capricious for the Commission to "grandfather" most existing combinations, and to leave opponents of these combinations to their remedies in individual renewal proceedings. In the latter connection we note that, while individual renewal proceedings are unlikely to accomplish any "overall restructuring" of the existing ownership patterns, the Order does make clear that existing combinations will be subject to challenge by competing applicants in renewal proceedings, to the same extent as they were prior to the instant rulemaking proceedings. [ ] That is, diversification of ownership will be a relevant but somewhat secondary factor. And, even in the absence of a competing applicant, license renewal may be denied if, *inter alia*, a challenger can show that a common owner has engaged in specific economic or programming abuses. [ ]

(2)

In concluding that the Commission acted unreasonably in not extending its divestiture requirement across-the-board, the Court of Appeals apparently placed heavy reliance on a "presumption" that existing newspaper-broadcast combinations "do not serve the public interest." [ ] The Court derived this presumption primarily from the Commission's own diversification policy, as "reaffirmed" by adoption of the prospective rules in this proceeding, and secondarily from "[t]he policies of the First Amendment," [ ], and the Commission's statutory duty to "encourage the larger and more effective use of radio in the public interest." 47 U.S.C. § 303(g). As explained in Part II above, we agree that diversification of ownership furthers statutory and constitutional policies, and, as the Commission recognized, separating existing newspaper-broadcast combinations would promote diversification. But the weighing of policies under the "public interest" standard is a task that Congress has delegated to the Commission in the first instance, and we are unable to find anything in the Communications Act, the First Amendment, or the Commission's past or present practices that would require the Commission to "presume" that its diversification policy should be given controlling weight in all circumstances.

Such a "presumption" would seem to be inconsistent with the Commission's long-standing and judicially approved practice of giving controlling weight in some circumstances to its more general goal of achieving "the best practicable service to the public." Certainly, as discussed in Part III–A(1) above, the Commission through its license renewal policy has made clear that it considers diversification of ownership to be a factor of less significance when deciding whether to allow an existing licensee to continue in operation than when evaluating applicants seeking initial licensing. Nothing in the language or the legislative history of § 303(g) indicates that Congress intended to foreclose all differences in treatment between new and existing licensees, and indeed, in amending § 307(d) of the Act in 1952, Congress appears to have lent its approval to the Commission's policy of evaluating existing licensees on a somewhat different basis than new applicants. Moreover, if enactment of the prospective rules in this proceeding itself were deemed to create a "presumption" in favor of divestiture, the Commission's ability to experiment with new policies would be severely hampered. One of the most significant advantages of the administrative process is its ability to adapt to new circumstances in a flexible manner, [ ], and we are unwilling to presume that the Commission acts unreasonably when it decides to try out a change in licensing policy primarily on a prospective basis.

The Court of Appeals also relied on its perception that the policies militating against divestiture were "lesser policies" to which the Commission had not given as much weight in the past as its divestiture policy. [ ] This perception is subject to much the same criticism as the "presumption" that existing co-located newspaper-broadcast combinations do not serve the public interest. The Commission's past concern with avoiding disruption of existing service is amply illustrated by its license renewal policies. In addition, it is worth noting that in the past when the Commission has changed its multiple ownership rules it has almost invariably tailored the changes so as to operate wholly or primarily on a prospective basis. . . .

The Court of Appeals apparently reasoned that the Commission's concerns with respect to disruption of existing service, economic dislocations, and decreases in local ownership necessarily could not be very weighty since the Commission has a practice of routinely approving voluntary transfers and assignments of licenses. [ ] But the question of whether the Commission should compel proven licensees to divest their stations is a different question from whether the public interest is served by allowing transfers by licensees who no longer wish to continue in the business. . . .

The Court of Appeals' final basis for concluding that the Commission acted arbitrarily in not giving controlling weight to its divestiture policy was the Court's finding that the rulemaking record did not adequately "disclose the extent to which divestiture would actually threaten" the competing policies relied upon by the Commission, [ ]. However, to the extent that factual determinations were involved in the Commission's decision to grandfather most existing combinations, they were primarily of a judgmental or predictive nature—e.g., whether a divestiture requirement would result in trading of stations with out-of-town owners; whether new owners would perform as well as existing cross-owners, either in the short run or in the long run; whether losses to existing owners would result from forced sales; whether such losses would discourage future investment in quality programming; and whether new owners would have sufficient working capital to finance local programming. In such circumstances complete factual support in the record for the Commission's judgment or prediction is not possible or required; "a forecast of the direction in which future public interest lies necessarily involves deductions based on the expert knowledge of the agency." [ ]

B

We also must conclude that the Court of Appeals erred in holding that it was arbitrary to order divestiture in the 16 "egregious cases" while allowing other existing combinations to continue in operation. The Commission's decision was based not—as the Court of Appeals may have believed, [ ]—on a conclusion that divestiture would be more harmful in the grandfathered markets than in the 16 affected markets, but rather on a judgment that the need for diversification was especially great in cases of local monopoly. This policy judgment was certainly not irrational, [ ], and indeed was founded on the very same assumption that underpinned the diversification policy itself and the prospective rules upheld by the Court of Appeals and now by this Court—that the greater the number of owners in a market, the greater the possibility of achieving diversity of program and service viewpoints.

As to the Commission's criteria for determining which existing newspaper-broadcast combinations have an "effective monopoly" in the "local marketplace of ideas as well as economically," we think the standards settled upon by the Commission reflect a rational legislative-type judgment. Some line had to be drawn, and it was hardly unreasonable for the Commission to confine divestiture to communities in which there is common ownership of the only daily newspaper and either the only television station or the only broadcast station of any kind encompassing the entire community with a clear signal. [ ] It was not irrational, moreover, for the Commission to disregard media sources other than newspapers and broadcast stations in setting its divestiture standards. The studies cited by the Commission in its notice of rulemaking unanimously concluded that newspapers and television are the two most widely utilized media sources for local news and discussion of public affairs; and, as the Commission noted in its Order, [ ], "aside from the fact that [magazines and other periodicals] often had only a tiny fraction in the market, they were not given real weight since they often dealt exclusively with regional or national issues and ignored local issues." Moreover, the differences in treatment between radio and television stations, [ ], were certainly justified in light of the far greater influence of television than radio as a source for local news. [ ]

The judgment of the Court of Appeals is affirmed in part and reversed in part.

It is so ordered.

Mr. Justice Brennan took no part in the consideration or decision of these cases.

Notes and Questions

1. As in *WNCN Listeners Guild,* p. ____, *supra,* the primary issue in this case is the scope of the appellate court's power to review Commission decisions. How does the Supreme Court's view of this differ from the appellate court's?

2. During the time between the appellate court decision and the Supreme Court decision, *The Washington Post* and the *Detroit Evening News* exchanged their locally-owned television stations to achieve compliance with the crossownership rule. If most crossowners had engaged in similar swaps, would requiring divestiture have served the public interest? As the Supreme Court noted, one obvious effect of such transactions would be to reduce local ownership of broadcast stations.

3. One important question for the application of the various FCC ownership rules concerns the level of ownership necessary to invoke the application of one of these rules. For example, should someone who buys five shares of stock in each of several publicly held corporations be considered in violation of an FCC ownership rule because the combined holdings of those corporations would violate that rule? Obviously, such a stock holding would not raise the concentration concerns underlying these rules. Furthermore, such an extreme reading of the rules would be unenforceable. The Commission has therefore set minimum ownership percentages for what it calls "cognizable" interests. Only cognizable interests subject the owner to the FCC ownership rules.

The current minimum ownership levels required to constitute cognizable interests were set in 1984. The basic level is 5 percent. However, for passive investors such as banks, investment companies and insurance companies, the level is 10 percent. Multiple Ownership Rules, 97 F.C.C.2d 997, 55 R.R.2d 1465 (1984). The Commission is now considering changes to these rules. Attribution of Broadcast Interests, 10 F.C.C.Rcd. 3606 (1995). An updated NPRM was issued to address the effect of the Telecommunications Act of 1996, 11 F.C.C.R. 19895 (1996).

4. When approval of an application for a new license or a license transfer would result in a violation of one of the Commission's media concentration rules, the new licensee is usually granted a temporary waiver of the rule. This gives such licensees a reasonable period of time to sell whatever is necessary to bring themselves into compliance. For example, when Rupert Murdoch's News America Corporation purchased six television stations from Metromedia, the Commission granted it a two-year waiver from the cross-ownership rule as applied to his properties in New York and Chicago. The two-year waiver was upheld on appeal. Health and Medicine Policy Research Group v. Federal Communications Commission, 807 F.2d 1038, 61 R.R.2d 1450 (D.C.Cir.1986).

The Commission granted a similar waiver when News America bought channel 25 in Boston. Twentieth Holdings Corp., 1 F.C.C.Rcd. 1201, 61 R.R.2d 1484 (1986). As of December 1987 the company had sold only the Chicago newspaper, and for months stories had been circulating that Murdoch planned to ask for a permanent waiver for the New York and Boston newspapers. Boston Business Journal, June 22, 1987 at 1. However, in December 1987 Congress included a provision in the FCC's budget authorization prohibiting the Commission from either altering the cross-ownership rules or extending temporary waivers. (The only two existing waivers were held by News America.)

News America appealed the FCC's subsequent denial of its petition for an extension of the temporary waivers. Noting that the continuing budget resolution struck at "Murdoch with the precision of a laser beam," the court of appeals found it fatally underinclusive. News America Publishing, Inc. v. Federal Communications Commission, 844 F.2d 800, 64 R.R.2d 1309, 15 Med.L.Rptr. 1161 (D.C.Cir.1988).

In the meantime News America had sold the *New York Post.* Although the court decision gave News America the option of seeking an extension of the waiver for the Boston newspaper and television station, the company decided instead to sell the television station.

5. Ironically, in 1993 News America reacquired the *New York Post.* At the time, no other parties were interested in acquiring the paper, which would have ceased publishing if it had not be sold. The FCC granted News America a waiver of the cross-ownership rules, apparently reasoning that even a cross-owned paper would provide more diversity than no paper at all. The waiver was upheld on appeal. Metropolitan Council of NAACP Branches v. Federal Communications Commission, 46 F.3d 1154, 76 R.R.2d 1604 (D.C.Cir.1995).

6. The 1997 budget bill, p. ___, *supra*, modified the crossownership rule to allow any newspaper in a city with 400,000 or more people as of the 1990 Census to bid on one of the returned analog channels.

3. CROSSOWNERSHIP RULES INVOLVING NEW MEDIA

As cable and other new communication technologies developed, the Commission sought to limit concentration within and across the various industries.

a. *Broadcast–Cable Crossownership*

One of the first of the new rules was a limitation on broadcast-cable crossownership. This was essentially codified by the 1984 Cable Act. 47 U.S.C.A. § 533(a). A television broadcast licensee cannot own a cable system within its primary signal coverage area. The statutory prohibition on broadcast-cable crossownership was eliminated by the 1996 Telecommunications Act. However, the FCC regulations are still in effect.

b. *Network–Cable Crossownership*

Similar rules governing network-cable crossownership were created at the same time as the original broadcast-cable rules. In the early 1990s, the Commission reexamined the network-cable crossownership rules. The new network-cable crossownership rules permit networks to own cable systems as long as a network's cable systems do not exceed 10 percent of the homes passed by cable nationwide or 50 percent of the homes passed by cable within any ADI. An ADI, Area of Dominant Influence, is comprised of those communities located within the primary coverage area of a television station. Affiliates, expressing concern that they would suddenly be in competition with their own networks if networks were to send top programs to cable instead of over the network, were told by the FCC that abuses would be handled as they arose. Common Ownership of Cable Television Systems and National Television Networks, 7 F.C.C.Rcd. 6156, 70 R.R.2d 1531 (1992). As we discussed in Chapter VIII, broadcast networks are already allowed to own cable programmers.

NBC and INTV filed petitions for reconsideration. NBC claimed that the new ownership limits still made it almost impossible for networks to enter the cable business. It was not cost-effective for a network to buy individual cable systems. Rather, the only effective way for networks to enter the cable business was to merge with or invest in major MSO's. This was precluded by the new rules.

In contrast, INTV argued that the new rules would result in "dangerous levels of horizontal concentration in local broadcast markets." INTV also claimed that "negative must carry" is "hopelessly inadequate" to protect against anticompetitive behavior. Finally, according to INTV, the network-cable crossownership rules, together with the changes in the financial interest and syndication rules (discussed later in this chapter) would result in off-network programming going directly to network-owned cable systems, as opposed to independent broadcast stations. The FCC denied the petitions. Common Ownership of Cable Television Systems and National Television Networks, 8 F.C.C.Rcd. 1184, 72 R.R.2d 39 (1993).

The 1996 Telecommunications Act required the FCC to eliminate its network-cable cross-ownership rules and replace them with rules designed to prevent network-owned cable systems from discriminating against non-affiliated television stations with regard to carriage-related matters. The elimination of the rule has not led to significant network ownership of cable systems due to the broadcast-cable crossownership rule. 1998 Biennial Regulatory Review–Streamlining of Mass Media Applications, Rules and Processes, 13 F.C.C.Rcd. 11349 (1998).

c. *Telephone–Cable Crossownership*

Still another crossownership rule prohibited a local exchange carrier (LEC) from owning a cable system within its telephone service area. 47

U.S.C.A. § 533(b). The latter restriction did not apply to rural areas. What was the reason for this exemption?

The FCC also relaxed the cable-telephone company crossownership rules in the early 1990s by authorizing telephone companies to transmit video programming on a common-carrier basis. Telephone companies could not exercise any editorial control over video programming carried under the new "video dialtone" rules, and had to offer their transmission capacity on a nondiscriminatory basis. However, they could own up to a five percent interest in video programmers. They could also provide nonregulated and enhanced services including billing and collection, order processing, equipment, and video processing services. The FCC, which had previously determined that the cross-ownership rules do not apply to long-distance carriers, also affirmed an earlier holding that neither a telephone company offering video dialtone services, nor its customer programmers were subject to the franchising requirements of the Communications Act. Telephone–Cable Cross–Ownership, 7 F.C.C.Rcd. 5781, 71 R.R.2d 70 (1992).

Around the same time the RBOCs began filing challenges to the telephone-cable crossownership rule. Although they could apply for permission to distribute video programming under the FCC's video dialtone rules, the RBOCs wanted the freedom to exercise editorial control. In 1993 a district court held § 533(b) unconstitutional as applied to a subsidiary of Bell Atlantic. The court determined that the appropriate analysis to be used was that originated in *O'Brien*, p. ___, *supra*. The government asserted that the rules served two government interests, "promoting competition in the video programming market and preserving diversity in the ownership of communications media." The court found that the rules actually decreased competition in the video programming market by reducing the number of outlets. As far as the ownership of communications media was concerned, the rules were undercut by the FCC's video dialtone decision, which already allowed telephone companies to enter the video transmission market. Chesapeake and Potomac Telephone Company of Virginia v. United States, 830 F.Supp. 909 (E.D.Va.1993).

In the first major case to rely on *Turner* I, p. ___, *supra*, the court of appeals affirmed. First, the court addressed the issue of the appropriate standard of scrutiny.

> . . . [T]he FCC and Congress have regulated the telephone companies' provision of cable service in light of the physical "bottleneck," [ ], peculiar to cable communications, see id., and the perception that the telephone companies, absent regulation, would have the incentive and ability to dominate that bottleneck and establish themselves as sole "gatekeeper[s]," [ ], thereof. Because Section 533(b)'s speaker distinction is thus justifiable entirely on the basis of the peculiar economic and physical venue inherent to cable communications, we conclude that it is not an improper content-based distinction.

The court therefore applied intermediate scrutiny. First it decided that the government's asserted interests, "restricting telephone company exercise of cross-subsidization and pole-access discrimination . . . in the cable medium, and preserving diversity of ownership of communications outlets and of the means of electronic access to homes and businesses," were substantial.

However, in the court's view, the rule was not narrowly tailored to serve those interests. Not only had Congress failed to support the rule with any factual findings, but there was an obvious, less-burdensome alternative that had been suggested by the FCC when it had previously recommended Congress eliminate the rule. "Congress could simply limit the telephone companies'editorial control over video programming to a fixed percentage of the channels available; the telephone companies would be required to lease the balance of the channels on a common carrier basis to various video programmers, without regard to content."

The rule also suffered from another fatal defect. It did not leave open ample alternative channels for communication. The effect of § 533(b) was to prevent the telephone companies from guaranteeing "that video programming they wish[ed] to transmit to their local audience via cable television, a protected form of speech, [would] reach their desired audience." Chesapeake and Potomac Telephone Company of Virginia v. United States, 42 F.3d 181, 76 R.R.2d. 986 (4th Cir.1994).

The Supreme Court granted *certiorari*, 515 U.S. 1157 (1995). Meanwhile, similar challenges to the constitutionality of the telco-cable crossownership restriction produced the same result in other jurisdictions. See, U.S. West, Inc. v. United States, 48 F.3d 1092, 76 R.R.2d 1239 (9th Cir.1994), Southern New England Telephone Co. v. United States, 886 F.Supp. 211 (D.Conn.1995), Ameritech Corp. v. United States, 867 F.Supp. 721 (N.D.Ill.1994), BellSouth Corp. v. United States, 868 F.Supp. 1335 (N.D.Ala.1994), Southwestern Bell Corp. v. United States, 1995 WL 444414 (N.D.Tex.), and Nynex Corp. v. United States, 1994 WL 779761 (D.Me.).

However, the entire issue became moot when the 1996 Telecommunications Act eliminated § 533(b), thus allowing LECs to offer cable service in their telephone service areas. Similarly, cable companies may now offer local phone service.

Under the new structure set up by the 1996 Act, LECs can choose among three regulatory structures for delivering cable service by wire. The first is to operate strictly as a common carrier, in which case the provisions of Title II of the Communications Act apply. The second option is to be a cable operator subject to the provisions of Title VI, the same as other cable operators.

The third option is a new structure called "open video systems" (OVS). This is meant to replace the video dialtone service created by the FCC. Therefore, VDT is abolished except for those systems approved prior to the enactment of the 1996 Act. 47 U.S.C.A. § 573

To distribute cable as an OVS operator, a common carrier must apply to the FCC for certification. To obtain certification the operator must comply with FCC regulations issued pursuant to the 1996 Act. Implementation of Section 302 of the Telecommunications Act of 1996 Open Video Systems, 11 F.C.C.Rcd. 18223 (1996).

(A) except as required pursuant to section 611, 614, or 615, prohibit an operator of an open video system from discriminating among video programming providers with regard to carriage on its open video system, and ensure that the rates, terms, and conditions for such carriage are just and reasonable, and are not unjustly or unreasonably discriminatory;

(B) if demand exceeds the channel capacity of the open video system, prohibit an operator of an open video system and its affiliates from selecting the video programming services for carriage on more than one-third of the activated channel capacity on such system, but nothing in this subparagraph shall be construed to limit the number of channels that the carrier and its affiliates may offer to provide directly to subscribers;

(C) permit an operator of an open video system to carry on only one channel any video programming service that is offered by more than one video programming provider (including the local exchange carrier's video programming affiliate), provided that subscribers have ready and immediate access to any such video programming service;

(D) extend to the distribution of video programming over open video systems the Commission's regulations concerning sports exclusivity (47 C.F.R. 76.67), network nonduplication (47 C.F.R. 76.92 et seq.), and syndicated exclusivity (47 C.F.R. 76.151 et seq.); and

(E)(i) prohibit an operator of an open video system from unreasonably discriminating in favor of the operator or its affiliates with regard to material or information (including advertising) provided by the operator to subscribers for the purposes of selecting programming on the open video system, or in the way such material or information is presented to subscribers;

(ii) require an operator of an open video system to ensure that video programming providers or copyright holders (or both) are able suitably and uniquely to identify their programming services to subscribers;

(iii) if such identification is transmitted as part of the programming signal, require the carrier to transmit such identification without change or alteration; and

(iv) prohibit an operator of an open video system from omitting television broadcast stations or other unaffiliated video programming services carried on such system from any navigational device, guide, or menu.

Certified OVS operators are not subject to Title II regulation of their cable service. In addition, they are exempt from the franchising, rate regulation (other than the negative option billing prohibition), consumer electronics compatibility and leased-access-channel requirements of Title VI, as well as the broadcast/MMDS/SMATV crossownership rules discussed later in this chapter. OVS operators are still subject to the other cable crossownership restrictions, must-carry rules and PEG channel requirements, as well as programming agreement restrictions discussed later in this chapter. Franchising authorities are not permitted to impose franchise fees, but may impose other fees in lieu of franchising fees. These fees may not exceed the maximum permissible for franchise fees.

The 1996 Act also prohibits an LEC from acquiring more than a 10 percent interest in a cable system providing service within the LEC's telephone service area. In addition, joint ventures between LECs and cable operators whose service areas are in the same market to provide either cable or telecommunications services are prohibited. There are exceptions to the buyout provisions for rural systems, acquisitions in competitive markets and certain small cable systems. In addition, LECs may contract to use the transmission facilities extending from the last multi-user terminal to the premises of the end user. 47 U.S.C.A. § 572.

d. *MMDS Restrictions*

Initially, there had been some ownership restrictions on MMDS, the most important of which was that a single operator could not acquire a license for more than four of the eight MDS channels in a market. (Remember that an operator could still exceed four channels by leasing other channels from ITFS operators.) The purpose of this restriction was to promote competition between MMDS operators. However, several years later, the Commission concluded that competition from other multichannel service providers such as cable was so strong that for even a single MMDS operator to survive in a given market it was necessary that the operator have access to as many channels as possible. Therefore, the Commission voted to eliminate the ownership restrictions. Wireless Cable Service, 68 R.R.2d 429 (1990).

The 1992 Cable Act added a prohibition on cable operators from holding multichannel multipoint distribution service (MMDS) licenses or offering satellite master antenna television (SMATV) service in any portion of a franchise area served by that cable operator. This provision does not apply to MMDS and SMATV services owned by the cable operator on Oct. 5, 1992. The 1996 Act included an exemption to that prohibition for LECs delivering cable by OVS.

e. *Open Access*

The advent of cable modems, which permit high-speed Internet access, has raised an interesting access question. The cable companies providing modem service require subscribers to this service to also subscribe to a specific online service provider (OSP). Subscribers can then access other providers such as AOL, but doing so is costly because they have to pay for both services. Although alternative high-speed-access technologies such as DSL are also being introduced, very few consumers currently have access to more than one high-speed access provider. Arguing that requiring cable modem subscribers to use the cable company's online service provider unfairly restricts consumers from choosing their own OSP, various industry and consumer groups have lobbied for rules requiring cable companies to provide open access to all. The FCC has rejected requests for such a requirement. It has also rejected a request to force cable companies to rent some of their leased access channels to ISPs.

However, some cities have passed open access regulations or made open access a condition for approving cable franchise transfers. For example, the city of Portland, Ore., as well as the neighboring county, conditioned approval of AT & T's acquisition of TCI's franchise on open access. AT & T sued the city and county claiming the requirement was preempted by federal statutes, as well as violating the First Amendment, the contract and commerce clauses of the U.S. Constitution, the Oregon Constitution and the franchise agreement. A federal district court rejected all of AT & T's claims.

The court of appeals reversed, finding that cable modem service is not cable service as defined by the Communications Act. Therefore, the city could not regulate cable modem service through its franchising authority. AT & T v. Portland, 216 F.3d 871 (9th Cir.2000).

B. NATIONAL CONCENTRATION

The Commission has proven equally concerned about the effects of concentration of ownership across different markets. Are the issues raised by national concentration different from those presented by local concentration? How is the marketplace of ideas in one city affected by a company's media holdings in other cities? Are there any potential benefits of a company's owning stations in other communities?

1. Multiple Ownership Rules

Beginning in 1940 the Commission adopted rules limiting the number of stations that might be held by a single owner. In 1953 the Commission resolved that the rules should prohibit the ownership or control, directly or indirectly, by any party of more than seven AM stations, seven FM stations and seven television stations of which not more than five could be VHF. The Commission explained its position as follows:

> The vitality of our system of broadcasting depends in large part on the introduction into this field of licensees who are prepared and qualified to serve the varied and divergent needs of the public for radio service. Simply stated, the fundamental purpose of this facet of

the multiple ownership rules is to promote diversification of owner-ship in order to maximize diversification of program and service viewpoints as well as to prevent any undue concentration of econom-ic power contrary to the public interest. In this connection, we wish to emphasize that by such rules diversification of program services is furthered without any governmental encroachment on what we recognize to be the prime responsibility of the broadcast licensee. (See Section 326 of the Communications Act.)

The Commission chose an equal number of AM and FM stations because at that time 538 of the 600 FM stations were owned by AM licensees, the result of a conscious Commission policy to encourage AM stations to put FM stations on the air since most of those operating FM stations alone were finding it extremely unprofitable. The number seven was chosen "in order that present holdings of such stations be not unduly disrupted." Few owners had holdings in excess of seven, and the Commission planned to hold a divestiture hearing for each of them. Rules and Regulations Relating to Multiple Ownership, 18 F.C.C. 288 (1953).

This limitation rule was challenged immediately by a group owner who claimed that the Commission was illegally using the rulemaking procedure to foreclose the right of an applicant to a hearing as to whether the license would be in the public interest, by making a categorical judgment linking the public interest with a given maximum concentration of holdings. The rules were upheld in United States v. Storer Broadcasting Co., 351 U.S. 192, 1 Med.L.Rptr. 1983 (1956). The Court rejected Storer's argument that § 309 of the Communications Act always requires a full hearing to determine whether granting additional licenses to the applicant would be in the public interest:

> We do not read the hearing requirement, however, as withdraw-ing from the power of the Commission the rule-making authority necessary for the orderly conduct of its business. As conceded by Storer, "Section 309(b) does not require the Commission to hold a hearing before denying a license to operate a station in ways contrary to those that the Congress has determined are in the public interest." The challenged Rules contain limitations against licensing not specifically authorized by statute. But that is not the limit of the Commission's rulemaking authority.

> This Commission, like other agencies, deals with the public interest. [ ] Its authority covers new and rapidly developing fields. Congress sought to create regulation for public protection with careful provision to assure fair opportunity for open competition in the use of broadcasting facilities. Accordingly, we cannot interpret § 309(b) as barring rules that declare a present intent to limit the number of stations consistent with a permissible "concentration of control." It is but a rule that announces the Commission's attitude on public protection against such concentration.

The opinion did state, however, that the Commission's responsibility to behave in the public interest required it to grant a hearing to an applicant who had already reached the maximum number of stations but nonetheless asserted sufficient reasons why the rule should be waived in its particular case.

In 1984 the Commission voted to expand the limits on multiple ownership from 7–7–7 to 12–12–12 with a six-year sunsetting provision (eliminating the rules entirely at the end of six years). Multiple Ownership, 100 F.C.C.2d 17, 56 R.R.2d 859 (1984). The new rule made no distinction between VHF and UHF television stations. Faced with mounting criticism of the new rule and threatened Congressional action, the Commission delayed implementation of the television portion of the order and reconsidered it. The revised order contained several new provisions:

> 33.   After reviewing the petitions for reconsideration filed in this proceeding, we now find it appropriate to modify certain aspects of our Report and Order. In this regard, we now find our modification of the rule should be revised to better account for the effect that this relaxation will have on population penetration. We also find that the Report and Order should be revised to take cognizance of the limitations inherent in UHF broadcasting and to promote our traditional policy of facilitating minority ownership. In addition, we find that a more appropriate approach is to eliminate the automatic sunset provision contained in our previous decision.

> . . .

> 36.   On reconsideration, we have become increasingly aware of the limitations of proceeding solely with a numerical multiple ownership limit in the event that there is a rapid expansion of group ownership in the wake of our relaxing of the national multiple ownership rules. As various parties have argued throughout this proceeding, a numerical approach may not give appropriate consideration to wide discrepancies in population coverage because a station in the largest market is deemed equivalent to a station in the smallest market for purposes of ownership regulation. As a consequence, relaxing the numerical cap from seven stations to twelve stations may provide an opportunity for a single group owner to increase its audience base substantially, particularly if acquisitions are made in the largest markets. A numerical cap does not affect this type of restructuring. While there is no evidence in the record that would lead us to believe that such an eventuality would necessarily have an adverse result, we now believe that the potential for this type of restructuring warrants a more cautious approach. To this extent, we now believe it is advisable to adopt an additional ownership limit based on audience reach.

The Commission settled on a 25 percent limit on audience reach. This limited the growth of the largest group owners without requiring any divestiture or grandfathering. (Metromedia had the largest combined reach at 23.89 percent.)

The FCC then turned to requests for special treatment for both UHFs and minorities. Due to the physical limitations inherent in the UHF band, UHF stations cannot compete on an equal basis. The original rules' stricter limitation on VHF ownership was part of the Commission's longstanding efforts to foster the development of UHF. There were no incentives for minorities in the original rules, but the Commission has adopted several other policies designed to increase minority ownership:

> 44. While we agree with the petitioners' assessment as to the need for a UHF incentive within the context of the audience reach limit, we do not believe that the incentive should be structured so as to merely increase the reach cap. Such an approach would not accurately represent the physical handicaps confronting UHF television. Consistent with the diversity objectives expressed in our ownership rules, we believe that a more appropriate indicator of the reach handicap of UHF stations is one that measures the actual coverage limitation inherent in the UHF signal. Therefore, with respect to the audience reach limit adopted herein, we believe that owners of UHF stations should be attributed with only 50 percent of an ADI market's theoretical audience reach to account for this disparity. For example, the theoretical ADI audience reach of the New York market comprises 7.72 percent of all television households. Under the system adopted today, the owner of a UHF station in the New York market would be attributed with an audience reach of only 50 percent of this amount which equals 3.86 percentage points. We find that the discount system adopted herein properly reflects the Commission's historical concern with UHF television. Furthermore, the discount approach provides a measure of the actual voice handicap and is therefore consistent with our traditional diversity objectives.

(b) Minority Incentives

> 45. In the Report and Order, we observed that the national multiple ownership rules were not primarily intended to function as a vehicle for promoting minority ownership in broadcasting. In this regard, we noted that the Commission has instituted various policies such as tax certificates, distress sale benefits and lottery preferences to promote minority ownership in communications. We continue to believe that these policies, as opposed to our multiple ownership rules, should serve as the primary mechanisms to promote minority ownership in television and radio broadcasting. We recognize, however, that our national multiple ownership rules may, in some circumstances, play a role in fostering minority ownership. Thus, while it would be inappropriate to retain multiple ownership regulations for the sole purpose of promoting minority ownership, we now believe that a minority incentive should be included in the rules

adopted by our action today. Accordingly, we are adopting rules today which permit group owners of television and radio stations to utilize a maximum numerical cap of 14 stations provided that at least two of the stations in which they hold cognizable interests are minority controlled. Group owners having a cognizable interest in at least one minority controlled television or radio station may utilize a maximum numerical cap of 13 stations. Extending this policy to the audience reach limit for television, we believe that a group owner having cognizable interests in minority controlled television stations should be allowed to reach a maximum of 30 percent of the national audience, provided that at least five percent of the aggregate reach of its stations is contributed by minority controlled stations.

Commissioners Dawson and Patrick each wrote separate statements to express disagreement with using the multiple ownership rules to promote minority ownership. Commissioner Dawson stated that she did not see how national "concentration is in any way ameliorated by the race of [an] entity's owners." Commissioner Patrick similarly observed, "If the public interest is threatened by concentrating ownership of 14 stations in a single owner, how is that threat obviated by the race of that owner?" Multiple Ownership (12–12–12 Reconsideration), 100 F.C.C.2d 74, 57 R.R.2d 966 (1985).

Both Commissioners seemed to be taking the position that any specific rule must serve only one interest. But remember the newspaper-broadcast crossownership case. Is the Commission allowed to apply rules differently to various groups as long as it can provide a rational basis for the unequal treatment?

At the same time the FCC relaxed the duopoly rules for radio, Radio Multiple Ownership Rules, p. ___, *supra,* it also relaxed the multiple ownership rules. After two reconsiderations, the FCC eventually settled on a limit of 20 AM and 20 FM stations. Licensees could acquire an attributable interest in an additional five AM and five FM stations as long as they were controlled by either minorities or small business (total revenues of less than $500,000 and total assets of less than $1 million.) Radio Multiple Ownership Rules, Recon., p. ___, *supra.* Radio Ownership Rules (Further Reconsideration), 9 F.C.C.Rcd. 7183, 76 R.R.2d 698 (1994).

The 1996 Telecommunications Act has eliminated all limits on the number of radio stations that one licensee can own nationally. It also eliminated the numerical cap on television stations and increased the national audience reach cap to 35 percent.

Thus, in just over a decade, the national ownership limits went from a strict limit of seven AM, seven FM and seven television stations to an unlimited number of stations subject only to a 35 percent audience reach cap for television stations. Is this change justified by changed conditions in the broadcast industry, or does it reflect a shift in regulatory philosophy?

2. Cable Subscriber Limits

The 1992 Cable Act required the FCC to conduct a rulemaking proceeding establishing reasonable limits on the number of subscribers a cable operator would be authorized to reach and on the number of channels that could be occupied by a program supplier in which the cable operator has an attributable interest.

For the purpose of the rules, the FCC adopted the same definition of "attributable interest" that is used for broadcast ownership rules, p. ___, *supra*. The Commission then "establishe[d] a 30 percent limit on the number of homes passed nationwide that any one entity can reach through cable systems in which such entity has an attributable interest." Ownership of additional systems, up to 35 percent of homes passed nationwide, would have been permitted, provided these systems were monopoly controlled. Cable Horizontal and Vertical Ownership Limits, 8 F.C.C.Rcd. 8565, 73 R.R.2d 1401 (1993).

Upon cross-motions for summary judgment, a federal district court found the subscriber limits provision unconstitutional, while holding the channel occupancy provision constitutional. *Daniels Cablevision*, p. ___, *supra*.

On appeal, both provisions were upheld. Relying on *Turner I*, p. ___, *supra*, the court determined that the appropriate standard to be applied was intermediate scrutiny. The court then found that both provisions served two important governmental interests, "promotion of diversity in ideas and speech, as well as the preservation of competition." Finally, the court found the provisions narrowly tailored. Time Warner Entertainment Co. v. United States, 211 F.3d 1313, 28 Med.L.Rptr. 1967, 20 C.R. 483 (D.C.Cir.2000).

Subsequently, the FCC enacted specific regulations to enforce these provisions. The regulations were challenged in a case that has implications for all of the Commission's ownership restrictions.

TIME WARNER ENTERTAINMENT CO. v. FEDERAL COMMUNICATIONS COMMISSION

United States Court of Appeals, District of Columbia Circuit, 2001.
240 F.3d 1126, 29 Med.L.Rptr. 1658.

Before: Williams, Randolph and Tatel, Circuit Judges.

Opinion for the Court filed by Circuit Judge Williams.

Stephen F. Williams, Circuit Judge:

Section 11(c) of the cable Television Consumer Protection and Competition Act of 1992, Pub.L. No. 102–385, 106 Stat. 1460 ("1992 Cable Act"), amends 47 U.S.C. § 533 to direct the Federal Communications Commission to set two types of limits on cable operators. The first type is horizontal, addressing operators' scale: "limits on the number of cable subscribers a person is authorized to reach through cable systems owned by such person, or in which such person has an attributable interest." 47 U.S.C. § 533(f)(1)(A). The second type is vertical, addressing operators' integration with "programmers" (suppliers of programs to be carried over cable systems): "limits on the number of channels on a cable system that can be occupied by a video programmer in which a cable operator has an attributable interest." 47 U.S.C. § 533(f)(1)(B). The FCC has duly promulgated regulations. See 47 C.F.R. § 76.503–04. . . .

     . . .

The horizontal rule imposes a 30% limit on the number of subscribers that may be served by a multiple cable system operator ("MSO"). See 47 C.F.R. § 76.503; Third Report 14 F.C.C.R. at 19119 § 55. Both the numerator and denominator of this fraction include only current subscribers to multichannel video program distributor ("MVPD") services. See *id.* at 19107–10 §§ 20–25. Subscribers include not only users of traditional cable services but also subscribers to non-cable MVPD services such as Direct Broadcast Satellite ("DBS"), a rapidly growing segment of the MVPD market. See *id.* at 19110–12 §§ 26–35. The Commission pointed out that under this provision the nominal 30% limit would allow a cable operator to serve 36.7% of the nation's cable subscribers if it served none by DBS. See *id.* at 19113 § 37 & n. 82.[3] In an express effort to encourage competition through new provision of cable, the Commission excluded from any MSO's numerator all new subscribers signed up by virtue of "overbuilding," the industry's term for cable laid in competition with a pre-existing cable operator. See *id.* at 19112–13 §§ 34, 37. Further, subscribers to a service franchised after the rule's adoption (October 20, 1999) do not go into an MSO's numerator, even if not the result of an overbuild. See *id.* at 19112 § 33. As a result, the rule's main bite is on firms obtaining subscribers through merger or acquisition.

The vertical limit is currently set at 40% of channel capacity, reserving 60% for programming by non-affiliated firms. [ ] Channels assigned to broadcast stations, leased access, and for public, educational, or governmental uses are included in the calculation of channel capacity. [ ] Capacity over 75 channels is not subject to the limit, so a cable operator is never required to reserve more than 45 channels for others (.60 x 75 = 45). [ ]

As cable operators, Time Warner and AT & T "exercise[ ] editorial discretion in selecting the programming [they] will make available to [their] subscribers," [*Time Warner I*, p. ___, *supra*], and are "entitled to the protection of the speech and press provisions of the First Amendment," [*Turner I*, p. ___, *supra*]. The horizontal limit interferes with petitioners' speech rights by restricting the number of viewers to whom

---

3. 30% of roughly 80 million MVPD subscribers would be about 24 million subscribers, which in turn would be 36.69% of roughly 66 million cable subscribers. Under the Commissions most recent subscriber es- timates, this provision would allow an MSO to serve 37.4% of cable subscribers, or approximately 1.1 million more customers than when the *Third Report* was written. [ ]

they can speak. The vertical limit restricts their ability to exercise their editorial control over a portion of the content they transmit.

In *Time Warner I* we upheld the statutory provisions against a facial attack, after finding them subject to intermediate rather than, as the cable firms argued, strict scrutiny. *Time Warner I*, [　]. The regulations here present a related but independent set of questions. Constitutional authority to impose some limit is not authority to impose any limit imaginable.

[The court decided to apply intermediate scrutiny.]

The interests asserted in support of the horizontal and vertical limits are the same interrelated interests that we found sufficient to support the statutory scheme in *Time Warner I*: "the promotion of diversity in ideas and speech" and "the preservation of competition." *Time Warner I*, [　]; see also *Turner I*, [　] (concluding that both qualify as important governmental interests). After a review of the legislative history, we concluded that Congress had drawn "reasonable inferences, based upon substantial evidence, that increases in the concentration of cable operators threatened diversity and competition in the cable industry." *Time Warner I*, 211 F.3d at 1319–20. But the FCC must still justify the limits that it has chosen as not burdening substantially more speech than necessary. In addition, in "demonstrat[ing] that the recited harms are real, not merely conjectural," *Turner I*, [　], the FCC must show a record that validates the *regulations,* not just the abstract statutory authority.

* * * * * *

The FCC asserts that a 30% horizontal limit satisfies its statutory obligation to ensure that no single "cable operator or group of cable operators can unfairly impede . . . the flow of video programming from the video programmer to the consumer," 47 U.S.C. § 533(f)(2)(A), while adequately respecting the benefits of clustering[4] and the economies of scale that are thought to come with larger size. [　] It interpreted this statutory language as a directive to prohibit large MSOs—either by the action of a single MSO or the coincidental or collusive actions of several MSOs—from precluding the entry into the market of a new cable programmer. [　] In setting the limit at 30%, it assumed there was a serious risk of collusion. [　] But while collusion is a form of anti-competitive behavior that implicates an important government interest, the FCC has not presented the "substantial evidence" required by *Turner I* and *Turner II* that such collusion has in fact occurred or is likely to occur; so its assumptions are mere conjecture. [　] The FCC alternatively relies on its supposed grant of authority to regulate the

---

4. "Clustering" refers to the strategy under which MSOs concentrate their operations within a particular geographic region, giving up scattered holdings around the country. The benefits are thought to be in achieving economies of both scale and scope, allowing MSOs to spread fixed investment costs over a larger customer base and to better compete with telephone companies owning local loops that are actual or potential substitutes. [　]

non-collusive actions of large MSOs. Congress may indeed, under certain readings of *Turner I* and *Turner II*, have the power to regulate the coincidental but independent actions of cable operators solely in the interest of diversity, but "[w]here an administrative interpretation of a statute invokes the outer limits of Congress' power, we expect a clear indication that Congress intended that result." [   ] The 1992 Cable Act, as we shall see, instead expresses the contrary intention.

Part VI of the Third Report lays out the calculations that lead the FCC to the 30% limit. [   ] First the FCC determines that the average cable network needs to reach 15 million subscribers to be economically viable. [   ] This is 18.56% of the roughly 80 million MVPD subscribers, and the FCC rounds it up to 20% of such subscribers. The FCC then divines that the average cable programmer will succeed in reaching only about 50% of the subscribers linked to cable companies that *agree* to carry its programming, because of channel capacity, "programming tastes of particular cable operators," or other factors. [   ] The average programmer therefore requires an "open field" of 40% of the market to be viable (.20/.50 = .40). [   ]

Finally, to support the 30% limit that it says is necessary to assure this minimum, the Commission reasons as follows: With a 30% limit, a programmer has an "open field" of 40% of the market even if the two largest cable companies deny carriage, acting "individually or collusively." [   ] A 50% rule is inadequate because, if a duopoly were to result, "[t]he probability of tacit collusion is higher with 2 competitors than 3 competitors." [   ] Even if collusion were not to occur, *independent* rejections by two MSOs could doom a new programmer, thwarting congressional intent as the Commission saw it. [   ] A 40% limit is insufficient for the same reason: "two MSOs, . . . representing a total of 80% of the market, might decline to carry the new network" and leave only 20% "open," which by hypothesis is not enough (because of the 50% success rate). [   ] Although the Commission doesn't spell out the intellectual process, it is necessarily defining the requisite "open field" as the residue of the market after a programmer is turned down either (1) by one cable company acting alone, or (2) by a set of companies acting either (a) collusively or (b) independently but nonetheless in some way that, because of the combined effect of their choices, threatens fulfillment of the statutory purposes. We address the FCC's authority to regulate each of these scenarios in turn.

The Commission is on solid ground in asserting authority to be sure that no single company could be in a position singlehandedly to deal a programmer a death blow. Statutory authority flows plainly from the instruction that the Commission's regulations "ensure that no cable operator or group of cable operators can unfairly impede, either because of *the size of any individual operator* or because of joint actions of operators of sufficient size, the flow of video programming from the video programmer to the consumer." 47 U.S.C. § 533(f)(2)(A) (emphasis added). Constitutional authority is equally plain. As the Supreme Court said in *Turner II*: "We have identified a corresponding 'governmental purpose of the highest order' in ensuring public access to 'a multiplicity of information sources.' " [   ]. If this interest in diversity is to mean anything in this context, the government must be able to ensure that a programmer have at least two conduits through which it can reach the number of viewers needed for viability—independent of concerns over anticompetitive conduct.

Assuming the validity of the premises supporting the FCC's conclusion that a 40% "open field" is necessary (a question that we need not answer here), the statute's express concern for the act of "any individual operator" would justify a horizontal limit of 60%. To reach the 30% limit, the FCC's action necessarily involves one or the other of two additional propositions: Either there is a material risk of collusive denial of carriage by two or more companies, or the statute authorizes the Commission to protect programmers against the risk of completely *independent* rejections by two or more companies leaving less than 40% of the MVPD audience potentially accessible. Neither proposition is sound.

First, we consider whether there is record support for inferring a non-conjectural risk of collusive rejection. Either Congress or the Commission could supply that record, and we take them in that order. We give deference to the predictive judgments of Congress, see *Turner II*, [   ], but Congress appears to have made no judgment regarding collusion. The statute plainly alludes to the *possibility* of collusion when it authorizes regulations to protect against "*joint* actions by a group of operators of sufficient size." 47 U.S.C. § 533(f)(2)(A) (emphasis added). But this phrase, while granting the Commission authority to take action in the event that it finds collusion extant or likely, is not itself a congressional finding of actual or probable collusion. Such findings have not been made. No reference to collusion appears in the Act's findings or policy, see 1992 cable Act § 2, 106 Stat. at 1460–63, nor in the legislative history discussing the horizontal or vertical limits. [   ] It was thus appropriate for the FCC to describe Congress's reference to "joint" action as merely a "legislative *assumption*." [   ]

The Commission's own findings amount to precious little. It says only:

> The legislative assumption [about joint action] is not unreasonable given an environment in which all the larger operators in the industry are vertically integrated so that all are both buyers and sellers of programming and have mutual incentives to reach carriage decisions beneficial to each other. Operators have incentives to agree to buy their programming from one another. Moreover, they have incentives to encourage one another to carry the same non-vertically integrated programming in order to share the costs of such programming.
>
> [   ]

None of these assertions is supported in the record. The Commission never explains why the vertical integration of MSOs gives them "mutual incentive to reach carriage decisions beneficial to each other," what may be the firms' "incentives to buy . . . from one another," or what the probabilities are that firms would engage in reciprocal buying (presumably to reduce each other's average programming costs). After all, the economy is filled with firms that, like MSOs, display partial upstream vertical integration. If that phenomenon implies the sort of collusion the Commission infers, one would expect the Commission to be able to point to examples. Yet it names none. . . .

The only justification that the FCC offers in support of its collusion hypothesis is the economic commonplace that, all other things being equal, collusion is less likely when there are more firms. [ ] This observation will always be true, although marginally less so for each additional firm; but by itself it lends no insight into the question of what the appropriate horizontal limit is. *Turner I* demands that the FCC do more than "simply 'posit the existence of the disease sought to be cured.'" *Turner I*, [ ]. It requires that the FCC draw "reasonable inferences based on substantial evidence." *Turner I*, [ ]. Substantial evidence does not require a complete factual record—we must give appropriate deference to predictive judgments that necessarily involve the expertise and experience of the agency. See *Turner II*, [ ]. But the FCC has put forth no evidence at all that indicates the prospects for collusion.

That having been said, we do not foreclose the possibility that there are theories of anti-competitive behavior other than collusion that may be relevant to the horizontal limit and on which the FCC may be able to rely on remand. See 47 U.S.C. § 533(f)(1). Indeed, Congress considered, among other things, the ability of MSOs dominant in specific cable markets to extort equity from programmers or force exclusive contracts on them. [ ]. A single MSO, acting alone rather than "jointly," might perhaps be able to do so while serving somewhat less than the 60% of the market (i.e., less than the fraction that would allow it unilaterally to lock out a new cable programmer) despite the existence of antitrust laws and specific behavioral prohibitions enacted as part of the 1992 cable Act, see 47 U.S.C. § 536, and the risk might justify a prophylactic limit under the statute. See *Time Warner I*, [ ]. So the absence of any showing of a serious risk of collusion does not *necessarily* preclude a finding of a sufficient governmental interest in preventing unfair competition. (We express no opinion on whether exploitation of a monopoly position in a specific cable market to extract rents that would otherwise flow to programmers alone gives rise to an "important governmental interest" justifying a burden on speech.) But the FCC made no attempt to justify its regulation on these grounds.

We pause here to address an aspect of petitioners' statutory challenge that is relevant to a showing of non-conjectural harm. Congress required that in setting the horizontal limit, the FCC "take particular account of the market structure . . . including the nature and market power of the local franchise." 47 U.S.C. § 533(f)(2)(C). Petitioners assert that the Commission's failure to take adequate account of the competitive pressures brought by the availability and increasing success of DBS make the horizontal limit arbitrary and capricious. Although DBS accounts for only 15.4% of current MVPD households, the annual increase in its total subscribership is almost three times that of cable (nearly three million additional subscribers over the period June 1999 to June 2000, as against one million for cable). [ ] To the extent petitioners argue that the horizontal limit must fail because market share does not *equal* market power, they misconstrue the statutory command. The Commission is not required to design a limit that falls solely on firms possessing market power. The provision is directed to the Commission's intellectual process, and requires it, in evaluating the harms posed by concentration and in setting the subscriber limit, to assess the determinants of market power in the cable industry and to draw a connection between market power and the limit set.

It follows naturally from our earlier discussion that we do not believe the Commission has satisfied this obligation. Having failed to identify a non-conjectural harm, the Commission could not possibly have addressed the connection between the harm and market power. But the assessment of a real risk of anti-competitive behavior—collusive or not— is itself dependent on an understanding of market power, and the Commission's statements in the Third Report seem to ignore the true relevance of competition. In changing the calculation of the horizontal limit to reflect subscribers instead of homes at which a service is available, for instance, the Commission wrote:

> [W]hether subscribership or homes passed data is used is largely a mechanical issue in terms of the market power issue. . . . As the market develops in terms of competition we believe . . . that an operator's actual number of subscribers more uniformly and accurately reflects power in the programming marketplace.

[ ]

But normally a company's ability to exercise market power depends not only on its share of the market, but also on the elasticities of supply and demand, which in turn are determined by the *availability* of competition. [ ] If an MVPD refuses to offer new programming, customers with access to an alternative MVPD may switch. The FCC shows no reason why this logic does not apply to the cable industry. . . .

. . . But whatever conclusions are to be drawn from the new data, it seems clear that in revisiting the horizontal rules the Commission will have to take account of the impact of DBS on that market power. Already when the Third Report was written, DBS could be considered to "pass every home in the country." [ ] The technological and regulatory changes since then appear only to strengthen petitioners' contention. [ ]

With the risk of collusion inadequately substantiated to support the 30% limit and no attempt to find other anticompetitive behavior, there remains the Commission's alternative ground—that programming choices made "unilaterally" by multiple cable companies, [ ], might reduce a programmer's "open field" below the 40% benchmark. The only support the Commission offered for regulation based on this possibility was the idea that every additional chance for a programmer to secure access would enhance diversity:

> [T]he 30% limit serves the salutary purpose of ensuring that there will be at least 4 MSOs in the marketplace. The rule thus maximizes the potential number of MSOs that will purchase programming. With more MSOs making purchasing decisions, this increases the likelihood that the MSOs will make different programming choices and a greater variety of media voices will therefore be available to the public.

[ ] Petitioners challenge the FCC's authority to regulate for this purpose on both constitutional and statutory grounds.

We have some concern how far such a theory may be pressed against First Amendment norms. Everything else being equal, each additional "voice" may be said to enhance diversity. And in this special context, every additional splintering of the cable industry increases the number of *combinations* of companies whose acceptance would in the aggregate lay the foundations for a programmer's viability. But at some point, surely, the marginal value of such an increment in "diversity" would not qualify as an "important" governmental interest. Is moving from 100 possible combinations to 101 "important"? It is not clear to us how a court could determine the point where gaining such an increment is no longer important. And it would be odd to discover that although a newspaper that is the only general daily in a metropolitan area cannot be subjected to a right of reply, [*Miami Herald*, p. ___, *supra*], it could in the name of diversity be forced to self-divide. Certainly the Supreme Court has not gone so far.

We need not face that issue, however, because we conclude that Congress has not given the Commission authority to impose, solely on the basis of the "diversity" precept, a limit that does more than guarantee a programmer two possible outlets (each of them a market adequate for viability). . . .

We begin with the statutory language. The relevant section requires the FCC to:

> ensure that no cable operator or group of cable operators can unfairly impede, either because of the size of any individual operator or because of joint actions by a group of operators of sufficient size, the flow of video programming from the video programmer to the consumer. 47 U.S.C. § 533(f)(2)(A).

The language addresses only "unfair[]" impediments to the flow of programming. The word "unfair" is of course extremely vague. Certainly, the action of several firms that is "joint," in the sense of collusive, may often entail unfairness of a conventional sort. The statute goes further, plainly treating exercise of editorial discretion by a single cable operator as "unfair" simply because that operator is the only game in town. (And *Time Warner I* authoritatively determines that the government is constitutionally entitled to impose limits solely on that ground.) But we cannot see how the word unfair could plausibly apply to the legitimate, independent editorial choices of multiple MSOs. A broad interpretation is plausible *only* for actions that impinge at least to some degree on the interest in competition that lay at the heart of Congress's concern.[6] The Commission's reading of the clause effectively deletes the word "joint" and opens the door to illimitable restrictions in the name of diversity.

Looking at the statute as a whole does little to support the FCC's position. The "interrelated interests" of promoting diversity and fair competition run throughout the 1992 Cable Act's various provisions. *Turner II,* [ ] But despite the duality of interests at work in this section, see *Time Warner I,* [ ], it is clear from the structure of the statute that Congress's *primary* concern in authorizing ownership limits is "fair" competition. The statute specifies, after all, that *these* regulations are to be promulgated "[i]n order to enhance effective competition." 47 U.S.C. § 533(f)(1). In only two of the other sections of the 1992 cable Act does Congress specify a dominant purpose. This statement of purpose supports a reading that sharply confines the authority to regulate solely in the interest of diversity.

. . .

On the record before us, we conclude that the 30% horizontal limit is in excess of statutory authority. While a 60% limit might be appropriate as necessary to ensure that programmers had an adequate "open field" even in the face of rejection by the largest company, the present record supports no more. In addition, the statute allows the Commission to act prophylactically against the risk of "unfair" conduct by cable operators that might unduly impede the flow of programming, either by the "joint" actions of two or more companies or the independent action of a single company of sufficient size. But the Commission has pointed to nothing in the record supporting a non-conjectural risk of anticompetitive behavior, either by collusion or other means. Accordingly, we reverse and remand with respect to the 30% rule.

*   *   *   *   *   *

The FCC presents its 40% vertical limit as advancing the same interests invoked in support of its statutory authority to adopt the rule: diversity in programming and fair competition. As with the horizontal rules the FCC must defend the rules themselves under intermediate

---

6. The Commission's economic theory— that cable operators have an incentive to contract with the same programmers in order to lower the programmers' average costs . . . —would seem to apply regardless of any horizontal limit. Putting various special cases aside, *any* profit-maximizing firm will have an incentive to lower its costs. In a market where a cable operator is a mo- nopolist, the resulting benefit to the firm would be classified as monopoly rents. In a market where an operator is in competition, it can be expected to pass the benefits on to its customers. But the FCC has not shown why such pursuit of lower costs, by the monopolist or the competitive firm, is by itself "unfair," and the statute allows for regulation only if unfairness can be shown.

scrutiny and justify its chosen limit as not burdening substantially more speech than necessary. Far from satisfying this test, the FCC seems to have plucked the 40% limit out of thin air.

The FCC relies almost exclusively on the congressional findings that vertical integration in the cable industry could "make it difficult for non-cable affiliated . . . programmers to secure carriage on vertically integrated cables systems" and that "vertically integrated program suppliers have the incentive and the ability to favor their affiliated cable operators . . . and program distributors." [   ] Regulatory limits in response to these consequences would "increase the diversity of voices available to the public." [   ] In *Time Warner I* we thought these findings strong enough to overcome the First Amendment challenge to the relevant provision of the 1992 cable Act. In doing so, we held that such a prophylactic rule was not "rendered unnecessary merely because preexisting statutes [such as the antitrust laws and the antidiscrimination provisions of the 1992 cable Act] impose behavioral norms." *Time Warner I*, [   ]. Beyond that we did not assess the appropriateness of the burden on speech. We upheld no specific vertical limit—none was before us.

We recognize that in drawing a numerical line an agency will ultimately indulge in some inescapable residue of arbitrariness; even if 40% is a highly justifiable pick, no one could expect the Commission to show why it was materially better than 39% or 41%. [   ] But to pass even the arbitrary and capricious standard, the agency must at least reveal " 'a rational connection between the facts found and the choice made.' " [   ] Here the FCC must also meet First Amendment intermediate scrutiny. Yet it appears to provide nothing but the conclusion that "we believe that a 40% limit is appropriate to balance the goals." [   ] What are the conditions that make 50% too high and 30% too low? How great is the risk presented by current market conditions? These questions are left unanswered by the Commission's discussion.

        . . .

In fairness, the FCC does make an attempt to review some relevant conditions. [   ] The FCC cites the House Report's conclusion that "some" vertically integrated MSOs favor their affiliates and "may" discriminate against others. [   ] But it also notes a report that none of the top five MSOs "showed a pattern" of favoring their affiliates. [   ] Indeed, the FCC concludes that "vertical relationships had increased both the quality and quantity of cable programming services." [   ] But still it settled on a limit of 40%. There is no effort to link the numerical limits to the benefits and detriments depicted. Further, given the pursuit of diversity, one might expect some inquiry into whether innovative independent originators of programming find greater success selling to affiliated or to unaffiliated programming firms, but there is none.

Quite apart from the numerical limit *vel non*, petitioners attack the Commission's refusal to exclude from the vertical limit cable operators that are subject to effective competition. The FCC had proposed exempting cable operators who met the definition of effective competition provided by § 623 of the Communications Act of 1934. [ ] Of course our decision in *Time Warner I* acknowledged the existence of incentives to use affiliated programming. [ ] For example, even where an unaffiliated supplier offered a better cost-quality trade-off, a company might be reluctant to ditch or curtail an inefficient in-house operation because of the impact on firm executives or other employees, or the resulting spotlight on management's earlier judgment. But petitioners argue, quite plausibly, that exposure to competition will have an impact on a cable company's *ability* to indulge in favoritism for in-house productions. After all, while reliance on in-house suppliers offering an inferior price-quality trade-off will reduce a monopolist's profits, it may threaten a competitive firm's very survival. This analysis is not foreign to the Commission, which endorsed it when proposing the exemption:

> We believe that this proposal is appropriate since effective competition will preclude cable operators from exercising the market power which originally justified channel occupancy limits. Where systems face effective competition, their incentive to favor an affiliated programmer will be replaced by the incentive to provide programming that is most valued by subscribers.

[ ]

The FCC makes two arguments to justify its refusal to exempt MVPDs that are subject to effective competition. First, it says that the definition of competition provided by 47 U.S.C. § 543 was "not adopted for this specific purpose" but rather for relief from rate regulation. [ ] Indeed, we have recognized that one of the ways in which the statutory standard is met may be surprisingly defective as a mark of real competition. [ ] But the Commission is free to carve out subsections that are truly pertinent to competition, as it had proposed. [ ]

Of course competition that is adequate to justify dispensing with rate regulation could still leave an undue likelihood of improper favoritism for affiliated programmers. But the possible failure of readily available criteria does not itself justify the use of so blunt a blade. Congress expressly directed the Commission to take "*particular* account of the market structure . . ., including the nature and market power of the local franchise." 47 U.S.C. § 533(f)(2)(C) (emphasis added). Because competition raises the stakes for a firm that sacrifices the optimal price-quality trade-off in its acquisition of programming, the issue seems to trigger the legislative directive. Yet the Commission seems to ignore its own conclusions about cable companies' incentives and constraints, and the dynamics of the programming industry. [ ] If the criteria of § 543(*l*)(1) are unsuitable, the Commission can consider concepts of effective competition that it finds more apt for these purposes.

Second, the FCC comments that if a competing MVPD favored *its* own affiliated programmers, the presence of competition would have no tendency to create room for independent programmers. [ ] But this theory seems contradicted by the Commission's own observation, mentioned earlier, that no vertically integrated MVPD has complained of reaching the 40% limit. Vertically integrated MVPDs evidently use loads of independent programming. Further, although cable operators continue to expand their interests in programmers, "[t]he *proportion* of vertically integrated channels . . . continue[d] to decline" for each of the last two years. [ ] Even if competing MSOs filled all of their channels with affiliates' products (as unlikely as that seems), the Commission nowhere explains why, in the pursuit of diversity, the independence of competing vertically integrated MVPDs is inferior to the independence of unaffiliated programmers. In any event, the Commission's point here does not respond to the intuition that competition spurs a firm's search for the best price-quality trade-off.

. . .

We find that the FCC has failed to justify its vertical limit as not burdening substantially more speech than necessary. Accordingly, we reverse and remand to the FCC for further consideration.

. . .

To summarize, we reverse and remand the horizontal and vertical limits, including the refusal to exempt cable operators subject to effective competition from the vertical limits, for further proceedings . . . . .

So ordered.

Notes and Questions.

1. A petition for *certiorari* was denied.

2. The court's decision raises questions regarding the continued viability of other concentration rules such as the television reach cap. The Commission has delayed hearings on some of these rules as a result.

3. The horizontal limits never went into effect because a federal district court found the section of the 1992 Cable Act authorizing them to be unconstitutional:

> Any governmentally ordained quota on the number of subscribers a cable operator may reach leaves the operator with absolutely no intra-medium means of speaking to the remainder of its potential audience. The First Amendment protects the right of every citizen to reach the minds of any willing listeners and, thus, the speaker's opportunity to win their attention.

Daniels Cablevision, p. ___, *supra*.

4. The court's decision raised questions regarding the continued viability of other concentration rules such as the television reach cap. The Commission is conducting a comprehensive review of these rules and is expected to issue new rules in mid–2003.

3. CONGLOMERATES IN BROADCASTING

Occasionally the problem has been raised, not in terms of multiple ownership of competing media, but in terms of concern about other businesses in which a prospective licensee is engaged. The prime example is a merger that was proposed between ABC, which, in its capacity as group owner, owned 17 broadcasting stations, and International Telephone and Telegraph, a vast conglomerate with manufacturing facilities, telecommunication operations and other activities in 66 countries throughout the world.

Critics were concerned that ITT would use the broadcasting facilities to further the interests of the parent corporation in ways that might include distorting the news and making editorial decisions on grounds other than professional journalism criteria. The Commission rejected these concerns on the ground that "it is too late in the day to argue that such outside business interests are disqualifying. . . . We cannot in this case adopt standards which when applied to other cases would require us to restructure the industry unless we are prepared to undertake that task. We could not, in good conscience, forbid ABC to merge with ITT without instituting proceedings to separate NBC from RCA, both of which are bigger than the respective principals in this case." The Commission granted the application for transferring of the 17 licenses by a 4 to 3 vote. ABC–ITT Merger, 7 F.C.C.2d 245, 9 R.R.2d 12 (1966).

While an appeal by the Justice Department on antitrust grounds was pending, the parties abandoned their proposed merger. Would there be any problem if, for example, General Motors sought to acquire a television station in Detroit? Are different questions raised if a book publisher or motion picture producer seeks a television license?

The Gannett–Combined Communications Merger. In 1979 the FCC approved what was at that time the largest deal in broadcasting history. The parties were Gannett, which at the time published 77 daily and 32 weekly newspapers and owned WHEC–TV in Rochester, N.Y., and Combined Communications Corp. which at the time owned newspapers in Cincinnati and Oakland, plus five VHF, two UHF, six AM and six FM stations. In addition, Gannett owned Louis Harris and Associates, the polling firm, and Combined was a major supplier of outdoor advertising. The deal called for $370 million in Gannett stock to go to Combined. After spin-offs to meet the FCC's crossownership policies, Gannett had 79 daily newspapers, seven television stations and 12 radio stations.

The final result, because of the spin-offs, violated no concentration rule. Nonetheless, the Commission considered whether granting the applications to transfer ownership of the stations would be in the "public interest." The majority concluded that the deal was not likely to affect competition adversely or raise antitrust concerns.

The First Amendment issue, however, raised harder questions. The FCC noted that Gannett had represented that "local autonomy will be the touchstone for the operation of each newspaper and broadcast property" and that the newspapers would operate separately from the broadcast properties. For example, Gannett asserted that in 1976, of its 35 papers that made endorsements, 22 endorsed Gerald Ford and 13 endorsed Jimmy Carter. Decentralized operation was the goal, although everyone recognized that under § 310 of the 1934 Act, Gannett had to retain ultimate control of its stations.

Some were concerned about the possibility that the size of the combination would lead advertisers and stock market investors to exercise more control over management than would occur with less centralized control. They feared that a large communications entity might "harm diversity of information and opinion through its institutional pressures rather than by any intentional acts of its corporate leadership."

The FCC stressed countervailing considerations: "Media chains may have more freedom and might be inclined to take more risks in their reporting of news and opinion because their financial health allows a degree of independence from the political views of their major advertisers." The size of the organization might permit more coverage of national news in competition with the wire services, the television networks, and the largest newspapers and magazines.

Because all of these newspapers and stations face "substantial local mixed-media competition," even if a "Gannett" view entered a new market, it was not eliminating other views available in that market. Affirmatively, the Commission noted that the deal had resulted in the break-up of cross-ownership interests in Phoenix and St. Louis, as well as sale of WHEC–TV to a buyer controlled by a minority group. This made WHEC–TV the first network-affiliated major market television station controlled by a minority group. The merger was approved 5–1.

The dissenter was greatly concerned by the "trend" toward placing "organs of information and news and opinion in this country in fewer and fewer hands. This is an unhealthy thing for a democracy: absentee ownership, on a vast scale, of newspapers and broadcasting stations. . . . Where are the William Allen Whites of 1979? Too many of them have been bought out, one by one, by the chains. They've been made offers they could not refuse."

In 1985 Gannett reached an agreement to purchase the Evening News Association, expanding both its newspaper and its broadcast holdings. As a result of the purchase, the audience reach of Gannett's television stations was increased from 6 to 10 percent.

The Capital Cities Communications–American Broadcasting Companies Merger. In 1985 Capital Cities Communications (CCC) acquired American Broadcasting Companies, Inc. (ABC) for $3.5 billion. This transaction, larger by far than any previous broadcast sale or merger, resulted in the formation of a new company, Capital Cities/ABC, Inc. (CC/ABC).

To meet the various FCC ownership rules, CC/ABC had to sell more than $1 billion worth of properties. However, the FCC did grant CC/ABC several waivers. A signal overlap between WABC–TV in New York and WPVI–TV in Philadelphia did not necessitate selling one of those stations because the Commission granted them a waiver of the duopoly rule. Also, the merger had produced ownership of TV–AM–FM combinations in New York City, Chicago, and Los Angeles and of an AM–FM combination in San Francisco. The FCC granted permanent waivers in all four cases because all four cities were in the top 25 television markets and each had over 30 separately owned and operated broadcast stations after the proposed waivers. The FCC found 94 separate licensees in New York, 105 in Chicago, 79 in Los Angeles and 57 in San Francisco. The Commission did not scrutinize each proposal for economic efficiencies because it had already concluded that such efficiencies generally exist. Allowing the combinations would not undermine the benefits that flow from the "Commission's traditional pro-competitive and diversity policies."

Commissioner Dennis concurred separately. She had suggested a two-tier approach in lieu of the 25 market–30 licensee approach. She would have restricted waivers to markets with at least 10 television stations, 45 separate owners and 65 broadcast stations. "In all other markets, we should not only retain the rule, but enforce it strictly." Because the four markets involved here met even her tighter requirements, she concurred. Capital Cities/ABC, Inc., 66 R.R.2d 1146 (1989).

The Disney Purchase of Capital Cities/ABC. Ten years later, CC/ABC was itself purchased by Walt Disney Co. for $18.5 billion, creating the largest media company in the U.S. Among the company's various holdings are 11 television stations, 21 radio stations, the ABC television network, the ABC radio networks, the Disney Channel, 80 percent of ESPN, 50 percent of Lifetime Television, 37.5 percent of Arts & Entertainment Network, Walt Disney Pictures, Touchstone Pictures, Caravan Pictures, Hollywood Pictures, Miramax Films, Buena Vista Pictures Distribution and Fairchild Publications.

The acquisition was approved by the FCC which granted six permanent waivers of the one-to-a-market rule, allowing Disney to retain radio-television combinations. Previously, Disney had agreed to divest one of its television stations in order to obtain Justice Department approval of the transaction. We will discuss the application of antitrust law to the broadcast industry later in this chapter.

The Westinghouse Electric Co. Purchase of CBS, Inc. In 1995, Westinghouse Electric Co. announced its plans to purchase CBS, Inc., for $5.4 billion. The transaction was approved with seven permanent waivers of the one-to-a-market rule, and twelve temporary waivers of various concentration rules. However, the 1996 changes to the national ownership limits, p. ___, *supra*, eliminated the need for some of the temporary waivers because the 16 television stations with a national audience reach of between 32 and 33 percent and the 21 FM stations owned by the new company no longer exceeded the maximum allowed. Stockholders of CBS, Inc., 1 C.R. 1114 (1995).

The Time Warner Purchase of Turner Broadcasting. In 1995 Time Warner announced its plans to purchase Turner Broadcasting System. However, the merger faced several major hurdles. The FTC was expected to subject the merger to close scrutiny. Not only did the two companies have combined holdings of two movie studios and a dozen cable channels, but TCI, the largest MSO in the country, owned 21 percent of Turner. Between them, Time Warner and TCI controlled almost 40 percent of all cable subscribers. Furthermore, as part of the deal, TCI also received preferential carriage agreements for both Time Warner and Turner programming.

Nevertheless, both the FTC and FCC approved the merger. However, the FTC required TCI to divest its shares in Time Warner (acquired in exchange for its shares in Turner) to a separate company, which will not be allowed to vote any stock in Time Warner. The FCC granted Time Warner a 12–month waiver for the Atlanta cable system. 1996 WL 580319.

Phone Company Purchases and Mergers. As expected, the 1996 Telecommunications Act quickly led to further consolidation in the communications industry. Less than one month after the bill's enactment, U.S. West announced the purchase of Continental Cablevision for $10.8 billion. This was soon followed by two other deals. SBC Communications merged with Pacific Telesis Group. The new company will have total assets of $16.7 billion. Also, Bell Atlantic merged with NYNEX to form a company with assets totalling $23 billion. The new company is Verizon.

Still another major merger occurred in 1998 with AT&T taking over TCI in a deal estimated at $48 billion. The merger was another example of the changing landscape of telecommunications, specifically the convergence of phone and cable service. AT&T was expected to use the cable MSO's wires to deliver local phone service in competition with the RBOC's. Broadcasting & Cable, June 29. 1998 at 6.

The merger was approved by the FCC, despite objections by AOL and various public interest groups. The opposition was to TCI's requirement that anyone using TCI's cable modem service also had to subscribe to its online service. Those opposing approval wanted approval of the merger conditioned on TCI allowing cable modem subscribers equal access to all online service providers. Although the FCC refused to to do so, several communities have conditioned approval of the transfer of TCI cable franchises to AT & T on an equal-access requirement.

Further questions regarding monopoly control of high-speed Internet Access were raised by AT&T's announcement that it will acquire MediaOne. When the deal was completed, AT&T became the largest cable MSO with 15 million subscribers. It will also own the only two cable Internet providers, AT&T's @Home and MediaOne's Road Runner. An additional concern for regulators was Microsoft's agreement as part of the deal to invest $5 billion in return for installation of its Windows CE operating system in 7.5–10 million AT&T set-top converters. Broadcastng & Cable, May 10, 1999 at 14–15.

However, the marriage of cable and phone service proved less successful than anticipated. Thus, within three years, AT&T sold its cable systems to Comcast, another large cable MSO.

DBS Consolidation. In late 1998, Hughes Corp., owner of DirectTV announced the acquisition of U.S.S.B. These deals left only two companies providing DBS service, DirectTV and Echostar. Then, in 2001, Echostar announced it was buying DirecTV. The announced deal caused a great deal of controversy. Proponents of the deal argued that it would produce a viable competitor for cable. Opponents argued that it would give Echostar a monopoly in the DBS industry. The FCC agreed with the latter and rejected the proposed deal.

4.   MINORITY OWNERSHIP

One of the FCC's concerns in recent years has been the dearth of minority broadcasters. The FCC developed several policies aimed at increasing minority ownership. One of these is the distress sale policy.

In 1978 in an effort to meet two concerns at once, the Commission announced steps to allow licensees whose renewals might be in jeopardy to sell their stations to minority groups for more than the value of the buildings and equipment but less than the going concern value. Statement of Policy on Minority Ownership of Broadcast Facilities, 68 F.C.C.2d 979, 42 R.R.2d 1689 (1978). The Commission announced that it would permit "licensees whose licenses have been designated for revocation hearings, or whose renewal applications have been designated for hearing on basic qualification issues . . . to transfer or assign their licenses at a 'distress sale' price to applicants with a significant minority ownership interest, assuming the proposed assignee or transferee meets our other qualifications." The distress price was expected to be "somewhat greater than the value of the unlicensed equipment, which could be realized even in the event of revocation."

In a clarifying statement, the Commission stated that the opportunity for distress sales applied only when no competing applicant was involved in the hearing.

The distress sale option was attractive to licensees who were ordered to hearings. The fact that allegations had been thought serious enough to warrant a hearing was a dangerous warning. To litigate and lose the renewal would leave the licensee with nothing except the buildings and equipment that it owned. The distress sale could yield the owner as much as 75 percent of the fair appraised value of a viable business.

The immediate social result of the distress sale policy has been to allow minority groups to enter the broadcasting industry in greater numbers. If the FCC's efforts to develop new stations, discussed in

Chapter II, work as expected, many minority broadcasters will use that route and the relatively limited distress sale route will become less important.

The distress sale policy explicitly limited "minority" to specific ethnic groups but indicated that "other clearly definable groups, such as women, may be able to demonstrate that they are eligible for similar treatment." But in Minority Ownership of Broadcast Facilities, 69 F.C.C.2d 1591, 44 R.R.2d 1051 (1978), the Commission ruled that although it had on occasion recognized female involvement as a merit in comparative proceedings, it would not extend the minority policy to women because it had "not concluded that the historical and contemporary disadvantagement suffered by women is of the same order, or has the same contemporary consequences" as those involving groups covered in the original policy statement.

In 1985 the Commission similarly refused to extend the minority preference in lottery proceedings. The FCC concluded that it did not have the authority and that, furthermore, extending it to women was inappropriate. Lottery Selection (Preference for Women), 58 R.R.2d 1077 (1985). The Commission's refusal to extend the preference to women was affirmed. *Pappas*, p. ___, *supra*.

In 1987, as a result of a court of appeals decision and the Commission's subsequent actions, all of the minority and female preference policies appeared to face possible elimination. The case was the appeal of the FCC's decision to grant an FM construction permit to Dale Bell in a comparative hearing. The primary factor in the decision was a female preference awarded to Bell.

The court of appeals held 2–1 that the Commission had exceeded its authority by adopting the female preference policy. The court subsequently granted Bell's petition for rehearing *en banc* and asked the parties to file briefs addressing two questions: "(1) whether the FCC has statutory authority to grant a limited preference for integrated ownership-management by women applicants in comparative licensing proceedings, and (2) whether such a grant is constitutional." The Commission's brief took many people by surprise:

> The racial and gender preference policies employed by the FCC in comparative licensing proceedings since 1978 are discriminatory classifications by government that are inherently suspect, presumptively invalid and subject to stringent scrutiny under the equal protection guarantee implicit in the due process clause of the Fifth Amendment. See Wygant v. Jackson Bd. of Educ., 476 U.S. 267 (1986); Lehr v. Robertson, 463 U.S. 248, 265–66 (1983). . . .
>
> . . .
>
> It has been suggested that one aspect of the justification for both the gender and race preference policies is that they serve as a remedy for past discrimination. . . .

Yet in a recent Supreme Court decision it was emphasized that "[t]his Court never has held that societal discrimination alone is sufficient to justify a racial classification. Rather, the Court has insisted upon some showing of prior discrimination by the governmental unit involved before allowing limited use of racial classifications in order to remedy such discrimination." *Wygant,* 476 U.S. at 274 (opinion of Powell, J.). There has never been a finding, nor so far as we know even an allegation, that the FCC engaged in prior discrimination against racial minorities or women in its licensing process. The general societal discrimination alluded to in some opinions is hence inadequate to support licensing preferences imposed by the FCC to remedy such general societal discrimination. Thus, there has been a clear failure to meet applicable constitutional standards to justify use of racial and gender licensing preferences as a remedy for prior discrimination.

The Commission did not go so far as to argue that the use of racial and gender licensing preferences to enhance diversity of programming was *per se* unconstitutional. Rather, it claimed that the requirement of strict scrutiny prohibited such preferences in the absence of a record demonstrating: (1) "that a race-or gender-based preference scheme to increase minority and female ownership is essential to achieving" diversity, and (2) "that a nexus exists between an owner's race or gender and program diversity." The Commission therefore asked the court to remand the case for further proceedings to determine whether "exceedingly persuasive justification" for the preferences could be established. The court granted the Commission's motion. Steele v. Federal Communications Commission, 806 F.2d 1126 (D.C.Cir.1986).

The Commission's other policies aimed at increasing minority ownership also came under attack. For example, in Faith Center, Inc., 57 R.R.2d 1185 (1984), an application for approval of a distress sale was challenged in part on the grounds that the distress sale policy is unconstitutional. The application was granted, and Shurberg Broadcasting of Hartford, Inc., appealed. After the remand in *Steele* was granted, the Commission requested a similar remand in Shurberg Broadcasting of Hartford, Inc. v. Federal Communications Commission, 876 F.2d 902 (D.C.Cir.1989). Although the remand request was initially denied, the court subsequently did remand *Shurberg* with instructions to decide it in accordance with the court's decision in *Steele.*

Following the remand in *Steele,* the Commission issued an NOI addressing these issues. Reexamination of the Commission's Comparative Licensing, Distress Sales and Tax Certificate Policies Premised on Racial, Ethnic or Gender Classifications, 1 F.C.C.Rcd. 1315 (1986).

However, Congress included a provision in the 1987 Omnibus Spending Bill prohibiting the Commission from repealing or continuing its reexamination of the minority ownership policies. In accordance with that mandate, the Commission terminated its proceedings and notified the court of appeals of its action. Pub. L. 100–202 (1987).

In 1988 a tentative settlement was reached in *Steele*. Despite the settlement in *Steele*, the court of appeals soon found itself addressing the issues raised in that case. In Winter Park Communications, Inc. v. Federal Communications Commission, 873 F.2d 347, 66 R.R.2d 575 (D.C.Cir.1989), the court upheld the minority preference policy. In Shurberg v. Federal Communications Commission, 876 F.2d 902, 66 R.R.2d 261 (D.C.Cir.1989), a different panel of the court found that the distress sale policy violated the equal protection clause of the Fifth Amendment. The Supreme Court granted *certiorari* in both cases.

METRO BROADCASTING, INC. v. FEDERAL COMMUNICATIONS COMMISSION

Supreme Court of the United States, 1990.
497 U.S. 547, 110 S.Ct. 2997, 67 R.R.2d 1353, 111 L.Ed.2d 445.

Justice Brennan delivered the opinion of the Court.

The issue in these cases, consolidated for decision today, is whether certain minority preference policies of the Federal Communications Commission violate the equal protection component of the Fifth Amendment. The policies in question are (1) a program awarding an enhancement for minority ownership in comparative proceedings for new licenses, and (2) the minority "distress sale" program, which permits a limited category of existing radio and television broadcast stations to be transferred only to minority-controlled firms. We hold that these policies do not violate equal protection principles.

I

A

The policies before us today can best be understood by reference to the history of federal efforts to promote minority participation in the broadcast industry.[1] . . . Although for the past two decades minorities have constituted at least one-fifth of the United States population, during this time relatively few members of minority groups have held broadcast licenses. In 1971, minorities owned only 10 of the approximately 7,500 radio stations in the country and none of the more than 1,000 television stations, [   ]; in 1978, minorities owned less than 1 percent of the Nation's radio and television stations, [   ]; and in 1986, they owned just 2.1 percent of the more than 11,000 radio and television stations in the United States. [   ] . . . Moreover, these statistics fail to reflect the fact that, as late entrants who often have been able to obtain only the less valuable stations, many minority broadcasters serve geographically limited markets with relatively small audiences.

---

1. The FCC has defined the term "minority" to include "those of Black, Hispanic Surnamed, American Eskimo, Aleut, American Indian and Asiatic American extrac- tion." Statement of Policy on Minority Ownership of Broadcasting Facilities, 68 F.C.C.2d 979, 980, n. 8 (1978). . . .

The Commission has recognized that the viewing and listening public suffers when minorities are underrepresented among owners of television and radio stations:

"Acute underrepresentation of minorities among the owners of broadcast properties is troublesome because it is the licensee who is ultimately responsible for identifying and serving the needs and interests of his or her audience. Unless minorities are encouraged to enter the mainstream of the commercial broadcasting business, a substantial portion of our citizenry will remain underserved and the larger, non-minority audience will be deprived of the views of minorities." [　]

The Commission has therefore worked to encourage minority participation in the broadcast industry. The FCC began by formulating rules to prohibit licensees from discriminating against minorities in employment. The FCC explained that "broadcasting is an important mass media form which, because it makes use of the airwaves belonging to the public, must obtain a federal license under a public interest standard and must operate in the public interest in order to obtain periodic renewals of that license." [　] Regulations dealing with employment practices were justified as necessary to enable the FCC to satisfy its obligation under the Communications Act to promote diversity of programming. [　] The United States Department of Justice, for example, contended that equal employment opportunity in the broadcast industry could " 'contribute significantly toward reducing and ending discrimination in other industries' " because of the " 'enormous impact which television and radio have upon American life.' " [　]

Initially, the FCC did not consider minority status as a factor in licensing decisions, maintaining as a matter of Commission policy that no preference to minority ownership was warranted where the record in a particular case did not give assurances that the owner's race likely would affect the content of the station's broadcast service to the public. [　] [This position was overruled in *TV 9*, p. ___, *supra*.]

. . . [T]he FCC adopted in May 1978 its *Statement of Policy on Minority Ownership of Broadcasting Facilities*, 68 F.C.C.2d 979. After recounting its past efforts to expand broadcast diversity, the FCC concluded:

"[W]e are compelled to observe that the views of racial minorities continue to be inadequately represented in the broadcast media. This situation is detrimental not only to the minority audience but to all of the viewing and listening public. Adequate representation of minority viewpoints in programming serves not only the needs and interests of the minority community but also enriches and educates the non-minority audience. It enhances the diversified programming which is a key objective not only of the Communications Act of 1934 but also of the First Amendment." [　]

Describing its actions as only "first steps," [　], the FCC outlined two elements of a minority ownership policy.

First, the Commission pledged to consider minority ownership as one factor in comparative proceedings for new licenses. [Here, the Court outlined the six comparative criteria used for mutually exclusive license applications, p. ___, *supra*.] In the Policy Statement on Minority Ownership, the FCC announced that minority ownership and participation in management would be considered as a "plus" to be weighed together with all other relevant factors. [   ] The "plus" is awarded only to the extent that a minority owner actively participates in the day-to-day management of the station.

Second, the FCC outlined a plan to increase minority opportunities to receive reassigned and transferred licenses through the so-called "distress sale" policy. [   ] As a general rule, a licensee whose qualifications to hold a broadcast license come into question may not assign or transfer the license until the FCC has resolved its doubts in a noncomparative hearing. The distress sale policy is an exception to that practice, allowing a broadcaster whose license has been designated for a revocation hearing, to assign the license to an FCC-approved minority enterprise. [   ] The assignee must meet the FCC's basic qualifications, and the minority ownership must exceed 50 percent or be controlling.[6] The buyer must purchase the license before the start of the revocation or renewal hearing, and the price must not exceed 75 percent of fair market value. These two Commission minority ownership policies are at issue today.

B

1

. . . [P]etitioner Metro Broadcasting, Inc. (Metro) challenges the Commission's policy awarding preferences to minority owners in comparative licensing proceedings. Several applicants, including Metro and Rainbow Broadcasting (Rainbow), were involved in a comparative proceeding to select among three mutually exclusive proposals to construct and operate a new UHF television station in the Orlando, Florida, metropolitan area. . . . [The Commission's Review Board considered] Rainbow's comparative showing and found it superior to Metro's. In so doing, the Review Board awarded Rainbow a substantial enhancement on the ground that it was 90 percent Hispanic-owned, whereas Metro had only one minority partner who owned 19.8 percent of the enterprise. The Review Board found that Rainbow's minority credit outweighed Metro's local residence and civic participation advantage. [   ] The Commission denied review of the Board's decision largely without discussion, stating merely that it "agree[d] with the Board's resolution of this case." [   ]

[The court of appeals affirmed the decision, 2–1, and petitions for rehearing were denied.]

---

6. In 1982, the FCC determined that a limited partnership could qualify as a minority enterprise if the general partner is a minority who holds at least 20 percent interest and who will exercise "complete control over a station's affairs." [   ]

2

[The other case] emerged from a series of attempts by Faith Center, Inc., the licensee of a Hartford, Connecticut television station, to execute a minority distress sale. In December 1980, the FCC designated for a hearing Faith Center's application for renewal of its license. [   ] [Faith Center obtained FCC approval for a distress sale, but the sale fell through due to financing problems. A second attempt at a distress sale was approved, this time over the objections of Alan Shurberg. The second sale also fell through due to financing problems.]

In December 1983, respondent Shurberg Broadcasting of Hartford, Inc. (Shurberg) applied to the Commission for a permit to build a television station in Hartford. The application was mutually exclusive with Faith Center's renewal application, then still pending. In June 1984, Faith Center again sought the FCC's approval for a distress sale, requesting permission to sell the station to Astroline Communications Company, Limited Partnership (Astroline), a minority applicant. Shurberg opposed the sale to Astroline on a number of grounds, including that the FCC's distress sale program violated Shurberg's right to equal protection. Shurberg therefore urged the Commission to deny the distress sale request and to schedule a comparative hearing to examine the application Shurberg had tendered alongside Faith Center's renewal request. In December 1984, the FCC approved Faith Center's petition for permission to assign its broadcast license to Astroline pursuant to the distress sale policy. [   ] The FCC rejected Shurberg's equal protection challenge to the policy as "without merit." [   ]

[The court of appeals, 2–1, held that the distress sale policy was unconstitutional. The majority found that the policy "unconstitutionally deprives Alan Shurberg and Shurberg Broadcasting of their equal protection rights under the Fifth Amendment because the program is not narrowly tailored to remedy past discrimination or to promote programming diversity."]

II

It is of overriding significance in these cases that the FCC's minority ownership programs have been specifically approved—indeed mandated—by Congress. . . .

. . . We hold that benign race-conscious measures mandated by Congress—even if those measures are not "remedial" in the sense of being designed to compensate victims of past governmental or societal discrimination—are constitutionally permissible to the extent that they serve important governmental objectives within the power of Congress and are substantially related to achievement of those objectives.

. . .

We hold that the FCC minority ownership policies pass muster under the test we announce today. First we find that they serve the important governmental objective of broadcast diversity. Second, we conclude that they are substantially related to the achievement of that objective.

A

Congress found that "the effects of past inequities stemming from racial and ethnic discrimination have resulted in a severe underrepresentation of minorities in the media of mass communications." [ ] Congress and the Commission do not justify the minority ownership policies strictly as remedies for victims of this discrimination, however. Rather, Congress and the FCC have selected the minority ownership policies primarily to promote programming diversity, and they urge that such diversity is an important governmental objective that can serve as a constitutional basis for the preference policies. We agree.

We have long recognized that "[b]ecause of the scarcity of [electromagnetic] frequencies, the Government is permitted to put restraints on licensees in favor of others whose views should be expressed on this unique medium." [*Red Lion*] The Government's role in distributing the limited number of broadcast licenses is not merely that of a "traffic officer," [*NBC*]; rather it is axiomatic that broadcasting may be regulated in light of the rights of the viewing and listening audience and that "the widest possible dissemination of information from diverse and antagonistic sources is essential to the welfare of the public." [*AP*] Safeguarding the public's right to receive a diversity of views and information over the airwaves is therefore an integral component of the FCC's mission. We have observed that " 'the "public interest" standard necessarily invites reference to First Amendment principles,' " [*NCCB*], and that the Communications Act has designated broadcasters as "fiduciaries for the public." [*League of Women Voters*]. "[T]he people as a whole retain their interest in free speech by radio [and other forms of broadcast] and their collective right to have the medium function consistently with the ends and purposes of the First Amendment," and "[i]t is the right of the viewers and listeners, not the right of the broadcasters, which is paramount." [*Red Lion*] "Congress may . . . seek to assure that the public receives through this medium a balanced presentation of information on issues of public importance that otherwise might not be addressed if control of the medium were left entirely in the hands of those who own and operate broadcasting stations." [*League of Women Voters*]

Against this background, we conclude that the interest in enhancing broadcast diversity is, at the very least, an important governmental objective and is therefore a sufficient basis for the Commission's minority ownership policies. . . . The benefits of such diversity are not limited to the members of minority groups who gain access to the broadcasting industry by virtue of the ownership policies; rather, the benefits redound to all members of the viewing and listening audience. . . .

B

We also find that the minority ownership policies are substantially related to the achievement of the Government's interest. One component of this inquiry concerns the relationship between expanded minority ownership and greater broadcast diversity; both the FCC and Congress have determined that such a relationship exists. Although we do not " 'defer' to the judgment of the Congress and the Commission on a constitutional question," and would not "hesitate to invoke the Constitution should we determine that the Commission has not fulfilled its task with appropriate sensitivity" to equal protection principles, [*CBS v. DNC*], we must pay close attention to the expertise of the Commission and the factfinding of Congress when analyzing the nexus between minority ownership and programming diversity. With respect to this "complex" empirical question, *ibid.*, we are required to give "great weight to the decisions of Congress and the experience of the Commission." *Id.*, at 102.

1

. . .

Furthermore, the FCC's reasoning with respect to the minority ownership policies is consistent with longstanding practice under the Communications Act. From its inception, public regulation of broadcasting has been premised on the assumption that diversification of ownership will broaden the range of programming available to the broadcast audience. . . . The Commission has never relied on the market alone to ensure that the needs of the audience are met. Indeed, one of the FCC's elementary regulatory assumptions is that broadcast content is not purely market-driven; if it were, there would be little need for consideration in licensing decisions of such factors as integration of ownership and management, local residence, and civic participation. . . .

2

[The Court then reviewed the various actions Congress had taken in support of the minority ownership policies. Most recently, for the past three years, Congress "specifically required the Commission, through appropriations legislation, to maintain the minority ownership policies without alteration."]

C

The judgment that there is a link between expanded minority ownership and broadcast diversity does not rest on impermissible stereotyping. Congressional policy does not assume that in every case minority ownership and management will lead to more minority-oriented programming or to the expression of a discrete "minority viewpoint" on the airwaves. Neither does it pretend that all programming that appeals to minority audiences can be labeled "minority programming" or that programming that might be described as "minority" does not appeal to nonminorities. Rather, both Congress and the FCC maintain simply that expanded minority ownership of broadcast outlets will, in the aggregate, result in greater broadcast diversity. A broadcasting industry with representative minority participation will produce more variation and diversity than will one whose ownership is drawn from a single racially and ethnically homogeneous group. . . .

Although all station owners are guided to some extent by market demand in their programming decisions, Congress and the Commission have determined that there may be important differences between the broadcasting practices of minority owners and those of their nonminority counterparts. This judgment—and the conclusion that there is a nexus between minority ownership and broadcasting diversity—is corroborated by a host of empirical evidence. Evidence suggests that an owner's minority status influences the selection of topics for news coverage and the presentation of editorial viewpoint, especially on matters of particular concern to minorities. "[M]inority ownership does appear to have specific impact on the presentation of minority images in local news," inasmuch as minority-owned stations tend to devote more news time to topics of minority interest and to avoid racial and ethnic stereotypes in portraying minorities. In addition, studies show that a minority owner is more likely to employ minorities in managerial and other important roles where they can have an impact on station policies. If the FCC's equal employment policies "ensure that . . . licensees' programming fairly reflects the tastes and viewpoints of minority groups," [ ], it is difficult to deny that minority-owned stations that follow such employment policies on their own will also contribute to diversity. While we are under no illusion that members of a particular minority group share some cohesive, collective viewpoint, we believe it a legitimate inference for Congress and the Commission to draw that as more minorities gain ownership and policymaking roles in the media, varying perspectives will be more fairly represented on the airwaves. The policies are thus a product of " 'analysis' " rather than a " 'stereotyped reaction' " based on " '[h]abit.' "

　　. . .

D

We find that the minority ownership policies are in other relevant respects substantially related to the goal of promoting broadcast diversity. First, the Commission adopted and Congress endorsed minority ownership preferences only after long study and painstaking consideration of all available alternatives. [ ] . . .

　　. . .

Moreover, the considered nature of the Commission's judgment in selecting the particular minority ownership policies at issue today is illustrated by the fact that the Commission has rejected other types of minority preferences. For example, the Commission has studied but refused to implement the more expansive alternative of setting aside certain frequencies for minority broadcasters. [ ] In addition, in a ruling released the day after it adopted the comparative hearing credit and the distress sale preference, the FCC declined to adopt a plan to require 45–day advance public notice before a station could be sold, which had been advocated on the ground that it would ensure minorities a chance to bid on stations that might otherwise be sold to industry insiders without ever coming on the market. [   ] . . .

The minority ownership policies, furthermore, are aimed directly at the barriers that minorities face in entering the broadcasting industry. The Commission's Task Force identified as key factors hampering the growth of minority ownership a lack of adequate financing, paucity of information regarding license availability, and broadcast inexperience. [   ] The Commission assigned a preference to minority status in the comparative licensing proceeding, reasoning that such an enhancement might help to compensate for a dearth of broadcasting experience. Most license acquisitions, however, are by necessity purchases of existing stations, because only a limited number of new stations are available, and those are often in less desirable markets or on less profitable portions of spectrum, such as the UHF band. Congress and the FCC therefore found a need for the minority distress sale policy, which helps to overcome the problem of lack of information by providing existing licensees with an incentive to seek out minority buyers. The Commission's choice of minority ownership policies thus addressed the very factors it had isolated as being responsible for minority underrepresentation in the broadcast industry.

   . . .

Finally, we do not believe that the minority ownership policies at issue impose impermissible burdens on nonminorities. Although the nonminority challengers in these cases concede that they have not suffered the loss of an already-awarded broadcast license, they claim that they have been handicapped in their ability to obtain one in the first instance. But just as we have determined that "[a]s part of this Nation's dedication to eradicating racial discrimination, innocent persons may be called upon to bear some of the burden of the remedy," [   ], we similarly find that a congressionally mandated benign race-conscious program that is substantially related to the achievement of an important governmental interest is consistent with equal protection principles so long as it does not impose *undue* burdens on nonminorities. [   ]

In the context of broadcasting licenses, the burden on nonminorities is slight. The FCC's responsibility is to grant licenses in the "public interest, convenience, or necessity," 47 U.S.C. §§ 307, 309 (1982 ed.), and the limited number of frequencies on the electromagnetic spectrum means that "[n]o one has a First Amendment right to a license." *Red Lion*, [   ]. Applicants have no settled expectation that their applications will be granted without consideration of public interest factors such as minority ownership. Award of a preference in a comparative hearing or transfer of a station in a distress sale thus contravenes "no legitimate firmly rooted expectation[s]" of competing applicants. [   ]

   . . .

III

The Commission's minority ownership policies bear the imprimatur of longstanding congressional support and direction and are substantially related to the achievement of the important governmental objective of broadcast diversity. The judgment in [*Metro*] is affirmed, the judgment in [*Shurberg*] is reversed, and the cases are remanded for proceedings consistent with this opinion.

JUSTICE STEVENS, concurring.

Today the Court squarely rejects the proposition that a governmental decision that rests on a racial classification is never permissible except as a remedy for a past wrong. [ ] I endorse this focus on the future benefit, rather than the remedial justification, of such decisions.

I remain convinced, of course, that racial or ethnic characteristics provide a relevant basis for disparate treatment only in extremely rare situations and that it is therefore "especially important that the reasons for any such classification be clearly identified and unquestionably legitimate." [ ] The Court's opinion explains how both elements of that standard are satisfied. Specifically, the reason for the classification—the recognized interest in broadcast diversity—is clearly identified and does not imply any judgment concerning the abilities of owners of different races or the merits of different kinds of programming. Neither the favored nor the disfavored class is stigmatized in any way. In addition, the Court demonstrates that this case falls within the extremely narrow category of governmental decisions for which racial or ethnic heritage may provide a rational basis for differential treatment. The public interest in broadcast diversity—like the interest in an integrated police force, diversity in the composition of a public school faculty or diversity in the student body of a professional school—is in my view unquestionably legitimate.

Therefore, I join both the opinion and judgment of the Court.

JUSTICE O'CONNOR, with whom THE CHIEF JUSTICE, JUSTICE SCALIA, and JUSTICE KENNEDY join, dissenting.

At the heart of the Constitution's guarantee of equal protection lies the simple command that the Government must treat citizens "as *individuals*, not 'as simply components of a racial, religious, sexual or national class.'" [ ] Social scientists may debate how peoples' thoughts and behavior reflect their background, but the Constitution provides that the Government may not allocate benefits and burdens among individuals based on the assumption that race or ethnicity determines how they act or think. To uphold the challenged programs, the Court departs from these fundamental principles and from our traditional requirement that racial classifications are permissible only if necessary and narrowly tailored to achieve a compelling interest. This departure marks a renewed toleration of racial classifications and a repudiation of our recent affirmation that the Constitution's equal protection guarantees extend equally to all citizens. The Court's application of a lessened equal protection standard to congressional action finds no support in our cases or in the Constitution. I respectfully dissent.

I

As we recognized last Term, the Constitution requires that the Court apply a strict standard of scrutiny to evaluate racial classifications such as those contained in the challenged FCC distress sale and comparative licensing policies. [   ] . . .

. . .

Nor does the congressional role in prolonging the FCC's policies justify any lower level of scrutiny. As with all instances of judicial review of federal legislation, the Court does not lightly set aside the considered judgment of a coordinate branch. Nonetheless, the respect due a coordinate branch yields neither less vigilance in defense of equal protection principles nor any corresponding diminution of the standard of review. . . .

. . .

II

Our history reveals the most blatant forms of discrimination have been visited upon some members of the racial and ethnic groups identified in the challenged programs. Many have lacked the opportunity to share in the Nation's wealth and to participate in its commercial enterprises. It is undisputed that minority participation in the broadcasting industry falls markedly below the demographic representation of those groups, [   ], and this shortfall may be traced in part to the discrimination and the patterns of exclusion that have widely affected our society. . . .

. . .

III

Under the appropriate standard, strict scrutiny, only a compelling interest may support the Government's use of racial classifications. Modern equal protection doctrine has recognized only one such interest: remedying the effects of racial discrimination. The interest in increasing the diversity of broadcast viewpoints is clearly not a compelling interest. It is simply too amorphous, too insubstantial, and too unrelated to any legitimate basis for employing racial classifications. The Court does not claim otherwise. Rather, it employs its novel standard and claims that this asserted interest need only be, and is, "important." . . .

An interest capable of justifying race-conscious measures must be sufficiently specific and verifiable, such that it supports only limited and carefully defined uses of racial classifications. . . .

. . . The [asserted] interest [in this case] is certainly amorphous: the FCC and the majority of this Court understandably do not suggest how one would define or measure a particular viewpoint that might be associated with race, or even how one would assess the diversity of broadcast viewpoints. . . . [T]he interest would support indefinite use of racial classifications, employed first to obtain the appropriate mixture of racial views and then to ensure that the broadcasting spectrum continues to reflect that mixture. We cannot deem to be constitutionally adequate an interest that would support measures that amount to the core constitutional violation of "outright racial balancing." [   ]

The asserted interest would justify discrimination against members of any group found to contribute to an insufficiently diverse broadcasting spectrum, including those groups currently favored. [We have previously] rejected as insufficiently weighty the interest in achieving role models in public schools, in part because that rationale could as readily be used to limit the hiring of teachers who belonged to particular minority groups. [   ] The FCC's claimed interest could similarly justify limitations on minority members' participation in broadcasting. It would be unwise to depend upon the Court's restriction of its holding to "benign" measures to forestall this result. Divorced from any remedial purpose and otherwise undefined, "benign" means only what shifting fashions and changing politics deem acceptable. Members of any racial or ethnic group, whether now preferred under the FCC's policies or not, may find themselves politically out of fashion and subject to disadvantageous but "benign" discrimination.

Under the majority's holding, the FCC may also advance its asserted interest in viewpoint diversity by identifying what constitutes a "Black viewpoint," an "Asian viewpoint," an "Arab viewpoint," and so on; determining which viewpoints are underrepresented; and then using that determination to mandate particular programming or to deny licenses to those deemed by virtue of their race or ethnicity less likely to present the favored views. Indeed, the FCC has, if taken at its word, essentially pursued this course, albeit without making express its reasons for choosing to favor particular groups or for concluding that the broadcasting spectrum is insufficiently diverse. [   ]

        . . .

Even considered as other than a justification for using race classifications, the asserted interest in viewpoint diversity falls short of being weighty enough. The Court has recognized an interest in obtaining diverse broadcasting viewpoints as a legitimate basis for the FCC, acting pursuant to its "public interest" statutory mandate, to adopt limited measures to increase the number of competing licensees and to encourage licensees to present varied views on issues of public concern. See, e.g., [NCCB; *Red Lion*; *Storer Broadcasting*; AP; NBC]. We have also concluded that these measures do not run afoul of the First Amendment's usual prohibition of Government regulation of the marketplace of ideas, in part because First Amendment concerns support limited but inevitable Government regulation of the peculiarly constrained broadcasting spectrum. [*Red Lion*] But the conclusion that measures adopted to further the interest in diversity of broadcasting viewpoints are neither beyond the FCC's statutory authority nor contrary to the First Amendment hardly establishes the interest as important for equal protection purposes.

The FCC's extension of the asserted interest in diversity of views in this case presents, at the very least, an unsettled First Amendment issue. The FCC has concluded that the American broadcasting public receives the incorrect mix of ideas and claims to have adopted the challenged policies to supplement programming content with a particular set of views. Although we have approved limited measures designed to increase information and views generally, the Court has never upheld a broadcasting measure designed to amplify a distinct set of views or the views of a particular class of speakers. Indeed, the Court has suggested that the First Amendment prohibits allocating licenses to further such ends. See [*NBC*] ("But Congress did not authorize the Commission to choose among [license] applicants on the basis of their political, economic or social views, or upon any other capricious basis. If it did, or if the Commission by these Regulations proposed a choice among applicants upon some such basis, the [First Amendment] issue before us would be totally different"). Even if an interest is determined to be legitimate in one context, it does not suddenly become important enough to justify distinctions based on race.

IV

Our traditional equal protection doctrine requires, in addition to a compelling state interest, that the Government's chosen means be necessary to accomplish and narrowly tailored to further the asserted interest. [ ] . . .

1

The FCC claims to advance its asserted interest in diverse viewpoints by singling out race and ethnicity as peculiarly linked to distinct views that require enhancement. The FCC's choice to employ a racial criterion embodies the related notions that a particular and distinct viewpoint inheres in certain racial groups, and that a particular applicant, by virtue of race or ethnicity alone, is more valued than other applicants because "likely to provide [that] distinct perspective." [ ] The policies directly equate race with belief and behavior, for they establish race as a necessary and sufficient condition of securing the preference. . . .

The FCC assumes a particularly strong correlation of race and behavior. The FCC justifies its conclusion that insufficiently diverse viewpoints are broadcast by reference to the percentage of minority owned stations. This assumption is correct only to the extent that minority owned stations provide the desired additional views, and that stations owned by individuals not favored by the preferences cannot, or at least do not, broadcast underrepresented programming. Additionally, the FCC's focus on ownership to improve programming assumes that preferences linked to race are so strong that they will dictate the owner's behavior in operating the station, overcoming the owner's personal inclinations and regard for the market. . . .

. . . The Court embraces the FCC's reasoning that an applicant's race will likely indicate that the applicant possesses a distinct perspective, but notes that the correlation of race to behavior is "not a rigid assumption about how minority owners will behave in every case." [ ] The corollary to this notion is plain: individuals of unfavored racial and ethnic backgrounds are unlikely to possess the unique experiences and background that contribute to viewpoint diversity. Both the reasoning and its corollary reveal but disregard what is objectionable about a stereotype: the racial generalization inevitably does not apply to certain individuals, and those persons may legitimately claim that they have been judged according to their race rather than upon a relevant criterion. [ ] Similarly disturbing is the majority's reasoning that different treatment on the basis of race is permissible because it is efficacious "in the aggregate." [ ] . . . This reliance on the "aggregate" and on probabilities confirms that the Court has abandoned heightened scrutiny, which requires a direct rather than approximate fit of means to ends. We would not tolerate the Government's claim that hiring persons of a particular race leads to better service "in the aggregate," and we should not accept as legitimate the FCC's claim in this case that members of certain races will provide superior programming, even if "in the aggregate." The Constitution's text, our cases, and our Nation's history foreclose such premises.

2

Moreover, the FCC's selective focus on viewpoints associated with race illustrates a particular tailoring difficulty. The asserted interest is in advancing the Nation's different "social, political, esthetic, moral, and other ideas and experiences," *Red Lion*, [ ], yet of all the varied traditions and ideas shared among our citizens, the FCC has sought to amplify only those particular views it identifies through the classifications most suspect under equal protection doctrine. Even if distinct views could be associated with particular ethnic and racial groups, focusing on this particular aspect of the Nation's views calls into question the Government's genuine commitment to its asserted interest. [ ]

. . . The policy is overinclusive: many members of a particular racial or ethnic group will have no interest in advancing the views the FCC believes to be underrepresented, or will find them utterly foreign. The policy is underinclusive: it awards no preference to disfavored individuals who may be particularly well versed in and committed to presenting those views. The FCC has failed to implement a case-by-case determination, and that failure is particularly unjustified when individualized hearings already occur, as in the comparative licensing process. [ ] . . .

Moreover, the FCC's programs cannot survive even intermediate scrutiny because race-neutral and untried means of directly accomplishing the governmental interest are readily available. The FCC could directly advance its interest by requiring licensees to provide programming that the FCC believes would add to diversity. The interest the FCC asserts is in programming diversity, yet in adopting the challenged policies, the FCC expressly disclaimed having attempted *any* direct efforts to achieve its asserted goal. [   ] . . . The FCC and the Court suggest that First Amendment interests in some manner should exempt the FCC from employing this direct, race-neutral means to achieve its asserted interest. They essentially argue that we may bend our equal protection principles to avoid more readily apparent harm to our First Amendment values. But the FCC cannot have it both ways: either the First Amendment bars the FCC from seeking to accomplish indirectly what it may not accomplish directly; or the FCC may pursue the goal, but must do so in a manner that comports with equal protection principles. And if the FCC can direct programming in any fashion, it must employ that direct means before resorting to indirect race-conscious means.

Other race-neutral means also exist, and all are at least as direct as the FCC's racial classifications. The FCC could evaluate applicants upon their ability to provide and commitment to offer whatever programming the FCC believes would reflect underrepresented viewpoints. If the FCC truly seeks diverse programming rather than allocation of goods to persons of particular racial backgrounds, it has little excuse to look to racial background rather than programming to further the programming interest. Additionally, if the FCC believes that certain persons by virtue of their unique experiences will contribute as owners to more diverse broadcasting, the FCC could simply favor applicants whose particular background indicates that they will add to the diversity of programming, rather than rely solely upon suspect classifications. Also, race-neutral means exist to allow access to the broadcasting industry for those persons excluded for financial and related reasons. The Court reasons that various minority preferences, including those reflected in the distress sale, overcome barriers of information, experience, and financing that inhibit minority ownership. [   ] Race-neutral financial and informational measures most directly reduce financial and informational barriers.

. . .

The FCC has posited a relative absence of "minority viewpoints," yet it has never suggested what those views might be, or what other viewpoints might be absent from the broadcasting spectrum. It has never identified any particular deficiency in programming diversity that should be the subject of greater programming, or that necessitates racial classifications.

. . .

The FCC seeks to avoid the tailoring difficulties by focusing on minority ownership rather than the asserted interest in diversity of broadcast viewpoints. The Constitution clearly prohibits allocating valuable goods such as broadcast licenses simply on the basis of race. [ ] Yet the FCC refers to the lack of minority ownership to support the existence of a lack of diversity of viewpoints, and has fitted its programs to increase ownership. [ ] This repeated focus on ownership supports the inference that the FCC seeks to allocate licenses based on race, an impermissible end, rather than to increase diversity of viewpoints, the asserted interest. And this justification that links the use of race preferences to minority ownership rather than to diversity of viewpoints ensure's that the FCC's programs . . . "cannot be tailored to any goal, except perhaps outright racial balancing." [ ]

3

. . .

Three difficulties suggest that the nexus between owners' race and programming is considerably less than substantial. First, the market shapes programming to a tremendous extent. Members of minority groups who own licenses might be thought, like other owners, to seek to broadcast programs that will attract and retain audiences, rather than programs that reflect the owner's tastes and preferences. [ ] Second, station owners have only limited control over the content of programming. The distress sale presents a particularly acute difficulty of this sort. Unlike the comparative licensing program, the distress sale policy provides preferences to minority owners who neither intend nor desire to manage the station in any respect. [ ] Whatever distinct programming may attend the race of an owner actively involved in managing the station, an absentee owner would have far less effect on programming.

Third, the FCC had absolutely no factual basis for the nexus when it adopted the policies and has since established none to support its existence. . . .

. . .

4

Finally, the Government cannot employ race classifications that unduly burden individuals who are not members of the favored racial and ethnic groups. [ ] The challenged policies fail this independent requirement, as well as the other constitutional requirements. The comparative licensing and distress sale programs provide the eventual licensee with an exceptionally valuable property and with a rare and unique opportunity to serve the local community. The distress sale imposes a particularly significant burden. The FCC has at base created a specialized market reserved exclusively for minority controlled applicants. There is no more rigid quota than a 100% set-aside. . . . The Court's argument that the distress sale allocates only a small percentage of all license sales, [ ], also misses the mark. This argument readily supports complete preferences and avoids scrutiny of particular programs: it is no response to a person denied admission at one school, or discharged from one job, solely on the basis of race, that other schools or employers do not discriminate.

The comparative licensing program, too, imposes a significant burden. The Court's emphasis on the multifactor process should not be confused with the claim that the preference is in some sense a minor one. It is not. The basic nonrace criteria are not difficult to meet, and, given the sums at stake, applicants have every incentive to structure their ownership arrangement to prevail in the comparative process. Applicants cannot alter their race, of course, and race is clearly the dispositive factor in a substantial percentage of comparative proceedings. Petitioner Metro asserts that race is overwhelmingly the dispositive factor. In reply, the FCC admits that it has not assessed the operation of its own program, [   ], and the Court notes only that "minority ownership does not guarantee that an applicant will prevail." [   ]

. . . I respectfully dissent.

JUSTICE KENNEDY, with whom JUSTICE SCALIA joins, dissenting.

[Justice Kennedy compared this case with Plessy v. Ferguson, in which the Court found constitutional a Louisiana law requiring "equal but separate accommodations" for railroad passengers of different races.]

. . . All that need be shown under the new approach . . . is that the future effect of discriminating among citizens on the basis of race will advance some "important" governmental interest.

Once the Government takes the step, which itself should be forbidden, of enacting into law the stereotypical assumption that the race of the owners is linked to broadcast content, it must decide which races to favor. While the Court repeatedly refers to the preferences as favoring "minorities," [   ], and purports to evaluate the burdens imposed on "nonminorities," [   ], it must be emphasized that the discriminatory policies upheld today operate to exclude the many racial and ethnic *minorities* that have not made the Commission's list. The enumeration of the races to be protected is borrowed from a remedial statute, but since the remedial rationale must be disavowed in order to sustain the policy, the race classifications bear scant relation to the asserted governmental interest. The Court's reasoning provides little justification for welcoming the return of racial classifications to our Nation's laws.

. . .

. . . Perhaps the Court can succeed in its assumed role of case-by-case arbiter of when it is desirable and benign for the Government to disfavor some citizens and favor others based on the color of their skin. Perhaps the tolerance and decency to which our people aspire will let the disfavored rise above hostility and the favored escape condescension. But history suggests much peril in this enterprise, and so the Constitution forbids us to undertake it. I regret that after a century of judicial opinions we interpret the Constitution to do no more than move us from "separate but equal" to "unequal but benign."

Notes and Questions

1. What effect does *Metro Broadcasting* have on the ongoing debate over the continuing viability of the scarcity rationale?

2. The constitutionality of the FCC's minority preference policies has once again become an open question as the result of a Supreme Court decision involving a constitutional challenge to a federal program designed to provide highway contracts to disadvantaged business enterprises. The definition of disadvantaged business enterprises was based in part on racial classifications. The key issue was the appropriate level of scrutiny to be applied to the program. The Court held, 5–4, that "all racial classifications, imposed by whatever federal, state, or local governmental actor, must be analyzed by a reviewing court under strict scrutiny. In other words, such classifications are constitutional only if they are narrowly tailored measures that further compelling governmental interests. To the extent that Metro Broadcasting is inconsistent with that holding, it is overruled." Adarand Constructors, Inc. v. Pena, 515 U.S. 200, 115 S.Ct. 2097 (1995).

3. *Adarand*, brought the constitutionality of the FCC's minority preference in comparative licensing proceedings and distress sale policies into question. The elimination of comparative renewals, p. ___, *supra*, rendered that part of the question moot. Prior to the Supreme Court decision in *Adarand*, the Commission had already instituted an NPRM aimed at increasing opportunities for minorities and females to enter the electronic media. Minority and Female Ownership, 10 F.C.C.Rcd. 2788 (1995).

4. Relying on *Adarand*, a court of appeals declared the Commission's affirmative action rules unconstitutional. The FCC had found the Lutheran Church–Missouri Synod violated those rules at the two radio stations it owned in Clayton, Mo. The FCC had asserted that "fostering diverse programming content" was a compelling government interest. The court rejected the FCC's contention that it was bound by the *Metro Broadcasting* approval of this interest because the Supreme Court had only found it to be an important interest. Characterizing the asserted interest as amorphous and quoting Justice O'Connor's dissent, the court of appeals found it was not compelling.

> The court then turned to the question of narrow tailoring:
>
> The Commission reprimanded the Church for preferring Lutheran secretaries, receptionists, business managers, and engineers precisely because it found these positions not "connected to the espousal of religious philosophy over the air." Yet it has defended its affirmative action rules on the ground that minority employees bring diversity to the airwaves. The FCC would thus have us believe that low-level employees manage to get their "racial viewpoint" on the air but lack the influence to convey their religious views. That contradiction makes a mockery out of the Commission's contention that its EEO

program requirements are designed for broadcast diversity purposes. The regulations could not pass the substantial relation prong of intermediate scrutiny, let alone the narrow tailoring prong of strict scrutiny.

Lutheran Church–Missouri Synod v. Federal Communications Commission, 141 F.3d 344 (D.C.Cir.1998). A petition for rehearing *en banc* was denied, 154 F.3d 487 (D.C.Cir.1998).

5. The *Metro Broadcasting* decision had stated that the FCC's "gender preference policy is not before us today." That issue was decided by the court of appeals in Lamprecht v. Federal Communications Commission, 958 F.2d 382, 70 R.R.2d 658 (D.C.Cir.1992). The court, 2–1, in an opinion by Thomas, Circuit Justice, recognized that Congress had ordered the Commission to continue granting gender preferences. Since it was impossible to find the Commission's action beyond statutory authorization, the court turned to constitutional questions—and concluded that the practice was unconstitutional on equal protection grounds. The government's methods were held not to be "substantially related" to the goal it hoped to achieve—more diverse programming if women were granted a preference in the licensing process.

The court understood that the Supreme Court had used a standard of "intermediate scrutiny" in situations such as *Metro*. This meant that "not only [must] sex-based generalizations be 'supported,' but [the support must] be strong enough to advance 'substantially' the legitimating government interest." Under that standard, the court could not find sufficient evidence in the FCC record to show that preferring women would have anything like the effect that the evidence in *Metro* suggested would occur if racial minority groups were granted preferences. There was no strong showing that women owners would program differently from men. The court concluded:

> When a government treats people differently because of their sex, equal-protection principles at the very least require that there be a meaningful factual predicate supporting a link between the government's means and its ends. In this case, the government has failed to show that its sex-preference policy is substantially related to achieving diversity on the airwaves. We therefore hold that the policy violated the Constitution.

The Commission decided not to seek further review, and ended preferences for women applicants.

6. An analysis of survey data by Professors Jeffrey Dubin and Matthew Spitzer suggests that minority ownership does affect broadcast programming content. The authors also found that to a lesser extent female ownership also affects content. J. Dubin and M. Spitzer, Testing Minority Preferences in Broadcasting, 68 So.Cal.L.Rev. 841 (1995).

7. Section 309(j) of the Communications Act requires the Commission to "ensure that small businesses, rural telephone companies, and businesses owned by members of minority groups and women are given the

opportunity to participate in the provision of spectrum-based services."
47 U.S.C.A. § 309(j)(4)(D). In addition, Section 309(j)(3)(B) instructs the
Commission, in establishing eligibility criteria and bidding methodolo-
gies, to promote "economic opportunity and competition . . . by avoiding
excessive concentration of licenses and by disseminating licenses among
a wide variety of applicants, including small businesses, rural telephone
companies, and businesses owned by members of minority groups and
women," collectively referred to as "designated entities." 47 U.S.C. s
309(j)(3)(B).

In its report and order establishing auction procedures for new
broadcast licenses, p. ___, *supra*, the Commission adopted a "new entrant" bidding credit, similar to that in use for LPTV and MDS licenses.
"[A]pplicants whose owners in the aggregate hold more than 50% of the
ownership interests [or a defacto controlling interest] in no other media
of mass communications" will receive a 35 percent bidding credit.
"[A]pplicants whose owners in the aggregate hold more than 50% of the
ownership interests [or a defacto controlling interest] in one, two or
three other media of mass communications" will receive a 25 percent
bidding credit. In addition, the Commission has started "a series of
studies to examine the barriers encountered by small, minority-and
women-owned businesses in the secondary markets and the auctions
process."

8.   The FCC had developed other techniques for encouraging minority
entry into broadcasting. In the *1978 Policy Statement*, p. ___, *supra*, the
Commission also announced that it would grant tax certificates, permitting a seller to defer payment of capital gains taxes, to owners who sell
their stations to groups controlled by members of minority groups.
Recall also the preference awarded minorities applying for the new FM
licenses created by the Commission in 1985.

9.   In 1995 Congress terminated the minority tax certificate program.
Congress' action was triggered by the revelation that Viacom would
receive a $600 million tax break from the sale of its cable systems. The
termination was made retroactive to the beginning of the year causing
18 broadcasters and cable operators, including Viacom, to lose tax breaks
for pending sales. Broadcasting and Cable, April 3, 1995 at 10.

10.   As of 1998, minority media ownership was only 3 percent. With the
elimination of various FCC programs such minority licensing preferences
and tax certificates, it is not expected to increase much in the near
future. The tax certificate program had been the most successful in
promoting minority ownership, accounting for 288 radio and 43 television stations transferred to minority ownership over a span of 15 years.
Broadcasting & Cable, July 20, 1998 at 7.

C.   PROGRAMMING DISTRIBUTION

Concentration of control problems are not limited, however, to
ownership issues. Control of programming supply and distribution is
equally, if not more, important.

1. Broadcast Networks

Initially, broadcast networks supplied much of the programming in the country, extending their influence far beyond the stations they own. The two primary legal avenues available to control or limit the actions of the networks are application of the antitrust laws and FCC regulation.

a. Antitrust Law

In its discussions of the various media concentration rules, the Commission often makes reference to antitrust concerns. The goals of American antitrust law were set in 1890, with the enactment of the Sherman Antitrust Act, 15 U.S.C.A. §§ 1 and 2. Section 1 states a desire to "protect trade and commerce against unlawful restraints and monopolies," and then declares illegal "every contract, combination in the form of trust or otherwise, or conspiracy, in restraint of trade, or commerce." Section 2 provides that "Every person who shall monopolize, or attempt to monopolize, or combine or conspire with any other person or persons, to monopolize any part of the trade or commerce . . . shall be guilty of a misdemeanor."

The quoted provisions of the Sherman Act have been applied against business enterprises engaged in manufacturing or marketing tangible products. In the early 1940s the Supreme Court decided that the First Amendment did not bar antitrust actions against media organizations. Associated Press v. United States, 326 U.S. 1 (1945). However, the special regulatory status of broadcasting under the Communications Act of 1934 raised two other important questions, both dealing with jurisdiction.

Because the antitrust laws are enforced by the Justice Department and the Federal Trade Commission, the first question was whether the Federal Communications Commission was barred from issuing regulations based on antitrust principles. In *NBC*, which we first considered in Chapter III and which we will examine further in this chapter, the Supreme Court concluded that the FCC was entitled to use antitrust principles in determining what constitutes the public interest.

The second jurisdictional question, whether an FCC ruling in a specific case barred action by other agencies, was raised in United States v. Radio Corporation of America, 358 U.S. 334 (1959). NBC, a wholly owned subsidiary of RCA, reached an agreement with Westinghouse to exchange NBC's Cleveland VHF television station plus $3 million for Westinghouse's Philadelphia VHF television station. Despite allegations that NBC had forced the transaction by threatening to withhold network affiliation from all Westinghouse stations, the FCC approved the transfer.

The Justice Department then filed an antitrust action against RCA and NBC asking among other things that NBC be forced to divest itself of the Philadelphia station. RCA argued that the FCC's approval of the sale had decided the antitrust questions, barring the government from bringing a separate antitrust action. The Supreme Court disagreed:

> . . . Appellees, like unregulated business concerns, made a business judgment as to the desirability of the exchange. Like unregulated concerns, they had to make this judgment with knowledge that the exchange might run afoul of the antitrust laws. Their decision varied from that of unregulated concern only in that they also had to obtain the approval of a federal agency. But [the] scope of that approval in the case of the FCC was limited to the statutory standard, "public interest, convenience, and necessity." . . . The monetary terms of the exchange were set by the parties, and were of concern to the Commission only as they might have affected the ability of the parties to serve the public. Even after approval, the parties were free to complete or not to complete the exchange as their sound business judgment dictated. In every sense, the question faced by the parties was solely one of business judgment (as opposed to regulatory coercion), save only that the Commission must have found that the "public interest" would be served by their decision to make the exchange. . . .

> This is not to imply that federal antitrust policy may not be considered in determining whether the "public interest, convenience, and necessity" will be served by proposed action of the broadcaster, for this Court has held to the contrary. National Broadcasting Co. v. United States, 319 U.S. 190, 222–224. Moreover, in a given case the Commission might find that antitrust considerations alone would keep the statutory standard from being met, as when the publisher of the sole newspaper in an area applies for a license for the only available radio and television facilities, which, if granted, would give him a monopoly of that area's major media of mass communication. [   ]

In 1972 the Justice Department, concerned with excessive network control over the market for television prime-time programming, filed antitrust suits against the three major networks. Six years later NBC entered into a consent decree that prohibited acquisition of syndication rights from independent producers and reciprocal dealings with the other networks and placed other limitations on dealings with independent producers. Subsequently the other networks signed similar consent decrees.

In 1992 the networks sought judicial review of the consent decrees. The district court granted the networks' request to eliminate sections IV and VI A of the consent decree. Section IV prohibited "NBC, ABC and CBS from acquiring financial interests or proprietary rights in nonnetwork uses of television programs produced by others or from engaging in the domestic syndication business." Section VI A prohibited "NBC, ABC and CBS from conditioning or tying the purchase of network rights to a program upon the supplier's grant of any other right or interest to NBC, ABC or CBS."

The court noted that the FCC had modified the financial interest and syndication rules (discussed later in this chapter) which were similar to sections IV and VI A of the consent decrees. Relying heavily on a staff report of the FTC's Bureau of Economics, which was originally prepared for the FCC's hearings on modifying the financial interest and syndication rules, the court found that the networks no longer had either monopsony or monopoly power. Thus, the underlying justifications for sections IV and VI A had been eliminated. United States v. National Broadcasting Company, Inc., 842 F.Supp. 402, 74 R.R.2d 986 (C.D.Cal. 1993).

b. *The Chain Broadcasting Rules*

By the late 1930s the three national network companies (NBC, CBS and Mutual) had almost half of the entire broadcast business in the country. In 1938, deeply concerned by this concentration of control, the Commission began an inquiry into the need for special regulations to curb the power of the networks by prohibiting certain common network practices. In 1941, after extensive public hearings at which nearly 100 witnesses testified, the Commission adopted eight regulations pertaining to chain broadcasting.

The first of these, Regulation 3.101 (Exclusive affiliation of station), prohibited networks from preventing affiliates from broadcasting the programs of other networks. The Commission believed that the effects of preventing affiliates from airing these programs included hindering the growth of new networks, depriving the listening public in many areas of service to which they were entitled, and preventing station licensees from exercising their statutory duty of determining which programs would best serve the needs of their community.

Regulation 3.102 (Territorial exclusivity) prohibited affiliation agreements that prevented networks from selling its programming to any other stations in the area, even where the local network affiliate chose not to broadcast a particular show. Again the Commission believed these agreements deprived the listening public of programming that might otherwise be available.

Regulation 3.103 (Term of affiliation) limited the length of affiliation agreements to two years. Common industry practice at the time was to use five-year agreements. Noting that broadcast license terms were only three years, the Commission found the five-year affiliation term to be contrary to the policy of the Act: "Regardless of any changes that may occur in the economic, political, or social life of the Nation or of the community in which the station is located, CBS and NBC affiliates are bound by contract to continue broadcasting the network programs of only one network for 5 years."

Regulation 3.104 (Option time) prohibited arrangements whereby a network reserved an option to use specified amounts of an affiliate's broadcast time. The Commission believed that these agreements hindered the development of local programming because regular schedules were disrupted whenever a network exercised its option.

Regulation 3.105 (Right to reject programs) prohibited clauses limiting the right of affiliates to reject network programming. In the Commission's view, such clauses constituted an inappropriate delegation of the licensee's duty to decide what programming should air.

Regulation 3.106 (Network ownership of stations) prohibited a network from owning stations in areas where the available facilities were so few or of such unequal coverage that competition would thereby be substantially restricted.

Regulation 3.107 (Dual network operation) prohibited one company from operating more than one network. This rule was aimed at preventing a single network from controlling too much programming. In response to this provision, NBC sold its Blue Network. The Blue Network subsequently became ABC.

Regulation 3.108 (Control by networks of station rates) prevented networks from controlling the rates charged for non-network national advertising by its affiliates. The FCC concluded that such control had an anticompetitive effect on advertising rates.

The networks then brought suit to enjoin enforcement of the chain broadcasting rules. We examined the arguments concerning the Commission's authority to regulate broadcasting at p. ___, *supra*. We now turn to the Court's consideration of the rules themselves.

In rejecting a claim that the regulations were arbitrary and capricious, the Court quoted with approval the Commission's stated rationale for these rules:

> "With the number of radio channels limited by natural factors, the public interest demands that those who are entrusted with the available channels shall make the fullest and most effective use of them. If a licensee enters into a contract with a network organization which limits his ability to make the best use of the radio facility assigned him, he is not serving the public interest. . . . The net effect [of the practices disclosed by the investigation] has been that broadcasting service has been maintained at a level below that possible under a system of free competition. Having so found, we would be remiss in our statutory duty of encouraging 'the larger and more effective use of radio in the public interest' if we were to grant licenses to persons who persist in these practices."

The Court also rejected two claims related to the FCC's jurisdiction in the area of antitrust. The first was that the regulations were an *ultra vires* attempt to enforce antitrust laws. The second that, because § 311 of the Communications Act authorizes the Commission to deny a broadcast license to anyone convicted of violating the antitrust laws, the FCC was precluded from considering any other issues regarding monopoly and competition. The Court held that FCC was making decisions regarding the public interest, convenience and necessity and that such decisions were certainly within the scope of the FCC's jurisdiction. *NBC*, p. ___, *supra*.

In 1977 the Commission re-examined the application of the Chain Broadcasting Regulations to radio and concluded that due to the high degree of competition that now existed, most of the Regulations were no longer necessary. Consequently, they eliminated all but a modified version of the territorial exclusivity regulation for both AM and FM stations.

> § 73.132　Territorial exclusivity. No licensee of an AM broadcast station shall have any arrangement with a network organization which prevents or hinders another station serving substantially the same area from broadcasting the network's programs not taken by the former station, or which prevents or hinders another station serving a substantially different area from broadcasting any program of the network organization: provided, however, that this section does not prohibit arrangements under which the station is granted first call within its primary service area upon the network's programs. The term "network organization" means any organization originating program material, with or without commercial messages, and furnishing the same to stations interconnected so as to permit simultaneous broadcast by all or some of them. However, arrangements involving only stations under common ownership, or only the rebroadcast by one station of programming from another with no compensation other than a lump-sum payment by the station rebroadcasting, are not considered arrangements with a network organization. The term "arrangement" means any contract, arrangement or understanding, express or implied.

Section 73.232 applies the same restrictions to FM stations. 47 C.F.R. § 73.232.

The Financial Interest and Syndication Rules. In 1965 the Commission adopted rules "designed to eliminate the networks from distribution and profit-sharing in domestic syndication and to restrict their activities in foreign markets to distribution of programs of which they are the sole producers." These rules were defended on the ground that networks had a conflict of interest in choosing programs. Independent producers who sought to exhibit their products on a network had to bargain with the networks, who were their "principal competitors in syndication and foreign sales." The Commission concluded that "networks do not normally accept new, untried packager-licensed programs for network exhibition unless the producer/packager is willing to cede a large part of the valuable rights and interests in subsidiary rights to the program to the network." There were also allegations of "warehousing," purchasing programs with no intention of showing them in order to keep them out of the marketplace.

In 1981, acting on a petition by CBS, Inc., the Commission ruled that the financial interest and syndication rules did not apply to non-broadcast rights to television programs. The decision opened the way for the networks to enter the cable, video cassette and video disc markets. An appeal by Viacom International, Inc., a major program syndicator, was denied. Viacom International Inc. v. Federal Communications Commission, 672 F.2d 1034, 50 R.R.2d 1641 (2d Cir.1982).

In 1982 the Commission issued an NPRM aimed at eliminating the financial interest and syndication rules. The NPRM was based on a 1980 report by the FCC Network Inquiry Special Staff that concluded the rules were unnecessary and ineffective. A year later the Commission issued a Tentative Decision proposing the deletion of the financial interest rule and modifying the syndication rule. 54 R.R.2d 457 (1983).

Bowing to Presidential, as well as legislative, pressure, Chairman Fowler indicated that he would not bring the matter before the Commission. Meanwhile, years of negotiations between the networks and syndicators were unable to resolve the issue.

Since adoption of the original financial interest and syndication rules and the Prime Time Access Rule (PTAR), discussed later in this chapter, the FCC had granted two permanent waivers. The first allowed the Christian Broadcast Network (CBN) to provide up to 30 hours of weekly programming without being subject to those rules. Christian Broadcasting Network, Inc., 87 F.C.C.2d 1076, 50 R.R.2d 359 (1981). The second exempted the Home Shopping Network (HSN) from the dual network rule and PTAR. Home Shopping, Inc., 4 F.C.C.Rcd. 2422, 66 R.R.2d 175 (1989). According to the Commission, the waivers were justified by the fact that neither CBN nor HSN was significantly involved in either the sale of national advertising or the production, acquisition or distribution of traditional entertainment programs to commercial stations for airing during the prime-time-access period.

The development of Fox Television as a fourth network, p. ___, *supra*, forced the Commission to return to the issue of the financial interest and syndication rules. The rules did not initially apply to Fox because its early programming was not sufficient to meet the existing FCC definition of a network, 47 C.F.R. § 73.658(j)(4). Although Fox was providing programming to more than 25 affiliates in more than 10 states, it was providing only nine hours a week of such programming. However, after announcing plans to increase its programming efforts to 18½ hours a week by the fall 1990 television season, Fox filed a petition asking the FCC to resume rulemaking in the financial interest and syndication rules proceeding.

In response the Commission terminated the old rulemaking proceeding as "stale" and issued a new NPRM on the financial interest and syndication rules. Evaluation of the Syndication and Financial Interest Rules, 5 F.C.C.Rcd. 1815 (1990). The NPRM elicited thousands upon thousands of pages of comments. These comments presented "alternative views of the television programming world so starkly and fundamentally at odds with each other that they virtually defy reconciliation." The Commission itself was sharply divided on the issue. Although the commissioners all agreed that the video marketplace had changed dramatically in the 20 years since the original rules were adopted, they did not agree on the degree to which that change rendered those rules unnecessary. By a 3–2 vote, the Commission decided to retain the rules, but with substantial modifications.

The two dissenters, Sykes and Quello, both felt that the Commission did not go nearly far enough in relaxing the rules. In separate dissents, each argued that the networks no longer have sufficient market power to exercise any significant control over the prime-time programming market. Thus, in their opinion, the Commission should have substantially, if not totally, repealed the rules. Financial Interest and Syndication Rules, 6 F.C.C.Rcd. 3094, 69 R.R.2d 341 (1991).

Numerous appeals were filed. The networks and their affiliates argued that the rules should have been eliminated rather than relaxed. Others, including Media Access Project and major studios, claimed that the rules were relaxed too much. Because the appeals were filed with more than one court, a lottery was used to choose which court would hear the case. The Seventh Circuit was chosen.

SCHURZ COMMUNICATIONS, INCORPORATED v. FEDERAL COMMUNICATIONS COMMISSION

United States Court of Appeals, Seventh Circuit, 1992.
982 F.2d 1043, 71 R.R.2d 693.

Before BAUER, CHIEF JUDGE, POSNER, CIRCUIT JUDGE, and FAIRCHILD, SENIOR CIRCUIT JUDGE.

POSNER, CIRCUIT JUDGE.

In 1970 the Federal Communications Commission adopted "financial interest and syndication" rules designed to limit the power of the then three television networks—CBS, NBC, and ABC—over television programming. [ ] Each of the three networks consisted (as they still do) of several television stations, in key markets, owned and operated by the network itself, plus about two hundred independently owned stations electronically connected to the network by cable or satellite. In exchange for a fee paid them by the network, these affiliated stations broadcast programs that the network transmits to them, as well as to its owned and operated stations, over the interconnect system. The networking of programs intended for the early evening hours that are the "prime time" for adult television viewing gives advertisers access to a huge number of American households simultaneously, which in turn enables the networks to charge the high prices for advertising time that are necessary to defray the cost of obtaining the programming most desired by television viewers.

The financial interest and syndication rules adopted in 1970 forbade a network to syndicate (license) programs produced by the network for rebroadcast by independent television stations—that is, stations that were not owned by or affiliated with the network—or to purchase syndication rights to programs that it obtained from outside producers, or otherwise to obtain a financial stake in such programs. If the network itself had produced the program it could sell syndication rights to an independent syndicator, but it could not retain an interest in the syndicator's revenue or profit.

Many syndicated programs are reruns, broadcast by independent stations, of successful comedy or dramatic series first shown on network television. Very few series are sufficiently successful in their initial run to be candidates for syndication. Independent stations like to air five episodes each week of a rerun series that originally had aired only once a week or less, so unless a series has a first run of several years—which few series do—it will not generate enough episodes to sustain a rerun of reasonable length. The financial interest and syndication rules thus severely limited the networks' involvement in supplying television programs other than for their own or their affiliated stations.

The concern behind the rules was that the networks controlling as they did through their owned and operated stations and their affiliates a large part of the system for distributing television programs to American households, would unless restrained use this control to seize a dominating position in the production of television programs. That is, they would lever their distribution "monopoly" into a production "monopoly." They would, for example, refuse to buy programs for network distribution unless the producers agreed to surrender their syndication rights to the network. For once the networks controlled those rights, the access of independent television stations, that is, stations not owned by or affiliated with one of the networks, to reruns would be at the sufferance of their networks, owners of a competing system of distribution. Market power in buying has the same misallocative effects as the more common market power in selling. The relation is especially close in this case because the networks can just as well be viewed as sellers of a distribution service as they can be as buyers of programs—the less they pay for programs, the more in effect they charge for distributing them.

The Commission hoped the rules would strengthen an alternative source of supply (to the networks) for independent stations—the alternative consisting of television producers not owned by the networks. The rules would do this by curtailing the ability of the networks to supply the program market represented by the independent stations, and by protecting the producers for that market for that market against being pressured into giving up potentially valuable syndication rights. And the rules would strengthen the independent stations (and so derivatively the outside producers, for whom the independent stations were an important market along with the networks themselves) by securing them against having to purchase reruns from their competitors the networks.

The basis for this concern that the networks, octopus-like, would use their position in distribution to take over programming, and would use the resulting control of programming to eliminate their remaining competition in distribution, was never very clear. If the networks insisted on buying syndication rights along with the right to exhibit a program on the network itself, they would be paying more for their programming. (So one is not surprised that in the decade before the rules were adopted, the networks had acquired syndication rights to no more than 35 percent of their prime-time series, although they had acquired a stake in the syndicator's profit in a considerably higher percentage of cases.) If the networks then turned around and refused to syndicate independent stations, they would be getting nothing in return for the money they had laid out for syndication rights except a long-shot chance—incidentally, illegal under the antitrust laws—to weaken the already weak competitors of network stations. Nor was it clear just how the financial interest and syndication rules would scotch the networks' nefarious schemes. If forbidden to buy syndication rights, networks would pay less for programs, so the outside producers would not come out clear winners— indeed many would be losers. Production for television is a highly risky undertaking, like wildcat drilling for gas and oil. Most television entertainment programs are money losers. The losses are offset by the occasional hit that makes it into syndication after completing a long first run. The sale of syndication rights to a network would enable a producer to shift risk to a larger, more diversified entity presumptively better able to bear it. The resulting reduction in the risks of production would encourage new entry into production and thus give the independent stations a more competitive supply of programs. Evidence introduced in this proceeding showed that, consistent with this speculation, networks in the pre–1970 era were more likely to purchase syndication rights from small producers than from large ones.

Whatever the pros and cons of the original financial interest and syndication rules, in the years since they were promulgated the structure of the television industry has changed profoundly. The three networks have lost ground, primarily as a result of the expansion of cable television, which now reaches 60 percent of American homes, and videocassette recorders, now found in 70 percent of American homes. Today each of the three networks buys only 7 percent of the total video and film programming sold each year, which is roughly a third of the percentage in 1970. The inclusion of films in the relevant market is appropriate because videocassettes enable home viewers to substitute a film for a television program. And each commands only about 12 percent of total television advertising revenues. Where in 1970 the networks had 90 percent of the prime-time audience, today they have 62 percent, and competition among as well as with the three networks is fierce. They are, moreover, challenged today by a fourth network, the Fox Broadcasting Corporation, which emerged in the late 1980s.

Notwithstanding the fourth network, which might have been expected to reduce the number of independent stations by converting many of them to network—Fox network—stations, the number of independent stations has increased fivefold since 1970. At the same time, contrary to the intention behind the rules yet an expectable result of them because they made television production a riskier business, the production of prime-time programming has become more concentrated. There are 40 percent fewer producers of prime-time programming today than there were two decades ago. And the share of that programming accounted for directly or indirectly by the eight largest producers, primarily Hollywood studios—companies large enough to bear the increased risk resulting from the Commission's prohibition against the sale of syndication rights to networks—has risen from 50 percent to 70 percent.

The original rules had been supported by the Antitrust Division of the Department of Justice. But as the years passed, antitrust thinking changed. The "leverage" theory, which taught that a firm having economic power in one market would use it to acquire a monopoly of another market, was widely discredited. The evolution of the television industry, sketched above, suggested that the rules, if they were having any effect at all, were working perversely from a competitive standpoint. . . .

. . . The question of what to do about the rules remained in limbo until 1990, when the Commission at the request of the Fox network initiated a fresh notice-and-comment rulemaking proceeding. After receiving voluminous submissions from the various segments of the television industry, the Commission held a one-day hearing, after which it issued an opinion, over dissents by two of the five Commissioners, including the chairman, promulgating a revised set of financial interest and syndication rules. . . .

The Commission's majority opinion describes them as "deregulatory," arguing that they expand the networks' opportunities to participate in the program market and promising to reexamine them in four years to see whether a further relaxation of restrictions might then be justifiable. . . .

. . .

Although the television industry is less complex than some and its product is well known even to federal judges, there are more than enough technical aspects to the industry, involving such things as the modes of financing and contracting and the effects of market structure and practices on television fare, to enforce judicial diffidence. Moreover, economists do not agree on the relation between monopoly or competition, on the one hand, and the quality or variety of an industry's output, on the other, so that it is difficult to obtain a theoretical perspective from which to evaluate the Commission's claims about that relation. If the Commission were enforcing the antitrust laws, it would not be allowed to trade off a reduction in competition against an increase in an intangible known as "diversity." Since it is enforcing the nebulous public interest standard instead, it is permitted, and maybe even required, to make such a tradeoff—at least we do not understand any of the parties to question the Commission's authority to do so. And although as an original matter one might doubt that the First Amendment authorized the government to regulate so important a part of the marketplace in ideas and opinions as television broadcasting, the Supreme Court has consistently taken a different view. [*National Citizens Committee for Broadcasting*, p. ___, *supra*; *Pacifica*, p. ___, *supra*; *National Broadcasting Co.*, p. ___, *supra*.] The challenged rules themselves, finally, are so complicated that it is unclear whether they are more or less restrictive than the rules they modified.

From what we have said so far, it should be apparent that the networks have no hope of proving to our satisfaction that the Commission is without *any* power to restrict the networks' participation in television programming. Even if we were persuaded that it would be irrational to impute to the networks even a smidgen of market power, the Commission could always take the position that it should carve out a portion of the production and distribution markets and protect them against the competition of the networks in order to foster, albeit at a higher cost to advertisers and ultimately to consumers, a diversity of programming sources and outlets that might result in a greater variety of perspectives and imagined forms of life than the free market would provide. That would be a judgment within the Commission's power to make.

The difficult question presented by the petitions to review is not whether the Commission is authorized to restrict the networks' participation in program production and distribution. It is whether the Commission has said enough to justify, in the face of the objections lodged with it, the particular restrictions that it imposed in the order here challenged. . . . [The standard for judicial review of administrative action requires more than that the rule be rational]; the statement accompanying its promulgation must show that it is rational—must demonstrate that a reasonable person upon consideration of all the points urged pro and con the rule would conclude that it was a reasonable response to a problem that the agency was charged with solving. . . .

The new rules flunk this test. The Commission's articulation of its grounds is not adequately reasoned. Key concepts are left unexplained, key evidence is overlooked, arguments that formerly persuaded the Commission and that time has only strengthened are ignored, contradictions within and among Commission decisions are passed over in silence. The impression created is of unprincipled compromises of Rube Goldberg complexity among contending interest groups viewed merely as clamoring suppliants who have somehow to be conciliated. The Commission said that it had been "confronted by alternative views of the television programming world so starkly and fundamentally at odds with each other that they virtually defy *reconciliation*" (emphasis added). The possibility of resolving a conflict in favor of the party with the stronger case, as distinct from throwing up one's hands and splitting the difference, was overlooked. The opinion contains much talk but no demonstration of expertise, and a good deal of hand-wringing over the need for prudence and the desirability of avoiding "convulsive" regulatory reform, yet these unquestioned goods are never related to the particulars of the rules—rules that could have a substantial impact on an industry that permeates the daily life of this nation and helps shape, for good or ill, our culture and our politics. The Commission must do better in articulating their justification. Perhaps the attempt to do so will result in significant modifications in the rules. Not all remands result in the reinstatement of the original decision with merely a more polished rationalization.

The Commission's majority opinion . . . is long, but much of it consists of boilerplate, the recitation of the multitudinous parties' multifarious contentions, and self-congratulatory rhetoric about how careful and thoughtful and measured and balanced the majority has been in evaluating those contentions and carrying out its responsibilities. Stripped of verbiage, the opinion, like a Persian cat with its fur shaved, is alarmingly pale and thin. It can be paraphrased as follows. The television industry has changed since 1970. There is more competition—cable television, the new network, etc. No longer is it clear that the networks have market power in an antitrust sense, which they could use to whipsaw the independent producers and strangle the independent stations. So there should be some "deregulation" of programming—some movement away from the 1970 rules. But not too much, because even in their decline the networks may retain some power to extort programs or program rights from producers. The networks offer advertisers access to 98 percent of American households; no competing system for the distribution of television programming can offer as much. Anyway the Commission's concern, acknowledged to be legitimate, is not just with market power in any antitrust sense but with diversity, and diversity is promoted by measures to assure a critical mass of outside producers and independent stations. So the networks must continue to be restricted—but less so than by the 1970 rules. The new rules will give the networks a greater opportunity to participate in programming than the old ones did, while protecting outside producers and independent stations from too much network competition.

All this is, on its face, plausible enough, but it is plausible only because the Commission, ostrich fashion, did not discuss the most substantial objections to its approach, though the objections were argued vigorously to it, by its own chairman among others. To begin with, the networks object that the new rules do not in fact increase their access to the programming market and may decrease it, in the face of the Commission's stated objective. The 40 percent limitation on the amount of prime-time entertainment that a network can supply from its in-house production is a new restriction on the networks, having no counterpart in the original rules. . . . The carving out of nonentertainment programming, from the restrictions imposed by the new rules is a throwaway, because there is no syndication market for news and sports programs. Also illusory, the networks argue, is the newly granted right to acquire syndication rights from outside producers, given the restrictions with which the new right is hedged about. A producer cannot wait until

30 days after negotiating the network license fee to sell off syndication rights, because the sale of those rights, the networks contend, is critical to obtaining the financing necessary to produce the program in the first place. These arguments may be right or wrong; our point is only that the Commission did not mention them. We are left in the dark about the grounds for its belief that the new rules will give the networks real, not imaginary, new opportunities in programming.

The new rules, like their predecessors, appear to harm rather than to help outside producers as a *whole* (a vital qualification) by reducing their bargaining options. It is difficult to see how taking away a part of a seller's market could help the seller. One of the rights in the bundle of rights that constitutes the ownership of a television program is the right to syndicate the program to nonnetwork stations. The new rules restrict—perhaps, as a practical matter, prevent—the sale of that right to networks. How could it help a producer to be *forbidden* to sell his wares to a class of buyers that may be the high bidders for them? . . . Since syndication is the riskiest component of a producer's property right—for its value depends on the distinctly low-probability event that the program will be smash hit on network television—restricting its sale bears most heavily on the smallest, the weakest, the newest, the most experimental producers, for they are likely to be the ones least able to bear the risk. It becomes understandable why the existing producers support the financial interest and syndication rules: the rules protect these producers against new competition both from the networks (because of the 40 percent cap) and from new producers. The ranks of the outside producers of prime-time programming have been thinned under the regime of financial interest and syndication rules. The survivors are the beneficiaries of the thinning. They do not want the forest restored to its pristine density. They consent to have their own right to sell syndication rights curtailed as the price of a like restriction on their potential competitors, on whom it is likely to bear more heavily.

This analysis of risk and its bearing on competition in the program industry is speculative, theoretical, and may for all we know be all wet—though it is corroborated by the increasing concentration of the production industry since the rules restricting the sale of syndication rights were first imposed in 1970. The Commission was not required to buy the analysis. But as the analysis was more than plausible and had been pressed upon it by a number of participants in the rulemaking proceeding—including a putatively disinterested Justice Department that in the past had frequently seen the bogeyman of monopoly lurking everywhere, as well as the Commission's own chairman—the Commission majority was not entitled to ignore it. Not even to consider the possibility that the unrestricted sale of syndication rights to networks would strengthen the production industry (the industry—not necessarily its present occupants) and thereby increase programming diversity by enabling a sharing between fledgling producers and the networks of the risks of new production was irresponsible. For if the argument about risk sharing is correct, the rules are perverse; by discouraging the entry of new producers into the high-risk prime-time entertainment, they are likely to reduce the supply of programs to the independent stations and so reduce diversity both of program sources and of program outlets. The Commission's stated desiderata are competition and diversity. The rules adopted by the Commission in order to achieve these desiderata have the remarkable property—if the risk-sharing argument that the Commission did not deign to address is correct—of disserving them both.

Central to the Commission's decision to continue restricting the networks' participation in programming is its belief that whether or not they have market power in some antitrust sense they have power to force producers to sell them programs for less than the programs would be worth in a fully competitive market. The networks call this a contradiction: either they have market power, or they don't; there is no middle ground. A rational commission could disagree. Market power is a matter of degree. Some firms have a lot of it, some a little, some none. It is plausible that each network, even when not colluding with the others (there is no evidence that they are colluding), has some market power and thus can drive a harder bargain than it could if it had none. Even though each of the three major networks has only about 20 percent of the prime-time audience and a producer who does not sell his program to a network can still hope to distribute it to the public via independent stations and cable networks, or for that matter movie theaters and videocassette dealers, network distribution offers advertisers unique simultaneous access to a large fraction of American households and increases the prospects for successful syndication, which apparently is where the real money in the creation of television entertainment is to be made.

The difficulty is that if the networks do have market power, the new rules (in this respect like the old) do not seem rationally designed to prevent its exercise. A rule telling a person he may not do business with some firm believed to have market power is unlikely to make the person better off. Suppose that in a competitive market a network would pay $2 million for first-run rights to some program and $1 million for syndication rights, for a total of $3 million, but that because of the lack of perfect substitutes for using this network to distribute his program the producer is willing to sell each of these rights to the network for half their competitive-market value (i.e., for $1 million and $500,000 respectively). The producer is made no better off by being forbidden to sell the syndication rights to the network. He gets the same meager first-run license fee ($1 million) and now must cast about for another buyer for the syndication rights. That other buyer is unlikely to pay more than the network would ($500,000); otherwise the producer would have sold the syndication rights to him in the first place. It is no answer that the network would not have given the producer the option of selling it only the first-run rights, that it would have insisted on the whole package so that it could control the program supply of the independent stations, which are heavily dependent on reruns and hence on syndication. The producer might indeed be desperate for network distribution, but that desperation would be reflected in the low price at which he was willing to sell the network whatever rights the network wanted. He cannot do better by being forbidden to make such a deal. If he could do better by selling syndication rights to someone else he would not accede to such unfavorable terms as the network offered.

If this is right, the new rules, at least insofar as they restrict network syndication, cannot increase the prices that producers receive. All they can do is increase the costs of production by denying producers the right to share risks with networks.

. . .

Everything that we have said about the effect of forbidding producers to sell syndication rights to networks may be wrong. That we freely grant. But the argument we have sketched—an argument vigorously pressed upon the Commission by the networks—is sufficiently persuasive to have placed a burden of explanation on the Commission. It did not carry the burden. It did not mention the objection.

And we have said nothing as yet of the treatment of the Fox network. That network is built around the production capability and film library of Twentieth Century Fox. At present the network supplies only 12 to 14 hours a week of prime-time programming to its owned and affiliated stations and is therefore exempt from the new rules. Should it reach 15 hours, however, it would be subject to them. Fox argues that, given the importance of program production in its overall corporate activity, the effect of the rules is to limit it to supplying fewer than 15 hours of prime-time programming and therefore limit its growth as a network. . . . By limiting Fox in this way the new financial interest and syndication rules limit competition with the major networks and thus entrench the market power that is the rules' principal rationale. Or so Fox argues; it may be bluffing; maybe the effect of the rules will be to induce Fox to divest its production or network arms, so that the network can grow without constraining Fox's production activities. But once again the Commission failed even to mention the argument that its rules perversely limit competition with the established networks.

More than competition in the economic sense is at stake. Fox's affiliates are for the most part the traditionally weak UHF stations. They do not consider themselves "network" stations in the same sense that a CBS or NBC or ABC affiliate does. Many of them are members of the trade association of independent television stations. Anything that weakens Fox's incentives to furnish prime-time programming weakens them, contrary to the Commission's desire, protectionist though it may be, to strengthen independent stations. This perverse consequence of the rules also went unmentioned.

The Commission's treatment of precedent was also cavalier. An administrative agency is no more straitjacketed by precedent than a court is. It can reject its previous decisions. But it must explain why it is doing so. . . . In 1983 in its tentative decision, the Commission rejected the proposition that the networks had significant market power, found that the financial interest and syndication rules were preventing efficient risk-sharing, and concluded that the rules should be phased out by 1990. [   ] In the eight years between that decision and the one under review the networks lost still more ground, with the continued rapid growth of cable television and the advent of the Fox network. The Commission majority cited the tentative decision but did not discuss it—did not explain what had happened in eight years to justify the Commission's about face or, if nothing had happened, why the tentative decision had been wrong from the start. The tentative decision had also laid down a general approach to the evaluation of network restrictions: "The Commission should not intervene in the market except where there is evidence of a market failure and a regulatory solution is available that is likely to improve the net welfare of the consuming public." [   ] That standard went unremarked in the present order.

. . .

We remarked earlier that even if the networks had zero market power, the Commission might in the discharge of its undefined, uncanalized responsibility to promote the public interest restrict the networks' programming activities in order to create a more diverse programming fare. What it could not do, consistent with the principles of reasoned decisionmaking, was pretend that it had never found that the networks had lost market power. . . .

Finally, while the word diversity appears with incantatory frequency in the Commission's opinion, it is never defined. At argument one of the counsel helpfully distinguished between source diversity and outlet diversity. . . . The former refers to programming sources, that is, producers, and the latter to distribution outlets, that is, television stations. The two forms of diversity are related because the station decides what programs to air and therefore affects producers' decisions about what to produce. A third and one might suppose the critical form of diversity is diversity in the programming itself; here "diversity" refers to the variety or heterogeneity of programs. The Commission neither distinguished among the types of diversity nor explained the interrelation among them. As it is very difficult to see how sheer *number* of producers or outlets could be thought a good thing—and anyway the rules seem calculated, however unwittingly, to decrease, or at least to freeze, but certainly not to increase, the number of producers—we assume that the Commission thinks of source diversity and outlet diversity as means to the end of programming diversity.

Are they? It has long been understood that monopoly in broadcasting could actually promote rather than retard programming diversity. If all the television channels in a particular market were owned by a single firm, its optimal programming strategy would be to put on a sufficiently varied menu of programs in each time slot to appeal to every substantial group of potential television viewers in the market, but not just the largest group. For that would be the strategy that maximized the size of the station's audience. Suppose, as a simple example, that there were only two television broadcast frequencies (and no cable television), and that 90 percent of the viewers in the market wanted to watch comedy from 7 to 8 p.m. and 10 percent wanted to watch ballet. The monopolist would broadcast comedy over one frequency and ballet over the other, and thus gain 100 percent of the potential audience. If the frequencies were licensed to two competing firms, each firm would broadcast comedy in the 7 to 8 p.m. time slot, because its expected audience share would be 45 percent (one half of 90 percent), which is greater than 10 percent. Each prime-time slot would be filled with "popular" programming targeted on the median viewer, and minority tastes would go unserved. Some critics of television believe that this is a fair description of prime-time network television. Each network vies to put on the most popular programs and as a result minority tastes are ill served.

. . .

[The Commission's] opinion, despite its length, is unreasoned and unreasonable, and therefore, in the jargon of judicial review of administrative action, arbitrary and capricious. The Commission's order is therefore vacated and the matter is returned to the Commission for further proceedings. The Commission may of course reopen the record of the rulemaking proceeding to receive additional comments if that will help it reach an articulate reasoned decision.

. . .

Vacated.

Notes and Questions

1. The court stayed the elimination of the new rules for 120 days in order to give the FCC an opportunity either to present better justification for them or to issue new rules.

2. The Commission responded by issuing new rules. Networks were prohibited from actively syndicating programs domestically. With programs syndicated domestically, networks could "hold financial interests and syndication rights only in programming produced solely in-house" and those shows had to be distributed by an independent distributor. To prevent warehousing, networks were required to release any program for which it held the syndication rights, "into the syndication market four years after the program's network debut or within six months following the end of the network run, whichever is sooner." The rules applied only to ABC, CBS and NBC. Syndication and Financial Interest Rules, 8 F.C.C.Rcd. 3282, 72 R.R.2d 1044 (1993).

On reconsideration, the Commission affirmed its decision except for a small adjustment to the network reporting requirements. Financial Interest and Syndication Rules (Reconsideration), 8 F.C.C.Rcd. 8270, 73 R.R.2d 1452 (1993). The court of appeals affirmed. Capital Cities/ABC, Inc. v. Federal Communications Commission, 29 F.3d 309 (7th Cir.1994).

3. The Commission also scheduled the rules to sunset two years after the financial interest and syndication provisions of the network consent

decrees were modified, p. ___, *supra*. As part of this provision, the FCC committed itself to "conducting a proceeding six months prior to the scheduled expiration date to give interested parties an opportunity to demonstrate that we should not allow these rules to expire as scheduled."

In 1995 the FCC issued an NPRM seeking comment on whether the rules should expire as scheduled. The Commission also asked for comments on whether the rules should be eliminated prior to their scheduled expiration in the event that those seeking to extend the rules are unable to "demonstrate 'an excellent, a compelling reason' why the restrictions should be continued." Syndication and Financial Interest Rules, 10 F.C.C.Rcd. 5672 (1995).

After reviewing the comments submitted, the FCC decided that those parties seeking to extend the restrictions had failed to meet their burden of proof. The FCC further concluded that the rules should be eliminated immediately rather than wait for the original sunset date. Syndication and Financial Interest Rules, 10 F.C.C.Rcd. 12165 (1995).

4. *The Prime Time Access Rule.* In 1965 the Commission issued a notice of proposed rulemaking in which it sought, among other things, to limit the networks' control over programming during prime time. After extensive comments and hearings, the Commission decided in 1970 to adopt a rule providing that after Sept. 1, 1971:

> . . . no television station, assigned to any of the top 50 markets in which there are three or more operating commercial television stations, shall broadcast network programs offered by any television network or networks for a total of more than 3 hours per day between the hours of 7 p.m. and 11 p.m. local time, except that in the Central time zone the relevant period shall be between the hours of 6 p.m. and 10 p.m.

Competition and Responsibility in Network Television Broadcasting, 23 F.C.C.2d 382, 18 R.R.2d 1825 (1970). This prime time access rule (PTAR I) exempted fast-breaking news events, on-the-spot coverage of news events and political broadcasts by candidates.

The Commission presented several reasons for its action. Primarily, it was concerned that during the 1960s the number of first-run syndicated entertainment series had fallen. The role of "off-network" entertainment series (programs that had been on the networks earlier and were now being syndicated to other stations) had grown enormously, as had the role of the networks in preparing new programs. Even among independent stations, "which should be the backbone of the syndication market," first-run syndications were being replaced by off-network programs. Only 14 of the top 50 markets had at least one independent VHF station.

Finally, the financial involvement of the networks in evening programming had doubled during the 1960s, and the independently produced programs had fallen by 90 percent. The Commission deplored this "unhealthy situation" and asserted that the new rule would provide a "healthy impetus to the development of independent program sources, with concomitant benefits in an increased supply of programs for independent (and, indeed, affiliated) stations. The entire development of UHF should be benefitted."

A constitutional and statutory challenge to the rules was rejected in Mt. Mansfield Television, Inc. v. Federal Communications Commission, 442 F.2d 470, 21 R.R.2d 2087, 1 Med.L.Rptr. 2020 (2d Cir.1971). The court relied on *Red Lion's* observations that the peculiar qualities of each medium must be considered in deciding the application of the First Amendment. It also quoted from cases, such as *Associated Press,* that stressed the virtues of "the widest possible dissemination of information from diverse and antagonistic sources," and observed:

> When viewed in the light of these principles, the prime time access rule, far from violating the First Amendment, appears to be a reasonable step toward fulfillment of its fundamental precepts, for it is the stated purpose of that rule to encourage the "[d]iversity of programs and development of diverse and antagonistic sources of program service" and to correct a situation where "[o]nly three organizations control access to the crucial prime time evening schedule." The specific arguments raised by the petitions reflect basic misconceptions of that purpose and of the First Amendment principles outlined above.

> For example, petitioner Columbia Broadcasting System, Inc. attempts an analogy between the prime time access rule and an imaginary governmental edict prohibiting newspapers in the 50 largest cities from devoting more than a given portion of their news space to items taken from national news services. This analogy completely overlooks the essential fact that "[w]here there are substantially more individuals who want to broadcast than there are frequencies to allocate, it is idle to posit an unabridgeable First Amendment right to broadcast comparable to the right of every individual to speak, write, or publish." Red Lion Broadcasting Co., supra, 395 U.S. at 388.

> To argue that the freedom of networks to distribute and licensees to select programming is limited by the prime time access rule, and that the First Amendment is thereby violated, is to reverse the mandated priorities which subordinate these interests to the public's right of access. The licensee is in many ways a "trustee" for the public in the operation of his channel. . . .

The Court found statutory authority to promulgate PTAR I in the power of the Commission to regulate in the public interest, citing *National Broadcasting Co.,* p. ___, *supra*. It also upheld the Commission's adoption of the syndication and financial interest rules, the first direct regulation of networks (rather than regulating licensees of stations), as within the Commission's statutory power because they were "reasonably ancillary to the effective performance of the Commission's various responsibilities for the regulation of television broadcasting." 442 F.2d at 481.

The Commission considered requests for waiver of the off-network programs to be presented during prime time without being counted toward the permissible three hours of network and off-network material each evening. What considerations might have led the Commission to grant waivers for "Wild Kingdom," "National Geographic," "Six Wives of Henry VIII" and "Animal World," but to deny waivers to "Lassie" and "Hogan's Heroes"?

5. Less than two years later, the Commission issued a combined NOI/ NPRM in which it announced its intention to consider whether to modify or repeal PTAR I. In 1973 the Commission adopted PTAR II, which modified PTAR I in several ways. The major change was to eliminate access time altogether on Sunday evenings and to reduce it to one half-hour other evenings. However, PTAR II was successfully challenged in court because the effective date did not allow sufficient time for independent producers to withdraw programs being produced in reliance on PTAR I. National Association of Independent Television Producers & Distributors v. Federal Communications Commission, 502 F.2d 249, 30 R.R.2d 887 (2d Cir.1974).

As a result, in January 1975 the Commission adopted PTAR III, effective September 1975. The provisions were similar to PTAR I, covering one hour per night, except for certain exemptions that reflected waivers regularly granted under PTAR I and new provisions for the use of feature films. Exemptions covered network or off-network "public affairs" programming, documentaries, and programs designed for children. The Commission also noted that it expected "that stations subject to the rule will devote an appropriate portion of 'cleared time' or at least of total prime time to material particularly directed to the needs or problems of the station's community . . ., including programming addressed to the special needs of minority groups." 50 F.C.C.2d at 852, 32 R.R.2d at 722.

It reaffirmed its view that the rule lessened network dominance by releasing a portion of prime time for licensees of individual stations to use to respond to their respective communities and by encouraging a new body of syndicated programming. It also denied that the rule led to a lack of diversity and to low quality programs, arguing that the rule had not yet been fully tested. Although the Justice Department argued that to assure stability the Commission should guarantee that PTAR III would remain in effect at least five years, the Commission refused to do so.

Another challenge followed. In National Association of Independent Television Producers & Distributors v. Federal Communications Commission, 516 F.2d 526, 33 R.R.2d 795 (2d Cir.1975), the court generally upheld PTAR III, but remanded it to the Commission for reconsideration of several aspects of the rule. The Commission responded and PTAR III became effective in September 1975. The court recognized that the rule's results had been mixed at best:

> The result has been, as could have been expected to some degree, that it is largely the cheaper productions, daytime fare, that have been put into cleared prime time slots. What was not anticipated by the Commission was the monotony of the product. A kind of Gresham's law seems to operate in first-run syndication—the cheaper tending to drive the dearer out of circulation. The fact is, as the Commission concedes, that the degree of diversity in programming for access time has been disappointing. In the entertainment area, the emphasis has largely been on game shows and animal shows, game shows constituting 41.9% of the 2,100 access half hours on 150 stations in one season. [ ] Comedies, dramas, and Westerns in access time have dropped significantly. Comedy has been virtually eliminated. The Commission notes a similar lack of diversity, however, with respect to the three networks themselves which all show a crime drama at the same hour in prime time, also giving the viewer no choice.

> On the other hand, as the Commission found, and as the public *amici* stress, programs of local interest, on matters of concern to the people served by local stations, have begun to obtain a foothold on commercial stations in the access time period. One may assume that in the long run game shows will pall to some extent and that independent producers will have to turn to more variegated fare if they wish to survive, but any prophecy on public taste, certainly by judges, would be hazardous indeed.

Under PTAR I, the Commission had to pass upon waivers for specific network programs, said to be in the public interest, that would preempt access time. As noted, these *ad hoc* decisions gave rise to contentions that the Commission was regulating program content in violation of the First Amendment. In PTAR III the Commission exempted public affairs, documentary and children's programs. This led to a major constitutional challenge to PTAR III. The court considered the problem at some length (516 F.2d at 536–38):

> This is said to be in violation of the First Amendment. It is true that the Commission has never before considered what types of program may be played at particular times. And it may be that *mandatory* programming by the Commission even in categories would raise serious First Amendment questions. On the other hand, the general power of the F.C.C. to interest itself in the kinds of programs broadcast by licensees has consistently been sustained by the courts against arguments that the supervisory power violates the First Amendment.

> . . .

> The only way that broadcasters can operate in the "public interest" is by broadcasting programs that meet somebody's view of what is in the "public interest." That can scarcely be determined by

the broadcaster himself, for it is an obvious conflict of interest. "There is no sanctuary in the First Amendment for unlimited private censorship operating in a medium not open to all." Red Lion, supra, 395 U.S. at 392. "It is the right of the viewers and listeners, not the right of the broadcasters, which is paramount." Id. at 390.

Since the public cannot through a million stifled yawns convey that their television fare, as a whole, is not in their interest, the Congress has made the F.C.C. the guardian of that public interest. All that the Commission can do about it is to encourage competitive fare. If a large segment of the public prefers game shows to documentaries, the Commission can hardly do more than admit paradoxically that taste *is* a matter for dispute. The Commission surely cannot do its job, however, without interesting itself in general program format and the kinds of programs broadcast by licensees. . . .

The Commission by this amendment of the rule is not ordering any program or even any type of program to be broadcast in access time. It has simply lifted a restriction on network programs if the licensee chooses to avail himself of such network programs in specified categories of programming. . . .

. . .

It is suggested that the Commission should have elected to force the stations to carve out *network* prime time for these programs. Whether or not the Commission could have done this—a course that would doubtless have evoked constitutional protests from the networks—it is not for this court to say. Nor is it for this court to say that the Commission had, in any event, no right to choose between reasonable alternatives.

6. In 1980, as part of a study of network power, the FCC staff reported that the prime time access rule had not increased local programming. Many major stations were "stripping" syndicated programs five nights per week. (Four NBC O & Os were running "Family Feud" five nights each week at 7:30 p.m.) A few creative local programs, particularly "Evening Magazine" on Westinghouse stations (syndicated as "PM Magazine" to non-Westinghouse stations), had emerged, but these were the rare exceptions. The staff suggested that if the Commissioners wanted local programming they should order it directly.

There were, however, other justifications for the prime time access rule. In the top 50 markets, the network affiliates were banned from using off-network programs during the access period. This allowed independent stations, primarily UHFs, to offer these popular programs as competition to the network affiliate offerings. As a result, the viability of the UHF stations was strengthened considerably.

At the same time the network affiliates came to appreciate the rule because they could make more money selling all the commercial availabilities in syndicated programming in contrast to the limited availabilities in network programming. Most affiliates opposed any proposals to eliminate the prime time access rule.

7.   In 1990, First Media, licensee of WCPX, filed a petition seeking the elimination of PTAR. The Commission failed to act for more than three years, but after First Media filed a petition asking the court of appeals to order the Commission to act, the FCC issued an NOI.

8.   Two years after its decision to sunset the financial interest and syndication rules, the Commission decided to eliminate PTAR:

> 3.   . . . [W]e conclude that PTAR should be extinguished. The three major networks do not dominate the markets relevant to PTAR. There are large numbers of sellers and buyers of video programming. Entry, even by small businesses, is relatively easy. There are a substantially greater number of broadcast programming outlets today than when PTAR was adopted in 1970 due to the growth in numbers of independent stations. In addition, nonbroadcast media have proliferated. Viewers can choose from program offerings on cable, so-called "wireless" cable, satellite television systems, and VCRs. Under these market conditions, PTAR is no longer needed to promote the development of non-network sources of television programming. We also find, given these market conditions, and the record before us, that the rule is not warranted as a means of promoting the growth of independent stations and new networks, or of safeguarding affiliate autonomy. Indeed, the rule generates costs and inefficiencies that are not now offset by substantial, if any, benefits.

> 4.   We thus find that the public interest warrants the repeal of PTAR. In scheduling repeal of the rule, we believe a one-year transition period is appropriate to provide parties time to adjust their programming strategies and business arrangements prior to the elimination of a regulatory regime that has been in place for 25 years. We consequently will make repeal of PTAR effective August 30, 1996. Review of The Prime Time Access Rule, 10 F.C.C.Rcd. 5672 (1995).

9.   The next business day after the Commission's decision on PTAR, the Disney–Capital Cities/ABC merger, p. ___, *supra*, was announced. One day later Westinghouse announced its agreement to purchase CBS, p. ___, *supra*.

10.   The Commission had eliminated the 2–year limit on network affiliation agreements several years earlier. The Commission decided that there is a significant public interest benefit to allowing networks and their affiliates, especially new networks and their affiliates, to choose the contractual duration best suited to their particular circumstances. Network Affiliation Agreements, 4 F.C.C.Rcd. 2755, 66 R.R.2d 190 (1989).

11.   In early 1995 the FCC eliminated two more of the chain broadcasting rules. Section 73.658(f), the "network station ownership" rule, prohibited "network ownership of television broadcast stations in mar-

kets that have so few stations, or stations of such unequal desirability (in terms of coverage, power, frequency, or other related matters), that 'competition would be substantially restrained' by permitting network ownership." Section 73.658(*l*), the "secondary affiliation" rule, limited "secondary affiliations in markets where two stations have affiliated with two of the three 'traditional' networks, and there is at least one independent station with comparable facilities." The Commission determined that, due to changes in the marketplace, both rules were obsolete. *Review of the Commission's Regulations Governing Television Broadcasting*, 10 F.C.C.Rcd. 4538, 77 R.R.2d 453 (1995).

12.   Deteriorating relations between the networks and their affiliates led to the National Affiliated Stations Alliance (NASA), a trade group representing more than 600 ABC, CBS and NBC affiliates, filing a complaint with the FCC that alleged multiple violations of the chain broadcasting rules. Among the violations alleged were efforts to restrict affiliates' ability to preempt network programming and interference with station sales. In addition, the complaint the Commission to investigate network practices that, although not in violation of the rules, are against the public interest. These included joint newsgathering ventures, "repurposing programming—also showing it on co-owned cable networks and websites—and favoring their O & Os over affiliates." *Broadcasting & Cable*, Mar. 6, 2001 at 6.

The networks responded by asking the FCC to relax some of the chain broadcasting rules arguing that without the right to insist affiliates air network programming, networks are unable to sell advertising in that programming. "A network cannot operate, let alone take the investment risks that networks necessarily take, if every significant programming decision must be made by 200 independent editors." *Broadcasting & Cable*, July 30, 2001 at 24.

13.   The Telecommunications Act of 1996 directed the FCC to modify the dual network rule, 47 C.F.R. § 73.3555, to limit the rule's application to acquisition by one of the major networks of either another major network or UPN or WB.

14.   In 2001, the Commission modified the dual-network rule to permit acquisition of UPN or the WB by one of the four major networks. The FCC based the decision on the increased competition for video programming and the continued growth of multichannel video programming distributors (MVPDs).

15.   The following are the current Chain Broadcasting Regulations for television:

§ 73.658 Affiliation agreements and network program practices; territorial exclusivity in non-network program arrangements.—(a) Exclusive affiliation of station. No license shall be granted to a television broadcast station having any contract, arrangement, or understanding, express or implied, with a network organization under which the station is prevented or hindered from, or penalized for, broadcasting the programs of any other network organization. (The term "network organization" as used in this section includes national and regional network organizations. [ ])

(b) Territorial exclusivity. No license shall be granted to a television broadcast station having any contract, arrangement, or understanding, express or implied, with a network organization which prevents or hinders another broadcast station located in the same community from broadcasting the network's programs not taken by the former station, or which prevents or hinders another broadcast station located in a different community from broadcasting any program of the network organization. This regulation shall not be construed to prohibit any contract, arrangement, or understanding between a station and a network organization pursuant to which the station is granted the first call in its community upon the programs of the network organization. As employed in this paragraph, the term "community" is defined as the community specified in the instrument of authorization as the location of the station.

(d) Station commitment of broadcast time. No license shall be granted to a television broadcast station having any contract, arrangement, or understanding, express or implied, with any network organization which provides for optioning of the station's time to the network organization, or which has the same restraining effect as time optioning. As used in this section, time optioning is any contract, arrangement, or understanding, express or implied, between a station and a network organization which prevents or hinders the station from scheduling programs before the network agrees to utilize the time during which such programs are scheduled, or which requires the station to clear time already scheduled when the network organization seeks to utilize the time.

(e) Right to reject programs. No license shall be granted to a television broadcast station having any contract, arrangement, or understanding, express or implied, with a network organization which, with respect to programs offered or already contracted for, pursuant to an affiliation contract, prevents or hinders the station from (1) rejecting or refusing network programs which the station reasonably believes to be unsatisfactory or unsuitable, or contrary to the public interest, or (2) substituting a program which, in the station's opinion, is of a greater local or national importance.

(g) Dual network operation. No license shall be issued to a television broadcast station affiliated with a network organization which maintains more than one network of television broadcast stations: provided, that this section shall not be applicable if such networks are not operated simultaneously, or if there is no substantial overlap in the territory served by the group of stations comprising each such network.

(h) Control by networks of station rates. No license shall be granted to a television broadcast station having any contract, arrangement, or understanding, express or implied, with a network organization under which the station is prevented or hindered from, or penalized for, fixing or altering its rates for the sale of broadcast time for other than the network's programs.

(i) No license shall be granted to a television broadcast station which is represented for the sale of non-network time by a network organization or by an organization directly or indirectly controlled by or under common control with a network organization, if the station has any contract, arrangement, or understanding, express or implied, which provides for the affiliation of the station with such network organization: provided, however, that this rule shall not be applicable to stations licensed to a network organization or to a subsidiary of a network organization.

2. CABLE- AND SATELLITE-DELIVERED PROGRAMMING

As we discussed in Chapter VIII, many of the early restrictions on cable were motivated by a concern for the effect that competition from cable would have on broadcast television stations. For example, one of the earliest restrictions, called the anti-leap-frogging rule, provided that when it was permissible to import distant signals, the system had to select from among those nearest to the city in which the system was operating. The FCC deleted this rule in 1976.

We have already discussed the most important of these signal carriage rules, the must-carry rules, in Chapter IX. We now consider the remainder of these rules.

a. *The Anti–Siphoning Rules*

After an erratic early history, the Commission began to regulate pay systems' programs. The first major challenge of these regulations involved subscription television (STV). In defending the regulations, the Commission noted that they were the result of a two-year test in Hartford, Conn. The rules generally barred STV from showing any sports that were regularly carried on conventional television and also restricted showing of feature films that were more than three but less than 10 years old. Also, commercials were barred, and no more than 90 percent of the programming could be movies and sports. The Commission decided that although it had the authority to allocate scarce channels to a pay service, such a service would not be justifiable unless it presented programs that were not readily available on conventional television. A second concern was that revenues from subscription operations might be sufficient to permit pay systems to bid away the most popular programs on conventional television, thus reducing the quality of conventional programming. These regulations were upheld in National Association of Theatre Owners v. Federal Communications Commission, 420 F.2d 194 (D.C.Cir.1969), certiorari denied 397 U.S. 922 (1970).

The next major development was the promulgation of similar restrictions for pay cable origination. These regulations, similar to those just mentioned for STV, were overturned in a lengthy opinion in Home

Box Office, Inc. v. Federal Communications Commission, 567 F.2d 9 (D.C.Cir.), certiorari denied 434 U.S. 829 (1977). In the consolidated proceeding, involving 15 cases, the Commission's pay cable regulations, previously aimed at preventing cable from "siphoning" programs from "free" commercial television, were now said to be intended to prevent the "migration" of such programs from "free" television to cable.

The Court in *Home Box Office* found that the connection between the perceived threat to broadcasting and the anti-siphoning rules was insufficient to justify them under the "reasonably ancillary to broadcasting" standard. Therefore, they held the rules were beyond the Commission's jurisdiction.

Although the lack of jurisdiction alone would necessitate rejection of the Commission's action, the court decided to consider the merits of the rules.

Here the court found insufficient evidence to support the claim that pay cable would bar popular programs to the conventional audience. Rather, the court assumed that pay cable would sell these programs for use by conventional broadcasters. The court was more concerned about the problem of the poor because pay cable would demand exclusive rights—at least for first presentation. But the court concluded that it was not clear that the popularity of films declined "with an increase in the interval between first theater exhibition and first television broadcast." The conclusion was that as to movies, at least, migration would not hurt the poor "very much." Also, the court noted that the Commission's exclusion of advertising on pay cable hurt the poor because it prevented cablecasters from experimenting with a combined revenue system that allowed lower program fees together with some advertising. But all this was speculation; the record was silent and could not support these restrictions on cable.

Addressing the constitutional question, the court started by rejecting the contention that cable's First Amendment rights were governed by *Red Lion*, p. ___, *supra*. This left the question of what constituted permissible restrictions on cable. "The absence in cable television of the physical restraints of the electromagnetic spectrum does not, however, automatically lead to the conclusion that no regulation of cable television is valid."

The court drew a distinction between regulation aimed at suppression of free speech and regulation where the restriction on speech is incidental to the purpose of the regulation. Having done so the court applied the *O'Brien* test, p. ___, *supra*. This was the first case applying *O'Brien* to cable regulation.

Applying the test to the anti-siphoning rules, the court found them "grossly overbroad." For example, the rules restricted the exhibition on cable of many films that were clearly unsuitable for broadcast television. Furthermore, there was no real evidence that siphoning was a serious threat to broadcasting. "Where the First Amendment is concerned, creation of such a rebuttable presumption of siphoning without clear record support is simply impermissible."

b. Network Exclusivity

To protect the local station when it was carrying network programs, the FCC promulgated exclusivity rules (formerly called non-duplication rules) to prevent cable from carrying an imported distant signal that was offering the same network program as the local network affiliate. First, the FCC required the cable system to black out the distant signal if the program was being broadcast on the same day as it was being presented by the local affiliate. Later, the FCC changed the rule to require blackout only if the two showings were at the same hour.

In the mid–1970s the Commission modified the black-out requirement, permitting cable systems to show the local station's signal (and its commercials) simultaneously on both the local channel and the channel that normally carries the distant signal, even though the local station might suffer if the local audience stays with the distant station after the program is over.

c. Syndication Exclusivity

Another regulation protecting local stations had provided that cable systems in large markets could not carry distant signals showing programs to which a local station had acquired exclusive future local rights. The obvious concern underlying the syndicated program exclusivity rule was that the increased availability of the program would fragment the audience for the show. As previously noted, p. ___, *supra*, this was repealed in 1980.

As an outgrowth of the 1986 must-carry proceedings, p. ___, *supra*, the Commission issued a combined NOI/NPRM proposing to reinstitute the syndicated exclusivity rule, expand the network exclusivity rule, and relax or delete the territorial exclusivity rule (one of the chain broadcasting rules discussed earlier in this chapter). Amendment of Parts 73 and 76 of the Commission's Rules Relating to Program Exclusivity in the Cable and Broadcast Industries, 2 F.C.C.Rcd. 2393 (1987):

> The public's *long-run* interests, we believe, will best be served by facilitating a competitive market that is not skewed in favor of any competitor. This, in turn, can only serve to encourage as full and diverse a supply of creative programming as the public is willing to pay for. Not only do the links between demand and production appear to be weakened, but the current regulatory scheme appears to put broadcasters at a disadvantage in competing with other media for product from which the programming producers can receive full value. Such a situation would be the antithesis of the fair competition on a level playing field that this Commission has attempted to provide in all of its industry regulation.

Following its inquiry, the Commission announced new syndication exclusivity rules and expanded the network exclusivity rules. The new rules allow stations to enforce exclusivity contracts against cable systems retransmitting distant signals with duplicative programming. Syndicators may also enforce exclusivity in all markets for the first year after their initial sale to a television station. Contracts in existence prior to the imposition of the new rules cannot be used to enforce exclusivity unless there is explicit language covering the reimposition of syndication exclusivity. Program Exclusivity in the Cable and Broadcast Industries, 3 F.C.C.Rcd. 5299, 64 R.R.2d 1818 (1988).

In addition, stations are allowed to negotiate national exclusivity. This provision, which is particularly valuable for superstations, includes a blanket exemption from the territorial exclusivity rule. Thus, a superstation such as WTBS can obtain national rights to a syndicated program and preclude any other broadcast station in the country from carrying that program.

Cable systems with fewer than 1,000 subscribers are exempted from the new rules as are programs carried on stations generally available off the air.

Network exclusivity was also expanded. The old provision that limited protection to simultaneously aired duplicative network programming was eliminated. Network affiliates are allowed to demand protection against all duplicative network programming.

Various cable companies and satellite retransmitters appealed the new rules.

UNITED VIDEO, INC. v. FEDERAL COMMUNICATIONS COMMISSION

United States Court of Appeals, District of Columbia Circuit, 1989.
890 F.2d 1173, 66 R.R.2d 1865.

Before WALD, CHIEF JUDGE, and EDWARDS and SILBERMAN, CIRCUIT JUDGES.

WALD, CHIEF JUDGE:

A syndicated television program is a program marketed from its supplier to local television stations by means other than a television network. In 1988, the FCC reinstated its "syndicated exclusivity" rules. These rules allow the supplier of a syndicated program to agree with a broadcast television station that the station shall be the exclusive presenter of the program in its local broadcast area. A broadcast station with exclusive rights to a syndicated program can forbid any cable television station from importing the program into its local broadcast area from a distant station.

Petitioners, mostly cable television companies whose distant signal offerings will be restricted under the new rules, challenge the rules as arbitrary and capricious, and as violative of the Copyright Act of 1976, the Cable Act of 1984, and the First Amendment. We find that the Commission's action is within its authority and is not arbitrary and capricious. Accordingly we deny the petition for review.

I. Background

This Court has had several opportunities to examine the checkered history of the regulation of cable television by the Federal Communications Commission. . . . *See e.g.,* [*Century Communications*, p. ___, *supra*]; [*Quincy Cable*, p. ___, *supra*]; [*Home Box Office*, p. ___, *supra*]. As a prelude to our analysis in this case, we review briefly highlights from the history of syndicated exclusivity regulation ("syndex").

The volatile relationship between cable and broadcast television has traditionally hinged on the ability of cable television stations to receive the signal that a broadcast station sends over the air, and to retransmit that signal to subscribers via a cable. This retransmission is not a "broadcast," for it is not a dissemination of radio communications intended to be received by the public. [ ] The Communications Act forbids a broadcast station from rebroadcasting another broadcast station's signal without permission, 47 USC § 325(a), but does not forbid cable retransmission.

Prior to the 1976 revision of the copyright laws, two Supreme Court decisions held that the distinction between broadcasting and cable transmission had important copyright law implications. [*Fortnightly*, p. ___, *supra*] held that when a cable company posted an antenna high on a hilltop, and ran a cable from the antenna into its subscribers' homes, it did nothing significantly different than an individual television owner does when she puts an antenna on her own roof, and runs a cable from it to her television inside. In particular, the cable company's retransmission was not a "performance" of the television program, and so did not violate the copyright on it. [*Teleprompter*, p. ___, *supra*] extended this reasoning to cases where the cable brought a program to a distant market. Accordingly, cable companies were free, as far as copyright law was concerned, to pick up signals aired by broadcasters and retransmit them throughout the country.

The distress felt by originating broadcasters whose signals were retransmitted in this way was matched only by the anger of local broadcasters in the receiving end communities, who watched the cable companies importing into their local markets the very programs that they were themselves showing, and to which they had purchased exclusive broadcast rights. [ ] Even before the *Fortnightly* decision validated this practice against copyright claims, the FCC decided that it was an unfair form of competition. Beginning in 1965, the Commission promulgated exclusivity rules that protected local broadcasters from the importation into their markets of distant signals that duplicated signals to which they had purchased exclusive rights. [ ] These rules provided nonduplication protection for both network and syndicated programs. In

1966, the Commission expanded the rules . . . and required all cable systems to notify the Commission before carrying any distant signal. [   ]

The Commission for some time attempted to review every importation of a distant signal into any of the top one hundred local television markets for consistency with "the establishment and healthy maintenance of television broadcast service in the area." [   ] This proved to be an administrative impossibility, however, and the Commission sought a more workable scheme. In 1972, the Commission adopted an industry "consensus agreement," that provided comprehensive regulation of the relationship between broadcast and cable television. [   ] The consensus agreement included syndex rules. [   ]

In 1976, Congress finally got around to addressing the question of the copyright liability of cable companies that carried distant signals. Congress provided, in the Copyright Revision Act of 1976, a compulsory licensing scheme whereby cable companies paid an administratively-set fee for such carriage. Subsequently, in 1980, the FCC decided that, given the new copyright regime, syndex protection was no longer in the public interest, although network exclusivity was retained. [   ] The Commission stated that the elimination of syndex would cause no significant harm to broadcast stations.

Broadcast stations petitioned the Commission for a reconsideration of its negative position on syndex in 1984, but the Commission refused to budge, saying that there had been no change in circumstances that would justify a change in its position. [   ] In 1987, however, the Commission began another review of its 1980 decision to eliminate syndex, and in 1988 it promulgated the rules challenged in this case. *In the Matter of Amendment of Parts 73 and 76 of the Commission's Rules Relating to Program Exclusivity in the Cable and Broadcast Industries*, 3 F.C.C.Rcd. 5299 [64 R.R.2d 1818] (1988), *on reh'g*, 4 F.C.C.Rcd. 2711 [66 R.R.2d 44] (1989) (rules codified at 47 C.F.R. §§ 73.658, 76.92–76.97, 76.151–76.163). The Commission decided that its 1980 decision reflected an imperfect understanding of the role cable was to assume in the ensuing decade as a full competitor to broadcast television. The Commission found that with the enormous growth in cable's audience and advertising revenues, the lack of syndex was harming broadcast stations, and might have been significantly affecting the supply of syndicated programs. The Commission decided to reinstate syndex in view of the changes in the cable television industry that occurred between 1980 and 1988.

II.   Arbitrariness and Caprice

A.   The Commission's Factual Findings

The Commission's decision to reinstate syndex rests on its finding that syndex rules will promote diversity in syndicated programming. In the report accompanying the rules, the Commission found that unrestricted importation of distant signals (*i.e.*, no syndex protection) leads to duplication of programming in local broadcasting areas; this duplication lessens the value of syndicated programs to broadcast stations; that loss of value in turn lowers the price syndicated program suppliers will receive for their programs; and all of this ultimately reduces the incentive for syndicated program suppliers to produce programs, which translates into a reduction in the diversity of programming available to the public. [   ] On the basis of this scenario the Commission concluded that syndex rules should be reinstated in order to promote diversity of programming.

The petitioners challenge the FCC's rule as arbitrary and capricious, for want of support in the rulemaking record. Our review on such a claim is narrow: the court must not substitute its judgment for that of the agency, but it must ensure that the agency has examined the relevant data and articulated a satisfactory explanation for its action, including a "rational connection between the facts found and the choice made." [   ] Since this action represents a change in agency policy, the court must also ensure that the agency supplied a "reasoned analysis indicating that its prior policies and standards are being deliberately changed, not casually ignored." [   ] We will examine each of the links in the Commission's alleged causal chain.

1. *Duplication*

The petitioners do not challenge the Commission's finding that unrestricted importation of distant signals leads to duplication of programming between broadcast and cable channels. . . .

2. *Lessening of Value of Syndicated Programs to Local Broadcast Stations*

The petitioners hotly contest the Commission's finding that program duplication lessens the value of syndicated programs purchased by local broadcast stations. However, the Commission's report cites substantial evidence from which it could reasonably draw this conclusion. The Commission discusses two related ways in which duplication lessens the value of syndicated programs: audience diversion and the loss of exclusivity as a competitive tool.

The Commission found that duplication of programming diverts a substantial portion of the broadcast audience to cable. The evidence was strongest regarding diversion caused by a cable station's *simultaneous* transmission of a program being aired by a broadcast channel, for such diversion can be gauged by ratings information. . . .

The Commission reasonably inferred that diversion lessened the value of the programming by lowering advertising revenues. The petitioners contest this finding, claiming it is based on a single study, which they attack as faulty. However, the report makes clear that the Commission relied on the study for only a rough approximation of the decrease in advertising revenue. More important was the hardly controversial conclusion that the amount that advertisers will pay depends on the size of the audience that a program attracts. [   ] This statement needs no detailed study to support it.

. . .

The Commission's report does not specify quite so clearly how it reached the conclusion that *non-simultaneous* transmission of duplicative programming (including transmission of different episodes of the same program) also causes audience diversion. The one sentence explicitly devoted to this question in the report says that "the quantity of non-simultaneous duplication documented in the record in this proceeding, taken as a whole, presents compelling evidence that substantial diversion is taking place." [   ] This sentence suggests that the Commission has simply assumed diversion from the conceded fact of non-simultaneous duplication. The Commission points to no specific empirical support for this statement in the record.

While it is intuitively reasonable to assume that simultaneous duplication causes diversion, the question of non-simultaneous duplication seems more varied and complex. . . . If the Commission had relied solely on its assumption of audience diversion as evidence that non-simultaneous duplication lessens the value of programs to broadcast stations, we might well have felt obliged to require some supplementation or further explanation of its reasoning.

However, the Commission relies on more solid evidence that duplication makes programming less valuable. The evidence is that all stations, broadcast and cable, want exclusivity. . . . The reason, as the FCC notes in its report, is that exclusivity gives stations the opportunity to promote themselves as the only presenter of a certain program. If a broadcaster spends money promoting a duplicated program, some of the value of the expenditure will be captured by the cable company that is importing the same program. Syndex will give the local broadcaster a competitive tool that it can use both to call attention to the particular program and to "alert viewers to the general attractiveness of the broadcaster's whole range of programming." [   ] The strong desire of all stations for complete exclusivity is evidence that even non-simultaneous duplication lessens the value of programming, whether because of audience diversion or for other reasons.

While the Commission's report may leave something to be desired in its detail on the dangers of non-simultaneous duplication, we do not think its conclusion that even this type of duplication lessens the value of programming for broadcast stations can be called arbitrary or capricious. The record as a whole shows that both broadcast and cable companies want complete exclusivity; the Commission did not act without reason in concluding that exclusivity must be a valuable commodity, and conversely that lack of exclusivity diminishes the value of a program.

B.   Effects on Program Supply

The weakest link in the FCC's causal chain is its claim that reinstating syndex will affect the supply of syndicated programming. And indeed, throughout the rule making proceeding, the Commission has always conceded that there is no direct, empirical evidence that syndex will actually increase program diversity, explaining that such evidence would be particularly difficult to obtain empirically. [   ]

We do not think that the absence of empirical evidence is fatal to the Commission's claim. Courts reviewing an agency's selection of means to accomplish policy goals are "not entitled to insist on empirical data for every proposition on which the selection depends." [   ] In [*Century Communications*], which struck down the FCC's must-carry regulations, this Court noted that an agency contention may be "so obvious or commonsensical that it needs no empirical support to stand up." [   ]

We think the Commission's conclusion about the link between lack of program diversity and lowered broadcast revenues due to lack of exclusivity is sufficiently in accord with accepted economic theory that it can stand without empirical support, particularly since we agree with the Commission that it would be very difficult for it to show the degree to which programs are currently *not* being produced because of the lack of syndex protection. . . . [T]he FCC has assumed only that increasing the value of programs to broadcast companies will increase the amount paid for them, and that these higher prices will improve product supply. The Commission explains that "[p]rogram suppliers, like other business people, respond to incentives. . . . Incentives to develop new programs are greatest when program suppliers are able to sell their programs wherever there are viewers (or advertisers) willing to pay for them." [   ] These claims, unlike the ones made by the FCC in *Century Communications*, do not "beg[   ] incredulity," 835 F.2d at 302; rather they are reasonable.

. . .

Having tested each link in the Commission's causal chain, we find that it used valid reasoning to conclude that syndex rules will increase the diversity of programming options available to the public. Its imposition of syndex was adequately supported by the rulemaking record.

C. Change in Agency Course

The petitioners complain that the Commission has not adequately explained why it is reinstating syndex rules only eight years after abandoning them, and only four years after reaffirming its decision to abandon them. However, the Commission's report, which examines in great detail its 1980 decision to eliminate syndex, meets this circuit's standard that an agency changing course must "supply a reasoned analysis indicating that its prior policies and standards are being deliberately changed, not casually ignored." [*Action for Children's Television*, p. ____, *supra*]

The Commission's report reviews in detail the history of the regulation of cable, including, in particular, the 1980 decision to eliminate syndex rules. [   ] The report notes several ways in which the Commission now feels the 1980 decision to have been inadequate. First, the report discusses how circumstances have changed since 1980. The principal change has been the unforeseen emergence of cable television as a full competitor to broadcast television. As the report documents, cable's audience and advertising revenues have increased dramatically and unexpectedly since 1980. In 1980, cable served 19% of television households, but in 1988 it served 51%, a percentage the FCC projected would rise to 60% by 1996. [ ] In 1980, the Commission had predicted that cable penetration would never go beyond 48%. [ ] Cable advertising revenues were $45.5 million in 1980, but they grew to over $1 billion in 1988; cable's share of total television advertising revenue climbed from less than 0.5% to more than 6%. [ ] This unexpected growth, the Commission notes, substantially undermines its 1980 findings that repeal of syndex would not cause significant audience diversion or otherwise harm broadcast stations.

The Commission also faults its earlier studies for focusing on the effects repeal of syndex would have on individual stations, rather than its effects on the competitive process and the incentive for production of new programs. . . .

. . .

The Commission in its report also acknowledges that the absence of syndex provides consumers with the benefit of "time and episode diversity." A cable station, free of syndex restraints, may import a different episode of a program than the one aired by a broadcast station, or the same episode at a different time of day. The Commission suggests, however, that this diversity must be balanced against the lack of diversity engendered by duplication, and by the reduced incentive for the production of new programs. The Commission also suggests that market forces will allow duplication where viewers value it sufficiently, since stations with exclusive rights to a program can always sell the right to duplicate it. Finally, the Commission notes that the value of cable in providing time diversity has been lessened by the significant increase in the penetration of video cassette recorders (up from 1.5% of television households in 1979 to 58.1% today), since VCRs allow viewers to provide time diversity for themselves. [ ]

The Commission's report *in toto* suggests it undertook a thoroughgoing review of the syndex question and came to a new result with full awareness of its prior choices. . . . Accordingly, we reject the petitioners' claim that the Commission's rules are arbitrary and capricious.

III.   The Commission's Authority

[Petitioners also argued that the syndex rules were an attempt to impose copyright liability and as such preempted by the Copyright Act of 1976. The court rejected this argument relying on both the text and legislative history of the Copyright Act as well as the fact that the previous syndex rules were in effect when the 1976 Act was passed.]

B.   The Cable Act

The Cable Communications Policy Act of 1984 amended the Communications Act to explicitly grant the FCC a power it had previously only inferred from its general authority to regulate television: the power to regulate cable television. [   ] However, the Act also set some limits on that power, and in particular it provided:

(1) Any Federal agency, State, or franchising authority may not impose requirements regarding the provision or content of cable television services, except as expressly provided in this subchapter.

. . .

47 U.S.C. § 544(f). The petitioners claim that this section forbids syndex rules.

The Commission argues that the legislative history of Section 544(f) shows that the term "requirements," as used in the section, refers only to *affirmative* requirements, that is, to rules that a cable station *must* carry a certain program or channel or type of program or channel, and does not prohibit negative requirements, that is, rules prohibiting cable stations from carrying certain signals. . . .

. . .

However, having consulted the legislative history, we cannot agree with the Commission's contention that, as used in Section 544(f), the word "requirements" was meant to distinguish between affirmative and negative obligations. Some "negative" rules would probably fall under Section 544(f)'s bar. For instance, a local franchising authority's attempt to *prohibit* the carriage of HBO would likely implicate the same Congressional concerns as an attempt to *require* carriage of HBO. We therefore think Section 544(f) would bar such a prohibition.

On the other hand, not every "affirmative" regulation implicates Section 544(f). Suppose, for instance, a cable company bidding for a local franchise indicated that it was planning to provide service on only Mondays, Tuesdays, and Wednesdays. If the local franchising authority decided that it would award the franchise only to a cable company that agreed to provide service seven days a week, it would not be, in the words of the House report, "dictat[ing] the specific programming to be provided over a cable system" even though the regulation would be affirmative in nature.

In short, we think that the affirmative/negative distinction suggested by the Commission fails to capture what Congress meant by the term "requirements" in Section 544(f). Rather, the examples given in the House report suggest that the key is whether a regulation is content-based or content-neutral. Section 544(f), one must note, does not simply forbid "requirements"; it forbids "requirements regarding the *provision* or *content* of cable services" (emphasis added). The House report suggests that Congress thought a cable company's owners, not government officials, should decide what sorts of programming the company would provide. But it does not suggest a concern with regulations of cable not based on the content of cable programming, and do not require that particular programs or types of programs be provided. Such regulations are not requirements "regarding the provision or content" of cable services.

Syndex is clearly different from a requirement or prohibition of the carriage of a particular program or channel. Although it will certainly affect the content of cable programming, it is content-neutral. . . .

We do not mean to suggest that the concept of content neutrality, as developed in First Amendment cases, can be freely imported into all cases construing the Communications Act. In this case, however, the history reviewed above explicitly shows that Congress's concern in enacting Section 544(f) was with content-based rules. We think it plain that Congress did not intend Section 544(f) to forbid syndex. . . .

. . .

C. The First Amendment

The petitioners argue that syndex rules, like the must-carry rules that this Court struck down in [*Century Communications*, p. ___, *supra*], cannot survive even the relaxed First Amendment scrutiny of [*O'Brien*, p. ___, *supra*]. However, the Commission was correct to find that the rules are not subject to such scrutiny.

The petitioners repeatedly claim that syndex restrains the expression of fully protected speech which has been paid for and authorized under the compulsory licensing scheme of Section 111 of the Copyright Act. [ ] The fact is, however, that because of the provisions of Section 111, cable companies will *not* be able to obtain a compulsory license to transmit a program if transmission would violate the syndex rules. As explained above, Congress deliberately chose to withhold a compulsory license from those transmissions that the FCC decides to prohibit for reasons of communications policy. The petitioners are therefore in the position of claiming that they have a First Amendment right to express themselves using the copyrighted materials of others.

. . .

In the present case, the petitioners desire to make commercial use of the copyrighted works of others. There is no First Amendment right to do so. Although there is some tension between the Constitution's copyright clause and the First Amendment, the familiar idea/expression dichotomy of copyright law, under which ideas are free but their particular expression can be copyrighted, has always been held to give adequate protection to free expression. [ ]

. . .

IV. Conclusion

"While the deregulation of the cable television industry raises serious policy questions, . . . these questions are best left to the agencies that were created, in large part, to resolve them." [*Malrite*] The Commission has considered anew the question of how to balance the rights of broadcast and cable television companies so as best to serve the public interest in receiving diverse programming. Congress decided that this question should be resolved by the agency, and on the record before us we uphold its resolution.

The petition for review is denied.

Notes and Questions

1. A provision of the Satellite Home Viewer Act, p. ___, *supra*, directed the FCC to extend the syndicated exclusivity rules to satellite carriers to the extent it was feasible. After conducting an inquiry into the matter, the FCC concluded that it was not technically or economically feasible to subject satellite carriers to the syndicated exclusivity rules. Among the reasons cited for this conclusion were the inability of existing decoders to delete programs selectively in over 200 markets and the much smaller subscriber base (53.9 million cable subscribers versus 678,000 HSD subscribers) from which to recover the developmental costs of implementing syndicated exclusivity. Syndicated Exclusivity Requirements for Satellite Carriers, 68 R.R.2d 1172 (1991).

2. In its initial decision on cable carriage of digital television, p. ___, *supra*, the Commission sought comment on how digital television affected the need for the cable carriage rules, as well as how they should apply to television stations broadcasting more than one program at a time. The FCC also sought comment on how digital cable carriage rules should be applied to DBS.

d. Cable Programmer Restrictions

By the late 1980s, both Congress and the FCC had grown concerned that vertical integration and concentration in the cable industry was leading to discrimination against TVRO dish owners, multichannel video program distributors such as MMDS and DBS, and against unaffiliated cable program producers.

In an inquiry mandated by the Satellite Home Viewer Act, p. ___, *supra*, the FCC found that there was no "pattern of discrimination by satellite carriers among the various distributors who market superstation and network station programming." However, the Commission did find differences in the rates charged to home dish distributors and cable operators raising the possibility that unlawful rate discrimination was taking place. After adopting the test for unlawful discrimination used in proceedings under Section 202(a) of the Communications Act (47 U.S.C.A. § 202(a)), the Commission issued a further notice on this issue. "The test in Section 202(a) has three components: (1) whether the services in question are like services; (2) whether discrimination has occurred; and (3) whether such discrimination is just and reasonable." Superstation and Network Station Programming (Discrimination in Distribution), 5 F.C.C.Rcd. 523, 67 R.R.2d 675 (1989).

Following that inquiry the Commission issued a report concluding that "there are significant disparities in some of the prices charged by some carriers to home dish distributors as compared to the prices charged to cable companies and other customers for superstation and network station programming. Some of these disparities are not justified by the cost of providing service as documented in this proceeding." However, the Commission left the final determination of whether or not these constitute violations of the Communications Act to hearings on specific complaints. At the same time the Commission noted that the Satellite Home Viewer Act provides aggrieved parties a private right of action in federal court under the Copyright Act. Superstation and Network Station Programming (Discrimination in Distribution), 69 R.R.2d 436 (1991).

The 1992 Cable Act contained a number of provisions aimed at multichannel video programming distributors and video programming vendors. Pursuant to one of these, the Commission established a 40 percent

> limit on the number of channels that can be occupied on a vertically integrated cable system by video programmers in which the cable operator has an attributable interest. In order to promote a diversity of views the Commission will allow carriage of vertically integrated programming services on two additional channels, or up to 45% of a system's channel capacity, whichever is greater, provided such video programming services are minority-controlled.

The vertical ownership restrictions apply only up to 75 channels. However, the FCC declined to adopt additional restrictions on the "ability of multichannel distributors to engage in the creation or production of video programming." *Cable Horizontal and Vertical Ownership Limits*, p. ___, *supra*. Various petitions for reconsideration are pending.

The 1992 Cable Act contained two sections on unfair or discriminatory practices in the sale of satellite cable and satellite broadcast programming. 47 U.S.C.A. § 628. Section 628(b) prohibits cable operators, satellite cable programming vendors in which a cable operator has an attributable interest, and satellite broadcast programming vendors from engaging in unfair methods of competition or unfair or deceptive acts or practices, "the purpose or effect of which is to hinder significantly or to prevent any multichannel video programming distributor from providing satellite cable programming or satellite broadcast programming to subscribers or consumers." Section 628(c) prohibits undue influence and price discrimination by vertically integrated cable operators, vertically integrated satellite cable programmers and all satellite broadcast programming vendors.

The FCC adopted rules implementing these provisions. Video Programming Distribution and Carriage (Implementation of 1992 Cable Act Provisions), 8 F.C.C.Rcd. 3359, 72 R.R.2d 649 (1993). For the purpose of determining vertical integration, the FCC set a strict 5 percent attribution rule. Attributable interests include all equity interests of 5 percent or more. Limited partnership interests of 5 or more percent will be attributable, even where the limited partners are insulated from management of the partnership's affairs. Also attributable are all officer and director positions and general partnership interests.

Exclusive programming arrangements between vertically integrated programming vendors and cable operators in areas not served by cable are illegal *per se*. In areas served by cable they are enforceable only after an FCC determination using criteria set forth in § 628(c)(4) that they serve the public interest. Thus, a program vendor or cable operator wishing to execute an exclusive contract must first petition the Commission for a declaration that the contract serves the public interest.

A successful § 628 complaint must show that a competing distributor has been offered or paid a lower price or received more favorable terms than the complainant. The complainant must also demonstrate that there is some overlap in actual or proposed service areas. The appropriate market for assessing competition will depend on how the distributors buys and sells programming. For example, a cable operator would be assessed on the basis of a local market, whereas a DBS operator would be assessed using a national market.

Program vendors may establish different prices, terms and conditions for different distributors as long as they are based on legitimate cost factors such as the cost of creation, sale, delivery or transmission of the programming. Volume discounts will be permitted if they reflect direct economic benefits to the vendor. Vendors may also establish price differences based on the creditworthiness or financial stability of the distributor.

When the first two petitions were filed pursuant to this 628(c)(4) of the Act, the FCC denied one and granted the other. The denial of Time Warner's petition regarding Court TV was based on several factors. The FCC found that Court TV was an established cable network, thus it could attract capital investment and financing without exclusivity. In addition, an opposition had been filed by Liberty Cable, an SMATV company competing with Time Warner in Manhattan. The Commission determined that exclusivity would limit Liberty Cable's ability to compete with Time Warner in the Manhattan multichannel video programming market. Time Warner Cable, 9 F.C.C.Rcd. 3221, 75 R.R.2d 350 (1994).

The approved petition concerned New England Cable News (NECN), a regional network. Unlike Court TV, NECN was not an established network. Exclusivity was needed to attract capital investment and financing. Within the six states constituting NECN's service area, there were very few multichannel video programming providers competing with the region's cable companies. Thus, in the FCC's opinion, exclusivity was necessary for NECN's survival and would have a negligible effect on competition in the relevant programming distribution markets. New England Cable News, 9 F.C.C.Rcd. 3231, 75 R.R.2d 360 (1994).

The second section governing program distribution agreements is § 616. 47 U.S.C.A. § 536. The distinction between § 628 and § 616 is that the former

. . . primarily restrict[s] the activities of vertically integrated programming vendors with respect to cable operators and other multichannel programming distributors. Section 616 restricts the activities of cable operators and other multichannel programming distributors when dealing with programming vendors.

4. Specifically, Section 616 requires the Commission to adopt regulations that prevent a multichannel distributor from: (1) requiring a programming vendor to provide it with a financial interest in the programming service as a condition of carrying the program service on its system; (2) coercing a programming vendor to provide it with exclusive rights as a condition of carriage, from retaliating against such a vendor for failing to provide exclusive rights; or (3) engaging in conduct that discriminates on the basis of affiliation of vendors in the selection, terms or conditions for carriage of video programming. In addition, the statute specifies procedures the Commission must adopt for implementation of the above provisions, including expedited review of complaints made by a programming vendor and assessment of appropriate penalties for violation of the carriage agreement rules as well as for the filing of frivolous claims.

Video Programming Distribution and Carriage (Implementation of 1992 Cable Act Provisions), 9 F.C.C.Rcd. 2642, 73 R.R.2d 1350 (1993).

The FCC adopted complaint procedures similar to those established for § 628 complaints. It also established a one-year statute of limitations.

Chapter XIII

COPYRIGHT AND TRADEMARK

There are several ways to protect a creative work product, but historically this protection was first achieved through copyright law. Copyright and trademark law provide protection for intellectual property—something akin to the protection of a patent for an invention. Copyright protects a literary or artistic creation, such as the script of a television program. Specifically, it protects the *expression* of ideas and facts rather than the *facts* or *ideas* themselves, because it is generally in the public interest to encourage dissemination of the latter. Trademark law, on the other hand, protects words or symbols associated with a company or product, such as the call letters of a broadcasting station or the name of a television show.

The right to own, to control and to profit from one's creative work is, of course, essential to people who make their living in the communications media.

As we shall see, a great deal of expression is in the *public domain*—not owned by any one owner—and can be used freely by anyone without permission. When one wants to use copyrighted work, however (with some exceptions to be noted later), one needs permission.

The laws of copyright are thus restraints on freedom of expression, but they are not generally condemned for being so.

Article I, § 8, of the Constitution of the United States gives Congress the power "to promote the progress of science and useful arts by securing for limited times to authors and inventors the exclusive right to their respective writings and discoveries. . . ." The first Congress utilized that authority to adopt copyright legislation, and it has been with us in some form ever since. The framers of the Constitution could hardly have envisioned the wide range of media with which copyright must today be concerned: broadcast, cable, print, computer, video recording, photocopying, jukeboxes, etc.

The copyright statute is found in Title 17 of the United States Code, §§ 101–118.

A. THE NATURE OF COPYRIGHT

1. BACKGROUND

The origins of copyright are interwoven with the history of English licensing procedures. One technique for controlling the printing press in England was to organize printers into a group that became known as the Stationers Company. The Crown granted to that company a monopoly of

790

all printing, with the power to seek out and suppress material published by non-members who violated the monopoly. The Crown's goal was to thwart seditious libel and other objectionable material. The printers, for their part, seized on the monopoly situation to control reproduction of whatever they printed. The result was the licensed printers' right to control copies based on the censorship of the 16th and 17th centuries. When licensing was discontinued in 1695, the rights of the printers were undermined. They petitioned Parliament to adopt protections resembling what they had had under the licensing schemes. In 1709 Parliament responded with the Statute of Anne, which set the pattern for copyright legislation both in England and in this country. The Stationers Company remained, but its new role was to register printed material, which would serve to protect that material against unauthorized copying.

The first U.S. Congress adopted a similar procedure: printed matter could be protected by filing a copy with the newly established copyright office, headed by the "Register of Copyrights." The types of writings protected and the period of protection have been expanded since the 1790 statute, which protected only books, maps and charts for 14 years plus renewal for a second 14–year term.

Under the 1909 statute, published works were protected by federal law while unpublished works were protected under state law. The 1909 federal statute was replaced in the 1970s by new legislation preserving the basic philosophical strands of copyright law, including the denial of copyright for federal government documents, and combining protection into a single national framework. Changes were made in legal technicalities and to accommodate newer media. The "new" statute went into effect in 1978.

2.   SUBJECT MATTER

Section 102 of the 1976 copyright statute sets out the basic pattern of protection when it states that protection subsists in "original works of authorship fixed in any tangible medium of expression, now known or later developed, from which they can be perceived, reproduced or otherwise communicated, either directly or with the aid of a machine or device." The types of "original works of authorship" that can be protected by copyright include:

> (1) literary works; (2) musical works, including any accompanying words; (3) dramatic works, including any accompanying music; (4) pantomimes and choreographic works; (5) pictorial, graphic, and sculptural works; (6) motion pictures and other audiovisual works; and (7) sound recordings.

Although one can copyright the way one *expresses* facts and ideas, one cannot copyright those facts and ideas themselves. As the statute says:

> In no case does copyright protection for an original work of authorship extend to any idea, procedure, process, system, method or operation, concept, principle, or discovery, regardless of the form

it which it is described, explained, illustrated, or embodied in such work. 17 U.S.C.A. § 102.

In a variety of cases, courts have had to decide whether specific works were (a) protected subject matter under the statute or (b) ideas or facts that were not protected. Sometimes works fall into the latter category because, although they required effort, or "sweat of the brow," they did not necessarily require creativity—thus they may not be considered to be *original.* Such a work, for example, may present only factual information that is not the kind of subject matter that can be copyrighted.

One case in which a court had to consider whether the subject matter was protectable under the copyright statute was a case involving an author's theory that a crew member had sabotaged the German dirigible Hindenburg in New Jersey in 1937—supposedly causing its explosion and crash to please a Communist girlfriend. Two other authors developed similar explanations for the disaster, and a suit resulted. Hoehling v. Universal City Studios, Inc., 618 F.2d 972 (2d Cir.), certiorari denied, 449 U.S. 841 (1980). The court began its discussion by placing copyright in its broader context:

> A grant of copyright in a published work secures for its author a limited monopoly over the expression it contains. The copyright provides a financial incentive to those who would add to the corpus of existing knowledge by creating original works. Nevertheless, the protection afforded the copyright holder has never extended to history, be it documented fact or explanatory hypothesis. The rationale for this doctrine is that the cause of knowledge is best served when history is the common property of all, and each generation remains free to draw upon the discoveries and insights of the past. Accordingly, the scope of copyright in historical accounts is narrow indeed, embracing no more than the author's original expression of particular facts and theories already in the public domain. As the case before us illustrates, absent wholesale usurpation of another's expression, claims of copyright infringement where works of history are at issue are rarely successful.

The court asserted that although plaintiff had a valid copyright on his book, to prove "infringement" he had to prove that defendants had "improperly appropriated" his "expression." Although plaintiff admitted that his idea was not copyrightable, he correctly argued that "his 'expression' of *his* idea is copyrightable." The court analyzed that claim as follows:

> He relies on Learned Hand's opinion in [Sheldon v. Metro–Goldwyn Pictures Corp., 81 F.2d 49 (2d Cir.), certiorari denied 298 U.S. 669 (1936)] holding that *Letty Lynton* infringed *Dishonored Lady* by copying its story of a woman who poisons her lover, and Augustus Hand's analysis in Detective Comics v. Bruns Publications, Inc., 111 F.2d 432 (2d Cir.1940), concluding that the exploits of "Wonderman" infringed the copyright held by the creators of

"Superman," the original indestructible man. Moreover, Hoehling asserts that, in both these cases, the line between "ideas" and "expression" is drawn, in the first instance, by the fact finder.

Sheldon and *Detective Comics,* however, dealt with works of fiction, where the distinction between an idea and its expression is especially elusive. But, where, as here, the idea at issue is an interpretation of an historical event, our cases hold that such interpretations are not copyrightable as matter of law. In Rosemont Enterprises, Inc. v. Random House, Inc., 366 F.2d 303 (2d Cir.1966), cert. denied, 385 U.S. 1009 (1967), we held that the defendant's biography of Howard Hughes did not infringe an earlier biography of the reclusive alleged billionaire. Although the plots of the two works were necessarily similar, there could be no infringement because of the "public benefit in encouraging the development of historical and biographical words and their public distribution." Id. at 307; accord, Oxford Book Co. v. College Entrance Book Co., 98 F.2d 688 (2d Cir.1938). To avoid a chilling effect on authors who contemplate tackling an historical issue or event, broad latitude must be granted to subsequent authors who make use of historical subject matter, including theories or plots. Learned Hand counseled in Myers v. Mail & Express Co., 36 C.O.Bull 487, 479 (S.D.N.Y. 1919), "[t]here cannot be any such thing as copyright in the order of presentation of the facts, nor, indeed, in their selection."

The court went further, however, and asserted that it may not even be possible to protect even some fictitious episodes:

The remainder of Hoehling's claimed similarities relate to random duplications of phrases and sequences of events. For example, all three works contain a scene in a German beer hall, in which the airship's crew engages in revelry prior to the voyage. Other claimed similarities concern common German greetings of the period, such as "Heil Hitler," or songs, such as the German National anthem. These elements, however, are merely *scenes a faire,* that is, "incidents, characters or settings which are as a practical matter indispensable, or at least standard, in the treatment of a given topic." [ ] Because it is virtually impossible to write about a particular historical era or fictional theme without employing certain "stock" or standard literary devices, we have held that *scenes a faire* are not copyrightable as a matter of law. See Reyher v. Children's Television Workshop, 533 F.2d 87, 91 (2d Cir.), cert. denied, 429 U.S. 980 (1976).

Finally, the court brought these several aspects of the case together and recognized that breaking the copyrighted work up into many little parts created a new danger:

All of Hoehling's allegations of copying, therefore, encompass material that is non-copyrightable as a matter of law, rendering summary judgment entirely appropriate. We are aware, however, that in distinguishing between themes, facts, and *scenes a faire* on the one hand, and copyrightable expression on the other, courts may lose sight of the forest for the trees. By factoring out similarities based on non-copyrightable elements, a court runs the risk of overlooking wholesale usurpation of a prior author's expression. A verbatim reproduction of another work, of course, even in the realm of nonfiction, is actionable as copyright infringement. See Wainwright Securities, Inc. v. Wall Street Transcript Corp., 558 F.2d 91 (2d Cir.1977), cert. denied, 434 U.S. 1014 (1978). Thus, in granting or reviewing a grant of summary judgment for defendants, courts should assure themselves that the works before them are not virtually identical. In this case, it is clear that all three authors relate the story of the Hindenburg differently.

In works devoted to historical subjects, it is our view that a second author may make significant use of prior work, so long as he does not bodily appropriate the expression of another. Rosemont Enterprises, Inc., *supra*, 366 F.2d at 310. This principle is justified by the fundamental policy undergirding the copyright laws—the encouragement of contributions to recorded knowledge. The "financial reward guaranteed to the copyright holder is but an incident of this general objective, rather than an act in itself." Berlin v. E.C. Publications, Inc., 329 F.2d 541, 543–44 (2d Cir.), cert. denied, 379 U.S. 822 (1964). Knowledge is expanded as well by granting new authors of historical works a relatively free hand to build upon the work of their predecessors.

The meaning of the words "original works of authorship" and "fixed," as used in § 102 of the 1976 Copyright Act, were critical to a case involving the telecasting of a parade. Production Contractors, Inc. v. WGN Continental Broadcasting Co., 622 F.Supp. 1500, 12 Med.L.Rptr. 1708 (N.D.Ill.1985). The plaintiff (PCI) planned, organized and promoted a parade on Michigan Avenue in Chicago. It sold exclusive Chicago area television broadcasting rights in the parade to the American Broadcasting Company, owner of WLS–TV in Chicago, designating WLS as the "Official Television Station of the 1985 McDonald's Charity Christmas Parade."

Knowing that another station, WGN–TV, planned to televise the parade, PCI sought a declaratory judgment concerning rights to broadcast the parade. The federal district court held that the parade itself was not a *work of authorship*. It said "[T]here is no case law supporting the proposition that the promotion and production of a parade is a work of authorship entitled to copyright protection." Further, the court held that "[T]he telecast of the parade is a work of authorship fixed simultaneously with its transmission only for purposes of copyright protection from videotaping, tape-delays, or secondary transmissions," none of which applied to WGN–TV, which planned to use its own equipment. The court granted summary judgment for WGN–TV.

Problems involving "exclusive" rights continue to arise in television, despite the basic premise that facts, ideas, information and events cannot be copyrighted—only the *expression* of them can. During the July 4, 1986, festivities at the Statue of Liberty, for example, there was disagreement over the extent of coverage by other networks of events for which ABC was the "official" network. Those differences were resolved without litigation.

A Supreme Court decision, Feist Publications, Inc. v. Rural Telephone Service Co., Inc., 499 U.S. 340 (1991), illustrates the principle that facts cannot be copyrighted. Rural Telephone Service, which provides telephone service to several communities in Kansas, publishes a telephone directory. It refused to license its white pages listings to Feist for a larger telephone directory covering 11 telephone service areas. Feist extracted the information from Rural's directory and used it in their own, altering some of the listings and using others identical to the listings in Rural's directory. Rural sued for copyright infringement. The Supreme Court decided in favor of Feist Publications.

Justice O'Connor wrote for the Court that "This case concerns the interaction of two well-established propositions. The first is that facts are not copyrightable; the other, that compilations of facts generally are. Each of these propositions possesses an impeccable pedigree. . . . [I]t is beyond dispute that compilations of facts are within the subject matter of copyright. Compilations were expressly mentioned in the Copyright Act of 1909, and again in the Copyright Act of 1976. . . . There is undeniable tension between these two propositions. . . . The key to resolving the tension lies in understanding why facts are not copyrightable. The *sine qua non* of copyright is originality. To qualify for copyright protection, a work must be original to the author."

"[T]he copyright in a factual compilation is thin," she wrote. "Notwithstanding a valid copyright, a subsequent compiler remains free to use the facts contained in [another's] publication to aid in preparing a competing work, so long as the competing work does not feature the same selection and arrangement." The Court has rejected, she said, "sweat of the brow" arguments that would give protection to factual compilations on the basis of hard work rather than originality. "Rural expended sufficient effort to make the white pages directory useful," she wrote, "but insufficient creativity to make it original," concluding that the names, towns and telephone numbers copied by Feist were not original to Rural and were therefore not protected by copyright.

Because of the Court's decision in *Feist,* it became possible later in the 1990s for companies to publish telephone directories and other factual compilations in CD–ROM format without infringing on copyrights.

In another case, the National Basketball Association claimed that Motorola and Sports Team Analysis and Tracking Systems ("STATS") infringed its copyrights by providing constant updates on professional basketball scores on a special pager. A federal district court in New York City held that the service constituted a misappropriation of NBA property, but the court of appeals reversed, holding that the scores are factual information and cannot be copyrighted. National Basketball Association v. Motorola, Inc., 105 F.3d 841, 25 Med.L.Rptr. 1385 (1997).

3. OWNERSHIP OF COPYRIGHT

The authors of a work are the initial copyright owners unless the work is a "work made for hire." This is defined as

(1) a work prepared by an employee within the scope of his or her employment; or

(2) a work specifically ordered or commissioned for use as a contribution to a collective work, as a part of a motion picture or other audiovisual work, as a translation, as a supplementary work, as a compilation, as an instructional text, as a test, as answer material for a test, or as an atlas, if the parties expressly agree in a written instrument signed by them that the work shall be considered a work made for hire. 17 U.S.C.A. § 101.

In the case of a "work made for hire," the original ownership belongs to the employer or person who commissioned the work. As is the case with any property right, ownership of a copyright can be left to the owner's heirs or sold.

In Community for Creative Non–Violence v. Reid, 490 U.S. 730 (1989), the Supreme Court was asked to avoid the rigors of section 101(2) by expansively interpreting the term "employee" in section 101(1). It declined. Reid had created a sculpture for CCNV in conformance with CCNV's concept and general design ideas. The parties did not discuss copyright ownership in advance. After the sculpture was finished, each filed a competing copyright claim. The trial judge held that CCNV owned the copyright, but the court of appeals reversed, holding that it was not a work for hire and therefore copyright was owned by Reid. 846 F.2d 1485 (D.C.Cir.1988).

The Supreme Court unanimously affirmed. CCNV did not claim the sculpture was a specially commissioned work under subsection (2); there was no written agreement to that effect, and even if there had been, a sculpture is not one of the types of works to which the subsection applies. Instead, CCNV argued that Reid should be considered an "employee" for purposes of subsection (1), on the ground that CCNV had retained the right to control Reid's product and had actually exercised such control. The Court, however, held that the legislative history of the Act required the term to be understood in light of the general common law of agency, which takes into account many factors in addition to control of the work. It concluded Reid was not an employee because he was engaged in a skilled occupation, supplied his own tools, worked in his own studio, was retained for a brief time for the project in question and no others, had control of his own working hours and the employment and compensation of assistants, and was not treated as an employee for purposes of benefits, social security and payroll taxes, worker's compensation or unemployment taxes.

The Court refused to allow the interpretation given to section 101(1) by the Second Circuit, which had held that freelancers were "employees" if the hiring party had actually wielded control during the creation of the work. See Aldon Accessories Ltd. v. Spiegel, Inc., 738 F.2d 548 (2d Cir.), certiorari denied 469 U.S. 982 (1984). Many publishing and communications companies headquartered in New York apparently had relied on that interpretation and therefore had failed to obtain contractual assignments from their freelance contributors. As a result, some industry sources said the CCNV decision put in question the ownership of millions of dollars in literary and entertainment properties, and might affect 40 percent of all existing copyrights. The CCNV decision generated concern about the ownership of millions of dollars in literary and entertainment properties and specifically about the effect on termination of copyrights. Licenses and transfers granted by authors generally may be terminated after 35 or 40 years by the authors or their survivors; companies that find themselves holding licenses rather than authorship as a result of *CCNV v. Reid* faced the possibility of having their interests terminated altogether.

Magazine publishers often commission freelance photographers or artists to illustrate specific articles. Sometimes they reuse the articles and/or illustrations in books, calendars, special anniversary editions, etc. After the decision in *CCNV v. Reid*, how may publishers protect their interest in future use of these illustrations? What is their potential liability for past reuses that may be infringing after *CCNV v. Reid*?

See Chapter XIII for a discussion of Baltimore Orioles v. Major League Baseball Players, in which it was decided that owners of baseball teams hold exclusive rights to games. In the court's view, the players, paid as team employees, create works for hire by their participation in games.

4. RIGHTS OF COPYRIGHT OWNER(S)

Section 106 states the nature of the protection extended to the copyright owner:

> Subject to sections 107 through 118, the owner of copyright under this title has the exclusive right to do and to authorize any of the following:
>
> > (1) to reproduce the copyrighted work in copies or phonorecords;
> >
> > (2) to prepare derivative works based upon the copyrighted work;
> >
> > (3) to distribute copies or phonorecords of the copyrighted work to the public by sale or other transfer of ownership, or by rental, lease, or lending;
> >
> > (4) in the case of literary, musical, dramatic, and choreographic works, pantomimes, and motion pictures and other

audiovisual works, to perform the copyrighted work publicly; and

(5) in the case of literary, musical, dramatic, and choreographic works, pantomimes, and pictorial, graphic, or sculptural works, including the individual images of a motion picture or other audiovisual work, to display the copyrighted work publicly. 17 U.S.C.A. § 106.

It is possible for a copyright owner to sell some rights and retain others. A famous novelist, for example, might first sell the rights to publish excerpts of a forthcoming novel to a national magazine, next sell the right to publish the hardcover first edition of the book to a publishing house, then sell the right for publication of a later paperback edition to another publishing house, and, finally, sell the right to make a movie based on the book to a studio.

It is important to note that the only protections accorded copyright are statutory and are listed in § 106. An unlicensed use that does not conflict with one of the exclusive rights enumerated in § 106 is not an infringement. Beyond that, § 106 is explicitly made subject to a series of limitations listed in §§ 107–118. We will discuss the most important of these limitations, fair use, later in this chapter.

One limitation on the § 106 rights that is not mentioned in the copyright statute is the first sale doctrine. A judicially-created rule, the doctrine provides that copyright owners who sell copies of their copyrighted works have no further control over the sale or lease of those particular copies. The original copyright owners' other rights remain unimpaired.

Under the first sale doctrine, for example, a video store can buy videotapes and then rent them to the public. However, under a 1984 amendment to § 109(b)(1) of the Copyright Act, phonograph records cannot be rented (except by nonprofit libraries or nonprofit educational institutions) without the permission of the copyright holders. The rationale is that there would be little or no purpose in renting a record other than to copy it. In contrast, one can presume that customers may rent videotapes to view them without illegally copying them. For a more complete discussion of the doctrine, see United States v. Atherton, 561 F.2d 747 (9th Cir.1977).

5. DURATION OF COPYRIGHT

The 1909 Copyright Act, which still governs the term of protection for many works, originally provided copyright protection for 28 years with one 28–year renewal. That renewal term was extended to 47 years by the Copyright Act of 1976—with the result that such works would be protected for a total of 75 years. The Sonny Bono Copyright Term Extension Act of 1998 (CTEA) extends protection of pre–1978 copyright works for another 20 years, to a total of 95 years.

For works created in 1978 (recall that Jan. 1, 1978, was the effective date of the Copyright Act of 1976) and later, the Copyright Act of 1976 provided protection for the life of the author plus 50 years—or, in the case of two or more authors, for the life of the last surviving author plus 50 years. The Sonny Bono Copyright Term Extension Act of 1998 extends that to the life of the last surviving author plus 70 years. European Union law already provided protection for life of the author plus 70 years, so the extension brings U.S. law into harmony with European Union law. All terms of copyright run to the end of the calendar year in which they would otherwise expire. 17 U.S.C.A. §§ 302–305.

Passage of the Term Extension Act of 1998 meant continued copyright protection for such musical works as "Who's Sorry Now" and "Rhapsody in Blue," which would have entered the public domain on Jan. 1, 1999, but was too late to protect "Toot Toot Tootsie, Goodbye" and "Carolina in the Morning," both of which entered the public domain in 1998. A number of media giants, including Time–Warner (owner of the Gershwin rights, for instance) and Disney were major proponents of the legislation. Disney expressed concern about the fact that its "Steamboat Willie" cartoon, containing the first appearance of the character who came to be known as Mickey Mouse, would otherwise have lost copyright protection soon. (Note, however, that Mickey and his name both have trademark protection anyway.)

Eric Eldred, a noncommercial Internet publisher of works in the public domain, along with others, including the American Association of Law Libraries and other users of public domain works, challenged the constitutionality of the Copyright Term Extension Act (CTEA) in a case that eventually reached the Supreme Court of the United States. The plaintiffs alleged that the Constitution gives Congress the authority to provide copyright protection only for *limited terms* and that the possibility of retroactive extensions would thwart the original intent of the Constitution, and that the CTEA failed to keep the appropriate balance between freedom of speech and the interests of copyright. The U.S. government, along with the Motion Picture Association of America, the Recording Industry Association of America, ASCAP, and Broadcast Music Incorporated (BMI), supported the act. In a 7–2 decision, the Supreme Court upheld the constitutionality of the CTEA. Justice Ruth Bader Ginsburg, writing for the majority, said the Constitution "gives Congress wide leeway to prescribe 'limited terms' for copyright protection and allows Congress to secure the same level and duration of protection for all copyright holders, present and future." Eldred v. Ashcroft, ___ U.S. ___, 123 S.Ct. 769 (2003).

6. STATUTORY FORMALITIES

Under the Copyright Act of 1976, any work is protected as soon as it is "fixed in a tangible medium." However, to retain this protection certain statutory formalities should be observed. Originally every copy was required to carry notice consisting of the full word copyright, the accepted abbreviation "copr.," or the internationally accepted symbol ©;

but the Berne Convention Implementation Act, Public Law 100–568, eliminated the requirement that domestic authors display a copyright notice, substituting the word "may" for "shall" in 17 U.S.C.A. 401(a). We will discuss the Berne Convention in the section of this chapter on international protection.

One requirement for obtaining *full* copyright protection is to register the work with the Register of Copyrights. Registration is a prerequisite for filing a copyright infringement suit and involves filling out a form, paying a small fee and providing a few copies of the work.

Forms and current fee schedules are available from the Copyright Office, Library of Congress, Washington, D.C. 20559. Much information is available at the Copyright Office's web site: http://lcweb.loc.gov/copyright/–including application forms that can be downloaded.

7. PREEMPTION OF STATE LAW

The Copyright Act of 1976 preempted all state law governing rights equivalent to copyright protection. As previously noted, this eliminated common-law copyright protection for unpublished works. It does not, however, mean that other state laws, such as those relating to defamation, cannot be applied to copyrighted works.

Sometimes, however, determining what constitutes a non-equivalent right is not easy. In Chapter XIV, in the discussion of the right of privacy, we will see the Supreme Court decision in Zacchini v. Scripps–Howard Broadcasting Co., which recognized a "right of publicity" for Hugo Zacchini, an entertainer known for his "human cannonball" act. Zacchini's 15–second act at a fair grounds was videotaped by a television station and broadcast on the evening news. The Court held that the broadcast posed a substantial threat to the economic value of the performance and that the performer was entitled to damages in an invasion of privacy suit.

Zacchini's act was not copyrighted. Had he "fixed" it by having it filmed or taped himself, he could have copyrighted it. Notice the similarities between copyright law and this special application of privacy law in protecting one's right to control one's own creation or performance.

It is difficult to generalize from *Zacchini* because so few entertainers' acts are so short that they can be recorded in substantial portion by news media and because this area of privacy law is so undeveloped.

8. INTERNATIONAL PROTECTION

Many countries—but not the United States—signed an agreement in 1886 in Berne, Switzerland, giving international copyright protection. That agreement, widely referred to as the Berne Convention, established the International Union for the Protection of Literary and Artistic Works. Although it was a member of an overlapping international treaty, the United States took more than a century to consider joining the other

Berne Convention countries but finally did so after Congress passed the Berne Convention Implementation Act of 1988 and President Reagan signed it. Membership took effect March 1, 1989.

It was hoped that membership in the treaty would help to curb international piracy of original works by Americans—at least in the 79 other countries that were members when the U.S. joined. International piracy has continued, however, to be a problem, particularly in developing countries with active commercial sectors. The Clinton Administration focused attention on the pirating of software, videotapes and music in China for months in 1996, including threatening trade sanctions by the U.S. Government if China did not stop violations of intellectual property rights, but the issue had been pushed into the background by the time President Clinton visited China in 1998. Although U.S. officials said China had closed down many illegal producers and made hundreds of arrests, industry experts said problems were still widespread, particularly with illegally copied video compact disks. The New York Times, June 24, 1998 at A–10.

The Berne Convention includes, in Article VI, a Moral Rights Clause adopted in 1928. That clause provides that, "independently of the author's copyright, and even after assignment of the said copyright, the author shall retain the right to claim authorship of the work, as well as the right to object to deformation, mutilation, or other modification of the said work with may be prejudicial to his honor or his reputation." Despite the fact that Congress asserted in the Berne Convention Implementation Act that the moral rights clause should *not* be explicitly enforced in American courts, experts viewed the Berne membership as a "moral statement" of the importance of protecting intellectual property and were optimistic that authors and creators whose works were altered would be better able to protect their works from alteration than they had been previously. New York Times, March 10, 1989 at B–7.

The U.S. has been criticized for not protecting the moral rights of authors and artists, but a Performers and Phonograms Treaty adopted in Geneva at a December 1996 conference added protection to some moral rights independent of economic rights.

The World Intellectual Property Organization (WIPO) Copyright Treaty and the WIPO Performances and Phonograms Treaty were signed by 160 nations, including the United States, in 1997, addressing issues such as the protection of copyrighted works in cyberspace. The treaties were implemented in the U.S. by the Digital Millennium Copyright Act (DMCA) of 1998 making it illegal to manufacture, import or in any way traffic in devices that circumvent technologies that protect copyrights in cyberspace. Passage of the legislation by Congress followed two years of difficult negotiations with strong proponents of improved copyright protection on one side of the debate and libraries and universities, fearing that protections would interfere with research, on the other. One of the more difficult issues involved legal protection for computer databases, including such things as telephone books (recall *Feist*, p. 795, *supra*) and compilations of sports statistics. Because of objections from educators, researchers, and libraries, protection for such databases— which would have been included in the version of the legislation approved by the House of Representatives—was *not* protected in the final version. Legal Backgrounder, Feb. 19, 1999.

B. ALLEGED OR ACTUAL INFRINGEMENTS

Infringements, real or imagined, can take a variety of forms. In some instances permission to use all or part of the copyrighted material may have been given, but the copyright holder may allege that the user has exceeded the permission. That may happen when the material is disseminated more widely (perhaps in another country) than originally envisioned, when the material used is more extensive than the copyright holder envisioned or when the purpose of the dissemination or the context in which the material is presented is not what the copyright holder expected.

More frequently, the problem may be that material is used with no permission having been granted at all. In some such instances, the material has been attributed correctly to the copyright holder (which still does not give the user any right to use it without permission); in other instances the material has not been attributed.

In cases involving such literary or artistic creative work as musical or dramatic presentations, the problem may involve the question of whether the user's reproduction of the copyright holder's work actually constituted a "performance" of it.

In other cases, such as those in which two writers or two composers have created similar works, the key question will be whether one author copied the other's work. The plaintiff in such a case attempts to prove that the defendant had access to the copyrighted work and that there is a *substantial similarity* between the copyrighted work and the defendant's work.

Copyright protection extends only to copying the work in question. If someone *independently creates* a similar work, there is no copyright infringement. Thus, in any copyright suit the plaintiff must show that the defendant had access to the plaintiff's work. However, as former Beatle George Harrison learned, plaintiff does not have to prove that defendant intentionally or even consciously copied it. Bright Tunes Music Corp. v. Harrisongs Music, Ltd., 420 F.Supp. 177 (S.D.N.Y.1976).

Two cases illustrate problems of protection of commercial rights to ideas—specifically excluded from copyright coverage under Section 102. When copyright protection is unavailable, plaintiffs sometimes sue under contract law. In one of the cases, Murray v. NBC, 844 F.2d 988, 15 Med.L.Rptr. 1284 (2d Cir.1988), a plaintiff claimed that, four years before "The Cosby Show" premiered on NBC, he had proposed to the network an idea for a half-hour situation comedy starring Cosby to be titled "Father's Day." Unable to sue for copyright infringement, the plaintiff sued for misappropriation, conversion, breach of contract and violation of the Lanham Act (on the theory that the program's origin was falsely designated). The court of appeals held that the plaintiff's idea for a program about an intact, middle-class black family was not novel and could not be protected.

In the second case, Buchwald v. Paramount Pictures Corp., 1990 WL 357611, 17 Med.L.Rptr. 1257 (1990), humorist Art Buchwald sued Paramount claiming that the Eddie Murphy movie "Coming to America" was based on a screen treatment he had sold to Paramount in 1983. Buchwald said he was entitled to a lump sum payment and a share of the net profits from the film. The case was in the courts for seven years and cost several million dollars in legal fees and expenses. A California court held that the similarity between Buchwald's screen treatment and the film, combined with evidence of Paramount's unlimited access to Buchwald's idea, warranted a finding that the movie was "based upon" Buchwald's work and awarded Buchwald $250,000 plus 19 percent of the profits. Paramount denied that there had been any profits, and more litigation followed. Buchwald and Paramount eventually settled the case in 1995. The New York Times, March 4, 1996 at D–1.

Unauthorized home copying of digital recordings has presented a problem because multi-generational copies of digitally formatted works have virtually the same quality as the original. Estimates are that the recording and music publishing industries lose more than $1 billion a year because of home copying. In response to those losses, Congress passed the Audio Home Recording Act of 1992, which provides for a tax on digital audio recording equipment (with certain exceptions) and a tax on blank digital tapes. The Recording Industry Association of America (RIAA) collects and distributes royalties resulting from the home copying through the Alliance of Artists and Recording Companies (AARC).

The MP3 technology, which makes it possible to compress digital audio files downloaded from the Internet so that a five-minute CD song uses only about five megabytes of storage space and retains its original digital quality sound, creates more issues. RIAA and AARC sued Diamond Multimedia systems in 1998, alleging in part that Diamond's Rio device, a hand-held machine that receives, stores, and plays digital audio files in the MP3 format, should be subject to the Audio Home Recording Act, with which Diamond had not complied. See discussion of the case at p. 854, *infra*.

1. REMEDIES

The Copyright Act of 1976 provides numerous remedies for copyright infringement. Sections 502–503 provide for an injunction against further infringement as well as destruction of all existing infringing materials. Under § 504, the copyright owner may elect to receive either the damages actually suffered plus any additional profits of the infringer or statutory damages of not less than $250 or more than $10,000. The court may also at its discretion award costs and attorney's fees.

In the case of willful infringement for commercial advantage or private financial gain, criminal sanctions are also available. Section 506 provides for fines of up to $50,000 and imprisonment for up to two years, depending on the type of work infringed and the prior record of the defendant.

2. Fair Use

As previously noted, the grant of rights to the owner of the copyright is conditioned on a series of limitations expressed in §§ 107–118. These include permitting libraries to make single photocopies of articles and permitting persons to make phonograph records of music without permission upon payment of certain royalties. As we saw earlier, p. 448, *supra*, § 111 deals with cable television. Probably the most important of these limitations is found in § 107, dealing with the question of fair use. Until the 1976 statute fair use had been left to develop as a judicially created exception to the rights of the copyright owner. There was great controversy over whether to recognize the defense explicitly and, if so, how to do it. The result is § 107:

> Notwithstanding the provisions of section 106, the fair use of a copyrighted work, including such use by reproduction in copies or phonorecords or by any other means specified by that section, for purposes such as criticism, comment, news reporting, teaching (including multiple copies for classroom use), scholarship, or research, is not an infringement of copyright. In determining whether the use made of a work in any particular case is a fair use the factors to be considered shall include—
>
> > (1) the purpose and character of the use, including whether such use is of a commercial nature or is for nonprofit educational purposes;
> >
> > (2) the nature of the copyrighted work;
> >
> > (3) the amount and substantiality of the portion used in relation to the copyrighted work as a whole; and
> >
> > (4) the effect of the use upon the potential market for or value of the copyrighted work. 17 U.S.C.A. § 107.

The following case involves two special fair use questions. One is the application of fair use to historical works. Remember our earlier discussion of historical works, p. 792, *supra*. The other question is whether fair use can be used if the copyrighted work was unpublished at the time of infringement. The case is also an excellent illustration of how courts approach fair use cases in general.

HARPER & ROW PUBLISHERS, INC. v. NATION ENTERPRISES

Supreme Court of the United States, 1985.

471 U.S. 539, 105 S.Ct. 2218, 85 L.Ed.2d 588, 11 Med.L.Rptr. 1969.

JUSTICE O'CONNOR delivered the opinion of the Court.

This case requires us to consider to what extent the "fair use" provision of the Copyright Revision Act of 1976, 17 U.S.C. § 107 (hereinafter the Copyright Act), sanctions the unauthorized use of quotations from a public figure's unpublished manuscript. In March 1979, an undisclosed source provided The Nation magazine with the unpublished manuscript of "A Time to Heal: The Autobiography of Gerald R. Ford." Working directly from the purloined manuscript, an editor of The Nation produced a short piece entitled "The Ford Memoirs—Behind the Nixon Pardon." The piece was timed to "scoop" an article scheduled shortly to appear in Time magazine. Time had agreed to purchase the exclusive right to print prepublication excerpts from the copyright holders. . . .

I

. . . The memoirs were to contain "significant hitherto unpublished material" concerning the Watergate crisis, Mr. Ford's pardon of Former President Nixon and "Mr. Ford's reflections on this period of history, and the morality and personalities involved." . . . In addition to the right to publish the Ford memoirs in book form, the agreement gave petitioners the exclusive right to license prepublication excerpts, known in the trade as "first serial rights." . . . [A]s the memoirs were nearing completion, petitioners negotiated a prepublication licensing agreement with Time, a weekly news magazine. Time agreed to pay $25,000, $12,500 in advance and an additional $12,500 at publication, in exchange for the right to excerpt 7,500 words from Mr. Ford's account of the Nixon pardon. The issue featuring the excerpts was timed to appear approximately one week before shipment of the full length book version to bookstores. Exclusivity was an important consideration; Harper & Row instituted procedures designed to maintain the confidentiality of the manuscript, and Time retained the right to renegotiate the second payment should the material appear in print prior to its release of the excerpts.

[Mr. Navasky received a copy of the manuscript.] Mr. Navasky knew that his possession of the manuscript was not authorized and that the manuscript must be returned to his "source" to avoid discovery. [   ] He hastily put together what he believed was a "real hot news story" composed of quotes, paraphrases and facts drawn exclusively from the manuscript. [   ] Mr. Navasky attempted no independent commentary, research or criticism, in part because of the need for speed if he was to "make news" by "publish[ing] in advance of publication of the Ford book." [   ] The 2,250 word article . . . appeared on April 3, 1979. As a result of The Nation's article, Time canceled its piece and refused to pay the remaining $12,500.

II

We agree with the Court of Appeals that copyright is intended to increase and not to impede the harvest of knowledge. But we believe the Second Circuit gave insufficient deference to the scheme established by the Copyright Act for fostering the original works that provide the seed and substance of this harvest. The rights conferred by copyright are designed to assure contributors to the store of knowledge a fair return for their labors. [   ]

Article I, § 8, of the Constitution provides that:

> "The Congress shall have Power . . . to Promote the Progress of Science and useful Arts, by securing for limited Times to Authors and Inventors the exclusive Right to their respective Writings and Discoveries."

As we noted last Term, "[this] limited grant is a means by which an important public purpose may be achieved. It is intended to motivate the creative activity of authors and inventors by the provision of a special reward, and to allow the public access to the products of their genius after the limited period of exclusive control has expired." Sony v. Universal City Studios, 464 U.S. 417 (1984). "The monopoly created by copyright thus rewards the individual author in order to benefit the public." [   ] This principle applies equally to works of fiction and nonfiction. The book at issue here, for example, was two years in the making, and began with a contract giving the author's copyright to the publishers in exchange for their services in producing and marketing the work. In preparing the book, Mr. Ford drafted essays and word portraits of hundreds of taped interviews that were later distilled to chronicle his personal viewpoint. It is evident that the monopoly granted by copyright actively served its intended purpose of inducing the creation of new material of potential historical value.

Section 106 of the Copyright Act confers a bundle of exclusive rights to the owner of the copyright. Under the Copyright Act, these rights—to publish, copy, and distribute the author's work—vest in the author of an original work from the time of its creation. In practice, the author commonly sells his rights to publishers who offer royalties in exchange for their services in producing and marketing the author's work. The copyright owner's rights, however, are subject to certain statutory exceptions. Among these is § 107, which codifies the traditional privilege of other authors to make "fair use" of an earlier writer's work. In addition, no author may copyright facts or ideas. The copyright is limited to those aspects of the work—termed "expression"—that display the stamp of the author's originality.

Creation of a nonfiction work, even a compilation of pure fact, entails originality. . . . The copyright holders of "A Time to Heal" complied with the relevant statutory notice and registration procedures. Thus, there is no dispute that the unpublished manuscript of "A Time to Heal," as a whole was protected by § 106 from unauthorized reproduction. Nor do respondents dispute that verbatim copying of excerpts of the manuscript's original form of expression would constitute infringement unless excused as fair use. [   ] Yet copyright does not prevent subsequent users from copying from a prior author's work those constituent elements that are not original—for example, quotations borrowed under the rubric of fair use from other copyrighted works, facts, or materials in the public domain—as long as such use does not unfairly appropriate the author's original contributions. [ ] Perhaps the controversy between the lower courts in the case over copyrightability is more aptly a dispute over whether The Nation's appropriation of unoriginal and uncopyrightable elements encroached on the originality embodied in the work as a whole. Especially in the realm of factual narrative, the law is currently unsettled regarding the ways in which uncopyrightable elements combine with the author's original contributions to form protected expression. . . .

We need not reach these issues, however, as The Nation has admitted to lifting verbatim quotes of the author's original language totalling between 300 and 400 words and constituting some 13% of The Nation article. In using generous verbatim excerpts of Mr. Ford's unpublished manuscript to lend authenticity to its account of the forthcoming memoirs, The Nation effectively arrogated to itself the right of first publication, an important marketable subsidiary right. For the reasons set forth below, we find that this use of the copyrighted manuscript, even stripped to the verbatim quotes conceded by The Nation as to be copyrightable expression, was not a fair use within the meaning of the Copyright Act.

III

A

Fair use was traditionally defined as "a privilege in others than the owner of the copyright to use the copyrighted material in a reasonable manner without his consent." [ ] The statutory formulation of the defense of fair use in the Copyright Act of 1976 reflects the intent of Congress to codify the common-law doctrine. Section 107 requires a case-by-case determination whether a particular use is fair, and the statute notes four nonexclusive factors to be considered. This approach was "intended to restate the [pre-existing] judicial doctrine of fair use, not to change, narrow, or enlarge it in any way." H.R.Rep. No. 94–1476, p. 66 (1976) (hereinafter House Report).

"[T]he author's consent to a reasonable use of his copyrighted works ha[d] always been implied by the courts as a necessary incident of the constitutional policy of promoting the progress of science and the useful arts, since a prohibition of such use would inhibit subsequent writers from attempting to improve upon prior works and thus . . . frustrate the very ends sought to be attained." . . .

. . .

Perhaps because the fair use doctrine was predicated on the author's implied consent to "reasonable and customary" use when he released his work for public consumption, fair use traditionally was not recognized as a defense to charges of copying from an author's as yet unpublished works. Under common-law copyright, "the property of the author . . . in his intellectual creation [was] absolute until he voluntarily part[ed] with the same." [ ] This absolute rule, however, was tempered in practice by the equitable nature of the fair use doctrine. In a given case, factors such as implied consent through *de facto* publication or performance or dissemination of a work may tip the balance of equities in favor of prepublication use. [   ] But it has never been seriously disputed that "the fact that the plaintiff's work is unpublished . . . is a factor tending to negate the defense of fair use." . . .

The Copyright Revision Act of 1976 represents the culmination of a major legislative reexamination of copyright doctrine. Among its other innovations, it eliminated publication "as a dividing line between common law and statutory protection," [   ], extending statutory protection to all works from the time of their creation. It also recognized for the first time a distinct statutory right of first publication, which had previously been an element of the common-law protections afforded unpublished works. . . .

Though the right of first publication, like the other rights enumerated in § 106, is expressly made subject to the fair use provision of § 107, fair use analysis must always be tailored to the individual case. The nature of the interest at stake is highly relevant to whether a given use is fair. From the beginning, those entrusted with the task of revision recognized the "overbalancing reasons to preserve the common law protection of undisseminated works until the author or his successor chooses to disclose them." [   ] The right of first publication implicates a threshold decision by the author whether and in what form to release his work. First publication is inherently different from other § 106 rights in that only one person can be the first publisher; as the contract with Time illustrates, the commercial value of the right lies primarily in exclusivity. Because the potential damage to the author from judicially enforced "sharing" of the first publication right with unauthorized users of his manuscript is substantial, the balance of equities in evaluating such a claim of fair use inevitably shifts.

　　. . .

. . . The author's control of first public distribution implicates not only his personal interest in creative control but his property interest in exploitation of prepublication rights, which are valuable in themselves and serve as a valuable adjunct to publicity and marketing. See Belushi v. Woodward, 598 F.Supp. 36 (D.C.1984) (successful marketing depends on coordination of serialization and release to public); Marks, Subsidiary Rights and Permissions, in What Happens in Book Publishing, 230 (C. Grannis ed. 1967) (exploitation of subsidiary rights is necessary to financial success of new books). Under ordinary circumstances, the author's right to control the first public appearance of his undisseminated expression will outweigh a claim of fair use.

B

Respondents, however, contend that First Amendment values require a different rule under the circumstances of this case. The thrust of the decision below is that "[t]he scope of [fair use] is undoubtedly wider when the information conveyed relates to matters of high public concern." . . . Respondents explain their copying of Mr. Ford's expression as essential to reporting the news story it claims the book itself represents. In respondents' view, not only the facts contained in Mr. Ford's memoirs, but "the precise manner in which [he] expressed himself was as newsworthy as what he had to say." [ ] Respondents argue that the public's interest in learning this news as fast as possible outweighs the right of the author to control its first publication.

The Second Circuit noted, correctly, that copyright's idea/expression dichotomy "strike[s] a definitional balance between the First Amendment and the Copyright Act by permitting free communication of facts while still protecting an author's expression." [ ] No author may copyright his ideas or the facts he narrates. . . . As this Court long ago observed: "[T]he news element—the information respecting current events contained in the literary production—is not the creation of the writer, but is a report of matters that ordinarily are *public juris;* it is history of the day." International News Service v. Associated Press, [ ]. But copyright assures those who write and publish factual narratives such as "A Time to Heal" that they may at least enjoy the right to market the original expression contained therein as just compensation for their investment.

. . . The promise of copyright would be an empty one if it could be avoided merely by dubbing the infringement a fair use "news report" of the book.

Nor do respondents assert any actual necessity for circumventing the copyright scheme with respect to the types of works and users at issue here.[6] Where an author and publisher have invested extensive resources in creating an original work and are poised to release it to the public, no legitimate aim is served by preempting the right of first publication. . . .

In our haste to disseminate news, it should not be forgotten that the Framers intended copyright itself to be the engine of free expression. . . .

It is fundamentally at odds with the scheme of copyright to accord lesser rights in those works that are of greatest importance to the public. Such a notion ignores the major premise of copyright and injures author and public alike. . . .

. . .

IV

. . . [W]hether The Nation article constitutes fair use under § 107 must be reviewed in light of the principles discussed above. The factors enumerated in the section are not meant to be exclusive: "[S]ince the

---

6. It bears noting that Congress in the Copyright Act recognized a public interest warranting specific exemptions in a number of areas not within traditional fair use, see, e.g., 17 U.S.C. § 115 (compulsory license for records); § 105 (no copyright in government works). No such exemption limits copyright in personal narratives written by public servants after they leave government service.

doctrine is an equitable rule of reason, no generally applicable definition is possible, and each case raising the question must be decided on its own facts." [ ] The four factors identified by Congress as especially relevant in determining whether the use was fair are: (1) the purpose and character of the use; (2) the nature of the copyrighted work; (3) the substantiality of the portion used in relation to the copyrighted work as a whole; (4) the effect on the potential market for or value of the copyrighted work. We address each one separately.

Purpose of the Use. The Second Circuit correctly identified news reporting as the general purpose of The Nation's use. News reporting is one of the examples enumerated in § 107 to "give some idea of the sort of activities the courts might regard as fair use under the circumstances." . . . The fact that an article arguably is "news" and therefore a productive use is simply one factor in a fair use analysis.

. . . The Nation has every right to seek to be the first to publish information. But The Nation went beyond simply reporting uncopyrightable information and actively sought to exploit the headline value of its infringement, making a "news event" out of its unauthorized first publication of a noted figure's copyrighted expression.

The fact that a publication was commercial as opposed to non-profit is a separate factor that tends to weigh against a finding of fair use. "[E]very commercial use of copyrighted material is presumptively an unfair exploitation of the monopoly privilege that belongs to the owner of the copyright." [*Sony*] In arguing that the purpose of news reporting is not purely commercial, The Nation misses the point entirely. The crux of the profit/nonprofit distinction is not whether the sole motive of the use is monetary gain but whether the user stands to profit from exploitation of the copyrighted material without paying the customary price.

In evaluating character and purpose we cannot ignore The Nation's stated purpose of scooping the forthcoming hardcover and Time abstracts. The Nation's use had not merely the incidental effect but the *intended purpose* of supplanting the copyright holder's commercially valuable right of first publication. Also relevant to the "character" of the use is "the propriety of the defendant's conduct." [ ] The trial court found that The Nation knowingly exploited a purloined manuscript. Unlike the typical claim of fair use, The Nation cannot offer up even the fiction of consent as justification. Like its competitor newsweekly, it was free to bid for the right of abstracting excerpts from "A Time to Heal." . . .

Nature of the Copyrighted Work. Second, the Act directs attention to the nature of the copyrighted work. "A Time to Heal" may be characterized as an unpublished historical narrative or autobiography. The law generally recognizes a greater need to disseminate factual works than works of fiction or fantasy. . . . Some of the briefer quotes from the memoir are arguably necessary adequately to convey the facts: for example, Mr. Ford's characterization of the White House tapes as the "smoking gun" is perhaps so integral to the idea expressed as to be inseparable from it. But The Nation did not stop at isolated phrases and instead excerpted subjective descriptions and portraits of public figures whose power lies in the author's individualized expression. Such use, focusing on the most expressive elements of the work, exceeds that necessary to disseminate the facts.

The fact that a work is unpublished is a critical element of its "nature." Our prior discussion establishes that the scope of fair use is narrower with respect to unpublished works. . . .

In the case of Mr. Ford's manuscript, the copyrightholders' interest in confidentiality is irrefutable; the copyrightholders had entered into a contractual undertaking to "keep the manuscript confidential" and required that all those to whom the manuscript was shown also "sign an agreement to keep the manuscript confidential." While the copyrightholders' contract with Time required Time to submit its proposed article seven days before publication, The Nation's clandestine publication afforded no such opportunity for creative or quality control. It was hastily patched together and contained "a number of inaccuracies." A use that so clearly infringes the copyrightholder's interests in confidentiality and creative control is difficult to characterize as "fair."

Amount and Substantiality of the Portion Used. Next, the Act directs us to examine the amount and substantiality of the portion used in relation to the copyrighted work as a whole. In absolute terms, the words actually quoted were an insubstantial portion of "A Time to Heal." The district court, however, found that "[T]he Nation took what was essentially the heart of the book." [ ] We believe the Court of Appeals erred in overruling the district judge's evaluation of the qualitative nature of the taking. See, e.g., Roy Export Co. Establishment v. Columbia Broadcasting System, Inc., [   ] (taking of 55 seconds out of one hour and twenty-nine minute film deemed qualitatively substantial). A Time editor described the chapters on the pardon as "the most interesting and moving parts of the entire manuscript." . . .

As the statutory language indicates, a taking may not be excused merely because it is insubstantial with respect to the *infringing* work. As Judge Learned Hand cogently remarked, "[N]o plagiarist can excuse the wrong by showing how much of his work he did not pirate." [*Sheldon*] Conversely, the fact that a substantial portion of the infringing work was copied verbatim is evidence of the qualitative value of the copied material, both to the originator and to the plagiarist who seeks to profit from marketing someone else's copyrighted expression.

Stripped to the verbatim quotes, the direct takings from the unpublished manuscript constitute at least 13% of the infringing article. See [*Meeropol*] (copyrighted letters constituted less than 1% of infringing work but were prominently featured). The Nation article is structured around the quoted excerpts which serve as its dramatic focal points. In view of the expressive value of the excerpts and their key role in the infringing work, we cannot agree with the Second Circuit that the "magazine took a meager, indeed an infinitesimal amount of Ford's original language." [   ]

Effect on the Market. Finally, the Act focuses on "the effect of the use upon the potential market for or value of the copyrighted work." This last factor is undoubtedly the single most important element of fair use. . . . [O]nce a copyrightholder establishes with reasonable probability the existence of a causal connection between the infringement and a loss of revenue, the burden properly shifts to the infringer to show that this damage would have occurred had there been no taking of copyrighted expression. Petitioners established a prima facie case of actual damage that respondent failed to rebut. The trial court properly awarded actual damages and accounting of profits.

. . .

It is undisputed that the factual material in the balance of The Nation's article, besides the verbatim quotes at issue here, was drawn exclusively from the chapters on the pardon. The excerpts were employed as featured episodes in a story about the Nixon pardon—precisely the use petitioners had licensed to Time. The borrowing of these verbatim quotes from the unpublished manuscript lent The Nation's piece a special air of authenticity—as Navasky [*The Nation*'s editor] expressed it, the reader would know it was Ford speaking and not The Nation. Thus, it directly competed for a share of the market for prepublication excerpts. . . .

V

. . . In sum, the traditional doctrine of fair use, as embodied in the Copyright Act, does not sanction the use made by The Nation of these copyrighted materials. Any copyright infringer may claim to benefit the public by increasing public access to the copyrighted work. But Congress has not designed, and we see no warrant for judicially imposing, a "compulsory license" permitting unfettered access to the unpublished copyrighted expression of public figures.

The Nation conceded that its verbatim copying of some 300 words of direct quotation from the Ford manuscript would constitute an infringement unless excused as a fair use. Because we find that The Nation's use of these verbatim excerpts from the unpublished manuscript was not a fair use, the judgment of the Court of Appeals is reversed and remanded for further proceedings consistent with this opinion.

It is so ordered.

Justice Brennan, with whom Justice White and Justice Marshall join, dissenting.

The Court holds that The Nation's quotation of 300 words from the unpublished 200,000-word manuscript of President Gerald R. Ford infringed the copyright in that manuscript, even though the quotations related to a historical event of undoubted significance—the resignation and pardon of President Richard M. Nixon. Although the Court pursues the laudable goal of protecting "the economic incentive to create and disseminate ideas," this zealous defense of the copyright owner's prerogative will, I fear, stifle the broad dissemination of ideas and information copyright is intended to nurture. Protection of the copyright owner's economic interest is achieved in this case through an exceedingly narrow definition of the scope of fair use. The progress of arts and sciences and the robust public debate essential to an enlightened citizenry are ill served by this constricted reading of the fair use doctrine. [   ] I therefore respectfully dissent.

I

A

This case presents two issues. First, did The Nation's use of material from the Ford manuscript in forms other than direct quotation from that manuscript infringe Harper & Row's copyright. Second, did the quotation of approximately 300 words from the manuscript infringe the copyright because this quotation did not constitute "fair use" within the meaning of § 107 of the Copyright Act. The Court finds no need to resolve the threshold copyrightability issue. The use of 300 words of quotation was, the Court finds, beyond the scope of fair use and thus a copyright infringement. Because I disagree with the Court's fair use holding, it is necessary for me to decide the threshold copyrightability question.

. . .

The "originality" requirement now embodied in § 102 of the Copyright Act is crucial to maintenance of the appropriate balance between these competing interests. Properly interpreted in the light of the legislative history, this section extends copyright protection to an author's literary form but permits free use by others of the ideas and information the author communicates. . . .

It follows that infringement of copyright must be based on a taking of literary form, as opposed to the ideas or information contained in a copyrighted work. Deciding whether an infringing appropriation of literary form has occurred is difficult for at least two reasons. First, the distinction between literary form and information or ideas is often elusive in practice. Second, infringement must be based on a *substantial* appropriation of literary form. This determination is equally challenging. Not surprisingly, the test for infringement has defied precise formulation. In general, though, the inquiry proceeds along two axes: *how closely* has the second author tracked the first author's particular language and structure of presentation; and *how much* of the first author's language and structure has the second author appropriated.

. . .

The Language. Much of the information The Nation conveyed was not in the form of paraphrase at all, but took the form of synopsis of lengthy discussions in the Ford manuscript. In the course of this summary presentation, The Nation did use occasional sentences that closely resembled language in the original Ford manuscript. But these linguistic similarities are insufficient to constitute an infringement. . . .

At most The Nation paraphrased disparate isolated sentences from the original. A finding of infringement based on paraphrase generally requires far more close and substantial a tracking of the original language than occurred in this case.

The Structure of Presentation. The article does not mimic Mr. Ford's structure. The information The Nation presents is drawn from scattered sections of the Ford work and does not appear in the sequence in which Mr. Ford presented it. . . . Also, it is difficult to suggest that a 2,000–word article could bodily appropriate the structure of a 200,000–word book. Most of what Mr. Ford created, and most of the history he recounted, was simply not represented in The Nation's article.

When The Nation was not quoting Mr. Ford, therefore, its efforts to convey the historical information in the Ford manuscript did not so closely and substantially track Mr. Ford's language and structure as to constitute an appropriation of literary form.

II

The Nation is thus liable in copyright only if the quotation of 300 words infringed any of Harper & Row's exclusive rights under § 106 of the Act. . . . The question here is whether The Nation's quotation was a noninfringing fair use within the meaning of § 107.

. . .

With respect to a work of history, particularly the memoirs of a public official, the statutorily-prescribed analysis cannot properly be conducted without constant attention to copyright's crucial distinction between protected literary form and unprotected information or ideas. The question must always be: was the subsequent author's use of *literary form* a fair use within the meaning of § 107, in light of the purpose for the use, the nature of the copyrighted work, the amount of literary form used, and the effect of this use of literary form on the value of or market for the original.

Limiting the inquiry to the propriety of a subsequent author's use of the copyrighted owner's literary form is not easy in the case of a work of history. Protection against only substantial appropriation of literary form does not ensure historians a return commensurate with the full value of their labors. . . . Copyright thus does not protect that which is often of most value in a work of history and courts must resist the tendency to reject the fair use defense on the basis of their feeling that an author of history has been deprived of the full value of his or her labor. A subsequent author's taking of information and ideas is in no sense piratical because copyright law simply does not create any property interest in information and ideas.

The urge to compensate for subsequent use of information and ideas is perhaps understandable. An inequity seems to lurk in the idea that much of the fruit of the historian's labor may be used without compensation. This, however, is not some unforeseen by-product of a statutory scheme intended primarily to ensure a return for works of the imagination. Congress made the affirmative choice that the copyright laws should apply in this way. . . .

. . . Application of the statutorily prescribed analysis with attention to the distinction between information and literary form leads to a straightforward finding of fair use within the meaning of § 107.

The Purpose of the Use. The Nation's purpose in quoting 300 words of the Ford manuscript was, as the Court acknowledges, news reporting. . . .

. . .

The Court concedes the validity of the news reporting purpose but then quickly offsets it against three purportedly countervailing considerations. First, the Court asserts that because The Nation publishes for profit, its publication of the Ford quotes is a presumptively unfair commercial use. Second, the Court claims that The Nation's stated desire to create a "news event" signalled an illegitimate purpose of supplanting the copyright owner's right of first publication. Third, The Nation acted in bad faith, the Court claims, because its editor "knowingly exploited a purloined manuscript."

The Court's reliance on the commercial nature of The Nation's use as "a separate factor that tends to weigh against a finding of fair use," is inappropriate in the present context. Many uses § 107 lists as paradigmatic examples of fair use, including criticism, comment and *news reporting,* are generally conducted for profit in this country, a fact of which Congress was obviously aware when it enacted § 107. To negate any argument favoring fair use based on news reporting or criticism because that reporting or criticism was published for profit is to render meaningless the congressional imprimatur placed on such uses.

Nor should The Nation's intent to create a "news event" weigh against a finding of fair use. Such a rule, like the Court's automatic presumption against news reporting for profit, would undermine the congressional validation of the news reporting purpose. . . . The record suggests only that The Nation sought to be the first to reveal the information in the Ford manuscript. The Nation's stated purpose of scooping the competition should under those circumstances have no negative bearing on the claim of fair use. Indeed the Court's reliance on this factor would seem to amount to little more than distaste for the standard journalistic practice of seeking to be the first to publish news.

The Court's reliance on The Nation's putative bad faith is equally unwarranted. No court has found that The Nation possessed the Ford manuscript illegally or in violation of any common law interest of Harper & Row; all common law causes of action have been abandoned or dismissed in this case. Even if the manuscript had been "purloined" by someone, nothing in this record imputes culpability to The Nation. On the basis of the record in this case, the most that can be said is that The Nation made use of the contents of the manuscript knowing the copyright owner would not sanction the use.

. . .

The Nature of the Copyrighted Work. . . .

The Court acknowledges that "[t]he law generally recognizes a greater need to disseminate factual works than works of fiction or fantasy," and that "some of the briefer quotations from the memoir are arguably necessary to convey the facts," ibid. But the Court discounts the force of this consideration, primarily on the ground that "the fact that a work is unpublished is a crucial element of its 'nature.' " At this point the Court introduces into analysis of this case a categorical presumption against prepublication fair use. ("Under ordinary circumstances, the author's right to control the first public appearance of his undisseminated expression will outweigh a claim of fair use.")

This categorical presumption is unwarranted on its own terms and unfaithful to congressional intent. Whether a particular prepublication use will impair any interest the Court identifies as encompassed within the right of first publication, will depend on the nature of the copyrighted work, the timing of prepublication use, the amount of expression used and the medium in which the second author communicates. Also, certain uses might be tolerable for some purposes and not others. . . .

. . .

The Amount and Substantiality of the Portion Used. More difficult questions arise with respect to judgments about the importance to this case of the amount and substantiality of the quotations used. . . .

. . .

At least with respect to the six particular quotes of Mr. Ford's observations and reflections about President Nixon, I agree with the Court's conclusion that The Nation appropriated some literary form of substantial quality. I do not agree, however, that the substantiality of the expression taken was clearly excessive or inappropriate to The Nation's news reporting purpose.

Had these quotations been used in the context of a critical book review of the Ford book, there is little question that such a use would be fair use within the meaning of § 107 of the Act. The amount and substantiality of the use—in both quantitative and qualitative terms— would have certainly been appropriate to the purpose of such a use. It is difficult to see how the use of these quoted words in a news report is less appropriate. . . .

. . .

The Effect on the Market. The Court correctly notes that the effect on the market "is undoubtedly the single most important element of fair use," and the Court properly focuses on whether The Nation's use adversely affected Harper & Row's serialization potential and not merely the market for sales of the Ford work itself. Unfortunately, the Court's failure to distinguish between the use of information and the appropriation of literary form badly skews its analysis of this factor.

The Nation's publication indisputably precipitated Time's eventual cancellation. But that does not mean that The Nation's use of the 300 quoted words caused this injury to Harper & Row. Wholly apart from these quoted words, The Nation published significant information and ideas from the Ford manuscript. If it was this publication of information, and not the publication of the few quotations, that caused Time to abrogate its serialization agreement, then whatever the negative effect on the serialization market, that effect was the product of wholly legitimate activity.

. . .

Balancing the Interests. Once the distinction between information and literary form is made clear, the statutorily prescribed process of weighing the four statutory fair use factors discussed above leads naturally to a conclusion that The Nation's limited use of literary form was not an infringement. . . .

III

The Court's exceedingly narrow approach to fair use permits Harper & Row to monopolize information. This holding "effect[s] an important extension of property rights and a corresponding curtailment in the free use of knowledge and of ideas." International News Service v. Associated Press, 248 U.S. at 263 (Brandeis, J. dissenting). The Court has perhaps advanced the ability of the historian—or at least the public official who has recently left office—to capture the full economic value of information in his or her possession. But the Court does so only by risking the robust debate of public issues that is the "essence of self-government." Garrison v. Louisiana, 379 U.S., at 74–75. The Nation was providing the grist for that robust debate. The Court imposes liability upon The Nation for no other reason than that The Nation succeeded in being the first to provide certain information to the public. I dissent.

Notes and Questions

1. How would the analysis change if *The Nation's* article had appeared a week after the book was published? A week after the *Time* publication?

2. During the oral argument counsel for *The Nation* asserted that "There are two words to describe what *The Nation* was doing: news reporting." Does the majority accept that view?

3. Although most commentators have concluded that the 1976 statute did not change the prior law of fair use, it seems safer to consider cases

decided since then. A sampling of post–1976 fair use cases follow in the notes below.

4. In Sony Corp. v. Universal City Studios, Inc., 464 U.S. 417 (1984), discussed in more detail later in this chapter, the Court, 5–4, held that home recording of broadcast television programs constitutes a fair use. "[A]lthough every commercial use of copyrighted material is presumptively an unfair exploitation of the monopoly privilege," a different rule applies for noncommercial uses. Here, plaintiff must show "either that the particular use is harmful, or that if it should become widespread, it would adversely affect the potential market for the copyrighted work. Actual present harm need not be shown. . . . Nor is it necessary to show with certainty that future harm will result. What is necessary is a showing by a preponderance of the evidence that *some* meaningful likelihood of future harm exists. If the intended use is for commercial gain, that likelihood may be presumed. But if it is for a noncommercial purpose, the likelihood must be demonstrated."

Two critical findings of the trial court led the majority to deny protection. "First, Sony demonstrated a significant likelihood that substantial numbers of copyright holders who license their works for broadcast on free television would not object to having their broadcasts time-shifted by private viewers. And second, respondents failed to demonstrate that time-shifting would cause any likelihood of nonminimal harm to the potential market for, or the value of, their copyrighted works." These led the Court to conclude that time-shifting, by far the most common use of the recorders, was fair use.

5. In Pacific and Southern Co., Inc. v. Duncan, 744 F.2d 1490, 56 R.R.2d 1620, 11 Med.L.Rptr. 1135 (11th Cir.1984), certiorari denied 471 U.S. 1004 (1985), plaintiff television station WXIA–TV presented four copyrighted local news programs daily. It audiotaped and videotaped each program. It retained the audiotape and the written transcript of the program for an indefinite time; it erased the videotape after seven days. WXIA did not market clips of its own stories, though it honored requests for tapes when made.

Defendant, doing business as TV News Clips, taped the news programs of television stations and tried to sell copies of the clips to those persons or groups covered by the news reports. The copies were not copyrighted and stated "for personal use only not for rebroadcast." Defendant erased tapes after one month.

The court of appeals found a valid copyright even though the only fixed copy was defendant's. The plaintiff's tapes satisfied the requirement that the work be fixed for a period of "more than transitory duration." On the fair use question, the court turned to the four factors. The commercial nature of defendant's practices "militates quite strongly against a finding of fair use." Moreover, defendant's use "is neither productive nor creative in any way. It does not analyze the broadcast or improve it at all. . . . TV News Clips only copies and sells." Because the court treated each story on the news as a "coherent narrative," it found that the defendant had taken the entire work. The fourth factor also cut against defendant since it "uses the broadcasts for a purpose that WXIA might use for its own benefit." The potential market is undermined.

The second factor might be seen to favor defendant because of the importance to society of access to the news. "But the courts should also take care not to discourage authors from addressing important topics for fear of losing their copyright protections."

Defendant argued that every copyright must further the ends of the copyright clause and that this one did not because of WXIA's systematic destruction of videotapes. (Although the defendant treated this as a First Amendment argument, the court thought it should be addressed under fair use.) Not every copyright holder "must offer benefits to society, for the copyright is an incentive rather than a command. And, *a fortiori,* a copyright holder need not provide the most complete public access possible. WXIA provides complete access for seven days and permanent access to everything except the visual images broadcast live from within the studio. The public benefits from this creative work; therefore, enforcing the copyright statute in this case does not violate the Copyright Clause."

The court held that the district court had abused its discretion by refusing to issue an injunction after finding an infringement.

6. Note that one of the considerations in determining fair use is whether the use is of an educational nature. Clearly, however, the fact that a use is educational does not give one free license to use another's copyrighted property and to infringe on another's ability to profit from his work. Recording of broadcast programming for classroom use presents particular problems which were addressed by a committee composed of representatives from both industry and education. Committee members agreed upon a set of "Guidelines for Off–Air Recording of Broadcast Programming for Educational Purposes." Copyright L.Rep. p. 20, 157 (Dec. 30, 1981).

> 1. The guidelines were developed to apply only to off-air recording by non-profit educational institutions.
>
> 2. A broadcast program may be recorded off-air simultaneously with broadcast transmission (including simultaneous cable retransmission) and retained by a non-profit educational institution for a period not to exceed the first forty-five (45) consecutive calendar days after date of recording. Upon conclusion of such retention period, all off-air recordings must be erased or destroyed immediately. "Broadcast programs" are television programs transmitted by television stations for reception by the general public without charge.
>
> 3. Off-air recordings may be used once by individual teachers in the course of relevant teaching activities, and repeated once only when instructional reinforcement is necessary, in classrooms and similar places devoted to instruction within a single building, cluster

or campus, as well as in the homes of students receiving formalized home instruction, during the first ten (10) consecutive school days in the forty-five (45) day calendar day retention period. "School days" are school session days—not counting weekends, holidays, vacations, examination periods, or other scheduled interruptions—within the forty-five (45) calendar day retention period.

4. Off-air recordings may be made only at the request of and used by individual teachers, and may not be regularly recorded in anticipation of requests. No broadcast program may be recorded in anticipation of requests. No broadcast program may be recorded off-air more than once at the request of the same teacher, regardless of the number of times the program may be broadcast.

5. A limited number of copies may be reproduced from each off-air recording to meet the legitimate needs of teachers under these guidelines. Each such additional copy shall be subject to all provisions governing the original recording.

6. After the first ten (10) consecutive school days, off-air recordings may be used up to the end of the forty-five (45) calendar day retention period only for teacher evaluation purposes, i.e., to determine whether or not to include the broadcast program in the teaching curriculum, and may not be used in the recording institution for student exhibition or any other non-evaluation purpose without authorization.

7. Off-air recordings need not be used in their entirety, but the recorded programs may not be altered from their original content. Off-air recordings may not be physically or electronically combined or merged to constitute teaching anthologies or compilations.

8. All copies of off-air recordings must include the copyright notice on the broadcast program as recorded. Educational institutions are expected to establish appropriate control procedures to maintain the integrity of these guidelines.

7. An appellate court ruled in 1993 that the book *Welcome to Twin Peaks* was *not* a fair use of the scripts for the television series "Twin Peaks." The book told plot details of the series. The court upheld a copyright infringement judgment but vacated a trademark infringement judgment. The court said that any finding of confusion between the parties' use of "Twin Peaks" must be particularly compelling. Twin Peaks Productions, Inc. v. Publications International Ltd., 996 F.2d 1366, 21 Med.L.Rptr. 1545 (2d Cir.1993).

8. The Supreme Court of the United States held in 1994 that Rapper Luther Campbell's parody of the late Roy Orbison's song "Oh, Pretty Woman" in "Pretty Woman" by the rap group "2 Live Crew," *may* be a fair use. The U.S. Court of Appeals for the Sixth Circuit had previously ruled that the parody was *not* a fair use, emphasizing the "wholly commercial" nature of the parody. Writing for all nine Supreme Court justices, David Souter said that, "The language of the [copyright] statute

makes clear that the commercial or nonprofit educational purpose of a work is only one element of the first factor enquiry into its purpose and character." He quoted Samuel Johnson's admonition that "no man but a blockhead ever wrote, except for money." Justice Souter found that, although the commercial use weighed against a finding of fair use, the other three factors must be considered. He found the second factor, "the nature of the copyrighted work," to be "not much help in this case, or ever likely to help much in separating the fair use sheep from the infringing goats in a parody case, since parodies almost invariably copy publicly known, expressive works." He thought the court of appeals had been "insufficiently appreciative of parody's need for recognizable sight or sound," and that market harm could not be readily inferred. Accordingly, the Supreme Court reversed the judgment of the court of appeals and remanded the case for further proceedings to determine if Campbell used too much of the original work and to evaluate the effect of the parody on the copyright holder's potential profits. Campbell v. Acuff–Rose Music Inc., 510 U.S. 569, 114 S.Ct. 1164, 22 Med.L.Rptr. 1353 (1994). No further proceedings had been reported as of April 1999.

9.   In 1986 Congress passed the Electronic Communications Privacy Act prohibiting unauthorized interception of network satellite feeds—and thus providing another kind of protection for the creators of works transmitted by electronic means. See discussion of the Electronic Communications Privacy Act in Chapter XIV.

10.   Controversy over the alteration of Hollywood films involves difficult questions over what can be done to copyrighted works once they have been sold. Beginning in the 1980s, "colorization" of old black and white films, some of them classics, and the compression of films (speeding them up almost imperceptibly) in order to shorten their showing time (and thus allow more time for television commercials) brought about charges of "desecration" of such films as "The Sound of Music" and "High Noon." Although some lobbyists favored legislation that would have disallowed the showing of films under their original titles if they had been altered, only limited protection—labeling on video copies of altered films saying they have been altered—was included when Congress passed The National Film Preservation Act of 1988, 2 U.S.C.A. §§ 178–178L. Three years later the Film Disclosure Act was proposed in Congress to requiring labeling of all movies "materially altered" for the home video market, commercial exhibition or for transmission over cable, satellite or broadcast television, but it was never enacted. Opponents argued that labeling could hurt the video business and discourage the showing of movies on television.

11.   The widely-shown videotape of truck driver Reginald Denny being attacked at the beginning of the 1992 Los Angeles riots was the subject of two cases that tested the limits of fair use for news purposes. Bob Tur, owner of Los Angeles News Service (LANS) taped the attack from a helicopter. LANS copyrighted the videotaped and licensed it to the media. KCAL–TV asked LANS for a license but was refused. KCAL obtained a copy of the tape from another station and broadcast it several

times. LANS sued for copyright infringement. A federal district court granted summary judgment for KCAL, holding that the use was a fair use, but the court of appeals reversed—pointing out that KCAL "rode LANS' copyrighted coattails" by not paying for the tape or investing in its own helicopter. The station did not credit LANS either, and, in fact, put its own logo on the tape. Los Angeles News Service v. KCAL–TV Channel 9, 108 F.3d 1119, 25 Med.L.Rptr. 1506 (9th Cir.1997). The parties settled.

In another case relating to the same tape, LANS sued Reuters, which admitted to providing the video to foreign subscribers without authorization on at least 1,200 occasions. A federal district court held that the transmissions of the tapes to other countries did not violate the 1976 Copyright Act because the transmissions were not completed until they were received aboard, so they did not constitute domestic infringements within the reach of U.S. copyright law. The court of appeals reversed, holding that the infringement took place when copying took place in New York to send the tapes around the world. And, the court of appeals affirmed the trial judge's analysis of the fair use, deciding that three of the four fair use factors favored LANS because the infringing uses were commercial, they took the heart of the work, and they negatively impacted the market for LANS' videotape. Los Angeles News Service v. Reuters Television International, 149 F.3d 987, 26 Med. L.Rptr. 2001 (1998). The Supreme Court denied *certiorari*, 525 U.S. 1141 (1999).

C. MUSIC LICENSING

The frequent use of copyrighted musical works by the electronic media requires special treatment. It would be difficult for individual music composers and performers to police the use of their own works, so performing rights societies have been organized for the protection of copyright holders. The groups include the American Society of Composers, Authors and Publishers (ASCAP), Broadcast Media, Inc. (BMI) and SESAC, Inc. (formerly the Society of European State Authors and Composers).

Getting permission to use copyrighted music is especially complicated. One must be concerned with both synchronization rights and performance rights. Synchronization rights allow the combining of the copyrighted music with a video to create a single work. Performance rights allow one to show the video work to others.

Whether you need to obtain the performance rights as well as the synchronization rights depends how you intend to use your video piece. If you intend to show it on broadcast television, performance rights are unnecessary. Because of the practical realities of the licensing system, broadcasters have little or no choice but to obtain blanket licenses from the major licensing societies. This means the broadcaster must either pay for a blanket license giving the right to all music licensed by that organization or refrain from using any material licensed by that organization. Even if the material is supplied by a network or syndicator and that supplier has rights to the material, the broadcaster must have the blanket license.

Thus, because the broadcaster has obtained the performing rights for almost any copyrighted piece of music, you will not need to obtain them. If you do the synchronizing, however, you must still obtain these rights.

This licensing scheme has survived several legal challenges, one of them in the case below. Performance and synchronization rights can be obtained either from the individual authors or from music licensing organizations. If you plan to use a record, the label will designate which organization (BMI, ASCAP or SESAC) licenses that piece of music.

The following case illustrates some of the music licensing problems.

BUFFALO BROADCASTING COMPANY, INC. v. AMERICAN SOCIETY OF COMPOSERS, AUTHORS AND PUBLISHERS

United States Court of Appeals, Second Circuit, 1984.744 F.2d 917.
Certiorari denied 469 U.S. 1211, 105 S.Ct. 1181, 84 L.Ed.2d 329 (1985).

JON O. NEWMAN, CIRCUIT JUDGE:

Once again we consider the lawfulness under section 1 of the Sherman Antitrust Act of the blanket license offered by the American Society of Composers, Authors and Publishers (ASCAP) and Broadcast Music, Inc. (BMI). The license permits the licensee to perform publicly any musical composition in the repertory of the licensor. In this litigation the blanket license is challenged by a class of licensees comprising all owners of "local" television stations in the United States, i.e., stations not owned by any of the three major television networks, ABC, CBS, and NBC. After a bench trial . . . the blanket license was held to be an unreasonable restraint of trade. [ ] ASCAP and BMI were enjoined from licensing to local television stations non-dramatic music performing rights for any "syndicated" program. For reasons that follow, we conclude that the evidence was insufficient as a matter of law to show that the blanket license is an unlawful restraint of trade in the legal and factual context in which it currently exists. We therefore reverse the judgment of the District Court.

Background

I. The Parties

The five named plaintiffs own and operate one or more local television stations. They represent a class of owners of local television stations in the United States who obtain music performing rights pursuant to license agreements with ASCAP and/or BMI. The class does not include the three major television networks, ABC, CBS, and NBC, each of which owns five television stations. The class includes approximately

450 owners who, because of multiple holdings, own approximately 750 local television stations. . . .

Defendant ASCAP is an unincorporated membership association of composers, authors, and publishers of music, formed in 1914. It has approximately 21,000 writer and 8,000 publisher members. It holds non-exclusive licenses for the non-dramatic performing rights to more than three million musical compositions. BMI is a non-profit corporation organized in 1939 by radio broadcasters. It has approximately 38,000 writer and 22,000 publisher affiliates. Its repertory, for which it holds non-exclusive licenses for non-dramatic performing rights, includes more than one million compositions. The eleven individual defendants represent two classes of defendants that include all persons from whom ASCAP and BMI have obtained the non-exclusive right to license non-dramatic music performing rights to others.

II.   Music, Rights, and Licenses

The subject matter of this litigation is music transmitted by television stations to their viewer-listeners. Television music is classified as either theme, background, or feature. Theme music is played at the start or conclusion of a program and serves to enhance the identification of the program. Background music accompanies portions of the program to heighten interest, underscore the mood, change the pace, or otherwise contribute to the overall effect of the program. Feature music is a principal focus of audience attention, such as a popular song sung on a variety show.

More particularly, we are concerned with the licensing of non-dramatic performing rights to copyrighted music, that is, the right to "perform" the music publicly by transmitting it, whether live or on film or tape, to television audiences.[1] This performance right is created by the Copyright Act as one of the exclusive rights enjoyed by the copyright owner. 17 U.S.C.A. § 106(4) (1982). Also pertinent to this litigation is the so-called synchronization right, or "synch" right, that is, the right to reproduce the music onto the soundtrack of a film or a videotape in synchronization with the action. The "synch" right is a form of the reproduction right also created by statute as one of the exclusive rights enjoyed by the copyright owner. Id. § 101.

Music performed by local television stations is selected in one of three ways. It may be selected by the station itself, or by the producer of a program that is sold to the station, or by a performer spontaneously. The stations select music for the relatively small portion of the program day devoted to locally produced programs. The vast majority of music aired by television stations is selected by the producers of programs supplied to the stations. In some instances these producers are the major

---

1. A non-dramatic performing right is the right to perform a musical composition other than in a dramatic performance, which the ASCAP blanket license defines as "a performance of a musical composition on a television program in which there is a definite plot depicted by action and where the performance of the musical composition is woven into and carries forward the plot and its accompanying action." See *3 Nimmer on Copyright* § 10.10[E] (1984).

television networks, but this litigation is not concerned with the performing rights to music on programs supplied to the local stations by the major networks because the networks have blanket licenses from ASCAP and BMI and convey performing rights to local stations when they supply network programs. Apart from network-produced programs, the producers of programs for local stations are "syndicators" supplying the stations with "syndicated" programs. Most syndicated programs are feature length movies or one-hour or half-hour films or videotapes produced especially for television viewing by motion picture studios, their television production affiliates, or independent television program producers. However, the definition of "syndicated program" that was stipulated to by the parties also includes live, non-network television programs offered for sale or license to local stations.[2] These syndicated programs are the central focus of this litigation. The third category of selected music, songs chosen spontaneously by a performer, accounts for a very small percentage of the music aired by the stations. These spontaneous selections of music can occur on programs produced either locally or by the networks or by syndicators.

Syndicators wishing to include music in their programs may either select pre-existing music (sometimes called "outside" music) or hire a composer to compose original music (sometimes called "inside" music). Most music on syndicated programs, up to 90% by plaintiffs' estimate, is inside music commissioned through the use of composer-for-hire agreements between the producer and either the composer alone or the composer and a corporation entitled to contract for a loan of the composer's services. Composer-for-hire agreements are normally standard form contracts. The salary paid to the composer, sometimes called "up front money," varies considerably from a few hundred dollars to several thousand dollars. The producer for whom a "work made for hire" was composed is considered by the Act to be the author and, unless the producer and composer have otherwise agreed, owns "all of the rights comprised in the copyright." [ ] However, composer-for-hire agreements for syndicated television programs typically provide that the producer assigns to the composer and to a music publishing company the performing right to the music composed pursuant to the agreement.[3]

When the producer wishes to use outside music in a film or videotape program, it must obtain from the copyright producer the "synch" right in order to record the music on the soundtrack of the film or tape. "Synch" rights vary in price, usually within a range of $150 to $500. When the producer wishes to use inside music, as is normally the case, it need not obtain the "synch" right because it already owns this right by virtue of the "work made for hire" provision of the Act.

---

2. The stipulation defines "syndicated program" as "a theatrical motion picture, pre-recorded television program or live television program which is offered for sale or license to a television station to be broadcast by that station as a non-network program."

3. The assignment of performing rights from the producer to the composer and publishing company is typically not an assignment of all performing rights, but the exceptions are not pertinent to this litigation.

Whether the producer decides to use outside or inside music, it need not acquire the television performing right since neither the making of the program nor the selling of the program to a television station is a "performance" of the music that would require a performing right. The producer is therefore free either to sell the program without the performing right and leave it to the station to obtain that right, or to obtain the performing right from the copyright proprietor, usually the composer and a publishing company, and convey that music performing right to the station along with the performing rights to all other copyrighted components of the program. If the producer obtains the music performing right from the copyright proprietor and conveys it to the station, the transaction is known as "source licensing" or "clearance at the source." If the station obtains the music right directly from the copyright proprietor, the transaction is known as "direct licensing."

The typical arrangement whereby local television stations acquire music performing rights in syndicated and all other programs is neither source licensing nor direct licensing. Instead, the stations obtain from ASCAP and BMI a blanket license permitting television performance of all of the music in the repertories of these organizations. The license is conveyed for a fee normally set as a percentage of the station's revenue. That fee, after deduction of administrative expenses, is distributed to the copyright proprietors on a basis that roughly reflects the extent of use of the music and the size of the audience for which the station "performed" the music. The royalty distribution is normally divided equally between the composer and the music publishing company.

In addition to offering stations a blanket license, ASCAP and BMI also offer a modified form of the blanket license known as a "program" or "per program" license. The program license conveys to the station the music performing rights to all of the music in the ASCAP or BMI repertory for use on the particular program for which the license is issued. The fee for a program license is a percent of the revenue derived by the station from the particular program, i.e., the advertising dollars paid to sponsor the program.

The blanket license contains a "carve-out" provision exempting from the base on which the license fee is computed the revenue derived by the station from any program presented by motion picture or transcription for which music performing rights have been licensed at the source by the licensor, i.e., ASCAP or BMI. The program license contains a more generous version of this provision, extending the exemption to music performing rights licensed at the source *either* by ASCAP/BMI *or* by the composer and publisher. Thus, for film and videotaped syndicated programs, a station can either obtain a blanket license for all of its music performing rights and reduce its fee for those programs licensed at the source by ASCAP/BMI, or obtain program licenses for each of its programs that use copyrighted music and avoid the fee for those programs licensed at the source by either ASCAP/BMI or by the composers and publishers.

III. Prior Litigation

[The opinion recounted previous litigation concerning the licensing of music performing rights back to a 1941 antitrust suit brought against ASCAP and BMI. That suit was settled by consent decrees that imposed some limitations on ASCAP and BMI but permitted them to obtain exclusive licenses for music performing rights from their members and affiliates. The consent decree was amended in 1950; there were suits in 1951 and 1961. CBS sued ASCAP in 1969, challenging the legality of blanket licenses taken by local television stations from ASCAP and BMI. The Supreme Court eventually held that the blanket license was not a *per se* violation of § 1 of the Sherman Anti–Trust Act, BMI, Inc. v. CBS, Inc., 441 U.S. 1 (1979). On remand, the United States Court of Appeals for the Second Circuit agreed that the blanket license had not been proven to be a restraint of trade. CBS, Inc. v. ASCAP, 620 F.2d 930 (2d Cir.1980), certiorari denied 450 U.S. 970 (1981) which the opinion subsequently refers to as "*CBS-remand.*" The local stations began this litigation in 1978.]

. . . We think the initial and, as it turns out, dispositive issue on the merits is whether the blanket licensing of performing rights to the local television stations has been proven to be a restraint of trade. [ ] Arguably the answer is *a fortiori* after the Supreme Court's decision and our decision on remand in the CBS litigation. The Supreme Court noted that "the necessity for and advantages of a blanket license for [television and radio networks] may be far less obvious than is the case when the potential users are individual television or radio stations. . . ." 441 U.S. at 21 [ ]. And on remand we upheld the blanket license against the claim of a network. However, for several reasons, it does not follow that the local stations lose simply because the CBS network lost. First, the Supreme Court's observation concerned the relative pro-competitive effects of the blanket license for a network compared to local stations. Even though the pro-competitive effects may be greater when the licensees are local stations, those pro-competitive effects do not necessarily outweigh the anti-competitive effects. Second, the Supreme Court's comparative statement does not determine the threshold issue of whether the blanket licensing of performing rights to local television stations is a restraint at all. The fact that CBS did not prove that blanket licensing of networks restrained competition does not necessarily mean that blanket licensing of local stations may not be shown to be a restraint. Finally, in *CBS-remand* we reviewed the District Judge's ruling that no restraint had been proved; here, we review a ruling that the local stations proved the existence of a restraint.

. . .

In reaching the conclusion that plaintiffs had proven the lack of realistically available alternatives to the blanket license, Judge Gagliardi gave separate consideration to three possibilities: the program license, . . . direct licensing, and source licensing. We consider each in turn.

Program License. Judge Gagliardi based his conclusion that a program license is not realistically available to the plaintiffs essentially on two circumstances: the cost of a program license and the reporting requirements that such a license imposes on a licensee. "The court therefore concludes that the per program license is too costly and burdensome to be a realistic alternative to the blanket license." [ ] Without rejecting any subsidiary factual finding concerning the availability of a program license, we reject the legal conclusion that it is not a realistic alternative to the blanket license.

. . .

. . . [T]he only valid test of whether the program license is "too costly" to be a realistic alternative is whether the price for such a license, in an objective sense, is higher than the value of the rights obtained. But plaintiffs presented no evidence that the price of the program license is "high" in terms of value received. . . .

. . .

. . . The fact that very few stations have elected to take program licenses is not evidence that they are priced beyond an objectively reasonable price range. It may simply reflect, as defendants believe, that the blanket license has virtues of convenience that make it a legitimate object of customer preference.

. . .

[The conclusion that the program license is not realistically available because of the burdens of required record-keeping that accompany its use] is similarly flawed by the lack of evidence. . . .

. . .

Direct Licensing. The District Court concluded that direct licensing is not a realistic alternative to the blanket license without any evidence that any local station ever offered any composer a sum of money in exchange for the performing rights to his music. . . . Judge Gagliardi concluded . . . that direct licensing could not occur without the intervention of some agency to broker the numerous transactions. . . . We have no quarrel with [that] proposition. . . .

However, we see no evidentiary support for the . . . proposition . . . that no one would undertake the brokering function for direct licensing. . . .

Source Licensing. As Judge Gagliardi noted, the "current availability and comparative efficiency of source licensing have been the focus of this lawsuit." [ ] The availability of source licensing is significant to the inquiry as to whether the blanket license is a restraint because so much of the stations' programming consists of syndicated programs for which the producer could, if so inclined, convey music performing rights. Most of these syndicated programs use composer-for-hire music. As to such music, the producer starts out with the rights of the copyright, including the performing right, by operation of law, 17 U.S.C. § 201(b), unless the hiring agreement otherwise provides. Thus it becomes important to determine whether the stations can obtain from the producer the music performing right, along with all of the other rights in a syndicated program that are conveyed to the stations when the program is licensed. . . .

. . .

Judge Gagliardi properly declined to give any probative weight to the plaintiffs' transparent effort to assemble in the midst of litigation evidence that they had seriously tried to obtain source licensing. . . . Nevertheless the District Court concluded that source was not a realistic alternative. . . . [But we conclude that plaintiffs have simply failed to produce sufficient evidence to support a conclusion that the blanket license is a restraint of trade.]

. . .

The Claimed Lack of Necessity. Plaintiffs earnestly advance the argument that the blanket license, as applied to syndicated programming, should be declared unlawful for the basic reason that it is unnecessary. In their view, the blanket license is suspect because, where it is used, no price competition occurs among songs when those who need performing rights decide which songs to perform. The resulting absence of price competition, plaintiffs urge, is justifiable only in some contexts such as night clubs, live and locally produced programming of television stations, and radio stations, which make more spontaneous choices of music than do television stations.

There are two fundamental flaws in this argument. First, it has not been shown on this record that the blanket license, even as applied to syndicated television programs, is not necessary. If all the plaintiffs mean is that a judicial ban on blanket licensing for syndicated television programs would not halt performance of copyrighted music on such programs and that some arrangement for the purchase of performing rights would replace the blanket license, we can readily agree. . . . But a licensing system may be "necessary" in the practical sense that it is far superior to other alternatives in efficiency. . . .

. . .

. . . Even if the evidence showed that most of the efficiencies of the blanket license could be achieved under source licensing, it would not follow that the blanket license thereby becomes unlawful. . . .

. . . [W]e hold that the local television stations have not presented evidence in this case permitting a conclusion that the blanket license is a restraint of trade in violation of section 1.

The judgment of the District Court is therefore reversed.

[Judge Winter wrote a separate opinion, concurring.]

Notes and Questions

1. If the court of appeals had upheld the district court ruling that ASCAP and BMI blanket licenses to local television stations constituted an unreasonable restraint of trade under section 1 of the Sherman Anti-Trust Act, the performing societies could have lost $80 million in annual local television performing rights revenues. That represented about 25 percent of the performing rights societies' total annual revenues. The Entertainment and Sports Lawyer, Winter 1985 at 10.

2. Do you agree with the court of appeals' conclusion that there was no violation of the Sherman Act, or would you be more inclined to agree with the district court? Does it seem reasonable to conclude that direct licensing and source licensing are viable alternatives to blanket licensing just because the plaintiffs had been unable to prove that they were not?

3. The playing of music in stores and restaurants has been the subject of several suits—partially because of the issue of whether playing the radio constitutes a performance.

The Supreme Court addressed the issue in Twentieth Century Music Corp. v. Aiken, 422 U.S. 151 (1975). The owner of a fast-service food shop in Pittsburgh ("George Aiken's Chicken") was sued for copyright infringement because he played a radio with four ceiling speakers in his shop each day. The plaintiffs complained that their copyrighted musical compositions were being "performed," but the Supreme Court held the opposite, noting the "practical unenforceability" of a ruling that businesses that do what Aiken did are copyright infringers.

Subsequent cases sometimes yielded different results, but Congress eventually addressed the issue. The Fairness in Music Licensing Act, passed simultaneously with the 1998 term extensions, p. 799, *supra* (giving the act the lengthy full name of the Sonny Bono Term Extension Fairness in Music Licensing Act) created an exemption for restaurants and small businesses that previously had to pay ASCAP, BMI, and other music licensing organizations for the privilege of playing the radio on their premises. The exemption applies to bars and restaurants of less than 3,750 square feet and retail stores of less than 2,000 square feet (such as mall boutique shops). In theory, copyright holders lost royalties by creation of the exemption but gained royalties by the term extension—thus the rationale for addressing the two issues in the same legislation.

4. The National Cable Television Association, Community Antenna Television Association and the Disney Channel filed suit in 1990 against BMI alleging antitrust violations. The plaintiffs said that the cable industry and its members confront "a cartelized industry in which non-negotiable demands for license fees and terms have been made by the cartel" and are "enforced through punitive copyright infringement litigation." The suit challenged the 50-year practice by BMI of granting, for a price, blanket licenses for public performance of the works of the

composers and publishers it represents. In other litigation, American Television & Communications and 16 other cable companies sued BMI and nine affiliates, alleging Sherman Antitrust Act violations. They alleged that BMI and its members are succeeding "in their anticompetitive scheme because of the monopolistic and illegal stranglehold" that they have on the performance rights to music. BMI countersued. The U.S. District Court for the District of Columbia decided in 1991 that the Disney Channel and Black Entertainment Television had infringed BMI's copyrights and levied a judgment of $1.98 million against the Disney Channel and $225,000 against BET. National Cable Television Association, Inc. v. Broadcast Music, Inc., 772 F.Supp. 614 (D.D.C.1991). The Disney Channel and Black Entertainment subsequently reached new licensing agreements with BMI. Billboard, Dec. 14, 1991 at 75.

D. PROBLEMS OF NEW TECHNOLOGIES

Perhaps the biggest problem Congress faced in drafting the Copyright Act of 1976 was providing for new technologies. The courts and Congress have faced difficult questions concerning the application of copyright law to a variety of technologies never envisioned with the Copyright Act of 1909 was passed. Recall from Chapter VIII, for example, discussion of cable television's liability for the retransmission of broadcast television programing. A wide range of other issues is suggested below.

1. VIDEOTAPE RECORDING

In Sony Corp. v. Universal City Studios, Inc., p. 818, *supra,* the Court, held 5–4, that the use of videotape recorders did not infringe the copyrights of the producers of the programs that were copied. The majority began by noting that the "monopoly privileges that Congress may authorize are neither unlimited nor primarily designed to provide a special private benefit. Rather, the limited grant is a means by which an important public purpose may be achieved. It is intended to motivate the creative activity of authors and inventors by the provision of a special reward, and to allow the public access to the products of their genius after the limited period of exclusive control has expired."

The Court also observed that the clause assigned Congress the primary responsibility for defining the scope of protection. "Because the task involves a difficult balance between the interests of authors and inventors in the control and exploitation of their writings and discoveries on the one hand, and society's competing interest in the free flow of ideas, information, and commerce on the other hand, our patent and copyright statutes have been amended repeatedly."

In this case, dealing with a new technology, the majority stressed that the "judiciary's reluctance to expand the protections afforded by the copyright without explicit legislative guidance is a recurring theme. [　] Sound policy, as well as history, supports our consistent deference to

Congress when major technological innovations alter the market for copyrighted materials."

. . .

2. USE OF COPYRIGHTED MATERIALS ON THE INTERNET

Inevitably, the courts and Congress have been dealing too with questions about intellectual property rights in cyberspace. In some cases, courts have considered alleged copyright infringements relating to text or photographs on the Internet. For example, the operator of a subscription bulletin board service was found to have infringed *Playboy*'s copyright and trademarks when subscribers to the service downloaded photographs from the copyrighted magazines. The court held the downloading was not a fair use. Playboy Enterprises Inc. v. Frena, 839 F.Supp. 1552, 22 Med.L.Rptr. 1301 (M.D.Fla.1993).

However, the Digital Millennium Copyright Act of 1998, p. 801, *supra*, now spells out detailed provisions as to when Internet service providers must remove materials that allegedly infringe copyrights in order to maintain an immunity from liability. The ISP is exempt from liability if it expeditiously removes or disables access to such material. There are specific requirements for notification and authorization to act on behalf of the complaining party, so the rights of the party who posted the material and the rights of the complaining party are both taken into consideration. (In the next chapter, we will consider whether ISPs are responsible for libelous material on their systems.)

The legal battle over the popular Internet music file-sharing site Napster attracted much news attention to the issue of distribution of copyrighted music over the Internet. The Recording Industry Association of America sued Napster on behalf of the major record companies claiming that its users were "exchanging pirated music."

A & M RECORDS, INC. v. NAPSTER, INC.

United States Court of Appeals for the Ninth Circuit, 2001
239 F.3d 1004.

Before SCHROEDER, CHIEF JUDGE, ROBERT R. BEEZER and RICHARD A. PAEZ, CIRCUIT JUDGES.

BEEZER, CIRCUIT JUDGE:

Plaintiffs are engaged in the commercial recording, distribution and sale of copyrighted musical compositions and sound recordings. The complaint alleges that Napster, Inc. ("Napster") is a contributory and vicarious copyright infringer. On July 26, 2000, the district court granted plaintiffs' motion for a preliminary injunction. The injunction was slightly modified by written opinion on August 10, 2000. [ ] The district court preliminarily enjoined Napster "from engaging in, or facilitating others in copying, downloading, uploading, transmitting, or distributing plaintiffs' copyrighted musical compositions and sound recordings, protected by either federal or state law, without express permission of the rights owner." [ ] Federal Rule of Civil Procedure 65(c) requires successful plaintiffs to post a bond for damages incurred by the enjoined party in the event that the injunction was wrongfully issued. The district court set bond in this case at $5 million.

We entered a temporary stay of the preliminary injunction pending resolution of this appeal. We have jurisdiction pursuant to 28 U.S.C. § 1292(a)(1). We affirm in part, reverse in part and remand.

I

We have examined the papers submitted in support of and in response to the injunction application and it appears that Napster has designed and operates a system which permits the transmission and retention of sound recordings employing digital technology.

In 1987, the Moving Picture Experts Group set a standard file format for the storage of audio recordings in a digital format called MPEG–3, abbreviated as "MP3." Digital MP3 files are created through a process colloquially called "ripping." Ripping software allows a computer owner to copy an audio compact disk ("audio CD") directly onto a computer's hard drive by compressing the audio information on the CD into the MP3 format. The MP3's compressed format allows for rapid transmission of digital audio files from one computer to another by electronic mail or any other file transfer protocol.

Napster facilitates the transmission of MP3 files between and among its users. Through a process commonly called "peer-to-peer" file sharing, Napster allows its users to: (1) make MP3 music files stored on individual computer hard drives available for copying by other Napster users; (2) search for MP3 music files stored on other users' computers; and (3) transfer exact copies of the contents of other users' MP3 files from one computer to another via the Internet. These functions are made possible by Napster's MusicShare software, available free of charge from Napster's Internet site, and Napster's network servers and server-side software. Napster provides technical support for the indexing and searching of MP3 files, as well as for its other functions, including a "chat room," where users can meet to discuss music, and a directory where participating artists can provide information about their music.

A. Accessing the System

In order to copy MP3 files through the Napster system, a user must first access Napster's Internet site and download . . . the MusicShare software to his individual computer. See http://www. Napster. com. Once the software is installed, the user can access the Napster system. A first-time user is required to register with the Napster system by creating a "user name" and password.

B. Listing Available Files

If a registered user wants to list available files stored in his computer's hard drive on Napster for others to access, he must first create a "user library" directory on his computer's hard drive. The user then saves his MP3 files in the library directory, using self-designated file names. He next must log into the Napster system using his user name and password. His MusicShare software then searches his user library and verifies that the available files are properly formatted. If in the correct MP3 format, the names of the MP3 files will be uploaded from the user's computer to the Napster servers. The content of the MP3 files remains stored in the user's computer.

Once uploaded to the Napster servers, the user's MP3 file names are stored in a server-side "library" under the user's name and become part of a "collective directory" of files available for transfer during the time the user is logged onto the Napster system. The collective directory is fluid; it tracks users who are connected in real time, displaying only file names that are immediately accessible.

C.   Searching For Available Files

Napster allows a user to locate other users' MP3 files in two ways: through Napster's search function and through its "hotlist" function.

Software located on the Napster servers maintains a "search index" of Napster's collective directory. To search the files available from Napster users currently connected to the net-work servers, the individual user accesses a form in the MusicShare software stored in his computer and enters either the name of a song or an artist as the object of the search. The form is then transmitted to a Napster server and automatically compared to the MP3 file names listed in the server's search index. Napster's server compiles a list of all MP3 file names pulled from the search index which include the same search terms entered on the search form and transmits the list to the searching user. The Napster server does not search the contents of any MP3 file; rather, the search is limited to "a text search of the file names indexed in a particular cluster. Those file names may contain typographical errors or otherwise inaccurate descriptions of the content of the files since they are designated by other users." [   ]

To use the "hotlist" function, the Napster user creates a list of other users' names from whom he has obtained MP3 files in the past. When logged onto Napster's servers, the system alerts the user if any user on his list (a "hotlisted user") is also logged onto the system. If so, the user can access an index of all MP3 file names in a particular hotlisted user's library and request a file in the library by selecting the file name. The contents of the hotlisted user's MP3 file are not stored on the Napster system.

D.   Transferring Copies of an MP3 file

To transfer a copy of the contents of a requested MP3 file, the Napster server software obtains the Internet address of the requesting user and the Internet address of the "host user" (the user with the available files). [   ] The Napster servers then communicate the host user's Internet address to the requesting user. The requesting user's computer uses this information to establish a connection with the host user and downloads a copy of the contents of the MP3 file from one computer to the other over the Internet, "peer-to-peer." A downloaded MP3 file can be played directly from the user's hard drive using Napster's Music–Share program or other software. The file may also be transferred back onto an audio CD if the user has access to equipment designed for that purpose. In both cases, the quality of the original sound recording is slightly diminished by transfer to the MP3 format.

This architecture is described in some detail to promote an understanding of transmission mechanics as opposed to the content of the transmissions. The content is the subject of our copyright infringement analysis.

II

We review a grant or denial of a preliminary injunction for abuse of discretion. [　] Application of erroneous legal principles represents an abuse of discretion by the district court. [　] If the district court is claimed to have relied on an erroneous legal premise in reaching its decision to grant or deny a preliminary injunction, we will review the underlying issue of law de novo. [　]

On review, we are required to determine, "whether the court employed the appropriate legal standards governing the issuance of a preliminary injunction and whether the district court correctly apprehended the law with respect to the underlying issues in the case." [　] "As long as the district court got the law right, 'it will not be reversed simply because the appellate court would have arrived at a different result if it had applied the law to the facts of the case.' " [　]

Preliminary injunctive relief is available to a party who demonstrates either: (1) a combination of probable success on the merits and the possibility of irreparable harm; or (2) that serious questions are raised and the balance of hardships tips in its favor. [　]. "These two formulations represent two points on a sliding scale in which the required degree of irreparable harm increases as the probability of success decreases." [　]

III

Plaintiffs claim Napster users are engaged in the wholesale reproduction and distribution of copyrighted works, all constituting direct infringement. . . . The district court agreed. We note that the district court's conclusion that plaintiffs have presented a prima facie case of direct infringement by Napster users is not presently appealed by Napster. We only need briefly address the threshold requirements.

A. Infringement

Plaintiffs must satisfy two requirements to present a prima facie case of direct infringement: (1) they must show ownership of the allegedly infringed material and (2) they must demonstrate that the alleged infringers violate at least one exclusive right granted to copyright holders under 17 U.S.C. § 106. [   ] Plaintiffs have sufficiently demonstrated ownership. The record supports the district court's determination that "as much as eighty-seven percent of the files available on Napster may be copyrighted and more than seventy percent may be owned or administered by plaintiffs." [   ]

The district court further determined that plaintiffs' exclusive rights under § 106 were violated: "here the evidence establishes that a majority of Napster users use the service to download and upload copyrighted music. . . . And by doing that, it constitutes—the uses constitute direct infringement of plaintiffs' musical compositions, recordings." [   ] The district court also noted that "it is pretty much acknowledged . . . by Napster that this is infringement." [   ] We agree that plaintiffs have shown that Napster users infringe at least two of the copyright holders' exclusive rights: the rights of reproduction, § 106(1); and distribution, 4229 § 106(3). Napster users who upload file names to the search index for others to copy violate plaintiffs' distribution rights. Napster users who download files containing copyrighted music violate plaintiffs' reproduction rights.

Napster asserts an affirmative defense to the charge that its users directly infringe plaintiffs' copyrighted musical compositions and sound recordings.

B. Fair Use

Napster contends that its users do not directly infringe plaintiffs' copyrights because the users are engaged in fair use of the material. [   ] Napster identifies three specific alleged fair uses: sampling, where users make temporary copies of a work before purchasing; space-shifting, where users access a sound recording through the Napster system that they already own in audio CD format; and permissive distribution of recordings by both new and established artists.

The district court considered factors listed in 17 U.S.C. § 107, which guide a court's fair use determination. These factors are: (1) the purpose and character of the use; (2) the nature of the copyrighted work; (3) the "amount and substantiality of the portion used" in relation to the work as a whole; and (4) the effect of the use upon the potential market for the work or the value of the work. [   ] The district court first conducted a general analysis of Napster system uses under § 107, and then applied its reasoning to the alleged fair uses identified by Napster. The district court concluded that Napster users are not fair users. . . . We agree. We first address the court's overall fair use analysis.

1. Purpose and Character of the Use

This factor focuses on whether the new work merely replaces the object of the original creation or instead adds a further purpose or different character. In other words, this factor asks "whether and to what extent the new work is 'transformative.'" [   ]

The district court first concluded that downloading MP3 files does not transform the copyrighted work. [   ] This conclusion is supportable.

Courts have been reluctant to find fair use when an original work is merely retransmitted in a different medium. [   ]

This "purpose and character" element also requires the district court to determine whether the allegedly infringing use is commercial or noncommercial. [   ] A commercial use weighs against a finding of fair use but is not conclusive on the issue. [   ] The district court determined that Napster users engage in commercial use of the copyrighted materials largely because (1) "a host user sending a file cannot be said to engage in a personal use when distributing that file to an anonymous requester" and (2) "Napster users get for free something they would ordinarily have to buy." [   ] The district court's findings are not clearly erroneous.

Direct economic benefit is not required to demonstrate a commercial use. Rather, repeated and exploitative copying of copyrighted works, even if the copies are not offered for sale, may constitute a commercial use. [   ] In the record before us, commercial use is demonstrated by a showing that repeated and exploitative unauthorized copies of copyrighted works were made to save the expense of purchasing authorized copies. [   ] Plaintiffs made such a showing before the district court. . . .

We also note that the definition of a financially motivated transaction for the purposes of criminal copyright actions includes trading infringing copies of a work for other items, "including the receipt of other copyrighted works." [   ]

2.   The Nature of the Use

Works that are creative in nature are "closer to the core of intended copyright protection" than are more fact-based works. [   ] The district court determined that plaintiffs' "copyrighted musical compositions and sound recordings are creative in nature . . . which cuts against a finding of fair use under the second factor." [   ] We find no error in the district court's conclusion.

3.   The Portion Used

"While 'wholesale copying does not preclude fair use per se,' copying an entire work 'militates against a finding of fair use.' " [   ] The district court determined that Napster users engage in "wholesale copying" of copyrighted work because file transfer necessarily "involves copying the entirety of the copyrighted work." [   ] We agree. We note, however, that under certain circumstances, a court will conclude that a use is fair even when the protected work is copied in its entirety. [   ]

4.   Effect of Use on Market

"Fair use, when properly applied, is limited to copying by others which does not materially impair the marketability of the work which is copied." [   ] The proof required to demonstrate present or future market harm varies with the purpose and character of the use: A challenge to a noncommercial use of a copy-righted work requires proof either that the particular use is harmful, or that if it should become wide-spread, it would adversely affect the potential market for the copyrighted work. . . . If the intended use is for commercial gain, that likelihood [of market harm] may be presumed. But if it is for a noncommercial purpose, the likelihood must be demonstrated. [   ]

Addressing this factor, the district court concluded that Napster harms the market in "at least" two ways: it reduces audio CD sales among college students and it "raises barriers to plaintiffs' entry into the market for the digital downloading of music." [   ] The district court relied on evidence plaintiffs submitted to show that Napster use harms the market for their copyrighted musical compositions and sound recordings. In a separate memorandum and order regarding the parties' objections to the expert reports, the district court examined each report, finding some more appropriate and probative than others. [   ] Notably, plaintiffs' expert, Dr. E. Deborah Jay, conducted a survey (the "Jay Report") using a random sample of college and university students to track their reasons for using Napster and the impact Napster had on their music purchases. [   ] The court recognized that the Jay Report focused on just one segment of the Napster user population and found "evidence of lost sales attributable to college use to be probative of irreparable harm for purposes of the preliminary injunction motion." [   ].

Plaintiffs also offered a study conducted by Michael Fine, Chief Executive Officer of Soundscan, (the "Fine Report") to determine the effect of online sharing of MP3 files in order to show irreparable harm. Fine found that online file sharing had resulted in a loss of "album" sales within college markets. After reviewing defendant's objections to the Fine Report and expressing some concerns regarding the methodology and findings, the district court refused to exclude the Fine Report insofar as plaintiffs offered it to show irreparable harm. [   ]

Plaintiffs' expert Dr. David J. Teece studied several issues ("Teece Report"), including whether plaintiffs had suffered or were likely to suffer harm in their existing and planned businesses due to Napster use. [   ]

Napster objected that the report had not undergone peer review. The district court noted that such reports generally are not subject to such scrutiny and overruled defendant's objections. [   ]

As for defendant's experts, plaintiffs objected to the report of Dr. Peter S. Fader, in which the expert concluded that Napster is beneficial to the music industry because MP3 music file-sharing stimulates more audio CD sales than it displaces. [   ] The district court found problems in Dr. Fader's minimal role in overseeing the administration of the survey and the lack of objective data in his report. The court decided the generality of the report rendered it "of dubious reliability and value." The court did not exclude the report, however, but chose "not to rely on Fader's findings in determining the issues of fair use and irreparable harm." [   ]

The district court cited both the Jay and Fine Reports in support of its finding that Napster use harms the market for plaintiffs' copyrighted musical compositions and sound recordings by reducing CD sales among college students. The district court cited the Teece Report to show the harm Napster use caused in raising barriers to plaintiffs' entry into the market for digital downloading of music. [   ] The district court's careful consideration of defendant's objections to these reports and decision to rely on the reports for specific issues demonstrates a proper exercise of discretion in addition to a correct application of the fair use doctrine. Defendant has failed to show any basis for disturbing the district court's findings.

We, therefore, conclude that the district court made sound findings related to Napster's deleterious effect on the present and future digital download market. Moreover, lack of harm to an established market cannot deprive the copyright holder of the right to develop alternative markets for the works. [ ] Here, similar to L.A. Times and UMG Recordings, the record supports the district court's finding that the "record company plaintiffs have already expended considerable funds and effort to commence Internet sales and licensing for digital downloads." [   ] Having digital downloads available for free on the Napster system necessarily harms the copyright holders' attempts to charge for the same downloads.

Judge Patel did not abuse her discretion in reaching the above fair use conclusions, nor were the findings of fact with respect to fair use considerations clearly erroneous. We next address Napster's identified uses of sampling and space-shifting.

5. Identified Uses

Napster maintains that its identified uses of sampling and space-shifting were wrongly excluded as fair uses by the district court.

a. Sampling

Napster contends that its users download MP3 files to "sample" the music in order to decide whether to purchase the recording. Napster argues that the district court: (1) erred in concluding that sampling is a commercial use because it conflated a noncommercial use with a personal use; (2) erred in determining that sampling adversely affects the market for plaintiffs' copyrighted music, a requirement if the use is noncommercial; and (3) erroneously concluded that sampling is not a fair use because it determined that samplers may also engage in other infringing activity.

The district court determined that sampling remains a commercial use even if some users eventually purchase the music. We find no error in the district court's determination. Plaintiffs have established that they are likely to succeed in proving that even authorized temporary downloading of individual songs for sampling purposes is commercial in nature. [   ] The record supports a finding that free promotional downloads are highly regulated by the record company plaintiffs and that the companies collect royalties for song samples available on retail Internet sites. [   ] Evidence relied on by the district court demonstrates that the free downloads provided by the record companies consist of thirty-to-sixty second samples or are full songs programmed to "time out," that is, exist only for a short time on the downloader's computer. [   ] In comparison, Napster users download a full, free and permanent copy of the recording. [   ] The determination by the district court as to the commercial purpose and character of sampling is not clearly erroneous.

The district court further found that both the market for audio CDs and market for online distribution are adversely affected by Napster's service. As stated in our discussion of the district court's general fair use analysis: the court did not abuse its discretion when it found that, overall, Napster has an adverse impact on the audio CD and digital download markets. Contrary to Napster's assertion that the district court failed to specifically address the market impact of sampling, the district court determined that "even if the type of sampling supposedly done on Napster were a non-commercial use, plaintiffs have demonstrated a substantial likelihood that it would adversely affect the potential market for their copy-righted works if it became widespread." [   ] The record supports the district court's preliminary determinations that: (1) the more music that sampling users download, the less likely they are to eventually purchase the recordings on audio CD; and (2) even if the audio CD market is not harmed, Napster has adverse effects on the developing digital download market.

Napster further argues that the district court erred in rejecting its evidence that the users' downloading of "samples" increases or tends to increase audio CD sales. The district court, however, correctly noted that "any potential enhancement of plaintiffs' sales . . . would not tip the fair use analysis conclusively in favor of defendant." [   ] We agree that increased sales of copyrighted material attributable to unauthorized use should not deprive the copyright holder of the right to license the material. [   ] Nor does positive impact in one market, here the audio CD market, deprive the copyright holder of the right to develop identified alternative markets, here the digital download market. [   ]

We find no error in the district court's factual findings or abuse of discretion in the court's conclusion that plaintiffs will likely prevail in establishing that sampling does not constitute a fair use.

b.   Space–Shifting

Napster also maintains that space-shifting is a fair use. Space-shifting occurs when a Napster user downloads MP3 music files in order to listen to music he already owns on audio CD. [   ] Napster asserts that we have already held that space-shifting of musical compositions and sound recordings is a fair use. [   ]

We conclude that the district court did not err when it refused to apply the "shifting" analyses of Sony and Diamond. Both Diamond and Sony are inapposite because the methods of shifting in these cases did not also simultaneously involve distribution of the copyrighted material to the general public; the time or space-shifting of copyrighted material exposed the material only to the original user. In Diamond, for example, the copyrighted music was transferred from the user's computer hard drive to the user's portable MP3 player. So too Sony, where "the majority of VCR purchasers . . . did not distribute taped television broadcasts, but merely enjoyed them at home." [   ] Conversely, it is obvious that once a user lists a copy of music he already owns on the Napster system in order to access the music from another location, the song becomes "available to millions of other individuals," not just the original CD owner. [   ]

c. Other Uses

Permissive reproduction by either independent or established artists is the final fair use claim made by Napster. The district court noted that plaintiffs did not seek to enjoin this and any other noninfringing use of the Napster system, including: chat rooms, message boards and Napster's New Artist Program. [   ] Plaintiffs do not challenge these uses on appeal.

We find no error in the district court's determination that plaintiffs will likely succeed in establishing that Napster users do not have a fair use defense. Accordingly, we next address whether Napster is secondarily liable for the direct infringement under two doctrines of copyright law: contributory copyright infringement and vicarious copyright infringement.

IV

We first address plaintiffs' claim that Napster is liable for contributory copyright infringement. Traditionally, "one who, with knowledge of the infringing activity, induces, causes or materially contributes to the infringing conduct of another, may be held liable as a 'contributory' infringer." [   ] Put differently, liability exists if the defendant engages in "personal conduct that encourages or assists the infringement." [   ]

The district court determined that plaintiffs in all likelihood would establish Napster's liability as a contributory infringer. The district court did not err; Napster, by its conduct, knowingly encourages and assists the infringement of plaintiffs' copyrights.

A. Knowledge

Contributory liability requires that the secondary infringer "know or have reason to know" of direct infringement. [   ] The district court found that Napster had both actual and constructive knowledge that its users exchanged copyrighted music. The district court also concluded that the law does not require knowledge of "specific acts of infringement" and rejected Napster's contention that because the company cannot distinguish infringing from noninfringing files, it does not "know" of the direct infringement. [   ].

It is apparent from the record that Napster has knowledge, both actual and constructive, . . . of direct infringement. Napster claims that it is nevertheless protected from contributory liability by the teaching of Sony Corp. v. Universal City Studios, Inc., [casebook, p. 732]. We disagree. We observe that Napster's actual, specific knowledge of direct infringement renders Sony's holding of limited assistance to Napster. We are compelled to make a clear distinction between the architecture of the Napster system and Napster's conduct in relation to the operational capacity of the system.

The Sony Court refused to hold the manufacturer and retailers of video tape recorders liable for contributory infringement despite evidence that such machines could be and were used to infringe plaintiffs' copyrighted television shows. Sony stated that if liability "is to be imposed on petitioners in this case, it must rest on the fact that they have sold equipment with constructive knowledge of the fact that their customers may use that equipment to make unauthorized copies of copyrighted material." Id. at 439 (emphasis added). The Sony Court declined to impute the requisite level of knowledge where the defendants made and sold equipment capable of both infringing and "substantial noninfringing uses." [   ]

We are bound to follow Sony, and will not impute the requisite level of knowledge to Napster merely because peer-to-peer file sharing technology may be used to infringe plaintiffs' copyrights. [   ] We depart from the reasoning of the district court that Napster failed to demonstrate that its system is capable of commercially significant noninfringing uses. [   ] The district court improperly confined the use analysis to current uses, ignoring the system's capabilities. [   ] Consequently, the district court placed undue weight on the proportion of current infringing use as compared to current and future noninfringing use. [   ] Nonetheless, whether we might arrive at a different result is not the issue here. [   ] The instant appeal occurs at an early point in the proceedings and "the fully developed factual record may be materially different from that initially before the district court. . . ." [   ] Regardless of the number of Napster's infringing versus noninfringing uses, the evidentiary record here supported the district court's finding that plaintiffs would likely prevail in establishing that Napster knew or had reason to know of its users' infringement of plaintiffs' copyrights.

This analysis is similar to that of Religious Technology Center v. Netcom On–Line Communication Services, Inc., which suggests that in an online context, evidence of actual knowledge of specific acts of infringement is required to hold a computer system operator liable for contributory copyright infringement. [   ] Netcom considered the potential contributory copyright liability of a computer bulletin board operator whose system supported the posting of infringing material. [   ] The court, in denying Netcom's motion for summary judgment of noninfringement and plaintiff's motion for judgment on the pleadings, found that a disputed issue of fact existed as to whether the operator had sufficient knowledge of infringing activity. [   ]

The court determined that for the operator to have sufficient knowledge, the copyright holder must "provide the necessary documentation to show there is likely infringement." [   ] If such documentation was provided, the court reasoned that Netcom would be liable for contributory infringement because its failure to remove the material "and thereby stop an infringing copy from being distributed worldwide constitutes substantial participation" in distribution of copyrighted material. [   ]

We agree that if a computer system operator learns of specific infringing material available on his system and fails to purge such material from the system, the operator knows of and contributes to direct infringement. [   ] Conversely, absent any specific information which identifies infringing activity, a computer system operator cannot be liable for contributory infringement merely because the structure of the system allows for the exchange of copyrighted material. [   ] To enjoin simply because a computer network allows for infringing use would, in our opinion, violate Sony and potentially restrict activity unrelated to infringing use.

We nevertheless conclude that sufficient knowledge exists to impose contributory liability when linked to demonstrated infringing use of the Napster system. [   ] The record supports the district court's finding that Napster has actual knowledge that specific infringing material is available using its system, that it could block access to the system by suppliers of the infringing material, and that it failed to remove the material. [   ] . . .

B. Material Contribution

Under the facts as found by the district court, Napster materially contributes to the infringing activity. Relying on Fonovisa, the district court concluded that "without the support services defendant provides, Napster users could not find and download the music they want with the ease of which defendant boasts." [   ] We agree that Napster provides "the site and facilities" for direct infringement. [   ] The district court correctly applied the reasoning in Fonovisa, and properly found that Napster materially contributes to direct infringement.

We affirm the district court's conclusion that plaintiffs have demonstrated a likelihood of success on the merits of the contributory copyright infringement claim. We will address the scope of the injunction in part VIII of this opinion.

V

We turn to the question whether Napster engages in vicarious copyright infringement. Vicarious copyright liability is an "outgrowth" of respondeat superior. [   ] In the context of copyright law, vicarious liability extends beyond an employer/employee relationship to cases in which a defendant "has the right and ability to supervise the infringing activity and also has a direct financial interest in such activities." [   ]

Before moving into this discussion, we note that Sony's "staple article of commerce" analysis has no application to Napster's potential liability for vicarious copyright infringement. [   ] The issues of Sony's liability under the "doctrines of 'direct infringement' and 'vicarious liability' " were not before the Supreme Court, although the Court recognized that the "lines between direct infringement, contributory infringement, and vicarious liability are not clearly drawn." [   ] Consequently, when the Sony Court used the term "vicarious liability," it did so broadly and outside of a technical analysis of the doctrine of vicarious copyright infringement. [   ]

A. Financial Benefit

The district court determined that plaintiffs had demonstrated they would likely succeed in establishing that Napster has a direct financial interest in the infringing activity. [   ] We agree. Financial benefit exists where the availability of infringing material "acts as a 'draw' for customers." [   ] Ample evidence supports the district court's finding that Napster's future revenue is directly dependent upon "increases in user-base." More users register with the Napster system as the "quality and quantity of available music increases." [   ] We conclude that the district court did not err in determining that Napster financially benefits from the availability of protected works on its system.

B. Supervision

The district court determined that Napster has the right and ability to supervise its users' conduct. [   ] We agree in part.

The ability to block infringers' access to a particular environment for any reason whatsoever is evidence of the right and ability to supervise. [   ] Here, plaintiffs have demonstrated that Napster retains the right to control access to its system. Napster has an express reservation of rights policy, stating on its website that it expressly reserves the "right to refuse service and terminate accounts in [its] discretion, including, but not limited to, if Napster believes that user conduct violates applicable law . . . or for any reason in Napster's sole discretion, with or without cause."

To escape imposition of vicarious liability, the reserved right to police must be exercised to its fullest extent. Turning a blind eye to detectable acts of infringement for the sake of profit gives rise to liability. [   ]

The district court correctly determined that Napster had the right and ability to police its system and failed to exercise that right to prevent the exchange of copyrighted material. The district court, however, failed to recognize that the boundaries of the premises that Napster "controls and patrols" are limited. [   ] Put differently, Napster's reserved "right and ability" to police is cabined by the system's current architecture. As shown by the record, the Napster system does not "read" the content of indexed files, other than to check that they are in the proper MP3 format.

Napster, however, has the ability to locate infringing material listed on its search indices, and the right to terminate users' access to the system. The file name indices, therefore, are within the "premises" that

Napster has the ability to police. We recognize that the files are user-named and may not match copyrighted material exactly (for example, the artist or song could be spelled wrong). For Napster to function effectively, however, file names must reasonably or roughly correspond to the material contained in the files, otherwise no user could ever locate any desired music. As a practical matter, Napster, its users and the record company plaintiffs have equal access to infringing material by employing Napster's "search function."

Our review of the record requires us to accept the district court's conclusion that plaintiffs have demonstrated a likelihood of success on the merits of the vicarious copyright infringement claim. Napster's failure to police the system's "premises," combined with a showing that Napster financially benefits from the continuing availability of infringing files on its system, leads to the imposition of vicarious liability. We address the scope of the injunction in part VIII of this opinion.

VI

We next address whether Napster has asserted defenses which would preclude the entry of a preliminary injunction.

Napster alleges that two statutes insulate it from liability. First, Napster asserts that its users engage in actions protected by § 1008 of the Audio Home Recording Act of 1992, 17 U.S.C. § 1008. Second, Napster argues that its liability for contributory and vicarious infringement is limited by the Digital Millennium Copyright Act, 17 U.S.C. § 512. We address the application of each statute in turn.

A. Audio Home Recording Act

The statute states in part:

No action may be brought under this title alleging infringement of copyright based on the manufacture, importation, or distribution of a digital audio recording device, a digital audio recording medium, an analog recording device, or an analog recording medium, or based on the noncommercial use by a consumer of such a device or medium for making digital musical recordings or analog musical recordings. [   ]

Napster contends that MP3 file exchange is the type of "noncommercial use" protected from infringement actions by the statute. Napster asserts it cannot be secondarily liable for users' nonactionable exchange of copyrighted musical recordings.

The district court rejected Napster's argument, stating that the Audio Home Recording Act is "irrelevant" to the action because: (1) plaintiffs did not bring claims under the Audio Home Recording Act; and (2) the Audio Home Recording Act does not cover the downloading of MP3 files. [   ]

We agree with the district court that the Audio Home Recording Act does not cover the downloading of MP3 files to computer hard drives. First, "under the plain meaning of the Act's definition of digital audio recording devices, computers (and their hard drives) are not digital audio recording devices because their 'primary purpose' is not to make digital audio copied recordings." [   ] Second, notwithstanding Napster's claim that computers are "digital audio recording devices," computers do not make "digital music recordings" as defined by the Audio Home Recording Act. [   ]

B.   Digital Millennium Copyright Act

Napster also interposes a statutory limitation on liability by asserting the protections of the "safe harbor" from copyright infringement suits for "Internet service providers" contained in the Digital Millennium Copyright Act, 17 U.S.C. § 512. [   ] The district court did not give this statutory limitation any weight favoring a denial of temporary injunctive relief. The court concluded that Napster "has failed to persuade this court that subsection 512(d) shelters contributory infringers." [   ]

We need not accept a blanket conclusion that § 512 of the Digital Millennium Copyright Act will never protect secondary infringers. [   ]

We do not agree that Napster's potential liability for contributory and vicarious infringement renders the Digital Millennium Copyright Act inapplicable per se. We instead recognize that this issue will be more fully developed at trial. At this stage of the litigation, plaintiffs raise serious questions regarding Napster's ability to obtain shelter under § 512, and plaintiffs also demonstrate that the balance of hardships tips in their favor. [   ]

Plaintiffs have raised and continue to raise significant questions under this statute, including: (1) whether Napster is an Internet service provider as defined by 17 U.S.C. § 512(d); (2) whether copyright owners must give a service provider "official" notice of infringing activity in order for it to have 4252 knowledge or awareness of infringing activity on its system; and (3) whether Napster complies with § 512(i), which requires a service provider to timely establish a detailed copyright compliance policy. [   ]

The district court considered ample evidence to support its determination that the balance of hardships tips in plaintiffs' favor:

Any destruction of Napster, Inc. by a preliminary injunction is speculative compared to the statistical evidence of massive, unauthorized downloading and uploading of plaintiffs' copyrighted works—as many as 10,000 files per second by defendant's own admission. [   ] The court has every reason to believe that, without a preliminary injunction, these numbers will mushroom as Napster users, and newcomers attracted by the publicity, scramble to obtain as much free music as possible before trial. [   ]

VII

Napster contends that even if the district court's preliminary determinations that it is liable for facilitating copyright infringement are correct, the district court improperly rejected valid affirmative defenses of waiver, implied license and copyright misuse. We address the defenses in turn.

A. Waiver

"Waiver is the intentional relinquishment of a known right with knowledge of its existence and the intent to relinquish it." [   ] In copyright, waiver or abandonment of copyright "occurs only if there is an intent by the copyright proprietor to surrender rights in his work." [   ]

Napster argues that the district court erred in not finding that plaintiffs knowingly provided consumers with technology designed to copy and distribute MP3 files over the Internet and, thus, waived any legal authority to exercise exclusive control over creation and distribution of MP3 files. The district court, however, was not convinced "that the record companies created the monster that is now devouring their intellectual property rights." [   ] We find no error in the district court's finding that "in hastening the proliferation of MP3 files, plaintiffs did nothing more than seek partners for their commercial downloading ventures and develop music players for files they planned to sell over the Internet." . . .

B. Implied License

Napster also argues that plaintiffs granted the company an implied license by encouraging MP3 file exchange over the Internet. Courts have found implied licenses only in "narrow" circumstances where one party "created a work at [the other's] request and handed it over, intending that [the other] copy and distribute it." [   ] The district court observed that no evidence exists to support this defense: "indeed, the RIAA gave defendant express notice that it objected to the availability of its members' copy-righted music on Napster." [   ] The record supports this conclusion.

C. Misuse

The defense of copyright misuse forbids a copyright holder from "securing an exclusive right or limited monopoly not granted by the Copyright Office." [   ] Napster alleges that online distribution is not within the copyright monopoly. According to Napster, plaintiffs have colluded to "use their copyrights to extend their control to online distributions."

We find no error in the district court's preliminary rejection of this affirmative defense. The misuse defense prevents copyright holders from leveraging their limited monopoly to allow them control of areas outside the monopoly. [   ] There is no evidence here that plaintiffs seek to control areas outside of their grant of monopoly. Rather, plaintiffs seek to control reproduction and distribution of their copyrighted works, exclusive rights of copyright holders. 17 U.S.C. § 106; [   ]. That the copyrighted works are transmitted in another medium—MP3 format rather than audio CD—has no bearing on our analysis. [   ]

VIII

The district court correctly recognized that a preliminary injunction against Napster's participation in copyright infringement is not only warranted but required. We believe, however, that the scope of the injunction needs modification in light of our opinion. Specifically, we reiterate that contributory liability may potentially be imposed only to the extent that Napster: (1) receives reasonable knowledge of specific infringing files with copyrighted musical compositions and sound recordings; (2) knows or should know that such files are available on the Napster system; and (3) fails to act to prevent viral distribution of the works. [ ] The mere existence of the Napster system, absent actual notice and Napster's demonstrated failure to remove the offending material, is insufficient to impose contributory liability. [ ]

Conversely, Napster may be vicariously liable when it fails to affirmatively use its ability to patrol its system and preclude access to potentially infringing files listed in its search index. Napster has both the ability to use its search function to identify infringing musical recordings and the right to bar participation of users who engage in the transmission of infringing files.

The preliminary injunction which we stayed is overbroad because it places on Napster the entire burden of ensuring that no "copying, downloading, uploading, transmitting, or distributing" of plaintiffs' works occur on the system. As stated, we place the burden on plaintiffs to provide notice to Napster of copyrighted works and files containing such works available on the Napster system before Napster has the duty to disable access to the offending content. Napster, however, also bears the burden of policing the system within the limits of the system. Here, we recognize that this is not an exact science in that the files are user named. In crafting the injunction on remand, the district court should recognize that Napster's system does not currently appear to allow Napster access to users' MP3 files.

Based on our decision to remand, Napster's additional arguments on appeal going to the scope of the injunction need not be addressed. We, however, briefly address Napster's First Amendment argument so that it is not reasserted on remand. Napster contends that the present injunction violates the First Amendment because it is broader than necessary. The company asserts two distinct free speech rights: (1) its right to publish a "directory" (here, the search index) and (2) its users' right to exchange information. We note that First Amendment concerns in copyright are allayed by the presence of the fair use doctrine. [ ] There was a preliminary determination here that Napster users are not fair users. Uses of copyrighted material that are not fair uses are rightfully enjoined. [ ]

IX

We address Napster's remaining arguments: (1) that the court erred in setting a $5 million bond, and (2) that the district court should have imposed a constructive royalty payment structure in lieu of an injunction.

A. Bond

Napster argues that the $5 million bond is insufficient because the company's value is between $1.5 and $2 billion. We review objections to the amount of a bond for abuse of discretion. [   ]

We are reluctant to dramatically raise bond amounts on appeal. [   ] The district court considered competing evidence of Napster's value and the deleterious effect that any injunction would have upon the Napster system. We cannot say that Judge Patel abused her discretion when she fixed the penal sum required for the bond.

B. Royalties

Napster contends that the district court should have imposed a monetary penalty by way of a compulsory royalty in place of an injunction. We are asked to do what the district court refused.

Napster tells us that "where great public injury would be worked by an injunction, the courts might . . . award damages or a continuing royalty instead of an injunction in such special circumstances." [   ] We are at a total loss to find any "special circumstances" simply because this case requires us to apply well-established doctrines of copyright law to a new technology. Neither do we agree with Napster that an injunction would cause "great public injury." Further, we narrowly construe any suggestion that compulsory royalties are appropriate in this context because Congress has arguably limited the application of compulsory royalties to specific circumstances, none of which are present here. [   ]

The Copyright Act provides for various sanctions for infringers. [   ] These statutory sanctions represent a more than adequate legislative solution to the problem created by copyright infringement.

Imposing a compulsory royalty payment schedule would give Napster an "easy out" of this case. If such royalties were imposed, Napster would avoid penalties for any future violation of an injunction, statutory copyright damages and any possible criminal penalties for continuing infringement. The royalty structure would also grant Napster the luxury of either choosing to continue and pay royalties or shut down. On the other hand, the wronged parties would be forced to do business with a company that profits from the wrongful use of intellectual properties. Plaintiffs would lose the power to control their intellectual property: they could not make a business decision not to license their property to Napster, and, in the event they planned to do business with Napster, compulsory royalties would take away the copyright holders' ability to negotiate the terms of any contractual arrangement.

X

We affirm in part, reverse in part and remand.

We direct that the preliminary injunction fashioned by the district court prior to this appeal shall remain stayed until it is modified by the district court to conform to the requirements of this opinion. We order a partial remand of this case on the date of the filing of this opinion for the limited purpose of permitting the district court to proceed with the settlement and entry of the modified preliminary injunction.

Even though the preliminary injunction requires modification, appellees have substantially and primarily prevailed on appeal. Appellees shall recover their statutory costs on appeal. [   ]

Affirmed in part, reversed in part and remanded.

Notes and Questions

1.   Napster took its service down in 2001 and filed for bankruptcy the next year. N.Y. Times, June 4, 2002.

2.   A Norwegian teenager developed a decryption program called "DeCSS" that circumvents copyright protection measures and allows DVDs to be played on unlicensed machines as well as to be copied. He put DeCSS on his own web site, and it was copied to hundreds of other web sites. Universal City Studios sued, citing the "anti-trafficking" provisions of the Digital Millennium Copyright Act that make it illegal to publish materials or programs that can be used to circumvent copyright protection measures.

In August 2000 a federal district court judge enjoined 2600.com, the online version of a popular hacker magazine, from publishing or linking to the DeCSS program. The company appealed, arguing that the injunction was unconstitutional because computer code was speech, entitled to full protection. The Court of Appeals held that, although computer code is protected speech, the First Amendment protection was limited by the fact that the decryption program had the capacity to accomplish unauthorized and unlawful access to materials for which the studios had intellectual property rights. The injunction was affirmed. Universal City Studios v. Corly, 273 F.3d 429 (2d Cir.2001).

3.   In another case, the DVD Copy Control Association (DVD CCA) argued that a Texas man, Matthew Pavlovich, violated California's law governing trade secrets when he posted a copy of the DeCSS (De–Content Scramble System) software on a web site. At the time, in 1991, he was a student at Purdue University in Indiana. The software was the same software written by the Norwegian student, *supra*. In December 2002, Justice Sandra Day O'Connor granted a temporary stay of a California ruling saying that Pavolovich could be sued in Texas or Indiana, but not California. But the stay was lifted on Jan. 3, 2003, essentially denying the DVD CCA further relief from the California ruling.

4.   Similar issues were raised by the arrest in Las Vegas of a Russian software writer on charges of trafficking in product designed to circumvent copyright protection measures. The FBI alleged that the man held

copyright on a software program, Advanced e-Book Processor (AEBPR), that decrypts copyright safeguards on Adobe's eBook Reader. It was believed to be the first case to apply criminal clauses of the Digital Millennium Copyright Act to electronic publishing. Consumer Electronics, July 23, 2001.

5. Still another issue involving the use of copyrighted materials on the Internet is the question of AM/FM streaming—the practice of transmitting broadcasts over the Internet in digital format by FCC licensed AM or FM broadcasters. The practice raises a number of questions, not the least of which relates to royalty fees on music. The Recording Industry Association of America, Inc., (RIAA) filed a Petition for Rulemaking in 2000, urging the Copyright office to rule that the AM/FM Webcasts of FCC-licensed stations are not exempt from copyright liability and are instead subject to licensing and would therefore have to pay royalties for music transmitted over the Internet. New York Law Journal, July 24, 2000 at S4.

The Copyright Office did then did make a rule that AM/FM broadcast signals transmitted simultaneously over a digital communications network, such as the Internet, are not exempted and thus are subject to the limited public performance right in sound recordings. A large number of broadcasters then initiated a legal action seeking to overturn the ruling. The Copyright Office and recording industry association moved for summary judgment, claiming that the final rule was reasonable. The district court granted summary judgement for the Copyright Office and recording industry association, holding that the Copyright Office had sufficient statutory authority to issue its final rule and that the rule was reasonable. Bonneville International Corp. v. Peters, 153 F.Supp.2d 763 (E.D.Pa. 2001).

6. A separate question involves Webcasters whose only transmission is via the Internet—so-called "Internet-only" stations. While they acknowledge that the 1998 federal legislation requires that they pay something for the music they transmit, they have argued that it should be only a small amount—less than two-tenths of a cent per listener per hour. RIAA, on the other hand, has asked for four-tenths of a cent per listener per song, which would amount to 5 or 6 cents per hour. Or, RIAA has said that an alternative would be for the Webcasters to pay 15 percent of their gross revenue. Webcasters say that that is much too high and that some Webcasters would be driven out of business by such a requirement. Los Angeles Times, May 3, 2001 at T2.

SoundExchange, a division of RIAA set up to collect royalties due for streaming under the Digital Millenium Copyright Act, has been the subject of some concern that royalties might be paid to the record companies without ever reaching the performers. Daily Variety, April 23, 2001 at A4.

7. In a situation that has been compared to the Napster situation, pirated copies of books are showing up on the Internet as well. Envisional, a Web monitoring company in Great Britain, reports research show-

ing that 7,267 pirated e-books could be accessed freely on the Internet, including those by internationally known authors such as John Grisham and J.K. Rowling and Tom Clancy. Some piracy results from disabling copy-protection systems for e-books, but most result from scanning paper copies of books, converting to e-formulas, downloading and printing. Reuters, Aug. 22, 2001.

8. In another attempt to deal with online piracy, the Recording Industry Association of America (RIAA) sought to learn the identity of a Verizon customer who was suspected of downloading more than 600 songs in one day over the Internet. Verizon objected to providing the alleged infringer's name because, it said, such a move would violate customer privacy and turn the company into an online copyright policeman. A federal court in Washington, D.C., ordered Verizon to cooperate, and the company said it would appeal. RIAA v. Verizon Internet Services, Inc. Reuters, Jan 21, 2003.

9. On the other hand, a federal judge in Los Angeles ruled in May that file-swapping services StreamCast Networks and Grokster were not liable for copyright infringements that took place using their software. The services had been sued by RIAA and the MPAA. The judge said, "Defendants distribute and support software, the users of which can and do choose to employ it for both lawful and unlawful ends.... Grokster and StreamCast are not significantly different from companies that sell home video recorders or copy machines, both of which can be and are used to infringe copyrights." The plaintiffs vowed to appeal. CNET news.com, May 18, 2003.

3. WRITERS' RIGHTS TO MATERIAL IN ELECTRONIC DATABASES

In a much-publicized case, the Supreme Court ruled in 2001 in favor of Jonathan Tasini and other freelance writers who contribute articles to the New York Times Co. and other publishers. The freelancers retain the copyright of their individual works and agree to the original hard-copy publication of their works. They claimed that republishing the articles in electronic databases constituted copyright infringement.

The publishers claimed they had a right to create a "collective work" of the material that had already been published elsewhere in hard-copy form and that they had a right to make revisions of the work. By a 7–2 vote, the Court held that the publishers were protected by no such "revision privilege" because users of databases are able to obtain individual articles, not intact periodicals. The Court found that databases were not analogous to microfilm or microfiche, because the latter typically contain continuous photographic reproductions of a periodical so that each article is seen in context—whereas the databases provide access to individual articles out of context. New York Times v. Tasini, 533 U.S. 483, 121 S.Ct. 2381, 29 Med.L.Rptr. 1865 (2001).

Similarly, a district court held that " 'the right to print, publish and sell the work[s] in book form' does not include the right to publish the works in the format that has come to be known as the 'ebook.'" The holding was part of a decision denying Random House a preliminary injunction prohibiting Rosetta Books from publishing certain works by William Styron, Kurt Vonnegut and Robert Parker in digital format on the Internet. Random House, Inc. v. Rosetta Books LLC, 150 F.Supp.2d 613, 29 Med.L.Rptr. 2025 (S.D.N.Y.2001).

4. DEEP LINKING OF WEB SITES

Ticketmaster Corp. sued Microsoft for providing a direct link from Microsoft's Sidewalk web site to Ticketmaster's ticket ordering page—thus bypassing Ticketmaster's opening pages and ads. Microsoft argued that there is an unwritten Internet code under which any Web site operator can link to anyone else's site. The parties reached a settlement in 1999. Although terms of the settlement were not revealed, Ticketmaster did say Microsoft had agreed to no longer link Sidewalk to pages deep within the Ticketmaster site. The New York Times, Feb. 15, 1999 at C–6.

5. SYSTEM CACHING

One of the provisions of the Digital Millennium Copyright Act (DMCA) protects the process known as system caching in which computer programs automatically store copies of recently accessed images and materials so that users can return to them quickly. Some copyright owners have objected that caching makes possible the making of copies not under their control—therefore, in their view, a copyright infringement. Caching may also result in an undercount of the number of hits at a site, which can negatively impact advertising revenue. Nonetheless, Congress protected caching but set up elaborate rules in the DMCA for refreshing, reloading or other updating of material. Cable TV and New Media Law & Finance, April 1999 at 1.

6. DIGITAL VIDEO AND AUDIO RECORDING

Intellectual property concerns relating to digital sound were addressed by Congress in the Digital Performance Right in Sound Recordings Act of 1995. The law, which became effective Feb. 1, 1996, added § 106(6) to the Copyright Act, granting copyright holders of sound recordings the exclusive right to perform their works publicly by digital audio transmission and expanded § 115's compulsory "mechanical" license to include delivery by digital transmission.

As the Register of Copyrights testified before the House Judiciary Committee Subcommittee on Court and Intellectual Property in 1997, "One of the most serious challenges to effective enforcement of copyright in the digital environment is the ease, speed and accuracy of copying at multiple, anonymous locations." Federal News Service, Sept. 16, 1997.

Congress has trod carefully in this area, however, and concerns that language could outlaw the popular and legal consumer recording functions of digital video and audio recording products and personal computers were part of the reason that the National Information Infrastructure (NII) Copyright Protection Act of 1995 died in committee.

Some of the greatest controversy has been over the technology that allows consumers to download digital audio files from the Internet without paying royalties to any copyright owners. The technology, MP3—shorthand for MPEG Layer 3—permits compression so that a 5–minute CD song that would normally take up about 50 megabytes of space on a computer's hard drive can be compressed to about 5 megabytes of space, and yet still retain its quality. In October 1998, the Recording Industry Association of America, Inc., sued Diamond Multimedia Systems Inc., manufacturer of the Rio, a lightweight, hand-held machine that receives, stores and replays digital audio files stored in the MP3 format. The plaintiffs sought to enjoin Diamond from manufacturing and distributing the Rio, arguing that it would lead to widespread music piracy. The plaintiffs also argued that Rio is a digital audio recording (DAR) device and is subject to the Audio Home Recording Act of 1992 (AHRA), with which Diamond had not complied. Under the AHRA, DAR devices are supposed to have copying controls, and royalties are to be paid on the sale of DAR devices.

In 2003 a number of major players in the music industry announced that they had reached agreement on a plan to combat digital privacy without government intervention. Joining the agreement were the Recording Industry Association of America (RIAA), the Business Software Alliance (whose members include Microsoft, Apple Computer Inc. and Adobe Systems Inc.), and the Computer Systems Policy Project (made up of chief executives of IBM, Intel, Hewlett–Packard and Dell). Calling it a "landmark consensus," proponents of the agreement said they would *not* seek new legislation, but will instead try to rely on the dynamics of an unregulated marketplace. The companies said, however, that they will support aggressive enforcement of existing laws against digital piracy. In exchange, the RIAA will argue against government requirements to build locking controls into future recording devices that might have made it more difficult for consumers to share music and movies. "Music Companies Agree to Antipiracy Plan," The New York Times, Jan. 14, 2003, and "Music Industry Won't Seek Government Aid on Piracy," The New York Times, Jan. 15, 2003.

7. SATELLITE RETRANSMISSION

The National Football League sought a permanent injunction to stop PrimeTime 24 Joint Venture, a satellite carrier that makes network television programming available to satellite dish owners and renters through secondary transmissions, from transmitting the NFL's copyrighted telecasts to its satellite subscribers in Canada. The U.S. Court of Appeals held that the transmissions constituted a "public performance" or "public display" within the meaning of the Copyright Act and therefore infringed on the NFL's rights. National Football League v.

PrimeTime 24 Joint Venture, 211 F.3d 10 (2d Cir.2000). PrimeTime 24 applied for certiorari arguing that the Copyright Act does not apply in Canada, but the Supreme Court denied certiorari. 532 U.S. 941 (2001).

In a separate case, the NFL and the National Basketball Association filed a copyright infringement suit against TVRadioNow Corp., a company that was allegedly taking telecasts of games from broadcast stations in Buffalo and Toronto and making them available via an Internet site—iCraveTV.com. The associations claimed that, not only was the quality of the Internet transmission poor, but defendants made other unauthorized changes in the content, including selling advertising in a frame surrounding the video on the web site. One of the principals of the company had lived in Pennsylvania prior to moving recently to Canada, and another still resided in Pennsylvania, so the complaint was filed in that state. National Football League v. TVRadioNow Corp., 2000 U.S.Dist. ___ LEXIS 1012.

E. TRADEMARKS

Trademarks and servicemarks, like copyright, protect intellectual property. Instead of protecting an entire movie script, an entire book or an entire magazine, as a copyright may, trademarks and servicemarks protect "identifying symbols"—words, names, symbols or devices.

The distinction between trademarks and servicemarks is that trademarks are symbols that identify goods whereas servicemarks are symbols that identify services. Because the law governing trademarks and servicemarks is essentially the same, we will use "trademark" to represent both.

Federal registration of trademarks is authorized under Congressional legislation. Unlike copyright and patents, trademarks are not specifically mentioned in the Constitution. The governing statute is the Federal Trademark Act of 1946, known as the Lanham Act after the late Rep. Fritz Garland Lanham. Registrations are filed with the United States Patent and Trademark Office.

Whether a term is eligible for trademark protection depends on how it is classified. For example, Miller Brewing was denied trademark protection for the term "LITE" because it was viewed as a descriptive term for a type of beer. "A term for which trademark protection is claimed will fit somewhere in the spectrum which ranges through (1) generic or common descriptive and (2) merely descriptive to (3) suggestive and (4) arbitrary or fanciful." Miller Brewing Co. v. G. Heileman Brewing Co., Inc., 561 F.2d 75, 79 (7th Cir.1977). Generic terms—those that describe a kind of good—can never become trademarks. Merely descriptive terms—those that describe a characteristic or ingredient—can become trademarks only by acquiring a secondary meaning "distinctive of the applicant's goods." Suggestive terms—ones that suggest rather than describe a characteristic or ingredient—can become trademarks without proof of a secondary meaning. Arbitrary or fanciful terms—ones that in no way suggest or describe a characteristic or ingredient of the product—can also become trademarks without proof of secondary meaning. Arbitrary or fanciful terms are better protected than suggestive terms because there is always a danger that a suggestive term will be viewed as a descriptive term, thus requiring proof of a secondary meaning.

Groups of letters, even an individual letter, can function as a trademark. If one uses an individual letter, the type style or design of the letter must be distinctive.

It is also possible to register titles, characters, names and "other distinctive features" of radio or television programs under § 45 of the Lanham Act. Section 43(a) of the Lanham Act permits protection of unregistered names of performers or sports teams, etc.

Cartoon characters and literary characters can be protected under either copyright or trademark, depending on the use. For example, a "Superman" cartoon would be copyrighted, but "Superman" products would be trademarked.

Manufacturers, for obvious reasons, want to protect their exclusive rights to use names and symbols associated with their products. Sometimes, if they are not sufficiently vigilant in their protection of their trademarks, the trademarks enter the *public domain* and can be used by anyone. Aspirin and cellophane are examples of trademarks that lost trademark protection because people came to use them as generic terms for the product as opposed to the name of a specific brand. The owners of the registered trademarks Xerox® and Kleenex®, knowing that people sometimes misuse their trademarks as though they were generic names, are among those that advertise in such magazines as *Editor & Publisher* and *Broadcasting & Cable,* emphasizing that their names are protected and should be capitalized.

Trademark owners particularly concerned about the problem emphasize the ® symbol next to their names or go to considerable lengths to emphasize that their names are brand names, as in broadcast commercials referring to "Sanka Brand" coffee.

Like copyright holders, trademark owners do not have unlimited, exclusive rights to the use of their trademarks. Trademark owners are protected against uses that could cause confusion between their products and other similar products (trademark infringement) as well as uses on dissimilar products that might cause deterioration of the distinctive aspect of the trademarks (trademark dilution). Such cases, however, can be difficult to win. For example, although the Boston Athletic Association registered the trademark "Boston Marathon" and licensed one television station to broadcast the race, it was unable to get an injunction prohibiting another station from also televising the event, because it failed to show sufficient evidence of relevant customer confusion. WCVB–TV v. Boston Athletic Association, 926 F.2d 42, 18 Med.L.Rptr. 1710 (1st Cir.1991).

Noncommercial uses of trademarks are generally considered protected by the First Amendment. For example, an injunction prohibiting the publication of a parody of the L.L. Bean Catalogue pursuant to Maine's anti-dilution statute was found to violate the First Amendment. L.L. Bean, Inc. v. Drake Publishers, Inc., 811 F.2d 26, 13 Med.L.Rptr. 2009 (1st Cir.1987). L.L. Bean had argued that the parody, *L.L. Beam's Back–To–School–Sex–Catalog,* would tarnish the goodwill and reputation associated with Bean's trademark:

> It offends the Constitution, however, to invoke the anti-dilution statute as a basis for enjoining the noncommercial use of a trademark by a defendant engaged in a protected form of expression. . . .
>
> If the anti-dilution statute were construed as permitting a trademark owner to enjoin the use of his mark in a noncommercial context found to be negative or offensive, then a corporation could shield itself from criticism by forbidding the use of its name in commentaries critical of its conduct. The legitimate aim of the anti-dilution statute is to prohibit the unauthorized use of another's trademark in order to market incompatible products or services. The Constitution does not, however, permit the range of the anti-dilution statute to encompass the unauthorized use of a trademark in a noncommercial setting such as an editorial or artistic context.

In 1996 President Clinton signed into law new federal anti-dilution legislation—§ 43(c) of the Lanham Act, providing in part for the protection from "dilution of the distinctive quality of [a] famous" trademark, notwithstanding the absence of a likelihood of confusion. The new section will provide uniform nationwide protection, but some critics fear it will stifle parodies. New York Law Journal, March 27, 1996.

Broadcasters may protect their stations' call letters by trademark. For years, under an assumption that the government owned the call letters, individuals could not trademark them, but the FCC protected them. After the FCC ended such protection, the issue of call letters arose in an appeal before the Trademark Trial and Appeal Board of the Patent and Trademark Office, U.S. Department of Commerce. WSM, Inc., an AM radio station, had used the call letters "WSM" since 1925 and claimed use of the call letters as a servicemark. The Examining Attorney in the Patent and Trademark Office had refused to register the letters as a servicemark on the assumption that the station did not own the call letters because they were used only with FCC approval. The Trademark Trial and Appeal Board reversed:

> The Examining Attorney has apparently misunderstood the nature of the relationship between the FCC and applicant. . . . It is clear that the FCC is not the owner of the call letters used by the broadcasters which it regulates. The right to broadcast is what the agency licenses to broadcasters. . . . In the case at hand the applicant obtained whatever rights it has in its service mark by adopting it and using it to identify its broadcasting services. The

FCC neither selected the mark for applicant nor used it to identify any services. . . . [A]s long as applicant uses the mark to identify its services which are lawfully rendered in commerce applicant is the owner of its service mark [and is therefore entitled to register it].

WSM, Inc., 225 U.S. Patent Quarterly 883 (1985).

Today, although it is possible to trademark call letters, problems still can arise when two stations have call letters which look or sound similar. An example involves a trademark infringement alleged by station WMEE(FM) of Fort Wayne, Ind., which in 1984 complained after a station in Decatur, Ind., whose signal overlapped with that of WMEE, changed its call letters from WADM to WMCZ(FM). On the request of WMEE, a federal district court judge issued a preliminary injunction prohibiting the new WMCZ from identifying itself by those call letters. Furthermore, the judge ordered WMCZ to air a disclaimer differentiating itself from WMEE. The judge, who said the two calls were "overwhelmingly phonetically and rhythmically similar," said that, "[i]mplicit in the FCC's relinquishment of its role as arbiter of call letter disputes is the conclusion that, when local courts resolve call letter disputes, the law of that local forum and circuit would apply." Pathfinder Communications Corp. v. Midwest Communications Co., 593 F.Supp. 281 (N.D.Ind.1984).

The issue of ownership of the word "olympic" was argued in San Francisco Arts and Athletics, Inc. v. United States Olympic Committee, 479 U.S. 1052 (1987). The Olympic Committee had sought to bar a gay rights group from sponsoring an athletic competition called the Gay Olympics. In a 5–4 decision, the Court held that Congress had granted the Olympic Committee exclusive commercial use of the word "olympic." The gay rights group had argued that by allowing "olympics" for handicapped children, police officers and others, but not for gays, the committee had enforced its trademark rights in a biased way, but Justice Powell, in the majority opinion, said that because the committee was not a government agency, it could not violate someone's constitutionally protected right to equal protection under the law.

The underlying purpose of the special protection given the word "olympic" appears to be more of an attempt to maintain dignity or "officialness" of the internationally-sanctioned games, than to protect their commercial value.

In another case of alleged trademark dilution, Mattel Inc., manufacturer of Barbie, sued MCA Records Inc. and the Danish band Aqua because of the 1997 dance hit "Barbie Girl" which referred to Barbie as a "blond bimbo." Mattel argued that preteen girls thought the song was an advertisement for Barbie or part of the official line of Barbie products. MCA defended the song, which sold 1.4 million copies, as "social commentary." The 9th Circuit Court of Appeals held in 2002 that consumers were *not* misled by the song. In his opinion, Judge Alex Kozinski said the original 1950s Barbie resembled a "German street walker" but was gradually transformed into a long-legged American with a "fictitious figure." He said, "With fame often comes unwanted attention." He concluded that the Trademark Dilution Act could not be extended to punish a parody and said, "The parties are advised to chill." Mattel v. MCA Records Inc., 296 F.3d 894 (9th Cir.2002), cert. denied, 71 U.S.L.W. 3503 (2003).

The 1988 Trademark Law Revision Act, amending the Lanham Act, overhauled the trademark system. Under its provisions, the term of registration and renewal was reduced from 20 to 10 years. The amendments also permit a company to receive trademark protection for as much as three years before it actually sells a product or service with that mark. Companies formerly could register trademarks only when they had put them into use. Language in Section 43(a) of the Act includes a provision making misrepresentations about another's product or service—so-called product disparagement—actionable.

The latter provision is directed at some forms of comparative advertising in which rival advertisers have sometimes been accused of maligning their competitors' goods or services. As a result of compromise with media organizations worried about threats to free speech, it applies only to business advertising and promotion and not to political advertising or editorial commentary.

F. DOMAIN NAMES

Recognizable domain names on the Internet can, of course, be of great economic value. For awhile, Network Solutions, Inc., (NSI) had sole control over the Domain Name System central database repository of domain names, and the company registered more than 4.2 million domain names. As a government contractor, NSI administered all domain names ending in ".com," ".net" or ".org." Trademark owners concerned about others' registrations of domain names that might infringe on their registered trademarks faced the choice of going to a court to challenge use of a domain name or to go to the administrative "court" run by NSI. Many chose the latter.

In a move ending NSI's sole control of the naming, in 1999, the Internet Corporation for Assigned Names and Numbers (ICANN) identified five competitors for NSI in the assignment of Internet domain names. Competing with NSI will be America Online Inc.; Oleane, a division of France Telecom; the Internet Council of Registrars; Melbourne IT; and Register.com, a division of Forman Interactive Corp. Later in 1999, AT & T and 28 other companies are also expected to be involved in the process.

A principal rule has been that domain names can not contain any of the seven words frowned on by the FCC and made famous in the George Carlin comedy skit, pp. 228–229, *supra*, but in mid–1999, NSI was facing lawsuits in both California and New Hampshire from plaintiffs who challenged on First Amendment grounds NSI's right to block such names. Some other words were found unacceptable as well. NSI, for example, which had registered Godhatesfags.com, finding it an acceptable Internet domain name, rejected Nigger.com. (An NSI customer-service representative reportedly told one caller that the latter term was one of the FCC's seven dirty words.)

Inevitably there have been threats of litigation and actual court cases involving domain names that are close to trademark-protected corporate names, and in some cases corporations have registered names they did not want others to use. Chase Manhattan Bank registered chasesucks.com, chasestinks.com, and IhateChase.com in order to make sure that no one else could use them and threatened to sue the owner of chasebanksucks.com for trademark infringement. Charles Schwab, General Electric and Hyatt are other big corporation said to have registered names to prevent their registration by others. Bally Total Fitness sued the owner of BallySucks—unsuccessfully. A general principle in trademark protection is that the protection extends only to the registered name, and, if an offensive word is attached to it on a Web site, there is no protection.

An additional problem raised by domain names is cybersquatting—the practice of registering domain names incorporating the names of companies or famous people, then attempting to sell the names to those companies or people. A variation on this practice is registering a name similar to a company that sells competing products with the intention of syphoning off some of that company's business (e.g., a discount store registering www.wallmart.com).

In 1999 Congress passed the Anticybersquatting Consumer Protection Act under which plaintiffs can sue alleged cyberpirates for damages. The Act creates a civil cause of action against someone who, in bad faith with intent to profit, registers, traffics or uses a domain name that is identical or confusingly similar to a distinctive or famous mark (including a personal name) or a registered trademark. A cause of action is also available, with certain limited exceptions, against anyone who "registers a domain name that consists of the name of another living person, or a name substantially and confusingly similar thereto, without that person's consent, with the specific intent to profit from such name by selling the domain name for financial gain to that person or any third party."

Chapter XIV

DEFAMATION

In this chapter and those that follow we will consider the range of legal arguments for prohibiting certain communications because of their substantive content. In each case we will consider, among other points, the justifications offered for restriction and the value of the communication. The justifications are as diverse as the situations to which they are applied. Arguments for limiting speech and press to protect privacy are unlikely to resemble the arguments based on national security.

Even if the speech is determined to be subject to governmental control, there is the further question of what types of sanctions may be imposed. Among the array are criminal prosecutions, civil damage remedies and bans on speech imposed by administrative techniques or by court injunction. Again, particular sanctions are used for specific kinds of speech. Even when speech is found to be defamatory, for example, it is regulated after the fact and is not enjoined. On the other hand, speech held to invade privacy has been barred from publication. In sum, the sanctions available are as diverse as the justifications offered to restrict the speech in the first place.

We begin our survey of restraints on communication with the state's interest in granting redress to persons whose reputations have been hurt by false statements. We start with defamation law in part because it was one of the earliest legal actions available against journalists and in part because even today it poses a significant legal danger for those in electronic media. It is certainly the most extensively litigated area of media law.

Harm to reputation is one of the earliest injuries recognized by virtually every legal system. Early societies were undoubtedly concerned that the failure to provide legal recourse to those whose reputations had been impugned would lead to breaches of the peace. Although that concern has eased as civilization has advanced, states may still be concerned about the potential for violence. Beyond that, however, traditional values emphasize the importance of an individual's good name. Whatever the justifications, the action for defamation has long had a place in the common law.

English law has redressed and punished attacks on reputation since the feudal days. During the 16th century, the authorities began using the law of defamation to punish political criticism of the government and its officials. These attacks were referred to as seditious libel.

Although it is doubtful that the English law of seditious libel was transplanted in this country, it seems clear that the tort law that provided damage remedies to individuals did cross the Atlantic. After independence, defamation law continued to be enforced. The First Amendment's statement that "Congress shall make no law . . . abridging the freedom of speech, or of the press . . ." had no apparent impact upon defamation law until the mid–1960s. Because defamation law was a creature of state law—the power to regulate defamation law was not delegated to Congress—the First Amendment had no immediate effect on the states' administration of that law.

Even after it became clear that the First Amendment applied to the states through the Fourteenth Amendment, these provisions were thought inapplicable to false statements that adversely affected an individual's reputation. The Supreme Court did not tie defamation and the First Amendment together until the seminal case of New York Times Co. v. Sullivan, decided in 1964. That case not only brought major change to the law of defamation, but also provided a philosophy that has led to many other recent developments in mass media law. We shall consider the impact of this case on defamation law shortly.

A. THE STATE LAW OF DEFAMATION

Before we can appreciate the significance of the constitutional developments, however, we must understand the common-law world of defamation. The constitutional developments have not created a totally new legal area; rather they have altered some of the pre-existing state rules and left the remaining ones in place. States remain free to protect reputation in whatever manner they see fit so long as they do so consistently with the First Amendment.

A second reason for inquiring into state law is that state law itself has a significant number of protections for those who are sued for defamation. It is often possible for a defendant to win a defamation case under the state's traditional rules without ever having to rely upon the protection of the First Amendment.

Why might a defendant who could win a case under First Amendment principles try to win that case under state rules? There are several practical explanations. Perhaps the major one is that, as a matter of procedure, the state defenses may permit a defendant to win the case earlier in the litigation (such as on a motion to dismiss, rather than on a motion for summary judgment or perhaps only after a trial is held). It is often faster and cheaper for a media defendant to succeed on state law grounds than to rely exclusively on the more glorious, but perhaps less expeditious, ground of the First and Fourteenth Amendments.

The point is that we must understand the basic operation of traditional state defamation law as well as the Constitution. We turn first to the state law and then to the impact of constitutional law.

1. THE REPUTATION ELEMENT

a. *Definition*

The essence of the action for defamation is the claim that defendant has uttered a false statement that has harmed the plaintiff's reputation. The modern view is that a statement is defamatory if it harms the plaintiff's reputation by lowering the plaintiff in the estimation of the community or by deterring others from associating or dealing with the plaintiff. It is easy to think of statements that will fit such a broad definition. It obviously covers charges that plaintiff committed a crime or that the plaintiff was inept in his or her chosen trade or profession. It is enough that the published statement be of the sort that would lead a segment of the community to think less of the plaintiff. That segment need not be large.

When the false statement is transmitted by electronic media, obviously, there is usually a large audience, but there need not be.

Most cases have involved charges of volitional behavior by plaintiff—committing a crime, lacking skill or writing an article. The broad sweep of the definition, however, extends to accusations that the plaintiff was of illegitimate birth, had been raped or was in dire financial straits. Even though the plaintiff cannot be blamed for a condition, the courts have nonetheless bowed to reality and recognized that these kinds of charges may in fact cause others to shun, or refrain from associating with, the plaintiff. Judges "take the world as we find it" even if the segment of the community that thinks less of the plaintiff can be characterized as "wrong-thinking"—as they would be in the illegitimacy and rape examples.

At the same time, there is a limit to that principle. Consider, for example, a false charge that the mob's gunman missed his target. Were the gunman to sue and assert that his reputation had been tarnished among the underworld, it is unlikely that a court would entertain the charge. Is it appropriate to redress a claim based on an audience segment that is criminal rather than simply wrong-thinking?

b. *Corporations*

Until now, the discussion has been directed to the question of protecting the reputation of a human being. Not infrequently, however, defamatory statements are made about corporations. It is generally held that corporations also have reputations that they may vindicate through actions for defamation. Usually the corporation must be attacked in a way that affects its credit or, if it is a corporation organized for profit, its profit-making ability.

A non-profit corporation may also be defamed if the charge is one that tends to interfere with its ability to obtain financial support from the public. A corporation that relies on public donations may be able to sue for defamation if the charge would interfere with its ability to obtain such funds.

c. *Ambiguity*

Statements are often ambiguous. In such cases the prevailing rule is to have the judge decide whether any of the statement's possible meanings can reasonably be understood to have a defamatory impact. If the judge decides that at least one of the possible meanings would be defamatory, it then becomes a function of the jury to decide the meaning that was in fact conveyed.

It should be noted here that the Supreme Court in one discussion of ambiguous statements resolved the question itself. The case arose from a tumultuous city council meeting involving the plaintiff, a local real estate developer, in a negotiation with the city council. Members of the audience characterized the plaintiff's bargaining position as "blackmail." The defendant newspaper accurately reported the meeting and included the blackmail charges—sometimes without quotation marks. The state courts granted plaintiff a judgment against the newspaper.

Justice Stewart concluded for the majority that "as a matter of constitutional law, the word 'blackmail' in these circumstances was not" defamatory:

> It is simply impossible to believe that a reader who reached the word "blackmail" in either article would not have understood exactly what was meant; it was Bresler's public and wholly legal negotiating proposals that were being criticized. No reader could have thought that either the speakers at the meeting or the newspaper articles reporting their words were charging Bresler with the commission of a criminal offense. On the contrary, even the most careless reader must have perceived that the word was no more than rhetorical hyperbole. . . .

Justice White dissented. He could not "join the majority claim of superior insight with respect to how the word 'blackmail' would be understood by the ordinary reader in Greenbelt, Maryland." Greenbelt Cooperative Publishing Association v. Bresler, 398 U.S. 6, 1 Med.L.Rptr. 1589 (1970).

Another problem arises when part of a story has a defamatory impact but another part of the story negates that impact. The lead-in to a story may be defamatory, but the story as a whole may be harmless. Normally, courts consider how a reasonable reader would respond.

Statements may be defamatory even though the thrust of the accusations is not clear from the words used. In such indirect defamation cases, plaintiffs' complaints must show the court how the plaintiffs have been defamed. The description of how plaintiffs do this involves the use of three technical words. If the plaintiffs themselves are not directly named, they must show by "colloquium" that the statements were "of and concerning" them. If it is still not clear how the plaintiffs have been defamed, they must plead extrinsic facts that would permit a defamatory meaning to be applied to defendants' words. Such an allegation of extrinsic facts is called the "inducement." Finally we have "innuendo." Where the statements are not clearly defamatory on their face, it is the function of the innuendo to assert the meanings that plaintiffs attach to the passages and any additions by colloquium and inducement. The innuendo is not a fact but is the plaintiffs' assertion of how the passages would be understood by those who heard the defendants' words and knew the additional unstated facts.

An example may help clarify the matter. Let us assume a defendant says, "The man who lives in the house two doors east of my house was the only person in the Smith home between 7 and 8 p.m. last night." If the plaintiff thinks that this statement defames him and wishes to sue, his pleading must establish how he has been defamed. For colloquium he might allege, "I am the only man who lives in the house two doors east of the speaker's house." This ties the plaintiff to the statement but does not clarify its defamatory nature. The defamation is clarified if the plaintiff alleges as inducement that the Smith house was burglarized between 7 and 8 p.m. that night. The plaintiff will then assert that the innuendo is that he is being accused of the crime of burglary.

d. "Of and Concerning Plaintiff"

In order for a defamatory statement to affect the plaintiff adversely, the reader must connect that statement with the plaintiff. As we said above, the plaintiff must show that the statement objected to was "of and concerning" him. Sometimes this is a problem because of the ambiguity of the statement or because the plaintiff is only indirectly identified. In those cases our discussion about ambiguous statements will help resolve the case. If readers could plausibly believe that the plaintiff was referred to, then a jury will decide whether the statement was in fact so understood.

e. Groups

Another aspect of this problem involves statements that attack large groups of people. In such cases is it possible for an individual member of that group to assert that the statement hurt his personal reputation? At the extreme, an attack on all lawyers in the United States or on all clergymen would be held to be such a general broadside that no individual lawyer or clergyman could sue. The same would be true of broadside attacks on racial, religious or ethnic groups.

At the other extreme it is generally accepted that a charge made against a small group may defame all members of that group. For example, a television newscast may assert that "the officers" of a corporation have embezzled funds. There are only four officers of the corporation. Each of them may be found to have been defamed. Even if the statement had said "one of the officers of the corporation" had embezzled funds, the group is small enough so that all four officials are put under a shadow and can sue.

As the group grows larger the impact of the statement may depend on the number accused. In one case, a defamatory charge was made against one unidentified member of a 21–member police force. All 21 sued. The court dismissed the case. It feared that allowing the action would permit a suit by an entire baseball team over a report that one member was disciplined for brawling. Such a result "would chill communication to the marrow." But suppose the charge had been against "all but one" of the members of that police force. Such a statement may reflect on each member of the force though the same charge made against only one of the 21 might not. Arcand v. Evening Call Publishing Co., 567 F.2d 1163, 3 Med.L.Rptr. 1748 (1st Cir.1977).

All states deny damage actions to large groups, but a few have attempted to use criminal statutes to prevent or punish such charges against racial or ethnic groups. We will discuss this later in this chapter.

f. Opinions—A Special Problem

At common law there was much confusion about whether opinion, as distinguished from fact, could be the basis for a defamation action. Because a strongly expressed unfavorable opinion could easily lower a person's reputation in the eyes of others, the courts usually held that such a statement could form the basis of a defamation action even though it could not be found to be true or false. Occasionally, the courts held that although truth was a defense to defamation, that did not mean that a statement could be defamatory only if it could be shown to be false. Courts held that those sued for publishing defamatory opinions might invoke the defense of fair comment—the privilege of stating opinions that they actually held and did not express solely for the purpose of hurting the object of the attack. We will discuss fair comment later in this chapter.

One indication of the Supreme Court's view of the protected status of opinion was dictum in Gertz v. Robert Welch, Inc., 418 U.S. 323, 1 Med.L.Rptr. 1633 (1974), reprinted at p. 895, *infra*: "Under the First Amendment there is no such thing as a false idea. However pernicious an opinion may seem, we depend for its correction not on the conscience of judges and juries but on the competition of other ideas." 418 U.S. at 339–40, 1 Med.L.Rptr. at 1640.

In Milkovich v. Lorain Journal Co., 497 U.S. 1, 17 Med.L.Rptr. 2009 (1990), the Supreme Court downplayed the importance of the "no such thing as a false statement" dictum in *Gertz*. Milkovich coached a high school wrestling team that had been involved in a brawl with a competing team. Controversy and a lawsuit about the team's having been put on probation ensued. A sports columnist wrote about a hearing on the suit, saying, "Anyone who attended the meet . . . knows in his heart that Milkovich . . . lied at the hearing after . . . having given his solemn oath to tell the truth." Milkovich sued, alleging that the column accused him of perjury.

The Supreme Court said that the court's dictum in *Gertz* about "no such thing as a false idea" was "merely a reiteration of Justice Holmes' classic 'marketplace of ideas' concept" and that it was not intended to "create a wholesale defamation exemption for anything that might be labeled 'opinion.' " Chief Justice Rehnquist wrote that "[T]he statement, 'In my opinion Jones is a liar,' can cause as much damage to reputation as the statement, 'Jones is a liar.' " The former statement, Rehnquist said, "implies a knowledge of facts which lead to the conclusion that Jones told an untruth." The court held that "[T]he connotation [in the sports column] that [Milkovich] committed perjury is sufficiently factual to be susceptible of being proved true or false," and remanded the case. Eventually Milkovich reached an undisclosed cash settlement with the newspaper.

In 1990 the Supreme Court vacated and remanded a lower court's decision in Immuno AG. v. Moor–Jankowski, 74 N.Y.2d 548, 549 N.Y.S.2d 938, 549 N.E.2d 129, 17 Med.L.Rptr. 1161 (1989) for further reconsideration in light of *Milkovich*. Immuno AG, an Austrian pharmaceutical company that performs tests on animals, had sued Moor–Jankowski, editor of the *Journal of Medical Primatology*, published in New York, over a letter to the editor from an animal rights activist concerned about a proposed research facility using chimpanzees for research. When the *Journal* had published the letter, it had included an editor's note saying that Immuno's lawyers had challenged the accuracy of the letter and identifying the writer as an animal rights activist. New York's highest court decided that the state's constitution offers more protection for freedom of the press than does the U.S. Constitution—and dismissed the case. 77 N.Y.2d 235, 566 N.Y.S.2d 906, 567 N.E.2d 1270, 18 Med.L.Rptr. 1625, certiorari denied, 500 U.S. 954 (1991).

The *Milkovich* distinction between fact and opinion was also an issue in Unelko Corp. v. Rooney, in which the maker of a car windshield treatment product sued Andy Rooney of "60 Minutes" for saying the product "Rain–X" "didn't work." Although Rooney's comment was held to imply an assertion of objective fact and, under *Milkovich*, was not shielded from liability, the court of appeals upheld a grant of summary judgment for Rooney due to the manufacturer's failure to demonstrate falsity. 912 F.2d 1049, 17 Med.L.Rptr. 2317 (9th Cir.1990).

g. *Vagueness*

Some courts have found language too imprecise to form the basis of a defamation action. An accusation that William F. Buckley, Jr., was a "fellow traveler" of fascist causes was too "loosely definable" and too "variously interpretable" to be actionable as a defamation. The court suggested that there might be a difference between that vague charge and a more specific charge that plaintiff was a member of a particular party or group that subscribed to that type of belief. Buckley v. Littell, 539 F.2d 882, 1 Med.L.Rptr. 1762 (2d Cir.1976), certiorari denied 429 U.S. 1062 (1977).

Similarly, a charge that a police union's collective bargaining efforts involved the "inroad of communism" was held too vague to support a suit. National Association of Government Employees, Inc. v. Central Broadcasting Corp., 379 Mass. 220, 396 N.E.2d 996, 5 Med.L.Rptr. 2078 (1979). The court thought it clear from the context and words used that no hearer in the community after even brief reflection would understand the speaker to be charging plaintiff with complicity in the "horrors distinctive of a totalitarian regime."

In contrast, a federal court held in 1993 that a plaintiff had a cause of action for defamation despite the defendant's claim that no statement had been made about her. The plaintiff, an actress, had appeared in a television commercial for Wasa crispbread from Sweden. In the commercial, she was shown in a towel, with a male companion in a bathrobe. Defendant Al Goldstein, executive producer of the sexually explicit late-night cable television program "Midnight Blue," asked his staff to "adapt" the commercial to include pornographic videotape of couples, apparently engaging in sex. In denying a motion to dismiss the case, the court held that the juxtaposition of the pornographic videotape with the commercial was a "statement" subject to defamatory interpretation. Geary v. Goldstein, 831 F.Supp. 269, 21 Med.L.Rptr. 1906 (S.D.N.Y. 1993).

h. *"Libel–proof" Plaintiffs*

Courts have long assumed that plaintiffs whose reputations were already bad prior to the publication of a libel should be treated differently than those who had previously had good reputations—whatever damages were suffered from incrementally lowering the reputation were unlikely to be significant. The doctrine was that "a libel-proof plaintiff is not entitled to burden a defendant with a trial in which the most favorable result the plaintiff could achieve is an award of nominal damages." Jackson v. Longcope, 394 Mass. 577, 476 N.E.2d 617 (1985). In *Jackson,* a convicted multiple murderer was challenging a statement that he had raped and strangled all of his victims. In another example, *Penthouse* magazine publisher Robert Guccione was held to be "libel proof" in connection with a 1983 article in *Hustler* that alleged that he was "married and has a live-in girlfriend." At the time the article appeared, Guccione had been divorced four years, but he had earlier lived with his girlfriend for 13 years while married to someone else. Guccione v. Hustler Magazine, Inc., 800 F.2d 298, 13 Med.L.Rptr. 1316 (2d Cir.1986), certiorari denied 479 U.S. 1091 (1987).

The extent to which plaintiffs may be found to be libel-proof in the future, however, is unpredictable after the decision of the Supreme Court of the United States in Masson v. New Yorker Magazine, Inc., 501 U.S. 496 (1991). In *Masson,* the Supreme Court noted that the court below had relied on the "incremental harm" doctrine—looking at the extent to which statements for which the plaintiff had sued damaged him beyond the extent to which he might have been damaged by statements for which he had not sued. The Supreme Court said that "[W]e reject any suggestion that the incremental harm doctrine is compelled as a matter of First Amendment protection for speech. The question of incremental harm does not bear upon whether a defendant has published a statement with knowledge of falsity or reckless disregard of whether it was false or not."

2. LIBEL AND SLANDER—THE DAMAGE QUESTION

So far we have been discussing the general subject of "defamation." Included within defamation are the subcategories of libel and slander. Historically, slanders were oral defamations and were handled by the common-law courts; libels were written defamations that, because of the development of printing, became a major concern of the crown. After the end of the days of the Star Chamber, a criminal court, oral and written defamations were redressed by the common-law courts. Those courts, however, preserved some distinctions between the two that have survived to our day.

The critical distinction relates to what types of damages a plaintiff must show in order to be allowed to bring an action for defamation. Two types of damages are central to this discussion. "Special damages" are specific identifiable losses that the plaintiff can prove he has sustained and can trace to the defendant's defamatory statement. "General damages" are damages to reputation that the plaintiff is presumed or proven to have sustained as a result of the defendant's statement. The jury is permitted to speculate on the extent of injury based on the words used, the medium used and the predicted response of the community.

The common law courts have treated libel as substantially more serious than slander. The distinction arose when relatively few people could read and the written word inspired awe and thus was more credible. A writing might be given more weight because it required more thought and planning than a spontaneous oral utterance. Furthermore, the writing was more lasting and was likely to reach a larger audience than most, if not all, slanders. Thus, libels as a class were more likely to cause harm than slanders, and courts declared that plaintiffs in libel cases were able to recover general damages without any showing of special damages. Therefore, a plaintiff proceeding under libel has always been at least as well off as, and often better off than, a plaintiff suing for slander for precisely the same words.

If an action is for slander, plaintiff must prove "special damages" unless the defamatory thrust fits into at least one of four categories. These categories are: the imputation of a serious crime involving moral turpitude; imputation of an existing loathsome disease; a charge that attacks the plaintiff's competence or honesty in business, trade or profession; or a charge of unchastity in a woman. Such a spoken charge is called "slander *per se*" and permits an action enabling the plaintiff to claim general damages to reputation without proving actual pecuniary harm. Here the jury may conclude that publication of the charge caused substantial harm in the community, and can measure damages according to the number and identity of those who learned of the charge, and their presumed reaction based on the seriousness and credibility of the charge. If a plaintiff can also establish special damages, these could be recovered in addition to any general damages.

If the slander is not within the four categories, then an action must be supported by proof of special damages, such as losing a job or a business deal.

The distinction between libel and slander has blurred with the development of new modes of communication. Until this century, it was likely that a written defamation would reach more people than an oral one. But with the development of electronic media, the odds have shifted. In analyzing new technologies should we stick to the traditional oral-written line or should we develop an approach that treats all modes of mass communication as libel and other modes of communication as slander? In a few states, legislation has resolved the matter. For example, California provides that broadcasting is slander. In the states that are resolving the question by common law, the tendency has been to treat broadcasting as libel.

The resulting libel-slander rules have sometimes permitted a plaintiff to recover enormous amounts in general damages. At other times they have barred a plaintiff from recovering anything whatever, because special damages were required but could not be proven although serious general harm seemed likely.

In addition to the critical distinction between general and special damages, two other classifications loom large in defamation law: nominal damages and punitive damages. Although nominal damages are unimportant in most tort actions, they may be central in defamation cases. The award of a symbolic amount such as six cents usually shows that the jury found the attack to be false but also found the words not to have hurt, either because the speaker was not credible or the plaintiff's strong reputation blunted the harm (or his reputation was so low nothing could really hurt it). For an example, see the suit by Quentin Reynolds against the Hearst Corporation and one of its columnists, upholding a jury award of $1 in compensatory damages and $175,000 in punitive damages against the various defendants. Reynolds v. Pegler, 223 F.2d 429 (2d Cir.), certiorari denied 350 U.S. 846 (1955)(Black, J., dissenting).

A few states declare that punitive damages, which are to punish defendants for serious misbehavior, are never recoverable. Most states allow them in appropriate cases.

3.   THE BASIS FOR LIABILITY—THE TROUBLE SPOT

Before one person is liable in tort law for hurting another, commonly, but not universally, some "fault" must be ascribed to the actor's conduct. For example, a plaintiff cannot win an automobile accident case simply by showing that the defendant's car hit the plaintiff. Instead, plaintiff must show that the defendant driver was "at fault" in his behavior. (It is, of course, different in so-called "no-fault" states, which emphasize the harm to plaintiff rather than the fault of the defendant.)

In defamation, the common law long took the view that fault played no part in the tort. In other words, historically, plaintiffs had only to show that the defendants' statements hurt the plaintiffs' reputations and prove whatever damages were required by the libel-slander rules. It was irrelevant that the defendants did not realize that their statements could hurt the plaintiffs or anyone.

Thus, a newspaper lost a case in which it published a birth announcement that was a hoax—the couple had been married only three months. Those who read the article and who knew the fact of plaintiff's recent marriage would have given the story a meaning the newspaper never intended. Even if the newspaper had tried unsuccessfully to check the story but failed to learn about the hoax, it would not have mattered. The common law asserted that defendants in defamation cases were subject to "strict liability"—a liability that was not based on fault. The peril to free speech is readily apparent today. But the response in earlier times was that the remedy was accuracy and refusal to write about things that were not known first hand.

As we shall see, this troubling aspect of the common law has become the focus of constitutional developments.

For the electronic media, the problem of determining liability can be particularly difficult in instances of live or near-live transmissions. In a Massachusetts case, a candidate for public office alleged that he had been libeled when the host of a radio talk show failed to take advantage of a seven-second delay to terminate the remarks of an anonymous caller. Pacella v. Milford Radio Corp., 18 Mass.App.Ct. 6, 462 N.E.2d 355 (1984), affirmed without opinion by an evenly divided court, 394 Mass. 1051, 476 N.E.2d 595, certiorari denied 474 U.S. 844 (1985). Under the common law, the candidate might have won. The common-law tradition was that media were responsible for libelous statements they transmitted, whether they originated them or not, and whether they were careful or not. Several states adopted a model statute giving broadcasters greater protection. As we shall see in the discussion of constitutional privilege, p. 885, *infra*, however, a different standard is imposed in cases involving public figures today. Thus, in the Pacella case, the court held that the broadcaster was not responsible because it had not been shown that failure to stop the allegedly libelous statement demonstrated "reckless disregard of truth or falsity," language to which we will return later in this chapter.

Traditionally, the plaintiff's action for defamation has been easy to establish. The plaintiff had to prove the publication to a third person of a statement of and concerning plaintiff that injured his reputation, and then had to meet whatever damage showing was required under the relevant libel-slander rules. These elements shown, it was up to the defendant to present a defense.

The Internet, however, poses new questions about liability, in part because of opposing views as to whether providers of on-line services are publishers or are merely passive distributors or conduits like bookstores or libraries. Several cases have dealt with this issue. In Cubby Inc. v. CompuServe Inc., 776 F.Supp. 135, 19 Med.L.Rptr. 1525 (S.D.N.Y.1991), the publisher of the electronic newsletter *Skuttlebut* sued CompuServe for allegedly defamatory statements in a competing electronic newsletter called *Rumorville USA*. The latter called *Skuttlebut* a "new start-up scam" that got its information "through some backdoor." CompuServe argued that it acted as a news distributor rather than a publisher and therefore could not be held liable for the statements in *Rumorville*. A federal district court agreed, calling the on-line service "in essence" an electronic for-profit Library with "little or no editorial control."

In contrast, in Stratton Oakmont, Inc. v. Prodigy Services Co., 1995 WL 323710, 23 Med.L.Rptr. 1794 (N.Y.Sup.1995), an unknown Prodigy user posted a message on Prodigy's "Money Talk" electronic bulletin board in October 1994 portraying a securities investment firm and its president as criminals and characterizing the firm's dealings as fraud. They sued for $200 million. Prodigy argued that it was not a publisher, but that argument was rejected by a New York trial court in May 1995. The trial judge indicated that Prodigy's use of human monitors and automated systems to remove objectionable material made it a publisher. The parties settled the lawsuit late in 1995, but the trial judge declined to withdraw his decision. Best's Review, March 1996 at 60.

As we shall see in the *Zeran* momentarily, § 230 of the Communications Decency Act of 1996, provides that "no provider or user of an interactive computer service shall be treated as the publisher or speaker of any information provided by another information content provider." 47 U.S.C.A. § 230(c)(1). However, another New York case—this one resulting from defamatory email messages and bulletin board postings in September 1994 (before the period covered by the CDA)—resulted in a 1997 decision in favor of defendant Prodigy Services. "Vile and obscene" email was sent by what has been described as "an infantile practical joker" to a leader in then—15–year-old Alex Lunney's Boy Scout troop. It was sent from a fictitious account in the name of Alex Lunney and included threats of rape, sodomy, and murder. The boy's troop leader then confronted him in the presence of the boy's mother. The boy eventually sued Prodigy for defamation, negligence, and intentional infliction of emotional distress. A New York appellate court, in finding for Prodigy, relied on a New York State court decision in Anderson v. New York Telephone Co., 35 N.Y.2d 746, 361 N.Y.S.2d 913, 320 N.E.2d 647 (1974), comparing Prodigy's service to that of a telephone company in which the company's employees play no part in the creation of messages, and said Prodigy, because it exercised no "editorial control" over the emails or bulletin board postings in September 1994 (Prodigy had discontinued pre-screening for offensive language and had discontinued "Board Leaders" or "Editors" for the bulletin boards earlier that year), could not be held liable. Lunney v. Prodigy Services, 250 A.D.2d 230, 27 Med.L.Rptr. 1373 (1998).

In Zeran v. America Online, the issue presented was slightly different, because AOL had received notice of defamatory material posted through their services.

ZERAN v. AMERICA ONLINE, INC.

United States Court of Appeals, Fourth Circuit, 1997.
129 F.3d 327, 25 Med.L.Rptr. 2526.

Before WILKINSON, CHIEF JUDGE, RUSSELL, CIRCUIT JUDGE, and BOYLE, CHIEF UNITED STATES DISTRICT JUDGE for the Eastern District of North Carolina, sitting by designation.

WILKINSON, CHIEF JUDGE:

Kenneth Zeran brought this action against America Online, Inc. ("AOL"), arguing that AOL unreasonably delayed in removing defamatory messages posted by an unidentified third party, refused to post retractions of those messages, and failed to screen for similar postings thereafter. The district court granted judgment for AOL on the grounds that the Communications Decency Act of 1996 ("CDA")—47 U.S.C. § 230—bars Zeran's claims. Zeran appeals, arguing that § 230 leaves intact liability for interactive computer service providers who possess notice of defamatory material posted through their services. He also contends that § 230 does not apply here because his claims arise from AOL's alleged negligence prior to the CDA's enactment. Section 230, however, plainly immunizes computer service providers like AOL from liability for information that originates with third parties. Furthermore, Congress clearly expressed its intent that § 230 apply to lawsuits, like Zeran's, instituted after the CDA's enactment. Accordingly, we affirm the judgment of the district court.

I.

"The Internet is an international network of interconnected computers," currently used by approximately 40 million people worldwide. Reno v. ACLU, 521 U.S. 844, 117 S.Ct. 2329, 2334, 138 L.Ed.2d 874 (1997). One of the many means by which individuals access the Internet is through an interactive computer service. These services offer not only a connection to the Internet as a whole, but also allow their subscribers to access information communicated and stored only on each computer service's individual proprietary network. Id. AOL is just such an interactive computer service. Much of the information transmitted over its network originates with the company's millions of subscribers. They may transmit information privately via electronic mail, or they may communicate publicly by posting messages on AOL bulletin boards, where the messages may be read by any AOL subscriber.

The instant case comes before us on a motion for judgment on the pleadings, [ ], so we accept the facts alleged in the complaint as true. [   ]

On April 25, 1995, an unidentified person posted a message on an AOL bulletin board advertising "Naughty Oklahoma T–Shirts." The posting described the sale of shirts featuring offensive and tasteless slogans related to the April 19, 1995, bombing of the Alfred P. Murrah Federal Building in Oklahoma City. Those interested in purchasing the shirts were instructed to call "Ken" at Zeran's home phone number in Seattle, Washington. As a result of this anonymously perpetrated prank, Zeran received a high volume of calls, comprised primarily of angry and derogatory messages, but also including death threats. Zeran could not change his phone number because he relied on its availability to the public in running his business out of his home. Later that day, Zeran called AOL and informed a company representative of his predicament. The employee assured Zeran that the posting would be removed from AOL's bulletin board but explained that as a matter of policy AOL would not post a retraction. The parties dispute the date that AOL removed this original posting from its bulletin board.

On April 26, the next day, an unknown person posted another message advertising additional shirts with new tasteless slogans related to the Oklahoma City bombing. Again, interested buyers were told to call Zeran's phone number, to ask for "Ken," and to "please call back if busy" due to high demand. The angry, threatening phone calls intensified. Over the next four days, an unidentified party continued to post messages on AOL's bulletin board, advertising additional items including bumper stickers and key chains with still more offensive slogans. During this time period, Zeran called AOL repeatedly and was told by company representatives that the individual account from which the messages were posted would soon be closed. Zeran also reported his case to Seattle FBI agents. By April 30, Zeran was receiving an abusive phone call approximately every two minutes.

Meanwhile, an announcer for Oklahoma City radio station KRXO received a copy of the first AOL posting. On May 1, the announcer related the message's contents on the air, attributed them to "Ken" at Zeran's phone number, and urged the listening audience to call the number. After this radio broadcast, Zeran was inundated with death threats and other violent calls from Oklahoma City residents. Over the next few days, Zeran talked to both KRXO and AOL representatives. He also spoke to his local police, who subsequently surveilled his home to protect his safety. By May 14, after an Oklahoma City newspaper published a story exposing the shirt advertisements as a hoax and after KRXO made an on-air apology, the number of calls to Zeran's residence finally subsided to fifteen per day.

[Suits against KRXO and AOL were transferred to the Eastern District of Virginia.] Zeran did not bring any action against the party who posted the offensive messages.[1] [The district court granted AOL

---

1. Zeran maintains that AOL made it impossible to identify the original party by failing to maintain adequate records of its users. The issue of AOL's record keeping practices, however, is not presented by this appeal.

judgment on the pleadings under Federal Rule 12(c), based on the claim that § 230 was a complete defense. This appeal followed.]

II.

A.

Because § 230 was successfully advanced by AOL in the district court as a defense to Zeran's claims, we shall briefly examine its operation here. Zeran seeks to hold AOL liable for defamatory speech initiated by a third party. He argued to the district court that once he notified AOL of the unidentified third party's hoax, AOL had a duty to remove the defamatory posting promptly, to notify its subscribers of the message's false nature, and to effectively screen future defamatory material. . . .

The relevant portion of § 230 states: "No provider or user of an interactive computer service shall be treated as the publisher or speaker of any information provided by another information content provider." 47 U.S.C. § 230(c)(1). By its plain language, § 230 creates a federal immunity to any cause of action that would make service providers liable for information originating with a third-party user of the service. Specifically, § 230 precludes courts from entertaining claims that would place a computer service provider in a publisher's role. Thus, lawsuits seeking to hold a service provider liable for its exercise of a publisher's traditional editorial functions—such as deciding whether to publish, withdraw, postpone or alter content—are barred.

The purpose of this statutory immunity is not difficult to discern. Congress recognized the threat that tort-based lawsuits pose to freedom of speech in the new and burgeoning Internet medium. The imposition of tort liability on service providers for the communications of others represented, for Congress, simply another form of intrusive government regulation of speech. Section 230 was enacted, in part, to maintain the robust nature of Internet communication and, accordingly, to keep government interference in the medium to a minimum. In specific statutory findings, Congress recognized the Internet and interactive computer services as offering "a forum for a true diversity of political discourse, unique opportunities for cultural development, and myriad avenues for intellectual activity." Id. § 230(a)(3). It also found that the Internet and interactive computer services "have flourished," to the benefit of all Americans, *with a minimum of government regulation.* Id. § 230(a)(4) (emphasis added). Congress further stated that it is "the policy of the United States . . . to preserve the vibrant and competitive free market that presently exists for the Internet and other interactive computer services, *unfettered by Federal or State regulation.*" Id. § 230(b)(2) (emphasis added).

None of this means, of course, that the original culpable party who posts defamatory messages would escape accountability. While Congress acted to keep government regulation of the Internet to a minimum, it also found it to be the policy of the United States "to ensure vigorous enforcement of Federal criminal laws to deter and punish trafficking in obscenity, stalking, and harassment by means of computer." Id. § 230(b)(5). Congress made a policy choice, however, not to deter harmful online speech through the separate route of imposing tort liability on companies that serve as intermediaries for other parties' potentially injurious messages.

Congress' purpose in providing the § 230 immunity was thus evident. Interactive computer services have millions of users. See Reno v. ACLU, [   ] (noting that at the time of the district court trial, "commercial online services had almost 12 million individual subscribers"). The amount of information communicated via interactive computer services is therefore staggering. The specter of tort liability in an area of such prolific speech would have an obvious chilling effect. It would be impossible for service providers to screen each of their millions of postings for possible problems. Faced with potential liability for each message republished by their services, interactive computer service providers might choose to severely restrict the number and type of messages posted. Congress considered the weight of the speech interests implicated and chose to immunize service providers to avoid any such restrictive effect.

Another important purpose of § 230 was to encourage service providers to self-regulate the dissemination of offensive material over their services. In this respect, § 230 responded to a New York state court decision, Stratton Oakmont, Inc. v. Prodigy Servs. Co., 1995 WL 323710 (N.Y.Sup.Ct. May 24, 1995). There, the plaintiffs sued Prodigy—an interactive computer service like AOL—for defamatory comments made by an unidentified party on one of Prodigy's bulletin boards. The court held Prodigy to the strict liability standard normally applied to original publishers of defamatory statements, rejecting Prodigy's claims that it should be held only to the lower "knowledge" standard usually reserved for distributors. The court reasoned that Prodigy acted more like an original publisher than a distributor both because it advertised its practice of controlling content on its service and because it actively screened and edited messages posted on its bulletin boards.

Congress enacted § 230 to remove the disincentives to self-regulation created by the Stratton Oakmont decision. Under that court's holding, computer service providers who regulated the dissemination of offensive material on their services risked subjecting themselves to liability, because such regulation cast the service provider in the role of a publisher. Fearing that the specter of liability would therefore deter service providers from blocking and screening offensive material, Congress enacted § 230's broad immunity "to remove disincentives for the development and utilization of blocking and filtering technologies that empower parents to restrict their children's access to objectionable or inappropriate online material." 47 U.S.C. § 230(b)(4). In line with this purpose, § 230 forbids the imposition of publisher liability on a service provider for the exercise of its editorial and self-regulatory functions.

B.

Zeran argues, however, that the § 230 immunity eliminates only publisher liability, leaving distributor liability intact. Publishers can be held liable for defamatory statements contained in their works even absent proof that they had specific knowledge of the statement's inclusion. W. Page Keeton et al., Prosser and Keeton on the Law of Torts § 113, at 810 (5th ed.1984). According to Zeran, interactive computer service providers like AOL are normally considered instead to be distributors, like traditional news vendors or book sellers. Distributors cannot be held liable for defamatory statements contained in the materials they distribute unless it is proven at a minimum that they have actual knowledge of the defamatory statements upon which liability is predicated. Id. at 811 (explaining that distributors are not liable "in the absence of proof that they knew or had reason to know of the existence of defamatory matter contained in matter published"). Zeran contends that he provided AOL with sufficient notice of the defamatory statements appearing on the company's bulletin board. This notice is significant, says Zeran, because AOL could be held liable as a distributor only if it acquired knowledge of the defamatory statements' existence.

Because of the difference between these two forms of liability, Zeran contends that the term "distributor" carries a legally distinct meaning from the term "publisher." Accordingly, he asserts that Congress' use of only the term "publisher" in § 230 indicates a purpose to immunize service providers only from publisher liability. He argues that distributors are left unprotected by § 230 and, therefore, his suit should be permitted to proceed against AOL. We disagree. Assuming arguendo that Zeran has satisfied the requirements for imposition of distributor liability, this theory of liability is merely a subset, or a species, of publisher liability, and is therefore also foreclosed by § 230.

The terms "publisher" and "distributor" derive their legal significance from the context of defamation law. Although Zeran attempts to artfully plead his claims as ones of negligence, they are indistinguishable from a garden variety defamation action. Because the publication of a statement is a necessary element in a defamation action, only one who publishes can be subject to this form of tort liability. Restatement (Second) of Torts § 558(b) (1977); [ ]. Publication does not only describe the choice by an author to include certain information. In addition, both the negligent communication of a defamatory statement and the failure to remove such a statement when first communicated by another party—each alleged by Zeran here under a negligence label— constitute publication. Restatement (Second) of Torts § 577; see also Tacket v. General Motors Corp., 836 F.2d 1042, 1046–47 (7th Cir.1987). In fact, every repetition of a defamatory statement is considered a publication. [ ]

In this case, AOL is legally considered to be a publisher. "[E]very one who takes part in the publication . . . is charged with publication."

[ ] Even distributors are considered to be publishers for purposes of defamation law:

> Those who are in the business of making their facilities available to disseminate the writings composed, the speeches made, and the information gathered by others may also be regarded as participating to such an extent in making the books, newspapers, magazines, and information available to others as to be regarded as publishers. They are intentionally making the contents available to others, sometimes without knowing all of the contents—including the defamatory content—and sometimes without any opportunity to ascertain, in advance, that any defamatory matter was to be included in the matter published.

[Prosser & Keeton] at 803. AOL falls squarely within this traditional definition of a publisher and, therefore, is clearly protected by § 230's immunity.

Zeran contends that decisions like Stratton Oakmont and Cubby, Inc. v. CompuServe Inc. [p. 872], recognize a legal distinction between publishers and distributors. He misapprehends, however, the significance of that distinction for the legal issue we consider here. It is undoubtedly true that mere conduits, or distributors, are subject to a different standard of liability. As explained above, distributors must at a minimum have knowledge of the existence of a defamatory statement as a prerequisite to liability. But this distinction signifies only that different standards of liability may be applied within the larger publisher category, depending on the specific type of publisher concerned. See Keeton et al., [   ] at 799–800 (explaining that every party involved is charged with publication, although degrees of legal responsibility differ). To the extent that decisions like Stratton and Cubby utilize the terms "publisher" and "distributor" separately, the decisions correctly describe two different standards of liability. Stratton and Cubby do not, however, suggest that distributors are not also a type of publisher for purposes of defamation law.

Zeran simply attaches too much importance to the presence of the distinct notice element in distributor liability. The simple fact of notice surely cannot transform one from an original publisher to a distributor in the eyes of the law. To the contrary, once a computer service provider receives notice of a potentially defamatory posting, it is thrust into the role of a traditional publisher. The computer service provider must decide whether to publish, edit, or withdraw the posting. In this respect, Zeran seeks to impose liability on AOL for assuming the role for which § 230 specifically proscribes liability—the publisher role.

Our view that Zeran's complaint treats AOL as a publisher is reinforced because AOL is cast in the same position as the party who originally posted the offensive messages. According to Zeran's logic, AOL is legally at fault because it communicated to third parties an allegedly defamatory statement. This is precisely the theory under which the original poster of the offensive messages would be found liable. If the original party is considered a publisher of the offensive messages, Zeran certainly cannot attach liability to AOL under the same theory without conceding that AOL too must be treated as a publisher of the statements.

Zeran next contends that interpreting § 230 to impose liability on service providers with knowledge of defamatory content on their services is consistent with the statutory purposes outlined in Part IIA. Zeran fails, however, to understand the practical implications of notice liability in the interactive computer service context. Liability upon notice would defeat the dual purposes advanced by § 230 of the CDA. Like the strict liability imposed by the Stratton Oakmont court, liability upon notice reinforces service providers' incentives to restrict speech and abstain from self-regulation.

If computer service providers were subject to distributor liability, they would face potential liability each time they receive notice of a potentially defamatory statement—from any party, concerning any message. Each notification would require a careful yet rapid investigation of the circumstances surrounding the posted information, a legal judgment concerning the information's defamatory character, and an on-the-spot editorial decision whether to risk liability by allowing the continued publication of that information. Although this might be feasible for the traditional print publisher, the sheer number of postings on interactive computer services would create an impossible burden in the Internet context. Cf. Auvil v. CBS 60 Minutes, 800 F.Supp. 928, 931 (E.D.Wash. 1992) (recognizing that it is unrealistic for network affiliates to "monitor incoming transmissions and exercise on-the-spot discretionary calls"). Because service providers would be subject to liability only for the publication of information, and not for its removal, they would have a natural incentive simply to remove messages upon notification, whether the contents were defamatory or not. See Philadelphia Newspapers, Inc. v. Hepps, 475 U.S. 767, 777, (1986) (recognizing that fears of unjustified liability produce a chilling effect antithetical to First Amendment's protection of speech). Thus, like strict liability, liability upon notice has a chilling effect on the freedom of Internet speech.

Similarly, notice-based liability would deter service providers from regulating the dissemination of offensive material over their own services. Any efforts by a service provider to investigate and screen material posted on its service would only lead to notice of potentially defamatory material more frequently and thereby create a stronger basis for liability. Instead of subjecting themselves to further possible lawsuits, service providers would likely eschew any attempts at self-regulation.

More generally, notice-based liability for interactive computer service providers would provide third parties with a no-cost means to create the basis for future lawsuits. Whenever one was displeased with the speech of another party conducted over an interactive computer service, the offended party could simply "notify" the relevant service provider, claiming the information to be legally defamatory. In light of the vast amount of speech communicated through interactive computer services, these notices could produce an impossible burden for service providers, who would be faced with ceaseless choices of suppressing controversial speech or sustaining prohibitive liability. Because the probable effects of distributor liability on the vigor of Internet speech and on service provider self-regulation are directly contrary to § 230's statutory purposes, we will not assume that Congress intended to leave liability upon notice intact.

Zeran finally contends that the interpretive canon favoring retention of common law principles unless Congress speaks directly to the issue counsels a restrictive reading of the § 230 immunity here. [ ] This interpretive canon does not persuade us to reach a different result. Here, Congress has indeed spoken directly to the issue by employing the legally significant term "publisher," which has traditionally encompassed distributors and original publishers alike.

. . .

Section 230 represents the approach of Congress to a problem of national and international dimension. . . . While Congress allowed for the enforcement of "any State law that is consistent with [§ 230]," 47 U.S.C. § 230(d)(3), it is equally plain that Congress' desire to promote unfettered speech on the Internet must supersede conflicting common law causes of action. Section 230(d)(3) continues: "No cause of action may be brought and no liability may be imposed under any State or local law that is inconsistent with this section." Here, Congress' command is explicitly stated. Its exercise of its commerce power is clear and counteracts the caution counseled by the interpretive canon favoring retention of common law principles.

III.

[The court held that § 230(d)(3) explicitly barred cases filed after the statute's enactment: "No cause of action may be brought and no liability may be imposed under any State or local law that is inconsistent with this section." Even if retroactivity were to be dated from the date of the publication, the court understood that its role was first "to determine whether Congress has expressly prescribed the statute's proper reach." Landgraf v. USI Film Prods., 511 U.S. 244, 280 (1994). "Congress clearly expressed its intent that the statute apply to any complaint instituted after its effective date, regardless of when the relevant conduct giving rise to the claims occurred." Thus, "Congress decided that free speech on the Internet and self-regulation of offensive speech were so important that § 230 should be given immediate, comprehensive effect."]

. . . Section 230 neither imposes any new liability on Zeran nor takes away any rights acquired under prior law. No person has a vested right in a nonfinal tort judgment, much less an unfiled tort claim. [ ] Furthermore, Zeran cannot point to any action he took in reliance on the law prior to § 230's enactment. Because § 230 has no untoward retroactive effect, even the presumption against statutory retroactivity absent an express directive from Congress is of no help to Zeran here.

IV.

For the foregoing reasons, we affirm the judgment of the district court.

AFFIRMED.

Notes and Questions

1. What is the relationship between "publisher" and "distributor" in defamation law? Is this a decision based on the common law distinction or on the court's reading of the statute?

2. How does AOL's situation after receiving notice differ from that of (1) a radio station that uses a live call-in format or (2) a newspaper that receives notice that an article it is considering publishing is in fact libelous?

3. What arguments justify the court's analysis of AOL's situation after it gets notice from Zeran? Was there reason to doubt Zeran's claim when it came in? Should that be relevant?

4. Might Zeran formulate a valid claim based on either (1) AOL's refusal to help him identify the (identifiable) person who posted the statements or (2) the claim that AOL's operating structure does not permit it to identify such posters?

5. Dendrite International Inc. sued four defendants, known only by their user names on a Yahoo! financial message board on which they had posted messages, for defamation as well as for breach of contract, breach of fiduciary duty and misappropriation of trade secrets. Dendrite asserted that it could tell from the messages that at least two of the defendants were current or former employees of Dendrite, and further asserted that their employees had signed confidentiality agreements that remained in effect for two years after an employee leaves the company. Yahoo! declined to identify the posters without a subpoena.

The court declined to issue the subpoena without expert analysis that the allegedly defamatory statements on the message board had caused fluctuations in the company's stock price. The judge cited Columbia Insurance Co. v. seescandy.com, 185 F.R.D. 573 (N.D.Cal.1999), requiring that the right to post on the Internet anonymously be balanced against the interest in allowing parties to sue for legitimate grievances. The court found the plaintiff had neither proved neither reputational injury nor proved that any trade secret existed. Dendrite International Inc. v. Doe, N.J. Super. Ct., Ch. Div., Morris County, No. MRS C–29–00 (2000).

4. COMMON LAW DEFENSES

Several common law libel defenses are typically recognized in state law. They include truth, the privilege accorded participants in certain official proceedings, the privilege accorded to those who quote accurately from such proceedings and the privilege of criticism, sometimes called "fair comment." These defenses were used by libel defendants under strict liability prior to 1964. We will discuss them first and then look at the important constitutional privilege of absence of malice in a separate section.

a. *Truth*

The most obvious defense, but one rarely used, is to prove the essential truth of the defamatory statement. Most states recognize truth as a complete defense regardless of the speaker's motives. Because the action is intended to compensate those whose reputations are damaged incorrectly, if the defendant has spoken the truth, the reputational harm is deemed to provide no basis for an action. A minority of states have required the truth to have been spoken with "good motives" or for "justifiable ends" or both, but in the wake of *New York Times* and its progeny, such requirements may not be constitutional.

The defendant need not prove literal truth but must establish the "sting" of his charge. Thus, if the defendant has charged the plaintiff with stealing $25,000 from a bank, truth will be established even if the actual amount was only $12,000. If the defendant cannot prove any theft whatever but can prove the plaintiff is a bigamist, this information will not support his defense of truth, but it may help mitigate damages to show that the plaintiff's reputation is already in low esteem for other reasons and, thus he has suffered less harm than might otherwise have occurred.

These matters can raise troublesome questions. In Hovey v. Iowa State Daily Publication Board, Inc., 372 N.W.2d 253, 12 Med.L.Rptr. 1035 (Iowa 1985), the defendant newspaper reported on a violent episode that took place while the female plaintiff was serving as a bartender at an American Legion Hall. One customer knocked the only other customer unconscious and forced the plaintiff to perform oral sex upon him. The man was charged with "sexual abuse." The newspaper, however, reported that the man had been charged with "raping a bartender." Another paragraph reported that he had been charged with "second degree sexual abuse, willful injury, and first degree robbery." The article also stated that bond for the "rape" and robbery charges had been set at $50,000.

The court rejected the plaintiff's claim that "rape" referred only to "forcible genital sexual intercourse." It agreed with the defendant that "rape" was broad enough to include "any forced sex act, including oral sex." The court referred to general dictionaries and to recent revisions in the Iowa criminal code that had subsumed rape into the crime of sexual abuse in 1978.

Finally, after adopting the substantial truth test, the court concluded that the "difference between the truth and the reported truth was not material enough for the inaccuracy to be actionable."

Truth ultimately was the critical issue in a highly publicized suit against "60 Minutes." A 1989 segment on the program focussed on the possible carcinogenic effect of pesticides, including one (daminozide) marketed under the trade name Alar, used on apples. Many stores stopped stocking Alar-treated apples, and growers claimed to have lost as much as $75 million as a result. Eleven apple growers sued the network for libel. Later in 1989 the Environmental Protection Agency classified daminozide as a probable carcinogen, and Alar's manufacturer asked the EPA to withdraw the food-use registrations of the chemical. A federal district court dismissed the libel suit, finding that the growers failed to present evidence sufficient to create a "genuine issue of material fact on the issue of whether the broadcast was false," and the court of appeals affirmed. Auvil v. CBS "60 Minutes," 67 F.3d 816, 23 Med.L.Rptr. 2454 (9th Cir.1995), certiorari denied 517 U.S. 1167 (1996).

Truth is little used as a defense because the defense may be very expensive to establish. A defendant relying on truth almost always bears the legal costs of a full-dress trial as well as the sometimes major expense of investigating the matter and gathering enough evidence to ensure the outcome.

b.   *State Privileges*

Not only were there disadvantages to the defense of truth, there were attractive alternatives. Over the centuries the law of defamation has developed several privileges to protect those who utter defamations. Some privileges are "absolute" in the sense that if the occasion gives rise to an absolute privilege, there will be no liability even if the speaker deliberately lied about the plaintiff. The most significant example is the federal and state constitutional privilege afforded legislators who may not be sued for defamation for any statement made during debate. High executive officials, judges and participants in judicial proceedings also have an absolute privilege to speak freely on matters relevant to their obligations. No matter how such a speaker abuses the privilege by lying, no tort liability will flow. See Barr v. Matteo, 360 U.S. 564 (1959). The main circumstance that gives absolute privilege to the media occurs when broadcasters are required to grant equal opportunity to all candidates for the same office. If a candidate commits defamation, the broadcaster is not liable for the defamation. See *WDAY*, p. 169, *supra.*

Most common law privileges serve individuals and do not specifically affect media—with two important exceptions. The first involves the conditional privilege to make fair and accurate reports of governmental proceedings. Under general defamation law, one who repeats another's statement is responsible for the truth of what he repeats. Thus, if X states that "Y told me that Z is a murderer," and Z sues X for defamation, X will be treated as the publisher who is responsible for his own statement. In order to prevail on the defense of truth, X must prove that Z is in fact a murderer—it is not enough for X to prove that in fact Y told him that Z was a murderer. The general reason underlying this view is the reluctance to protect gossip.

It was not long, however, before the courts and the legislatures began to realize that sometimes speakers should be encouraged to repeat others' statements. The federal and state constitutions had already provided that members of the legislative branch could quote others in debate with absolute protection against legal sanctions.

The major example of the value of repetition was found in the reporting of how government was functioning and what government officials were saying. Thus, observers were to be encouraged to report what legislators said on the floor or in the committee as well as events in court. It would put reporters in a hopeless situation to be able to report safely only the truthful statements of government officials or of witnesses at a trial. As a result of these considerations, a privilege developed, sometimes called the privilege of "record libel," under which reports of what occurs in governmental proceedings are privileged even if some of those quoted have spoken falsely—so long as the report is accurate or a fair summary of what transpired.

The second major common law privilege of value to the media was the privilege of fair comment upon matters of public interest. When the privilege was applied in cases of literary and artistic criticism it caused little confusion. Problems raised by such comment are discussed in the classic Cherry v. Des Moines Leader, 114 Iowa 298, 86 N.W. 323 (1901) in which a reviewer scathingly described a performance by the Cherry sisters. But at the turn of the century cases arose in which the privilege of fair comment was claimed with regard to other matters of public interest, including the conduct of politicians. This was not the privilege of reporting what certain public officials were doing in their official capacity. Rather the privilege claimed would permit citizens to criticize and argue about the conduct of their officials, and these cases presented the problem of distinguishing between facts and opinion. In the literary criticism area the application of the privilege could depend upon the accuracy of the "facts" because they were usually readily apparent. When dealing with politics, however, the "facts" were often elusive. This new problem created a judicial split.

Most state courts decided that in order for criticism of government officials and others to be privileged, the facts upon which the comments were based had to be true. A minority of courts, including Coleman v. MacLennan, 78 Kan. 711, 98 P. 281 (1908), disagreed. They decided that facts relating to matters of public interest could not form the basis for a defamation case even if the facts were incorrect, so long as the speaker honestly believed them to be true.

It was from this disagreement among the states that the constitutional developments sprang.

B. CONSTITUTIONAL PRIVILEGE

So long as state law controlled, publishers and broadcasters could try to persuade state courts and legislatures to alter the defamation rules. As we have seen, their success varied in different states. Early efforts to gain further protection in defamation cases by invoking federal constitutional law to limit state power did not fare well.

In *Near*, p. 25, *supra*, the case that perhaps first reinforced the protection of the press in this country, the majority observed, "But it is recognized that punishment for the abuse of the liberty accorded to the press is essential to the protection of the public, and that the common-law rules that subject the libeler to responsibility for the public offense, as well as for the private injury, are not abolished by the protection extended in our Constitution."

In *Chaplinsky*, p. 22, *supra*, the Court said:

> There are certain well-defined and narrowly limited classes of speech, the prevention and punishment of which have never been thought to raise any Constitutional problem. These include the lewd and obscene, the profane, the libelous, and the insulting or "fighting" words—those that by their very utterance inflict injury or tend to incite an immediate breach of the peace. It has been well observed that such utterances are no essential part of any exposition of ideas, and are of such slight social value as a step to truth that any benefit that may be derived from them is clearly outweighed by the social interest in order and morality.

This language was often quoted approvingly. Justice Frankfurter, writing for a 5–4 majority in Beauharnais v. Illinois, 343 U.S. 250 (1952), to sustain a state criminal libel law, relied on *Chaplinsky* for the proposition that libelous utterances were not "within the area of constitutionally protected speech."

This sequence set the stage for the following case from Alabama, a state that had long followed the majority rule that there was no privilege for incorrect facts, even in stories of public importance.

NEW YORK TIMES CO. v. SULLIVAN

Together with Abernathy v. Sullivan

Supreme Court of the United States, 1964.

376 U.S. 254, 84 S.Ct. 710, 11 L.Ed.2d 686, 1 Med.L.Rptr. 1527.

[This action was based on a full-page advertisement in *The New York Times* on behalf of several individuals and groups protesting a "wave of terror" against blacks involved in non-violent demonstrations in the South. Plaintiff, one of three elected commissioners of Montgomery, the capital of Alabama, was in charge of the police department.

When he demanded a retraction, as state law required, *The Times* instead responded that it failed to see how he was defamed. He then filed suit against *The Times* and four clergymen whose names appeared as sponsors—although they denied having authorized this—in the ad. Plaintiff alleged that the third and the sixth paragraphs of the advertisement libelled him:

> "In Montgomery, Alabama, after students sang 'My Country, 'Tis of Thee' on the State Capitol steps, their leaders were expelled from school, and truckloads of police armed with shotguns and tear-gas ringed the Alabama State College Campus. When the entire student body protested to state authorities by refusing to re-register, their dining hall was padlocked in an attempt to starve them into submission."

>   . . .

> "Again and again the Southern violators have answered Dr. King's peaceful protests with intimidation and violence. They have bombed his home almost killing his wife and child. They have assaulted his person. They have arrested him seven times—for 'speeding,' 'loitering' and similar 'offenses.' And now they have charged him with 'perjury'—a *felony* under which they could imprison him for *ten years*. . . ."

Plaintiff claimed that he was libelled in the third paragraph by the reference to the police, since his responsibilities included supervision of the Montgomery police. He asserted that the paragraph could be read as charging the police with ringing the campus and seeking to starve the students by padlocking the dining hall. As to the sixth paragraph, he contended that the word "they" referred to his departments since arrests are usually made by the police and the paragraph could be read as accusing him of committing the acts charged. Several witnesses testified that they read the statements as referring to plaintiff in his capacity as commissioner.

The defendants admitted several inaccuracies in these two paragraphs; the students sang "The Star Spangled Banner," not "My Country, 'Tis of Thee"; nine students were expelled, not for leading the demonstration, but for demanding service at a lunch counter in the county courthouse; the dining hall was never padlocked; police at no time ringed the campus though they were deployed nearby in large numbers; they were not called to the campus in connection with the demonstration; Dr. King had been arrested only four times; and officers disputed his account of the alleged assault. Plaintiff proved that he had not been commissioner when three of the four arrests occurred and that he had nothing to do with procuring the perjury indictment.

The trial judge charged that the statements were libel *per se*, that the jury should decide whether they were made "of and concerning" the plaintiff, and, if so, general damages were to be presumed. Although noting that punitive damages required more than carelessness, he refused to charge that they required a finding of actual intent to harm or "gross negligence and recklessness." He also refused to order the jury to separate its award of general and punitive damages. The jury returned a verdict for $500,000—the full amount demanded. The Alabama Supreme Court affirmed, holding that malice could be found in several aspects of *The Times*'s conduct.

The Supreme Court began by disposing of the assertion that the Fourteenth Amendment is directed against State action and not private action, holding that "[t]he test is not the form in which state power has been applied but, whatever the form, whether such power has in fact been exercised." It also rejected the argument that constitutional guarantees were inapplicable because the statements were part of an advertisement.]

JUSTICE BRENNAN delivered the opinion of the Court.

. . .

II.

. . .

The question before us is whether [Alabama's] rule of liability, as applied to an action brought by a public official against critics of his official conduct, abridges the freedom of speech and of the press that is guaranteed by the First and Fourteenth Amendments.

Respondent relies heavily, as did the Alabama courts, on statements of this Court to the effect that the Constitution does not protect libelous publications. Those statements do not foreclose our inquiry here. None of the cases sustained the use of libel laws to impose sanctions upon expression critical of the official conduct of public officials. . . . In deciding the question now, we are compelled by neither precedent nor policy to give any more weight to the epithet "libel" than we have to other "mere labels" of state law. NAACP v. Button, 371 U.S. 415, 429 (1963). Like insurrection, contempt, advocacy of unlawful acts, breach of the peace, obscenity, solicitation of legal business, and the various other formulae for the repression of expression that have been challenged in this Court, libel can claim no talismanic immunity from constitutional limitations. It must be measured by standards that satisfy the First Amendment.

The general proposition that freedom of expression upon public questions is secured by the First Amendment has long been settled by our decisions. . . . Mr. Justice Brandeis, in his concurring opinion in Whitney v. California, 274 U.S. 357, 375–376 (1927), gave the principle its classic formulation:

"Those who won our independence believed . . . that public discussion is a political duty; and that this should be a fundamental principle of the American government. . . . Believing in the power of reason as applied through public discussion, they eschewed silence coerced by law—the argument of force in its worst form. Recognizing the occasional tyrannies of governing majorities, they amended the Constitution so that free speech and assembly should be guaranteed."

Thus we consider this case against the background of a profound national commitment to the principle that debate on public issues should be uninhibited, robust, and wide-open, and that it may well include vehement, caustic, and sometimes unpleasantly sharp attacks on government and public officials. [   ] The present advertisement, as an expression of grievance and protest on one of the major public issues of our time, would seem clearly to qualify for the constitutional protection. The question is whether it forfeits that protection by the falsity of some of its factual statements and by its alleged defamation of respondent.

. . .

Injury to official reputation affords no more warrant for repressing speech that would otherwise be free than does factual error. Where judicial officers are involved, this Court has held that concern for the dignity and reputation of the courts does not justify the punishment as criminal contempt of criticism of the judge or his decision. Bridges v. California, 314 U.S. 252 (1941). . . . There is no force in respondent's argument that the constitutional limitations implicit in the history of the Sedition Act apply only to Congress and not to the States. It is true that the First Amendment was originally addressed only to action by the Federal Government, and that Jefferson, for one, while denying the power of Congress "to control the freedom of the press," recognized such a power in the States. [   ] But this distinction was eliminated with the adoption of the Fourteenth Amendment and the application to the States of the First Amendment's restrictions. [   ]

What a State may not constitutionally bring about by means of a criminal statute is likewise beyond the reach of its civil law of libel. . . .

[The Court quoted James Madison, suggesting the need for breathing space in public discussion, and the fear that even speakers of the truth will be chilled when the law is too restrictive.]

The constitutional guarantees require, we think, a federal rule that prohibits a public official from recovering damages for a defamatory falsehood relating to his official conduct unless he proves that the statement was made with "actual malice"—that is, with knowledge that it was false or with reckless disregard of whether it was false or not. An oft-cited statement of a like rule, which has been adopted by a number of state courts, is found in the Kansas case of Coleman v. MacLennan, 78 Kan. 711, 98 P. 281 (1908). . . .

Such a privilege for criticism of official conduct is appropriately analogous to the protection accorded a public official when *he* is sued for libel by a private citizen. In Barr v. Matteo, 360 U.S. 564, 575 (1959), this Court held the utterance of a federal official to be absolutely privileged if made "within the outer perimeter" of his duties. The States accord the same immunity to statements of their highest officers, although some differentiate their lesser officials and qualify the privilege they enjoy. But all hold that all officials are protected unless actual malice can be proved. The reason for the official privilege is said to be that the threat of damage suits would otherwise "inhibit the fearless, vigorous, and effective administration of policies of government" and "dampen the ardor of all but the most resolute, or the most irresponsible, in the unflinching discharge of their duties." Barr v. Matteo, supra, 360 U.S., at 571. Analogous considerations support the privilege for the citizen-critic of government. It is as much his duty to criticize as it is the official's duty to administer. . . .

We conclude that such a privilege is required by the First and Fourteenth Amendments.

III.

We hold today that the Constitution delimits a State's power to award damages for libel in actions brought by public officials against critics of their official conduct. Since this is such an action, the rule requiring proof of actual malice is applicable. While Alabama law apparently requires proof of actual malice for an award of punitive damages, where general damages are concerned malice is "presumed." Such a presumption is inconsistent with the federal rule. . . . Since the trial judge did not instruct the jury to differentiate between general and punitive damages, it may be that the verdict was wholly an award of one or the other. But it is impossible to know, in view of the general verdict returned. Because of this uncertainty, the judgment must be reversed and the case remanded. [   ]

Since respondent may seek a new trial we deem that considerations of effective judicial administration require us to review the evidence in the present record to determine whether it could constitutionally support a judgment for respondent. . . .

Applying these standards, we consider that the proof presented to show actual malice lacks convincing clarity which the constitutional standard demands, and hence that it would not constitutionally sustain the judgment for respondent under the proper rule of law. The case of the individual petitioners requires little discussion. Even assuming that they could constitutionally be found to have authorized the use of their names on the advertisement, there was no evidence whatever that they were aware of any erroneous statements or were in any way reckless in that regard. The judgment against them is thus without constitutional support.

As to the Times, we similarly conclude that the facts do not support a finding of actual malice. . . .

. . .

We also think the evidence was constitutionally defective in another respect: it was incapable of supporting the jury's finding that the allegedly libelous statements were made "of and concerning" respondent. Respondent relies on the words of the advertisement and the testimony of six witnesses to establish a connection between it and himself. . . . There was no reference to respondent in the advertisement, either by name or official position. . . .

This proposition has disquieting implications for criticism of governmental conduct. For good reason, "no court of last resort in this country has ever held, or even suggested, that prosecutions for libel on government have any place in the American system of jurisprudence." City of Chicago v. Tribune Co., 307 Ill. 595, 601, 139 N.E. 86, 88 (1923). The present proposition would sidestep this obstacle by transmuting criticism of government, however impersonal it may seem on its face, into personal criticism, and hence potential libel, of the officials of whom the government is composed. . . . We hold that such a proposition may not constitutionally be used to establish that an otherwise impersonal attack on governmental operations was a libel of an official responsible for those operations. Since it was relied on exclusively here, and there was no evidence to connect the statements with respondent, the evidence was constitutionally insufficient to support a finding that the statements referred to respondent.

The judgment of the Supreme Court of Alabama is reversed and the case is remanded to that court for further proceedings not inconsistent with this opinion.

Reversed and remanded.

MR. JUSTICE BLACK, with whom MR. JUSTICE DOUGLAS joins, concurring.

I concur in reversing this half-million-dollar judgment against the New York Times Company and the four individual defendants. In reversing the Court holds that "the Constitution delimits a State's power to award damages for libel in actions brought by public officials against critics of their official conduct." I base my vote to reverse on the belief that the First and Fourteenth Amendments not merely "delimit" a State's power to award damages to "public officials against critics of their official conduct" but completely prohibit a State from exercising such a power. The Court goes on to hold that a State can subject such critics to damages if "actual malice" can be proved against them. "Malice," even as defined by the Court, is an elusive, abstract concept, hard to prove and hard to disprove. The requirement that malice be proved provides at best an evanescent protection for the right critically to discuss public affairs and certainly does not measure up to the sturdy safeguard embodied in the First Amendment. Unlike the Court, therefore, I vote to reverse exclusively on the ground that the Times and the individual defendants had an absolute, unconditional constitutional right to publish in the Times advertisement their criticisms of the Montgomery agencies and officials. . . .

. . .

We would, I think, more faithfully interpret the First Amendment by holding that at the very least it leaves the people and the press free to criticize officials and discuss public affairs with impunity. . . . An unconditional right to say what one pleases about public affairs is what I consider to be the minimum guarantee of the First Amendment.[6]

I regret that the Court has stopped short of this holding indispensable to preserve our free press from destruction.

MR. JUSTICE GOLDBERG, with whom MR. JUSTICE DOUGLAS joins, concurring in the result.

. . .

In my view, the First and Fourteenth Amendments to the Constitution afford to the citizen and to the press an absolute, unconditional privilege to criticize official conduct despite the harm which may flow from excesses and abuses. . . .

. . .

. . . It may be urged that deliberately and maliciously false statements have no conceivable value as free speech. That argument, however, is not responsive to the real issue presented by this case, which is whether that freedom of speech which all agree is constitutionally protected can be effectively safeguarded by a rule allowing the imposition of liability upon a jury's evaluation of the speaker's state of mind. If individual citizens may be held liable in damages for strong words, which a jury finds false and maliciously motivated, there can be little doubt that public debate and advocacy will be constrained. And if newspapers, publishing advertisements dealing with public issues, thereby risk liability, there can also be little doubt that the ability of minority groups to secure publication of their views on public affairs and to seek support for their causes will be greatly diminished. . . .

. . .

If the government official should be immune from libel actions so that his ardor to serve the public will be dampened and "fearless, vigorous, and effective administration of policies of government" not be inhibited, [   ], then the citizen and the press should likewise be immune from libel actions for their criticism of official conduct. . . .

The conclusion that the Constitution affords the citizen and the press an absolute privilege for criticism of official conduct does not leave the public official without defenses against unsubstantiated opinions or deliberate misstatements. "Under our system of government, counterargument and education are the weapons available to expose these matters, not abridgment . . . of free speech. . . ." Wood v. Georgia, 370 U.S. 375, 389 (1962). The public official certainly has equal if not greater access than most private citizens to media of communication. . . .

. . .

Notes and Questions

1.   What is the justification for the majority position?

---

6.   Cf. Meiklejohn, Free Speech and Its Relation to Self–Government (1948).

2. The majority twice observes that deliberate falsity is used in argument. Why is such behavior not protected here?

3. Do you consider either of the concurring opinions preferable to the majority approach? Would it be desirable to enable a public official to have a jury assess the truth of charges against him—without seeking damages?

4. Commenting after the *Times* case, Professor Kalven speculated on the case's future:

> The closing question, of course, is whether the treatment of seditious libel as the key concept for development of appropriate constitutional doctrine will prove germinal. It is not easy to predict what the Court will see in the *Times* opinion as the years roll by. It may regard the opinion as covering simply one pocket of cases, those dealing with libel of public officials, and not destructive of the earlier notions that are inconsistent only with the large reading of the Court's action. But the invitation to follow a dialectic progression from public official to government policy to public policy to matters in the public domain, like art, seems to me to be overwhelming. If the Court accepts the invitation, it will slowly work out for itself the theory of free speech that Alexander Meiklejohn has been offering us for some fifteen years now.

Kalven, The New York Times Case: A Note on "The Central Meaning of the First Amendment," 1964 Sup.Ct.Rev. 191, 221. Does his prediction seem sound? Keep it in mind as we consider the cases decided since *Times*.

5. The majority in the *New York Times* case did not explicitly condemn the concurring approaches. A few months later, in Garrison v. Louisiana, 379 U.S. 64, 1 Med.L.Rptr. 1548 (1964), the Court, in an opinion by Justice Brennan, extended the *Times* rule to cases of criminal libel and also held that truth must be a defense in cases brought by public officials. The majority explained its refusal to protect deliberate falsity:

> Although honest utterance, even if inaccurate, may further the fruitful exercise of the right of free speech, it does not follow that the lie, knowingly and deliberately published about a public official, should enjoy a like immunity. At the time the First Amendment was adopted, as today, there were those unscrupulous enough and skillful enough to use the deliberate or reckless falsehood as an effective political tool to unseat the public servant or even topple an administration. [ ] That speech is used as a tool for political ends does not automatically bring it under the protective mantle of the Constitution. For the use of the known lie as a tool is at once at odds with the premises of democratic government and with the orderly manner in which economic, social, or political change is to be effected. Calculated falsehood falls into that class of utterances which "are no essential part of any exposition of ideas, and are of such slight social value as a step to truth that any benefit that may be derived from them is clearly outweighed by the social interest in order and

morality. . . ." [ ] Hence the knowingly false statement and the false statement made with reckless disregard of the truth, do not enjoy constitutional protection.

6. The next major case was Rosenblatt v. Baer, 383 U.S. 75, 1 Med. L.Rptr. 1558 (1966). Plaintiff Baer had been hired to be Supervisor of a public recreation facility owned by Belknap County, N.H. Defendant, in his weekly newspaper column, noted that a year after plaintiff's discharge the facility was doing much better financially. The column could be understood as charging either inefficiency or dishonesty. In reversing plaintiff's state court judgment, the Supreme Court said that the vague language could be read as an attack on government—and that Baer could not sue unless he showed that he had been singled out for attack. Justice Brennan's majority opinion said that it is clear that the public official designation from *New York Times* applies all the way down the hierarchy of government employees "who have, or appear to the public to have, substantial responsibility for or control over the conduct of governmental affairs."

7. The Supreme Court next considered two cases together, Curtis Pub. Co. v. Butts, and Associated Press v. Walker, 388 U.S. 130, 1 Med. L.Rptr. 1568 (1967). In *Butts,* the defendant magazine had accused the plaintiff athletic director of disclosing his game plan to an opposing coach before their game. Although he was on the staff of a state university, Butts was paid by a private alumni organization. In *Walker,* the defendant news service reported that the plaintiff, a former United States Army general who resigned to engage in political activity, had personally led students in an attack on federal marshals who were enforcing a desegregation order at the University of Mississippi.

In both cases, lower courts had affirmed substantial jury awards against the defendants and had refused to apply the *Times* doctrine on the ground that public officials were not involved. The Supreme Court divided several ways on several issues, affirming *Butts,* 5–4, and reversing *Walker,* 9–0. Chief Justice Warren wrote the pivotal opinion in which he concluded that both men were "public figures" and that the standard developed in *New York Times* should apply to "public figures" as well. He found that on the merits the standard had not been met in *Walker.* In *Butts,* he found that defendant's counsel had deliberately waived the *Times* doctrine and he also found evidence establishing reckless behavior. He thus voted to reverse *Walker* and affirm *Butts.*

> To me, differentiation between "public figures" and "public officials" and adoption of separate standards of proof for each has no basis in law, logic, or First Amendment policy. Increasingly in this country, the distinctions between governmental and private sectors are blurred. . . . [A]lthough they are not subject to the restraints of the political process, "public figures," like "public officials," often play an influential role in ordering society. And surely as a class these "public figures" have as ready access as "public officials" to mass media of communication, both to influence policy and to

counter criticism of their views and activities. Our citizenry has a legitimate and substantial interest in the conduct of such persons, and freedom of the press to engage in uninhibited debate about their involvement in public issues and events is as crucial as it is in the case of "public officials." The fact that they are not amenable to the restraints of the political process only underscores the legitimate and substantial nature of the interest, since it means that public opinion may be the only instrument by which society can attempt to influence their conduct.

8.   In St. Amant v. Thompson, 390 U.S. 727, 1 Med.L.Rptr. 1586 (1968), the defendant, a candidate for public office, read on television a series of statements he had received from Mr. Albin, a member of a Teamsters' Union local. The statements, made under oath, falsely implied that the plaintiff, a deputy sheriff, had taken bribes. The defendant had not checked the facts stated by Albin, nor had he investigated Albin's reputation for veracity. The state court ruled that these failures to inquire further sufficed to meet the required standard of reckless disregard for the truth. The Supreme Court reversed and concluded that the standard of "reckless disregard" had not been met. It recognized that the term could receive no single "infallible definition" and that its outer limits would have to be developed in "case-to-case adjudication, as is true with so many legal standards for judging concrete cases, whether the standard is provided by the Constitution, statutes or case law." There "must be sufficient evidence to permit the conclusion that the defendant in fact entertained serious doubts as to the truth of his publication" in order for recklessness to be found.

9.   Next the Court unanimously extended the *Times* rationale to candidates because "it can hardly be doubted that the constitutional guarantee has its fullest and most urgent application precisely to the conduct of campaigns for political office." Monitor Patriot Co. v. Roy, 401 U.S. 265, 1 Med.L.Rptr. 1619 (1971) and Ocala Star–Banner Co. v. Damron, 401 U.S. 295, 1 Med.L.Rptr. 1624 (1971).

10.   A plurality of the Court took the next step in Rosenbloom v. Metromedia, Inc., 403 U.S. 29, 1 Med.L.Rptr. 1597 (1971), involving a broadcaster's charge that a magazine distributor sold obscene material and was arrested in a police raid. Justice Brennan, joined by Chief Justice Burger and Justice Blackmun, held that the *Times* standard should be extended to "all discussion and communication involving matters of public or general concern, without regard to whether the persons involved are famous or anonymous." The arrest and the distributor's subsequent claims against the police were thought to fit this category, and the *Times* standard was applied. In reaching that position, Justice Brennan concluded that the focus on the plaintiff's status begun in the *Times* case bore "little relationship either to the values protected by the First Amendment or to the nature of our society. . . . Thus, the idea that certain 'public' figures have voluntarily exposed their entire lives to public inspection, while private individuals have kept theirs carefully shrouded from public view is, at best, a legal fiction." Discus-

sion of a matter of public concern must be protected even when it involves an unknown person. If the states fear that private citizens will be unable to respond to adverse publicity, "the solution lies in the direction of ensuring their ability to respond, rather than in stifling public discussion of matters of public concern," a reference to possible use of a right for people attacked in the media to reply. 403 U.S. at 47.

Justice White concurred on the narrow ground that the press is privileged to report "upon the official actions of public servants in full detail." Justice Black provided the fifth vote against liability for the reasons stated in his earlier opinions. Justices Harlan, Stewart and Marshall dissented on various grounds, but they agreed that the private plaintiff should be required to prove no more than negligence in this case. Justice Douglas did not participate.

Because there was no majority opinion from the Court in *Rosenbloom,* the case provided little guidance for future defamation cases. Three years later, in Gertz v. Robert Welch, Inc., the Court handed down a major libel decision, considered by many to be the most important since *Sullivan.* As you will see, *Gertz* attempts to clarify the difference between public and private figure libel plaintiffs. It also lifts from many private figure plaintiffs—depending on the state in which they sue—the burden of proving "actual malice" to collect compensatory damages.

GERTZ v. ROBERT WELCH, INC.

Supreme Court of the United States, 1974.
418 U.S. 323, 94 S.Ct. 2997, 41 L.Ed.2d 789, 1 Med.L.Rptr. 1633.

[Plaintiff, an attorney, was retained to represent the family of a youth killed by Nuccio, a Chicago policeman. In that capacity, plaintiff attended the coroner's inquest and filed an action for damages but played no part in a criminal proceeding in which Nuccio was convicted of second degree murder. Respondent publishes *American Opinion,* a monthly outlet for the views of the John Birch Society. As part of its efforts to alert the public to an alleged nationwide conspiracy to discredit local police, the magazine's editor engaged a regular contributor to write about the Nuccio episode. The article that appeared charged a frame-up against Nuccio and portrayed plaintiff as a "major architect" of the plot. It also falsely asserted that he had a long police record, was an official of the Marxist League for Industrial Democracy, and was a "Leninist" and a "Communist-fronter." The editor made no effort to verify the story.

Gertz filed an action for libel in District Court because of the diversity of citizenship. The trial judge first ruled that Gertz was not a public official or public figure and that under Illinois law there was no defense. The jury awarded $50,000. On further reflection, the judge decided that since a matter of public concern was being discussed, the *Times* rule should apply, and he granted the defendant judgment notwithstanding the jury's verdict. He thus anticipated the plurality's approach in Rosenbloom v. Metromedia, Inc. The court of appeals, relying on the intervening decision in *Rosenbloom,* affirmed because of the absence of "clear and convincing" evidence of "actual malice." Gertz appealed.]

MR. JUSTICE POWELL delivered the opinion of the Court.

. . .

II

The principal issue in this case is whether a newspaper or broadcaster that publishes defamatory falsehoods about an individual who is neither a public official nor a public figure may claim a constitutional privilege against liability for the injury inflicted by those statements. The Court considered this question on the rather different set of facts presented in Rosenbloom v. Metromedia, Inc., 403 U.S. 29 (1971). . . .

. . .

In his opinion for the plurality in Rosenbloom v. Metromedia, Inc., [ ], Mr. Justice Brennan took the *New York Times* privilege one step further. He concluded that its protection should extend to defamatory falsehoods relating to private persons if the statements concerned matters of general or public interest. . . .

. . .

III

We begin with the common ground. Under the First Amendment there is no such thing as a false idea. However pernicious an opinion may seem, we depend for its correction not on the conscience of judges and juries but on the competition of other ideas. But there is no constitutional value in false statements of fact. Neither the intentional lie nor the careless error materially advances society's interest in "uninhibited, robust, and wide-open" debate on public issues. . . .

Although the erroneous statement of fact is not worthy of constitutional protection, it is nevertheless inevitable in free debate. . . . And punishment of error runs the risk of inducing a cautious and restrictive exercise of the constitutionally guaranteed freedoms of speech and press. Our decisions recognize that a rule of strict liability that compels a publisher or broadcaster to guarantee the accuracy of his factual assertions may lead to intolerable self-censorship. Allowing the media to avoid liability only by proving the truth of all injurious statements does not accord adequate protection to First Amendment liberties. . . . The First Amendment requires that we protect some falsehood in order to protect speech that matters.

The need to avoid self-censorship by the news media is, however, not the only societal value at issue. If it were, this Court would have embraced long ago the view that publishers and broadcasters enjoy an unconditional and indefeasible immunity from liability for defamation.

The legitimate state interest underlying the law of libel is the compensation of individuals for the harm inflicted on them by defamatory falsehood. . . . Some tension necessarily exists between the need for a vigorous and uninhibited press and the legitimate interest in redressing wrongful injury. . . .

The *New York Times* standard defines the level of a constitutional protection appropriate to the context of defamation of a public person. Those who, by reason of the notoriety of their achievements or the vigor and success with which they seek the public's attention, are properly classed as public figures and those who hold governmental office may recover for injury to reputation only on clear and convincing proof that the defamatory falsehood was made with knowledge of its falsity or with reckless disregard for the truth. This standard administers an extremely powerful antidote to the inducement to media self-censorship of the common-law rule of strict liability for libel and slander. And it exacts a correspondingly high price from the victims of defamatory falsehood. Plainly many deserving plaintiffs, including some intentionally subjected to injury, will be unable to surmount the barrier of the *New York Times* test. Despite this substantial abridgment of the state law right to compensation for wrongful hurt to one's reputation, the Court has concluded that the protection of the *New York Times* privilege should be available to publishers and broadcasters of defamatory falsehood concerning public officials and public figures. [ ] We think that these decisions are correct, but we do not find their holdings justified solely by reference to the interest of the press and broadcast media in immunity from liability. Rather, we believe that the *New York Times* rule states an accommodation between this concern and the limited state interest present in the context of libel actions brought by public persons. For the reasons stated below, we conclude that the state interest in compensating injury to the reputation of private individuals requires that a different rule should obtain with respect to them.

Theoretically, of course, the balance between the needs of the press and the individual's claim to compensation for wrongful injury might be struck on a case-by-case basis. As Mr. Justice Harlan hypothesized, "it might seem, purely as an abstract matter, that the most utilitarian approach would be to scrutinize carefully every jury verdict in every libel case, in order to ascertain whether the final judgment leaves fully protected whatever First Amendment values transcend the legitimate state interest in protecting the particular plaintiff who prevailed." Rosenbloom v. Metromedia, Inc., 403 U.S., at 63 (footnote omitted). But this approach would lead to unpredictable results and uncertain expectations, and it could render our duty to supervise the lower courts unmanageable. Because an *ad hoc* resolution of the competing interests at stake in each particular case is not feasible, we must lay down broad rules of general application. Such rules necessarily treat alike various cases involving differences as well as similarities. Thus it is often true that not all of the considerations which justify adoption of a given rule will obtain in each particular case decided under its authority.

With that caveat we have no difficulty in distinguishing among defamation plaintiffs. The first remedy of any victim of defamation is self-help—using available opportunities to contradict the lie or correct the error and thereby to minimize its adverse impact on reputation. Public officials and public figures usually enjoy significantly greater access to the channels of effective communication and hence have a more realistic opportunity to counteract false statements than private individuals normally enjoy.[9] Private individuals are therefore more vulnerable to injury, and the state interest in protecting them is correspondingly greater.

More important than the likelihood that private individuals will lack effective opportunities for rebuttal, there is a compelling normative consideration underlying the distinction between public and private defamation plaintiffs. An individual who decides to seek governmental office must accept certain necessary consequences of that involvement in public affairs. He runs the risk of closer public scrutiny than might otherwise be the case. And society's interest in the officers of government is not strictly limited to the formal discharge of official duties. As the Court pointed out in Garrison v. Louisiana, 379 U.S., at 77, the public's interest extends to "anything which might touch on an official's fitness for office. . . . Few personal attributes are more germane to fitness for office than dishonesty, malfeasance, or improper motivation, even though these characteristics may also affect the official's private character."

Those classed as public figures stand in a similar position. Hypothetically, it may be possible for someone to become a public figure through no purposeful action of his own, but the instances of truly involuntary public figures must be exceedingly rare. For the most part those who attain this status have assumed roles of especial prominence in the affairs of society. Some occupy positions of such persuasive power and influence that they are deemed public figures for all purposes. More commonly, those classed as public figures have thrust themselves to the forefront of particular public controversies in order to influence the resolution of the issues involved. In either event, they invite attention and comment.

Even if the foregoing generalities do not obtain in every instance, the communications media are entitled to act on the assumption that the public officials and public figures have voluntarily exposed themselves to increased risk of injury from defamatory falsehood concerning them. No such assumption is justified with respect to a private individual. . . . Thus, private individuals are not only more vulnerable to injury than public officials and public figures; they are also more deserving of recovery.

For these reasons we conclude that the States should retain substantial latitude in their efforts to enforce a legal remedy for defamatory falsehood injurious to the reputation of a private individual. The exten-

9. Of course, an opportunity for rebuttal seldom suffices to undo harm of defamatory falsehood. Indeed, the law of defamation is rooted in our experience that the truth rarely catches up with a lie. But the fact that the self-help remedy of rebuttal, standing alone, is inadequate to its task does not mean that it is irrelevant to our inquiry.

sion of the *New York Times* test proposed by the *Rosenbloom* plurality would abridge this legitimate state interest to a degree that we find unacceptable. And it would occasion the additional difficulty of forcing state and federal judges to decide on an *ad hoc* basis which publications address issues of "general or public interest" and which do not—to determine, in the words of Mr. Justice Marshall, "what information is relevant to self-government." Rosenbloom v. Metromedia, Inc., 403 U.S., at 79. We doubt the wisdom of committing this task to the conscience of judges. . . .

We hold that, so long as they do not impose liability without fault, the States may define for themselves the appropriate standard of liability for a publisher or broadcaster of defamatory falsehood injurious to a private individual. This approach provides a more equitable boundary between the competing concerns involved here. It recognizes the strength of the legitimate state interest in compensating private individuals for wrongful injury to reputation, yet shields the press and broadcast media from the rigors of strict liability for defamation. . . .

IV

Our accommodation of the competing values at stake in defamation suits by private individuals allows the States to impose liability on the publisher or broadcaster of defamatory falsehood on a less demanding showing than that required by *New York Times*. This conclusion is not based on a belief that the considerations which prompted the adoption of the *New York Times* privilege for defamation of public officials and its extension to public figures are wholly inapplicable to the context of private individuals. Rather, we endorse this approach in recognition of the strong and legitimate state interest in compensating private individuals for injury to reputation. But this countervailing state interest extends no further than compensation for actual injury. For the reasons stated below, we hold that the States may not permit recovery of presumed or punitive damages, at least when liability is not based on a showing of knowledge of falsity or reckless disregard for the truth.

The common law of defamation is an oddity of tort law, for it allows recovery of purportedly compensatory damages without evidence of actual loss. Under the traditional rules pertaining to actions for libel the existence of injury is presumed from the fact of publication. Juries may award substantial sums as compensation for supposed damage to reputation without any proof that such harm actually occurred. The largely uncontrolled discretion of juries to award damages where there is no loss unnecessarily compounds the potential of any system of liability for defamatory falsehood to inhibit the vigorous exercise of First Amendment freedoms. Additionally, the doctrine of presumed damages invites juries to punish unpopular opinion rather than to compensate individuals for injury sustained by the publication of a false fact. More to the point, the States have no substantial interest in securing for plaintiffs such as this petitioner gratuitous awards of money damages far in excess of any actual injury.

We would not, of course, invalidate state law simply because we doubt its wisdom, but here we are attempting to reconcile state law with a competing interest grounded in the constitutional command of the First Amendment. It is therefore appropriate to require that state remedies for defamatory falsehood reach no farther than is necessary to protect the legitimate interest involved. It is necessary to restrict defamation plaintiffs who do not prove knowledge of falsity or reckless disregard for the truth to compensation for actual injury. We need not define "actual injury," as trial courts have wide experience in framing appropriate jury instructions in tort actions. Suffice it to say that actual injury is not limited to out-of-pocket loss. Indeed, the more customary types of actual harm inflicted by defamatory falsehood include impairment of reputation and standing in the community, personal humiliation, and mental anguish and suffering. Of course, juries must be limited by appropriate instructions, and all awards must be supported by competent evidence concerning the injury, although there need be no evidence which assigns an actual dollar value to the injury.

We also find no justification for allowing awards of punitive damages against publishers and broadcasters held liable under state-defined standards of liability for defamation. In most jurisdictions jury discretion over the amounts awarded is limited only by the gentle rule that they not be excessive. Consequently, juries assess punitive damages in wholly unpredictable amounts bearing no necessary relation to the actual harm caused. And they remain free to use their discretion selectively to punish expressions of unpopular views. Like the doctrine of presumed damages, jury discretion to award punitive damages unnecessarily exacerbates the danger of media self-censorship, but, unlike the former rule, punitive damages are wholly irrelevant to the state interest that justifies a negligence standard for private defamation actions. They are not compensation for injury. Instead, they are private fines levied by civil juries to punish reprehensible conduct and to deter its future occurrence. In short, the private defamation plaintiff who establishes liability under a less demanding standard than that stated by *New York Times* may recover only such damages as are sufficient to compensate him for actual injury.

V

Notwithstanding our refusal to extend the *New York Times* privilege to defamation of private individuals, respondent contends that we should affirm the judgment below on the ground that petitioner is either a public official or a public figure. There is little basis for the former assumption. Several years prior to the present incident, petitioner had served briefly on housing committees appointed by the mayor of Chicago, but at the time of publication he had never held any remunerative governmental position. Respondent admits this but argues that petitioner's appearance at the coroner's inquest rendered him a "de facto public official." Our cases recognize no such concept. Respondent's suggestion would sweep all lawyers under the *New York Times* rule as officers of the court and distort the plain meaning of the "public official" category beyond all recognition. We decline to follow it.

Respondent's characterization of petitioner as a public figure raises a different question. That designation may rest on either of two alternative bases. In some instances an individual may achieve such pervasive fame or notoriety that he becomes a public figure for all purposes in all contexts. More commonly, an individual voluntarily injects himself or is drawn into a particular public controversy and thereby becomes a public figure for a limited range of issues. In either case such persons assume special prominence in the resolution of public questions.

Petitioner has long been active in community and professional affairs. He has served as an officer of local civic groups and of various professional organizations, and he has published several books and articles on legal subjects. Although petitioner was consequently well known in some circles, he had achieved no general fame or notoriety in the community. None of the prospective jurors called at the trial had ever heard of petitioner prior to this litigation, and respondent offered no proof that this response was atypical of the local population. We would not lightly assume that a citizen's participation in community and professional affairs rendered him a public figure for all purposes. Absent clear evidence of general fame or notoriety in the community, and pervasive involvement in the affairs of society, an individual should not be deemed a public personality for all aspects of his life. It is preferable to reduce the public-figure question to a more meaningful context by looking to the nature and extent of an individual's participation in the particular controversy giving rise to the defamation.

In this context it is plain that petitioner was not a public figure. He played a minimal role at the coroner's inquest, and his participation related solely to his representation of a private client. He took no part in the criminal prosecution of Officer Nuccio. Moreover, he never discussed either the criminal or civil litigation with the press and was never quoted as having done so. He plainly did not thrust himself into the vortex of this public issue, nor did he engage the public's attention in an attempt to influence its outcome. We are persuaded that the trial court did not err in refusing to characterize petitioner as a public figure for the purpose of this litigation.

We therefore conclude that the *New York Times* standard is inapplicable to this case and that the trial court erred in entering judgment for respondent. Because the jury was allowed to impose liability without fault and was permitted to presume damages without proof of injury, a new trial is necessary. We reverse and remand for further proceedings in accord with this opinion.

It is so ordered.

MR. JUSTICE BLACKMUN, concurring.

[Although I joined the *Rosenbloom* plurality opinion,] I am willing to join, and do join, the Court's opinion and its judgment for two reasons:

1. By removing the specters of presumed and punitive damages in the absence of *New York Times* malice, the Court eliminates significant and powerful motives for self-censorship that otherwise are present in the traditional libel action. By so doing, the Court leaves what should prove to be sufficient and adequate breathing space for a vigorous press. What the Court has done, I believe, will have little, if any, practical effect on the functioning of responsible journalism

2. The Court was sadly fractionated in *Rosenbloom*. A result of that kind inevitably leads to uncertainty. I feel that it is of profound importance for the court to come to rest in the defamation area and to have a clearly defined majority position that eliminates the unsureness engendered by *Rosenbloom*'s diversity. If my vote were not needed to create a majority, I would adhere to my prior view. A definitive ruling, however, is paramount. [   ]

For these reasons, I join the opinion and the judgment of the Court.

MR. CHIEF JUSTICE BURGER, dissenting.

.   .   .

Agreement or disagreement with the law as it has evolved to this time does not alter the fact that it has been orderly development with a consistent basic rationale. In today's opinion the Court abandons the traditional thread so far as the ordinary private citizen is concerned and introduces the concept that the media will be liable for negligence in publishing defamatory statements with respect to such persons. Although I agree with much of what Mr. Justice White states, I do not read the Court's new doctrinal approach in quite the way he does. I am frank to say I do not know the parameters of a "negligence" doctrine as applied to the news media. Conceivably this new doctrine could inhibit some editors, as the dissents of Mr. Justice Douglas and Mr. Justice Brennan suggest. But I would prefer to allow this area of law to continue to evolve as it has up to now with respect to private citizens rather than embark on a new doctrinal theory which has no jurisprudential ancestry.

The petitioner here was performing a professional representative role as an advocate in the highest tradition of the law, and under that tradition the advocate is not to be invidiously identified with his client. The important public policy which underlies this tradition—the right to counsel—would be gravely jeopardized if every lawyer who takes an "unpopular" case, civil or criminal, would automatically become fair game for irresponsible reporters and editors who might, for example, describe the lawyer as a "mob mouthpiece" for representing a client with a serious prior criminal record, or as an "ambulance chaser" for representing a claimant in a personal injury action.

I would reverse the judgment of the Court of Appeals and remand for reinstatement of the verdict of the jury and the entry of an appropriate judgment on that verdict.

MR. JUSTICE DOUGLAS, dissenting.

.   .   .

. . . The standard announced today leaves the States free to "define for themselves the appropriate standard of liability for a publisher or broadcaster" in the circumstances of this case. This of course leaves the simple negligence standard as an option with the jury free to impose damages upon a finding that the publisher failed to act as "a reasonable man." With such continued erosion of First Amendment protection, I fear that it may well be the reasonable man who refrains from speaking.

Since in my view the First and Fourteenth Amendments prohibit the imposition of damages upon respondent for this discussion of public affairs, I would affirm the judgment below.

Mr. Justice Brennan, dissenting.

I agree with the conclusion, expressed in Part V of the Court's opinion, that, at the time of publication of respondent's article, petitioner could not properly have been viewed as either a "public official" or "public figure"; instead, respondent's article, dealing with an alleged conspiracy to discredit local police forces, concerned petitioner's purported involvement in "an event of public or general interest." . . .

. . .

[Justice Brennan restated the views he expressed in *Rosenbloom.*]

. . . Under a reasonable-care regime, publishers and broadcasters will have to make pre-publication judgments about juror assessment of such diverse considerations as the size, operating procedures, and financial condition of the newsgathering system, as well as the relative costs and benefits of instituting less frequent and more costly reporting at a higher level of accuracy. [ ] Moreover, in contrast to proof by clear and convincing evidence required under the *Times* test, the burden of proof for reasonable care will doubtless be the preponderance of the evidence. . . .

The Court does not discount altogether the danger that jurors will punish for the expression of unpopular opinions. This probability accounts for the Court's limitation that "the States may not permit recovery of presumed or punitive damages, at least when liability is not based on a showing of knowledge of falsity or reckless disregard for the truth." [ ] But plainly a jury's latitude to impose liability for want of due care poses a far greater threat of suppressing unpopular views than does a possible recovery of presumed or punitive damages. Moreover, the Court's broad-ranging examples of "actual injury," including impairment of reputation and standing in the community, as well as personal humiliation, and mental anguish and suffering, inevitably allow a jury bent on punishing expression of unpopular views a formidable weapon for doing so. Finally, even a limitation of recovery to "actual injury"— however much it reduces the size or frequency of recoveries—will not provide the necessary elbowroom for First Amendment expression. . . .

. . .

Mr. Justice White, dissenting.

. . .

The impact of today's decision on the traditional view of libel is immediately obvious and indisputable. No longer will the plaintiff be able to rest his case with proof of a libel defamatory on its face or proof of a slander historically actionable *per se.* In addition, he must prove some further degree of culpable conduct on the part of the publisher, such as intentional or reckless falsehood or negligence. And if he succeeds in this respect, he faces still another obstacle: recovery for loss of reputation will be conditioned upon "competent" proof of actual injury to his standing in the community. This will be true regardless of the nature of the defamation and even though it is one of those particularly reprehensible statements that have traditionally made slanderous words actionable without proof of fault by the publisher or of the damaging impact of his publication. The Court rejects the judgment of experience that some publications are inherently capable of injury, and actual injury so difficult to prove, that the risk of falsehood should be borne by the publisher, not the victim. . . .

. . .

These are radical changes in the law and severe invasions of the prerogatives of the States%. . . .

. . .

The central meaning of *New York Times,* and for me the First Amendment as it relates to libel laws, is that seditious libel—criticism of government and public officials—falls beyond the police power of the State. . . .

. . .

The Court evinces a deep-seated antipathy to "liability without fault." But this catch-phrase has no talismanic significance and is almost meaningless in this context where the Court appears to be addressing those libels and slanders that are defamatory on their face and where the publisher is no doubt aware from the nature of the material that it would be inherently damaging to reputation. He publishes notwithstanding, knowing that he will inflict injury. With this knowledge, he must intend to inflict that injury, his excuse being that he is privileged to do so—that he has published the truth. But as it turns out, what he has circulated to the public is a very damaging falsehood. Is he nevertheless "faultless?" Perhaps it can be said that the mistake about his defense was made in good faith, but the fact remains that it is he who launched the publication knowing that it could ruin a reputation.

In these circumstances, the law has heretofore put the risk of falsehood on the publisher where the victim is a private citizen and no grounds of special privilege are invoked. The Court would now shift this risk to the victim, even though he has done nothing to invite the calumny, is wholly innocent of fault, and is helpless to avoid his injury. I doubt that jurisprudential resistance to liability without fault is sufficient ground for employing the First Amendment to revolutionize the law of libel, and in my view, that body of legal rules poses no realistic threat to the press and its service to the public. The press today is vigorous and robust. To me, it is quite incredible to suggest that threats of libel suits from private citizens are causing the press to refrain from publishing the truth. I know of no hard facts to support that proposition, and the Court furnishes none.

The communications industry has increasingly become concentrated in a few powerful hands operating very lucrative businesses reaching across the Nation and into almost every home. Neither the industry as a whole nor its individual components are easily intimidated, and we are fortunate that they are not. Requiring them to pay for the occasional damage they do to private reputation will play no substantial part in their future performance or their existence.

In any event, if the Court's principal concern is to protect the communications industry from large libel judgments, it would appear that its new requirements with respect to general and punitive damages would be ample protection.

. . .

For the foregoing reasons, I would reverse the judgment of the Court of Appeals and reinstate the jury's verdict.

Notes and Questions

1. Why did the majority adhere to the *Times* rule for public officials? Public figures? Some have argued that *Gertz* was a public figure and that the case should have been analyzed along the lines of *Butts* and *Walker*.

2. Why does the majority in *Gertz* prefer its approach to the plurality's approach in *Rosenbloom*?

3. What criteria might be relevant in deciding whether a broadcaster has been at fault in broadcasting a false statement?

4. If a private citizen proves fault, why can he not recover traditional damages for defamation?

5. The Supreme Court has not decided finally whether libel plaintiffs may recover punitive damages, but *Harte-Hanks Communications*, p. 913, *infra*, indicates that some can.

6. *Three Attempts to Apply Gertz.* The first significant application of *Gertz* occurred in Time, Inc. v. Firestone, 424 U.S. 448, 1 Med.L.Rptr. 1665 (1976), in which *Time* magazine reported, perhaps incorrectly, that a member of "one of America's wealthier families" had received a divorce because of his wife's adultery. The divorce decree was probably based on either "extreme cruelty" or "lack of domestication" but the judge was not explicit. The state court upheld the wife's defamation award of $100,000. *Time* argued that the "actual malice" standard should apply for two reasons. First, it asserted that the plaintiff was a public figure, but the majority disagreed: "Respondent did not assume any role of especial prominence in the affairs of society, other than

perhaps Palm Beach society, and she did not thrust herself to the forefront of any particular public controversy in order to influence the resolution of the issues involved in it." The Court rejected the argument that because the case was of great public interest, the respondent must have been a public figure: "Dissolution of a marriage through judicial proceedings is not the sort of 'public controversy' referred to in *Gertz,* even though the marital difficulties of extremely wealthy individuals may be of interest to some portion of the reading public." Moreover, plaintiff was compelled to go to court to seek relief in a marital dispute and her involvement was not voluntary. The fact that she held "a few" press conferences during the case did not change her otherwise private status. She did not attempt to use them to influence the outcome of the trial or to thrust herself into an unrelated dispute.

The second claim was that negligent errors in the reporting of judicial proceedings should never lead to liability. Justice Rehnquist's opinion for the Court rejected the contention:

> It may be that all reports of judicial proceedings contain some informational value implicating the First Amendment, but recognizing this is little different from labeling all judicial proceedings matters of "public or general interest," as that phrase was used by the plurality in *Rosenbloom.* Whatever their general validity, use of such subject matter classifications to determine the extent of constitutional protection afforded defamatory falsehoods may too often result in an improper balance between the competing interests in this area.

Plaintiff had withdrawn her claim of damages to reputation before trial, but the Court held that the award could be sustained on proof of anxiety and concern over the impact of the adultery charge on her young son. The Court vacated the judgment for lack of consideration of fault by either the jury or any of the state courts. Justice White, believing that the state courts had found negligence, would have affirmed the award. Justice Brennan dissented on the ground that reports of judicial proceedings should not lead to liability unless the errors are deliberate or reckless. He also thought the damage limits of *Gertz* had been "subverted" by the recovery allowed here with no showing of reputational harm. Justice Marshall, dissenting, thought that plaintiff was a public figure; he also doubted the existence of negligence. Justice Stevens took no part.

The Florida Supreme Court ordered a new trial, but plaintiff dropped the case, saying that she had been vindicated.

Recall that under the common law "record libel" privilege, reports of governmental proceedings were privileged if they were fair and accurate reports of what had happened—even if the speaker being quoted had committed a defamation. Under the common law privilege, *Time*'s report, if incorrectly reporting the basis of the divorce decree, would not have been protected. For this reason *Time* had to assert a constitutional privilege.

7. *Neutral reportage.* One federal case suggests the possibility of a First Amendment privilege that differs from the *Times–Gertz* variety. In the case, Edwards v. National Audubon Society, Inc., 556 F.2d 113, 2 Med.L.Rptr. 1849 (2d Cir.), certiorari denied sub nom. Edwards v. New York Times Co., 434 U.S. 1002 (1977), Devlin, a *Times* nature reporter, was following the continuing dispute between the Audubon Society and the chemical industry over the impact of various pesticides on birds. Based in part on the fact that annual bird counts conducted by the Audubon Society showed increasing numbers, some scientists retained by the industry argued that pesticides were not harmful. The Society believed that the higher numbers were due to more watchers with more skill using better observation areas.

An editorial in a Society publication asserted that whenever members heard a scientist use the bird count in an argument "you are in the presence of someone who is being paid to lie, or is parroting something he knows little about." The reporter called the Society and, the jury found, was told the names of five scientists that Society officials had in mind. The reporter then wrote a story accurately reporting the dispute and stating that a Society official had said that the scientists referred to in the editorial included five the reporter then named. In a suit by the scientists, the court held that an accurate report of this nature could not constitutionally lead to a libel judgment against the newspaper.

What are the limits of the *Edwards* principle? Are there times when the public should be informed of charges that are not made by a "responsible, prominent organization"? What is the test for whether a report of a particular charge is "newsworthy"? What level of error in the report, if any, should deprive the reporter of the privilege? Should it be restricted to public figures?

Some courts have rejected the neutral reportage defense as inconsistent with *St. Amant,* because *Edwards* would allow one who reports a story that he knows to be false or has serious doubts about, to be protected from liability.

One can only conjecture about whether the neutral reportage privilege retains much vitality. In the 1970s and 1980s, some courts adopted the standard and some flatly rejected it. An example of the former is Barry v. Time, Inc., 584 F.Supp. 1110 (N.D.Cal.1984). An example of the latter is Postill v. Booth Newspapers, Inc., 118 Mich.App. 608, 325 N.W.2d 511 (1982).

Note that the record libel privilege discussed earlier is a state privilege that can be limited by state statutes and decisions. In New York, for example, the relevant statute requires "official proceedings" before a privilege comes into play—and the New York courts have not expanded that privilege. Thus, in *Edwards,* the state statute did not apply.

A more recent neutral reportage case was the suit brought by Khalid Khawar, who was in the Ambassador Hotel in Los Angeles as a reporter-photographer for a Pakistani magazine the night Robert Kennedy was shot there in 1968. A 1988 book, *The Senator Must Die*, by conspiracy theorist Robert Morrow, claimed that Kennedy was murdered by the Iranian secret police and the Mafia. A photo in the book shows Khawar with an arrow pointing to him as the killer. The supermarket tabloid *The Globe* published a story about the book and, although it did not use Khawar's name, reproduced the photo from the book. Khawar sued *The Globe* for libel, saying he was recognized by people in his home town and that his family received death threats. *The Globe*, supported by a number of major national news organizations, argued that it accurately reported on a matter of public interest. Lower courts rejected the neutral reportage defense, and the California Supreme Court ruled in favor of Khawar, upholding a $1.2 million verdict against *The Globe*. The court held that California does not recognize a neutral reportage privilege for republication of a libel concerning a *private* figure, which it found Khawar to be. Khawar's attorney called neutral reportage "simply an excuse to titillate by knowing repetition of falsehoods." (Khawar also sued the book publisher. That case was settled.) Khawar v. Globe International, Inc., 19 Cal. 4th 254, 26 Med.L.Rptr. 2505 (1998), certiorari denied, 199 S.Ct. 1760 (1999).

8. In Wolston v. Reader's Digest Association, Inc., 443 U.S. 157, 5 Med.L.Rptr. 1273 (1979), defendant published a book in 1974 that included plaintiff's name on a list of "Soviet agents identified in the United States." A footnote said that the list consisted of agents "who were convicted of espionage or falsifying information or perjury and/or contempt charges following espionage indictments or who fled to the Soviet bloc to avoid prosecution."

Plaintiff had been convicted of contempt of court in 1958 for failing to appear before a grand jury investigating Soviet espionage. He was never indicted for any of the listed offenses. At the time, plaintiff did not attempt to debate the propriety of his behavior. During the six weeks between his failure to appear and his sentencing, plaintiff's case was the subject of 15 stories in Washington and New York newspapers. "This flurry of publicity subsided" following the sentencing and plaintiff "succeeded for the most part in returning to the private life he had led" prior to the subpoena.

When plaintiff sued for libel, the lower courts held that in both 1958 and 1974 he was a public figure and that summary judgment was properly granted against him because he had presented no evidence of actual malice. (In the Supreme Court, plaintiff abandoned the argument that even if he was a public figure in 1958, he was no longer in 1974.)

The Supreme Court reversed. For the majority, Justice Rehnquist reviewed the "self-help" and the "assumption of risk" explanations developed in *Gertz* to support the public-private distinction, and concluded that the second was the more important.

Justice Rehnquist concluded that plaintiff had neither "voluntarily thrust" nor "injected" himself into the forefront of the controversy surrounding the investigation of Soviet espionage in the United States:

It would be more accurate to say that petitioner was dragged unwillingly into the controversy. The government pursued him in its investigation. . . .

Petitioner's failure to appear before the grand jury and citation for contempt no doubt were "newsworthy," but the simple fact that these events attracted media attention also is not conclusive of the public figure issue. A private individual is not automatically transformed into a public figure just by becoming involved in or associated with a matter that attracts public attention. . . .

Nor do we think that petitioner engaged the attention of the public in an attempt to influence the resolution of the issues involved. . . . He did not in any way seek to arouse public sentiment in his favor and against the investigation. Thus, this case is not a case where a defendant invites a citation for contempt in order to use the contempt citation as a fulcrum to create public discussion about the methods being used in connection with an investigation or prosecution. . . . In short, we find no basis whatsoever for concluding that petitioner relinquished, to any degree, his interest in the protection of his own name.

This reasoning leads us to reject the further contention of respondents that any person who engages in criminal conduct automatically becomes a public figure for purposes of comment on a limited range of issues relating to his conviction. [   ] We declined to accept a similar argument in Time, Inc. v. Firestone.

Justice Rehnquist concluded that, "[t]o hold otherwise would create an 'open season' for all who sought to defame persons convicted of a crime."

9. Hutchinson v. Proxmire, 443 U.S. 111, 5 Med.L.Rptr. 1279 (1979), arose from Senator Proxmire's awarding of one of his Golden Fleece awards—made to government agencies that he believed engaged in wasteful spending. In this case he awarded it to agencies that had funded the plaintiff-scientist's research work on aggression in animals. The Senator had uttered the alleged defamation in several forums, including a speech prepared for delivery on the Senate floor; advance press releases; a newsletter sent to 100,000 people; and a television interview program. The Court first decided that in this case Article I, Section 6 of the Constitution—the so-called Speech or Debate Clause—protected only a speech delivered on the floor.

The Court then turned to the First Amendment issue. Chief Justice Burger concluded that neither the fact that plaintiff had successfully applied for federal funds nor that he had access to media after Senator Proxmire's charges, "demonstrates that Hutchinson was a public figure prior to the controversy. . . ."

In a footnote, the Chief Justice observed that "[t]he Court has not provided precise boundaries for the category of 'public official'; it cannot be thought to include all public employees, however."

Senator Proxmire subsequently made a public retraction, before television cameras, of his comments about Hutchinson.

10. *Public and Private Figures.* In Dameron v. Washington Magazine, Inc., 779 F.2d 736, 12 Med.L.Rptr. 1508 (D.C.Cir.1985), certiorari denied 476 U.S. 1141 (1986), plaintiff had been the only air traffic controller on duty in 1974 when a plane approaching Dulles crashed into Mt. Weather. The episode received much attention: plaintiff testified in hearings and a claim under the Federal Torts Claims Act was litigated. In that case the court dismissed claims based on controller negligence. In 1982 a plane crashed into the Potomac River. Part of the story on the 1982 crash in defendant's city magazine was a sidebar on earlier plane crashes and their causes. In that list the 1974 crash was attributed to "controller" failure. Plaintiff sued for libel.

The court held that although plaintiff had not injected himself into any controversy, persons "can become involved in public controversies and affairs without their consent or will. Air-controller Dameron, who had the misfortune to have a tragedy occur on his watch, is such a person. We conclude that Dameron did become an involuntary public figure for the limited purpose of discussions of the Mt. Weather crash."

Although the Supreme Court had said that "the instances of truly involuntary public figures must be exceedingly rare," the court thought that "within the very narrow framework represented by the facts of this case, such has been Dameron's fate."

11. *Proving Actual Malice.* One case on proving "actual malice" raised the issue of what types of questions the plaintiff could ask the media defendants during the pretrial effort to obtain evidence for the trial. The normal rule in civil cases is that any evidence that would be admissible at the trial may be obtained by "discovery" beforehand—usually either by deposition (oral testimony given by a prospective witness with only the lawyers for the parties present) or by interrogatories (written answers to written questions). This exchange of information allows the parties to know the strengths and weaknesses of their cases and avoids surprises at trial.

In Herbert v. Lando, 441 U.S. 153, 4 Med.L.Rptr. 2575 (1979), Anthony Herbert, an admitted public figure, sued the producer and reporter of the television program "60 Minutes" and the CBS network for remarks on the program about his behavior while in military service in Vietnam. During his deposition, Barry Lando, the producer, generally responded, but he refused to answer some questions about why he made certain investigations and not others, what he concluded about the honesty of certain people he interviewed for the program, and about conversations he had with Mike Wallace, the reporter, in preparation for the segment. Lando contended that these thought processes and internal editorial discussions were protected from disclosure by the First Amendment. The Supreme Court disagreed.

Justice White, for the Court, understood the defendants to be arguing that "the defendant's reckless disregard of truth, a critical element, could not be shown by direct evidence through inquiry into the thoughts, opinions, and conclusions of the publisher but could be proved only by objective evidence from which the ultimate fact could be inferred." This was a barrier of some substance "particularly when defendants themselves are prone to assert their good-faith belief in the truth of their publications, and libel plaintiffs are required to prove knowing or reckless falsehood with 'convincing clarity.'"

Justice White concluded that permitting plaintiffs "to prove their cases by direct as well as indirect evidence is consistent with the balance struck by our prior decisions." He "found it difficult to believe that error-avoiding procedures will be terminated or stifled simply because there is liability for culpable error and because the editorial process will itself be examined in the tiny percentage of instances in which error is claimed and litigation ensues."

On remand, Herbert's $44 million libel suit was dismissed by the court of appeals, which said that CBS had presented sufficient evidence to defend its overall view of him and that a libel action cannot be based on minor subsidiary statements that merely support the story's overall conclusion. 781 F.2d 298, 12 Med.L.Rptr. 1593 (2d Cir.1986).

This case indirectly suggests problems when a reporter is asked to identify the source of a story. That subject is discussed at length in Chapter XV.

12. Wayne Dolcefino, a reporter for KTRK television in Texas, broadcast a report during an election campaign questioning whether Sylvester Turner, a state representative and candidate for Mayor of Houston, was involved in a multi-million-dollar insurance scam. The reporter had received a tip about an insurance swindle. In a 5:30 p.m. newscast six days before a runoff election, the reporter told viewers that a life-long friend of Turner's, Sylvester Foster, had attempted to fake his own death in a conspiracy to collect insurance money and went on to say,

> ". . . What role did Houston mayoral candidate Sylvester Turner play in this tale of multi-million dollar fraud? We have been investigating Turner's role in this attempted insurance scandal since we first heard about it on the day before the Thanksgiving holiday. Our focus, what did Sylvester Turner know and when did he know it? . . . Both Dwight Thomas and Sylvester Turner were deeply involved in the Sylvester Foster case and the attempt to get life insurance companies to pay off 6.5 million dollars in the wake of the disappearance. But did they know it was all a hoax, a scheme to swindle millions?" Thomas was then shown denying that he and Turner would have dealt with Foster had they known of any illegality, "But," the reporter stated, "Thomas and Turner did deal with Sylvester Foster, even after learning he was the target of criminal investigations in early 1986, and they pursued the estate money even after significant evidence of a possible scam in Foster's death had already surfaced."

At 8 p.m., Turner held a news conference denying any wrongdoing, and was supported by a judge and the insurance company's lawyer. The station rebroadcast its original story at 10 p.m., but the news anchor added a statement that Turner had attacked the story's allegations as false and misleading at a news conference. The trial court awarded Turner $550,000 in actual damages and $4.5 million in exemplary damages against KTRK and $500,000 in exemplary damages against the reporter. A state appellate court reversed, holding that the plaintiff had failed to present clear and convincing proof that the reporter or station acted with actual malice. The Texas Supreme Court held that the report as a whole was false and defamatory because it omitted critical facts and juxtaposed others leaving a substantially false impression that Turner had participated in insurance fraud. But the Supreme Court agreed that there was no clear and convincing proof of actual malice:

> ". . . [We] cannot say that Dolcefino's failure to include [some facts] is clear and convincing evidence that he knew the broadcast would present a false impression or that he entertained serious doubts to that effect. It is not apparent from the record whether Dolcefino, as a non-lawyer, understood the significance of Foster's naming Thomas as executor or knew that his description of the reasons for Turner's disqualification was incomplete. . . . Further, because of the upcoming election, the story was clearly 'hot news'. . . . Dolcefino had only five days to research and write a complicated story, a primary source of which was court documents. Moreover, the story had to be edited to fit the time demands of a news segment. Dolcefino's failure to include all the relevant details regarding Turner's participation in the estate suggests negligence, but under these circumstances we cannot conclude that it establishes actual malice with convincing clarity. . . ." Turner v. KTRK Television Inc., 38 S.W.3d 103, 29 Med.L.Rptr. 1673 (2000).

13. *Appellate Review*. In Bose Corp. v. Consumers Union, 466 U.S. 485, 10 Med.L.Rptr. 1625 (1984), the Supreme Court held in favor of the publisher of *Consumer Reports* magazine in a product disparagement suit filed by the manufacturer of loudspeakers criticized in the magazine. The magazine said that Bose 901 speakers produced sounds that "tended to wander about the room" and that a violin "appeared to be 10 feet wide and a piano stretched from wall to wall."

The Supreme Court held that appeals courts, when reviewing findings of actual malice in libel cases and other cases governed by New York Times v. Sullivan, must exercise their own judgment in determining whether actual malice was shown with convincing clarity. Thus, the court of appeals' decision in favor of Consumers Union was affirmed.

14.   A case involving the libel of a judicial candidate in Ohio provided an opportunity for the Supreme Court to clarify the decision in *Bose* regarding independent appellate review—and simultaneously provided parallels to *Butts*. Daniel Connaughton was an unsuccessful candidate for municipal judge in Hamilton, Ohio, in 1983. A local newspaper, the

Journal News, supported his opponent, who was the incumbent. A week prior to the election, the newspaper ran a front-page story quoting a grand jury witness as saying that Connaughton had used "dirty tricks" and offered her and her sister jobs and a trip to Florida "in appreciation" for their help in the investigation of the director of court services who had worked for the incumbent. At a libel trial in federal district court, the jury found by a preponderance of the evidence that the story in question was defamatory and false, and by clear and convincing proof that the story was published with actual malice, and awarded Connaughton $5,000 in compensatory damages and $195,000 in punitive damages.

The court of appeals affirmed. It separately considered the evidence supporting each of the jury's special verdicts, concluding that the findings were not clearly erroneous. It did not attempt to make an independent evaluation of the credibility of conflicting oral testimony concerning facts underlying the finding of actual malice but identified 11 subsidiary facts that the jury "could have" found and held that such findings would not have been clearly erroneous, and, based on its independent review, held that when considered cumulatively they provided clear and convincing evidence of actual malice. Harte–Hanks Communications appealed to the Supreme Court. Although the latter held that a showing of "highly unreasonable conduct constituting an extreme departure from the standards of investigation and reporting ordinarily adhered to by responsible publishers" cannot alone support a verdict in favor of a public figure plaintiff in a libel action, that the rule applied by the court of appeals nonetheless was supportive of the court's ultimate conclusion that the *Journal News* acted with actual malice. The Court said that a reviewing court in a public figure libel case must "exercise independent judgment and determine whether the record establishes actual malice with convincing clarity" to ensure that the verdict is consistent with *New York Times* and subsequent cases. Harte–Hanks Communications, Inc. v. Connaughton, 491 U.S. 657, 16 Med.L.Rptr. 1881 (1989).

15. *Truth and Falsity.* Although the Court's focus was on the fault requirement, questions still lingered about who had the burden of proof on the question of truth or falsity. In Philadelphia Newspapers, Inc. v. Hepps, 475 U.S. 767, 12 Med.L.Rptr. 1977 (1986), the Court, 5–4, held that the plaintiff had the burden of proving falsity at least in cases brought by private plaintiffs where the speech was of public concern. For the majority, Justice O'Connor concluded that to "ensure that true speech on matters of public concern is not deterred, we hold that the common-law presumption that defamatory speech is false cannot stand when a plaintiff seeks damages against a media defendant for speech of public concern." (Two of the five joining the majority opinion rejected the limitation to "media" defendants.) Even though this burden would "insulate from liability some speech that is false, but unprovably so," that result is essential to avoid the "chilling" effect that would otherwise accompany true speech on matters of public concern.

The majority asserted that its conclusion added "only marginally to the burdens" on libel plaintiffs because a jury is more likely to accept a "contention that the defendant was at fault in publishing the statements at issue if convinced that the relevant statements were false. As a practical matter, then, evidence offered by plaintiffs on the publisher's fault . . . will generally encompass evidence of the falsity of the matters asserted." The majority reserved the question of the quantity of proof of falsity that a plaintiff must present.

Justice Stevens, for the dissenters, thought the majority result "pernicious." He posited a situation in which a defendant, knowing that the plaintiff could not prove the statement false, deliberately lied about the plaintiff. This situation might occur due to the passage of time, the loss of critical records, or the absence of an eyewitness. The majority's analysis was an "obvious blueprint for character assassination." In his view, as long as publishers are protected by the fault requirement, "there can be little, if any, basis for a concern that a significant amount of true speech will be deterred unless the private person victimized by a malicious libel can also carry the burden of proving falsity."

16.   In Anderson v. Liberty Lobby, Inc., 477 U.S. 242, 12 Med.L.Rptr. 2297 (1986), the Supreme Court held, 6–3, that the standard for considering summary judgment motions must take into account the burden the plaintiff will have to meet at trial. Because the plaintiff in the case was held to be a public figure, the Court held that on the summary judgment motion, the judge must decide "whether the evidence in the record could support a reasonable jury finding either that the plaintiff has shown actual malice by clear and convincing evidence or that the plaintiff has not."

In response to the argument that at the summary judgment stage the plaintiff need show only enough to prevail on a "preponderance of the evidence" standard, the Court responded that it "makes no sense to say that a jury could reasonably find for either party without some benchmark as to what standards govern its deliberations and within what boundaries its ultimate decision must fall, and these standards and boundaries are in fact provided by the applicable evidentiary standards."

The Court denied that its holding denigrated the role of the jury. "Credibility determinations, the weighing of the evidence, and the drawing of legitimate inferences from the facts are jury functions, not those of a judge, whether he is ruling on a motion for summary judgment or for a directed verdict."

In a footnote, the Court addressed footnote 9 in *Hutchinson,* p. 909, *supra,* in which the Court had suggested that proof of actual malice "does not readily lend itself to summary disposition." That sentence "was simply an acknowledgment of our general reluctance" to grant special procedural protections to the media in addition to the substantive standards announced in cases like *Times* and *Gertz.* This was not relevant here because the Court in *Liberty Lobby* was announcing a general approach to all civil cases—that the summary judgment standard was to be the same as the one that the plaintiff must meet at the trial itself.

Justice Brennan dissented out of concern that the majority's decision "may erode the constitutionally enshrined role of the jury, and also undermine the usefulness of summary judgment procedure." On the latter point, he was concerned that the decision would confuse the lower courts.

Justice Rehnquist, joined by Chief Justice Burger, also dissented. He offered some examples that he thought showed that the majority's decision would have no effect on a large class of cases. His examples follow:

(1) On a summary judgment motion, "the plaintiff concedes that his only proof of malice is the testimony of witness A. Witness A testifies at his deposition that the reporter who wrote the story in question told him that she, the reporter, had done absolutely no checking on the story and had real doubts about whether or not it was correct as to the plaintiff. The defendant's examination of witness A brings out that he has a prior conviction for perjury." Justice Rehnquist said that summary judgment must be denied if the majority meant what it said about the jury judging credibility.

(2) At trial, after plaintiff's case the defendant moves for a directed verdict. The trial testimony repeats the deposition testimony except that now the trial judge has seen A's demeanor—"and noticed that he fidgets when answering critical questions, his eyes shift from the floor to the ceiling, and he manifests all other indicia traditionally attributed to perjurers." Justice Rehnquist asserted that no directed verdict may be entered.

(3) The defense puts on its case which includes three disinterested witnesses who were present at the alleged conversation. Each "categorically denies that the reporter made the claimed statement" to A. Justice Rehnquist asserted that a directed verdict must be denied to the defendant.

The lesson he drew was that the standard does not matter in a credibility case. Even in cases based on documentary evidence he asserted that inferences from the documents are "as much the prerogative of the finder of fact as inferences as to the credibility of witnesses." He thought the line between "evidence which should satisfy reasonable men, and the evidence which should satisfy reasonable men beyond a reasonable doubt, . . . in the long run . . . is too thin for day to day use" (quoting Judge Learned Hand). If that was true, it was even more true where the standard was convincing clarity.

17. A 1991 case presented the Supreme Court with the question of whether a journalist's use of quotation remarks around words that are not provably the plaintiff's should be treated as reckless disregard for the truth under the actual malice standard. Psychoanalyst Jeffrey Masson sued writer Janet Malcolm for defamation in a two-part *New Yorker* magazine profile of him published in 1983. The profile was based on a series of interviews and phone calls with Masson. The unflattering profile included numerous lengthy passages in quotation marks report-

ing Masson's comments. Among them, for example, was a statement attributed to Masson in which he supposedly referred to himself as being "like an intellectual gigolo." Masson denied making many of the statements. Malcolm's tape recordings of the interviews lacked many of the passages complained of by Masson, but Malcolm said that not all of her conversations with Masson were on tape and that she had discarded handwritten notes of some of the conversations. At the relevant place on the tape recording, there was no use of the words "intellectual gigolo," for example, but instead Masson had said that acquaintances considered him "much too junior within the hierarchy of analysts for these important training analysts to be caught dead with me."

The trial court in *Masson* held that the allegedly fabricated quotations were either substantially true or represented "possible rational interpretations" of ambiguous conversations and were thus entitled to constitutional protection. The court of appeals, on the other hand, assumed that Malcolm had deliberately altered each quotation not found on the tape recordings but held that Masson had failed to raise a question of actual malice, so it affirmed the decision in favor of Masson.

The Supreme Court reversed, noting that, "In general, quotation marks around a passage indicate to the reader that the passage reproduces the speaker's words verbatim." The Court acknowledged that some altering of quotes is accepted—such as those necessary to, in the Court's words, "eliminate grammatical and syntactical infelicities," but nonetheless concluded that the published passages differed sufficiently from the tape recorded statements so as to create an issue of fact for a jury as to falsity, and therefore remanded the case for further proceedings. Masson v. New Yorker Magazine, Inc., 501 U.S. 496, 18 Med. L.Rptr. 2241 (1991). Two libel trials followed. At the first, in 1993, jurors found that Malcolm had fabricated five quotations and that two of them were libelous, but a mistrial was declared when jurors were unable to reach a unanimous decision on damages. At the second, in 1994, a jury decided that Malcolm had not libeled Masson, and, in 1996, the court of appeals affirmed. 85 F.3d 1394, 24 Med.L.Rptr. 1787 (9th Cir.1996).

18.　One of the most publicized libel trials in American history was the one pursued by cattlemen (Texas Beef Group) against popular television talk show host Oprah Winfrey. Winfrey, during a show on "Dangerous Foods," had vowed never to eat another hamburger, and the cattlemen blamed her for causing cattle prices to plummet, costing them about $11 million. The suit was originally seen as a test of the constitutionality of "veggie libel" laws designed to protect perishable agricultural products from unsubstantiated attacks about their safety, and national attention was insured when Winfrey moved her television show to Amarillo for the trial. But the federal district judge ruled that the case could not continue under the agriculture disparagement law. That move reduced the suit to a basic business defamation suit, and the cattlemen would have needed to prove actual malice to win. After a six-week trial, the jury decided in Winfrey's favor. The defendant pointed out, however, that the case had already cost her $500,000 to $1 million. The New York Times, Feb. 17, 1998 at A–10, and The Washington Post, Feb. 27, 1998 at A03.

C. REMEDIES FOR DEFAMATION

1. INJUNCTIONS

Injunctions are generally unavailable for reasons discussed in Chafee's Government and Mass Communication 91–92 (1947): "One man's judgment is not to be trusted to determine what people can read. . . . So our law thinks it better to let the defamed plaintiff take his damages for what they are worth than to intrust a single judge (or even a jury) with the power to put a sharp check on the spread of possible truth."

2. REPLY

If the plaintiff completes the obstacle course we have described, damages are the only available remedy of any importance. The right of reply mentioned by Justice Brennan in *Rosenbloom* and *Gertz* would allow the victim of the defamation to respond in his own words in the offending publication, but states rarely require this, and such a requirement has constitutional problems. As to the role of reply in broadcasting, see Chapters III and V.

3. RETRACTION

The common law had some rules that tended to reduce the amount of damages recoverable in defamation. They were called "partial defenses" because they did not defeat liability but only reduced the size of the award. At common law if the defendant voluntarily retracted the statement, that fact was admissible to show that the plaintiff had not been damaged as badly as he claimed. It might also show that the defendant had not acted maliciously in the first place.

As a practical matter, however, retractions generally are effective only in media with frequent dissemination to the same audience. Thus retractions make little sense for defamatory statements in books or films, and retractions are generally believed to be more effective when placed in the same space in a newspaper than when they are run on radio or television. Although some state statutes require that prospective plaintiffs demand retractions, those statutes are more likely to apply to print media than to electronic media.

A "Uniform Correction or Clarification of Defamation Act" intended to encourage prompt retractions was proposed in 1993 by the National Conference of Commissioners on Uniform State Laws. Media attorneys generally applauded the proposal, under which media that ran prompt retractions would be protected from awards for loss of reputation and awards for punitive damages. Instead, plaintiffs in such instances would be able to collect only for "provable economic loss." Plaintiffs' attorneys criticized the proposal on the grounds that damage awards provide one of the few ways the public an punish the press. Despite the fact that the American Bar Association's House of Delegates approved the proposal at its 1994 meeting and North Dakota enacted the legislation in 1995, attention to it faded later in the 1990s.

D. CRIMINAL LIBEL AND GROUP LIBEL

1. CRIMINAL LIBEL

Criminal libel is not generally available although it is part of the law in most states. The New York State Constitution, for example, provides that, "In all criminal prosecutions or indictments for libels, the truth may be given in evidence to the jury; and if it shall appear to the jury that the matter charged as libelous is true, and was published with good motives and for justifiable ends, the party shall be acquitted; and the jury shall have the right to determine the law and the fact." McKinney's Const. Art. 1, § 8.

Criminal libel had already fallen into disuse before *Garrison,* p. 892, *supra*. The strictures placed on the action in that case diminished still further its usefulness. The role of the action is even more doubtful when it is used by prosecutors on behalf of famous or powerful persons who do not wish to bring a civil action themselves. This was the situation in 1976 when a state court declared the California criminal libel law unconstitutional because of its limitations on the defense of truth and its presumption of malice. Because some states have taken the same path and others are not enforcing statutes, criminal libel no longer appears to be a serious risk to the media.

Recall *R.A.V.,* p. 22, *supra,* in which the Supreme Court in 1992 struck down as unconstitutionally overbroad a St. Paul ordinance making it a crime to engage in speech or behavior likely to arouse "anger or alarm" on the basis of "race, color, creed, religion or gender."

2. GROUP LIBEL STATUTES AND HATE SPEECH

The main concern in the debate over group libel has been the hazards of unrestricted hate propaganda. Curbs on group defamation have been advocated to reduce friction among racial, religious and ethnic groups. As early as 1917 some states enacted criminal group libel laws for that purpose. The Nazi defamation of minority groups, and conspicuous racial tensions in the United States, brought renewed attention to group libel laws in the 1940s and 1950s.

The most common method of confronting group libel has been the enactment of criminal laws directed specifically at the problem. Such laws typically prohibit communications that are abusive or offensive toward a group or that tend to arouse hatred, contempt or ridicule of the group. Penalties have ranged from a fine of $50 or 30 days imprisonment, to $10,000 or two years in prison.

Beauharnais v. Illinois, 343 U.S. 250 (1952), is the only Supreme Court decision to review the constitutionality of group libel legislation. The Court, 5–4, affirmed a conviction under Illinois's 1917 group libel statute. The law prohibited publications portraying "depravity, criminality, unchastity, or lack of virtue of a class of citizens, of any race, color, creed, or religion" that subjected those described to "contempt, derision, or obloquy or which is productive of breach of the peace or riots." Beauharnais, the president of an organization called the "White Circle League," had distributed leaflets calling on the Mayor and City Council to halt the "further encroachment, harassment and invasion of white people, their property, neighborhoods and persons, by the Negro."

Justice Frankfurter's opinion for the Court treated the statute as "a form of criminal libel law" and accepted the *dictum* of *Chaplinsky*, p. 22, *supra*, that libel was one of those "well-defined and narrowly limited classes of speech, the prevention and punishment of which has never been thought to raise any constitutional problem." He traced the history of violent and destructive racial tension in Illinois and concluded that it would "deny experience" to say that the statute was without reason. He disposed of the First Amendment question in a single paragraph near the end of his opinion.

> Libelous utterances not being within the area of constitutionally protected speech, it is unnecessary, either for us or for the State courts, to consider the issue behind the phrase "clear and present danger." Certainly no one would contend that obscene speech, for example, may be punished only upon a showing of such circumstances. Libel, as we have seen, is in the same class.

Of the four dissenters, only Justices Black and Douglas addressed the First Amendment problems that the majority had cast aside by excluding the whole area of libel from First Amendment protection. Justice Black analyzed the decision as extending the scope of the law of criminal libel from "the narrowest of areas" involving "purely private feuds" to "discussions of matters of public concern." This was an invasion of the First Amendment's absolute prohibition of laws infringing the freedom of public discussion. Justice Douglas concurred in Justice Black's opinion and wrote separately to emphasize that he would have required a demonstration that the "peril of speech" was "clear and present." He agreed with Justice Black that allowing a legislature to regulate "within reasonable limits" the right of free speech was "an ominous and alarming trend." Only a half-dozen states retain group defamation statutes.

Group libel statutes also raise practical objections. Group libel prosecutions normally involve issues on which the community is sharply divided. The incidence as well as the outcome of prosecutions may thus depend on which segments of the community are represented in the office of the prosecuting attorney and on the jury. Moreover, a defendant could use the trial to promote his views and might well benefit regardless of the result: an acquittal would validate his viewpoint, while a conviction would make him a martyr whose civil liberties have been violated. These difficulties have led most commentators and many representatives of minority groups to oppose group libel litigation.

The Internet, of course, provides ample opportunity for those who want to use it to defame groups as well as individuals, businesses and others. While much of the debate over hate speech on the Internet has focused on possible threat to health and safety (as in the posting of names and addresses of abortion providers at the Nuremberg Files web site, p. 649, *supra*) and on problems created for companies whose stock is publicly traded (as in "cybersmearing" by posting false information on Internet bulletin boards intended for investors), a substantial amount of hate speech is directed at racial and ethnic groups and presents all of the usual problems of dealing with such speech through group libel statutes.

E. PRACTICAL CONSIDERATIONS FOR MEDIA DEFENDANTS

1. HEADING OFF LIBEL SUITS

Recent research among libel plaintiffs suggests that many of them, unhappy though they may be when they realize that something harmful and erroneous has been published about them, are not immediately inclined to sue the media. Too frequently, people who have been defamed become angry enough to sue only after they have been treated curtly or even rudely when they tried to get the errors corrected.

Keeping this in mind, media attorneys and managers are today trying harder to prepare their employees for better handling of complaints. Such complaints should be taken seriously, and the complainer should be handled with courtesy and care. Usually, that means that the complaint should be referred to a senior staff member trained in handling such complaints.

Apologies and retractions, when appropriate, can help to head off law suits before they occur. That is normally to the advantage of both the potential plaintiff and the media defendant. Defendants will, of course, have to use care in making apologies or retractions; should the potential plaintiff become an actual plaintiff, the admission may be used against the defendant in court. Publication of the correct information without embellishment is sometimes the best approach.

2. MEGAVERDICTS

As recently as the mid–1980's, no appellate court had ever upheld a libel verdict for damages in excess of $1 million, but the amounts sought by plaintiffs in the late 1980's and 1990's in many kinds of tort actions soared. Juries started awarding larger amounts of money, and appellate courts upheld larger verdicts. The business community sounded a public alarm about what it viewed as a national problem. In one highly publicized case, a jury awarded $2.7 million in punitive damages to a woman who spilled hot coffee from a McDonald's in her lap in a moving car, but the trial judge reduced the award to $480,000. Media companies joined other businesses in briefs submitted to the Supreme Court in several non-media cases in which allegedly excessive damage awards were appealed on due process grounds.

In one highly publicized defamation case, former District Attorney Vic Feazell sued WFAA–TV in Dallas for television reports alleging the taking of payments to quash drunken driving cases and won a $58 million libel judgement, but, before any appeal, the parties settled for an undisclosed amount of money. Similarly, Attorney Richard Sprague settled for an undisclosed amount of money his suit against Philadelphia Newspapers that had originally resulted in a $34 million award to him. In a case that never came to trial, Philip Morris garnered big headlines by suing ABC for $10 *billion* following a 1994 report alleging that the tobacco company spiked some of its products with extra nicotine. That case too was settled out of court.

A federal judge in 1997 set aside a damage award of $200 million in punitive damages against Dow Jones & Company, publisher of *The Wall St. Journal*, in a libel suit resulting from a 1993 article that said an investment firm, Money Management Analytic Research Group, Inc., (MMAR) was reckless in dealing with its clients and was under investigation by regulatory agencies. The judge had ordered Dow Jones to pay a $22.7 million award in actual damages, but in April 1999 he set aside the verdict and ordered a new trial after finding that the plaintiff had withheld important evidence that would have bolstered Dow Jones' defense. National Law Journal, April 19, 1999 at A8.

3. Libel Insurance

When a court awards damages against a media defendant in a libel suit, it is legally irrelevant whether that defendant carries libel insurance. As a practical matter, of course, it is extremely important. Media employers are often reluctant to be candid about their insurance, even with their own employees. Certainly employers do not want their employees to take unnecessary risks, and media employers typically value their reputations for accuracy so they do not want to lose libel suits even if they do carry insurance. Media libel insurance policies typically provide for a deductible amount that is paid by the insured before the insurance coverage comes into play. The higher the deductible, the lower the premiums that the employer pays for the insurance. Media employers who could afford to sustain losses of $50,000 or $100,000 on each damage award against them or who can afford the legal expenses might elect to be "self-insured" for those amounts and to carry insurance policies with the $50,000 or $100,000 deductible clause to cover them for any awards or expenses greater than those amounts. The increasing size of trial court awards for libel damages has, inevitably, led to an increase in libel insurance premiums; that increase in the premiums in turn has a negative effect on virtually every insured media organization—not just those that are sued.

Libel insurance policies are offered through some trade associations such as the National Association of Broadcasters.

4. DEFENSE COSTS

Even the media defendants who win their cases in trial or appellate courts may spend large sums of money defending themselves. In major cases some defendants have spent several million dollars defending themselves. Although vindication in court may seem ideal, the cost of lawyers and the cost in terms of one's own employees' time may make it tempting tosettle out of court with the plaintiff—even where there is a substantial likelihood that the defendant would ultimately prevail should the case be decided by an appellate court. A media defendant who developed the reputation of settling out of court too easily could become a target for nuisance suits brought by plaintiffs who do not really expect to win but hope defendants will buy them off by settling out of court without ever going to trial. Some major media organizations have adopted the position of never settling out of court for just that reason, but such a posture is difficult to maintain in an instance where the media organization really did publish a false statement, particularly where the plaintiff is a private figure who does not need to prove actual malice and who has real damages. The defendant's own insurance carrier may apply pressure to settle, and the size of the verdicts of recent years makes the risk of going to trial all the greater and increases the temptation to settle out of court.

5. EVIDENCE AND WITNESSES

Attorneys representing media clients sometimes have a difficult choice to make: if they scare the journalists too much about possible libel suits, they may create their own chilling effect; but if they ignore the subject, the journalists may fall into traps that can make the defense of a libel suit more troubling. Plaintiffs who are public officials or public figures will, of course, be seeking evidence that the defendant published with knowledge of falsity or with a high degree of awareness of probable falsity. Internal memos or margin notes written on copy expressing doubts about the facts in a story can be just the kind of evidence the plaintiff will seek. Newsroom conversations about doubts—even doubts in one's own mind—may be discoverable (see discussion of *Herbert,* p. 910, *supra*).

In an age in which libel litigation is common, journalists publishing material that may damage a person's reputation would be wise to think of the story subject as a potential plaintiff and to be as sure of their facts as possible. Just as such nationally-known journalists as Dan Rather and Mike Wallace have been called to discuss their stories from the witness stand, younger journalists may have to do the same and should be unafraid to do so if they have followed accepted journalistic practices. (The latter can present interesting questions, because professional standards in journalism vary. Codes of ethics—like the code of The Society of Professional Journalists—may be of some use. Principles such as getting at least two independent sources before disseminating damaging information may be widely followed but still are not provably a part of a universally accepted code of conduct for the journalist.)

F. INFLICTION OF EMOTIONAL DISTRESS

When Rev. Jerry Falwell sued *Hustler* magazine publisher Larry Flynt in a highly publicized case, he sued for libel and invasion of privacy and a separate but related tort—infliction of emotional distress. The possibility that public figure libel plaintiffs, frustrated by their inability to win libel suits under *New York Times,* would sue in great numbers for infliction of emotional distress was a serious concern for the media as the Falwell case went to the Supreme Court.

The case was precipitated by the inside front cover of the November 1983 issue of *Hustler*—what may have looked at first like an advertisement for Campari Liqueur but was actually a parody with a headline saying, "Jerry Falwell talks about his first time." In sometimes crude language, the parody "quoted" Falwell as saying his first sexual experience was with his mother in an outhouse and that he could only preach when he was drunk. At the bottom, in small type, was a disclaimer: "Ad parody—not to be taken seriously."

In pre-trial discovery, Larry Flynt identified himself as "Christopher Columbus Cornwallis I.P.Q. Harvey H. Apache Pugh" and testified that the parody was written by Yoko Ono and Billy Idol. In answers to other questions, he testified that he had been attempting to characterize Falwell as a liar and hypocrite and to "assassinate" Falwell's character. (Flynt's attorneys subsequently claimed that Flynt was unable to give a correct account of the events.)

Falwell's defamation and privacy claims had been disposed of by the time the case reached the Supreme Court, which needed only to address the infliction of emotional distress claim. Chief Justice Rehnquist, writing for the Court, said "[I]n the world of debate about public affairs, many things done with motives that are less than admirable are protected by the First Amendment," and that even "outrageous" satire can be deserving of protection. "We conclude," he wrote,

> "that public figures and public officials may not recover for the tort of intentional infliction of emotional distress . . . without showing in addition that the publication contains a false statement of fact which was made with 'actual malice,' i.e., with knowledge that the statement was false or with reckless disregard as to whether or not it was true."

Without such showing, Falwell lost. Hustler Magazine, Inc. v. Falwell, 485 U.S. 46, 14 Med.L.Rptr. 2281 (1988).

Although not Supreme Court cases, intentional infliction of emotional distress cases have also been brought as a result of radio and television attempts at humor. For example, a superior court in Los Angeles held for the defendant in Raye v. Letterman, 14 Med.L.Rptr. 2047 (Cal.Super.1987). David Letterman had said, "I saw the most terrifying commercial on television last night, featuring Martha Raye, actress, condom user." The court noted that Martha Raye is well known for a denture product commercial in which she is introduced as "Martha Raye, actress, denture wearer," and that a parody/satire of the line could not reasonably be understood as statement of fact and thus could not be defamatory.

A 1997 New York suit for intentional infliction of emotional distress resulted from a radio station's "Ugliest Bride" contest. The complaint alleged that on the day the plaintiff's bridal photograph was published in a local newspaper, the station's disk jockeys engaged in a routine in which they made derogatory and disparaging comments about the plaintiff's appearance and invited their listening audience to do the same. She alleged that because she worked for a rival station, defendants deviated from the ordinary routine of this "contest" by disclosing her full name, place of employment and job supervisors. She said she and her supervisors heard this broadcast and that it caused her extreme emotional distress, exacerbated by the fact that it happened when she was a newlywed.

The court held that plaintiff could maintain a claim for emotional distress even though a defamation claim on the same facts would be barred by the special protection that the New York constitution provides for opinion. "[W]e observe that the tort of intentional infliction of emotional distress has received very little judicial solicitude.... [We affirm the trial court's denial of defendant's motion to dismiss the case.] ... [We attach particular significance to several factors. First, plaintiff is a private individual and not a 'public figure.' Second, the nature of the communications made by defendants involved a matter of virtually no 'public interest'; there is an inference that defendants' conduct represented a deliberate intent to inflict injury upon plaintiff based upon the claimed unprecedented expansion of its standard 'routine' of the 'Ugliest Bride' contest to include particulars concerning plaintiff's name, employer, supervisors and the like, and the fact that the parties are business competitors in the radio broadcast industry.

"We are not unmindful of the constitutional issues implicated in this case and in our resolution thereof. In the quest for the proper accommodation between the right of redress for infliction of injury and the freedoms of speech and expression protected by the First Amendment, we have determined that the State's relatively strong interest in compensating individuals for harm outweighs the relatively weak First Amendment protection to be accorded defendants." Esposito–Hilder v. SFX Broadcasting, Inc., 236 A.D.2d 186, 26 Med.L.Rptr. 1541 (1997).

Chapter XV

PRIVACY

Defamation, which we discussed in the last chapter, and invasion of privacy, which we discuss in this one, are sometimes treated together in law courses as related rights to protect one's dignity. In defamation, we balance the right of freedom of expression against the right of individuals to protect their reputations. In privacy, we balance the right of freedom of expression against the right of individuals to be let alone. Although many people tend to think of privacy as a basic human right and many assume that it is constitutional, the word privacy never appears in the Constitution. Compared to defamation, privacy is a relatively new legal concept with many facets.

Concerns for privacy in the 1980s have been diverse—involving such varied issues as the dissemination of personal credit information via computerized systems, electronic eavesdropping, the protection of newsrooms from police searches, release of personal information about individuals by the government and a right to know what is in one's own academic records. Some of these issues we will address elsewhere in this book, because they are related to other topics; the protection of newsrooms from police searches, for example, is dealt with in Chapter XV because the "privacy" of the newsroom is directly related to the confidentiality of journalists' sources and their notes. Other privacy issues are beyond the scope of this book.

In this chapter we will be concerned primarily with invasion of privacy as a tort—a civil wrong or injury. Although the recognition of privacy torts varies from state to state, scholars generally have recognized four different torts or branches of invasion of privacy. One of these relates to the newsgathering stage of the communications process: intruding on the plaintiff's physical solitude. It is akin to the tort of trespass. The other three torts or branches of invasion of privacy relate to the publication stage of the communications process. They are publication of embarrassing private (true) facts; putting the plaintiff in a false light in the public eye; and appropriation of another's name or likeness for commercial or trade purposes. Of the four branches, the "false-light" tort comes closest to the tort of defamation, because it is the only one that involves falsity.

Because of the similarities between defamation and false-light invasion of privacy, some of the traditional defenses in defamation are sometimes applicable to this branch of invasion of privacy—including truth. Truth is obviously not a defense for publication of embarrassing private facts, because the fact that an embarrassing publication is true just makes it all the more embarrassing. Because the applicability of defenses varies with the branch of invasion of privacy being considered, we shall touch on defenses at several different points in this chapter.

A. INTRUSION ON THE PLAINTIFF'S PHYSICAL SOLITUDE

As indicated above, intrusion on the plaintiff's physical solitude is the only one of the four branches of privacy that comes up in the context of *newsgathering* rather than in the context of dissemination. In the absence of any Supreme Court decision involving such an invasion of privacy by the mass media, we will look here at some cases decided by the lower courts as examples.

The major divisions of this branch of invasion of privacy reflect the type of consent problem involved. Within each subsection we consider the types of invasions that plaintiff may complain about. The most traditional are trespass (unpermitted entry) on land and theft of personal property. The claim is that the physical zone of privacy that surrounds each of us has been intruded upon—usually in an effort to obtain information that would otherwise not be available.

1.   INTRUSIONS WITHOUT EXPRESS CONSENT

a.   *Trespass*

For centuries, the act of intentionally entering the land of another without consent has made the entrant liable for trespass. The civil damages include any actual harm done to the property and some damages for the symbolic invasion of the owner's or occupier's legal interest. If accompanied by ill will or spite or a desire to harm the owner, perhaps punitive damages as well are awarded. Comparable rules apply to a person who legally enters land but then remains on it against the wishes of the owner or occupier of the land.

In one clear case, the plaintiff alleged that his wife had committed suicide during the day; that when he returned to the house that evening he discovered that the screen over the kitchen window had been cut and that a photograph of his wife that had been on a table in the living room that morning had been taken. Although the plaintiff failed to prove that the defendant's reporters had committed the trespass, the court indicated that the only problem in the case was one of identification. The trespass and theft could not be defended even if there had been great public interest in the photograph. Metter v. Los Angeles Examiner, 35 Cal.App.2d 304, 95 P.2d 491 (1939).

Sometimes reporters lack express consent to enter properties from the owners but have consent—or may even have been invited onto the property—by public officials. As we shall see, this has been a particular problem in the context of "ride-alongs" in which journalists accompany police.

In Florida Publishing Co. v. Fletcher, 340 So.2d 914, 2 Med.L.Rptr. 1088 (Fla.1976), the plaintiff alleged that after she had left town on a trip, a fire broke out in her house that killed her 17–year-old daughter; that after the daughter's body was removed from the floor a silhouette was revealed; that defendant newspaper's photographer took a photograph of the silhouette; and that plaintiff first learned of the tragedy by reading the story in a newspaper and seeing the accompanying photographs. In her claim for trespass, the depositions revealed that police and fire officials, as was their standard practice, invited press photographers and reporters to enter the house; that the media representatives entered through an open door without objection; and that they entered quietly and did no damage to the property. The fire marshal wanted a clear picture of the silhouette to show that the body had been on the floor before the heat of the fire damaged the room. After the official took one picture, he ran out of film and asked the newspaper photographer to take pictures for the official investigation. He did so and also made copies for his own paper, which published them.

The defendant moved for summary judgment on the trespass claims. Affidavits from various government and media sources stated that entering private property and inviting the press in this type of situation was common practice. Plaintiff filed only her own affidavit and none from media or other experts. She conceded that it was proper for the police and fire officials to enter and also admitted that no one had objected to the entry of the press. The trial judge granted summary judgment because the affidavits "attest to the fact that it is common usage, custom, and practice for news media to enter private premises and homes to report on matters of public interest or a public event."

The Florida Supreme Court agreed that implied consent covered the case. Research showed that implied consent by custom and usage "do not rest upon the previous nonobjection to entry by the particular owner of the property in question but rest upon custom and practice generally." In addition to the fact that here the press entered in response to an express invitation from public officials, the court stressed that this was the first case presenting the question. "This, in itself, tends to indicate that the practice has been accepted by the general public since it is a widespread practice of longstanding." One judge dissented on jurisdictional grounds. The Supreme Court denied *certiorari*, 431 U.S. 930 (1977).

Compare Green Valley School, Inc. v. Cowles Florida Broadcasting, Inc., 327 So.2d 810 (Fla.App.1976). State officials planned a midnight raid, under a properly issued warrant, to search the premises of a controversial local private boarding school. The head of the party of 50 raiders invited reporters and photographers from several local media organizations to accompany the party. The defendant television station presented an extensive report of the raid on the evening news the following night, suggesting that the raid had turned up evidence of mistreatment of the students, rampant sexual misbehavior and use of drugs. The school sued the station for defamation and trespass.

The trial judge granted summary judgment to the station on the trespass claim. The court of appeals reversed, addressing the question entirely in the following passage.

> To uphold appellees' assertion that their entry upon appellant's property at the time, manner, and circumstances as reflected by this record was as a *matter of law* sanctioned by "the request of and with the consent of the State Attorney" and with the "common usage and custom in Florida" could well bring to the citizenry of this state the hobnail boots of a Nazi stormtrooper equipped with glaring lights invading a couple's bedroom at midnight with the wife hovering in her nightgown in an attempt to shield herself from the scanning TV camera. In this jurisdiction, a law enforcement officer is not as a *matter of law* endowed with the right or authority to invite people of his choosing to invade private property and participate in a midnight raid of the premises.

On the same day that it decided *Fletcher,* the Florida Supreme Court dismissed an appeal in the Green Valley case, indicating that it found no conflict between the results in the two cases. Can they be reconciled?

As suggested earlier, journalists' attempts to show real people in crisis situations—police raids, emergency medical operations or fires, sometimes in residential settings—raise additional questions. Although these issues seem to arise most frequently in the context of television, they can arise out of situations involving print journalists as well.

In a case involving the CBS program "Street Stories," Secret Service agents invited a camera crew to film them executing a search warrant at the home of a man suspected of credit card fraud. The man was not at home, but when his wife opened the door four agents, followed by a producer, camera operator, and sound technician, pushed their way inside. The agents ransacked the house and questioned the wife accusingly while the television crew filmed. They seized no evidence other than a family photograph. The film showed the woman, wearing only a dressing gown, objecting to the filming and trying to console her crying four-year-old son. She testified that the crew never identified themselves as news media and she assumed they were part of the official search party. Apparently the footage was never shown on "Street Stories."

The woman and her son sued the agents, CBS and the show's producer for intrusion. The agents claimed they were immune from suit as officials carrying out governmental duties. CBS and the producer claimed immunity on the ground they were acting with the government's permission. The district judge rejected both defenses, noting that no official immunity extends to violations of well established constitutional rights:

> [The lead agent's] act of allowing the CBS camera crew to enter the apartment and film the search far exceeded the scope of the warrant. It was in clear violation of then well established Fourth Amendment principles. For this purpose it is the equivalent of a

rogue policeman using his official position to break into a home in order to steal objects for his own profit or that of another.

. . .

CBS had no greater right than that of a thief to be in the home, to take pictures and to remove the photographic record. CBS claims no First Amendment right to be present.

. . .

CBS [and the producer] are not entitled to a qualified immunity. Even were they entitled to the same defense as a government official, as already noted, the complaint alleges a violation of a then clearly established constitutional right which precludes grant of qualified immunity to the official.

Ayeni v. CBS Inc., 848 F.Supp. 362, 22 Med.L.Rptr. 1466 (E.D.N.Y.1994). CBS settled the case by paying compensation to the plaintiffs. The Secret Service agents appealed, but the Second Circuit affirmed the trial judge's ruling that the plaintiffs were entitled to proceed against the agents. See Ayeni v. Mottola, 35 F.3d 680, 22 Med.L.Rptr. 2225 (2d Cir.1994). After the affirmance, a CBS spokesman said the network would no longer send camera crews into homes with officers unless it had the occupant's permission.

The Supreme Court of the United States heard oral arguments in 1999 on two ride-along cases—one involving journalists accompanying law enforcement officials into a private residence (as in *Ayeni*) and the other involving journalists accompanying federal marshals onto a privately-owned ranch. In the residence case, U.S. marshals and Montgomery County, Md., deputy sheriffs were searching for Dominic Wilson, a 27–year-old fugitive. A *Washington Post* reporter and a photographer, invited by the U.S. Marshals Service, accompanied them. They entered his parents' home at dawn, as the parents slept, on April 16, 1992, but the son was not there. The father, photographed in his undershorts, and the mother, photographed in a sheer nightgown, sued, alleging violation of their Fourth Amendment rights to avoid unreasonable searches and seizures. Without reaching the question of whether the parents had a right of privacy, the court of appeals ruled that the officers were immune to the lawsuit because it was not clear at the time of the incident that their actions were unconstitutional. The court pointed out, for instance, that *Ayeni* had not been decided yet at the time of the 1992 search, and that there were few relevant case precedents. The court said, "Where an intrusion is justified, whether by warrant or by probable cause and exigent circumstances, police are temporarily placed in control of the premises and its occupants. . . . When these officers [in *Wilson*] acted . . . the smidgen of case law that had considered the constitutionality of permitting the media to accompany officers into a private residence while they executed a warrant had found no constitutional infirmity with the practice." Wilson v. Layne, 110 F.3d 1071, 25 Med.L.Rptr. 1555 (4th Cir.1997). We will discuss the oral arguments before the Supreme Court shortly.

The ranch case presents a slightly different issue in that an intrusion may seem less offensive outdoors rather than in the sanctity of one's home. In that case, U.S. Fish and Wildlife Service agents had suspected that Paul Berger had poisoned federally protected eagles that were preying on sheep at his Montana ranch. The agents allowed a CNN crew to accompany them on a 1993 raid. There was a written contract between the federal authorities and CNN and Turner Broadcasting System, authorizing the filming and recording of the search for broadcast on environmental television shows "Earth Matters" and "Network Earth." As the court of appeals said, "The media wanted footage of the discovery of evidence showing that Paul Berger was poisoning eagles, and the government wanted the publicity." Berger was subsequently convicted of a misdemeanor offense of misusing a pesticide but acquitted of felony charges of killing eagles. He sued both CNN and the agents for trespass, conversion, intentional infliction of emotional distress and violation of the federal wiretapping statute. The court of appeals held that the federal officers were *not* entitled to qualified immunity and held that the media acted jointly with the federal authorities and therefore reversed a previous judgement in favor of the media. Berger v. Hanlon, 129 F.3d 505, 25 Med.L.Rptr. 2505 (9th Cir.1997).

In *Wilson*, the Supreme Court held, in an opinion by Chief Justice Rehnquist, that "it is a violation of the Fourth Amendment for police to bring members of the media or other third parties into a home during the execution of a warrant when the presence of the third parties in the home was not in aid of the execution of the warrant." But the majority went on to hold that it was not unreasonable for officers to have believed in April 1992 that bringing along media observers was lawful—in fact, the official marshal's service ride-along policy had explicitly contemplated that media who engaged in ride-alongs might enter private homes with their cameras as part of fugitive arrests—so the Supreme Court affirmed the judgment of the court of appeals ordering summary judgement for the defendant law enforcement officers. The Court's decision in *Wilson* obviously makes it likely that law enforcement officials will in the future be much less likely to bring media into homes with them. Wilson v. Layne, 526 U.S. 603, 27 Med.L.Rptr. 1705 (1999).

In *Berger*, the Supreme Court denied CNN's petition for *certiorari* but granted that of the officers and then vacated the appellate court's decision and ruled against the plaintiffs on the basis of the qualified immunity recognized by *Wilson v. Layne*. Note that *Berger* involved intrusion only into the Bergers' 75,000–acre ranch, not into their home. Nevertheless, the Court in its per curiam opinion said the Bergers "alleged a Fourth Amendment violation under our decision today in *Wilson v. Layne*." Hanlon v. Berger, 526 U.S. 808, 27 Med.L.Rptr. 1716 (1999). Should that be understood as meaning *Wilson v. Layne* is not confined to intrusions into homes?

On remand, despite the Supreme Court's holding that the officers were entitled to qualified immunity, the Ninth Circuit held that the media defendants were not, citing cases holding that private actors who conspire with federal officers do not share the immunity granted to the latter. The court held that the Bergers' state-law claims against CNN for trespass and intentional infliction of emotional distress also could proceed to trial. It affirmed summary judgement for the defendants on the federal wiretap claim. See Berger v. Hanlon, 188 F.3d 1155, 27 Med. L.Rptr. 2213 (9th Cir.1999).

An older case illustrates a different situation—that in which unwelcome media enter premises that are privately owned but that are open to the public. In Le Mistral, Inc. v. Columbia Broadcasting System, 61 A.D.2d 491, 402 N.Y.S.2d 815, 3 Med.L.Rptr. 1913 (1978), CBS, as owner and operator of WCBS–TV in New York City, directed reporter Rich and a camera crew to visit restaurants that had been cited for health code variations. Plaintiff was on the list. The crew entered plaintiff's restaurant with cameras "rolling" and using bright lights that were necessary to get the pictures. The jury found CBS liable for trespass and awarded plaintiff $1,200 in compensatory damages and $250,000 in punitive damages. After the verdict (in a passage approved on appeal), the trial judge stated:

> The instructions given to the crew, whether specific to this event or as standing operating procedure, were to avoid seeking an appointment or permission to enter any of the premises where a story was sought, but to enter unannounced catching the occupants by surprise; "with cameras rolling" in the words of CBS' principal witness, Rich. From the evidence the jury was entitled to conclude that following this procedure the defendant's employees burst into plaintiff's restaurant in noisy and obtrusive fashion and following the loud commands of the reporter, Rich, to photograph the patrons dining, turned their lights and camera upon the dining room. Consternation, the jury was informed, followed. Patrons waiting to be seated left the restaurant. Others, who had finished eating, left without waiting for their checks. Still others hid their faces behind napkins or table cloths or hid themselves beneath tables. . . . [The] president of the plaintiff and manager of its operations, refused to be interviewed, and as the camera continued to "roll" he pushed the protesting Miss Rich and her crew from the premises. All told, the CBS personnel were in the restaurant not more than ten minutes, perhaps as little as one minute, depending on the testimony the jury chose to credit. The jury by its verdict clearly found the defendant guilty of trespass and from the admissions of CBS' own employees they were guilty of trespass. The witness Rich sought to justify her crew's entry into the restaurant by calling it, on a number of occasions, a "place of public accommodation", but, as she acknowledges, they did not seek to avail themselves of the plaintiff's "accommodation"; they had no intention of purchasing food or drink.

The trial judge upheld the determination of liability but set aside both damage awards because he had erroneously barred a defense witness from testifying as to CBS's motive and purpose in entering the premises. On appeal, the court held that its review of the record "demonstrates an adequate basis to justify the compensatory damage award rendered by the jury and, accordingly, such award must stand." As to punitive damages, the court agreed that the judge had erred in excluding the testimony because all "circumstances immediately connected with the transaction tending to exhibit or explain the motive of the defendant are admissible." One judge thought it clear that the defendants were "not motivated by actual malice or such an intentional disregard of plaintiff's rights as would justify the imposition of punitive damages. [ ] The defendant was merely pursuing a newsworthy item in the overly aggressive but good faith manner that characterizes the operation of the news media today. . . . In this sensitive and evolving First Amendment area, I would permit this precedent-setting opinion to stand as a warning to all newsgatherers that future trespasses may well be met with an award of punitive damages."

CBS, dissatisfied with the decision, sought to appeal to New York's highest court to argue that no trespass had been committed and also that, in any event, punitive damages were improper. That court ultimately refused to hear the case for jurisdictional reasons.

The case is complicated by the disruptive presence of the television cameras. If newspaper reporters had entered the restaurant, would they have been trespassers from the moment they entered—or only from the moment they refused to leave? If, while the newspaper reporters were leaving, they continued watching the scene and making mental notes of what they saw, would that be improper? If the court is suggesting that the premises were open only to those seriously considering purchasing food or drink, why should it matter whether the entry was disruptive?

b. *Other Intrusions Without Consent*

We turn now to alleged invasions of privacy that do not fit into the trespass mold. These involve issues of how far persons may use cameras or high-technology equipment to obtain information about a subject; wiretapping; and secretly recording conversations to which the person is a party.

Galella v. Onassis, 487 F.2d 986, 1 Med.L.Rptr. 2425 (2d Cir.1973), involved aggressive efforts by a "paparazzo" photographer to obtain photographs of the widow and children of President John Kennedy. Galella brought his power boat close to Mrs. Onassis as she was swimming, jumped out of bushes as she was walking past, jumped into her son's path to take a photograph of him riding his bicycle, and invaded the children's private schools. Those acts that reasonably put the subject in fear of personal safety would create tort liability under longstanding rules. But those that involved annoyance presented harder questions.

Mrs. Onassis claimed that when she went through the streets to go shopping or to visit a friend, or walked alone in Central Park, she was engaged in private activities that should not be the subject of any unwanted photography. The court disagreed. Mrs. Onassis was "a public figure and thus subject to news coverage" although the First Amendment provided no "wall of immunity protecting newsmen" from liability for torts committed while gathering news. The court balanced Mrs. Onassis's concern about intrusion with the legitimate interests of photography by ordering Galella to stay 25 feet from Mrs. Onassis at all times; not to block her movement in public places; and not to do "any act foreseeably or reasonably calculated" to place Mrs. Onassis in jeopardy or frighten her. Any further restriction on his taking and selling photographs of her would be improper.

Galella was subsequently charged with criminal contempt for violating the order, but he avoided paying a $120,000 fine for contempt by agreeing not to take any more pictures of Mrs. Onassis.

In 1979 a TV camera crew trailed a man as he was trying to pay a ransom to persons who had kidnaped his wife. Despite his pleas, the crew followed the man, apparently along public ways. The episode attracted much press discussion after the FBI said the action had "put that woman's life in danger." An editorial in *Editor & Publisher*, July 28, 1979 at 6, asserted that although the TV crew might have considered its actions "enterprising reporting . . . it was more like sheer stupidity. . . . It is this sort of arrogance and brashness that gets media in trouble with the public."

After the woman was released, the couple sued the station for endangering the woman's life. Because no harm actually occurred in the case the suit might be difficult. Should the husband be able to sue for mental anguish he suffered as a result of the crew's actions? Criminal liability might be possible if it was shown that the crew learned of the man's movements by making unauthorized interceptions of messages on a nonbroadcast frequency in violation of what was then § 605 of the Communications Act (now § 705), 47 U.S.C.A. § 605. Should the law impose a sanction against reporters whose gathering efforts in fact lead to harm because kidnappers panic or get angry because their instructions apparently are not being followed?

Where solitude is invaded, the courts speak of the subject's reasonable expectations of privacy as the guide to available protection. Thus, one who leaves his curtains open, knowing that persons in the building across the street can look inside his apartment, can claim no reasonable expectation of privacy. But if the only vantage point from which the inside of the apartment can be seen is a hilltop two miles away, a court might well find that a reporter who set up a powerful telescope on that hill and looked through the open window has invaded privacy.

Similarly, a person inside a dwelling can make no reasonable claim of invasion of privacy if he shouts at his spouse and is overheard by others outside. But if he speaks in a normal or hushed voice—and is overheard because a highly sensitive microphone in the next apartment or across the street has picked up the communication, a court would probably find an invasion.

Wiretapping and other forms of intercepting messages frequently have been involved in litigation. Although some early cases did impose tort liability in these cases, the major development occurred when Congress passed The Omnibus Crime Control and Safe Streets Act of 1968, 18 U.S.C.A. §§ 2510–2520. The basic provision subjects to criminal liability "any person" who without a warrant "willfully intercepts" any "wire or oral communication." Section 2520 provides that violators are liable for compensatory and punitive damages. Some exclusions apply, but none specially to reporters.

Revisions in 18 U.S.C.A. §§ 2510–2520 were made in 1986, in the Electronic Communications Privacy Act (ECPA). Section 2511 now provides, in part, that any person who, unless authorized by one or both parties to the communication, intentionally intercepts, uses or discloses any "wire, oral, or electronic communication" is subject to punishment.

The ECPA also prohibits unauthorized interception of network satellite feeds—specifically news and sports backhauls. The legislation reaffirmed existing prohibitions against interception of scrambled broadcast signals. The House accepted the Senate version of the bill, under which government can seek an injunction for a first offense, and repeat offenders can be fined up to $500. For intentional or malicious interference with communications and weather satellites, possible penalties are prison terms up to 10 years and fines up to $250,000.

In *Bartnicki v. Vopper*, an unknown person recorded a cell phone conversation between a union negotiator (Gloria Bartnicki) and the head of a teachers union (Anthony Kane) during a period of difficult labor negotiations between the teachers union and a school board. The tape of the conversation, containing threats against local school board members, was eventually provided by an intermediary to radio talk-show host Fred Vopper, who played it on two local radio stations. The plaintiffs, Bartnicki and Kane, sued the intermediary (an opponent of the union) and also sued the media under the federal wiretap act and the comparable Pennsylvania statute.

The Supreme Court held in 2001 in favor of the media defendants, emphasizing that they did not participate in the interception, they obtained the tape lawfully, and they disclosed the contents of a conversation that concerned a public matter, even though they had reason to know the tape was illegally intercepted. Justice Stevens, writing for the majority, quoted *Smith v. Daily Mail* [the casebook, p. 29]: "As a general matter, 'state action to punish the publication of truthful information seldom can satisfy constitutional standards.' . . . '[If] a newspaper lawfully obtains truthful information about a matter of public significance then state officials may not constitutional punish publication of the information, absent a need . . . of the highest order.' " Essentially, then, the court found the First Amendment to outweigh the privacy interest. Bartnicki v. Vopper, 532 U.S. 514, 29 Med.L.Rptr. 1737 (2001).

Despite Congress's attempts to protect the privacy rights of wireless communications, apparent loopholes in the statutes seem to have permitted some eavesdropping because of problems with proving intent on the part of the interceptors of wireless conversations or because the eavesdroppers have not "disclosed" the contents of a conversation. The Wireless Privacy Enhancement Act was before Congress in 1999. It would expand the definition of the frequencies that may not be scanned to include digital PCS frequencies as well as cellular, and it would prohibit either the interception or the divulgence of wireless communications without requiring both.

Two television cases exemplify litigation of the 1980s. In one, a woman who was alleged to have traded sexual favors for a light sentence by an Ohio judge agreed to be interviewed by ABC in her home, but she refused to appear on camera. The network made surreptitious video and voice recordings, and she sued. Although the court held that there was no criminal or tortious purpose, it held that the plaintiff was entitled to try to prove in court that ABC intended to injure her. Boddie v. American Broadcasting Companies, Inc., 731 F.2d 333, 10 Med.L.Rptr. 1923 (6th Cir.1984). In the other, ABC had surreptitiously recorded a meeting between congressional investigators and a cancer insurance salesman—with the consent of the investigators. The court ruled that ABC must show that its *only* purpose was to aid Congress or that it must demonstrate that it had no injurious purpose in secretly recording the encounter. Benford v. American Broadcasting Companies, Inc., 502 F.Supp. 1159, 6 Med.L.Rptr. 2489 (D.Md.1980), affirmed 661 F.2d 917 (4th Cir.), certiorari denied 454 U.S. 1060 (1981).

In Ribas v. Clark, 38 Cal.3d 355 (1985), a woman with marital difficulties had a friend listen in on a telephone call with her husband; the court awarded no common law damages, but there was a statutory penalty. The court quoted a law review comment:

> There is a qualitative as well as a quantitative difference between secondhand repetition by the listener and simultaneous dissemination to a second auditor, whether that auditor be a tape recorder or a third party. In the former situation the speaker retains control over the extent of his immediate audience. Even though that audience may republish his words, it will be done secondhand, after the fact, probably not in entirety, and the impact will depend upon the credibility of the teller. Where electronic monitoring is involved, however, the speaker is deprived of the right to control the extent of his own firsthand dissemination. . . . In this regard participant monitoring closely resembles third-party surveillance; both practices deny the speaker a most important aspect of privacy of communication—the right to control the extent of first instance dissemination of his statements.

Florida has a statute that reaches participant monitoring by barring persons "not acting under color of law" from intercepting a wire or oral communication unless all parties to the communication had given their prior consent. An important lawsuit arose from a general attack on the statute by reporters who claimed that the use of concealed recording equipment was essential to investigative reporting for three reasons: it aided accuracy of reporting; persons being interviewed would not be candid if they knew they were being recorded; and the recording provided corroboration in case of suit for defamation.

The Florida Supreme Court upheld the statute's constitutionality. The statute allows "each party to a conversation to have an expectation of privacy from interception by another party to the conversation. It does not exclude any source from the press, intrude upon the activities of the news media in contacting sources, prevent the parties to the communication from consenting to the recording, or restrict the publication of any information gained from the communication. First Amendment rights do not include a constitutional right to corroborate news gathering activities when the legislature has statutorily recognized the private rights of individuals."

In response to the argument that secret recording may be the only way to get credible information about crime, the court stated that protection against intrusion might protect even a person "reasonably suspected of committing a crime." Shevin v. Sunbeam Television Corp., 351 So.2d 723, 3 Med.L.Rptr. 1312 (Fla.1977).

Based on the briefs and without argument, the Supreme Court dismissed the appeal by the press for want of a substantial federal question, 435 U.S. 920 (1978). Three justices dissented.

The Florida court had relied to some extent on the case of Dietemann v. Time, Inc., 449 F.2d 245, 1 Med.L.Rptr. 2417 (9th Cir.1971). In that case, two reporters obtained access to plaintiff's home to find out whether he was a medical quack. While plaintiff was diagnosing the alleged ailment of one reporter, the other secretly took photographs with a hidden camera. The entire conversation was transmitted to confederates outside by means of a transmitter hidden in one reporter's purse. In this part of the case, the court concluded that California would impose liability for invasion of privacy:

> [One who invites others to his home] does not and should not be required to take the risk that what is heard and seen will be transmitted by photograph or recording, or in our modern world, in full living color and hi-fi to the public at large or to any segment of it that the visitor may select. A different rule could have a most pernicious effect upon the dignity of man and it would surely lead to guarded conversations and conduct where candor is most valued, e.g., in the case of doctors and lawyers.

> The defendant claims that the First Amendment immunizes it from liability for invading plaintiff's den with a hidden camera and its concealed electronic instruments because its employees were gathering news and its instrumentalities "are indispensable tools of investigative reporting." We agree that newsgathering is an integral part of news dissemination. We strongly disagree, however, that the hidden mechanical contrivances are "indispensable tools" of newsgathering. Investigative reporting is an ancient art; its successful

practice long antecedes the invention of miniature cameras and electronic devices. The First Amendment has never been construed to accord newsmen immunity from torts or crimes committed during the course of newsgathering. The First Amendment is not a license to trespass, to steal, or to intrude by electronic means in the precincts of another's home or office. It does not become such a license simply because the person subjected to the intrusion is reasonably suspected of committing a crime.

Defendant relies upon the line of cases commencing with [*New York Times*] . . . to sustain its contentions that (1) publication of news, however tortiously gathered, insulates defendant from liability for the antecedent tort. . . .

As we previously observed, publication is not an essential element of plaintiff's cause of action. Moreover, it is not the foundation for the invocation of a privilege. Privilege concepts developed in defamation cases and to some extent in privacy actions in which publication is an essential component are not relevant in determining liability for intrusion conduct antedating publication. [ ] Nothing in *New York Times* or its progeny suggests anything to the contrary. Indeed, the Court strongly indicates that there is no First Amendment interest in protecting news media from calculated misdeeds. [ ]

In a more recent case, Wolfson v. Lewis, 924 F.Supp. 1413, 24 Med.L.Rptr. 1609 (E.D.Pa.1996), a federal district court enjoined broadcast journalists associated with "Inside Edition" from "harassing, hounding, following, intruding, frightening, terrorizing or ambushing" Richard and Nancy Wolfson and their children. For a story on high salaries paid to executives of U.S. Healthcare, "Inside Edition" was said to have engaged in surveillance of the home of Leonard Abramson (chairman of U.S. Healthcare and father of Mrs. Wolfson, who, like her husband and father, was an executive of U.S. Healthcare) and to have followed members of the family leaving the Wolfson home in Pennsylvania, then to have gone to the Abramson home in Florida, where the Wolfsons had gone, and to have used a rented motor boat, "shotgun mike" and television camera equipped with zoom lens to pick up sounds and images from the waterfront house there. The district court found that the plaintiffs were "likely to succeed on the merits of their claim for invasion of privacy," and therefore entered the preliminary injunction requested by the Wolfsons. The Wolfson case was settled, reportedly without the payment of any money, just as appellate arguments were about to begin. "As part of the resolution, the court dissolved the injunction, the Wolfsons withdrew an amended complaint they filed, and Inside Edition and the reporters agreed not to follow or go to the homes of the Wolfsons and certain family members." Philadelphia Inquirer, Jan. 28, 1997, at B3.

In Shulman v. Group W Productions, 18 Cal.4th 200, 26 Med.L.Rptr. 1737 (1998), the California Supreme Court held that the media can be held liable for intrusion for taping an accident victim's conversations with emergency personnel at the site of a wreck, even if the event occurs on public property with many bystanders observing. A television camera-man accompanied a helicopter rescue crew to a site where Ruth Shulman and her son were trapped in an overturned automobile at the bottom of an embankment. The cameraman outfitted the flight nurse with a microphone and videotaped the rescue. Portions of the audio and video-tape were later broadcast on a program titled "On Scene: Emergency Rescue." Shulman suffered severe back injuries which left her paraple-gic.

The Shulmans sued for both intrusion and disclosure of private facts (the latter to be discussed at p. 949, *infra*). The California Supreme Court held 5–2 that summary judgment for defendants on the intrusion claims was improper. The majority said the plaintiffs could have reason-able expectations of privacy not only within the helicopter, but also with respect to conversations with the nurse at the accident site. The majority said it was not clear whether these conversations were in fact overheard by bystanders standing at the top of the embankment, and that it was therefore for a jury to determine whether defendants had intruded into a situation in which plaintiffs had a reasonable expectation of privacy. The majority rejected defendants' claim that the First Amendment barred intrusion claims for newsgathering as long as the information was about a matter of legitimate public concern and was obtained lawfully. On the private facts claim, the vote was 5–2 against the plaintiffs. The majority said First Amendment protection for disseminating newsworthy informa-tion is far stronger than for newsgathering and precluded liability for the broadcast of plaintiffs' words and images because they were of legitimate public concern.

In another case, plaintiff Beverly Deteresa sued ABC for unlawful eavesdropping on or recording of confidential communications under California law, for physical intrusion of solitude, and for other torts. Deteresa was an flight attendant on the flight O.J. Simpson took to Chicago shortly after the murders of his wife and Ronald Goldman. When an ABC producer came to her door and said he wanted her to appear on an ABC show, she said she wasn't interested in appearing on the show but she discussed flight with him. The next day he told her he had audiotaped their conversation and had had a cameraperson video-tape them from a public street adjacent to her home. A five-second clip of the video was shown on "Day One," but none of the audiotape was broadcast. A district court granted summary judgment for defendants; that decision was affirmed by the court of appeals. The Supreme Court denied *certiorari*. Deteresa v. American Broadcasting Companies, Inc., 121 F.3d 460, 25 Med.L.Rptr. 2038 (9th Cir.1997), certiorari denied 523 U.S. 1137 (1998).

2. Consent Has Been Obtained

We turn now to cases in which the reporter contends that what might otherwise be a tort is not because the plaintiff consented to the conduct in question. The basic legal principle is not in doubt. Occasionally, the cases involve such neat situations as a plaintiff who signs a written consent. Usually, the cases are more complex.

In Cassidy v. American Broadcasting Companies, Inc., 60 Ill.App.3d 831, 17 Ill.Dec. 936, 377 N.E.2d 126, 3 Med.L.Rptr. 2449 (1978), an undercover policeman was sent to a massage parlor. After paying $30 he was escorted to a room to watch "de-luxe lingerie modeling." On entering the warm room he observed camera lights. He asked, "What are we on, TV?" The model replied, "Yes, we're making a movie." As plaintiff reclined on the bed watching the model change her lingerie several times, he made suggestive remarks and advances. He then arrested the model for solicitation. The entire scene was in fact being photographed from an adjacent room by a local television station through a two-way mirror. The manager of the parlor had asked the defendant to film the episode to show that police were harassing him.

Plaintiff's suit failed because, among other reasons, the plaintiff apparently did not intend his conduct to be private because he knew that someone might be making a movie of his conduct. He testified his actions were in the line of duty as an officer and that if the model wished to sell him a completed film he would use it as evidence in his investigation. Plaintiff had no expectation of privacy.

Although plaintiff had not explicitly consented to being filmed, his conduct after being informed that a film was being made amounted to consent. But should the same rule apply if a jury could reasonably find that the model made her statement jokingly or sardonically so that a reasonable person in plaintiff's position would not have believed what she said?

The most common problems reporters face in consent cases appear to involve consents that are obtained by some type of misrepresentation. Since reporters often investigate alleged misdeeds they are unlikely to get consent to do interviews, go to certain places or record interviews if they identify themselves as reporters. In such cases, what is the role of consent?

In *Dietemann,* the reporters posed as a couple seeking medical advice from the plaintiff, who lived a quiet life and did not advertise or even have a telephone. They went to his gate and rang the bell. When plaintiff appeared, the reporters falsely said that they had been sent by a certain person and wanted to see plaintiff because the female visitor had a lump in her breast that she wanted diagnosed. Plaintiff admitted the pair to his den and made his diagnosis. On this part of the case the court observed:

> Plaintiff's den was a sphere from which he could reasonably expect to exclude eavesdropping newsmen. He invited two of defendant's employees to the den. One who invites another to his home or office takes a risk that the visitor may not be what he seems, and that the visitor may repeat all he hears and observes when he leaves. But he does not and should not be required to take the risk

that what is heard and seen will be transmitted by photograph or recording. . . .

Why does plaintiff take the risk that a visitor may not be who he claims to be, or that a visitor may repeat what he hears inside, but not take the risk that secret recordings and photographs are being made? Is it that the plaintiff does in fact intend to deal with the persons who are standing before him—whatever names they give or whatever reasons they give for coming?

ABC's "Primetime Live" was found by a Federal jury in Greensboro, N.C., to have trespassed and committed fraud while researching a 1992 segment about the Food Lion grocery chain. Despite general complaints about the accuracy of the report, Food Lion did *not* sue for defamation, instead basing their suit on the network's newsgathering—specifically the network's misrepresentation on employment applications of the backgrounds of ABC employees who submitted phony resumes in order to get hired as Food Lion employees. The jury decided that Food Lion should receive more than $5 million in damages—almost all punitive— igniting heated debate on concealed-identity tactics, particularly by television news magazines.

In interviews in the days following the verdict, the jurors insisted that they had no objection to ABC's use of hidden cameras but that committing fraud in the course of newsgathering was illegal, and that Food Lion therefore deserved to win. New York Times, Dec. 23, 1996 at 1.

The trial judge subsequently reduced the punitive damages to a total of $315,000. The case subsequently went to the court of appeals, which held that Food Lion could not recover for fraud, and affirmed the judgment for breach of a duty of loyalty to Food Lion and for trespass but awarded only $2 in damages for those claims. Food Lion, Inc. v. Capital Cities/ABC, Inc., 194 F.3d 505, 27 Med.L.Rptr. 2409 (4th Cir. 1999).

Courts generally rule that consent to enter one section of land does not authorize entering any other part; and that consent to do one thing, such as reading the gas meter, does not authorize removal of the gas meter. In these cases, it is apparent that the actor has exceeded the consent. In *Dietemann,* however, the plaintiff gave consent to enter the land and come to the den—and that is precisely what the reporters did. His misunderstanding about identity did not lead him to consent to one thing but to be hit with another. (A person who wants legal protection against someone who is told a secret and then reveals it may obtain it by entering into a contract in which the recipient makes legally enforceable promises about his future behavior.)

If misrepresenting identity doesn't raise major legal problems, it does raise ethical questions that are much discussed among journalists. The matter is reviewed at length in Zimmerman, "By Any Other Name . . .," *Washington Journalism Review* (Nov./Dec. 1979) at 32.

The matter received much attention in 1979 when the Pulitzer prize for local investigative reporting was denied to a newspaper that uncovered massive official corruption after it bought and ran a bar in Chicago under a false name. At about the same time, a reporter posed as a Congressman to obtain a seat at the signing of the Egyptian–Israeli peace treaty. The reporter said that the episode involved telling "only one lie." *Editor & Publisher*, June 9, 1979 at 6, responded, "But *how many lies* are too many? Are we getting back to the no-holds-barred philosophy that the story should be gotten at any cost?" Noting that the press complains loudly when someone impersonates a newsman, the editorial continued, "We believe that newsmen's impersonations of others in order to get a story [are] equally damaging to their believability and should be scrupulously avoided." Some have suggested that if reporters will lie to get a story, readers may believe that they would also lie in writing the story if they thought the matter important enough.

The argument the other way, of course, stresses that uncovering crime or other misbehavior is very hard—that it would have been virtually impossible to have demonstrated the corruption in Chicago without setting up the fake business. An example involved a reporter who got a job as a guard at the Three Mile Island nuclear plant after the malfunctioning and then took photographs while on the job. His goal was to show how easy it was to get a job—his asserted background and references were never checked—and to show how lax security was inside the plant. Are there other ways to obtain this information? How important is it to obtain the information? Does such behavior damage the credibility of the press?

Although civil actions by persons deceived in these cases may not be likely, some of the cases may well involve potential criminal liability— particularly cases involving impersonation of government officials or lying to government officials.

Should different principles apply if reporters knowingly accept material improperly obtained by others? In one case, aides to a United States Senator removed numerous documents from his files, copied them and passed the copies to columnists who knew how they had been obtained. The court held that the columnists had committed no tort:

> If we were to hold appellants liable for invasion of privacy on these facts, we would establish the proposition that no one who receives information from an intruder, knowing it has been obtained by improper intrusion, is guilty of a tort. In an untried and developing area of tort law, we are not prepared to go so far. A person approached by an eavesdropper with an offer to share in the information gathered through the eavesdropping would perhaps play the nobler part should he spurn the offer and shut his ears. However, it seems to us that at this point it would place too great a strain on human weakness to hold one liable in damages who merely succumbs to temptation and listens. Pearson v. Dodd, 410 F.2d 701 (D.C.Cir.) certiorari denied 395 U.S. 947 (1969).

Should the result change if a reporter had said to the aide "I'd sure love to see your file on" a particular matter—and three days later the aide presented the file?

"Street Stories" included a 1992 segment in which a distraught Oakland, Calif., mother told a victim counselor and a police officer that her husband had beaten and kicked her. She subsequently sued CBS for $10 million for invasion of privacy, fraud, and intentional infliction of emotional distress, charging that members of the "Street Stories" production crew failed to identify themselves and agreed not to film her and her daughter when they accompanied a mobile crisis intervention team to her house. The mother said the crew members had told her that they were shooting a story on the crisis intervention team for the San Francisco district attorney's office. In response to CBS's request for summary judgment, Judge Smith said too many facts could not be resolved without further discovery and possible trial but urged that the parties attempt to work out a settlement. Baugh v. CBS Inc., 828 F.Supp. 745, 21 Med.L.Rptr. 2065 (1993). The two sides subsequently settled, with terms of the agreement not being revealed. San Francisco Chronicle, July 22, 1993 at A26.

Despite the fact that "Prime Time Live" sent "patients" equipped with concealed cameras into an eye clinic to obtain evidence of unnecessary cataract operations, the Seventh Circuit held that the television program had committed no trespass, invasion of privacy or actionable fraud, because the clinic and two of its surgeons had agreed to allow the network to film a cataract operation and interview clinic personnel, and the alleged fraud of posing as patients to gain access to the clinic did not vitiate the owners' consent because the entry did not violate any interest protected by the law of trespass. See Desnick v. American Broadcasting Cos., 44 F.3d 1345, 23 Med.L.Rptr. 1161 (7th Cir.1995).

The clinic said it had agreed to allow the network in only after the producer promised that no ambush interviews or undercover surveillance would be used. The program used both techniques. However, in an opinion by Judge Posner, the court said that the owner's objection was not to the physical presence of the intruders, but to their purpose. The opinion suggested the result might be different if the intruders observed personal rather than professional activities, if the premises were a home rather than a business, or if there was an intrusion into a "private space" such as a hospital room. The court distinguished *Dietemann* on the ground that "he was not in business, and did not advertise his services or charge for them." The same analysis applied to the intrusion claim under the law of privacy.

The allegedly fraudulent promises not to use ambush interviews or surveillance were not actionable as promissory fraud because Illinois law provided that remedy only where the promises were part of a "scheme to defraud." "The only scheme here was a scheme to expose publicly any bad practices that the investigative team discovered, and that is not a fraudulent scheme." The court thought the facts might support a claim for breach of contract, but the plaintiffs had abandoned that theory.

Defenses. As discussed above, consent (if not exceeded) can be a defense for a suit for an intrusion on physical solitude. Such defamation defenses as truth and absence of malice have no relevance because neither falsity nor its cause is part of an intrusion suit. It should be noted specifically that newsworthiness is not a defense for intrusion: the fact that the public wants news is no justification for violating another's rights in order to obtain it.

3. CRIMINAL LIABILITY

At several points during the foregoing discussion of civil liability, we have had occasion to touch on related criminal sanctions. In this section we draw together the likely sources of criminal liability that may confront newsgatherers.

At the outset, federal and state governments have statutes punishing such acts as the theft of government property and the concealment or removal of official records and documents. See, e.g., 18 U.S.C.A. §§ 641, 2071. In addition, conspiracy to commit criminal acts is also a crime. Other statutes directly relate to property or information in specific areas, such as national security or nuclear energy. Knowingly receiving stolen property may also be criminal even though the recipient had nothing to do with the original theft.

Other crimes involving direct harm to government may include impersonating an officer not obeying a lawful order of a police officer or bribing a government employee. The latter was involved when a news photographer paid a prison guard to take secret photographs of the accused killer known as "Son of Sam."

The government also uses criminal legislation to support the civil law in protecting individual property and privacy. We have seen some in operation already, such as the criminal punishment for intercepting communications whether by wiretapping or otherwise. Breaking into a home and stealing a photograph from the table would involve several criminal offenses as well as tort liability. Other protections are available. In one episode, a publisher was charged with extortion by allegedly threatening to write untrue stories about people in the community unless they supplied information for forthcoming stories or agreed to advertise in the paper.

In one case, reporters covering a demonstration at a construction site for a nuclear plant in Oklahoma were convicted of trespassing on private property. The utility, Public Service Company of Oklahoma (PSO), did not want extensive coverage of the marchers—as had occurred at an earlier demonstration. This time, PSO warned all reporters that they would be arrested if they entered the fenced property at any point not permitted by PSO. PSO then set up a viewing area that reporters might use on its otherwise closed property. It was not clear in advance whether the demonstration or any confrontation would be visible from that point.

Several reporters used the viewing area. Others followed the demonstrators and entered the land when the demonstrators went through the fence. These reporters were the ones convicted of trespass. Each was fined $25.

The Oklahoma Court of Criminal Appeals held that the First Amendment does not shield newspersons from state criminal prosecution in their newsgathering function and affirmed the convictions. Stahl v. State, 665 P.2d 839, 9 Med.L.Rptr. 1945 (Okl.Crim.App.1983), certiorari denied 464 U.S. 1069 (1984).

B. INVASION OF PRIVACY BY PUBLICATION

As indicated above, there are several ways the media may invade privacy through the publication or dissemination of information rather than through its gathering.

The idea that a right of privacy from the media should be legally protected can be traced to a law review article by Louis D. Brandeis and his law partner, Samuel D. Warren, The Right to Privacy, 4 Harv.L.Rev. 193 (1890), often considered the most influential law review article ever published. The authors, reacting to the editorial practices of Boston newspapers, made clear their concerns:

> The press is overstepping in every direction the obvious bounds of propriety and of decency. Gossip is no longer the resource of the idle and of the vicious, but has become a trade, which is pursued with industry as well as effrontery. To satisfy a prurient taste the details of sexual relations are spread broadcast in the columns of the daily papers. To occupy the indolent, column upon column is filled with idle gossip, which can only be procured by intrusion upon the domestic circle.

Working with a variety of rather remote precedents from other areas of law, the authors developed an argument that courts should recognize an action for invasion of privacy by media publication.

The theory was rejected in the first major case to consider it. In Roberson v. Rochester Folding Box Co., 171 N.Y. 538, 64 N.E. 442 (1902), the defendants, a flour company and a box company, obtained a good likeness of the plaintiff, a pretty girl, and reproduced it on their advertising posters. Plaintiff said she was humiliated and suffered great distress. The court, 4–3, rejected a common law privacy action on grounds that suggested concern about innovating after so many centuries; an inability to see how the doctrine, once accepted, could be judicially limited to appropriate situations; and skepticism about finding liability for behavior that might actually please some potential "victims." The Warren and Brandeis article was discussed at length, but the court concluded that the precedents relied upon were too remote to sustain the proposed rights.

The outcry was immediate. At its next session, the New York legislature created a statutory right of privacy (New York Civil Rights Law, §§ 50 and 51). The basic provision was that "a person, firm or corporation that uses for advertising purposes, or the purposes of trade, the name, portrait or picture of any living person without having first obtained the written consent of such person, or if a minor or his or her parent or guardian, is guilty of a misdemeanor." The other section provided for an injunction and created an action for compensatory and punitive damages. The meaning of "advertising purposes" was clear, but the phrase "purposes of trade" was not self-explanatory. Eventually it came to mean that an accurate story carried as editorial (non-advertising) content did not violate the statute.

Other states, perhaps learning from the New York experience, slowly began to develop a common law right to privacy that was not influenced by statutory language and not limited to advertising invasions. In addition to an action for commercial use of one's name, the courts also developed actions for truthful uses of plaintiff's name that were thought to be outside the areas of legitimate public concern. The action for invasion of privacy by publication of true editorial material began to take hold during the 1920s and early 1930s.

Courts in the late 1930s became more attentive to the Supreme Court's expanding protection of expression. Operating on a common-law level, they tended to expand protection for the media by taking a narrow view of what were legitimately private areas.

For the embarrassing private facts tort, the courts allowed a defense of newsworthiness to be expanded, because they were reluctant to impose normative standards of what should be newsworthy. Instead, they leaned toward a descriptive definition of newsworthiness that protected whatever editors had decided would interest their readers. By the 1960s some doubted whether the action for invasion of privacy had any remaining vitality.

It was precisely, during the last part of the 1960s and the beginning of the 1970s, however, that privacy as a general social value was perceived to be threatened in different ways by the encroachment of computers, data banks and electronic devices, as well as the media. The concept of privacy also expanded as the Supreme Court dealt with birth control, abortion and other problems in the context of a right of privacy. This was bound to have an impact on the media aspects of privacy as well.

One result of the new thinking was to broaden the area of privacy protection.

1.   PUTTING THE PLAINTIFF IN A FALSE LIGHT

As indicated earlier, the tort of putting the plaintiff in a false light in the public eye is the privacy tort closest to defamation, because both involve publication of falsity. There is a critical difference between the two, however: the publication that results in a successful defamation action is *harmful* as well as false. The publication that results in a successful false light invasion of privacy action may not be harmful in the sense of harming the plaintiff's reputation. It may be just the opposite—a publication that falsely portrays the plaintiff to be better than he is in real life (i.e., a hero) or simply *different* than he is in real life.

In one example, a group used the plaintiff's name without authorization on a petition to the governor to veto a bill. Although falsely stating that plaintiff had signed the petition would not be defamatory, the court found the situation actionable because it cast plaintiff in a false light.

The first two Supreme Court decisions involving alleged invasions of privacy by the mass media both happened to be false light cases. They were Time, Inc. v. Hill, 385 U.S. 374, 1 Med.L.Rptr. 1791 (1967) and Cantrell v. Forest City Publishing Co., 419 U.S. 245, 1 Med.L.Rptr. 1815 (1974).

In 1952 James Hill and his family were held hostage in their Pennsylvania home for 19 hours by escaped convicts who apparently treated them decently. The incident received nationwide coverage. Thereafter the Hills moved to Connecticut, sought seclusion, and refused to make public appearances. A novel—*The Desperate Hours*—modeled partially on the event was published the following year. In 1955 *Life* magazine in a short article announced that a play and motion picture were being made from the novel, which they said was "inspired" by the Hill episode. The play, "a heartstopping account of how a family rose to heroism in a crisis," would enable the public to see the Hill story "re-enacted." Photographs showed actors performing scenes from the play at the house at which the original events had occurred. The Hills claimed the story was inaccurate because the novel and play showed convicts committing violence on the father and uttering a "verbal sexual insult" at the daughter.

Suit was brought under the New York statute requiring plaintiff to show the article was being used for advertising purposes or purposes of trade. A truthful article, no matter how unpleasant for the Hills, would not have been actionable. The state courts had previously indicated that falsity would show that the article was really for the purposes of trade and not for public enlightenment. The state courts allowed recovery after lengthy litigation.

The Supreme Court, in a plurality opinion, decided that the privilege to comment on matters of public interest had constitutional protection and could not be lost by the introduction of falsity unless actual malice could be proved. Thus, the Hill family lost.

The decision should be viewed in the context of what was happening in the court's defamation decisions in the same period. This was only three years after the Court had decided, in *New York Times*, p. 885, *supra*, that public officials would be required to prove actual malice in defamation cases. By 1967 thinking, the members of the Hill family were public figures—having become so involuntarily as the result of having been part of a newsworthy event. And 1967 was the same year in which the Court extended the actual malice rule of *New York Times* to public figures like Wally Butts and former Army Gen. Edwin Walker.

One should not miss the irony that the attorney who represented the Hill family before the Supreme Court was a man with a strong sense of privacy and considerable distaste for the media: then former Vice President, not-yet-President Richard M. Nixon.

The next false-light privacy case decided by the Supreme Court was Cantrell v. Forest City Publishing Co. A reporter for *The Cleveland Plain Dealer* had written a prize-winning story about a bridge collapse that had killed 44 people, including Melvin Cantrell. Some months later the reporter returned to the Cantrell home for a follow-up on how the family coped with the disaster. Although Mrs. Cantrell was not present, her children were. The reporter's story failed to make clear that Mrs. Cantrell had been absent, and a reader presumably would have concluded just the opposite from the story, which said she "will talk neither about what happened nor about how they are doing. She wears the same mask of non-expression she wore at the funeral. She is a proud woman. Her world has changed. She says that after it happened, the people in town offered to help them out with money and they refused to take it." The family sought damages on a false-light privacy theory.

The Court, in an opinion by Justice Stewart, held that the First Amendment did not protect deliberate or reckless falsity. He also observed that because the actual malice standard was met in this case, it was not an appropriate case in which to consider the hypothetical question of whether private figure plaintiffs like the Cantrells *had* to prove actual malice or might merely be asked to prove simple negligence. As Justice Stewart put it, it was not an appropriate occasion to "consider whether a State may constitutionally apply a more relaxed standard of liability for a publisher . . . of false statements injurious to a private individual under a false-light theory of privacy, or whether the constitutional standard announced in Time, Inc. v. Hill applies to all false-light cases."

Justice Douglas was the sole dissenter in *Cantrell*: "Those who write the current news seldom have the objective, dispassionate point of view—or the time—of scientific analysts. They deal in fast-moving events and the need for 'spot reporting.' . . . [I]n matters of public import such as the present news reporting, there must be freedom from damages lest the press be frightened into playing a more ignoble role than the Framers visualized."

The stories that resulted in the *Cantrell* and *Hill* cases purported to tell the truth. A different sort of false light problem arises in the context of "docudramas," which openly mix fact and fiction. Actress Elizabeth Taylor held a nationally-publicized news conference to say she would sue ABC if it dared to broadcast a docudrama based on her life. The network canceled the docudrama.

However, in Hicks v. Casablanca Records, 464 F.Supp. 426 (S.D.N.Y. 1978), a motion picture and novel about an incident in the life of mystery-writer Agatha Christie was held to be protected under the First Amendment so long as it was not presented to be taken as true.

A particular problem for broadcasters is contextual false light, in which something truthful becomes misleading because of the context in which it is used. Broadcasters must be especially careful of juxtaposing pictures with unrelated audio and of using file footage which viewers may mistake as current.

See p. 923, *supra,* for a discussion of the *Hustler* case, in which Rev. Jerry Falwell sued for libel, invasion of privacy and intentional infliction of emotional distress.

John Charles Heekin sued CBS for false light invasion of privacy because of a 60 Minutes segment about domestic violence. An interview with Heekin's former wife was juxtaposed with stories of battered and abused women. Heekin claimed that the specific facts about him in the story were true but that the juxtaposition of those facts with the other stories created a false impression that he had abused his wife and children. The Florida trial court held that the state's fair reporting privilege barred the action against the network because the facts came from public records. But a Florida appellate court reversed, holding that the false light claim was based not on the *source* of the facts, but instead on the network's *use* of the facts.

The court held that *Time, Inc. v. Hill*, p. 946, *supra,* was inapplicable to the Heekin case for two reasons:

. . . First, *Time* involved allegations by a limited public figure that the publication of false facts about his family portrayed them in a false light—thus, the action was essentially one for defamation. The *Time* analysis does not apply to Heekin's action, which involves allegations by a private plaintiff that the publication of true facts portrayed him in a false light. Second, the issue in *Time* was whether New York's right of privacy statute, which created a statutory cause of action for misappropriation of a plaintiff's likeness, was unconstitutional as applied to actions against the press. Given that the case dealt with the interpretation and application of a New York misappropriation statute, the holding and analysis of *Time* is of questionable applicability to Heekin's false light claim under Florida common law.

The court reversed the lower court's dismissal of the action. Heekin v. CBS Broadcasting Inc., 29 Med.L.Rptr. 1795 (Fla.Dist.Ct.App 2001).

Defenses. Many of the same defenses that can be used by media defendants in defamation cases might also be argued to have application in a false-light privacy case. Truth would be a strong defense. Qualified privilege might be offered as a defense if one had quoted accurately from a record of an official proceeding. Privileged criticism or fair comment might work as a defense if the publication alleged to put the plaintiff in a false light was actually a statement of opinion rather than a statement of fact. If the plaintiff is a public official or public figure, absence of malice could be a strong defense. To a large extent, the applicability of the libel defenses in privacy cases is yet to be determined in the courts and there would be special problems in applying some of those to contextual false light.

2. Publication of Embarrassing Private Facts

Publication of embarrassing private facts (which we address in this section) and appropriation of another's name or likeness for commercial or trade purposes (which we address in the next section) are the two branches of invasion of privacy that have to do with truthful publication—either by electronic media or by print—that interferes with someone's right to be let alone. Redundant though it may seem, it may be helpful to think of the former as publication of embarrassing private *true* facts.

a. *Categories*

The cases of publication of embarrassing private facts fall into a small number of categories—those dealing with sexual matters, commission of crime, poverty, idiosyncratic qualities and other embarrassing stories.

The important point is not whether the state cases are decided "correctly." The area is so new and unformed that the cases do not fit into a neat pattern—except that plaintiffs rarely win. The results are given in capsule form at the end of each case, without reasons, simply to satisfy curiosity—not to suggest the proper resolution. Below, we will explore approaches to this very troublesome area. The law aside, prospective reporters and news directors should consider how the facts of each story should be handled.

Sexual Matters. 1. In a study of official misconduct at a county home, a newspaper reported that among the misconduct was the involuntary sterilization of a named 18–year-old young woman seven years earlier. Howard v. Des Moines Register and Tribune Co., 283 N.W.2d 289, 5 Med.L.Rptr. 1667 (Iowa 1979), certiorari denied 445 U.S. 904 (1980) (case dismissed).

2. Television cameras went to the scene of a report that a man was threatening harm to his housekeeper's sister. The crew arrived and began filming as police led the stark-naked man from the house. In a news report the following evening, plaintiff's "buttocks and genitals were visible to television viewers for a time period of approximately eight-to-nine-tenths of one second." Taylor v. KTVB Inc., 96 Idaho 202, 525 P.2d 984 (1974) (case remanded to determine defendant's reasons for using the film; settled out of court).

3. A television station reported the identity of a deceased rape victim. Cox Broadcasting Corp. v. Cohn, 420 U.S. 469, 1 Med.L.Rptr. 1819 (1975). The case is included later in this chapter.

4. Plaintiff was kidnaped by her estranged husband and taken to an apartment. He forced her to disrobe and then beat her. Police came. Following the suicide of the husband, police hurried plaintiff from the apartment nude "save for a mere towel." Photographers on the scene took photographs and turned them over to defendant newspaper, which ran several of them. Cape Publications, Inc. v. Bridges, 423 So.2d 426, 8 Med.L.Rptr. 2535 (Fla.App.1982), certiorari denied 464 U.S. 893 (1983) (judgment for $10,000 reversed on appeal and case dismissed).

5. During an assassination attempt on President Ford in San Francisco, Oliver Sipple knocked the arm of the assailant as she sought to aim a second shot at the President. Sipple was the object of extensive media attention, including stories that identified him as homosexual. Sipple, asserting that relatives who lived in the Midwest did not know of his orientation, sued the *San Francisco Chronicle.* The newspaper defended in part on the argument that privacy was not involved because Sipple had marched in gay parades and had acknowledged that at least 100 to 500 people in San Francisco knew he was homosexual. The newspaper argued that his sexual orientation was relevant to the story because, although some stereotyped gays as sissies, Sipple was an ex-marine who acted heroically. The court held that the newspaper articles' references to Sipple's homosexuality did not constitute unlawful public disclosure of private facts, because Sipple's sexual orientation was well known and the articles about him were of legitimate public interest. Sipple v. Chronicle Publishing Co., 154 Cal.App.3d 1040, 201 Cal.Rptr. 665, 10 Med.L.Rptr. 1690 (1984).

6. A woman on the "Phil Donahue Show" disclosed that her husband had raped her 11–year-old daughter by another marriage and that the daughter had become pregnant, and the daughter's child had been "adopted" by the woman and her husband. The woman and the show's producers were sued by the now adult daughter and the daughter's husband, on behalf of the daughter's child. Anonsen v. Donahue, 857 S.W.2d 700 (Tex.App.1993), certiorari denied 511 U.S. 1128 (1994) (summary judgment for defendants based on the revelations' being protected under the First Amendment).

Prison and Criminal Behavior. 7. The plaintiff—an attorney and former municipal judge—was arrested for driving while intoxicated and using profane and abusive language. At the police station, he was "hitting and banging on his cell door, hollering and cursing from the time of his arrest" until he was released about five hours later. He was aware that a local journalist was in the cell block a short distance away with a tape recorder. The journalist taped some of the noise and played excerpts from it on the air. Holman v. Central Arkansas Broadcasting Co., Inc., 610 F.2d 542, 5 Med.L.Rptr. 2217 (8th Cir.1979) (case dismissed).

Idiosyncracies. 8. *Sports Illustrated* planned an article about the "Wedge," a California beach reputed to be the world's most dangerous site for body surfing. Mike Virgil, known as the most daring surfer at the site, was interviewed and was referred to in the story as one who extinguished cigarettes in his mouth, ate spiders and other insects and was perceived by other surfers as "abnormal." He was quoted in the article as saying, "Every summer I'd work construction and dive off billboards to hurt myself or drop loads of lumber on myself to collect unemployment compensation so I could surf at the Wedge. Would I fake injuries? No, I wouldn't fake them. I'd be damn injured. But I would recover. I guess I used to live a pretty reckless life. I think I might have been drunk most of the time." (Although Virgil had once consented to be interviewed, he withdrew the consent when he learned the shape the story would take. The court rejected the defense of consent.) Virgil v. Time, Inc., 527 F.2d 1122, 1 Med.L.Rptr. 1835 (9th Cir.1975), certiorari denied 425 U.S. 998 (1976) (affirming denial of summary judgment, two justices dissenting).

Embarrassment or Ridicule. 9. A newspaper article reported that the basketball team at the state university was in trouble because four named players, of the eight who were returning, "are on academic probation and in danger of flunking." Bilney v. Evening Star Newspaper Co., 43 Md.App. 560, 406 A.2d 652 (1979) (case dismissed).

Suicide. 10. Electronic journalists faced a particularly difficult decision involving ethics and privacy when the Pennsylvania state treasurer, R. Budd Dwyer, shot himself during a news conference in January 1987. Several stations, after warning viewers, showed the entire suicide— Dwyer putting a .357 Magnum pistol into his mouth and pulling the trigger. Others showed an edited version period. Enraged viewers complained that children, home from school because of a snowstorm, saw the videotape before parents could switch the channel. The incident points up the difficulty of balancing full disclosure in news coverage against respect for the privacy of a suicide victim's family and viewers' sensitivities. Editor & Publisher, Jan. 31, 1987, at 9.

b. *Legal Analysis*

As the law has been developing, the plaintiff must show that the information made public was in fact "private," that the disclosure would be "highly offensive to a reasonable person" and that the revelation was not newsworthy. We look at each element in turn.

Private Information. The courts have not been very attentive to this aspect of the matter—perhaps because in most cases the information is clearly something that the plaintiff has held closely and did not want bandied about. Our examples ranged from one extreme to the other. The plaintiff in the sex-change case had not publicized the surgery. On the other hand, private facts are unlikely to exist as to the exterior of a home, or when someone at a police station shouts so loudly that others cannot help but hear what is said.

Between these extremes we have cases like that of Oliver Sipple, whose sexual orientation was not a secret among his friends and his immediate community, and who was willing to march in gay parades, but who wanted the information kept inside San Francisco. Although some cases should be eliminated on the ground that the information published had not been "private" at the time of the publication, most do seem to involve matters that most people would attempt to keep secret.

"Highly Offensive to a Reasonable Person." This formulation has received much more attention. Although the specific language is taken from the Restatement of Torts (Second) § 652D, similar expressions have been used in the cases during this tort's development. The single most important consideration appears to be the substance of the statement. In some cases it appears difficult to argue that the revelation would be highly offensive to a reasonable person.

It is no coincidence that the cases commonly involve sexual, health and financial topics that are generally thought to involve the most intimate matters. Another area has involved revelations about rehabilitated criminals. As we shall see, simply showing that the revelation would be highly offensive to a reasonable person does not guarantee that the defendant will be held liable for an invasion of privacy. It is, however, an essential first step.

Note that no complex damage rules, such as exist in defamation, have emerged in privacy. The plaintiff who can successfully demonstrate an invasion of privacy will recover damages measured by the emotional harm suffered. Obviously, damages here cannot rehabilitate the plaintiff in the way that damages in defamation might pay for the reputational harm caused by the false statement.

"Newsworthiness" or *"Legitimate Concern" Defense.* In addition to requiring that the publicized matter be private and "highly offensive to a reasonable person," the courts demand that the matter be "not of legitimate concern to the public." Most litigation has revolved around this or similar phrases, such as claims that the article in question was "newsworthy" or that it was of "general or public concern." It should be emphasized at the outset that this requirement exists under state common law and has been applied with greater or lesser rigor in every major state case in which a privacy claim has been raised.

As noted in the introduction to this section, there was a period in which the courts seemed to treat "newsworthy" or "of legitimate concern" as descriptive terms. Any article appearing in a newspaper would meet that requirement because if an editor chose to include it, it must be newsworthy. Such an approach would soon eliminate the privacy action. More recently, the courts have shifted and now attempt to develop normative guidelines to determine when the information might be of "legitimate concern to the public."

Although the public figure definitions from defamation are not used in privacy, voluntary and involuntary public figures may be treated differently in privacy. Not surprisingly, people who see the limelight may be viewed differently than those who are victims of an accident or crime or are otherwise swept up in media coverage of an event through no choice of their own.

Virgil, the body surfer, for example, voluntarily brought himself into the public eye by his prowess, his continued attendance at a particular beach and his engaging in a particular type of activity. Sipple, on the other hand, although he had participated in gay parades in San Francisco, had kept his sexual orientation from relatives in the Midwest and could never have expected the national attention he received when he became part of the news of the Ford assassination attempt. Neither Virgil nor Sipple, of course, ultimately prevailed in his privacy suit.

A 1986 case decided by the Supreme Court of Oregon demonstrates the problems in balancing "newsworthiness" and "legitimate concern" against concerns over material which is "highly offensive to a reasonable person." Anderson v. Fisher Broadcasting Companies, Inc., 300 Or. 452, 712 P.2d 803, 12 Med.L.Rptr. 1604 (1986), involved television coverage of the scene of an automobile accident. A camera crew for KATU–TV in Portland videotaped events at the scene, including shots of the plaintiff bleeding and in pain while receiving emergency treatment. The tape was never used as part of a news broadcast, but the station later used a brief excerpt in promotional spots advertising a special news report about a new system for dispatching emergency medical help.

Plaintiff Richard Anderson sued for general damages for mental anguish, and said he was pictured in a condition "offensive to a reasonable person" and not of legitimate public concern. The broadcaster claimed the use of the plaintiff's picture occurred in advertising another news program and that such use was constitutionally privileged.

The Oregon Supreme Court found it unnecessary to reach the constitutional issue. The court held that "[g]enerally, Oregon decisions have not allowed recovery for injury to a stranger's feelings as such, unless the infliction of psychic distress was the object of defendant's conduct or the conduct violated some legal duty apart from causing the distress."

Further, the court said:

> What is "private" so as to make its publication offensive likely differs among communities, between generations, and among ethnic, religious, or other social groups, as well as among individuals. Likewise, one reader's or viewer's "news" is another's tedium or trivia. The editorial judgment of what is "newsworthy" is not . . . properly a community standard. Even when some editors themselves vie to tailor "news" to satisfy popular tastes, others may believe that the community should see or hear facts or ideas that the majority finds uninteresting or offensive.

The court concluded that in Oregon, ". . . [t]he truthful presentation of facts concerning a person, even facts that a reasonable person would wish to keep private and that are not 'newsworthy,' does not give rise to common law tort liability for damages for mental or emotional distress, unless the manner or purpose of defendant's conduct is wrongful in some respect apart from causing the plaintiff's hurt feelings," and reinstated the judgment of the circuit court for the defendant television station.

c. *Constitutional Privilege Defense*

So few plaintiffs win suits for publication of embarrassing private facts that there have been few opportunities for the Supreme Court to speak to the issue. Defendants have almost always prevailed under state law. In *Cox,* however, the Georgia Supreme Court had held for a plaintiff with regard to a television station's naming of a deceased rape victim—resulting in the first Supreme Court decision in this area of the law.

COX BROADCASTING CORP. v. COHN

Supreme Court of the United States, 1975.
420 U.S. 469, 95 S.Ct. 1029, 43 L.Ed.2d 328, 1 Med.L.Rptr. 1819.

[Mr. Cohn's 17–year-old daughter was raped in Georgia and did not survive the occurrence. In Georgia it was a misdemeanor for "any news media or any other person to print and publish, broadcast, televise or disseminate through any other medium of public dissemination . . . the name or identity of any female who may have been raped. . . ." Ga.Code Ann. § 26–9901. Similar statutes exist in a few other states. The girl was not identified at the time. Eight months later, appellant's reporter, Wassell, also an appellant, attended a hearing for the six youths charged with the rape and murder. He learned the girl's name by inspecting the indictment in the courtroom. His report naming the girl was telecast.

The Georgia Supreme Court held that the complaint stated a common law action for damages for invasion of the father's own privacy. Defendant's First Amendment argument was rejected on the ground that the statute was an authoritative declaration that Georgia considered a rape victim's name not to be a matter of public concern. The court could discern "no public interest or general concern about the identity of the victim of such a crime as will make the right to disclose the identity of the victim rise to the level of First Amendment protection."

On appeal, the Supreme Court first decided that the decision below was a "final" judgment so as to give the court jurisdiction. The Court then turned to the First Amendment issue.]

Mr. Justice White delivered the opinion of the Court.

. . .

Georgia stoutly defends both § 26–9901 and the State's common-law privacy action challenged here. Her claims are not without force, for powerful arguments can be made, and have been made, that however it may be ultimately defined, there *is* a zone of privacy surrounding every individual, a zone within which the State may protect him from intrusion by the press, with all its attendant publicity. Indeed, the central thesis of the root article by Warren and Brandeis, The Right to Privacy, 4 Harv.L.Rev. 193, 196 (1890), was that the press was overstepping its prerogatives by publishing essentially private information and that there should be a remedy for the alleged abuses.

More compellingly, the century has experienced a strong tide running in favor of the so-called right of privacy. . . .

. . . Because the gravamen of the claimed injury is the publication of information, whether true or not, the dissemination of what is embarrassing or otherwise painful to an individual, it is here that claims of privacy most directly confront the constitutional freedoms of speech and press. The face-off is apparent, and the appellants urge upon us the broad holding that the press may not be made criminally or civilly liable for publishing information that is neither false nor misleading but absolutely accurate, however damaging it may be to reputation or individual sensibilities.

. . .

Rather than address the broader question whether truthful publications may ever be subjected to civil or criminal liability consistently with the First and Fourteenth Amendments, or to put it another way, whether the State may ever define and, protect an area of privacy free from unwanted publicity in the press, it is appropriate to focus on the narrower interface between press and privacy that this case presents, namely, whether the State may impose sanctions on the accurate publication of the name of a rape victim obtained from public records—more specifically, from judicial records which are maintained in connection with a public prosecution and which themselves are open to public inspection. We are convinced that the State may not do so.

In the first place, in a society in which each individual has but limited time and resources with which to observe at first hand the operations of his government, he relies necessarily upon the press to bring to him in convenient form the facts of those operations. Great responsibility is accordingly placed upon the news media to report fully and accurately the proceedings of government, and official records and documents open to the public are the basic data of governmental operations. Without the information provided by the press most of us and many of our representatives would be unable to vote intelligently or to register opinions on the administration of government generally. With respect to judicial proceedings in particular, the function of the press serves to guarantee the fairness of trials and to bring to bear the beneficial effects of public scrutiny upon the administration of justice. See Sheppard v. Maxwell, 384 U.S. 333, 350 (1966).

Appellee has claimed in this litigation that the efforts of the press have infringed his right to privacy by broadcasting to the world the fact that his daughter was a rape victim. The commission of crime, prosecutions resulting from it, and judicial proceedings arising from the prosecution, however, are without question events of legitimate concern to the public and consequently fall within the responsibility of the press to report the operations of government.

The special protected nature of accurate reports of judicial proceedings has repeatedly been recognized. This Court, in an opinion written by Mr. Justice Douglas, has said:

> "A trial is a public event. What transpires in the court room is public property. If a transcript of the court proceedings had been published, we suppose none would claim that the judge could punish the publisher for contempt. And we can see no difference though the conduct of the attorneys, of the jury, or even of the judge himself, may have reflected on the court. *Those who see and hear what transpired can report it with impunity.* There is no special perquisite of the judiciary which enables it, as distinguished from other institutions of democratic government, to suppress, edit, or censor events which transpire in proceedings before it." Craig v. Harney, 331 U.S. 367, 374 (1947) (emphasis added).

. . .

The developing law surrounding the tort of invasion of privacy recognizes a privilege in the press to report the events of judicial proceedings. The Warren and Brandeis article, supra, noted that the proposed new right would be limited in the same manner as actions for libel and slander where such a publication was a privileged communication: "the right to privacy is not invaded by any publication made in a court of justice . . . and (at least in many jurisdictions) reports of any such proceedings would in some measure be accorded a like privilege."

. . .

Thus, even the prevailing law of invasion of privacy generally recognizes that the interests in privacy fade when the information involved already appears on the public record. The conclusion is compelling when viewed in terms of the First and Fourteenth Amendments and in light of the public interest in a vigorous press. The Georgia cause of action for invasion of privacy through public disclosure of the name of a rape victim imposes sanctions on pure expression—the content of a publication—and not conduct or a combination of speech and non-speech elements that might otherwise be open to regulation or prohibition. See United States v. O'Brien, 391 U.S. 367, 376–377 (1968). The publication of truthful information available on the public record contains none of the indicia of those limited categories of expression, such as "fighting" words, which "are no essential part of any exposition of ideas, and are of such slight social value as a step to truth that any benefit that may be derived from them is clearly outweighed by the social interest in order and morality." Chaplinsky v. New Hampshire, 315 U.S. 568, 572 (1942) (footnote omitted).

By placing the information in the public domain on official court records, the State must be presumed to have concluded that the public interest was thereby being served. Public records by their very nature are of interest to those concerned with the administration of government, and a public benefit is performed by the reporting of the true contents of the records by the media. The freedom of the press to publish that information appears to us to be of critical importance to our type of government in which the citizenry is the final judge of the proper conduct of public business. In preserving that form of government the First and Fourteenth Amendments command nothing less than that the States may not impose sanctions on the publication of truthful information contained in official court records open to public inspection.

We are reluctant to embark on a course that would make public records generally available to the media but forbid their publication if offensive to the sensibilities of the supposed reasonable man. Such a rule would make it very difficult for the media to inform citizens about the public business and yet stay within the law. The rule would invite timidity and self-censorship and very likely lead to the suppression of many items that would otherwise be published and that should be made available to the public. At the very least, the First and Fourteenth Amendments will not allow exposing the press to liability for truthfully publishing information released to the public in official court records. If there are privacy interests to be protected in judicial proceedings, the States must respond by means which avoid public documentation or other exposure of private information. Their political institutions must weigh the interests in privacy with the interests of the public to know and of the press to publish.[26] Once true information is disclosed in public court documents open to public inspection, the press cannot be sanctioned for publishing it. In this instance as in others reliance must rest upon the judgment of those who decide what to publish or broadcast. See Miami Herald Pub. Co. v. Tornillo, 418 U.S., at 258.

Appellant Wassell based his televised report upon notes taken during the court proceedings and obtained the name of the victim from the indictments handed to him at his request during a recess in the hearing. Appellee has not contended that the name was obtained in an improper fashion or that it was not on an official court document open to public inspection. Under these circumstances, the protection of freedom of the press provided by the First and Fourteenth Amendments bars the State of Georgia from making appellants' broadcast the basis of civil liability.[27]

Reversed.

Mr. Chief Justice Burger concurs in the judgment.

26. We mean to imply nothing about any constitutional questions which might arise from a state policy not allowing access by the public and press to various kinds of official records, such as records of juvenile court proceedings.

27. Appellants have contended that whether they derived the information in question from public records or instead through their own investigation, the First and Fourteenth Amendments bar any sanctions from being imposed by the State because of the publication. Because appellants have prevailed on more limited grounds, we need not address this broader challenge to the validity of § 26–9901 and of Georgia's right of action for public disclosure.

Mr. Justice Powell, concurring.

. . .

Mr. Justice Douglas, concurring.

On the merits, . . . there is no power on the part of the government to suppress or penalize the publication of "news of the day."

Mr. Justice Rehnquist, dissenting.

Because I am of the opinion that the decision which is the subject of this appeal is not a[reviewable] "final" judgment or decree, . . . I would dismiss this appeal for want of jurisdiction.

Notes and Questions

1. What issues does the majority opinion avoid deciding? Why do you think the majority took the approach it did?

2. The principal opinion in *Howard,* the involuntary sterilization case, p. 949, *supra,* responded to the argument that plaintiff's name was unnecessary as follows:

> Here the disclosure of plaintiff's involuntary sterilization was closely related to the subject matter of the news story. It documented the article's theme of maladministration and patient abuses at the Jasper County Home. . . .
>
> In the sense of serving an appropriate news function, the disclosure contributed constructively to the impact of the article. It offered a personalized frame of reference to which the reader could relate, fostering perception and understanding. Moreover, it lent specificity and credibility to the report.
>
> In this way the disclosure served as an effective means of accomplishing the intended news function. It had positive communicative value in attracting the reader's attention to the article's subject matter and in supporting expression of the underlying theme.
>
> Examined in the light of the first amendment, we do not believe the disclosure could reasonably be held to be devoid of news value. [ ]
>
> Assuming, as plaintiff argues, the newspaper had a right to print an article that documented extrastatutory involuntary sterilizations at the Jasper County Home, the editors also had a right to buttress the force of their evidence by naming names. We do not say it was necessary for them to do so, but we are certain they had a right to treat the identity of victims of involuntary sterilizations as matters of legitimate public concern. . . .
>
> This is a far cry from embarrassing people by exposing their medical conditions or treatment when identity can add nothing to the probity of the account. [ ]

The disclosure of plaintiff's identity in this case could not reasonably be viewed as the spreading of gossip solely for its own sake. . . .

Would *Cox* reach the same result?

3. In *Virgil*, p. 951, *supra*, involving the body surfer, the publisher, citing *Cox*, argued in its brief that the First Amendment protected almost all true statements from liability:

A press which must depend upon a governmental determination as to what facts are of 'public interest' in order to avoid liability for their truthful publication is not free at all. . . . A constitutional rule can be fashioned which protects all the interests involved. This goal is achieved by providing a privilege for truthful publications which is defeasible only when the court concludes as a matter of law that the truthful publication complained of constitutes a clear abuse of the editor's constitutional discretion to publish and discuss subjects and facts which in his judgment are matters of public interest.

The court rejected the argument and adopted the view of the *Restatement (Second) of Torts*, that liability may be imposed if the matter published is "not of legitimate concern to the public." Then the court relied on a passage from the *Restatement* that was quoted earlier in this section—that "in the last analysis what is proper becomes a matter of the community mores."

In libel and obscenity cases juries utilize community standards, and the court thought they should do so here, too, "subject to close judicial scrutiny to ensure that the jury resolutions comport with First Amendment principles." What is the difference between *Time*'s position and that adopted by the court? Is the court's view consistent with *Cox*? Over the dissents of Justices Brennan and Stewart, the Supreme Court denied *certiorari* in *Virgil*. 425 U.S. 998 (1976). The case was remanded for trial.

On remand, the trial judge held that the magazine was entitled to summary judgment. First, the judge concluded that the facts revealed were not "highly offensive." Even if they were, the facts were "included as a legitimate journalistic attempt to explain Virgil's extremely daring and dangerous style of body surfing at the Wedge. There is no possibility that a juror would conclude that the personal facts were included for any inherent morbid, sensational, or curiosity appeal they might have." Virgil v. Sports Illustrated, 424 F.Supp. 1286, 2 Med.L.Rptr. 1271 (S.D.Cal.1976).

4. Although the courts have tended to take this area case-by-case, editors complain that such an approach breeds intolerable uncertainty. An editor must decide today what might happen in court in several years—and the standards are said to be vague. What will be found "highly offensive to a reasonable person" or to violate "community standards and mores"? Juries given these questions may punish unpopular broadcasters and publishers.

Compare this situation with that confronting an editor in the defamation area. There the editor, with advice from lawyers, must decide whether the *Times* or *Gertz* rule applies and then decide whether the publication's conduct meets that standard. And truth is always a defense. Do you see a sharp difference between the editor's position there and where the case involves privacy?

5. A rare successful privacy case resulted in an award of $1,500 actual and $25,000 punitive damages, affirmed by the South Carolina Supreme Court. Hawkins v. Multimedia, Inc., 288 S.C. 569, 344 S.E.2d 145, 12 Med.L.Rptr. 1878 (1986). In a sidebar article to a story on teenage pregnancies, defendant's newspaper identified plaintiff as the teenage father of an illegitimate child. The majority of the article focused on the teenage mother. After the mother identified plaintiff as the father, the reporter called plaintiff twice to obtain comments. The first time she spoke with plaintiff's mother. The second time she spoke with the reluctant plaintiff for three or four minutes. "In neither call did the reporter request permission to identify or quote [plaintiff]."

Over defendant's objection, the trial judge charged that a minor cannot consent to an invasion of privacy. The appellate court did not reach the issue because it found that defendant had failed to establish consent in the first place. Although plaintiff did not hang up immediately, he was "very shy." He never agreed to the use of his name.

The court rejected defense arguments that the article was of "general interest" because that defense requires "legitimate" public interest. "Public or general interest does not mean mere curiosity, and newsworthiness is not necessarily the test." This issue was properly submitted to the jury.

Finally, the trial judge refused the defendant's charge that "malice must be shown by clear and convincing evidence." The appellate court concluded that malice "need not be shown to recover for invasion of privacy." It is relevant only for punitive damages. The proper burden for punitive damages was not raised at trial and could not be raised on appeal.

The Supreme Court denied *certiorari*, 479 U.S. 1012 (1986).

6. In some instances publication may lead to emotional distress or may even jeopardize the safety of a person identified in the media—and may, therefore, precipitate a privacy suit. In Times-Mirror Co. v. Superior Court (Doe), 198 Cal.App.3d 1420, 244 Cal.Rptr. 556, 15 Med.L.Rptr. 1129 (1988), stay denied, 488 U.S. 1036, certiorari dismissed 489 U.S. 1094 (1989), the complaint alleged that plaintiff Jane Doe returned home at midnight to find her roommate dead on the floor. She looked up to confront a man. She then fled the apartment and called the police. The newspaper published a story that identified the plaintiff by name as having discovered the body. After several intervening paragraphs, the article stated that "one witness" had given police a description of a man seen fleeing the apartment.

The plaintiff's suit centered on the claim that the story had told the murderer the identity of the only witness in the case and had thus subjected her to an increased risk of harm. The trial court's denial of summary judgment was affirmed, 2–1. The majority rejected an "absolute" First Amendment defense for printing the name of a witness. (There was a dispute as to whether the name had come from an official source or from the reporter's work.) Next, the newspaper argued that the fact reported was not private because plaintiff had told some friends, neighbors and relatives that she had discovered the body and confronted the murderer. The court responded that "[t]alking to selected individuals does not render private information public . . . On the record before us we cannot say Doe rendered otherwise private information public by cooperating in the criminal investigation and seeking solace from friends and relatives."

Next, the newspaper contended that the publication was newsworthy. The court relied on privacy cases for the proposition that community mores controlled and that jurors could find that Doe's name was not newsworthy by balancing the public benefit of knowing the name against the effect publication of her name might have on her safety and emotional well-being. The jury, the court said, must also "consider the seriousness of the intrusion and the extent to which Doe voluntarily exposed herself to notoriety."

Finally, the paper relied on cases like [*Daily Mail,* p. 29, *supra*] for the proposition that, absent an interest of the highest order, the state may not punish a defendant for publishing lawfully obtained truthful information. The court rejected the newspaper's claim: "The state must investigate violent crimes and protect witnesses. Already reluctant witnesses will be more hesitant to provide information if their names will appear in the morning paper. The state's interest is particularly strong when the criminal is still at large. The state's interest is reflected in the regular police policy not to release the identity of witnesses. . . . The interest of the state to protect witnesses and to conduct criminal investigations is sufficient to overcome the Times' First Amendment right to publish Doe's name."

The dissenter contended that plaintiff "unhappily, became an involuntary public figure. As a matter of law, the publication of Doe's name was newsworthy." Nor did the mention of Doe in the story offend community notions of decency. The majority was rejecting the reactions of the reasonable person and substituting the "subjective reaction" of the plaintiff. "The reporter and the editor are now hostage to the paranoiac, the psychotic, the schizophrenic, whose reactions to publication now determine the scope of First Amendment media immunity."

When the defendant sought *certiorari,* The Florida Star v. B.J.F. (the next case we shall address) was already before the Court. The defendant contended that its case was also worthy of *certiorari* or that the state court action should be stayed until the Court decided *Florida Star.* The Court denied the stay although it had not yet decided the

Florida Star case, and the Doe case was settled shortly after the stay was denied. Editor & Publisher, March 18, 1989 at 22.

7.   The Supreme Court addressed the problem of identification of rape victims for a second time in The Florida Star v. B.J.F., 491 U.S. 524, 16 Med.L.Rptr. 1801 (1989). *The Florida Star,* a small weekly newspaper in Jacksonville, Fla., whose policy was not to publish the names of sexual offense victims, sent a "reporter-trainee" to the sheriff's department to gather information for the newspaper's "Police Reports" section. The sheriff's department, which did not normally release the names of sexual offense victims, placed in its press room a copy of a police report of a rape, including the full name of the victim (referred to in the Supreme Court's opinion as "B.J.F.").

The reporter-trainee, apparently unaware of the newspaper's policy, copied the police report verbatim, including B.J.F.'s full name. The item appeared in the newspaper as one of 54 police blotter stories in that issue:

> "[B.J.F.] reported on Thursday, October 20, she was crossing Brent-
> wood Park, which is in the 500 block of Golfair Boulevard, en route
> to her bus stop, when an unknown black man ran up behind the
> lady and placed a knife to her neck and told her not to yell. The
> suspect then undressed the lady and had sexual intercourse with her
> before fleeing the scene with her 60 cents, Timex watch and gold
> necklace. Patrol efforts have been suspended concerning this inci-
> dent because of a lack of evidence."

The victim sued both the sheriff's department (which settled before trial for $2,500) and the newspaper. She testified that she heard about the article from fellow workers and acquaintances, that her mother received phone calls from a man who said he would rape B.J.F. again, that she had to change her phone number and that she had to seek police protection and counseling. The newspaper responded that it had obtained B.J.F.'s name from the police report and that its violation of its own non-publication rule was inadvertent.

The Supreme Court decided for the newspaper, holding that, where a newspaper publishes truthful, lawfully obtained information, "punish-ment may lawfully be imposed, if at all, only when narrowly tailored to a state interest of the highest order," and that no such interest would be satisfactorily served by imposing liability under the facts of the B.J.F. case.

8.   The decision in *Florida Star* led to a petition seeking review of a case involving an alleged invasion of privacy by a television statement which disclosed the identity of a rape victim. Ross v. Midwest Communications Inc., 870 F.2d 271, 16 Med.L.Rptr. 1463 (5th Cir.1989), certiorari denied 493 U.S. 935. Marla Ross was raped in 1983 by an assailant who was never apprehended. Police assured her her name would be held in strict confidence. In a documentary about the possible innocence of a man accused of another rape, Minneapolis television station WCCO–TV men-tioned Ross as "Marla" and showed a photograph of the house in which

she lived at the time of the rape. A federal district court granted summary judgment for the television station, holding that the details of the rape were a matter of legitimate public interest, and the U.S. Court of Appeals for the Fifth Circuit affirmed. In his petition for review following the *Florida Star* case, Ross's attorney told the Supreme Court that its decision in *Florida Star* "shattered the fragile confidence rape survivors possessed in law enforcement promises that their identities would not be disclosed." Med.L.Rptr. News Notes, Sept. 26, 1989. The Supreme Court denied *certiorari*, 493 U.S. 935 (1989).

9.   The highly publicized sexual assault charges against William Kennedy Smith, along with decisions by a London tabloid, an American supermarket tabloid (*The Globe*), *The New York Times* and NBC to identify Patricia Bowman, the woman who made the allegations against him, raised anew the concerns about the proper ways of treating complainants in sexual assault cases prior to any court determination that they are, in fact, victims. Public disclosure of Bowman's history, particularly in a profile of her in the *Times*, generated a national controversy over identification of rape complainants.

The day after NBC first used Bowman's name, *The New York Times* published its profile of her, including comments by unnamed sources that she had had a poor academic record and "a little wild streak" in high school, had borne a child out of wedlock, and frequented expensive bars in Palm Beach. The story was accompanied by an editor's note saying that *The Times* ordinarily did not publish rape victims' names, "but editors said yesterday that NBC's broadcast took the matter out of their hands." See Butterfield and Tabor, Leap up Social Ladder for Woman in Rape Inquiry, New York Times, April 17, 1991 at A17. (In later editions the headline was changed to "Woman in Florida Rape Inquiry Fought Adversity and Sought Acceptance").

The *Times* story set off a furor within the newspaper's own staff and around the country. A week later *The Times* ran an editor's note saying it had not intended to challenge the veracity of the woman's accusations and that the story should have included such a statement. See New York Times, April 26, 1991 at A3. The same issue of the *Times* contained a story reporting that 100 *Times* employees had signed a petition objecting to the original story about the woman and that a staff meeting of *Times* editors with 300 staffers "quickly turned confrontational." The story quoted one of the *Times* editors who approved the story as saying *Times* editors expected much of the mainstream press to follow its lead in identifying the woman, but that most news organizations did not do so. Glaberson, "Times Article Naming Rape Accuser Ignites Debate on Journalistic Values," New York Times, April 26, 1991 at A12.

The only news outlet prosecuted for violating Florida's "rape shield statute" was the *Globe,* which is published in Boca Raton. The Florida Supreme Court, relying on *Florida Star,* held that the statute was unconstitutional on its face but declined to "rule out the possibility that the legislature could fashion a statute that would pass constitutional muster." State v. Globe Communications Corp., 648 So.2d 110 (Fla. 1994).

After Smith's acquittal, Patricia Bowman gave press interviews and made television appearances.

NBC similarly identified the accuser of boxer Mike Tyson. The executive producer of NBC News said that not naming her would open NBC up to criticism from people who would say, "How come you used Bowman's name, but not this one's?" USA Today, Feb 3, 1992 at 3D. In an interview on NBC Today two months later, Bowman made a personal appeal to then-NBC News President Michael Gartner to stop the policy of naming alleged rape victims. She called the policy "frightening" and said disclosure inhibits victims from coming forward. An NBC spokesperson said the network had no plans to change the policy of making decisions on naming rape victims on a case-by-case basis. The spokesperson said Gartner believed "the more we tell our viewers, the better informed they'll be in making up their own minds about the issues involved." USA Today, Apr. 29, 1992 at 3D.

d. *Enjoining Violations of Privacy*

Many commentators have observed that damages in defamation are a more adequate remedy than in truthful invasion of privacy cases. In defamation the award of damages, especially special damages, may compensate the plaintiff for a loss of reputation that has in fact injured him financially. Even a judgment for nominal damages may have a vital symbolic function. In privacy, however, once the invasion has occurred the embarrassing truth is out and a judgment or an award of money does not resurrect a sullied reputation or undo other harm caused by the publication. Counterattack and counterspeech are not useful here.

Thus, courts have looked more seriously at alternatives in privacy suits and have been somewhat more responsive to a plea for an injunction to prevent the utterance of the invasion in the first place. Often the plaintiff learns about the invasion only after actual broadcast or publication, but in some situations prevention is feasible. Because the privacy action is so recent in origin, it lacks a long history like that of defamation. In the latter, the injunction came to be totally rejected.

The Supreme Court has never passed on the constitutionality of injunctions in this area. Despite three cases taken on appeal, the Court has yet to come to grips with the issue. In the first, a famous baseball player persuaded the New York courts to enjoin the publication of an unauthorized biography that contained false dialogue. Spahn v. Julian Messner, Inc., 21 N.Y.2d 124, 286 N.Y.S.2d 832, 233 N.E.2d 840 (1967). The defendants compromised and settled their dispute while it was being appealed to the Supreme Court.

The second chance came in a case involving a motion picture about conditions in a Massachusetts institution for the criminally insane. The state court barred showing of the picture except to selected groups because of the producer's invasion of the privacy of the inmates, assertedly in violation of an agreement he signed in order to get permission to make the film. Commonwealth v. Wiseman, 356 Mass. 251, 249 N.E.2d 610 (1969). The Supreme Court denied *certiorari* to Frederick Wiseman, the producer, 398 U.S. 960 (1970), over the lengthy dissent of Justice Harlan, joined by Justices Douglas and Brennan:

> Petitioners seek review in this Court of a decision of the Massachusetts Supreme Judicial Court enjoining the commercial distribution to general audiences of the film "Titticut Follies." Petitioners' film is a "documentary" of life in Bridgewater State Hospital for the criminally insane. Its stark portrayal of patient routine and treatment of the inmates is at once a scathing indictment of the inhumane conditions that prevailed at the time of the film and an undeniable infringement of the privacy of the inmates filmed, who are shown nude and engaged in acts that would unquestionably embarrass an individual of normal sensitivity. . . .

> The balance between these two interests, that of the individual's privacy and the public's right to know about conditions in public institutions, is not one that is easily struck, particularly in a case like that before us where the importance of the issue is matched by the extent of the invasion of privacy. . . .

In 1991 the judge revised the order to require only that names and addresses of inmates be kept confidential. At the Boston Film Festival in September 1991, the film was shown to a general audience for the first time since its suppression in 1967. See "Judge Lifts Bar on 'Titticut Follies' Film," News Media and the Law, Fall 1991, at 36.

The third Supreme Court case involved a claim by a former patient trying to enjoin her analyst from publishing a book the analyst had written about the patient's treatment. Although names and other facts were changed in the book, plaintiff alleged that she and her family were easily identifiable. The state courts granted a preliminary injunction enjoining all distribution until the litigation concluded. The defendants, including the book's publisher, sought *certiorari*, claiming that the injunction against publishing concededly true statements of medical and scientific importance violated the First Amendment. The Court granted *certiorari*, Roe v. Doe, 417 U.S. 907 (1974), and heard oral arguments. It then decided not to decide the case by dismissing the writ of *certiorari* as having been "improvidently granted." 420 U.S. 307 (1975). The complication of the confidential relationship between the parties and the murky record caused by the use of the names "Doe" and "Roe" might have dissuaded the Court from deciding the case.

The case then went to trial on the merits. The trial judge found that the plaintiff was entitled to a remedy because of defendant's violation of an implied agreement to treat the plaintiff in confidence. He awarded damages for the harm plaintiff suffered from the release of 220 copies of the book before the preliminary injunction was issued. He also permanently enjoined distribution of the remaining stock. Doe v. Roe, 93

Misc.2d 201, 400 N.Y.S.2d 668 (1977). By subsequent order, the remaining volumes were destroyed.

In 1976 a television crew entered an institution for the care of neglected children and filmed some of the children. Questions "which could fairly be described as leading or suggestive were directed to the children with respect to drugs, assaults, etc. to which the children responded." The institutions director sought to enjoin the televising of the film. The trial judge denied a preliminary injunction and vacated his temporary restraining order, but granted a stay pending appeal. The appellate court concluded after viewing the film that they were "not persuaded that its sole or even its chief object is to provide information which could lead to a correction of the conditions it claims exists." Nonetheless, nothing in the film warranted a ban on its showing. If appropriate, the defendants could be "called to account" after the fact. Quinn v. Johnson, 51 A.D.2d 391, 381 N.Y.S.2d 875 (1976). At this point, the case was resolved when the broadcaster decided that it could blur the faces of the children to make them unrecognizable. One newspaper noted, "Here was a case where the large principle against prior restraint or censorship was upheld; and yet, where a humane judgment could be made at the same time. Nothing in the First Amendment prevents the exercise of good taste and compassion." New York Times, May 10, 1976 at 26.

How might one analyze the competing interests in these invasion of privacy cases when the issue becomes one of a remedy for a true statement that is adjudged an invasion? How do these cases square with concern about prior restraint?

3.   APPROPRIATION

The fourth branch of invasion of privacy is appropriation of another's name or likeness for commercial or trade purposes. Its major impact is on the field of advertising, because news reports have generally been held not to be "for commercial or trade purposes." But see Zacchini v. Scripps–Howard Broadcasting, *infra*. As is the case with other branches of invasion of privacy, truth is not a defense. A manufacturer who advertises that John Smith uses his product may not be able to defend himself merely by proving that John Smith does use his product, although that is important for other reasons.

What must be demonstrated to avoid a successful appropriation action is consent. This usually comes in the form of a written "release" because many states require that consent to appropriation be written. Indeed, it is common for advertising agencies and even news organizations to have standard release forms available for use. Many release forms are limited in that they restrict the uses that can be made of a particular name or likeness or the period of time during which the use will be permitted. Numerous appropriation cases have been the result of using a picture in a manner not covered by the original release.

Determining what constitutes commercial or trade purposes has not always proved easy for the courts. In one case, a television station that telephoned a couple during the program "Dialing for Dollars," and aired the ensuing conversation found itself liable for appropriation. Jeppson v. United Television, Inc., 580 P.2d 1087, 3 Med.L.Rptr. 2513 (Utah 1978). Does the following case offer any guidance?

ZACCHINI v. SCRIPPS–HOWARD BROADCASTING CO.

Supreme Court of the United States, 1977.
433 U.S. 562, 97 S.Ct. 2849, 53 L.Ed.2d 965, 2 Med.L.Rptr. 2089.

Mr. Justice White delivered the opinion of the Court.

Petitioner, Hugo Zacchini, is an entertainer. He performs a "human cannonball" act in which he is shot from a cannon into a net some 200 feet away. Each performance occupies some 15 seconds. In August and September 1972, petitioner was engaged to perform his act on a regular basis at the Geauga County Fair in Burton, Ohio. He performed in a fenced area, surrounded by grandstands, at the fair grounds. Members of the public attending the fair were not charged a separate admission fee to observe his act.

On August 2, a freelance reporter for Scripps–Howard Broadcasting Co., the operator of a television broadcasting station and respondent in this case, attended the fair. He carried a small movie camera. Petitioner noticed the reporter and asked him not to film the performance. The reporter did not do so on that day; but on the instructions of the producer of respondent's daily newscast, he returned the following day and videotaped the entire act. This film clip, approximately 15 seconds in length, was shown on the 11 o'clock news program that night, together with favorable commentary.[1]

Petitioner then brought this action for damages, alleging that he is "engaged in the entertainment business," that the act he performs is one "invented by his father and . . . performed only by his family for the last fifty years," that respondent "showed and commercialized the film of his act without his consent," and that such conduct was an "unlawful appropriation of plaintiff's professional property." App. 4–5. Respondent answered and moved for summary judgment, which was granted by the trial court.

. . .

. . . Insofar as the Ohio Supreme Court held that the First and Fourteenth Amendments of the United States Constitution required judgment for respondent, we reverse the judgment of that court.

---

1. The script of the commentary accompanying the film clip read as follows:

"This . . . now . . . is the story of a *true spectator* sport . . . the sport of human cannonballing . . . in fact, the great *Zacchini* is about the only human cannonball around, these days . . . just happens that, *where* he is, is the Great Geauga County Fair, in Burton . . . and believe me, although it's not a *long* act, it's a thriller . . . and you really need to see it *in person* . . . to appreciate it. . . ." (Emphasis in original.)

. . .

Even if the judgment in favor of respondent must nevertheless be understood as ultimately resting on Ohio law, it appears that at the very least the Ohio court felt compelled by what it understood to be federal constitutional considerations to construe and apply its own law in the manner it did. In this event, we have jurisdiction and should decide the federal issue; for if the state court erred in its understanding of our cases and of the First and Fourteenth Amendments we should so declare, leaving the state court free to decide the privilege issue solely as a matter of Ohio law. [ ] If the Supreme Court of Ohio "held as it did because it felt under compulsion of federal law as enunciated by this Court so to hold, it should be relieved of that compulsion. It should be freed to decide . . . these suits according to its own local law." [ ]

The Ohio Supreme Court relied heavily on [*Hill*], but that case does not mandate a media privilege to televise a performer's entire act without his consent. Involved in [*Hill*] was a claim under the New York "Right of Privacy" statute that Life Magazine, in the course of reviewing a new play, had connected the play with a long-past incident involving petitioner and his family and had falsely described their experience and conduct at that time. The complaint sought damages for humiliation and suffering flowing from these nondefamatory falsehoods that allegedly invaded Hill's privacy. The Court held, however, that the opening of a new play linked to an actual incident was a matter of public interest and that Hill could not recover without showing that the Life report was knowingly false or was published with reckless disregard for the truth— the same rigorous standard that had been applied in [*New York Times*].

[*Hill*], which was hotly contested and decided by a divided Court, involved an entirely different tort from the "right of publicity" recognized by the Ohio Supreme Court. . . .

The differences between these two torts are important. First, the State's interests in providing a cause of action in each instance are different. "The interest protected" in permitting recovery for placing the plaintiff in a false light "is clearly that of reputation, with the same overtones of mental distress as in defamation." Prosser, supra, 48 Calif.L.Rev., at 400. By contrast, the State's interest in permitting a "right of publicity" is in protecting the proprietary interest of the individual in his act in part to encourage such entertainment. As we later note, the State's interest is closely analogous to the goals of patent and copyright law, focusing on the right of the individual to reap the reward of his endeavors and having little to do with protecting feelings or reputation. Second, the two torts differ in the degree to which they intrude on dissemination of information to the public. In "false light" cases the only way to protect the interests involved is to attempt to minimize the publication of the damaging matter, while in "right of publicity" cases the only question is who gets to do the publishing. An entertainer such as petitioner usually has no objection to the widespread publication of his act as long as he gets the commercial benefit of such publication. Indeed, in the present case petitioner did not seek to enjoin the broadcast of his act; he simply sought compensation for the broadcast in the form of damages.

. . .

Moreover, [*Hill*], *New York Times, Metromedia, Gertz,* and *Firestone* all involved the reporting of events; in none of them was there an attempt to broadcast or publish an entire act for which the performer ordinarily gets paid. It is evident, and there is no claim here to the contrary, that petitioner's state-law right of publicity would not serve to prevent respondent from reporting the newsworthy facts about petitioner's act. Wherever the line in particular situations is to be drawn between media reports that are protected and those that are not, we are quite sure that the First and Fourteenth Amendments do not immunize the media when they broadcast a performer's entire act without his consent. The Constitution no more prevents a State from requiring respondent to compensate petitioner for broadcasting his act on television than it would privilege respondent to film and broadcast a copyrighted dramatic work without liability to the copyright owner, [ ], or to film and broadcast a prize fight, [ ], or a baseball game, [ ], where the promoters or the participants had other plans for publicizing the event. There are ample reasons for reaching this conclusion.

The broadcast of a film of petitioner's entire act poses a substantial threat to the economic value of that performance. As the Ohio court recognized, this act is the product of petitioner's own talents and energy, the end result of much time, effort, and expense. Much of its economic value lies in the "right of exclusive control over the publicity given to his performance"; if the public can see the act free on television, it will be less willing to pay to see it at the fair.[12] The effect of a public broadcast of the performance is similar to preventing petitioner from charging an admission fee. . . . Moreover, the broadcast of petitioner's entire performance, unlike the unauthorized use of another's name for purposes of trade or the incidental use of a name or picture by the press, goes to the heart of petitioner's ability to earn a living as an entertainer. Thus, in this case, Ohio has recognized what may be the strongest case for a "right of publicity"—involving, not the appropriation of an entertainer's reputation to enhance the attractiveness of a commercial product, but the appropriation of the very activity by which the entertainer acquired his reputation in the first place.

Of course, Ohio's decision to protect petitioner's right of publicity here rests on more than a desire to compensate the performer for the time and effort invested in his act; the protection provides an economic incentive for him to make the investment required to produce a perfor-

---

12. It is possible, of course, that respondent's news broadcast increased the value of petitioner's performance by stimulating the public's interest in seeing the act live. In these circumstances, petitioner would not be able to prove damages and thus would not recover. But petitioner has alleged that the broadcast injured him to the extent of $25,000, App. 5, and we think the State should be allowed to authorize compensation of this injury if proved.

mance of interest to the public. This same consideration underlies the patent and copyright laws long enforced by this Court. . . .

There is no doubt that entertainment, as well as news, enjoys First Amendment protection. It is also true that entertainment itself can be important news. [*Hill*] But it is important to note that neither the public nor respondent will be deprived of the benefit of petitioner's performance as long as his commercial stake in his act is appropriately recognized. Petitioner does not seek to enjoin the broadcast of his performance; he simply wants to be paid for it. Nor do we think that a state-law damages remedy against respondent would represent a species of liability without fault contrary to the letter or spirit of [*Gertz*]. Respondent knew exactly that petitioner objected to televising his act but nevertheless displayed the entire film.

We conclude that although the State of Ohio may as a matter of its own law privilege the press in the circumstances of this case, the First and Fourteenth Amendments do not require it to do so.

Reversed.

Mr. Justice Powell, with whom Mr. Justice Brennan and Mr. Justice Marshall join, dissenting.

Disclaiming any attempt to do more than decide the narrow case before us, the Court reverses the decision of the Supreme Court of Ohio based on repeated incantation of a single formula: "a performer's entire act." The holding today is summed up in one sentence:

> "Wherever the line in particular situations is to be drawn between media reports that are protected and those that are not, we are quite sure that the First and Fourteenth Amendments do not immunize the media when they broadcast a performer's entire act without his consent."

I doubt that this formula provides a standard clear enough even for resolution in this case.[1] In any event, I am not persuaded that the Court's opinion is appropriately sensitive to the First Amendment values at stake, and I therefore dissent.

Although the Court would draw no distinction, I do not view respondent's action as comparable to unauthorized commercial broadcasts of sporting events, theatrical performances, and the like where the broadcaster keeps the profits. There is no suggestion here that respon-

---

1. Although the record is not explicit, it is unlikely that the "act" commenced abruptly with the explosion that launched petitioner on his way, ending with the landing in the net a few seconds later. One may assume that the actual firing was preceded by some fanfare, possibly stretching over several minutes, to heighten the audience's anticipation: introduction of the performer, description of the uniqueness and danger, last-minute checking of the apparatus, and entry into the cannon, all accompanied by suitably ominous commentary from the master of ceremonies. If this is found to be the case on remand, then respondent could not be said to have appropriated the "entire act" in its 15–second newsclip—and the Court's opinion then would afford no guidance for resolution of the case. Moreover, in future cases involving different performances, similar difficulties in determining just what constitutes the "entire act" are inevitable.

dent made any such use of the film. Instead, it simply reported on what petitioner concedes to be a newsworthy event, in a way hardly surprising for a television station—by means of film coverage. The report was part of an ordinary daily news program, consuming a total of 15 seconds. It is a routine example of the press fulfilling the informing function so vital to our system.

The Court's holding that the station's ordinary news report may give rise to substantial liability has disturbing implications, for the decision could lead to a degree of media self-censorship. [ ] Hereafter whenever a television news editor is unsure whether certain film footage received from a camera crew might be held to portray an "entire act," he may decline coverage—even of clearly newsworthy events—or confine the broadcast to watered-down verbal reporting, perhaps with an occasional still picture. The public is then the loser. This is hardly the kind of news reportage that the First Amendment is meant to foster. [ ]

In my view the First Amendment commands a different analytical starting point from the one selected by the Court. Rather than begin with a quantitative analysis of the performer's behavior—is this or is this not his entire act?—we should direct initial attention to the actions of the news media: what use did the station make of the film footage? When a film is used, as here, for a routine portion of a regular news program, I would hold that the First Amendment protects the station from a "right of publicity" or "appropriation" suit, absent a strong showing by the plaintiff that the news broadcast was a subterfuge or cover for private or commercial exploitation.[4]

. . . In a suit like the one before us, however, the plaintiff does not complain about the fact of exposure to the public, but rather about its timing or manner. He welcomes some publicity, but seeks to retain control over means and manner as a way to maximize for himself the monetary benefits that flow from such publication. But having made the matter public—having chosen, in essence, to make it newsworthy—he cannot, consistent with the First Amendment, complain of routine news reportage. Cf. Gertz v. Robert Welch, Inc., [ ] (clarifying the different liability standards appropriate in defamation suits, depending on whether or not the plaintiff is a public figure).

Since the filmclip here was undeniably treated as news and since there is no claim that the use was subterfuge, respondent's actions were constitutionally privileged. I would affirm.

[Mr. Justice Stevens dissented on the ground that he could not tell whether the Ohio Supreme Court had relied on federal constitutional issues in deciding the case. He would have remanded the case to that

---

4. This case requires no detailed specification of the standards for identifying a subterfuge, since there is no claim here that respondent's news use was anything but bona fide. [ ] I would point out, however, that selling time during a news broadcast to advertisers in the customary fashion does not make for "commercial exploitation" in the sense intended here. [ ]

court "for clarification of its holding before deciding the federal constitutional issue."]

Notes and Questions

1. On remand, the Ohio Supreme Court took advantage of the opportunity afforded by the majority opinion and decided that nothing in the Ohio Constitution protected the behavior of the media defendant. The case was remanded for trial. Zacchini v. Scripps–Howard Broadcasting Co., 54 Ohio St.2d 286, 376 N.E.2d 582, 3 Med.L.Rptr. 2444 (1978). The case was subsequently settled.

2. How important is it that the majority treats the 15 seconds as the "entire act"?

3. Does this case involve an aspect of "privacy"? Does it resemble the Cox case in that both involved lawfully obtained information of interest or concern to the public? Can you explain why the defendant in *Cox* did not have to pay while the defendant in *Zacchini* might have to pay?

4. After *Zacchini,* what would happen in a case in which a street artist who survives on contributions from passersby—a mime, an accordionist, a dancer—is photographed by the local television station and shown in a story about summer diversions on the streets of the city? Is the street artist's claim as strong as Zacchini's?

5. *Right of publicity.* The Zacchini case is an example of an offshoot of appropriation known as right of publicity. This particular right was once defined as follows:

> The distinctive aspect of the common-law right of publicity is that it recognizes the commercial value of the picture or representation of a prominent person or performer and protects his proprietary interest in the profitability of his public reputation or persona. Ali v. Playgirl, Inc., 447 F.Supp. 723, 3 Med.L.Rptr. 2540 (S.D.N.Y.1978).

Unlike the traditional tort of appropriation, right of publicity is exclusively the province of well-known individuals. Also, whereas the original tort was at least partially rooted in the concept of the right to be let alone and not to be exploited for commercial or trade purposes, this new variation seems only concerned with who should reap the financial benefits. In essence it is a property right, as opposed to a personal right in some states. Thus, Johnny Carson was able to sue a manufacturer of portable toilets that were marketed under the name, "Here's Johnny." Carson v. Here's Johnny Portable Toilets, Inc., 698 F.2d 831, 9 Med. L.Rptr. 1153 (6th Cir.1983), reversing 498 F.Supp. 71 (E.D.Mich.1980). Similarly, the estate of Elvis Presley won a claim against the producers of THE BIG EL SHOW, an imitation of Presley's performances. Estate of Presley v. Russen, 513 F.Supp. 1339 (D.N.J.1981).

In some cases it is not even the true name or likeness of a person, but rather some character or role that is at issue. In Groucho Marx Productions, Inc. v. Day and Night Co., Inc., 523 F.Supp. 485, 7 Med.

L.Rptr. 2030 (S.D.N.Y.1981), reversed on other grounds 689 F.2d 317, 8 Med.L.Rptr. 2201 (2d Cir.1982), the court held that the play, "A Day in Hollywood, a Night in the Ukraine," appropriated the Marx brothers' characters. In this context, a suit for appropriation has become a new method of protecting creative work—even characters created by comedians. Is this a right equivalent to copyright? Should it be preempted by the federal copyright statute, especially in this context? How does it differ from copyright?

6.   Baltimore Orioles, Inc. v. Major League Baseball Players Association, 805 F.2d 663, 13 Med.L.Rptr. 1625 (7th Cir.1986), certiorari denied 480 U.S. 941 (1987), raised the question of professional baseball players' right of publicity in the context of televised games. The court of appeals held that the team owners' copyright in videotaped telecasts preempted the players' right of publicity in their performances because the performances were fixed in tangible form and because the players' rights of publicity were equivalent to rights embraced in copyright.

7.   In another case, Stephano v. News Group Publications, 64 N.Y.2d 174, 485 N.Y.S.2d 220, 474 N.E.2d 580, 11 Med.L.Rptr. 1303 (1984), a model sued for invasion of privacy under New York State's statute prohibiting appropriation for "advertising or trade purposes." The model had posed in a "bomber jacket" for a 1981 article on men's fall fashions for *New York* magazine. Contending that he had agreed to model for one article only, he sued, claiming a breach of his "right of publicity" because one of the photos was used in a "Best Bets" magazine column, giving an approximate price for the jacket and listing several stores at which it would be available. The New York Court of Appeals held that the magazine's use of the photo in the "Best Bets" column was of general public interest and that it was not used for advertising or trade purposes as defined by New York law. Despite the unusual result in *Zacchini,* the principle seems clear that the media will usually win such cases unless their claims of newsworthiness or public interest are exceptionally weak. Stephano's suit was *not,* of course, a copyright action, but the similarities to copyright—attempting to control or profit from what one perceives as one's property—are worth noting.

8.   As noted in the *Hustler* case, p. 923, *supra,* the Rev. Jerry Falwell's suit against *Hustler* magazine alleged invasion of privacy as well as libel. Falwell alleged, in his privacy claim, that the "ad" constituted an unauthorized use of his name or likeness for trade purposes under the Virginia invasion of privacy statute. The court of appeals, noting that there were no decisions of the Virginia courts construing the statute, but that it was substantially similar to the New York statute, held that because the jury found that the parody in Falwell's case was not believable and because it contained a disclaimer, publication of the parody did not constitute a use of Falwell's name and likeness for purposes of trade.

9.   When advertising agency Young & Rubicam contacted the agent of singer Bette Midler to ask whether she would be interested in doing a

television commercial for the Ford Motor Company, the agent declined on Midler's behalf. The agency subsequently sought out Ula Hedwig, who had been a backup singer for Midler for 10 years, to do a sound-alike rendition of Midler's recording of "Do You Want to Dance." After the commercial aired, Midler sued under both copyright law and privacy law. The court of appeals held that the deliberate, unconsented imitation of the distinctive voice of a professional singer in order to sell a product constitutes an unlawful appropriation of identity under California law. Midler v. Ford Motor Co., 849 F.2d 460, 15 Med.L.Rptr. 1620 (9th Cir.1988). The Supreme Court denied *certiorari* in the case and a companion case, 503 U.S. 951 (1992), leaving in place an award to Midler of $400,000 in compensatory damages.

10.   In Waits v. Frito–Lay, Inc., 978 F.2d 1093, 20 Med.L.Rptr. 1585 (9th Cir.1992), certiorari denied 506 U.S. 1080 (1993), singer Tom Waits sued the snack food manufacturer and its advertising agency for voice misappropriation and false endorsement as a result of a Doritos radio commercial featuring an imitation of Waits' distinctive singing voice. The court of appeals held that there was sufficient evidence to support the jury's findings that Frito–Lay and the advertising agency acted with malice and that consumers were likely to be misled by the commercial into believing that Waits endorsed the product. It upheld all but $100,000 of the jury verdict and award of $2.6 million.

11.   The "New Kids on the Block" sued *USA Today* and *Star* magazine for violating their right of publicity—along with trademark infringement and misappropriation, when the "New Kids" trademark was used in articles which asked readers to participate, via a "900" telephone number, in a survey to determine the group's most popular member. The district court held that the use of the trademark was related to news-gathering and was not mere commercial exploitation, so the First Amendment barred the claims. The court of appeals affirmed. The New Kids on the Block v. News America Publishing, Inc., 971 F.2d 302, 20 Med.L.Rptr. 1468 (9th Cir.1992).

12.   Game show hostess Vanna White sued Samsung Electronics America, Inc., for using, in an advertisement, a robot dressed in a wig, gown and jewelry reminiscent of White and posed next to a game board like the one in "Wheel of Fortune." A panel decision by the court of appeals held that the right of publicity is *not* limited solely to the appropriation of a name or likeness. Instead, the panel said, the right of publicity encompasses the appropriation of "identity." The court of appeals refused to rehear the panel decision. Three judges dissented from the order rejecting the suggestion for rehearing *en banc*, saying that the decision "erects a property right of remarkable and dangerous breadth." "I don't see how," said Judge Alex Kozinski, one of the dissenters, "giving White the power to keep others from evoking her image in the public's mind can be squared with the First Amendment." White v. Samsung, 989 F.2d 1512, 21 Med.L.Rptr. 1330 (9th Cir.), certiorari denied 508 U.S. 951 (1993).

13.   What do the pre-Internet cases suggest about celebrities' rights in an era when computer manipulation of photographs and the ease of posting photos on the Web make it possible to create sites full of celebrity photos—some nude, some not, some real, some not, and some used for "what's real and what's not" games?

14.   *Descendability*. Personal rights such as those protected by defamation and invasion of privacy law terminate at death. Thus, for example, one can publish defamatory statements about deceased individuals with impunity (unless the same statement also defames people who are still alive). Because the right of publicity is a property right, a great controversy has developed as to whether it survives the death of its creator.

Currently, there seem to be three distinct approaches being taken by various courts and legislatures. One is that the right terminates upon death. Under this view, as soon as people die, their names, likenesses and characterizations are available for anyone to use without legal liability. At the other extreme is the position that death has no effect on the right of publicity. In jurisdictions adhering to this view, the consent of whoever owns the property in question (perhaps the individual's heirs or someone who has purchased the right) is always necessary. Finally, there is an intermediate approach that holds the right of publicity to survive death only if it was commercially exploited during the person's lifetime.

If the right of publicity continues beyond death (either because it always does or because it was commercially exploited during the person's lifetime), the next question is how long it lasts. A state statute might stipulate a specific number of years, or the right of publicity might last as long as it continues to be exploited by the individual's heirs or forever. State statutes that provide for survivability do so for varying periods of time ranging from 50 years after death in California to 10 years after death in Tennessee.

15.   Los Angeles Magazine published a fashion spread that used computer technology to merge famous still photos of actors and actresses from classic films with images of the latest spring fashions. The spread was called "Grand Illusions," and the copy read: "By using state-of-the-art digital magic, we clothed some of the cinema's most enduring icons in fashions by the hottest designers." One photo combined the face and head of actor Dustin Hoffman with a photo of the body of a male model wearing a silk gown and high heels designed by contemporary fashion designers. The composite was an allusion to Hoffman's title role in the movie Tootsie, in which he dressed as a woman. The court awarded Hoffman $1.5 million in compensatory damages, $1.5 million in punitive damages, and $270,0000 in attorneys fees for violation of his right of publicity under common law, a California statute and the federal Lanham Act.

The trial court found the magazine's purpose to be commercial because the photo was used "to sell magazines, advertise and promote designer clothing." Its First Amendment defenses were rejected because the feature "provided no commentary about fashions" but "merely used randomly selected designer clothes to attract attention when 'worn' by the computer–manipulated, involuntary, celebrity models." The judge also said the photo could receive no First Amendment protection because the magazine knew it "falsely" depicted Hoffman as wearing clothing he never wore. The Ninth Circuit, however, reversed the lower court's decision and held that the use of Hoffman's photo was not "pure commercial speech," noting that the magazine "did not use Hoffman's image in a traditional advertisement printed merely for the purpose of selling a particular product: nor 'did the article simply advance a commercial message. The court held that the article was entitled to "full First Amendment protection." Hoffman v. Capital Cities/ABC, 255 F.3d 1180, 29 Med.L.Rptr. 1993 (9th Cir. 2001).

C. PRIVACY ISSUES RELATING TO THE INTERNET

The ability of both companies and the government to gather, correlate and distribute detailed information concerning individuals is a major privacy concern. Some methods of gathering such information are open and voluntary such as filling out questionnaires. Others are trade-offs for convenience or financial incentives. For example, an online grocer stores previous orders to allow a consumer to duplicate common purchases, or a bookstore keeps a record of purchases in order to notify customers of new books by their favorite authors.

More surreptitious methods include the use of cookies, small data files stored on peoples' hard drives which can be used to keep track of the sites visited during browsing. Although it is possible to block cookies, many Internet users were unaware of the existence of cookies or how they can be used until the media began writing about them. Some users are no doubt still unaware. Cookies in many ways benefit the Internet surfers but also provide information of commercial value to the companies that use them. Sen. John Edwards (D.,N.C.) introduced legislation in October 2000 and reintroduced it in 2001, to protect the privacy of consumers by forcing the companies that use cookies to disclose what information they gather. "Technology makes our lives easier in so many ways, but that convenience can compromise our privacy," he said. The New York Times, Jan. 31, 2001 at C4.

Finally, although difficult, it is possible to intercept material sent over the Internet. In addition, anything sent over the Internet also resides on various computers. Many people and companies have learned this the hard way when copies of E-mails have been used as evidence against them.

One approach to safeguarding privacy is the use of encryption software. However, as discussed later in this chapter, the government has opposed some uses of strong encryption because it restricts the ability of security and law enforcement agencies to gather information.

The other primary approach is to pass laws restricting data collection and distribution. Although, efforts to do so have been largely unsuccessful in this country, other countries have extensive privacy regulation. With the developing emphasis on international E-commerce, the gap between the U.S. position and that of other countries presents the potential for a major trade conflict.

In 1998 the European Union Data Protection Directive took effect. Under the directive, member states must take a number of specific measures to protect individuals' privacy. The most important measure from a U.S. perspective is one prohibiting businesses in E.U. countries from transferring data to countries that don't have adequate privacy protection. The problem is that the U.S. approach relies almost exclusively on self-regulation. After more than a year of negotiation, the U.S. and the E.U. have been unable to resolve the conflict, although negotiations continue.

Hindering the U.S. position has been a series of revelations concerning companies gathering information contrary to their publicly declared policies. The most recent of these involves Double Click, the leading provider of banner ads to Web sites. Using cookies, Double Click tracks Internet users across the approximately 1500 sites where the company has placed ads. When Double Click merged with Abacus Direct, the country's largest catalog database firm, its SEC registration statement referred to plans to combine Double Click's tracking information with detailed personal information contained in the Abacus database. Highlighting the potential privacy problems was the revelation that a number of medical and health information sites that guaranteed user privacy carried ads placed by Double Click.

When the statement was publicized and complaints had been filed with the FTC against Double Click, the company issued a revised privacy policy allowing people to opt out of the data-gathering process. Critics of the policy argue that the opt-out approach is ineffective because many people are unaware of the privacy problem and others find the opt-out procedure too burdensome. Privacy advocates prefer an opt-in policy that requires an individual to affirmatively agree to participate in the data collection.

One type of data collection that has provoked U.S. legislative action involves children. The Children's Online Privacy Protection Act required the FTC to establish regulations governing data collection from children. The regulations which take effect in early 2000, impose extensive notice and parental consent requirements on commercial Web sites or online services that are primarily directed at children under 13. It applies to individually identifiable personal information obtained directly or through the use of cookies or other tracking mechanisms.

Parental consent must be verifiable. Acceptable methods of verification vary, depending on how the company uses the information. If only used for internal purposes such as subsequent promotions, a follow-up e-mail, letter or phone call will suffice. For other uses such as distribution to third parties, more reliable verification procedures are required. These include "getting a signed form from the parent via postal mail or facsimile; accepting and verifying a credit card number; taking calls from parents, through a toll-free telephone number staffed by trained personnel; email accompanied by digital signature; email accompanied by a PIN or password obtained through one of the verification methods above." Two years from the original effective date, the more reliable methods of verification will be required for all uses.

Chapter XVI

SPECIAL PROBLEMS OF ELECTRONIC
MEDIA JOURNALISTS

Whereas defamation and invasion of privacy problems can arise in the context of entertainment programming on the electronic media (as well as in the context of electronic journalism), the special problems we consider in this chapter are ones that are typically limited to news and documentary programming. Among the problems are protection of government interests, news coverage of the administration of justice, journalist's privilege and newsgathering from public sources.

A. THE PROTECTION OF GOVERNMENT INTERESTS

In the discussion in Chapter I of abridgment of freedom of the press, we examined the question of prior restraint on dissemination of messages. In *Near*, p. 25, *supra*, we saw an example of a restraint imposed on a publication that had, in part, accused public officials in Minneapolis of involvement in bootlegging and gambling. In *New York Times*, p. 885, *supra*, we saw the federal government's Vietnam era attempt to restrain publication of the "Pentagon Papers," the secret study of U.S. decision-making in Southeast Asia. Recall that the Supreme Court found that the heavy burden of showing justification for the imposition of a prior restraint was met in neither case. In *The Progressive*, p. 26, *supra*, we saw the federal government's attempt to stop dissemination of the "secret of the H-bomb." That case, recall, ended with publication of the "secret" in publications other than *The Progressive*, and the case never reached the Supreme Court.

There are a variety of other contexts in which the government may want to use prior restraint or some other means to discourage or stop dissemination of messages that may present problems for the government, its officials, or its citizens.

For example, a 1972 case exemplifies the problems of authors who have had access to national security information. United States v. Marchetti, 466 F.2d 1309, 1 Med.L.Rptr. 1051 (4th Cir.1972), involved an injunction obtained by the government against publication of Marchetti's book about the Central Intelligence Agency, his former employer. At the time Marchetti joined, he promised not to divulge any classified information unless specifically authorized in writing by the director, and when he resigned from the CIA he signed a loyalty oath. The court upheld the restraint, and the Supreme Court denied *certiorari*, 409 U.S. 1063 (1972).

Sometimes the government's interest is with the protection of the private rights of its citizens—as in an instance in which a judge may seek to restrain dissemination of information in order to protect the fair trial rights of an accused individual.

Recall also from Chapter I the discussion of *Landmark Communications*, p. 29, *supra*, and *Daily Mail*, p. 29, *supra*, both of which involved attempts to protect a state or public interest through discouraging or restraining publication of facts that most electronic media journalists would certainly consider to be news.

Our long legal tradition against censorship and the difficulty of justifying such a restraint in court discourage most attempts to protect public or private interests through such restraints. Instead, as we have seen in defamation and privacy, we usually rely on the ability of persons who are damaged to sue *after* the dissemination has taken place.

B. PRESS COVERAGE OF THE ADMINISTRATION OF JUSTICE

Press coverage of the administration of justice poses special problems both for the press and for the courts. It is easy to generalize about the openness of the judicial system and about Americans' distaste for secret courts, and it is easy to generalize about our proud tradition of protecting the fairness of civil and criminal trials. The generalizations too often ignore the reality: the First Amendment right to freedom of the press and the Sixth Amendment right to a fair trial sometimes appear to give rise to conflict.

As journalists tell the story of a crime or arrest prior to trial, they inevitably influence opinions in the area, and it can be difficult—perhaps even impossible—to find jurors who can ignore press reports and come to a fair verdict based solely on evidence presented in court. On the other hand, if judges try to shape or stop news coverage of the administration of justice, they may be interfering with the First Amendment rights of journalists.

Note that most of the discussion of the fair trial/free press issue has traditionally revolved around protecting the rights of people formally accused of crimes—i.e., arrested. Most of the usual "remedies" (including postponing the trial, granting a change of venue or sequestering the jury) would do little to protect someone identified in the media as a suspect but never charged with any crime. Richard Jewell, the Atlanta man whose name was leaked by an FBI source as a suspect in the 1996 Olympic Centennial Park bombing, is the most obvious example. Although the fair trial/free press remedies did not help him, Jewell sued for libel. A couple of months after the bombing, the Society of Professional Journalists' Code of Ethics was amended to recommend that the press "be judicious about naming criminal suspects before the formal filing of charges." Editor & Publisher, Oct. 19, 1996 at 8.

1. BACKGROUND

The judicial branch has been the object of considerable litigation as to which of its functions are to be open to public scrutiny. A specific constitutional provision, held to be solely for the benefit of the accused and not addressed to the press, is basic to our discussion. The Sixth Amendment to the United States Constitution provides: "In all criminal prosecutions, the accused shall enjoy the right to a speedy and public trial, by an impartial jury of the State and district wherein the crime shall have been committed. . . ."

Problems arise primarily in the context of press and public interest in dramatic criminal cases involving either sensational crimes or prominent persons, and less frequently in the context of highly-publicized civil lawsuits. The resulting problems between journalists and lawyers/judges over pre-trial and trial news accounts have been referred to as "fair trial-free press" by the bar and "free press-fair trial" by the press.

In several Supreme Court cases of the 1960s, criminal convictions were reversed because the Court found that prejudicial press coverage had resulted in possible unfairness. Judges, realizing their responsibilities to protect defendants from such unfairness, reached for means of protection—ordering the press not to report certain information, closing pre-trial hearings to the press, keeping cameras out of the courtrooms, closing trials, etc. The press viewed such steps as intrusions on First Amendment rights. The Supreme Court decided cases involving these issues in the 1970s and 1980s.

The Supreme Court confronted the problem at the constitutional level in *Irvin v. Dowd*, 366 U.S. 717, 1 Med.L.Rptr. 1178 (1961). Defendant Leslie Irvin had been arrested in Indiana following a series of murders attributed to the "Mad Dog Killer." He was convicted and sentenced to death; his appeal included 46 exhibits indicating that, as Justice Clark put it, ". . . a barrage of newspaper headlines, articles, cartoons and pictures were unleashed against him during the six or seven months preceding his trial."

Typically in such appeals, newspaper headlines and stories receive greater emphasis than broadcast news accounts because of the easier availability of the former. The majority opinion in *Irvin* did, however, note that in the area "radio and TV stations . . . also carried extensive newscasts covering the same incidents."

Prominent in the telling evidence of trouble at the trial was the fact that the panel of potential jurors included 430 persons, of whom 268 were excused by the court itself as having fixed opinions as to the guilt of Irvin. At least 370 of the prospective jurors entertained some opinion as to Irvin's guilt. Finding a "pattern of deep and bitter prejudice," the Court vacated the conviction and remanded the case for retrial, at which Irvin was convicted again.

Another troubling case occurred when Wilbert Rideau was arrested in Louisiana for bank robbery, kidnapping and murder. The sheriff invited a film crew from the local television station to film the sheriff's "interview" with Rideau. During the 20–minute interrogation, Rideau confessed to the crimes. The station showed the interview three times. After a requested change of venue was denied, Rideau was convicted and sentenced to death. The Supreme Court overturned the conviction, noting that after drawing a jury from people who could have been exposed to the confession, any "court proceedings . . . could be but a hollow formality." The Court implied that nothing could have overcome the effects of the television film and that specific proof of juror prejudice was not necessary under such circumstances. Rideau v. Louisiana, 373 U.S. 723, 1 Med.L.Rptr. 1183 (1963). (Rideau was ultimately retried and convicted a second time.)

Perhaps the most famous of the 1960s cases in this area was Sheppard v. Maxwell, 384 U.S. 333, 1 Med.L.Rptr. 1220 (1966). Dr. Sam Sheppard was accused of the 1954 murder of his pregnant wife, Marilyn, and tried in the light of national publicity. He was convicted and spent a number of years in prison before his attorney, a young, relatively unknown F. Lee Bailey, successfully carried Sheppard's appeal to the Supreme Court. Justice Clark delivered the opinion of the Court:

> Much of the material printed or broadcast during the trial was never heard from the witness stand, such as the charges that Sheppard had purposely impeded the murder investigation and must be guilty since he had hired a prominent criminal lawyer; that Sheppard was a perjurer; that he had sexual relations with numerous women; that his wife had characterized him as a "Jekyll–Hyde"; that he was "a bare-faced liar" because of his testimony as to police treatment; and finally, that a woman convict claimed Sheppard to be the father of her illegitimate child. As the trial progressed, the newspapers summarized and interpreted the evidence, devoting particular attention to the material that incriminated Sheppard, and often drew unwarranted inferences from testimony. At one point, a front-page picture of Mrs. Sheppard's blood-stained pillow was published after being "doctored" to show more clearly an alleged imprint of a surgical instrument.

> Nor is there doubt that this deluge of publicity reached at least some of the jury. On the only occasion that the jury was queried, two jurors admitted in open court to hearing the highly inflammatory charge that a prison inmate claimed Sheppard as the father of her illegitimate child. Despite the extent and nature of the publicity to which the jury was exposed during trial, the judge refused defense counsel's other requests that the jurors be asked whether they had read or heard specific prejudicial comment about the case, including the incidents we have previously summarized. In these circumstances, we can assume that some of this material reached members of the jury. [   ]

. . .

The carnival atmosphere at trial could easily have been avoided since the courtroom and courthouse premises are subject to the control of the court. . . .

Concluding that the trial court judge had failed to protect the defendant's rights adequately, the Court ordered Sheppard released unless the state gave him a new trial. Ohio retried him, and Sheppard (unlike Irvin or Rideau) was acquitted at the second trial.

(The Sheppard murder story continues to generate interest years later. It inspired the popular television series "The Fugitive" in the 1960's and the 1993 Harrison Ford film of the same name. Sheppard died in 1970 without clearing his name. The case became news again in 1996 as Sheppard's son, focusing attention on Richard Eberling, a one-time window washer at the Sheppard home who was subsequently convicted of murder, made his own effort to clear his father. A court ruling that Sheppard was innocent would clear the way for Sheppard's estate to sue for wrongful incarceration. A former nurse allegedly told *The Cleveland Plain Dealer* that Eberling once confessed to having murdered Marilyn Sheppard. Newsday, April 30, 1996 at A21.)

Some would argue that the overturned convictions of Irvin, Rideau and Sheppard reflected the strong protection of defendants' rights by the Warren Court. A 1975 case, Murphy v. Florida, 421 U.S. 794, 1 Med. L.Rptr. 1232 (1975), in which a criminal conviction was upheld, could be seen simply as reflecting the Court's changing attitudes toward defendants, but that analysis would fail to recognize that the circumstances of *Murphy* were quite different from those of the earlier cases. In *Murphy* the jurors in defendant's robbery trial had learned through news stories about some or all of Jack "Murph the Surf" Murphy's earlier convictions for murder, securities theft and the 1964 theft of the Star of India sapphire from a New York museum. The majority stated that qualified jurors need not be totally ignorant of the facts surrounding the case. The Court found in the *voir dire*—the examination of the potential jurors—no showing of hostility to the defendant. Four of the six jurors volunteered that defendant's past was irrelevant. Only 20 of the 78 persons examined were excused because of an opinion of guilt. (Note that this is quite unlike *Irvin.*) "This may indeed be 20 more than would occur in the trial of a totally obscure person, but it by no means suggests a community with sentiment so poisoned against the petitioner as to impeach the indifference of jurors who displayed no animus of their own." Only Justice Brennan dissented.

It is understatement to say that the extraordinary media coverage of the O. J. Simpson murder case generated much renewed interest in the fair trial-free press problem. Much has been said and written about leaked information, erroneous information, public statements by prosecutors, the release of Nicole Simpson's 911 phone calls, public statements by defense attorneys, celebrity status of the attorneys, witnesses, and judges associated with the case, payments to news sources for their stories, manipulation of photographs, the effects of live television coverage of the chase, the effects of live television coverage of court proceedings, editorial cartoons, mentions of the Simpson case in comedy routines and comic strips, etc.

It may be useful to remember, in reading this section of Chapter XV, that most of the traditional concerns about fair trial-free press revolved around the nature and extent of *news* coverage by newspapers and by broadcasters in the area in which the defendant would be tried. Certainly the *news* coverage of the Simpson case—both in Los Angeles and elsewhere—was the topic of much conversation, and the case provided countless examples of the increased blurring of *news* and *entertainment* by the media. The so-called tabloid TV shows and talk shows devoted countless hours to the case. "A Current Affair," the day after Nicole Simpson and Ronald Goldman were slain, asked viewers to phone a 900 number if they thought O.J. Simpson "had something to do with his ex-wife's murder" and another number if they did not. Rolanda Watts scheduled five live shows from Los Angeles in one week on the Simpson case—including two to discuss the possibility of his getting a fair trial.

The distinction between the tabloid TV shows and the networks' news magazines has become more difficult to see. Co-anchor Deborah Norville, on "America Tonight" in July 1994, invited viewers to call a 900 number (each call costing 50 cents) to vote for Simpson's receiving a death penalty *if* he should be convicted. The distinction between reporting *news that has occurred* and *speculating* about what might occur has also been lost. The case may engender some serious discussion of the question of "When is the possibility that something *may* occur in a high-profile case *news*, and when is it merely gossip?"

The fair trial free press problems in the Simpson case were so atypical—at least in scale—of those encountered in most trials that it is difficult to generalize from the Simpson case, but it will undoubtedly be cited for years to come in debates about fair trial-free press problems.

2. So-Called Remedies for the Fair Trial–Free Press Problem

a. *The Standard Remedies*

Although the judge's failure to maintain proper decorum during the trial was viewed as his major error in *Sheppard,* the Court devoted extensive consideration to the behavior of the media and suggested techniques by which the judge might better have insulated the trial. Some of those suggestions are included below. Note that most of the "remedies" have limitations or drawbacks that preclude their being used widely.

Cautioning Police, Prosecutors, etc. Cutting off information at its source is an obvious way of trying to curtail dissemination by the news media, and prosecutors sometimes are the sources of news stories about confessions and probable guilt, but gags on police and attorneys may be challenged by those gagged on the ground that they interfere with the First Amendment rights of the police and attorneys to express themselves. Furthermore, to the extent that the process of newsgathering may be protected by the First Amendment (see discussion of *Richmond Newspapers* later in this section), such restrictive orders may be unconstitutional.

In 1991 the Supreme Court of the United States reversed a judgment against Attorney Dominic P. Gentile, who had held a press conference the day after his client was indicted on criminal charges. The client was acquitted by a jury six months later, and the Disciplinary Board of the State Bar of Nevada subsequently found that Gentile had violated a Nevada Supreme Court Rule prohibiting lawyers from making extrajudicial statements to the press that they know or reasonably should know would have a "substantial likelihood of materially prejudicing" a proceeding. The Nevada Supreme Court had affirmed, rejecting Gentile's contention that the rule violated his right to free speech.

The Supreme Court of the United States reversed, holding that the "substantial likelihood of material prejudice" test applied by Nevada and most other states satisfies the First Amendment but that the Nevada rule was nonetheless void for vagueness: its grammatical structure and the absence of clarifying interpretation failed to provide fair notice to lawyers. Gentile v. State Bar of Nevada, 501 U.S. 1030 (1991).

Encouraging the Use of Voluntary Guidelines. In the 1960s the American Bar Association responded to the fair trial-free press concern by creating a committee that came to be known as the Reardon Committee to recommend guidelines for pre-trial and trial news coverage. The committee recommended that, prior to trial, lawyers release no extrajudicial statements relating to (1) prior criminal record of the accused, (2) existence or contents of any confession, (3) performance of any examinations or tests or the defendant's refusal to undergo them, (4) identity, testimony or credibility of prospective witnesses, (5) possibility of a guilty plea to the charge or a lesser offense or (6) any opinion as to the accused's guilt or innocence. Other recommendations dealt with other facets of the fair trial-free press issue. Many journalists resented what they viewed as an attempt by the legal profession to tell them how to do their jobs and ignored the Reardon Committee's recommendations.

Guidelines of state bench-bar-press organizations may have fared somewhat better because they were generally adopted by joint committees of members of the journalism and legal professions. These guidelines typically suggest that journalists *think carefully* before revealing information that the Reardon Committee cautioned against, but they also express recognition of a right of the journalist to access to information about the criminal justice system.

The effectiveness of the guidelines is directly related to their voluntariness. Even in states in which the guidelines are followed with some regularity in routine cases, they tend to lose their effectiveness when sensational crimes are committed. There is also some danger that courts may use the guidelines in ways the journalists never envisioned. We will see examples of this later in this chapter.

Shielding Witnesses. Shielding witnesses from the press similarly may interfere with the witnesses' own First Amendment rights and may interfere with a press right to gather news. On the other hand, of course, witnesses are under no obligation to answer questions from journalists.

Granting a Continuance. Postponing ("continuing") the trial until publicity dies down may interfere with the defendant's right to a speedy trial. Also, when the trial finally does take place, it becomes a news event all over again.

Granting Change of Venue. Where news accounts in an area may have created a situation in which it is unlikely that the accused can obtain a fair trial, a judge can transfer a trial to another area less touched by the publicity. A constitutional problem may arise in some instances, because the Sixth Amendment provides for one's trial "by an impartial jury of the State and district wherein the crime shall have been committed." Furthermore, such changes of venue are costly and bothersome to both the prosecution and the defense. If news accounts have already been state-wide or national, the change is unlikely to do much to mitigate the damage. Even if the new site of the trial has been untouched by earlier news accounts, the scheduling of the trial there becomes a news event in that area, and the problem may begin anew, though with less attention because the victim(s) are not local people.

Granting Change of Venire. Rather than moving the trial, it is theoretically possible to import a panel of jurors—or veniremen—from another area where they are less likely to have formed opinions about the case. In practice this is extremely rare, and it too raises Sixth Amendment questions. In 1993, as preparations were being made for the trial of two white men accused of setting afire a black New York tourist, estimates showed that up to $1 million might be saved by flying in the jury from outside the area rather than moving the trial. At the last minute, however, a Florida appellate court blocked the change of venire by ruling that the judge lacked authority to split the jury *selection from the trial.* Kohut v. Evans, 623 So.2d 569 (Fla.App.1993). A change of venire was granted, however, in the case of three suburban police officers charged with involuntary manslaughter in the 1995 death of a black motorist near Pittsburgh. Jurors were chosen from Chester County, rather than Allegheny County, where the death took place. Pennsylvania Law Weekly, Oct. 20, 1997 at 15.

Relying on the Voir Dire. During the voir dire, the process under which the prospective jurors are screened, attempts are made to exclude from the jury those people whose previously formed opinions will preclude their reaching a fair verdict based on the evidence presented during the trial. The voir dire may be successful in keeping truly biased people off a jury, but it is less successful when potential jurors have heard a specific piece of information. Also, the criticism is made that it can tend to eliminate from the jury those potential jurors who follow the news in their community most closely and who form intelligent opinions based on what they read or hear.

Cautioning Journalists. If the court cautions journalists in advance of publication of prejudicial information, the warning can seem to imply a threat of punishment by the contempt powers and may seem like an unconstitutional form of prior restraint (see Chapter I). If the warning is made after prejudicial information has already been revealed, the warning is likely to be ineffective.

Cautioning Jurors. The Court in *Sheppard* was critical of the trial judge for failing to give the jurors sufficient instruction about not reading media accounts of the trial or listening to comment outside the courtroom. Despite the fact that most judges today can be expected to give careful instructions, and most have faith in jurors to follow those instructions, there are undoubtedly instances in which jurors fail to heed those instructions and do see prejudicial news accounts outside the courtroom.

Sequestering the Jury. Sequestering the jury—keeping them in a hotel during the trial—greatly reduces the risk of improper exposure to media accounts of the trial. Because the public reads about sequestration in some highly publicized cases, it seems to perceive sequestration as a more common practice than it is. Its high cost precludes its use in all but a few cases, and defense attorneys are sometimes reluctant even to suggest it because of uncertainty about the effect on the jury. As some say, jurors who are unhappy about being confined for the duration of a trial cannot take out their frustrations on the judge and just may take them out on the accused.

b. *Restraints on Publication*

Because the First Amendment has traditionally been seen as a protection for the freedom to publish, restraints on the publication of information are undoubtedly the least desirable and most constitutionally suspect of the theoretically-available remedies for the fair trial-free press problem. Two cases that illustrate the problem are *Dickinson*, p. 27, *supra*, and Nebraska Press Association v. Stuart, 427 U.S. 539, 1 Med.L.Rptr. 1064 (1976).

The press calls them gag orders; lawyers and judges call them restrictive orders or protective orders. By whatever name, such an order directs the press (and often others) not to disseminate information a judge thinks may prejudice jurors in a forthcoming or present trial. Violating such an order can result in a citation for contempt.

A major case involving a restrictive order is *Nebraska Press Association*. Six members of the Kellie family were found murdered in their rural home in 1975. A neighbor, Erwin Charles Simants, was an immediate suspect, and the crime attracted widespread news coverage by electronic and print media. Three days after the crime, the prosecutor and the defense attorney joined in asking the trial court to enter a restrictive order relating to "matters that may or may not be publicly reported or disclosed to the public" because of the "mass coverage of news media" and the "reasonable likelihood of prejudicial news which would make difficult, if not impossible, the impaneling of an impartial jury and tend to prevent a fair trial."

The county court entered such an order, also requiring the members of the press to observe the Nebraska Bar–Press Guidelines, a set of voluntary guidelines of the type mentioned above. Attempts by the media to get the restrictive order lifted were unsuccessful. Simants was convicted, but the case brought by the Nebraska Press Association and other media organizations continued to the Supreme Court.

Chief Justice Burger, writing for the majority, said that in order to determine whether the danger posed by the media justified the restrictive order, "we must examine the evidence before the trial judge when the order was entered to determine (a) the nature and extent of pretrial news coverage; (b) whether other measures would be likely to mitigate the effects of unrestrained pretrial publicity; (c) how effectively a restraining order would operate to prevent the threatened danger." Finding that the trial judge's conclusion as to the impact of publicity on prospective jurors was "of necessity speculative" because he was dealing with "factors unknown and unknowable," the Court concluded that "the heavy burden imposed as a condition to securing a prior restraint was not met . . ." The judgment of the Nebraska Supreme Court was therefore reversed.

If a trial judge waits until unrestrained pretrial news accounts seem dangerous enough to justify a restraint, would such an order then be unacceptable because it would be largely ineffective?

In Goldblum v. National Broadcasting Corp., 584 F.2d 904, 4 Med. L.Rptr. 1718 (9th Cir.1978), plaintiff, former executive officer of Equity Funding Corp., was serving a sentence for fraudulent activity in connection with the corporation's insolvency. NBC produced a "docudrama" based on the case, using the names of plaintiff and the corporation. Plaintiff, alleging that the program was inaccurate, sought an injunction against the showing of the program on the ground that it might inflame public opinion against him, jeopardize his release on parole and adversely affect jury selection in any future criminal or civil cases arising out of the episode.

The district judge ordered NBC to produce the movie for review the day its presentation was scheduled. When NBC refused the judge ordered counsel for the network imprisoned until the film was produced. A few hours later a panel of the court of appeals granted an application for relief and freed the attorney. In a subsequent opinion, the court said that it found "no authority which is even a remote justification" for issuing a prior restraint on the theory that parole officials might become inflamed or that jury selection in some "wholly speculative criminal prosecution" might be adversely affected. The order to produce and the imprisonment were invalid.

In State v. Coe, 101 Wash.2d 364, 679 P.2d 353, 10 Med.L.Rptr. 1465 (1984), a trial judge's order holding a broadcaster in contempt for playing tapes that had been played in open court was reversed on appeal. The judge had ordered that the tapes not be played on the air because the defendant might be suicidal. The appellate court majority held that the state permitted those cited for contempt to violate the order and then challenge it if the order was "patently invalid or 'void' as outside the court's power."

Recall *Noriega*, p. 27, *supra,* in which a temporary restraint was imposed on CNN to stop the network from broadcasting taperecorded telephone calls between Noriega and members of his defense team. CNN was subsequently convicted with criminal contempt of court as a result of its 1990 airing of Noriega's conversations with his attorneys.

Gag Orders on Litigants. A special problem arises when the media are themselves parties to litigation and want to report on the case. Part of the problem, in fact, is that the courts treat the press like any other litigant. In Seattle Times Co. v. Rhinehart, 467 U.S. 20, 10 Med.L.Rptr. 1705 (1984), the Supreme Court held that a protective order by a trial court in the state of Washington did not violate the First Amendment even though it prohibited the Seattle Times newspaper from publishing certain information related to a libel case against them. The information in question had been obtained by the newspaper as part of the discovery process prior to the libel trial, and the Court reasoned that there was a sufficient showing of good cause for the order and that the rights of a litigant do not necessarily include the right to disseminate information obtained through the "legislative grace" of the discovery process. Although most journalists and attorneys representing media clients consider it a disturbing trend, lower courts in other cases have also affirmed orders gagging litigants or trial participants.

Gags on Counsel. A federal judge concerned about possible prejudice to the trials of individuals charged in the World Trade Center bombing case entered an order prohibiting counsel for all parties in the case from publicly discussing any aspect of the case. The U.S. Court of Appeals for the Second Circuit held that the order was not narrowly tailored, that it was entered without any finding that alternatives to such blanket prohibition would be inadequate to protect the defendants' fair trial rights, and that it violated the First Amendment. The per curiam opinion said, "There is no indication in the record that the court explored any alternatives or at all considered imposing any less broad proscription; indeed the court discouraged counsel from even proffering possible alternatives." United States v. Salameh, 992 F.2d 445, 21 Med.L.Rptr. 1376 (2d Cir.1993). The trial was eventually held in New York City, despite the heavy media attention, and four men were convicted of the bombing. The New York Times, May 25, 1994 at A–1.

Gags on Grand Jurors. In another attempt to cut off information at its source, a Florida law prohibited grand jury witnesses from disclosing their testimony. When a journalist was himself a grand jury witness, the statute effectively became a restraint on publication. In a 1990 case, the Supreme Court found the statute to violate the First Amendment. Michael Smith, a reporter for the Charlotte Herald–News in Charlotte County, Fla., had been called to testify before a special grand jury about information he had obtained while writing a series of newspaper stories about alleged improprieties committed by the Charlotte County state attorney's office and sheriff's department. He had been warned that any disclosure of his testimony would violate the Florida statute. Writing for a unanimous court, Chief Justice Rehnquist acknowledged various state interests in keeping grand jury testimony secret but concluded that they were insufficient "to overcome [Smith's] First Amendment right to make a truthful statement of the information he had acquired on his own." Butterworth v. Smith, 494 U.S. 624, 17 Med.L.Rptr. 1569 (1990).

c. *Denials of Access to the Courtroom and Conditional Access*

As judges faced the reality that other means of solving the fair trial-free press problems were either undesirable or ineffective, some turned to excluding the press and public from the courtroom during pretrial hearings or during trials themselves, or granted access to the courtroom only on the acceptance of conditions.

Journalists, of course, are also members of the public. But more, they see themselves as the eyes and ears of the public—surrogates for those who cannot attend a hearing or trial. They brought the first major challenge to closed pretrial hearings.

Gannett Co. v. DePasquale, 443 U.S. 368, 5 Med.L.Rptr. 1337 (1979), presented the question of whether members of the public are constitutionally entitled to attend a pretrial hearing. The issue arose out of a murder prosecution in upstate New York. The murder victim disappeared in 1976 after last having been seen fishing with two men. The victim's truck was found in Michigan, and the two young men were arrested there. Newspapers in New York State reported the arrest and police theories of the crime. Brought back to New York, the two men moved to suppress statements they had made to Michigan police, claiming the statements were given involuntarily. They also moved to suppress the gun that had been found as a result of the confession in Michigan.

The motions came before Judge DePasquale, and defense counsel asked the judge to close the hearing because "the unabated buildup of adverse publicity" had jeopardized the ability of the defendants to receive a fair trial. Neither the prosecutor nor the Gannett reporter in the courtroom objected. The judge removed press and public from the courtroom. The next day the reporter complained to the judge, but the hearing had concluded and the judge refused to release a transcript. Three days later counsel for Gannett appeared and asked that the ruling be vacated and that a transcript of the hearing be provided. The judge refused, the New York Court of Appeals upheld the judge's action, and the Supreme Court affirmed, 5–4, in an opinion by Justice Stewart.

Justice Stewart concluded that the Sixth Amendment's provision that "the accused shall enjoy the right to a speedy and public trial by an impartial jury" extended no rights whatever to the public. He said the right to a public trial is a personal right of the accused. He also said that any First and Fourteenth Amendment rights of Gannett to attend a criminal trial were not violated because the trial judge made an appraisal of the situation and concluded that, under the circumstances of this particular case, any right to attend the proceeding was outweighed by the defendants' right to a fair trial.

After the *Gannett* decision, many thought the matter was left to each state. The decision caused considerable confusion, with its references to both pretrial hearings and trials, and there was speculation that the majority opinion had been drafted as a dissenting opinion before one of the justices was persuaded to join it as the majority opinion.

Following the decision, news directors, editors and professional associations circulated "Gannett cards" among their reporters. The cards, worded so that a reporter can read them on the spot should a judge be considering a closure, ask that such a decision be delayed until the reporter's media employer has an opportunity to be represented by legal counsel to argue on behalf of the right of the media and public to observe the proceedings.

Months before the Supreme Court's decision in *Gannett,* a trial judge in Hanover County, Va., closed a murder trial—setting the stage for Richmond Newspapers, Inc. v. Virginia, 448 U.S. 555, 6 Med.L.Rptr. 1833 (1980).

The defendant had been convicted of second-degree murder, and his conviction had been overturned on appeal because improper evidence had been admitted. The second and third trials resulted in mistrials. At the start of the fourth trial, defense counsel moved to exclude the press and public from the courtroom. He did not want witnesses to compare stories or information to leak out and be learned by the jurors, who had not been sequestered. The prosecutor offered no objection, and the judge closed the courtroom.

The newspaper appealed the reporter's exclusion, and the Supreme Court eventually held that the trial should have been open. The vote was 7–1, but the reasoning behind the decision is difficult to explain because the seven justices in the majority wrote six opinions and there was no majority opinion. Chief Justice Burger wrote the plurality opinion, stressing that *Gannett* had involved "pretrial" proceedings while this case involved a trial. He traced at length the history of public trials that ran back at least to the 13th century in England, mentioning as reasons for openness the greater likelihood that witnesses would tell the truth, the therapeutic value of having open criminal trials as an outlet for community concern, hostility, and emotion, and the opportunity for understanding the system and its workings in a particular case.

The Chief Justice then recognized a First Amendment right to attend criminal trials. Writing that it was not crucial whether the right be called a "right of access" or a "right to gather information," he said "The explicit, guaranteed rights to speak and to publish concerning what takes place at a trial would lose much meaning if access to observe the trial could, as it was here, be foreclosed arbitrarily." This recognition of a right to gather information is significant because the far more traditional view of the First Amendment had been that it protected one's right to disseminate information one had already obtained, not one's right to obtain information.

Although some confusion about closures of either pretrial hearings or trials remained after *Richmond,* many fewer judges closed courtrooms. In Globe Newspaper Co. v. Norfolk County Superior Court, 457 U.S. 596, 8 Med.L.Rptr. 1689 (1982), however, the Supreme Court had to examine *The Boston Globe's* challenge to a state statute providing for automatic closure of rape and other sexual assault trials during the testimony of minors who are victims. Justice Brennan wrote for the six-member majority, "We agree with respondent that the first interest—safe-guarding the physical and psychological well-being of a minor—is a compelling one. But as compelling as that interest is, it does not justify a mandatory-closure rule, for it is clear that the circumstances of the particular case may affect the significance of the interest. A trial court can determine on a case-by-case basis whether closure is necessary to protect the welfare of a minor victim."

In such closure decisions, the First Amendment requires that any such restriction on access to criminal trials be necessitated by compelling state interest and be narrowly tailored to serve that interest.

In Press–Enterprise Co. v. Superior Court (I), 464 U.S. 501, 10 Med.L.Rptr. 1161 (1984), the Supreme Court dealt with the issue of the closing of the *voir dire* examination of potential jurors. Holding that such proceedings in criminal trials are presumptively open to the public, the Court said that closure would be justified only where there is an overriding interest, where the closure is narrowly tailored and where alternatives to closure have been considered. The court found no support for the trial court's conclusion that an open proceeding would have threatened the prospective jurors' interests in privacy in this case. (The problem was compounded, from the press's point of view, by the fact that the trial court had refused to release the transcript of the *voir dire* as well.)

In Waller v. Georgia, 467 U.S. 39, 10 Med.L.Rptr. 1714 (1984), the Supreme Court addressed the problem of a closure of pretrial suppression hearings over the objection of the defendant. The case involved allegations of racketeering and gambling, and a pretrial hearing was held to consider suppression of wiretaps and evidence seized during searches at the defendants' homes. The hearing was closed when the prosecution moved for closure alleging that unnecessary "publication" of information obtained under the wiretaps would render the information inadmissible as evidence, and that the wiretap evidence would "involve" the privacy interests of some persons who were indicted but were not then on trial, and some who were not then indicted. Citing *Press–Enterprise (I),* the court held the closure of the suppression hearing was unjustified, noting that the entire seven-day hearing had been closed even though the tapes were played for less than 2½ hours.

Concern for the *voir dire* process arose again in Press–Enterprise Co. v. Superior Court (II), 478 U.S. 1, 13 Med.L.Rptr. 1001 (1986). The case involved a preliminary hearing in the case of Robert Diaz, a nurse charged with murdering 12 patients. Acting on a motion from the defense, the magistrate had closed the hearing, noting that the case had attracted national publicity and that "only one side may get reported in the media."

The hearing continued for 41 days, during which much of the testimony was medical and scientific. The record of the hearing was sealed. The California Supreme Court held that if a defendant established a "reasonable likelihood of substantial prejudice," the burden shifted to the prosecution or the media to show by a preponderance of evidence that there was no such reasonable probability of prejudice. The Supreme Court of the United States reversed.

Chief Justice Burger, writing for a seven-member majority, said that, "The considerations that led the Court to apply the First Amendment right of access to criminal trials in *Richmond Newspapers* and *Globe* and the selection of jurors in *Press–Enterprise I* lead us to conclude that the right of access applies to preliminary hearings as conducted in California."

He wrote:

> Since a qualified First Amendment right of access attaches to preliminary hearings in California . . ., the proceedings cannot be closed unless specific, on the record findings are made demonstrating that "closure is essential to preserve higher values and is narrowly tailored to serve that interest." . . .
>
> . . . [The] risk of prejudice does not automatically justify refusing public access to hearings on every motion to suppress. Through voir dire, cumbersome as it is in some circumstances, a court can identify those jurors whose prior knowledge of the case would disable them from rendering an impartial verdict. And even if closure were justified for the hearings on a motion to suppress, closure of an entire 41–day proceeding would rarely be warranted. The First Amendment right of access cannot be overcome by the conclusory assertion that publicity might deprive the defendant of [the right to a fair trial]. And any limitation " 'must be narrowly tailored to serve that interest.' " [   ]

The fact that nine out of 10 criminal prosecutions are concluded before they reach trial makes the decision in *Press–Enterprise II* particularly important to the news media.

Conditional Access. With a variety of precedents holding that trial court judges should not gag journalists and should not keep them or other members of the public out of the courtroom, it was perhaps inevitable that trial judges would seek another way of trying to solve fair trial-free press problems. A trial court judge in the State of Washington decided to use the voluntary bench-bar-media guidelines adopted in that state as a basis for granting access to his courtroom, allowing only reporters who agreed to abide by the guidelines into the room.

The Washington Supreme Court upheld the trial judge's order in Federated Publications, Inc. v. Swedberg, 96 Wash.2d 13, 633 P.2d 74, 7 Med.L.Rptr. 1865 (1981), certiorari denied 456 U.S. 984 (1982). Critics of bench-bar-press guidelines said that one of the envisioned dangers of such guidelines—their misuse by the courts—had become a reality. Early predictions of a trend toward such conditions on access to courtrooms proved premature, however. Adoption of amendments to state bench-bar-press guidelines, specifically precluding their use by courts for any purpose, lessened the likelihood that the guidelines, which media representatives had adopted in good faith, might be used against them in this way.

Conditional access also arises in juvenile proceedings. In many states, hearings in juvenile cases are confidential on the ground that they are primarily to rehabilitate and are clinical rather than punitive. The Supreme Court has said that a state may "continue, if it deems it appropriate, to provide and to improve provision for the confidentiality of records of police contracts and court action relating to juveniles." In re Gault, 387 U.S. 1, 25 (1967). In Mayer v. State, 523 So.2d 1171, 15 Med.L.Rptr. 2255 (Fla.App.1988), a newspaper reporter was held in contempt for writing about a child custody hearing.

d.   Denials of Access to Court Records

Although there is a tradition of openness of court records, there are instances in which courts have withheld certain information during and sometimes after trials. Judges may bar release of the names of jurors in notorious cases to protect their privacy and impartiality. Or, as in *Press–Enterprise (I)*, p. 993, *supra*, part or all of a transcript may be withheld.

In one case, a trial court judge in Iowa, concerned about retaliation against jurors, ordered reporters not to print the names, addresses or phone numbers of jurors in a murder trial involving the widow of a slain motorcycle gang member. The judge also barred photographs of the jurors entering and leaving the courthouse. The press appealed the order, and it was overturned in light of *Nebraska Press*. Des Moines Register & Tribune Co. v. Osmundson, 248 N.W.2d 493, 2 Med.L.Rptr. 1321 (Iowa 1976).

If a judge cannot prevent the press from reporting the names of jurors that have become public, the next step might be to try to prevent the names from becoming public in a state in which jurors' names are not public property. This was approved in a criminal prosecution of major narcotics suspects in New York City. The trial judge gave prospective jurors numbers and never released their names and addresses. After conviction defendants appealed, asserting, as one ground, that the lack of names and addresses meant the defendants could not question neighbors and learn on their own about the prospective jurors. The court affirmed the convictions. United States v. Barnes, 604 F.2d 121 (2d Cir.1979), certiorari denied 446 U.S. 907 (1980). The court, in a decision called disturbing by *The New York Times* and others, said if an anonymous juror feels less pressure as the result of anonymity "this is as it should be—a factor contributing to his impartiality."

The presumption of openness of court records does not necessarily extend to making copies of videotape evidence used at trials. The Maryland Court of Special Appeals held July 1, 1993, that a Maryland trial court did not abuse its discretion when it refused to allow news media to copy a videotape that had been played in open court at a murder trial. The prosecution alleged that the two defendants were the same two men shown in the videotape in a car. The tape showed the carjacking-murder victim, Pamela Basu, and her daughter getting into the car. The appellate court held that the presumption of access was overcome by the compelling governmental interest in preserving the fair trial rights of the two defendants, only one of whom was being tried when the videotape was first admitted into evidence. Group W Television, Inc. v. State, 96 Md.App. 712, 626 A.2d 1032, 21 Med.L.Rptr. 1697 (1993).

e. Use of the Contempt Power

Courts have long been concerned about efforts by the parties and press to influence judges to decide pending cases in a certain way. The traditional approach was that such efforts either influenced the judge or appeared to influence the judge—and that either view seriously impaired the functioning of the judicial branch. The technique for handling the problem was to hold the perpetrator in contempt of court and impose appropriate sanctions.

Contempt of court involves a variety of actions that obstruct the administration of justice. These include disturbance of a judicial proceeding by shouting in the courtroom, willful refusal to obey a court order to pay alimony, and refusal to answer a grand jury question after a judge has ordered the witness to do so. If a court were to punish a member of the press for contempt, it would be more likely to be for disobeying an order of the court (not to bring equipment into the courtroom, for instance), for interfering with the administration of justice by broadcasting or publishing something prejudicial (the power is generally *not* used in such instances but might be) or for refusing to answer a question about a secret source or secret notes. (We will discuss confidentiality in the next section of this chapter).

f. Restrictions on Cameras and Other Equipment

For most of the last half century, cameras and sound-recording equipment have been kept out of courtrooms—partially because of the canons of ethics of judges, partially because of Supreme Court decisions, and partially because of tradition. During those years electronic equipment has become less and less obtrusive, and television has become commonplace in most other places in which newsworthy events are taking place. Experimentation with cameras in the last 10 years has led to changes in the rules in many states, but some others still forbid them. To understand the situation, one must look at its history.

When Bruno Hauptmann was brought to trial for kidnapping and slaying the son of famous aviator Charles Lindbergh in 1932, journalists and photographers packed the courtroom. Hauptmann, found guilty and sentenced to death, may not have gotten a fair trial because of the adverse publicity. In response, the American Bar Association adopted Canon 35, banning radio and television broadcasting and still cameras from courtrooms, in 1937. The canon's successor, Canon 3A(7), was amended in 1982, reflecting changing state practices. The canon now says a judge should prohibit broadcasting, reporting and photographing, except when they are authorized by supervising appellate courts or other authorities and are consistent with fair trial rights—being unobtrusive, not distracting, and not interfering with the administration of justice.

In a Supreme Court case, Estes v. Texas, 381 U.S. 532, 1 Med. L.Rptr. 1187 (1965), defendant had been indicted in the Texas state courts for "swindling"—inducing farmers to buy nonexistent fertilizer tanks and then to deliver to him mortgages on the tanks. The nature of the charges and the large sums of money involved attracted national interest. Texas was one of two states that then permitted televised trials (the other, Colorado, required the defendant's permission). Over Estes' objection, the trial judge permitted televising of a two-day hearing before trial.

Estes was convicted, but the Supreme Court eventually reversed the conviction, 5–4. In his majority opinion Justice Clark concluded that the use of television at the trial involved "such a probability that prejudice will result that it is deemed inherently lacking in due process" even without any showing of specific prejudices. He was concerned about the impact on jurors, judges, parties, witnesses and lawyers.

Justice Harlan, who provided the crucial fifth vote for reversal, joined the majority opinion only to the extent that it applied to televised coverage of "courtroom proceedings of a criminal trial of widespread public interest," "a criminal trial of great notoriety" and "a heavily publicized and highly sensational affair." In such cases he was worried about the impact on jurors.

Despite the fact that there had not been five votes on the court for the notion that cameras were inherently unfair, the *Estes* decision was frequently and erroneously cited as standing for that principle during the years when cameras were almost universally banned from courtrooms. When some states began experimenting again with cameras, it was inevitable that the Supreme Court would again face this issue. The Court did so in Chandler v. Florida, 449 U.S. 560, 7 Med.L.Rptr. 1041 (1981), unanimously rejecting the view that televising a criminal trial over the objections of the defendant *automatically* rendered the trial unfair. (In Florida, only the consent of the trial judge was required to allow the trial to be televised.) The defendants had argued that the impact of television on the participants introduced potentially prejudicial, but unidentifiable, aspects into the trial. The majority, in an opinion by Chief Justice Burger, first concluded that *Estes* did not stand for the proposition that broadcasting was barred "in all cases and under all circumstances." Because of Justice Harlan's narrow views in that case, the ruling of *Estes* should apply only to cases of widespread interest. (On this point, two Justices insisted that *Chandler* overruled *Estes* and should say so.)

Then, Chief Justice Burger continued that the risk of prejudice from press coverage of a trial was not limited to broadcasting. "The risk of juror prejudice in some cases does not justify an absolute ban on news coverage of trials by the printed media; so also the risk of such prejudice does not warrant an absolute constitutional ban on all broadcast coverage." A case attracts attention because of its intrinsic interest to the public. The "appropriate safeguard" against prejudice in such cases "is the defendant's right to demonstrate that the media's coverage of his case—be it printed or broadcast—compromised the ability of the particular jury that heard the case to adjudicate fairly." The Court also observed that the changes in technology since *Estes* supported the state's argument that it now be permitted to allow television in the courtroom.

One manifestation of the public interest in observing the court process is the success of the Courtroom Television Network, "Court TV," which began in 1991 and in 1999 reaches 35–million households.

Because the defendants in *Chandler*—two former city policemen accused of burglarizing a restaurant—showed no adverse impact from the televising, the convictions were upheld.

Notice that this case involved criminal defendants attacking their convictions. It did *not* involve a First Amendment claim by broadcasters to bring their equipment into the courtroom in a state that barred such entry. The Court did not discuss the impact of *Richmond Newspapers* or other First Amendment cases. As of the time *Chandler* was decided, more than half the states were permitting television in the courtroom either on an experimental basis or on a permanent basis after a successful experiment had ended. In many of these states, the consent of a criminal defendant was required before entry could be allowed. Many states that barred entry or required consent of a party before entry have continued their practices after *Chandler*. Forty-seven states now permit cameras in courtrooms, but rules vary, and some states continue to struggle with the issue.

In New York State for example, trial courts began audiovisual coverage with an 18–month experiment that ended in 1989. Despite support from the state's governor and chief judge, legislative attempts to establish permanent rules allowing cameras in trial courts failed in 1989. There was on-and-off coverage during a series of experiments (with an interval between), but coverage ended June 30, 1997, because the state legislature had enacted no new enabling legislation. Some observers were quick to point out the lasting distaste for television in courts following the O.J. Simpson criminal trial.

The much-publicized trial of New York City police officers involved int the shooting of Amadou Diallo was moved from New York City to Albany, and, in a move that surprised many observers, a judge there granted a petition by Court TV to cover the trial, saying that the ban on the cameras was unconstitutional. Some other judges in the state then followed the precedent and admitted cameras amid differing opinions as to whether the practice could continue without action by the legislature. The New York Times, March 17, 2000 at B–7. The uncertainty continued into 2001. A New York trial court, for example, ruled March 30, 2001, that, "[S]ince no appellate Division has ruled on the substantive issue, the decision to allow cameras in the courtroom . . . rests with the sound discretion of the trial judge." The court held that the public's right to know in a death penalty case outweighs the defendant's privacy rights under a state law that bars use of audiovisual equipment in the court-room and that the statute is therefore unconstitutional. People v. Schroedel, N.Y. County Court, Sullivan County, 29 Med.L.Rptr. 1805 (2001).

Similarly, there was experimental audiovisual coverage of civil proceedings in a few district and appellate federal courts beginning in 1991, but the U.S. Judicial Conference decided in 1994 against permitting cameras in federal courts. In 1996 the conference authorized coverage in the appellate courts, but the media generally have less interest in covering appellate proceedings than in covering trials. In the spring of 1999, Congress had before it the "Sunshine in the Courtroom Act," which would grant federal judges discretion to allow electronic coverage of their courts.

The Supreme Court continues to ban audiovisual coverage. The Chief Justice has made few public comments on the subject. Although he said at a Senate hearing on his nomination as Chief Justice that he would give "sympathetic consideration" to a request for broadcast coverage of the Court, he said shortly after becoming Chief Justice that he was concerned about the possible loss of institutional "mystique and moral authority" of the Court. "I hope we don't get to the time where the members of the Court are trying to get on the 6:00 news every night," he said. Observers note that the Supreme Court justices too were probably less than impressed by the coverage of the O.J. Simpson trial, and the Chief Justice is suspected of being less than pleased about the coverage of his role at the impeach proceedings of President Clinton— including the heavy emphasis on the gold stripes on his judicial robes and numerous jokes on late-night shows.

Among the arguments in favor of cameras in courtrooms are educational value, the opportunity to let more people see the administration of justice, the "neutral" way the camera views the scene without necessity of human narration, the possibility that witnesses will testify more truthfully because others who know the truth may be watching, the creation of a video record for appellate purposes and the possibility of closed circuit viewing by spectators elsewhere in the courthouse.

Among arguments against cameras in courtrooms are the danger that excerpts of trials will be used sensationally, threats to the privacy or safety of the jurors, the possibility that participants (judge, lawyers, witnesses) may behave differently with cameras present, the fear that camera angles and choices of shots will influence viewers' perceptions of the scene, and the creation of disruption in the courtroom.

Courtroom Sketching. Where television has not been permitted in courtrooms, television news directors have resorted to sketches of the courtroom scene to provide a visual dimension to their reports of judicial proceedings. That practice came under attack during the pretrial proceedings involving the trial of the "Gainesville Eight," who were charged with conspiring to disrupt the 1972 Republican National Convention. The trial judge decreed that no sketches be drawn in the courtroom. On appeal, the court refused to accept "a sweeping prohibition of in-court sketching where there has been no showing whatsoever that sketching is any way obtrusive or disruptive." United States v. Columbia Broadcasting System, Inc., 497 F.2d 102, 1 Med.L.Rptr. 1351 (5th Cir.1974).

The Nixon Tapes in the Courts. As we will see later, the saga of the Nixon tapes reached its first significant stage when the Supreme Court ordered President Nixon to honor a subpoena from the Watergate special prosecutor to deliver tapes of a large group of conversations for use in the so-called Watergate trial. United States v. Nixon, 418 U.S. 683 (1974). In 1974 Congress passed the Presidential Recordings and Materials Preservation Act, directing the Administrator of General Services to take custody of the former President's tapes and documents. The Administrator was directed to submit to Congress regulations governing access to Presidential materials of historical value. The act was upheld in Nixon v. Administrator of General Services, 433 U.S. 425, 2 Med.L.Rptr. 2025 (1977). That was chapter two.

The third episode took shape during the Watergate trial. The tape reels obtained from the President were played in the judge's chambers before trial. Some conversations were declared irrelevant or privileged and were not reproduced. The other conversations were rerecorded on new tapes designated Copy A for the district court and Copy B for the special prosecutor. Some, but not all, of the conversations on Copy A were admitted into evidence. Some, but not all, of these were played to the jury. Some were played in full; others only in part. "Deletions were effected not by modifying the exhibit itself, but by skipping deleted portions on the tape or by interrupting the sound transmission to the jurors' headphones." Written transcripts of the conversations being played to the jurors were provided to the jurors and others in the court— all of whom heard the tapes over headphones.

During the trial broadcasters approached Judge Sirica to obtain copies of the 22 hours of tapes played to the jury. After extensive proceedings he denied the request for immediate access to the tapes on the ground that the convicted defendants had appeals pending, and release of the tapes might prejudice their rights.

The court of appeals reversed, relying on the importance of the common-law privilege of inspecting and copying judicial records. The fear of prejudice to the defendants did not outweigh the public's right to access.

The Supreme Court reversed the court of appeals. Nixon v. Warner Communications, Inc., 435 U.S. 589, 3 Med.L.Rptr. 2074 (1978). Justice Powell, writing for the majority, began by discussing the asserted common-law right to inspect judicial records. Although he found some case support, the right was not absolute. "Every court has supervisory power over its own records and files and access has been denied where court files might have become a vehicle for improper purposes." Common-law rights to inspect had given way in cases in which the record might be used to "gratify private spite or promote public scandal" as in divorce cases; where the record contained libelous statements; and where the record contained "business information that might harm a litigant's competitive standing." Although he thought the cases showed that the decision was "one best left to the sound discretion of the trial court," Justice Powell was willing to assume that some right to inspect the tapes existed.

The Court then reviewed Nixon's arguments against disclosure. First, he argued that he had a property interest in his voice that the broadcasters should not be allowed to exploit for commercial gain. Second, he asserted a right of privacy. (The court of appeals had rejected that argument on the grounds that the passage of the Presidential Recordings Act contemplated release of the tapes at some time, and that presidential documents are not subject to ordinary privacy claims. The broadcasters added that the privacy claim was overridden by the fact that the tapes, with the nuances and inflections, would provide added understanding. Nixon disagreed on the ground that out of 22 hours of tapes, broadcasters and record makers would use fractions, necessarily taken out of context.) Third, Nixon argued that United States v. Nixon authorized use of the tapes only for the trial since they were obtained from a third party. Finally, he argued that it would be unseemly for the courts to "facilitate the commercialization" of the tapes for presentation "at cocktail parties" or in "comedy acts or dramatic productions." Justice Powell continued:

At this point, we normally would be faced with the task of weighing the interests advanced by the parties in light of the public interest and the duty of the courts.[14] On respondents' side of the scales is the incremental gain in public understanding of an immensely important historical occurrence that arguably would flow from the release of aural copies of these tapes, a gain said to be not inconsequential despite the already widespread dissemination of printed transcripts. Also on respondents' side of the scales is the presumption—however gauged—in favor of public access to judicial records. On petitioner's side are the arguments identified above, which must be assessed in the context of court custody of the tapes. Underlying each of petitioner's arguments is the crucial fact that respondents require a court's cooperation in furthering their commercial plans. The court—as custodian of tapes obtained by subpoena over the opposition of a sitting President, solely to satisfy "fundamental demands of due process of law in the fair administration of criminal justice," United States v. Nixon, 418 U.S., at 713— has a responsibility to exercise an informed discretion as to release of the tapes, with a sensitive appreciation of the circumstances that led to their production. This responsibility does not permit copying upon demand. Otherwise, there would exist a danger that the court could become a partner in the use of the subpoenaed material "to gratify private spite or promote public scandal," [ ], with no corresponding assurance of public benefit.

Having set the stage, Justice Powell announced that the Court need not decide the case because of a "unique element that was neither advanced by the parties nor given appropriate consideration by the courts below." Although the parties argued that the Presidential Recordings Act did not cover these tapes, the Court found a Congressional intent to create an administrative procedure for processing all the Nixon documents, including these recordings. (Why might each party have argued against the Act's relevance?) "The presence of an alternative means of public access tips the scales in favor of denying release." Questions concerning the regulations prepared by the Administrator of General Services were reserved "for future consideration in appropriate proceedings."

The broadcasters argued that even the presence of the Act could not destroy their constitutional claims to inspect the documents. First, the broadcasters relied on *Cox*, p. 954, *supra*, which barred damage liability against a broadcaster that named a rape victim whose name was obtained from official court records. The broadcasters argued that this gave them a right to copy anything displayed in open court. Justice Powell disagreed: the case gave the press only the right to copy records "open to the public." Here, reporters heard the tapes and were given transcripts, and could comment on each. *Cox* did not require that copies of the tapes

---

14. Judge Sirica's principal reason for refusing to release the tapes—fairness to the defendants, who were appealing their convictions—is no longer a consideration. All appeals have been resolved.

"to which the public has never had *physical* access" be made available for copying. "The First Amendment generally grants the press no right to information about a trial superior to that of the general public."

In their second constitutional argument, the broadcasters relied on the Sixth Amendment's guarantee of a public trial, asserting that public understanding of the trial is incomplete if the public cannot hear the tapes that the jury heard. Justice Powell thought this proved too much—because it would require recording testimony of live witnesses at trials. Also, the guarantee is to avoid the use of "courts as instruments of persecution" and confers no special benefit on the press. Finally, the right to public trial does not require that the trial be broadcast or recorded for the public. The requirement "is satisfied by the opportunity of members of the public and the press to attend the trial and to report what they have observed. [ ] That opportunity abundantly existed here."

Although the lower court decision favoring the broadcasters was reversed, the Court did not decide how the district court should dispose of the tapes. Justices White and Brennan dissented in part on the reading of the Recordings Act and would have ordered the tapes delivered immediately to the Administrator. Justices Marshall and Stevens, in separate opinions, would have affirmed the court of appeals.

The Watergate tapes continued to be the subject of litigation throughout Nixon's life and afterwards. Of 3,700 hours of tape, only 63 hours had been released by 1993, and only 545 hours by 1998. A federal appeals court ruled that 820 hours of the tapes were private and could be destroyed. Kutler v. Carlin, 329 U.S.App.D.C. 100, 139 F.3d 237 (1998). But by 2001, 1284 hours had been released, and the Nixon estate had agreed to allow the National Archives and Record Service to permit sale or copying of the released tapes.

A separate dispute over the tapes involved their value. The government confiscated approximately 40 million pages of documents at the same time it confiscated the tapes. Originally the government estimated the materials' worth at $2.2 million, but the Nixon estate estimated their worth at $30 million or more, which, allowing for interest, could have brought the amount the government might owe to the Nixon estate to more than $200 million. The government and the estate settled the matter in 2000, with the government paying $18 million. Lawyers got $7.4 million, the Nixon Foundation (which runs the presidential library) received $6 million, $3.75 million went for taxes, and Nixon's daughters received $90,000. San Francisco Examiner, June 16, 2000, p. A-22.

C. CONFIDENTIALITY IN NEWSGATHERING

The administration of justice depends upon access to information relevant to court disputes. When the only apparent way to obtain such information is by asking a journalist to reveal a confidential source or turn over unpublished notes, documents or outtakes, problems between the media and the courts can occur. Constitutional guarantees of a fair trial are meant to allow the parties a complete, objective hearing on the issues. What if a journalist refuses to divulge certain information? What about tapes in a television station's newsroom that shed light on an incident being considered by a court?

Journalists traditionally have sought recognition of a special privilege not to have to reveal their confidential sources, even when the identity of the source is part of the evidence sought by a court, a grand jury or a legislative committee; but confidential sources are just part of a larger problem. In addition to being asked to reveal sources, journalists have been asked for their notes, for documents and other evidence that they obtained in the course of newsgathering, for unpublished materials (negatives of photos not used and outtakes of television productions) and for testimony as to their thoughts during the newsgathering and editing processes. In addition, there have been attempts to gather evidence by police searches of newsrooms or by obtaining reporters' travel records or telephone records in an attempt to deduce their sources.

1. THE ROLE OF CONFIDENTIALITY

a. *Background*

It has been generally accepted that persons thought to have relevant information may be subpoenaed to testify as witnesses at certain governmental proceedings. Nevertheless, some relationships have been held to give rise to "privileges" permitting a party to withhold information he has learned in a confidential relationship. The most venerable of these relationships have been those of physician and patient, lawyer and client, and priest and penitent. In each of these the recipient may be prevented by the source from testifying as to information learned in confidence in that professional capacity.

Under common law, an assertion by journalists of a similar privilege from testifying was generally rejected. Critics of a privilege for journalists sometimes point out that professionals in medicine and law typically must meet certain educational requirements, be certified to practice and be subject to disciplinary action if they fail to adhere to professional standards. Journalists, on the other hand, have no minimum educational requirements, require no certification or license to be journalists, and are not subject to the same kinds of peer review to which doctors and lawyers are subject. So long as freedom of press belongs to everyone, not just to a few licensed to be journalists, professional standards are difficult to police. Although one likes to believe that the vast majority of journalists are ethical and truthful, such incidents as that involving the Janet Cooke Pulitzer Prize-winning story on the juvenile heroin addict (who turned out not to be a real child) in *The Washington Post* attract public attention and are sometimes pointed to by critics of a privilege for journalists.

Despite the rejection of the privilege at common law, it has made headway as a statutory protection. Since the first reporter's privilege statute was enacted in Maryland in 1896, half the states have enacted so-called "shield" laws. As we shall see, these statutes may have limited utility in certain situations.

In states without privilege statutes, reporters tried, with little success, to claim such a privilege under common law. Then, in 1958, columnist Marie Torre tried a different approach. She had reported that a CBS executive had made certain disparaging remarks about entertainer Judy Garland. Garland sued CBS for defamation and sought by deposition to get Torre to identify the executive. Torre attacked the effort as a threat to freedom of the press, refused to answer the question, and asserted that the First Amendment protected her refusal. The court, though seeing some constitutional implications, held that even if the First Amendment were to provide some protection, the reporter must testify when the information sought goes to the "heart" of the plaintiff's claim. Garland v. Torre, 259 F.2d 545, 1 Med.L.Rptr. 2541 (2d Cir.), certiorari denied 358 U.S. 910 (1958). Torre ultimately served 10 days in jail for criminal contempt.

After *Garland,* reporters continued to assert First Amendment claims, still with little success. In the late 1960s, the situation became more serious as the federal government began to serve subpoenas on reporters more frequently. The media asserted that this made previously willing sources of information unwilling because of fear that the courts would not protect the reporter or the source, and reporters would violate confidences when pressed by the government.

b.   *The Supreme Court Considers the Privilege*

The first Supreme Court case to consider whether the First Amendment supports privileges claimed by reporters involved grand jury testimony. A grand jury is a group of citizens who receive evidence of alleged crimes brought to them by a prosecutor. If the grand jury believes that this evidence, uncontroverted by the accused, would justify conviction, it will return an "indictment"—a formal accusation of crime. This will set the criminal prosecution in operation. The Fifth Amendment to the United States Constitution provides that no one be brought to trial for "a capital, or otherwise infamous crime" unless first indicted by a grand jury. States need not, and some do not, use grand juries. (Where the grand jury is not used, the prosecutor instead files an "information" against the accused to get the case started.) Grand juries are able to subpoena witnesses, and all testimony before grand juries is supposed to be kept secret. In part, this confidentiality requirement is to prevent a stigma from attaching to those whom the grand jury refuses to indict.

The Supreme Court's decision in Branzburg v. Hayes, 408 U.S. 665, 1 Med.L.Rptr. 2617 (1972) was actually a decision in three cases, one of which involved a television reporter, Paul Pappas. Pappas recorded and photographed statements of Massachusetts Black Panther Party officials during a period of racial turmoil. He was allowed to enter the Party's headquarters to cover an expected police raid in return for his promise to disclose nothing he observed within. He stayed three hours, no raid occurred, and he wrote no story. He was summoned before the county grand jury but refused to answer any questions about what had taken place while he was there. When he was called a second time, he moved to quash the second summons. The motion was denied by the trial judge, who noted the absence of a statutory journalist's privilege in Massachusetts and denied the existence of a constitutional privilege. The Supreme Judicial Court of Massachusetts affirmed, and the case was appealed to the Supreme Court of the United States.

(The other two cases considered with *Pappas* involved print reporters. Paul Branzburg, a Kentucky newspaper reporter, had been called before a grand jury and directed to identify two individuals mentioned in an article he wrote about marijuana and hashish. Earl Caldwell, a *New York Times* reporter, had been subpoenaed to appear before a federal grand jury in California investigating the Black Panthers and to bring with him notes and tape recordings of interviews given to him for publication by the Panthers.)

The Supreme Court split 5–4. Justice White's opinion for the Court said, "The sole issue before us is the obligation of reporters to respond to grand jury subpoenas as other citizens do and to answer questions relevant to an investigation into the commission of a crime. . . . It is clear that the First Amendment does not invalidate every incidental burdening of the press that may result from the enforcement of civil or criminal statutes of general applicability. . . . A number of States have provided newsmen a statutory privilege of varying breadth, but the majority have not done so, and none has been provided by federal statute. Until now the only testimonial privilege for unofficial witnesses that is rooted in the Federal Constitution is the Fifth Amendment privilege against compelled self-incrimination. We are asked to create another by interpreting the First Amendment to grant newsmen a testimonial privilege that other citizens do not enjoy. This we decline to do. . . . The argument that the flow of news will be diminished by compelling reporters to aid the grand jury in a criminal investigation is not irrational, nor are the records before us silent on the matter. But we remain unclear how often and to what extent informers are actually deterred from furnishing information when newsmen are forced to testify before a grand jury."

The opinion invited legislative action: "At the federal level, Congress has freedom to determine whether a statutory newsman's privilege is necessary and desirable and to fashion standards and rules as narrow or broad as deemed necessary to deal with the evil discerned and, equally important, to refashion those rules as experience from time to time may dictate. There is also merit in leaving state legislatures free, within First Amendment limits, to fashion their own standards."

Accordingly, the Court affirmed the decision that Pappas must appear before the grand jury and made similar decisions in the cases of the print reporters.

Justice Powell, who provided the critical fifth vote for the majority, wrote a concurring opinion that was read by some as undercutting the majority opinion:

> I add this brief statement to emphasize what seems to me to be the limited nature of the Court's holding. The Court does not hold that newsmen, subpoenaed to testify before a grand jury, are without constitutional rights with respect to the gathering of news or in safeguarding their sources. Certainly, we do not hold, as suggested in Mr. Justice Stewart's dissenting opinion, that state and federal authorities are free to "annex" the news media as "an investigative arm of government." The solicitude repeatedly shown by this Court for First Amendment freedoms should be sufficient assurance against any such effort, even if one seriously believed that the media—properly free and untrammeled in the fullest sense of these terms—were not able to protect themselves.

> . . . [T]he Court states that no harassment of newsmen will be tolerated. If a newsman believes that the grand jury investigation is not being conducted in good faith he is not without remedy. Indeed, if the newsman is called upon to give information bearing only a remote and tenuous relationship to the subject of the investigation, or if he has some other reason to believe that his testimony implicates confidential source relationships without a legitimate need of law enforcement, he will have access to the court on a motion to quash and an appropriate protective order may be entered. The asserted claim to privilege should be judged on its facts by the striking of a proper balance between freedom of the press and the obligation of all citizens to give relevant testimony with respect to criminal conduct. The balance of these vital constitutional and societal interests on a case-by-case basis accords with the tried and traditional way of adjudicating such questions. . . .

> In short, the courts will be available to newsmen under circumstances where legitimate First Amendment interest require protection.

Justice Stewart, dissenting, wrote that "The Court's crabbed view of the First Amendment reflects a disturbing insensitivity to the critical role of an independent press in our society. . . . The right to gather news implies, in turn, a right to a confidential relationship between a reporter and his source."

Justice Stewart's dissent suggested three possible qualifications that might be incorporated into a qualified privilege for journalists: "[W]hen a reporter is asked to appear before a grand jury and reveal confidences, I would hold that the government must (1) show that there is probable cause to believe that the newsman had information that is clearly relevant to a specific probable violation of law; (2) demonstrate that the information sought cannot be obtained by alternative means less destructive of First Amendment rights; and (3) demonstrate a compelling and overriding interest in the information."

Outtakes. The problem of reporter's privilege arises most frequently in the context of material that has been published without attribution to a source, but the electronic media (and, less frequently, the print media) also face problems with "outtakes," parts of film or videotape that have been cut and not transmitted. The term might also refer to notes taken by a reporter that are not used in a story or even to perceptions or observations not even written down. Are government efforts to obtain this unpublished or unrecorded information different from the more conventional effort to get a reporter to identify a source of published information? Outtakes are essential when the goal is to try to judge the fairness of what was actually presented.

The issue of outtakes arose in the dispute involving "60 Minutes," the Brown & Williamson tobacco company, and Brown & Williamson's former research executive Jeffrey Wigand. Much public attention was given to CBS's decision late in 1995 not to run an interview with Wigand on advice of its legal department because of fears the network might face a "multi-billion dollar" lawsuit for influencing Wigand to violate a confidentiality agreement he had once signed with Brown & Williamson. After *The Wall Street Journal* published Mr. Wigand's accusations (from written testimony in a Mississippi lawsuit), CBS went ahead and aired its Wigand interview early in February 1996. Later that same month a New York State judge threw out a subpoena seeking outtakes and other information from CBS regarding the "60 Minutes" interview. The judge ruled that Brown & Williamson had failed to show that the information requested was "highly material" or "critical" to its lawsuit against Wigand, in part because Brown & Williamson already had sufficient evidence to prove Wigand's breach of the confidentiality agreement. New York Law Journal, Feb. 29, 1996 at 1.

Unsolicited information. The courts are even less sympathetic when unsolicited information has been thrust on the reporter. See Lewis v. United States, 517 F.2d 236 (9th Cir.1975), upholding the contempt conviction of a manager of a radio station for refusing to produce the original of a "communique" he received from an underground group that claimed responsibility for a bombing. Does this situation differ greatly from those presented in *Branzburg?*

State Protection. Although there is still no federal shield law, about half of the states now have shield laws. Journalists might have been more effective in lobbying for such shield laws had they been in agreement about whether to lobby for absolute shield laws (that would be "airtight" but difficult to "sell" to legislators) or for qualified shield laws (that would be easier to sell but would be considerably weakened by the qualifications built into them). Some journalists, believing that the First Amendment should automatically protect confidentiality despite the Supreme Court decision in *Branzburg*, maintain that seeking shield laws from legislatures would be an inappropriate recognition of the legislators' right to pass such laws. Shield laws vary in detail but generally are statutory attempts to exempt journalists from divulging certain information—usually confidential sources or the information itself.

States also may find protection for confidentiality in their own state constitutions. In O'Neill v. Oakgrove Construction, Inc., 71 N.Y.2d 521, 528 N.Y.S.2d 1, 523 N.E.2d 277, 15 Med.L.Rptr. 1219 (1988), New York State's highest court held that the Gannett Newspapers in Rochester had a qualified privilege under the state constitution and the First Amendment to decline to produce unpublished photographs of a traffic accident scene. The photographs had been sought as part of a suit by a man injured when his car slid off a roadway under construction. The newspaper photographer had taken 58 photographs, of which one was published. Note that this is an example of the outtakes problem discussed above.

c. *After Branzburg: Seeking Information From Journalists*

Criminal Trials and Shield Laws. The conflict between the Sixth Amendment rights of defendants in criminal trials and First Amendment claims to testimonial privilege is illustrated in the Farber case.

Myron Farber, a reporter for *The New York Times,* began investigating a series of mysterious deaths that had occurred several years earlier at a hospital in New Jersey. His investigations led to a series of articles and to murder indictments against a physician. During the six-month-long murder trial, the defendant's attorney had subpoenas served on the reporter and the newspaper demanding that they produce certain documents relating to interviews with witnesses at the trial. Motions to quash the subpoenas were denied, but the trial judge did order that the documents be delivered to him for *in camera* inspection. Farber and the *Times* refused. Efforts to stay the order pending appeals were denied by the state appellate courts and Justices White and Marshall.

Farber and the *Times* refused to comply and were held in civil and criminal contempt. The civil contempt involved a fine of $5,000 per day on the *Times* and a flat $1,000 on Farber, who was sentenced to jail until he complied. The criminal penalties were $100,000 on the newspaper, and $1,000 on Farber plus six months in jail. On review, the New Jersey Supreme Court affirmed, 5–2. Matter of Farber, 78 N.J. 259, 394 A.2d 330, 4 Med.L.Rptr. 1360 (1978).

The court rejected the argument that the First Amendment protected Farber's refusal because of the need to keep newsgathering and dissemination from being substantially impaired. It concluded that *Branzburg* "squarely held that no such First Amendment right exists." "Thus we do no weighing or balancing of societal interest in reaching our determination that the First Amendment does not afford appellants the privilege they claim."

The court held that the state constitutional provision affording a criminal defendant the right to compel witnesses to produce documents prevailed over the shield law. There is also a Sixth Amendment right under the U.S. Constitution to compulsory process. The Supreme Court of the United States denied *certiorari sub nom.* New York Times Co. v. New Jersey, 439 U.S. 997 (1978). Justice Brennan took no part in the decision.

Farber spent a total of 40 days in jail, and the *Times* was fined $285,000, part of which was refunded several years later when the governor of New Jersey pardoned both Farber and the *Times*. The physician was acquitted. The New Jersey Legislature subsequently strengthened its shield law by requiring more clearly that a showing of need must be made before the reporter can be required to reveal confidential information even to the trial judge in chambers, much less the litigants. The state's Supreme Court twice upheld the statute shortly thereafter.

In most confidentiality cases, it is the plaintiff or the prosecutor who seeks additional information from the journalist. *Farber* was unusual in that it was the defendant—a murder defendant at that—seeking the information. Under the Sixth Amendment, the defendant is entitled to compulsory process to seek information.

CBS, Inc. v. Superior Court, 85 Cal.App.3d 241, 149 Cal.Rptr. 421, 4 Med.L.Rptr. 1568 (1978), involved an arrangement between CBS and the Santa Clara County sheriff's department under which CBS was permitted to photograph meetings between undercover agents and two men. The meetings led to the arrest of both men for selling controlled substances, and CBS showed the arrest sequence on its program "60 Minutes." Before the criminal trial, the attorney for one defendant sought the CBS outtakes. CBS refused. The trial judge ordered the outtakes turned over to the defense.

On appeal, the court concluded that under state law, "where a criminal defendant has demonstrated a *reasonable possibility* that evidence sought to be discovered might result in his exoneration, he is entitled to its discovery." The court ordered the judge to conduct a preliminary screening of the film and to consider whether delivery of voice clips alone would satisfy the defendant's needs.

On remand, the tapes were made available to the parties. As a result, the prosecutor dropped the charges against the defendant who had sought the film. The defendant's attorney is reported to have said that the film clips showed that although the defendant was present, "he didn't participate" in the transaction, contrary to the officers' version. San Francisco Chronicle, Feb. 24, 1979 at 4.

In People v. Korkala, 99 A.D.2d 161, 472 N.Y.S.2d 310, 10 Med. L.Rptr. 1355 (1984), the state sought outtakes from an interview that interviewers from CBS's "60 Minutes" had held with the defendant. CBS had broadcast 22 minutes from interviews that were said to have lasted several hours. CBS argued that the New York shield law gave reporters an "absolute privilege" against having to turn over such information. The court disagreed on the ground that the statute covered only cases in which the source had an expectation of confidentiality. Here the defendant had spoken openly with others on the subject.

On the First Amendment issue, the court balanced and concluded that although relevance was clear, it was not yet clear that the information would actually be needed in the prosecution. That would depend on the tack taken by defendant at the trial. The court ordered that the outtakes be shown to the trial judge *in camera.* If the defense had taken a turn that made delivery relevant, then the judge could have ordered production of the relevant material.

CBS did not appeal further. It made the outtakes available to the judge, who viewed them in a CBS screening room. CBS asserted that if the judge were to order any material to be delivered to the prosecutor, CBS might again take legal action. N.Y. Times, Apr. 6, 1984, at 25.

Civil cases. When we turn to civil cases the justifications change for insisting on a reporter's testimony. Because the case is not criminal, society's interest may be less direct, and no one's freedom or life is at stake. Instead, a private person or group is suing for injury to person, property, privacy or reputation.

A qualified privilege was found in Democratic National Committee v. McCord, 356 F.Supp. 1394 (D.D.C.1973). The Committee for the Re-election of the President (President Nixon's reelection committee) was defending several suits arising out of the Watergate break-in. To obtain evidence for use in the trials, the Committee caused subpoenas to be issued against a number of journalists. On motions to quash the subpoenas, a federal court held that since all other means had not been used to obtain the material before requesting it from reporters, and since the Committee had not shown clearly that the material was relevant to the trials, the subpoenas should not be issued. In so ruling, the court discussed "the right of the press to gather and publish, and that of the public to receive, news from . . . ofttimes confidential sources." The court also noted that the suits in question were civil, not criminal, and that the media were not parties to the suits.

The courts thus adapted to civil cases the thrust of Justice Stewart's dissent in *Branzburg,* in which he contended that three conditions be met before a journalist is forced to testify or submit material, p. 1004, *supra.* A number of federal cases involving subpoenas to reporters in civil suits have followed the *McCord* approach.

The Reporter as Plaintiff. What if the reporter is a party in the case? Syndicated columnist Jack Anderson sued several officials of the Nixon administration for trying to harass him. The defendants asserted that the statute of limitations had run and denied the merits of the claims. As part of their defense, they asked plaintiff when and how he learned about the alleged harassment and also sought information on other aspects of his claims. Several of these questions required disclosure of confidential sources, but plaintiff refused to reveal them. The judge ordered Anderson to reveal the sources on the ground that they were central to the defenses being raised:

> Here the newsman is not being obliged to disclose his sources. Plaintiff's pledge of confidentiality would have remained unchallenged had he not invoked the aid of the Court seeking compensatory and punitive damages based on his claim of conspiracy. Plaintiff is attempting to use the First Amendment simultaneously as a sword and a shield. He believes he was wronged by a conspiracy that sought to retaliate against the sources and to undermine his reliability and professional standing before the public because what he said was unpopular with the conspirators. But when those he accuses seek to defend by attempting to discover who his sources were, so that they may find out what the sources knew, their version of what they told him and how they were hurt, plaintiff says this is off limits—a forbidden area of inquiry. He cannot have it both ways. Plaintiff is not a bystander in the process but a principal. He cannot ask for justice and deny it to those he accuses.

The judge rejected plaintiff's claim that the conflicting claims should be "balanced." This was "most unrealistic. Having chosen to become a litigant, the newsman is not exempt from those obligations imposed by the rule of law on all litigants." The choice was plaintiff's: reveal the sources or have the case dismissed. Anderson v. Nixon, 444 F.Supp. 1195, 3 Med.L.Rptr. 1687 (D.D.C.1978). The case was subsequently dismissed.

The Press as Defendant. One complex question that cuts across several areas we have discussed is whether media defendants in defamation cases are privileged to refuse to identify confidential sources who gave them allegedly defamatory information. The philosophy of New York Times v. Sullivan counsels that debate should be open and robust— but that the press should be liable for defamations that are deliberately or recklessly false. What if the public figure plaintiff must know the source of the story to prove that the falsehood was deliberate or reckless? On the other hand, if the plaintiff can expose confidential sources simply by the expedient of suing for libel, such sources may disappear. Is *Branzburg* relevant on this aspect of reporters' privilege?

Several courts struggled with this matter in the 1970s. (Recall that in the Judy Garland case, the newspaper was not sued.) In 1979 *Herbert*, p. 910, *supra*, shed some light on the question. Recall that the Supreme Court held that the First Amendment did not protect a journalist from having to testify about his thoughts, opinions and conclusions as he was researching and preparing a story, and about his intra-office communications with others working on the story. The Court stressed that a plaintiff operating under the *New York Times* standard had a difficult task and should be able to seek direct evidence of constitutional malice.

The Court's suggestion that relevant evidence should be available to the plaintiff would suggest that confidential sources not be protected. On the other hand, the Herbert case involved little or no potential for chilling confidential sources, because it involved only the professional journalist's thoughts and communications. The compelled revelation of confidential sources would raise a different question.

Identifying Violators of Judicial Orders. Another issue of privilege arises when a judge or grand jury wants to learn who told a reporter information that was supposed to be secret. The problem is illustrated by the case of the late William Farr, a newspaper reporter who covered the lurid Manson trial in Los Angeles. To reduce potentially prejudicial publicity in that case, the trial judge ordered the attorneys and certain others not to speak about specific phases of the case. Farr reported certain facts that he could only have learned from a person covered by the judge's order. The judge demanded that Farr identify his source despite the California privilege statute: "A publisher, editor, reporter . . . cannot be adjudged in contempt by a court . . . for refusing to disclose the source of any information procured for publication and published in a newspaper. . . ." Farr stated that the information had come from forbidden sources including two of the six attorneys. Each attorney denied having been a source. The judge again asked Farr to identify the individuals. Farr refused and was held in contempt.

The statute was held inapplicable because the legislature had no power to prohibit the court from seeking to preserve the integrity of its own operations. The legislature's efforts to immunize persons from punishment for violation of court orders violated the separation of powers. To immunize Farr "would severely impair the trial court's discharge of a constitutionally compelled duty to control its own officers. The trial court was enjoined by controlling precedent of the United States Supreme Court to take reasonable action to protect the defendants in the Manson case from the effects of prejudicial publicity." Farr v. Superior Court, 22 Cal.App.3d 60, 99 Cal.Rptr. 342, 1 Med.L.Rptr. 2545 (1971). The Supreme Court of California denied a hearing and the Supreme Court of the United States denied *certiorari*, 409 U.S. 1011 (1972).

In a later proceeding, Farr argued that a contempt citation upon him was essentially a sentence of imprisonment for life because he clearly would not comply. The court noted that an order committing a person until he complies with a court order is "coercive and not penal in nature." The purpose of this sanction is not to punish but to obtain compliance with the order. Where an individual demonstrates conclusively that the coercion will fail, the contempt power becomes penal and comes within a five-day maximum sentence set by California statute. The case was remanded to determine whether coercion could be justified. In re Farr, 36 Cal.App.3d 577, 111 Cal.Rptr. 649 (1974). Farr was released.

Disclosing Information to Other Bodies. Not only do courts ask journalists for information, so do legislatures and administrative agencies. In 1971 the House of Representatives Commerce Committee subpoenaed then-CBS president Frank Stanton, ordering him to produce portions of film shot for, but not shown on, the documentary, "The Selling of the Pentagon." When Stanton refused to give the outtakes to the Committee, it voted 25–13 to recommend that Congress issue a contempt citation. The House refused to do so.

The Justice Department in 1985 subpoenaed the three major television networks, the Cable News Network and the national news magazines to turn over all video and audio tapes and photographs (including outtakes) of the 17–day hostage crisis at Beirut International Airport. Government lawyers said the evidence they hoped to gather would be used for presentation to a grand jury that would be asked to indict the hijackers. Despite protests that the request amounted to a "fishing expedition," most of the media turned over copies of at least some of their tapes and photographs.

Department of Justice Guidelines. After *Branzburg*, the Attorney General of the United States in 1973 adopted guidelines to regulate the issuance of subpoenas to members of the news media. The main point was that, except for cooperating reporters, no subpoena could be issued to any member of the news media "without the express authorization of the Attorney General." In requesting such authorization, subordinates were told to do so in criminal cases only if there is reasonable ground to believe that a crime has occurred and that the information sought is essential to a successful investigation, particularly with respect to guilt or innocence, and only after efforts to obtain the information from alternative nonmedia sources have failed. In civil cases, the litigation must be "of substantial importance." Even subpoena authorization requests for publicly disclosed information "should be treated with care to avoid claims of harassment." All requests should be directed at limited subject matter, should cover a limited period of time, and "should avoid requiring production of a large volume of unpublished material."

After the Department of Justice in 1979 obtained records of a reporter's toll calls from the local telephone company, the press urged government attention to the problem. The result was the promulgation in 1980 of amendments to the subpoena guidelines to provide that discussions with the reporter should precede any subpoena to the telephone company where the appropriate Assistant Attorney General concludes that such disclosure would not jeopardize the investigation. Before any subpoena is issued, the "express authorization of the Attorney General" is required. Such authorization should not be requested from the Attorney General unless there is reason to believe a crime has been committed, the need is clear, and alternative investigation steps have been unsuccessfully explored. The reporter should be informed within 45 days (though that may be delayed another 45 days) and the information obtained shall be closely held to prevent unauthorized persons from learning what the records reveal. The amended guidelines, which may be altered by any successor Attorney General, are in 45 Fed.Reg. 76,436

(Nov. 19, 1980), are codified in 28 C.F.R. § 50.10, and are reprinted in 6 Med.L.Rptr. 2153 (1980).

Vanessa Leggett, a professor and freelance writer, served 168 days in prison in 2001–2002 for refusing to hand over notes, tape recordings and transcripts of interviews to a federal grand jury investigating a murder. Leggett had obtained the material during a series of interviews with a prisoner who subsequently committed suicide, leaving a note claiming responsibility for the murder. She had previously provided copies of some of the material to state investigators, subject to an agreement limiting their use and disclosure. When federal investigators sought the originals without any limit as to their use, Leggett refused and was jailed for contempt. She was released on January 4, 2002, when the grand jury's term expired.

The Fifth Circuit refused to order Leggett's release. The court expressed skepticism as to whether Leggett was a "journalist," but even assuming for purposes of its decision that she was, found that while "the strength of this journalist's privilege is at its apex in the context of civil cases where the disclosure of confidential information is at issue ... the privilege is far weaker in criminal cases, reaching its nadir in grand jury proceedings." The appellate court concluded that the privilege is "ineffectual against a grand jury subpoena absent evidence of governmental harassment or oppression," neither of which, the court asserted, had Leggett demonstrated. In re Grand Jury Subpoenas, 29 Med. L. Rptr. 2301 (5th Cir. 2001) (unpublished opinion). The Supreme Court declined to review the case. Leggett v. United States, 122 S. Ct. 1593 (2002).

Press groups disagreed sharply with the Fifth Circuit's decision, noting that there was ample evidence of "government harassment or oppression." They noted, for example, that the U.S. Attorney (the prosecutor rather than the FBI appeared to be calling the shots in this case) failed to follow the Justice Department's own guidelines for seeking information intended for publication and sought the material only after Leggett declined a request to serve as an FBI informant, the material requested concerned a suspect who was dead and who had been in police custody and therefore subject to police questioning, the prosecutor was unwilling to negotiate limits on the material sought or uses to which it would be put as state officials had, and the fact that a second grand jury met only 16 days before bringing indictments without any need for Leggett's material. Guillermo X. Garcia, The Vanessa Leggett Saga, Am. Journ. Rev., March 2002 at 20.

d. The Breach of Contract Problem: Journalists Willing to Provide Information

Cohen v. Cowles Media Co., 501 U.S. 663, 18 Med.L.Rptr. 2273 (1991), presented a quite different problem. Whereas earlier cases involved situations in which journalists wanted to protect confidential sources, *Cohen* is about a situation in which two newspapers decided to identify a source. Dan Cohen, a Republican associated with a Minnesota gubernatorial campaign, offered to provide documents about the Democratic candidate for lieutenant governor to reporters from two newspapers. Both reporters promised to keep his identity anonymous. Cohen then provided them with copies of public court records indicating that the Democratic candidate had been charged in 1969 with unlawful assembly and that she had been convicted in 1970 of petit theft (for leaving a store without paying for $6 worth of sewing materials).

The two newspapers, the *St. Paul Pioneer Press Dispatch* and the *Minneapolis Star and Tribune,* then interviewed the Democratic candidate. It turned out that the unlawful assembly charge arose out of her participation in a protest of an alleged failure to hire minority workers on municipal construction projects, and the charges were eventually dropped, and the sewing materials incident happened at a time when she was apparently emotionally distraught, and that conviction had been vacated. Both newspapers, after "consultation and debate" decided to identify Cohen as their source. Cohen sued both newspapers, alleging fraudulent misrepresentation and breach of contract.

The case took a variety of twists and turns. A jury first awarded $200,000 in compensatory damages and $500,000 in punitive damages. A state appellate court reversed the award of punitive damages, and the Minnesota Supreme Court reversed the compensatory damages award ("a contract cause of action is inappropriate for these particular circumstances."). The Supreme Court of the United States concluded that, "[T]he First Amendment does not confer on the press a constitutional right to disregard promises that would otherwise be enforced under state law," but still declined to reinstate the jury verdict awarding him the $200,000 in compensatory damages—choosing instead to remand the case to the Minnesota Supreme Court, which then held that Cohen was entitled to $200,000 in damages. Cohen v. Cowles Media Co., 479 N.W.2d 387, 19 Med.L.Rptr. 1858 (Minn.1992).

In another breach of promise case, a Minnesota resident alleged that she had agreed to be interviewed by *Glamour* magazine concerning her sexual abuse by a therapist only on the condition that she not be identified. The magazine changed her last name, but she contended that the use of her actual first name, profession and other details made her identifiable. The U.S. Court of Appeals for the 8th Circuit ruled that the plaintiff could proceed with her lawsuit: "When the promise was made not to identify plaintiff, the plain meaning of the promise was that [the free-lance writer who wrote the article] would mask the identity of the plaintiff in such a way that a reasonable reader could not identify Jill Ruzicka by factual description. . . . There is nothing vague or ambiguous about such a promise." Ruzicka v. Conde Nast Publications, Inc., 999 F.2d 1319, 21 Med.L.Rptr. 1821 (8th Cir.1993).

2. Use of Search Warrants Against the Press

Basically, law enforcement officials may choose from among three methods for obtaining relevant evidence. The first is simply to ask the person who probably has it to turn it over. The lack of formality simplifies and expedites the process. The drawback is that a possessor of information who decides not to cooperate may legally destroy or transfer possession of the material after learning that the police want it.

The second procedure is the subpoena, discussed above. Prosecutorial officials ask either the court or grand jury for authority to issue a subpoena for evidence sought in connection with an investigation, or act under delegated authority. The recipient may not legally destroy the material after being served with the subpoena. A recipient who thinks the subpoena asks something illegal may challenge it. A recipient who claims not to have the material or information being sought may make a statement to that effect under oath. It may be difficult to prove whether the person illegally destroyed the material after receiving the subpoena.

The third method, the search warrant, played the central role in a case involving *The Stanford Daily,* the campus newspaper at Stanford University. A magistrate must decide whether a police request for a search warrant establishes probable cause to believe that the material sought is at the named location. If the magistrate is persuaded, the police may execute the warrant by appearing at the specified location without prior notice and may search the premises until they find the identified material.

Police believed that *Stanford Daily* photographers had taken photographs that would aid in identifying persons who had assaulted policemen during a violent demonstration. The police obtained a search warrant and served it on the *Daily.* After the search, the *Daily* brought an action against the chief of police and other local officials, and the case, Zurcher v. Stanford Daily, 436 U.S. 547, 3 Med.L.Rptr. 2377 (1978), eventually reached the Supreme Court. Justice White wrote for the majority that valid warrants may be issued to search *any* property, and that even though the Fourth Amendment may protect the materials sought to be seized, nothing in the First Amendment bars searches of newspaper offices.

After the decision a few states enacted bans on the issuance of search warrants against the media, and Congress passed the Privacy Protection Act of 1980, making it unlawful for an official of any government to search or seize "any work product material possessed by a person reasonably believed to have a purpose to disseminate to the public a newspaper, book, broadcast, or other similar form of public communication, in or affecting interstate or foreign commerce," except in special circumstances.

Despite the protection afforded the media by the 1980 federal statute and similar provisions in state statutes, problems can still arise. Washoe County District Attorney Richard Gammick obtained search warrants from a Nevada judge to search four newsrooms in Reno looking for videotaped interviews and notes of interviews with a man who had led police on a long chase following a shooting spree in January 1999. The media objected to the searches, but Gammick said the search warrants fell under a Privacy Protection Act exception because he believed the materials would be destroyed before they could be obtained by subpoena. Gammick returned videotape to KOLO–TV after the station threatened to sue him under the Privacy Protection Act, but he did so under the condition that the tape would be preserved. The News Media & The Law, Winter 1999 at 3.

Telephone Records. The government may learn about reporters' sources or activities in ways that do not involve search warrants or subpoenas. Reporters Committee for Freedom of the Press v. American Telephone & Telegraph Co., 593 F.2d 1030, 4 Med.L.Rptr. 1177 (D.C.Cir. 1978), involved government requests for records of long distance calls charged to (but perhaps not made to or from) certain telephone numbers. Reporters charged that the First and Fourteenth Amendments required that subscribers be given notice before AT & T honored the government's request for toll-call records. The court, 2–1, concluded that balancing was not appropriate because "Government access to third-party evidence in the course of a good faith felony investigation in no sense 'abridges' plaintiffs' information-gathering activities." The possibility of bad-faith investigations (to harass reporters) did not warrant prior judicial intervention unless the reporter could establish "a clear and imminent threat of such future misconduct." The dissenter would have afforded reporters the opportunity to have prior judicial decisions made on such requests on a case-by-case basis. *Certiorari* was denied, 440 U.S. 949, 4 Med.L.Rptr. 2536 (1979), Brennan, Marshall and Stewart, JJ., dissenting.

3. IMPLICATIONS FOR JOURNALISTS

Journalists would not want to go through their careers in constant fear of a subpoena or a jail term; that sort of "chill" would seriously damage the newsgathering process and the free flow of information to the public. On the other hand, journalists handling sensitive material or dealing with confidences would be foolish not to make themselves aware of the shield law protection or lack thereof in the state(s) in which they work. Journalists sometimes will find that their sources, particularly those in official positions who are experienced at dealing with the press, are themselves familiar with the state shield laws.

Legalities aside, identifiable sources and attributable quotes strengthen good news stories. That is enough reason not to promise confidentiality to every source who asks for such a promise. Even in those instances in which reporters believe pledges of confidentiality are the only way they can get information from a source, they should be certain they have authorization from their employers before making such promises. As we have seen from the cases, reporters and their employer publications or stations are often "in it together" when a court seeks evidence in their hands. News organizations are well advised to be sure that news directors, editors, reporters and others are aware of the organization's policy on confidential sources and information before promises are made or subpoenas are served.

Although journalists can reasonably expect their employers to be supportive when subpoena problems arise, legal problems can create stress. When reporters' notes are subpoenaed, who owns the notes—the reporters or their employers? Absent any formal understanding to the contrary, employers may assert that they have "bought" them as part of the reporters' work product when the reporters endorsed their pay checks, even though the employers do not normally ask for the notes. Journalists may be more likely to feel they have "sold" only their finished stories and that the notes are still their personal property. Should it make any difference whether the reporters have taken notes in notebooks from their employers' supply rooms or in notebooks they bought themselves?

Obviously, where sensitive material is concerned, journalists should be careful about what materials they create and where they store them. Generating photocopies of confidential materials or writing memos within the news organization that might reveal or tend to reveal confidential information are examples of creating additional pieces of paper that could be subject to subpoena and should therefore not be done unnecessarily. Despite the protection against newsroom searches afforded by 1980 Congressional action, journalists may prefer to keep their most confidential notes or documents away from their offices—even away from their homes—in safe deposit boxes, for instance. This is not to suggest that paranoia should be the order of the day, and most reporters will never face such problems, but caution is in order for those handling the most sensitive information.

Computers also raise questions. If the confidential information is stored in the computer, can the journalist be compelled to create a printout? In the event of a newsroom search, could the journalist be compelled to give law enforcement agents the password?

Even where there is no subpoena or search, journalists will sometimes find themselves having to make difficult decisions about the release of unpublished (not necessarily confidential) information. Suppose, for example, a television newsperson takes several minutes of videotape at the scene of a fatal auto accident, but only a few seconds are used on the air. An insurance company, involved in subsequent litigation, asks the television station if it can buy the complete tape, because it believes the tape will show some details of the accident scene better than the official police photos. Should the station turn over the tape? Would doing so be a harmless extension of the station's usual role in disseminating the truth about events. Would the fact that the station last week turned over unaired tapes of a children's Halloween party play any part in the decision? Would accident victims or other news subjects be less cooperative with television cameramen if they thought the latter might give or sell tapes for non-journalistic purposes, including use in litigation?

These questions and others relating to the confidentiality problems are difficult to answer. Although it may at first be easy for journalists to say they would go to jail rather than to reveal a source or break a confidence, that becomes more difficult when relatives, neighbors and friends outside of journalism ask how journalists think they are "above the law" and not subject to the same obligations that other citizens have. And, although a few journalists have briefly become famous by going to jail and have written about the experience, the fact is that the experience is inconvenient and disruptive at the least and quite difficult at the worst.

The Reporters Committee for Freedom of the Press reported in March 2001 that, although the average number of subpoenas issued to media organizations has dropped since 1999, broadcasters receive a much larger share of subpoenas served than do newspapers. Television stations received 71 percent of subpoenas in the reporting period. Several of those who responded to the survey offered explanations, including the comment that, "for trial lawyers, video is more compelling." Media Law Reporter News Notes, April 10, 2001.

D. NEWSGATHERING FROM PUBLIC SOURCES

Journalists obtain news from government sources and government-controlled places the same way they obtain news of other kinds—by cultivating sources, making phone calls, asking questions, observing. Sometimes government and the people in it are reluctant sources, and the journalist can use legal help in obtaining access to the information. The recognition by the Supreme Court in *Richmond Newspapers*, p. 991, *supra*, of a First Amendment right of the public to attend trials is still an unusual recognition of a constitutional protection for newsgathering; more typically, the First Amendment has been recognized only as a right to publish news that one already possesses. Because a constitutional right of newsgathering was far from clearly established, journalists and others interested in observing the workings of government lobbied successfully in the 1960s and later for legislation at both the federal and state levels to provide access to government information.

In this section we consider access to public records, access to public meetings and access to public places. Refer to the related discussion at p. 990, *supra*, on access to courtrooms and to Chapter XIV for a discussion of access to private places.

1. Access to Public Records

a. *Freedom of Information Act*

As long as legislatures were the preeminent lawmakers in the country, persons concerned with government actions could follow the process. With the New Deal, however, vast numbers of administrative agencies and organizations emerged. Congress empowered most of them to promulgate their own internal rules, to issue substantive regulations, to enforce laws, to adjudicate some controversies and to take other action of great importance to citizens. The sheer number of regulations and orders being promulgated made it difficult to keep track of the process. In addition, some of the agencies were not open about their operations.

In 1946 Congress passed the Administrative Procedure Act to require all administrative agencies to follow certain procedures in the adoption of regulations and in their adjudicative hearings. Congress also sought to make the internal rules and procedures of agencies more readily available to the public.

For a variety of reasons, this first effort at openness was not notably successful. In 1967 Congress responded to growing criticism by adopting the first version of the Freedom of Information Act. The FOIA was amended in 1974 to expand its scope. 5 U.S.C.A. § 552.

Congress passed the Freedom of Information Reform Act in October 1986—adopting a number of changes the media had sought for years. The amendments were inserted by the Senate in an anti-drug bill and subsequently accepted by the House of Representatives. The changes reflected a compromise: Senate Republicans led by Sen. Orrin Hatch (R.– Utah) wanted amendments curtailing public access to law enforcement records and informant files, while Senate Democrats successfully negotiated changes in the Act's fee structure as part of the package. [H.R. 5484, 99th Cong., 2nd Sess., 132 Cong.Rec. S14033 (daily ed. Sept. 27, 1986)].

The FOIA applies to all federal government agencies except Congress, the courts, the government of the District of Columbia and courts martial or the military during wartime. The Act requires each agency to publish in the *Federal Register* a description of its organization and a list of its personnel through whom the public can obtain information. Each agency must also explain the procedures by which it will furnish information. Each agency must make available to the public staff manuals and internal instructions that affect members of the public, final opinions in adjudicated cases, and current indexes.

Agencies may set reasonable fees for finding and copying material requested by the public. These fees are to be waived when the information will be of benefit to the general public.

Agencies are supposed to respond quickly to requests for information. Should an agency not comply with the FOIA, a member of the public may ask a federal district court to enforce the Act. The court may review in private the material the agency wishes to withhold, but it is the agency that bears the burden of showing that the material may be withheld under one of the exemptions to the Act discussed below. If the court decides the information should be released, it can order the government to pay all costs associated with the court action. Additionally, the agency employee who authorized the improper withholding of the information may be punished.

The FOIA contains nine exemptions—categories of material that need not be made available to the public. Several of these exemptions were amended in 1974 and 1989 to require more material to be given to the public. The exemptions are:

(b) This section does not apply to matters that are—

(1)(A) specifically authorized under criteria established by an Executive order to be kept secret in the interest of national defense or foreign policy and (B) are in fact properly classified pursuant to such Executive order;

(2) related solely to the internal personnel rules and practices of an agency;

(3) specifically exempted from disclosure by statute (other than [the Privacy Act]), provided that such statute (A) requires that the matters be withheld from the public in such a manner as to leave no discretion on the issue, or (B) establishes particular criteria for withholding or refers to particular types of matters to be withheld;

(4) trade secrets and commercial or financial information obtained from a person and privileged or confidential;

(5) inter-agency or intra-agency memorandums or letters which would not be available by law to a party other than an agency in litigation with the agency;

(6) personnel and medical files and similar files the disclosure of which would constitute a clearly unwarranted invasion of personal privacy;

(7) records or information compiled for law enforcement purposes, but only to the extent that the production of such law enforcement records or information (A) could reasonably be expected to interfere with enforcement proceedings, (B) would deprive a person of a right to a fair trial or an impartial adjudication, (C) could reasonably be expected to constitute an unwarranted invasion of personal privacy, (D) could reasonably be expected to disclose the identity of a confidential source, including a State, local, or foreign agency or authority or any private institution which furnished information on a confidential basis, and, in the case of a record or information compiled by criminal law enforcement authority in the course of a criminal investigation or by an agency conducting a lawful national security intelligence investigation, information furnished by a confidential source, (E) would disclose techniques and procedures for law enforcement investigations or prosecutions, or would disclose guidelines for law enforcement investigations or prosecutions if such disclosure could reasonably be expected to risk circumvention of the law, or (F) could reasonably be expected to endanger the life or physical safety of any individual;

(8) contained in or related to examination, operating, or condition reports prepared by, on behalf of, or for the use of an agency

responsible for the regulation or supervision of financial institutions; or

(9) geological and geophysical information and data, including maps, concerning wells.

[Any reasonably segregable portion of a record must be provided to any person requesting such record after deletion of the portions that are exempt under this subsection.]

Notes and Questions

1. Notice that nothing in the original Act gave any special rights to the press as opposed to the public generally. Is that surprising?

2. What appear to be the crucial limitations of the Act?

3. Each exemption has produced its share of litigation. Those causing the most difficulty appear to be the first, third, fifth and seventh exemptions. In some cases amendments have already altered interpretations when Congress disagreed with a judicial interpretation. The procedures under the Act can get quite complicated. The Reporters Committee for Freedom of the Press and other organizations have prepared publications on how to use the Act.

The Supreme Court has had occasion to pass on several cases interpreting the Act. These are often technical in nature and not particularly useful for our purposes. For example, the Supreme Court held that names and other identifying information could be deleted from State Department documents, sought under the Freedom of Information Act, concerning Haitian nationals who had attempted to emigrate illegally to the U.S. The documents had been requested under the FOIA by a Florida lawyer, but the State Department had cited exemption six, which applies to privacy interests. United States Department of State v. Ray, 502 U.S. 164, 19 Med.L.Rptr. 1641 (1991).

4. Critics of the Act argue that compliance with it costs the government and the taxpayers too much money, that it endangers some law enforcement personnel and informants, and that it is an example of too much government, but the Act appears to have weathered most of the attempts to weaken it.

5. The broadened definition of investigatory records after the 1986 amendments covers any information compiled for law enforcement purposes and permits secrecy if public access "could reasonably be expected to cause" harm to law enforcement efforts. Previous language allowed secrecy only if disclosure "would" cause such harm.

The amendments also exempt informant files from the FOI Act's disclosure requirements, except where the government has officially confirmed that a person is an informant. Also, when revealing information about an ongoing investigation would tip off the targets, government agencies are not required to disclose.

6. The structure for fees and fee waivers included in the 1986 amendments provide that "news media," educational and scientific institutions are to be charged duplication fees for FOI Act requests only when the request exceeds 100 pages. These "non-commercial" requestors are also exempt from charges for the first two hours of search time. Commercial requesters are normally charged for both search time and duplication charges, but they can request fee waivers if they can demonstrate that disclosure is in the public interest and would "contribute significantly to public understanding of the operations or activities of the government."

Under orders from Congress, the Office of Management and Budget (OMB) issued guidelines in 1987 to help federal agencies develop fee schedules in accordance with the 1986 amendments.

Congress had not defined the term "news media," but OMB defined "Representatives of the News Media" to include persons gathering information for organizations that publish or broadcast news (defining "news" as information about current events). Examples of news media cited in the guidelines include "television or radio stations and publishers of periodicals (but only in those instances when they can qualify as disseminators of 'news') who make their products available for purchase or subscription by the general public." Would Matt Drudge, compiler of the "Drudge Report" for AOL qualify as a representative of the news media?

7. The Supreme Court of the United States held in 1989 that third party requests for law enforcement records or information about a private citizen (even one charged with or convicted of a crime) "can reasonably be expected to invade that citizen's privacy," and that the FBI's criminal identification or "rap sheet" records are therefore exempt from disclosure under the Freedom of Information Act. United States Department of Justice v. Reporters Committee for Freedom of the Press, 489 U.S. 749, 16 Med.L.Rptr. 1545 (1989).

8. The Supreme Court held in 1993 that the federal government is not entitled to presume that confidentiality—and exemption 7(d) of the Freedom of Information Act—applies to *all* sources supplying information to the FBI during a criminal investigation, but the Court said the FBI may rely on an inference of confidentiality from more narrowly defined circumstances. The Court said that a source should be deemed "confidential" if the source furnished information with the understanding that the FBI would not divulge it except to the extent it thought necessary for law enforcement purposes. United States Department of Justice v. Landano, 508 U.S. 165, 21 Med.L.Rptr. 1513 (1993).

9. In 1993 President Clinton called on all federal departments and agencies to "renew their commitment to the Freedom of Information Act." Attorney General Janet Reno rescinded the Justice Department's 1981 FOIA guidelines and instead said in an Oct. 4, 1993, memo that a "presumption of disclosure" applies to information requested under the FOIA.

10. After several years of delays, the Electronic Freedom of Information Improvement Act was enacted in 1996. It requires increased electronic access to federal agency records and makes it clear that the Freedom of Information Act applies to electronic data as well as to printed material.

In the aftermath of the Sept. 11, 2001, terrorist attacks, both federal and state governments adopted new restrictions on public—and press—access to previously open public records. Some of these new restrictions—for example, removing information on nuclear and chemical facilities, utilities, and other sensitive sites from government Web pages and federal document depositories—plainly respond to national security concerns. Other restrictions arguably do not.

For example, in October 2001, Attorney General John Ashcroft issued a memorandum to federal agencies announcing a new interpretation of the Freedom of Information Act that would permit officials to withhold information from the public on any "sound legal basis." "When you carefully consider FOIA requests and decide to withhold records," the attorney general wrote, "you can be assured that the Department of Justice will defend your decisions." Jim Oliphant, War on Terror is Reshaping Legal Landscape, The Recorder, Nov. 19, 2001, at 3.

On Nov. 1, 2001, President Bush issued an executive order allowing either a former president or the sitting president to block public access to the former president's papers. Under the order, any request for a former president's papers must not be granted until the former president and the sitting president have an opportunity to review the material and determine whether they wish to grant access. The order specifies a 90–day limit in which those reviews must take place, but either president may extend the 90–day limit. Presidential Documents, 66 Fed. Reg. 56,023 (2001).

In December 2001, 16 groups sued the Justice Department for failing to release the names and other information about the more than 1,100 people detained in the United States as part of the investigation into the terrorist attacks. The Justice Department ultimately released the names of 93 of the detainees, and places of birth, charges against them, and dates of arrest for the others still in custody. The district court denied the plaintiffs' request for discovery. Center for National Security Studies v. Department of Justice, 2002 U.S. Dist. LEXIS 2983 (D.D.C. 2002).

Many states have similarly reduced access to previously public records. Many of these new restrictions are detailed in a report from the Reporters Committee for Freedom of the Press, Homefront Confidential: How the War on Terrorism Affects Access to Information and the Public's Right to Know (Spring 2002) <www.rcfp.org>.

b. The Privacy Act

The movement toward openness in government has been tempered by growing concern about the dangers to individual privacy resulting from the growing number of records and federal agencies keeping records. In response to these concerns, Congress passed the Privacy Act of 1974. 5 U.S.C.A. § 522a. One major part of the Act permits subjects of records to see their files, obtain copies and correct inaccuracies. Individuals are not required to give the agencies any reasons for wanting to see their files. Civil actions may be brought for improper refusals to provide the file and for improper refusals to make corrections.

The part of the Act of most interest to the press, however, is the part that restricts disclosure of the contents of records unless certain conditions are met:

(b) Conditions of disclosure.—No agency shall disclose any record which is contained in a system of records by any means of communication to any person, or to another agency, except pursuant to a written request by, or with the prior written consent of, the individual to whom the record pertains, unless disclosure of the record would be—

(1) to those officers and employees of the agency which maintains the record who have a need for the record in the performance of their duties;

(2) required under section 552 of this title [FOIA];

(3) for a routine use as defined . . .;

(4) to the Bureau of the Census for purposes of planning or carrying out a census or survey or related activity . . .;

(5) to a recipient who has provided the agency with advance adequate written assurance that the record will be used solely as a statistical research or reporting record, and the record is to be transferred in a form that is not individually identifiable;

(6) to the National Archives of the United States as a record which has sufficient historical or other value to warrant its continued preservation by the United States Government, or for evaluation by the Administrator of General Services or his designee to determine whether the record has such value;

(7) to another agency or to an instrumentality of any governmental jurisdiction within or under the control of the United States for a civil or criminal law enforcement activity if the activity is authorized by law, and if the head of the agency or instrumentality has made a written request to the agency which maintains the record specifying the particular portion desired and the law enforcement activity for which the record is sought;

(8) to a person pursuant to a showing of compelling circumstances affecting the health or safety of an individual if upon such disclosure notification is transmitted to the last known address of such individual;

(9) to either House of Congress, or, to the extent of matter within its jurisdiction, any committee or subcommittee thereof, any joint committee of Congress or subcommittee of any such joint committee;

(10) to the Comptroller General, or any of his authorized representatives, in the course of the performance of the duties of the General Accounting Office; or

(11) pursuant to the order of a court of competent jurisdiction.

c. State Open Records Statutes

Although they vary a great deal, state access to information statutes exist in every state and they are frequently parallel to the federal statute by beginning with a premise that all government records should be publicly available and then listing a series of exceptions or exemptions. These statutes are generally still new enough that they are subject to frequent amendment, and journalists are well advised to obtain copies of their open records statutes for their states to see just what is available.

d. Using the Statutes

Freedom of information legislation can sometimes be helpful to a journalist—or, for that matter, any other member of the public seeking information—but that is not to say that it is frequently relied upon by the average journalist covering government. Establishing a good relationship with friendly sources inside government is a much more common way of obtaining information than using the statutes. When, however, the information would otherwise be unavailable, the reporter needs to know how to use the statute.

Freedom of information requests often have to be put into writing. Persons requesting information are advised to make their requests as simple as possible, specify the records wanted as specifically as possible, cite the statute under which the records are sought, ask to whom an appeal should be addressed should access to the records be denied and either put a dollar limit on the amount they are willing to pay or ask to be advised of the cost before the request is filled.

Even with attempts to strengthen the federal and state statutes at various times, a number of problems remain. Among those most frequently cited are (1) charging excessive fees for the records, (2) delaying the filling of requests, (3) demanding unreasonable specificity in identifying the records sought, (4) contaminating otherwise releasable records by filing them with classified information and (5) applying the exemptions too broadly.

Regrettable though it may be, it is a fact of life that the level of compliance with the state statutes is sometimes a factor of the level of government from which information is sought. Small town officials are still heard to deny access to information and to respond to mention of their states' freedom of information laws by saying, "That's just some law passed in the state capital. What are they going to do to me about it?" With few penalties built into the state laws for non-compliance and enforcement, the freedom of information legislation still has a long way to go before it becomes very helpful from the journalists' point of view.

From government's viewpoint, one problem with freedom of information legislation has been so-called "reverse FOIA" lawsuits. At issue has been whether the exemptions in the statute are mandatory or discretionary. The Supreme Court held in Chrysler Corporation v. Brown, 441 U.S. 281, 4 Med.L.Rptr. 2441 (1979), that FOIA does *not* create a private right of action to stop an agency from releasing documents covered by exemptions. A submitter of confidential business information, however, might attempt to stop disclosure by asserting that release would constitute an abuse of an agency's discretion under the Trade Secrets Act, 18 U.S.C.A. § 1905.

2. Access to Public Meetings

Guidelines for access to meetings of Congress or its committees and access to information about Congressional proceedings are prescribed initially in the Constitution. (Art. I, § 5):

> Each House may determine the Rules of its Proceedings. . . . Each House shall keep a Journal of its Proceedings, and from time to time publish the same, excepting such Parts as may in their Judgment require Secrecy; and the Yeas and Nays of the Members of either House on any question shall, at the Desire of one fifth of those Present, be entered on the Journal.

From the earliest days, sessions of the full House or Senate have usually been open to the public. Senate sessions were occasionally closed for discussion of treaties or nominations, and in the 30 years between 1945 and 1975, the Senate held 17 closed sessions, devoted usually to foreign relations or defense questions. Guide to the Congress of the United States 73 (2d ed. 1976).

Although most sessions of the full House and Senate have been open, most committee meetings were closed unless hearings were being held. Since 1970 there has been a sharp increase in open committee meetings, extending first to mark-up sessions (in which a pending bill may be approved, amended or rewritten), and later to conference committee meetings in which representatives of the two houses try to reconcile two different versions of proposed legislation. In 1975 the House and Senate voted to require open conferences unless a majority of conferees from either chamber vote in public to close a session. Can such negotiations be conducted effectively in open sessions? Should all meetings of all committees and subcommittees be open?

A different problem arises out of the conduct of Congressional investigations. The power to legislate implies the power to inquire into subjects that may require legislation, and allows Congress to conduct investigations and hold hearings. Congress may compel the attendance of witnesses and the production of documents at these hearings under threat of citation for contempt. The arguments against open hearings do not involve national security or the inhibiting effect of publicity on legislative compromise. Rather they reflect a concern for the privacy of witnesses and those whose behavior is under scrutiny. The advent of television coverage of some Congressional hearings has made this concern more significant.

Note that the Senate closed parts of the Clinton impeachment proceedings to the public in 1999—first to debate a motion to dismiss articles of impeachment, again to discuss whether to allow the prosecution to call witnesses, and again to deliberate on whether to convict the President. The latter discussion, of course, was analogous to jury deliberations in a criminal trial, but the decision in favor of closure was controversial nonetheless because of the importance of the history-making proceedings.

a.   The "Sunshine Act"

At the urging of Congressmen and Senators from Florida, which had had good experience with its "Sunshine Law," Congress in 1976 passed a federal "Government in the Sunshine Act." 5 U.S.C.A. § 552b. The statement of purpose accompanying the Act declares that "the public is entitled to the fullest practicable information regarding the decision-making processes of the Federal Government." The Act seeks to "provide the public with such information while protecting the rights of individuals and the ability of the Government to carry out its responsibilities."

Essentially, the Act provides that all federal agencies headed by boards of two or more persons appointed by the President—approximately 50 agencies—must hold "every portion of every meeting" open to the public unless there is a valid reason for closure. Adequate advance notice must be given of each meeting. If a meeting is closed because it falls within one of the 10 exemptions to be noted, the agency must make public a transcript or minutes of all parts of the meeting that do not contain exempt material. Meetings may be closed only after a publicly recorded vote of a majority of the full membership of the agency.

The exemptions apply where the agency "properly determines" that a portion of the meeting "is likely to" result in the disclosure of specified information. The exemptions include verbatim copies of several FOIA exemptions—(1) involving national defense or foreign policy; (2) involving internal rules and practices of the agency; (3) matters specifically exempted from disclosure by another statute; (4) trade secrets; (7) law enforcement investigatory records; and (8) involving financial institutions. In addition, another exemption tracks closely the "clearly unwarranted invasion of personal privacy" language of the sixth exemption of the FOIA. Given the similar goals of the two statutes, it is not surprising that they contain similar exemptions.

In addition, the Sunshine Act contains the following summarized exemptions not found in the FOIA:

(5) disclosures that "involve accusing any person of a crime, or formally censuring any person;"

(9) "premature disclosures" involving agencies that regulate currencies, securities, commodities, or financial institutions, where the disclosure would be likely to (i) lead to "significant financial speculation" in these items or (ii) "significantly endanger the financial stability of any financial institution" or where the disclosure would be likely to "significantly frustrate implementation of a proposed agency action."

(10) information concerning an agency's issuance of a subpoena or its participation in a civil action or proceeding.

b.   *State Open Meetings Statutes*

Clearly, less governmental business is conducted by the state legislature than by the multitude of agencies created by the legislature or by the executive branch under legislative authorization. In an effort to bring these agencies and their decision-making processes under public scrutiny many state legislatures have adopted "open meeting" or "sunshine" laws. These statutes and their enforcement provisions vary greatly. Some statutes provide that actions improperly taken in closed meetings can be declared null and void. Journalists generally favor fines or other penalties for public officials who disregard the open meetings statutes.

3.   ACCESS TO PUBLIC PLACES

In addition to keeping records and holding meetings, governments also control access to their own buildings and grounds and sometimes to privately-owned property as well. No general legislation covers these situations. Instead, each has been handled under regulations issued by the person in control or by specific governmental departments such as the Bureau of Prisons.

For example, in 1974 President Ford excluded all reporters from mingling with guests at White House receptions. In 1975 he announced new rules under which a small pool of reporters, carrying only notebooks, might circulate at such events "with the understanding that the pool reporters will respect the privacy of personal communications between myself or Mrs. Ford and our guests." Editor & Publisher, Sept. 13, 1975 at 15.

In 1979, when President Carter took a steamer trip down the Mississippi River, he set rules for reporters who wished to accompany him: that the White House must approve all photographs, that no photos be bought from tourists, and that national organizations not distribute photos taken by local photographers along the way. As a result, several organizations refused to send their staffs on the trip. New York Times, Aug. 15, 1979 at A18.

On Oct. 25, 1983, the United States began a military operation on the island nation of Grenada. Press representatives were excluded from entry to the island until October 27, when a limited number of reporters were transported to the island by military aircraft. By November 7 all travel restrictions had been lifted and the press had unlimited access to the island. After conditions had returned to normal, Larry Flynt, publisher of *Hustler* magazine, sued the Secretary of Defense and others for declaratory and injunctive relief. Damages were not sought. The district judge granted a government motion to dismiss the case on the ground of mootness. Because the district court's opinion had also discussed the merits and had dismissed the complaint with prejudice, the court vacated that opinion and ordered the dismissal solely on the ground of mootness. Flynt v. Weinberger, 762 F.2d 134, 11 Med.L.Rptr. 2118 (D.C.Cir.1985). The request for injunctive relief was clearly moot because the events had passed. The request for declaratory relief was also moot because the complaint was addressed solely to the constitutionality of the ban in Grenada. There was no "reasonable expectation" that the Grenada controversy would recur.

Judge Edwards, concurring, asserted that the court had no occasion to consider "whether it is unconstitutional for the government to ban the press from covering military actions where the sole or principal justification offered by the government is the safety of the press (and especially where an allegation is made that the government's actual motivation is to prevent unfavorable press coverage which might influence public opinion)." Because that issue was not encompassed in the complaint, there was no need to "decide whether this issue, if properly raised, would be moot."

After the outcry over the episode, the Defense Department created a panel under Maj. Gen. Winant Sidle to consider alternatives. That panel proposed, and the Defense Department put into effect, a limited pool to cover the early stages of surprise military operations. The Defense Department picks the organizations to participate in the pool, but the organizations pick the specific reporters.

When U.S. troops were sent to Saudi Arabia in 1990 following Iraq's invasion of Kuwait, the complaints about the pool arrangements surfaced again. Two pools were called nearly a week after the first U.S. troops arrived. One went to Saudi Arabia and the other pool members were sent to U.S. Navy ships in the area. The Secretary of Defense attributed the delay in sending the pools to Saudi objections to the media presence. Editor & Publisher, Aug. 18, 1990 at 11.

In the months leading up to the start of the air war in 1991, the Pentagon came up with new regulations for combat pool reporters, including a requirement that the reporters pass a physical fitness test involving push-ups, sit-ups and a mile-and-a-half run. Requirements were adjusted according to age and sex, and reportedly few journalists had trouble with them. Editor & Publisher, Jan. 12, 1991 at 8. During the air war there were numerous press complaints about required "security review" of their stories and about allegations that their military escorts took them to unnewsworthy locations and sometimes picked the soldiers to be interviewed. There were also complaints that pool reports—particularly reports by print media reporters—sometimes took hours to be reviewed, even though broadcast journalists sometimes were able to send live transmissions with little or no interference from their military escorts.

Press concerns over problems in war coverage continued long after the war ended. After eight months of talks with news organizations, the Pentagon issued a set of principles to give journalists greater access to military operations than they had in the Persian Gulf war. The guidelines say journalists "will be provided access to all major military units." The news organizations and the Pentagon could not agree on the critical issue of the military's "security review" of articles and broadcasts. New York Times, May 22, 1992 at A–15.

Access and Terrorism. Terrorist activities and other crime events that unfold over a period of time present special problems with regard to the conflict between efforts of the media to cover the breaking news live and the desire of law enforcement officials to prevent the terrorists or other criminals from learning, through media reports, about law enforcement actions. The problem is, of course, aggravated when there are hostages. A prime example is the April 1999 school shootings in Littleton, Colo. During the hours in which that drama was unfolding, some students hiding in the school spoke by cell phone to the local television station. The television station and CNN broadcast the conversations live, thereby revealing students' hiding places—without knowing whether the shooters, like other students in the school, might be hearing the broadcasts over classroom television sets. Criticism of the media resulted. A CNN executive said CNN already has rules about such instances. "our primary guideline," he said, "is don't do anything that could endanger human life or human safety, and don't endanger an ongoing law enforcement effort." The infamous chase of O.J. Simpson on the California freeways, and the 10–hour siege in 1982 at the Washington Monument, where Norman Mayer had driven a truck supposedly loaded with explosives, are other examples of multi-hour events that attracted widespread, live media attention and raised issues about what Simpson or Mayer might learn from media.

Access to Police and Fire Scenes. As for local situations, almost all states have statutes that authorize police to bar access and provide that failure to obey an order to remain outside is punishable as failing to obey lawful police orders. Press passes that frequently permit journalists to cross police or fire lines at the scene of an accident, crime, or tragedy are typically subject to the control of the police and do not give the reporter a privilege to disregard police orders directed to them.

Access to Prisons. In 1974 the Supreme Court decided two companion cases involving efforts to obtain information from inmates confined in prisons. Pell v. Procunier, 417 U.S. 817, 1 Med.L.Rptr. 2379 (1974), involved a ban on press interviews with named inmates in the California prison system. Saxbe v. Washington Post Co., 417 U.S. 843, 1 Med. L.Rptr. 2314 (1974) involved a similar ban in the federal prison system. The Court concluded in *Pell* that the security and penological considerations of incarceration were sufficient to justify rejection of the inmates' claims that the interview ban violated their First Amendment rights.

Justice Stewart, writing for the Court in *Pell* and in *Saxbe,* then turned to the claims raised by the press. He noted that "this regulation is not part of an attempt by the State to conceal the conditions in its prisons or to frustrate the press' investigation and reporting of those conditions." Reporters could visit the institutions and "speak about any subject to any inmates whom they might encounter." Interviews with inmates selected at random were also permitted and both the press and public could take tours through the prisons. "In short, members of the press enjoy access to California prisons that is not available to other members of the public." Indeed, the only apparent restriction was the one being challenged.

Relying in part on the logic of *Branzburg,* Justice Stewart said that ". . . [N]ewsmen have no constitutional right of access to prisons or their inmates beyond that afforded the general public." Four justices dissented.

A few years later the Supreme Court returned to the prison question in a slightly different context in Houchins v. KQED, Inc., 438 U.S. 1, 3 Med.L.Rptr. 2521 (1978). A suicide had occurred at a jail in Santa Rita, Calif. KQED, licensee of a television station in San Francisco, reported the story and quoted a psychiatrist as saying that conditions at part of the jail were responsible for the illnesses of some prisoners there. Earlier, a federal judge had ruled that conditions at part of the jail constituted cruel and unusual punishment. Houchins, the county sheriff, refused to admit a KQED camera crew to the jail, and no public tours of the jail were permitted.

KQED and the NAACP filed suit under 42 U.S.C.A. § 1983 claiming violation of their First Amendment rights. The NAACP claimed that information about the jail was essential to permit public debate on jail conditions in the county. After the suit was filed, the sheriff permitted monthly tours. Although he barred cameras and tape recorders, he allowed several reporters, including one from KQED, to tour. Tour members "were not permitted to interview inmates and inmates were generally removed from view."

KQED argued that the tours were unsatisfactory because advance scheduling prevented timely access and because photography and interviewing were barred. The sheriff defended his policy on grounds of "inmate privacy," the danger of creating "jail celebrities," and the concern that there would be a disruption of jail operations.

Chief Justice Burger announced the judgment of the Supreme Court and delivered an opinion joined by Justices White and Rehnquist. In it, he wrote, "The media are not a substitute for or an adjunct of government, and like the courts, they are 'ill-equipped' to deal with problems of prison administration. . . . The public importance of conditions in penal facilities and the media's role of providing information afford no basis for reading into the Constitution a right of the public or the media to enter these institutions, with camera equipment, and take moving and still pictures of inmates for broadcast purposes. This Court has never intimated a First Amendment guarantee of a right of access to all sources of information within government control."

Access to Executions. Questions sometimes arise about media access to executions. Phil Donahue sued to videotape and show the 1994 execution of David Lawson, a North Carolina convict who wanted his execution to be televised. The Supreme Court of the United States ultimately denied the request. Los Angeles Times, June 17, 1994 at F–2. Later in the year, an Ohio judge said he wanted television to show the execution of a convicted double murderer to show that "swift and certain punishment" awaits criminals. Broadcasting, Dec. 5, 1994 at 89.

Access to Voting Sites. Public concerns have been raised periodically about early network television predictions of winners on election days. Part of the fear was that, because of different time zones, predictions from the East would affect voting in the West. A law against such predictions would clearly be a prior restraint, but 24 states enacted laws regulating exit polling—thus trying to solve the problem through a denial of access to the areas immediately surrounding the voting places. The networks and other media organizations challenged such statutes. In Daily Herald Co. v. Munro, 838 F.2d 380, 14 Med.L.Rptr. 2332 (9th Cir.1988), the court of appeals ruled unanimously that exit polling is a form of speech protected by the First Amendment, not only because the broadcasting of results is speech, but because conducting the polls requires discussion between pollsters and voters. Federal courts in other jurisdictions have also blocked enforcement of exit polling laws. News Media & The Law, Summer 1988 at 51. Lyle Denniston, however, pointed out that the Supreme Court's decision in Burson v. Freeman, 504 U.S. 191, 20 Med.L.Rptr. 1137 (1992), upholding a Tennessee law barring campaigning within 100 feet of the entrance to any polling place could lead to laws banning others in the same area. Says Denniston, "Politicians would invite constitutional trouble if they persuaded legislatures to put limits on press activity near polling places. But the Supreme Court's ruling in the Tennessee case suggests an alternative: passing laws to ban everyone but voters from the 'free zone' around the polls." "Are Exit Polls an Endangered Species?," Washington Journalism Review, Sept. 1992 at 50.

4. DISCRIMINATORY ACCESS TO INFORMATION

Our focus has been on the question of whether any statute or constitutional provision requires unwilling government officials to reveal information or to permit the press or public to gather information from government files, meetings, or areas under government control. (Occasionally, a statute like the Privacy Act bars willing officials from supplying information.) In such a situation, government officials want nobody to learn certain information.

A quite different question arises when government officials are willing to part with information that they are not required to divulge—but want to discriminate among the prospective gatherers. The government's interest in this situation is no longer that the material should remain confidential or that secrecy is needed, because the official is quite prepared to divulge the information. The claim of government secrecy has been replaced by the desire of a government official to play favorites in the disclosure process, either for personal or political reasons.

Reporters have no right to force unwilling private persons to reveal information. If the private sources do decide to speak, there is no reason why they cannot sell their stories to the highest bidders or give them first to reporters who are close friends. But government traditionally must not behave in a discriminatory fashion. Even though government officials may not be required by statute or constitution to reveal certain information, they do not have unlimited control over the method of dissemination.

The starting point in general is that unless an official can demonstrate some reason for treating two apparently similar persons differently, the one who is being treated less well is not receiving equal protection of the laws. Notice that this constitutional protection in the Fourteenth Amendment applies broadly to all government action. If a government welfare program were arbitrarily to pay more money to redheads than to other recipients, the others would be able to claim a denial of equal protection.

Not all distinctions are invidious. When press cards must be limited for some reasons, some government agencies may prefer media organizations that regularly cover the situations in which the cards will be needed. For example, if media representatives need press cards to get through police lines at emergencies, the police might give cards to media that regularly cover such events but not give cards to specialized newspapers or magazines that do not. Drawing these lines is sometimes difficult. The situation is explored in Los Angeles Free Press, Inc. v. City of Los Angeles, 9 Cal.App.3d 448, 88 Cal.Rptr. 605 (1970), certiorari denied 401 U.S. 982 (1971), Justices Black, Douglas and Brennan dissenting.

Sometimes gender differences between reporters have been asserted to justify unequal treatment. The question of admitting women sports reporters to men's locker rooms went to court when the New York Yankees refused to allow them in after games. (This was not a case of private discrimination because Yankee Stadium is located on property owned by the city and thus involved governmental action.) The judge ordered that the women be admitted when the men were admitted. The players' privacy could be protected in less restrictive ways than by totally excluding women reporters. "The other two interests asserted by defendants, maintaining the status of baseball as a family sport and conforming to traditional notions of decency and propriety, are clearly too insubstantial to merit serious consideration." Ludtke v. Kuhn, 461 F.Supp. 86, 4 Med.L.Rptr. 1625 (S.D.N.Y.1978).

Sometimes different treatment may be based on characteristics of the individual. For example, in Sherrill v. Knight, 569 F.2d 124, 3 Med.L.Rptr. 1514 (D.C.Cir.1977), Sherrill, Washington correspondent for *The Nation,* had credentials for the House and Senate press galleries but was denied a White House press pass because of Secret Service objections. He was said to be a security risk because he had assaulted the press secretary to the governor of Florida and also faced assault charges in Texas.

The Secret Service had been ordered by the trial court to formulate "narrow and specific" standards for deciding who posed a sufficient danger to the President to be denied a press card. Security officials were the appellants in the court of appeals.

The court recognized that the safety of a President was a compelling, indeed overwhelming, interest that would justify restrictions on a reporter's access to the White House, but it said that simply telling the reporter that he was barred "for reasons of security" did not meet the procedural safeguards that were required. The court ordered the Secret Service to "publish or otherwise make publicly known the actual standard employed in determining whether an otherwise eligible journalist will obtain a White House pass," but did not require the "detailed articulation" the trial judge would have required. It is enough if the Service is guided by the standard of whether the applicant "presents a potential source of physical danger . . . so serious as to justify his exclusion." In addition, a reporter who is barred must get notice of the facts the Service is relying on and have a chance to rebut them.

Occasionally, the basis for the different treatment is to be found in the nature of the media involved. Some states have barred journalists with tape recorders from legislative chambers, though they have allowed reporters to use pencil and pad. These limits, which have rarely been challenged, have usually been upheld.

Television has presented special problems. Earlier in this chapter, we considered the question of television cameras in courtrooms. Television has also raised questions in connection with the coverage of executions. In Garrett v. Estelle, 556 F.2d 1274, 2 Med.L.Rptr. 2265 (5th Cir.1977), certiorari denied 438 U.S. 914 (1978), the court upheld Texas' refusal to allow cameras or tape recorders into the execution chamber.

The state was willing to allow press pool reporters into the chamber and to permit other reporters to view the events over simultaneous closed-circuit television. The court held, following *Pell* and *Saxbe*, that "the first amendment does not accompany the press where the public may not go." There was no public right to entry or to film the event.

The final argument was that Texas had already chosen to make executions public by televising them over a closed circuit. Texas responded that legislation closing executions had already been upheld, Holden v. Minnesota, 137 U.S. 483 (1890), and that the limited televising of the execution should not be equated with making the event public. The court agreed that the closed circuit television was for those allowed to be present and should not be used to justify opening the event to the public.

Because Texas executes more people (more than 200 between 1976 and 2000) than any other state, it continues to be a focal point for discussions about the advisability of televising executions. Opponents suggest that such a practice would be the worst kind of reality television—voyeurism at its extreme. Some proponents of the death penalty favor televising because they believe it would tend to deter criminals from committing crimes. Some opponents of the death penalty favor televising because they believe it might persuade more people to oppose the death penalty. Legally, however, conventional thought is that the prison systems do not wish to permit television coverage, and there is no First Amendment reading that would obligate them to do so. Austin American–Statesman, Oct. 9, 2000 at E1.

A federal court held that media organizations who had wanted to film or broadcast live over the Internet the execution of Oklahoma City bomber Timothy McVeigh failed to demonstrate that the federal statute prohibiting such televising of federal executions is unconstitutional. The court held that because the statute is content-neutral and is supported by substantial governmental interest, it is not unreasonable. The Entertainment Network and Liveontheweb.com wanted to show the execution. Entertainment Network Inc. v. Lappin, U.S. District Court (S.D.Ind.), 29 Med.L.Rptr. 1769 (2001).

Televising Congress. The House of Representatives first permitted television coverage of its proceedings in 1979 and the Senate in 1986, and since then, live coverage of Congressional proceedings has become a staple on C–SPAN. Criticism has been directed at the rule that requires the government employees who operate the cameras to show only the persons speaking (rather than showing empty seats or inattentive members of Congress), but the rule was a condition of the permission for coverage. The house approved a "sunshine rule" in 1995 requiring all committee meetings to remain open to the public and media unless the entire committee votes for closure because of national security or ethical issues. Recall that the Senate closed its session while debating the impeachment of President Clinton in 1999.

Appendix A

THE CONSTITUTION OF THE UNITED STATES OF AMERICA

We the People of the United States, in Order to form a more perfect Union, establish Justice, insure domestic Tranquility, provide for the common defence, promote the general Welfare, and secure the Blessings of Liberty to ourselves and our Posterity, do ordain and establish this Constitution for the United States of America.

ARTICLE I.

SECTION 1. All legislative Powers herein granted shall be vested in a Congress of the United States, which shall consist of a Senate and House of Representatives.

SECTION 2. The House of Representatives shall be composed of Members chosen every second Year by the People of the several States, and the Electors in each State shall have the Qualifications requisite for Electors of the most numerous Branch of the State Legislature.

No Person shall be a Representative who shall not have attained to the Age of twenty five Years, and been seven Years a Citizen of the United States, and who shall not, when elected, be an inhabitant of that State in which he shall be chosen.

Representatives and direct Taxes shall be apportioned among the several States which may be included within this Union, according to their respective Numbers, which shall be determined by adding to the whole Number of free Persons, including those bound to Service for a Term of Years, and excluding Indians not taxed, three fifths of all other Persons. The actual Enumeration shall be made within three Years after the first Meeting of the Congress of the United States, and within every subsequent Term of ten Years, in such Manner as they shall by Law direct. The Number of Representatives shall not exceed one for every thirty Thousand, but each State shall have at Least one Representative; and until such enumeration shall be made, the State of New Hampshire shall be entitled to chuse three, Massachusetts eight, Rhode Island and Providence Plantations one, Connecticut five, New York six, New Jersey four, Pennsylvania eight, Delaware one, Maryland six, Virginia ten, North Carolina five, South Carolina five, and Georgia three.

When vacancies happen in the Representation from any State, the Executive Authority thereof shall issue Writs of Election to fill such Vacancies.

The House of Representatives shall chuse their Speaker and other Officers; and shall have the sole Power of Impeachment.

SECTION 3. The Senate of the United States shall be composed of two Senators from each State, chosen by the Legislature thereof, for six Years; and each Senator shall have one Vote.

Immediately after they shall be assembled in Consequence of the first Election, they shall be divided as equally as may be into three Classes. The Seats of the Senators of the first Class shall be vacated at the Expiration of the second Year, of the second Class at the Expiration of the fourth Year, and of the third Class at the Expiration of the sixth Year, so that one third may be chosen every second Year; and if Vacancies happen by Resignation, or otherwise, during the Recess of the Legislature of any State, the Executive thereof may make temporary Appointments until the next Meeting of the Legislature, which shall then fill such Vacancies.

No Person shall be a Senator who shall not have attained to the Age of thirty Years, and been nine Years a Citizen of the United States, and who shall not, when elected, be an Inhabitant of that State for which he shall be chosen.

The Vice President of the United States shall be President of the Senate, but shall have no Vote, unless they be equally divided.

The Senate shall chuse their other Officers, and also a President pro tempore, in the Absence of the Vice President, or when he shall exercise the Office of President of the United States.

The Senate shall have the sole Power to try all Impeachments. When sitting for that Purpose, they shall be on Oath or Affirmation. When the President of the United States is tried the Chief Justice shall preside: And no Person shall be convicted without the Concurrence of two thirds of the Members present.

Judgment in Cases of Impeachment shall not extend further than to removal from Office, and disqualification to hold and enjoy any Office of honor, Trust, or Profit under the United States: but the Party convicted shall nevertheless be liable and subject to Indictment, Trial, Judgment, and Punishment, according to Law.

SECTION 4. The Times, Places and Manner of holding Elections for Senators and Representatives, shall be prescribed in each State by the Legislature thereof; but the Congress may at any time by Law make or alter such Regulations, except as to the Places of chusing Senators.

The Congress shall assemble at least once in every Year, and such Meeting shall be on the first Monday in December, unless they shall by Law appoint a different Day.

SECTION 5. Each House shall be the Judge of the Elections, Returns, and Qualifications of its own Members, and a Majority of each shall constitute a Quorum to do Business; but a smaller Number may adjourn from day to day, and may be authorized to compel the Attendance of absent Members, in such Manner, and under such Penalties as each House may provide.

Each House may determine the Rules of its Proceedings, punish its Members for disorderly Behaviour, and, with the Concurrence of two thirds, expel a Member.

Each House shall keep a Journal of its Proceedings, and from time to time publish the same, excepting such Parts as may in their Judgment require Secrecy; and the Yeas and Nays of the Members of either House on any question shall, at the Desire of one fifth of those Present, be entered on the Journal.

Neither House, during the Session of Congress, shall, without the Consent of the other, adjourn for more than three days, nor to any other Place than that in which the two Houses shall be sitting.

SECTION 6. The Senators and Representatives shall receive a Compensation for their Services, to be ascertained by Law, and paid out of the Treasury of the United States. They shall in all Cases, except Treason, Felony and Breach of the Peace, be privileged from Arrest during their Attendance at the Session of their respective Houses, and in going to and returning from the same; and for any Speech or Debate in either House, they shall not be questioned in any other Place.

No Senator or Representative shall, during the Time for which he was elected, be appointed to any civil Office under the Authority of the United States, which shall have been created, or the Emoluments whereof shall have been encreased during such time; and no Person holding any Office under the United States, shall be a Member of either House during his Continuance in Office.

SECTION 7. All Bills for raising Revenue shall originate in the House of Representatives; but the Senate may propose or concur with amendments as on other Bills.

Every Bill which shall have passed the House of Representatives and the Senate, shall, before it becomes a Law, be presented to the President of the United States; If he approve he shall sign it, but if not he shall return it, with his Objections to that House in which it shall have originated, who shall enter the Objections at large on their Journal, and proceed to reconsider it. If after such Reconsideration two thirds of that House shall agree to pass the Bill, it shall be sent, together with the Objections, to the other House, by which it shall likewise be reconsidered, and if approved by two thirds of that House, it shall become a Law. But in all such Cases the Votes of both Houses shall be determined by Yeas and Nays, and the Names of the Persons voting for and against the Bill shall be entered on the Journal of each House respectively. If any Bill shall not be returned by the President within ten Days (Sunday excepted) after it shall have been presented to him, the Same shall be a Law, in like Manner as if he had signed it, unless the Congress by their Adjournment prevent its Return, in which Case it shall not be a Law.

Every Order, Resolution, or Vote to which the Concurrence of the Senate and House of Representatives may be necessary (except on a question of Adjournment) shall be presented to the President of the

United States; and before the Same shall take Effect, shall be approved by him, or being disapproved by him, shall be repassed by two thirds of the Senate and House of Representatives, according to the Rules and Limitations prescribed in the Case of a Bill.

SECTION 8. The Congress shall have Power To lay and collect Taxes, Duties, Imposts and Excises, to pay the Debts and provide for the common Defence and general Welfare of the United States; but all Duties, Imposts and Excises shall be uniform throughout the United States;

To borrow Money on the credit of the United States;

To regulate Commerce with foreign Nations, and among the several States, and with the Indian Tribes;

To establish an uniform Rule of Naturalization, and uniform Laws on the subject of Bankruptcies throughout the United States;

To coin Money, regulate the Value thereof, and of foreign Coin, and fix the Standard of Weights and Measures;

To provide for the Punishment of counterfeiting the Securities and current Coin of the United States;

To establish Post Offices and post Roads;

To promote the Progress of Science and useful Arts, by securing for limited Times to Authors and Inventors the exclusive Right to their respective Writings and Discoveries;

To constitute Tribunals inferior to the supreme Court;

To define and punish Piracies and Felonies committed on the high Seas, and Offences against the Law of Nations;

To declare War, grant Letters of Marque and Reprisal, and make Rules concerning Captures on Land and Water;

To raise and support Armies, but no Appropriation of Money to that Use shall be for a longer Term than two Years;

To provide and maintain a Navy;

To make Rules for the Government and Regulation of the land and naval Forces;

To provide for calling forth the Militia to execute the Laws of the Union, suppress Insurrections and repel Invasions;

To provide for organizing, arming, and disciplining, the Militia, and for governing such Part of them as may be employed in the Service of the United States, reserving to the States respectively, the Appointment of the Officers, and the Authority of training the Militia according to the discipline prescribed by Congress;

To exercise exclusive Legislation in all Cases whatsoever, over such District (not exceeding ten Miles square) as may, by Cession of particular States, and the Acceptance of Congress, become the Seat of the Government of the United States, and to exercise like Authority over all Places purchased by the Consent of the Legislature of the State in which the Same shall be, for the Erection of Forts, Magazines, Arsenals, dock-Yards, and other needful Buildings;—And

To make all Laws which shall be necessary and proper for carrying into Execution the foregoing Powers, and all other Powers vested by this Constitution in the Government of the United States, or in any Department or Officer thereof.

SECTION 9. The Migration or Importation of such Persons as any of the States now existing shall think proper to admit, shall not be prohibited by the Congress prior to the Year one thousand eight hundred and eight, but a Tax or duty may be imposed on such Importation, not exceeding ten dollars for each Person.

The Privilege of the Writ of Habeas Corpus shall not be suspended, unless when in Cases of Rebellion or Invasion the public Safety may require it.

No Bill of Attainder or ex post facto Law shall be passed.

No Capitation, or other direct, Tax shall be laid, unless in Proportion to the Census or Enumeration herein before directed to be taken.

No Tax or Duty shall be laid on Articles exported from any State.

No Preference shall be given by any Regulation of Commerce or Revenue to the Ports of one State over those of another; nor shall Vessels bound to, or from, one State, be obliged to enter, clear, or pay Duties in another.

No Money shall be drawn from the Treasury, but in Consequence of Appropriations made by Law; and a regular Statement and Account of the Receipts and Expenditures of all public Money shall be published from time to time.

No Title of Nobility shall be granted by the United States: And no Person holding any Office of Profit or Trust under them, shall, without the Consent of the Congress, accept of any present, Emolument, Office, or Title, of any kind whatever, from any King, Prince or foreign State.

SECTION 10. No State shall enter into any Treaty, Alliance, or Confederation; grant Letters of Marque and Reprisal; coin Money; emit Bills of Credit; make any Thing but gold and silver Coin a Tender in Payment of Debts; pass any Bill of Attainder, ex post facto Law, or Law impairing the Obligation of Contracts, or grant any Title of Nobility.

No State shall, without the Consent of the Congress, lay any Imposts or Duties on Imports or Exports, except what may be absolutely necessary for executing its inspection Laws: and the net Produce of all Duties and Imposts, laid by any State on Imports or Exports, shall be for the Use of the Treasury of the United States; and all such Laws shall be subject to the Revision and Controul of the Congress.

No State shall, without the Consent of Congress, lay any Duty of Tonnage, keep Troops, or Ships of War in time of Peace, enter into any Agreement or Compact with another State, or with a foreign Power, or engage in War, unless actually invaded, or in such imminent Danger as will not admit of delay.

ARTICLE II.

SECTION 1. The executive Power shall be vested in a President of the United States of America. He shall hold his Office during the Term of four Years, and, together with the Vice President, chosen for the same Term, be elected, as follows

Each State shall appoint, in such Manner as the Legislature thereof may direct, a Number of Electors, equal to the whole Number of Senators and Representatives to which the State may be entitled in the Congress: but no Senator or Representative, or Person holding an Office of Trust or Profit under the United States, shall be appointed an Elector.

The Electors shall meet in their respective States, and vote by Ballot for two Persons, of whom one at least shall not be an Inhabitant of the same State with themselves. And they shall make a List of all the Persons voted for, and of the Number of Votes for each; which List they shall sign and certify, and transmit sealed to the Seat of the Government of the United States, directed to the President of the Senate. The President of the Senate shall, in the Presence of the Senate and House of Representatives, open all the Certificates, and the Votes shall then be counted. The Person having the greatest Number of Votes shall be the President, if such Number be a Majority of the whole Number of Electors appointed; and if there be more than one who have such Majority, and have an equal Number of Votes, then the House of Representatives shall immediately chuse by Ballot one of them for President; and if no Person have a Majority, then from the five highest on the List the said House shall in like Manner chuse the President. But in chusing the President, the Votes shall be taken by States, the Representation from each State having one Vote; a quorum for this Purpose shall consist of a Member or Members from two thirds of the States, and a Majority of all the States shall be necessary to a Choice. In every Case, after the Choice of the President, the Person having the greatest Number of Votes of the Electors shall be the Vice President. But if there should remain two or more who have equal Votes, the Senate shall chuse from them by Ballot the Vice President.

The Congress may determine the Time of chusing the Electors, and the Day on which they shall give their Votes; which Day shall be the same throughout the United States.

No Person except a natural born Citizen, or a Citizen of the United States, at the time of the Adoption of this Constitution, shall be eligible to the Office of President; neither shall any Person be eligible to that Office who shall not have attained to the Age of thirty five Years, and been fourteen Years a Resident within the United States.

In Case of the Removal of the President from Office, or of his Death, Resignation, or Inability to discharge the Powers and Duties of the said Office, the Same shall devolve on the Vice President, and the Congress may by Law provide for the Case of Removal, Death, Resignation or Inability, both of the President and Vice President, declaring what Officer shall then act as President, and such Officer shall act accordingly, until the Disability be removed, or a President shall be elected.

The President shall, at stated Times, receive for his Services, a Compensation, which shall neither be encreased nor diminished during the Period for which he shall have been elected, and he shall not receive within that Period any other Emolument from the United States, or any of them.

Before he enter on the Execution of his Office, he shall take the following Oath or Affirmation:—"I do solemnly swear (or affirm) that I will faithfully execute the Office of President of the United States, and will to the best of my Ability, preserve, protect and defend the Constitution of the United States."

SECTION 2. The President shall be Commander in Chief of the Army and Navy of the United States, and of the Militia of the several States, when called into the actual Service of the United States; he may require the Opinion, in writing, of the principal Officer in each of the executive Departments, upon any Subject relating to the Duties of their respective Offices, and he shall have Power to grant Reprieves and Pardons for Offences against the United States, except in Cases of Impeachment.

He shall have Power, by and with the Advice and Consent of the Senate, to make Treaties, provided two thirds of the Senators present concur; and he shall nominate, and by and with the Advice and Consent of the Senate, shall appoint Ambassadors, other public Ministers and Consuls, Judges of the supreme Court, and all other Officers of the United States, whose Appointments are not herein otherwise provided for, and which shall be established by Law: but the Congress may by Law vest the Appointment of such inferior Officers, as they think proper, in the President alone, in the Courts of Law, or in the Heads of Departments.

The President shall have Power to fill up all Vacancies that may happen during the Recess of the Senate, by granting Commissions which shall expire at the End of their next Session.

SECTION 3. He shall from time to time give to the Congress Information of the State of the Union, and recommend to their Consideration such Measures as he shall judge necessary and expedient; he may, on extraordinary Occasions, convene both Houses, or either of them, and in Case of Disagreement between them, with Respect to the Time of Adjournment, he may adjourn them to such Time as he shall think proper; he shall receive Ambassadors and other public Ministers; he shall take Care that the Laws be faithfully executed, and shall Commission all the Officers of the United States.

SECTION 4. The President, Vice President and all civil Officers of the United States, shall be removed from Office on Impeachment for, and Conviction of, Treason, Bribery, or other high Crimes and Misdemeanors.

ARTICLE III.

SECTION 1. The judicial Power of the United States, shall be vested in one supreme Court, and in such inferior Courts as the Congress may from time to time ordain and establish. The Judges, both of the supreme and inferior Courts, shall hold their Offices during good Behaviour, and shall, at stated Times, receive for their Services, a Compensation, which shall not be diminished during their Continuance in Office.

SECTION 2. The judicial Power shall extend to all Cases, in Law and Equity, arising under this Constitution, the Laws of the United States, and Treaties made, or which shall be made, under their Authority;—to all Cases affecting Ambassadors, other public Ministers and Consuls;—to all Cases of admiralty and maritime Jurisdiction;—to Controversies to which the United States shall be a Party;—to Controversies between two or more States;—between a State and Citizens of another State;—between Citizens of different States;—between Citizens of the same State claiming Lands under Grants of different States, and between a State, or the Citizens thereof, and foreign States, Citizens or Subjects.

In all Cases affecting Ambassadors, other public Ministers and Consuls, and those in which a State shall be Party, the supreme Court shall have original Jurisdiction. In all the other Cases before mentioned, the supreme Court shall have appellate Jurisdiction, both as to Law and Fact, with such Exceptions, and under such Regulations as the Congress shall make.

The Trial of all Crimes, except in Cases of Impeachment, shall be by Jury; and such Trial shall be held in the State where the said Crimes shall have been committed; but when not committed within any State, the Trial shall be at such Place or Places as the Congress may by Law have directed.

SECTION 3. Treason against the United States, shall consist only in levying War against them, or in adhering to their Enemies, giving them Aid and Comfort. No Person shall be convicted of Treason unless on the Testimony of two Witnesses to the same overt Act, or on Confession in open Court.

The Congress shall have Power to declare the Punishment of Treason, but no Attainder of Treason shall work Corruption of Blood, or Forfeiture except during the Life of the Person attainted.

ARTICLE IV.

SECTION 1. Full Faith and Credit shall be given in each State to the public Acts, Records, and judicial Proceedings of every other State. And the Congress may by general Laws prescribe the Manner in which such Acts, Records and Proceedings shall be proved, and the Effect thereof.

SECTION 2. The Citizens of each State shall be entitled to all Privileges and Immunities of Citizens in the several States.

A Person charged in any State with Treason, Felony, or other Crime, who shall flee from Justice, and be found in another State, shall on Demand of the executive Authority of the State from which he fled, be delivered up, to be removed to the State having Jurisdiction of the Crime.

No Person held to Service or Labour in one State, under the Laws thereof, escaping into another, shall, in Consequence of any Law or Regulation therein, be discharged from such Service or Labour, but shall be delivered up on Claim of the Party to whom such Service or Labour may be due.

SECTION 3. New States may be admitted by the Congress into this Union; but no new State shall be formed or erected within the Jurisdiction of any other State; nor any State be formed by the Junction of two or more States, or Parts of States, without the Consent of the Legislatures of the States concerned as well as of the Congress.

The Congress shall have Power to dispose of and make all needful Rules and Regulations respecting the Territory or other Property belonging to the United States; and nothing in this Constitution shall be so construed as to Prejudice any Claims of the United States, or of any particular State.

SECTION 4. The United States shall guarantee to every State in this Union a Republican Form of Government, and shall protect each of them against Invasion; and on Application of the Legislature, or of the Executive (when the Legislature cannot be convened) against domestic Violence.

ARTICLE V.

The Congress, whenever two thirds of both Houses shall deem it necessary, shall propose Amendments to this Constitution, or, on the Application of the Legislature of two thirds of the several States, shall call a Convention for proposing Amendments, which, in either Case, shall be valid to all Intents and Purposes, as Part of this Constitution, when ratified by the Legislatures of three fourths of the several States, or by Conventions in three fourths thereof, as the one or the other Mode of Ratification may be proposed by the Congress; Provided that no Amendment which may be made prior to the Year One thousand eight hundred and eight shall in any Manner affect the first and fourth Clauses in the Ninth Section of the first Article; and that no State, without its Consent, shall be deprived of its equal Suffrage in the Senate.

ARTICLE VI.

All Debts contracted and Engagements entered into, before the Adoption of this Constitution, shall be as valid against the United States under this Constitution, as under the Confederation.

This Constitution, and the Laws of the United States which shall be made in Pursuance thereof; and all Treaties made, or which shall be made, under the Authority of the United States, shall be the supreme Law of the Land; and the Judges in every State shall be bound thereby, any Thing in the Constitution or Laws of any State to the Contrary notwithstanding.

The Senators and Representatives before mentioned, and the Members of the several State Legislatures, and all executive and judicial Officers, both of the United States and of the several States, shall be bound by Oath or Affirmation, to support this Constitution; but no religious Test shall ever be required as a Qualification to any Office or public Trust under the United States.

ARTICLE VII.

The Ratification of the Conventions of nine States, shall be sufficient for the establishment of this Constitution between the States so ratifying the Same.

ARTICLES IN ADDITION TO, AND AMENDMENTS OF, THE CONSTITUTION OF THE UNITED STATES OF AMERICA, PROPOSED BY CONGRESS, AND RATIFIED BY THE SEVERAL STATES, PURSUANT TO THE FIFTH ARTICLE OF THE ORIGINAL CONSTITUTION.

AMENDMENT I [1791]

Congress shall make no law respecting an establishment of religion, or prohibiting the free exercise thereof; or abridging the freedom of speech, or of the press; or the right of the people peaceably to assemble, and to petition the Government for a redress of grievances.

AMENDMENT II [1791]

A well regulated Militia, being necessary to the security of a free State, the right of the people to keep and bear Arms, shall not be infringed.

AMENDMENT III [1791]

No Soldier shall, in time of peace be quartered in any house, without the consent of the Owner, nor in time of war, but in a manner to be prescribed by law.

AMENDMENT IV [1791]

The right of the people to be secure in their persons, houses, papers, and effects, against unreasonable searches and seizures, shall not be violated, and no Warrants shall issue, but upon probable cause, supported by Oath or affirmation, and particularly describing the place to be searched, and the persons or things to be seized.

AMENDMENT V [1791]

No person shall be held to answer for a capital, or otherwise infamous crime, unless on a presentment or indictment of a Grand Jury, except in cases arising in the land or naval forces, or in the Militia, when in actual service in time of War or public danger; nor shall any person be subject for the same offence to be twice put in jeopardy of life or limb; nor shall be compelled in any criminal case to be a witness against himself, nor be deprived of life, liberty, or property, without due process of law; nor shall private property be taken for public use, without just compensation.

AMENDMENT VI [1791]

In all criminal prosecutions, the accused shall enjoy the right to a speedy and public trial, by an impartial jury of the State and district wherein the crime shall have been committed, which district shall have been previously ascertained by law, and to be informed of the nature and cause of the accusation; to be confronted with the witnesses against him; to have compulsory process for obtaining Witnesses in his favor, and to have the Assistance of Counsel for his defence.

AMENDMENT VII [1791]

In Suits at common law, where the value in controversy shall exceed twenty dollars, the right of trial by jury shall be preserved, and no fact tried by a jury be otherwise re-examined in any Court of the United States, than according to the rules of the common law.

AMENDMENT VIII [1791]

Excessive bail shall not be required, nor excessive fines imposed, nor cruel and unusual punishments inflicted.

AMENDMENT IX [1791]

The enumeration in the Constitution, of certain rights, shall not be construed to deny or disparage others retained by the people.

AMENDMENT X [1791]

The powers not delegated to the United States by the Constitution, nor prohibited by it to the States, are reserved to the States respectively, or to the people.

AMENDMENT XI [1798]

The Judicial power of the United States shall not be construed to extend to any suit in law or equity, commenced or prosecuted against one of the United States by Citizens of another State, or by Citizens or Subjects of any Foreign State.

AMENDMENT XII [1804]

The Electors shall meet in their respective states and vote by ballot for President and Vice-President, one of whom, at least, shall not be an inhabitant of the same state with themselves; they shall name in their ballots the person voted for as President, and in distinct ballots the person voted for as Vice–President, and they shall make distinct lists of all persons voted for as President, and of all persons voted for as Vice–President, and of the number of votes for each, which lists they shall sign and certify, and transmit sealed to the seat of the government of the United States, directed to the President of the Senate;—The President of the Senate shall, in the presence of the Senate and House of Representatives, open all the certificates and the votes shall then be counted;—The person having the greatest number of votes for President, shall be the President, if such number be a majority of the whole number of Electors appointed; and if no person have such majority, then from the persons having the highest numbers not exceeding three on the list of those voted for as President, the House of Representatives shall choose immediately, by ballot, the President. But in choosing the President, the votes shall be taken by states, the representation from each state having one vote; a quorum for this purpose shall consist of a member or members from two-thirds of the states, and a majority of all the states shall be necessary to a choice. And if the House of Representatives shall not choose a President whenever the right of choice shall devolve upon them, before the fourth day of March next following, then the Vice–President shall act as President, as in the case of the death or other constitutional disability of the President—The person having the greatest number of votes as Vice–President, shall be the Vice–President, if such number be a majority of the whole number of Electors appointed, and if no person have a majority, then from the two highest numbers on the list, the Senate shall choose the Vice–President; a quorum for the purpose shall consist of two-thirds of the whole number of Senators, and a majority of the whole number shall be necessary to a choice. But no person constitutionally ineligible to the office of President shall be eligible to that of Vice–President of the United States.

AMENDMENT XIII [1865]

SECTION 1. Neither slavery nor involuntary servitude, except as a punishment for crime whereof the party shall have been duly convicted, shall exist within the United States, or any place subject to their jurisdiction.

SECTION 2. Congress shall have power to enforce this article by appropriate legislation.

AMENDMENT XIV [1868]

SECTION 1. All persons born or naturalized in the United States and subject to the jurisdiction thereof, are citizens of the United States and of the State wherein they reside. No State shall make or enforce any law which shall abridge the privileges or immunities of citizens of the United States; nor shall any State deprive any person of life, liberty, or property, without due process of law; nor deny to any person within its jurisdiction the equal protection of the laws.

SECTION 2. Representatives shall be apportioned among the several States according to their respective numbers, counting the whole number of persons in each State, excluding Indians not taxed. But when the right to vote at any election for the choice of electors for President and Vice President of the United States, Representatives in Congress, the Executive and Judicial officers of a State, or the members of the Legislature thereof, is denied to any of the male inhabitants of such State, being twenty-one years of age, and citizens of the United States, or in any way abridged, except for participation in rebellion, or other crime, the basis of representation therein shall be reduced in the proportion which the number of such male citizens shall bear to the whole number of male citizens twenty-one years of age in such State.

SECTION 3. No person shall be a Senator or Representative in Congress, or elector of President and Vice President, or hold any office, civil or military, under the United States, or under any State, who, having previously taken an oath, as a member of Congress, or as a member of any State legislature, or as an executive or judicial officer of any State, to support the Constitution of the United States, shall have engaged in insurrection or rebellion against the same, or given aid or comfort to the enemies thereof. But Congress may by a vote of two-thirds of each House, remove such disability.

SECTION 4. The validity of the public debt of the United States, authorized by law, including debts incurred for payment of pensions and bounties for services in suppressing insurrection or rebellion, shall not be questioned. But neither the United States nor any State shall assume or pay any debt or obligation incurred in aid of insurrection or rebellion against the United States, or any claim for the loss or emancipation of any slave; but all such debts, obligations and claims shall be held illegal and void.

SECTION 5. The Congress shall have power to enforce, by appropriate legislation, the provisions of this article.

AMENDMENT XV [1870]

SECTION 1. The right of citizens of the United States to vote shall not be denied or abridged by the United States or by any State on account of race, color, or previous condition of servitude.

SECTION 2. The Congress shall have power to enforce this article by appropriate legislation.

AMENDMENT XVI [1913]

The Congress shall have power to lay and collect taxes on incomes, from whatever source derived, without apportionment among the several States, and without regard to any census or enumeration.

AMENDMENT XVII [1913]

The Senate of the United States shall be composed of two Senators from each State, elected by the people thereof, for six years; and each

Senator shall have one vote. The electors in each State shall have the qualifications requisite for electors of the most numerous branch of the State legislatures.

When vacancies happen in the representation of any State in the Senate, the executive authority of such State shall issue writs of election to fill such vacancies: *Provided,* That the legislature of any State may empower the executive thereof to make temporary appointments until the people fill the vacancies by election as the legislature may direct.

This amendment shall not be so construed as to affect the election or term of any Senator chosen before it becomes valid as part of the Constitution.

AMENDMENT XVIII [1919]

SECTION 1. After one year from the ratification of this article the manufacture, sale, or transportation of intoxicating liquors within, the importation thereof into, or the exportation thereof from the United States and all territory subject to the jurisdiction thereof for beverage purposes is hereby prohibited.

SECTION 2. The Congress and the several States shall have concurrent power to enforce this article by appropriate legislation.

SECTION 3. This article shall be inoperative unless it shall have been ratified as an amendment to the Constitution by the legislatures of the several States, as provided in the Constitution, within seven years from the date of the submission hereof to the States by the Congress.

AMENDMENT XIX [1920]

The right of citizens of the United States to vote shall not be denied or abridged by the United States or by any State on account of sex.

Congress shall have power to enforce this article by appropriate legislation.

AMENDMENT XX [1933]

SECTION 1. The terms of the President and Vice President shall end at noon on the 20th day of January, and the terms of Senators and Representatives at noon on the 3d day of January, of the years in which such terms would have ended if this article had not been ratified; and the terms of their successors shall then begin.

SECTION 2. The Congress shall assemble at least once in every year, and such meeting shall begin at noon on the 3d day of January, unless they shall by law appoint a different day.

SECTION 3. If, at the time fixed for the beginning of the term of the President, the President elect shall have died, the Vice President elect shall become President. If a President shall not have been chosen before the time fixed for the beginning of his term, or if the President elect shall have failed to qualify, then the Vice President elect shall act as President until a President shall have qualified; and the Congress may by law provide for the case wherein neither a President elect nor a Vice President elect shall have qualified, declaring who shall then act as President, or the manner in which one who is to act shall be selected, and such person shall act accordingly until a President or Vice President shall have qualified.

SECTION 4. The Congress may by law provide for the case of the death of any of the persons from whom the House of Representatives may choose a President whenever the right of choice shall have devolved upon them, and for the case of the death of any of the persons from whom the Senate may choose a Vice President whenever the right of choice shall have devolved upon them.

SECTION 5. Sections 1 and 2 shall take effect on the 15th day of October following the ratification of this article.

SECTION 6. This article shall be inoperative unless it shall have been ratified as an amendment to the Constitution by the legislatures of three-fourths of the several States within seven years from the date of its submission.

AMENDMENT XXI [1933]

SECTION 1. The eighteenth article of amendment to the Constitution of the United States is hereby repealed.

SECTION 2. The transportation or importation into any State, Territory, or possession of the United States for delivery or use therein of intoxicating liquors, in violation of the laws thereof, is hereby prohibited.

SECTION 3. This article shall be inoperative unless it shall have been ratified as an amendment to the Constitution by conventions in the several States, as provided in the Constitution, within seven years from the date of the submission hereof to the States by the Congress.

AMENDMENT XXII [1951]

SECTION 1. No person shall be elected to the office of the President more than twice, and no person who has held the office of President, or acted as President, for more than two years of a term to which some other person was elected President shall be elected to the office of the President more than once. But this Article shall not apply to any person holding the office of President when this Article was proposed by the Congress, and shall not prevent any person who may be holding the office of President, or acting as President, during the term within which this Article becomes operative from holding the office of President or acting as President during the remainder of such term.

SECTION 2. This article shall be inoperative unless it shall have been ratified as an amendment to the Constitution by the legislatures of three-fourths of the several States within seven years from the date of its submission to the States by the Congress.

AMENDMENT XXIII [1961]

SECTION 1. The District constituting the seat of Government of the United States shall appoint in such manner as the Congress may direct:

A number of electors of President and Vice President equal to the whole number of Senators and Representatives in Congress to which the District would be entitled if it were a State, but in no event more than the least populous State; they shall be in addition to those appointed by the States, but they shall be considered, for the purposes of the election of President and Vice President, to be electors appointed by a State; and they shall meet in the District and perform such duties as provided by the twelfth article of amendment.

SECTION 2. The Congress shall have power to enforce this article by appropriate legislation.

AMENDMENT XXIV [1964]

SECTION 1. The right of citizens of the United States to vote in any primary or other election for President or Vice President, for electors for President or Vice President, or for Senator or Representative in Congress, shall not be denied or abridged by the United States or any State by reason of failure to pay any poll or other tax.

SECTION 2. The Congress shall have power to enforce this article by appropriate legislation.

AMENDMENT XXV [1967]

SECTION 1. In case of the removal of the President from office or of his death or resignation, the Vice President shall become President.

SECTION 2. Whenever there is a vacancy in the office of the Vice President, the President shall nominate a Vice President who shall take office upon confirmation by a majority vote of both Houses of Congress.

SECTION 3. Whenever the President transmits to the President pro tempore of the Senate and the Speaker of the House of Representatives his written declaration that he is unable to discharge the powers and duties of his office, and until he transmits to them a written declaration to the contrary, such powers and duties shall be discharged by the Vice President as Acting President.

SECTION 4. Whenever the Vice President and a majority of either the principal officers of the executive department or of such other body as Congress may by law provide, transmit to the President pro tempore of the Senate and the Speaker of the House of Representatives their written declaration that the President is unable to discharge the powers and duties of his office, the Vice President shall immediately assume the powers and duties of the office as Acting President.

Thereafter, when the President transmits to the President pro tempore of the Senate and the Speaker of the House of Representatives his written declaration that no inability exists, he shall resume the powers and duties of his office unless the Vice President and a majority of either the principal officers of the executive department or of such other body as Congress may by law provide, transmit within four days to the President pro tempore of the Senate and the Speaker of the House of Representatives their written declaration that the President is unable to discharge the powers and duties of his office. Thereupon Congress shall decide the issue, assembling within forty-eight hours for that purpose if not in session. If the Congress, within twenty-one days after receipt of the latter written declaration, or, if Congress is not in session, within twenty-one days after Congress is required to assemble, determines by two-thirds vote of both Houses that the President is unable to discharge the powers and duties of his office, the Vice President shall continue to discharge the same as Acting President; otherwise, the President shall resume the powers and duties of his office.

AMENDMENT XXVI [1971]

SECTION 1. The right of citizens of the United States, who are eighteen years of age or older, to vote shall not be denied or abridged by the United States or by any State on account of age.

SECTION 2. The Congress shall have power to enforce this article by appropriate legislation.

AMENDMENT XXVII [1992]

No law varying the compensation for the services of the senators and representatives shall take effect until an election of representatives shall have intervened.

Appendix B

COMMUNICATIONS ACT OF 1934

48 Stat. 1064 (1934), as amended, 47 U.S.C.A.
§ 151 et seq. (as of April 1, 1996)

TITLE I—GENERAL PROVISIONS

PURPOSES OF ACT; CREATION OF FEDERAL COMMUNICATIONS COMMISSION

Sec. 1. [47 U.S.C.A. § 151.]

For the purpose of regulating interstate and foreign commerce in communication by wire and radio so as to make available, so far as possible, to all the people of the United States without discrimination on the basis of race, color, religion, national origin, or sex, a rapid, efficient, Nation-wide, and world-wide wire and radio communication service with adequate facilities at reasonable charges, for the purpose of the national defense, for the purpose of promoting safety of life and property through the use of wire and radio communication, and for the purpose of securing a more effective execution of this policy by centralizing authority heretofore granted by law to several agencies and by granting additional authority with respect to interstate and foreign commerce in wire and radio communication, there is hereby created a commission to be known as the "Federal Communications Commission," which shall be constituted as hereinafter provided, and which shall execute and enforce the provisions of this Act.

. . .

APPLICATION OF ACT

Sec. 2. [47 U.S.C.A. § 152.]

(a) The provisions of this Act shall apply to all interstate and foreign communication by wire or radio and all interstate and foreign transmission of energy by radio, which originates and/or is received within the United States, and to all persons engaged within the United States in such communication or such transmission of energy by radio, and to the licensing and regulating of all radio stations as hereinafter provided. . . . The provisions of this Act shall apply with respect to cable service to all persons engaged within the United States in providing such service, and to the facilities of cable operators which relate to such service as provided in title VI.

DEFINITIONS

Sec. 153. [47 U.S.C. § 153.]

(1) The term "affiliate" means a person that (directly or indirectly) owns or controls, is owned or controlled by, or is under

common ownership or control with, another person. For purposes of this paragraph, the term "own" means to own an equity interest (or the equivalent thereof) of more than 10 percent.

. . .

(3) The term "AT & T Consent Decree" means the order entered August 24, 1982, in the antitrust action styled United States v. Western Electric, Civil Action No. 82–0192, in the United States District Court for the District of Columbia, and includes any judgment or order with respect to such action entered on or after August 24, 1982.

(4) The term "Bell operating company"—

(A) means any of the following companies: Bell Telephone Company of Nevada, Illinois Bell Telephone Company, Indiana Bell Telephone Company, Incorporated, Michigan Bell Telephone Company, New England Telephone and Telegraph Company, New Jersey Bell Telephone Company, New York Telephone Company, US West Communications Company, South Central Bell Telephone Company, Southern Bell Telephone and Telegraph Company, Southwestern Bell Telephone Company, The Bell Telephone Company of Pennsylvania, The Chesapeake and Potomac Telephone Company, The Chesapeake and Potomac Telephone Company of Maryland, The Chesapeake and Potomac Telephone Company of Virginia, The Chesapeake and Potomac Telephone Company of West Virginia, The Diamond State Telephone Company, The Ohio Bell Telephone Company, The Pacific Telephone and Telegraph Company, or Wisconsin Telephone Company; and

(B) includes any successor or assign of any such company that provides wireline telephone exchange service; but

(C) does not include an affiliate of any such company, other than an affiliate described in subparagraph (A) or (B).

(5) The term "broadcast station", "broadcasting station", or "radio broadcast station" means a radio station equipped to engage in broadcasting as herein defined.

(6) The term "broadcasting" means the dissemination of radio communications intended to be received by the public, directly or by the intermediary of relay stations.

(7) The term "cable service" has the meaning given such term in section 602.

(8) The term "cable system" has the meaning given such term in section 602.

(9) The term "chain broadcasting" means simultaneous broadcasting of an identical program by two or more connected stations.

(10) The term "common carrier" or "carrier" means any person engaged as a common carrier for hire, in interstate or foreign communication by wire or radio or in interstate or foreign radio transmission of energy, except where reference is made to common carriers not subject to this chapter; but a person engaged in radio broadcasting shall not, insofar as such person is so engaged, be deemed a common carrier.

. . .

(12) The term "construction permit" or "permit for construction" means that instrument of authorization required by this chapter or the rules and regulations of the Commission made pursuant to this chapter for the construction of a station, or the installation of apparatus, for the transmission of energy, or communications, or signals by radio, by whatever name the instrument may be designated by the Commission.

(13) The term "corporation" includes any corporation, joint-stock company, or association.

. . .

(17) The term "foreign communication" or "foreign transmission" means communication or transmission from or to any place in the United States to or from a foreign country, or between a station in the United States and a mobile station located outside the United States.

. . .

(21) The term "interstate communication" or "interstate transmission" means communication or transmission (A) from any State, Territory, or possession of the United States (other than the Canal Zone), or the District of Columbia, to any other State, Territory, or possession of the United States (other than the Canal Zone), or the District of Columbia, (B) from or to the United States to or from the Canal Zone, insofar as such communication or transmission takes place within the United States, or (C) between points within the United States but through a foreign country; but shall not, with respect to the provisions of subchapter II of this chapter (other than section 223 of this title), include wire or radio communication between points in the same State, Territory, or possession of the United States, or the District of Columbia, through any place outside thereof, if such communication is regulated by a State commission.

. . .

(24) The term "licensee" means the holder of a radio station license granted or continued in force under authority of this chapter.

. . .

(32) The term "Person" includes an individual, partnership, association, joint-stock company, trust, or corporation.

(33) The term "radio communication" or "communication by radio" means the transmission by radio of writing, signs, signals, pictures, and sounds of all kinds, including all instrumentalities, facilities, apparatus, and services (among other things, the receipt, forwarding, and delivery of communications) incidental to such transmission.

. . .

(35) The term "radio station" or "station" means a station equipped to engage in radio communication or radio transmission of energy.

. . .

(41) The term "state" includes the District of Columbia and the Territories and possessions.

(42) The term "station license", "radio station license", or "license" means that instrument of authorization required by this chapter or the rules and regulations of the Commission made pursuant to this chapter, for the use or operation of apparatus for transmission of energy, or communications, or signals by radio, by whatever name the instrument may be designated by the Commission.

. . .

(49) The term "transmission of energy by radio" or "radio transmission of energy" includes both such transmission and all instrumentalities, facilities, and services incidental to such transmission.

(50) The term "United States" means the several States and Territories, the District of Columbia, and the possessions of the United States, but does not include the Canal Zone.

(51) The term "wire communication" or "communication by wire" means the transmission of writing, signs, signals, pictures, and sounds of all kinds by aid of wire, cable, or other like connection between the points of origin and reception of such transmission, including all instrumentalities, facilities, apparatus, and services (among other things, the receipt, forwarding, and delivery of communications) incidental to such transmission.

TITLE II—COMMON CARRIER PROVISIONS

. . .

OBSCENE OR HARASSING USE OF TELECOMMUNICATIONS FACILITIES [UNDER THE COMMUNICATIONS ACT OF 1934]

Sec. 223. [47 U.S.C.A. 223.]*

(a) Whoever—

(1) in interstate or foreign communications—

---

* [The 1996 Telecommunications Act amended 18 U.S.C.A. §§ 1462, 1465 to read as follows.]

18 U.S.C.A. § 1462. Importation or transportation of obscene matters

    (A) by means of a telecommunications device knowingly—

        (i) makes, creates, or solicits, and

        (ii) initiates the transmission of,

any comment, request, suggestion, proposal, image, or other communication which is obscene, lewd, lascivious, filthy, or indecent, with intent to annoy, abuse, threaten, or harass another person;

    (B) by means of a telecommunications device knowingly—

        (i) makes, creates, or solicits, and

        (ii) initiates the transmission of,

any comment, request, suggestion, proposal, image, or other communication which is obscene or indecent, knowing that the recipient of the communication is under 18 years of age, regardless of whether the maker of such communication placed the call or initiated the communication;

Whoever brings into the United States, or any place subject to the jurisdiction thereof, or knowingly uses any express company or other common carrier or interactive computer service (as defined in section 230(e)(2) of the Communications Act of 1934), for carriage in interstate or foreign commerce—

(a) any obscene, lewd, lascivious, or filthy book, pamphlet, picture, motion-picture film, paper, letter, writing, print, or other matter of indecent character; or

(b) any obscene, lewd, lascivious, or filthy phonograph recording, electrical transcription, or other article or thing capable of producing sound; or

(c) any drug, medicine, article, or thing designed, adapted, or intended for producing abortion, or for any indecent or immoral use; or any written or printed card, letter, circular, book, pamphlet, advertisement, or notice of any kind giving information, directly or indirectly, where, how, or of whom, or by what means any of such mentioned articles, matters, or things may be obtained or made; or

Whoever knowingly takes or receives from such express company or other common carrier or interactive computer service (as defined in section 230(e)(2) of the Communications Act of 1934) any matter or thing the carriage or importation of which is herein made unlawful—

Shall be fined under this title or imprisoned not more than five years, or both, for the first such offense and shall be fined under this title or imprisoned not more than ten years, or both, for each such offense thereafter.

18 U.S.C.A. § 1465. Transportation of obscene matters for sale or distribution

Whoever knowingly transports or travels in, or uses a facility or means of interstate or foreign commerce or an interactive computer service (as defined in section 230(e)(2) of the Communications Act of 1934) in or affecting commerce for the purpose of sale or distribution of obscene material in interstate or foreign commerce, any obscene, lewd, lascivious, or filthy book, pamphlet, picture, film, paper, letter, writing, print, silhouette, drawing, figure, image, cast, phonograph recording, electrical transcription or other article capable of producing sound or any other matter of indecent or immoral character, shall be fined under this title or imprisoned not more than five years, or both.

The transportation as aforesaid of two or more copies of any publication or two or more of any article of the character described above, or a combined total of five such publications and articles, shall create a presumption that such publications or articles are intended for sale or distribution, but such presumption shall be rebuttable.

(C) makes a telephone call or utilizes a telecommunications device, whether or not conversation or communication ensues, without disclosing his identity and with intent to annoy, abuse, threaten, or harass any person at the called number or who receives the communications;

(D) makes or causes the telephone of another repeatedly or continuously to ring, with intent to harass any person at the called number; or

(E) makes repeated telephone calls or repeatedly initiates communication with a telecommunications device, during which conversation or communication ensues, solely to harass any person at the called number or who receives the communication; or

(2) knowingly permits any telecommunications facility under his control to be used for any activity prohibited by paragraph (1) with the intent that it be used for such activity,

shall be fined under title 18, United States Code, or imprisoned not more than two years, or both.; and

. . .

(d) Whoever—

(1) in interstate or foreign communications knowingly—

(A) uses an interactive computer service to send to a specific person or persons under 18 years of age, or

(B) uses any interactive computer service to display in a manner available to a person under 18 years of age,

any comment, request, suggestion, proposal, image, or other communication that, in context, depicts or describes, in terms patently offensive as measured by contemporary community standards, sexual or excretory activities or organs, regardless of whether the user of such service placed the call or initiated the communication; or

(2) knowingly permits any telecommunications facility under such person's control to be used for an activity prohibited by paragraph (1) with the intent that it be used for such activity,

shall be fined under title 18, United States Code, or imprisoned not more than two years, or both.

(e) In addition to any other defenses available by law:

(1) No person shall be held to have violated subsection (a) or (d) solely for providing access or connection to or from a facility, system, or network not under that person's control, including transmission, downloading, intermediate storage, access software, or other related capabilities that are incidental to providing such access or connec-

tion that does not include the creation of the content of the communication.

(2) The defenses provided by paragraph (1) of this subsection shall not be applicable to a person who is a conspirator with an entity actively involved in the creation or knowing distribution of communications that violate this section, or who knowingly advertises the availability of such communications.

(3) The defenses provided in paragraph (1) of this subsection shall not be applicable to a person who provides access or connection to a facility system, or network engaged in the violation of this section that is owned or controlled by such person.

(4) No employer shall be held liable under this section for the actions of an employee or agent unless the employee's or agent's conduct is within the scope of his or her employment or agency and the employer (A) having knowledge of such conduct, authorizes or ratifies such conduct, or (B) recklessly disregards such conduct.

(5) It is a defense to a prosecution under subsection (a)(1)(B) or (d), or under subsection (a)(2) with respect to the use of a facility for an activity under subsection (a)(1)(B) that a person—

(A) has taken, in good faith, reasonable, effective, and appropriate actions under the circumstances to restrict or prevent access by minors to a communication specified in such subsections, which may involve any appropriate measures to restrict minors from such communications, including any method which is feasible under available technology; or

(B) has restricted access to such communication by requiring use of a verified credit card, debit account, adult access code, or adult personal identification number.

(6) The Commission may describe measures which are reasonable, effective, and appropriate to restrict access to prohibited communications under subsection (d). Nothing in this section authorizes the Commission to enforce, or is intended to provide the Commission with the authority to approve, sanction, or permit, the use of such measures. The Commission shall have no enforcement authority over the failure to utilize such measures. The Commission shall not endorse specific products relating to such measures. The use of such measures shall be admitted as evidence of good faith efforts for purposes of paragraph (5) in any action arising under subsection (d). Nothing in this section shall be construed to treat interactive computer services as common carriers or telecommunications carriers.

(f)(1) No cause of action may be brought in any court or administrative agency against any person on account of any activity that is not in violation of any law punishable by criminal or civil penalty, and that the person has taken in good faith to implement a defense authorized under this section or otherwise to restrict or prevent the transmission of, or access to, a communication specified in this section.

(2) No State or local government may impose any liability for commercial activities or actions by commercial entities, nonprofit libraries, or institutions of higher education in connection with an activity or action described in subsection (a)(2) or (d) that is inconsistent with the treatment of those activities or actions under this section: Provided, however, That nothing herein shall preclude any State or local government from enacting and enforcing complementary oversight, liability, and regulatory systems, procedures, and requirements, so long as such systems, procedures, and requirements govern only intrastate services and do not result in the imposition of inconsistent rights, duties or obligations on the provision of interstate services. Nothing in this subsection shall preclude any State or local government from governing conduct not covered by this section.

(g) Nothing in subsection (a), (d), (e), or (f) or in the defenses to prosecution under subsection (a) or (d) shall be construed to affect or limit the application or enforcement of any other Federal law.

(h) For purposes of this section—

(1) The use of the term "telecommunications device" in this section—

(A) shall not impose new obligations on broadcasting station licensees and cable operators covered by obscenity and indecency provisions elsewhere in this Act; and

(B) does not include an interactive computer service.

(2) The term "interactive computer service" has the meaning provided in section 230(e)(2).

(3) The term "access software" means software (including client or server software) or enabling tools that do not create or provide the content of the communication but that allow a user to do any one or more of the following:

(A) filter, screen, allow, or disallow content;

(B) pick, choose, analyze, or digest content; or

(C) transmit, receive, display, forward, cache, search, subset, organize, reorganize, or translate content.

(4) The term "institution of higher education" has the meaning provided in section 1201 of the Higher Education Act of 1965 (20 U.S.C. 1141).

(5) The term "library" means a library eligible for participation in State-based plans for funds under title III of the Library Services and Construction Act (20 U.S.C. 355e et seq.).

. . .

PROTECTION FOR PRIVATE BLOCKING AND
SCREENING OF OFFENSIVE MATERIAL

Sec. 230. [47 U.S.C.A. § 230.]*

§ 2422.   Coercion and enticement

(a) The Congress finds the following:

(1) The rapidly developing array of Internet and other interactive computer services available to individual Americans represent an extraordinary advance in the availability of educational and informational resources to our citizens.

(2) These services offer users a great degree of control over the information that they receive, as well as the potential for even greater control in the future as technology develops.

(3) The Internet and other interactive computer services offer a forum for a true diversity of political discourse, unique opportunities for cultural development, and myriad avenues for intellectual activity.

(4) The Internet and other interactive computer services have flourished, to the benefit of all Americans, with a minimum of government regulation.

(5) Increasingly Americans are relying on interactive media for a variety of political, educational, cultural, and entertainment services.

(b) It is the policy of the United States—

(1) to promote the continued development of the Internet and other interactive computer services and other interactive media;

(2) to preserve the vibrant and competitive free market that presently exists for the Internet and other interactive computer services, unfettered by Federal or State regulation;

(3) to encourage the development of technologies which maximize user control over what information is received by individuals, families, and schools who use the Internet and other interactive computer services;

(4) to remove disincentives for the development and utilization of blocking and filtering technologies that empower parents to

---

* [Section 508 of the 1996 Telecommunications Act amended 18 U.S.C.A. § 2422 to read as follows.]

(a) Whoever knowingly persuades, induces, entices, or coerces any individual to travel in interstate or foreign commerce, or in any Territory or Possession of the United States, to engage in prostitution, or in any sexual activity for which any person can be charged with a criminal offense, shall be fined under this title or imprisoned not more than five years, or both.

(b) Whoever, using any facility or means of interstate or foreign commerce, including the mail, or within the special maritime and territorial jurisdiction of the United States, knowingly persuades, induces, entices, or coerces any individual who has not attained the age of 18 years to engage in prostitution or any sexual act for which any person may be criminally prosecuted, or attempts to do so, shall be fined under this title or imprisoned not more than 10 years or both.

restrict their children's access to objectionable or inappropriate online material; and

(5) to ensure vigorous enforcement of Federal criminal laws to deter and punish trafficking in obscenity, stalking, and harassment by means of computer.

(c)(1) No provider or user of an interactive computer service shall be treated as the publisher or speaker of any information provided by another information content provider.

(2) No provider or user of an interactive computer service shall be held liable on account of—

(A) any action voluntarily taken in good faith to restrict access to or availability of material that the provider or user considers to be obscene, lewd, lascivious, filthy, excessively violent, harassing, or otherwise objectionable, whether or not such material is constitutionally protected; or

(B) any action taken to enable or make available to information content providers or others the technical means to restrict access to material described in paragraph (1).

(d)(1) Nothing in this section shall be construed to impair the enforcement of section 223 of this Act, chapter 71 (relating to obscenity) or 110 (relating to sexual exploitation of children) of title 18, United States Code, or any other Federal criminal statute.

(2) Nothing in this section shall be construed to limit or expand any law pertaining to intellectual property.

(3) Nothing in this section shall be construed to prevent any State from enforcing any State law that is consistent with this section. No cause of action may be brought and no liability may be imposed under any State or local law that is inconsistent with this section.

(4) Nothing in this section shall be construed to limit the application of the Electronic Communications Privacy Act of 1986 or any of the amendments made by such Act, or any similar State law.

(e) As used in this section:

(1) The term "Internet" means the international computer network of both Federal and non-Federal interoperable packet switched data networks.

(2) The term "interactive computer service" means any information service, system, or access software provider that provides or enables computer access by multiple users to a computer server, including specifically a service or system that provides access to the Internet and such systems operated or services offered by libraries or educational institutions.

(3) The term "information content provider" means any person or entity that is responsible, in whole or in part, for the creation or

development of information provided through the Internet or any other interactive computer service.

(4) The term "access software provider" means a provider of software (including client or server software), or enabling tools that do any one or more of the following:

(A) filter, screen, allow, or disallow content;

(B) pick, choose, analyze, or digest content; or

(C) transmit, receive, display, forward, cache, search, subset, organize, reorganize, or translate content.

. . .

ELECTRONIC PUBLISHING BY BELL OPERATING COMPANIES
Sec. 274. [47 U.S.C.A. 274.]

(a) No Bell operating company or any affiliate may engage in the provision of electronic publishing that is disseminated by means of such Bell operating company's or any of its affiliates' basic telephone service, except that nothing in this section shall prohibit a separated affiliate or electronic publishing joint venture operated in accordance with this section from engaging in the provision of electronic publishing.

(b) A separated affiliate or electronic publishing joint venture shall be operated independently from the Bell operating company. Such separated affiliate or joint venture and the Bell operating company with which it is affiliated shall—

(1) maintain separate books, records, and accounts and prepare separate financial statements;

(2) not incur debt in a manner that would permit a creditor of the separated affiliate or joint venture upon default to have recourse to the assets of the Bell operating company;

(3) carry out transactions (A) in a manner consistent with such independence, (B) pursuant to written contracts or tariffs that are filed with the Commission and made publicly available, and (C) in a manner that is auditable in accordance with generally accepted auditing standards;

(4) value any assets that are transferred directly or indirectly from the Bell operating company to a separated affiliate or joint venture, and record any transactions by which such assets are transferred, in accordance with such regulations as may be prescribed by the Commission or a State commission to prevent improper cross subsidies;

(5) between a separated affiliate and a Bell operating company—

(A) have no officers, directors, and employees in common after the effective date of this section; and

(B) own no property in common;

(6) not use for the marketing of any product or service of the separated affiliate or joint venture, the name, trademarks, or service marks of an existing Bell operating company except for names, trademarks, or service marks that are owned by the entity that owns or controls the Bell operating company;

(7) not permit the Bell operating company—

(A) to perform hiring or training of personnel on behalf of a separated affiliate;

(B) to perform the purchasing, installation, or maintenance of equipment on behalf of a separated affiliate, except for telephone service that it provides under tariff or contract subject to the provisions of this section; or

(C) to perform research and development on behalf of a separated affiliate;

(8) each have performed annually a compliance review—

(A) that is conducted by an independent entity for the purpose of determining compliance during the preceding calendar year with any provision of this section; and

(B) the results of which are maintained by the separated affiliate or joint venture and the Bell operating company for a period of 5 years subject to review by any lawful authority; and

(9) within 90 days of receiving a review described in paragraph (8), file a report of any exceptions and corrective action with the Commission and allow any person to inspect and copy such report subject to reasonable safeguards to protect any proprietary information contained in such report from being used for purposes other than to enforce or pursue remedies under this section.

(c)(1) Except as provided in paragraph (2)—

(A) a Bell operating company shall not carry out any promotion, marketing, sales, or advertising for or in conjunction with a separated affiliate; and

(B) a Bell operating company shall not carry out any promotion, marketing, sales, or advertising for or in conjunction with an affiliate that is related to the provision of electronic publishing.

(2)(A) A Bell operating company may provide inbound telemarketing or referral services related to the provision of electronic publishing for a separated affiliate, electronic publishing joint venture, affiliate, or unaffiliated electronic publisher: Provided, That if such services are provided to a separated affiliate, electronic publishing joint venture, or affiliate, such services shall be made available to all electronic publishers on request, on nondiscriminatory terms.

(B) A Bell operating company may engage in nondiscriminatory teaming or business arrangements to engage in electronic publishing with any separated affiliate or with any other electronic publisher if (i) the Bell operating company only provides facilities, services, and basic telephone service information as authorized by this section, and (ii) the Bell operating company does not own such teaming or business arrangement.

(C) A Bell operating company or affiliate may participate on a nonexclusive basis in electronic publishing joint ventures with entities that are not a Bell operating company, affiliate, or separated affiliate to provide electronic publishing services, if the Bell operating company or affiliate has not more than a 50 percent direct or indirect equity interest (or the equivalent thereof) or the right to more than 50 percent of the gross revenues under a revenue sharing or royalty agreement in any electronic publishing joint venture. Officers and employees of a Bell operating company or affiliate participating in an electronic publishing joint venture may not have more than 50 percent of the voting control over the electronic publishing joint venture. In the case of joint ventures with small, local electronic publishers, the Commission for good cause shown may authorize the Bell operating company or affiliate to have a larger equity interest, revenue share, or voting control but not to exceed 80 percent. A Bell operating company participating in an electronic publishing joint venture may provide promotion, marketing, sales, or advertising personnel and services to such joint venture.

(d) A Bell operating company under common ownership or control with a separated affiliate or electronic publishing joint venture shall provide network access and interconnections for basic telephone service to electronic publishers at just and reasonable rates that are tariffed (so long as rates for such services are subject to regulation) and that are not higher on a per-unit basis than those charged for such services to any other electronic publisher or any separated affiliate engaged in electronic publishing.

(e)(1) Any person claiming that any act or practice of any Bell operating company, affiliate, or separated affiliate constitutes a violation of this section may file a complaint with the Commission or bring suit as provided in section 207 of this Act, and such Bell operating company, affiliate, or separated affiliate shall be liable as provided in section 206 of this Act; except that damages may not be awarded for a violation that is discovered by a compliance review as required by subsection (b)(7) of this section and corrected within 90 days.

(2) In addition to the provisions of paragraph (1), any person claiming that any act or practice of any Bell operating company, affiliate, or separated affiliate constitutes a violation of this section may make application to the Commission for an order to cease and desist such violation or may make application in any district court of the United States of competent jurisdiction for an order enjoining

such acts or practices or for an order compelling compliance with such requirement.

(f) Any separated affiliate under this section shall file with the Commission annual reports in a form substantially equivalent to the Form 10–K required by regulations of the Securities and Exchange Commission.

(g)(1) Any electronic publishing service being offered to the public by a Bell operating company or affiliate on the date of enactment of the Telecommunications Act of 1996 shall have one year from such date of enactment to comply with the requirements of this section.

(2) The provisions of this section shall not apply to conduct occurring after 4 years after the date of enactment of the Telecommunications Act of 1996.

(h)(1) The term "electronic publishing" means the dissemination, provision, publication, or sale to an unaffiliated entity or person, of any one or more of the following: news (including sports); entertainment (other than interactive games); business, financial, legal, consumer, or credit materials; editorials, columns, or features; advertising; photos or images; archival or research material; legal notices or public records; scientific, educational, instructional, technical, professional, trade, or other literary materials; or other like or similar information.

(2) The term "electronic publishing" shall not include the following services:

(A) Information access, as that term is defined by the AT & T Consent Decree.

(B) The transmission of information as a common carrier.

(C) The transmission of information as part of a gateway to an information service that does not involve the generation or alteration of the content of information, including data transmission, address translation, protocol conversion, billing management, introductory information content, and navigational systems that enable users to access electronic publishing services, which do not affect the presentation of such electronic publishing services to users.

(D) Voice storage and retrieval services, including voice messaging and electronic mail services.

(E) Data processing or transaction processing services that do not involve the generation or alteration of the content of information.

(F) Electronic billing or advertising of a Bell operating company's regulated telecommunications services.

(G) Language translation or data format conversion.

(H) The provision of information necessary for the management, control, or operation of a telephone company telecommunications system.

(I) The provision of directory assistance that provides names, addresses, and telephone numbers and does not include advertising.

(J) Caller identification services.

(K) Repair and provisioning databases and credit card and billing validation for telephone company operations.

(L) 911–E and other emergency assistance databases.

(M) Any other network service of a type that is like or similar to these network services and that does not involve the generation or alteration of the content of information.

(N) Any upgrades to these network services that do not involve the generation or alteration of the content of information.

(O) Video programming or full motion video entertainment on demand.

(i) As used in this section—

(1) The term "affiliate" means any entity that, directly or indirectly, owns or controls, is owned or controlled by, or is under common ownership or control with, a Bell operating company. Such term shall not include a separated affiliate.

(2) The term "basic telephone service" means any wireline telephone exchange service, or wireline telephone exchange service facility, provided by a Bell operating company in a telephone exchange area, except that such term does not include—

(A) a competitive wireline telephone exchange service provided in a telephone exchange area where another entity provides a wireline telephone exchange service that was provided on January 1, 1984, or

(B) a commercial mobile service.

(3) The term "basic telephone service information" means network and customer information of a Bell operating company and other information acquired by a Bell operating company as a result of its engaging in the provision of basic telephone service.

(4) The term "control" has the meaning that it has in 17 C.F.R. 240.12b–2, the regulations promulgated by the Securities and Exchange Commission pursuant to the Securities Exchange Act of 1934 (15 U.S.C. 78a et seq.) or any successor provision to such section.

(5) The term "electronic publishing joint venture" means a joint venture owned by a Bell operating company or affiliate that engages in the provision of electronic publishing which is dissemi-

nated by means of such Bell operating company's or any of its affiliates' basic telephone service.

(6) The term "entity" means any organization, and includes corporations, partnerships, sole proprietorships, associations, and joint ventures.

(7) The term "inbound telemarketing" means the marketing of property, goods, or services by telephone to a customer or potential customer who initiated the call.

(8) The term "own" with respect to an entity means to have a direct or indirect equity interest (or the equivalent thereof) of more than 10 percent of an entity, or the right to more than 10 percent of the gross revenues of an entity under a revenue sharing or royalty agreement.

(9) The term "separated affiliate" means a corporation under common ownership or control with a Bell operating company that does not own or control a Bell operating company and is not owned or controlled by a Bell operating company and that engages in the provision of electronic publishing which is disseminated by means of such Bell operating company's or any of its affiliates' basic telephone service.

(10) The term "Bell operating company" has the meaning provided in section 3, except that such term includes any entity or corporation that is owned or controlled by such a company (as so defined) but does not include an electronic publishing joint venture owned by such an entity or corporation.

. . .

GENERAL POWERS OF THE COMMISSION

Sec. 303. [47 U.S.C.A. § 303.]*

Except as otherwise provided in this Act, the Commission from time to time, as public convenience, interest, or necessity requires shall:

(a) Classify radio stations;

(b) Prescribe the nature of the service to be rendered by each class of licensed stations and each station within any class;

(c) Assign bands of frequencies to the various classes of stations, and assign frequencies for each individual station and determine the power which each station shall use and the time during which it may operate;

---

* [Section 207 of the 1996 Telecommunications Act directed the FCC to take the following steps:] Within 180 days after the date of enactment of this Act, the Commission shall, pursuant to section 303 of the Communications Act of 1934, promulgate regulations to prohibit restrictions that impair a viewer's ability to receive video programming services through devices designed for over-the-air reception of television broadcast signals, multichannel multipoint distribution service, or direct broadcast satellite services.

(d) Determine the location of classes of stations or individual stations;

(e) Regulate the kind of apparatus to be used with respect to its external effects and the purity and sharpness of the emissions from each station and from the apparatus therein;

(f) Make such regulations not inconsistent with law as it may deem necessary to prevent interference between stations and to carry out the provisions of this Act: *Provided, however,* That changes in the frequencies, authorized power, or in the times of operation of any station, shall not be made without the consent of the station licensee unless, after a public hearing, the Commission shall determine that such changes will promote public convenience or interest or will serve public necessity, or the provisions of this Act will be more fully complied with;

(g) Study new uses for radio, provide for experimental uses of frequencies, and generally encourage the larger and more effective use of radio in the public interest;

(h) Have authority to establish areas or zones to be served by any station;

(i) Have authority to make special regulations applicable to radio stations engaged in chain broadcasting;

(j) Have authority to make general rules and regulations requiring stations to keep such records of programs, transmissions of energy, communications, or signals as it may deem desirable;

. . .

(m)(1) Have authority to suspend the license of any operator upon proof sufficient to satisfy the Commission that the licensee—

(A) has violated any provision of any Act, treaty, or convention binding on the United States, which the Commission is authorized to administer, or any regulation made by the Commission under any such Act, treaty, or convention; or

. . .

(D) has transmitted superfluous radio communications or signals or communications containing profane or obscene words, language, or meaning. . . .

. . .

(r) Make such rules and regulations and prescribe such restrictions and conditions, not inconsistent with law, as may be necessary to carry out the provisions of this Act, or any international radio or wire communications treaty or convention, or regulations annexed thereto, including any treaty or convention insofar as it relates to the use of radio, to which the United States is or may hereafter become a party.

(s) Have authority to require that apparatus designed to receive television pictures broadcast simultaneously with sound be capable of adequately receiving all frequencies allocated by the Commission to television broadcasting when such apparatus is shipped in interstate commerce, or is imported from any foreign country into the United States, for sale or resale to the public.

. . .

(v) Have exclusive jurisdiction to regulate the provision of direct-to-home satellite services. As used in this subsection, the term "direct-to-home satellite services" means the distribution or broadcasting of programming or services by satellite directly to the subscriber's premises without the use of ground receiving or distribution equipment, except at the subscriber's premises or in the uplink process to the satellite.

(w) Prescribe*—(1) on the basis of recommendations from an advisory committee established by the Commission in accordance with section 551(b)(2) of the Telecommunications Act of 1996, guidelines and recommended procedures for the identification and rating of video programming that contains sexual, violent, or other indecent material about which parents should be informed before it is displayed to children: Provided, That nothing in this paragraph shall be construed to authorize any rating of video programming on the basis of its political or religious content; and

(2) with respect to any video programming that has been rated, and in consultation with the television industry, rules requiring distributors of such video programming to transmit such rating to permit parents to block the display of video programming that they have determined is inappropriate for their children.

(x) Require, in the case of an apparatus designed to receive television signals that are shipped in interstate commerce or manufactured in the United States and that have a picture screen 13 inches or greater in size (measured diagonally), that such apparatus be equipped with a feature designed to enable viewers to block display of all programs with a common rating, except as otherwise permitted by regulations pursuant to section 330(c)(4).

---

* Section 551(e) of the 1996 Telecommunications Act provided as follows:

(e)(1) The [provision of subsection w] of this section shall take effect 1 year after the date of enactment of this Act [February 8, 1996], but only if the Commission determines, in consultation with appropriate public interest groups and interested individuals from the private sector, that distributors of video programming have not, by such date—

(A) established voluntary rules for rating video programming that contains sexual, violent, or other indecent material about which parents should be informed before it is displayed to children, and such rules are acceptable to the Commission; and

(B) agreed voluntarily to broadcast signals that contain ratings of such programming.

(2) In prescribing regulations to implement the [provisions of subsection (x)], the Federal Communications Commission shall, after consultation with the television manufacturing industry, specify the effective date for the applicability of the requirement to the apparatus covered by such amendment, which date shall not be less than two years after the date of enactment of this Act.

TECHNOLOGY FUND

Sec. 303 Note. [47 U.S.C.A. § 303 Note.]

It is the policy of the United States to encourage broadcast television, cable, satellite, syndication, other video programming distributors, and relevant related industries (in consultation with appropriate public interest groups and interested individuals from the private sector) to—

(1) establish a technology fund to encourage television and electronics equipment manufacturers to facilitate the development of technology which would empower parents to block programming they deem inappropriate for their children and to encourage the availability thereof to low income parents;

(2) report to the viewing public on the status of the development of affordable, easy to use blocking technology; and

(3) establish and promote effective procedures, standards, systems, advisories, or other mechanisms for ensuring that users have easy and complete access to the information necessary to effectively utilize blocking technology and to encourage the availability thereof to low income parents.

. . .

ALLOCATION OF FACILITIES; TERM OF LICENSES

Sec. 307. [47 U.S.C.A. § 307.]

(a) The Commission, if public convenience, interest, or necessity will be served thereby, subject to the limitations of this Act, shall grant to any applicant therefor a station license provided for by this Act.

(b) In considering applications for licenses, and modifications and renewals thereof, when and insofar as there is demand for the same, the Commission shall make such distribution of licenses, frequencies, hours of operation, and of power among the several States and communities as to provide a fair, efficient, and equitable distribution of radio service to each of the same.

(c)(1) Each license granted for the operation of a broadcasting station shall be for a term of not to exceed 8 years. Upon application therefor, a renewal of such license may be granted from time to time for a term of not to exceed 8 years from the date of expiration of the preceding license, if the Commission finds that public interest, convenience, and necessity would be served thereby. Consistent with the foregoing provisions of this subsection, the Commission may by rule prescribe the period or periods for which licenses shall be granted and renewed for particular classes of stations, but the Commission may not adopt or follow any rule which would preclude it, in any case involving a station of a particular class, from granting or renewing a license for a shorter period than that prescribed for stations of such class if, in its judgment, the public interest, convenience, or necessity would be served by such action.

(2) In order to expedite action on applications for renewal of broadcasting station licenses and in order to avoid needless expense to applicants for such renewals, the Commission shall not require any such applicant to file any information which previously has been furnished to the Commission or which is not directly material to the considerations that affect the granting or denial of such application, but the Commission may require any new or additional facts it deems necessary to make its findings.

(3) Pending any hearing and final decision on such an application and the disposition of any petition for rehearing pursuant to section 405, the Commission shall continue such license in effect.

(d) No renewal of an existing station license in the broadcast or the common carrier services shall be granted more than thirty days prior to the expiration of the original license.

APPLICATIONS FOR LICENSES . . .

Sec. 308. [47 U.S.C.A. § 308.]

. . .

(b) All applications for station licenses, or modifications or renewals thereof, shall set forth such facts as the Commission by regulation may prescribe as to the citizenship, character, and financial, technical, and other qualifications of the applicant to operate the station; the ownership and location of the proposed station and of the stations, if any, with which it is proposed to communicate; the frequencies and the power desired to be used; the hours of the day or other periods of time during which it is proposed to operate the station; the purposes for which the station is to be used; and such other information as it may require. . . .

. . .

(d) Each applicant for the renewal of a commercial or noncommercial television license shall attach as an exhibit to the application a summary of written comments and suggestions received from the public and maintained by the licensee (in accordance with Commission regulations) that comment on the applicant's programming, if any, and that are characterized by the commentor as constituting violent programming.

ACTION UPON APPLICATIONS; FORM OF AND CONDITIONS ATTACHED TO LICENSES

Sec. 309. [47 U.S.C.A. § 309.]

(a) Subject to the provisions of this section, the Commission shall determine, in the case of each application filed with it to which section 308 applies, whether the public interest, convenience, and necessity will be served by the granting of such application, and, if the Commission, upon examination of such application and upon consideration of such other matters as the Commission may officially notice, shall find that public interest, convenience, and necessity would be served by the granting thereof, it shall grant such application.

. . .

(d)(1) Any party in interest may file with the Commission a petition to deny any application. . . .

(2) If the Commission finds on the basis of the application, the pleadings filed, or other matters which it may officially notice that there are no substantial and material questions of fact and that a grant of the application would be consistent with subsection (a) (or subsection (k) in the case of renewal of any broadcast station license), it shall make the grant, deny the petition, and issue a concise statement of the reasons for denying the petition, which statement shall dispose of all substantial issues raised by the petition. If a substantial and material question of fact is presented or if the Commission for any reason is unable to find that grant of the application would be consistent with subsection (a) (or subsection (k) in the case of renewal of any broadcast station license), it shall proceed as provided in subsection (e).

(e) If, in the case of any application to which subsection (a) of this section applies, a substantial and material question of fact is presented or the Commission for any reason is unable to make the finding specified in such subsection, it shall formally designate the application for hearing on the ground or reasons then obtaining and shall forthwith notify the applicant and all other known parties in interest of such action and the grounds and reasons therefor, specifying with particularity the matters and things in issue but not including issues or requirements phrased generally. . . .

. . .

(h) Such station licenses as the Commission may grant shall be in such general form as it may prescribe, but each license shall contain, in addition to other provisions, a statement of the following conditions to which such license shall be subject: (1) The station license shall not vest in the licensee any right to operate the station nor any right in the use of the frequencies designated in the license beyond the term thereof nor in any other manner than authorized therein; (2) neither the license nor the right granted thereunder shall be assigned or otherwise transferred in violation of this Act; (3) every license issued under this Act shall be subject in terms to the right of use or control conferred by section 606 of this Act.*

. . .

(k)(1) STANDARDS FOR RENEWAL.—If the licensee of a broadcast station submits an application to the Commission for renewal of such license, the Commission shall grant the application if it finds, with respect to that station, during the preceding term of its license—

---

* [Section 606 grants substantial powers to the President to utilize communications facilities during wartime or a national emergency.]

(A) the station has served the public interest, convenience, and necessity;

(B) there have been no serious violations by the licensee of this Act or the rules and regulations of the Commission; and

(C) there have been no other violations by the licensee of this Act or the rules and regulations of the Commission which, taken together, would constitute a pattern of abuse.

(2) If any licensee of a broadcast station fails to meet the requirements of this subsection, the Commission may deny the application for renewal in accordance with paragraph (3), or grant such application on terms and conditions as are appropriate, including renewal for a term less than the maximum otherwise permitted.

(3) If the Commission determines, after notice and opportunity for a hearing as provided in subsection (e), that a licensee has failed to meet the requirements specified in paragraph (1) and that no mitigating factors justify the imposition of lesser sanctions, the Commission shall—

(A) issue an order denying the renewal application filed by such licensee under section 308; and

(B) only thereafter accept and consider such applications for a construction permit as may be filed under section 308 specifying the channel or broadcasting facilities of the former licensee.

(4) In making the determinations specified in paragraph (1) or (2), the Commission shall not consider whether the public interest, convenience, and necessity might be served by the grant of a license to a person other than the renewal applicant.

LIMITATION ON HOLDING AND TRANSFER OF LICENSES
Sec. 310. [47 U.S.C.A. § 310.]

(a) The station license required hereby shall not be granted to or held by any foreign government or representative thereof.

(b) No broadcast or common carrier . . . license shall be granted to or held by—

(1) Any alien or the representative of any alien;

(2) Any corporation organized under the laws of any foreign government;

(3) Any corporation of which more than one-fifth of the capital stock is owned of record or voted by aliens or their representatives or by a foreign government or representative thereof or by any corporation organized under the laws of a foreign country;

(4) any corporation directly or indirectly controlled by any other corporation of which more than one-fourth of the capital stock is owned of record or voted by aliens, their representatives or by a

foreign government or representative thereof or by any corporation organized under the laws of a foreign country, if the Commission finds that the public interest will be served by the refusal or revocation of such license.

. . .

(d) No construction permit or station license, or any rights thereunder, shall be transferred, assigned, or disposed of in any manner, voluntarily or involuntarily, directly or indirectly, or by transfer of control of any corporation holding such permit or license, to any person except upon application to the Commission and upon finding by the Commission that the public interest, convenience, and necessity will be served thereby. Any such application shall be disposed of as if the proposed transferee or assignee were making application under section 308 for the permit or license in question; but in acting thereon the Commission may not consider whether the public interest, convenience, and necessity might be served by the transfer, assignment, or disposal of the permit or license to a person other than the proposed transferee or assignee.

SPECIAL REQUIREMENTS WITH RESPECT TO CERTAIN APPLICATIONS IN THE BROADCASTING SERVICE
Sec. 311. [47 U.S.C.A. § 311.]

. . .

(c)(1) If there are pending before the Commission two or more applications for a permit for construction of a broadcasting station, only one of which can be granted, it shall be unlawful, without approval of the Commission, for the applicants or any of them to effectuate an agreement whereby one or more of such applicants withdraws his or their application or applications.

(2) The request for Commission approval in any such case shall be made in writing jointly by all the parties to the agreement. Such request shall contain or be accompanied by full information with respect to the agreement, set forth in such detail, form, and manner as the Commission shall by rule require.

(3) The Commission shall approve the agreement only if it determines (A) that the agreement is consistent with the public interest, convenience, or necessity; and (B) no party to the agreement filed its application for the purpose of reaching or carrying out such agreement. If the agreement does not contemplate a merger, but contemplates the making of any direct or indirect payment to any party thereto in consideration of his withdrawal of his application, the Commission may determine the agreement to be consistent with the public interest, convenience, or necessity only if the amount or value of such payment, as determined by the Commission, is not in excess of the aggregate amount determined by the Commission to have been legitimately and prudently expended and

to be expended by such applicant in connection with preparing, filing, and advocating the granting of his application.

. . .

ADMINISTRATIVE SANCTIONS

Sec. 312. [47 U.S.C.A. § 312.]

(a) The Commission may revoke any station license or construction permit—

(1) for false statements knowingly made either in the application or in any statement of fact which may be required pursuant to section 308;

(2) because of conditions coming to the attention of the Commission which would warrant it in refusing to grant a license or permit on an original application;

(3) for willful or repeated failure to operate substantially as set forth in the license;

(4) for willful or repeated violation of, or willful or repeated failure to observe any provision of this Act or any rule or regulation of the Commission authorized by this Act or by a treaty ratified by the United States;

(5) for violation of or failure to observe any final cease and desist order issued by the Commission under this section;

(6) for violation of section 1304, 1343, or 1464 of title 18 of the United States Code;* or

§ 1304.   Broadcasting lottery information

§ 1343.   Fraud by wire, radio, or television

* [Relevant provisions read as follows:

Whoever broadcasts by means of any radio station for which a license is required by any law of the United States, or whoever, operating any such station, knowingly permits the broadcasting of, any advertisement of or information concerning any lottery, gift enterprise, or similar scheme, offering prizes dependent in whole or in part upon lot or chance, or any list of the prizes drawn or awarded by means of any such lottery, gift enterprise, or scheme, whether said list contains any part or all of such prizes, shall be fined not more than $1,000 or imprisoned not more than one year, or both.

Each day's broadcasting shall constitute a separate offense.

Whoever, having devised or intending to devise any scheme or artifice to defraud, or for obtaining money or property by means of false or fraudulent pretenses, representations, or promises, transmits or causes to be transmitted by means of wire, radio, or television communication in interstate or foreign commerce, any writings, signs, signals, pictures, or sounds for the purpose of executing such scheme or artifice, shall be fined not more than $1,000 or imprisoned not more than five years, or both.

Whoever utters any obscene, indecent, or profane language by means of radio communications shall be fined not more than

$10,000 or imprisoned not more than two years, or both.

(a) The provisions of sections 1301, 1302, 1303, and 1304 shall not apply to an advertisement, list of prizes, or information concerning a lottery conducted by a State acting under the authority of State law—

(1) contained in a newspaper published in that State, or

(2) broadcast by a radio or television station licensed to a location in that State or an adjacent State which conducts such a lottery. . . .]

§ 1464.   Broadcasting obscene language

§ 1307.   State-conducted lotteries

     (7) for willful or repeated failure to allow reasonable access to or to permit purchase of reasonable amounts of time for the use of a broadcasting station by a legally qualified candidate for Federal elective office on behalf of his candidacy.

     (b) Where any person (1) has failed to operate substantially as set forth in a license, (2) has violated or failed to observe any of the provisions of this Act, or section 1304, 1343, or 1464 of title 18 of the United States Code, or (3) has violated or failed to observe any rule or regulation of the Commission authorized by this Act or by a treaty ratified by the United States, the Commission may order such person to cease and desist from such action.

     (c) Before revoking a license or permit pursuant to subsection (a), or issuing a cease and desist order pursuant to subsection (b), the Commission shall serve upon the licensee, permittee, or person involved an order to show cause [at a hearing] why an order of revocation or a cease and desist order should not be issued. . . .

     (d) In any case where a hearing is conducted pursuant to the provisions of this section, both the burden of proceeding with the introduction of evidence and the burden of proof shall be upon the Commission.

    . . .

     (g) If a broadcasting station fails to transmit broadcast signals for any consecutive 12–month period, then the station license granted for the operation of that broadcast station expires at the end of that period, notwithstanding any provision, term, or condition of the license to the contrary.

APPLICATION OF ANTITRUST LAWS; REFUSAL OF LICENSES AND PERMITS IN CERTAIN CASES

Sec. 313. [47 U.S.C.A. § 313.]

     (a) All laws of the United States relating to unlawful restraints and monopolies and to combinations, contracts, or agreements in restraint of trade are hereby declared to be applicable to the manufacture and sale of and to trade in radio apparatus and devices entering into or affecting interstate or foreign commerce and to interstate or foreign radio communications. Whenever in any suit, action, or proceeding, civil or criminal, brought under the provisions of any of said laws or in any proceedings brought to enforce or to review findings and orders of the Federal Trade Commission or other governmental agency in respect of any matters as to which said Commission or other governmental agency is by law authorized to act, any licensee shall be found guilty of the violation of the provisions of such laws or any of them, the court, in addition to the penalties imposed by said laws, may adjudge, order, and/or decree that the license of such licensee shall, as of the date the decree or judgment becomes finally effective or as of such other date as the said decree shall fix, be revoked and that all rights under such license shall thereupon cease: *Provided, however,* That such licensee shall have the same right of appeal or review, as is provided by law in respect of other decrees and judgments of said court.

(b) The Commission is hereby directed to refuse a station license and/or the permit hereinafter required for the construction of a station to any person (or to any person directly or indirectly controlled by such person) whose license has been revoked by a court under this section.

. . .

FACILITIES FOR CANDIDATES FOR PUBLIC OFFICE

Sec. 315. [47 U.S.C.A. § 315.]

(a) If any licensee shall permit any person who is a legally qualified candidate for any public office to use a broadcasting station, he shall afford equal opportunities to all other such candidates for that office in the use of such broadcasting station: *Provided,* That such licensee shall have no power of censorship over the material broadcast under the provisions of this section. No obligation is imposed under this subsection upon any licensee to allow the use of its station by any such candidate. Appearance by a legally qualified candidate on any—

(1) Bona fide newscast,

(2) Bona fide news interview,

(3) Bona fide news documentary (if the appearance of the candidate is incidental to the presentation of the subject or subjects covered by the news documentary), or

(4) On-the-spot coverage of bona fide news events (included but not limited to political conventions and activities incidental thereto), shall not be deemed to be use of a broadcasting station within the meaning of this subsection. Nothing in the foregoing sentence shall be construed as relieving broadcasters, in connection with the presentation of newscasts, news interviews, news documentaries, and on-the-spot coverage of news events, from the obligation imposed upon them under this Act to operate in the public interest and to afford reasonable opportunity for the discussion of conflicting views on issues of public importance.

(b) The charges made for the use of any broadcast station by any person who is a legally qualified candidate for any public office in connection with his campaign for nomination for election, or election, to such office shall not exceed—

(1) During the 45 days preceding the date of a primary or primary runoff election and during the 60 days preceding the date of a general or special election in which such person is a candidate, the lowest unit charge of the station for the same class and amount of time for the same period; and

(2) At any other time, the charges made for comparable use of such station by other users thereof.

(c) For the purposes of this section:

(1) The term "broadcasting station" includes a community antenna television system.

(2) The terms "licensee" and "station licensee" when used with respect to a community antenna television system, mean the operator of such system.

(d) The Commission shall prescribe appropriate rules and regulations to carry out the provisions of this section.

MODIFICATION BY COMMISSION OF CONSTRUCTION PERMITS OR LICENSES

Sec. 316. [47 U.S.C.A. § 316.]

(a) Any station license or construction permit may be modified by the Commission either for a limited time or for the duration of the term thereof, if in the judgment of the Commission such action will promote the public interest, convenience, and necessity, or the provisions of this Act or of any treaty ratified by the United States will be more fully complied with. No such order of modification shall become final until the holder of the license or permit shall have been notified in writing of the proposed action and the grounds and reasons therefor, and shall have been given reasonable opportunity, in no event less than thirty days, to show cause by public hearing, if requested, why such order of modification should not issue. . . .

(b) In any case where a hearing is conducted pursuant to the provisions of this section, both the burden of proceeding with the introduction of evidence and the burden of proof shall be upon the Commission.

ANNOUNCEMENT WITH RESPECT TO CERTAIN MATTER BROADCAST

Sec. 317. [47 U.S.C.A. § 317.]

(a)(1) All matter broadcast by any radio station for which any money, service or other valuable consideration is directly or indirectly paid, or promised to or charged or accepted by, the station so broadcasting, from any person, shall, at the time the same is so broadcast, be announced as paid for or furnished, as the case may be, by such person: *Provided,* That "service or other valuable consideration" shall not include any service or property furnished without charge or at a nominal charge for use on, or in connection with, a broadcast unless it is so furnished in consideration for an identification in a broadcast of any person, product, service, trademark, or brand name beyond an identification which is reasonably related to the use of such service or property on the broadcast.

. . .

CONSTRUCTION PERMIT

Sec. 319. [47 U.S.C.A. § 319.]

. . .

(d) A permit for construction shall not be required for Government stations, amateur stations, or mobile stations. A permit for construction shall not be required for public coast stations, privately owned fixed microwave stations, or stations licensed to common carriers, unless the Commission determines that the public interest, convenience, and necessity would be served by requiring such permits for any such stations. With respect to any broadcasting station, the Commission shall not have any authority to waive the requirement of a permit for construction, except that the Commission may by regulation determine that a permit shall not be required for minor changes in the facilities of authorized broadcast stations. With respect to any other station or class of stations, the Commission shall not waive the requirement for a construction permit unless the Commission determines that the public interest, convenience, and necessity would be served by such a waiver.

FALSE DISTRESS SIGNALS; REBROADCASTING . . .

Sec. 325. [47 U.S.C.A. § 325.]

(a) No person within the jurisdiction of the United States shall knowingly utter or transmit, or cause to be uttered or transmitted, any false or fraudulent signal of distress, or communication relating thereto, nor shall any broadcasting station rebroadcast the program or any part thereof of another broadcasting station without the express authority of the originating station.

(b) Consent to retransmission of broadcasting station signals.

(1) Following the date that is one year after October 5, 1992, no cable system or other multichannel video programming distributor shall retransmit the signal of a broadcasting station, or any part thereof, except—

(A) with the express authority of the originating station; or

(B) pursuant to section 614 of this title, in the case of a station electing, in accordance with this subsection, to assert the right to carriage under such section.

(2) The provisions of this subsection shall not apply to—

(A) retransmission of the signal of a noncommercial broadcasting station;

(B) retransmission directly to a home satellite antenna of the signal of a broadcasting station that is not owned or operated by, or affiliated with, a broadcasting network, if such signal was transmitted by a satellite carrier on May 1, 1991;

(C) retransmission of the signal of a broadcasting station that is owned or operated by, or affiliated with, a broadcasting network directly to a home satellite antenna, if the household receiving the signal is an unserved household; or

(D) retransmission by a cable operator or other multichannel video programming distributor of the signal of a superstation if such signal was obtained from a satellite carrier and the originating station was a superstation on May 1, 1991.

(3)(A) Within 45 days after October 5, 1992, the Commission shall commence a rulemaking proceeding to establish regulations to govern the exercise by television broadcast stations of the right to grant retransmission consent under this subsection and of the right to signal carriage under section 614 of this title, and such other regulations as are necessary to administer the limitations contained in paragraph (2). The Commission shall consider in such proceeding the impact that the grant of retransmission consent by television stations may have on the rates for the basic service tier and shall ensure that the regulations prescribed under this subsection do not conflict with the Commission's obligation under section 623(b)(1) of this title to ensure that the rates for the basic service tier are reasonable. Such rulemaking proceeding shall be completed within 180 days after October 5, 1992.

(B) The regulations required by subparagraph (A) shall require that television stations, within one year after October 5, 1992, and every three years thereafter, make an election between the right to grant retransmission under this subsection and the right to signal carriage under section 614 of this title. If there is more than one cable system which services the same geographic area, a station's election shall apply to all such cable systems.

(4) If an originating television station elects under paragraph (3)(B) to exercise its right to grant retransmission consent under this subsection with respect to a cable system, the provisions of section 534 of this title shall not apply to the carriage of the signal of such station by such cable system.

(5) The exercise by a television broadcast station of the right to grant retransmission consent under this subsection shall not interfere with or supersede the rights under section 614 or 615 of this title of any station electing to assert the right to signal carriage under that section.

(6) Nothing in this section shall be construed as modifying the compulsory copyright license established in section 111 of Title 17 or as affecting existing or future video programming licensing agreements between broadcasting stations and video programmers.

. . .

CENSORSHIP . . .

Sec. 326. [47 U.S.C.A. § 326.]

Nothing in this Act shall be understood or construed to give the Commission the power of censorship over the radio communications or signals transmitted by any radio station, and no regulation or condition shall be promulgated or fixed by the Commission which shall interfere with the right of free speech by means of radio communication.

PROHIBITION AGAINST SHIPMENT OF CERTAIN TELEVISION RECEIVERS

Sec. 330. [47 U.S.C.A. § 330.]

(a) No person shall ship in interstate commerce, or import from any foreign country into the United States, for sale or resale to the public, apparatus described in paragraph (s) of section 303 unless it complies with rules prescribed by the Commission pursuant to the authority granted by that paragraph: *Provided,* That this section shall not apply to carriers transporting such apparatus without trading in it.

. . .

(c)(1) Except as provided in paragraph (2), no person shall ship in interstate commerce or manufacture in the United States any apparatus described in section 303(x) of this Act except in accordance with rules prescribed by the Commission pursuant to the authority granted by that section.

(2) This subsection shall not apply to carriers transporting apparatus referred to in paragraph (1) without trading in it.

(3) The rules prescribed by the Commission under this subsection shall provide for the oversight by the Commission of the adoption of standards by industry for blocking technology. Such rules shall require that all such apparatus be able to receive the rating signals which have been transmitted by way of line 21 of the vertical blanking interval and which conform to the signal and blocking specifications established by industry under the supervision of the Commission.

(4) As new video technology is developed, the Commission shall take such action as the Commission determines appropriate to ensure that blocking service continues to be available to consumers. If the Commission determines that an alternative blocking technology exists that—

(A) enables parents to block programming based on identifying programs without ratings,

(B) is available to consumers at a cost which is comparable to the cost of technology that allows parents to block programming based on common ratings, and

(C) will allow parents to block a broad range of programs on a multichannel system as effectively and as easily as technology that allows parents to block programming based on common ratings, the Commission shall amend the rules prescribed pursuant to section 303(x) to require that the apparatus described in such section be equipped with either the blocking technology described in such section or the alternative blocking technology described in this paragraph.

. . .

DIRECT BROADCAST SATELLITE SERVICE OBLIGATIONS
Sec. 335. [47 U.S.C.A. § 335.]

(a) The Commission shall, within 180 days after October 5, 1992, initiate a rulemaking proceeding to impose, on providers of direct broadcast satellite service, public interest or other requirements for providing video programming. Any regulations prescribed pursuant to such rulemaking shall, at a minimum, apply the access to broadcast time requirement of section 312(a)(7) of this title and the use of facilities requirements of section 315 of this title to providers of direct broadcast satellite service providing video programming. Such proceeding also shall examine the opportunities that the establishment of direct broadcast satellite service provides for the principle of localism under this chapter, and the methods by which such principle may be served through technological and other developments in, or regulation of, such service.

(b)(1) The Commission shall require, as a condition of any provision, initial authorization, or authorization renewal for a provider of direct broadcast satellite service providing video programming, that the provider of such service reserve a portion of its channel capacity, equal to not less than 4 percent nor more than 7 percent, exclusively for noncommercial programming of an educational or informational nature.

(2) A provider of such service may utilize for any purpose any unused channel capacity required to be reserved under this subsection pending the actual use of such channel capacity for noncommercial programming of an educational or informational nature.

(3) A provider of direct broadcast satellite service shall meet the requirements of this subsection by making channel capacity available to national educational programming suppliers, upon reasonable prices, terms, and conditions, as determined by the Commission under paragraph (4). The provider of direct broadcast satellite service shall not exercise any editorial control over any video programming provided pursuant to this subsection.

(4) In determining reasonable prices under paragraph (3)—

(A) the Commission shall take into account the nonprofit character of the programming provider and any Federal funds used to support such programming;

(B) the Commission shall not permit such prices to exceed, for any channel made available under this subsection, 50 percent of the total direct costs of making such channel available; and

(C) in the calculation of total direct costs, the Commission shall exclude—

(i) marketing costs, general administrative costs, and similar overhead costs of the provider of direct broadcast satellite service; and

(ii) the revenue that such provider might have obtained by making such channel available to a commercial provider of video programming.

. . .

BROADCAST SPECTRUM FLEXIBILITY

Sec. 336. [47 U.S.C.A. § 336]

(a) If the Commission determines to issue additional licenses for advanced television services, the Commission—

(1) should limit the initial eligibility for such licenses to persons that, as of the date of such issuance, are licensed to operate a television broadcast station or hold a permit to construct such a station (or both); and

(2) shall adopt regulations that allow the holders of such licenses to offer such ancillary or supplementary services on designated frequencies as may be consistent with the public interest, convenience, and necessity.

(b) In prescribing the regulations required by subsection (a), the Commission shall—

(1) only permit such licensee or permittee to offer ancillary or supplementary services if the use of a designated frequency for such services is consistent with the technology or method designated by the Commission for the provision of advanced television services;

(2) limit the broadcasting of ancillary or supplementary services on designated frequencies so as to avoid derogation of any advanced television services, including high definition television broadcasts, that the Commission may require using such frequencies;

(3) apply to any other ancillary or supplementary service such of the Commission's regulations as are applicable to the offering of analogous services by any other person, except that no ancillary or supplementary service shall have any rights to carriage under section 614 or 615 or be deemed a multi-channel video programming distributor for purposes of section 628;

(4) adopt such technical and other requirements as may be necessary or appropriate to assure the quality of the signal used to provide advanced television services, and may adopt regulations that stipulate the minimum number of hours per day that such signal must be transmitted; and

(5) prescribe such other regulations as may be necessary for the protection of the public interest, convenience, and necessity.

(c) If the Commission grants a license for advanced television services to a person that, as of the date of such issuance, is licensed to operate a television broadcast station or holds a permit to construct such a station (or both), the Commission shall, as a condition of such license, require that either the additional license or the original license held by the licensee be surrendered to the Commission for reallocation or reassignment (or both) pursuant to Commission regulation.

(d) Nothing in this section shall be construed as relieving a television broadcasting station from its obligation to serve the public interest, convenience, and necessity. In the Commission's review of any application for renewal of a broadcast license for a television station that provides ancillary or supplementary services, the television licensee shall establish that all of its program services on the existing or advanced television spectrum are in the public interest. Any violation of the Commission rules applicable to ancillary or supplementary services shall reflect upon the licensee's qualifications for renewal of its license.

(e)(1) If the regulations prescribed pursuant to subsection (a) permit a licensee to offer ancillary or supplementary services on a designated frequency—

(A) for which the payment of a subscription fee is required in order to receive such services, or

(B) for which the licensee directly or indirectly receives compensation from a third party in return for transmitting material furnished by such third party (other than commercial advertisements used to support broadcasting for which a subscription fee is not required),

the Commission shall establish a program to assess and collect from the licensee for such designated frequency an annual fee or other schedule or method of payment that promotes the objectives described in subparagraphs (A) and (B) of paragraph (2).

(2) The program required by paragraph (1) shall—

(A) be designed (i) to recover for the public a portion of the value of the public spectrum resource made available for such commercial use, and (ii) to avoid unjust enrichment through the method employed to permit such uses of that resource;

(B) recover for the public an amount that, to the extent feasible, equals but does not exceed (over the term of the license) the amount that would have been recovered had such services been licensed pursuant to the provisions of section 309(j) of this Act and the Commission's regulations thereunder; and

(C) be adjusted by the Commission from time to time in order to continue to comply with the requirements of this paragraph.

(3)(A) Except as provided in subparagraph (B), all proceeds obtained pursuant to the regulations required by this subsection shall be deposited in the Treasury in accordance with chapter 33 of title 31, United States Code.

(B) Notwithstanding subparagraph (A), the salaries and expenses account of the Commission shall retain as an offsetting collection such sums as may be necessary from such proceeds for the costs of developing and implementing the program required by this section and regulating and supervising advanced television services. Such offsetting collections shall be available for obligation subject to the terms and conditions of the receiving appropriations account, and shall be deposited in such accounts on a quarterly basis.

(4) Within 5 years after the date of enactment of the Telecommunications Act of 1996, the Commission shall report to the Congress on the implementation of the program required by this subsection, and shall annually thereafter advise the Congress on the amounts collected pursuant to such program.

(f) Within 10 years after the date the Commission first issues additional licenses for advanced television services, the Commission shall conduct an evaluation of the advanced television services program. Such evaluation shall include—

(1) an assessment of the willingness of consumers to purchase the television receivers necessary to receive broadcasts of advanced television services;

(2) an assessment of alternative uses, including public safety use, of the frequencies used for such broadcasts; and

(3) the extent to which the Commission has been or will be able to reduce the amount of spectrum assigned to licensees.

(g) As used in this section:

(1) The term "advanced television services" means television services provided using digital or other advanced technology as further defined in the opinion, report, and order of the Commission entitled "Advanced Television Systems and Their Impact Upon the Existing Television Broadcast Service", MM Docket 87–268, adopted September 17, 1992, and successor proceedings.

(2) The term "designated frequency" means each of the frequencies designated by the Commission for licenses for advanced television services.

(3) The term "high definition television" refers to systems that offer approximately twice the vertical and horizontal resolution of receivers generally available on the date of enactment of the Tele-

communications Act of 1996, as further defined in the proceedings described in paragraph (1) of this subsection.

TITLE V—PENAL PROVISIONS—FORFEITURES
FORFEITURES

Sec. 503. [47 U.S.C.A. § 503.]

. . .

(b)(1) Any person who is determined by the Commission, in accordance with paragraph (3) or (4) of this subsection, to have—

(A) willfully or repeatedly failed to comply substantially with the terms and conditions of any license, permit, certificate, or other instrument or authorization issued by the Commission;

(B) willfully or repeatedly failed to comply with any of the provisions of this Act or of any rule, regulation, or order issued by the Commission under this Act or under any treaty convention, or other agreement to which the United States is a party and which is binding upon the United States;

(C) violated any provision of section 317(c) or 509(a) of this Act; or

(D) violated any provision of sections 1304, 1343, or 1464 of Title 18, United States Code;

shall be liable to the United States for a forfeiture penalty. A forfeiture penalty under this subsection shall be in addition to any other penalty provided for by this Act; except that this subsection shall not apply to any conduct which is subject to forfeiture under . . . section 507 of this Act.

(2)(A) If the violator is (i) a broadcast station licensee or permittee, (ii) a cable television operator, or (iii) an applicant for any broadcast or cable television operator license, permit, certificate, or other instrument or authorization issued by the Commission, the amount of any forfeiture penalty determined under this section shall not exceed $25,000 for each violation or each day of a continuing violation, except that the amount assessed for any continuing violation shall not exceed a total of $250,000 for any single act or failure to act described in paragraph (1) of this subsection.

(B) If the violator is a common carrier subject to the provisions of this chapter or an applicant for any common carrier license, permit, certificate, or other instrument of authorization issued by the Commission, the amount of any forfeiture penalty determined under this subsection shall not exceed $100,000 for each violation or each day of a continuing violation, except that the amount assessed for any continuing violation shall not exceed a total of $1,000,000 for any single act or failure to act described in paragraph (1) of this subsection.

. . .

(D) The amount of such forfeiture penalty shall be assessed by the Commission, or its designee, by written notice. In determining the amount of such a forfeiture penalty, the Commission or its designee shall take into account the nature, circumstances, extent, and gravity of the prohibited acts committed and, with respect to the violator, the degree of culpability, any history of prior offenses, ability to pay, and such other matters as justice may require.

. . .

PROHIBITED PRACTICES IN CASES OF CONTESTS OF INTELLECTUAL KNOWLEDGE, INTELLECTUAL SKILL OR CHANCE

Sec. 509. [47 U.S.C.A. § 509.]

(a) It shall be unlawful for any person, with intent to deceive the listening or viewing public—

(1) To supply to any contestant in a purportedly bona fide contest of intellectual knowledge or intellectual skill any special and secret assistance whereby the outcome of such contest will be in whole or in part prearranged or predetermined.

(2) By means of persuasion, bribery, intimidation, or otherwise, to induce or cause any contestant in a purportedly bona fide contest of intellectual knowledge or intellectual skill to refrain in any manner from using or displaying his knowledge or skill in such contest, whereby the outcome thereof will be in whole or in part prearranged or predetermined.

. . .

TITLE VI—CABLE COMMUNICATIONS
PURPOSES

Sec. 601. [47 U.S.C.A. § 521.]

The purposes of this title are to

(1) establish a national policy concerning cable communications;

(2) establish franchise procedures and standards which encourage the growth and development of cable systems and which assure that cable systems are responsive to the needs and interests of the local community;

(3) establish guidelines for the exercise of Federal, State, and local authority with respect to the regulation of cable systems;

(4) assure and encourage that cable communications provide and are encouraged to provide the widest possible diversity of information sources and services to the public;

(5) establish an orderly process for franchise renewal which protects cable operators against unfair denials of renewal where the operator's

past performance and proposal for future performance meet the standards established by this title; and

(6) promote competition in cable communications and minimize unnecessary regulation that would impose an undue economic burden on cable systems.

. . .

DEFINITIONS

Sec. 602. [47 U.S.C.A. § 522.]*

For purposes of this subchapter—

(1) the term "activated channels" means those channels engineered at the headend of a cable system for the provision of services generally available to residential subscribers of the cable system, regardless of whether such services actually are provided, including any channel designated for public, educational, or governmental use;

(2) the term "affiliate," when used in relation to any person, means another person who owns or controls, is owned or controlled by, or is under common ownership or control with, such person;

(3) the term "basic cable service" means any service tier which includes the retransmission of local television broadcast signals;

(4) the term "cable channel" or "channel" means a portion of the electromagnetic frequency spectrum which is used in a cable system and which is capable of delivering a television channel (as television channel is defined by the Commission by regulation);

(5) the term "cable operator" means any person or group of persons (A) who provides cable service over a cable system and directly or through one or more affiliates owns a significant interest in such cable system, or (B) who otherwise controls or is responsible for, through any arrangement, the management and operation of such a cable system;

(6) the term "cable service" means—

(A) the one-way transmission to subscribers of (i) video programming, or (ii) other programming service, and

(B) subscriber interaction, if any, which is required for the selection or use of such video programming or other programming service;

(7) the term "cable system" means a facility, consisting of a set of closed transmission paths and associated signal generation, reception, and control equipment that is designed to provide cable service which includes video programming and which is provided to multiple subscribers within a community, but such term does not include (A) a facility that serves only to retransmit the television signals of 1 or more

---

* In permitting telephone companies to provide video programming services § 302(b)(3) of the 1996 Telecommunications Act repealed existing FCC video dialtone rules and policies; but grandfathered video dialtone systems approved prior to the enactment of the 1996 Act.

television broadcast stations; (B) a facility that serves subscribers without using any public right-of-way; (C) a facility of a common carrier which is subject, in whole or in part, to the provisions of subchapter II of this chapter, except that such facility shall be considered a cable system (other than for purposes of section 621(c) of this title) to the extent such facility is used in the transmission of video programming directly to subscribers; or (D) any facilities of any electric utility solely for operating its electric utility system;

(8) the term "Federal agency" means any agency of the United States, including the Commission;

(9) the term "franchise" means an initial authorization, or renewal thereof (including a renewal of an authorization which has been granted subject to section 626 of this title), issued by a franchising authority, whether such authorization is designated as a franchise, permit, license, resolution, contract, certificate, agreement, or otherwise, which authorizes the construction or operation of a cable system;

(10) the term "franchising authority" means any governmental entity empowered by Federal, State, or local law to grant a franchise;

(11) the term "grade B contour" means the field strength of a television broadcast station computed in accordance with regulations promulgated by the Commission.

(12) the term "multichannel video programming distributor" means a person such as, but not limited to, a cable operator, a multichannel multipoint distribution service, a direct broadcast satellite service, or a television receive-only satellite program distributor, who makes available for purchase, by subscribers or customers, multiple channels of video programming;

(13) the term "other programming service" means information that a cable operator makes available to all subscribers generally;

(14) the term "person" means an individual, partnership, association, joint stock company, trust, corporation, or governmental entity;

(15) the term "public, educational, or governmental access facilities" means—

(A) channel capacity designated for public, educational, or governmental use; and

(B) facilities and equipment for the use of such channel capacity;

(16) the term "service tier" means a category of cable service or other services provided by a cable operator and for which a separate rate is charged by the cable operator;

(17) the term "State" means any State, or political subdivision, or agency thereof;

(18) the term "usable activated channels" means activated channels of a cable system, except those channels whose use for the distribution of

broadcast signals would conflict with technical and safety regulations as determined by the Commission; and

(19) the term "video programming" means programming provided by, a television broadcast station.

CABLE CHANNELS FOR PUBLIC, EDUCATIONAL OR GOVERNMENTAL USE

Sec. 611. [47 U.S.C.A. § 531.]

(a) A franchising authority may establish requirements in a franchise with respect to the designation or use of channel capacity for public, educational, or governmental use only to the extent provided in this section.

(b) A franchising authority may in its request for proposals require as part of a franchise, and may require as part of a cable operator's proposal for a franchise renewal, subject to section 626, that channel capacity be designated for public, educational, or governmental use, . . .

(c) A franchising authority may enforce any requirement in any franchise regarding the providing or use of such channel capacity. Such enforcement authority includes the authority to enforce any provisions of the franchise for services, facilities, or equipment proposed by the cable operator, which relate to public, educational, or governmental use of channel capacity, whether or not required by the franchising authority pursuant to subsection (b).

. . .

(e) Subject to section 624(d), a cable operator shall not exercise any editorial control over any public, educational, or governmental use of channel capacity provided pursuant to this section, except a cable operator may refuse to transmit any public access program or portion of a public access program which contains obscenity, indecency, or nudity.

. . .

CABLE CHANNELS FOR COMMERCIAL USE

Sec. 612. [47 U.S.C.A. § 532.]

(a) The purpose of this section is to assure that the widest possible diversity of information sources are made available to the public from cable systems in a manner consistent with growth and development of cable systems.

(b)(1) A cable operator shall designate channel capacity for commercial use by persons unaffiliated with the operator in accordance with the following requirements:

(A) An operator of any cable system with 36 or more (but not more than 54) activated channels shall designate 10 percent of such channels which are not otherwise required for use (or the use of which is not prohibited) by Federal law or regulation.

(B) An operator of any cable system with 55 or more (but not more than 100) activated channels shall designate 15 percent of such channels which are not otherwise required for use (or the use of which is not prohibited) by Federal law or regulation.

(C) An operator of any cable system with more than 100 activated channels shall designate 15 percent of all such channels.

(D) An operator of any cable system with fewer than 36 activated channels shall not be required to designate channel capacity for commercial use by persons unaffiliated with the operator, unless the cable system is required to provide such channel capacity under the terms of a franchise in effect on the date of the enactment of this title.

. . .

(c)(1) If a person unaffiliated with the cable operator seeks to use channel capacity designated pursuant to subsection (b) for commercial use, the cable operator shall establish, consistent with the purpose of this section, the price, terms, and conditions of such use which are at least sufficient to assure that such use will not adversely affect the operation, financial condition, or market development of the cable system.

(2) A cable operator shall not exercise any editorial control over any video programming provided pursuant to this section, or in any other way consider the content of such programming, except that a cable operator may refuse to transmit any leased access program or portion of a leased access program which contains obscenity, indecency, or nudity and may consider such content to the minimum extent necessary to establish a reasonable price for the commercial use of designated channel capacity by an unaffiliated person.

. . .

(d) Any person aggrieved by the failure or refusal of a cable operator to make channel capacity available for use pursuant to this section may bring an action in the district court of the United States for the judicial district in which the cable system is located to compel that such capacity be made available. If the court finds that the channel capacity sought by such a person has not been made available in accordance with this section, or finds that the price, terms, or conditions established by the cable operator are unreasonable, the court may order such system to make available to such person the channel capacity sought, and further determine the appropriate price, terms, or conditions for such use consistent with subsection (c), and may award actual damages if it deems such relief appropriate. . . .

(e)(1) Any person aggrieved by the failure or refusal of a cable operator to make channel capacity available pursuant to this section may petition the Commission for relief under this subsection upon a showing of prior adjudicated violations of this section. . . . If the Commission finds that the channel capacity sought by such person has not been made available in accordance with this section, or that the price, terms, or conditions established by such system are unreasonable under subsection (c), the Commission shall, by rule and order, require such operator to make available such channel capacity under price, terms, and conditions consistent with subsection (c).

. . .

(h) Any cable service offered pursuant to this section shall not be provided, or shall be provided subject to conditions, if such cable service in the judgment of the franchising authority is obscene, or is in conflict with community standards in that it is lewd, lascivious, filthy, or indecent or is otherwise unprotected by the Constitution of the United States. This subsection shall permit a cable operator to enforce prospectively a written and published policy of prohibiting programming that the cable operator reasonably believes describes or depicts sexual or excretory activities or organs in a patently offensive manner as measured by contemporary community standards.

(i)(1) Notwithstanding the provisions of subsections (b) and (c) of this section, a cable operator required by this section to designate channel capacity for commercial use may use any such channel capacity for the provision of programming from a qualified minority programming source or from any qualified educational programming source, whether or not such source is affiliated with the cable operator. The channel capacity used to provide programming from a qualified minority programming source or from any qualified educational programming source pursuant to this subsection may not exceed 33 percent of the channel capacity designated pursuant to this section. No programming provided over a cable system on July 1, 1990, may qualify as minority programming or educational programming on that cable system under this subsection.

(2) For purposes of this subsection, the term "qualified minority programming source" means a programming source which devotes substantially all of its programming to coverage of minority viewpoints, or to programming directed at members of minority groups, and which is over 50 percent minority-owned, as the term "minority" is defined in section 309(i)(3)(C)(ii) of this title.

(3) For purposes of this subsection, the term "qualified educational programming source" means a programming source which devotes substantially all of its programming to educational or instructional programming that promotes public understanding of mathematics, the sciences, the humanities, and the arts and has a documented annual expenditure on programming exceeding $15,-000,000. . . .

(4) Nothing in this subsection shall substitute for the requirements to carry qualified noncommercial educational television stations as specified under section 615 of this title.

(j)(1) Within 120 days following October 5, 1992, the Commission shall promulgate regulations designed to limit the access of children to indecent programming, as defined by Commission regulations, and which cable operators have not voluntarily prohibited under subsection (h) of this section by—

    (A) requiring cable operators to place on a single channel all indecent programs, as identified by program providers, intended for carriage on channels designated for commercial use under this section;

    (B) requiring cable operators to block such single channel unless the subscriber requests access to such channel in writing; and

    (C) requiring programmers to inform cable operators if the program would be indecent as defined by Commission regulations.

(2) Cable operators shall comply with the regulations promulgated pursuant to paragraph (1).

OWNERSHIP RESTRICTIONS

Sec. 613. [47 U.S.C.A. § 533.]

(a) It shall be unlawful for a cable operator to hold a license for multichannel multipoint distribution service, or to offer satellite master antenna television service separate and apart from any franchised cable service, in any portion of the franchise area served by that cable operator's cable system. The Commission—

    (1) shall waive the requirements of this paragraph for all existing multichannel multipoint distribution services and satellite master antenna television services which are owned by a cable operator on October 5, 1992;

    (2) may waive the requirements of this paragraph to the extent the Commission determines is necessary to ensure that all significant portions of a franchise area are able to obtain video programming; and

    (3) shall not apply the requirements of this subsection to any cable operator in any franchise area in which a cable operator is subject to effective competition as determined under section 623(1).

. . .

(c) The Commission may prescribe rules with respect to the ownership or control of cable systems by persons who own or control other media of mass communications which serve the same community served by a cable system.

(d) Any State or franchising authority may not prohibit the ownership or control of a cable system by any person because of such person's ownership or control of any media of mass communications or other media interests. Nothing in this section shall be construed to prevent any State or franchising authority from prohibiting the ownership or control of a cable system in a jurisdiction by any person (1) because of such person's ownership or control of any other cable system in such jurisdiction; or (2) in circumstances in which the State or franchising authority determines that the acquisition of such a cable system may eliminate or reduce competition in the delivery of cable service in such jurisdiction.

(e)(1) Subject to paragraph (2), a State or franchising authority may hold any interest in any cable system.

(2) Any State or franchising authority shall not exercise any editorial control regarding the content of any cable service on a cable system in which such governmental entity holds ownership interest (other than programming on any channel designated for educational or governmental use), unless such control is exercised through an entity separate from the franchising authority.

(f)(1) In order to enhance effective competition, the Commission shall, within one year after October 5, 1992, conduct a proceeding—

(A) to prescribe rules and regulations establishing reasonable limits on the number of cable subscribers a person is authorized to reach through cable systems owned by such person, on in which such person has an attributable interest;

(B) to prescribe rules and regulations establishing reasonable limits on the number of channels on a cable system that can be occupied by a video programmer in which a cable operator has an attributable interest; and

(C) to consider the necessity and appropriateness of imposing limitations on the degree to which multichannel video programming distributors may engage in the creation or production of video programming.

(2) In prescribing rules and regulations under paragraph (1), the Commission shall, among other public interest objectives—

(A) ensure that no cable operator or group of cable operators can unfairly impede, either because of the size of any individual operator or because of joint actions by a group of operators of sufficient size, the flow of video programming from the video programmer to the consumer;

(B) ensure that cable operators affiliated with video programmers do not favor such programmers in determining carriage on their cable systems or do not unreasonably restrict the flow of the video programming of such programmers to other video distributors;

(C) take particular account of the market structure, ownership patterns, and other relationships of the cable television industry, including the nature and market power of the local franchise, the joint ownership of cable systems and video programmers, and the various types of non-equity controlling interests;

(D) account for any efficiencies and other benefits that might be gained through increased ownership or control;

(E) make such rules and regulations reflect the dynamic nature of the communications marketplace;

(F) no impose limitations which would bar cable operators from serving previously unserved rural areas; and

(G) not impose limitations which would impair the development of diverse and high quality video programming.

(g) This section shall not apply to prohibit any combination of any interests held by any person on July 1, 1984, to the extent of the interests so held as of such date, if the holding of such interests was no inconsistent with any applicable Federal or State law or regulations in effect on that date.

(h) For purposes of this section, the term "media of mass communications" shall have the meaning given such term under Section 309(I)(3)(C)(I) of this title.

CARRIAGE OF LOCAL COMMERCIAL TELEVISION SIGNALS

Sec. 614. [47 U.S.C.A. § 534.]

(a) Each cable operator shall carry, on the cable system of that operator, the signals of local commercial television stations and qualified low power stations as provided by this section. Carriage of additional broadcast television signals on such system shall be at the discretion of such operator, subject to section 325(b) of this title.

(b)(1)(A) A cable operator of a cable system with 12 or fewer usable activated channels shall carry the signals of at least three local commercial television stations, except that if such a system has 300 or fewer subscribers, it shall not be subject to any requirements under this section so long as such system does not delete from carriage by that system any signal of a broadcast television station.

(B) A cable operator of a cable system with more than 12 usable activated channels shall carry the signals of local commercial television stations, up to one-third of the aggregate number of usable activated channels of such system.

(2) Whenever the number of local commercial television stations exceeds the maximum number of signals a cable system is required to carry under paragraph (1), the cable operator shall have discretion in selecting which such stations shall be carried on its cable system, except that—

(A) under no circumstances shall a cable operator carry a qualified low power station in lieu of a local commercial television station; and

(B) if the cable operator elects to carry an affiliate of a broadcast network (as such term is defined by the Commission by regulation), such cable operator shall carry the affiliate of such broadcast network whose city of license reference point . . . is closest to the principal headend of the cable system.

(3)(A) A cable operator shall carry in its entirety, on the cable system of that operator, the primary video, accompanying audio, and line 21 closed caption transmission of each of the local commercial television stations carried on the cable system and, to the extent technically feasible, program-related material in the vertical blanking interval or on subcarriers. Retransmission of other material in the vertical blanking interval or other nonprogram-related material (including teletext and other subscription and advertiser-supported information services) shall be at the discretion of the cable operator. Where appropriate and feasible, operators may delete signal enhancements, such as ghost-canceling, from the broadcast signal and employ such enhancements at the system headend or headends.

(B) The cable operator shall carry the entirety of the program schedule of any television station carried on the cable system unless carriage of specific programming is prohibited, and other programming authorized to be substituted, . . .

(4)(A) The signals of local commercial television stations that a cable operator carries shall be carried without material degradation. The Commission shall adopt carriage standards to ensure that, to the extent technically feasible, the quality of signal processing and carriage provided by a cable system for the carriage of local commercial television stations will be no less than that provided by the system for carriage of any other type of signal.

(B) At such time as the Commission prescribes modifications of the standards for television broadcast signals, the Commission shall initiate a proceeding to establish any changes in the signal carriage requirements of cable television systems necessary to ensure cable carriage of such broadcast signals of local commercial television stations which have been changed to conform with such modified standards.

Notwithstanding paragraph (1), a cable operator shall not be required to carry the signal of any local commercial television that substantially duplicates the signal of another local commercial television station which is carried on its cable system, or to carry the signals of more than one local commercial television station affiliated with a particular broadcast network (as such term is defined by regulation). If a cable operator elects to carry on its cable system a signal which substantially duplicates the signal of another local commercial television station carried on the cable system, or to carry on its system the signals of more than one local commercial television station affiliated with a particular broadcast network, all such signals shall be counted toward the number of signals the operator is required to carry under paragraph (1).

(6) Each signal carried in fulfillment of the carriage obligations of a cable operator under this section shall be carried on the cable system channel number on which the local commercial television station is broadcast over the air, or on the channel on which it was carried on July 19, 1985, or on the channel on which it was carried on January 1, 1992, at the election of the station, or on such other channel as is mutually agreed upon by the station and the cable operator. Any dispute regarding the positioning of a local commercial television shall be resolved by the Commission.

(7) Signals carried in fulfillment of the requirements of this section shall be provided to every subscriber of a cable system. Such signals shall be viewable via cable on all television receivers of a subscriber which are connected to a cable system by a cable operator or for which a cable operator provides a connection. If a cable operator authorizes subscribers to install additional receiver connections, but does not provide the subscriber with such connections, or with the equipment and materials for such connections, the operator shall notify such subscribers of all broadcast stations carried on the cable system which cannot be viewed via cable without a converter box, and shall offer to sell or lease such a converter box to such subscribers at rates in accordance with section (b)(3) of this title.

. . .

(10) A cable operator shall not accept or request monetary payment or other valuable consideration in exchange either for carriage of local commercial television stations in fulfillment of the requirements of this section or for the channel positioning rights provided to such stations under this section, except that—

(c)(1) If there are not sufficient signals of full power local commercial television stations to fill the channels set aside under subsection (b) of this section—

    (A) a cable operator of a cable system with a capacity of 35 or fewer usable activated channels shall be required to carry one qualified low power station; and

    (B) a cable operator of a cable system with a capacity of more than 35 usable activated channels shall be required to carry two qualified low power stations.

(2) A cable operator required to carry more than one signal of a qualified low power station under this subsection may do so, subject to approval by the franchising authority pursuant to section 611 of this title, by placing such additional station on public, educational, or governmental channels not in use for their designated purposes.

. . .

(g)(1) Pending the outcome of the proceeding under paragraph (2), nothing in this chapter shall require a cable operator to carry on any tier, or prohibit a cable operator to carry on any tier, the signal of any commercial television station or video programming service that is predominately utilized for the transmission of sales presentations or program length commercials.

(2) Within 270 days after October 5, 1992, the Commission, notwithstanding prior proceedings to determine whether broadcast television stations that are predominantly utilized for the transmission of sales presentations or program length commercials are serving the public interest, convenience, and necessity, shall complete a proceeding in accordance with this paragraph to determine whether broadcast television stations that are predominantly utilized for the transmission of sales presentations or program length commercials are serving the public interest, convenience, and necessity . . . In the event that the Commission concludes that one or more of such stations are serving the public interest, convenience, and necessity, the Commission shall qualify such stations as local commercial television stations for purposes of subsection (a) of this section. In the event that the Commission concludes that one or more of such stations are not serving the public interest, convenience, and necessity, the Commission shall allow the licensees of such stations a reasonable period within which to provide different programming, and shall not deny such stations a renewal expectancy solely because their programming consisted predominately of sales presentations or program length commercials.

. . .

(h)(1)(C)(i) For purposes of this section, a broadcasting station's market shall be determined by the Commission by regulation or order using, where available, commercial publications which delineate television markets based on viewing patterns, except that following written request, the Commission may, with respect to a particular television broadcast station, include additional communities within its television market or exclude communities from such station's television market to better effectuate the purposes of this section. In considering such requests, the Commission may determine that particular communities are part of more than one television market.

. . .

(iv) Within 120 days after the date on which a request is filed under this subparagraph (or 120 days after the date of enactment of the Telecommunications Act of 1996, if later), the Commission shall grant or deny the request.

CARRIAGE OF NONCOMMERCIAL EDUCATIONAL TELEVISION
Sec. 615. [47 U.S.C.A. § 535.]

(a) In addition to the carriage requirements set forth in section 614 of this title, each cable operator of a cable system shall carry the signals of qualified noncommercial educational television stations in accordance with the provisions of this section.

(b)(1) Subject to paragraphs (2) and (3) and subsection (e) of this section, each cable operator shall carry, on the cable system of that cable operator, any qualified local noncommercial educational television station requesting carriage.

(2)(A) Notwithstanding paragraph (1), a cable operator of a cable system with 12 or fewer usable activated channels shall be required to carry the signal of one qualified local noncommercial educational television station; except that a cable operator of such system shall comply with subsection (c) of this section and may, in its discretion, carry the signals of other qualified noncommercial educational television stations.

(B) In the case of a cable system described in subparagraph (A) which operates beyond the presence of any qualified local noncommercial educational television station—

(i) the cable operator shall import and carry on that system the signal of one qualified noncommercial educational television station;

(ii) the selection for carriage of such a signal shall be at the election of the cable operator; and

(iii) in order to satisfy the requirements for carriage specified in this subsection, the cable operator of the system shall not be required to remove any other programming service actually provided to subscribers on March 29, 1990; except that such cable operator shall use the first channel available to satisfy the requirements of this subparagraph.

(3)(A) Subject to subsection (c) of this section, a cable operator of a cable system with 13 to 36 usable activated channels—

(i) shall carry the signal of at least one qualified local noncommercial educational television but shall not be required to carry the signals of more than three such stations, and

(ii) may, in its discretion, carry additional such stations.

(B) In the case of a cable system described in this paragraph which operates beyond the presence of any qualified local noncommercial educational television station, the cable operator shall import and carry on that system the signal of at least one qualified noncommercial educational television station to comply with subparagraph (A)(i).

(C) The cable operator of a cable system described in this paragraph which carries the signal of a qualified local noncommercial educational station affiliated with a State public television network shall not be required to carry the signal of any additional qualified local noncommercial educational television stations affiliated with the same network if the programming of such additional stations is substantially duplicated by the programming of the qualified local noncommercial educational television station receiving coverage.

(D) A cable operator of a system described in this paragraph which increases the usable activated channel capacity of the system to more than 36 channels on after March 29, 1990, shall, in accordance with the other provisions of this section, carry the signal of each qualified local noncommercial educational television station requesting carriage, subject to subsection (e) of this section.

(c) Notwithstanding any other provision of this section, all cable operators shall continue to provide carriage to all qualified local noncommercial educational television stations whose signals were carried on their systems as of March 29, 1990. The requirements of this subsection may be waived with respect to a particular cable operator and a particular such station, upon the written consent of the cable operator and the station.

(d) A cable operator required to add the signals of qualified local noncommercial educational television stations to a cable system under this section may do so, subject to approval by the franchising authority pursuant to section 611 of this title, by placing such additional stations on public, educational, or governmental channels not in use for their designated purposes.

(e) A cable operator of a cable system with a capacity of more than 36 usable activated channels which is required to carry the signals of three qualified local noncommercial educational television stations shall not be required to carry the signals of additional such stations the programming of which substantially duplicates the programming broadcast by another qualified local noncommercial educational television station requesting carriage. Substantial duplication shall be defined by the Commission in a manner that promotes access to distinctive noncommercial educational television services.

(i)(1) A cable operator shall not accept monetary payment or other valuable consideration in exchange for carriage of the signal of any qualified local noncommercial educational television station carried in fulfillment of the requirements of this section, except that such a station may be required to bear the cost associated with delivering a good quality signal or a baseband video signal to the principal headend of the cable system.

(2) Notwithstanding the provisions of this section, a cable operator shall not be required to add the signal of a qualified local noncommercial educational television station not already carried under the provisions of subsection (c) of this section, where such signal would be considered a

distant signal for copyright purposes unless such station indemnifies the cable operator for any increased copyright costs resulting from carriage of such signal.

. . .

REGULATION OF CARRIAGE AGREEMENTS

Sec. 616. [47 U.S.C.A. § 536.]

(a) Within one year after October 5, 1992, the Commission shall establish regulations governing program carriage agreements and related practices between cable operators or other multichannel video programming distributors and video programming vendors. Such regulations shall—

(1) include provisions designed to prevent a cable operator or other multichannel video programming distributor from requiring a financial interest in a program service as a condition for carriage on one or more of such operator's systems;

(2) include provisions designed to prohibit a cable operator or other multichannel video programming distributor from coercing a video programming vendor to provide, and from retaliating against such a vendor for failing to provide, exclusive rights against other multichannel video programming distributors as a condition of carriage on a system;

(3) contain provisions designed to prevent a multichannel video programming distributor from engaging in conduct the effect of which is to unreasonably restrain the ability of an unaffiliated video programming vendor to compete fairly by discriminating in video programming distribution on the basis of affiliation or nonaffiliation of vendors in the selection, terms, or conditions for carriage of video programming provided by such vendors;

. . .

SALES OF CABLE SYSTEMS

Sec. 617. [47 U.S.C.A. § 617.]

(a) Except as provided in this section, no cable operator may sell or otherwise transfer ownership in a cable system within a 36–month period following either the acquisition or initial construction of such system by such operator.

(b) In the case of a sale of multiple systems, if the terms of the sale require the buyer to subsequently transfer ownership of one or more such systems to one or more third parties, such transfers shall be considered a part of the initial transaction.

. . .

(d) The Commission may, consistent with the public interest, waive the requirement of subsection (a) of this section, except that, if the franchise requires franchise authority approval of a transfer, the Com-

mission shall not waive such requirements unless the franchise authority
has approved the transfer. The Commission shall use its authority under
this subsection to permit appropriate transfers in the cases of default,
foreclosure, or other financial distress.

   . . .

GENERAL FRANCHISE REQUIREMENTS

Sec. 621. [47 U.S.C.A. § 541.]

(a)(1) A franchising authority may award, in accordance with the
provisions of this title, one or more franchises within its jurisdiction.

   . . .

   (3) In awarding a franchise or franchises, a franchising authority shall assure that access to cable service is not denied to any group
of potential residential cable subscribers because of the income of
the residents of the local area in which such group resides.

(b)(1) Except to the extent provided in paragraph (2) and subsection
(f) of this section, a cable operator may not provide cable service without
a franchise.

   . . .

   (3)(A) If a cable operator or affiliate thereof is engaged in the
provision of telecommunications services—

      (i) such cable operator or affiliate shall not be required
   to obtain a franchise under this title for the provision of
   telecommunications services; and

      (ii) the provisions of this title shall not apply to such
   cable operator or affiliate for the provision of telecommunications services.

   (B) A franchising authority may not impose any requirement under this title that has the purpose or effect of prohibiting, limiting, restricting, or conditioning the provision of a
telecommunications service by a cable operator or an affiliate
thereof.

   (C) A franchising authority may not order a cable operator
or affiliate thereof—

      (i) to discontinue the provision of a telecommunica-
   tions service, or

      (ii) to discontinue the operation of a cable system, to
   the extent such cable system is used for the provision of a
   telecommunications service, by reason of the failure of such
   cable operator or affiliate thereof to obtain a franchise or
   franchise renewal under this title with respect to the provision of such telecommunications service.

   (D) Except as otherwise permitted by sections 611 and 612,
a franchising authority may not require a cable operator to

provide any telecommunications service or facilities, other than institutional networks, as a condition of the initial grant of a franchise, a franchise renewal, or a transfer of a franchise.

(c) Any cable system shall not be subject to regulation as a common carrier or utility by reason of providing any cable service.

. . .

FRANCHISE FEES

Sec. 622. [47 U.S.C.A. § 542.]

(a) Subject to the limitation of subsection (b), any cable operator may be required under the terms of any franchise to pay a franchise fee.

(b) For any 12–month period, the franchise fees paid by a cable operator with respect to any cable system shall not exceed 5 percent of such cable operator's gross revenues derived in such period from the operation of the cable system to provide cable services. . . .

. . .

REGULATION OF RATES

Sec. 623. [47 U.S.C.A. § 543.]

(a)(1) In general.—No Federal agency or State may regulate the rates for the provision of cable service except to the extent provided under this section and section 612 of this title. Any franchising authority may regulate the rates for the provision of cable service, or any other communications service provided over a cable system to cable subscribers, but only to the extent provided under this section. No Federal agency, State, or franchising authority may regulate the rates for cable service of a cable system that is owned or operated by a local government or franchising authority within whose jurisdiction that cable system is located and that is the only cable system located within such jurisdiction.

(2) Preference for competition.—If the Commission finds that a cable system is subject to effective competition, the rates for the provision of cable service by such system shall not be subject to regulation by the Commission or by a State or franchising authority under this section. . . .

. . .

(7)(A) The Commission shall allow cable operators, pursuant to any rules promulgated under subsection (b)(3), to aggregate, on a franchise, system, regional, or company level, their equipment costs into broad categories, such as converter boxes, regardless of the varying levels of functionality of the equipment within each such broad category. Such aggregation shall not be permitted with respect to equipment used by subscribers who receive only a rate regulated basic service tier.

(B) Within 120 days of the date of enactment of the Tele-communications Act of 1996, the Commission shall issue revisions to the appropriate rules and forms necessary to implement subparagraph (A)

. . .

(b)(1) The Commission shall, by regulation, ensure that the rates for the basic service tier are reasonable. Such regulations shall be designed to achieve the goal of protecting subscribers of any cable system that is not subject to effective competition from rates for the basic service tier if such cable system were subject to effective competition.

. . .

(7)(A) Each cable operator of a cable system shall provide its subscribers a separately available basic service tier to which subscription is required for access to any other tier of service. Such basic tier shall, at a minimum, consist of the following:

(i) All signals carried in fulfillment of the requirements of sections 614 and 615 of this title.

(ii) Any public, educational, and governmental access programming required by the franchise of the cable system to be provided to subscribers.

(iii) Any signal of any television broadcast station that is provided by the cable operator to any subscriber, except a signal which is secondarily transmitted by a satellite carrier beyond the local service area of such station.

(B) A cable operator may add additional video programming signals or services to the basic service tier. Any such additional signals or services provided on the basic service tier shall be provided to subscribers at rates determined under the regulations prescribed by the Commission under this subsection.

(8)(A) A cable operator may not require the subscription to any tier other than the basic service tier required by paragraph (7) as a condition of access to video programming offered on a per channel or per program basis. A cable operator may not discriminate between subscribers to the basic service tier and other subscribers with regard to the rates charged for video programming offered on a per channel or per program basis.

(B) The prohibition in subparagraph (A) shall not apply to a cable system that, by reason of the lack of addressable converter boxes or other technological limitations, does not permit the operator to offer programming on a per channel or per program basis in the same manner required by subparagraph (A). This subparagraph shall not be available to any cable operator after—

(i) the technology utilized by the cable system is modified or improved in a way that eliminates such technological limitation; or

(ii) 10 years after October 5, 1992, subject to subparagraph (C).

(C) If, in any proceeding initiated at the request of any cable operator, the Commission determines that compliance with the requirements of subparagraph (A) would require the cable operator to increase its rates, the Commission may, to the extent consistent with the public interest, grant such cable operator a waiver from such requirements for such specified period as the Commission determines reasonable and appropriate.

(c)(1) Within 180 days after October 5, 1992, the Commission shall, by regulation, establish the following:

(A) criteria prescribed in accordance with paragraph (2) for identifying, in individual cases, rates for cable programming services that are unreasonable;

(B) fair and expeditious procedures for the receipt, consideration, and resolution of complaints from any franchising authority (in accordance with paragraph 3) alleging that a rate for cable programming services charged by a cable operator violates the criteria prescribed under subparagraph (A), which procedures shall include the minimum showing that shall be required for a complaint to obtain Commission consideration and resolution of whether the rate in question is unreasonable. . . .

. . .

(3) The Commission shall review any complaint submitted by a franchising authority after the date of enactment of the Telecommunications Act of 1996 concerning an increase in rates for cable programming services and issue a final order within 90 days after it receives such a complaint, unless the parties agree to extend the period for such review. A franchising authority may not file a complaint under this paragraph unless, within 90 days after such increase becomes effective it receives subscriber complaints.

(4) This subsection shall not apply to cable programming services provided after March 31, 1999.

(d) This subsection does not apply to (1) a cable operator with respect to the provision of cable service over its cable system in any geographic area in which the video programming services offered by the operator in that area are subject to effective competition, or (2) any video programming offered on a per channel or per program basis. Bulk discounts to multiple dwelling units shall not be subject to this subsection, except that a cable operator of a cable system that is not subject to effective competition may not charge predatory prices to a multiple dwelling unit. Upon a prima facie showing by a complainant that there are reasonable grounds to believe that the discounted price is predatory, the cable system shall have the burden of showing that its discounted price is not predatory.

. . .

(*l*) As used in this section—

(1) The term "effective competition" means that—

(A) fewer than 30 percent of the households in the franchise area subscribe to the cable service of a cable system;

(B) the franchise area is—

(i) served by at least two unaffiliated multichannel video programming distributors each of which offers comparable video programming to at least 50 percent of the households in the franchise area; and

(ii) the number of households subscribing to programming services offered by multichannel video programming distributors other than the largest multichannel video programming distributor exceeds 15 percent of the households in the franchise area; or

(C) a multichannel video programming distributor operated by the franchising authority for that franchise area offers video programming to at least 50 percent of the households in that franchise area; or a local exchange carrier or its affiliate (or any multichannel video programming distributor using the facilities of such carrier or its affiliate) offers video programming services directly to subscribers by any means (other than direct-to-home satellite services) in the franchise area of an unaffiliated cable operator which is providing cable service in that franchise area, but only if the video programming services so offered in that area are comparable to the video programming services provided by the unaffiliated cable operator in that area.

(2) The term "cable programming service" means any video programming provided over a cable system, regardless of service tier, including installation or rental of equipment used for the receipt of such video programming, other than (A) video programming carried on the basic service tier, and (B) video programming offered on a per channel or per program basis.

(m)(1) Subsections (a), (b), and (c) do not apply to a small cable operator with respect to—

(A) cable programming services, or

(B) a basic service tier that was the only service tier subject to regulation as of December 31, 1994,

any franchise area in which that operator services 50,000 or fewer subscribers.

(2) For purposes of this subsection, the term "small cable operator" means a cable operator that, directly or through an affiliate, serves in the aggregate fewer than 1 percent of all subscribers in the United States and is not affiliated with any entity or

entities whose gross annual revenues in the aggregate exceed $250,000,000.

(n) Notwithstanding any other provision of this section or of section 612, losses associated with a cable system (including losses associated with the grant or award of a franchise) that were incurred prior to September 4, 1992, with respect to a cable system that is owned and operated by the original franchisee of such system shall not be disallowed, in whole or in part, in the determination of whether the rates for any tier of service or any type of equipment that is subject to regulation under this section are lawful.

REGULATION OF SERVICES, FACILITIES, AND EQUIPMENT

Sec. 624. [47 U.S.C.A. § 544.]

(a) Any franchising authority may not regulate the services, facilities, and equipment provided by a cable operator except to the extent consistent with this title.

(b) In the case of any franchise granted after the effective date of this title, the franchising authority, to the extent related to the establishment or operation of a cable system—

(1) in its requests for proposals for a franchise (including requests for renewal proposals, subject to Section 626), may establish requirements for facilities and equipment, but may not establish requirements for video programming or other information services; and

(2) subject to Section 625, may enforce any requirements contained within the franchise—

(A) for facilities and equipment; and

(B) for broad categories of video programming or other services.

(c) In the case of any franchise in effect on the effective date of this title, the franchising authority may, subject to Section 625, enforce requirements contained within the franchise for the provision of services, facilities, and equipment, whether or not related to the establishment or operation of a cable system.

(d)(1) Nothing in this title shall be construed as prohibiting a franchising authority and a cable operator from specifying, in a franchise or renewal thereof, that certain cable services shall not be provided or shall be provided subject to conditions, if such cable services are obscene or are otherwise unprotected by the Constitution of the United States.

(2)(A) In order to restrict the viewing of programming which is obscene or indecent, upon the request of a subscriber, a cable operator shall provide (by sale or lease) a device by which the subscriber can prohibit viewing of a particular cable service during periods selected by that subscriber.

. . .

(e) Within one year after October 5, 1992, the Commission shall prescribe regulations which establish minimum technical standards relating to cable systems' technical operation and signal quality. The Commission shall update such standards periodically to reflect improvements in technology. No State or franchising authority may prohibit, condition, or restrict a cable system's use of any type of subscriber equipment or any transmission technology.

(f)(1) Any Federal agency, State, or franchising authority may not impose requirements regarding the provision or content of cable services, except as expressly provided in this title.

. . .

CONSUMER ELECTRONICS EQUIPMENT COMPATIBILITY
Sec. 624a. [47 U.S.C.A. § 544a.]

. . .

(b)(1) Within 1 year after October, 1992, the Commission, in consultation with representatives of the cable industry and the consumer electronics industry, shall report to Congress on means of assuring compatibility between televisions and video cassette recorders and cable systems, consistent with the need to prevent theft of cable service, so that cable subscribers will be able to enjoy the full benefit of both the programming available on cable systems and the functions available on their televisions and video cassette recorders. Within 180 days after the date of submission of the report required by this subsection, the Commission shall issue such regulations as are necessary to assure such compatibility.

MODIFICATION OF FRANCHISE OBLIGATIONS
Sec. 625. [47 U.S.C.A. § 545.]

(a)(1) During the period a franchise is in effect, the cable operator may obtain from the franchising authority modifications of the requirements in such franchise—

> (A) in the case of any such requirement for facilities or equipment, including public, educational, or governmental access facilities or equipment, if the cable operator demonstrates that (i) it is commercially impracticable for the operator to comply with such requirement, and (ii) the proposal by the cable operator for modification of such requirement is appropriate because of such commercial impracticability; or

> (B) in the case of any such requirement for services, if the cable operator demonstrates that the mix, quality, and level of services required by the franchise at the time it was granted will be maintained after such modification.

. . .

(c) A cable operator may provide notice of service and rate changes to subscribers using any reasonable written means at its sole discretion. Notwithstanding section 623(b)(6) or any other provision of this Act, a cable operator shall not be required to provide prior notice of any rate change that is the result of a regulatory fee, franchise fee, or any other fee, tax, assessment, or charge of any kind imposed by any Federal agency, State, or franchising authority on the transaction between the operator and the subscriber.

. . .

RENEWAL

Sec. 626. [47 U.S.C.A. § 546.]

(a)(1) A franchising authority may, on its own initiative during the 6th month period which begins with the 36th month before the franchise expiration, commence a proceeding which affords the public in the franchise area appropriate notice and participation for the purpose of (A) identifying the future cable-related community needs and interests, and (B) reviewing the performance of the cable operator under the franchise during the then current franchise term. If the cable operator submits, during such 6–month period, a written renewal notice requesting the commencement of such a proceeding, the franchising authority shall commence such a proceeding not later than 6 months after the date such notice is submitted.

(2) The cable operator may not invoke the renewal procedures set forth in subsections (b) through (g) of this section unless—

(A) such a proceeding is requested by the cable operator by timely submission of such notice; or

(B) such a proceeding is commenced by the franchising authority on its own initiative.

(b)(1) Upon completion of a proceeding under subsection (a), a cable operator seeking renewal of a franchise may, on its own initiative or at the request of a franchising authority, submit a proposal for renewal.

(2) Subject to section 624, any such proposal shall contain such material as the franchising authority may require, including proposals for an upgrade of the cable system.

(3) The franchising authority may establish a date by which such proposals shall be submitted.

(c)(1) Upon submittal by a cable operator of a proposal to the franchising authority for the renewal of a franchise, the franchising authority shall provide prompt public notice of such proposal and, during the 4–month period which begins on the completion of any proceedings under subsection (a), renew the franchise or, issue a preliminary assessment that the franchise should not be renewed and, at the request of the operator or on its own initiative, commence an administrative proceeding after providing prompt public notice of such proceeding in accordance with paragraph (2) to consider whether—

(A) the cable operator has substantially complied with the material terms of the existing franchise and with applicable law;

(B) the quality of the operator's service including signal quality, response to consumer complaints, and billing practices, but without regard to the mix, quality, or level of cable services or other services provided over the system, has been reasonable in light of community needs;

(C) the operator has the financial, legal, and technical ability to provide the services, facilities, and equipment as set forth in the operator's proposal; and

(D) the operator's proposal is reasonable to meet the future cable-related community needs and interests, taking into account the cost of meeting such needs and interests.

. . .

(3) At the completion of a proceeding under this subsection, the franchising authority shall issue a written decision granting or denying the proposal for renewal based upon the record of such proceeding, and transmit a copy of such decision to the cable operator. Such decision shall state the reasons therefor.

(d) Any denial of a proposal for renewal shall be based on one or more adverse findings made with respect to the factors described in subparagraphs (A) through (D) of subsection (c)(1). . . .

DEVELOPMENT OF COMPETITION AND DIVERSITY IN VIDEO PROGRAMMING DISTRIBUTION

Sec. 628. [47 U.S.C.A. § 548.]

(a) The purpose of this section is to promote the public interest, convenience, and necessity by increasing competition and diversity in the multichannel video programming market, to increase the availability of satellite cable programming and satellite broadcast programming to persons in rural and other areas not currently able to receive such programming, and to spur the development of communications technologies.

(b) It shall be unlawful for a cable operator, a satellite cable programming vendor in which a cable operator has an attributable interest, or a satellite broadcast programming vendor to engage in unfair methods of competition or unfair or deceptive acts or practices, the purpose or effect of which is to hinder significantly or to prevent any multichannel video programming distributor from providing satellite cable programming or satellite broadcast programming to subscribers or consumers.

(c)(1) Within 180 days after October 5, 1992, the Commission shall, in order to promote the public interest, convenience, and necessity by increasing competition and diversity in the multichannel video programming market and the continuing development of communications technologies, prescribe regulations to specify particular conduct that is prohibited by subsection (b) of this section.

(2) The regulations to be promulgated under this section shall—

(A) establish effective safeguards to prevent a cable operator which has an attributable interest in a satellite cable programming vendor or a satellite broadcast programming vendor from unduly or improperly influencing the decision of such vendor to sell, or the prices, terms, and conditions of sale of, satellite cable programming or satellite broadcast programming to any unaffiliated multichannel video programming distributor;

(B) prohibit discrimination by a satellite cable programming vendor in which a cable operator has an attributable interest or by a satellite broadcast programming vendor in the prices, terms, and conditions of sale or delivery of satellite cable programming or satellite broadcast programming among or between cable systems, cable operators, or other multichannel video programming distributors, or their agents or buying groups, . . .

. . .

(C) prohibit practices, understandings, arrangements, and activities, including exclusive contracts for satellite cable programming or satellite broadcast programming between a cable operator and a satellite cable programming vendor or satellite broadcast programming vendor, that prevent a multichannel video programming vendor in which a cable operator has an attributable interest or any satellite broadcast programming vendor in which a cable operator has an attributable in interest for distribution to persons in areas not served by a cable operator as of October 5, 1992; and

(D) with respect to distribution to persons in areas served by a cable operator, prohibit exclusive contracts for satellite cable programming or satellite broadcast programming between a cable operator and a satellite cable programming vendor in which a cable operator has an attributable interest or a satellite broadcast programming vendor in which a cable operator has an attributable interest, unless the Commission determines (in accordance with paragraph (4)) that such contract is in the public interest.

(3)(A) Nothing in this section shall require any person who is engaged in the national or regional distribution of video programming to make such programming available in any geographic area beyond which such programming has been authorized or licensed for distribution.

(B) Nothing in this section shall apply

(i) to the signal of any broadcast affiliate of a national television network or other television signal that is retransmitted by satellite but that is not satellite broadcast programming, or

(ii) to any internal satellite communication of any broadcast network or cable network that is not satellite broadcast programming.

(4) In determining whether an exclusive contract is in the public interest for purposes of paragraph (2)(D), the Commission shall consider each of the following factors with respect to the effect of such contract on the distribution of video programming in areas that are served by a cable operator:

(A) the effect of such exclusive contract on the development of competition in local and national multichannel video programming distribution markets;

(B) the effect of such exclusive contract on competition from multichannel video programming distribution technologies other than cable;

(C) the effect of such exclusive contract on the attraction of capital investment in the production and distribution of new satellite cable programming;

(D) the effect of such exclusive contract on diversity of programming in the multichannel video programming distribution market; and

(E) the duration of the exclusive contract.

. . .

(j) Any provision that applies to a cable operator under this section shall apply to a common carrier or its affiliate that provides video programming by any means directly to subscribers. Any such provision that applies to a satellite cable programming vendor in which a cable operator has an attributable interest shall apply to any satellite cable programming vendor in which such common carrier has an attributable interest. For the purposes of this subsection, two or fewer common officers or directors shall not by itself establish an attributable interest by a common carrier in a satellite cable programming vendor (or its parent company).

CONSUMER PROTECTION AND CUSTOMER SERVICE

Sec. 632. [47 U.S.C.A. § 552.]

(a) A franchising authority may establish and enforce—

(1) customer service requirements of the cable operator; and

(2) construction schedules and other construction-related requirements, including construction-related performance requirements, of the cable operator.

(b) The Commission shall, within 180 days of enactment of the Cable Consumer Protection and Competition Act of 1992, establish standards by which cable operators may fulfill their customer service requirements. Such standards shall include, at a minimum, requirements governing—

(1) cable system office hours and telephone availability;

(2) installations, outages, and service calls; and

(3) communications between the cable operator and the subscriber (including standards governing bills and refunds).

(c)(1) Nothing in this subchapter shall be construed to prohibit any State or any franchising authority from enacting or enforcing any consumer protection law, to the extent not specifically preempted by this subchapter.

(2) Nothing in this section shall be construed to preclude a franchising authority and a cable operator from agreeing to customer service requirements that exceed the standards established by the Commission under subsection (b) of this section. Nothing in this subchapter shall be construed to prevent the establishment or enforcement of any municipal law or regulation, or any State law, concerning customer service that imposes customer service requirements that exceed the standards set by the Commission under this section, or that addresses matters not addressed by the Commission under this section.

COMPETITIVE AVAILABILITY OF NAVIGATION DEVICES

Sec. 629. [47 U.S.C.A. § 549]

(a) The Commission shall, in consultation with appropriate industry standard-setting organizations, adopt regulations to assure the commercial availability, to consumers of multichannel video programming and other services offered over multichannel video programming systems, of converter boxes, interactive communications equipment, and other equipment used by consumers to access multichannel video programming and other services offered over multichannel video programming systems, from manufacturers, retailers, and other vendors not affiliated with any multichannel video programming distributor. Such regulations shall not prohibit any multichannel video programming distributor from also offering converter boxes, interactive communications equipment, and other equipment used by consumers to access multichannel video programming and other services offered over multichannel video programming systems, to consumers, if the system operator's charges to consumers for such devices and equipment are separately stated and not subsidized by charges for any such service.

(b) The Commission shall not prescribe regulations under subsection (a) which would jeopardize security of multichannel video programming and other services offered over multichannel video programming systems, or impede the legal rights of a provider of such services to prevent theft of service.

(c) The Commission shall waive a regulation adopted under subsection (a) for a limited time upon an appropriate showing by a provider of multichannel video programming and other services offered over multichannel video programming systems, or an equipment provider, that such waiver is necessary to assist the development or introduction of a new or improved multichannel video programming or other service offered over multichannel video programming systems, technology, or products. Upon an appropriate showing, the Commission shall grant any such waiver request within 90 days of any application filed under this subsection, and such waiver shall be effective for all service providers and products in that category and for all providers of services and products.

(d)(1) Determinations made or regulations prescribed by the Commission with respect to commercial availability to consumers of converter boxes, interactive communications equipment, and other equipment used by consumers to access multichannel video programming and other services offered over multichannel video programming systems, before the date of enactment of the Telecommunications Act of 1996 shall fulfill the requirements of this section.

(2) Nothing in this section affects section 64.702(e) of the Commission's regulations (47 C.F.R. 64.702(e)) or other Commission regulations governing interconnection and competitive provision of customer premises equipment used in connection with basic common carrier communications services.

(e) The regulations adopted under this section shall cease to apply when the Commission determines that—

(1) the market for the multichannel video programming distributors is fully competitive;

(2) the market for converter boxes, and interactive communications equipment, used in conjunction with that service is fully competitive; and

(3) elimination of the regulations would promote competition and the public interest.

(f) Nothing in this section shall be construed as expanding or limiting any authority that the Commission may have under law in effect before the date of enactment of the Telecommunications Act of 1996.

UNAUTHORIZED RECEPTION OF CABLE SERVICE

Sec. 633. [47 U.S.C.A. § 553.]

(a)(1) No person shall intercept or receive or assist in intercepting or receiving any communications service offered over a cable system, unless specifically authorized to do so by a cable operator or as may otherwise be specifically authorized by law.

(2) For the purpose of this section, the term "assist in intercepting or receiving" shall include the manufacture or distribution of equipment intended by the manufacturer or distributor (as the case may be) for unauthorized reception of any communications service offered over a cable system in violation of subparagraph (1).

. . .

LIMITATION OF FRANCHISING AUTHORITY LIABILITY
Sec. 635a. [47 U.S.C.A. § 555a.]

(a) In any court proceeding pending on or initiated after October 5, 1992, involving any claim against a franchising authority or other governmental entity, or any official, member, employee, or agent of such authority or entity, arising from the regulation of cable service or from a decision of approval or disapproval with respect to a grant, renewal, transfer, or amendment of a franchise, any relief, to the extent such relief is required by any other provision of Federal, State, or local law, shall be limited to injunctive relief and declaratory relief.

(b) The limitation contained in subsection (a) of this section shall not apply to actions that, prior to such violation, have been determined by a final order of a court of binding jurisdiction, no longer subject to appeal, to be in violation of a cable operator's rights.

. . .

CRIMINAL AND CIVIL LIABILITY
Sec. 638. [47 U.S.C.A. § 558.]

Nothing in this title shall be deemed to affect the criminal or civil liability of cable programmers or cable operators pursuant to the Federal, State, or local law of libel, slander, obscenity, incitement, invasions of privacy, false or misleading advertising, or other similar laws, except that cable operators shall not incur any such liability for any program carried on any channel designated for public, educational, governmental use or any other channel obtained under Section 612 or under similar arrangements.

OBSCENE PROGRAMMING
Sec. 639. [47 U.S.C.A. § 559.]

Whoever transmits over any cable system any matter which is obscene or otherwise unprotected by the Constitution of the United States shall be fined under Title 18, United States Code, or imprisoned not more than two years, or both.

SCRAMBLING OF CABLE CHANNELS FOR NONSUBSCRIBERS
Sec. 640. [47 U.S.C.A. § 560]

(a) Upon request by a cable service subscriber, a cable operator shall, without charge, fully scramble or otherwise fully block the audio and video programming of each channel carrying such programming so that one not a subscriber does not receive it.

(b) As used in this section, the term "scramble" means to rearrange the content of the signal of the programming so that the programming cannot be viewed or heard in an understandable manner.

SCRAMBLING OF SEXUALLY EXPLICIT ADULT VIDEO SERVICE PROGRAMMING

Sec. 641. [47 U.S.C.A. § 561]

(a) In providing sexually explicit adult programming or other programming that is indecent on any channel of its service primarily dedicated to sexually-oriented programming, a multichannel video programming distributor shall fully scramble or otherwise fully block the video and audio portion of such channel so that one not a subscriber to such channel or programming does not receive it.

(b) Until a multichannel video programming distributor complies with the requirement set forth in subsection (a), the distributor shall limit the access of children to the programming referred to in that subsection by not providing such programming during the hours of the day (as determined by the Commission) when a significant number of children are likely to view it.

(c) As used in this section, the term "scramble" means to rearrange the content of the signal of the programming so that the programming cannot be viewed or heard in an understandable manner.

REGULATORY TREATMENT OF VIDEO PROGRAMMING SERVICES

Sec. 651. [47 U.S.C.A. § 571]

(a)(1) To the extent that a common carrier (or any other person) is providing video programming to subscribers using radio communication, such carrier (or other person) shall be subject to the requirements of title III and section 652, but shall not otherwise be subject to the requirements of this title.

(2) To the extent that a common carrier is providing transmission of video programming on a common carrier basis, such carrier shall be subject to the requirements of title II and section 652, but shall not otherwise be subject to the requirements of this title. This paragraph shall not affect the treatment under section 602(7)(C) of a facility of a common carrier as a cable system.

(3) To the extent that a common carrier is providing video programming to its subscribers in any manner other than that described in paragraphs (1) and (2)—

(A) such carrier shall be subject to the requirements of this title, unless such programming is provided by means of an open video system for which the Commission has approved a certification under section 653; or

(B) if such programming is provided by means of an open video system for which the Commission has approved a certification under section 653, such carrier shall be subject to the requirements of this part, but shall be subject to parts I through IV of this title only as provided in 653(c).

(4) A common carrier that is providing video programming in a manner described in paragraph (1) or (2), or a combination thereof, may elect to provide such programming by means of an open video system that complies with section 653. If the Commission approves such carrier's certification under section 653, such carrier shall be subject to the requirements of this part, but shall be subject to parts I through IV of this title only as provided in 653(c).

(b) A local exchange carrier that provides cable service through an open video system or a cable system shall not be required, pursuant to title II of this Act, to make capacity available on a nondiscriminatory basis to any other person for the provision of cable service directly to subscribers.

(c) A common carrier shall not be required to obtain a certificate under section 214 with respect to the establishment or operation of a system for the delivery of video programming.

PROHIBITION ON BUY OUTS

Sec. 652. [U.S.C.A. § 572]

(a) No local exchange carrier or any affiliate of such carrier owned by, operated by, controlled by, or under common control with such carrier may purchase or otherwise acquire directly or indirectly more than a 10 percent financial interest, or any management interest, in any cable operator providing cable service within the local exchange carrier's telephone service area.

(b) No cable operator or affiliate of a cable operator that is owned by, operated by, controlled by, or under common ownership with such cable operator may purchase or otherwise acquire, directly or indirectly, more than a 10 percent financial interest, or any management interest, in any local exchange carrier providing telephone exchange service within such cable operator's franchise area.

(c) A local exchange carrier and a cable operator whose telephone service area and cable franchise area, respectively, are in the same market may not enter into any joint venture or partnership to provide video programming directly to subscribers or to provide telecommunications services within such market.

(d)(1) Notwithstanding subsections (a), (b), and (c) of this section, a local exchange carrier (with respect to a cable system located in its telephone service area) and a cable operator (with respect to the facilities of a local exchange carrier used to provide telephone exchange service in its cable franchise area) may obtain a controlling interest in, management interest in, or enter into a joint venture or partnership with the operator of such system or facilities for the use of such system or facilities to the extent that—

(A) such system or facilities only serve incorporated or unincorporated—

(i) places or territories that have fewer than 35,000 inhabitants; and

(ii) are outside an urbanized area, as defined by the Bureau of the Census; and

(B) in the case of a local exchange carrier, such system, in the aggregate with any other system in which such carrier has an interest, serves less than 10 percent of the households in the telephone service area of such carrier.

(2) Notwithstanding subsection (c), a local exchange carrier may obtain, with the concurrence of the cable operator on the rates, terms, and conditions, the use of that part of the transmission facilities of a cable system extending from the last multi-user terminal to the premises of the end user, if such use is reasonably limited in scope and duration, as determined by the Commission.

(3) Notwithstanding subsections (a) and (c), a local exchange carrier may obtain a controlling interest in, or form a joint venture or other partnership with, or provide financing to, a cable system (hereinafter in this paragraph referred to as "the subject cable system"), if—

(A) the subject cable system operates in a television market that is not in the top 25 markets, and such market has more than 1 cable system operator, and the subject cable system is not the cable system with the most subscribers in such television market;

(B) the subject cable system and the cable system with the most subscribers in such television market held on May 1, 1995, cable television franchises from the largest municipality in the television market and the boundaries of such franchises were identical on such date;

(C) the subject cable system is not owned by or under common ownership or control of any one of the 50 cable system operators with the most subscribers as such operators existed on May 1, 1995; and

(D) the system with the most subscribers in the television market is owned by or under common ownership or control of any one of the 10 largest cable system operators as such operators existed on May 1, 1995.

(4) Subsection (a) does not apply to any cable system if—

(A) the cable system serves no more than 17,000 cable subscribers, of which no less than 8,000 live within an urban area, and no less than 6,000 live within a nonurbanized area as of June 1, 1995;

(B) the cable system is not owned by, or under common ownership or control with, any of the 50 largest cable system operators in existence on June 1, 1995; and

(C) the cable system operates in a television market that was not in the top 100 television markets as of June 1, 1995.

(5) Notwithstanding subsections (a) and (c), a local exchange carrier with less than $100,000,000 in annual operating revenues (or any affiliate of such carrier owned by, operated by, controlled by, or under common control with such carrier) may purchase or otherwise acquire more than a 10 percent financial interest in, or any management interest in, or enter into a joint venture or partnership with, any cable system within the local exchange carrier's telephone service area that serves no more than 20,000 cable subscribers, if no more than 12,000 of those subscribers live within an urbanized area, as defined by the Bureau of the Census.

(6) The Commission may waive the restrictions of subsections (a), (b), or (c) only if—

(A) the Commission determines that, because of the nature of the market served by the affected cable system or facilities used to provide telephone exchange service—

(i) the affected cable operator or local exchange carrier would be subjected to undue economic distress by the enforcement of such provisions;

(ii) the system or facilities would not be economically viable if such provisions were enforced; or

(iii) the anticompetitive effects of the proposed transaction are clearly outweighed in the public interest by the probable effect of the transaction in meeting the convenience and needs of the community to be served; and

(B) the local franchising authority approves of such waiver.

(e) For purposes of this section, the term "telephone service area" when used in connection with a common carrier subject in whole or in part to title II of this Act means the area within which such carrier provided telephone exchange service as of January 1, 1993, but if any common carrier after such date transfers its telephone exchange service facilities to another common carrier, the area to which such facilities provide telephone exchange service shall be treated as part of the telephone service area of the acquiring common carrier and not of the selling common carrier.

ESTABLISHMENT OF OPEN VIDEO SYSTEMS.

Sec. 653. [47 U.S.C.A. § 573]

(a)(1) A local exchange carrier may provide cable service to its cable service subscribers in its telephone service area through an open video system that complies with this section. To the extent permitted by such regulations as the Commission may prescribe consistent with the public interest, convenience, and necessity, an operator of a cable system or any other person may provide video programming through an open video system that complies with this section. An operator of an open video system shall qualify for reduced regulatory burdens under subsection (c) of this section if the operator of such system certifies to the Commission that such carrier complies with the Commission's regulations under subsection (b) and the Commission approves such certification. The Commission shall publish notice of the receipt of any such certification and shall act to approve or disapprove any such certification within 10 days after receipt of such certification.

(2) The Commission shall have the authority to resolve disputes under this section and the regulations prescribed thereunder. Any such dispute shall be resolved within 180 days after notice of such dispute is submitted to the Commission. At that time or subsequently in a separate damages proceeding, the Commission may, in the case of any violation of this section, require carriage, award damages to any person denied carriage, or any combination of such sanctions. Any aggrieved party may seek any other remedy available under this Act.

(b)(1) Within 6 months after the date of enactment of the Telecommunications Act of 1996, the Commission shall complete all actions necessary (including any reconsideration) to prescribe regulations that—

(A) except as required pursuant to section 611, 614, or 615, prohibit an operator of an open video system from discriminating among video programming providers with regard to carriage on its open video system, and ensure that the rates, terms, and conditions for such carriage are just and reasonable, and are not unjustly or unreasonably discriminatory;

(B) if demand exceeds the channel capacity of the open video system, prohibit an operator of an open video system and its affiliates from selecting the video programming services for carriage on more than one-third of the activated channel capacity on such system, but nothing in this subparagraph shall be construed to limit the number of channels that the carrier and its affiliates may offer to provide directly to subscribers;

(C) permit an operator of an open video system to carry on only one channel any video programming service that is offered by more than one video programming provider (including the local exchange carrier's video programming affiliate): Provided, That subscribers have ready and immediate access to any such video programming service;

(D) extend to the distribution of video programming over open video systems the Commission's regulations concerning sports exclusivity (47 C.F.R. 76.67), network nonduplication (47 C.F.R. 76.92 et seq.), and syndicated exclusivity (47 C.F.R. 76.151 et seq.); and

(E)(i) prohibit an operator of an open video system from unreasonably discriminating in favor of the operator or its affiliates with regard to material or information (including advertising) provided by the operator to subscribers for the purposes of selecting programming on the open video system, or in the way such material or information is presented to subscribers;

(ii) require an operator of an open video system to ensure that video programming providers or copyright holders (or both) are able suitably and uniquely to identify their programming services to subscribers;

(iii) if such identification is transmitted as part of the programming signal, require the carrier to transmit such identification without change or alteration; and

(iv) prohibit an operator of an open video system from omitting television broadcast stations or other unaffiliated video programming services carried on such system from any navigational device, guide, or menu.

(2) Subject to the requirements of paragraph (1) and the regulations thereunder, nothing in this section prohibits a common carrier or its affiliate from negotiating mutually agreeable terms and conditions with over-the-air broadcast stations and other unaffiliated video programming providers to allow consumer access to their signals on any level or screen of any gateway, menu, or other program guide, whether provided by the carrier or its affiliate.

(c)(1) Any provision that applies to a cable operator under—

(A) sections 613 (other than subsection (a) thereof), 616, 623(f), 628, 631, and 634 of this title, shall apply,

(B) sections 611, 614, and 615 of this title, and section 325 of title III, shall apply in accordance with the regulations prescribed under paragraph (2), and

(C) sections 612 and 617, and parts III and IV (other than sections 623(f), 628, 631, and 634), of this title shall not apply,

to any operator of an open video system for which the Commission has approved a certification under this section.

(2)(A) In the rulemaking proceeding to prescribe the regulations required by subsection (b)(1), the Commission shall, to the extent possible, impose obligations that are no greater or lesser than the obligations contained in the provisions described in paragraph (1)(B) of this subsection. The Commission shall complete all action (including any reconsideration) to prescribe such regulations no later than

6 months after the date of enactment of the Telecommunications Act of 1996.

(B) An operator of an open video system under this part may be subject to the payment of fees on the gross revenues of the operator for the provision of cable service imposed by a local franchising authority or other governmental entity, in lieu of the franchise fees permitted under section 622. The rate at which such fees are imposed shall not exceed the rate at which franchise fees are imposed on any cable operator transmitting video programming in the franchise area, as determined in accordance with regulations prescribed by the Commission. An operator of an open video system may designate that portion of a subscriber's bill attributable to the fee under this subparagraph as a separate item on the bill.

(3) With respect to the establishment and operation of an open video system, the requirements of this section shall apply in lieu of, and not in addition to, the requirements of title II.

(4) Nothing in this Act precludes a video programming provider making use of an open video system from being treated as an operator of a cable system for purposes of section 111 of title 17, United States Code.

(d) For purposes of this section, the term "telephone service area" when used in connection with a common carrier subject in whole or in part to title II of this Act means the area within which such carrier is offering telephone exchange service.

UNAUTHORIZED PUBLICATION OR USE OF COMMUNICATIONS
Sec. 705. [47 U.S.C.A. § 605.]

(a) Except as authorized by Chapter 119, Title 18, no person receiving, assisting in receiving, transmitting, or assisting in transmitting, any interstate or foreign communication by wire or radio shall divulge or publish the existence, contents, substance, purport, effect, or meaning thereof, except through authorized channels of transmission or reception, (1) to any person other than the addressee, his agent, or attorney, (2) to a person employed or authorized to forward such communication to its destination, (3) to proper accounting or distributing officers of the various communicating centers over which the communication may be passed, (4) to the master of a ship under whom he is serving, (5) in response to a subpoena issued by a court of competent jurisdiction, or (6) on demand of other lawful authority. No person not being authorized by the sender shall intercept any radio communication and divulge or publish the existence, contents, substance, purport, effect, or meaning of such intercepted communication to any person. No person not being entitled thereto shall receive or assist in receiving any interstate or foreign communication by radio and use such communication (or any information therein contained) for his own benefit or for the benefit of another not entitled thereto. No person having received any intercepted radio communication or having become acquainted with the contents, substance, purport, effect, or meaning of such communication (or any part thereof) knowing that such communication was intercepted, shall divulge or publish the existence, contents, substance, purport, effect, or meaning of such communication (or any part thereof) or use such communication (or any information therein contained) for his own benefit or for the benefit of another not entitled thereto. This section shall not apply to the receiving, divulging, publishing, or utilizing the contents of any radio communication which is transmitted by any station for the use of the general public, which relates to ships, aircraft, vehicles or persons in distress, or which is transmitted by an amateur radio station operator or by a citizens band radio operator.

(b) The provisions of subsection (a) shall not apply to the interception or receipt by any individual, or the assisting (including the manufacture or sale) of such interception or receipt, of any satellite cable programming for private viewing if—

(1) the programming involved is not encrypted; and

(2)(A) a marketing system is not established under which—

(i) an agent or agents have been lawfully designated for the purpose of authorizing private viewing by individuals; and

(ii) such authorization is available to the individual involved from the appropriate agent or agents; or

(B) a marketing system described in subparagraph (A) is established and the individuals receiving such programming have obtained authorization for private viewing under that system.

(c) No person shall encrypt or continue to encrypt satellite delivered programs included in the National Program Service of the Public Broadcasting Service and intended for public viewing by retransmission by television broadcast stations; except that as long as at least one unencrypted satellite transmission of any program subject to this subsection is provided, this subsection shall not prohibit additional encrypted transmissions of the same program.

(d) For purposes of this section—

(1) the term "satellite cable programming" means video programming which is transmitted via satellite and which is primarily intended for the direct receipt by cable operators for their retransmission to cable subscribers;

(2) the term "agent," with respect to any person, includes an employee of such person;

(3) the term "encrypt," when used with respect to satellite cable programming, means to transmit such programming in a form whereby the aural and visual characteristics (or both) are modified or altered for the purpose of preventing the unauthorized receipt of

such programming by persons without authorized equipment which is designed to eliminate the effects of such modification or alteration;

(4) the term "private viewing" means the viewing for private use in an individual's dwelling unit by means of equipment, owned or operated by such individual, capable of receiving satellite cable programming directly from a satellite; and

(5) the term "private financial gain" shall not include the gain resulting to any individual for the private use in such individual's dwelling unit of any programming for which the individual has not obtained authorization for that use.

(e)(1) Any person who willfully violates subsection (a) shall be fined not more than $1,000 or imprisoned for not more than 6 months or both.

(2) Any person who violates subsection (a) willfully and for purposes of direct or indirect commercial advantage or private financial gain shall be fined not more than $25,000 or imprisoned for not more than 1 year, or both, for the first such conviction and shall be fined not more than $50,000 or imprisoned for not more than 2 years, or both, for any subsequent conviction.

(3)(A) Any person aggrieved by any violation of subsection (a) may bring a civil action in a United States district court or in any other court of competent jurisdiction.

(B) The court may—

(i) grant temporary and final injunctions on such terms as it may deem reasonable to prevent or restrain violations of subsection (a);

(ii) award damages as described in subparagraph (C); and

(iii) direct the recovery of full costs, including awarding reasonable attorneys' fees to an aggrieved party who prevails.

(C)(i) Damages awarded by any court under this section shall be computed, at the election of the aggrieved party, in accordance with either of the following subclauses;

(I) the party aggrieved may recover the actual damages suffered by him as a result of the violation and any profits of the violator that are attributable to the violation which are not taken into account in computing the actual damages; in determining the violator's profits, the party aggrieved shall be required to prove only the violator's gross revenue, and the violator shall be required to prove his deductible expenses and the elements of profit attributable to factors other than the violation; or

(II) the party aggrieved may recover an award of statutory damages for each violation involved in the action in a sum of not less than $250 or more than $10,000, as the court considers just.

(ii) In any case in which the court finds that the violation was committed willfully and for purposes of direct or indirect commercial advantage or private financial gain, the court in its discretion may increase the award of damages, whether actual or statutory, by an amount of not more than $50,000.

(iii) In any case where the court finds that the violator was not aware and had no reason to believe that his acts constituted a violation of this section, the court in its discretion may reduce the award of damages to a sum of not less than $100.

(4) Any person who manufactures, assembles, modifies, imports, exports, sells, or distributes any electronic, mechanical, or other device or equipment, knowing or having reason to know that the device or equipment is primarily of assistance in the unauthorized decryption of satellite cable programming or direct-to-home satellite services, or is intended for any other activity prohibited by subsection (a) of this section, shall be fined not more than $500,000 for each violation or imprisoned for not more than 5 years for each violation, or both. For purposes of all penalties and remedies established for violations of this paragraph, the prohibited activity established herein as it applies to each such device shall be deemed a separate violation.

(5) The penalties under this subsection shall be in addition to those prescribed under any other provision of this title.

(6) Nothing in this subsection shall prevent any State, or political subdivision thereof, from enacting or enforcing any laws with respect to the importation, sale, manufacture, or distribution of equipment by any person with the intent of its use to assist in the interception or receipt of radio communications prohibited by subsection (a).

(e) Nothing in this section shall affect any right, obligation, or liability under Title 17, United States Code, any rule, regulation, or order thereunder, or any other applicable Federal, State, or local law.

VIDEO PROGRAMMING ACCESSIBILITY

Sec. 713. [47 U.S.C.A. § 613]

(a) Within 180 days after the date of enactment of the Telecommunications Act of 1996, the Federal Communications Commission shall complete an inquiry to ascertain the level at which video programming is closed captioned. Such inquiry shall examine the extent to which existing or previously published programming is closed captioned, the size of the video programming provider or programming owner providing closed captioning, the size of the market served, the relative audience shares achieved, or any other related factors. The Commission shall submit to the Congress a report on the results of such inquiry.

(b) Within 18 months after such date of enactment, the Commission shall prescribe such regulations as are necessary to implement this section. Such regulations shall ensure that—

(1) video programming first published or exhibited after the effective date of such regulations is fully accessible through the provision of closed captions, except as provided in subsection (d); and

(2) video programming providers or owners maximize the accessibility of video programming first published or exhibited prior to the effective date of such regulations through the provision of closed captions, except as provided in subsection (d).

(c) Such regulations shall include an appropriate schedule of deadlines for the provision of closed captioning of video programming.

(d) Notwithstanding subsection (b)—

(1) the Commission may exempt by regulation programs, classes of programs, or services for which the Commission has determined that the provision of closed captioning would be economically burdensome to the provider or owner of such programming;

(2) a provider of video programming or the owner of any program carried by the provider shall not be obligated to supply closed captions if such action would be inconsistent with contracts in effect on the date of enactment of the Telecommunications Act of 1996, except that nothing in this section shall be construed to relieve a video programming provider of its obligations to provide services required by Federal law; and

(3) a provider of video programming or program owner may petition the Commission for an exemption from the requirements of this section, and the Commission may grant such petition upon a showing that the requirements contained in this section would result in an undue burden.

(e) The term "undue burden" means significant difficulty or expense. In determining whether the closed captions necessary to comply with the requirements of this paragraph would result in an undue economic burden, the factors to be considered include—

(1) the nature and cost of the closed captions for the programming;

(2) the impact on the operation of the provider or program owner;

(3) the financial resources of the provider or program owner; and

(4) the type of operations of the provider or program owner.

(f) Within 6 months after the date of enactment of the Telecommunications Act of 1996, the Commission shall commence an inquiry to examine the use of video descriptions on video programming in order to ensure the accessibility of video programming to persons with visual impairments, and report to Congress on its findings. The Commission's report shall assess appropriate methods and schedules for phasing video descriptions into the marketplace, technical and quality standards for video descriptions, a definition of programming for which video descriptions would apply, and other technical and legal issues that the Commission deems appropriate.

(g) For purposes of this section, "video description" means the insertion of audio narrated descriptions of a television program's key visual elements into natural pauses between the program's dialogue.

(h) Nothing in this section shall be construed to authorize any private right of action to enforce any requirement of this section or any regulation there under. The Commission shall have exclusive jurisdiction with respect to any complaint under this section.

Appendix C

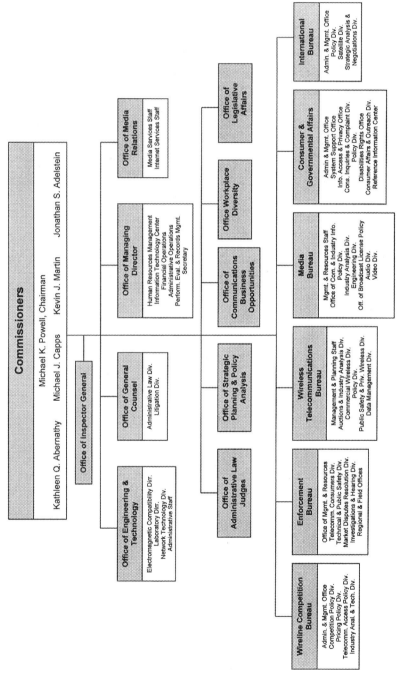

Appendix D

SUMMARY OF THE BROADCAST OWNERSHIP RULES ADOPTED ON JUNE 2, 2003

As this book went to press the FCC had not yet issued the text of the Report and Order for the new ownership rules. The following is a summary of the rules issued by the FCC.

DUAL NETWORK OWNERSHIP PROHIBITION: *(originally adopted 1946)*

The FCC retained its ban on mergers among any of the top four national broadcast networks.

Prohibition Promotes Competition and Localism

The FCC determined that its existing dual network prohibition continues to be necessary to promote competition in the national television advertising and program acquisition markets. The rule also promotes localism by preserving the balance of negotiating power between networks and affiliates. If the rule was eliminated and two of the top four networks were to merge, affiliates of those two networks would have fewer networks to turn to for affiliation.

LOCAL TV MULTIPLE OWNERSHIP LIMIT: *(originally adopted in 1964)*

The new rule states:

> In markets with five or more TV stations, a company may own two stations, but only one of these stations can be among the top four in ratings.

> In markets with 18 or more TV stations, a company can own three TV stations, but only one of these stations can be among the top four in ratings.

In deciding how many stations are in the market, both commercial and non-commercial TV stations are counted.

The FCC adopted a waiver process for markets with 11 or fewer TV stations in which two top-four stations seek to merge. The FCC will evaluate on a case-by-case basis whether such stations would better serve their local communities together rather than separately.

TV Limit Enhances Competition and Preserves Viewpoint Diversity

The FCC determined that its prior local TV ownership rule could not be justified on diversity or competition grounds. The FCC found that Americans rely on a variety of media outlets, not just broadcast television, for news and information. In addition, the prior rule could not be justified as necessary to promote competition because it failed to reflect the significant competition now faced by local broadcasters from cable and satellite TV services. This is the first local TV ownership rule to acknowledge that competition.

The new rule permits local television combinations that are proven to enhance competition in local markets and to facilitate the transition to digital television through economic efficiencies. Finally, the new rule's continued ban on mergers among the top-four stations will have the effect of preserving viewpoint diversity in local markets. The record showed that the top four stations each typically produce an independent local newscast.

Because viewpoint diversity is fostered when there are multiple independently owned media outlets, the FCC's competition-based limits on local TV ownership also advance the goal of promoting the widest dissemination of viewpoints.

NATIONAL TV OWNERSHIP LIMIT: (*originally adopted in 1941*)

The FCC incrementally increased the 35% limit to a 45% limit on national ownership.

A company can own TV stations reaching no more than a 45% share of U.S. TV households.

The share of U.S. TV households is calculated by adding the number of TV households in each market that the company owns a station. Regardless of the station's ratings, it is counted for all of the potential viewers in the market. Therefore, a 45% share of U.S. TV households is not equal to a 45% share of TV stations in the U.S.

On March 31, 2003, there were 1,340 commercial TV stations in the U.S. Of these 1,340 stations, Viacom owns 39 TV stations (2.9%), Fox owns 37 (2.8%), NBC owns 29 (2.2%) and ABC owns 10 (0.8%).

National Cap Protects Localism and Preserves Free Television

The FCC determined that a national TV ownership limit is needed to protect localism by allowing a body of network affiliates to negotiate collectively with the broadcast networks on network programming decisions.

The FCC also found that the current 35% level did not strike the right balance of promoting localism and preserving free over-the-air television for several reasons.

1. The record showed that the 35% cap did not have any meaningful effect on the negotiating power between individual networks and their affiliates with respect to program-by-program preemption levels.

2. The record showed the broadcast network owned-and-operated stations ("O & Os") served their local communities better with respect to local news production. Network-owned stations aired more local news programming than did affiliates.

3. The record showed that the public interest is served by regulations that encourage the networks to keep expensive programming, such as sports, on free, over-the-air television.

Record Supports Maintaining UHF Discount

The FCC decided to maintain the "UHF Discount" when calculating a company's national reach because it currently serves the public interest. The FCC said that more than 40 million Americans still have access only to free, over-the-air television.

Evidence in the record demonstrates that UHF stations have smaller signal coverage areas than VHF stations, which has a very real impact on UHF stations' ability to compete.

The UHF discount has promoted the entry of new broadcast networks into the market. These new networks have improved consumer choice and program diversity for all Americans, including those with and without cable and satellite TV service.

For these reasons, the FCC maintained a 50% discount for calculating the national reach of UHF stations. However, the FCC determined that when the transition to digital television is complete, the UHF discount would be eliminated for the stations owned by the four largest broadcast networks. The FCC will determine, in a future biennial review, whether to include any other networks and station group owners in the UHF discount sunset. The FCC drew this distinction to ensure that its resolution of the UHF discount issue will properly account for its goal of encouraging the formation of new, over-the-air broadcast networks.

LOCAL RADIO OWNERSHIP LIMIT: *(originally adopted in 1941)*

The FCC found that the current limits on local radio ownership continue to be necessary in the public interest, but that the previous methodology for defining a radio market did not serve the public interest. The radio caps remain at the following levels:

> In markets with 45 or more radio stations, a company may own 8 stations, only 5 of which may be in one class, AM or FM.

> In markets with 30–44 radio stations, a company may own 7 stations, only 4 of which may be in one class, AM or FM.

> In markets with 15–29 radio stations, a company may own 6 stations, only 4 of which may be in one class, AM or FM.

> In markets with 14 or fewer radio stations, a company may own 5 stations, only 3 of which may be in one class, AM or FM.

Radio Limit Promotes Competition and Viewpoint Diversity

Although Americans rely on a wide variety of outlets in addition to radio for news, the FCC found that the current radio ownership limits continue to be needed to promote competition among local radio stations. Competitive radio markets ensure that local stations are responsive to local listener needs and tastes. By guaranteeing a substantial number of independent radio voices, this rule will also promote viewpoint diversity among local radio owners.

Geographic Arbitron Markets Implemented

The FCC replaced its signal contour method of defining local radio markets with a geographic market approach assigned by Arbitron. The FCC said that its signal contour method created anomalies in ownership of local radio stations that Congress could not have intended when it established the local radio ownership limits in 1996. The FCC closed that loophole by applying a more rational market definition than radio signal contours. The FCC said applying Arbitron's geographic markets method will better reflect the true markets in which radio stations compete.

All radio stations licensed to communities in an Arbitron market are counted in the market as well as stations licensed to other markets but considered "home" to the market.

Both commercial and noncommercial stations are counted in the market. The FCC determined that the current rule improperly ignores the impact that noncommercial stations can have on competition for listeners in radio markets.

For non-Arbitron markets, the FCC will conduct a short-term rulemaking to define markets comparable to Arbitron markets. These new markets will be specifically designed to prevent any unreasonable aggregation of station ownership by any one company.

As an interim procedure for non-Arbitron markets, the FCC will apply a modified contour method for counting the number of stations in the market. This modified contour approach minimizes the potential for additional anomalies to occur during this transition period, while providing the public a clear rule for determining the relevant radio markets.

In using the contour-overlap market definition on an interim basis, the FCC made certain adjustments to minimize the more notorious anomalies of that system. Specifically, the FCC will exclude from the market any radio station whose transmitter site is more than 92 kilometers (58 miles) from the perimeter of the mutual overlap area. This will alleviate some of the gross distortions in market size that can occur when a large signal contour that is part of a proposed combination overlaps the contours of distant radio stations and thereby brings them into the market.

CROSS-MEDIA LIMITS:

This rule replaces the broadcast-newspaper and the radio-television cross-ownership rules. The new rule states:

In markets with three or fewer TV stations, no cross-ownership is permitted among TV, radio and newspapers. A company may obtain a waiver of that ban if it can show that the television station does not serve the area served by the cross-owned property (*i.e.* the radio station or the newspaper).

In markets with between 4 and 8 TV stations, combinations are limited to <u>one</u> of the following:

(A) A daily newspaper; one TV station; and up to half of the radio station limit for that market (*i.e.* if the radio limit in the market is 6, the company can only own 3) **OR**

(B) A daily newspaper; and up to the radio station limit for that market; (*i.e.* no TV stations) **OR**

(C) Two TV stations (if permissible under local TV ownership rule); up to the radio station limit for that market (*i.e.* no daily newspapers).

In markets with nine or more TV stations, the FCC eliminated the newspaper-broadcast cross-ownership ban and the television-radio cross-ownership ban.

Promotes Diversity and Localism

The FCC concluded that neither the newspaper-broadcast prohibition nor the TV-radio cross-ownership prohibition could be justified for larger markets in light of the abundance of sources that citizens rely on for news. Nor were those rules found to promote competition because radio, TV and newspapers generally compete in different economic markets. Moreover, the FCC found that greater participation by newspaper publishers in the television and radio business would improve the quality and quantity of news available to the public.

Therefore, the FCC replaced those rules with a set of Cross–Media Limits (CML). These limits are designed to protect viewpoint diversity by ensuring that no company, or group of companies, can control an inordinate share of media outlets in a local market.

The FCC developed a Diversity Index to measure the availability of key media outlets in markets of various sizes. The FCC concluded that there were three tiers of markets in terms of "viewpoint diversity" concentration, each warranting different regulatory treatment.

In the tier of smallest markets (3 or fewer TV stations), the FCC found that key outlets were sufficiently limited such that any cross-ownership among the three leading outlets for local news—broadcast TV, radio, and newspapers—would harm viewpoint diversity.

In the medium-sized tier (4–8 TV stations), markets were found to be less concentrated today than in the smallest markets and that certain media outlet combinations could safely occur without harming viewpoint diversity. Certain other combinations would threaten viewpoint diversity and are thus prohibited.

In the largest tier of markets (9 or more TV stations), the FCC concluded that the large number of media outlets, in combination with ownership limits for local TV and radio, were more than sufficient to protect viewpoint diversity.

RADIO AND TV TRANSFERABILITY LIMITED TO SMALL BUSINESSES:

The FCC's new TV and radio ownership rules may result in a number of situations where current ownership arrangements exceed ownership limits. The FCC grand-fathered owners of those clusters, but generally prohibited the sale of such above-cap clusters. The FCC made a limited exception to permit sales of grand-fathered combinations to small businesses as defined in the *Order*.

In taking this action, the FCC sought to respect the reasonable expectations of parties that lawfully purchased groups of local radio stations that today, through redefined markets, now exceed the applicable caps. The FCC also attempted to promote competition by permitting station owners to retain any above-cap local radio clusters but not transfer them intact unless there is a compelling public policy justification to do so. The FCC found two such justifications: (1) avoiding undue hardships to cluster owners that are small businesses; and (2) promoting the entry into the broadcasting business by small businesses, many of which are minority- or female-owned.

INDEX

References are to Pages.

---

†